HANDBOOK OF
PREJUDICE, STEREOTYPING, AND DISCRIMINATION

HANDBOOK OF
PREJUDICE, STEREOTYPING, AND DISCRIMINATION

EDITED BY
TODD D. NELSON

Psychology Press
Taylor & Francis Group
New York   Hove

Psychology Press
Taylor & Francis Group
270 Madison Avenue
New York, NY 10016

Psychology Press
Taylor & Francis Group
27 Church Road
Hove, East Sussex BN3 2FA

© 2009 by Taylor & Francis Group, LLC
Psychology Press is an imprint of Taylor & Francis Group, an Informa business

Printed in the United States of America on acid-free paper
10 9 8 7 6 5 4 3

International Standard Book Number-13: 978-0-8058-5952-2 (Hardcover)

Library of Congress Cataloging-in-Publication Data

Handbook of prejudice, stereotyping, and discrimination / editor, Todd D. Nelson.
    p. cm.
  Includes bibliographical references and index.
  ISBN 978-0-8058-5952-2 (alk. paper)
  1. Prejudices. 2. Stereotypes (Social psychology) 3. Social perception. 4. Discrimination. I. Nelson, Todd D., 1966-

BF575.P9H36 2009
303.3'85--dc22

2008044022

Visit the Taylor & Francis Web site at
http://www.taylorandfrancis.com

and the Psychology Press Web site at
http://www.psypress.com

Contents

Preface

Research on prejudice has been a cornerstone of social psychology from the inception of the field. From our early attempts to understand the contents of racial stereotypes, to neuroimaging the brain as we process information about outgroups, researchers have learned much over the last nine decades about the factors that give rise to the birth of prejudice, how it is maintained, and why prejudice is often difficult to eliminate. In any scientific field, there are points in time when researchers can be spurred on in new directions as the state of the literature is summarized, or via pioneering new theory. In prejudice research, such touchstones as Allport's (1954) *Nature of Prejudice,* Dovidio and Gaertner's (1986) *Prejudice, Discrimination and Racism,* and Mackie and Hamilton's (1993) *Affect, Cognition, and Stereotyping* have been invaluable in terms of summarizing what we know, advancing new theoretical perspectives, and pointing out new directions for future research. However, surprisingly, there has not yet been a concerted effort to specifically produce a volume that is designed to showcase the range and depth of the field of prejudice research. In other words, there is no "Handbook of Prejudice and Stereotyping." I found this rather astonishing, because research on prejudice has always been a high priority among social psychologists. There are handbooks for many other fields in social psychology (e.g., handbooks of motivation and cognition, affect, attitudes, etc.), but nothing on one of the most-researched topics in social psychology. This led to the idea for this volume.

This volume is intended as a scholarly resource for researchers and students alike, as they seek to understand the current state of the field of prejudice research. Each chapter is written by distinguished leading prejudice researchers. The structure and scope of the volume is loosely based on the esteemed *Handbook of Social Psychology,* in that each chapter author was given a goal to produce a snapshot of the field in that specific subarea of prejudice research, and to advance, where applicable, new theory. I am grateful to each of the chapter authors for agreeing to contribute to this volume, and for producing such outstanding chapters. Their work has made this a reference volume that will be invaluable for experienced and new prejudice researchers alike.

The volume is organized into five main parts. First, Charles Stangor reviews the history of research on prejudice, stereotyping, and discrimination. The second section, "Cognitive, Affective, and Neurological Processes Involved in Prejudice," is further divided into five subsections. First, the processes by which we form prejudice are discussed in chapters by Levy and Hughes, and also by Stephan, Ybarra, and Morrison. In the next subsection, "Cognitive Processes," we find the bulk of the handbook represented with 10 chapters in this area. This may reflect the strong social cognition emphasis of many of the field's top prejudice researchers. Devine and Sharp lead off this section with an outstanding chapter on automaticity in prejudice and stereotyping. Major and Sawyer follow with a fascinating paper on the causes and consequences for those who make attributions of other's behavior to discrimination. Next, Bodenhausen, Todd, and Richeson discuss the processes used and situations in which we control stereotypes and prejudice.

Biernat follows with a discussion of how stereotyping is affected by shifting anchors and standards that bias and guide whether and what stereotype is applied to a target. Aronson and McGlone then present an excellent chapter on both stereotype threat and social identity threat. Next, Hamilton, Sherman, Crump, and Spencer-Rodgers discuss the fascinating work on the role of entitativity in stereotyping. Jussim and his colleagues follow with a detailed, excellent discussion of the work on understanding stereotype accuracy. Crocker and Garcia then discuss intergroup interactions in terms of how they typically can start off negative and get increasingly negative as a result of each individual's own suspicions and interaction goals.

The influence of power on the powerful and how they interact with the powerless (or those with less power) is explored next by Vescio and her colleagues. Finally, this subsection is concluded by Dasgupta's discussion of a topic that has been hot in prejudice research since the early 1990s: implicit prejudice and stereotyping.

The next subsection, "Affective Processes," contains two excellent chapters. Mackie, Maitner, and Smith discuss their interesting and useful intergroup emotions theory. Next, Greenberg and his colleagues discuss how terror management theory nicely explains a wide array of prejudice and stereotyping.

The following subsection, "The Neurobiology of Prejudice," contains two chapters. This area of research is still very much in its infancy, but many are excited about the possibility that new brain imaging technology and methods can bring new understanding about the brain structures involved in prejudice and stereotyping. Kubota and Ito lead with their chapter on the use of event-related potential to understand prejudice and stereotyping. Amodio and Lieberman then follow with a discussion of the use of fMRI techniques to map brain activity when one thinks about ingroups and outgroups.

The next subsection only contains one chapter, but it is a very important one on the measurement of prejudice. Olson discusses the various ways researchers have measured it in the past, and the advantages and pitfalls of various popular methods and instruments used to measure prejudice.

The third main section of the volume is "Targets of Prejudice." Simply put, who are people mostly prejudiced against, and why? On what dimensions do people stereotype others? These five chapters represent the bulk of research on those frequently researched targets of prejudice. This in no way is a comprehensive list however (e.g., neither religious prejudice nor handicapism are listed). Some of those that have been left out are due to a dearth of research in that area. Zaraté leads off with an outstanding chapter on racism, the dimension on which most research on prejudice has been centered. Swim and Hyers then present the current state of the art in our understanding of sexism. Nelson then discusses prejudice against older adults in his chapter on ageism. Next is an outstanding chapter by Herek on our understanding of prejudice against people based on their sexual orientation. The section concludes with a chapter by Crandall, Nierman, and Hebl, on a type of prejudice—antifat prejudice—that is akin to ageism in its institutionalized, socially condoned nature in the United States.

The fourth main section, "Reducing Prejudice," presents two excellent chapters addressing this subject. Gaertner and Dovidio discuss the research on the common ingroup identity approach to prejudice reduction between groups. Monteith and Mark follow with their chapter on reducing prejudice through self-regulation processes.

The fifth main section, like the opening section, contains just one chapter, an epilogue, in which Fiske and her colleagues discuss their ideas for future empirical and theoretical directions in prejudice and stereotyping.

This volume owes much to those in the editorial process and production team at Taylor & Francis who helped guide it to its completion. First, I would like to thank Debra Riegert, who offered the contract for the book when she was at Lawrence Erlbaum Associates (now a part of Taylor & Francis) in the fall of 2005. Her early faith and enthusiasm in the volume was fantastic and much appreciated. At Taylor & Francis, Editor Paul Dukes was also an enthusiastic advocate for the volume, and I'd like to thank him for his patience as some chapters came in later (or much later!) than anticipated. Finally, I'd like to thank editorial assistant Lee Transue and everyone else at Taylor & Francis for helping to get the book into production. I hope you find this volume interesting, fascinating, useful, and invaluable in your own journey to learn more about prejudice and stereotyping.

Todd D. Nelson
November 2008

REFERENCES

Allport, G. W. (1954). *The nature of prejudice.* Reading, MA: Addison-Wesley.

Dovidio, J.F., & Gaertner, S. L. (1986). *Prejudice, discrimination, and racism.* New York: Academic Press.

Mackie, D. M., & Hamilton, D. L. (Eds.), (2003). *Affect, cognition, and stereotyping: Interactive processes in group perception.* New York: Academic Press.

Contributors

David M. Amodio
New York University

Joshua Aronson
New York University

Monica Biernat
University of Kansas

Brittany Bloodhart
Pennsylvania State University

Galen V. Bodenhausen
Northwestern University

Thomas R. Cain
Rutgers University – New Brunswick campus

Christian S. Crandall
University of Kansas

Jarret T. Crawford
Rutgers University – New Brunswick campus

Florette Cohen
Rutgers University – New Brunswick campus

Jennifer Crocker
University of Michigan

Sara A. Crump
University of California, Santa Barbara

Nilanjana Dasgupta
University of Massachusetts

Patricia G. Devine
University of Wisconsin – Madison

John F. Dovidio
Yale University

Susan T. Fiske
Princeton University

Samuel L. Gaertner
University of Delaware

Julie A. Garcia
Stanford University

Sarah J. Gervais
Pennsylvania State University

Jeff Greenberg
University of Arizona

David L. Hamilton
University of California, Santa Barbara

Kent Harber
Rutgers University – Newark campus

Lasana T. Harris
Princeton University

Michelle Hebl
Rice University

Larisa Heiphetz
Pennsylvania State University

Gregory M. Herek
University of California – Davis

Julie Milligan Hughes
University of Texas at Austin

Lauri L. Hyers
West Chester University

Tiffany A. Ito
University of Colorado

Lee Jussim
Rutgers University – New Brunswick campus

Spee Kosloff
University of Arizona

Jennifer T. Kubota
University of Colorado

Mark Landau
University of Kansas

Tiane L. Lee
Princeton University

Sheri R. Levy
State University of New York – Stony Brook

Matthew D. Lieberman
University of California – Los Angeles

Diane M. Mackie
University of California – Santa Barbara

Angela T. Maitner
University of California – Santa Barbara

Brenda Major
University of California, Santa Barbara

Aimee Y. Mark
University of Southern Indiana

Matthew S. McGlone
University of Texas, Austin

Margo J. Monteith
Purdue University

Kimberly Rios Morrison
Ohio State University

Todd D. Nelson
California State University – Stanislaus

Angela Nierman
University of Kansas

Michael A. Olson
University of Tennessee

Jennifer A. Richeson
Northwestern University

Ann Marie Russell
Princeton University

Pamela J. Sawyer
University of California, Santa Barbara

Lindsay B. Sharp
University of Wisconsin – Madison

Steven J. Sherman
Indiana University

Eliot R. Smith
Indiana University

Sheldon Solomon
Skidmore College

Julie Spencer-Rodgers
University of Victoria

Charles Stangor
University of Maryland

Walter G. Stephan
University of Hawaii

Janet K. Swim
Pennsylvania State University

Andrew R. Todd
Northwestern University

Theresa K. Vescio
Pennsylvania State University

Oscar Ybarra
University of Michigan

Michael A. Zárate
University of Texas – El Paso

1 The Study of Stereotyping, Prejudice, and Discrimination Within Social Psychology

A Quick History of Theory and Research

Charles Stangor
University of Maryland

The history of the empirical study of stereotyping, prejudice, and discrimination is a young one, but nevertheless one that is rich, exciting, and potentially useful in informing public policy. It is a history that has happened incredibly fast—indeed it is a great pleasure for me to personally know pretty much everyone who has helped to create the excellent research that I try to summarize in this chapter. This literature has been developed and presented in the myriad journal articles that we have published on these topics, and summarized in a substantial number of comprehensive reviews (Brewer & Brown, 1998; Crocker, Major, & Steele, 1998; Fiske, 1998; Hamilton & Sherman, 1994; Mackie & Smith, 1998; Major & O'Brien, 2005; Major, Quinton, & McCoy, 2003; Messick & Mackie, 1989; Nelson, 2002; Stangor & Lange, 1994; Wilder, 1986), as well as innumerable edited books. This work has also been improved and refined through the many enjoyable conferences that we have shared together.

We should be extremely proud of the accomplishments that we have made in this field. When we began our enterprise, less than 100 years ago, it was not clear how stereotypes and prejudice should be conceptually considered, or that they could be effectively operationalized. In less than a century we have created a generally accepted conceptualization of these important ideas, which we routinely assess using sophisticated implicit reaction time measures and brain imaging techniques, in addition to our standard repertoire of behavior and self-report. We understand, at least to some extent, the sources of these beliefs and attitudes, and we have made some progress in understanding how to effectively change them. Most important, we have developed a substantial understanding of the influence of stereotypes and prejudice—as social expectations—on behavior. This represents a major conceptual advance in only a short period of time.

Our research has also been widely incorporated into other fields, including clinical, developmental, educational, legal, and organizational psychology. This suggests that the results of our endeavors are important and useful. On the other hand, we have had a tendency to focus on the easy problems and ignore the more difficult ones. Despite some important exceptions, we have tended to work in our labs rather than hitting the field, we study college students who by and large are not prejudiced, and we refrain from making many public statements about the implications of our research. These limitations have probably prevented us from advancing as quickly or effecting as much social change as we might like. I think we should try to do more in this regard.

I hope you will enjoy my review, and will not be offended where I have included my own unique, and potentially debatable, interpretations of some of these topics. Let me be the first to acknowledge,

1

however, that in many ways there is little point in either reading or writing it. The chapter represents, in essence, an abridged version of what to me is the *real* history of the social psychology of stereotyping and prejudice, which is David Schneider's (2004) amazing book, *The Psychology of Stereotyping*. In all honesty, you don't have time to read my chapter—you should take the time instead to read the real story—from Professor Schneider.

DEFINING STEREOTYPES AND PREJUDICE

The definitions that we find most consensual regarding stereotyping and prejudice have changed over time as the field itself has changed. Most important, our definitions have generally simplified with the years. We now define prejudice as a negative attitude toward a group or toward members of the group. Defining stereotyping has been more problematic—there are tens, if not hundreds of definitions in the literature, although they are mostly based on the general idea of stereotypes as knowledge structures that serve as mental "pictures" of the groups in question (Lippmann, 1922). With some exceptions, I'd say that we generally agree that stereotypes represent the traits that we view as characteristic of social groups, or of individual members of those groups, and particularly those that differentiate groups from each other. In short, they are the traits that come to mind quickly when we think about the groups.

The tendency to simplify things has led us to discard some of the presumed characteristics of stereotypes and prejudice that were integral to early conceptualizations, such as those of Allport (1954), including *inaccuracy, negativity,* and *overgeneralization.* It is unfortunate that we have let those original requirements go—after all, they really are the heart of why we care about the topic at all. Our concepts should be simple, but also not so simple that they lose their essence. Stereotypes are problematic because they are negative, inaccurate, and unfair—they would simply be part of the study of person perception more broadly if they weren't.

In terms of negativity, the data are clear, and we probably should acknowledge it more fully, as we generally do regarding prejudice. Although they can be positive, stereotypes are primarily negative. We generate many more negative than positive stereotypes when asked to do so, and even expressing positive stereotypes is not seen positively. Consider how we might react to people who have claimed that African Americans have the positive traits of being athletic and musical. The problem, in part, is that if we express positive stereotypes, it is assumed that we hold the negative ones, too.

It is more difficult to get a good handle on the accuracy question. Although some have tried (Judd, Ryan, & Park, 1991; Lee, Jussim, & McCauley, 1995; McCauley, Stitt, & Segal, 1980; Ryan, Park, & Judd, 1996), the conclusions they have drawn have not been consistent. Suffice it to say that there is a good kernel of truth to most group beliefs—there is a correlation between perception and reality (Swim, 1994). Whether stereotypes are in general over- or underestimated is not so clear. In any case, it is the process of using stereotypes (overgeneralization), more than holding them, that is problematic, because it is so unfair (Fiske, 1989; Stangor, 1995). No matter how accurate our belief is, it does not describe every member of the group—therefore, basing judgments of individuals on category level knowledge is just plain wrong. The idea that categorization is less fair than individuation is a major contribution of this literature, and one that I think has also made some difference outside of the field.

Over the years, the participants that we use in our studies have become much less willing to admit that they are prejudiced or hold stereotypes, perhaps in part because their beliefs have in fact changed (Devine & Elliot, 1995; Gaertner & McLaughlin, 1983a). This creates some conceptual issues, most notably in terms of measurement, as I discuss later. Another outcome of this change, however, is that we really rarely see prejudice in the populations that we tend to study. The evaluations of most outgroups are overall positive—at least above a neutral point (Brewer, 1999; Brewer & Silver, 1978). This creates a conceptual question regarding whether positive evaluations of outgroups (evaluations that are nevertheless more negative than evaluations of ingroups) represent prejudice: Is ingroup favoritism really a problem if it is not accompanied by outgroup derogation? There may not be a good answer to the question, but it must make us wonder if we are really studying prejudice (the "negative evaluation of members of outgroups") at all. In any case it is clear that we must compare attitudes toward outgroups to those of relevant ingroups, and that these two sets of attitudes may be quite independent (Brewer, 1999; Brewer & Silver, 1978).

Group attitudes and beliefs are, of course, in large part about cognition, and this has remained, as far back as Lippmann (1922) and D. Katz and Braly (1933), the focus of our approach. Most fundamental is social categorization—a natural process that occurs spontaneously in our everyday perception (Macrae, Bodenhausen, Milne, Thorn, & Castelli, 1997; Taylor, Fiske, Etcoff, & Ruderman, 1978). Stereotypes, the traits associated with social categories, represent an important form of social knowledge, and we have learned, through an extensive line of research, much about how they are mentally represented. Most generally, stereotypes exist as cognitive structures, such as schemas (Augoustinos & Innes, 1990; Fiske & Linville, 1980; Martin & Halverson, 1981; Woll & Graesser, 1982), prototypes (Brewer, Dull, & Lui, 1981), and exemplars (Bodenhausen, Schwarz, Bless, & Wanke, 1995; Smith & Zárate, 1992). This does not mean that these beliefs are rigid; they are not— they change fluidly across social context (Oakes, Haslam, & Turner, 1994; Smith et al., 1992; Smith & Zárate, 1990). The study of stereotypes has informed person perception more broadly, just as the study of person perception has informed our understanding of stereotypes.

Other conceptualizations of stereotypes, although not as common, are potentially useful. For instance, we can also think about group beliefs in terms of their variability, in addition to their means (Linville, Salovey, & Fischer, 1986; Ostrom & Sedikides, 1992; B. Park, Judd, & Ryan, 1991). This seems important, and it would be good to more regularly measure this dimension of group perception. We may more frequently change stereotypes by changing perceived variability than by changing perceived means. Group beliefs can be conceptualized as theories about the world of social groups and group relations—our beliefs about the essence of social groups (Rothbart & Taylor, 1992; Yzerbyt, Schadron, Leyens, & Rocher, 1994). Theories about responsibility, for instance, explain why negative attitudes are stronger for people who we see as responsible for their negative characteristics (Crandall & Biernat, 1990).

We have focused primarily on process, but there has been some work on content (Maner et al., 2005). Fiske and her colleagues (Fiske, Cuddy, Glick, & Xu, 2002) have attempted to categorize the fundamental components of stereotypes, focusing on the dimensions of warmth and competence. These two dimensions are basic to social psychology (Osgood, Suci, & Tannenbaum, 1957), and capture a good proportion of the variance in perceived stereotypes. Attempting to develop models of the content of our group beliefs, in addition to our focus on process, is an important goal that we need to spend more time on.

Categorization is driven by desires for simplicity (Ford & Stangor, 1992; Macrae, Hewstone, & Griffiths, 1993; Macrae, Milne, & Bodenhausen, 1994; Tajfel, 1981; Tajfel & Wilkes, 1963). We desire, as much as possible, to differentiate individuals from different categories from each other, and to view individuals within categories as maximally similar. These desires can distort perceptions and create biases even in minimal settings, and these distortions are particularly powerful when the categorization dimension involves differentiating ingroup from outgroup members, under concerns of maintaining one's social identity in the presence of competing groups (Brewer & Campbell, 1976; Fein & Spencer, 1997; A. Haslam, Oakes, Reynolds, & Turner, 1999; S. Haslam et al., 1998; Mummendey, 1995). Indeed social identity is a—perhaps *the*—fundamental underlying motivation behind prejudice and discrimination, although the results of this vast literature are complex, often conflicting, and difficult to simply summarize (Abrams & Hogg, 1990; Deaux, Reid, Mizrahi, & Ethier, 1995; Ellemers, Spears, & Doosje, 1999; Jackson & Smith, 1999; Roccas & Brewer, 2002).

Categorization also involves the self—the principle of *self-categorization* (Hogg & McGarty, 1990; Turner, 1987; Turner, Oakes, Haslam, & McGarty, 1994; Turner & Oakes, 1989). Self-categorization concerns the ways in which the individual perceives his or her interactions with other people. We may sometimes act as individuals, but at other times we may act more as a representative of a social group. The dynamic between perceiving and interacting as individuals versus group members is fundamental, and has contributed broadly to our understanding of group relations.

In addition to their cognitive components, our attitudes are based in large part on our emotional responses to social groups (Bodenhausen, Kramer, & Sasser, 1994; Fiske, 1982; Mackie, Devos, & Smith, 2000; Mackie & Hamilton, 1993). Affect predicts attitudes as well or better than does cognition (Stangor, Sullivan, & Ford, 1991), can influence categorization (Dovidio, Gaertner, Isen, & Lowrance, 1995), and indeed has a variety of effects on stereotyping and prejudice, depending in part on the particular affect (Bodenhausen, Gabriel, & Lineberger, 2000; Bodenhausen et al., 1994; J. Park & Banaji, 2000). The relationship between stereotypes (cognition) and prejudice (affect) is not always strong, but is reliable (Dovidio, Brigham, Johnson, & Gaertner, 1996). This is reasonable, because affect and cognition represent different components of the same underlying attitudes, and because stereotypes are in part rationalizations for our prejudices (Jost & Major, 2001; Sinclair & Kunda, 2000).

Although we know that emotion matters, probably more than cognition, we have focused to a large extent on the latter, perhaps in part because our samples are generally made up of college students who are highly cognitively focused (Sears, 1986), and for whom cognition probably explains a relatively large part of their social judgment and behavior. And, of course, we have taken most of our paradigms from cognitive psychology. More important, perhaps, is the difficulty of measuring emotion. People do experience emotions when we respond to and interact with social group members, but they have more trouble expressing them on self-report measures. Our arsenal of measurement techniques is poor, in comparison to those for assessing cognition. Indeed, it is probably not wrong to say that at this point we have no measures of emotion other than self-report. The ability to pinpoint emotion-related brain activity through newly developed social neuroscience techniques will likely help us in this regard (Olsson & Phelps, 2007).

We can think of group beliefs at both the individual ("I believe. . . .") as well as at the social ("We believe. . . .") level (Stangor & Schaller, 1996). We have tended to focus on the former, because this is in general what we all do, although we also acknowledge that the latter is fundamental. Indeed, if there is not general agreement within our participant populations about which beliefs are associated with which social groups (who is good or bad; who has which traits), then our studies, even though they are individual in orientation, won't work. On some measures it is difficult to determine whether we are measuring personal or collective beliefs (Karpinski & Hilton, 2001).

There have been some important attempts to focus on the social side of prejudice, particularly by studying how individuals communicate their stereotypes and prejudices, and the effects of communication on beliefs (Kashima, 2000; Lyons & Kashima, 2003; Ruscher, 1998, 2001; Schaller, Conway, & Tanchuk, 2002). Perhaps most impressive is the work by Crandall (Crandall & Stangor, 2005) showing how strongly group beliefs correlate with perceived social norms. This work suggests that, most fundamentally, stereotypes and prejudice are social norms. This is an old idea (Pettigrew, 1959) , and one that perhaps isn't that sexy in today's context—but it is in fact the most important way we think about social stereotypes. In short, people hold and express stereotypes and prejudice to the extent that they see it as appropriate, within their social contexts, to do so.

It is my feeling, taking it all together, that we need to focus more on prejudice and stereotypes as social rather than individual constructions. Stereotypes represent our relationships with our groups and our cultures—with those we know and care about. This was the initial argument of the original stereotype researchers—D. Katz and Braly and Allport, for instance. In short, we are prejudiced because we feel that others that we care about are, too—that it is okay to be so. Similarly, we are tolerant when we feel that being so is socially acceptable. Conceptualizing stereotypes and prejudice within their social and cultural context is essential, and we frequently do not.

MEASUREMENT

We can measure stereotypes in many ways, both self-report and behavioral. These measures may be more or less reactive. Our major approach has been self-report, including thought listings (Stangor et al., 1991), trait check-offs (D. Katz & Braly, 1933), probability judgments (McCauley & Stitt, 1978), and, of course, Likert scales. These measures are reliable and generally predictive of discrimination—they are the best measures we have, in my opinion. We need to be careful in our interpretation of these measures, however, because no social group is ever evaluated out of its social context. Variations in subjective perceptions of scale meanings and of the implied reference groups may distort group judgments (Biernat & Fuegen, 2001; Biernat & Vescio, 2002; Collins, Crandall, & Biernat, 2006).

Nonreactive, indirect, or unobtrusive (Crosby, Bromley, & Saxe, 1980) behavioral measures such as seating distance (Macrae et al., 1994) and "implicit" reaction time measures (Banaji & Hardin, 1996; Cunningham, Preacher, & Banaji, 2001; Dasgupta, McGhee, Greenwald, & Banaji, 2000; Devine, 1989; Dovidio, Evans, & Tyler, 1986; Gaertner & McLaughlin, 1983b; Payne, Cheng, Govorun, & Stewart, 2005; Perdue, Dovidio, Gurtman, & Tyler, 1990; Rudman, Greenwald, Mellott, & Schwartz, 1999) have also been prevalent, although until recently less popular overall because they are more difficult to collect. Physiological and neurological measures of prejudice are also available (Cooper, 1956; Ito, 2006; Mendes, 2002; Phelps, 2000).

We have tended to measure using whatever technology is most current. When Likert scales were first developed, they were used to good stead. When physiological measures were created, we started to use them (Cooper & Singer, 1956). When we got PCs in our labs, reaction time measures predominated (Banaji & Hardin, 1996; Devine, 1989; Dovidio et al., 1986). Now, as functional magnetic resonance imaging (fMRI) magnets get cheaper they will naturally become more popular, and we will be able to view stereotypes and prejudice in the brain.

A limitation of these changes is that it is not always clear that newer measures tell us much more about the core social constructs of stereotyping and prejudice than older measures do. The street has run in large part one way—we adapt the measures that others have developed, but do not provide much in return. It seems to me that any of these many measurement techniques will likely predict behavior, but it is not clear that any one predicts any better than any other. In short, creating new measurement techniques has not always produced much insight into the underlying processes of interest.

The really social aspect of the measurement issue involves the presumed contaminating role of self-presentation. It is bad to hold and to express prejudice, and the assumption is that indirect measures therefore represent more valid responses. This general belief has been historically prevalent, beginning perhaps with the "bogus pipeline" (Sigall & Page, 1971), and has guided the development of unobtrusive measures of all sorts, and more recently the implicit approach to measurement. Indeed, some of our most important theories about racism and sexism have been based on the idea that we are more prejudiced than we care to show ourselves or others (Crandall & Eshleman, 2003; Gaertner & Dovidio, 1981, 1986; Monteith, Deneen, & Tooman, 1996; Zuwerink, Devine, Monteith, & Cook, 1996), and that we express those prejudices more when they can be covered up by other external excuses (Gaertner & Dovidio, 1977).

We have developed a number of nonobvious sexism and racism measures to try to assess beliefs among the "well-intentioned" (Gaertner & Dovidio, 1981). These measures include aversive, ambivalent, modern, and symbolic racism and sexism (Gaertner & Dovidio, 1986; Glick & Fiske, 1996; McConahay, 1986; Pettigrew, 1998b; Sears & Henry, 2005; Swim, Aikin, Hall, & Hunter, 1995). In large part these measures have been developed as a result of our focus on those who are not really prejudiced, and who live in a climate of political correctness. If we were to study the really bigoted, then perhaps we would feel more comfortable using more direct measures. More important, these ideas are important because they allow us to learn something about the content of prejudice—that prejudice is in fact multifaceted and takes on different forms for different groups.

We are not uniquely negative to outgroups, and in some cases quite the opposite; in short, simple liking–disliking measures are not always sufficient to really capture the full meaning of prejudice.

Yet other researchers seem to not have worried about the self-presentation issue so much, going instead for direct questioning regarding the underlying constructs. For instance, a popular and highly predictive measure of prejudice (I believe it is the best overall measure of prejudice that we have) is social dominance orientation (Sidanius & Pratto, 1999)—a measure that directly asks about group differences. Similarly, Devine and her colleagues ask their participants how hard they try to avoid being prejudiced—again a direct and useful measure that creates variability and predictive power (Plant & Devine, 1998).

What can we conclude in this regard? My reading of the literature leads me to think that we do not need to worry so much about being indirect. Yes, indirect measures can be useful—but implicit measures are no "truer" than are explicit measures. To be really useful, indirect or unobtrusive measures must either predict the same outcome measure above and beyond direct measures, they must predict different outcome measures, or they must otherwise differentiate attitude components. Some research has demonstrated these properties (Dovidio, Kawakami, Johnson, Johnson, & Howard, 1997; Gregg, Seibt, & Banaji, 2006) but by and large we have not addressed these issues. The approach is generally to correlate implicit and explicit measures (Brauer, Wasel, & Niedenthal, 2000; Karpinski & Hilton, 2001; Nosek, 2005), perhaps looking at the moderators of the relationship, without much concern for how these measures differentially predict the important outcome variables. This is not to argue that implicit measures are irrelevant or unimportant—they may be, but they also have limitations (Arkes & Tetlock, 2004). In many cases implicit and explicit measures show similar effects. Consider, for instance, the large-scale Web-based research of Nosek and his colleagues (Nosek et al., 2007), who find, across millions of participants, shockingly similar results on implicit and explicit measures.

My gut feeling is that explicit measures (or perhaps implicit measures that are truly social) are going to take us farther in the long term. Because prejudice and discrimination are highly influenced by social norms, and perhaps especially by the proscriptive ones, the relationship between attitude and action will be higher for measures that are indeed influenced themselves by these norms—and these are generally the explicit ones. We want people, when they express prejudice, to do it *within* a social context. People may lie on direct measures such as social dominance orientation just as they lie on any other self-report measure (consider the Rosenberg self-esteem scale, hugely influenced by self-promotion, and yet highly valid). In these cases we expect that self-promotion represents an overall main effect that does not interact with the predictive correlations. The distribution of scores, although inflated, is nevertheless predictive of the outcomes that we care about. In any case, no matter what measures we use, we need to validate them on broader populations than we generally use (Biernat & Crandall, 1999).

PREDICTING PREJUDICE: THE PREJUDICED PERSONALITY

A small cottage industry has developed around the goal of discovering the individual difference variables that predict prejudice. This interest has come in large part out of Allport's and others' claims about the "prejudiced personality," and has continued to expand with new measures virtually every year. Individual difference variables that are known to predict prejudice include social dominance orientation (Sidanius & Pratto, 1999), the authoritarian personality (Adorno, Frenkel-Brunswik, Levinson, & Sanford, 1950; Altemeyer, 1981, 1988; Backstrom & Bjorklund, 2007), need for closure or structure (Jost, Glaser, Kruglanski, & Sulloway, 2003; Schaller, Boyd, Yohannes, & O'Brien, 1995; Shah, Kruglanski, & Thompson, 1998), internal and external motivations to control prejudice (Plant & Devine, 1998), humanism and the Protestant work ethic (I. Katz & Hass, 1988), egalitarianism (Moskowitz, Wasel, Schaal, & Gollwitzer, 1999), implicit attributional theories (Chiu, Dweck, Tong, & Fu, 1997; Plaks, Stroessner, Dweck, & Sherman, 2001), and religious fundamentalism (Rowatt et al., 2006).

This approach seems informative—we can learn about the fundamental motives of prejudice by understanding the personality variables that relate to it—indeed, our beliefs about social groups represent an essential part of our underlying political and social value orientations (Biernat, Vescio, & Theno, 1996; Biernat, Vescio, Theno, & Crandall, 1996; Jost et al., 2003; Schwartz, 1992). I think we have been better off when we think broadly about the topic, and that we can do more in this regard. The many individual difference measures naturally factor into fewer dimensions, and understanding these dimensions can help us get to the core of prejudice. Perhaps the best progress in this regard has been made by Altemeyer and his colleagues (Altemeyer, 1981, 1988), who find that attitudes toward outgroups are determined in large part by two personality dimensions, indexed broadly by authoritarianism and social dominance orientation. Stangor and Leary (2006) found similar results—the various personality variables that we studied factored into an egalitarianism and a traditionalism dimension, and egalitarianism uniquely predicted attitudes toward outgroups, whereas traditionalism uniquely predicted attitudes toward ingroups. It will be important to continue to link our conceptualizations of intergroup attitudes to fundamental human motives, and I think there will be excellent payoffs here.

WHY STEREOTYPES AND PREJUDICE MATTER

The direct social and health impact of prejudice and discrimination on members of minority ethnic groups has been extensively studied, although not particularly by social psychologists. Discrimination has been blamed for the large percentage of Blacks living in poverty, and their lack of access to high-paying jobs (Williams & Rucker, 2000; Williams & Williams-Morris, 2000). Discrimination also has negative effects on the physical and mental health of those who experience it. African Americans have elevated mortality rates for virtually all of the leading causes of death in the United States (Williams, 1999). Racial minorities have less access to and receive poorer quality health care than Whites, even controlling for other variables such as level of health insurance status (Williams, 1999; Williams & Rucker, 2000). Blacks are less likely to receive major therapeutic procedures for many conditions and often do not receive necessary treatments, have delayed diagnoses, or fail to manage chronic diseases (Bach, Cramer, Warren, & Begg, 1999).

Existing research also suggests that discrimination may have negative effects on the mental health of its victims. Stigmatized individuals who report experiencing frequent exposure to discrimination or other forms of unfair treatment also report more psychological distress, depression, and lower levels of life satisfaction and happiness (N. Anderson & Armstead, 1995; Corning, 2002; Glauser, 1999; Kessler, Mickelson, & Williams, 1999; Klonoff, Landrine, & Ullman, 1999; Landrine & Klonoff, 1996; Schultz et al., 2000; Swim, Hyers, Cohen, & Ferguson, 2001; Williams, Spencer, & Jackson, 1999; Williams & Williams-Morris, 2000). Social psychologists should take better note of these health-related findings, because this is a domain where we can put our expertise to important use (Ottati, Bodenhausen, & Newman, 2005).

In addition to their effects on mental and physical health, there are a variety of other potential outcomes of perceiving or misperceiving discrimination. There are substantial effects of discrimination on job hiring and performance evaluations (Glick, Zion, & Nelson, 1988; Riach & Rich, 2004). Members of minority groups feel rejected when they experience discrimination (Schmitt, Branscombe, Kobrynowicz, & Owen, 2002). Individuals who believe that they are the victims of discrimination may begin to avoid or distrust members of the relevant social category—a sense of "cultural mistrust" (Terrell, Terrell, & Miller, 1993; Watkins, Terrell, Miller, & Terrell, 1989). In some cases this avoidance may be adaptive and appropriate, but in other cases it may cause individuals to overestimate the extent of discrimination directed at them, leading them to see prejudice as inevitable (Pinel, 2002). The perceived possibility that perceivers are acting on their stereotypes and prejudice tends to poison social interactions (Crocker & Major, 1989; Crocker, Voelkl, Testa, & Major, 1991). Thus prejudice and stereotyping create a variety of stressors for their victims (Inzlicht, McKay, & Aronson, 2006).

Self-expectations matter—just thinking about our own social category memberships, which naturally activates the stereotypes associated with the categories, can create self-fulfilling prophecies that influence behavior (Aronson, Lustina, Good, Keough, & Steele, 1999; Cadinu, Maass, Frigerio, Impagliazzo, & Latinotti, 2003; Sekaquaptewa & Thompson, 2003; Steele & Aronson, 1995). It appears that we do not need to accept the negative connotations of a self-stereotype for it to matter—just making stereotypes accessible, salient, and self-relevant is sufficient to influence behavior. Although these effects seem relatively strong in laboratory settings, creating both positive outcomes (stereotype lift; Walton & Cohen, 2003) as well as negative outcomes (stereotype threat), there is less evidence that they matter that much in real life. Although we have again been reluctant to really look outside the lab to see how these things are really playing out, some of the research in this regard suggests that stereotype threat effects may be weaker in the field than in the lab (Stricker & Bejar, 2004; Stricker & Ward, 2004).

A particularly important aspect of this phenomenon, and one that helps explain the maintenance of status differences within cultures, is that individuals from stigmatized groups may also internalize and accept the negative beliefs associated with their groups (Jost, Banaji, & Nosek, 2004; Jost & Hunyady, 2005). As a consequence it becomes very difficult to overcome them. Lines of research such as this one by Jost and his colleagues, which integrate social, cultural, and political psychology, are among the most important ones for us to pursue.

Although it can be and usually is, being the target of discrimination is not always negative. For one, the stigmatized may at least in some cases completely miss that they are victims (Stangor et al., 2003). Although this of course makes it difficult to confront the discrimination, it does protect the self. Believing that one has been the victim of discrimination can increase identification with the ingroup, which can have positive outcomes (Branscombe, Schmitt, & Harvey, 1999; Schmitt, Spears, & Branscombe, 2003). Believing that one is a victim can also provide a method of buffering self-worth (Major, Kaiser, & McCoy, 2003). Individuals with more positive outcomes and higher group identity are less affected by stereotyping and prejudice (Kaiser, Major, & McCoy, 2004; Major, Kaiser, et al., 2003).

ETIOLOGY

Where do our stereotypes and prejudices come from? They are, of course, developed as all cognitive representations are developed, and we have a good idea of the cognitive process involved in this regard (Bigler, 1995; Bigler & Liben, 1992). Children have an active and seemingly innate interest in learning about social categories and stereotypes, and in understanding how to fit themselves into this categorization system (Ruble & Martin, 1998; Stangor & Ruble, 1989). As a result children learn stereotypes very early and become confident in them, such that they are initially highly resistant to change. Children soften their beliefs and become more flexible after age 10 or so (Bigler & Liben, 1992; Signorella, Bigler, & Liben, 1993).

But what about the content? Most likely this knowledge comes from our parents, from our peers, and from the media. Again, we have not been particularly interested in the issues of content, and the evidence about its development remains ambiguous. Frances Aboud, the world's expert on stereotype development, argues that there is virtually no relationship between the racial attitudes of children and their parents (Aboud, 1988; Aboud & Amato, 2001). Other data suggest at least some correlation (Stangor & Leary, 2006). We really need to know more about the influence of parents on children in this regard, and it is disappointing that the question has not been pursued. Indeed, it would seem important to do the studies that could really tell us—in comparison to other beliefs—the extent to which stereotypes and prejudice come from nature and from nurture. We don't know if parents can have any influence at all on their children's stereotypes, and some theoretical approaches suggest that they cannot (Harris, 2002). One important approach would be to do the relevant twin studies (e.g., Olson, Vernon, Harris, & Jang, 2001).

Perhaps prejudice is primarily evolutionary—we like those who we see as similar and thus more likely to be helpful and benign, stigmatizing and avoiding those who appear to be poor partners for social exchange, who may be likely to be diseased, or who threaten important group values (Collins et al., 2006; Maner et al., 2005). This seems possible, at least for the social groups that have an evolutionary history of difference and conflict. That we perceive people differently in the dark rather than in the light seems consistent with the idea (Schaller, Park, & Mueller, 2003).

Of course we also must learn our intergroup beliefs from the media. Film, television, and the Web not only create the relevant stereotypes, but more important, they provide us with the relevant social norms—who we can and cannot like (Ruscher, 2001). Gays were the most recent bastions in this normative progression, now being accepted by many as part of mainstream media. We have not really focused on the media, in part because the relevant questions are more content than process, but doing so is critical; we should conduct the appropriate longitudinal panel studies to assess the role of the media on group beliefs, as we have done to assess the role of viewing violent media on aggression (e.g., C. A. Anderson et al., 2003).

Some group beliefs are the result of purely random factors—fortunate happenstance for some and unfortunate happenstance for others. One possible example of this is the data-based illusory correlation, which suggests that—because minority information and negative information are both highly salient—minority members will be disliked just for being minorities. This idea spawned a generation of research (Hamilton, 1981; Hamilton & Rose, 1980; McGarty, Haslam, Turner, & Oakes, 1993; Mullen & Johnson, 1990; Schaller & Maass, 1989), but again it was a program that never left the lab. We have no idea whether any real stereotypes or real prejudices form as the result of illusory correlations.

Stereotypes also stem from the existing distributions of the roles played by social category members, for instance men and women (Eagly & Kite, 1987; Eagly & Mladinic, 1989; Eagly & Steffen, 1984). This idea is also consistent with the fact that stereotypes change as a result of changes in social context (Devine & Elliot, 1995). In many cases, however, the roles are determined by the stereotypes, too—so our expectations come from our perceptions of existing social conditions, but the expectations may also create these conditions.

INFLUENCE: USING STEREOTYPES AND PREJUDICE

Stereotypes matter because they are part and parcel of our everyday life—they influence our judgments and behavior toward individuals, often entirely out of our awareness (Bargh, Chen, & Burrows, 1996; Dijksterhuis, Aarts, Bargh, & van Knippenberg, 2000; Wheeler & Petty, 2001). They become part of our everyday language (Maass & Arcuri, 1996; Maass, Salvi, Arcuri, & Semin, 1989). These behaviors create self-fulfilling prophecies that bring out the stereotypes in their targets (Chen & Bargh, 1999; Word, Zanna, & Cooper, 1974). They are the cognitive "monsters" that poison many of our social interactions (Bargh, 1999).

One of the important, and perhaps discouraging, discoveries is the extent to which social categorization and the accompanying activation of stereotypic material occurs quickly when we first see another person, and without any real intention or awareness on the part of the person who is doing the categorizing. This quick spontaneous or automatic categorization (Banaji & Hardin, 1996; Uleman & Bargh, 1989) suggests that these activated stereotypes may be applied to judgments of others, and certainly this can happen. We tend to use our categories more when we are fatigued, distracted, or ego-depleted (Bodenhausen & Macrae, 1998; Govorun & Payne, 2006; Kruglanski & Freund, 1983), when the going gets tough (Stangor & Duan, 1991), or when we are little motivated to do more (Fiske & Neuberg, 1990; Neuberg & Fiske, 1987). Thus using our stereotypes to size up another person might simply make our life easier (Allport, 1954; Fiske & Taylor, 1991; Macrae et al., 1993; Macrae et al., 1994; Tajfel & Forgas, 1981; van Knippenberg & van Knippenberg, 1994).

We are particularly likely to categorize people who we do not know very well or do not care about. In short, we may use our stereotypes almost exclusively when the category is all the information we have about someone (Brodt & Ross, 1998), or if we are not particularly interested in getting to know the person better. In other cases when we know the individual well (for instance, as classroom teachers know their students), we may ignore people's group memberships almost completely, responding to them entirely at the individual level (Madon et al., 1998).

Even when responding to people we do not know well, we can and do get beyond initial activation to control our responses to others. This takes work, but is the right thing to do (Fiske, 1989). Just as we hold and express stereotypes that are normatively appropriate, we tend to use stereotypes when we think it is acceptable to do so—for instance when we think we have some valid knowledge about the group in question (Yzerbyt et al., 1994).

We are also more likely to categorize people using categories that are perceptually salient. As a result, categorization occurs frequently on the basis of people's sex, race, age, and physical attractiveness, in part because these features are immediately physically apparent to us when we see other people (Brewer, 1988). Categories also become particularly salient when individuals are in the context of members of other, different, categories—that is, when they are solos or when they are in the minority (Cota & Dion, 1986; Kanter, 1977; Oakes, Turner, & Haslam, 1991; Taylor, 1981; Taylor & Crocker, 1981).

Social categories, like any other knowledge structure, can be more or less cognitively accessible, and thus more or less used in information processing (Stangor, 1988). For instance, members of minority groups might find ethnicity to be a more important category than members of majority groups, and, because it is highly accessible, these individuals might be particularly likely to think about others in terms of their ethnicity. Similarly, highly prejudiced people may also be particularly likely to categorize by race (Stangor, Lynch, Duan, & Glass, 1992), and women who are active in the feminist movement might be particularly likely to think about people in terms of gender (Bem, 1981; Pinel, 1999).

REDUCING STEREOTYPING AND PREJUDICE

Perhaps the most important contributions that social psychologists have made involve the potential for improving intergroup relations. This is an important, but also very difficult topic, and one that has been cracked in large part on the theoretical and not the applied level. We have developed excellent models to work from, but know little about how to implement programs that will make a real difference. The recent focus on cognition, conducted primarily in controlled lab studies, has moved us away in large part from the original empirical approaches that defined the domain of inquiry. It was the historically earlier field studies—generally intensive in orientation and scope (Cook, 1978, 1984; Sherif & Sherif, 1953)—that still allow us to make our most important statements regarding stereotype and prejudice change, and that still form the foundations of our textbooks. Since then, our approaches have been more limited in scope—although there have been some exceptions to this rule (e.g., Aronson, Blaney, Stephan, Sikes, & Snapp, 1978).

One thing that is clear is that we are not going to stop categorization entirely. Forcing a color-blind perspective is not that useful, and can even be harmful (Schofield, 1986; Wolsko, Park, Judd, & Wittenbrink, 2000). People have a natural tendency to categorize, and this is not likely to go away soon. Given this inherent limitation, it seems therefore that there are three ways in which we might proceed.

First, we can attempt to change the beliefs themselves. This is perhaps the most common approach, but perhaps also the most difficult. The problem is one of inertia—expectancies tend to support themselves in virtually every possible way. As a result, providing the stereotype holder with stereotype-inconsistent information generally tends to be ineffective because the conflicting knowledge is ignored (Trope & Thompson, 1997), distorted (Darley & Gross, 1983), forgotten (Fyock & Stangor, 1994; Stangor & McMillan, 1992), attributed away (Hewstone, 1990; Swim & Sanna, 1996), or if it has influence, that influence is very limited (Rothbart & John, 1992; Weber & Crocker, 1983). An alternative approach, and one that deserves more attention, is to attempt to change the perceived variability of groups such that the perceiver sees that the stereotypes, although perhaps true, are far from true for every group member and thus not that diagnostic.

Positive intergroup contact can change beliefs (Cook, 1978; Desforges et al., 1991; Pettigrew, 1998a; Pettigrew & Tropp, 2006; Wright, Aron, McLaughlin-Volpe, & Ropp, 1997), but this approach has substantial problems. For one, contact is not always positive; indeed situations that provide opportunities for positive attitude change are limited—bad situations make things worse (Stangor, Jonas, Stroebe, & Hewstone, 1996)—and the conditions that create good situations are very difficult to achieve (Hewstone, 1996; Hewstone & Brown, 1986). Second is the issue of generalization. We change our beliefs about the individuals we contact much faster than we change our beliefs about the group as a whole, particularly because we tend to "subtype" individuals who do not match our expectations into lower level group memberships (Brewer et al., 1981; Deaux & Lewis, 1984; Gaertner, Mann, Murrell, & Dovidio, 1989; Taylor, 1981; Weber & Crocker, 1983). Generalization is more likely when the targets provide information that is relevant to existing beliefs such that the conflicting information is more difficult to ignore (Desforges et al., 1991; Rothbart & John, 1985).

Another approach to changing beliefs, and one that avoids the issue of generalization, is to attempt to convince people that their prejudiced beliefs are nonnormative (Sechrist & Stangor, 2001; Stangor, Sechrist, & Jost, 2001). Although this technique has been successful in the lab, again we do not know if it will work outside of laboratory settings.

Second, we can allow the beliefs to remain intact, but help people avoid applying them to individuals. This also is hard—because stereotyping is so well-practiced, and because it occurs often out of awareness, it is difficult to stop (Bargh, 1999). However, some social situations, including repeated practice in denying beliefs (Kawakami, Dovidio, Moll, Hermsen, & Russin, 2000), awareness of one's moral hypocrisy (Son Hing, Li, & Zanna, 2002), the presence of counteracting exemplars (Bodenhausen et al., 1995), and instructional sets (Lowery, Hardin, & Sinclair, 2001), seem to be able to reduce automatic as well as explicit stereotyping.

Legal remedies are designed in large part to force us to stop using our stereotypes and prejudices, and these approaches are successful. More generally, we must try to convince people to do the right thing—to make the hard choices—in this regard (Fiske, 1989). We must individuate or personalize others, rather than categorizing them (Brewer, 1988; Fiske & Neuberg, 1990). In some cases, learning about others as individuals will completely overwhelm the influence of their group memberships on our impressions of them (Locksley, Borgida, Brekke, & Hepburn, 1980).

Finally, and perhaps most likely to be successful, is the possibility of leaving both the beliefs and their use intact, but reducing the categorization process itself. Our cognitive approach has taught us much about the determinants and outcomes of categorization, and this provides a powerful tool in our arsenal. Stereotyping and prejudice are reduced significantly when the members of the different groups are able to perceive themselves as members of a common group, to see each other similarly, and to make friends with each other (Gaertner & Dovidio, 2000; Gaertner, Dovidio, et al., 2000; Gaertner et al., 1989; Gaertner, Mann, Dovidio, Murrell, & Pomare, 1990, 2000; Wright et al., 1997). This change can be accomplished perceptually, but is most effective through intergroup contact. Through fostering perceptions of shared identities, encouraging meaningful contact that defies group boundaries, and highlighting similarities on other dimensions unrelated to group distinctions, the ingroup and an outgroup can begin to see each other as more similar than different, thereby reducing negative intergroup actions and promoting positive ones (Gaertner et al., 1989; Gaertner et al., 1990).

Again, our paradigms have been in large part lab-based. We know much less about actually changing beliefs through recategorization in real-world contexts. An exception is our study of forced contact through school busing. Our data suggest that this seems to have worked (Pettigrew & Tropp, 2006), although it also did not work very quickly.

SUMMARY AND IMPLICATIONS

If there is a single theme that runs through this review, it is my opinion that we have spent too much time on the easier questions, with a relative neglect of the harder ones. One could argue that this is an issue of basic versus applied, and perhaps that is true. We have focused on the basic cognitive and affective processes that guide social perception, we have made huge progress in understanding these topics, and these findings have been applied in other domains. However, the tendency to ignore content, to keep our research in the lab, and to base our findings on the responses of college students has not come without some cost. In the end we know little about the truly prejudiced and bigoted—they are not in our domain of investigation. This could have some real consequences. For instance, some fundamental underlying assumptions, such as the idea that "true" attitudes are more negative than expressed attitudes may not be true across the population at large.

Our research has also tended to be individual rather than social, and has tended to ignore the playing out of intergroup attitudes in real life. There are some exceptions. For instance, some recent studies have investigated the costs and outcomes of intergroup contact using real time intergroup interactions (Shelton, Richeson, Salvatore, & Hill, 2006; Smart & Wegner, 1999; Vorauer, 2006; Vorauer & Sakamoto, 2006), and other research has focused on underlying implicit processes to better understand the tough decisions that law enforcement personnel must make (Correll, Park, Judd, & Wittenbrink, 2002; Correll et al., 2007). These are very important studies, and represent the kind of research that we must do more of. We also need to keep contributing to social policy—we have done some of this, including the *Brown v. Board of Education,* 347 U.S.483 (1954) decision and others (Fiske, Bersoff, Borgida, Deaux, & Heilman, 1991).

These are important contributions, but we really should do more. For instance, our research should have taught us a lot about how to make the best use of racial diversity in the classroom and in working groups, but we have not really tested these things (McCauley, Wright, & Harris, 2000). We should be contributing to the creation of diversity training programs, to prejudice-reduction programs in schools, and to the political discourse on discrimination. We know more about these topics than anyone else.

I make these statements because I feel that our reluctance to go out of our labs has in large part led us in many ways to be ignored by the world around us, and more recently by granting agencies. It is not seen as important by many to study stereotyping and prejudice, perhaps in part because we have not well linked our theories with policy and real social change. I have no doubt that the next 100 years will see us making substantial contributions to this issue.

ACKNOWLEDGMENT

The writing of this chapter was supported by grant BCS0240877 from the U.S. National Science Foundation.

REFERENCES

Aboud, F. E. (1988). *Children and prejudice.* New York: Basil Blackwell.
Aboud, F. E., & Amato, M. (2001). Developmental and socialization influences on intergroup bias. In R. Brown & S. Gaertner (Eds.), *Blackwell handbook in social psychology:* Vol. 4. Intergroup processes (pp. 65–85). New York: Blackwell.
Abrams, D., & Hogg, M. A. (Eds.). (1990). *Social identity theory: Constructive and critical advances.* New York: Springer-Verlag.
Adorno, T. W., Frenkel-Brunswik, E., Levinson, D. J., & Sanford, R. N. (1950). *The authoritarian personality.* New York: Harper.
Allport, G. W. (1954). *The nature of prejudice.* Reading, MA: Addison-Wesley.
Altemeyer, B. (1981). *Right-wing authoritarianism.* Winnipeg, MB: University of Manitoba Press.

Altemeyer, B. (1988). *Enemies of freedom: Understanding right-wing authoritarianism.* San Francisco: Jossey-Bass.

Anderson, C. A., Berkowitz, L., Donnerstein, E., Huesmann, L. R., Johnson, J. D., Linz, D., et al. (2003). The influence of media violence on youth. *Psychological Science in the Public Interest, 4*(3), 81–110.

Anderson, N., & Armstead, C. (1995). Toward understanding the association of socioeconomic status and health: A new challenge for the biopsychosocial approach. *Psychosomatic Medicine, 57,* 213–225.

Arkes, H. R., & Tetlock, P. E. (2004). Attributions of implicit prejudice, or "would Jesse Jackson 'fail' the implicit association test?" *Psychological Inquiry, 15*(4), 257–278.

Aronson, E., Blaney, N., Stephan, C., Sikes, J., & Snapp, M. (1978). *The jigsaw classroom.* London: Sage.

Aronson, J., Lustina, M. J., Good, C., Keough, K., & Steele, C. M. (1999). When white men can't do math: Necessary and sufficient factors in stereotype threat. *Journal of Experimental Social Psychology, 35,* 29–46.

Augoustinos, M., & Innes, J. M. (1990). Towards an integration of social representations and social schema theory. *British Journal of Social Psychology, 29,* 213–231.

Bach, P. B., Cramer, L. D., Warren, J. L., & Begg, C. B. (1999). Racial differences in the treatment of early-stage lung cancer. *New England Journal of Medicine, 341*(16), 1198–1205.

Backstrom, M., & Bjorklund, F. (2007). Structural modeling of generalized prejudice: The role of social dominance, authoritarianism, and empathy. *Journal of Individual Differences, 28*(1), 10–17.

Banaji, M. R., & Hardin, C. D. (1996). Automatic stereotyping. *Psychological Science, 7,* 136–141.

Bargh, J. (Ed.). (1999). *The cognitive monster: The case against the controllability of automatic stereotype effects.* New York: Guilford.

Bargh, J. A., Chen, M., & Burrows, L. (1996). Automaticity of social behavior: Direct effects of trait construct and stereotype activation on action. *Journal of Personality & Social Psychology, 71*(2), 230–244.

Bem, S. L. (1981). Gender schema theory: A cognitive account of sex typing. *Psychological Review, 88,* 354–364.

Biernat, M., & Crandall, C. S. (Eds.). (1999). *Racial attitudes.* San Diego, CA: Academic.

Biernat, M., & Fuegen, K. (2001). Shifting standards and the evaluation of competence: Complexity in gender-based judgment and decision making. *Journal of Social Issues, 57*(4), 707–724.

Biernat, M., & Vescio, T. K. (2002). She swings, she hits, she's great, she's benched: Implications of gender-based shifting standards for judgment and behavior. *Personality and Social Psychology Bulletin, 28*(1), 66–77.

Biernat, M., Vescio, T. K., & Theno, S. A. (1996). Violating American values: A "value congruence" approach to understanding outgroup attitudes. *Journal of Experimental Social Psychology, 32,* 387–410.

Biernat, M., Vescio, T. K., Theno, S. A., & Crandall, C. S. (1996). Values and prejudice: Toward understanding the impact of American values on outgroup attitudes. In J. H. O. C. Seligman & M. P. Zanna (Eds.), *Values: The Ontario Symposium* (Vol. 8, pp. 153–159). Hillsdale, NJ: Erlbaum.

Bigler, R. (1995). The role of classification skill in moderating environmental influences on children's gender stereotyping: A study of the functional use of gender in the classroom. *Child Development, 66,* 1072–1087.

Bigler, R., & Liben, L. (1992). Cognitive mechanisms in children's gender stereotyping: Theoretical and educational implications of a cognitive-based intervention. *Child Development, 63,* 1351–1363.

Bodenhausen, G. V., Gabriel, S., & Lineberger, M. (2000). Sadness and susceptibility to judgmental bias: The case of anchoring. *Psychological Science, 11*(4), 320–323.

Bodenhausen, G. V., Kramer, G. P., & Sasser, K. (1994). Happiness and stereotypic thinking in social judgment. *Journal of Personality & Social Psychology, 66*(4), 621–632.

Bodenhausen, G. V., & Macrae, C. N. (1998). Stereotype activation and inhibition. In R. Wyer (Ed.), *Advances in social cognition* (Vol. 11, pp. 1–52). Mahwah, NJ: Erlbaum.

Bodenhausen, G. V., Schwarz, N., Bless, H., & Wanke, M. (1995). Effects of atypical exemplars on racial beliefs: Enlightened racism or generalized appraisals? *Journal of Experimental Social Psychology, 31,* 48–63.

Branscombe, N. R., Schmitt, M. T., & Harvey, R. D. (1999). Perceiving pervasive discrimination among African Americans: Implications for group identification and well-being. *Journal of Personality & Social Psychology, 77*(1), 135–149.

Brauer, M., Wasel, W., & Niedenthal, P. (2000). Implicit and explicit components of prejudice. *Review of General Psychology, 4,* 79–101.

Brewer, M. B. (1988). A dual process model of impression formation. In T. K. Srull & R. S. Wyer (Eds.), *Advances in social cognition* (Vol. 1, pp. 1–36). Hillsdale, NJ: Erlbaum.

Brewer, M. B. (1999). The psychology of prejudice: Ingroup love or outgroup hate? *Journal of Social Issues, 55*(3), 429–444.

Brewer, M., & Brown, R. (1998). Intergroup relations. In S. Fiske, D. Gilbert, & G. Lindzey (Eds.), *Handbook of social psychology* (4th ed., Vol. 2, pp. 554–594). Boston: McGraw-Hill.

Brewer, M. B., & Campbell, D. T. (1976). *Ethnocentrism and intergroup attitudes: East African evidence.* New York: Sage.

Brewer, M. B., Dull, L., & Lui, L. (1981). Perceptions of the elderly: Stereotypes as prototypes. *Journal of Personality and Social Psychology, 41,* 656–670.

Brewer, M. B., & Silver, M. (1978). Ingroup bias as a function of task characteristics. *European Journal of Social Psychology, 8,* 393–400.

Brodt, S. E., & Ross, L. D. (1998). The role of stereotyping in overconfident social prediction. *Social Cognition, 16,* 225–252.

Cadinu, M., Maass, A., Frigerio, S., Impagliazzo, L., & Latinotti, S. (2003). Stereotype threat: The effect of expectancy on performance. *European Journal of Social Psychology, 33*(2), 267–285.

Chen, M., & Bargh, J. A. (1999). Consequences of automatic evaluation: Immediate behavioral predispositions to approach or avoid the stimulus. *Personality and Social Psychology Bulletin, 25*(2), 215–224.

Chiu, C.-Y., Dweck, C. S., Tong, J. Y.-Y., & Fu, J. H.-Y. (1997). Implicit theories and conceptions of morality. *Journal of Personality and Social Psychology, 73*(5), 923–940.

Collins, E. C., Crandall, C. S., & Biernat, M. (2006). Stereotypes and implicit social comparison: Shifts in comparison-group focus. *Journal of Experimental Social Psychology, 42*(4), 452–459.

Cook, S. W. (1978). Interpersonal and attitudinal outcomes in cooperating interracial groups. *Journal of Research in Developmental Education, 12,* 97–113.

Cook, S. W. (1984). Cooperative interaction in multiethnic contexts. In N. Miller & M. B. Brewer (Eds.), *Groups in contact* (pp. 77–96). New York: Academic.

Cooper, J. B., & Singer, D. N. (1956). The role of emotion in prejudice. *Journal of Social Psychology, 44,* 241–247.

Corning, A. F. (2002). Self-esteem as a moderator between perceived discrimination and psychological distress among women. *Journal of Counseling Psychology, 49*(1), 117–126.

Correll, J., Park, B., Judd, C. M., & Wittenbrink, B. (2002). The police officer's dilemma: Using ethnicity to disambiguate potentially threatening individuals. *Journal of Personality and Social Psychology, 83*(6), 1314–1329.

Correll, J., Park, B., Judd, C. M., Wittenbrink, B., Sadler, M. S., & Keesee, T. (2007). Across the thin blue line: Police officers and racial bias in the decision to shoot. *Journal of Personality and Social Psychology, 92*(6), 1006–1023.

Cota, A. A., & Dion, K. L. (1986). Salience of gender and sex composition of ad hoc groups: An experimental test of distinctiveness theory. *Journal of Personality and Social Psychology, 50*(4), 770–776.

Crandall, C., & Biernat, M. (1990). The ideology of anti-fat attitudes. *Journal of Applied Social Psychology, 20,* 227–243.

Crandall, C. S., & Eshleman, A. (2003). A justification-suppression of the expression and experience of prejudice. *Psychological Bulletin, 129*(3), 414–446.

Crandall, C. S., & Stangor, C. (Eds.). (2005). *Conformity and prejudice.* Malden, MA: Blackwell.

Crocker, J., & Major, B. (1989). Social stigma and self-esteem: The self-protective properties of stigma. *Psychological Review, 96,* 608–630.

Crocker, J., Major, B., & Steele, C. (1998). Social stigma. In D. T. Gilbert & S. T. Fiske (Eds.), *The handbook of social psychology* (4th ed., Vol. 2, pp. 504–553). New York: McGraw-Hill.

Crocker, J., Voelkl, K., Testa, M., & Major, B. (1991). Social stigma: The affective consequences of attributional ambiguity. *Journal of Personality and Social Psychology, 60,* 218–228.

Crosby, F., Bromley, S., & Saxe, L. (1980). Recent unobtrusive studies of black and white discrimination and prejudice: A literature review. *Psychological Bulletin, 87,* 546–563.

Cunningham, W., Preacher, K., & Banaji, M. (2001). Implicit attitude measures: Consistency, stability, and convergent validity. *Psychological Science, 12,* 163–170.

Darley, J. M., & Gross, P. H. (1983). A hypothesis-confirming bias in labeling effects. *Journal of Personality and Social Psychology, 44,* 20–33.

Dasgupta, N., McGhee, D. E., Greenwald, A. G., & Banaji, M. R. (2000). Automatic preference for White Americans: Eliminating the familiarity explanation. *Journal of Experimental Social Psychology, 36*(3), 316–328.

Deaux, K., & Lewis, L. (1984). The structure of gender stereotypes: Interrelationships among components and gender label. *Journal of Personality and Social Psychology, 46,* 991–1004.

Deaux, K., Reid, A., Mizrahi, K., & Ethier, K. A. (1995). Parameters of social identity. *Journal of Personality & Social Psychology, 68*(2), 280–291.

Desforges, D. M., Lord, C. G., Ramsey, S. L., Mason, J. A., Van Leeuwen, M. D., West, S. C., et al. (1991). Effects of structured cooperative contact on changing negative attitudes toward stigmatized social groups. *Journal of Personality & Social Psychology, 60*(4), 531–544.

Devine, P. G. (1989). Stereotypes and prejudice: Their automatic and controlled components. *Journal of Personality and Social Psychology, 56,* 5–18.

Devine, P. G., & Elliot, A. J. (1995). Are racial stereotypes really fading? The Princeton Trilogy revisited. *Personality and Social Psychology Bulletin, 21,* 1139–1150.

Dijksterhuis, A., Aarts, H., Bargh, J. A., & van Knippenberg, A. (2000). On the relation between associative strength and automatic behavior. *Journal of Experimental Social Psychology, 36*(5), 531–544.

Dovidio, J. F., Brigham, J. C., Johnson, B. T., & Gaertner, S. L. (1996). Stereotyping, prejudice, and discrimination: Another look. In C. N. Macrae, C. Stangor, & M. Hewstone (Eds.), *Stereotypes and stereotyping* (pp. 276–322). New York: Guilford.

Dovidio, J., Evans, N., & Tyler, R. (1986). Racial stereotypes: The contents of their cognitive representations. *Journal of Experimental Social Psychology, 22,* 22–37.

Dovidio, J. F., Gaertner, S. L., Isen, A. M., & Lowrance, R. (1995). Group representations and intergroup bias: Positive affect, similarity, and group size. *Personality and Social Psychology Bulletin, 21*(8), 856–865.

Dovidio, J. F., Kawakami, K., Johnson, C., Johnson, B., & Howard, A. (1997). On the nature of prejudice: Automatic and controlled processes. *Journal of Experimental Social Psychology, 33,* 510–540.

Eagly, A. H., & Kite, M. E. (1987). Are stereotypes of nationalities applied to both women and men? *Journal of Personality and Social Psychology, 53,* 451–462.

Eagly, A. H., & Mladinic, A. (1989). Gender stereotypes and attitudes toward women and men. *Personality and Social Psychology Bulletin, 15,* 543–558.

Eagly, A. H., & Steffen, V. J. (1984). Gender stereotypes stem from the distribution of women and men into social roles. *Journal of Personality and Social Psychology, 46,* 735–754.

Ellemers, J., Spears, R., & Doosje, B. (Eds.). (1999). *Social identity: Context, commitment, content.* Oxford, UK: Blackwell.

Fein, S., & Spencer, S. J. (1997). Prejudice as self-image maintenance: Affirming the self through derogating others. *Journal of Personality and Social Psychology, 73,* 31–44.

Fiske, S. T. (1982). Schema-triggered affect: Applications to social perception. In M. S. Clark & S. T. Fiske (Eds.), *Affect and cognition: The 17th annual Carnegie Symposium on Cognition* (pp. 55–78). Hillsdale, NJ: Erlbaum.

Fiske, S. T. (1989). Examining the role of intent: Toward understanding its role in stereotyping and prejudice. In J. S. Uleman & J. A. Bargh (Eds.), *Unintended thought* (pp. 253–286). New York: Guilford.

Fiske, S. T. (1998). Stereotyping, prejudice and discrimination. In D. T. Gilbert, S. T. Fiske, & G. Lindzey (Eds.), *Handbook of social psychology* (4th ed., Vol. 2, pp. 357–414). New York: McGraw-Hill.

Fiske, S. T., Bersoff, D. N., Borgida, E., Deaux, K., & Heilman, M. E. (1991). Social science research on trial: The use of sex stereotyping research in Price Waterhouse vs. Hopkins. *American Psychologist, 46,* 1049–1060.

Fiske, S. T., Cuddy, A. J. C., Glick, P., & Xu, J. (2002). A model of (often mixed) stereotype content: Competence and warmth respectively follow from perceived status and competition. *Journal of Personality & Social Psychology, 82*(6), 878–902.

Fiske, S. T., & Linville, P. W. (1980). What does the schema concept buy us? *Personality and Social Psychology Bulletin, 6,* 543–557.

Fiske, S. T., & Neuberg, S. L. (1990). A continuum of impression formation, from category based to individuating processes: Influences of information and motivation on attention and interpretation. In M. P. Zanna (Ed.), *Advances in experimental social psychology* (Vol. 23, pp. 1–74). New York: Academic.

Fiske, S. T., & Taylor, S. E. (1991). *Social cognition* (2nd ed.). New York: McGraw-Hill.

Ford, T. E., & Stangor, C. (1992). The role of diagnosticity in stereotype formation: Perceiving group means and variances. *Journal of Personality and Social Psychology, 63*(3), 356–367.

Fyock, J., & Stangor, C. (1994). The role of memory biases in stereotype maintenance. *British Journal of Social Psychology, 33*(3), 331–343.

Gaertner, S. L., & Dovidio, J. F. (1977). The subtlety of White racism, arousal, and helping behavior. *Journal of Personality and Social Psychology, 35*(10), 691–707.

Gaertner, S. L., & Dovidio, J. F. (1981). Racism among the well intentioned. In E. Clausen & J. Bermingham (Eds.), *Pluralism, racism and public policy: The search for equality* (pp. 208–222). Boston: G. K. Hall.

Gaertner, S. L., & Dovidio, J. F. (1986). The aversive form of racism. In S. L. Gaertner & J. F. Dovidio (Eds.), *Prejudice, discrimination and racism* (pp. 1–34). Orlando, FL: Academic.

Gaertner, S. L., & Dovidio, J. F. (2000). *Reducing intergroup bias: The common ingroup identity model.* New York: Psychology Press.

Gaertner, S. L., Dovidio, J. F., Nier, J. A., Banker, B. S., Ward, C. M., Houlette, M., et al. (Eds.). (2000). *The common ingroup identity model for reducing intergroup bias: Progress and challenges.* Thousand Oaks, CA: Sage.

Gaertner, S. L., Mann, J. A., Dovidio, J. F., Murrell, A. J., & Pomare, M. (1990). How does cooperation reduce intergroup bias? *Journal of Personality and Social Psychology, 59*(4), 692–704.

Gaertner, S. L., Mann, J. A., Dovidio, J. F., Murrell, A. J., & Pomare, M. (Eds.). (2000). *How does cooperation reduce intergroup bias?* New York: Psychology Press.

Gaertner, S. L., Mann, J., Murrell, A., & Dovidio, J. F. (1989). Reducing intergroup bias: The benefits of recategorization. *Journal of Personality & Social Psychology, 57*(2), 239–249.

Gaertner, S. L., & McLaughlin, J. P. (1983a). Changing not fading: Racial stereotypes revealed by a nonreactive, reaction time measure. *Social Psychology Quarterly, 46,* 23–30.

Gaertner, S. L., & McLaughlin, J. P. (1983b). Racial stereotypes: Associations and ascriptions of positive and negative characteristics. *Social Psychology Quarterly, 46*(1), 23–30.

Glauser, A. S. (1999). Legacies of racism. *Journal of Counseling & Development, 77,* 62–67.

Glick, P., & Fiske, S. (1996). The Ambivalent Sexism Inventory: Differentiating hostile and benevolent sexism. *Journal of Personality and Social Psychology, 70,* 491–512.

Glick, P., Zion, C., & Nelson, C. (1988). What mediates sex discrimination in hiring decisions? *Journal of Personality and Social Psychology, 55*(2), 178–186.

Govorun, O., & Payne, B. K. (2006). Ego-depletion and prejudice: Separating automatic and controlled components. *Social Cognition, 24*(2), 111–136.

Gregg, A. P., Seibt, B., & Banaji, M. R. (2006). Easier done than undone: Asymmetry in the malleability of implicit preferences. *Journal of Personality and Social Psychology, 90*(1), 1–20.

Hamilton, D. L. (1981). Illusory correlation as a basis for stereotyping. In D. L. Hamilton (Ed.), *Cognitive processes in stereotyping and intergroup behavior* (pp. 115–144). Hillsdale, NJ: Erlbaum.

Hamilton, D. L., & Rose, T. L. (1980). Illusory correlation and the maintenance of stereotypic beliefs. *Journal of Personality and Social Psychology, 39,* 832–845.

Hamilton, D. L., & Sherman, J. W. (1994). Stereotypes. In R. S. Wyer & T. K. Srull (Eds.), *Handbook of social cognition* (Vol. 2, pp. 1–68). Hillsdale, NJ: Erlbaum.

Harris, J. R. (Ed.). (2002). *Beyond the nurture assumption: Testing hypotheses about the child's environment.* Mahwah, NJ: Erlbaum.

Haslam, A., Oakes, P. J., Reynolds, K. J., & Turner, J. C. (1999). Social identity salience and the emergence of stereotype consensus. *Personality and Social Psychology Bulletin, 25,* 809–818.

Haslam, S., Turner, J., Oakes, P., Reynolds, K., Eggins, R., Nolan, M., et al. (1998). When do stereotypes become really consensual? Investigating the group-based dynamics of the consensualization process. *European Journal of Social Psychology, 28,* 755–776.

Hewstone, M. (1990). The "ultimate attribution error"? A review of the literature on intergroup causal attribution. *European Journal of Social Psychology, 20*(4), 311–335.

Hewstone, M. (1996). Contact and categorization: Social psychological interventions to change intergroup relations. In C. N. Macrae, C. Stangor, & M. Hewstone (Eds.), *Stereotypes and stereotyping* (pp. 323–368). New York: Guilford.

Hewstone, M., & Brown, R. (1986). Contact is not enough: An intergroup perspective on the "Contact Hypothesis." In M. Hewstone & R. J. Brown (Eds.), *Contact and conflict in intergroup encounters* (pp. 1–44). London: Basil-Blackwell.

Hogg, M. A., & McGarty, C. (1990). Self-categorzation and social identity. In D. Abrams & M. A. Hogg (Eds.), *Social identity theory: Constructive and critical advances* (pp. 10–27). London and New York: Harvester Wheatsheaf and Springer-Verlag.

Inzlicht, M., McKay, L., & Aronson, J. (2006). Stigma as ego depletion: How being the target of prejudice affects self-control. *Psychological Science, 17*(3), 262–269.

Ito, T. A., Urland, G. R., Willadsen-Jensen, & E., Correll, J. (2006). The social neuroscience of stereotyping and prejudice: Using event-related potentials to study social perception. In J. T. Cacioppo, P. S. Visser, & C. L. Pickett (Eds.), *Social neuroscience: People thinking about thinking people* (pp. 189-212). Cambridge, MA: MIT Press.

Jackson, J. W., & Smith, E. R. (1999). Conceptualizing social identity: A new framework and evidence for the impact of different dimensions. *Personality & Social Psychology Bulletin, 25*(1), 120–135.

Jost, J. T., Banaji, M. R., & Nosek, B. A. (2004). A decade of system justification theory: Accumulated evidence of conscious and unconscious bolstering of the status quo. *Political Psychology, 25*(6), 881–920.

Jost, J. T., Glaser, J., Kruglanski, A. W., & Sulloway, F. J. (2003). Political conservatism as motivated social cognition. *Psychological Bulletin, 129*(3), 339–375.

Jost, J. T., & Hunyady, O. (2005). Antecedents and consequences of system-justifying ideologies. *Current Directions in Psychological Science, 14*(5), 260–265.

Jost, J. T., & Major, B. (Eds.). (2001). *The psychology of legitimacy: Emerging perspectives on ideology, justice, and intergroup relations.* New York: Cambridge University Press.

Judd, C. M., Ryan, C. S., & Park, B. (1991). Accuracy in the judgment of in-group and out-group variability. *Journal of Personality and Social Psychology, 61,* 366–379.

Kaiser, C. R., Major, B., & McCoy, S. K. (2004). Expectations about the future and the emotional consequences of perceiving prejudice. *Personality & Social Psychology Bulletin, 30*(2), 173–184.

Kanter, R. M. (1977). Some effects of proportions on group life: Skewed sex ratios and responses to token women. *American Journal of Sociology, 82,* 965–990.

Karpinski, A., & Hilton, J. L. (2001). Attitudes and the Implicit Association Test. *Journal of Personality and Social Psychology, 81*(5), 774–788.

Kashima, Y. (2000). Maintaining cultural stereotypes in the serial reproduction of narratives. *Personality & Social Psychology Bulletin, 26*(5), 594–604.

Katz, D., & Braly, K. W. (1933). Racial stereotypes of one hundred college students. *Journal of Abnormal and Social Psychology, 28,* 280–290.

Katz, I., & Hass, R. G. (1988). Racial ambivalence and American value conflict: Correlational and priming studies of dual cognitive structures. *Journal of Personality and Social Psychology, 55,* 893–905.

Kawakami, K., Dovidio, J. F., Moll, J., Hermsen, S., & Russin, A. (2000). Just say no (to stereotyping): Effects of training in the negation of stereotypic associations on stereotype activation. *Journal of Personality and Social Psychology, 78*(5), 871–888.

Kessler, R. C., Mickelson, K. D., & Williams, D. R. (1999). The prevalence, distribution, and mental health correlated of perceived discrimination in the United States. *Journal of Health and Social Behavior, 40,* 208–230.

Klonoff, E. A., Landrine, H., & Ullman, J. B. (1999). Racial discrimination and psychiatric symptoms among blacks. *Cultural Diversity and Ethnic Minority Psychology, 5*(4), 329–339.

Kruglanski, A. W., & Freund, T. (1983). The freezing and unfreezing of lay inferences: Effects on impressional primacy, ethnic stereotyping, and numerical anchoring. *Journal of Experimental Social Psychology, 19,* 448–468.

Landrine, H., & Klonoff, E. (1996). The schedule of racist events: A measure of racial discrimination and a study of its negative physical and mental health consequences. *Journal of Black Psychology, 22,* 144–168.

Lee, Y. T., Jussim, L. J., & McCauley, C. R. (1995). *Stereotype accuracy: Toward appreciating group differences.* Washington, DC: American Psychological Association.

Linville, P. W., Salovey, P., & Fischer, G. W. (1986). Stereotyping and perceived distributions of social characteristics: An application to ingroup–outgroup perception. In J. F. Dovidio & S. L. Gaertner (Eds.), *Prejudice, discrimination and racism* (pp. 165–208). Orlando, FL: Academic.

Lippman, W. (1922). *Public opinion.* New York: Harcourt & Brace.

Locksley, A., Borgida, E., Brekke, N., & Hepburn, C. (1980). Sex stereotypes and judgments of individuals. *Journal of Personality and Social Psychology, 39,* 821–831.

Lowery, B. S., Hardin, C. D., & Sinclair, S. (2001). Social influence effects on automatic racial prejudice. *Journal of Personality and Social Psychology, 81*(5), 842–855.

Lyons, A., & Kashima, Y. (2003). How are stereotypes maintained through communication? The influence of stereotype sharedness. *Journal of Personality & Social Psychology, 85*(6), 989–1005.

Maass, A., & Arcuri, L. (1996). Language and stereotyping. In C. N. Macrae, C. Stangor, & M. Hewstone (Eds.), *Stereotypes and stereotyping* (pp. 193–226). New York: Guilford.

Maass, A., Salvi, D., Arcuri, L., & Semin, G. (1989). Language use in intergroup contexts: The linguistic intergroup bias. *Journal of Personality and Social Psychology, 57,* 981–993.

Mackie, D. M., Devos, T., & Smith, E. R. (2000). Intergroup emotions: Explaining offensive action tendencies in an intergroup context. *Journal of Personality & Social Psychology, 79*(4), 602–616.

Mackie, D. M., & Hamilton, D. L. (1993). *Affect, cognition and stereotyping: Interactive processes in group perception.* Orlando, FL: Academic.

Mackie, D. M., & Smith, E. R. (1998). Intergroup relations: Insights from a theoretically integrative approach. *Psychological Review, 105*(3), 499–529.

Macrae, C. N., Bodenhausen, G. V., Milne, A. B., Thorn, T. M. J., & Castelli, L. (1997). On the activation of social stereotypes: The moderating role of processing objectives. *Journal of Experimental Social Psychology, 33*(5), 471–489.

Macrae, C. N., Hewstone, M., & Griffiths, R. J. (1993). Processing load and memory for stereotype-based information. *European Journal of Social Psychology, 23,* 77–87.

Macrae, C. N., Milne, A. B., & Bodenhausen, G. V. (1994). Stereotypes as energy-saving devices: A peek inside the cognitive toolbox. *Journal of Personality and Social Psychology, 66,* 37–47.

Madon, S., Jussim, L., Keiper, S., Eccles, J., Smith, A., & Palumbo, P. (1998). The accuracy and power of sex, social class, and ethnic stereotypes: A naturalistic study in person perception. *Personality & Social Psychology Bulletin, 24*(12), 1304–1318.

Major, B., Kaiser, C. R., & McCoy, S. K. (2003). It's not my fault: When and why attributions to prejudice protect self-esteem. *Personality & Social Psychology Bulletin, 29*(6), 772–781.

Major, B., & O'Brien, L. T. (2005). The social psychology of stigma. *Annual Review of Psychology, 56,* 393–421.

Major, B., Quinton, W., & McCoy, S. (2003). Antecedents and consequences of attributions to discrimination: Theoretical and empirical advances. *Advances in Experimental Social Psychology, 34,* 251–329.

Maner, J. K., Kenrick, D. T., Becker, D. V., Robertson, T. E., Hofer, B., Neuberg, S. L., et al. (2005). Functional projection: How fundamental social motives can bias interpersonal perception. *Journal of Personality & Social Psychology, 88*(1), 63–78.

Martin, C. L., & Halverson, C. F., Jr. (1981). A schematic processing model of sex typing and stereotyping in children. *Child Development, 52,* 1119–1134.

McCauley, C., & Stitt, C. L. (1978). An individual and quantitative measure of stereotypes. *Journal of Personality and Social Psychology, 36,* 929–940.

McCauley, C., Stitt, C. L., & Segal, M. (1980). Stereotyping: From prejudice to prediction. *Psychological Bulletin, 87,* 195–208.

McCauley, C., Wright, M., & Harris, M. E. (2000). Diversity workshops on campus: A survey of current practice at U.S. colleges and universities. *College Student Journal, 34*(1), 100–114.

McConahay, J. B. (1986). Modern racism, ambivalence, and the modern racism scale. In S. Gaertner & J. Dovidio (Eds.), *Prejudice, discrimination, and racism* (pp. 91–126). Orlando, FL: Academic.

McGarty, C., Haslam, S. A., Turner, J. C., & Oakes, P. J. (1993). Illusory correlation as accentuation of actual intercategory difference: Evidence for the effect with minimal stimulus information. *European Journal of Social Psychology, 23,* 391–410.

Mendes, W. B., Blascovich, J., Lickel, B., & Hunter, S. (2002). Challenge and threat during social interaction with white and black men. *Personality and Social Psychology Bulletin, 28*(7), 939-952.

Messick, D. M., & Mackie, D. (1989). Intergroup relations. *Annual Review of Psychology, 40,* 45–81.

Monteith, M. J., Deneen, N. E., & Tooman, G. D. (1996). The effect of social norm activation on the expression of opinions concerning gay men and Blacks. *Basic & Applied Social Psychology, 18*(3), 267–288.

Moskowitz, G. B., Wasel, W., Schaal, B., & Gollwitzer, P. M. (1999). Preconscious control of stereotype activation through chronic egalitarian goals. *Journal of Personality and Social Psychology, 77,* 167–184.

Mullen, B., & Johnson, C. (1990). Distinctiveness-based illusory correlations and stereotyping: A meta-analytic integration. *British Journal of Social Psychology, 29,* 11–28.

Mummendey, A. (1995). Positive distinctiveness and social discrimination: An old couple living in divorce. *European Journal of Social Psychology, 25*(6), 657–670.

Nelson, T. D. (2002). *The psychology of prejudice.* Needham Heights, MA: Allyn & Bacon.

Neuberg, S. L., & Fiske, S. T. (1987). Motivational influences on impression formation: Outcome dependency, accuracy-driven attention, and individuating processes. *Journal of Personality and Social Psychology, 53,* 431–444.

Nosek, B. A. (2005). Moderators of the Relationship Between Implicit and Explicit Evaluation. *Journal of Experimental Psychology: General, 134*(4), 565-584.

Nosek, B. A., Smyth, F. L., Hansen, J. J., Devos, T., Lindner, N. M., Ranganath, K. A., et al. (2007). Pervasiveness and correlates of implicit attitudes and stereotypes. *European Review of Social Psychology, 16,* 335–390.

Oakes, P. J., Haslam, S. A., & Turner, J. C. (1994). *Stereotyping and social reality.* Oxford, UK: Blackwell.

Oakes, P. J., Turner, J. C., & Haslam, S. A. (1991). Perceiving people as group members: The role of fit in the salience of social categorizations. *British Journal of Social Psychology, 30,* 125–144.

Olson, J. M., Vernon, P. A., Harris, J. A., & Jang, K. L. (2001). The heritability of attitudes: A study of twins. *Journal of Personality and Social Psychology, 80*(6), 845–860.

Olsson, A., & Phelps, E. A. (Eds.). (2007). *Understanding social evaluations: What we can (and cannot) learn from neuroimaging.* New York: Guilford.

Osgood, C. E., Suci, G. J., & Tannenbaum, P. H. (1957). *The measurement of meaning.* Urbana: University of Illinois Press.

Ostrom, T. M., & Sedikides, C. (1992). Out-group homogeneity effects in natural and minimal groups. *Psychological Bulletin, 112*(3), 536–552.

Ottati, V., Bodenhausen, G. V., & Newman, L. S. (Eds.). (2005). *Social psychological models of mental illness stigma.* Washington, DC: American Psychological Association.

Park, B., Judd, C. M., & Ryan, C. S. (1991). Social categorization and the representation of variability information. *European Review of Social Psychology, 2,* 221–245.

Park, J., & Banaji, M. R. (2000). Mood and heuristics: The influence of happy and sad states on sensitivity and bias in stereotyping. *Journal of Personality and Social Psychology, 78*(6), 1005–1023.

Payne, B. K., Cheng, C. M., Govorun, O., & Stewart, B. D. (2005). An inkblot for attitudes: Affect misattribution as implicit measurement. *Journal of Personality and Social Psychology, 89*(3), 277–293.

Perdue, C. W., Dovidio, J. F., Gurtman, M. B., & Tyler, R. B. (1990). Us and them: Social categorization and the process of intergroup bias. *Journal of Personality and Social Psychology, 59,* 475–486.

Pettigrew, T. F. (1959). Regional differences in anti-Negro prejudice. *Journal of Abnormal and Social Psychology, 59,* 28–36.

Pettigrew, T. F. (1998a). Intergroup contact theory. *Annual Review of Psychology, 49,* 65–85.

Pettigrew, T. (1998b). Reactions toward the new minorities of Western Europe. *Annual Review of Sociology, 24,* 77–103.

Pettigrew, T. F., & Tropp, L. R. (2006). A meta-analytic test of intergroup contact theory. *Journal of Personality and Social Psychology, 90*(5), 751–783.

Phelps, E. A., O'Connor, K. J., Cunningham, W. A., Funayama, E. S., Gatenby, J. C., Gore, J. C., & Banaji, M. R. (2000). Performance on indirect measures of race evaluation predicts amygdala activation. *Journal of Cognitive Neuroscience, 12*(5), 729-738.

Pinel, E. (1999). Stigma-consciousness: The psychological legacy of social stereotypes. *Journal of Personality and Social Psychology, 76,* 114–128.

Pinel, E. C. (2002). Stigma consciousness in intergroup contexts: The power of conviction. *Journal of Experimental Social Psychology, 38*(2), 178–185.

Plaks, J. E., Stroessner, S. J., Dweck, C. S., & Sherman, J. W. (2001). Person theories and attention allocation: Preferences for sterotypic versus counterstereotypic information. *Journal of Personality and Social Psychology, 80*(6), 876–893.

Plant, E. A., & Devine, P. G. (1998). Internal and external motivation to respond without prejudice. *Journal of Personality & Social Psychology, 75*(3), 811–832.

Riach, P. A., & Rich, J. (2004). Fishing for discrimination. *Review of Social Economy, 62*(4), 465–486.

Roccas, S., & Brewer, M. (2002). Social identity complexity. *Personality & Social Psychology Review, 6*(2), 88–106.

Rothbart, M., & John, O. P. (1985). Social categorization and behavioral episodes: A cognitive analysis of the effects of intergroup contact. *Journal of Social Issues, 41,* 81–104.

Rothbart, M., & John, O. (1992). Intergroup relations and stereotype change: A social-cognitive analysis and some longitudinal findings. In P. Sniderman & P. Tetlock (Eds.), *Prejudice, politics and the American dilemma* (pp. 32–59). Stanford, CA: Stanford University Press.

Rothbart, M., & Taylor, M. (Eds.). (1992). *Category labels and social reality: Do we view social categories as natural kinds?* Thousand Oaks, CA: Sage.

Rowatt, W. C., Tsang, J.-A., Kelly, J., LaMartina, B., McCullers, M., & McKinley, A. (2006). Associations between religious personality dimensions and implicit homosexual prejudice. *Journal for the Scientific Study of Religion, 45*(3), 397–406.

Ruble, D., & Martin, C. (1998). Gender development. In W. Damon (Ed.), *Handbook of child psychology* (5th ed., pp. 933–1016). New York: Wiley.

Rudman, L. A., Greenwald, A. G., Mellott, D. S., & Schwartz, J. L. K. (1999). Measuring the automatic components of prejudice: Flexibility and generality of the Implicit Association Test. *Social Cognition, 17*(4), 437–465.

Ruscher, J. B. (1998). Prejudice and stereotyping in everyday communication. In M. P. Zanna (Ed.), *Advances in experimental social psychology* (Vol. 30, pp. 241–307). San Diego, CA: Academic.

Ruscher, J. B. (2001). *Prejudiced communication: A social psychological perspective.* New York: Guilford.

Ryan, C., Park, B., & Judd, C. (1996). Assessing stereotype accuracy: Implications for understanding the stereotyping process. In C. N. Macrae, C. Stangor, & M. Hewstone (Eds.), *Stereotypes and stereotyping* (pp. 121–157). New York: Guilford.

Schaller, M., Boyd, C., Yohannes, J., & O'Brien, M. (1995). The prejudiced personality revisited: Personal need for structure and formation of erroneous group stereotypes. *Journal of Personality and Social Psychology, 68,* 544–555.

Schaller, M., Conway, L. G., & Tanchuk, T. L. (2002). Selective pressures on the once and future contents of ethnic stereotypes: Effects of the communicability of traits. *Journal of Personality and Social Psychology, 82*(6), 861–877.

Schaller, M., & Maass, A. (1989). Illusory correlation and social categorization: Toward an integration of motivational and cognitive factors in stereotype formation. *Journal of Personality and Social Psychology, 56,* 709–721.

Schaller, M., Park, J. H., & Mueller, A. (2003). Fear of the dark: Interactive effects of beliefs about danger and ambient darkness on ethnic stereotypes. *Personality and Social Psychology Bulletin, 29*(5), 637–649.

Schmitt, M. T., Branscombe, N. R., Kobrynowicz, D., & Owen, S. (2002). Perceiving discrimination against one's gender group has different implications for well-being in women and men. *Personality and Social Psychology Bulletin, 28*(2), 197–210.

Schmitt, M. T., Spears, R., & Branscombe, N. R. (2003). Constructing a minority group identity out of shared rejection: The case of international students. *European Journal of Social Psychology, 33*(1), 1–12.

Schneider, D. J. (2004). *The psychology of stereotyping.* New York: Guilford.

Schofield, J. (1986). Causes and consequences of the colorblind perspective. In J. F. Dovidio & S. L. Gaertner (Eds.), *Prejudice, discrimination, and racism* (pp. 231–253). San Diego, CA: Academic.

Schultz, A., Israel, B., Williams, D., Parker, E., Becker, A., & James, S. (2000). Social inequalities, stressors and self reported health status among African American and white women in the Detroit metropolitan area. *Social Science and Medicine, 51,* 1639–1653.

Schwartz, S. H. (1992). Universals in the content and structure of values: Theoretical advances and empirical tests in 20 countries. *Advances in Experimental Social Psychology, 25,* 1–65.

Sears, D. O. (1986). College sophomores in the laboratory: Influences of a narrow data base on social psychology's view of human nature. *Journal of Personality and Social Psychology, 51,* 515–530.

Sears, D. O., & Henry, P. J. (2005). Over thirty years later: A contemporary look at symbolic racism. *Advances in Experimental Social Psychology, 37,* 95–150.

Sechrist, G., & Stangor, C. (2001). Perceived Consensus Influences Intergroup Behavior and Stereotype Accessibility. *Journal of Personality and Social Psychology, 80,* 645-654.

Sekaquaptewa, D., & Thompson, M. (2003). Solo status, stereotype threat, and performance expectancies: Their effects on women's performance. *Journal of Experimental Social Psychology, 39*(1), 68–74.

Shah, J. Y., Kruglanski, A. W., & Thompson, E. P. (1998). Membership has its (epistemic) rewards: Need for closure effects on intergroup favoritism. *Journal of Personality and Social Psychology, 75,* 383–393.

Shelton, J. N., Richeson, J. A., Salvatore, J., & Hill, D. M. (Eds.). (2006). *Silence is not golden: The intrapersonal consequences of not confronting prejudice.* Mahwah, NJ: Erlbaum.

Sherif, M., & Sherif, C. W. (1953). *Groups in harmony and tension.* New York: Harper & Row.

Sidanius, J., & Pratto, F. (1999). *Social dominance: An intergroup theory of social hierarchy and oppression.* New York: Cambridge University Press.

Sigall, H., & Page, R. (1971). Current stereotypes: A little fading, a little faking. *Journal of Personality & Social Psychology, 18*(2), 247–255.

Signorella, M., Bigler, R., & Liben, L. (1993). Developmental differences in children's gender schemata about others: A meta-analytic review. *Developmental Review, 13,* 147–183.

Sinclair, L., & Kunda, Z. (2000). Motivated stereotyping of women: She's fine if she praised me but incompetent if she criticized me. *Personality & Social Psychology Bulletin, 26*(11), 1329–1342.

Smart, L., & Wegner, D. M. (1999). Covering up what can't be seen: Concealable stigma and mental control. *Journal of Personality and Social Psychology, 77*(3), 474–486.

Smith, E. R. (1992). The role of exemplars in social judgment. In L. L. Martin & A. Tesser (Eds.), *The construction of social judgments* (pp. 107-132). Hillsdale, NJ: Erlbaum.

Smith, E. R., & Zárate, M. A. (1990). Exemplar and prototype use in social categorization. *Social Cognition, 8*(3), 243–262.

Smith, E. R., & Zárate, M. A. (1992). Exemplar-based model of social judgment. *Psychological Review, 99*(1), 3–21.

Son Hing, L. S., Li, W., & Zanna, M. P. (2002). Inducing hypocrisy to reduce prejudicial responses among aversive racists. *Journal of Experimental Social Psychology, 38*(1), 71–78.

Stangor, C. (1988). Stereotype accessibility and information processing. *Personality and Social Psychology Bulletin, 14,* 694–708.

Stangor, C. (1995). Content and application inaccuracy in social stereotyping. In Y. T. Lee, L. J. Jussim, & C. R. McCauley (Eds.), *Stereotype accuracy: Toward appreciating group differences* (pp. 275–292). Washington, DC: American Psychological Association.

Stangor, C., & Duan, C. (1991). Effects of multiple task demands upon memory for information about social groups. *Journal of Experimental Social Psychology, 27,* 357–378.

Stangor, C., Jonas, K., Stroebe, W., & Hewstone, M. (1996). Development and change of national stereotypes and attitudes. *European Journal of Social Psychology, 26,* 663–675.

Stangor, C., & Lange, J. (1994). Mental representations of social groups: Advances in conceptualizing stereotypes and stereotyping. *Advances in Experimental Social Psychology, 26,* 357–416.

Stangor, C., & Leary, S. (2006). Intergroup beliefs: Investigations from the social side. *Advances in Experimental Social Psychology, 38,* 243–283.

Stangor, C., Lynch, L., Duan, C., & Glass, B. (1992). Categorization of individuals on the basis of multiple social features. *Journal of Personality and Social Psychology, 62*(2), 207–218.

Stangor, C., & McMillan, D. (1992). Memory for expectancy-congruent and expectancy-incongruent information: A review of the social and social developmental literatures. *Psychological Bulletin, 111*(1), 42–61.

Stangor, C., & Ruble, D. N. (1989). Differential influences of gender schemata and gender constancy on children's information processing and behavior. *Social Cognition, 7,* 353–372.

Stangor, C., & Schaller, M. (1996). Stereotypes as individual and collective representations. In C. N. Macrae, C. Stangor, & M. Hewstone (Eds.), *Stereotypes and stereotyping* (pp. 3–40). New York: Guilford.

Stangor, C., Sechrist, G., & Jost, J. (2001). Changing Racial Beliefs by Providing Consensus Information. *Personality and Social Psychology Bulletin, 27,* 484-494.

Stangor, C., Sullivan, L. A., & Ford, T. E. (1991). Affective and cognitive determinants of prejudice. *Social Cognition, 9*(4), 359–380.

Stangor, C., Swim, J. K., Sechrist, G. B., deCoster, J., Van Allen, K., & Ottenbreit, A. (2003). Ask, answer and announce: Three stages in perceiving and responding to discrimination. *European Review of Social Psychology, 14,* 277–311.

Steele, C. M., & Aronson, J. (1995). Stereotype threat and the intellectual performance of African Americans. *Journal of Personality and Social Psychology, 69,* 797–811.

Stricker, L. J., & Bejar, I. I. (2004). Test difficulty and stereotype threat on the GRE General test. *Journal of Applied Social Psychology, 34*(3), 563–597.

Stricker, L. J., & Ward, W. C. (2004). Stereotype threat, inquiring about test takers' ethnicity and gender, and standardized test performance. *Journal of Applied Social Psychology, 34*(4), 665–693.

Swim, J. K. (1994). Perceived versus meta-analytic effect sizes: An assessment of the accuracy of gender stereotypes. *Journal of Personality Social Psychology, 66*(1), 21–36.

Swim, J., Aikin, K., Hall, W., & Hunter, B. (1995). Sexism and racism: Old-fashioned and modern prejudices. *Journal of Personality and Social Psychology, 68,* 199–214.

Swim, J. K., Hyers, L. L., Cohen, L. L., & Ferguson, M. J. (2001). Everyday sexism: Evidence for its incidence, nature, and psychological impact from three daily diary studies. *Journal of Social Issues, 57*(1), 31–53.

Swim, J. K., & Sanna, L. J. (1996). He's skilled, she's lucky: A meta-analysis of observers' attributions for women's and men's successes and failures. *Personality and Social Psychology Bulletin, 22*(5), 507–519.

Tajfel, H. (1981). *Human groups and social categories: Studies in social psychology.* Cambridge, UK: Cambridge Univesity Press.

Tajfel, H., & Forgas, J. P. (1981). Social categorization: Cognitions, values and groups. In J. P. Forgas (Ed.), *Social cognition* (pp. 113–140). New York: Academic.

Tajfel, H., & Wilkes, A. L. (1963). Classification and quantitative judgment. *British Journal of Psychology, 54,* 101–114.

Taylor, S. E. (1981). A categorization approach to stereotyping. In D. L. Hamilton (Ed.), *Cognitive processes in stereotyping and intergroup behavior* (pp. 83–114). Hillsdale, NJ: Erlbaum.

Taylor, S. E., & Crocker, J. (1981). Schematic bases of social information processing. In E. T. Higgins, C. P. Herman, & M. P. Zanna (Eds.), *Social cognition: The Ontario Symposium* (Vol. 1, pp. 89–134). Hillsdale, NJ: Erlbaum.

Taylor, S. E., Fiske, S. T., Etcoff, N. L., & Ruderman, A. J. (1978). Categorical and contextual bases of person memory and stereotyping. *Journal of Personality and Social Psychology, 36*(7), 778–793.

Terrell, F., Terrell, S. L., & Miller, F. (1993). Level of cultural mistrust as a function of educational and occupational expectations among Black students. *Adolescence, 28,* 573–578.

Trope, Y., & Thompson, E. (1997). Looking for truth in all the wrong places? Asymmetric search of individuating information about stereotyped group members. *Journal of Personality and Social Psychology, 73,* 229–241.

Turner, J. C. (1987). *Rediscovering the social group: A self-categorization theory.* Oxford, UK: Basil Blackwell.

Turner, J. C., & Oakes, P. J. (Eds.). (1989). *Self-categorization theory and social influence* (2nd ed.). Hillsdale, NJ: Erlbaum.

Turner, J. C., Oakes, P. C., Haslam, S. A., & McGarty, C. (1994). Self and collective: Cognition and social context. *Personality and Social Psychology Bulletin, 20,* 454–463.

Uleman, J. S., & Bargh, J. A. (1989). *Unintended thought.* New York: Guilford.

van Knippenberg, D., & van Knippenberg, A. (1994). Social categorization, focus of attention and judgements of group opinions. *British Journal of Social Psychology, 33,* 477–489.

Vorauer, J. D. (2006). An information search model of evaluative concerns in intergroup interaction. *Psychological Review, 113*(4), 862–886.

Vorauer, J. D., & Sakamoto, Y. (2006). I thought we could be friends, but….Systematic miscommunication and defensive distancing as obstacles to cross-group friendship formation. *Psychological Science, 17*(4), 326–331.

Walton, G. M., & Cohen, G. L. (2003). Stereotype lift. *Journal of Experimental Social Psychology, 39*(5), 456–467.

Watkins, C., Terrell, F., Miller, F. S., & Terrell, S. L. (1989). Cultural mistrust and its effects on expectational variables in Black client–White counselor relationships. *Journal of Counseling Psychology, 36,* 447–450.

Weber, R., & Crocker, J. (1983). Cognitive processes in the revision of stereotypic beliefs. *Journal of Personality and Social Psychology, 45,* 961–977.

Wheeler, S. C., & Petty, R. E. (2001). The effects of stereotype activation on behavior: A review of possible mechanisms. *Psychological Bulletin, 127*(6), 797–826.

Wilder, D. A. (1986). Social categorization: Implications for creation and reduction of intergroup bias. In L. Berkowitz (Ed.), *Advances in experimental social psychology* (Vol. 19, pp. 241–355). New York: Academic.

Williams, D. R. (1999). Race, socioeconomic status, and health: The added effect of racism and discrimination. In N. E. Adler & M. Marmot (Eds.), *Socioeconomic status and health in industrial nations: Social, psychological, and biological pathways* (Vol. 896, pp. 173–188). New York: New York Academy of Sciences.

Williams, D. R., & Rucker, T. D. (2000). Understanding and addressing racial disparities in health care. *Health Care Financing Review, 21*(4), 75–91.

Williams, D. R., Spencer, M. S., & Jackson, J. S. (1999). Race, stress, and physical health: The role of group identity. In R. J. Contrada & R. D. Ashmore (Eds.), *Self, social identity, and physical health: Interdisciplinary explorations* (Vol. 2, pp. 71–100). New York: Oxford University Press.

Williams, D. R., & Williams-Morris, R. (2000). Racism and mental health: The African American experience. *Ethnicity and Health, 5*(3–4), 243–269.

Woll, S., & Graesser, A. (1982). Memory discrimination for information typical or atypical of person schemata. *Social Cognition, 1,* 287–310.

Wolsko, C., Park, B., Judd, C. M., & Wittenbrink, B. (2000). Framing interethnic ideology: Effects of multicultural and color-blind perspectives on judgments of groups and individuals. *Journal of Personality and Social Psychology, 78*(4), 635–654.

Word, C. O., Zanna, M. P., & Cooper, J. (1974). The nonverbal mediation of self-fulfilling prophecies in interracial interaction. *Journal of Experimental Social Psychology, 10,* 109–120.

Wright, S., Aron, A., McLaughlin-Volpe, T., & Ropp, S. (1997). The extended contact effect: Knowledge of cross-group friendships and prejudice. *Journal of Personality and Social Psychology, 73,* 73–90.

Yzerbyt, V., Schadron, G., Leyens, J., & Rocher, S. (1994). Social judgeability: The impact of meta-informational cues on the use of stereotypes. *Journal of Personality and Social Psychology, 66,* 48–55.

Zuwerink, J., Devine, P., Monteith, J., & Cook, D. (1996). Prejudice toward blacks: With and without compunction? *Basic and Applied Social Psychology, 18,* 131–150.

2 Development of Racial and Ethnic Prejudice Among Children

Sheri R. Levy
State University of New York at Stony Brook

Julie Milligan Hughes
University of Texas at Austin

A 5-year old girl refuses to work with a classmate of a different ethnic group. A 9-year-old boy mutters a racial slur about a different-race peer. Such acts do not typically capture national and international headlines as instances of pervasive intergroup conflict. Although most of the headlines capture the intergroup struggles of adults, prejudice is expressed among children as early as 4 years of age (e.g., Aboud, 1988; Bar-Tal, 1996).

Researchers, educators, parents, and other concerned individuals have long tried to understand and reduce prejudice among children. Some would suggest that the behaviors of the 5-year-old and 9-year-old children just described do not represent the children's true attitudes, but rather reflect their oblivious mimicry of the behavior of others. Thus, there is no prejudice to reduce and the acts should be ignored. In contrast, others would argue these behaviors reflect the children's true attitudes as taught in their environment; consequently, children's prejudice could be reduced by additional teaching, such as learning about the cultural traditions and customs of different racial and ethnic groups, as well as by learning about historical and contemporary racial and ethnic injustices. An additional interpretation is that children's negative racial attitudes and behaviors grow out of perceiving other groups (outgroups) as too different, and therefore outgroup attitudes could be greatly improved by focusing on shared identities (e.g., as students from the same school). Yet another interpretation is that children's attitudes and behaviors in part reflect their lack of social sophistication or ability to be tolerant; thus, reducing children's prejudice requires developmentally appropriate training toward more sophisticated thought processes. These interpretations reflect some of the main theories of the development of prejudice among children and some of the allied techniques for reducing prejudice among children.

The goal of this chapter is to provide a summary of the tremendous strides researchers, mainly developmental and social psychologists, have made in understanding and reducing negative racial attitudes and behaviors among children. We begin by defining key concepts and measurement tools relevant to children's racial attitudes and behavior. We then elaborate on the main theories of the origins of racial attitudes and behaviors among children, describing traditional theories and then highlighting more contemporary theories. We discuss the empirical research relevant to these theories including, when relevant, prejudice-reduction techniques that have grown out of these theories. Finally, future directions for research on understanding and addressing racial attitudes and behaviors among youth are discussed.

DEFINITIONS AND MEASURES

Most research on children's racial and ethnic attitudes has focused on prejudice. *Prejudice* has been defined as holding negative feelings toward a group and its members or exhibiting hostile or negative treatment directed at a group and its members (e.g., Brown, 1995). Although there are distinctions between race and ethnicity (e.g., Quintana, 1998), racial and ethnic group memberships appear to have similar implications for prejudice; thus, we discuss the findings of research on race and ethnicity together. We focus only on ethnic and racial prejudice because of the combined set of features differentiating it from other prejudices. For example, the category of race is less malleable (e.g., people may move in and out of the category of overweight), more visible (e.g., people's sexual orientation is not a visible category), and allows for social separation more readily (e.g., people may be biased toward members of the other gender, while also engaging in intimate relationships with them) than other prejudices. Because research on racial and ethnic prejudice may not, therefore, generalize to other forms of prejudice, the focus of this chapter is research that contributes to our understanding of the development of racial and ethnic prejudice in children.

Developmentally appropriate assessments of children's racial and ethnic attitudes are critically important. Whereas older children can complete surveys on their own, most younger children complete surveys with the help of an experimenter.

Prejudice measures typically assess affect toward an outgroup with the use of "liking" or emotion words. One of the early measures of prejudice among young children, for example, was the doll preference task developed by Clark and Clark (1947). Experimenters asked children to select a black or white doll that best fit several attributes, such as goodness and niceness.

Whereas prejudice is considered an affective component of intergroup attitudes (Aboud, 1988), stereotyping is considered a cognitive component of intergroup attitudes and refers to associating attributes (e.g., personality and morality traits) with a group (Allport, 1954). Yet, there are very few "pure" stereotyping measures in the children's literature. Many of the measures that assess attributes concern evaluative traits (good, bad), which suggests they should be classified as prejudice measures. Others have evaluative traits (e.g., good, bad) along with stereotypical traits (e.g., smart, aggressive). For example, in the Preschool Racial Attitude Measure (PRAM) designed by John Williams and colleagues (Williams, Best, & Boswell, 1975), children were shown a series of line drawings of two children (e.g., African American and European American), and asked to select the figure that best completed the story: "Here are two girls; One of them is happy and smiles almost all the time. Which one is the happy girl?" The Multi-Response Racial Attitude Measure (MRA; Aboud, 2003; Doyle & Aboud, 1995), which builds on the PRAM and uses similar attributes, requires children to distribute positive and negative attributes to members of the ingroup, outgroup, both, or neither.

One relatively new measure of racial stereotyping and prejudice developed for use with children is the Black/White Intergroup Attitude Scale (BIAS; Hughes, Bigler, & Levy, 2007). The stereotyping component of the BIAS assesses children's stereotyping of African American and European American groups in three domains—occupations, activities, and traits—similar to measures of gender stereotyping (e.g., Children's Occupations, Attitudes, and Traits; Liben & Bigler, 2002). The prejudice component of the BIAS, the Black/White Evaluative Trait Scale, assesses children's positive and negative views of African American and European American groups. The BIAS differs from other prejudice and stereotyping measures in two ways. The first is that the stereotyping and prejudice items included in the BIAS were chosen specifically not to conflate the cognitive and affective components of children's racial attitudes, but instead to assess them independently. A second unique characteristic of the BIAS is that it assesses children's attitudes toward African Americans and attitudes toward European Americans independently, by asking children to evaluate one racial group on all of the scale items, and then the other racial group on all of the items. Thus, children's racial attitudes toward the two groups are scored independently, in line with recent theorizing that ingroup and outgroup attitudes are in fact independent constructs (e.g., Aboud, 2003; Brewer, 1999; Cameron, Alvarez, Ruble, & Fuligni, 2001).

Another cognitive measure of intergroup attitudes, group knowledge, assesses the participants' existing knowledge of a group (e.g., customs, heritage; see Gimmestad & de Chiara, 1982), but unlike stereotyping measures does not assess knowledge of associated traits. As is the case with the BIAS, measures of group knowledge face the challenge of maintaining construct validity over time and across samples, given appreciable temporal variation in the stereotypes and knowledge that people hold regarding various ethnic groups (see Allport, 1954; Karlins, Coffman, & Walters, 1969).

Discrimination is considered the behavioral component of prejudice, and refers to partial or biased treatment of people based on group membership (Aboud & Amato, 2001). Measures of discrimination assess behavior toward a group or group member, such as reward allocation, or punishment (Aboud, 1988; Aboud & Amato, 2001). There are also measures of preferred social distance (i.e., Bogardus Social Distance Scale; Hartley, 1946), particularly willingness to play with a member of the ingroup or outgroup (e.g., Abrams, Rutland, & Cameron 2003; Karafantis & Levy, 2004; Katz, 1973; Levy & Dweck, 1999). For example, in a recent measure by Levy, West, Bigler, et al. (2005), children were shown a sheet of 16 black-and-white photographs (balanced by race—in this case, African Americans and European Americans—and gender) in yearbook format (e.g., "Who would you rather *NOT* sit next to at a movie theater? Circle as many pictures of people who you would rather *NOT* sit next to at a movie theatre. If you would be willing to sit next to all these people, do not circle any pictures."). This measure allows for assessment of ingroup and one or more outgroup attitudes, and is covert because it is unclear to participants that race is the key variable under study.

Most measures of children's racial attitudes are overt measures. Although a straightforward technique has advantages, there are also disadvantages. Straightforward questions, for example, may be offensive to some children. In addition, the socially desirable response may be obvious to older children. Although some research suggests that social desirability issues are not problematic (e.g., Doyle, Beaudet, & Aboud, 1988), other studies show its effect increases with age (Rutland, Cameron, Milne, & McGeorge, 2005). However, most developmental researchers, like researchers with adults studying sensitive topics, take steps (e.g., ensuring confidentiality, using anonymous responding, providing some privacy) to reduce social desirability effects, because such effects cannot be eliminated.

Indirect measures of prejudice also exist. For example, in some assessments, children are asked to make judgments about ambiguous situations involving members of different racial groups (e.g., Katz, Sohn, & Zalk, 1975; Margie, Killen, & Sinno, 2005; McGlothlin, Killen, & Edmonds, 2005; Sagar & Schofield, 1980). An early indirect measure is the Katz–Zalk projective test, in which elementary school children were shown ambiguous interracial slides of common school situations and asked to select which child is likely to receive a good outcome (e.g., win a trophy) and which one is likely to receive a bad outcome (e.g., get reprimanded by a teacher). More recently, in Killen and colleagues' Ambiguous Pictures Task (Margie et al., 2005; McGlothlin et al., 2005), children are presented with colored pencil drawings of African American and European American children, potentially performing moral transgressions (e.g., stealing money from someone, pushing someone off a swing). Children evaluate two versions of the story (one in which a member of each racial group is the potential transgressor) and describe their understanding of the scene and evaluate the characters' motivations. Such measures are unique and advantageous in that the context of the intergroup judgment is taken into account.

There are also measures of children's implicit intergroup attitudes (i.e., attitudes outside their awareness). Rutland et al. (2005) and Baron and Banaji (2006) have adapted the Implicit Association Test (Greenwald & Banaji, 1995), which was developed with adults, for use with children. The measure assesses children's positive and negative association with racial groups (e.g., African American, European American) by measuring how quickly children classify a word as positive or negative when it is paired with a particular racial group. For example, quick responses to the pairing of African American and positive evaluative words suggests a positive association to African Americans.

THEORIES OF THE ORIGINS OF PREJUDICE AMONG CHILDREN

PSYCHODYNAMIC APPROACH

Early theories of the development of prejudice suggested that prejudice among children was a rare, abnormal problem. This limited viewpoint was put forth by the psychodynamic approach to prejudice as articulated by Adorno, Frenkel-Brunswick, Levinson, and Sanford (1950) in their classic book *The Authoritarian Personality*. Adorno and colleagues' research was an attempt to understand the atrocities of Nazi Germany. Adorno and colleagues proposed that parenting styles characterized by punishment and threats created racial prejudice in children. They suggested that children exposed to threat and punishment in response to expressions of unconventional behavior developed inadequate egos. In an environment forcefully promoting conventionalism and submission to authority, children relied on defense mechanisms to release their aggressive impulses, such as projecting their anger onto social deviants, rather than onto their "powerful" parents (on whom they relied). Children projected their anger onto social deviants because authority figures approved of aggression toward these targets. The projection of anger onto social deviants, which in some contexts could include members of racial or ethnic minorities, was thought to give rise to prejudice toward certain outgroups. The *authoritarian personality* was thought to develop during adolescence, based on these childhood experiences.

The original psychodynamic theorizing suggested that therapy is the appropriate treatment for children who exhibit prejudice (Cotharin & Mikulas, 1975), but such therapeutic techniques are not common today. This is in part because the psychodynamic approach to prejudice has been criticized on theoretical (nonrefutable theory) and methodological grounds (subjective interviews of adults about their past; see Altemeyer, 1981). Contemporary research as discussed later has made it clear that the authoritarian personality does not reflect any one national climate (e.g., a "German personality"). Prejudice is pervasive, and atrocities have occurred all over the world at the hands of many different groups. Prejudice, then, is no longer considered an abnormal occurrence (although acts of discrimination are, in many countries, illegal).

Contemporary work on the authoritarian personality has shed most of the psychodynamic framework, and instead focuses more on a social learning framework. Although this work has established a conceptual link between racial and ethnic prejudice and authoritarianism as a learned belief system including excessive conformity, submission to authority, and hostility toward those deviating from authority-sanctioned standards of behavior (e.g., Altemeyer, 1981), this work is typically done with college-age samples. Thus, there is little understanding of the potential contributing role of authoritarianism to prejudice among children.

SOCIAL LEARNING APPROACH

Another early theory of the development of prejudice among children is social learning theory, originally proposed in Allport's classic (1954) work, *The Nature of Prejudice*. According to this theory, children learn prejudice by observing and imitating role models such as parents. Similar to the psychodynamic approach to prejudice, the social learning approach suggests that children's prejudice increases with age. Allport suggested, however, that children mimic, and then come to believe, what they are exposed to in their environments.

There is much evidence supporting social learning theory more generally (e.g., Bandura, 1977). Research, however, has provided inconsistent evidence regarding the relation between children's racial attitudes and the racial attitudes of others in their environment, such as parents. For example, a positive relation was found between the racial attitudes of European American fathers and their adolescent sons, but not for African American father–son pairs (Carlson & Iovini, 1985). Other research has revealed that as African American children age, their attitudes toward African Americans and European Americans gradually become more like their parents' attitudes (Branch & Newcombe, 1986). Further, approximately 8-year-old White Canadian children's racial attitudes were not strongly related to their mothers' racial attitudes (Aboud & Doyle, 1996b).

Another potential source of prejudice, according to social learning theory, is children's peers. One study found little overlap between the racial attitudes and behaviors of approximately 14-year-old European American and African American children and those of their peers (Patchen, 1983). Other studies have shown school-aged European American children and their peers do not generally possess similar racial attitudes, although the children *perceived* their peers to hold attitudes similar to their own (Aboud & Doyle, 1996b; Ritchey & Fishbein, 2001).

Why might children not share their racial attitudes with many of their role models? Some evidence suggests that parents, particularly members of race-majority groups, rarely discuss prejudice with their children (see Aboud & Amato, 2001). Ironically, it appears that more racially tolerant parents may not discuss racial issues with their children for fear of bringing attention to race. Yet, it has been shown that when adults and peers address prejudice, it is decreased (Aboud & Doyle, 1996a).

For example, Aboud and Doyle (1996a) found that low-prejudice (as assessed at pretest) White Canadian third and fourth graders who discussed their racial attitudes with a high-prejudice peer actually lowered their peer's prejudice. Thus, the lack of strong relation between attitudes of children and their role models may stem from a lack of explicit discussion, not a lack of influence. Indeed, cognitive developmental work suggests that when children are actively engaged in the learning strategy, it is more likely that the information will be internalized, generalized, and acted on (e.g., Teasley, 1995).

Linguistic Connotation Theorizing

Linguisitic connotation is one subtheory of social learning theory that has specifically focused on very young children. Williams and colleagues (e.g., Williams & Edwards, 1969) hypothesized that racial attitudes developed in part from the connotative meaning of color names in U.S. culture. They showed that European American preschoolers tend to evaluate the color white positively and to evaluate the color black negatively. Further, other research has demonstrated a causal relation between color associations and racial attitudes. Williams and Edwards (1969; also see Elliot & Tyson, 1983) used positive reinforcement (e.g., "all right"; receipt of three small candies) and negative reinforcement (e.g., "no"; loss of two pennies) to train preschoolers to make positive associations with the color black (black animals) and negative ones with the color white (white animals). The training weakened, but did not reverse, the children's original color concepts, and promoted less negative evaluations of African Americans on the PRAM measure described earlier. Thus, interventions that target evaluative dimensions of racial labels have the potential to increase tolerance among this age group. Such techniques may be less effective among older children who have more sophisticated understandings that are not addressed by simple reconditioning of color concepts. The findings do suggest, however, that if children learn prejudice from their environment, they can unlearn prejudice, too.

Merely replacing old beliefs with new beliefs may be an overly simplistic approach (e.g., Bigler, 1999) especially among older children. Active teaching strategies may be necessary to counter children's preexisting biases. Unfortunately, many of the studies in which children are given counterstereotypic information about socially stigmatized groups apply a passive learning strategy such as direct instruction from the socializer to the participant (e.g., Elliot & Tyson, 1983) or viewing material from the media (see Graves, 1999). These strategies have a minimal effect on children's racial attitudes. The information may need to be rich and complex, reflecting the reality of racial and ethnic issues, and to be communicated in ways that facilitate children's active processing of the information.

Multicultural Theorizing

Multicultural education is one popular approach to prejudice reduction, derived from social learning theories. Multicultural education theorizing suggests that prejudice develops because of a lack of both knowledge and understanding of diverse groups. Multicultural theory suggests that through learning about cultural groups, individuals will understand and respect other cultures, thereby reducing negative attitudes (Banks, 1995). Often, multicultural education involves children's participation in and out of the classroom, such as class art projects in observance of a cultural holiday, or trips to museums with a cultural focus as well as direct learning about the culture.

Although laudable in many ways, a criticism of the multicultural approach is that the celebration of cultural "differences" may increase the likelihood that children and adolescents will place individuals into rigid categories, thereby increasing racial and ethnic stereotyping and prejudice. This is especially true among children who lack the cognitive sophistication to recognize that individuals fit into multiple categories (e.g., age, race, or gender; Bigler, 1999). Similarly, Bigler and colleagues (e.g., Bigler, Brown, & Markell, 2001; Patterson & Bigler, 2006) have demonstrated that explicit mention of perceptually salient social categories results in the development of biased attitudes. Educational curricula that focus specifically on the history of certain racial groups within a racially diverse society may, by highlighting race and racial differences, inadvertently increase children's racial biases. For example, the presentation of race-related educational material during Black History Month differentiates people according to racial group membership. Children exposed to this information may conclude that race is an important dimension along which individuals differ—thus, stereotyping and prejudice will increase rather than decrease. This work points to limiting the use of race as a differentiating characteristic in the classroom, or, when discussing race, to emphasize the similarities across, and differences within, racial groups.

Banks (1995) further suggested that effective multicultural education requires that the total school environment reflect the cultural diversity of American society and to help children all experience educational equality. Banks suggested that changes be made in the "values and attitudes of the school staff, curricula and teaching materials, assessment and testing procedures, teaching and motivational styles, and values and norms sanctioned by the school" (p. 329). Banks's multicultural school reform proposal appears less susceptible to some of the concerns raised about proposals that include minimal additions to school curricula (e.g., inclusion of race-related material only as part of a month-to-month recognition of nonmajority groups).

Antiracist Theorizing

Similar to multicultural education theorizing, antiracist education theorizing suggests prejudice derives in part from a lack of intergroup knowledge, namely an awareness and understanding of the history and roots of inequality (e.g., McGregor, 1993). Antiracist education often goes hand in hand with multicultural education efforts in elementary and secondary schools. Antiracist teaching involves descriptions of past and contemporary racial discrimination and inequalities, pointing out the forces that maintain racism. This may increase empathy and at the same time discourage future racism. However, if not done carefully, such teaching could be counterproductive for both perpetrators and targets of racism. Providing insight into the prejudice of the students' ingroup and the students' own prejudiced reactions may make students feel angry or self-righteous (Kehoe & Mansfield, 1993). In addition, "classroom materials and activities used to illustrate the existence of racism may appear stereotyped, threatening, or humiliating from the point of view of minority children" (McGregor, 1993, p. 216). Yet, a reaction of guilt may have positive outcomes in older adolescents. For example, research with college-age students suggests that guilt can be a motivating force in reducing people's expression of prejudice (Monteith, 1993). Therefore, although perhaps a powerful intervention, it is necessary that steps be taken to minimize potentially negative side effects of antiracist education, for example, by providing examples of majority group members who are working to end racism and by pointing out similarities between groups to avoid stereotyping (see Hughes, Bigler, and Levy, 2007).

One pair of studies reported by Hughes and colleagues (2007) examined the effects of learning about historical racism on the racial attitudes of European American and African American children. The experimental groups in these studies received lessons about famous African American leaders, and embedded in these lessons were examples of the racial discrimination they experienced. Children in control groups received the same biographical information about the leaders, with the exception of any mention or examples of racism. Posttest examinations of European American children's racial attitudes revealed significantly lower degrees of anti-African American prejudice among children in the experimental group compared to the control group, which exhibited significantly more negative than positive evaluations of African Americans. Although there were no differences between conditions among African American children, both they and the European American children also exhibited greater valuing of interracial fairness in the antiracism condition than in the control condition. Thus, these studies are one example of positive consequences of teaching children about the pernicious effects of racial discrimination.

In the preceding studies, children were more or less passive recipients of antiracist messages. In other studies, researchers have tested the impact of direct engagement in the emotional experience of being the target of prejudice on children's racial attitudes and behaviors. Firsthand experiences with prejudice may motivate children to alleviate others' distress as if it were their own—that is, by acting in a less biased way toward racial outgroups (Underwood & Moore, 1982). One of the earliest examples of antiracist empathy training was a classroom demonstration devised by Jane Elliot in the late 1960s. In response to the assassination of Martin Luther King, Jr., Elliot, a teacher in a predominately European American rural town, taught her approximately 8-year-old students how it would feel to be a target of discrimination. Elliot chose eye color as a characteristic that would differentiate the students, telling students on one day that blue-eyed children were superior, and on the next day, that brown-eyed children were superior. She enhanced the lesson by showing preferential treatment to the "superior" group the entire day, and pointing out the successes and failures of group members as evidence of the group's superior or inferior position. Therefore, for one day, each group of children had a firsthand experience with discrimination on the basis of an arbitrary characteristic.

However, actual evidence of the effectiveness of the blue eyes/brown eyes simulation is minimal. Weiner and Wright (1973), as an exception, tested a variation of the blue eyes/brown eyes simulation with approximately 8-year-old European American students. In this case, the classroom teacher told children that they were members of "green" or "orange" groups and asked to them to wear colored armbands. Like Elliot, the teacher encouraged discrimination against each group for 1 day. Compared to the control classroom, participants in the simulation reported more willingness to attend a picnic with Black children. These results provide encouraging support for the impact of antiracism role-playing on intergroup attitudes.

One caveat with empathy training is that age-related cognitive and affective skills are necessary to benefit from the training. Older, more cognitively sophisticated children generally have more sophisticated empathy skills than younger children (McGregor, 1993). Thus, it is possible that if children lack the sophistication to engage in perspective taking, as well as the ability to properly interpret the emotional arousal induced by experiencing discrimination, empathic activities may not effectively reduce children's prejudice. Rather, it is possible for cognitively unsophisticated children to experience increased negativity or avoidance of other racial groups as a result of intervention efforts.

Colorblind Theorizing

The aforementioned work on the social learning approach suggests prejudice can be reduced by highlighting social categories such as race and ethnicity and directly countering some of the learned prejudice. A contrasting hypothesis, offered by the colorblind approach, is that prejudice derives from people's emphasis on race, and therefore prejudice can be decreased by deemphasizing race. Researchers have long suggested that the colorblind theory should facilitate social harmony in the racially diverse U.S. society. It is captured by the "melting pot" metaphor, which suggests that differences between people immigrating to a country such as the United States eventually melt away such that there is "no longer any visible or psychological basis for prejudice" (Allport, 1954, p. 517).

The main thrust of the colorblind approach that suggests that race should not be emphasized has been tested in various interventions with children with some success. One way to implement the colorblind theory—or the notion of deemphasizing race—to reduce racial prejudice is to turn people's attention toward the universal qualities of humans instead of racial group membership. Houser (1978), for example, examined whether stereotyping toward several ethnic groups would be reduced among 5- to 9-year-old children who watched (vs. did not watch) films promoting the message that it is important to focus on universally shared qualities. For example, one film called *The Toymaker* depicted the story of two puppets who were best friends until they looked in the mirror and realized that one had stripes and the other had spots. The toymaker pointed out that they were both created by the same person and were essentially connected to each other (each covering one hand of the toymaker). Although the film clips were brief (approximately 10 to 15 minutes), children who watched them reported a decrease in stereotyping toward several ethnic groups from pretest to posttest, relative to children who did not view any films but rather participated in regular classroom activities.

Alternatively, children's focus on racial group membership could be redirected to the unique internal characteristics of individuals such as likes and dislikes. Aboud and Fenwick (1999), for example, found that 10-year-old White Canadian children who participated (vs. did not participate) in an 11-week school-based program that trained them to focus on the internal attributes of people demonstrated a decrease in prejudice toward Blacks. Experiments that deemphasize race by directing children's attention to individual differences within a group have also showed promise for reducing prejudice (e.g., Katz, 1973). For example, Katz (1973) trained 7- and 11-year-old African American and European American children to attend to the unique characteristics of people. In one condition, the uniqueness of individuals within a racial group was highlighted by having children associate names with photographs of children of a different race. In the other condition, children were explicitly prompted to determine whether pairs of photographs were the same (thus to attend to individual differences). Both experimental conditions led to reduced reported social distance and prejudice among both African American and European American children of both age groups studied, when compared to a control condition in which children simply viewed the photographs.

Several experiments (e.g., Jones & Foley, 2003) have used a combination approach in which attention is diverted from social group category information to how people are both similar and unique (all people are the same in a way, but each person is also unique). In one experiment, Levy, West, Bigler, et al. (2005) had African American and Latino children, 11 to 14 years old, read two science readers (one about the weather, the other about recycling), which featured an equal number of light- and dark-skinned males and females. For example, in a scene in the "weather" book in which the depicted children appeared frightened by thunder and lightning, the similar–unique combined message was: "All humans are the same. Everyone gets scared sometimes, but each person also is a unique individual. Different things scare different individuals." Children who were randomly assigned to the control condition read only about the main topic of the book (e.g., weather). Children in the similar–unique condition reported greater levels of egalitarianism and greater desired social closeness to unfamiliar European American peers compared to those in the control condition. The combination message, suggesting that people are both similar and unique, was most successful in increasing participants' beliefs in social equality and treatment, also leaving positive views of their own group intact. The combined message may be the most effective and appealing, because it is the most realistic and serves people's needs to be both similar and different from others (e.g., see Brewer, 1991).

In sum, diverting attention from racial and ethnic categories shows some promise. Yet, a total colorblind approach to education is controversial because race and other grouping characteristics do affect people's lives. For example, efforts to assimilate immigrants and ethnic groups into the dominant culture often do not work (Garcia & Hurtado, 1995). The colorblind approach may facilitate intolerance by glossing over the rich histories of less dominant cultures and by ignoring past and present U.S. racism (e.g., Schofield, 1986). When racism occurs, the colorblind theory can be used to justify inaction through denial, thereby helping maintain the current power structure and preserving the privileges of the dominant group (e.g., Schofield, 1986). This more intolerant aspect of the colorblind theory appears to develop with age and reveal itself in late adolescence and adulthood (Levy, West, & Ramirez, 2005).

Mere Exposure Theorizing

Another variation of the social learning approach is captured by mere exposure theorizing. This theory suggests that negative attitudes arise from a lack of exposure to outgroup members. Allport (1954) referred to this as "fear of the strange" (p. 300). Through repeated vicarious exposure to and observation of outgroup members via multiethnic readers, pictures, and television (e.g., Graves, 1999; Litcher & Johnson, 1969), positive intergroup attitudes presumably will emerge (Graves, 1999; Litcher & Johnson, 1969). The results from studies based on the theory of mere exposure have not been encouraging. For instance, there was no significant reduction in negative attitudes among sixth graders exposed to excerpts from children's stories about Mexican Americans (Koeller, 1977); thus, mere exposure may not be adequate to change negatively held attitudes (see Banks, 1995; Bigler, 1999; Bigler & Liben, 1993). Additional challenge to the theory is posed by continuing existence of prejudice among children even in contemporary times (e.g., Black-Gutman & Hickson, 1996; Hughes et al., 2007), when media provide much exposure to racially diverse characters.

Extended Contact Theory

Extended contact theory goes beyond mere exposure theorizing. The "extended contact effect" or "indirect cross friendship hypothesis" (e.g., Cameron & Rutland, 2006, 2008; Cameron, Rutland, Brown, & Douch, 2006) suggests that knowing that members of one's own group (e.g., Latinos) are friends with members of another group (e.g., European Americans) leads to more positive attitudes toward that group (e.g., European Americans). Support for the extended contact hypothesis is widespread, with applications across development from childhood to adulthood (see Cameron & Rutland, 2008).

For example, in studies by Cameron and Rutland (2006), children read and discuss several fiction books in which members of their ingroup have close friendships with outgroup members. Afterward, children tend to show more positive outgroup attitudes (a measure similar to the MRA discussed earlier) and more willingness to interact with an outgroup member in the future (a measure similar to the intended behavior ones discussed earlier), whereas their attitudes and intended behavior toward the ingroup are not changed. Optimal conditions of extended contact include the salience and typicality of the ingroup and outgroup members, as well as high ingroup identification on the part of the participant or the observer (e.g., Cameron & Rutland, 2006). Also, Cameron and Rutland showed that among children, one avenue through which extended contact can lead to more positive outgroup attitudes is through psychologically including members of the outgroup in the recipient's self-concept.

Intergroup Contact Theory

Intergroup contact theory goes one step further by suggesting that interacting with outgroups facilitates developing positive concepts about them. According to intergroup contact theory originally proposed by Allport (1954; Pettigrew, 1998), prejudice, develops, in part, out of a lack of personal, positive contact among members of different groups. It became clear after the initial desegregation of U.S. schools that simply providing the opportunity for intergroup contact did not always lead to improved intergroup relations. That is, even though there was racial diversity in the schools, students continued to segregate themselves socially according to race, and to express racial prejudice. Unfortunately, schools help create "resegregation" by "tracking" children according to ability, which tends to occur in discriminatory ways, separating children across race lines, thereby reducing opportunities for positive contact in the classroom, which transfers to the lunchroom and schoolyard (Khmelkov & Hallinan, 1999).

There is now a large literature with children and adults showing that intergroup contact that is individualized and cooperative, maintains equal status between individuals, and is sanctioned by authorities tends to promote intergroup understanding and friendships (e.g., Pettigrew & Tropp, 2006; Tropp & Prenovost, 2008). Researchers have shown that intergroup harmony can be promoted by altering features of the classroom environment in accordance with these principles. For instance, Aronson and Gonzalez (1988) designed what is called the *jigsaw classroom,* in which students work cooperatively to learn and teach each other components of an academic lesson. This technique replaces competitive aspects of the classroom with cooperative ones. For example, students in a classroom are divided into six racially and academically mixed groups, each consisting of six students. Each group learns one sixth of the information that is unique, valuable, and necessary to understand the full lesson. Then, participants in each of the original groups are divided so that new groups are composed of one member of each of the original groups, thereby allowing them to teach each other the entire lesson. Thus, the jigsaw technique promotes interdependence and cooperation in a racially diverse classroom. This form of cooperative learning successfully improved children's relationships with each other and increased self-esteem, and provided the fortunate side effect of enhancing students' academic success. Other variations of cooperative learning have been successful at increasing intergroup harmony (e.g., Johnson & Johnson, 2000), including bilingual education (e.g., Wright & Tropp, 2005).

One unfortunate weakness of the cooperative learning strategy in improving intergroup relations is that cross-race friendships may not persist after cooperative learning ends. In general, cross-race friendships tend to decrease with age (e.g., Khmelkov & Hallinan, 1999; Mendelson & Aboud, 1999). This trend is somewhat surprising, given that there do not appear to be qualitative differences between cross-race and same-race friendships, which would warrant a greater reduction in cross-race friendships (Mendelson & Aboud, 1999). However, some have suggested that cross-race friendships are generally more fragile (Khmelkov & Hallinan, 1999), leaving them more likely to end when peer groups shrink and dating begins. Research on social reasoning by Killen and colleagues (Killen, Lee-Kim, McGlothlin, & Stangor, 2002) suggests that shifts in children's reasoning may in part account for why cross-race friendships decline. Killen and colleagues' work has shown that, with increasing age, children think that it is more acceptable to exclude other-race peers from friendships because they believe that groups function better when everyone is of the same race (presuming that they share interests).

Summary

Many theories fit under the heading of social learning approach to the development of prejudice. Research to date suggests that being raised in a prejudiced environment does not necessarily translate into developing prejudiced attitudes, nor does a tolerant environment necessarily lead to tolerant attitudes. This is likely because children are socialized by many agents in their environment (e.g., parents, peers, media). There is some evidence that those messages that are communicated in the most direct and interactive ways are the most relevant and effective. Simply reconditioning or providing counterstereotypic information is overly simplistic and thus not effective, especially among older children. When the environment is racially diverse, implementing a cooperative learning technique is an effective vehicle for reducing prejudice and also for enhancing academic success. Other interventions based on social learning theory, such as multicultural education and antiracist teaching, do not rely on a racially diverse setting; but they include some counterintuitive traps that could actually increase prejudice. Social learning theorizing continues, but is also being increasingly incorporated into other theories, as discussed later.

COGNITIVE APPROACH

Research on cognitive theories, like social learning theories, suggests prejudice derives from fundamental, normal psychological processes. The cognitive-developmental theory was originally articulated by Piaget (Piaget & Weil, 1951) and was applied to the understanding of prejudice by Katz (1973), Aboud (1988), and Bigler and Liben (1993), among others. The cognitive-developmental theory suggests that children's attitudes toward racial and ethnic groups are influenced by their ability to think about group information in complex ways. For example, a child cannot express empathy for another person until he or she has the ability to see the world through another person's perspective.

According to cognitive-developmental theorizing, prejudice is inevitable among young children because they lack the skills necessary to view people as individuals. Cognitive-developmental theory suggests that children are initially focused on themselves and then on social categories in which they tend to focus on surface features and to exaggerate differences among groups (such as assuming that all members of group A do X). Only later, as their cognitive systems mature, can children recognize similarities across groups (e.g., some members of group A *and* of group B do X) and differences within the same group (some members of group A do X, and some members of group A do Y). As children obtain these skills, they are more able to judge people as individuals and thus their prejudice is reduced. With age, presumably all children obtain the cognitive skills that allow for reduced prejudice. These skills are apparently obtained between the ages of 7 and 11. However, prejudice is not perpetually reduced with age.

There is some research to support this theorizing. As early as preschool and kindergarten, race-majority group children exhibit prejudice; examples include prejudice of English Canadians toward French Canadians (Doyle et al., 1988), Euro-Australians toward Aboriginal Australians (Black-Gutman & Hickson, 1996), and Jewish Israelis toward Arabs (Bar-Tal, 1996). Young majority children typically assign more positive and fewer negative attributes to their own groups (*ingroups*) than to other groups (*outgroups*), but show a decline in prejudice at around age 7 (e.g., Doyle & Aboud, 1995; Doyle et al., 1988). Research indeed shows that shifts toward reduced prejudice levels are explained in part by acquisition of the social cognitive skills thought to enable prejudice reduction, such as the ability to classify others on multiple dimensions (Bigler & Liben, 1993; Katz et al., 1975), the ability to perceive similarities between members of different groups (Black-Gutman & Hickson, 1996; Doyle & Aboud, 1995), and the ability to perceive differences within the same group (Doyle & Aboud, 1995; Katz et al., 1975). There is some evidence that these age-related differences cannot be easily explained by increased concerns with appearing prejudiced (Doyle & Aboud, 1995).

The cognitive-developmental approach has much in common with adult social psychological literature on motivated social cognition. This line of work has shown, consistent with the developmental work, that mature social perceivers who exhibit lower levels of stereotyping are high in their perception of similarities across groups, high in attributional complexity, high in need for cognition, and low in need for simple cognitive structure (see Levy, 1999). Thus, cognitive skills that are acquired with age are also known to express themselves as individual differences among adults and influence levels of stereotyping. Thus, after developing cognitive-developmental skills, children may not necessarily use them. Differential use of these skills or differential accessibility of such conceptions over time may account for stable individual differences (see Levy, 1999).

The causal role of cognitive-developmental skills in prejudice among children has been tested. Katz (1973) trained children to perceive differences among members of the same group. This intervention targeted children who were just obtaining this ability (7-year-olds) and those who likely had already obtained the ability (10-year-olds). In this brief intervention lasting approximately 15 minutes, Katz taught European American children to differentiate among photographs of either African American children (experimental condition) or European American children (control condition). Two weeks later, children in the experimental condition gave fewer prejudiced responses than those in the control condition, regardless of age.

It is notable that the aforementioned experiments incorporated aspects of cognitive-developmental theory in addition to social learning theory. That is, focusing on the evolving social-cognitive ability of noticing cross-group similarities overlaps with teaching shared qualities. Likewise, similar to the evolving social-cognitive ability of noticing within-group differences is focusing on unique qualities of individuals. This overlap is an important one, and suggests that social cognitive skills can be taught and strengthened through antibias messages.

Other experiments to test the causal role of cognitive-developmental skills in children's prejudice roles have been less successful. These have focused on the multiple classification skill training. Bigler and Liben (1992) trained 5- to 10-year-old children to sort or to classify photographs of people into piles based on salient features of the group (in this case, gender and occupation). Although in this case less gender stereotyping was observed in the training condition, the impact of multiple classification training on levels of prejudice has not been demonstrated (see Bigler et al., 2001; Cameron et al., 2006).

Summary

Accumulating evidence indicates that cognitive-developmental skills play a role in prejudice development. Thus, cognitive-developmental theory has served as a base for several interventions, generally involving cognitive skill training. More work is needed. The cognitive-developmental theory, despite supportive evidence, is not currently defined in a way that explains individual differences in prejudice among children exhibiting similar cognitive skill levels; thus, both environmental and cognitive factors may need to be considered (e.g., Black-Gutman & Hickson, 1996; Levy, 1999; Levy & Dweck, 1999), as discussed in the next section.

SOCIAL-COGNITIVE DEVELOPMENTAL APPROACHES

Social-cognitive developmental approaches combine key elements from the aforementioned social and cognitive approaches and, thus, represent hybrid approaches that emphasize both aspects of the person (e.g., age, cognitive skills) and aspects of the social environment (e.g., influences in the immediate context, broader context).

Social Identity Development Theory

As noted, according to cognitive developmental theory, a key shift in children's focus is from themselves to social categories (ingroups, outgroups). Social identity theory (e.g., Turner, Brown, & Tajfel, 1979), a prominent theory in social psychological research with adults and more recently with children, focuses on the pivotal role of people's numerous social identities (e.g., gender, nationality, social class, race), which become salient in different situations and impact social judgment and behavior. Unlike cognitive-developmental theory, social identity theory highlights the role of context in eliciting one or more social identities more than others and thereby highlights the interaction between the person and the situation. People are motivated to see their salient ingroups as positive and distinct from outgroups, which can help maintain positive self-esteem and coherence of one's self-image (e.g., Abrams & Hogg, 2001).

To elaborate, social identity research with adults has been expanded and applied to children via social identity development theory (SIDT; Nesdale, 1999; Nesdale, Maass, Durkin & Griffiths, 2005). Consistent with the adult literature on social identity theory, SIDT focuses on the pivotal role that context plays in eliciting a particular valued social identity, leading people to favor their ingroup, derogate the outgroup, or both. For example, Nesdale (1999) found that children's intergroup bias, like that of adults, is likely to be dependent on other factors, such as the extent, stability, and legitimacy of intergroup status differences. Children's subjective identification with social groups, for example, may not be a necessary precondition for exhibiting preference for one's social ingroups. Bennett, Lyons, Sani, and Barrett (1998) found that children (ages 6, 9, 12, and 15 years) who did not identify with their national group, but who were immersed in a culture that exposed them to positive information about their national group, evidenced a preference for that group. This suggests that in a context that strongly favors one's ingroup, ingroup favoritism can emerge in the absence of ingroup identification.

Common Ingroup Identity Model

According to the common ingroup identity model by Gaertner and Dovidio (e.g., Gaertner & Dovidio, 2000; see Gaertner et al., 2008), another prominent theory in social psychological research with adults and more recently with children, prejudice can be reduced by increasing the salience of common superordinate memberships (e.g., a school) or shared features relevant to the shared group membership (e.g., common goals). A shared common identity suggests that previous outgroup members are now ingroup members, receiving the rewards of ingroup favoritism—similar to the extended contact hypothesis reviewed earlier.

In a study with almost 1,000 6- and 7-year-old U.S. elementary school children (approximately two thirds European American, one third African American), Houlette, Gaertner, and Johnson (2004) examined the impact of a widespread U.S. intervention program in which children engaged in a variety of activities with the overall message that all people belong to the human family. The intervention led to greater interest in playing with hypothetical outgroup peers. Further, in studies with 9- and 10-year-old African Portuguese and European Portuguese students and 13- to 17-year-old U.S. students (e.g., African American, Chinese, European American, Hispanic, Japanese, Jewish, and Vietnamese students), the more students felt like they shared an identity, the lower their level of intergroup bias (see Gaertner et al., 2008).

Developmental Model of Subjective Group Dynamics

As noted earlier, an important focus of several theories (cognitive-developmental theory, SIDT) is understanding when and why children favor their ingroups, derogate outgroups, or both. In that work, there is little discussion of the processes that may lead to favoring the outgroup or derogating the ingroup. Abrams, Rutland, Cameron, and Marques (2003) proposed a developmental model of subjective group dynamics (DSGD), which focuses on such processes in the context of social exclusion and inclusion. Their work builds on adult research on small group processes, namely the subjective group dynamics model and the "black sheep effect" in which unlikable or excluded ingroup members are evaluated more negatively than unlikable outgroup members (see Abrams, Rutland, Cameron, et al., 2003). According to the DSGD model, the ingroup needs to be validated to ensure the subjective superiority of the ingroup over relevant outgroups. A deviant outgroup member, who expresses loyalty to the ingroup, can validate the ingroup more than a deviant (or disloyal) ingroup member. Thus, the outgroup member can be favored over the ingroup member. Compared to other models, DSGD focuses on both intergroup processes (evaluations of the ingroup as a whole compared to the outgroup) and on intragroup processes (evaluations of individual members of both ingroup and outgroup).

For example, Abrams, Rutland, and Cameron (2003) had children aged 5 to 12 years evaluate ingroup (English) and outgroup (German) members, including members of these groups who were normative (supported England's soccer team in the 2002 soccer World Cup) or deviant (supported Germany's soccer team). As expected, older children were more sophisticated in their understanding of group loyalty, and exhibited subjective group dynamics. Although favoring the normative over the deviant ingroup member, older children also favored the deviant outgroup member over the deviant ingroup member. Also, older children who identified more strongly with England exhibited greater subjective group dynamics. This research shows that with age, children do not simply use category memberships when they judge group members. DSGD highlights that context, the characteristics of individual group members in relation to group norms, also drives older children's group attitudes.

Social Domain Model

Another prominent theory that has emerged and expanded on children's understanding of group-based exclusion is the social domain model (SDM; e.g., Killen et al., 2002). However, unlike DSGD and SIDT, SDM has its origins in developmental psychology. According to SDM, children's social judgments from a young age are context-specific and influenced by three types of reasoning: moral (e.g., justice, rights, others' welfare), social-conventional (e.g., traditions, rules, norms, including ensuring group functioning), and psychological (e.g., personal choice). In applying this model to the intergroup domain, Killen and colleagues have tested children's application of these three forms of reasoning to intergroup contexts. For instance, Killen and Stangor (2001) found that most children reported that straightforward exclusion of a child from a club because of his or her race (excluding an African American child from the chess club) was wrong for moral reasons, and Killen and colleagues (2002) found that almost all children and adolescents thought excluding a child from school because of race was morally wrong. However, when the context was multifaceted, for example, when the children learned the qualifications of a stereotypic and nonstereotypic child who wanted to join a club, children (particularly older children) used social-conventional reasons (e.g., group functioning) in addition to moral reasons for excluding some other-race children from the club. In a friendship context, sometimes participants (namely older children) tended to judge exclusion as okay because of psychological reasons (personal choice to select friends). This line of research, then, also highlights the need to study context, but also to focus on the reasoning children bring to intergroup contexts.

Social-Developmental Perspective on Lay Theories

Complementary to other work that has emphasized the interaction of person variables and context variables in intergroup judgments, Levy and colleagues have tested a social-developmental perspective on the role of children's and adults' pervasive lay (everyday) theories on their intergroup judgments. Their social-developmental perspective, drawing on ecological perspectives (e.g., Bronfenbrenner, 1979), social identity theories (e.g., Turner et al., 1979), and social domain theory (e.g., Killen et al., 2002), emphasizes that people interact with and are nested within many potentially different environments; further, this perspective highlights the role that personal characteristics (e.g., age, race, psychological motivations) play in the interpretation of lay theories children receive from their environments. For example, African American and European American children (ages 10–15) tend to see the Protestant work ethic (PWE), the pervasive lay theory that people who work hard succeed (e.g., "All people can pull themselves up by their bootstraps"), as a belief about social equality—everyone can put forth effort and succeed, so everyone is equal (Levy, West, Bigler, et al., 2005; Levy, West, Ramirez, & Karafantis, 2006). With age, greater exposure to the intolerant meaning of the PWE was expected. One example of exposure to the intolerant meaning of PWE is hearing others argue that disadvantaged groups and their members are to blame for their disadvantage for not working hard enough. Indeed, college students who were led to think about past instances of others using PWE in support of such arguments were less egalitarian (reported less support for social equality and donated less money to a homeless shelter) compared to students in a control condition (Levy et al., 2006). Although with experience, all adults may have greater exposure to the prejudice-justifying meaning of PWE than do children, the justifying meaning should be most relevant to advantaged U.S. group members in that it justifies their advantaged place in society. Indeed, consistent with this notion, European American adults endorsed the justifying meaning of PWE more than African American adults. Thus, this work shows that context along with person factors (age, race, psychological needs) help shape people's use of lay theories to support prejudice or tolerance.

Developmental Intergroup Theory

Developmental intergroup theory (DIT; Bigler & Liben, 2006) is a recently developed and integrated approach to ethnic attitude development that combines social identity theory, cognitive-developmental theory, and other empirical findings. According to DIT, intergroup biases develop if a social dimension acquires psychological salience. Four factors contribute to a dimension's psychological salience: perceptual salience of groups, unequal group size, explicit labeling of group membership, and implicit segregation. These four factors characterize society's treatment of race and ethnicity, and thus children are presumed to be likely to view race and ethnicity as an important dimension along which individuals vary. Given the psychological salience of race, the development of racial biases is facilitated by several additional factors, such as essentialist thinking about race and ethnicity (see Hirschfeld, 1995). Additionally, according to DIT, exogenous factors (e.g., stereotypic environmental models) and endogenous factors (e.g., self-esteem, cognitive development) contribute to the maintenance of prejudice and stereotyping. Much developmental research supports DIT, demonstrating, for example, that labeling and other environmental markers of group membership increase the salience of groups to children and lead to the formation of intergroup biases (e.g., Patterson & Bigler, 2006).

Summary

Several theoretical accounts of the development of children's prejudice have integrated social and cognitive-developmental approaches to explain both developmental and individual differences in levels of prejudice among children. Developmental and social mechanisms include: children's self-identification in a racial group (SIDT; Nesdale, 1999; common ingroup identity model, Gaertner & Dovidio, 2000; DIT, Bigler & Liben, 2006), the developmental shift in children's interpersonal focus from self to group to others (SIDT; Nesdale, 1999), intragroup reasoning (DSGD; Abrams, Rutland, Cameron, et al., 2003), moral and social reasoning (SDM; Killen et al., 2002), and children's lay theories (social-developmental perspective; Levy et al., 2006). Further integration is needed, however, to establish a cohesive explanation of the multifaceted nature of children's attitudes, reasoning, and behaviors related to race and ethnicity.

EVOLUTIONARY APPROACH

According to an evolutionary perspective, prejudice and discrimination are nearly inevitable and difficult to change. Fishbein (1996), for example, suggested that the roots of prejudice began in hunter-gatherer tribes and continue universally today because of their success in that period of human evolution. One such proposed evolutionary mechanism relies on a history of related tribe members showing greater preference for each other than for tribe members to whom they were not related, therefore helping and protecting them, which would then maximize the percentage of one's genes that were transmitted to successive generations. Fishbein offers this as evidence that humans are currently predisposed to show favoritism toward individuals who are most genetically similar to themselves. Another such mechanism that may set the stage for prejudice is the human reliance on authority figures to transmit information to their young. This process encourages children to accept unquestioningly what they are told by authority figures, including information about outgroup members. The final mechanism that Fishbein proposes is the hostility that humans have developed to protect their children, females, and resources from outsiders. Fishbein argues that the development of prejudice is closely linked to the development of a group identity around ages 3 or 4.

Another evolutionary perspective suggests that children's thinking about social groups is organized according to inherent theories about humans, which guide the way they gather and interpret information about social groups (Hirschfeld, 1995, 2001). These inherent theories help children attend to important group information and ignore unimportant information. According to this perspective, because the concept of race resonates quite well with children's preexisting cognitive structures for differentiating social groups (i.e., race is visually salient), race becomes a powerful organizing factor for humans.

Despite interest in evolutionary theories of racial prejudice, these approaches have generally been criticized for suggesting that prejudice is natural and thus should be condoned. Still, it seems that certain aspects of evolutionary thought overlap with other approaches to prejudice. For instance, similar to the evolutionary mechanism that favors categorization according to similarities to oneself, the aforementioned cognitive theories propose that such categorization helps individuals simplify the wealth of social information that they encounter. Also, there are obvious similarities between sociocultural and evolutionary explanations that suggest that prejudice grows out of limited resources and social forces. Further, the evolutionary emphasis on accepting information from authority figures complements social learning theory, which suggests that children learn prejudiced views from their parents and other important people in their lives. Evolutionary approaches may be best suited to explaining the history of mechanisms currently facilitating prejudice (e.g., the methods humans use to categorize groups of people), whereas approaches focusing directly on the current mechanisms, such as the social learning theory or cognitive-developmental models, are best suited to understanding the more immediate and hence more relevant (i.e., for the reduction of biases) causes of prejudice.

CONCLUSION AND FUTURE DIRECTIONS

Prejudice is not exclusively a problem that concerns adult populations. Children exhibit racial and ethnic prejudice from a young age. Prejudice is to some degree inevitable because of people's limited cognitive resources and social forces (e.g., hierarchical society, limited environmental resources). Yet, this is an exciting and promising time in the field. It is clear that prejudice is multifaceted and is more likely to be understood by combining elements from different approaches. Further, even from this selective review, it is clear that experiments testing causal mechanisms have revealed many innovative intervention strategies. It seems that in the near future, interventions, like theories, will be increasingly multifaceted, drawing on elements from multiple perspectives.

There are some limitations of the research and some gaps that need to be filled. Much research has focused on Whites or on White–Black relations, and thus the findings are likely limited to those populations. The work that has examined multiple person variables (age, race, gender) makes it clear that a "one size fits all" theory is not sufficient. Another gap in most theoretical work on racial attitudes is the development of prejudice through adolescence. Few empirical investigations have applied the theoretical accounts presented here to research with adolescents. One exception to this is research on social identity theories, which has often focused on adolescent samples. Nonetheless, many aspects of the development of racial prejudice during adolescence, such as the emergence of politically relevant lay theories about race or the link between racial identity and intergroup prejudice, have yet to be examined.

Another issue in future research is the need to study students at schools with overt racial problems. Not surprisingly, many of the schools that are most willing to participate in studies are the schools that are already implementing prejudice-reducing strategies and, relative to other schools, have fewer race problems (e.g., Gimmestad & de Chiara, 1983). This limits the conclusions that can be drawn from studies and fails to accomplish the goal of this work—to understand the roots of prejudice and ways to reduce prejudice. Researchers have lamented the difficulty of securing participation from schools, an obstacle made even more threatening as the recent emphasis on standardized testing in the United States has reduced the time available for nonacademic school-based activities. A key to success in the design and implementation of effective research is a strong partnership among researchers, educators, and parents.

In conclusion, decades of research have provided diverse and informative theoretical approaches to studying the development and reduction of racial prejudice in children. With the increasing diversity of youth in the United States and abroad, it is particularly timely and important to continue making progress toward understanding and reducing racial and ethnic prejudice among children.

REFERENCES

Aboud, F. E. (1988). *Children and prejudice.* New York: Blackwell.

Aboud, F. E. (2003). The formation of ingroup favoritism and outgroup prejudice in young children: Are they distinct attitudes? *Developmental Psychology, 39,* 48–60.

Aboud, F. E., & Amato, M. (2001). Developmental and socialization influences on intergroup bias. In R. Brown & S. Gaertner (Eds.), *Blackwell handbook in social psychology: Vol. 4. Intergroup processes* (pp. 65–85). Oxford, UK: Blackwell.

Aboud, F. E., & Doyle, A. B. (1996a). Does talk of race foster prejudice or tolerance in children? *Canadian Journal of Behavioral Science, 28,* 161–170.

Aboud, F. E., & Doyle, A. B. (1996b). Parental and peer influences on children's racial attitudes. *International Journal of Intercultural Relations, 20,* 371–383.

Aboud, F. E., & Fenwick, V. (1999). Evaluating school-based interventions to reduce prejudice in pre-adolescents. *Journal of Social Issues, 55,* 767–785.

Abrams, D., & Hogg, M. A. (2001). Comments on the motivational status of self-esteem in social identity and intergroup discrimination. In M. A. Hogg & D. Abrams (Eds.), *Intergroup relations: Essential readings* (pp. 232–244). New York: Psychology Press.

Abrams, D., Rutland, A., & Cameron, L. (2003). The development of subjective group dynamics: Children's judgments of normative and deviant in-group and out-group individuals. *Child Development, 74,* 1840–1856.

Abrams, D., Rutland, A., Cameron, L., & Marques, J. M. (2003). The development of subjective group dynamics: When in-group bias gets specific. *British Journal of Developmental Psychology, 21,* 155–176.

Adorno, T. W., Frenkel-Brunswick, E., Levinson, D. J., & Sanford, R. N. (1950). *The authoritarian personality.* New York: Harper.

Allport, G. W. (1954). *The nature of prejudice.* Cambridge, MA: Addison-Wesley.

Altemeyer, B. (1981). *Right-wing authoritarianism.* Winnipeg: University of Manitoba Press.

Aronson, E., & Gonzalez, A. (1988). Desegregation, jigsaw and the Mexican American experience. In P. A. Katz & D. A. Taylor (Eds.), *Eliminating racism: Profiles in controversy* (pp. 301–314). New York: Plenum.

Bandura, A. (1977). *Social learning theory.* Englewood, NJ: Prentice-Hall.

Banks, J. A. (1995). Multicultural education for young children: Racial and ethnic attitudes and their modification. In W. D. Hawley & A. W. Jackson (Eds.), *Toward a common destiny: Improving race and ethnic relations in America* (pp. 236–250). San Francisco: Jossey-Bass.

Baron, A. S., & Banaji, M. R. (2006). The development of implicit attitudes: Evidence of race evaluations from ages 6 and 10 and adulthood. *Psychological Science, 17,* 53–58.

Bar-Tal, D. (1996). Development of social categories and stereotypes in early childhood: The case of "the Arab" concept formation, stereotype and attitudes by Jewish children in Israel. *International Journal of Intercultural Relations, 20,* 341–370.

Bennett, M., Lyons, E., Sani, F., & Barrett, M. (1998). Children's subjective identification with the group and in-group favoritism. *Developmental Psychology, 34,* 902–909.

Bigler, R. S. (1999). The use of multicultural curricula and materials to counter racism in children. *Journal of Social Issues, 55,* 687–705.

Bigler, R. S., Brown, C. S., & Markell, M. (2001). When groups are not created equal: Effects of group status on the formation of intergroup attitudes in children. *Child Development, 72,* 1151–1162.

Bigler, R. S., & Liben, L. S. (1992). Cognitive mechanisms in children's gender stereotyping: Theoretical and educational implications of a cognitive-based intervention. *Child Development, 63,* 1351–1363.

Bigler, R. S., & Liben, L. S. (1993). A cognitive-developmental approach to racial stereotyping and reconstructive memory in Euro-American children. *Child Development, 64,* 1507–1518.

Bigler, R. S., & Liben, L. S. (2006). A developmental intergroup theory of social stereotypes and prejudice. In R. V. Kail (Ed.), *Advances in child development and behavior* (Vol. 34, pp. 38–89). San Diego, CA: Elsevier.

Black-Gutman, D., & Hickson, F. (1996). The relationship between racial attitudes and social-cognitive development in children: An Australian study. *Developmental Psychology, 32,* 448–456.

Branch, C. W., & Newcombe, N. (1986). Racial attitude development among black children as a function of parental attitudes: A longitudinal and cross-sectional study. *Child Development, 57,* 712–721.

Brewer, M. B. (1991). The social self: On being the same and different at the same time. *Personality and Social Psychology Bulletin, 17,* 475–482.

Brewer, M. B. (1999). The psychology of prejudice: Ingroup love or outgroup hate? *Journal of Social Issues, 55,* 429–444.

Bronfenbrenner, U. (1979). Contexts of child rearing: Problems and prospects. *American Psychologist, 34,* 844–850.

Brown, R. (1995). *Prejudice: Its social psychology.* Cambridge, MA: Blackwell.

Cameron, J. A., Alvarez, J. M., Ruble, D. N., & Fuligni, A. J. (2001). Children's lay theories about ingroups and outgroups: Reconceptualizing research on prejudice. *Personality and Social Psychology Review, 5,* 118–128.

Cameron, L., & Rutland, A. (2006). Extended contact through story reading in school: Reducing children's prejudice towards the disabled. *Journal of Social Issues, 62,* 469–488.

Cameron, L., & Rutland, A. (2008). An integrative approach to changing children's intergroup attitudes. In S. R. Levy & M. Killen (Eds.), *Intergroup relations: An integrative developmental and social psychological perspective* (pp. 191–203). New York: Oxford University Press.

Cameron, L., Rutland, A., Brown, R., & Douch, R. (2006). Changing children's intergroup attitudes towards refugees: Testing different models of extended contact. *Child Development, 77,* 1208–1219.

Carlson, J. M., & Iovini, J. (1985). The transmission of racial attitudes from fathers to sons: A study of blacks and whites. *Adolescence, 20,* 233–237.

Clark, K. E., & Clark, M. B. (1947). Racial identification and preference in Negro education. In T. M. Newcomb & E. L. Hartley (Eds.), *Readings in social psychology.* New York: Holt, Rinehart, & Winston.

Cotharin, R. L., & Mikulas, W. L. (1975). Systematic desensitization of racial emotional responses. *Journal of Behavior Therapy & Experimental Psychiatry, 6,* 347–348.

Doyle, A. B., & Aboud, F. E. (1995). A longitudinal study of white children: Racial prejudice as a social-cognitive development. *Merrill-Palmer Quarterly, 41,* 209–228.

Doyle, A. B., Beaudet, J., & Aboud, F. E. (1988). Developmental patterns in the flexibility of children's ethnic attitudes. *Journal of Cross-Cultural Psychology, 19,* 3–18.

Elliot, G. A., & Tyson, G. A. (1983). The effects of modifying color-meaning concepts on the racial attitudes of Black and White South African preschool children. *Journal of Social Psychology, 121,* 181–190.

Fishbein, H. D. (1996). *Peer prejudice and discrimination: Evolutionary, cultural, and developmental dynamics.* Boulder, CO: Westview.

Gaertner, S. L., & Dovidio, J. F. (2000). *Reducing intergroup bias: The common ingroup identity model.* New York: Psychology Press.

Gaertner, S. L., Dovidio, J. F., Guerra, R., Rebelo, M., Monteiro, M. B., Riek, B. M., & Houlette, M. A. (2008). The Common Ingroup Identity model: Applications to children and adults. In S. R. Levy & M. Killen (Eds.), *Intergroup relations: An integrative developmental and social psychological perspective* (pp. 204–219). New York: Oxford University Press.

Garcia, E. E., & Hurtado, A. (1995). Becoming American: A review of current research on the development of racial and ethnic identity in children. In W. D. Hawley & A. W. Jackson (Eds.), *Toward a common destiny* (pp. 163–184). San Francisco: Jossey-Bass.

Gimmestad, B. J., & de Chiara, E. (1982). Dramatic plays: A vehicle for prejudice reduction in the elementary school. *Journal of Educational Research, 76,* 45–49.

Graves, S. B. (1999). Television and prejudice reduction: When does television as a vicarious experience make a difference? *Journal of Social Issues, 55,* 707–727.

Greenwald, A. G., & Banaji, M. R. (1995). Implicit social cognition: Attitudes, self-esteem, and stereotypes. *Psychological Review, 102,* 4–27.

Hartley, E. (1946). *Problems in prejudice.* Oxford, UK: King's Crown Press.

Hirschfeld, L. A. (1995). Do children have a theory of race? *Cognition, 54,* 209–252.

Hirschfeld, L. A. (2001). On a folk theory of society: Children, evolution, and mental representations of social groups. *Personality and Social Psychology Review, 5,* 107–117.

Houlette, M. A., Gaertner, S. L., & Johnson, K. M. (2004). Developing a more inclusive social identity: An elementary school intervention. *Journal of Social Issues, 60,* 35–55.

Houser, B. B. (1978). An examination of the use of audiovisual media in reducing prejudice. *Psychology in the Schools, 15,* 116–122.

Hughes, J. M., Bigler, R. S., & Levy, S. R. (2007). Consequences of learning about historical racism among European American and African American children. *Child Development, 78,* 1689–1705.

Johnson, D. W., & Johnson, R. T. (2000). The three Cs of reducing prejudice and discrimination. In S. Oskamp (Ed.), *Reducing prejudice and discrimination.* Mahwah, NJ: Erlbaum.

Jones, L. M., & Foley, L. A. (2003). Educating children to decategorize racial groups. *Journal of Applied Social Psychology, 33,* 554–564.

Karafantis, D. M., & Levy, S. R. (2004). The role of children's lay theories about the malleability of human attributes in beliefs about and volunteering for disadvantaged groups. *Child Development, 75,* 236–250.

Karlins, M., Coffman, T. L., & Walters, G. (1969). On the fading of social stereotypes: Studies in three generations of college students. *Journal of Personality and Social Psychology, 13,* 1–16.

Katz, P. A. (1973). Stimulus predifferentiation and modification of children's racial attitudes. *Child Development, 44,* 232–237.

Katz, P. A., Sohn, M., & Zalk, S. R. (1975). Perceptual concomitants of racial attitudes in urban grade-school children. *Developmental Psychology, 11,* 135–144.

Kehoe, J. W., & Mansfield, E. (1993). The limitations of multicultural education and anti-racist education. In K. A. McLeod (Ed.), *Multicultural education: The state of the art* (pp. 3–8). Toronto, ON: University of Toronto.

Khmelkov, V. T., & Hallinan, M. T. (1999). Organizational effects on race relations in schools. *Journal of Social Issues, 55,* 627–645.

Killen, M., Lee-Kim, J., McGlothlin, H., & Stangor, C. (2002). How children and adolescents evaluate gender and racial exclusion. *Monographs of the Society for Research in Child Development, 67,* 1–119.

Killen, M., & Stangor, C. (2001). Children's social reasoning about inclusion and exclusion in gender and race peer group contexts. *Child Development, 72,* 174–186.

Koeller, S. (1977). The effect of listening to excerpts from children's stories about Mexican-Americans on the attitudes of sixth graders. *Journal of Educational Research, 70,* 329–334.

Levy, S. R. (1999). Reducing prejudice: Lessons from social-cognitive factors underlying perceiver differences in prejudice. *Journal of Social Issues, 55,* 745–766.

Levy, S. R., & Dweck, C. S. (1999). The impact of children's static versus dynamic conceptions of people on stereotype formation. *Child Development, 70,* 1163–1180.

Levy, S. R., West, T. L., Bigler, R. S., Karafantis, D. M., Ramirez, L., & Velilla, E. (2005). Messages about the uniqueness and similarities of people: Impact on U.S. Black & Latino youth. *Journal of Applied Developmental Psychology, 26,* 714–733.

Levy, S. R., West, T., & Ramirez, L. (2005). Lay theories and intergroup relations: A social developmental perspective. *The European Review of Social Psychology, 16,* 189–220.

Levy, S. R., West, T. L., Ramirez, L., & Karafantis, D. M. (2006). The Protestant work ethic: A lay theory with dual intergroup implications. *Group Processes & Intergroup Relations, 9,* 95–115.

Liben, L. S., & Bigler, R. S. (2002). The developmental course of gender differentiation: Conceptualizing, measuring, and evaluating constructs and pathways. *Monographs of the Society for Research in Child Development, 67,* vii–47.

Litcher, J. H., & Johnson, D. W. (1969). Changes in attitudes toward Negroes of white elementary school students after use of multiethnic readers. *Journal of Educational Psychology, 60,* 148–152.

Margie, N. G., Killen, M., & Sinno, S. (2005). Minority children's intergroup attitudes about peer relationships. *British Journal of Developmental Psychology, 23,* 251–269.

McGlothlin, H., Killen, M., & Edmonds, C. (2005). European-American children's intergroup attitudes about peer relationships. *British Journal of Developmental Psychology, 23,* 227–249.

McGregor, J. (1993). Effectiveness of role playing and anti-racist teaching in reducing student prejudice. *The Journal of Educational Research, 86,* 215–226.

Mendelson, M. J., & Aboud, F. E. (1999). Measuring friendship quality in late adolescents and young adults: McGill friendship questionnaires. *Canadian Journal of Behavioural Science, 31,* 130–132.

Monteith, M. (1993). Self-regulation of prejudiced responses: Implications for progress in prejudice-reduction efforts. *Journal of Personality and Social Psychology, 65,* 469–485.

Nesdale, D. (1999). Developmental changes in children's ethnic preferences and social cognitions. *Journal of Applied Developmental Psychology, 20,* 501–519.

Nesdale, D., Maass, A., Durkin, K., & Griffiths, J. (2005). Group norms, threat, and children's racial prejudice. *Child Development, 76,* 652–663.

Patchen, M. (1983). Students' own racial attitudes and those of peers of both races, as related to interracial behavior. *Sociology & Social Research, 68,* 59–77.

Patterson, M. M., & Bigler, R. S. (2006). Preschool children's attention to environmental messages about groups: Social categorization and the origins of intergroup bias. *Child Development, 77,* 847–860.

Pettigrew, T. F. (1998). Intergroup contact theory. *Annual Review of Psychology, 49,* 65–85.

Pettigrew, T. F., & Tropp, L. R. (2006). A meta-analytic test of intergroup contact theory. *Journal of Personality and Social Psychology, 90,* 751–783.

Piaget, J., & Weil, A. M. (1951). The development in children of the idea of the homeland and of relations to other countries. *International Social Science Journal, 3*, 561–578.

Quintana, S. M. (1998). Children's developmental understanding of ethnicity and race. *Applied and Preventive Psychology, 7*, 27–45.

Ritchey, P. N., & Fishbein, H. D. (2001). The lack of an association between adolescent friends' prejudices and stereotypes. *Merrill-Palmer Quarterly, 47*, 188–206.

Rutland, A., Cameron, L., Milne, A., & McGeorge, P. (2005). Social norms and self-presentation: Children's implicit and explicit intergroup attitudes. *Child Development, 76*, 451–466.

Sagar, H. A., & Schofield, J. W. (1980). Racial and behavioral cues in Black and White children's perceptions of ambiguously aggressive acts. *Journal of Personality and Social Psychology, 39*, 590–598.

Schofield, J. W. (1986). Causes and consequences of the colorblind perspective. In J. F. Dovidio & S. L. Gaertner (Eds.), *Prejudice, discrimination, and racism* (pp. 231–253). Orlando, FL: Academic.

Teasley, S. D. (1995). The role of talk in children's peer collaborations. *Developmental Psychology, 31*, 207–220.

Tropp, L. R., & Prenovost, M. A. (2008). The role of intergroup contact in predicting children's inter-ethnic attitudes: Evidence from meta-analytic and field studies. In S. R. Levy & M. Killen (Eds.), *Intergroup relations: An integrative developmental and social psychological perspective* (pp. 236–248). New York: Oxford University Press.

Turner, J. C., Brown, R. J., & Tajfel, H. (1979). Social comparison and group interest in ingroup favouritism. *European Journal of Social Psychology, 9*, 187–204.

Underwood, B., & Moore, B. (1982). Perspective taking and altruism. *Psychological Bulletin, 91*, 143–173.

Weiner, M. J., & Wright, F. E. (1973). Effects of undergoing arbitrary discrimination upon subsequent attitudes toward a minority group. *Journal of Applied Psychology, 3*, 94–102.

Williams, J. E., Best, D. L., & Boswell, D. A. (1975). The measurement of children's racial attitudes in the early school years. *Child Development, 46*, 494–500.

Williams, J. E., & Edwards, C. D. (1969). An exploratory study of the modification of color and racial concept attitudes in preschool children. *Child Development, 40*, 737–750.

Wright, S. C., & Tropp, L. R. (2005). Language and intergroup contact: Investigating the impact of bilingual instruction on children's intergroup attitudes. *Group Processes & Intergroup Relations, 8*, 309–328.

3 Intergroup Threat Theory

Walter G. Stephan
University of Hawaii

Oscar Ybarra
University of Michigan

Kimberly Rios Morrison
Stanford University

We live in a world polarized by religion, nationality, political ideology, race, ethnicity, sex, social class, and many more divisions too numerous to mention. These social groups shape our identities and our lives. All of these social groups are characterized by membership criteria and boundaries—they include some people and exclude others. Although it is not logically necessary for these boundaries to imply any tension between groups, in practice relations between groups are far more likely to be antagonistic than complementary. Social identity theorists argue that one reason for intergroup antagonism is the psychological benefits conferred on group members, particularly those associated with identification with ingroups (Tajfel & Turner, 1986). These benefits include acceptance, belonging, and social support, as well as a system of roles, rules, norms, values, and beliefs to guide behavior. Groups also provide our lives with meaning by boosting our self-esteem (Crocker & Luhtanen, 1990), increasing our sense of distinctiveness from others (Turner, Hogg, Oakes, Reicher, & Wetherell, 1987), and making us more certain of the social world and our place within it (Abrams & Hogg, 1988). Because of the needs they fill, groups are as dear to us as life itself, and we fear their destruction almost as much as we fear our own. As a result, we tend to favor our own group and exhibit hostility toward other groups, especially during dangerous or contentious times (Branscombe, Ellemers, Spears, & Doosje, 1999; Tajfel & Turner, 1986).

Similarly, the philosopher Barbara Ward (1959) contended that since the dawn of time, humans have been fundamentally "tribal" in nature. Membership in these "tribal" social groups provides people with traditions, customs, myths, religion, and common language, as well as access to basic subsistence (see also Brewer, 1997; Brewer & Caporael, 1990). A corollary of the unified system of meaning provided by people's own "tribes" is the existence of "tribes" of strangers beyond the ingroup's boundaries. Because their own "tribes" are so important to them, people often regard these other "tribes" as a threat (see also Alexander, 1974; Dunbar, 1988). Specifically, tribes that possess the power to harm or destroy the ingroup are a threat to the very existence of the ingroup, whereas tribes that possess different values are a threat to the unified meaning system of the ingroup. One outcome of the tribal psychology mindset is that people may be inclined to perceive threats where none exist, a tendency consistent with the more general bias people display toward avoiding costly errors (Haselton & Buss, 2003). Perceiving threats when none exist may be a less costly error than not perceiving threats when in fact they do exist. Thus, by default people may be predisposed to perceive threats from outgroups.

In the context of intergroup threat theory, an intergroup threat is experienced when members of one group perceive that another group is in a position to cause them harm. We refer to a concern about physical harm or a loss of resources as realistic threat, and to a concern about the integrity or validity of the ingroup's meaning system as symbolic threat. The primary reason intergroup threats are important is because their effects on intergroup relations are largely destructive. Even when a threat from an outgroup leads to nonhostile behavioral responses (e.g., negotiation, compromise, deterrence), the cognitive and affective responses to threat are likely to be negative.

In the remainder of this chapter, we explore the nature of the intergroup threats people experience, why and when people feel threatened by other groups, and how they respond to them. We also review some of the research that has been done to test this and related theories of threat, as well as formulate some hypotheses to stimulate future research.

INTERGROUP THREAT THEORY

In the original version of intergroup threat theory, labeled integrated threat theory (Stephan & Stephan, 2000), four types of threat were included, but this number has since been reduced to two basic types—realistic and symbolic threats (Stephan & Renfro, 2002). Negative stereotypes, which were initially considered to be a separate type of threat, now seem to us to be a cause of threat involving characteristics of the outgroup that could have a negative impact on the ingroup (e.g., aggressiveness, deviousness, immorality). Indeed, negative stereotypes have been found to be a significant predictor of both realistic and symbolic threats (Stephan et al., 2002). Intergroup anxiety, which involves the anticipation of negative outcomes from intergroup interaction, was also initially considered to be a separate threat but now seems to us to be a subtype of threat centering on apprehensions about interacting with outgroup members. These apprehensions arise from a number of different sources, including concerns that the outgroup will exploit the ingroup, concerns that the outgroup will perceive the ingroup as prejudiced, and concerns that the outgroup will challenge the ingroup's values (Stephan & Stephan, 1985).

In addition to focusing on realistic and symbolic threats, the first revision of the theory (Stephan & Renfro, 2002) made a distinction between threats to the ingroup as a whole and threats to individual members, in which individuals experience threat as a function of their membership in a particular ingroup. For example, a European American man with a good job might believe affirmative action threatens his group, but feel no individual threat. Conversely, an African American man on the streets of a European American neighborhood may feel his own welfare is threatened, but at that moment may not be concerned about the threats that European Americans pose to African Americans more generally.

In the revised theory, realistic group threats are threats to a group's power, resources, and general welfare. Symbolic group threats are threats to a group's religion, values, belief system, ideology, philosophy, morality, or worldview. Realistic individual threats concern actual physical or material harm to an individual group member such as pain, torture, or death, as well as economic loss, deprivation of valued resources, and threats to health or personal security. Symbolic individual threats concern loss of face or honor and the undermining of an individual's self-identity or self-esteem.

The conflict between the Israelis and Arabs provides a stark illustration of the various types of threat. For both groups, realistic group threats are omnipresent in the form of the possibility of open warfare. This is a struggle involving land, economics, power, and blood, where each group threatens the very existence of the other. Symbolic group threats are nearly as obvious. The two groups differ in religion and culture and speak different languages. Each group is perceived to pose a fundamental threat to the cultural worldview and way of life of the other. Threats also exist at the individual level. Realistic individual threats exist in the form of terrorism for the Israelis. For the Arabs, such threats are present as targeted assassinations in which civilians are often casualties. Individual symbolic threats occur when individuals feel they are being dishonored, disrespected, or dehumanized by members of the other group.

Our conceptualization of threat is related to that of social identity theorists, who posit that the actions of outgroups often lead ingroups to feel as though their group's status is threatened (Branscombe et al., 1999). However, the social identity definition of "status threat" involves both tangible resources (e.g., bleak prospects on the job market; see Jetten, Postmes, & McAuliffe, 2002) and group esteem (e.g., believing that other group views the ingroup negatively; see Branscombe, Spears, Ellemers, & Doosje, 2002; Cameron, Duck, Terry, & Lalonde, 2005). From our perspective, threats to tangible resources can be considered realistic, whereas threats to group esteem can be considered symbolic.

Before proceeding to a discussion of the antecedents and consequences of threat, we would like to comment on an important issue with respect to the type of threats of concern to us. Intergroup threat theory is a social psychological theory in that is it primarily concerned with perceptions of threat. Perceived threats have real consequences, regardless of whether or not the perceptions of threat are accurate. Thus, intergroup threat theory is not as concerned with the actual threat posed by outgroups (e.g., rising rates of unemployment or immigration) as it is with the degree to which threats to the ingroup are perceived to exist. To illustrate this point, consider a survey study on attitudes toward immigrants in Germany, conducted by Semyonov, Raijman, Tov, and Schmidt (2004). This study examined four variables: (a) the actual proportion of immigrants in counties across Germany, (b) the respondents' perceptions of the proportion of immigrants in their counties, (c) the respondents' perceptions of the threats posed by immigrants, and (d) the respondents' exclusionary attitudes toward immigrants. It was found that the actual proportion of immigrants in the respondents' localities did not predict exclusionary attitudes toward immigrants. Instead, the perceived proportion of immigrants predicted both perceived threats and exclusionary attitudes. In addition, the relationship between perceived proportion of immigrants and exclusionary attitudes was mediated by perceived threats.

ANTECEDENTS OF THREAT

In the first revision of integrated threat theory, it was argued that the degree to which people perceive threats from another group depends on prior relations between the groups, the cultural values of the group members, the situations in which the groups interact with one another, and individual difference variables. In the next section, we mention the variables included in earlier versions of the theory, but we will also discuss additional variables that now seem important to us. We review the antecedents of threat in the manner that Allport (1954) might have chosen, based on his lens model of the causes of prejudice. He argued that there are four basic categories of antecedents of prejudice, ranging from more distal factors (e.g., historical and sociocultural antecedents) to more proximal factors (e.g., situational and personality antecedents). Likewise, we begin by discussing the distal intergroup and cultural antecedents of threat, followed by the more proximal situational and individual-level antecedents.

Intergroup Relations

One factor that affects the perception of intergroup threats is the relative power of the groups. In the original theory, it was argued that both high and low power groups are susceptible to perceiving they are under threat. We now believe that, in general, low power groups are more likely than high power groups to *experience* threats, but that high power groups (to the extent that they actually perceive they are threatened) will react more strongly to threat. Low power groups are highly susceptible to perceiving threats because they are at the mercy of more powerful groups. Consistent with this idea, Stephan and colleagues have demonstrated that low power racial and ethnic groups (e.g., Black Americans, Native Canadians) perceive higher levels of threat from high power groups (e.g., European Americans, Anglo Canadians) than high power groups perceive from low power groups (Corenblum & Stephan, 2001; Stephan et al., 2002). High power groups react strongly to feeling threatened because they have a great deal to lose and, unlike low power groups, they possess the resources to respond to the threats. This idea finds support in research showing that the relationship between threat and intergroup attitudes (e.g., prejudice) is stronger for high power groups than for low power groups (Johnson, Terry, & Louis, 2005; Riek, Mania, & Gaertner, 2006).

Under some conditions, perceptions of threat may also be high when the ingroup and outgroup are believed to be relatively equal in power. When equal power groups are in open conflict or are competing with one another for valued resources, their equal power makes them evenly matched as opponents (Esses, Dovidio, Jackson, & Armstrong, 2001). In a study providing suggestive evidence in support of this idea, members of a high power group (European Americans) who assessed the *similarities* between their ingroup and a lower power outgroup (Mexican Americans) on work-related traits reported higher levels of threat than did those who assessed the *differences* between their ingroup and the outgroup on these traits. Presumably, thinking about work-related similarities (e.g., "They are just as hard-working as we are") caused ingroup members to view the outgroup as more equal in power and hence able to compete effectively with the ingroup for resources such as jobs (Zárate, Garcia, Garza, & Hitlan, 2004). Similarly, research on social comparison processes indicates that more closely ranked groups behave more competitively with one another and thus pose greater threats to one another than do less closely ranked groups (Garcia, Tor, & Gonzalez, 2006).

Two other antecedents of intergroup threat are a history of group conflict and group size. The groups that are most prone to perceiving intergroup threats are those that believe the groups have a long history of conflict (Shamir & Sagiv-Schifter, 2006; Stephan et al., 2002), as well as those that are small in size relative to the outgroup (Campbell, 2006; Corneille, Yzerbyt, Rogier, & Buidin, 2001; McLaren, 2003; Quillian, 1995; Schaller & Abeysinghe, 2006). The results of an experiment examining threats by political parties illustrate the latter condition. This study demonstrated that members of a particular political party felt more threatened by an opposing party if they believed that the opposing party constituted 40% (relative to 4%) of the population in their voting district (Corneille et al., 2001).

Israeli–Palestinian relations serve as an example of the influence of group size and intergroup conflict on perceived threat. Perceptions of the size of the ingroup may lead both Israelis and Palestinians to feel threatened by one another, but for somewhat different reasons. Specifically, the Palestinians may feel threatened by the Israelis because the Palestinians are the smaller group numerically. The Israelis, however, may feel threatened by the Palestinians because the Israelis see themselves as a minority in an otherwise predominantly Muslim region of the world (i.e., they employ different reference groups to arrive at similar conclusions). Prior relations between the groups have been characterized by intense conflict, which may trigger high levels of threat in both groups. In a study supporting this reasoning, Israelis reported higher levels of perceived threat from Palestinians after a violent confrontation between the two groups (the Al-Aqsa Intifada in 2000) than before the confrontation (Shamir & Sagiv-Schifter, 2006).

In general, we would expect issues of group power, prior conflict, and relative group size to elicit realistic threats to a greater degree than symbolic threats. The reason is that these factors are more closely related to the groups' abilities to harm one another or control valued resources than they are to differences in values and beliefs. Similarly, because these factors are all associated with the ability of the outgroup to inflict harm on the ingroup as a whole, they would be more likely to elicit group threats than individual threats.

It is also likely that historically created cultural value differences predict perceptions of threat. For example, according to the concordance model of acculturation (Piontkowski, Rohman, & Florack, 2002; Rohman, Florack, & Piontkowski, in press; Rohman, Piontkowski, & van Randenborgh, 2006), groups are especially likely to perceive one another as threatening when they believe their cultural values and characteristics differ from those of the outgroup (see also Zárate et al., 2004). A host culture may prefer that an immigrant group give up its culture and assimilate to the host culture, but worry that the immigrant group wants to maintain its culture. The immigrant group's desire to maintain its own culture would constitute a threat to the values of the host culture. Conversely, immigrant groups often feel threatened by the prospect of having to assume the values of the host culture, which may conflict with their own values (Crisp, Stone, & Hall, 2006).

We would expect value differences to be better predictors of symbolic threats than realistic threats, and to be better predictors of group threats than individual threats. For example, in a recent experiment, German participants read about a fictitious immigrant group whose values were depicted as either similar to or different from those of the ingroup (Rohman et al., 2006, Study 2). The authors found that reading about the group with different values increased participants' perceptions of symbolic threat, but it did not affect their perceptions of realistic threat.

Although prior relations between two groups can create threats, it is also important to keep in mind that different types of social groups may pose different types of threats. For instance, economically competitive outgroups (e.g., for European Americans this might be Asian Americans) may pose realistic threats related to potential losses of resources (see Maddux, Polifroni, & Galinsky, 2006). Outgroups that carry diseases (e.g., people with AIDS), in contrast, may pose realistic threats related to fear of contamination (Berrenberg, Finlay, Stephan, & Stephan, 2003; Faulkner, Schaller, Park, & Duncan, 2004; Navarrete & Fessler, 2006). Other groups, such as those that are perceived as socially deviant (e.g., cults), may more easily elicit symbolic threats (see also Cottrell & Neuberg, 2005, for a related discussion).

Cultural Dimensions

The revised threat theory argued that certain constellations of cultural values can influence the perception of threats. Among the cultural dimensions included in the revised theory, which we elaborate on presently, were individualism–collectivism (Triandis, 1995), power distance (Hofstede, 1980), and uncertainty avoidance (Gudykunst, 1995; Hofstede, 1980, 1991). Individualism refers to cultures in which the self is defined in terms of each individual's unique and distinct characteristics, whereas collectivism refers to cultures in which the self is defined in terms of affiliations with particular groups (Triandis, 1995). Members of collectivistic cultures, given their emphasis on group memberships, may be especially prone to experiencing threats from outgroups. Power distance refers to cultures in which there is an expectation that some individuals will be more powerful than others (Hofstede, 1980). Because cultures with high power distance are characterized by higher rates of conflict and violence than cultures with low power distance (Hofstede, 2001), we would expect the former to be more susceptible to perceiving threats than the latter. We would also expect threat to be more prevalent in cultures with high uncertainty avoidance, as such cultures are likely to value the reduction of uncertainty and the preservation of social order (Hofstede, 1980).

It is also possible that cultural tightness versus looseness (Triandis, 1989), the need for security (Schwartz & Bilsky, 1987; see also Rickett, 2006), and having a benevolent worldview (Schwartz & Boehnke, 2004) would affect perceptions of threat from outgroups. "Tight" cultures emphasize the importance of conformity to group norms and values, whereas "loose" cultures are relatively tolerant of deviations from social norms (Triandis, 1989). Thus, generally speaking, "tight" cultures are likely to experience higher levels of threat than "loose" cultures because nonconformity threatens their values. Cultures that are characterized by a high need for security (i.e., whose members have a strong desire to avoid threats to their physical safety), or by a belief that the world is an unsafe and dangerous place (i.e., not benevolent; Schwartz & Bilsky, 1987), should also be particularly vulnerable to experiencing intergroup threats.

Another cultural-level dimension that may relate to threat is low versus high context communication style (Hall, 1955). Cultures with low context communication styles stress direct communication where the message is in the words spoken. High context communication involves deciphering the meaning behind the spoken or unspoken words and requires extensive knowledge of cultural rules, roles, norms, history, and context. Because there is a greater potential for conflict and misunderstanding when people from high context cultures communicate with people from other cultures, they may be apprehensive about interacting with cultural outgroups. These apprehensions concern core symbolic elements of their culture, their use of words, images, metaphors, allusions, and their unique cultural myths in everyday communication. Concerns about being able to communicate effectively may cause them to feel more threatened by cultural outgroups than people from cultures favoring more direct communication styles.

In the case of cultural dimensions, the underlying premise is that some cultures may predispose people to feel threatened by outgroups, particularly those cultures that emphasize close ingroup ties (a specific aspect of collectivism), rules, and hierarchy that may be jeopardized by outgroups: uncertainty avoidance, tightness, power distance, and mistrust (security/low benevolence). To test these predictions in the context of cultural differences, it would be necessary to have samples consisting of a large number of cultures that vary along these dimensions. However, many of these cultural dimensions can be measured as individual difference variables and in this form are conceptually similar to the personality variables that we describe later. We provide more detail on these similarities in the individual differences section.

Because the cultural dimensions refer primarily to values, standards, rules, norms, and beliefs of social groups, they should be more closely related to symbolic than realistic threats, as the following example illustrates. For the last two generations one group, militant Muslim fundamentalists, has been responsible for more international terrorism than any other. There are many reasons for this, including historical, geopolitical, and economic issues, but one basic reason is that they feel threatened by Western culture. Intergroup threat theory can shed some light on why they feel so threatened. Muslim culture is collectivistic, high in power distance, high on cultural tightness and uncertainty avoidance, emphasizes high context communication, and is characterized by mistrust of other groups. These aspects of Muslim culture may make fundamentalist Muslims particularly prone to feeling threatened by other cultures, especially Western culture, because it is so dramatically different. Fundamentalist Muslims are deeply concerned about the continued existence of their culture in its traditional form. Although the threats posed by Western culture are primarily symbolic, realistic threats are present as well, due in part to the acts of terrorism that militant Muslim fundamentalists have employed to defend their way of life. These acts of terrorism have led the West to engage in violent attacks against Muslims (e.g., in Afghanistan and Iraq), causing Muslims to fear that their safety and well-being, as well as their way of life, are in jeopardy.

Situational Factors

The revised threat theory drew on contact theory (Pettigrew, 1998, 2001; Stephan, 1985) to specify a number of variables that would be expected to influence perceptions of threat, including the setting in which the intergroup interaction occurs, how structured the interaction is, the degree to which norms exist for intergroup relations, the ratio of ingroup and outgroup members in this context, the goals of the interaction, the relative power of ingroup and outgroup members in this context, the degree of support for the interaction from relevant authority figures, and the cooperative or competitive nature of the interaction. The actual power to do harm that the other group possesses in the specific context under consideration should also be taken into account—as well, of course, as any actual threats they have made to the ingroup. These situational variables are specific to interpersonal contexts in which members of two groups interact with one another (e.g., school and work settings). Thus, they can be distinguished from the intergroup variables discussed earlier, which concern historical relations between the groups as a whole (e.g., past religious and political conflicts).

The situations most likely to create perceptions of threat are those in which people are uncertain how to behave, are in unfamiliar settings, believe they are outnumbered and "outgunned" (have lower power than the other group), feel unsupported by authority figures, and are competing against an outgroup that can harm them or has threatened to do so. For example, minority group members who work in a factory owned and dominated by the majority group would likely feel threatened because the situational factors put them at such a disadvantage. They are at a disadvantage both numerically and in terms of power, they are competing with majority group members for advancement, they are unlikely to feel supported by the majority group management, and they may face harassment or even physical violence on the job.

Because situational factors refer primarily to conditions affecting immediate tangible outcomes of intergroup interaction, we would expect them to be more closely related to realistic than symbolic threats. Furthermore, because these factors are more likely to elicit concerns about the outcomes of individual group members (e.g., whether a worker will lose his or her job) than they are to elicit concerns about the group's outcomes as a whole (e.g., whether the trade union to which the worker belongs will lose power), they should be more closely related to realistic individual than realistic group threats.

It is clear that these situational factors vary over time and across contexts to a greater extent than the other types of antecedent variables. These fluctuations make the experience of threat highly dynamic, as members of the same two groups may feel very threatened in some contexts but not in others. The extent to which the two groups experience threat in different contexts has important implications for how they respond to and interact with one another, a point we revisit in the section on consequences of threat.

Individual Difference Variables

The original version of threat theory included strength of ingroup identity, amount and type of contact, and outgroup knowledge as individual difference variables. Highly identified group members, like members of collectivist cultures (Triandis, 1995), consider the ingroup important to their self-definition. As a result, they should be more likely than less-identified group members to both perceive and react to threats from an outgroup (Riek et al., 2006; Stephan et al., 2002). In addition, group members who have had less personal contact with outgroups are more inclined to experience threat than those who have had more personal contact with the outgroup (Tropp & Pettigrew, 2000; Voci & Hewstone, 2003), although personal contact with the outgroup in negative settings can heighten perceptions of threat (see Plant & Devine, 2003; Stephan et al., 2002). Similarly, group members who are relatively unfamiliar with the outgroup tend to be more susceptible to threat than those who have extensive knowledge of the outgroup (Chasteen, 2005; Corenblum & Stephan, 2001).

The revised theory added social dominance orientation (SDO), a measure of support for group-based inequality (Pratto, Sidanius, Stallworth, & Malle, 1994) and right-wing authoritarianism (RWA), a measure of desire for social order (Altemeyer, 1981), as antecedents of threat. Both SDO and RWA bear some resemblance to the hierarchy-related cultural dimensions described earlier, such as power distance (Hofstede, 1980) and "tightness" (Triandis, 1989). Previous research has shown that whereas SDO predicts beliefs that outgroups are a source of competition to the ingroup (Duckitt, 2006; Esses et al., 2001), RWA predicts beliefs that outgroups threaten the ingroup's way of life (Duckitt, 2006). Thus, SDO may be an antecedent of realistic threat, whereas RWA may be an antecedent of symbolic threat.

It is also likely that both individual self-esteem (Rosenberg, 1965) and collective self-esteem (Crocker & Schwartz, 1985; Luhtanen & Crocker, 1992) are related to predispositions to perceive threats, but in opposite ways. Low individual self-esteem makes people susceptible to experiencing threats from outgroups because people with low self-esteem, relative to people with high self-esteem, are likely to be less confident that they can deal with threats (McFarlin & Blascovich, 1981). We should note, however, that the actual experience of threat may be particularly aversive to people high in individual self-esteem, who have a strong need to maintain their positive self-image (Baumeister, Smart, & Boden, 1996). With regard to collective self-esteem, or people's feelings of attachment to the ingroup (Crocker & Luhtanen, 1990), high collective self-esteem should lead to the greatest perceptions of threat because it is these individuals who care most about what happens to their group and its members.

It is possible that chronic mortality salience (Greenberg, Solomon, & Pyszczynski, 1997) and paranoid worldviews (Kramer, 1998; Ybarra, 2002; Ybarra & Stephan, 1996; Ybarra, Stephan, & Schaberg, 2000) also predict perceptions of threat. The reasoning behind this prediction is that both of these constructs, like low individual self-esteem (Rosenberg, 1965) and the cultural dimension of low benevolence (Schwartz & Bilsky, 1987), involve a lack of personal security and a feeling of being vulnerable to harm.

Thus, the people who are most susceptible to feeling threatened by outgroups are those who are insecure, are suspicious, fear death, are inexperienced with outgroups, are strongly drawn to their ingroups, desire an ordered society, and support social inequality. Using these criteria, lower echelon members of the all-volunteer American military who are sent abroad might be expected to experience high levels of threat. They usually lack experience with and knowledge of other cultures, they have a commitment to hierarchical military command structures, they have been trained to be wary, they have reason to fear for their lives, and they typically have a strong espirit de corps.

Those individual difference variables tied to a concern for the self, including individual self-esteem, fear of death, suspiciousness, and lack of experience with the outgroup, would be expected to be more closely related to the perception of individual than group threats. In contrast, the individual difference variables that are linked to the group as an entity, including collective self-esteem and valuing social order, would be expected to be more closely related to group than individual threat.

To summarize briefly, it appears that across these domains of antecedents, there are five recurring conditions that foster perceived intergroup threat. First, the ingroup is highly valued. Second, the ingroup has low power or control vis-a-vis the outgroup (in the past or the present). Third, relations with the outgroup have been negative. Fourth, ingroup members mistrust or are suspicious of the outgroup. Fifth, rules, order, and social hierarchies are valued by ingroup members. We turn next to the consequences of perceiving intergroup threats.

CONSEQUENCES OF THREAT

Although the original version of threat theory focused primarily on changes in attitudes toward the outgroup (Stephan & Stephan, 2000), it is apparent that there are a number of other cognitive, affective, and behavioral outcomes of threat.

Cognitive Responses

Cognitive responses to intergroup threat include changes in perceptions of the outgroup such as changes in stereotypes (Quist & Resendez, 2003); ethnocentrism, intolerance, hatred, and dehumanization of the outgroup (Shamir & Sagiv-Schifter, 2006; Skitka, Bauman, & Mullen, 2004); changes in attributions for the outgroup's behavior (Costarelli, 2005); perceived outgroup homogeneity (Rothgerber, 1997); and an increased likelihood of perceiving threat-related emotions (e.g., anger) in others (Maner et al., 2005).

Cognitive biases in intergroup perceptions should also be triggered or amplified by threat. For example, threat may increase the occurrence of the ultimate attribution error (Pettigrew, 1979; Stephan, 1977), in which negative acts of the outgroup (and positive ingroup acts) are explained in terms of member characteristics, whereas positive outgroup acts (and negative ingroup acts) are attributed to the situation. Related to this effect are communicative and memory biases that are likely to be amplified by threat, such that people provide more abstract descriptions of negative outgroup than ingroup behavior (e.g., Maass, Ceccarelli, & Rudin, 1996) and are more likely to make misanthropic memory errors (Ybarra et al., 2000). That is, they will be especially likely to remember negative behaviors perpetrated by outgroup members when those behaviors have been attributed to their dispositional qualities, and positive outgroup behaviors when these behaviors have been attributed to situational factors (Ybarra et al., 2000). Threat may also contribute to an increase in the stereotype disconfirmation bias, in which outgroup stereotypes are thought to be more difficult to disconfirm than ingroup stereotypes (Ybarra, Stephan, Schaberg, & Lawrence, 2003), and the overestimation bias, in which the size of the outgroup is judged to be bigger than it really is (Gallagher, 2003).

In addition, people may respond to threats by opposing policies that favor the outgroup (Renfro, Duran, Stephan, & Clason, 2006; Sawires & Peacock, 2000), as well as by condoning extreme behaviors that they would not ordinarily condone (e.g., the use of torture against prospective terrorists). Attitudes toward the ingroup may become more favorable, and ingroup cohesiveness—for example, as indicated by perceptions of similarity among ingroup members (Karasawa, Karasawa, & Hirose, 2004; Rothgerber, 1997; Wilder, 1984)—would be expected to increase in the face of threat. One common consequence shared by all of these cognitive biases is that they make violence against the outgroup more likely and easier to justify.

Finally, it should be noted that perceiving grave threats is potentially so disruptive to group life that members of threatened groups may at times also try to minimize or deny the existence of threats from outgroups. For example, a recent study found that when members of low status groups made judgments about their ingroup and an outgroup, they acknowledged the lower status of the ingroup on status-defining traits, yet they buttressed their evaluations of the ingroup on status-irrelevant traits (Karasawa et al., 2004). By affirming themselves and the ingroup in this way, people may be able to downplay the reasons for the status differences and the actual threat that such differences may pose (see also Brewer, Manzi, & Shaw, 1993; Mullen, Brown, & Smith, 1992; Sachdev & Bourhis, 1991).

Emotional Responses

The emotional reactions to threat are likely to be negative. They include fear, anxiety, anger, and resentment (Stephan, Renfro, & Davis, 2008; Renfro et al., 2006); contempt and disgust (Mackie, Devos, & Smith, 2000); vulnerability (MacLeod & Hagan, 1992); collective guilt (Doosje, Branscombe, Spears, & Manstead, 1998); and in all likelihood other emotions such as rage, hatred, humiliation, dread, helplessness, despair, righteous indignation, and panic. Also, threat may undermine emotional empathy for outgroup members and increase emotional empathy for ingroup members. The relationship between threat and (lack of) empathy for outgroups is corroborated by a set of studies showing that threats to a group's status lead group members to feel *schadenfreude,* or pleasure at the suffering of an outgroup (Leach, Spears, Branscombe, & Doosje, 2003).

Threats directed at individual group members would be expected to evoke emotions tied to a concern for the self (e.g., for one's personal security or self-image), such as fear and vulnerability. Threats directed at the group as a whole, by contrast, would be expected to evoke emotions tied to a concern for the welfare of the group (e.g., for the group's resources and reputation), such as anger, resentment, and collective guilt. Supporting this idea, research has shown that different types of threat trigger different types of emotions. For instance, perceived threats to the ingroup's property and economic resources (a realistic group threat) induce self-reported anger, whereas perceived threats to physical safety (a form of realistic individual threat) induce self-reported fear (Cottrell & Neuberg, 2005). In another study, facial electromyography was used to measure emotions (Stephan, Renfro, & Davis, 2008). This study found that individual threats led to greater activation of facial muscles associated with fear (relative to anger), whereas group threats led to greater activation of facial muscles associated with anger (relative to fear). The authors argue that the basic reason for the different patterns of responses is that when an individual is feeling threatened by an outgroup, it is generally more adaptive to respond with fear than anger because fear is more likely to lead to avoidance. In contrast, when the entire ingroup has been threatened, anger is likely to be a more adaptive response than fear because it may mobilize the ingroup to respond to the threat (see Smith, 1993).

In addition, different types of outgroups may elicit different emotional reactions. For example, gay men elicit disgust among heterosexuals, and African Americans and Mexican Americans elicit fear as well as anger among European Americans (Cottrell & Neuberg, 2005; see also Rickett, 2006). A possible reason for these differences is that gay men are a source of symbolic threat, but both African Americans and Mexican Americans are sources of realistic threat (Cottrell & Neuberg, 2005). Thus, the constellation of emotions that different outgroups elicit may be a function of the characteristics of the outgroup and the types of threat it is perceived to pose.

Intergroup threats also may increase the tendency to infrahumanize outgroups (Leyens et al., 2001). Infrahumanization involves an unwillingness to attribute the capacity to experience the same types of subtle human emotions felt by the ingroup (e.g., nostalgia, guilt) to members of the outgroup. Instead, the outgroup is thought to be capable of experiencing only the same basic emotions as animals (e.g., anger, pleasure).

Behavioral Responses

Behavioral responses to threat range from withdrawal, submission, and negotiation to aggression (direct or displaced), discrimination, lying, cheating, stealing, harassment, retaliation, sabotage, protests, strikes, warfare, and other forms of open intergroup conflict. In some cases, threat leads to direct hostility against the outgroup that is closely related to the source of the threat. For instance, research has shown that men who experienced a threat to their gender identity are especially likely to sexually harass a female confederate (Maass, Cadinu, Guarnieri, & Grasselli, 2003). However, in other cases, threat may lead to displaced hostility against an outgroup that is unrelated to the source of the threat. In an experiment illustrating this point, psychology students whose status was threatened by an outgroup (medical students) subsequently discriminated against another, lower status outgroup (social work students; Cadinu & Reggiori, 2002).

Although threats usually induce hostile behavior (be it direct or displaced) toward outgroup members, threats sometimes trigger seemingly positive behaviors toward outgroup members. Positive behaviors are particularly likely to emerge when people are motivated to appear nonprejudiced and hence maintain a positive image of themselves or their ingroup (see Devine, Monteith, Zuwerink, & Elliot, 1991; Gaertner & Dovidio, 1986). In one study, for example, heterosexual male participants were told that they would converse with a gay male about either dating (threat condition) or life on campus (control condition). Participants in the threat condition sat closer to their conversation partner than did those in the control condition, apparently because the former were more concerned than the latter that their partner would perceive them as prejudiced (Bromgard & Stephan, 2006).

Behavioral responses also include negative reactions to the stress created by threat. For example, the academic performance of stigmatized group members (e.g., African Americans) suffers when they believe that others view their ingroup negatively (Cohen & Garcia, 2005), or when they believe that they themselves might confirm the negative stereotype associated with their ingroup (Spencer, Steele, & Quinn, 1999; Steele & Aronson, 1995). We would argue that these beliefs are forms of symbolic group threat and symbolic individual threat, respectively. In addition, the potential threats posed by interracial interactions have been found to impair both the problem-solving skills (Mendes, Blascovich, Lickel, & Hunter, 2002) and executive functioning (e.g., performance on the Stroop color-naming task; Richeson & Trawalter, 2005) of European Americans, presumably due to a fear of seeming racist (see Shelton, 2000). Such intergroup anxieties can lead to increases in threat-related physiological responses as well (Littleford, Wright, & Sayoc-Parial, 2005; Matheson & Cole, 2004; Mendes et al., 2002).

Intergroup threats may also have consequences for group dynamics. For instance, threats from outgroups may lead to more negative reactions to defectors or deviants within the ingroup, as well as a greater policing of intergroup boundaries (e.g., defining criteria for membership in the group, drawing sharper distinctions between the ingroup and outgroup, and rejecting prospective members who do not fully meet the membership criteria). Indeed, threats to the ingroup's status (Marques, Abrams, & Serodio, 2001) and core values (Eidelman, Silvia, & Biernat, 2006) have both been found to trigger derogation of deviant ingroup members. However, in some cases (e.g., when the outgroup is larger, more powerful, and more desirable than the ingroup), threats may lead to disaffiliation with the ingroup (Tajfel & Turner, 1986). The ability of minorities within the ingroup to influence the majority should generally decrease under threat, and groupthink should increase. In fact, groupthink may be at its strongest during times of threat, as Janis (1982) advanced in his original theory. At a more general level, it is not difficult to envision situations in which a threat from an outgroup throws the ingroup into disarray, greatly reducing its capacity to function effectively.

Overall, the nature of the cognitive, emotional, and behavioral responses to threat may depend on whether the perceived threats are symbolic or realistic in nature. Symbolic threats would seem to be more likely than realistic threats to lead to dehumanization, delegitimation, moral exclusion of the outgroup, and reduced empathy for the outgroup. In addition, symbolic threats should be particularly likely to result in increased conformity to the ingroup's norms and values (see Jetten et al., 2002; Vaes & Wicklund, 2002). It is also possible that symbolic threats lead to the most vicious behavioral responses to outgroups such as genocide, torture, and mutilation. In the context of immigration policy, symbolic threats would be expected to be linked to a preference for the assimilation of outgroups.

Realistic threats would be expected to lead to more pragmatic responses to the outgroup—that is, behaviors designed to cope with the threat. These behaviors might include withdrawal, avoidance, and aggression. Realistic threats are also more likely to lead to negotiation than symbolic threats because most groups strongly resist changing their core values (Azar & Burton, 1986). In the context of immigration policy, realistic threats may lead to a preference for separatism. Responses to realistic threats are probably influenced more by the relative power of the outgroup than are responses to symbolic threats.

Responses to threat should also be affected by whether the threat is perceived to be directed at the group or at individual members of the group. Group threats may be more likely than individual threats to be related to increases in group cohesion, groupthink, expressions of anger and aggression, reductions in collective guilt (if there was any to begin with), and collective responses to the other group such as strikes, boycotts, and warfare. Individual threats may be more likely than group threats to be related to cognitive biases, fear, helplessness, avoidance, appeasement, ingratiation, decrements in performance, disaffiliation with the ingroup, and identification with the aggressor. For example, in a recent study of Israeli Jews' attitudes toward Israeli–Palestinian relations, Maoz and McCauley (2005) found that zero-sum perceptions of realistic group threat (i.e., beliefs that more power for the Palestinians signified less power for the Israelis) were associated with negative attitudes toward compromise with the Palestinians, but perceptions of realistic individual threat (i.e., fears that the Palestinians would inflict personal harm on participants and their families) were not. That is, group threat was linked to attitudes toward compromise with Palestinians as a group, but individual threat was not.

In sum, people react to threat in a wide variety of ways. Their cognitive responses will most likely make it difficult for them to think clearly, carefully, or accurately about the outgroup and how to respond to it. Their internal emotional reactions are likely to be negative, which may also interfere with responding thoughtfully to the threats that exist. Their behavioral reactions to the other groups are likely to be oriented toward approach (e.g., aggression) or avoidance (e.g., withdrawal, appeasement), but it is also possible that threat will immobilize the ingroup, hence leading to inaction. Threats can also provoke the full range of stress reactions. In most cases, threat is not responsible in and of itself for creating these responses; rather, it serves to amplify them. For instance, a large body of research indicates that merely categorizing people into groups elicits intergroup biases (see Ellemers, Spears, & Doosje, 2002), but we would anticipate that adding threat to the categorization process would magnify these biases (Branscombe et al., 1999).

Although this picture of the outcomes of threats is almost exclusively negative, it may be well to bear in mind that threats can sometimes have positive consequences. Threats may serve to improve subgroup relations within a larger group. For instance, threats to a superordinate group (e.g., Americans) can reduce prejudice toward those who are ordinarily seen as outgroup members (e.g., perceptions of African Americans by European Americans and vice versa), thus leading all members of the superordinate category to unite in the face of a common threat (Dovidio et al., 2004). Moreover, with great threats come opportunities for great courage. Courage does not always take the form of aggression toward the other group, but may consist of leadership toward more equitable relations. Mahatma Gandhi and Martin Luther King are good examples of leaders who successfully employed nonaggression in the face of lethal threat.

CONCLUDING COMMENTS

In this chapter we have reviewed research that has been inspired by, is related to, or can be understood from the perspective of intergroup threat theory. We have also expanded the purview of the theory, put forth new hypotheses, and made many suggestions for future research. In its newest version, the theory considers two main types of threats that ingroups experience from outgroups. These are realistic threats, which refer to the physical welfare or resources of the ingroup, and symbolic threats, which refer to the ingroup's system of meaning. These two types of threats can be experienced at the group level or individual level. We have reviewed many antecedents of threat, which funnel down from distal factors (e.g., the history of the relations between groups, cultural characteristics) to more specific factors (e.g., characteristics of the group members themselves, the situations in which group members find themselves). The latest version of the theory is also more explicit in terms of people's responses to perceived threat from outgroups. These responses can occur at the individual level (e.g., cognitive, emotional, and behavioral responses), but can also include responses that influence the dynamics and relations between the ingroup and the outgroup (e.g., hostility and aggression).

It is important to keep in mind that threats occur in the ongoing relations between groups. Therefore, their antecedents and consequences are interactive and recursive. That is, the behavior of each group affects the responses and perceptions of the other group. For instance, if people respond to threats by acting aggressively toward the outgroup, the outgroup will be forced to respond. If the outgroup responds with counteraggression, this will change the ingroup's perceptions of the level of conflict between the groups and increase their perceptions of threat. Similarly, the responses of the outgroup can affect other variables considered to be antecedents of threat in the theory. Recent research, for example, has shown that threats can lead to increases in group identification (Moskalenko, McCauley, & Rozin, 2006), authoritarianism (Duckitt & Fisher, 2003), social dominance orientation (Morrison, & Ybarra, 2008), and power distance (Olivas-Lujan, Harzing, & McCoy, 2004). Thus, threats to an ingroup can influence attitudes, beliefs, and ideologies that are typically thought to remain invariant over time and across situations. Moreover, the ingroup's own responses to threat will feed back into its perceptions of the outgroup, usually augmenting them (when their reactions lead them to perceive the outgroup as more threatening), although sometimes attenuating them (when their reactions lead to reduced perceptions of threat).

As the research we have cited indicates, much is now known about the causes and consequences of intergroup threat, yet there is much to learn. In addition to exploring some of the new possibilities we have suggested for both the antecedents and consequences of threat, there are other aspects of threat that are worthy of investigation. We have little information, for instance, about the time course of intergroup threats. When does the experience of threat escalate, and what causes it to do so? Does the perception of threat typically decrease over time as people adapt to it? Do people respond differently to acute versus chronic threats? To what degree are threats consciously appraised, and to what degree do they affect people in the absence of conscious awareness? What is the subjective experience of threat, beyond the emotions we have suggested? Are there societal conditions that consistently lead to the perception of threat, such as high unemployment, the existence of neighboring states with different ideologies, or the imminence of terrorist attacks? What actions on the part of outgroups cause the greatest perceptions of threat? Do the responses to threat vary as a function of whether the threat is posed by a single outgroup member or the outgroup as a whole? Are there individual differences in responses to threat that parallel or are different from those that influence the perception of threat? Do different elements of realistic or symbolic threat have different consequences (e.g., do threats to physical well-being have different consequences than economic or political threats)? How are threats affected by multiple cross-cutting identities (e.g., would the outcomes differ for an Asian American woman who feels threatened by a European American woman or another Asian American woman) or hierarchical identities (e.g., how would the outcomes differ for an American Republican woman if a similar type of threat was directed at only one of her identity groups)?

If the foregoing discussion seems terribly depressing with respect to the possibility of improving intergroup relations, we can only say that understanding the nature of the problems created by threat is a step forward in searching for solutions to deal with these problems. We believe we have identified threat as a cause of problems in intergroup relations that has not received the attention it deserves, at least until quite recently. We are hopeful that as the field continues to strive for a more complete understanding of the problems created by threat, we will all be in a better position to devise ways of reducing threats and their negative consequences.

REFERENCES

Abrams, D., & Hogg, M. A. (1988). Comments on the motivational status of self-esteem in social identity and intergroup discrimination. *European Journal of Social Psychology, 18,* 317–334.

Alexander, R. D. (1974). The evolution of social behavior. *Annual Review of Ecology and Systematics, 4,* 325–384.

Allport, G. W. (1954). *The nature of prejudice.* Reading, MA: Addison-Wesley.

Altemeyer, B. (1981). *Right wing authoritarianism.* Winnipeg: University of Manitoba Press.

Azar, E. E., & Burton, J. W. (1986). *International conflict resolution: Theory and practice.* Boulder, CO: Rienner.

Baumeister, R., Smart, L., & Boden, J. (1996). Relation of threatened egotism to violence and aggression: The dark side of self-esteem. *Psychological Review, 103,* 5–33.

Berrenberg, J. L., Finlay, K. A., Stephan, W. G., & Stephan, C. (2003). Prejudice towards people with cancer or AIDS: Applying the integrated threat model. *Journal of Biobehavioral Research, 7,* 75–86.

Branscombe, N. R., Ellemers, N., Spears, R., & Doosje, B. (1999). The context and content of social identity threats. In N. Ellemers, R. Spears, & B. Doosje (Eds.), *Social identity: Context, commitment, content* (pp. 35–58). Oxford, UK: Blackwell.

Branscombe, N. R., Spears, R., Ellemers, N., & Doosje, B. (2002). Intragroup and intergroup evaluation effects on group behavior. *Personality and Social Psychology Bulletin, 28,* 744–753.

Brewer, M. B. (1997). On the social origins of human nature. In C. McGarty & S. A. Haslam (Eds.), *The message of social psychology: Perspectives on mind in society* (pp. 54–62). Cambridge, MA: Blackwell.

Brewer, M. B., & Caporael, L. R. (1990). Selfish genes vs. selfish people: Sociobiology as origin myth. *Motivation and Emotion, 14,* 237–242.

Brewer, M. B., Manzi, J. M., & Shaw, J. S. (1993). In-group identification as a function of depersonalization, distinctiveness, and status. *Psychological Science, 4,* 88–92.

Bromgard, G, & Stephan, W. G. (2006). Responses to the stigmatized: Disjunctions in affect, cognitions, and behavior. *Journal of Applied Social Psychology, 36*(10), 2436-2448.

Cadinu, M., & Reggiori, C. (2002). Discrimination of a low-status outgroup: The role of ingroup threat. *European Journal of Social Psychology, 32,* 501–515.

Cameron, J. E., Duck, J. M., Terry, D. J., & Lalonde, R. N. (2005). Perceptions of self and group in the context of a threatened national identity: A field study. *Group Processes and Intergroup Relations, 8,* 73–88.

Campbell, D. E. (2006). Religious "threat" in contemporary presidential elections. *Journal of Politics, 68,* 104–115.

Chasteen, A. L. (2005). Seeing eye-to-eye: Do intergroup biases operate similarly for younger and older adults? *International Journal of Aging & Human Development, 61,* 123–139.

Cohen, G. L., & Garcia, J. (2005). "I am us": Negative stereotypes as collective threats. *Journal of Personality and Social Psychology, 89,* 566–582.

Corenblum, B., & Stephan, W. G. (2001). White fears and native apprehensions: An integrated threat theory approach to intergroup attitudes. *Canadian Journal of Behavioral Science, 33,* 251–268.

Corneille, O., Yzerbyt, V. Y., Rogier, A., & Buidin, G. (2001). Threat and the group attribution error: When threat elicits judgments of extremity and homogeneity. *Personality and Social Psychology Bulletin, 27,* 437–446.

Costarelli, S. (2005). Social identity threat and experienced affect: The distinct roles of intergroup attributions and social identification. *Current Research in Social Psychology, 10*(10). No pagination specified.

Cottrell, C. A., & Neuberg, S. L. (2005). Different emotional reactions to different groups: A sociofunctional threat-based approach to "prejudice." *Journal of Personality and Social Psychology, 88,* 770–789.

Crisp, R. J., Stone, C. H., & Hall, N. R. (2006). Recategorization and subgroup identification: Predicting and preventing threats from common ingroups. *Personality and Social Psychology Bulletin, 32,* 230–243.

Crocker, J., & Luhtanen, R. (1990). Collective self-esteem and ingroup bias. *Journal of Personality and Social Psychology, 58,* 60–67.

Crocker, J., & Schwartz, I. (1985). Prejudice and ingroup favoritism in a minimal intergroup situation: Effects of self-esteem. *Journal of Personality and Social Psychology, 11,* 379–386.

Devine, P. G., Monteith, M. J., Zuwerink, J. R., & Elliot, A. J. (1991). Prejudice with and without compunction. *Journal of Personality and Social Psychology, 60,* 817–830.

Doosje, B. E. J., Branscombe, N. R., Spears, R., & Manstead, A. S. R. (1998). Antecedents and consequences of group-based guilt: The effects of ingroup identification. *Group Processes and Intergroup Relations, 9,* 325–338.

Dovidio, J. F., ten Vergert, M., Stewart, T. L., Gaertner, S. L., Johnson, J. D., Esses, V. M., et al. (2004). Perspective and prejudice: Antecedents and mediating mechanisms. *Personality and Psychology Bulletin, 30,* 1537–1549.

Duckitt, J. (2006). Differential effects of right wing authoritarianism and social dominance orientation on outgroup attitudes and their mediation by threat from and competitiveness to outgroups. *Personality and Social Psychology Bulletin, 32,* 684–696.

Duckitt, J., & Fisher, K. (2003). The impact of social threat on world view and ideological attitudes. *Political Psychology, 24,* 199–222.

Dunbar, R. I. M. (1988). *Primate social systems.* Ithaca, NY: Cornell University Press.

Eidelman, S., Silvia, P. J., & Biernat, M. (2006). Responding to deviance: Target exclusion and differential devaluation. *Personality and Social Psychology Bulletin, 32,* 1153–1164.

Ellemers, N., Spears, R., & Doosje, B. (2002). Self and social identity. *Annual Review of Psychology, 53*(1), 161-186.

Esses, V. M., Dovidio, J. F., Jackson, L. M., & Armstrong, T. L. (2001). The immigration dilemma: The role of perceived group competition, ethnic prejudice, and national identity. *Journal of Social Issues, 57,* 389–412.

Faulkner, J., Schaller, M., Park, J. H., & Duncan, L. A. (2004). Evolved disease-avoidance mechanisms and contemporary xenophobic attitudes. *Group Processes and Intergroup Relations, 7,* 333–353.

Gaertner, S. L., & Dovidio, J. F. (1986). The aversive form of racism. In J. F. Dovidio & S. L. Gaertner (Eds.), *Prejudice, discrimination, and racism* (pp. 315–332). Orlando, FL: Academic.

Gallagher, C. A. (2003). Miscounting race: Explaining whites' misperceptions of racial group size. *Sociological Perspectives, 46,* 381–396.

Garcia, S. M., Tor, A., & Gonzalez, R. (2006). Ranks and rivals: A theory of competition. *Personality and Social Psychology Bulletin, 32,* 970–982.

Greenberg, J., Solomon, S., & Pyszczynski, T. (1997). Terror management theory of self-esteem and cultural worldviews: Empirical assessments and conceptual refinements. *Advances in Experimental Social Psychology, 29,* 61–139.

Gudykunst, W. B. (1995). Anxiety/uncertainty management (AUM) theory: Development and current status. In R. L. Wiseman (Ed.), *Intercultural communication theory* (pp. 8–51). Thousand Oaks, CA: Sage.

Hall, E. T. (1955). The anthropology of manners. *Scientific American, 192,* 85–89.

Haselton, M. G., & Buss, D. M. (2003). Biases in social judgment: Design flaws or design features? In J. P. Forgas, K. D. Williams, & W. von Hippel (Eds.), *Social judgments: Implicit and explicit processes* (pp. 23–43). New York: Cambridge University Press.

Hofstede, G. (1980). *Culture's consequences.* Beverly Hills, CA: Sage.

Hofstede, G. (1991). *Cultures and organizations.* London: McGraw-Hill.

Hofstede, G. (2001). *Culture's consequences: Comparing values, behaviors, institutions and organizations across nations.* Thousand Oaks, CA: Sage.

Janis, I. L. (1982). *Groupthink.* Boston: Houghton Mifflin.

Jetten, J., Postmes, T., & McAuliffe, B. J. (2002). "We're *all* individuals": Group norms of individualism and collectivism, levels of identification and identity threat. *European Journal of Social Psychology, 32,* 189–207.

Johnson, D., Terry, D. J., & Louis, W. R. (2005). Perceptions of the intergroup structure and anti-Asian prejudice among White Australians. *Group Processes and Intergroup Relations, 8,* 53–71.

Karasawa, M., Karasawa, K., & Hirose, Y. (2004). Homogeneity perception as a reaction to identity threat: Effects of status difference in a simulated society game. *European Journal of Social Psychology, 34,* 613–625.

Kramer, R. M. (1998). Paranoid cognition in social systems: Thinking and acting in the shadow of doubt. *Personality and Social Psychology Review, 2,* 251–275.

Leach, C. W., Spears, R., Branscombe, N. R., & Doosje, B. (2003). Malicious pleasure: Schadenfreude at the suffering of another group. *Journal of Personality and Social Psychology, 84,* 932–943.

Leyens, J. P., Rodriguez-Perez, A., Rodriguez-Torres, R., Gaunt, R., Paladino, M. P., Vaes, J., et al. (2001). Psychological essentialism and the differential attribution of uniquely human emotions to ingroups and outgroups. *European Journal of Social Psychology, 31*(4), 395–411.

Littleford, L. N., Wright, M. O., & Sayoc-Parial, M. (2005). White students' intergroup anxiety during same-race and interracial interactions: A multimethod approach. *Basic and Applied Social Psychology, 27,* 85–94.

Luhtanen, R., & Crocker, J. (1992). A collective self-esteem scale: Self-evaluation of one's own identity. *Personality and Social Psychology Bulletin, 18,* 302–318.

Maass, A., Cadinu, M., Guarnieri, G., & Grasselli, A. (2003). Sexual harrassment under social identity threat: The computer harassment paradigm. *Journal of Personality and Social Psychology, 85,* 853–870.

Maass, A., Ceccarelli, R., & Rudin, S. (1996). Linguistic intergroup bias: Evidence for in-group protective motivation. *Journal of Personality and Social Psychology, 71,* 512–526.

Mackie, D. M., Devos, T., & Smith, E. R. (2000). Intergroup emotions: Explaining offensive action tendencies in an intergroup context. *Journal of Personality and Social Psychology, 79,* 602–616.

MacLeod, C., & Hagan, R. (1992). Individual differences in the selective processing of threatening information, and emotional responses to a stressful life event. *Behaviour Research and Therapy, 30,* 151–161.

Maddux, W. W., Polifroni, M., & Galinsky, A. D. (2006). *When being good is good . . . and bad: Realistic threat explains negativity resulting from the model minority stereotype.* Manuscript submitted for publication.

Maner, J. K., Kenrick, D. T., Becker, D. V., Robertson, T. E., Hofer, B., Neuberg, S. L., et al. (2005). Functional projection: How fundamental social motives can bias interpersonal perception. *Journal of Personality and Social Psychology, 88,* 63–78.

Maoz, I., & McCauley, C. (2005). Psychological correlates of support for compromise: A polling study of Jewish-Israeli attitudes toward solutions to the Israeli–Palestinian conflict. *Political Psychology, 26,* 791–807.

Marques, J. M., Abrams, D., & Serodio, R. G. (2001). Being better by being right: Subjective group dynamics and derogation of in-group deviants when generic norms are undermined. *Journal of Personality and Social Psychology, 81,* 436–447.

Matheson, K., & Cole, B. M. (2004). Coping with a threatened group identity: Psychosocial and neuroendocrine responses. *Journal of Experimental Social Psychology, 40,* 777–786.

McFarlin, D. B., & Blascovich, J. (1981). Effects of self-esteem and performance feedback on future affective preferences and cognitive expectations. *Journal of Personality and Social Psychology, 40,* 521–531.

McLaren, L. M. (2003). Anti-immigrant prejudice in Europe: Contact, threat perception, and preferences for the exclusion of migrants. *Social Forces, 81,* 909–936.

Mendes, W. B., Blascovich, J., Lickel, B., & Hunter, S. (2002). Challenge and threat during social interaction with white and black men. *Personality and Social Psychology Bulletin, 28,* 939–952.

Morrison, K. R., & Ybarra, O. (2008). The effects of realistic threat and group identification on social dominance orientation. *Journal of Experimental Social Psychology, 44,* 156-163.

Moskalenko, S., McCauley, C., & Rozin, P. (2006). Group identification under conditions of threat: College students' attachment to country, family, ethnicity, religion, and university before and after September 11, 2001. *Political Psychology, 27,* 77–97.

Mullen, B., Brown, R., & Smith, C. (1992). Ingroup bias as a function of salience, relevance, and status: An integration. *European Journal of Social Psychology, 22,* 103–122.

Navarrete, C. D., & Fessler, D. M. T. (2006). Disease avoidance and ethnocentrism: The effects of disease vulnerability and disgust sensitivity on intergroup attitudes. *Evolution and Human Behavior, 27,* 270–282.

Olivas-Lujan, M. R., Harzing, A., & McCoy, S. (2004). September 11, 2001: Two quasi-experiments on the influence of threats on cultural values and cosmopolitanism. *International Journal of Cross-Cultural Management, 4,* 211–228.

Pettigrew, T. F. (1979). The ultimate attribution error: Extending Allport's cognitive analysis of prejudice. *Personality and Social Psychology Bulletin, 5,* 461–476.

Pettigrew, T. F. (1998). Intergroup contact theory. *Annual Review of Psychology, 49,* 65–85.

Pettigrew, T. F. (2001). Personality and sociocultural factors in intergroup attitudes: A cross-national comparison. In M. A. Hogg & D. Abrams (Eds.), *Intergroup relations: Essential readings* (pp. 18–29). New York: Psychology Press.

Piontkowski, U., Rohman, A., & Florack, A. (2002). Concordance of acculturation attitudes and perceived threat. *Group Processes and Intergroup Relations, 5,* 221–232.

Plant, E. A., & Devine, P. G. (2003). The antecedents and implications of interracial anxiety. *Personality and Social Psychology Bulletin, 29,* 790–801.

Pratto, F., Sidanius, J., Stallworth, L. M., & Malle, B. F. (1994). Social dominance orientation: A personality variable predicting social and political attitudes. *Journal of Personality and Social Psychology, 67,* 741–763.

Quillian, L. (1995). Prejudice as a response to perceived group threat: Population composition and anti-immigrant and racial prejudice in Europe. *American Sociological Review, 60,* 586–611.

Quist, R. M., & Resendez, M. G. (2003). Social dominance threat: Examining social dominance theory's explanation of prejudice as legitimizing myths. *Basic and Applied Social Psychology, 24,* 287–293.

Renfro, C. L., Duran, A., Stephan, W. G., & Clason, D. L. (2006). The role of threat in attitudes toward affirmative action and its beneficiaries. *Journal of Applied Social Psychology, 36,* 41–74.

Richeson, J. A., & Trawalter, S. (2005). Why do interracial interactions impair executive function? A resource depletion account. *Journal of Personality and Social Psychology, 88,* 934–947.

Rickett, E. M. (2006). A culture of security: Implications of the salience of security on intergroup relations. *Dissertation Abstracts International: Section B: The Sciences and Engineering, 66*(11-B), 6338.

Riek, B. M., Mania, E. W., & Gaertner, S. L. (2006). Intergroup threat and outgroup attitudes: A meta-analytic review. *Personality and Social Psychology Review, 10,* 336–353.

Rohman, A., Florack, A., & Piontkowski, U. (2006). The role of discordant acculturation attitudes in perceived threat: An analysis of host and immigrant attitudes in Germany. *International Journal of Intercultural Relations., 30*(6), 683–702.

Rohmann, A., Piontkowski, U., & van Randnborgh, A. (2008). When attitudes do not fit: Discordance of acculturation attitudes as an antecedent of intergroup threat. *Personality and Social Psychology Bulletin, 34*(3), 337-352.

Rosenberg, M. (1965). *Society and the adolescent self-image.* Princeton, NJ: Princeton University Press.

Rothgerber, H. (1997). External intergroup threat as an antecedent to perceptions of in-group and out-group homogeneity. *Journal of Personality and Social Psychology, 73,* 1206–1212.

Sachdev, I., & Bourhis, R. Y. (1991). Power and status differentials in minority and majority group relations. *European Journal of Social Psychology, 1991,* 1–24.

Sawires, J. N., & Peacock, M. J. (2000). Symbolic racism and voting behavior on Proposition 209. *Journal of Applied Social Psychology, 30,* 2092–2099.

Schaller, M., & Abeysinghe, A. M. N. D. (2006). Geographical frame of reference and dangerous intergroup attitudes: A double-minority study in Sri Lanka. *Political Psychology, 27,* 615–631.

Schwartz, S. H., & Bilsky, W. (1987). Toward a theory of the universal content and structure of values: Extensions and cross-cultural replications. *Journal of Personality and Social Psychology, 58,* 878–891.

Schwartz, S. H., & Boehnke, K. (2004). Evaluating the structure of human values with confirmatory factor analysis. *Journal of Research in Personality, 38*(3), 230-255.

Semyonov, M., Raijman, R., Tov, A. Y., & Schmidt, P. (2004). Population size, perceived threat, and exclusion: A multiple-indicators analysis of attitudes toward foreigners in Germany. *Social Science Research, 33,* 681–701.

Shamir, M., & Sagiv-Schifter, T. (2006). Conflict, identity, and tolerance: Israel in the Al-Aqsa intifada. *Political Psychology, 27,* 569–595.

Shelton, J. N. (2000). A reconceptualization of how we study issues of racial prejudice. *Personality and Social Psychology Review, 4,* 374–390.

Skitka, L. J., Bauman, C. W., & Mullen, E. (2004). Political tolerance and coming to psychological closure following the September 11, 2001 terrorist attacks: An integrative approach. *Personality and Social Psychology Bulletin, 30,* 743–756.

Smith, E. R. (1993). Social identity and social emotions: Toward new conceptualizations of prejudice. In D. M. Mackie & D. L. Hamilton (Eds.), *Affect, cognition, and stereotyping: Interactive processes in group perception* (pp. 297–315). San Diego, CA: Academic.

Spencer, S. J., Steele, C. M., & Quinn, D. M. (1999). Stereotype threat and women's math performance. *Journal of Experimental Social Psychology, 35,* 4–28.

Steele, C. M., & Aronson, J. (1995). Stereotype threat and the intellectual test performance of African Americans. *Journal of Personality and Social Psychology, 69,* 797–811.

Stephan, W. (1977). Stereotyping: The role of ingroup–outgroup differences in causal attribution for behavior. *Journal of Social Psychology, 101,* 225–266.

Stephan, W. G. (1985). Intergroup relations. In G. Lindzey & E. Aronson (Eds.), *Handbook of social psychology* (Vol. 3, pp. 599–658). New York: Addison-Wesley.

Stephan, W. G., Boniecki, K. A., Ybarra, O., Bettencourt, A., Ervin, K. S., Jackson, L. A., et al. (2002). The role of threats in the racial attitudes of Blacks and Whites. *Personality and Social Psychology Bulletin, 28,* 1242–1254.

Stephan, W. G., & Renfro, C. L. (2002). The role of threats in intergroup relations. In D. Mackie & E. R. Smith (Eds.), *From prejudice to intergroup emotions* (pp. 191–208). New York: Psychology Press.

Stephan, W. G., Renfro, L. C., & Davis, M. (2008). The role of threat in intergroup relations. In U. Wagner, L. Tropp, G. Finchilescu, & C. Tredoux (Eds.), *Improving intergroup relations: Building on the legacy of Thomas F. Pettigrew* (pp. 56-71). Malden, MA: Blackwell.

Stephan, W. G., & Stephan, C. W. (1985). Intergroup anxiety. *Journal of Social Issues, 41,* 157–175.

Stephan, W. G., & Stephan, C. W. (2000). An integrated threat theory of prejudice. In S. Oskamp (Ed.), *Reducing prejudice and discrimination* (pp. 23–45). Mahwah, NJ: Erlbaum.

Tajfel, H. C., & Turner, J. C. (1986). The social identity theory of intergroup behavior. In S. Worchel & W. G. Austin (Eds.), *Psychology of intergroup relations* (pp. 7–24). Chicago: Nelson-Hall.

Triandis, H. C. (1989). The self and social behavior in differing cultural contexts. *Psychological Review, 96,* 506–520.

Triandis, H. C. (1995). *Individualism and collectivism.* Boulder, CO: Westview.

Tropp, L. R., & Pettigrew, T. F. (2000). Intergroup contact and the central role of affect in intergroup prejudice. In L. Z. Tiedens & C. W. Leach (Eds.), *The social life of emotions: Studies in emotion and social interaction* (pp. 246–269). New York: Cambridge University Press.

Turner, J. C., Hogg, M. A., Oakes, P. J., Reicher, S. D., & Wetherell, M. S. (1987). *Rediscovering the social group: A self-categorization theory.* Cambridge, MA: Basil Blackwell.

Vaes, J., & Wicklund, R. A. (2002). General threat leading to defensive reactions: A field experiment on linguistic features. *British Journal of Social Psychology, 41,* 271–280.

Voci, A., & Hewstone, M. (2003). Intergroup contact and prejudice toward immigrants in Italy: The mediational role of anxiety and the moderational role of group salience. *Group Processes and Intergroup Relations, 6,* 37–54.

Ward, B. (1959). *Five ideas that change the world.* New York: Norton.

Wilder, D. A. (1984). Predictions of belief homogeneity and similarity following social categorization. *British Journal of Social Psychology, 23,* 323–333.

Ybarra, O. (2002). Naïve causal understanding of valenced behaviors and its implications for social information processing. *Psychological Bulletin, 128,* 421–441.

Ybarra, O., & Stephan, W. G. (1996). Misanthropic person memory. *Journal of Personality and Social Psychology, 70,* 691–700.

Ybarra, O., Stephan, W. G., & Schaberg, L. A. (2000). Misanthropic memory for the behavior of group members. *Personality and Social Psychology Bulletin, 26,* 1515–1525.

Ybarra, O., Stephan, W. G., Schaberg, L., & Lawrence, J. (2003). Beliefs about the disconfirmability of stereotypes: The stereotype disconfirmability effect. *Journal of Applied Social Psychology, 33,* 2630–2646.

Zárate, M. A., Garcia, B., Garza, A. A., & Hitlan, R. T. (2004). Cultural threat and perceived realistic group conflict as dual predictors of prejudice. *Journal of Experimental Social Psychology, 40,* 99–105.

4 Automaticity and Control in Stereotyping and Prejudice

Patricia G. Devine and Lindsay B. Sharp
University of Wisconsin–Madison

Throughout the history of the study of stereotyping and prejudice, theorists have wrestled in one way or another with the idea that stereotyping is easy, if not natural, and that responding without bias is more difficult and effortful. Early theorists like Lippman (1922) and Allport (1954) suggested that stereotypes play a central and pervasive role in social perception. It has been argued for example, that stereotypes ease the burden of the social perceiver in responding to a potentially overwhelming and complex social environment (see Hamilton & Sherman, 1994, for a review). Allport (1954) suggested that "the mind tends to categorize environmental events in the 'grossest' manner compatible with action" (p. 21), reflecting a now common assumption that such categorizations take little effort and facilitate adjustment to the environment. More contemporarily, Macrae, Milne, and Bodenhausen (1994) suggested that stereotypes "serve to simplify perception, judgment, and action. As energy saving devices, they spare perceivers the ordeal of responding to an almost incomprehensively complex social world" (p. 37). As early as 1954, Allport suggested that "It seems a safe generalization to say that an ethnic label arouses a stereotype which in turn leads to rejective behavior" (p. 333). As such, stereotypes came to be viewed as cognitive structures that were easily activated and then applied to members of stigmatized groups.

Following in the tradition of Allport's (1954) classic writings, many theorists have assumed that stereotype activation occurred effortlessly when people come in contact with members of the stereotyped group (Brewer, 1988; Devine, 1989; Dovidio, Evans, & Tyler, 1986; Fiske & Neuberg, 1990). Emerging from this type of analysis was the discouraging possibility that stereotype activation ultimately results in biased and prejudiced responses that are not easily avoided. That is, stereotype application was also assumed to be rather spontaneous and nondeliberative. This type of reasoning led some to argue that prejudice is an inevitable consequence of these normal, even adaptive, categorization processes (Billig, 1985; Fox, 1992). Indeed, the research literature is replete with evidence that stereotypes often result in biased judgments of and behaviors toward targets of stereotypes (see Fiske, 1998, and Hamilton & Sherman, 1994, for reviews).

Others, however, were more reluctant to accept the fatalism implied by the inevitability of prejudice conclusions. The inevitability of prejudice perspective functionally eliminates the possibility that the potentially destructive and biasing effects of stereotypes on social perception and behavior could be controlled or otherwise avoided. A review of the stereotyping literature reveals an ongoing tension between the apparently adaptive functions stereotypes play in simplifying social perception and the potentially destructive and biasing effects of stereotypes. That is, however easily stereotypes are activated, there are many circumstances under which, and some social perceivers for whom, stereotype application is considered unacceptable. Allport (1954) also anticipated that such quick categorizations may not always be compatible with one's goals and, thus, anticipated more contemporary concerns over whether and how control over automatically activated stereotypes is accomplished. According to Allport (1954), perceivers will sometimes "put the brakes on their prejudices" (p. 332). More recently, Fiske (1989) echoed Allport's suggestion when she wrote, "The idea that categorization is a natural and adaptive, even dominant, way of understanding other people does not mean that it is the only option available" (p. 277). Although the process of preventing the biasing effects of stereotyping was not specified, the suggestion that there are alternatives to stereotyping was noted in several theorists' writings.

Although the early literature alluded to the possibility of spontaneous and deliberative processes each playing a role in the expression or prevention of intergroup biases, the formal study of automatic and controlled processes in the area of stereotyping and prejudice began with efforts to understand persisting evidence of prejudice against a backdrop of societal trends toward liberalism and individual rejection of cultural stereotypes and prejudice. That is, in the middle of the 20th century, it became apparent to at least some people that stereotyping and prejudice directed toward others based simply on group membership had negative effects that run counter to the guiding principle on which our nation was founded (i.e., that all people are created equally and deserve equal treatment). During this period, our nation's leaders enacted legislation that prohibited overt discrimination and social norms concerning the acceptability of stereotyping and prejudice also underwent a major transformation. These legal and normative changes led to enormous challenges for individuals as they tried to change old, familiar ways of thinking and behaving. Indeed, to avoid responding in such biased ways seemed to require overcoming socialization experiences or unlearning what were once not only accepted but encouraged ways of responding to members of various groups. The challenge to social scientists was to develop conceptual analyses that could explain why people who proclaim prejudice and stereotyping are wrong sometimes respond in stereotypic or prejudiced ways.

Building on models in cognitive psychology that drew a distinction between intentional (conscious) and unintentional (unconscious) components of human thought and behavior (Neely, 1977; Posner & Snyder, 1975; Shiffrin & Schneider, 1977), Devine (1989) proposed that group-based responses are governed by a combination of controlled, consciously held beliefs about groups and automatic, preconscious stereotyping processes and that these two processes are dissociable (i.e., may operate and be measured independently). According to these models, automatic processes were defined as processes that occurred without intention, effort, awareness, and without interfering with other concurrent cognitive processes (Jacoby, Lindsay, & Toth, 1992; Johnson & Hasher, 1987; Logan & Cowan, 1984; Posner & Snyder, 1975; Shiffrin & Schneider, 1977). In short, they were thought to be involuntary and inescapable. Controlled processes, in contrast, were considered to be intentional, under the individual's control, effortful, and to entail conscious awareness. Although controlled processes were thought to be capacity limited, they were considered to be more flexible than automatic processes and thus useful for decision making and the initiation of new behaviors.

More specifically, Devine (1989) suggested that during socialization, a culture's beliefs about various social groups are frequently activated and become well learned. As a result, these deep-rooted stereotypes and evaluative biases are automatically activated, without conscious awareness or intention, in the presence of members of stereotyped groups (or their symbolic equivalent) and can consequently influence social thought and behavior. Devine noted, however, that although virtually all people know society's stereotypes and, thus, are affected by them at the automatic level, many people are opposed to these stereotypes and consciously reject stereotyping, prejudice, and discrimination. Devine argued that people's personal beliefs about stigmatized groups are less accessible and not necessarily consistent with automatic stereotypes. Devine proposed that the influence of automatic stereotype activation can be diminished through controlled processing, which requires intentionally inhibiting stereotypes and deliberately replacing them with belief-based responses. Thus, people with nonprejudiced beliefs may exert controlled processing to inhibit the unwanted influence of stereotypes on their responses.

Although possible, exerting control successfully is not always easy and Devine (1989) likened the process to breaking a bad habit, suggesting that overcoming prejudice would likely be an arduous process that required time and sustained effort. After making a decision to renounce prejudice, according to Devine's model, successful control requires (a) motivation to respond without bias; (b) awareness that the stereotype has been activated; and (c) cognitive resources (i.e., attention and working memory capacity) to inhibit the influence of stereotypes and to replace any race-biased response tendencies with an intentional nonprejudiced response (Bodenhausen & Macrae, 1998; Monteith, 1993). If any of these conditions is not met, stereotypes are likely to influence responses producing what appear to be prejudiced responses even among those who renounce prejudice. In this sense, prejudice could persist among those who renounce prejudice because of spontaneous, unintentional stereotype activation and use.

Devine's (1989) conceptual analysis of the role of automatic and controlled processes in stereotyping and prejudice proved to be highly influential and these issues have been at the center of the ever-burgeoning literature devoted to understanding when stereotypes will and will not exert an influence on social thought and behavior. In many ways, it is not surprising that numerous researchers became interested in these issues and we would suggest that sustained interest in exploring automaticity and control in the stereotyping and prejudice context likely reflects both practical and theoretical concerns. Practically, the extent to which stereotype activation and application can be prevented or otherwise controlled has implications for a variety of social and interpersonal settings in which stereotypes can have serious and pernicious consequences, particularly for those who are the objects of stereotypes (Fiske, 1989; Jones, Farina, Hasatrof, Markus, & Scott, 1984). Understanding these processes could lead to effective interventions to reduce prejudice and stereotyping. Theoretically, understanding these processes is just as exciting. That is, studying such socially significant issues in theoretically sophisticated and methodologically rigorous ways may help to unlock some of the puzzling aspects of how information is represented in memory, accessed, and used (or not used) in social judgment and behavior.

As reflected in Devine's (1989) model, early work on automaticity and control in stereotyping and prejudice was strongly influenced by the dual process conceptualization of automaticity and control. That is, consistent with the then-contemporary models in cognitive psychology, early work depicted automatic and controlled processes as mutually exclusive processes. Any given response was typically characterized as being influenced by automatic *or* controlled processes. In the stereotyping literature, this approach led to the study of automaticity that was largely separate from the study of control. This strategy was partly influenced by theoretical considerations and partly by methodological ones. As noted previously, theoretically, the distinction followed directly from the then contemporary models in cognitive psychology that laid the foundation for studying automaticity and control (e.g., Posner & Snyder, 1975; Shiffrin & Schneider, 1977). Methodologically, in the study of stereotyping and prejudice some tasks lent themselves well to revealing the effects of automatic processes related to stereotyping and prejudice, whereas other tasks were presumed to reflect the influence of controlled processes. As such, the influence of automatic and controlled processes was typically examined in separate tasks and the focus of study was typically on automatic or controlled processes.

In the decade following the publication of Devine's article, dual process conceptions of stereotype activation and use (or control over use) witnessed an explosion of research activity. Devine and Monteith (1999) provided a review of this literature that reflected the rather independent study of automaticity and control in the study of stereotyping and prejudice, with the first part of their review focused on issues of automaticity of stereotype activation and use and the second part of the review devoted to issues of control of stereotype activation and use. It was clear at the time that substantial progress had been made in understanding issues of automaticity and control in stereotyping and prejudice. It was also clear, however, that there were areas in which our understanding of these issues was rather preliminary and incomplete. For example, Devine and Monteith, building on Bargh's (1989, 1994) analysis of conditional automaticity, suggested that in the study of stereotyping and prejudice, the dual process approach perpetuated a false dichotomy between automatic and controlled processes (see Bargh, 1989, 1994). In closing their chapter, Devine and Monteith (1999) argued that they believed "the most exciting developments . . . are likely to be forthcoming as we move beyond strict dual process conceptions to more elaborated analyses of the ways in which automatic and controlled processes interact to affect thought, judgment, and behavior" (p. 356).

In the years following Devine and Monteith's (1999) review, a great deal of work has been done addressing both the nature of automaticity and control and how we understand these processes in stereotyping and prejudice has changed substantially. Consistent with their prophecy, one of the most important and exciting developments in this literature has been a move away from the either–or reasoning (i.e., a process is either automatic or controlled) toward an understanding that no response is process pure. Current conceptualizations recognize that any given response is best thought of as arising from automatic and controlled processes, to differing degrees. This more nuanced way of thinking about automaticity *and* control grew out of conceptual advances that enabled the development of single tasks that simultaneously indexed both automatic and controlled components of a response. Indeed, in the late 1990s and into the new millennium, breakthroughs in methods as well as synthesis with conceptual and empirical work in cognitive neuroscience have yielded new insights about the nature of automatic and controlled processes in stereotyping and prejudice. Specifically, methods have been developed that enable estimation of the extent to which any given response is affected by automatic and controlled processes as well as examination of these processes as they unfold over time and in dynamic and reciprocal ways.

In what follows, we build on and extend Devine and Monteith's (1999) review. Our primary objective is to illustrate the progress that has been made in the study of automaticity and control in stereotyping and prejudice, but also to review the latest generation of research exploring the more nuanced and interactive nature of automatic and controlled processes. In each section of the chapter, we identify the major issues and questions that captured researchers' interest and led to developments in our understanding of automaticity and control. As noted previously, the literature is ever-burgeoning and has become quite voluminous. A comprehensive review of all relevant literature is beyond the scope of this chapter. As such, our review is meant to be illustrative of the central themes and developments rather than an exhaustive review of the literature. Before concluding, we identify areas in which our understanding is still rather preliminary in the hope of identifying new and productive areas for future research.

AUTOMATICITY

EVIDENCE OF AUTOMATIC STEREOTYPE ACTIVATION

Early demonstrations of automatic stereotype activation began with the assumption that stereotype activation did not require intention, attention, or capacity. Thus when appropriate cues are present (e.g., race, gender, age), stereotype activation should inevitably follow (Devine, 1989). Once activated, the stereotype could influence subsequent responses. To illustrate how stereotypes could be automatically activated, researchers used a variety of priming methods that in one way or another bypassed or otherwise prevented the possibility for controlled processes to affect responses. For example, in Devine's original demonstration, stereotype-related primes were presented to participants very rapidly (e.g., 80 msec) and parafoveally (outside of one's central area of visual acuity) so that participants were not consciously aware of the content of the primes. Nevertheless the construct would be made accessible. Using this type of method, Devine found that stereotypes were activated and influenced subsequent judgments of a target person without the participant ever becoming aware that the stereotype had been activated (see also Chen & Bargh, 1997).

Other researchers similarly interested in demonstrating how stereotypes could be automatically activated and affect judgment of target words used masked priming paradigms to prevent participants from being aware of primes (e.g., Purdue & Gurtman, 1990). The logic, of course, was that if participants were not aware of the primes, their reactions to target words could not reflect controlled processes. Still, other researchers, rather than trying to prevent conscious awareness of the primes, used procedures that that limited the possibility for controlled processing by using extremely brief intervals between the primes and the targets (e.g., 300-msec stimulus-onset asynchrony [SOA]; e.g., Banaji & Hardin, 1996). These priming effects were typically independent of participants' explicit beliefs and were generally considered to be powerful demonstrations of automatic stereotype activation effects. Such biases, although often unintended, were thought to be inevitable and their influence nearly impossible to avoid (Bargh, 1999; Devine, 1989).

Although there was clear evidence to support the idea that intergroup biases could be automatically activated, research quickly began to accumulate to suggest there were limits to the idea that such biases are activated automatically and unconditionally in response to group members (or related cues). Some of the major advances in the study of automaticity in stereotyping and prejudice arose in the form of challenges to specific assumptions laid out in Devine's (1989) model. The first assumption to be challenged was the inevitability of stereotype activation. Devine argued that stereotype activation would be equally strong and inescapable for all people, regardless of their conscious beliefs or reported level of prejudice. As reviewed later, several studies have by now challenged the notion that intergroup biases (i.e., stereotypes or evaluative biases) are unconditionally activated in response to group members. The other assumption to be challenged concerned the malleability of automatic intergroup biases. According to Devine's model, stereotype change (or reducing automatic biases more generally) was a time-consuming, arduous process that required intentional effort guided by conscious beliefs (i.e., breaking the prejudice habit was hard, deliberative work). In recent years, several programs of research have shown that situational or contextual manipulations can produce reductions in automatic intergroup biases with little or no intentional effort to overcome such biases, suggesting that such biases may be much easier to change than originally assumed.

VARIABILITY OF AUTOMATIC INTERGROUP BIASES

The literature addressing variability in automatic intergroup biases reveals that a variety of factors moderate the tendency to show automatic biases. For example, one line of research documenting variability in the activation of automatic intergroup biases has focused on creating situations to test the boundary conditions for Devine's (1989) original assertion that stereotypes are automatically activated in the presence of group members. One important moderator identified in this line of research is attentional resources of the perceiver. Individuals who are preoccupied with other matters tend to not experience automatic stereotypes, and social category cues that are outside of the focus of attention may not automatically activate the category.

Attentional Processes

Gilbert and Hixon (1991) reported one of the first studies to show that stereotype activation is not unconditionally automatic when individuals are exposed to members of stereotyped groups. Specifically, they demonstrated that stereotype activation could be prevented when perceivers' attentional resources were drained. In Gilbert and Hixon's study, participants completed a word fragment completion task while made either cognitively busy (i.e., told to remember an eight-digit number) or while not busy. The word fragments were presented via videotape by an Asian assistant. Some of the words could be completed in a stereotypic manner (e.g., s_y could be shy; r_ce could be rice, etc.) and, hence, this task was used as a measure of stereotype activation. Gilbert and Hixon reasoned that, to the extent that the presence of the Asian assistant automatically activated stereotypes, the number of stereotypic completions should be equivalent for the busy and not busy participants. In contrast with the automaticity of stereotype activation analysis, Gilbert and Hixon found that cognitively busy participants generated fewer stereotypic completions than participants who were not cognitively busy during the word fragment completion task. Spencer, Fein, Wolfe, Fong, and Dunn (1998) have since replicated that effect for stereotypes of Blacks. Specifically, participants who were cognitively busy produced fewer stereotypic word completions following subliminal exposure to Black faces, compared to participants who did not have the added task of rehearsing digits.

Macrae and colleagues (Macrae, Bodenhausen, Milne, Thorn, & Castelli, 1997; Macrae, Hood, Milne, Rowe, & Mason, 2002) have shown that automatic stereotype activation is likely only when stereotyped group members are processed in a socially meaningful way. To explore this issue, Macrae et al. (1997) manipulated attentional focus during a sequential priming task in which the primes were pictures of common inanimate objects or women and the targets were stereotypic or counterstereotypic traits. While completing the task, participants were asked to either decide whether each picture was of an animate object (i.e., social judgment) or decide whether a white dot was present (i.e., nonsocial task). This secondary task served to manipulate attention to the features of the photographed women, as such features would be useful for judging whether objects were animate but not for judging the presence of a dot. Pictures of women facilitated responses to stereotypic traits only in the social judgment task; automatic stereotypes were not activated when attention was focused on detecting a white dot. In other studies, Macrae, Hood, et al. (2002) presented primes of faces whose eye gaze was direct, averted (to the side), or absent (closed eyes). It was argued that a person's eye gaze is a central cue in social interactions and that direct eye gaze signals that the person has intentions in relation to oneself and is thus a potentially meaningful social object. In accordance with this reasoning, findings indicated stronger automatic activation of stereotypes for faces with direct eye gaze compared to those whose gaze was averted or absent.

In general, these findings suggest that an individual must be perceived as a social object for stereotypes associated with that person's group membership to be activated. These findings indicate that automatic stereotype activation does not unconditionally follow the presentation of cues related to a social category, and, as such, have identified a boundary condition for Devine's assertion, namely being that others must be perceived as social objects for automatic stereotype activation to occur. Of course, the fact remains that others are typically perceived as social objects and thus stereotypes are often, although not always, automatically activated in the presence of stigmatized group members.

Social Context and Social Roles

Even when perceived as a social being, a stigmatized group member may not unconditionally elicit automatic bias. A variety of investigations suggest that the surrounding context can moderate the activation of automatic intergroup biases in response to stigmatized group members. For example, Wittenbrink, Judd, and Park (2001; see also Mitchell, Nosek, & Banaji, 2003) examined how different social contexts can moderate automatic intergroup biases. Participants who viewed a video of Blacks at an outdoor barbecue or a church displayed less automatic bias on a sequential priming task than those who viewed a video of Blacks in a gang or ghetto street context. The target group was the same, yet it elicited very different automatic evaluations, depending on the context within which it was embedded.

Barden, Maddux, Petty, and Brewer (2004) used extant knowledge of subtypes (Devine & Baker, 1991) to select social and professional roles that moderate the activation of automatic race bias. In their first study, a picture of an Asian, Black, or White individual was displayed with either a basketball court or classroom in the background. An evaluative priming procedure indicated that an automatic evaluative bias favoring Asians relative to Blacks was found for the classroom context, presumably resulting from the activation of different stereotypes for each group associated with the student role. The opposite pattern was observed for the basketball court background, with automatic evaluative bias favoring Blacks relative to Asians, presumably because Blacks are stereotypically considered to be more athletic than Asians. In both roles, automatic evaluations associated with Whites fell in between Asians and Blacks. In a second study, pictures of Blacks and Whites were displayed with a prison, church, and factory background. The prison context elicited automatic evaluations favoring Whites relative to Blacks. The church context elicited automatic evaluations favoring neither race, with Whites and Blacks being evaluated equally, consistent with previous findings reported by Wittenbrink et al. (2001). The factory context elicited automatic evaluations favoring Blacks relative to Whites. These findings supported findings from the first study and findings by Wittenbrink et al. (2001) suggesting the contextual moderation of automatic racial bias. It was thought that these different contexts likely implied different roles, and thus a third study was conducted using a common (prison) context, but different roles. White and Black individuals were portrayed in a prison context as either a lawyer or a prisoner. When portrayed as prisoners, an evaluative bias favoring Whites relative to Blacks emerged. However, when portrayed as lawyers, an evaluative bias favoring Blacks relative to Whites was observed.

Similar research by Richeson and Ambady (2001) demonstrated how situation-specific roles related to the relative status of the perceiver can moderate the activation of automatic bias. White participants learned that they would be working with a Black student and were given the goal of evaluating their partner's performance (superior role), getting along with their partner (equal-status role), or receiving a positive evaluation from their partner (subordinate role). Assignment to the superior role produced a higher level of automatic bias than assignment to the equal-status role, and assignment to the subordinate role produced the least amount of automatic bias.

These findings are important in that they illustrate that race is not a static construct that will always be associated with the same stereotypes or evaluations; rather, the meaning of group membership and associated stereotypes changes depending on contextual information indicative of a person's more specific social role. Race has different implications, for different people, in different places. This idea has long been reflected in theory and research exploring the phenomenon of subtyping, and now seems consequential for understanding when (and which) stereotypes should be expected to be automatically activated.

In a related vein of research, Livingston and Brewer (2002) showed that automatic bias may be moderated by the appearance of targets. Blacks possessing more "Negroid" facial features (e.g., darker skin) evoked more automatic bias than those with less Negroid features, despite being rated as members of the same group in a pretest. Similar to Livingston and Brewer (2002), Macrae, Mitchell, and Pendry (2002) found that members of the same group can elicit different automatic responses, depending on the familiarity of their names. Specifically, familiar male and female names (e.g., John and Sarah) facilitated faster responses to stereotypic attributes compared to unfamiliar names (Isaac and Glenda). These findings suggest that automatic processes are more complicated than was once conceived. Rather than a group-related stimulus serving to trigger the activation of group stereotypes and evaluation, it appears that the degree to which a target is typical of a group influences automatic evaluation. Widespread automatic bias and stereotyping may not apply to all group members equally.

Individual Differences

Other research has explored the extent to which individual difference variables moderate the tendency to display automatic intergroup biases (e.g., Devine, Plant, Amodio, Harmon-Jones, & Vance, 2002; Fazio, Jackson, Dunton, & Williams, 1995; Lepore & Brown, 1997; Moskowitz, Gollwitzer, Wasel, & Schaal, 1999; Wittenbrink, Judd, & Park, 1997). For instance, Devine et al. (2002; Amodio, Harmon-Jones, & Devine, 2003) found that the degree of implicit evaluative bias expressed on the Implicit Association Test (IAT) was jointly determined by the extent to which their participants were internally (personally) or externally (normatively) motivated to respond without prejudice (Plant & Devine, 1998). Participants who reported high levels of internal motivation to respond without prejudice and little external motivation to respond without prejudice showed much lower levels of IAT bias favoring Whites over Blacks than did any of the other participants. Similarly, Moskowitz et al. (1999; Moskowitz, Salomon, & Taylor, 2000) found that those who reported chronic egalitarian values showed very little stereotype activation compared to others lacking chronically accessible egalitarian values and goals.

Fazio et al. (1995) found an interaction between automatic evaluations and individual differences in motivation to control prejudiced reactions when predicting explicitly reported racial attitudes. These findings led Fazio et al. to distinguish among three types of individuals according to differences in automatically activated evaluation and subsequent controlled process. According to Fazio et al., some Whites are "truly nonprejudiced" and do not experience an automatically activated negative evaluation in response to Blacks, and may actually experience activation of a positive evaluation. For other "truly prejudiced" individuals, negative evaluations are automatically activated and applied in response to Blacks. Finally, for some individuals, negative evaluations are automatically activated on encountering a Black person, but motivation, be it sincere or strategic, leads to attempts to monitor and avoid the effects of that negativity.

Later research by Maddux, Barden, Brewer, and Petty (2005) documented an interaction between contextual factors and individual differences in motivation to control prejudice on automatic responses toward Blacks and Whites. No automatic bias was observed when a church context was used in an evaluative priming procedure; however, when a jail context was used, those with low motivation to control prejudiced responses showed an automatic bias favoring Whites, whereas those with high motivation to control prejudiced responses showed an automatic bias favoring Blacks. This outgroup bias exhibited by highly motivated individuals was driven primarily by the inhibition of automatic negative responses to Blacks, triggered by the contextual cue of person threat. Those lacking motivation showed an ingroup bias whenever contextual threat was present, be it target-relevant (jail) or general (tornado). However, highly motivated individuals showed an outgroup bias only when the context implied that targets themselves were threatening (jail). These contexts seem to serve as prejudice-control cues for individuals motivated to be less prejudiced, leading them to automatically inhibit negative responses toward Blacks in such situations.

Situationally Induced Motivational Factors

Rather than focusing on individual differences in values and motivations, some researchers have more specifically explored how situationally induced motives may moderate the activation and inhibition of stereotypes. Inspired by shared reality theory (Hardin & Conley, 2001; Hardin & Higgins, 1996), Lowery, Hardin, and Sinclair (2001; S. Sinclair, Lowery, Hardin, & Colangelo, 2005) examined the effect of affiliative motives. These researchers argued that implicit responses are sensitive to the social demands of interpersonal interactions. They hypothesized that individuals achieve common ground by adjusting their perspectives and communicative attempts according to inferences about the knowledge and attitudes of interaction partners. Consistent with this reasoning, Lowery et al. (2001) found that Whites exhibited less automatic bias in the presence of a Black experimenter than a White experimenter (tacit social influence) and when instructed to avoid prejudice (expressed social influence). These results were interpreted as providing support for shared reality theory, which posits that social tuning of attitudes occurs automatically to meet the social relationship demands of any given interaction (i.e., negative race bias would be less evident when one needs to regulate a social relationship with the Black person). Such findings suggest that the social motivation to create a positive interaction and connect with others may moderate automatic stereotype activation.

Similar research by L. Sinclair and Kunda (1999) suggests that a self-protective motivation to form a particular impression of an individual can prompt the inhibition of stereotypes that contradict one's desired impression and the activation of stereotypes that support it. Participants praised by a Black professional subsequently inhibited the Black stereotype and activated the professional doctor stereotype. However, those who were criticized displayed the opposite pattern, activating the Black stereotype and inhibiting the doctor stereotype. These effects appear to have been driven by situation-specific self-protective motives; they only manifested in recipients of feedback and were not evident in detached observers.

In sum, a number of researchers have documented that stereotypes and biases are not unconditionally automatically activated as Devine (1989) originally suggested. Individual differences related to egalitarian values, situationally induced information processing goals and social motivations, and relevant contextual factors have been demonstrated to moderate the automatic activation of stereotypes. Accompanying this research pertaining to variability in stereotype activation, related investigations have likewise explored the nature of automatic processes in stereotyping and prejudice by focusing on the plasticity of automatic stereotypes and biases.

MALLEABILITY OF AUTOMATIC INTERGROUP BIASES

Whereas early theorists argued that reducing stereotyping tendencies would require effort and time and would be initiated by conscious intentions to be nonprejudiced (e.g., Devine, 1989; Monteith, 1993), more recent work has demonstrated that, in some cases, implicit stereotyping and prejudice can be altered without the benefit of deliberate attempts to reduce such biases. Indeed, the potential strength of such techniques is that they can produce bias reduction without being linked to deliberate prejudice-reducing efforts. Several programs of research have demonstrated that situational manipulations can produce reductions in automatic bias, and have thus suggested that intergroup biases and stereotypic thoughts may be more amenable to change than Devine had originally predicted. In what follows, we review relevant research. As will become clear, some manipulations require more conscious and deliberate attempts at regulation than others.

Effects of Practice

If changing stereotypic thoughts is indeed similar to breaking a habit, it would involve more than just a decision; it should also take practice. Consistent with this reasoning, research by Kawakami, Dovidio, and their colleagues has focused on how various training programs may be used to influence automatic biases (e.g., Kawakami, Dovidio, & Van Kamp, 2005; Kawakami, Phills, Steele, & Dovidio, 2007). In one such study, Kawakami, Dovidio, Moll, Hermsen, and Russin (2000) examined the effect of training in negating stereotype associations related to skinhead and racial categories on subsequent stereotype activation. Extensive training, involving hundreds of trials requiring the overt rejection of the stereotypes related to a specific category, reduced subsequent automatic stereotype activation, and this effect was observed 24 hours after training. Similar longitudinal research suggests that a college diversity course has the potential to alter students' automatic associations. Rudman, Ashmore, and Gary (2001) observed changes in implicit bias and stereotyping among students enrolled in a semester-long prejudice and conflict seminar. Across the semester, students enrolled in the seminar exhibited significant reductions in automatic bias and stereotype activation, whereas students enrolled in control courses (research methods) did not.

Thinking About Counterstereotypic Exemplars

Other research suggests that mere exposure to counterstereotypic exemplars or engaging in counterstereotypic imagery may influence automatic associations in the same way. Blair, Ma, and Lenton (2001) found that engaging in counterstereotypic mental imagery produced weaker automatic stereotype activation compared with participants who engaged in neutral, stereotypic, or no mental imagery. A study conducted by Dasgupta and Asgari (2004) provided similar support for the notion that social environments containing stereotypical or counterstereotypical exemplars can impact automatic stereotypic beliefs. Women in social contexts that exposed them to female leaders were less likely to express automatic stereotypic beliefs about their ingroup. The effect of social environment (women's college vs. coed college) on automatic beliefs was mediated by the frequency of exposure to women leaders (i.e., female faculty).

In related research, Dasgupta and Greenwald (2001) exposed participants to either liked Black and disliked White individuals, disliked Black and liked White individuals, or nonracial exemplars. Conscious exposure to liked Blacks (e.g., Denzel Washington) and disliked Whites (e.g., Jeffrey Dahmer) decreased subsequently measured implicit bias against Blacks. Notably, this effect on implicit attitudes persisted 24 hours after the exposure, but did not affect explicit racial attitudes. These findings suggest a spreading attitude effect; such positive associations with Blacks may be generalized beyond initial specific exemplars to the general social category.

Motor Processes and Spreading Attitudes

Other research exploring the malleability of implicit associations has likewise focused on promoting positive associations with stigmatized group members, but did not focus on the accessibility of specific exemplars or declarative information. Rather, Ito, Chiao, Devine, Lorig, and Cacioppo (2006) demonstrated that subtle changes in motor processes, specifically feedback from surreptitiously being induced to smile while viewing unfamiliar Black faces, led to diminished implicit racial bias for novel Black faces presented later. Ito et al. likewise suggested that this type of moderation of implicit bias occurred through a spreading attitude effect arising out of evaluative conditioning processes (Walther, 2002). Further, they argued that this type of process may be particularly powerful because it does not rely on conscious awareness of the contingency between conditioned and unconditioned stimuli and does not require prior familiarity with individuals whose faces are used in the experimental task.

These various malleability findings imply that appropriate environmental pairings and mental representations have the potential to counter the associations that have been learned in the past. However, whether these observed effects persist over extended time and generalize across situations is also unknown. Research of this type is exciting in that it suggests that automatic associations can be dramatically influenced by fairly simple alterations (see Blair, 2002, for an excellent review), and has led to an appreciation that although a response may be difficult to control, it is not necessarily immutable or impossible to regulate. However, consideration of such optimistic implications should be tempered with at least a modicum of skepticism. The mechanisms underlying these apparent changes in automatic associations have not been elucidated fully, and thus it is still unclear whether the automatic operation of stereotypes and prejudice is being truly modified (i.e., the associations being eliminated), or if these observed effects reflect the activation of another social category subtype or the temporary activation of an alternative information processing rule or goal (see Devine, 2001). Further research will be needed to illuminate the processes responsible for these apparent changes in automatic associations, and such investigations will have major implications for how we interpret the role of awareness, motivation, skill, and cognitive resources in the context of stereotype activation and application (Bargh, 1992, 1999; Devine, 1989).

IMPACT AND PERVASIVENESS OF AUTOMATIC BIASES

If automatic associations are as easily modified as these studies suggest, one must wonder why implicit biases are still so pervasive, even in many low-prejudiced individuals. In stark contrast to these investigations documenting the supposed malleability of automatic attitudes is other research indicating that automatic associations are not so readily extinguished, that the effects of automatic biases are difficult to monitor and control, and that high levels of implicit ingroup favoritism are evident across ages and cultures.

For example, Hugenberg and Bodenhausen (2003) recently found that higher implicit (but not explicit) racial bias was associated with a readiness to perceive anger in Black faces. These findings suggest that Whites with high levels of implicit racial bias are predisposed to perceive threat in Black but not White faces, and therefore indicate that the harmful effects of automatic stereotype activation may exert their influence extremely early in social interactions. Other research has explored how automatic bias may relate to other stereotypes, such as academic performance. Ashburn-Nardo, Knowles, and Monteith (2003) found that Blacks' implicit preference for their ingroup predicted their preference for a Black (compared to White) partner on an intellectually challenging task. In general, research suggests that implicit racial attitudes influence responses that are more difficult to monitor and control. For example, Fazio et al. (1995) found that Whites' automatic bias was predictive of nonverbal behaviors and a Black Confederates ratings of the quality of an interracial interaction. Other investigations have likewise indicated that automatic bias and stereotyping are related to subtle factors in interaction quality such as physical closeness (Bessenoff & Sherman, 2000), touch (Wilson, Lindsey, & Schooler, 2000), speech errors and hesitations (McConnell & Liebold, 2001), and other nonverbal behaviors related to friendliness such as visual contact, smiling, and speaking time (Dovidio, Gaertner, Kawakami, & Hodson, 2002; Dovidio, Kawakami, Johnson, Johnson, & Howard, 1997; McConnell & Liebold, 2001).

Gregg, Seibt, and Banaji (2006) conducted a series of studies focused on the formation and modification of automatic associations and self-reported preferences. They found that both automatic and self-reported preferences could be induced by abstract supposition and by concrete learning. However, unlike self-reported preferences, and in contrast to previous malleability findings, newly formed automatic preferences could not be readily reversed by either abstract supposition or concrete learning. In short, Gregg et al. provided empirical support that automatic associations are "easier done than undone." Although both implicit evaluations and explicit attitudes may be swiftly formed, implicit evaluations seem to be especially insensitive to modification once created. Similarly, Rydell and McConnell (2006) found that explicit conscious attitudes were shaped in a manner consistent with fast-changing processes, were affected by explicit processing goals, and were predictive of more deliberate behavior. In contrast, more automatic implicit attitudes reflected an associative system characterized by a slower process of repeated pairings between an attitude object and evaluations, were unaffected by explicit processing goals, and were predictive of more spontaneous behaviors. In addition, Ashburn-Nardo, Voils, and Monteith (2001) found implicit ingroup favoritism emerged even in minimal group settings, suggesting a readiness of the human mind to favor one's ingroup.

Related to these investigations into the formation of automatic biases, other studies have used a developmental perspective to learn more about the origin and development of racial bias across the life span. Although influential dissociation theories (e.g., Devine, 1989) have posited that implicit racial attitudes develop via socialization early in life, research on children's race-related attitudes and reasoning has been scarce. One exception is an investigation conducted by S. Sinclair, Dunn, and Lowery (2005) that documented evidence of implicit bias favoring Whites over Blacks (similar to the pattern observed in adults) for fourth- and fifth-grade children. Also, a correspondence between parents' explicit prejudice and children's explicit and implicit attitudes was found among children who were highly identified with their parents. Also, Baron and Banaji (2006) conducted a cross-sectional study exploring the origins and development of race-related implicit and explicit preferences. High levels of implicit ingroup favoritism were apparent at young ages (6 years old) and stable levels were observed across age groups. However, although explicit ingroup favoritism was initially high for young children, it declined with development and was essentially nonexistent in adulthood. Consistent with Devine's (1989) dissociation model, these findings suggest that explicit attitudes related to race become less prejudiced across development whereas implicit attitudes are formed very early in life and remain influential.

Finally, Dunham, Baron, and Banaji (2006) conducted a similar cross-sectional investigation exploring the development of implicit race attitudes in Americans and Japanese. Implicit ingroup bias was present early in life (6 years old) for both populations, and stable high levels were observed across development (10 years old and adulthood). The magnitude and developmental trajectory was similar for both cultures, suggesting that implicit intergroup bias is a fundamental feature of social cognition. Relevant research by Livingston (2002) explored the implicit attitudes of Blacks within American culture. Although Whites generally display implicit ingroup favoritism, many Blacks do not show a similar ingroup preference, but rather exhibit an implicit evaluative preference for Whites relative to Blacks. These findings support Devine's (1989) reasoning that automatic associations reflect the pervasive influence of cultural evaluations associated with social groups.

In sum, although not unconditionally automatic and perhaps more flexible than was once thought, automatic bias is still pervasive, often unintended, efficient, and in short, very likely. As a result, low-prejudice responses generally require regulation to inhibit automatically activated stereotypes and implement the intended response. The findings on malleability of automatic biases are impressive, and although volitional processes in the form of direct efforts to reduce intergroup biases were not necessary to produce these effects, we strongly suspect that deliberative processes would likely be required for these procedures to have sustained effects over time. For example, individuals who want to be low-prejudiced must *choose* to practice "saying no" to stereotypes, or engage in counterstereotypic imagery. In addition, although local environments that encourage reduction of biases can be powerful, people most often choose their social environments. For local environments to produce long-lasting change, people would need to self-select these environments as was the case in Dasgupta and Agussi's studies involving single-sex or mixed-sex colleges. Questions concerning who is likely to engage in these regulatory efforts and how automatic biases may be effectively managed over time have led some researchers to more specifically consider the various mechanisms of control people deploy to reduce automatic intergroup biases or in Allport's (1954) terms "to put the brakes on their prejudice" (p. 332). It is to a consideration of this literature that we now turn.

CONTROL

Although automatic stereotypic associations are activated with discouraging frequency and ease, several theorists have posited that automatic stereotypic reactions can be overridden under favorable conditions (e.g., Allport, 1954; Devine, 1989; Fazio et al., 1995; Fiske, 1989; Wegener & Petty, 1997; Wilson & Brekke, 1994). Indeed, given the potential to unduly bias intergroup thought and behavior and the recognition that perceivers have a choice in how they respond to others (Bargh, 1994; Fiske, 1989), a great deal of research has been done to identify the ways in which automatic race-related responses may be controlled or otherwise regulated. By and large, this work has developed in parallel to research focused on automatic processes in stereotyping and prejudice. Shaped by dual-processing approaches to social cognition, research of this nature has focused on the ways in which automatic modes of information processing may be refined, corrected, or overridden by more controlled processes. Such dual process models have generally put forth that awareness, motivation, and ability are necessary for the controlled regulation of automatic stereotyping and evaluation (Bargh, 1992, 1999; Devine, 1989; Neuberg & Fiske, 1987). In what follows, we review the major control strategies explored in the regulation of intergroup biases (see Amodio & Devine, in press, for a more detailed analysis of control mechanisms).

INDIVIDUATION: GATHERING ADDITIONAL INFORMATION

According to classic dual process models of person perception (e.g., Brewer, 1988; Brewer & Harasty, 1999; Fiske & Neuberg, 1990; Fiske, Lin, & Neuberg, 1999), perceivers start with category-based impressions of others and proceed to forming individuated impressions of others only when sufficiently motivated. In the absence of such motivation, intergroup biases arising from activated stereotypes occur. Although they differ in some details, these models contend that social perceivers categorize or stereotype others initially but can avoid stereotypic biases by replacing such categorical processing with more individuated, highly personalized processing. This more controlled, intentional type of processing is only likely to occur, however, when sufficient motivation and ability are present. Thus, in such models, stereotyping is the default, quickly and effortlessly applied process, which precedes any conscious, goal-driven processes. Such efficient processing can only be corrected or nullified, according to these models, by more careful, elaborated processing.

CORRECTION: OVERCOMING POTENTIAL BIAS

Correction is a control process, the goal of which is to regulate the impact of automatically activated biases to correct for their potential influence on judgments or behavior (Fazio, 1990; Wegener & Petty, 1997; Wilson & Brekke, 1994). That is, if automatic stereotype activation cannot be avoided, a person may attempt to estimate the effects of the activated stereotype and make appropriate adjustments to his or her responses to correct for the presumed influence of the stereotype. For accurate adjustments to be made, an individual must believe bias is operating (awareness), be motivated to make corrections, and have correct naive theories about direction and magnitude of the biasing effect of stereotypes on responses. However, given the necessary condition of awareness of bias, mental correction may pertain to a subset of situations (i.e., conscious awareness of potential bias) and response types (i.e., deliberative judgments, self-reported responses). Of course, motivation to make adjustments must also be present. To the extent that these requirements can realistically be met, postactivation bias correction holds promise for remedying the negative effects of unintended stereotyping and bias.

SUPPRESSION: BANISHING STEREOTYPES FROM CONSCIOUSNESS

Other research on the control of automatic prejudice has focused on the efficacy of deliberate attempts to banish unwanted thoughts or feelings from the mind (Wegner, 1994). Specifically, in an attempt to avoid unwanted bias, people may attempt to suppress prejudiced thoughts (Macrae, Bodenhausen, & Milne, 1998; Macrae, Bodenhausen, Milne, & Jetten, 1994; Monteith, Sherman, & Devine, 1998; Monteith, Spicer, & Tooman, 1998) and replace them with more desirable distracter thoughts. Although such a strategy may seem reasonable, research suggests that attempts to suppress stereotypic thoughts often result in a rebound effect in which the unwanted thoughts become hyperaccessible subsequent to suppression (e.g., Macrae, Bodenhausen, et al., 1994; Wyer, Sherman, & Stroessner, 1998, 2000). Thus, suppressing stereotypic thoughts may lead to their unwittingly exerting influence on later thoughts and actions. Such paradoxical outcomes have been explained in terms of Wegner's model of mental control (Macrae, Bodenhausen, et al., 1994; Wegner, 1994).

According to this model, control is effectively achieved as long as the perceiver is able to persist in an effortful search for distracter thoughts to replace the unwanted (stereotypic) thoughts. However, while this search-and-replace process occurs, an ironic monitoring process supposedly searches consciousness for evidence of the stereotypic thoughts, which causes these thoughts to be repeatedly primed, and thus increases their accessibility. Therefore, if the functioning of the operating process is undermined (e.g., due to cognitive load; Wegner, 1994), or if the conscious intention to avoid the unwanted thought is relaxed (Macrae, Bodenhausen, et al., 1994), stereotypic thoughts may rebound. The interesting findings obtained in this line of research suggest that the more people try to reduce their stereotypic thinking through suppression, the more they will fail to do so (e.g., Macrae, Bodenhausen, et al., 1994).

Most of the work on the (in)effectiveness of suppression as a control strategy has examined the influence of experimenter-supplied instructions to suppress stereotypes. Recent research suggests, however, that there are individual differences in the motivation and ability to regulate and suppress stereotypic thoughts. Monteith and her colleagues (Monteith, Spicer, & Tooman, 1998; Monteith, Sherman, & Devine, 1998) demonstrated that low-prejudiced individuals (i.e., who have internalized egalitarian values) do not appear to be as susceptible to rebound effects as high-prejudiced individuals. In addition, Wyer et al. (1998) examined the roles of situationally induced motivations to respond without prejudice on the use and effectiveness of stereotype suppression. Wyer et al. found that under conditions in which stereotype use might elicit social disapproval (e.g., when their responses would be evaluated by an African American organization), participants spontaneously suppressed the use of race stereotypes and showed stronger rebound effects when later forming impressions of a race-unspecified individual, relative to a control condition (Wyer et al., 1998). Those who spontaneously suppressed the stereotype showed equally strong rebound effects as participants who were explicitly instructed to suppress. These findings help to identify situations when "spontaneous" suppression is likely to occur and might suggest that external motivation to suppress (be it derived from experimental instructions or normative pressure) is likely to result in rebound. Taken together, these findings imply that moderators such as egalitarian goals and social context may be important for understanding the (un)successful suppression of stereotypes.

INDIRECT AND UNINTENTIONAL CONTROL STRATEGIES

Recently researchers have examined the effectiveness of means to reduce automatic stereotyping that, although they clearly involve effortful processing, are not presented as strategies to reduce stereotyping. Galinsky and Moskowitz (2000), for example, examined the effectiveness of perspective taking compared with stereotype suppression in reducing stereotyping. Specifically, in the perspective taking condition participants were instructed to take the perspective of a stimulus person (e.g., effectively step into the person's shoes and experience the world from his vantage point). Although this was a consciously driven process, participants in the perspective taking condition were not told anything about trying not to stereotype. Galinsky and Moskowitz found that whereas participants in the suppression condition showed evidence of rebound (i.e., heightened stereotype accessibility in a postsuppression period), those in the perspective taking condition did not. Galinsky and Ku (2004) extended this work and found that perspective taking decreased stereotyping and ingroup favoritism, and further, these effects were moderated by self-esteem. Perspective takers with temporarily or chronically high self-esteem evaluated an outgroup more positively than those with low self-esteem. Perspective taking seems to facilitate self–other overlap and thus uses the natural propensity to think well of oneself, a process typically thought to induce and perpetuate intergroup bias (Tajfel & Turner, 1986), to extend favorable associations related to oneself to the evaluation of others.

Sassenberg and Moskowitz (2005) explored the possibility that changing people's mindsets, and hence the way they processed information about members of a stigmatized group, affected the extent to which stereotypes were automatically activated. As with the perspective taking work, there was no mention of stereotyping or concern over prejudiced responding in these studies. Prior to the assessment of stereotypes in a lexical decision task, participants were assigned to a creative mindset (i.e., write about three instances in which they had behaved creatively), thoughtful mindset (i.e., write about three instances in which they had behaved thoughtfully), or no mindset control group. Although automatic stereotype activation was evident for those in the control and thoughtful mindset conditions, it was not evident in the creative mindset condition. These findings support Sassenberg and Moskowitz's hypothesis that priming creativity activates the mindset to "think different," which prevents stereotypes in general from becoming automatically activated, and thus may be an indirect control strategy that, unlike others, is not tailored to a specific group or situation.

A final stereotype regulation strategy focuses on lateral inhibition processes that do not rely on deliberatively mediated processes. Macrae, Bodenhausen and Milne (1995), for example, demonstrated that stereotype activation can be reduced through a process referred to as lateral inhibition. This type of inhibition process operates, for example, when a person could be stereotyped in multiple ways, as most people can be (e.g., according to both gender and ethnicity). Under such circumstances, alternative relevant stereotypes could be simultaneously activated and exert an inhibiting influence on each other. Macrae et al. demonstrated that a slight change in context that affects the salience of the alternate categories can have a large effect on which stereotype gets activated and which gets inhibited.

In their studies, participants were exposed to a Chinese woman, and automatic stereotypes of both Chinese and women were subsequently measured in a lexical decision task. In one condition, the Chinese woman was putting on makeup, whereas in another condition she was using chopsticks. Compared to control participants, those who saw the person put on makeup were faster to respond to traits stereotypic of women and slower to respond to traits stereotypic of Chinese, whereas those who saw her use chopsticks produced the opposite pattern and were faster to respond to traits stereotypic of Chinese and slower to respond to traits stereotypic of women. According to Macrae and colleagues, lateral inhibition processes produced the differential stereotype activation effects. Because the process is assumed to occur automatically, it is believed to reflect a "preconscious" or "spontaneous" mechanism of control (see Bodenhausen & Macrae, 1998, for an excellent discussion of lateral inhibition). Although not directly tested, this type of process may be relevant for understanding some of the previously reviewed findings on variability in automatic stereotyping effects in which activation of stereotypes was moderated by social contexts (e.g., Wittenbrink et al., 1997) and social roles (e.g., Barden et al., 2004; Maddux et al., 2005) or how automatically activated chronic egalitarian goals may exert an inhibitory influence on stereotype activation (e.g., Moskowitz et al., 1999; Moskowitz et al., 2000).

SELF-REGULATION: INTENTIONAL INHIBITION AND REPLACEMENT

Inhibition of unacceptable responses and replacement with acceptable responses is the cornerstone of Devine's (1989) original application of dual process ideas to the study of intergroup biases. In this form of control, self-defining, internalized values determine acceptable behavior and any response (i.e., thought, feeling, or behavior) that conflicts with these values is considered unacceptable and to be eliminated. For example, for a low-prejudice person, automatic stereotype activation and application would be particularly troubling as it conflicts with egalitarian ideals. As such, the goal to be egalitarian and to respond without prejudice would lead to inhibition of automatically activated stereotypes or prejudiced feelings and the companion process of replacing biased responding with more acceptable low-prejudice thoughts and behavior (Devine, 1989).

In support of this conceptualization, Devine (1989) found that low-prejudice individuals provided nonstereotypic, egalitarian descriptions of their beliefs about Blacks when they had ample time to generate those descriptions. In contrast, when the opportunity for controlled processing was bypassed, low-prejudiced participants showed evidence of stereotype application. These findings led Devine to hypothesize that achieving effective and consistent low-prejudiced responding may be likened to breaking a habit. Devine proposed that overcoming the effects of automatically activated bias was an effortful and extended process whereby repeated inhibition of stereotypic responses and implementation of low-prejudiced beliefs would eventually lead to internalization and automatic activation of low-prejudiced standards instead of cultural stereotypes. Although her model suggested that intentions derived from egalitarian values must compete with automatic stereotyping to affect responses (Logan & Cowan, 1984), Devine did not precisely lay on the mechanisms that produced this inhibition and replacement process.

Subsequent research by Montieth and colleagues (Monteith, 1993; Monteith, Ashburn-Nardo, Voils, & Czopp, 2002) has examined these mechanisms in more detail. Rooted in Gray's (1982) neuropsychological model of motivation and learning, the work of Monteith and colleagues has examined the consequences of recognizing that one's stereotyping responses are at odds with one's nonprejudiced values (see Monteith & Mark, chap. 25, this volume, for a detailed summary of the model). According to the model, low-prejudice people learn to overcome their automatic prejudiced tendencies through self-regulatory outcomes that follow from an awareness of the failure to control stereotyping or prejudice. Specifically, this program of research has revealed that awareness that one has responded with prejudice elicits guilt along with other outcomes that help low-prejudice people to exert control over potentially prejudiced responses in future situations. These other outcomes include heightened self-focus, a momentary disruption of ongoing behavior coupled with retrospective reflection on why the failure occurred, and careful attention to the stimuli or cues present when the failure occurred.

Learning to associate a prejudice-related failure with guilt and self-regulatory mechanisms establishes *cues for control* that may serve as warning signals in the future to increase arousal and behavioral inhibition when the potential for prejudiced responding is present (Monteith et al., 2002). When these cues are present in future situations, they lead to an immediate interruption in ongoing behavior and prospective reflection, which leads to response slowing and a careful consideration of how to respond with the goal of preventing a discrepant (prejudiced) response. Essentially, Monteith posited that environmental stimuli serve as cues for punishment associated with prejudiced responding and trigger inhibitory mechanisms. This work is important because it provides a theoretical account of how controlled processes may be recruited to disrupt automatic processes in the presence of cues for control such that prejudiced responses are prevented and replaced with belief-based responses. Across a number of experiments, Monteith and colleagues have provided compelling evidence that low-prejudice people learn from their mistakes and become effective in regulating future prejudiced responses.

LIMITS TO DELIBERATIVE CONTROL STRATEGIES

As the literature suggests, deliberatively mediated control mechanisms can be quite powerful in combating intergroup biases. Perhaps the greatest strength of the control strategies reviewed, namely that they engage thoughtful regulation of responses, is also their potentially greatest weakness in the regulation of automatic intergroup biases. That is, a central assumption of these regulatory strategies is that control mechanisms are deployed only when people are aware of bias or potential bias. Perceivers must first be aware that ingroup biases may influence their responses before efforts to correct such responses can be instigated. Indeed, a major challenge in the intergroup bias literature concerns how to develop sensitivity to bias that arises from automatic processes. To the extent that automatic processes go undetected, as so often they do, they may serve as a potent source of intergroup biases and discrimination (Bargh, 1999; Banaji & Hardin, 1996).

THE INTERPLAY BETWEEN AUTOMATIC AND CONTROLLED PROCESSES

Traditionally, the separate contributions of automatic and controlled processes to race bias have been compared using performance on tasks that preclude the possibility of deliberative controlled response versus tasks on which control is extremely easy (e.g., self-reported responses). A drawback of this approach is that it confounds process mode with the measurement instrument. As a number of theorists have now noted, this methodology is somewhat misleading because no one task is likely to be indicative of purely automatic or purely controlled processing (Amodio et al., 2004; Bargh, 1994; Conrey, Sherman, Gawronski, Hugenberg, & Groom, 2005; Jacoby, 1991; Payne, 2001; Payne, Jacoby, & Lambert, 2005). Indeed, in recent years, there has been a growing recognition that both automatic and control processes are involved in the generation of any given behavior. The application of methods from computation modeling and from cognitive and behavioral neuroscience have made it possible to estimate the independent impact of automatic and controlled processes and to examine these processes as they unfold over time and in a reciprocal and dynamic way. This newer generation of work on automaticity and control has allowed for a more precise testing of some of the process assumptions laid out only very generally in early models of automaticity and control. In this regard, the newer work is both exciting and encouraging about the role of control to dampen or otherwise override automatic processes.

COMPUTATIONAL MODELING: SEPARATE ESTIMATES OF AUTOMATIC AND CONTROLLED PROCESSES

Building on Jacoby's (1991) process dissociation (PD) procedure, Payne was the first to take a computational modeling approach to estimate the extent to which race bias involves automatic and controlled processes. The basic idea underlying the PD approach is that behavioral responses, such as those commonly used in the reaction time assessment of intergroup biases, reflect a combination of automatic and controlled processes. To explore these processes in the context of race biases, Payne designed the weapon's identification task, a sequential priming paradigm in which Black or White faces are presented briefly, followed by a picture of a gun or tool. Participants are instructed to ignore the face and to categorize whether the subsequent object is a gun or tool by pressing one of two response keys. According to the PD model, the independent effects of automatic (e.g., stereotype-based) and controlled (e.g., accuracy-based) processes can be dissociated using tasks that place these processes in opposition to one another. In the weapons identification task, for example, when a correct response is congruent with automatic tendencies (e.g., choosing "gun" when a gun follows a Black face), automatic and controlled processes act in concert. When a correct response is incongruent with automatic tendencies (e.g., choosing "tool" when a tool follows a Black face), automatic and controlled processes act in opposition (see Payne, 2001, for PD formulas). By assessing accuracy performance across congruent (Black-gun) and incongruent (Black-tool) trial types, independent estimates of automatic and controlled processes may be obtained.

Using this procedure, Payne documented the existence of racial bias related to weapons and experimentally dissociated the automatic and controlled processes that contribute to that bias. Specifically, findings indicated that social category primes biased the perception of weapons through relatively automatic processes and did not influence controlled processes (see also Correll, Park, Judd, & Wittenbrink, 2002; Greenwald, Oakes, & Hoffman, 2003). Moreover, requiring participants to respond quickly reduced ability to control responses, but did not influence automatic activation, thus resulting in biased responses as evidenced by greater error rates than when categorization time was unlimited.

In a related paradigm, researchers have examined the extent to which race affects people's decision to shoot criminal suspects and whether training designed to reduce race biases affects automatic (reducing the race–criminality link) or controlled processes (improving one's accuracy on the task). For example, Correll et al. (2002) had participants complete a computer task in which male "suspects" appeared on a screen and were either holding handguns or neutral objects (e.g., cell phone, wallet). They were told to press a "shoot" button if the suspect had a gun or a "don't shoot" button if the suspect was unarmed. Consistent with Payne's (2001) work, participants were more likely to mistakenly shoot an unarmed suspect if he was Black than if he was White. With training, however, such biases can be reduced. For example, Plant, Peruche, and Butz (2005; Plant & Peruche, 2005) provided participants with experience with a shooter bias task in which suspect race is unrelated to the presence of the gun. Although participants' early responses revealed a bias toward mistakenly shooting unarmed Black rather than White suspects, after training, this bias was eliminated. Moreover, using the PD approach, Plant and colleagues showed that training led to increases in control from early to later trials and particularly for Black faces. Further, training led participants to inhibit racial stereotypes. Such work promises to shed light on what processes are involved in overcoming intergroup biases.

Expanding the process dissociation analysis, Conrey et al. (2005) argued that behavioral tasks to assess intergroup biases likely involve a broader set of processes than automatic and controlled processes. According to their quadruple process model, implicit measures of social cognition do not reflect only automatic processes but rather the joint contributions of four qualitatively different processes: activation of an automatic association, determination of the correct response, ability to overcome bias, and guessing. Conrey et al. demonstrated across a series of studies that each of these parameters can be manipulated independently and that they have dissociable effects on a range of outcomes. Conrey et al.'s model essentially suggests that control can be thought of in distinct ways (i.e., determination of a correct response and an ability to overcome bias). Previous models of control have typically conflated these constructs and Conrey et al.'s findings suggest that a more nuanced analysis of mechanisms of control may prove fruitful.

Social Neuroscience Approach to the Study of Automaticity and Control

Social psychological models of regulation of automatically activated race-biased tendencies suggest that regulatory processes are initiated only on conscious reflection of a biased response (e.g., Bodenhausen & Macrae, 1998; Devine, 1989; Devine & Monteith, 1993; Monteith, 1993). As noted previously, without awareness of bias (or potential for bias), regulatory efforts are not engaged. Although Monteith's model nicely anticipated the possibility that regulation may be deployed rapidly in the course of an unfolding response to preempt a race-biased behavior, the model focuses on the process of self-regulation that arises following a prejudiced response to prevent future transgressions. Previous social psychological models have not addressed the regulatory process by which race bias is detected and overridden in a single, rapidly unfolding response. We suspect that the major reason this step has received little attention is that the traditional tools of the social psychologist—self-reports, behavioral observations, computerized reaction-time tasks—are poorly equipped for measuring rapid changes in underlying cognitive processes (see Amodio, Devine, & Harmon-Jones, 2007). Such processes can, however, be studied by measuring neural activity and, in recent years, social psychologists have applied neuroscientific methods to explore the specific brain mechanisms underlying the activation and control of race bias. This approach has offered new glimpses into the nature of automatic race bias and its control that were heretofore not possible. This endeavor has been quite productive and a number of studies have shown that, although automatic race biases are activated quickly, mechanisms of control may also be deployed very rapidly and without awareness or deliberative processes. We briefly review a sampling of these exciting findings.

For example, research using startle eye-blink methodology and functional magnetic resonance imaging (fMRI) studies have indicated that the amygdala, a neural structure associated with the detection of threat and fear learning, was more strongly activated when participants viewed outgroup (vs. ingroup) faces (Amodio et al., 2003; Hart et al., 2000; Phelps et al., 2000). These findings have been thought to indicate that Whites automatically perceive unfamiliar Blacks as potentially threatening and fear relevant. In other research, event-related potential (ERP) studies of expectancy violation and multiple categorization have revealed forms of implicit stereotyping (Bartholow, Fabiani, Gratton, & Bettencourt, 2001) and evaluation (Ito, Thompson, & Cacioppo, 2004) in rapidly activated patterns of neural activity. By using ERPs to track changes in brain activity on the order of milliseconds, these researchers have gained new insights into the time course of automatic and controlled forms of race bias activation, and have shown that stereotype-based processing is evident within 100 msec of encountering a stigmatized group member (e.g., Ito et al., 2004). Consistent with the literature on automatic race biases reviewed previously, it appears that intergroup biases are quickly activated.

Using fMRI and ERP methods, a number of researchers have begun to study the neural components control (as well as automaticity) in intergroup bias (Amodio et al., 2004; Cunningham et al., 2004; Richeson et al., 2003). Cunningham et al. (2004) suggested that regulation of automatic race bias should involve cortical override of amygdala activity. To test this hypothesis, Cunningham et al. presented research participants with faces of Black and White individuals for either 30 msec or 525 msec. They argued that a 30-msec exposure would preclude conscious awareness of the face and, thus, would reveal brain activity associated with automatic race bias; at the longer duration because faces would be consciously perceived, controlled processes would be engaged to inhibit automatically activated amygdala activity. Consistent with expectations, Cunningham et al. (2004) found greater amygdala activation for Black than White faces when presented for a brief duration (30 msec). At the longer exposure duration (525 msec), however, this difference was reduced and there was greater activity in the regions of the prefrontal cortex (PFC) associated with inhibition and control. Consistent with the notion that cortical processes override amygdala activity, Cunningham et al. found a negative correlation between activity in the right ventromedial PFC and activity in the amygdala (see also Lieberman, Hariri, & Jarcho, 2005; Richeson et al., 2003). These findings corroborate social psychological theory, indicating that controlled processes may modulate automatic evaluation. However, they suggest that this adjustment may occur more quickly and efficiently than was once thought possible.

Research using fMRI to explore brain regions associated with automatic and controlled processes in race bias is exciting, innovative, and the findings are provocative. However, there are some important limitations of the research done to date that should be considered when interpreting this research and debating its utility more broadly in the study of control. For example, control in these studies is quite different from the type of control in behavioral tasks in which one can assess whether a response is consistent with intentions. That is, in the studies no active control response was required from participants, as they passively viewed faces (or judged whether faces appeared on the left or right side of the screen). Although it is clear that there was activity in brain regions known to be associated with self-regulation, the extent to which this activity reflects the same type of active controlled regulation when one's prepotent responses conflict with intended responses (i.e., as when automatic intergroup biases conflict with egalitarian responding based nonprejudiced values) over prejudiced reactions must await future research.

Further, fMRI studies have also been limited in the insight they can provide about the processes underlying automaticity and control of intergroup bias because of method constraints on temporal resolution that preclude investigations of quickly unfolding processes. In contrast to fMRI, which typically measures changes in neural activity on the order of seconds, ERPs, derived from electroencephalography (EEG) measure changes on the order of milliseconds. As such, this methodology, which affords high temporal resolution, is better suited to test predictions about the time course associated with rapidly unfolding processes. ERPs refer to patterns of neuronal activity that are detectable using electrodes placed on the scalp (see Fabiani, Gratton, & Coles, 2000). To observe ERPs, very subtle electrical changes on the scalp are recorded using EEG while a participant responds to events of an experimental task. By collecting EEG using a high sampling rate, ERPs can track real-time changes in brain activity as regulatory processes unfold.

In the cognitive neuroscience literature, the process of control has been characterized as two mechanisms, each associated with activity in separate neural structures (e.g., Botvinick, Nystrom, Fissel, Carter, & Cohen, 1999). The first is a conflict detection system, which monitors ongoing responses and is sensitive to completion between prepotent (e.g., automatic) and consciously intended responses. The conflict detection system, which has been associated with activity in the anterior cingulate cortex (ACC), is constantly active, requires few resources, and may operate below the level of awareness. When the ACC detects conflict, it alerts a second, resource-dependent system designed to inhibit unintended responses and replace them with intended responses. This regulatory system has been shown to involve PFC activity. An ERP component that has been shown previously to reflect conflict-related activity in the ACC is the *error-related negativity* (ERN; Falkenstein, Hohnsbein, Hoorman, & Blanke, 1991; Gehring & Fencsik, 2001). ERNs are specifically sensitive to conflicts that lead to response errors (i.e., failed control), making them particularly useful for examining failures in response regulation.

Amodio et al. (2004) had participants complete the weapons identification task while EEG was recorded so that ERNs could be examined to explore the role of conflict monitoring during the process of prejudice control. Given past work in which participants tended to respond more accurately on Black-gun trials, on which the Black faces prime the correct "gun" response, but make more errors on Black-tool trials, on which the Black faces prime the incorrect response (Payne, 2001), Amodio et al. (2004) reasoned that responding accurately on Black-tool trials requires greater controlled processing relative to Black-gun trials and that the ERN for errors that reflect prejudiced responding (i.e., responding gun on a Black-tool trial) would be enhanced. Although participants in their study reported low-prejudice attitudes on average, they exhibited a pattern of automatic race bias on the weapons identification task, such that Black faces facilitated responses to guns and interfered with responses to tools, relative to White faces. These results suggested that enhanced control was needed to override the prepotent tendency to erroneously choose "gun" on Black-tool trials. ERN amplitudes were significantly larger on errors on Black-tool trials, on which automatic stereotypes created high response conflict, compared with the other trial types, supporting the hypothesis that the need to control stereotypes elicits activity of the neural system for conflict detection. Lending credence to the idea that ERN amplitudes signal the need for controlled processing, Amodio et al. found that ERN amplitudes correlated with PD estimates of control (as well as other indicators that control was initiated). ERNs, however, were not correlated with the PD estimate of automatic processing, consistent with the idea that all participants would show similar levels of automatic bias, independent of whether they engaged in controlled processing.

In subsequent work, Amodio, Devine, and Harmon-Jones (2008) explored the extent to which their conflict detection framework could account for previously puzzling findings among low-prejudice individuals. That is, although all truly low-prejudice people desire to respond without prejudice, as our review made clear, some low-prejudice people appear to be good at regulating race biases, whereas other are poor at regulating such biases (e.g., Devine et al., 2002; Dovidio, Kawakami, & Gaertner, 2002; Moskowitz et al., 1999). Amodio et al. hypothesized that the neural systems of poor regulators may be less sensitive to conflict between an automatic race-biased tendency and an egalitarian response intention compared with good regulators. To test this hypothesis, they recruited good, poor, and nonregulators (i.e., high-prejudice people who were not personally motivated to respond without prejudice) and tested for differences in these groups' average ERN responses as they completed the weapons identification task. Replicating past research (Amodio et al., 2004; Payne, 2001), all participants showed evidence of automatic stereotyping (i.e., elevated PD-automatic scores for Black vs. White faces), yet good and poor regulators reported equally positive attitudes toward Black people. However, an examination of response control (PD-control estimate) showed that good regulators were significantly better at responding without bias than poor regulators. Consistent with expectations, the difference between good and poor regulators in behavioral control corresponded to their difference in conflict monitoring on trials in which control was needed to overcome bias. That is, good regulators exhibited an enhancement in ERN amplitudes when responses required the control of automatic stereotypes (i.e., on Black-tool trials) but poor regulators did not. Indeed, the difference in behavioral control between good and poor regulators was found to be fully mediated by their ERN amplitudes, suggesting that poor regulators are less effective in regulating their intergroup responses because their conflict-monitoring systems were relatively insensitive to discrepancies between a tendency to use stereotypes and their intention to respond without bias.

Taken together, these findings demonstrated that conflict-detection processes are activated in response to automatic race-biased tendencies and mechanisms of control are set in motion very early in the response stream and do not necessarily require conscious appraisals for the engagement of control. In this sense, Amodio et al.'s findings suggest that "putting the brakes on prejudice" can involve preconscious mechanisms that both detect the potential for failure and recruit the needed controlled processes to avert the biased response and replace it with intended responses. In this regard, social perceivers may be capable of "fighting automatic fire with automatic fire" (Bargh, 1999, p. 378), in that both stereotype activation and motivated inhibition are automatically unfolding at a preconscious level.

The social neuroscience approach has begun to make important strides in unpacking the sub-processes involved in response control and our understanding of control extends beyond corrective functions to include preconscious processes to prevent the expression of activated biases. However, critical questions are now emerging pertaining to the origin and development of preconscious regulation. Is such regulation learned as the result of continuous practice inhibiting unwanted stereotypical thoughts? Does preconscious regulation follow from personal beliefs and automatic goals? Future work will be needed to integrate postconscious control mechanisms (in which people effectively learn from their mistakes to avoid future discrepant responses) and the rapid onset of preconscious mechanisms that function to prevent a prejudice response as it unfolds. Is it the case, for example, that good regulators identified by Amodio et al. (2008; Devine et al., 2002) have established strong cues for control through the postconscious processes outlined by Monteith and colleagues and that, over time, these cues engage the preconscious conflict detection processes explored by Amodio and colleagues? Future research investigating the unfolding dynamics of automatic and controlled processes in social cognition will likely inform such questions.

CONCLUDING COMMENTS

In reviewing the state of knowledge regarding automatic and controlled processes in stereotyping and prejudice almost a decade ago, Devine and Monteith (1999) noted the frequency and efficiency of automatic biased processing, but also took great care to outline the nature of controlled processes and a model for self-regulation. Devine and Monteith's (1999) optimistic view of the role of control and inhibition in the regulation of intergroup biases seems to have been largely supported in the wealth of research in this area conducted since their review. As the field's understanding of the nature of automatic and controlled processes has developed, investigations exploring the effects of practice in low-prejudiced responding, egalitarian goal setting, and self-regulation seem to support the notion that automatic biases need not be thought of as inevitable. Technological advances have led to new techniques that have helped us better define what it means for a process to be "automatic" and "controlled," and have led to a better appreciation for both automatic and controlled contributions to psychological events and behavioral responses.

From the application of ERP technology for mapping processes in milliseconds (Amodio et al., 2004) to the use of developmental methodology in looking at changes across a lifetime (Baron & Banaji, 2006), exploiting technological advances and synthesizing relevant reasoning and methods across a variety of related disciplines has provided leverage for understanding the complex nature of automatic and controlled processes underlying stereotyping and prejudice. Although substantial progress is being made, much remains to be learned. In closing we wish to highlight a couple of important issues that will require attention as our collective efforts to understand the origins and reduction of intergroup biases continue.

The reader may have noted that through the chapter, we have used the general label intergroup biases to refer to automatic biases that arise from cognitive sources (e.g., stereotypes) and from affective sources (e.g., evaluation). This word choice was deliberate because in some of the research on race biases the measures focused primarily on stereotypes (e.g., Blair, 2001; Devine, 1989; Gilbert & Hixon, 1991; Lepore & Brown, 1997; Macrae et al., 1997; Monteith et al., 2002; Payne, 2001; L. Sinclair & Kunda, 1999), others focused primarily on evaluation (e.g., Dasgupta & Greenwald, 2001; Fazio et al., 1995; Greenwald, McGhee, & Schwartz, 1998; Ito et al., 2006; Lowery et al., 2001), and still others focused on some combination of stereotypes and evaluation (e.g., Dovidio et al., 1986; Rudman et al., 2001; Wittenbrink et al., 1997). As the literature review suggests, both forms of automatic intergroup biases are prevalent and can lead to pernicious effects for those stigmatized by such biases. Although cognitive and affective processes typically function in concert to produce intergroup biases, recent work suggests that these two forms of bias are independent and likely arise from distinct neural substrates associated with semantic (stereotypes) and affective (evaluation) memory systems (Amodio & Devine, 2006). Further, considering them separately may yield new insights into the nature, consequences, and (potential) regulation of such biases.

Amodio and Devine (2006) argued that to the extent that automatic stereotyping and evaluation reflect independent cognitive and affective systems, respectively, they should be uniquely associated with different types of discriminatory responses. Specifically, they suggested that automatic stereotyping should predict instrumental behaviors (e.g., impression judgments), which are driven primarily by cognitive processes, whereas automatic evaluation should predict consummatory behaviors that are driven primarily by affective-evaluative processes (e.g., interpersonal preferences and social distance). To obtain relatively pure measures of automatic stereotyping and evaluation, Amodio and Devine used separate IATs to measure implicit stereotyping and evaluation and examined the extent to which each IAT predicted instrumental and consummatory forms of behavior in double dissociation designs. Across three studies, although participants showed significant levels of bias on both implicit measures, their scores on the measures were not correlated. In addition, consistent with expectations, Amodio and Devine (2006) found that implicit stereotyping and evaluation have unique effects on alternative forms of race-biased behavior. That is, implicit stereotyping but not evaluation was predictive of impression ratings (i.e., instrumental behaviors). In contrast, implicit evaluative race bias but not stereotyping was predictive of interpersonal preference and social distance measures (i.e., consummatory behaviors).

Amodio and Devine (2006) suggested that attending to the distinction between implicit stereotyping and evaluation may help to clarify the construct of implicit race bias and its role in the prediction of behavior. For example, to date the evidence regarding the effects of implicit race bias on behavior is mixed (Blair, 2001). Amodio and Devine suggested that these mixed findings may arise from a mismatch between the implicit process assessed and the classes of discriminatory behaviors predicted. Overall, consideration of alternative forms of race bias may enhance predictive validity and allow more refined hypotheses of how implicit bias should affect behavior. Their analysis, because it links implicit stereotyping and evaluation to physiological and neural system models of the brain and behavior, suggests specific physiological indicators for different forms of race bias. For example, previous work has linked indexes of amygdala activity with measures of implicit evaluation (e.g., Amodio et al., 2003; Phelps et al., 2000). Although neural correlates of implicit race-based stereotyping have not yet been determined, ERP research on stereotype-based expectancy violation is consistent with a neocortical (vs. subcortical) substrate (e.g., Bartholow et al. 2001).

Finally, Amodio and Devine's analysis has implications for issues concerning the origin and malleability of intergroup biases. If implicit stereotyping and implicit evaluation arise from distinct neural substrates, as Amodio and Devine suggested, it is possible that they are learned and unlearned through different mechanisms. For example, human and animal models of learning and memory suggest that implicit evaluations may be learned more quickly and unlearned more slowly than implicit stereotypes. By integrating the extant work on intergroup biases with the broader literature on learning and memory, we may begin to develop a more complete understanding of what reduced bias on implicit measures in the literature showing malleability of intergroup biases really means. As noted previously, although the effects reported are impressive, whether they reflect real, enduring change is still an open question. Overall this approach encourages a new look at regulatory mechanisms and may offer an overarching framework in which to organize the various mechanisms of control previously reviewed. We suspect that this is an area in which important advances will be forthcoming.

Most of the literature examining automatic intergroup biases and their regulation has focused on intrapersonal processes (i.e., Do implicit biases get activated? Are these biases malleable? Can such biases be controlled?). However, the most important implications of intergroup biases are played out in interpersonal arenas where their effects can be the most destructive. Years ago one of us (Devine, 1998) argued that for a field with the nature and consequences of intergroup biases as its primary concern, the literature is somewhat strangely focused on intrapersonal processes. Indeed, some of the most exciting developments have arisen in the context of the examination of brain mechanisms involved in the activation and control of intergroup biases. Yet, such methods encourage a focus on increasingly microlevel processes. As research on automaticity and control of intergroup biases moves forward, we would like to encourage researchers to increasingly move beyond the isolated social perceiver into the interpersonal and dynamic social world in which the unchecked use of stereotypes and evaluative biases leads to the pernicious effects for those who are targets of intergroup biases. In closing, we echo Devine's (1998) observation that a complete analysis of the activation and regulation of intergroup biases will be forthcoming only when we recognize the challenges created for social perceivers by needing to manage and negotiate their cognitive and their social worlds.

REFERENCES

Allport, G. W. (1954). *The nature of prejudice.* Reading, MA: Addison-Wesley.
Amodio, D. M., & Devine, P. G. (2006). Stereotyping and evaluation in implicit race bias: Evidence for independent constructs and unique effects on behavior. *Journal of Personality and Social Psychology, 91,* 652–661.
Amodio, D. M., & Devine, P. G. (in press). Regulating behavior in the social world: Control in the context of intergroup bias. In R. Hassin, K. Ochsner, & Y. Trope (Eds.), *Self-control.* New York: Oxford University Press.
Amodio, D. M., Devine, P. G., & Harmon-Jones, E. (2007). Mechanisms for the regulation of intergroup responses: Insights from a social neuroscience approach. In E. Harmon-Jones & P. Winkielman (Eds.), *Social neuroscience: Integrating biological and psychological explanations of social behavior* (pp. 353–375). New York: Guilford.
Amodio, D. M., Devine, P. G., & Harmon-Jones, E. (2008). Individual differences in the regulation of intergroup bias: The role of conflict monitoring. *Journal of Personality and Social Psychology, 94,* 60–74.
Amodio, D. M., Harmon-Jones, E., & Devine, P. G. (2003). Individual differences in the activation and control of race bias as assessed by startle eyeblink responses and self-report. *Journal of Personality and Social Psychology, 84,* 738–753.

Amodio, D. M., Harmon-Jones, E., Devine, P. G., Curtin, J. J., Hartley, S. L., & Covert, A. E. (2004). Neural signals for the detection of unintentional race bias. *Psychological Science, 15,* 88–93.

Ashburn-Nardo, L., Knowles, M. L., & Monteith, M. J. (2003). Black Americans' implicit racial associations and their implications for intergroup judgment. *Social Cognition, 21,* 61–87.

Ashburn-Nardo, L., Voils, C. I., & Monteith, M. J. (2001). Implicit associations as the seeds of intergroup bias: How easily do they take root? *Journal of Personality and Social Psychology, 81,* 789–799.

Banaji, M. R., & Hardin, C. D. (1996). Automatic stereotyping. *Psychological Science, 7,* 136–141.

Barden, J., Maddux, W. W., Petty, R. E., & Brewer, M. B. (2004). Contextual moderation of racial bias: The impact of social roles on controlled and automatically activated attitudes. *Journal of Personality and Social Psychology, 87,* 5–22.

Bargh, J. A. (1989). Conditional automaticity: Varieties of automatic influence in social perception and cognition. In J. S. Uleman & J. A. Bargh (Eds.), *Unintended thought* (pp. 3–51). New York: Guilford.

Bargh, J. A. (1992). The ecology of automaticity: Toward establishing the conditions needed to produce automatic processing effects. *American Journal of Psychology, 105,* 181–199.

Bargh, J. A. (1994). The four horsemen of automaticity: Awareness, intention, efficiency, and control in social cognition. In R. S. Wyer & T. K. Srull (Eds.), *Handbook of social cognition: Vol. 1. Basic processes* (2nd ed., pp. 1–40). Hillsdale, NJ: Erlbaum.

Bargh, J. A. (1999). The cognitive monster: The case against the controllability of automatic stereotype effects. In S. Chaiken & Y. Trope (Eds.), *Dual-process theories in social psychology* (pp. 361–382). New York: Guilford.

Baron, A. S., & Banaji, M. R. (2006). The development of implicit attitudes: Evidence of race evaluations from ages 6 and 10 and adulthood. *Psychological Science, 17,* 53–58.

Bartholow, B., Fabiani, M., Gratton, G., & Bettencourt, B. A. (2001). A psychophysiological analysis of cognitive processing of and affective responses to social expectancy violations. *Psychological Science, 12,* 197–204.

Bessenoff, G. R., & Sherman, J. W. (2000). Automatic and controlled components of prejudice toward fat people: Evaluation versus stereotype activation. *Social Cognition, 18,* 329–353.

Billig, M. (1985). Prejudice, categorization, and particularization: From a perceptual to a rhetorical approach. *European Journal of Social Psychology, 15,* 79–103.

Blair, I. (2001). Implicit stereotypes and prejudice. In G. Moskowitz (Ed.), *Cognitive social psychology: On the tenure and future of social cognition* (pp. 359–374). Mahwah, NJ: Erlbaum.

Blair, I. (2002). The malleability of automatic stereotypes and prejudice. *Personality and Social Psychology Review, 6,* 242–261.

Blair, I., Ma., J., & Lenton, A. (2001). Imagining stereotypes away: The moderation of automatic stereotypes through mental imagery. *Journal of Personality and Social Psychology, 81,* 828–841.

Bodenhausen, G. V., & Macrae, C. N. (1998). Stereotype activation and inhibition. In R. Wyer, Jr. (Ed.), *Stereotype activation and inhibition* (pp. 1–52). Mahwah, NJ: Erlbaum.

Botvinick, M. M., Nystrom, L. E., Fissel, K., Carter, C. S., & Cohen, J. D. (1999). Conflict monitoring versus selection-for-action in anterior cingulate cortex. *Nature, 402,* 179–181.

Brewer, M. B. (1988). A dual-process model of impression formation. In T. K. Srull & R. S. Wyer (Eds.), *Advances in social cognition* (Vol. 1, pp. 1–36). Hillsdale, NJ: Erlbaum.

Brewer, M. B., & Harasty, A. S. (1999). Dual processes in the cognitive representation of persons and social categories. In S. Chaiken & Y. Trope (Eds.), *Dual process theories in social psychology* (pp. 255–270). New York: Guilford.

Chen, M., & Bargh, J. A. (1997). Nonconscious behavioral confirmation processes: The self-fulfilling consequences of automatic stereotype activation. *Journal of Experimental Social Psychology, 33,* 541–560.

Conrey, F. R., Sherman, J. W., Gawronski, B., Hugenberg, K., & Groom, C. J. (2005). Separating multiple processes in implicit social cognition: The quad model of implicit task performance. *Journal of Personality and Social Psychology, 89,* 469–487.

Correll, J., Park, B., Judd, C. M., & Wittenbrink, B. (2002). The police officer's dilemma: Using ethnicity to disambiguate potentially threatening individuals. *Journal of Personality and Social Psychology, 83*(6), 1314–1329.

Cunningham, W. A., Johnson, M. K., Raye, C. L., Gatenby, J. C., Gore, J. C., & Banaji, M. R. (2004). Separable neural components in the processing of Black and White faces. *Psychological Science, 15,* 806–813.

Dasgupta, N., & Asgari, S. (2004). Seeing is believing: Exposure to counterstereotypic women leaders and its effect on the malleability of automatic gender stereotyping. *Journal of Experimental Social Psychology, 40,* 642–658.

Dasgupta, N., & Greenwald, A. G. (2001). On the malleability of automatic attitudes: Combating automatic prejudice with images of admired and disliked individuals. *Journal of Personality and Social Psychology, 81,* 800–814.

Devine, P. G. (1989). Stereotypes and prejudice: Their automatic and controlled components. *Journal of Personality and Social Psychology, 56,* 5–18.

Devine, P. G. (1998). Beyond the isolated social perceiver: Why inhibit stereotypes? In R. S. Wyer (Ed.), *Stereotype activation and inhibition: Advances in social cognition* (Vol. 18, pp. 69–81). Hillsdale, NJ: Erlbaum.

Devine, P. G. (2001). Implicit prejudice and stereotyping: How automatic are they? *Journal of Personality and Social Psychology, 81*(5), 757–868.

Devine, P. G., & Baker, S. M. (1991). Measurement of racial stereotype subtyping. *Personality and Social Psychology Bulletin, 17,* 44–50.

Devine, P. G., & Monteith, M. J. (1993). The role of discrepancy-associated affect in prejudice reduction. In D. Mackie & D. Hamilton (Eds.), A*ffect, cognition, and stereotyping: Interactive processes in group perception* (pp. 317-344). San Diego: Academic Press.

Devine, P. G., & Monteith, M. J. (1999). Automaticity and control in stereotyping. In S. Chaiken & Y. Trope (Eds.), *Dual process theories in social psychology* (pp. 339–360). New York: Guilford.

Devine, P. G., Plant, E. A., Amodio, D. M., Harmon-Jones, E., & Vance, S. L. (2002). The regulation of explicit and implicit race bias: The role of motivations to respond without prejudice. *Journal of Personality and Social Psychology, 82,* 835–848.

Dovidio, J. F., Evans, N., & Tyler, R. B. (1986). Racial stereotypes: The contents of their cognitive representations. *Journal of Experimental Social Psychology, 22,* 22–37.

Dovidio, J. F., Gaertner, S. L., Kawakami, K., & Hodson, G. (2002). Why can't we just get along? Interpersonal biases and interracial distrust. *Cultural Diversity and Ethnic Minority Psychology, 8,* 88–102.

Dovidio, J. F., Kawakami, K., & Gaertner, S. L. (2002). Implicit and explicit prejudice and interracial interaction. *Journal of Personality and Social Psychology, 82,* 62–68.

Dovidio, J., Kawakami, K., Johnson, C., Johnson, B., & Howard, A. (1997). On the nature of prejudice: Automatic and controlled processes. *Journal of Experimental Social Psychology, 33,* 510–540.

Dunham, Y., Baron, A. S., & Banaji, M. R. (2006). From American city to Japanese village: A cross-cultural investigation of implicit race attitudes. *Child Development, 77,* 1268–1281.

Fabiani, M., Gratton, G., & Coles, M. G. H. (2000). Event-related brain potentials. In J. T. Cacioppo, L. G. Tassinary, & G. G. Berntson (Eds.), *Handbook of psychophysiology* (2nd ed., pp. 53–84). New York: Cambridge University Press.

Falkenstein, M., Hohnsbein, J., Hoorman, J., & Blanke, L. (1991). Effects of crossmodal divided attention on late ERP components: II. Error processing in choice reaction tasks. *Encephalography and Clinical Neurophysiology, 78,* 447–455.

Fazio, R. H. (1990). Multiple processes by which attitudes guide behavior: The MODE model as an integrative framework. In M. Zanna (Ed.), *Advances in experimental social psychology* (Vol. 23, pp. 75–109). San Diego, CA: Academic.

Fazio, R., Jackson, J., Dunton, B., & Williams, C. (1995). Variability in automatic activation as an unobtrusive measure of racial attitudes: A bona fide pipeline? *Journal of Personality and Social Psychology, 69,* 1013–1027.

Fiske, S. T. (1989). Examining the role of intent: Toward understanding its role in stereotyping and prejudice. In J. S. Uleman & J. A. Bargh (Eds.), *Unintended thought* (pp. 253–286). New York: Guilford.

Fiske, S. T. (1998). Stereotyping, prejudice, and discrimination. In D. T. Gilbert, S. T. Fiske, & G. Lindzey (Eds.), *The handbook of social psychology* (Vol. 2, pp. 357–411). New York: McGraw-Hill.

Fiske, S. T., Lin, M., & Neuberg, S. L. (1999). The continuum model: Ten years later. In S. Chaiken & Y. Trope (Eds.), *Dual process theories in social psychology* (pp. 231–254). New York: Guilford.

Fiske, S. T., & Neuberg, S. L. (1990). A continuum of impression formation, from category-based to individuating processes: Influences of information and motivation on attention and interpretation. In M. Zanna (Ed.), *Advances in experimental social psychology* (Vol. 23, pp. 1–74). San Diego: Academic.

Fox, R. (1992). Prejudice and the unfinished mind. *Psychological Inquiry, 3,* 137–152.

Galinsky, A. D., & Ku, G. (2004). The effects of perspective-taking on prejudice: The moderating role of self-evaluation. *Personality and Social Psychology Bulletin, 30,* 594–604.

Galinsky, A. D., & Moskowitz, G. B. (2000). Perspective-taking: Decreasing stereotype expression, stereotype accessibility, and in-group favoritism. *Journal of Personality and Social Psychology, 78,* 708–724.

Gehring, W. J., & Fencsik, D. E. (2001). Functions of the medial frontal cortex in the processing of conflict and errors. *Journal of Neuroscience, 21,* 9430–9437.

Gilbert, D. T., & Hixon, J. G. (1991). The trouble of thinking: Activation and application of stereotypic beliefs. *Journal of Personality and Social Psychology, 60,* 509–517.

Gray, J. A. (1982). *The neuropsychology of anxiety: An enquiry into the function of the septohippocampal system.* New York: Oxford University Press.

Greenwald, A., McGhee, D., & Schwartz, J. (1998). Measuring individual differences in implicit cognition: The Implicit Association Test. *Journal of Personality and Social Psychology, 74,* 1464–1480.

Greenwald, A. G., Oakes, M. A., & Hoffman, H. G. (2003). Targets of discrimination: Effects of race on responses to weapons holders. *Journal of Experimental Social Psychology, 39,* 399–405.

Gregg, A. P., Seibt, B., & Banaji, M. R. (2006). Easier done than undone: Asymmetry in the malleability of implicit preferences. *Journal of Personality and Social Psychology, 90,* 1–20.

Hamilton, D. L., & Sherman, J. W. (1994). Stereotypes. In R. S. Wyer, Jr., & T. K. Srull (Eds.), *Handbook of social cognition* (2nd ed., Vol. 2, pp. 1–68). Hillsdale, NJ: Erlbaum.

Hardin, C. D., & Conley, T. D. (2001). A relational approach to cognition: Shared experience and relationship affirmation in social cognition. In G. B. Moskowitz (Ed.), *Cognitive social psychology: The Princeton symposium on the legacy and future of social cognition* (pp. 3–17). Mahwah, NJ: Erlbuam.

Hardin, C. D., & Higgins, E. T. (1996). Shared reality theory: How social verification makes the subjective objective. In R. Sorrentino & E. T. Higgins (Eds.), *Handbook of motivation and cognition* (pp. 28–64). New York: Guilford.

Hart, A. J., Whalen, P. J., Shin, L. M., McInerney, S. C., Fischer, H., & Rauch, S. L. (2000). Differential response in the human amygdala to racial outgroup vs ingroup face stimuli. *Neuroreport: For Rapid Communication of Neuroscience Research, 11,* 2351–2355.

Hugenberg, K., & Bodenhausen, G. V. (2003). Facial prejudice: Implicit prejudice and the perception of facial threat. *Psychological Science, 14,* 640–643.

Ito, T. A., Chiao, K. W., Devine, P. G., Lorig, T. S., & Cacioppo, T. (2006). The influence of facial feedback on race bias. *Psychological Science, 17,* 256–261.

Ito, T. A., Thompson, E., & Cacioppo, J. T. (2004). Tracking the timecourse of social perception: The effects of racial cues on event-related brain potentials. *Personality and Social Psychology Bulletin, 30,* 1267–1280.

Jacoby, L. L. (1991). A process dissociation framework: Separating automatic from intentional uses of memory. *Journal of Memory and Language, 30,* 513–541.

Jacoby, L. L., Lindsay, D., & Toth, J. P. (1992). Unconscious influences revealed: Attention, awareness, and control. *American Psychologist, 47,* 802–809.

Johnson, M. K., & Hasher, L. (1987). Human learning and memory. *Annual Review of Psychology, 38,* 631–668.

Jones, E. E., Farina, A., Hasatrof, A. H., Markus, H., & Scott, R. A. (1984). *Social stigma: The psychology of marked relationships.* New York: Freeman.

Kawakami, K., Dovidio, J. F., Moll, J., Hermsen, S., & Russin, A. (2000). Just say no (to stereotyping): Effects of training in negation of stereotypic associations on stereotype activation. *Journal of Personality and Social Psychology, 78,* 871–888.

Kawakami, K., Dovidio, J. F., & Van Kamp, S. (2005). Kicking the habit: Effects of nonstereotypic association training and correction processes on hiring decisions. *Journal of Experimental Social Psychology, 41,* 68–75.

Kawakami, K., Phills, C. E., Steele, J. R., & Dovidio, J. F. (2007). (Close) distance makes the heart grow fonder: Improving implicit racial attitudes and interracial interactions through approach behaviors. *Journal of Personality and Social Psychology, 92,* 957–971.

Lepore, L., & Brown, R. (1997). Category and stereotype activation: Is prejudice inevitable? *Journal of Personality and Social Psychology, 72,* 275–287.

Lieberman, M. D., Hariri, A., & Jarcho, J. M. (2005). An fMRI investigation of race-related amygdala activity in African-American and Caucasian-American individuals. *Nature Neuroscience, 8,* 720–722.

Lippman, W. (1922). *Public opinion.* New York: Harcourt & Brace.

Livingston, R. W. (2002). The role of perceived negativity in the moderation of African Americans' implicit and explicit racial attitudes. *Journal of Experimental Social Psychology, 38,* 405–413.

Livingston, R. W., & Brewer, M. B. (2002). What are we really priming? Cue-based versus category-based processing of facial stimuli. *Journal of Personality and Social Psychology, 82,* 5–18.

Logan, G. D., & Cowan, W. B. (1984). On the ability to inhibit thought and action: A theory of act control. *Psychological Review, 91,* 295–327.

Lowery, B. S., Hardin, C. D., & Sinclair, S. (2001). Social influence effects on automatic racial prejudice. *Journal of Personality and Social Psychology, 81,* 842–855.

Macrae, C. N., Bodenhausen, G. V., & Milne, A. B. (1995). The dissection of selection in person perception: Inhibitory processes in social stereotyping. *Journal of Personality and Social Psychology, 69,* 397–407.

Macrae, C. N., Bodenhausen, G. V., & Milne, A. B. (1998). Saying no to unwanted thoughts: Self-focus and the regulation of mental life. *Journal of Personality and Social Psychology, 74,* 578–589.

Macrae, C. N., Bodenhausen, G. V., Milne, A. B., & Jetten, J. (1994). Out of mind but back in sight: Stereotypes on the rebound. *Journal of Personality and Social Psychology, 67,* 808–817.

Macrae, C. N., Hood, B. M., Milne, A. B., Rowe, A., & Mason, M. (2002). Are you looking at me? Eye gaze and person perception. *Psychological Science, 13,* 460–464.

Macrae, C. N., Milne, A. B., & Bodenhausen, G. V. (1994). Stereotypes as energy-saving devices: A peek inside the cognitive toolbox. *Journal of Personality and Social Psychology, 66,* 37–47.

Macrae, C. N., Bodenhausen, G. V., Milne, A. B., Thorn, T. M. J., & Castelli, L. (1997). On the activation of social stereotypes: The moderating role of processing objectives. *Journal of Experimental Social Psychology, 33,* 471–489.

Macrae, C. N., Mitchell, J. P., & Pendry, L. F. (2002). What's in a forename? Cue familiarity and stereotypical thinking. *Journal of Experimental Social Psychology, 38,* 186–193.

Maddux, W. W., Barden, J., Brewer, M. B., & Petty, R. E. (2005). Saying no to negativity: The effects of context and motivation to control prejudice on automatic evaluative responses. *Journal of Experimental Social Psychology, 41,* 19–35.

McConnell, A. R., & Liebold, J. M. (2001). Relations between the Implicit Association Test, explicit racial attitudes, and discriminatory behavior. *Journal of Experimental Social Psychology, 37,* 435–442.

Mitchell, J. A., Nosek, B. A., & Banaji, M. R. (2003). Contextual variations in implicit evaluation. *Journal of Experimental Psychology: General, 132,* 455–469.

Monteith, M. J. (1993). Self-regulation of prejudiced responses: Implications for progress in prejudice reduction efforts. *Journal of Personality and Social Psychology, 65,* 469–485.

Monteith, M. J., Ashburn-Nardo, L., Voils, C. I., & Czopp, A. M. (2002). Putting the brakes on prejudice: On the development and operation of cues for control. *Journal of Personality and Social Psychology, 83,* 1029–1050.

Monteith, M. J., Sherman, J. W., & Devine, P. G. (1998). Suppression as a stereotype control strategy. *Personality and Social Psychology Review, 2,* 63–82.

Monteith, M. J., Spicer, C. V., & Tooman, G. D. (1998). Consequences of stereotype suppression: Stereotypes on AND not on the rebound. *Journal of Experimental Social Psychology, 34,* 355–377.

Moskowitz, G. B., Gollwitzer, P. M., Wasel, W., & Schaal, B. (1999). Preconscious control of stereotype activation through chronic egalitarian goals. *Journal of Personality and Social Psychology, 77,* 167–184.

Moskowitz, G. B., Salomon, A. R., & Taylor, C. M. (2000). Preconsciously controlling stereotyping: Implicitly activated egalitarian goals prevent the activation of stereotypes. *Social Cognition, 18,* 151–177.

Neely, J. H. (1977). Semantic priming and retrieval from lexical memory: Roles of inhibitionless spreading activation and limited-capacity attention. *Journal of Experimental Psychology: General, 106,* 226–254.

Neuberg, S. L., & Fiske, S. T. (1987). Motivational influences on impression formation: Outcome dependency, accuracy-driven attention, and individuating processes. *Journal of Personality and Social Psychology, 53,* 431–444.

Payne, B. K. (2001). Prejudice and perception: The role of automatic and controlled processes in misperceiving a weapon. *Journal of Personality and Social Psychology, 81,* 181–192.

Payne, B. K., Jacoby, L. L., & Lambert, A. J. (2005). Attitudes as accessibility bias: Dissociating automatic and controlled processes. In R. R. Hassin, J. S. Uleman, & J. A. Bargh (Eds.), *The new unconscious* (pp. 393–420). New York: Oxford University Press.

Phelps, E. A., O'Connor, K. J., Cunningham, W. A., Funayama, E. S., Gatenby, J. C., Gore, J. C., et al. (2000). Performance on indirect measures of race evaluation predicts amygdala activation. *Journal of Cognitive Neuroscience, 12,* 729–738.

Plant, E. A., & Devine, P. G. (1998). Internal and external motivation to respond without prejudice. *Journal of Personality and Social Psychology, 75,* 811–832.

Plant, E. A., & Peruche, B. M. (2005). The consequences of race for police officers' responses to criminal suspects. *Psychological Science, 16,* 180–183.

Plant, E. A., Peruche, B. M., & Butz, D. A. (2005). Eliminating automatic race bias: Making race non-diagnostic for responses to criminal suspects. *Journal of Experimental Social Psychology, 41,* 141–156.

Posner, M. I., & Snyder, C. R. R. (1975). Attention and cognitive control. In R. Solso (Ed.), *Information processing and cognition: The Loyola symposium* (pp. 55–85). Hillsdale, NJ: Erlbaum.

Purdue, C. W., & Gurtman, M. B. (1990). Evidence for automatic ageism. *Journal of Experimental Social Psychology, 26,* 199–216.

Richeson, J. A., & Ambady, N. (2001). When roles reverse: Stigma, status, and self-evaluation. *Journal of Applied Social Psychology, 31,* 1350–1378.

Richeson, J. A., Baird, A. A., Gordon, H. L., Heatherton, T. F., Wyland, C. L., Trawalter, S., & Shelton, J. N. (2003). An fMRI investigation of the impact of interracial contact on executive function. *Nature Neuroscience, 6,* 1323-1328.

Rudman, L. A., Ashmore, R. D., & Gary, M. L. (2001). "Unlearning" automatic biases: The malleability of implicit prejudice and stereotypes. *Journal of Personality and Social Psychology, 81,* 856–868.

Rydell, R. J., & McConnell, A. R. (2006). Understanding implicit and explicit attitude change: A system of reasoning analysis. *Journal of Personality and Social Psychology, 91,* 995–1008.

Sassenberg, K., & Moskowitz, G. B. (2005). Don't stereotype, think different! Overcoming automatic stereotype activation by mindset priming. *Journal of Experimental Social Psychology, 41,* 506–514.

Shiffrin, R. M., & Schneider, W. (1977). Controlled and automatic human information processing: II. Perceptual learning, automatic attending and a general theory. *Psychological Review, 84,* 127–190.

Sinclair, L., & Kunda, Z. (1999). Reactions to a black professional: Motivated inhibition and activation of conflicting stereotypes. *Journal of Personality and Social Psychology, 77,* 885–904.

Sinclair, S., Dunn, E., & Lowery, B. S. (2005). The relationship between parental racial attitudes and children's implicit prejudice. *Journal of Experimental Social Psychology, 41,* 283–289.

Sinclair, S., Lowery, B. S., Hardin, C. D., & Colangelo, A. (2005). Social tuning of automatic racial attitudes: The role of affiliative motivation. *Journal of Personality and Social Psychology, 89*(4), 583–592.

Spencer, S., Fein, S., Wolfe, C. T., Fong, C., & Dunn, M. (1998). Automatic activation of stereotypes: The role of self-image threat. *Personality and Social Psychology Bulletin, 24,* 1139–1152.

Tajfel, H., & Turner, J. C. (1986). The social identity theory of inter-group behavior. In S. Worchel & L. W. Austin (Eds.), *Psychology of intergroup relations* (pp. 7–24). Chicago: Nelson-Hall.

Walther, E. (2002). Guilt by mere association: Evaluative conditioning and the spreading attitude effect. *Journal of Personality and Social Psychology, 82,* 919–954.

Wegener, D. T., & Petty, R. E. (1997). The flexible correction model: The role of naive theories of bias in bias correction. In M. P. Zanna (Ed.), *Advances in experimental social psychology* (Vol. 29, pp. 141–208). San Diego, CA: Academic.

Wegner, D. M. (1994). Ironic processes of mental control. *Psychological Review, 101,* 34–52.

Wilson, T. D., & Brekke, N. (1994). Mental contamination and mental correction: Unwanted influences on judgments and evaluations. *Psychological Review, 116,* 117–142.

Wilson, T. D., Lindsey, S., & Schooler, T. Y. (2000). A model of dual attitudes. *Psychological Review, 107,* 101–126.

Wittenbrink, B., Judd, C. M., & Park, B. (1997). Evidence for racial prejudice at the implicit level and its relationship with questionnaire measures. *Journal of Personality and Social Psychology, 72,* 262–274.

Wittenbrink, B., Judd, C. M., & Park, B. (2001). Spontaneous prejudice in context: Variability in automatically activated attitudes. *Journal of Personality and Social Psychology, 81,* 815–827.

Wyer, N. A., Sherman, J. W., & Stroessner, S. J. (1998). The spontaneous suppression of racial stereotypes. *Social Cognition, 16,* 340–352.

Wyer, N. A., Sherman, J. W., & Stroessner, S. J. (2000). The roles of motivation and ability in controlling the consequences of stereotype suppression. *Personality and Social Psychology Bulletin, 26,* 13–25.

5 Attributions to Discrimination
Antecedents and Consequences

Brenda Major and Pamela J. Sawyer
University of California, Santa Barbara

Mary Bates had been employed at Alliance Sterling for 14 years. When her boss, Harold Pinker, retired, she applied for his job. Ms. Bates had an excellent performance record and had been a loyal and reliable employee. She believed she deserved the promotion. Instead of choosing Ms. Bates as his replacement, however, Mr. Pinker chose her coworker, Mark Fitzsimmons. Mr. Fitzsimmons not only was younger than Ms. Bates, but also had worked for the firm fewer years than she. When Ms. Bates demanded to know why she was passed over for the promotion, Mr. Pinker told her that Mr. Fitzsimmons had better managerial skills than she and that he thought the other workers would respond better to Mr. Fitzsimmons than to her. Was Ms. Bates a victim of sex (or age or race) discrimination? Or was she in fact not as well qualified or talented as Mr. Fitzsimmons?

This example illustrates the predicament faced by individuals who are targets of discrimination. Discrimination is often ambiguous and difficult to establish with certainty. Considered in isolation, actions usually have a number of potential causes. Objective standards by which to establish discrimination are rarely available. Thus, judgments of discrimination are often subjective, subject to human error, and prone to dispute. Furthermore, the consequences of this judgment are substantial. Failing to see discrimination when it is present can be psychologically and physically costly. If Mary decides that her managerial skills are indeed deficient, for example, she may reevaluate her skills and abilities downward and reduce her aspirations. Seeing discrimination that does not exist, however, is also costly. It can engender hostility, suspicion, and conflict. How do people resolve predicaments like this? What are the consequences of perceiving oneself as a victim of discrimination?

The last two decades have seen a surge of research devoted to these questions. Research focuses on three main issues: (a) the extent to which targets recognize when they have been victims of discrimination (e.g., Crosby, 1982); (b) factors that influence the likelihood of attributing events (directed either at the self or others) to discrimination (e.g., Inman & Baron, 1996; Major, Quinton & Schmader, 2003); and (c) the psychological, interpersonal, and physical consequences of perceiving oneself as a victim of discrimination (e.g., Crocker, Voelkl, Testa & Major, 1991; Sellers & Shelton, 2003). In this chapter we review research examining each of these issues.

Understanding antecedents and consequences of perceived discrimination is important for both theoretical and practical reasons. Attribution processes play a central role in theories concerned with how people respond to social disadvantage (e.g., Allport, 1954/1979; Crocker & Major, 1989; Crosby, 1976, 1982). Yet we still know relatively little about the nature of these attributions and their consequences. Theories differ, for example, in their predictions regarding people's readiness to attribute their outcomes to discrimination, as well as in their predictions regarding the consequences of these attributions, especially for self-esteem. At a practical level, despite concerted efforts at remediation, discrimination continues to pose significant problems for society. In the decade following passage of the Civil Rights Act of 1991, the number of lawsuits claiming employment discrimination grew more than 20 percent annually (Sharf & Jones, 1999). Discrimination is increasingly viewed as a significant stressor with damaging health consequences (Krieger, 1990).

There is a pressing need to identify factors that lead people to regard themselves or others as victims of discrimination and the consequences of these judgments.

We focus in this chapter primarily on perceptions and attributions of personal rather than group discrimination. In addition, we focus primarily, although not exclusively, on the perceptions, attributions, and responses of individuals who are targets rather than observers or perpetrators of discrimination. Given page restrictions, our review of this literature is of necessity brief (see Major & Kaiser, 2005; Major, McCoy, Kaiser, & Quinton, 2003; Major & O'Brien, 2005; Major, Quinton, & McCoy, 2002; Stangor et al., 2003, for more extensive reviews). Before beginning our review, it is useful to clarify our terminology.

When people say that they have been a victim of discrimination (or that someone else has been), what do they mean? In our view, an attribution to discrimination has two essential components: (a) a judgment that treatment was based on social identity or group membership, and (b) a judgment that treatment was unjust or undeserved (Major, Quinton, & McCoy, 2002). Both of these judgments underlie the perception that discrimination is responsible for an outcome. That is, at a phenomenological level, when a person believes that he or she was discriminated against, that person believes he or she was unfairly treated on the basis of a social category or group membership. Targets (or observers or perpetrators) of negative treatment can believe that treatment was based on aspects of personal identity and was deserved (e.g., "I (he or she) did not get the job because I am (he or she was) not the most qualified") or was based on personal identity and was undeserved (e.g., "I (he or she) did not get the job because I am (he or she is) not well-connected"). Neither of these explanations for negative treatment is an attribution to discrimination because both lack the judgment that the person's social category was responsible for his or her treatment. Importantly, individuals can also recognize that their own, or someone else's, social identity was responsible for negative treatment but not see this as unjust. For example, several airlines now charge heavyweight flyers that "overflow" their seat more money for their tickets than they charge average weight flyers. The airlines consider this to be *justifiable differential treatment,* rather than discrimination. In our view, individuals who do not judge treatment on the basis of category membership as undeserved are unlikely to judge that discrimination has occurred. Only treatment judged as both undeserved and as based on social identity is likely to be perceived as discrimination.

Scholars often use the terms *attributions to discrimination* and *perceptions of discrimination* interchangeably. Sometimes these terms are used to refer to the same judgment, as when someone who does not get a job "perceives herself to be a victim of discrimination" or "attributes his rejection to discrimination." Sometimes, however, these terms refer to different judgments. For example, perceived discrimination often is used to refer to the level or frequency of discriminatory incidents to which people perceive they (or members of their group) have been exposed. Attributions to discrimination, in contrast, typically refer to how specific events are explained. Thus it is possible for a person to perceive that she frequently has been or will be a victim of discrimination, yet not attribute a specific event to discrimination. It is also possible for a person to attribute a specific event to discrimination even though he does not perceive himself to have been a victim of discrimination in the past or expect to be one in the future.

Researchers examining perceptions of and attributions to discrimination employ several different methodological approaches. Researchers studying perceived discrimination often ask participants the extent to which they or members of their group have experienced instances of discrimination (e.g., Crosby, 1982). Their resulting response reflects both their perceived exposure to negative events and their attributions of those events to discrimination. Researchers studying attributions to discrimination typically experimentally control for exposure to a negative event across participants, manipulate the plausibility that prejudice could have caused the event (or measure individual difference variables that might predict this attribution), and measure the extent to which participants attribute the negative event to discrimination (e.g., Crocker, Voelkl, Testa, & Major, 1991). In yet a third approach, participants are asked to indicate the likelihood that hypothetical events or scenarios are caused by prejudice or discrimination (e.g., Branscombe, Schmitt, & Harvey, 1999; Marti, Bobier, & Baron, 2000).

The distinction between perceptions of and attributions to discrimination becomes blurred when discussing factors that predict people's likelihood of perceiving themselves (or others) as a victim of discrimination or attributing their own (or others') outcomes to discrimination, as these factors are often the same. In contrast, attention to how perceptions of and attributions to discrimination are conceptualized and measured becomes important when considering the psychological or physical consequences of these different judgments. When people are asked how often they experience discrimination, their resulting response confounds perceived exposure to negative events with attributions for those events. This confounding makes it difficult to disentangle the effects of exposure from the effects of attributions when examining the relation between perceived discrimination and other outcome variables. In contrast, experimental studies in which the negative event to which people were exposed—a rejection, poor evaluation, or bad test grade—occurs independently of the perception of prejudice are better able to separate the consequences of being exposed to a negative event from the psychological implications of attributing that event to prejudice. We return to this issue later (see Major, Quinton, & McCoy, 2002).

In the following sections we review research examining the extent to which individuals perceive themselves as victims of discrimination, attribute outcomes to discrimination, or both, and factors that predict these perceptions and attributions. We then review research examining the implications of these perceptions and attributions for self-esteem, emotion, and interpersonal interactions.

PERCEIVING AND ATTRIBUTING OUTCOMES TO DISCRIMINATION: VIGILANCE OR MINIMIZATION?

How accurate are people at recognizing when they are targets of discrimination? If they err, do they tend to err on the side of overestimating or underestimating the extent to which they are victims of discrimination? A considerable amount of attention has focused on this issue.

Minimization

The prevailing view among scholars is that members of disadvantaged groups typically fail to recognize, underestimate, or even deny the extent to which they are personally targets of prejudice. This view is reflected in many social scientists' observations that social systems of inequality persist in large part because members of low-status groups fail to recognize the illegitimacy of the status system and of their own disadvantaged position within it (e.g., Jost, 1995; Major, 1994; Marx & Engels, 1846/1970; Sidanius & Pratto, 1999). Crosby (1982, 1984) perhaps best articulated this view. In her study of job satisfaction among working women, Crosby found that even though women were objectively being discriminated against in the workplace in terms of pay, they nonetheless denied personally being a victim of sex discrimination. Furthermore, they denied being a victim of personal discrimination even though they recognized that women as a group were discriminated against in the workplace. This reduced perception of personal relative to group discrimination has since been observed among a wide variety of groups in society, both advantaged and disadvantaged (e.g., Taylor, Wright, Moghaddam, & Lalonde, 1990). Evidence of minimization also emerges from studies showing that women and ethnic minorities often have difficulty recalling times when they were targets of prejudice (Stangor et al., 2003), and avoid labeling negative treatment that they have received as discrimination, even when the treatment objectively qualifies as such (Magley, Hulin, Fitzgerald, & DeNardo, 1999; Vorauer & Kumhyr, 2001).

What might motivate an individual to minimize or deny the extent to which he or she is a victim of discrimination? Crosby (1982, 1984) suggested that people may deny personal discrimination because they do not wish to label themselves as victims or others as villains. Individuals also may be reluctant to report discrimination out of self-presentational concerns. Specifically, because individuals who claim discrimination are often viewed as troublemakers or whiners (e.g., Kaiser & Miller, 2001, 2003), people may avoid reporting discrimination out of a desire to avoid creating a negative impression on others. Indeed, situations that make self-presentational concerns salient lead targets to minimize discrimination as a cause of their outcomes (e.g., Shelton & Stewart, 2004; Swim & Hyers, 1999). For example, women and African Americans were less likely to attribute rejection to discrimination when they made their attributions publicly in the presence of a member of the opposite, higher status social category, than privately or in the presence of a member of their own group (Stangor, Swim, Van Allen, & Sechrist, 2002). These findings illustrate that willingness to make an attribution to discrimination varies as a function of the perceived social costs of doing so. In a subsequent study, Sechrist, Swim, and Stangor (2004) showed that under public reporting conditions, women (targets) were less likely to attribute a negative evaluation from a blatantly sexist male evaluator to discrimination than were female observers of the same incident. Under private conditions, however, targets were just as likely to attribute their evaluation to discrimination as were observers. This finding is important, in that it illustrates that in private, targets neither underestimated nor exaggerated discrimination as a cause of their outcomes compared to observers of the same event.

Because of the social costs and risks of rejection involved with claiming one is a victim of discrimination, Carvallo and Pelham (2006) posited that acknowledging discrimination threatens an even more fundamental motive—the need to belong. Hence, they believed that the drive to bond and feel connected with others causes people to minimize personal discrimination. Consistent with this hypothesis, Carvallo and Pelham (2006) found that male and female participants dispositionally high in need to belong were less likely to report that they had personally been a target of gender discrimination than participants lower in need to belong. In a second study they manipulated the need to belong with a priming task intended to create feelings of acceptance. When the need to belong was satiated by the acceptance prime, men and women were more willing to acknowledge that they personally had experienced gender discrimination than when they had not been primed. A third study showed that women who were motivated to be accepted by a bogus male partner (because he was attractive and single) were less likely to attribute his negative evaluations of their work to prejudice than were women who were less motivated to be accepted (because the partner was married).

Interestingly, Carvallo and Pelham (2006) found the opposite results for perceptions of group discrimination. That is, men and women high in need to belong or who were not primed with acceptance were more likely to report that their gender group was the target of chronic prejudice than men and women low in need to belong or who were primed with acceptance. Carvallo and Pelham (2006) speculate that making group-level attributions might contribute to a sense of belongingness with the ingroup because it validates an important belief of many ingroup members (but see Garcia, Reser, Amo, Redersdorff, & Branscombe, 2005).

Adams, Tormala, and O'Brien (2006) examined minimization of prejudice from a different perspective. They hypothesized that self-esteem motives among dominant groups, in particular their desire to see themselves as unprejudiced, lead them to minimize or underestimate the extent to which minority groups are targets of discrimination. Hence, they predicted that satiating the self-esteem motive should increase the extent to which dominant groups (Whites) perceive discrimination against minorities, but should not have a similar effect on minorities. To test this prediction, Whites and Latinos completed a questionnaire manipulation of self-affirmation (Steele, 1988) prior to completing a survey measuring the extent to which they attributed a series of events to racism. In general, Latinos were more likely to attribute the events to racism than were Whites. However, the self-affirmation manipulation attenuated (Study 1) or eliminated (Study 2) this gap. Being self-affirmed significantly increased Whites' perceptions of racism against minorities. Interestingly, it tended to decrease Latinos' perceptions of racism against minorities, although this trend was not significant.

Vigilance

Although most scholars assert that targets minimize discrimination, others observe that people who are chronic targets of discrimination also can become vigilant for cues in their environment that signal that they are targets of prejudice, discrimination, or negative stereotypes (e.g., Barrett & Swim, 1998; Major, Quinton, & McCoy, 2002; Steele, Spencer, & Aronson, 2002). Allport (1954/1979) reflected this view, remarking that members of minority groups become "on guard" to signs of prejudice in others and "hypersensitive" to even the smallest of cues indicating prejudice to defend their egos against anticipated or experienced rejection (p. 144). This view is also implicit in Crocker and Major's (1989) observation that members of stigmatized groups are aware of their possibility of being a victim of prejudice, and hence may experience attributional ambiguity in their interactions with nonstigmatized others. That is, they may be unsure whether treatment they receive is based on their personal deservingness or on prejudice against their social identity.

Research confirms that members of chronically oppressed groups are more likely to say that they have been victims of discrimination than are members of dominant groups. This does not necessarily demonstrate vigilance, however, as the former are objectively more likely to be targets of prejudice and discrimination than the latter. Research also shows that members of chronically oppressed groups are more likely than members of dominant groups to label negative actions committed by a high-status perpetrator against a low-status victim as discrimination (Rodin, Price, Bryson, & Sanchez, 1990) and to attribute attributionally ambiguous events to discrimination (Adams et al., 2006; Marti, Bobier, & Baron, 2000). However, when members of high- and low-status groups experience the same circumstances (e.g., when they are personally rejected by a member of the other group), they are equally likely to attribute their rejection to discrimination (e.g., Major, Gramzow, et al., 2002; O'Brien, Kinias, & Major, 2008).

What might motivate individuals to be vigilant for or overestimate the extent to which they are a target of discrimination? One possibility is self-preservation. Vigilance is likely to be highly adaptive in social environments that are hostile or life threatening. Under such circumstances, a "false alarm" (seeing discrimination where none exists) is less dangerous than a "miss" (failing to see discrimination when it is present). Hence, people may be motivated to look for evidence that they are at risk of being discriminated against, so as to protect themselves from harm (Barrett & Swim, 1998). The motive to protect self-esteem from threat (ego defense) also may motivate vigilance for discrimination (Allport, 1954/1979). Blaming negative outcomes on the prejudice of others, rather than on internal causes such as one's own lack of ability, can help to buffer self-esteem from negative events and disadvantage (e.g., Crocker & Major, 1989; Crocker, Voelkl, Testa, and Major, 1991; Major, Kaiser, & McCoy, 2003). The finding of Adams et al. (2006) that a self-affirmation manipulation tended to *decrease* Latinos' attributions to racism is suggestive that self-esteem motives may influence perceptions of racism among minority groups.

Summary

In sum, there are compelling reasons why members of devalued groups may minimize as well as be vigilant for discrimination directed against them. We believe that rather than debating which one of these perspectives is correct, more can be learned by addressing who is more likely to make attributions to discrimination, or perceive themselves as victims of discrimination, and under what conditions attributions to discrimination occur. Research focusing on these questions can clarify when and why targets sometimes are vigilant for discrimination and at other times minimize or deny its presence. We review research on these issues in the following section.

MODERATORS OF PERCEPTIONS AND ATTRIBUTIONS TO DISCRIMINATION

As noted earlier, an attribution to discrimination reflects the judgment that treatment is based on group membership and is undeserved. Hence, factors that heighten either the accessibility of group membership or the accessibility of injustice as a cause of behavior are likely to increase attributions to discrimination (Major, Quinton, & McCoy, 2002). Characteristics of the event, the situation, and the person can do so.

CHARACTERISTICS OF THE EVENT

People appear to have prototypes (or expectancies) about what types of events constitute discrimination (Baron, Burgess, & Kao, 1991; Rodin et al., 1990). People compare events against their prototype for discrimination and the more closely the event in question fits the prototype, the more likely it is to be labeled discrimination. Thus, certain events are more easily recognized as discrimination than others. Discrimination is prototypically viewed as an *intergroup* phenomenon, that is, as occurring between members of different groups rather than within the same group (Inman & Baron, 1996; Rodin et al., 1990). For example, targets are more likely to report that they have been discriminated against when they are treated negatively by an outgroup member than by an ingroup member (Dion, 1975; Major, Gramzow, et al., 2002).

Certain *targets* and *bases* of discrimination are also more prototypical than others. Observers in the United States more readily attribute differential treatment on the basis of race and gender to discrimination than they do differential treatment on the basis of age or weight (Marti et al., 2000). In general, people judge differential treatment on the basis of social identities over which people have no personal control as discriminatory more than differential treatment on the basis of social identities over which people are perceived to have control (over onset, maintenance, or elimination). People see it as more justifiable to discriminate against people with controllable stigmas (Rodin et al., 1990), and judge them as more responsible and blameworthy than people whose stigmas are perceived as less controllable (Weiner, Perry, & Magnusson, 1988). Because these beliefs are shared even by those who are themselves stigmatized (Crandall, 1994), people who believe they have been treated negatively on the basis of a controllable attribute (e.g., obesity) are relatively unlikely to say they are victims of discrimination. For example, compared to average weight women, overweight women who were rejected by a male partner were significantly more likely to attribute their rejection to their weight, but were not more likely to attribute their rejection to their partner's concern with appearance or his personality (Crocker, Cornwell, & Major, 1993). Crocker and Major (1994) argued that because weight is viewed as controllable, overweight women regarded rejection on the basis of their weight as justified differential treatment rather than discrimination.

Discrimination prototypes also reflect *status-asymmetry* (Rodin et al., 1990). That is, observers are more likely to attribute an action to discrimination when the perpetrator is from a higher status group (e.g., Whites, men) than the victim (Blacks, women) as compared to when the perpetrator is from a lower status group than the victim (Inman & Baron, 1996; Rodin et al., 1990). Baron et al. (1991), for example, asked participants to read vignettes depicting possible acts of anti-female sexism and then list the two or three traits they felt were displayed by the perpetrator. Male perpetrators were far more likely than female perpetrators to be labeled as prejudiced given the same behavior. Other studies have found similar effects (Flournoy, Prentice-Dunn, & Klinger, 2002; Harris, Lievens, & Van Hoye, 2004; Inman & Baron, 1996; Inman, Huerta, & Oh, 1998; Morera, Dupont, Leyens, & Desert, 2004).

O'Brien et al. (2008) demonstrated that the discrimination prototype also reflects *stereotype-asymmetry*. That is, people expect that victims of discrimination are negatively stereotyped relative to perpetrators of discrimination. This expectation leads to greater judgments of discrimination in contexts in which the victim is negatively stereotyped relative to the perpetrator than in contexts in which the victim is positively stereotyped relative to the perpetrator. O'Brien et al. (2008, Study

1) asked participants to read a vignette about a job interview in which a man or woman rejected an opposite-sex applicant for a job. The job required skills that were either stereotypically feminine, masculine, or irrelevant to gender stereotypes. As predicted, when the job required stereotypically masculine skills, participants (observers) made more attributions to discrimination when the male manager rejected the female applicant than when the female manager rejected the male applicant. The reverse was true when the job required stereotypically feminine skills.

In a second study, male and female participants experienced a personal rejection by a member of the other sex on a task that required either stereotypically masculine or feminine skills (O'Brien et al., 2008, Study 2). When targets were rejected on the masculine task, women made more attributions to discrimination than men. However, when targets were rejected on the feminine task, men made more attributions to discrimination than women. There were no differences between women's and men's attributions to discrimination when they were rejected on a task in which the other gender was stereotyped as more competent. These studies are important for several reasons. First, they demonstrate that discrimination prototypes affect observers and targets similarly. Second, they illustrate that contextual stereotypes about the competence of the perpetrator relative to the victim are more influential determinants of attributions to discrimination than are the chronic statuses of the perpetrator and the victim. Finally, they show that when rejection occurs in contexts in which the higher status group is negatively stereotyped relative to the lower status group, (e.g., when a man is rejected by a woman in a feminine domain) observers and members of high-status groups are just as willing to say that the rejection was due to discrimination as when low-status groups are rejected by a higher status group.

The prototype of discrimination also is that it is *intentional* and *harmful* to the victim (Swim, Scott, Sechrist, Campbell, & Stangor, 2003). Thus, actions, events, or evaluations that cause harm to the target are more likely than those that lead to positive outcomes to be attributed to discrimination (Crocker et al., 1991). Swim et al. (2003) found that people who read about, observed, or experienced a potentially discriminatory action committed by a man toward a woman were more likely to judge the actor as prejudiced and the actor's behavior as discriminatory when the actor intended the action than when it was unintentional, and when the action caused harm to a target, especially when information about the intent of the actor was limited or absent. They also found that harm was a more influential determinant of targets' attributions than observers' attributions.

CHARACTERISTICS OF THE SITUATION

Besides prototypicality of the event, situational factors that increase the *accessibility* of discrimination as a construct or cause increase the likelihood that discrimination will be perceived and events will be attributed to discrimination. The more explicit or clear prejudice cues are in a situation, the more likely people are to report that they have been a target of discrimination (e.g., Major, Quinton, & Schmader, 2003). For example, women were more likely to blame a negative evaluation on discrimination if they learned the evaluator held very traditional (sexist) rather than liberal attitudes toward women's roles (Crocker et al., 1991), and ethnic minorities were more likely to attribute negative treatment from a White partner to discrimination if they had learned that their partner held antidiversity rather than prodiversity views (Operario & Fiske, 2001, Study 2). Women led to believe that a male partner had traditional attitudes toward women also allocated more of their attention toward subliminally presented sexism-related words relative to women led to believe their partner held liberal attitudes toward women (Kaiser, Vick, & Major, 2006). This latter study suggests that making prejudice accessible can increase vigilance at a preconscious level.

Similarly, alerting people to the possibility of discrimination in a situation increases their likelihood of attributing negative outcomes (either their own or others') to discrimination. For example, observers evaluating a series of hiring decisions in which a less qualified applicant was hired over a more qualified applicant were more likely to attribute the hiring decision to prejudice when primed to look for discrimination than when not primed (Marti et al., 2000). Women (targets) who were led to expect that their work would be evaluated by a panel of male judges in which 50% were known to discriminate against women were more likely to blame a subsequent negative evaluation on discrimination than women who were told that none of the men discriminated, and just as likely to blame the evaluation on discrimination as women who were told that all of the judges discriminated against women (Inman, 2001; Kaiser & Miller, 2001).

Because an attribution to discrimination involves the judgment that treatment is linked to group membership, situational cues that make group membership salient as a possible cause of outcomes also increase the likelihood that individuals will make attributions to discrimination. Thus, observers find discrimination easier to detect when data are aggregated across a number of individuals, thereby making the link between treatment and group membership salient, than when it is encountered on a case-by-case basis (Crosby, Clayton, Alksnis, & Hemker, 1986). Targets are also more likely to claim that they were discriminated against when they know that their group membership is known rather than unknown to an outgroup evaluator (Crocker et al., 1991; Dion & Earn, 1975).

Social comparison information also can influence attributions to discrimination. Perceptions of discrimination require comparing an individual's or group's contributions and outcomes with the contributions and outcomes of others who belong to different groups. Social comparison biases may work against detecting discrimination by reducing people's likelihood of realizing that their outcomes are linked to their group membership. People tend to affiliate and work with others like themselves and to compare their own situations with similar others. Hence, people who belong to disadvantaged groups are likely to compare with others who are similarly disadvantaged, and thus be unaware of the extent to which they and others like them are unfairly treated (Major, 1994).

CHARACTERISTICS OF THE PERSON

Affect

Targets' chronic or temporary affective state or mood can affect their likelihood of seeing themselves as victims of prejudice or attributing rejection to discrimination, perhaps by serving as an informational source that helps to interpret ambiguous situations. For example, compared to women in whom a positive mood was induced, women in whom a negative mood was induced perceived more discrimination against themselves and against other women, but only when they had not been provided with an external attribution for their mood (Sechrist, Swim, & Mark, 2003). In another study, women were primed to feel either sadness or anger in advance of being exposed to a gender-based rejection. After the rejection they were told to express or suppress their emotional reactions. Women primed to feel angry and told to express themselves were most likely to say that they had been discriminated against in an experiment. Women primed to feel sad and told to suppress their emotions reported the least discrimination (Gill & Matheson, 2006).

Chronic affective tendencies also can shape attributions to and perceptions of discrimination (Major, Quinton, & McCoy, 2002). Individuals chronically high in hostility and neuroticism are more likely to perceive themselves as victims of discrimination than are those who score lower on these measures (Huebner, Nemeroff, & Davis, 2005), as are individuals high in interpersonal rejection sensitivity (Major & Eccleston, 2002).

Prejudice Expectations

People also differ in the extent to which they are chronically aware of or sensitive to the possibility of being a target of negative stereotypes and discrimination because of their group membership. For example, individuals high in "stigma consciousness" (Pinel, 1999) expect that their behavior will be interpreted in light of their group membership. Among African Americans, Latino(a) Americans, Asian Americans, and women, stigma consciousness is strongly and positively correlated with perceived personal and group discrimination and negatively correlated with trust of others in general (Pinel, 1999). Women who are high in stigma consciousness allocate more of their attention toward subliminally presented sexism-related words relative to women who are low in stigma consciousness (Kaiser, Vick, et al., 2006), suggesting that they may be more vigilant for discrimination cues at a preconscious level.

A related construct is race-based rejection sensitivity, defined as a personal dynamic whereby individuals anxiously expect, readily perceive, and intensely react to rejection that has a possibility of being due to race (Mendoza-Denton, Downey, Purdie, Davis, & Pietrzac, 2002). Race-based rejection sensitivity is assessed by asking people to read attributionally ambiguous scenarios and to indicate, for each scenario, how concerned they are that a negative outcome would be due to their race and the likelihood that a negative outcome would be due to their race. In a longitudinal diary study, race-based rejection sensitivity assessed among African American students before they entered a predominately White university predicted the frequency with which they reported a negative race-related experience (e.g., feeling excluded, insulted, or receiving poor service because of one's race) during their first 3 weeks at university (Mendoza-Denton et al., 2002). Race-based rejection sensitivity also predicted their tendency to feel less belonging at the university and greater negativity toward both peers and professors.

Group Identification

The extent to which individuals chronically identify themselves in terms of their group memberships also influences their likelihood of perceiving and attributing outcomes to discrimination. Group identification is typically conceptualized as how important the group is to self-definition (centrality) and how strong feelings of attachment to the group are (Tajfel & Turner, 1986). Among socially devalued groups, group identification is positively correlated with perceptions of personal, as well as group discrimination (e.g., Branscombe et al., 1999; Crosby, Pufall, Snyder, O'Connell, & Whalen, 1989; Dion, 1975; Eccleston & Major, 2006; Gurin & Townsend, 1986). Cross-sectional, correlational studies, however, cannot determine whether higher group identification is an antecedent or consequent of perceived discrimination. Several experimental studies have shown that group identification assessed at a prior time predicted attributions of rejection to discrimination within an experimental context, particularly in attributionally ambiguous situations (Major, Quinton, & Schmader, 2003; Operario & Fiske, 2001). Furthermore, in a longitudinal study, Sellers and Shelton (2003) showed that group identification (centrality of racial group to the self) assessed among African American freshmen shortly after arrival at college (Time 1) predicted an increase in perceived frequency of exposure to racial discrimination several months later (Time 2), controlling for perceived discrimination at Time 1. This suggests that when a group membership is highly central to one's identity, it may lead one to interpret ambiguous events through a group lens (see Eccleston & Major, 2006). Another study showed that women high in group consciousness (feminism) perceived more discrimination directed against themselves and their group in general over the course of several weeks (Swim, Hyers, Cohen, & Ferguson, 2001). Group consciousness incorporates aspects of group identification as well as elements of perceived injustice directed against the group (Gurin, Miller, & Gurin, 1980).

Status-Related Beliefs

Individuals' beliefs about why status differences exist in society also influence their likelihood of seeing their own or others' outcomes as deserved or undeserved. Some beliefs encourage the perception that people deserve their outcomes, such as the belief in a just world (Lerner, 1980), the belief that status is based on merit (Sidanius & Pratto, 1999), the belief that status is permeable (Tajfel & Turner, 1986), and the belief that success is based on hard work (Mirels & Garrett, 1971). Although these are distinct beliefs, each locates causality within the individual and holds people personally responsible for their outcomes. Collectively, they contribute to a worldview in which unequal status relations among individuals and groups in society are perceived as just, fair, deserved, and based on individual merit. Hence, they have been called status-justifying beliefs (SJBs; Jost, 1995; O'Brien & Major, 2005).

High endorsement of SJBs can lead members of disadvantaged groups to minimize discrimination as a cause of their outcomes. Working women who strongly endorse the belief in a just world, for example, report less discontent with the employment situation of working women than do women who endorse this belief less strongly (Hafer & Olson, 1993). The more members of disadvantaged groups (e.g., ethnic minorities, women) believe that status systems are permeable and allow for individual mobility, the less they perceive themselves or their group as victims of discrimination. Furthermore, in a laboratory-based study, Major, Gramzow, et al. (2002) found that the more ethnic minority students believed in individual mobility, the less likely they were to say that an interpersonal rejection by a same-sex European American student was due to discrimination. Likewise, the more women believed in individual mobility, the less likely they were to say they were discriminated against when rejected by a same-race man.

In contrast, high endorsement of SJBs is associated with increased attributions to discrimination among members of advantaged groups. Endorsement of SJBs by members of advantaged groups is associated with feelings of relative superiority and entitlement (O'Brien & Major, in press). When these individuals are passed over in favor of members of lower status groups, they are likely to view it as a violation of equity, and hence as unjust. In the preceding experiments by Major, Gramzow, et al. (2002), the more European American students endorsed the belief in individual mobility, the more they attributed rejection by a Latino/a student (who chose, instead, another Latino/a) to racial discrimination. Likewise, the more men endorsed the belief in individual mobility, the more they attributed rejection by a woman (who chose another woman) to discrimination (Major, Gramzow, et al., 2002, Study 3). Collectively, these studies demonstrate that individual differences in endorsement of status justifying beliefs are an important determinant of how potentially discriminatory situations are construed and explained.

SUMMARY

In summary, characteristics of the event, the situation, and the person shape the likelihood that events are perceived as or attributed to discrimination. People have a prototype of what constitutes discrimination. An event or action is more likely to be attributed to discrimination when it is intergroup (i.e., the perpetrator and target are from different social categories) than intragroup, when the target's category membership is perceived as uncontrollable than controllable, when the perpetrator is higher status than the target, when the event or action is intentional and causes harm to the target, and when it occurs in a domain in which the target is negatively stereotyped relative to the perpetrator. Because an attribution to discrimination is based on the judgment that treatment is group based and unjust, situational cues that increase the accessibility of group membership or injustice as a cause of an event also increase perceptions of and attributions to discrimination. Finally, chronic individual differences in group identification, status beliefs, and prejudice expectations influence individuals' likelihood of perceiving themselves and their group as victims of discrimination in general, and attributing specific events to discrimination.

The foregoing implies that events and actions that are objectively discriminatory might not be perceived as such if they do not match our discrimination prototype. Thus, when an ethnic minority boss objectively discriminates against another ethnic minority employee (violating the intergroup rule), an institutional policy unintentionally but unfairly disadvantages members of one social category relative to others (violating the intentionality rule), or a qualified overweight woman is passed over for promotion (violating the uncontrollability rule), the action may not be seen as discrimination. Discrimination that violates our prototype may not only be harder to detect, but also may be held to a higher standard of evidence to prove. Even in the face of objective evidence of distributive injustice, situations that make it difficult to see links between group membership and outcomes, such as when income is not coded by race or gender, can decrease detection of discrimination, as can situational cues that foster perceived procedural fairness (e.g., giving a person "voice"; Major & Schmader, 2001). Individual beliefs and predispositions held by targets, observers, and perpetrators can blind them from seeing discrimination directed at themselves or others. In the next section, we consider the social and psychological consequences of perceiving prejudice and discrimination directed against oneself or one's group.

CONSEQUENCES OF PERCEPTIONS OF AND ATTRIBUTIONS TO DISCRIMINATION

Consider the scenario with which we began this chapter. Will Mary Bates be more upset if she decides she was passed over for promotion because of her lack of qualifications or ability or will she feel worse if she thinks it was due to discrimination? Will attributing her rejection to discrimination buffer or protect her self-esteem? Will she experience more stress if she believes she is not qualified or if she believes she was discriminated against? Questions such as these inspired a considerable amount of research over the last two decades. Researchers examined the impact of perceived discrimination and attributions to discrimination on outcomes such as motivation, task performance, self-stereotyping, social interactions, emotions, self-esteem, mental health, and physical health, among others. A full review of this extensive literature is beyond the scope of this chapter (see Crocker, Major, & Steele, 1998; Major, McCoy, et al., 2003; Major & O'Brien, 2005; Major, Quinton, & McCoy, 2002). Here, we focus our attention on the impact of attributions to discrimination on self-esteem, emotional well-being, and interpersonal relationships.

IMPACT OF PERCEIVED DISCRIMINATION ON SELF-ESTEEM AND EMOTIONAL WELL-BEING

Many studies have examined the implications of perceived discrimination for targets' self-esteem and emotional well-being. A variety of theoretical perspectives lead to the prediction that perceiving one's group to be devalued in society will result in negative self-evaluations and low self-esteem (e.g., Cartwright, 1950; Cooley, 1956; Mead, 1934). Studies comparing the self-esteem of members of stigmatized groups (i.e., targets of prejudice and discrimination) to the self-esteem of members of nonstigmatized groups, however, often reveal little support for this prediction (see Crocker & Major, 1989; Porter & Washington, 1979; Rosenberg & Simmons, 1972; Simpson & Yinger, 1985, for reviews). Indeed, some groups who perceive themselves as targets of pervasive and severe discrimination, such as African Americans, have higher self-esteem on average than groups who are rarely targets of prejudice, such as European Americans (Twenge & Crocker, 2002).

To explain this paradox, Crocker and Major (1989) theorized that members of stigmatized groups employ several cognitive strategies linked to their stigma that may protect their self-esteem from rejection and negative outcomes. In particular, members of stigmatized groups may attribute negative outcomes and rejection to prejudice based on their social identity rather than to internal, stable qualities of themselves. That is, awareness that prejudice is a plausible cause of their outcomes may enable them to discount the diagnosticity of negative feedback (Kelley, 1973). Drawing on theories of emotion (e.g., Weiner, 1995), Crocker and Major (1989) hypothesized that attributing negative events to others' prejudice (a cause external to the self) would protect affect and self-esteem relative to attributing negative events to causes internal to the self (such as a lack of ability or skill).

Major, Quinton, and McCoy (2002) subsequently refined and elaborated this theory. First, they defined an attribution to prejudice or discrimination as an attribution of *blame* because it involves attributing responsibility to another person whose actions are unjustified. This definitional clarification is important because attributions to justifiable differential treatment lack the self-protective properties sometimes associated with attributions to discrimination (e.g., Crocker at al., 1993). Second, because attributing outcomes to prejudice implicates an individual's social identity, such attributions have a strong internal component. Thus, they observed that attributing negative outcomes to discrimination protects self-esteem relative to blaming internal, stable aspects of the personal self, but not relative to blaming other purely external or random causes (Major, Kaiser, &

McCoy, 2003; Schmitt & Branscombe, 2002). Third, they acknowledged that discounting does not always occur; that is, perceiving that another person is prejudiced does not preclude attributing an outcome to one's own lack of deservingness, or vice versa (McClure, 1998). Thus, it is important to examine *discrimination-blame relative to self-blame* when considering the link between perceptions of or attributions to discrimination and self-esteem (e.g., Major, Kaiser, & McCoy, 2003). This is particularly true when discrimination is ambiguous (Major, Quinton, & Schmader, 2003). For example, women and ethnic minorities who report experiencing more negative events because of their gender or race also report experiencing more negative events because of their personality (Major, Henry, & Kaiser, 2006). Fourth, they emphasized the importance of differentiating emotional responses to perceived discrimination. Attributing outcomes to discrimination may protect against negative self-directed emotions such as depression, shame, and loss of self-esteem, but is unlikely to protect from negative other-directed emotions such as anger and hostility (Major, Kaiser, & McCoy, 2003; Major, Quinton, & McCoy, 2002).

A number of studies demonstrate that attributing negative outcomes to discrimination rather than to internal aspects of the self can buffer self-esteem. For example, Crocker et al. (1991) found that women who were negatively evaluated by a man with traditional attitudes toward women were more likely to attribute the evaluation to sexism, and reported significantly less depressed affect and marginally higher self-esteem than women who received negative feedback from an evaluator with more liberal attitudes toward women. Similarly, African Americans who received a negative evaluation from a White evaluator who they thought was aware of their race discounted the feedback by attributing it to discrimination and reported marginally higher self-esteem than African American participants who thought the evaluator was unaware of their race. Major, Kaiser, and McCoy (2003) found that the more women discounted rejection (i.e., blamed it on discrimination rather than on themselves), the higher their self-esteem. The buffering effects of attributing negative feedback to prejudice on self-esteem have been observed in several other studies (e.g., Dion, 1975; Dion & Earn; 1975; Hoyt, Agular, Kaiser, Blascovich, & Lee, 2007; Major, Quinton, & Schmader, 2003; McCoy & Major, 2003).

The idea that perceiving oneself to be a target of discrimination could buffer self-esteem proved to be highly controversial. Branscombe and colleagues (e.g., Branscombe et al., 1999; Schmitt & Branscombe, 2001), for example, argued that because prejudice signals rejection and exclusion on the part of the dominant group, "attributions to prejudice . . . are detrimental to the psychological well-being of the disadvantaged" (Schmitt & Branscombe, 2001 p. 193). This claim is supported by correlational studies, many of which show that the more members of disadvantaged groups perceive themselves (or their group) as a target of discrimination, the lower their self-esteem, the more negative their emotions, and the poorer their psychological well-being (see Major, Quinton, & McCoy, 2002, for a review).

How can we reconcile these seemingly disparate findings? Methodological differences contribute in part. As discussed at the outset of this chapter, researchers and reviewers of the literature frequently do not distinguish between perceptions of pervasive discrimination and attributions of specific negative events to discrimination. When perceived discrimination is assessed retrospectively on questionnaires, self-reports of experiences with discrimination (e.g., "I am a victim of society because of my gender") confound attributional processes with frequency and severity of exposure to discrimination. This makes it difficult to isolate the consequences for well-being of exposure to negative events from the consequences of attributing those events to discrimination. Studies correlating perceived discrimination with self-esteem and well-being also rarely control for important dispositional variables (e.g., hostility, rejection sensitivity) that might influence both perceptions of discrimination and self-esteem or psychological well-being. When they do, the relationship between discrimination and psychological well-being may be attenuated or even reversed. For example, Huebner et al. (2005) found that the relationship between perceived discrimination and depressive symptoms among gay and bisexual men was attenuated when they controlled for hostility and neuroticism. Major et al. (2006) found that the relationship between ethnic minority students' perceptions of having experienced negative events due to discrimination and their self-esteem was negative when they did not control for the extent to which these students also perceived themselves to have experienced negative events due to their personality, but was positively correlated with self-esteem when they did. Such findings underscore the point that because emotional well-being may influence perceptions of discrimination as well as the reverse (e.g., Sechrist et al., 2003), it is inappropriate to draw causal inferences from correlations among self-report measures collected at the same point in time.

Longitudinal studies examining the relationship between perceptions of discrimination and emotional well-being, self-esteem, or both are rare. One study that did so (Sellers & Shelton, 2003) followed African American students from three U.S. schools over two semesters to assess the impact of perceived racial discrimination and racial identity on psychological distress (depression, anxiety, and perceived stress). Controlling for distress and perceived discrimination at Time 1, the more racial discrimination students reported experiencing, the higher their psychological distress at Time 2. This relationship was moderated, however, by students' racial ideology and beliefs about how African Americans are viewed in society. Specifically, the relationship between perceived discrimination and psychological distress was weaker among African Americans who held a nationalist racial ideology and believed others regard African Americans negatively than it was among those who did not hold these views. The authors suggest that this may be because those participants who are highest in nationalistic ideology are also most likely to see the world as an unfair place for African Americans. Thus, experiencing discrimination may come as less of a shock to the worldview of those people than those that are low in this ideology. We return to this issue later.

Most experiments showing the buffering effects of attributions to discrimination on self-esteem or emotion have been conducted within laboratory environments. In these settings, exposure to a negative event is controlled across participants and the plausibility that prejudice could have caused the event is manipulated. Because the negative event to which people are exposed occurs independently of the attribution to prejudice, these studies are better able to separate the psychological implications of being exposed to a negative event from the psychological implications of attributing that event to prejudice.

Within a stress and coping framework, perceptions of pervasive discrimination and attributions of specific events to discrimination may be tapping different processes (Major, Quinton, & McCoy, 2002). The perception that one or one's group is a victim of pervasive prejudice can be conceptualized as a threat appraisal, in that individuals who report that they are frequent or severe victims of discrimination are describing their environment as hostile, dangerous, and potentially harmful to self. In contrast, attributing a specific negative event to discrimination can be viewed as a cognitive reappraisal coping strategy. That is, blaming an event on discrimination mitigates the threat to personal self-esteem that might arise from blaming the event on internal, stable aspects of the self. A stress and coping framework further predicts that all individuals will not respond in the same way to perceptions of discrimination. Rather, responses vary as a function of appraisals and coping (Lazarus & Folkman, 1984). Consistent with this framework, researchers have begun to identify personal, situational, and structural factors that moderate the implications of perceiving and making attributions to discrimination for psychological well-being. Following, we discuss several important moderators (see Major, Quinton, & McCoy, 2002; Major, McCoy, et al., 2003, for reviews).

Threat to Personal Identity

One important moderator is whether or not the person has experienced a threat to his or her personal identity. Personal identity refers to a person's sense of his or her *unique* self; that is, the self based in an individual's unique characteristics and traits. Personal identity can be distinguished from social identity (i.e., the self derived from membership in social categories or groups), which is shared to some extent with others. People may experience threat (e.g., rejection; a poor evaluation) based on aspects of their personal identity (e.g., their personality or ability) or social identity (e.g., their gender or ethnic group membership), or may experience both types of identity threat. For example, people who are told that their group is lazy (a threat to social identity) may also be told that they are personally incompetent (a threat to personal identity). Attributing outcomes to discrimination is likely to buffer self-esteem primarily when an individual experiences a threat to an internal, stable aspect of the personal self (Major, Kaiser, & McCoy, 2003), and is unlikely to do so in the absence of such a personal threat.

Clarity of Discrimination

A second factor that moderates the relationship between attributions to prejudice and self-esteem is the clarity, or intensity, of prejudice cues in the environment. Blatant prejudice leaves no uncertainty about who is to blame for a negative event, whereas ambiguous prejudice does. Crocker and Major (1989) speculated that blatant prejudice protects self-esteem from threat more than does prejudice that is hidden or disguised. Evidence of this was found in a study in which women received negative feedback from a male evaluator who was described as blatantly sexist, ambiguously sexist, or in no manner regarding sexism (Major, Quinton, & Schmader, 2003). Women reported significantly higher self-esteem when the negative feedback came from a clearly sexist man than when his sexism was ambiguous or no cues to his sexism were mentioned. As well, women in the blatant sexism condition discounted the negative feedback more (i.e., attributed the feedback more to discrimination than to their lack of ability) than did women in the ambiguous cues condition or the no cues condition, and discounting was positively associated with self-esteem.

Group Identification

A third variable that moderates the impact of perceived and attributed discrimination on personal self-esteem is the extent to which the target individual is identified with the group that is the basis for discrimination. When individuals are highly identified with their group, negative group-related events are more likely to be appraised as self-relevant. Negative events that are more self-relevant are more threatening (Lazarus & Folkman, 1984). Thus, McCoy and Major (2003) hypothesized that the more central and important a social identity is to an individual, the more threatening it is for that individual to perceive discrimination against that social identity. In their first experiment, women, all of whom had previously completed a measure of gender identification (gender centrality), received negative feedback from a male evaluator who they believed had clearly sexist or nonsexist attitudes. Women low in gender identification reported less depressed emotion and higher self-esteem in the sexist than nonsexist condition following receipt of the feedback. In contrast, among highly gender-identified women, self-esteem and depressed emotions did not differ between the sexist and nonsexist conditions. This interaction suggests that attributing negative outcomes to prejudice against one's social identity protects personal self-esteem only when that social identity is not a core aspect of self.

In a second experiment, greater ethnic group identification (centrality) was positively associated with depressed affect among Latino/a American students who read an article describing pervasive prejudice against Latino/as, but was negatively associated with depressed affect among Latino/a students who read a control article describing prejudice against a non-self-relevant group. This interaction is consistent with the claim that when social identity is a core aspect of the self, encountering prejudice against that social identity is more personally threatening than when social identity is less central to the self.

Although group identification may make an individual temporarily vulnerable to threats to that group, it may also serve as a resource that an individual can draw on later to cope with discrimination. A number of cross-sectional, correlational studies show a positive association between group identification and self-esteem among disadvantaged groups (e.g., Branscombe et al., 1999; Eccleston & Major, 2006). There are a variety of reasons why one might expect to observe a positive relationship: groups can provide emotional, informational, and instrumental support, social validation for one's perceptions, and social consensus for one's attributions.

Perceived discrimination against the ingroup also can increase identification with the ingroup, especially among those who are highly identified with the group (Allport, 1954/1979). By increasing ingroup identification, perceived discrimination may have an indirect, positive effect on self-esteem (Branscombe et al., 1999). A study by Spencer-Rodgers and Collins (2006) illustrated that perceived group disadvantage can be both negatively and positively related to self-esteem, through different pathways. Using structural equation modeling, they showed that perceived group disadvantage among Latino Americans was negatively associated with personal self-esteem via the mediator of perceived negative public regard (the belief that others look down on Latinos), a concept closely related to perceived discrimination. Perceived group disadvantage also was positively associated with personal self-esteem via the mediator of increased group identification (increased group centrality, increased attachment to the group, and increased liking for the group). Taken together, the total effect of perceived group disadvantage on self-esteem was nonsignificant, suggesting that the positive benefits of increased ingroup identification completely alleviated the detrimental effects of perceived group discrimination.

Beliefs

Stable beliefs and characteristics of persons also moderate the relationship between perceived prejudice and self-esteem. These beliefs are likely to moderate reactions to prejudice and discrimination by influencing people's threat appraisals. For example, Kaiser, Major, & McCoy (2009) showed that dispositional optimism moderated the impact of perceived prejudice on self-esteem. Among men and women who read about pervasive sexism directed toward their own gender group, an optimistic outlook on life was associated with significantly higher self-esteem and less depression. Among participants who read control information, optimism was unrelated to depressed emotions and still significantly, but more weakly, positively related to self-esteem. These effects were mediated by perceived threat such that optimists were less threatened by prejudice than were pessimists.

The impact of perceived discrimination on self-esteem also depends on the target's assumptions and beliefs about the way the world works, his or her worldview (Major, Kaiser, O'Brien, & McCoy, 2007; Sellers & Shelton, 2003). People's beliefs about and explanation for the unequal distribution of social and material goods in society, or their status ideology, is a core component of their worldview. Like other aspects of people's worldview, status ideologies provide a meaningful description of and explanation for reality and describe standards necessary to be a person of social and material value (Greenberg, Solomon, & Pyszczynski, 1997). Because worldviews serve to reduce uncertainty and allow individuals to function more effectively (Bowlby, 1969; Hogg, 2001; van den Bos & Lind, 2002), people are highly motivated to confirm and to defend their worldview from threat. Self-relevant information that confirms one's worldview should increase feelings of security, certainty, and self-esteem, whereas self-relevant information that threatens one's worldview should increase feelings of vulnerability and uncertainty and decrease self-esteem (Janoff-Bulman, 1989; Kaiser, Vick, & Major, 2004; Lerner, 1980).

Based on this reasoning, Major et al. (2007) recently proposed *worldview verification theory* (WVT) to explain responses to discrimination among disadvantaged groups. According to WVT, perceiving discrimination directed against the ingroup (or self) threatens the worldview of individuals who endorse SJBs, such as the belief that the status hierarchy is permeable and based on merit. Because perceiving discrimination directed against themselves or their group threatens their worldview, and hence their sense of meaning and value, it leads to decreased self-esteem. In contrast, perceiving discrimination directed against the ingroup (or self) confirms the worldview of individuals who reject SJBs such as the belief that the status hierarchy is permeable and based on merit. Perceived discrimination both corroborates their status ideology and provides an alternative explanation for their ingroup's (or their own) disadvantage. Consequently, WVT predicts that for individuals who reject a meritocracy worldview, perceiving discrimination against the ingroup or (self) will buffer or bolster their self-esteem.

Across three studies, Major et al. (2007) found support for these predictions. Overall, perceived discrimination against the ingroup, whether measured as an individual difference variable or manipulated experimentally, was unrelated to personal self-esteem among women and Latino/a Americans (see also Foster, Sloto, & Ruby, 2006; Kaiser, Major, & McCoy, 2004; Major, Kaiser et al., 2003; McCoy & Major, 2003, for similar findings). Perceived discrimination interacted with SJBs (worldview) to shape self-esteem. Consistent with WVT, among women and ethnic minorities who strongly embraced a meritocracy worldview, perceiving discrimination against their ethnic or gender group led to lowered self-esteem. This pattern is consistent with the idea that perceived devaluation of one's social identity will result in lower personal self-esteem (e.g., Branscombe et al., 1999). In contrast, for Latino/a American and female participants who rejected a meritocracy worldview, perceived discrimination against their ethnic or gender group led to higher self-esteem. This pattern is consistent with theories that predict that perceiving others to be prejudiced against one's social identity can serve a self-esteem protective function to the extent that it provides a more external attribution for one's own or one's groups' social disadvantage (e.g., Crocker & Major, 1989). Support for WVT predictions also emerge from several other studies (Foster et al., 2006; Foster & Tsarfati, 2005; Sellers & Shelton, 2003).

Summary

Personal, situational, and structural factors moderate the impact of perceptions of and attributions to discrimination on personal self-esteem and emotions. In the context of a personally threatening negative event, attributions to and perceptions of discrimination based on one's social identity may protect against a loss of personal self-esteem or an increase in depressed emotion by providing a less threatening explanation for the event. Attributions to discrimination also protect self-esteem when the contextual cues to prejudice are clear, thereby facilitating discounting of self-blame. Personal resources, such as dispositional optimism and endorsing a worldview that challenges the legitimacy of the status hierarchy, can buffer personal self-esteem from perceived prejudice against the group by reducing the extent to which prejudice is appraised as a personal threat. In contrast, a pessimistic outlook on life, high identification with the targeted group, and endorsing a worldview that justifies status differences in society can make an individual more vulnerable to perceived prejudice against themselves or their ingroup.

IMPLICATIONS FOR INTERPERSONAL RELATIONSHIPS

Although the vast majority of research on the psychological implications of perceived discrimination focuses on self-esteem, emotions, and mental health, researchers have begun to examine other potential outcomes. One emerging area of research centers on the interpersonal consequences of attributing one's outcomes to discrimination. This research indicates that claiming that outcomes are due to discrimination may have detrimental social costs for the person who does so. Because Western cultures tend to devalue individuals who fail to take responsibility for their outcomes (Jellison & Green, 1981), individuals who claim that their treatment is the result of discrimination (an external cause) are often perceived more negatively than those who make internal attributions for their poor performance and may be subject to retaliation from their peers (Feagin & Sikes, 1994). Whites view African Americans who blame unfavorable test results on discrimination more negatively than African Americans who blame themselves (e.g., lack of ability) or an external factor unrelated to discrimination (e.g., difficulty of the test; Kaiser & Miller, 2001, 2003). They see the former as complainers, hypersensitive, emotional, argumentative, irritating, and trouble-making compared to the latter, regardless of the validity of the claim. That is, even when racism was overt, observers rated targets who blamed discrimination more negatively than those who blamed other factors.

People are more likely to label targets who blame unfavorable outcomes on discrimination as complainers than they are to so label those blaming other causes, and they are particularly likely to dislike members of their own group who blame discrimination. Garcia et al. (2005) found that men and women disliked ingroup members (members of their own gender) who blamed a failure on discrimination more than they disliked members of the other gender who made an identical claim, and more than ingroup members who blamed the failure on themselves. In addition, the greater disliking of ingroup members who blamed discrimination was mediated by perceptions that ingroup targets who blamed discrimination were avoiding personal responsibility for their outcomes. The authors explain this in terms of a *black-sheep effect,* whereby people are more critical of ingroup members who claim discrimination because they are seen as disregarding the socially desirable norm of taking responsibility for their own failures.

This finding can be contrasted with the finding discussed earlier, that a higher need to belong was associated with greater perceptions of discrimination against the ingroup among both men and women (Carvallo & Pelham, 2006). Carvallo and Pelham (2006) speculated this occurred because perceiving discrimination against the ingroup validates an important belief of many ingroup members. We believe that whether or not ingroup members who claim discrimination are likely to be more derogated than outgroup members who do so depends on the observer's worldview.

Several studies indicate that the interpersonal costs of blaming negative outcomes on discrimination (vs. on other factors) are most severe when targets are evaluated by persons who strongly endorse a meritocratic worldview. Jost and Burgess (2000, Study 2) asked men and women to read about a young woman who sued her university after failing to be accepted to the honors program, which was known to differentially accept males. Results indicated that the more participants endorsed the belief in a just world, the more likely they were to discount and disfavor the woman in question. Kaiser, Dyrenforth, and Hagiwara (2006, Study 1) also demonstrated that endorsement of SJBs predicted negative appraisals of others who blame negative outcomes on discrimination. White participants who strongly endorsed SJBs were more likely to derogate a Black individual who blamed a poor evaluation on discrimination than a Black individual who blamed his poor evaluation on either his poor answers or test difficulty. The same pattern did not emerge among participants low in SJB endorsement. They did not differ in their evaluation of the participant based on his attributions for his performance. A second study found similar results and identified process variables by which SJBs lead to target evaluations. The relationship between SJBs and negative appraisals was mediated by perceived similarity of values between the perceiver and the target, as well as the belief that the participant had taken personal responsibility for his outcomes (Kaiser, Dyrenforth, & Hagiwara, 2006).

In summary, blaming one's outcomes on discrimination, at least in public, is costly. Those who claim discrimination are labeled as complainers and troublemakers, and likely to be ostracized by others, including members of their own group. Hence, it is not surprising that members of devalued groups often minimize the extent to which they are targets of discrimination. To do otherwise is just too costly.

CONCLUSIONS

Because discrimination is frequently ambiguous and difficult to prove with certainty, making an attribution to discrimination is often a highly subjective judgment. Personal, situational, and structural factors can increase or decrease the likelihood than people will judge that an event is due to discrimination, and can lead to overestimation or underestimation of prejudice. Similar factors appear to influence observers' and targets' attributions to discrimination. Increasingly, scholars have come to recognize that perceptions of discrimination can be as important as exposure to discrimination in predicting interpersonal relationships, self-esteem, and psychological well-being. Attributing personally threatening events to discrimination rather than to internal qualities of the self can protect against depressed affect and losses in self-esteem. It can also be an important anticipatory defense strategy for those who are chronically exposed to prejudice (Major et al., 2006; Sellers & Shelton, 2003). Nevertheless, attributing one's outcomes to discrimination can be costly. It can lead to social rejection both from members of one's own group as well as members of other groups. Chronically expecting to be a target of prejudice can lead to more negative interpersonal interactions with members of outgroups and avoidance of domains in which prejudice is expected (cf. Mendoza-Denton et al., 2002; Pinel, 1999). Perceiving pervasive discrimination against oneself or one's group can lead to increased psychological distress. Thus, like Mary Bates in the scenario with which we began this chapter, members of devalued groups who suspect they are targets of discrimination face a dilemma. When they are unsure, they must weigh the costs of falsely seeing discrimination that does not exist against the costs of missing discrimination when it does. When they are sure, they must weigh the costs of claiming discrimination against the costs of silence.

ACKNOWLEDGMENTS

Preparation of this chapter was supported by a grant from the National Institute of Heart, Lung and Blood (#R01 HL079383) to Brenda Major.

REFERENCES

Adams, G., Tormala, T. T., & O'Brien, L. T. (2006). The effect of self-affirmation on perception of racism. *Journal of Experimental Social Psychology, 42*(5), 616–626.
Allport, G. W. (1979). *The nature of prejudice.* Reading, MA: Addison-Wesley. (Original work published 1954)
Baron, R. S., Burgess, M. L., & Kao, C. F. (1991). Detecting and labeling prejudice: Do female perpetrators go undetected? *Personality and Social Psychology Bulletin, 17*(2), 115–123.
Barrett, L. F., & Swim, J. K. (1998). Appraisals of prejudice and discrimination. In J. K. Swim, & C. S. Stangor (Eds.), *Prejudice: The target's perspective* (pp. 11-36). San Diego, CA: Academic Press.
Bowlby, J. (1969). Disruption of affectional bonds and its effect on behavior. *Canada's Mental Health Supplement, 59,* 12.
Branscombe, N. R., Schmitt, M. T., & Harvey, R. D. (1999). Perceiving pervasive discrimination among African-Americans: Implications for group identification and well-being. *Journal of Personality and Social Psychology, 77*(1), 135–149.
Cartwright, D. (1950). Emotional dimensions of group life. In M. L. Reymert (Ed.), *Feelings and emotions: The Mooseheart Symposium* (pp. 439–447). New York: McGraw-Hill.
Carvallo, M., & Pelham, B. W. (2006). When fiends become friends: The need to belong and perceptions of personal and group discrimination. *Journal of Personality and Social Psychology, 90,* 94–108.
Cooley, C. H. (1956). *Two major works: Social organization. Human nature and the social order.* Glencoe, IL: The Free Press.
Crandall, C. S. (1994). Prejudice against fat people: Ideology and self-interest. *Journal of Personality and Social Psychology, 24*(6), 659–677.
Crocker, J., Cornwell, B., & Major, B. (1993). The stigma of overweight: Affective consequences of attributional ambiguity. *Journal of Personality and Social Psychology, 64,* 60–70.
Crocker, J., & Major, B. (1989). Social stigma and self-esteem: The self-protective properties of stigma. *Psychological Review, 96,* 608–630.
Crocker, J., Major, B., & Steele, C. (1998). Social stigma. In D. T. Gilbert, S. T. Fiske, & G. Lindzey (Eds.), *The handbook of social psychology* (Vol. 2, 4th ed., pp. 504–553). New York: McGraw-Hill.
Crocker, J., Voelkl, K., Testa, M., & Major, B. (1991). Social stigma: The affective consequences of attributional ambiguity. *Journal of Personality and Social Psychology, 60,* 218–228.
Crosby, F. A. (1976). Model of egoistical relative deprivation. *Psychological Review, 83,* 85–113.
Crosby, F. (1982). *Relative deprivation and working women.* New York: Oxford University Press.
Crosby, F. (1984). The denial of personal discrimination. *American Behavioral Scientist, 27,* 371–386.
Crosby, F., Clayton, S., Alksnis, O., & Hemker, K. (1986). Cognitive biases in the perception of discrimination: The importance of format. *Sex Roles, 14,* 637–646.
Crosby, F. J., Pufall, A., Snyder, R. C., O'Connell, M., & Whalen, P. (1989). The denial of personal disadvantage among you, me, and all the other ostriches. In M. Crawford & M. Gentry (Eds.), *Gender and thought: Psychological perspectives* (pp. 79–99). New York: Springer-Verlag.
Dion, K. L. (1975). Women's reactions to discrimination from members of the same or opposite sex. *Journal of Research in Personality, 9*(4), 294–306.

Dion, K. L., & Earn, B. M. (1975). The phenomenology of being a target of prejudice. *Journal of Personality and Social Psychology, 32*(5), 944–950.

Eccleston, C. P., & Major, B. N. (2006). Attributions to discrimination and self-esteem: The role of group identification and appraisals. *Group Processes and Intergroup Relations, 9,* 147–162.

Feagin, J. R., & Sikes, M. P. (1994). *Living with racism: The black middle-class experience.* Boston: Beacon Press.

Feldman, L. B., & Swim, J. K. (1998). Appraisals of prejudice and discrimination. In J. K. Swim & C. Stangor (Eds.), *Prejudice: The target's perspective* (pp. 11–36). San Diego, CA: Academic.

Flournoy, J. M., Jr., Prentice-Dunn, S., & Klinger, M. R. (2002). The role of prototypical situations in the perceptions of prejudice of African Americans. *Journal of Applied Social Psychology, 32*(2), 406–423.

Foster, M. D., Sloto, L., & Ruby, R. (2006). Responding to discrimination as a function of meritocracy beliefs and personal experiences: Testing the model of shattered assumptions. *Group Processes and Intergroup Relations, 9*(3), 401–411.

Foster, M. D., & Tsarfati, E. M. (2005). The effects of meritocracy beliefs on women's well being after first-time gender discrimination. *Personality and Social Psychology Bulletin, 31*(12), 1730–1738.

Garcia, D. M., Reser, A. H., Amo, R. B., Redersdorff, S., & Branscombe, N. R. (2005). Perceivers' responses to in-group and out-group members who blame a negative outcome on discrimination. *Personality and Social Psychology Bulletin, 31*(6), 769–780.

Gill, R., & Matheson, K. (2006). Responses to discrimination: The role of emotion and expectations for emotional regulation. *Personality and Social Psychology Bulletin, 32*(2), 149–161.

Greenberg, J., Solomon, S., & Pyszczynski, T. (1997). Terror management theory of self-esteem and cultural worldviews: Empirical assessments and conceptual refinements. In M. P. Zanna (Ed.), *Advances in experimental social psychology* (Vol. 29, pp. 61–139). San Diego, CA: Academic.

Gurin, P., Miller, A. H., & Gurin, G. (1980). Stratum identification and consciousness. *Social Psychology Quarterly, 43*(1), 30–47.

Gurin, P., & Townsend, A. (1986). Properties of gender identity and their implications for gender consciousness. *British Journal of Social Psychology, 25*(2), 139–148.

Hafer, C. L., & Olson, J. M. (1993). Beliefs in a just world, discontent, and assertive actions by working women. *Personality and Social Psychology Bulletin, 19,* 30–38.

Harris, M. M., Lievens, F., & Van Hoye, G. (2004). "I think they discriminated against me": Using prototype theory and organizational justice theory for understanding perceived discrimination in selection and promotion situations. *International Journal of Selection and Assessment, 12,* 54–65.

Hogg, M. A. (2001). Self-categorization and subjective uncertainty resolution: Cognitive and motivational facets of social identity and group membership. In J. P. Forgas, K. D. Williams, & L. Wheeler (Eds.), *The social mind: Cognitive and motivational aspects of interpersonal behavior* (pp. 323–349). New York: Cambridge University Press.

Hoyt, C. L., Agular, L., Kaiser, C. R., Blascovich, J., & Lee, K. (2007). The self-protective and undermining effects of attributional ambiguity. *Journal of Experimental Social Psychology, 43,* 884–893.

Huebner, D. M., Nemeroff, C. J., & Davis, M. C. (2005). Do hostility and neuroticism confound associations between perceived discrimination and depressive symptoms? *Journal of Social and Clinical Psychology, 24*(5), 723–740.

Inman, M. L. (2001). Do you see what I see?: Similarities and differences in victims' and observers' perceptions of discrimination. *Social Cognition, 19*(5), 521–546.

Inman, M. L., & Baron, R. S. (1996). Influence of prototypes on perception of prejudice. *Journal of Personality and Social Psychology, 70,* 727–739.

Inman, M. L., Huerta, J., & Oh, S. (1998). Perceiving discrimination: The role of prototypes in norm violation. *Social Cognition, 16*(4), 418–450.

Janoff-Bulman, R. (1989). Assumptive worlds and the stress of traumatic events: Applications of the schema construct. *Social Cognition, 7*(2), 113–136.

Jellison, J. M., & Green, J. (1981). A self-presentational approach to the fundamental attribution error: The norm of intentionality. *Journal of Personality and Social Psychology, 40*(4), 643–649.

Jost, J. T. (1995). Negative illusions: Conceptual clarification and psychological evidence concerning false consciousness. *Political Psychology, 16*(2), 397–424.

Jost, J. T., & Burgess, D. (2000). Attitudinal ambivalence and the conflict between group and system justification motives in low status groups. *Personality and Social Psychology Bulletin, 26*(3), 293–305.

Kaiser, C. R., Dyrenforth, P. S., & Hagiwara, N. (2006). Why are attributions to discrimination interpersonally costly? A test of system- and group-justifying motivations. *Personality and Social Psychology Bulletin, 32*(11), 1523–1536.

Kaiser, C. R., Major, B., & McCoy, S. K. (2004). Expectations about the future and the emotional consequences of perceiving prejudice. *Personality and Social Psychology Bulletin, 30,* 173–184.

Kaiser, C. R., & Miller, C. T. (2001). Stop complaining! The social costs of making attributions to discrimination. *Personality and Social Psychology Bulletin, 27,* 254–263.

Kaiser, C. R., & Miller, C. T. (2003). Derogating the victim: The interpersonal consequences of blaming events on discrimination. *Group Processes and Intergroup Relations, 6*(3), 227–237.

Kaiser, C. R., Vick, S. B., & Major, B. (2004). A prospective investigation of the relationship between just-world beliefs and the desire for revenge after September 11, 2001. *Psychological Science, 15*(7), 503-506.

Kaiser, C. R., Vick, S. B., & Major, B. (2006). Prejudice expectations moderate preconscious attention to cues that are threatening to social identity. *Psychological Science, 17*(4), 332–338.

Kelley, H. H. (1973). The process of causal attribution. *American Psychologist, 28*(2), 107–128.

Krieger, N. (1990). Racial and gender discrimination: Factors for high blood pressure? *Social Science Medicine, 30,* 1273–1281.

Lazarus, R. S., & Folkman, S. (1984). *Stress, appraisal, and coping.* New York: Springer.

Lerner, M. J. (1980). *The belief in a just world: A fundamental delusion.* New York: Plenum.

Magley, V. J., Hulin, C. L., Fitzgerald, L. F., & DeNardo, M. (1999). Outcomes of self-labeling sexual harassment. *Journal of Applied Psychology, 84*(3), 390–402.

Major, B. (1994). From social inequality to personal entitlement: The role of social comparisons, legitimacy appraisals, and group membership. In M. Zanna (Ed.), *Advances in experimental social psychology* (Vol. 26, pp. 293–355). San Diego, CA: Academic.

Major, B., & Eccleston, C. (2002). *Perceiving prejudice and self-esteem: Theoretical and empirical advances.* Address given at annual meeting, in October 2002, of the Society for Experimental Social Psychology, Columbus, Ohio.

Major, B., Gramzow, R. H., McCoy, S. K., Levin, S., Schmader, T., & Sidanius, J. (2002). Perceiving personal discrimination: The role of group status and legitimizing ideology. *Journal of Personality and Social Psychology, 82,* 269–282.

Major, B., Henry, P. J., & Kaiser, C. (2006). *Implications of perceived discrimination for self-esteem: It's relative.* Manuscript in preparation.

Major, B., & Kaiser, C. R. (2005). Perceiving and claiming discrimination. In L. B. Nielson & R. Nielson (Eds.), *The handbook of research on employment discrimination: Rights and realities* (pp. 279–293). New York: Springer.

Major, B., Kaiser, C. R., & McCoy, S. K. (2003). It's not my fault: When and why attributions to prejudice protect self-esteem. *Personality and Social Psychology Bulletin, 29,* 772–781.

Major, B., Kaiser, C. R., O'Brien, L. T., & McCoy, S. K. (2007). Perceived discrimination as worldview threat or worldview confirmation: Implications for self-esteem. *Journal of Personality and Social Psychology, 92*(6), 1068-1086.

Major, B., McCoy, S. K., Kaiser, C. R., & Quinton, W. J. (2003). Prejudice and self-esteem: A transactional model. In W. Stroebe & M. Hewstone (Eds.), *European review of social psychology* (Vol. 14, pp. 77–104). Hove, UK: Psychology Press/Taylor & Francis.

Major, B., & O'Brien, L. T. (2005). The social psychology of stigma. *Annual Review of Psychology, 56,* 393–421.

Major, B., Quinton, W. J., & McCoy, S. K. (2002). Antecedents and consequences of attributions to discrimination: Theoretical and empirical advances. In M. P. Zanna (Ed.), *Advances in experimental social psychology* (Vol. 34, pp. 251–330). San Diego, CA: Academic.

Major, B., Quinton, W. J., & Schmader, T. (2003). Attributions to discrimination and self-esteem: Impact of group identification and situational ambiguity. *Journal of Experimental Social Psychology, 39,* 220–231.

Major, B., & Schmader, T. (2001). Legitimacy and the construal of social disadvantage In J. Jost & B. Major (Eds.), *The psychology of legitimacy: Emerging perspectives on ideology, justice, and intergroup relationships* (pp. 363–388). New York: Cambridge University Press.

Marti, M. W., Bobier, D. M., & Baron, R. S. (2000). Right before our eyes: The failure to recognize non-prototypical forms of prejudice. *Group Processes and Intergroup Relations, 3*(4), 403-418.

Marx, K., & Engels, F. (1970). *The German ideology* (C. J. Arthur, Ed.). New York: International Publishers. (Original work published 1846)

McClure, J. (1998). Discounting causes of behavior: Are two reasons better than one? *Journal of Personality & Social Psychology, 74,* 7–20.

McCoy, S. K., & Major, B. (2003). Group identification moderates emotional responses to perceived prejudice. *Personality and Social Psychology Bulletin, 29,* 1005–1017.

Mead, G. H. (1934). *Mind, self and society: From the standpoint of a social behaviorist.* Chicago: University of Chicago Press.

Mendoza-Denton, R., Downey, G., Purdie, V. J., Davis, A., & Pietrzak, J. (2002). Sensitivity to status-based rejection: Implications for African American students' college experience. *Journal of Personality and Social Psychology, 83,* 896–918.

Mirels, H., & Garrett, J. (1971). The Protestant ethnic as a personality variable. *Journal of Consulting and Clinical Psychology, 36,* 40–44.

Morera, M. D., Dupont, E., Leyens, J. P., & Desert, M. (2004). When prototypicality makes "maybes" look more certain: Another look at targets' vigilance towards prejudice cues. *European Journal of Social Psychology, 34*(4), 437–457.

O'Brien, L., T., Kinias, Z., & Major, B. (2008). The role of status and stereotypes in attributions to discrimination. *Journal of Experimental Social Psychology, 44,* 405–412.

O'Brien, L. T., & Major, B. (2005). System-justifying beliefs and psychological well-being: The roles of group status and identity. Personality and Social Psychology Bulletin, 31(12), 1718-1729.

O'Brien, L., T., & Major, B. (in press). Group status and feelings of personal entitlement: The roles of social comparison and system justifying beliefs. In J. T. Jost, A. Kay, & H. Thorosdottir (Eds.), *Social and psychological bases of ideology and system justification.* New York: Cambridge University Press.

Operario, D., & Fiske, S. T. (2001). Ethnic identity moderates perceptions of prejudice: Judgments of personal versus group discrimination and subtle versus blatant bias. *Personality and Social Psychology Bulletin, 27,* 550–561.

Pinel, E. C. (1999). Stigma consciousness: The psychological legacy of social stereotypes. *Journal of Personality and Social Psychology, 76,* 114–128.

Porter, J. R., & Washington, R. E. (1979). Black identity and self-esteem: A review of studies of Black self-concept, 1968–1978. *Annual Review of Sociology, 5,* 53–74.

Rodin, M. J., Price, J. M., Bryson, J. B., & Sanchez, F. J. (1990). Asymmetry in prejudice attribution. *Journal of Experimental Social Psychology, 26,* 481–504

Rosenberg, M., & Simmons, R. G. (1972). *Black and white self-esteem: The urban school child.* Washington, DC: American Sociological Association.

Schmitt, M. T., & Branscombe, N. R. (2002). The meaning and consequences of perceived discrimination in disadvantaged and privileged social groups. *European Review of Social Psychology, 12,* 167–199.

Sechrist, G. B., Swim, J. K., & Mark, M. M. (2003). Mood as information in making attributions to discrimination. *Personality and Social Psychology Bulletin, 29,* 524–531.

Sechrist, G. B., Swim, J. K., & Stangor, C. (2004). When do the stigmatized make attributions to discrimination occurring to the self and others? The roles of self-presentation and need for control. *Journal of Personality and Social Psychology, 87,* 111–122.

Sellers, R. M., & Shelton, J. N. (2003). The role of racial identity in perceived racial discrimination. *Journal of Personality and Social Psychology, 84*(5), 1079–1092.

Sharf, J. C., & Jones, D. P. (1999). Employment risk management. In J. F. Kehoe (Ed.), *Managing selection in changing organizations* (pp. 271–318). New York: Jossey-Bass.

Shelton, J. N., & Stewart, R. E. (2004). Confronting perpetrators of prejudice: The inhibitory effects of social costs. *Psychology of Women Quarterly, 28,* 215–223.

Sidanius, J., & Pratto, F. (1999). *Social dominance: An intergroup theory of social hierarchy and oppression.* New York: Cambridge University Press.

Simpson, G. E., & Yinger, J. M. (1985). The consequences of prejudice and discrimination. In L. Susskind & L. Rodwin (Eds.), *Racial and cultural minorities: An analysis of prejudice and discrimination* (5th ed., pp. 111–136). New York: Plenum.

Spencer-Rodgers, J., & Collins, N. L. (2006). Risk and resilience: Dual effects of perceptions of group disadvantage among Latinos. *Journal of Experimental Social Psychology, 42*(6), 729–737.

Stangor, C., Swim, J. K., Sechrist, G. B., DeCoster, J., Van Allen, K. L., & Ottenbrit, A. (2003). Ask, answer, and announce: Three stages in perceiving and responding to discrimination. *European Review of Social Psychology, 14,* 277–311.

Stangor, C., Swim, J. K., Van Allen, K., & Sechrist, G. B. (2002). Reporting discrimination in public and private contexts. *Journal of Personality and Social Psychology, 82,* 69–74.

Steele, C. M. (1988). The psychology of self-affirmation: Sustaining the integrity of the self. In L. Berkowitz (Ed.), *Advances in experimental social psychology* (Vol. 21, pp. 261–302.). New York: Academic.

Steele, C. M., Spencer, S. J., & Aronson, J. (2002). Contending with group image: The psychology of stereo-type and social identity threat. In M. P. Zanna (Ed.), *Advances in experimental social psychology* (Vol. 34, pp. 379–440). San Diego, CA: Academic.

Swim, J. K., & Hyers, L. L. (1999). Excuse me—What did you say?! Women's public and private responses to sexist remarks. *Journal of Experimental Social Psychology, 35,* 68–88.

Swim, J. K., Hyers, L. L., Cohen, L. L., & Ferguson, M. J. (2001). Everyday sexism: Evidence for its incidence, nature, and psychological impact from three daily diary studies. *Journal of Social Issues, 57,* 31–53.

Swim, J. K., Scott, E. D., Sechrist, G. B., Campbell, B., & Stangor, C. (2003). The role of intent and harm in judgments of prejudice and discrimination. *Journal of Personality and Social Psychology, 84,* 944–959.

Tajfel, H., & Turner, J. C. (1986). The social identity theory of intergroup behavior. In S. Worchel & W. G. Austin (Eds.), *The psychology of intergroup relations* (pp. 7–24). Chicago: Nelson-Hall.

Taylor, D. M., Wright, S. C., Moghaddam, F. M., & Lalonde, R. N. (1990). The personal/group discrimina-tion discrepancy: Perceiving my group, but not myself, to be a target for discrimination. *Personality and Social Psychology Bulletin, 16,* 254–262.

Twenge, J. M., & Crocker, J. (2002). Race and self-esteem: Meta-analyses comparing Whites, Blacks, Hispanics, Asians, and American Indians and comments on Gray-Little and Hafdahl (2000). *Psychological Bulletin, 128*(3), 371–408.

van den Bos, K., & Lind, E. A. (2002). Uncertainty management by means of fairness judgments. In M. P. Zanna (Ed.), *Advances in experimental social psychology* (Vol. 34, pp. 1–60). San Diego, CA: Academic.

Vorauer, J. D., & Kumhyr, S. M. (2001). Is this about you or me? Self-versus other-directed judgments and feel-ings in response to intergroup interaction. *Personality and Social Psychology Bulletin, 27,* 706–719.

Weiner, B. (1985). An attributional theory of achievement motivation and emotion. *Journal of Personality and Social Psychology, 92,* 548–573.

Weiner, B., Perry, R. P., & Magnusson, J. (1988). An attributional analysis of reactions to stigmas. *Journal of Personality and Social Psychology, 55,* 738–748.

6 Controlling Prejudice and Stereotyping
Antecedents, Mechanisms, and Contexts

*Galen V. Bodenhausen, Andrew R. Todd,
and Jennifer A. Richeson*
Northwestern University

With a depressing degree of regularity, national attention in the United States becomes focused on prominent individuals who are caught in the act of making racist, sexist, homophobic, or otherwise prejudiced remarks, "jokes," or tirades. Such exposés are frequently paired with adamant assertions by the purveyors of these commentaries that they are not prejudiced people; indeed, they hold themselves to be good people, and they sometimes even seem to experience a sense of surprise at their own behavior, being unsure about the origins of their prejudiced remarks. However, they are quite sure that, whatever the origins of their unsavory comments, they do not reflect any personal endorsement of prejudice or derogatory stereotypes. To judge by the flurry of apologies that typically follow such incidents, it seems reasonable to infer that the people involved would have wished that they could have stopped themselves from making the remarks they made, not only because it landed them in hot water, but presumably also because it threatened their identities as civilized, unbigoted persons.

In this chapter we review research on the psychology of controlling prejudice and stereotyping. As a starting point, we discuss the central problem of the automatic activation of prejudice and stereotyping. In other words, we begin by describing what it is that is in need of control. Then, we consider the motivational antecedents of control—the psychological forces that lead people to want to control the prejudice and stereotypes that arise in their own minds. Next, we survey the cognitive mechanisms of self-regulation by which people attempt to control their prejudices, and we evaluate their adequacy for meeting the challenges posed by the operation of automatic or reflexive stereotypes and prejudice. Finally, we consider how these processes play out in a variety of personal, interpersonal, and societal contexts.

AUTOMATIC ACTIVATION OF STEREOTYPES AND PREJUDICE

WHAT ARE AUTOMATIC INTERGROUP BIASES?

In her seminal dissertation research, Devine (1989) argued that intergroup bias can be manifested in two distinct forms: automatic and controlled. Controlled prejudice is produced by conscious, intentional, deliberative mental processes, and has become much less common in contemporary society, at least with respect to many social groups. In contrast, automatic prejudice is produced by the spontaneous activation of mental associations that are not necessarily personally endorsed, but that are ubiquitously found in contemporary society, owing to ongoing cultural representations of minority groups that perpetuate negative or stereotypic associations with the groups. If the members of minority groups are consistently presented in negative social contexts (e.g., crime, terrorism, dependency, etc.), then classical and evaluative conditioning processes would certainly be expected to produce prejudiced mental associations with these groups and their members (e.g., Walther, Nagengast, & Trasselli, 2005). It is typically assumed that these associations build up slowly over the course of socialization (e.g., Rudman, 2004; Rydell & McConnell, 2006), becoming firmly entrenched over time. Devine (1989) argued that, at least in American culture, with its historical legacy of social inequality, racial (and perhaps other types of intergroup) associations are commonly, perhaps inevitably, infused with prejudice.

Once established, stereotypical or prejudiced mental associations can begin to function automatically. As Bargh (1994) outlined, automatic mental processes are characterized by some or all of the following criteria: (a) spontaneity, in that they happen in the absence of any intention; (b) efficiency, in that they do not require much in the way of attentional resources for their execution; (c) uncontrollability, in that they operate in a ballistic fashion and are hard to stop once they have been initiated; and (d) unconsciousness, in that they can operate in a manner that is not subject to awareness or conscious monitoring. The activation of mental associations, as one specific type of automatic cognitive process, also has one other important defining characteristic, namely the fact that such associations are agnostic with respect to the validity, or truth value, of the association (Gawronski & Bodenhausen, 2006). That is, mental associations can be triggered independently of a person's belief in or endorsement of the association. Taken together, these considerations imply that associations such as "women are dependent" or "Arabs are bad" can become activated in one's mind without any intention, even if one's conscious views are that "most women are strong" and "most Arabs are good"—as long as one has been consistently exposed to cultural images that reinforce the automatic, prejudiced associations.

Automatic mental associations about social groups are likely to be activated whenever a group member is encountered (and categorized in terms of his or her group membership). Certainly, there is abundant evidence that automatic evaluations can be activated without intention and without requiring much cognitive capacity (e.g., Bargh, Chaiken, Raymond, & Hymes, 1996; Cunningham, Raye, & Johnson, 2004). Once activated, prejudiced associations can exert a number of effects on the ongoing stream of information processing (for a review, see Bodenhausen & Macrae, 1998). Many of these effects can be subsumed under the rubric of "assimilation," in that the activation of the associations results in perceptions and responses that are biased in the direction of the association.[1] For example, if an "Arabs are bad" association gets activated on encountering an Arab person, then any ambiguous information about the person may be given a negative spin and be interpreted in the light of confirmatory mechanisms of biased attention, interpretation, and memory. A number of studies show that automatic associations may influence not only our perceptions and judgments, but also our overt behaviors, particularly spontaneous behaviors such as nonverbal reactions (e.g., Dovidio, Kawakami, Johnson, Johnson, & Howard, 1997; for reviews, see Gawronski & Bodenhausen, 2007; Strack & Deutsch, 2004). These behavioral effects also show an "assimilative" pattern; for example, negative evaluative associations tend to produce colder, less friendly kinds of nonverbal displays (Dovidio et al., 1997).

With respect to more verbal or consciously controlled behavior, when people have the luxury of abundant time and free attention, they can carefully consider how they wish to respond and make conscious, intentional choices to guide their social reactions. Under such circumstances, any automatic prejudicial associations that are activated are quite likely to be trumped by propositional attitudes and beliefs (i.e., those attitudes and beliefs that are consciously endorsed and personally held to be valid) at least as long as the person possesses countervailing egalitarian values

---

[1] Contrast effects, in which an activated expectancy results in judgments that are more extreme in the direction opposite to the expectation, are also possible, but such effects tend to occur primarily when available information about the target is unambiguously inconsistent with the expectancy (see Biernat, 2003).

(Gawronski & Bodenhausen, 2006). In many circumstances, however, we are obliged to generate social responses in the absence of abundant temporal and cognitive resources. When this is the case, even verbal behavior, judgments, and (ostensibly) more conscious forms of action can be biased by automatic associations (e.g., Macrae & Bodenhausen, 2000). Persons who find themselves in such circumstances, but who desire not to express prejudice in their own behavior, must then be on guard against the intrusion of unwanted associations, and to the extent that they creep into mind, they must attempt to control their expression.

How Inevitable Are Automatic Prejudice and Stereotypes?

As previously mentioned, Devine (1989) portrayed automatic prejudice as a culturally ubiquitous phenomenon, whereas she expected variability in the controlled side of prejudice (see also Bargh, 1999). From this perspective, it is viewed as essentially inevitable that automatic prejudice and stereotypes will be at least initially activated on encountering members of a relevant group. In contrast to this view, a number of studies have shown meaningful individual differences in the automatic activation of stereotypes in response to the presentation of a group exemplar (or group label). For example, Kawakami, Dion, and Dovidio (1998; see also Castelli, Macrae, Zogmaister, & Arcuri, 2004; Lepore & Brown, 1997; Wittenbrink, Judd, & Park, 1997) showed that individual differences in explicit racial prejudice predicted differences in the automatic activation of racial stereotypes, even under task conditions that effectively minimized any role of controlled processes. Two interpretations of this pattern seem most viable. First, it may be that, in contrast to Devine's original assertions, low-prejudice persons simply do not possess automatic stereotypic associations, so when they encounter members of the target group, there is little that is stereotypic, in terms of automatic associations, to be activated. Alternatively, it may be that low-prejudice persons still do have stereotypic associations come into their minds, but they have become exceedingly skilled at rapidly suppressing their activation. We return to this issue in a subsequent section.

In addition to individual differences, there is also evidence of situational differences in stereotype activation that may challenge the view that stereotypes are inevitably activated when group members are encountered. Among the most well-known studies in this category are those conducted by Gilbert and Hixon (1991), who found that perceivers failed to activate stereotypes about an Asian target when they were mentally busy rehearsing a long number. In their studies, participants completed a series of word fragments that were presented on cards that were held either by an Asian or a European woman. On critical trials, the word fragments could be completed with words that were stereotypically associated with Asians (or, alternatively, by nonstereotypic words). They found that when the cards were held by the Asian woman, the word fragments were more likely to be completed with Asian stereotype words, unless the participants had been given an additional cognitive task (i.e., rehearsing the long number) that kept them mentally busy. In this condition, although participants did notice the ethnicity of the card holder, they did not show greater frequency of Asian-stereotypic word completions. This study is usually reported as showing that cognitive resources are required for stereotype activation and that when people are busy, they might not be able to activate their stereotypes.

Subsequent research calls this idea into question. The key to stereotype activation seems to lie more in the motivations of the perceiver rather than in the availability of cognitive resources. For example, in a replication of Gilbert and Hixon's (1991) study, Spencer, Fein, Wolfe, Fong, and Dunn (1998) showed that cognitively busy participants indeed do activate stereotypes, as long as there is some motivational incentive for doing so (in this case, a self-esteem boost). More generally, research suggests that stereotypes are activated only when perceivers care about the social meaning of the target person for some reason (Macrae, Bodenhausen, Milne, Thorne, & Castelli, 1997; see Kunda & Spencer, 2003, for a review). From this perspective, it may be the case that the busy participants in Gilbert and Hixon's study never generated any interest in the card holder because they were already so busy with the two experimental tasks they were working on. (Participants in the nonbusy condition would have had more time to think about the card turner: Who is she? What is she like?) If the busy participants indeed had any reason to be interested in the card turner, they would likely be readily able to activate their stereotypes about her, even while busy, given the abundant evidence showing the efficiency involved in the activation of stereotypic and evaluative mental associations.

Whether or not stereotypes and prejudice are activated on encountering a member of a minority group also depends crucially on how the person is categorized. Any given person can be categorized in seemingly innumerable ways, including on the basis of sex, race, age, hair color, occupation, body shape, and so on. Research suggests that not all of the potentially applicable categories will be invoked in construing the target; instead, only the contextually meaningful or focally relevant categorical identities will be selected for activation (e.g., Bodenhausen & Macrae, 1998; Macrae, Bodenhausen, & Milne, 1995; Quinn & Macrae, 2005). Although some have suggested that the most basic, visually marked demographic categories, such as sex and race, will routinely provide the basis for categorizing targets (e.g., Stangor, Lynch, Duan, & Glass, 1992), there are now several studies that qualify this conclusion. For example, in a lexical decision paradigm, Macrae et al. (1995) provided evidence that when both race and sex information are visually available, but the experimental context orients perceivers toward one of these dimensions over the other, only that focal dimension (and its associated stereotypes) appears to be activated; the alternative categorical dimension was not merely disregarded, but rather was actively inhibited. Specifically, an Asian woman eating rice with chopsticks elicited automatic Asian associations, whereas female associations were even less cognitively accessible than under baseline conditions. In contrast, the same Asian woman applying makeup in a mirror activated automatic gender associations, whereas Asian associations were even less cognitively accessible than under baseline conditions. Similarly, in a repetition priming paradigm, Quinn and Macrae (2005) showed that when participants were required to categorize a set of faces on the basis of their age, they did not appear also (spontaneously) to categorize them on the basis of their sex. These studies show that categorizing a target in terms of race or sex is not inevitable, and if a target is not categorized in terms of these categories, then the prejudice and stereotypes associated with the categories will also not be activated.

Other studies show that the context within which a target is encountered can shift the focus of categorization from broad demographic groupings to more circumscribed subtypes. These studies rely on the premise that people's social beliefs are often organized into relatively fine-tuned, differentiated knowledge structures that represent recurring conjunctions of salient features. For example, rather than categorizing someone as "African American," a person might utilize a more focused subtype such as "Black businessman" or "ghetto Black" (Devine & Baker, 1991). It may, of course, be the case that the automatic evaluations and descriptive associations that go with these subtypes may not coincide with one another, nor with those attached to the broader, superordinate category. In line with this possibility, Wittenbrink, Judd, and Park (2001) showed that the automatic racial attitudes activated by Black faces differed, depending on whether the faces were presented in the context of a church or an urban street corner (with more positive automatic evaluations in the former condition). In a similar vein, Barden, Maddux, Petty, and Brewer (2004) showed that automatic evaluative racial biases could be reversed, depending on the social role occupied by the target. For example, whereas a Black prisoner elicited negative automatic racial evaluations, relatively to evaluations of Whites, a Black lawyer (visiting a prison) elicited relatively positive automatic evaluations (see also Richeson & Ambady, 2003).

It has thus become apparent from several lines of investigation that there is considerable flexibility to the patterns of categorization in which individuals engage when perceiving social targets, with corresponding flexibility in the automatic attitudes and stereotypes that are activated in the course of forming impressions of these targets. Part of the variance is captured by individual differences in the explicit endorsement of prejudice and stereotypes, and another part is captured by situational differences in the meaningfulness and relevance of particular categorical identities that could potentially be ascribed to a target. The problem of controlling automatic prejudice and stereotypes, then, is not an issue that is inevitably evoked in intergroup encounters. Rather, it is a problem that is most relevant in those situations in which perceivers do in fact categorize others in terms of categories for which they are aware of undesirable cultural associations (whether or not the perceiver would admit to the possibility of those associations coloring his or her own perceptions). In those conditions, prejudice control can become a concern of considerable significance to social perceivers—or at least some of them. When and why people care about controlling prejudice is the topic we next consider.

MOTIVATIONAL ANTECEDENTS OF PREJUDICE CONTROL

Dramatic social change over the course of the 20th century resulted in a shift in the endorsement of principles of racial and gender equality, such that they went from being a minority viewpoint to becoming the overwhelming majority position (e.g., Schuman, Steeh, Bobo, & Krysan, 1997). Moreover, growing awareness of the destructive potential of prejudice, as manifested saliently in Nazi Germany but also in increasing awareness of the criminal injustices historically associated with racial prejudice in America (e.g., the ongoing legacy of slavery and the oppression of Native Americans), led prejudice and stereotypes to acquire an unsavory character that they had previously managed to elude. These changes unleashed two motivational forces that underlie the arrival on the social scene of the desire to control prejudice and stereotypes.

The first force concerns changes in societal norms that make the expression of prejudice a source of social devaluation. Because there are now social penalties associated with unchecked prejudices, ranging all the way from receiving disapproving looks, to being labeled a bigot, to being fired from one's job, people develop a desire to control automatic biases to avoid the costs of nonconformity with the robust norms of egalitarianism that have come to dominate many contemporary societies. Plant and Devine (1998) have termed this form of motivation *external motivation* to control prejudice, because it arises primarily from external, social norms. When this motivation dominates, prejudice control involves mere compliance (Kelman, 1958), and the strength of the motivation may wax and wane, depending on one's situational vulnerability to sanction for expressing prejudice.

Social norms against the expression of prejudice may serve as a deterrent to intergroup bias not only by holding out the threat of sanction, should individuals happen to deviate from the norm, but also by becoming internalized within the individual (e.g., Etzioni, 2000). That is, people may become personally persuaded that prejudice is wrong, and the goal to avoid expressing it may become directly linked to one's own personal values. The desire to act on these values, independent of any external incentives or sanctions, constitutes an *internal motivation* to control prejudice, in Plant and Devine's (1998) terminology. When this motivation dominates, prejudice control becomes internalized (Kelman, 1958), and the strength of the motivation should vary as a function of the salience of one's personal values (e.g., Wicklund, 1982), not the salience of potential sanction. Given that either (or both) of the motives is active, then prejudice control processes may be implemented whenever the perceiver (a) encounters a relevant social target and (b) categorizes the target in terms of membership in a group that is not considered a suitable target for automatic negative attitudes and stereotypes. This latter point highlights the fact that motivation to control prejudice can vary across stigmatized social groups, with some groups eliciting relatively high motivation among many if not most people (e.g., African Americans), some eliciting very low motivation (e.g., skinheads or pedophile priests), and others varying greatly across perceivers (e.g., gays or overweight people). When the motive is activated, how do perceivers attempt to control their biases? How successful are they in this endeavor? It is toward these questions that we now turn our attention.

COGNITIVE MECHANISMS OF PREJUDICE CONTROL

The seeming regularity of incidents of "unwitting" prejudice expression recently captured in the popular media notwithstanding, to be seen as prejudiced—in one's own eyes or in the eyes of others—is, at the very least, irksome to most individuals (Dovidio & Gaertner, 2004; Gaertner &

Dovidio, 1986). As such, individuals will often dispatch one or more regulatory strategies to insulate their thoughts and actions from the potential influence of bias. In this section, we consider several of these control strategies as well as their implications for the activation and application of mental associations and the expression of (non)discriminatory behavior. Before we plunge into our discussion of the cognitive mechanisms involved in controlling prejudice, however, we first give some attention to the collection of cognitive operations involved in bringing about any goal-relevant outcome.

EXECUTIVE FUNCTION AND SELF-REGULATION

In the opening section, we highlighted the factors believed to be responsible for the automatization of tendencies toward intergroup bias. However, we were also careful to note that (a) even if prejudicial associations are activated on encountering a particular social target, it is not inevitable that these activated associations will result in biased responding; and (b) under the right conditions, it is possible for social perceivers to control the initial activation of these associations. To better understand how perceivers are able to ward off the impact of automatically activated bias on their perceptions, judgments, and overt behaviors, it is first necessary to understand the vital role played by the mind's executive function in the realization of any regulatory objective.

The term *executive function* refers to the constellation of higher order cognitive processes involved in the planning, execution, and regulation of behavior. Among these processes are the selective activation of information that facilitates attainment of one's objectives, the active inhibition of interfering information, and the monitoring of one's progress toward attainment of these objectives, including the overriding of automatic responses that might otherwise thwart their attainment (Baddeley, 1986; Norman & Shallice, 1986). Evidence gathered from neuroscience research points to the prefrontal cortex and associated structures as the seat of executive functioning and self-regulation (Banfield, Wyland, Macrae, Münte, & Heatherton, 2004; MacDonald, Cohen, Stenger, & Carter, 2000; Richeson et al., 2003), with damage to these regions resulting in impairments on tasks requiring executive control (Shallice & Burgess, 1991). Executive function within psychology has traditionally been associated with research on the cognitive processing of relatively nonsocial information; undeniably, however, a great deal of planning, problem solving, and other forms of self-regulation takes place within social contexts. For this reason, social psychologists have recently begun to recognize the importance of executive functioning in social judgment and behavior (e.g., Bodenhausen, Todd, & Becker, 2007; Cunningham, Johnson, et al., 2004; Feldman Barrett, Tugade, & Engle, 2004; Macrae, Bodenhausen, Schloerscheidt, & Milne, 1999; Payne, 2001, 2005; Richeson & Trawalter, 2005; von Hippel & Gonsalkorale, 2005).

For instance, research by Payne (2001, 2005; see also Conrey, Sherman, Gawronski, Hugenberg, & Groom, 2005) has sought to examine the independent influences of automatically activated bias and executive control processes on a weapon-identification task. In this task, participants are presented with images of guns and tools and are asked to identify each object. Preceding the images are brief (but nonetheless visible) presentations of Black and White male faces. Thus, some trials consist of a stereotype-consistent pairing (i.e., White-tool, Black-gun), whereas others consist of a stereotype-inconsistent pairing (i.e., White-gun, Black-tool). With the aid of Jacoby's (1991) process dissociation procedure, Payne (2001, 2005) was able to estimate an automatic bias (A) parameter, which reflects an automatic association between Black and guns, and a control (C) parameter, which reflects an ability to respond based on the target information alone and thus to avoid the influence of race. Recently, Payne (2005) discovered that individuals' C parameter estimates were correlated with their performance on a measure of general executive ability (i.e., antisaccade task; see Kane, Bleckley, Conway, & Engle, 2001). In another study, Payne (2005) examined participants' impressions of a Black target as a function of their automatic bias and their ability to exert executive control over this bias. Somewhat unsurprisingly, he discovered that people's impressions became significantly more negative as their A increased. However, this was only true for participants with relatively poor cognitive control (i.e., low C). The impressions formed by individuals higher in C were significantly less affected by A, suggesting that highly proficient executive functioning can act as a buffer against the adverse effects of automatic biases on impression formation.

These individual differences in general executive capacity aside, it appears that executive functioning is also limited by the demands made of it. There is an abundance of evidence from both cognitive and social psychology that supports this contention. According to Norman and Shallice (1986), the executive function (or supervisory attention system in their terminology) is a limited-capacity resource that can only focus on a limited number of tasks at one time (see also Engle, Conway, Tuholski, & Shisler, 1995). Consequently, it is susceptible to overload in certain resource-demanding (e.g., dual-task, cognitive load) situations. Similarly, Baumeister and colleagues' self-regulatory strength model (e.g., Baumeister, Muraven, & Tice, 2000; Schmeichel & Baumeister, 2004) also holds that executive functioning draws on a limited resource, but unlike Norman and Shallice's (1986) model, which is concerned with impairments due to concurrent task demands, it focuses on impairments resulting from the consecutive expenditure of regulatory resources. Taken together, these models suggest that executive control resources are limited and, therefore, the efficacy of prejudice control efforts that rely on such resources will also be limited.

Thus far, we have discussed several sources of motivation for controlling prejudiced responding and the importance of executive functioning for achieving this control. Aside from having the motivation, ability, and opportunity to exert control over unwanted bias, people must also be aware of its potential emergence (e.g., Strack & Hannover, 1996). It is only after acknowledging the existence of such a possibility that one or more regulatory procedures can be deployed to counteract its influence. Assuming people are cognizant of the potential for bias and they are motivated and able to engage in a regulatory attempt, what types of regulatory strategies can people implement to control the initial activation of biased associations? How effective are these strategies?

CONTROLLING THE INITIAL ACTIVATION OF BIASED ASSOCIATIONS

As previously noted, some theorists have asserted that the automatic activation of stereotypic mental associations on encountering a relevant group member is unavoidable (Allport, 1954; Bargh, 1999; Devine, 1989). Recently, however, researchers have accumulated evidence showing that even the initial activation of biased associations will fluctuate as a function of chronic individual differences (e.g., Kawakami et al., 1998; Lepore & Brown, 1997), contextual variation (e.g., Barden et al., 2004; Wittenbrink et al., 2001), temporary processing goals (e.g., Macrae et al., 1997; Wheeler & Fiske, 2005), and strategic debiasing attempts (e.g., Galinsky & Moskowitz, 2000; Kawakami, Dovidio, Moll, Hermsen, & Russin, 2000). In this section, we focus on the last of these potential moderators of bias activation. In doing so, we highlight several deliberately enacted regulatory strategies and discuss the cognitive mechanisms involved in each.

One of the most well-studied bias regulation procedures, stereotype suppression, involves the deliberate attempt by perceivers to deny the entrance of prejudicial or stereotypic thoughts into consciousness (Bodenhausen & Macrae, 1998; Macrae, Bodenhausen, Milne, & Jetten, 1994; Monteith, Sherman, & Devine, 1998). Wegner's (1994) general model of mental control offers an appropriate point of departure for considering the mechanisms involved in stereotype suppression. This model posits that the decision to engage in thought suppression initiates two separate cognitive processes. The first is a monitoring process that inspects the mental landscape for traces of the to-be-avoided thought. If any are detected, a second operating process is engaged; its job is to direct attention away from the unwanted thought by actively seeking distracter items. Whereas the monitoring process is hypothesized to function relatively effortlessly, the operating process is presumed to be much more effortful in that an abundant supply of cognitive resources is necessary for its successful execution. Consequently, any concurrent demand on a perceiver's attentional resources will severely diminish the effectiveness of the operating process, essentially leaving the resource-independent monitoring process running unattended. In its attempt to detect unwanted thoughts, the monitoring process necessarily activates—at some (preconscious) level—these thoughts as criteria on which to base its search. As a result, these thoughts are primed repeatedly such that they become more accessible than if no suppression attempt had been made (Wegner & Erber, 1992). In other words, even though the act of thought suppression (and stereotype suppression in particular) is undoubtedly initiated with the best of intentions, ironically, it can lead to the hyperaccessibility of the to-be-suppressed thoughts.

A substantial body of research has documented the unintended consequences associated with stereotype suppression (for a review, see Monteith et al., 1998). In one of the first demonstrations of stereotype hyperaccessibility following stereotype suppression, Macrae et al. (1994) had participants compose a "day-in-the-life" essay about a skinhead under one of two sets of task instructions: stereotype suppression versus control. Following the essay task, participants' accessibility for skinhead-relevant stereotypes was assessed using a lexical decision task. Consistent with Wegner's (1994) theorizing, stereotype suppressors exhibited significantly greater stereotype activation than control participants, a clear rebound effect. More recently, research by Payne, Lambert, and Jacoby (2002) examined the influence of a "prejudice avoidance" goal on participants' performance on a weapon-identification task (Payne, 2001). In this study, some of the participants were instructed to "try not to let the race of the face influence your decisions" (Payne et al., 2002, p. 388), whereas others were given no further instructions.[2] Results indicated that stereotype-consistent errors were more likely than stereotype-inconsistent errors in both conditions. Furthermore, this difference was stronger in the "avoid race" condition than in the control condition, suggesting once again that deliberate attempts to suppress biased associations often lead to exacerbated bias.

Considered as a whole, the literature on stereotype suppression paints a less than favorable picture of its viability as a self-regulatory strategy for overcoming the activation of unwanted associations. However, other research suggests that, under the right conditions, perceivers may be able to eschew suppression's ironic effects (Monteith et al., 1998). For instance, Gollwitzer, Trotschel, and Sumner (2002; cited in Gollwitzer, Fujita, & Oettingen, 2004) found that when suppression instructions were accompanied by a specific implementation intention ("When I see a person from group X, I tell myself: Don't stereotype!"), no rebound effects emerged.

Although stereotype suppression may be the most intuitively appealing bias control strategy, several others have proven more successful, at least with respect to the initial activation of prejudicial associations. One such strategy, perspective taking, involves the active attempt by perceivers to imagine the thoughts, feelings, and experiences of a social target. Because perspective taking does not entail the active suppression of unwanted associations, it should be less vulnerable to ironic rebound effects. Galinsky and Moskowitz (2000) tested this hypothesis by pitting stereotype suppression and perspective taking against each other. Adopting the procedure of Macrae and colleagues (1994), they discovered that whereas participants instructed to suppress stereotypes regarding a stereotyped group member (i.e., an elderly man) exhibited increased stereotype activation, those instructed to adopt the perspective of this target showed no evidence of stereotype hyperaccessibility. In fact, stereotype accessibility among perspective takers was no different from that of a group of control participants who were never exposed to the target. Furthermore, Galinsky and Moskowitz (2000) found that the mechanism responsible for decreased stereotype activation among perspective takers was an increase in self–target overlap, wherein the perspective taker's mental representation of the target is merged with his or her own self-representation (Davis, Conklin, Smith, & Luce, 1996).

Another strategy aimed at reducing the activation of negative associations is stereotype negation training. In a series of studies, Kawakami and her colleagues (2000) found that individuals given extensive practice at negating stereotypes exhibited a subsequent reduction in stereotype activation. The training itself consisted of a number of trials in which participants were presented with pictures of a Black or White person paired with a stereotype-consistent or stereotype-inconsistent word.

---

[2] The study by Payne and colleagues (2002) also had a condition in which participants were asked to "use the race of the faces to help you identify the gun or tool in question" (p. 388). Task performance in the "use race" condition was nearly identical to that of the "avoid race" condition, suggesting that making race salient increases the tendency to make stereotype-consistent errors.

Participants' task was to respond "no" on trials consisting of a Black or White person paired with a stereotype-consistent word and to respond "yes" on trials consisting of a Black or White person paired with a stereotype-inconsistent word. Prior to the training session, participants were presented with a sequential priming task (see Blair & Banaji, 1996) to obtain baseline levels of stereotype activation. Following the training session, participants completed this same sequential priming task. Results suggested a significant effect of the negation training on stereotype activation: Whereas participants' pretraining scores on the sequential priming task were indicative of stereotype activation, this pattern of biased responding was no longer evident following the training session. What's more, this reduction in stereotype activation was still evident 24 hours after the training session.

Because the training program of Kawakami and colleagues (2000) consisted of both negation (responding "no" to a stereotype-consistent pairing) and affirmation (responding "yes" to a stereotype-inconsistent pairing) trials, it is unclear what the mechanism driving their effects is. Although it is possible that repeatedly responding "no" to stereotype-consistent pairs may have diminished the strength of stereotypic associations, it is also possible that repeatedly responding "yes" to stereotype-inconsistent pairs led to the formation of new, nonstereotypic associations (cf. Blair & Banaji, 1996). In a recent test of these two possibilities, Gawronski, Deutsch, Mbirkou, Seibt, and Strack (2008) presented participants with a series of trials consisting of stereotypic and counterstereotypic target-word pairs. Half of the participants were instructed to respond "no" to stereotypic pairs and to give no response to the counterstereotypic pairs (negation training). The remaining participants were given the opposite instructions: Respond "yes" to counterstereotypic pairs and show no response to stereotypic pairs (affirmation training). Results indicated that whereas the affirmation training led to a reduction in stereotype activation (Study 1) and automatic evaluations (Study 2; see also Olson & Fazio, 2006), the negation training actually led to an increase in these associations. In other research looking at the affirmation of counterstereotypes, Blair, Ma, and Lenton (2001) found that participants instructed to spend several minutes creating a mental image of a strong woman exhibited a reduction in automatic stereotype activation, as compared to those asked to create a neutral image (see also Blair & Banaji, 1996; Dasgupta & Greenwald, 2001).

Finally, recent research by Sassenberg and Moskowitz (2005) found that priming individuals with a "creative" mindset (i.e., "describe three situations in which you behaved creatively") reduces automatic stereotype activation. Employing a lexical decision task with sequential priming, they found that whereas individuals primed with a "thoughtful" mindset (i.e., "describe three situations in which you behaved thoughtfully") were quicker in responding to stereotypic concepts related to African Americans following African American (vs. European American) face primes, those instilled with a "creative" mindset did not exhibit this activation pattern. To account for their findings, Sassenberg and Moskowitz (2005) argue that "[b]eing creative implies, by definition, the attempt to avoid the conventional routes of thinking and, therefore, the avoidance of the activation of typical associations" (p. 507). Taken together, the research reviewed here suggests that negation-focused strategies (e.g., suppression and negation training) may be less effective than strategies that promote broader thinking (e.g., perspective taking, affirmation training, counterstereotypic mental imagery, and "creative" mindsets).

CAN THE INHIBITION OF BIASED ASSOCIATIONS BECOME AUTOMATIZED?

At one time, self-regulation was considered to be largely effortful, conscious, and deliberative. However, researchers have since come to recognize the ways in which regulatory processes can become automatized, requiring little to no cognitive deliberation for their implementation and even occurring outside of a person's conscious awareness (Bargh, 1990; Moskowitz, 2001). For instance, Bargh's (1990) auto-motive model argues that temporary goals can become chronic, relatively automatic ones if they are frequently and consistently pursued. That is, the repeated pairing of a particular goal with a goal-triggering stimulus should, over time, lead to the goal's automatic activation on exposure to that stimulus. Applying this logic to the domain of prejudice regulation, it is possible that a frequent and consistent pairing of the goal of "being an egalitarian person" and the presence of a stereotyped group member (i.e., goal-triggering stimulus) could eventually result in the automatic initiation of this goal whenever a relevant group member is encountered (cf. Bargh & Gollwitzer, 1994).

In a recent test of this hypothesis, Moskowitz, Salomon, and Taylor (2000) found that individuals with chronic egalitarian goals were more likely than nonchronics to show heightened activation of egalitarian concepts following African American face primes. In another study using a word pronunciation task, Moskowitz et al. (2000) found that whereas nonchronics were faster in pronouncing stereotypic concepts following an African American face prime than a European American face prime, those with the chronic goal of being egalitarian displayed no evidence of stereotype activation—they were equally fast in their pronunciations of stereotypic concepts following African American and European American face primes (see also Moskowitz, Gollwitzer, Wasel, & Schaal, 1999). Moskowitz and colleagues (Moskowitz et al., 1999; Moskowitz et al., 2000) argue that because their measures assessed responses at speeds at which conscious control is not possible (cf. Neely, 1977), individuals with chronic egalitarian goals were exhibiting preconscious control of stereotype activation.

More recently, research employing neuroscience techniques has provided suggestive evidence for the automatization of bias regulation (Amodio et al., 2004; Cunningham, Johnson, et al., 2004). For example, Amodio et al. (2004) found that stereotype-consistent errors (i.e., mistaking a tool for a gun following an African American face prime) on Payne's (2001) weapon-identification task were associated with an event-related negativity (ERN) brain wave generated in the anterior cingulate gyrus. This area of the brain is believed to be involved in conflict detection, an important prerequisite for initiating executive control (see Botvinick, Braver, Barch, Carter, & Cohen, 2001). Moreover, it was those participants who showed the highest ERNs who exhibited the greatest amount of cognitive control (i.e., C parameter estimates) on the weapon-identification task. Thus, it appears that—at least for certain individuals—the commission of stereotype-consistent errors sets off an "alarm," signaling the need for control processes. This is consistent with theorizing by Monteith and colleagues (Monteith, Ashburn-Nardo, Voils, & Czopp, 2002), who posit that to effectively control bias, individuals must first develop a sensitivity to environmental cues that signal the potential for bias and thus the need for control.

Taken together, these findings suggest that perceivers may be able to inhibit biased associations automatically. In light of Bargh's (1990) auto-motive model, it seems that the frequent and consistent pairing of control goals (e.g., nonbiased responding) with goal-relevant stimuli (e.g., the presence of bias-eliciting group members) is the most tenable route to automatizing the bias reduction process. Indeed, the affirmation training study by Gawronski and colleagues (2008) reported earlier suggests that the frequent and consistent pairing of stereotype-inconsistent concepts with Black faces does lead to a reduction in the activation of stereotypes and negative evaluations. Although this study offers a compelling empirical demonstration of reduced stereotype activation, its practical implications for regulating stereotype activation in real-world contexts are still uncertain—an issue to which we return in the final section of the chapter.

CONTROLLING THE APPLICATION OF BIASED ASSOCIATIONS

From the preceding sections it should be obvious that the automatic activation of biased associations on encountering a relevant group member is far from inevitable. Nevertheless, we concede that the initial activation of these associations represents the default and inhibition the exception. Assuming, then, that perceivers do activate unwanted associations, what regulatory strategies might they employ to counteract the influence of these associations on their judgments and behavior? In this section, we consider three potential strategies—correction, individuation, and recategorization—and discuss the viability of each. Once again, the implementation of any of these strategies requires that perceivers be aware of the potential for bias and that they have sufficient motivation and (executive) capacity.

On detection of the potential for unwanted bias, people may strategically try to correct for its influence (e.g., Wegener & Petty, 1997; Wilson & Brekke, 1994). According to Wegener and Petty's (1997) flexible correction model, perceivers rely on their naive theories to determine the direction and magnitude of potential bias. From here, they actively attempt to remove the influence of the bias by adjusting their judgments and overt responses in a direction opposite and in an amount proportionate to the presumed bias. For example, a male math instructor may have a theory that negative stereotypes about female math students could cause him to underestimate their classroom contributions. To correct for this (perceived) bias, the math instructor may respond to the class participation of female students with effusive praise. Although it is possible that perceivers can effectively correct for bias, this example offers an illustration of how a miscalibrated correction attempt could actually backfire—the effusiveness of the praise may be viewed as disingenuous by its recipients. Thus, unless perceivers are skillful enough to identify precisely the magnitude of their bias, they are vulnerable to both under- and overcorrection (Wegener & Petty, 1995).

Another strategy for overcoming unwanted biases involves shifting the categorical basis of one's impressions and judgments from a proscribed category to one that is more socially "permissible." This recategorization can take several forms. For instance, perceivers might recategorize a target by accessing a desirable subtype of an initial category. Alternatively, they might call on a more self-inclusive or superordinate category. A notable example of this latter type of recategorization can be found in Gaertner and Dovidio's (2000) common ingroup identity model, which proposes that increasing the salience of a shared identity among members of different groups should lead to more favorable intergroup judgments and interactions. More specifically, this model contends that if members of different groups come to see themselves as members of a more inclusive, superordinate group, then beliefs about and actions toward (former) outgroup members should start to resemble those regarding the ingroup. According to this model, perceivers who wish to avoid unwanted biases could seek out and accentuate categorical identities they share with targets, essentially focusing on what they have in common.

One means of achieving this common ingroup identity is through perspective taking (Dovidio et al., 2004). Research has shown that adopting another's perspective fosters a self–target merging whereby one's cognitive representations of targets become more "self-like" and self-representations become more "other-like" (Davis et al., 1996; Galinsky, Ku, & Wang, 2005; Galinsky & Moskowitz, 2000). With this shift in cognitive representations comes a reduction in the salience of intergroup boundaries, which, in turn, should reduce the possibility that targets will be considered in terms of the negative stereotypes associated with their groups. Indeed, studies have shown that perspective taking does lead to decreases in both the activation (as described above) and the application of stereotypic associations (Galinsky & Moskowitz, 2000). Furthermore, in circumstances in which the target's social group membership is salient, the same ingroup benefits extended to targets should also get extended to other members of the target's social group—an "ingroup–outgroup merging" (Batson et al., 1997; Dovidio et al., 2004; Vescio, Sechrist, & Paolucci, 2003).

Finally, perceivers may evade the influence of unwanted associations by considering a target's personal attributes (i.e., individuation). That is, rather than focusing on just one categorical dimension (e.g., ethnicity) and its mental associates, perceivers might instead try to take into account other identity dimensions, such as gender, occupation, personality traits, or other perceptually salient characteristics. Attending to multiple aspects of a target's identity simultaneously should give rise to more complex, integrated (i.e., personalized) impressions that are less likely to be dominated by unwanted mental associations (Bodenhausen, Macrae, & Sherman, 1999; Brewer, 1988; Fiske & Neuberg, 1990). According to Fiske and Neuberg's (1990) continuum model of impression formation, stereotypic responses and individuated responses represent opposite ends of a continuum, with the major difference being that individuated responses result from considering the unique constellation of targets' attributes and stereotypic responses from considering only a single category as a basis for target construal (see also Bodenhausen et al., 1999). It should be noted, however, that individuation is not always feasible. In many circumstances (e.g., minimal encounters), perceivers have little more than targets' demographic characteristics on which to rely, making individuated impressions. Clearly, the efficacy of this strategy depends on the availability of target information.

In sum, the presence of members of culturally devalued groups often triggers the activation of stereotypical thoughts and negative evaluations. The expression of these beliefs and emotional reactions, however, is certainly not obligatory. Rather, a number of factors ranging from individuals' goals and motivations, their executive capacity, and their affective reactions to features of the particular group members present serve to shape the extent to which biased beliefs are expressed. Furthermore, recent research suggests that both chronic motivation and counterstereotype affirmation training can undermine the activation of stereotypical thoughts and prejudiced evaluations. Although the demonstration of such processes is critical to our understanding of how individuals can control biases and become truly nonprejudiced individuals should they aspire to do so, it is equally important to consider the situations and contexts in which bias activation and expression are likely to play out. We turn to this issue in the third, and final, section of the chapter.

SOCIAL CONTEXTS OF CONTROL

In the previous section on mechanisms of control, the majority of processes reviewed pertain to situations in which individuals are alone and have been confronted with cues or information suggesting that the judgments they are currently making could be influenced by prejudice. But what situational factors make control more or less feasible? How do control efforts translate into behavior with members of culturally devalued groups? Although extant research has found that control efforts can undermine both the activation and expression of bias in judgments of members of culturally devalued groups, less attention has been paid to how such efforts influence behavior during intergroup interactions. Furthermore, what facets of larger social and societal contexts are likely to facilitate the control processes outlined in the previous section? To address these concerns, in this final section of the chapter we consider the roles that various social contexts play in the control of intergroup bias. Specifically, we examine the control (and, thus, the expression) of intergroup bias in interpersonal interactions and larger situational and societal contexts.

INTERPERSONAL INTERACTIONS

Unlike any other social context, contact with outgroup members presents a high-stakes situation for the expression of bias. Recently, researchers have begun to examine the extent to which Whites and other members of dominant, high-status groups behave in biased ways during intergroup interactions with renewed interest. This research suggests that relevant relational concerns become active during interethnic interactions, at least for some members of dominant groups (see Shelton & Richeson, 2006). In other words, this new wave of research has found that interracial interactions arouse concerns about appearing prejudiced in members of dominant groups (Vorauer, Hunter, Main, & Roy, 2000). Vorauer et al. (2000) reported, for instance, that meta-stereotypical concepts such as "prejudiced," "biased," and "selfish" became active for Whites when they expected to have an interaction with an ethnic minority, but not with another White interaction partner. In other words, in addition to the activation of stereotypes, expecting to interact with an outgroup member also seems to trigger concerns about how one will be evaluated by that outgroup interaction partner (for reviews, see Shelton & Richeson, 2006; Vorauer, 2006).

How do concerns about appearing prejudiced influence the dynamics of intergroup interactions? Concerns about appearing prejudiced can result in quite varied behavior both in anticipation of, as well as during, intergroup interactions. Specifically, concerns can result in more approach-related behavior or, ironically, in more avoidant behavior. For instance, one way to reduce the possibility of appearing prejudiced is simply to avoid interracial contact all together (Snyder, Kleck, Strenta,

& Mentzer, 1979). Consistent with this line of reasoning, Plant and colleagues (Plant, 2004) found that individuals who are motivated to respond without prejudice for primarily external reasons (e.g., politically correct norms), rather than out of internal motivations and concerns (e.g., their values), are particularly likely to avoid interracial contact.

Even when interactions are not avoidable, however, concerns about appearing prejudiced can arouse avoidant behavior during the interaction. For instance, Goff, Steele, and Davies (2005) found that White participants sat farther away from a Black interaction partner when they believed they would discuss racial profiling, rather than love and relationships. Further, the more prejudice-related concepts (i.e., metastereotypes) associated with White Americans (e.g., racist, bigoted) were activated for these participants, the farther away they sat. In other words, these participants' concerns about being perceived as prejudiced led them to distance themselves from their potential Black interaction partner.

Rather than yielding avoidant behavior, however, concerns about prejudice can also result in more prosocial behavior. For many White individuals, concerns about appearing prejudiced motivate egalitarian behavior during interactions with ethnic minorities (Dunton & Fazio, 1997). For instance, Shelton (2003) examined the effects of explicit instructions to avoid prejudice on White individuals' behavior during interracial interactions. Interestingly, although Whites who were instructed to avoid prejudice reported that they felt quite anxious during the interaction, analyses of their nonverbal behavior revealed that they behaved less anxiously (they fidgeted less) than White participants who were not instructed to avoid prejudice. Thus, although participants felt more anxious during the interaction, their motivation (or, perhaps, determination) not to appear prejudiced was seemingly able to shunt the behavioral expression of their anxiety. In turn, Shelton also found that Black interaction partners liked Whites who were instructed to avoid appearing prejudiced more than they liked Whites who were not attempting to avoid appearing prejudiced.

Interestingly, research suggests that a conscious motivation to behave in nonprejudiced ways can moderate the influence that implicit evaluations are likely to have on behavior, even when those automatic associations are largely negative. Dasgupta and Rivera (2006) found, for instance, that participants with high levels of implicit antigay bias behaved no differently during interactions with gay men than participants lower in antigay bias, if they held nontraditional, egalitarian beliefs about gender roles. In other words, individuals' desire to behave in egalitarian ways was able to override the influence that negative implicit attitudes typically have on behavior.

Moreover, recent work suggests that motivation to respond without prejudice can completely reverse the relation between attitudes and behavior. That is, preoccupation with controlling prejudice can lead low-prejudice individuals to behave more negatively during intergroup interactions and high-prejudice individuals to behave less negatively. This hypothesis stems from work on choking under pressure, noting that monitoring and controlling behavior tends to disrupt the performance of experts, but enhance the performance of novices (Baumeister, 1984; Beilock & Carr, 2001). Because prejudice concerns trigger the monitoring and control of behavior (Monteith, 1993; Monteith et al., 2002), they are likely to disrupt the expression of positive behavior by low-prejudice individuals (relative experts), but enhance the expression of positive behavior by high-prejudice individuals (relative novices). Consistent with the choking hypothesis, Vorauer and Turpie (2004) found that low-prejudice White participants displayed fewer intimacy-building behaviors toward First Nations interaction partners when concerns about being perceived as prejudiced were heightened for them, compared with control participants for whom such concerns had not been made salient. Similarly, Shelton, Richeson, Salvatore, and Trawalter (2005) found that during an interaction that involved discussing race-related topics with a Black partner and, thus, activated Whites' concerns about appearing prejudiced, Whites with lower levels of automatic racial bias were less engaged (as judged by their interaction partners) than Whites with higher levels of automatic racial bias. Taken together, this work suggests that attempts to control bias can bring out the best behavior in more biased individuals, but also undermine the successful communication of egalitarian behavior by those lower in bias.

Verbal Versus Nonverbal Behavior

Much as our understanding of bias has shifted to consider attitudes and beliefs that are explicitly acknowledged as separable from those that individuals are either unable or unwilling to report (automatic or implicit beliefs and evaluations), our understanding of behavioral manifestations of bias during intergroup interactions has shifted to consider both overt, often verbal, components and subtle, often nonverbal, components of behavior. Indeed, recent work suggests that the control of stereotyping and prejudice during interracial interactions may be limited to the behaviors that individuals are actually able to control. Specifically, motivation can shape behavior when people have both the opportunity and sufficient psychosocial resources to consider various courses of action. Consequently, efforts to control bias are typically reflected in behaviors that are relatively controllable, such as judgments regarding how favorably a Black or gay job candidate is evaluated (Dovidio et al., 1997). By contrast, efforts to control the influence of bias often fail to influence behavior that is relatively difficult to monitor and control. For instance, although explicit judgments of a Black or gay job candidate may be quite positive, the manner or quality with which nonstigmatized individuals interact with that job candidate may reveal their biased attitudes. In other words, individuals may not rate Black and White job candidates differently, but they are likely to behave more negatively toward Black candidates, as assessed by nonverbal measures of interest (e.g., eye contact), anxiety (rate of blinking), and friendliness (e.g., smiling and nodding), compared to their behavior with White candidates (Dovidio, Kawakami, & Gaertner, 2002; Dovidio et al., 1997; Fazio, Jackson, Dunton, & Williams, 1995; Hebl & Kleck, 2000; McConnell & Liebold, 2001).

Rather than resulting in either more positive or negative behavior, therefore, concerns about appearing prejudiced may contribute to mixed messages during intergroup interactions. Specifically, efforts to control the expression of bias during interracial interactions are likely to result in relatively positive verbal messages, but also in more negative nonverbal behaviors. Research has shown that such mixed messages are apt to result in miscommunications during intergroup interactions, wherein majority and minority interaction partners have very different experiences (Dovidio et al., 2002; Shelton, Dovidio, Hebl, & Richeson, in press). Specifically, Dovidio and colleagues (2002) found that White participants of an interracial interaction judged their behavior based on the positivity of their verbal messages, whereas the Black participants of the interactions judged their White partners based on the positivity of their nonverbal messages. Hence, after interactions in which White participants' verbal behavior was relatively positive but their nonverbal behavior was relatively negative, the White participant is likely to exit the interaction thinking that it went quite well, but the Black partner will leave thinking that it went quite poorly. To the extent that the divergence of verbal and nonverbal behavior results from concerns about appearing prejudiced, such concerns may prove to hinder effective communication between members of low- and high-status sociocultural groups. Perhaps, furthermore, this is one mechanism through which intergroup divides regarding the state of race relations in the United States are maintained (Shelton et al., in press).

Affective and Cognitive Consequences of Control

In addition to affecting behavior during intergroup interactions, individuals' concerns that they will express prejudice are certain also to contribute to their affective experiences during intergroup interactions. A growing body of work now supports the notion that Whites' concerns with appearing prejudiced often contribute to negative affective reactions during interracial encounters (Plant & Devine, 1998, 2003). As mentioned previously, Whites who were instructed to try not to be prejudiced during an interaction with a Black partner reported experiencing more anxiety compared to those who were not given these instructions (Shelton, 2003). Similarly, Vorauer, Main, and O'Connell (1998) found that the more Whites thought that a First Nations interaction partner expected them to be prejudiced, the more negative their feelings about the upcoming interaction, and the lower their self-esteem after the interaction. Taken together, these findings suggest that nonstigmatized individuals' prejudice concerns can have deleterious consequences for their affective experiences in anticipation of, during, and after, interracial interactions.

Concerns about appearing prejudiced can also result in a number of important cognitive outcomes. Individuals are known to carefully monitor their thoughts, feelings, and behaviors to avoid being perceived as prejudiced (Monteith, 1993). Recent research has found, however, that such regulation of thoughts, feelings, and behavior is cognitively demanding, and, thus, can result in the temporary depletion of important cognitive resources (Richeson et al., 2003; Richeson & Shelton, 2003; Trawalter & Richeson, 2006). To illustrate this phenomenon, Richeson and Trawalter (2005) heightened the prejudice concerns of White individuals prior to an interethnic interaction. Specifically, after completing an implicit measure of racial bias, Whites were told either, "most people are more prejudiced than they think they are" (prejudice feedback condition), or "most people perform worse than they think they did" (control condition). They then made comments on a number of somewhat controversial topics, including racial profiling, with either a same-race or cross-race experimenter, and then completed the Stroop color-naming task to measure cognitive functioning. Results revealed that after an interracial interaction, participants who received the prejudice feedback performed significantly worse on the Stroop task than participants who received the performance feedback. This same feedback did not influence participants' performance on the Stroop task after a same-race interaction. In other words, this research suggests that concerns about behaving in prejudiced or stereotypical ways during intergroup interactions can tax individuals' cognitive resources, leaving them less able to manage the challenging cognitive tasks that they may face subsequently (see also Richeson & Shelton, 2007).

INSTITUTIONAL AND CULTURAL CONTEXTS

Although intergroup interaction is certainly a potent trigger of prejudice control, the frequency with which individuals participate in this setting is relatively low, in part due to the persistence of residential segregation. Hence, it is important to consider the roles of larger social and societal contexts in shaping the control of bias. Specifically, how do social norms, cultural ideologies, and diverse contexts influence the activation and control (if necessary) of biased thoughts?

Social Norms

Given the relative infrequency of intergroup contact, how can we account for the rapid decline of incidents of explicit, overt bias in North America? One explanation is the role that the social context often plays in constraining behavior. When overt discrimination is prohibited under the law or discouraged by norms in a particular context or situation, individuals are unlikely to respond in an overtly prejudicial fashion (but see also Pager, 2003). Consistent with this perspective, in a study of employment discrimination against gay men and lesbians, Hebl, Foster, Mannix, and Dovidio (2002) found no evidence of bias in formal actions made by potential employers. Employers, for instance, did not discriminate against confederates portrayed as gay or lesbian on formal employment behaviors, such as permission to complete a job application and callbacks for further consideration. Bias was revealed, however, in the more spontaneous (less controllable) aspects of employers' behaviors; they spent less time, used fewer words, and smiled less when interacting with the gay applicants compared with presumed heterosexual applicants. In a similar study involving obese and average-weight female confederates who sought help in a clothing store, customer service representatives revealed no evidence of formal discrimination against the obese female confederates, but they behaved in ways that communicated subtle bias, such as smiling less, displaying less direct eye contact, and ending the interactions prematurely (King, Hebl, Shapiro, Singletary, & Turner, 2006).

Although social norms can indeed result in more egalitarian behavior, the pressure to behave in nonprejudiced ways because of contextual pressure can also backfire. For instance, Monin and Miller (2001) argued that alleviating the pressure to respond without prejudice can actually lead individuals to behave in more biased ways subsequently. Specifically, they first allowed individuals to respond to a series of sexist statements in a manner that affirmed their antisexist attitudes. After, these participants responded to a scenario in which they had the opportunity to recommend a female or a male candidate for a traditionally male occupation. Results revealed that participants who had been given the opportunity to affirm their antisexist attitudes earlier in the study were less likely to recommend the woman for the position, compared to participants who had not been given the opportunity to affirm their antisexist attitudes. In other words, participants who were able to credential themselves as nonprejudiced were subsequently more likely to discriminate, compared with participants who were not able to demonstrate their nonprejudiced credentials.

In addition to the unintended effects of credentialing, the societal change that has made explicit and overt forms of prejudice toward many culturally devalued groups unacceptable may have unwittingly resulted in a tendency to deny that discrimination is still a problem in modern U.S. society. Indeed, rather than expressing compunction after making comments that could be construed as prejudiced, some individuals and their supporters simply state that their actions were not prejudiced. Consistent with this sentiment, there is a growing debate regarding whether the automatic activation of stereotypes and negative evaluations should be construed as bias or prejudice (Arkes & Tetlock, 2004). Although such a discussion is beyond the scope of this chapter, research suggests that the denial of discrimination offers a means by which individuals are able to protect their self-concepts from the threat of being prejudiced (Adams, Tormala, & O'Brien, 2006). Presumably, because thinking about prejudice evokes feelings of collective guilt for, and threatens the egalitarian self-concepts of, many nonstigmatized group members (Doosje, Branscombe, Spears, & Manstead, 1998), they minimize the presence of discrimination. Clearly, denying discrimination to avoid appearing (or feeling) prejudiced is not the best recipe for actually reducing prejudice.

External pressure to control prejudice can also result in responses to outgroup members that are more, rather than less, biased. For instance, Plant and Devine (2001) found that externally motivated individuals often feel constrained and bothered by pressure to be politically correct. When pressured to comply with such norms, they respond with increased negativity toward members of stigmatized groups and with angry or threatened affect. Lambert and colleagues (Lambert et al., 2003) found, furthermore, that public pressure to respond to an automatic stereotyping task in egalitarian ways resulted in the expression of greater bias. They argued that public pressure increased participants' physiological arousal, which, in turn, facilitated their dominant responses to members of devalued groups on the task. Consequently, the expression of implicit stereotypical biases on the task was more pronounced when individuals completed it in public rather than in private. Taken together, this research suggests that the social context can both increase, as well as attenuate, biased responding, but on some occasions the restriction of overt bias ironically may serve to undermine individuals' ability to behave in egalitarian ways.

Diversity Ideology

The research reviewed thus far reveals the profound influence that social contexts can have on prejudice control. In many, if not most countries and cultures, prejudice is a societal problem and, thus, in need of addressing at the societal level. Indeed, the rise of the modern civil rights movement in North America brought about many prescriptions for how to resolve anti-Black prejudice that were espoused by national public officials as well as influential nongovernmental figures. One response to prejudice and intergroup tension, especially when it involves interethnic or ethno-religious bias, has been the advocacy of models of diversity that reduce the importance and salience of social categories. Indeed, a colorblind ideology regarding racial and ethnic relations has gained preeminence in U.S. society, often explicitly communicated and affirmed in organizational contexts as varied as elementary schools and corporate workplaces (Plaut & Markus, 2005). Colorblind ideologies, by definition, deemphasize the importance of different cultural perspectives that are linked to racial or ethnic group membership in favor of thinking of people as individuals. By contrast, multicultural ideologies acknowledge and appreciate both the cultural differences between, as well as the similarities among, members of different groups.

Recent research has begun to examine the relations among colorblind and multicultural models of diversity and racial bias. Although the literature is somewhat mixed regarding the efficacy of colorblindness (Park & Judd, 2005; Wolsko, Park, Judd, & Wittenbrink, 2000), research largely suggests that the endorsement of multiculturalism predicts more positive racial attitudes, at least for members of culturally valued groups (Plaut, 2007; Richeson & Nussbaum, 2004; Verkuyten, 2005; Wolsko et al., 2000). Wolsko et al. (2000) found, for instance, that exposure to a statement endorsing a multicultural perspective on race relations led to less ingroup favoritism among White participants on a stereotyping task, compared with exposure to a statement endorsing a color-blind perspective. Similarly, Richeson and Nussbaum (2004) exposed Whites to the same prompts and found that exposure to the multiculturalism prompt led to the expression of less automatic racial bias against both African Americans (Richeson & Nussbaum, 2004) and Asian Americans (Richeson, Trawalter, & Nussbaum, 2007), compared with exposure to the colorblind prompt (but see Smyth & Nosek, 2007). Moreover, Verkuyten (2005) found that Dutch individuals for whom multiculturalism was salient derogated Turkish individuals in the Netherlands less than Dutch individuals for whom assimilation (colorblindness) was salient. To the extent that colorblindness is endorsed as a strategy to avoid intergroup conflict, this research suggests that prejudice may be exacerbated rather than attenuated.

Consistent with this possibility, recent research suggests that colorblindness may result in negative, inefficient communication during intergroup interactions. For instance, Norton, Sommers, Apfelbaum, Pura, and Ariely (2006) videotaped White participants playing a modified version of the "Guess Who?" game with either a White or Black confederate partner. The goal of the game was to guess which photo from an array consisting of individuals who differed by race, gender, and age (among other dimensions) the confederate had chosen by asking as few "yes" or "no" questions as possible. On the critical trials, the array consisted of 50% White and 50% Black individuals, and thus the most efficient strategy was to ask about the race of the target. Results suggested, however, that participants were significantly less willing to ask about the race of the target when they played the game with a Black partner compared to with a White partner. Furthermore, the extent to which participants were reluctant to ask about race was significantly correlated with their endorsement of a colorblind ideology regarding race relations. In other words, participants who believed that it is appropriate to behave in a colorblind manner with racial minorities persisted in doing so even when faced with a task that was ill suited for such colorblind behavior.

Interestingly, Norton et al. (2006) also found that the more individuals behaved in a colorblind way, the less positive was their nonverbal behavior during interracial interactions. Similarly, Leyens, Demoulin, Désert, Vaes, and Philippot (2002) found that prompting White students in Belgium to behave in a colorblind way with a Black photographer, rather than suggesting that they be "color-conscious," resulted in less effective communication of emotion. Specifically, participants were asked to pose several emotions for either a Black or a White photographer. White students in Belgium who were told to be colorblind experienced greater anxiety and appeared less friendly when they posed emotions for the Black, but not the White, photographer. Similar to the results of the Norton et al. (2006) study, Leyens et al. (2002) proposed that the cognitive effort and uneasiness associated with inhibiting biased responses in the colorblind condition led participants who typically do not express high levels of prejudice toward Blacks to appear less open and friendly with a Black person. Taken together, these results suggest that concerns about appearing prejudiced give rise to colorblind approaches to intergroup interaction that can result in awkward behavior, which may be interpreted as bias by ethnic minority interaction partners.[3]

---

[3] Research also suggests that colorblind approaches to interracial contact can threaten the self-concepts of members of ethnic minority groups (Plaut & Markus, 2005; Verkuyten, 2005), which, of course, is also unlikely to result in positive intergroup relations.

Diverse Environments

Just like efforts to control the expression of bias will always be suboptimal to situations in which biased thoughts and evaluations were never activated to begin with, we believe it important in this chapter to devote some attention to the role of diverse environments in undermining prejudice and discrimination. Why are diverse environments helpful in undermining biased responding? There is compelling evidence to suggest that increased, interpersonal interaction across group lines substantially attenuates biased attitudes as well as automatic negative emotional and physiological reactions to outgroup members, especially for members of dominant cultural groups (Blascovich, Mendes, Hunter, Lickel, & Kowai-Bell, 2001; Pettigrew & Tropp, 2006).

In addition to these established effects on attitudes, however, diverse environments can shape as well as alter automatic stereotypes and attitudes regarding members of socially important groups. Recall our previous discussion of the effects of counterstereotypical outgroup members on the activation and application of stereotypes. Specifically, research has consistently found more positive attitude and stereotype activation in response to counterstereotypical exemplars of devalued groups (Blair et al., 2001; Dasgupta & Greenwald, 2001). This work suggests, quite clearly, one prescription for prejudice—increase exposure to such counterstereotypical exemplars.

Outside of the lab, however, where might such counterstereotypical exemplars be found? In a compelling study, Dasgupta and Asgari (2004) examined one such context and its subsequent effects. Specifically, they examined the extent to which college-age women harbor negative stereotypical associations between gender and leadership as a function of attending a single-sex or a coeducational college. Because elite single-sex colleges typically employ a number of women in leadership roles, including female professors in traditionally male disciplines, Dasgupta and Asgari predicted that the female students at these colleges would be less likely to automatically associate male, more than female, with leadership. Consistent with this prediction, although women at single-sex compared with coeducational colleges did not differ in their implicit endorsement of gender stereotypes regarding leadership on entering college, by their sophomore year the groups' implicit beliefs had significantly diverged. The coeducational college women were more likely to associate men with leadership than women, but not the single-sex college women. Furthermore, this effect was mediated by the proportion of female professors the students had encountered. In other words, the presence of larger numbers of female leaders at the single-sex college seems to have bolstered these students' beliefs from the effects of a traditional college environment wherein men are more likely to be in positions of authority relative to women. Indeed, this research makes clear the profound import of diverse environments in which counterstereotypical exemplars are present and visible (see also Eagly & Steffen, 1984).

CONCLUSIONS

Prejudice and stereotypes can be deeply conditioned in the human mind, even among individuals who find them to be aversive and wish not to be influenced by them. Although the automatic activation of prejudiced attitudes and stereotypic beliefs may not be inevitable in all situations, most people are likely to find themselves having unwanted thoughts and feelings in intergroup contexts at least some of the time. In those circumstances, a desire to inhibit or control these unwanted reactions is also likely to emerge, especially when it is clear that the feelings violate personal or societal standards.

Unfortunately, controlling the expression of intergroup bias is not a simple and straightforward matter. As we have seen, a variety of strategies exist for controlling prejudice and stereotyping, varying in their efficacy and consequences. Some strategies, such as suppression, have the potential to backfire, ultimately producing even more of the unwanted thoughts. Yet with consistent effort, many of these approaches can produce the desired result. Indeed, for those who pursue egalitarian objectives consistently, relatively automatic forms of bias control may emerge and operate in ways that are not especially taxing to the self-regulatory system.

Although laboratory research has painted a potentially encouraging picture with respect to controlling intergroup bias, it is vitally important to examine how the relevant processes play out in the crucible of real social interactions. For many individuals, both the cues that trigger stereotype activation and those that promote inhibition and control are embedded within rich social contexts. For instance, for many individuals, intergroup interactions simultaneously activate negative stereotypes and concepts reflecting concern about appearing prejudiced. Similarly, the norms of particular social contexts often eschew overt forms of bias expression, raising concerns about appearing (but, perhaps, not actually being) prejudiced in these settings. The current state of research on the influence of prejudice concerns on actual behavior, however, is quite complicated; prejudice concerns can result in behavior that is more egalitarian or less egalitarian. Furthermore, irrespective of the influence of concerns on behavior, the effort to control bias also seems to result in relatively negative affective and cognitive outcomes for some individuals.

Research also suggests that concerns about responding in prejudiced ways may invoke suboptimal strategies for actual prejudice reduction. For instance, the threat associated with appearing prejudiced may result in a tendency to deny that biased responding is actually prejudiced. Furthermore, efforts to appear nonprejudiced that engage colorblind strategies can backfire, resulting in awkward behavior during intergroup interactions and, possibly also, a tendency to express more rather than less prejudice more generally. Taken together, this work makes clear the need to consider interventions that curtail biased responding without the various unexpected, unintended, ironic, and backlash reactions that have been revealed in the literature. Perhaps the creation of diverse environments is the best avenue for long-term prejudice reduction. To increase the diversity of many environments (e.g., businesses, universities) it is necessary to increase the participation of members of underrepresented and typically devalued groups. The presence of such individuals, however, serves also to strengthen the association between the groups and counterstereotypical or otherwise positive evaluations, which has been found to be a more promising mechanism of bias control than the negation or suppression of stereotypical thinking.

The fact that so many people in contemporary society have the desire to control the prejudice and stereotypes that have been historically so commonplace is a cause for celebration, but it is certainly not an occasion for complacency. Clearly much more remains to be learned about how and when people can move beyond their increasingly archaic intergroup biases and realize their aspirations to live harmoniously in a world of diversity.

REFERENCES

Adams, G., Tormala, T. E. T., & O'Brien, L. T. (2006). The effect of self-affirmation on perceptions of racism. *Journal of Experimental Social Psychology, 42,* 616–626.

Allport, G. W. (1954). *The nature of prejudice.* Reading, MA: Addison-Wesley.

Amodio, D. M., Harmon-Jones, E., Devine, P. G., Curtin, J. J., Hartley, S. L., & Covert, A. E. (2004). Neural signals for the detection of unintentional race bias. *Psychological Science, 15,* 88–93.

Arkes, H., & Tetlock, P. E. (2004). Attributions of implicit prejudice, or would Jesse Jackson fail the Implicit Association Test? *Psychological Inquiry, 15,* 257–278.

Baddeley, A. D. (1986). *Working memory.* London: Oxford University Press.

Banfield, J., Wyland, C. L., Macrae, C. N., Münte, T. F., & Heatherton, T. F. (2004). The cognitive neuroscience of self-regulation. In R. F. Baumeister & K. D. Vohs (Eds.), *The handbook of self-regulation* (pp. 62–83). New York: Guilford.

Barden, J., Maddux, W., Petty, R. E., & Brewer, M. B. (2004). Contextual moderation of racial bias: The impact of social roles on controlled and automatically activated attitudes. *Journal of Personality and Social Psychology, 87,* 5–22.

Bargh, J. A. (1990). Automotives: Preconscious determinants of thought and behavior. In E. T. Higgins & R. M. Sorrentino (Eds.), *Handbook of motivation and cognition* (Vol. 2, pp. 93–130). New York: Guilford.

Bargh, J. A. (1994). Four horsemen of automaticity: Awareness, intention, efficiency, and control in social cognition. In R. S. Wyer, Jr., & T. K. Srull (Eds.), *Handbook of social cognition* (2nd ed., Vol. 1, pp. 1–40). Mahwah, NJ: Erlbaum.

Bargh, J. A. (1999). The cognitive monster: The case against the controllability of automatic stereotype effects. In S. Chaiken & Y. Trope (Eds.), *Dual process theories in social psychology* (pp. 361–382). New York: Guilford.

Bargh, J. A., Chaiken, S., Raymond, P., & Hymes, C. (1996). The automatic evaluation effect: Unconditional automatic attitude activation with a pronunciation task. *Journal of Experimental Social Psychology, 32,* 104–128.

Bargh, J. A., & Gollwitzer, P. M. (1994). Environmental control of goal-directed action: Automatic and strategic contingencies between situations and behavior. In W. D. Spaulding (Ed.), *Integrative views of motivation, cognition, and emotion* (pp. 71–124). Lincoln: University of Nebraska Press.

Batson, C. D., Polycarpou, M. P., Harmon-Jones, E, Imhoff, H. J., Mitchener, E. C., Bednar, L. L., et al. (1997). Empathy and attitudes: Can feeling for a member of a stigmatized group improve feelings toward the group? *Journal of Personality and Social Psychology, 72,* 105–118.

Baumeister, R. F. (1984). Choking under pressure: Self-consciousness and paradoxical effects of incentives on skillful performance. *Journal of Personality and Social Psychology, 46,* 610–620.

Baumeister, R. F., Muraven, M., & Tice, D. M. (2000). Ego depletion: A resource model of volition, self-regulation, and controlled processing. *Social Cognition, 18,* 130–150.

Beilock, S. L., & Carr, T. H. (2001). On the fragility of skilled performance: What governs choking under pressure? *Journal of Experimental Psychology: General, 130,* 701–725.

Biernat, M. (2003). Toward a broader view of social stereotyping. *American Psychologist, 58,* 1019–1027.

Blair, I. V., & Banaji, M. R. (1996). Automatic and controlled processes in stereotype priming. *Journal of Personality and Social Psychology, 70,* 1142–1163.

Blair, I. V., Ma, J. E., & Lenton, A. P. (2001). Imagining stereotypes away: The moderation of implicit stereotypes through mental imagery. *Journal of Personality and Social Psychology, 81,* 828–841.

Blascovich, J., Mendes, W. B., Hunter, S. B., Lickel, B., & Kowai-Bell, N. (2001). Perceiver threat in social interactions with stigmatized individuals. *Journal of Personality and Social Psychology, 80,* 253–267.

Bodenhausen, G. V., & Macrae, C. N. (1998). Stereotype activation and inhibition. In R. S. Wyer, Jr. (Ed.), *Stereotype activation and inhibition: Advances in social cognition* (Vol. 11, pp. 1–52). Mahwah, NJ: Erlbaum.

Bodenhausen, G. V., Macrae, C. N., & Sherman, J. S. (1999). On the dialectics of discrimination: Dual processes in social stereotyping. In S. Chaiken & Y. Trope (Eds), *Dual-process theories in social psychology* (pp. 271–290). New York: Guilford.

Bodenhausen, G. V., Todd, A. R., & Becker, A. P. (2007). Categorizing the social world: Affect, motivation, and self-regulation. In B. H. Ross & A. B. Markman (Eds.), *Psychology of learning and motivation* (Vol. 47, pp. 123–155). Amsterdam: Elsevier.

Botvinick, M. M., Braver, T. S., Barch, D. M., Carter, C. S., & Cohen, J. D. (2001). Conflict monitoring and cognitive control. *Psychological Review, 108,* 624–652.

Brewer, M. B. (1988). A dual-process model of impression formation. In T. K. Srull & R. S. Wyer, Jr. (Eds.), *A dual-process model of impression formation: Advances in social cognition* (Vol. 1, pp. 1–36). Hillsdale, NJ: Erlbaum.

Castelli, L., Macrae, C. N., Zogmaister, C., & Arcuri, L. (2004). A tale of two primes: Contextual limits on stereotype activation. *Social Cognition, 22,* 233–247.

Conrey, F. R., Sherman, J. W., Gawronski, B., Hugenberg, K., & Groom, C. (2005). Separating multiple processes in implicit social cognition: The quad-model of implicit task performance. *Journal of Personality and Social Psychology, 89,* 469–487.

Cunningham, W. A., Johnson, M. K., Raye, C. L., Gatenby, J. C., Gore, J. C., & Banaji, M. R. (2004). Separable neural components in the processing of Black and White faces. *Psychological Science, 15,* 806–813.

Cunningham, W. A., Raye, C. I., & Johnson, M. K. (2004). Implicit and explicit evaluation: fMRI correlates of valence, emotional intensity, and control in the processing of attitudes. *Journal of Cognitive Neuroscience, 16,* 1717–1729.

Dasgupta, N., & Asgari, S. (2004). Seeing is believing: Exposure to counterstereotypic women leaders and its effect on automatic gender stereotyping. *Journal of Experimental Social Psychology, 40,* 642–658.

Dasgupta, N., & Greenwald, A. G. (2001). Exposure to admired group members reduces automatic intergroup bias. *Journal of Personality and Social Psychology, 81,* 800–814.

Dasgupta, N., & Rivera, L. M. (2006). From automatic anti-gay prejudice to behavior: The moderating role of conscious beliefs about gender and behavioral control. *Journal of Personality and Social Psychology, 91,* 268–280.

Davis, M. H., Conklin, L., Smith, A., & Luce, C. (1996). Effect of perspective taking on the cognitive representation of persons: A merging of self and other. *Journal of Personality and Social Psychology, 70,* 713–726.

Devine, P. G. (1989). Stereotypes and prejudice: Their automatic and controlled components. *Journal of Personality and Social Psychology, 56,* 5–18.

Devine, P. G., & Baker, S. M. (1991). Measurement of racial stereotype subtyping. *Personality and Social Psychology Bulletin, 17,* 44–50.

Doosje, B., Branscombe, N. R., Spears, R., & Manstead, S. R. (1998). Guilty by association: When one's group has a negative history. *Journal of Personality and Social Psychology, 75,* 872–886.

Dovidio, J. F., & Gaertner, S. L. (2004). Aversive racism. In M. P. Zanna (Ed.), *Advances in experimental social psychology* (Vol. 36, pp. 1–52). Amsterdam: Elsevier.

Dovidio, J. F., Kawakami, K., & Gaertner, S. L. (2002). Implicit and explicit prejudice and interracial interaction. *Journal of Personality and Social Psychology, 82,* 62–68.

Dovidio, J. F., Kawakami, K., Johnson, C., Johnson, B., & Howard, A. (1997). On the nature of prejudice: Automatic and controlled processes. *Journal of Experimental Social Psychology, 33,* 510–540.

Dovidio, J. F., ten Vergert, M., Stewart, T. L., Gaertner, S. L., Johnson, J. D., Esses, V. M., et al. (2004). Perspective and prejudice: Antecedents and mediating mechanisms. *Personality and Social Psychology Bulletin, 29,* 1537–1549.

Dunton, B. C., & Fazio, R. H., (1997). An individual difference measure of motivation to control prejudiced reactions. *Personality and Social Psychology Bulletin, 23,* 316–326.

Eagly, A. H., & Steffen, V. J. (1984). Gender stereotypes stem from the distribution of women and men into social roles. *Journal of Personality and Social Psychology, 46,* 735–754.

Engle, R. W., Conway, A. R. A., Tuholski, S. W., & Shisler, R. J. (1995). A resource account of inhibition.

Etzioni, A. (2000). *Psychological Science, 6,* 122–125. Social norms: Internalization, persuasion, and history. *Law and Society Review, 34,* 157–178.

Fazio, R. H., Jackson, J. R., Dunton, B. C., & Williams, C. J. (1995). Variability in automatic activation as an unobtrusive measure of racial attitudes: A bona fide pipeline? *Journal of Personality and Social Psychology, 69,* 1013–1027.

Feldman Barrett, L., Tugade, M. M., & Engle, R. W. (2004). Individual differences in working memory capacity and dual-process theories of the mind. *Psychological Bulletin, 130,* 553–573.

Fiske, S. T., & Neuberg, S. L. (1990). A continuum model of impression formation, from category-based to individuating processes: Influence of information and motivation on attention and interpretation. In M. P. Zanna (Ed.), *Advances in experimental social psychology* (Vol. 23, pp. 1–74). New York: Academic.

Gaertner, S. L., & Dovidio, J. F. (1986). The aversive form of racism. In J. F. Dovidio & S. L. Gaertner (Eds.), *Prejudice, discrimination, and racism* (pp. 61–89). Orlando, FL: Academic.

Gaertner, S. L., & Dovidio, J. F. (2000). *Reducing intergroup bias: The common ingroup identity model.* New York: Psychology Press.

Galinsky, A. D., Ku, G., & Wang, C. S. (2005). Perspective-taking and self–other overlap: Fostering social bonds and facilitating social coordination. *Group Processes & Intergroup Relations, 8,* 109–124.

Galinsky, A. D., & Moskowitz, G. B. (2000). Perspective-taking: Decreasing stereotype expression, stereotype accessibility, and in-group favoritism. *Journal of Personality and Social Psychology, 78,* 708–724.

Gawronski, B., & Bodenhausen, G. V. (2006). Associative and propositional processes in evaluation: An integrative review of implicit and explicit attitude change. *Psychological Bulletin, 132,* 692–731.

Gawronski, B., & Bodenhausen, G. V. (2007). Unraveling the processes underlying evaluation: Attitudes from the perspective of the APE model. *Social Cognition, 25,* 687–717.

Gawronski, B., Deutsch, R., Mbirkou, S., Seibt, B., & Strack, F. (2008). When "just say no" is not enough: Affirmation versus negation training and the reduction of automatic stereotype activation. *Journal of Experimental Social Psychology, 44,* 370–377.

Gilbert, D. T., & Hixon, J. G. (1991). The trouble of thinking: Activation and application of stereotypic beliefs. *Journal of Personality and Social Psychology, 60,* 509–517.

Goff, P. A., Steele, C. M., & Davies, P. G. (2005). *The space between us: Stereotype threat and avoidance for Whites in interethnic domains.* Unpublished manuscript, Stanford University, Palo Alto, CA.

Gollwitzer, P. M., Fujita, K., & Oettingen, G. (2004). Planning and the implementation of goals. In R. F. Baumeister & K. D. Vohs (Eds.), *Handbook of self-regulation: Research, theory and applications* (pp. 211–228). New York: Guilford.

Gollwitzer, P. M., Trotschel, R., & Sumner, M. (2002). *Mental control via implementation intentions is void of rebound effects.* Unpublished manuscript, University of Konstanz, Germany.

Hebl, M. R., Foster, J., Mannix, L. M., & Dovidio, J. F. (2002). Formal and interpersonal discrimination: A field study understanding of applicant bias. *Personality and Social Psychological Bulletin, 28,* 815–825.

Hebl, M. R., & Kleck, R. E. (2000). The social consequences of physical disability. In T. F. Heatherton, R. E. Kleck, M. R. Hebl, & J. G. Hull (Eds.), *The social psychology of stigma* (pp. 419–439), New York: Guilford.

Jacoby, L. L. (1991). A process dissociation framework: Separating automatic from intentional uses of memory. *Journal of Memory and Language, 30,* 513–541.

Kane, M. J., Bleckley, M. K., Conway, A. R. A., & Engle, R. W. (2001). A controlled-attention view of working memory capacity. *Journal of Experimental Psychology: General, 130,* 169–183.

Kawakami, K., Dion, K. L., & Dovidio, J. F. (1998). Racial prejudice and stereotype activation. *Personality and Social Psychology Bulletin, 24,* 407–416.

Kawakami, K., Dovidio, J. F., Moll, J., Hermsen, S., & Russin, A. (2000). Just say no (to stereotyping): Effects of training in the negation of stereotypic associations on stereotype activation. *Journal of Personality and Social Psychology, 78,* 871–888.

Kelman, H. C. (1958). Compliance, identification, and internalization: Three processes of attitude change. *Journal of Conflict Resolution, 2,* 51–60.

King, E. B., Shapiro, J. R., Hebl, M. R., Singletary, S. L., & Turner, S. (2006). The stigma of obesity in customer service: A mechanism for remediation and bottom-line consequences of interpersonal discrimination. *Journal of Applied Social Psychology, 91,* 579–593.

Kunda, Z., & Spencer, S. J. (2003). When do stereotypes come to mind and when do they color judgment? A goal-based theoretical framework for stereotype activation and application. *Psychological Bulletin, 129,* 522–544.

Lambert, A. J., Payne, B. K., Jacoby, L. L., Shaffer, L. M., Chasteen, A. L., & Khan, S. R. (2003). Stereotypes as dominant responses: On the "social facilitation" of prejudice in anticipated public contexts. *Journal of Personality and Social Psychology, 84,* 277–295.

Lepore, L., & Brown, R. (1997). Category and stereotype activation: Is prejudice inevitable? *Journal of Personality and Social Psychology, 72,* 275–287.

Leyens, J.-P., Demoulin, S., Désert, M., Vaes, J., & Philippot, P. (2002). Expressing emotions and decoding them: Ingroups and outgroups do not share the same advantages. In D. M. Mackie & E. R. Smith (Eds.), *From prejudice to intergroup emotions: Differentiated reactions to social groups* (pp. 139–151). New York: Psychology Press.

MacDonald, A. W., III, Cohen, J. D., Stenger, V. A., & Carter, C. S. (2000). Dissociating the role of the dorsolateral prefrontal and anterior cingulate cortex in cognitive control. *Science, 288,* 1835–1838.

Macrae, C. N., & Bodenhausen, G. V. (2000). Social cognition: Thinking categorically about others. *Annual Review of Psychology, 51,* 93–120.

Macrae, C. N., Bodenhausen, G. V., & Milne, A. B. (1995). The dissection of selection in person perception: Inhibitory processes in social stereotyping. *Journal of Personality and Social Psychology, 69,* 397–407.

Macrae, C. N., Bodenhausen, G. V., Milne, A. B., & Jetten, J. (1994). Out of mind but back in sight: Stereotypes on the rebound. *Journal of Personality and Social Psychology, 67,* 808–817.

Macrae, C. N., Bodenhausen, G. V., Milne, A. B., Thorne, T. M. J., & Castelli, L. (1997). On the activation of social stereotypes: The moderating role of processing objectives. *Journal of Experimental Social Psychology, 33,* 471–489.

Macrae, C. N., Bodenhausen, G. V., Schloerscheidt, A. M., & Milne, A. B. (1999). Tales of the unexpected: Executive function and person perception. *Journal of Personality and Social Psychology, 76,* 200–213.

McConnell, A. R., & Leibold, J. M. (2001). Relations between the Implicit Association Test, explicit racial attitudes, and discriminatory behavior. *Journal of Experimental Social Psychology, 37,* 435–442.

Monin, B., & Miller, D. T. (2001). Moral credentials and the expression of prejudice. *Journal of Personality and Social Psychology, 81,* 33–43.

Monteith, M. J. (1993). Self-regulation of prejudiced responses: Implications for progress in prejudice reduction efforts. *Journal of Personality and Social Psychology, 65,* 469–485.

Monteith, M. J., Ashburn-Nardo, L., Voils, C. I., & Czopp, A. M. (2002). Putting the brakes on prejudice: On the development and operation of cues for control. *Journal of Personality and Social Psychology, 83,* 1029–1050.

Monteith, M. J., Sherman, J. W., & Devine, P. G. (1998). Suppression as a stereotype control strategy. *Personality and Social Psychology Review, 2,* 63–82.

Moskowitz, G. B. (2001) Preconscious control and compensatory cognition. In G. B. Moskowitz (Ed.). Cognitive social psychology: *The Princeton symposium on the legacy and future of social cognition* (pp. 333-358). Hillsdale, NJ: Erlbaum.

Moskowitz, G. B., Gollwitzer, P. M., Wasel, W., & Schaal, B. (1999). Preconscious control of stereotype activation through chronic egalitarian goals. *Journal of Personality and Social Psychology, 77,* 167–184.

Moskowitz, G. B., Salomon, A. R., & Taylor, C. M. (2000). Preconsciously controlling stereotyping: Implicitly activated egalitarian goals prevent the activation of stereotypes. *Social Cognition, 18,* 151–177.

Neely, J. H. (1977). Semantic priming and retrieval from lexical memory: Roles of inhibitionless spreading activation and limited-capacity attention. *Journal of Experimental Psychology: General, 106,* 226–254.

Norman, D. A., & Shallice, T. (1986). Attention to action: Willed and automatic control of behavior. In R. J. Davidson, G. E. Schwartz, & D. Shapiro (Eds.), *Consciousness and self-regulation: Advances in research and theory* (Vol. 4, pp. 1–18). New York: Plenum.

Norton, M. I., Sommers, S. R., Apfelbaum, E. P., Pura, N., & Ariely, D. (2006). Colorblindness and interracial interaction: Playing the political correctness game. *Psychological Science, 17,* 949–953.

Olson, M. A., & Fazio, R. H. (2006). Reducing automatically activated racial prejudice through implicit evaluative conditioning. *Personality and Social Psychology Bulletin, 32,* 421–433.

Pager, D. (2003). The mark of a criminal record. *American Journal of Sociology, 108,* 937–975.

Park, B., & Judd, C. M. (2005). Rethinking the link between categorization and prejudice within the social cognition perspective. *Personality and Social Psychology Review, 9,* 108–130.

Payne, B. K. (2001). Prejudice and perception: The role of automatic and controlled processes in misperceiving a weapon. *Journal of Personality and Social Psychology, 81,* 181–192.

Payne, B. K. (2005). Conceptualizing control in social cognition: How executive control modulates the expression of automatic stereotyping. *Journal of Personality and Social Psychology, 89,* 488–503.

Payne, B. K., Lambert, A. J., & Jacoby, L. L. (2002). Best laid plans: Effects of goals on accessibility bias and cognitive control in race-based misperceptions of weapons. *Journal of Experimental Social Psychology, 38,* 384–396.

Pettigrew, T., & Tropp, L. (2006). A meta-analytic test of intergroup contact theory. *Journal of Personality and Social Psychology, 90,* 751–783

Plant, E. A. (2004). Responses to interracial interactions over time. *Personality and Social Psychology Bulletin, 30,* 1458–1471.

Plant, E. A., & Devine, P. G. (1998). Internal and external motivation to respond without prejudice. *Journal of Personality and Social Psychology, 75,* 811–832.

Plant, E. A., & Devine, P.G. (2001). Responses to other-imposed pro-Black pressure: Acceptance or backlash? *Journal of Experimental Social Psychology, 37,* 486–501.

Plant, E. A., & Devine, P.G. (2003). Antecedents and implications of intergroup anxiety. *Personality and Social Psychology Bulletin, 29,* 790–801.

Plaut, V. C. (2007, January). Attitudes toward diversity: What do race and status buy you? In V. C. Plaut & S. R. Sommers (Chairs), *When difference becomes us: Racial diversity, cognition, and group processes.* Symposium conducted at the annual meeting of the Society for Personality and Social Psychology, Memphis, TN.

Plaut, V. C., & Markus, H. R. (2005). *Basically we're all the same? Models of diversity and the dilemma of difference.* Unpublished manuscript, Stanford University, Palo Alto, CA.

Quinn, K. A., & Macrae, C. N. (2005). Categorizing others: The dynamics of person construal. *Journal of Personality and Social Psychology, 88,* 467–479.

Richeson, J. A., & Ambady, N. (2003). Effects of situational power on automatic racial prejudice. *Journal of Experimental Social Psychology, 39,* 177–183.

Richeson, J. A., Baird, A. A., Gordon, H. L., Heatherton, T. F., Wyland, C. L., Trawalter, S., et al. (2003). An fMRI examination of the impact of interracial contact on executive function. *Nature Neuroscience, 6,* 1323–1328.

Richeson, J. A., & Nussbaum, R. J. (2004). The impact of multiculturalism versus color-blindness on racial bias. *Journal of Experimental Social Psychology, 40,* 417–423.

Richeson, J. A., & Shelton J. N. (2003). When prejudice does not pay: Effects of interracial contact on executive function: *Psychology Science, 14,* 287-290.

Richeson, J. A., & Shelton, J. N. (2007). Negotiating interracial interactions: Costs, consequences, and possibilities. *Current Directions in Psychological Science, 16,* 316–320.

Richeson, J. A., & Trawalter, S. (2005). Why do interracial interactions impair executive function? A resource depletion account. *Journal of Personality and Social Psychology, 88,* 934–947.

Richeson, J. A., Trawalter, S., & Nussbaum, R. J. (2006). *Colorblind racial bias.* Unpublished manuscript, Northwestern University, Evanston, IL.

Rudman, L. A. (2004). Sources of implicit attitudes. *Current Directions in Psychological Science, 13,* 79–82.

Rydell, R. J., & McConnell, A. R. (2006). Understanding implicit and explicit attitude change: A systems of reasoning analysis. *Journal of Personality and Social Psychology, 91,* 995–1008.

Sassenberg, K. & Moskowitz, G. B. (2005). Do not stereotype, think different! Overcoming automatic stereotype activation by mindset priming. *Journal of Experimental Social Psychology, 41,* 506–514.

Schmeichel, B. J., & Baumeister, R. F. (2004). Self-regulatory strength. In R. Baumeister & K. Vohs (Eds.), *Handbook of self-regulation: Research, theory, and applications* (pp. 84–98). New York: Guilford.

Schuman, H., Steeh, C., Bobo, L., & Krysan, M. (1997). *Racial attitudes in America: Trends and interpretations* (2nd ed.). Cambridge, MA: Harvard University Press.

Shallice, T., & Burgess, P. W. (1991). Higher-order cognitive impairments and frontal lobe lesions in man. In H. S. Levin, H. M. Eisenberg, & A. L. Benton (Eds.), *Frontal lobe function and dysfunction* (pp. 125–138). New York: Oxford University Press.

Shelton, J. N. (2003). Interpersonal concerns in social encounters between majority and minority group members. *Group Processes and Intergroup Relations, 6,* 171–185.

Shelton, J. N., Dovidio, J. F., Hebl, M., & Richeson, J. A. (in press). Prejudice and intergroup interaction. In S. Demoulin, J. P. Leyens, & J. F. Dovidio (Eds.), *Intergroup misunderstandings: Impact of divergent social realities.* New York: Psychology Press.

Shelton, J. N., & Richeson, J. A. (2006). Interracial interactions: A relational approach. In M. P. Zanna (Ed.), *Advances in experimental social psychology* (Vol. 38, pp. 121–181). New York: Academic.

Shelton, J. N., Richeson, J. A., Salvatore, J., & Trawalter, S. (2005). Ironic effects of racial bias during interethnic interactions. *Psychological Science, 16,* 397–402.

Smyth, F. L., & Nosek, B. A. (2007, January). *The impact of multiculturalism versus color-blindness on racial bias revisited.* Poster presented at the annual meeting of the Society for Personality and Social Psychology, Memphis, TN.

Snyder, M. L., Kleck, R. E., Strenta, A., & Mentzer, S. J. (1979). Avoidance of the handicapped: An attributional ambiguity analysis. *Journal of Personality and Social Psychology, 37,* 2297–2306.

Spencer, S. J., Fein, S., Wolfe, C. T., Fong, C., & Dunn, M. A. (1998). Automatic activation of stereotypes: The role of self-image threat. *Personality and Social Psychology Bulletin, 24,* 1139–1152.

Stangor, C., Lynch, L., Duan, C., & Glass, B. (1992). Categorization of individuals on the basis of multiple social features. *Journal of Personality and Social Psychology, 62,* 207–218.

Strack, F., & Deutsch, R. (2004). Reflexive and impulsive determinants of social behavior. *Personality and Social Psychology Review, 8,* 220–247.

Strack, F., & Hannover, B. (1996). Awareness of influence as a precondition for implementing correctional goals. In P. M. Gollwitzer & J. A. Bargh (Eds.), *The psychology of action: Linking cognition and motivation to behavior* (pp. 579–596). New York: Guilford.

Trawalter, S., & Richeson, J. A. (2006). Regulatory focus and executive function after interracial interactions. *Journal of Experimental Social Psychology, 42,* 406–412.

Verkuyten, M. (2005). Ethnic group identification and group evaluation among minority and majority groups: Testing the multiculturalism hypothesis. *Journal of Personality and Social Psychology, 88,* 121–138.

Vescio, T. K., Sechrist, G. B., & Paolucci, M. P. (2003). Perspective taking and prejudice reduction: The mediational role of empathy arousal and situational attributions. *European Journal of Social Psychology, 33,* 455–472.

von Hippel, W., & Gonsalkorale, K. (2005). "That is bloody revolting!" Inhibitory control of thoughts better left unsaid. *Psychological Science, 16,* 497–500.

Vorauer, J. D. (2006). An information search model of evaluative concerns in intergroup interaction. *Psychological Review, 113,* 862–886.

Vorauer, J. D., Hunter, A., Main, K., & Roy, S. (2000). Concerns with evaluation and meta-stereotype activation. *Journal of Personality and Social Psychology, 78,* 690–707.

Vorauer, J. D., Main, K., & O'Connell, G. (1998). How do individuals expect to be viewed by members of lower status groups? Content and implications of meta-stereotypes. *Journal of Personality and Social Psychology, 75,* 917–937.

Vorauer, J. D., & Turpie, C. (2004). Disruptive effects of vigilance on dominant group members' treatment of outgroup members: Choking versus shining under pressure. *Journal of Personality and Social Psychology, 27,* 706–709.

Walther, E., Nagengast, B., & Trasselli, C. (2005). Evaluative conditioning in social psychology: Facts and speculations. *Cognition & Emotion, 19,* 175–196.

Wegener, D. T., & Petty, R. E. (1995). Flexible correction processes in social judgment: The role of naive theories in corrections for perceived bias. *Journal of Personality and Social Psychology, 68,* 36–51.

Wegener, D. T., & Petty, R. E. (1997). The flexible correction model: The role of naive theories of bias in bias correction. In M. P. Zanna (Ed.), *Advances in experimental social psychology* (Vol. 29, pp. 141–208). Mahwah, NJ: Erlbaum.

Wegner, D. M. (1994). Ironic processes of mental control. *Psychological Review, 101,* 34–52.

Wegner, D. M., & Erber, R. (1992). The hyperaccessibility of suppressed thoughts. *Journal of Personality and Social Psychology, 63,* 903–912.

Wheeler, M. E., & Fiske, S. T. (2005). Controlling racial prejudice and stereotyping: Social cognitive goals affect amygdala and stereotype activation. *Psychological Science, 16,* 56–63.

Wicklund, R. A. (1982). Self-focused attention and the validity of self-reports. In M. P. Zanna, E. T. Higgins, & C. P. Herman (Eds.), *Consistency in social behavior: The Ontario symposium* (Vol. 2, pp. 149–172). Hillsdale, NJ: Erlbaum.

Wilson, T. D., & Brekke, N. (1994). Mental contamination and mental correction: Unwanted influences on judgments and evaluations. *Psychological Bulletin, 116,* 117–142.

Wittenbrink, B., Judd, C. M., & Park, B. (1997). Evidence for racial prejudice at the implicit level and its relationship with questionnaire measures. *Journal of Personality and Social Psychology, 72,* 262–274.

Wittenbrink, B., Judd, C. M., & Park, B. (2001). Spontaneous prejudice in context: Variability in automatically activated attitudes. *Journal of Personality and Social Psychology, 81,* 815–827.

Wolsko, C., Park, B., Judd, C. M., & Wittenbrink, B. (2000). Framing interethnic ideology: Effects of multicultural and color-blind perspectives on judgments of groups and individuals. *Journal of Personality and Social Psychology, 78,* 635–654.

7 Stereotypes and Shifting Standards

Monica Biernat
University of Kansas

When Mary Shelley published her novel, *Frankenstein,* in 1818, she did so anonymously, perhaps to disguise her gender. When it was later discovered that the author was, indeed, a young woman, one reviewer wrote about the novel, "For a man, it was excellent, but for a woman, it was wonderful" (*Blackwood's,* 1823, as cited in Hindle, 1985). This comment reflects the explicit acknowledgment that gender can affect the standards against which a work product is evaluated. In this case, the standard for women is likely lower than the standard for men (work product is expected to be less good in women than in men), but it is also *qualitatively* different. Although both "excellent" and "wonderful" signify greatness, "wonderful" suggests something astonishing—perhaps especially so given the philosophical and violent nature of the novel.

Subjective descriptors such as "wonderful" or "excellent" are always used with reference to some standard (Kraut & Higgins, 1984). When we describe a package as "huge" or a day as "hot," there is an assumption that the audience of our communication will understand roughly what those terms mean, objectively. The huge package is presumably not so huge that it does not fit in a car's trunk, and the hot day is hot relative to expectations; hot in Tucson is very different than hot in Anchorage.[1] This slipperiness of subjective language is particularly interesting as it applies to descriptions of people, as one likely referent for these descriptions is the social category membership of the individual being described. As in Mary Shelley's case, gendered expectations can provide the framework against which descriptions can be interpreted, as can expectations based on race, age, or any number of other features of the person. Although we typically do not include the tag line, " . . . for a woman" or " . . . for an African American," our impressions and descriptions of others are likely to be based, in part, on reference to the group stereotype as a judgment standard.

This is the basic premise behind the shifting standards model of stereotype-based judgment (Biernat, 2003; Biernat & Manis, 1994; Biernat, Manis, & Nelson, 1991). According to this model, stereotypes—generally defined as expectations about the attributes of a group—provide judgment standards for evaluating individual group members. Because different groups have different stereotypes associated with them, standards *shift* depending on the social category membership of the individual being judged. Thus, a woman and man who engage in identical behavior might be described differently because different standards have been invoked, or the same subjective description might mean something substantively different because it was made with reference to shifting standards. For example, because of shifting standards, a woman who steals a parking space might be rated a 6 on a 7-point scale of aggressiveness whereas a man who does the same might be described as a 5. Additionally, a man rated a 5 in aggressiveness would likely be judged to be more objectively aggressive than a woman rated identically.

In this chapter, I first review evidence documenting the tendency to shift standards when judging individual group members on stereotyped dimensions. I then consider how this tendency plays out in communication and the translation of others' judgments. Next, I examine the effects of stereotypes on the setting of standards, and how those standards affect behavior toward individual members of stereotyped groups. The chapter concludes with a consideration of the link between shifting

---

[1] As I write this during a Kansas summer, a day with an expected high of *only* 87 degrees is being described as "cool."

standards and outgroup prejudice, and highlights the complexity inherent in charting the impact of stereotypes on social life.

SHIFTING STANDARDS IN SOCIAL JUDGMENT

A schematic depiction of the basic idea behind the shifting standards model is presented in Figure 7.1. The model is particularly concerned with understanding how stereotypes affect judgments of individual members of stereotyped groups on stereotyped dimensions. In this example, we assume that a perceiver holds the stereotype that men are better leaders than women. The perceiver also knows some information about an individual male or female target, in this case, that the target is a manager (i.e., in a leadership role). Now the perceiver is asked, "How skillful a leader is Katherine/Kenneth?"

One key assumption of the model is that the stereotype provides a standard against which the perceiver can make this judgment. Stereotypes include representations of the mean level of an attribute that members of a given group possess, as well as a likely range that members of the group will exhibit (Judd & Park, 1993). In this way, stereotypes serve an "endpoint setting" function: They allow perceivers to fix the endpoints of a subjective rating scale to reflect the expected distribution of a class of targets on the dimension of interest (see this theme in the classic judgment models of Parducci, 1963; Upshaw, 1962; and Volkmann, 1951). Thus, in Figure 7.1, the standard for women's leadership is lower than that for men, some range of leadership skill is expected within each group (the degree of variability within men and women is equated in this example), and there is some overlap in the expected distributions.

The result of this differential standard setting, along with a stereotyped expectation about Katherine's and Kenneth's leadership skill, is that Katherine is judged a subjectively better leader than Kenneth (she receives a mean rating above 5; he receives a 4.9). This is a *contrast effect*, as it reflects an apparently counterstereotypical pattern of judgment. However, the shifting standards argument suggests this contrast is more apparent than real—it is based on the male and female target

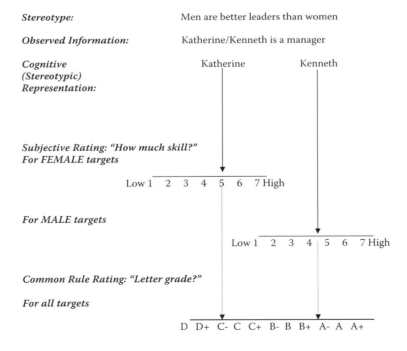

FIGURE 7.1 Schematic depiction of stereotypes influencing judgment standards and evaluations of male and female targets.

being judged in units with very different, gender-specific, meaning. One way we can determine that this is the case is by comparing judgments made on these "slippery" subjective rating scales to those made on a rating scales that are anchored in some external reality. We have typically referred to such scales as *objective* or *common rule* in nature, in that the units of judgment mean the same thing, regardless of attributes of the target being judged. In the example of heat discussed earlier, "hot" and "cool" judgments are subjective, but estimated temperature in degrees Fahrenheit is an objective or common rule index. In the example presented in Figure 7.1, a common rule judgment of leadership skill might include assigning a "letter grade" to indicate the target's performance. By these metrics, Tucson would pretty solidly be judged "hotter" than Anchorage, and Kenneth would be judged a better leader than Katherine. These are classic examples of *assimilation* to stereotypes, and such effects tend to emerge most strongly on objective or common rule response scales that do not allow for shifts in meaning from one target to another (Tucson to Anchorage; Katherine to Kenneth).

Based on these examples, the "signature" shifting standards effect is evidence of assimilation to stereotypes on common rule response scales, but reductions or reversals of this pattern when judgments are made in subjective units. Statistically, this is a target category X response scale interaction, and research from my laboratory has documented such a pattern for a number of social groups on a number of stereotyped dimensions. For example, in one study, participants viewed 40 photographs of men and women and were asked to judge their "financial success." Half of the participants made these estimates in objective units (dollars earned per year), whereas the other half made subjective judgments of financial success on a scale ranging from 1 (*financially unsuccessful*) to 7 (*financially successful*). Objective judgments clearly revealed assimilation to the (accurate) stereotype that men earn more money than women, but subjective judgments revealed a reliable contrast effect: Women were judged more financially successful than men (Biernat et al., 1991, Study 2).

The scatter plot depicted in the top panel of Figure 7.2 presents the mean objective and subjective financial success ratings attributed to each of the 40 photographs. It is clear that separate regression lines can be fit to the sets of male and female targets, such that a woman could earn objectively less money than a man to achieve any given subjective rating. For example, for a woman to be rated a 4 on financial success, she could earn about $9,000 less per year than a man with the same rating. For comparison purposes, the bottom panel of Figure 7.2 presents a scatter plot based on the same 40 targets, in this case judged on age in either objective (years) or subjective (young–old) units. There is no stereotype that "men are older than women," so standards need not shift when one is judging men versus women on this dimension. Indeed, as the scatter plot indicates, a single regression line captures the relationship between subjective and objective age judgments, across female and male targets. This finding supports the idea that differential group stereotypes are necessary to trigger the use of shifting standards to judge individual group members (Biernat et al., 1991).

Beliefs about men's better financial standing relative to women's may strike some as only tangential to understanding stereotyping. After all, this belief is based in reality, and it does not have the pernicious quality that many social stereotypes have. Additional research from our laboratory, however, has demonstrated that a comparable pattern of shifting standards emerges when one considers the kinds of stereotypes that are of greater social concern. For example, evidence of shifting standards emerges in judgments of men's and women's job-related competence, verbal ability, writing quality, athleticism, and leadership competence (as well as height, weight, and income; Biernat, Crandall, Young, Kobrynowicz, & Halpin, 1998; Biernat & Manis, 1994; Biernat et al., 1991; Biernat & Vescio, 2002). Similarly, evidence of assimilation to racial stereotypes is stronger when judgments are made in common rule rather than subjective units in the domains of verbal and math ability, athleticism, and job-related competence (Biernat & Kobrynowicz, 1997; Biernat & Manis, 1994; Kobrynowicz & Biernat, 1997). For example, when judging the athleticism of Black and White targets, rankings (a common rule indicator that invites cross-category judgment) produced stronger evidence than subjective ratings that Blacks were perceived as more athletic than Whites. Furthermore, when Black and White targets were "tied" in terms of the subjective athleticism ratings they received, rankings clearly indicated that the Black targets were seen as objectively more athletic than the similarly rated

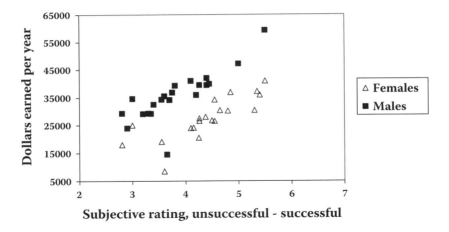

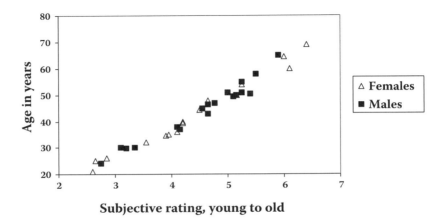

FIGURE 7.2   Scatter plots depicting subjective × objective judgments of targets on financial success (top panel) and age (bottom); data from Biernat et al. (1991).

White targets (Biernat & Manis, 1994, Study 3). In sum, across a variety of domains, gender and racial stereotypes prompt the use of shifting standards to judge individual targets. Recent research has also documented that the tendency to shift standards remains stable across the life span (at least in the domain of height judgments; Hoessler & Chasteen, 2008), but is enhanced under conditions of cognitive busyness (Biernat, Kobrynowicz, & Weber, 2003).

Evidence consistent with the shifting standards perspective has also emerged in research on judgments of "real" people, as in the literature on workplace performance appraisal. In a recent meta-analysis examining the effects of employee race on the evaluations they receive from supervisors, Roth, Huffcutt, and Bobko (2003) found that race bias is greater on objective than subjective indicators. For example, for measures of job quality, the effect size (Whites evaluated more favorably than Blacks) was $d = .24$ for objective measures (objective indicators of work product, errors, complaints) and $d = .20$ for subjective measures (subjective ratings of quality). For measures of job quantity, the objective $d = .32$ (e.g., number of units produced, sales volume), and the subjective $d = .09$. On measures of job knowledge (which included ratings [subjective] or tests [objective] of mastery of training material) the objective $d = .55$; subjective $d = .15$. On measures of absenteeism, the objective $d = .23$; subjective $d = .13$. Several studies also indicated comparable patterns with regard to White–Hispanic differences (for job knowledge, objective $d = .67$, subjective $d = .04$). Furthermore, in the two studies reviewed in which supervisors made both objective and subjective judgments of the same employees, the same pattern emerged (Campbell, Crooks, Mahoney, & Rock, 1973).

In short, judgments of real employees also indicate that evaluation standards may shift based on the target's race, and that the observed pattern is consistent with the shifting standards model predictions about the differences between objective (common rule, cross-category) and subjective (within-category) appraisals. In research on gender-based stereotypes of leadership competence, U.S. Army captains' judgments of each other also demonstrated a pattern consistent with shifting standards— evidence that men were perceived as better leaders than women was stronger in rankings (a cross-category judgment) than subjective ratings (Biernat, Crandall, et al., 1998). Both race and gender stereotypes seem to invoke the use of different, shifting standards to make subjective judgments.

TRANSLATION AND THE COMMUNICATION OF SUBJECTIVE LANGUAGE

When we talk to other people about other people, our conversation is peppered with subjective language. We might discuss the "really tall" woman we saw, or the "obnoxious" sales clerk, or the "aggressive" driver we encountered. Given our facility with making within-category adjustments of meaning for object descriptions (e.g., large cats vs. large elephants; fast cars vs. fast bicycles), one question is whether we do the same for evaluations of different groups of people. Do listeners "decode" subjective language in a manner that takes into account stereotype-based shifting standards?

We know from studies on height estimation that when asked "How tall is tall?" respondents indicate a height of about 6'3" for men, but only 5'9" for women (Roberts & Herman, 1986). Does the same within-category translation occur with respect to nonphysical attributes of the sort that characterize most social stereotypes? In one relevant study, participants listened to an audiotape of a man or woman describing himself or herself as a "very good" or "all right" parent (Kobrynowicz & Biernat, 1997, Study 2). Participants were asked to "decode" those descriptions by estimating the frequency with which the parent engaged in a wide variety of parenting behaviors (including physical care, emotional care, engagement in play, etc.). At both levels of quality ("very good" and "all right"), mothers were perceived to have objectively more involvement than fathers. That is, "very good" for a mom translated into more than twice as much physical care (diaper changes, baths, meal preparations) as "very good" for a dad; in fact, "all right" mothers were estimated to engage in slightly more physical care of children than "very good" fathers. In another study, "good at math" translated into a higher objective grade point average (GPA) performance for Asian than for White or Black students (Kobrynowicz & Biernat, 1997, Study 3). Identical subjective language in these cases was interpreted, or decoded, to mean objectively more evidence of the attribute (involved parenting, math skill) among individuals stereotyped as having the attribute (women, Asian students).

Subjective language is also prevalent in an important means of written communication—the letter of recommendation. Such letters are often key to admission and hiring decisions (e.g., Breland, 1983; Lopez, Oehlert, & Moberly, 1997), and a number of studies have examined whether their content may or may not be biased against women (e.g., Bronstein, Black, Pfennig, & White, 1986; Colarelli, Hechanova-Alampay, & Canali, 2002; Lunneborg & Lillie, 1973). Yet little is known about how these letters are interpreted by others, and whether equivalent content used to describe women and men is decoded differentially. In a series of studies, Biernat and Eidelman (2007) exposed participants to a favorable letter of recommendation supposedly written for a man or a woman applying to a graduate program in physics (a male domain in which women would likely be stereotyped as less competent than men). Participants were asked to translate what the professor writing the letter meant about the student's qualifications, and what they themselves thought about the student's qualifications (estimates were made in objective units such as estimated GPA and Graduate Record Exam (GRE) scores, as well as subjective ratings). Consistent with the shifting standards model, the woman about whom favorable things were written was assumed to be less academically accomplished than the comparable man (both in translating the professor's thoughts and estimating one's own).

However, in two other conditions of the study, we provided participants with additional information about the male professor—his gender attitudes. Specifically, in one condition, participants were led to believe the professor was sexist and that he did not think women were as competent in science as men; in another condition, the professor was portrayed as antisexist, and he viewed women and men as equally competent in physics. We expected these manipulations would be suggestive of lower or higher standards for women, respectively. That is, a sexist professor would be assumed to have low expectations for women; a nonsexist professor would be expected to have higher expectations. Thus, according to a standards-based prediction, positive comments about a woman would be translated to mean lower academic standing when provided by a sexist, and equal or higher academic standing when provided by a nonsexist writer (relative to the male student). These predictions are at odds with what might be predicted according to attributional rules of augmenting and discounting (Kelley, 1971). According to this perspective, if a sexist says something nice about a woman, this must mean she is really good (having overcome the writer's negative inclinations), and if an antisexist says something nice, she might not be all that good (the positive views of the writer provide a discounting cue).

Results were consistent with the standards-based interpretation: Relative to the male student, the female student was assumed to be significantly less objectively competent in the sexist writer condition, and nonsignificantly more competent in the antisexist writer condition (Biernat & Eidelman, 2007). That is, knowledge of the writer's sexism enhanced the pattern of translation that emerged in the control condition of the study. At the same time, however, respondents seemed to distance their own views from those of the sexist professor: Although they "translated" the positive letter to mean less objective quality for the female than male student, they themselves thought more highly of the female student. This suggests that individuals may understand others' communications by referencing the likely standards the communicator employed to make judgments; however, they may reject those judgments when the perspective of the communicator is viewed as inappropriate, or as a "mental contaminant" (Wilson & Brekke, 1994).

Recent work in my lab has also explored dyadic communication chains, in which one partner receives "objective" information about a target individual, then communicates a subjective impression to another individual, who then "back-translates" the subjective impression into (perceived) objective standing of the target. In a doctoral dissertation, Collins (2006) reported a series of studies in which "communicators" viewed academic performance information (e.g., a college transcript) that was attributed to a Black or White male student. Their task was to communicate their impression of the student, in writing, to another study participant. Consistent with the shifting standards model, subjective impressions were more favorable in the case of the Black than the White student. Yoked participants were then asked to read the communications and to estimate the objective academic attributes of the student (e.g., GPA, American College Testing [ACT] scores, etc.); that is, to reproduce key parts of the college transcript. Despite the greater positivity of the impressions formed of the Black student, back-translations either revealed no difference in perceived Black–White standing, or in two studies, judgments that the Black student was academically worse than the White student.[2]

That is, equal objective standing was communicated in more favorable terms when the student was Black than White. This could be based on shifting standards ("for a Black student, this record is pretty good"), but admittedly could also reflect the operation of "political correctness" norms or the desire to appear unbiased on the part of communicators. However, the fact that interpreters

---

[2] Consistent with the general finding that stereotyping effects are stronger when the target to be judged is ambiguous as opposed to clear-cut or extreme in his or her attributes (e.g., see Kunda & Thagard, 1996, for a review), Black targets were back-translated to be less objectively good than White targets when academic credentials were mediocre in quality (as opposed to very good).

understood more favorable subjective language to mean less strong academic credentials for the Black student argues against the "norms" interpretation. Instead, it seems more consistent with the central argument of the shifting standards model—that stereotypes affect the standards we use to judge individual members of stereotyped groups, and that these judgments are interpreted by others (who presumably share the same cultural knowledge of stereotypes) with reference to those differential standards.

SETTING STANDARDS

In the research discussed thus far, the role of standards in judgment has been assumed rather than directly assessed. Gender stereotypes about aggression, financial standing, or competence in masculine work domains are assumed to mean that standards are lower for women than men on these dimensions; racial stereotypes about academic ability similarly mean lower standards for Blacks than Whites. As Figure 7.1 indicates, lower standards for a group indicate lower expectations, which lead to anchoring of within-group subjective rating scales at lower levels of a stereotyped dimension. In turn, this pattern of standard setting can give rise to contrast effects in social judgment. This idea is stated eloquently in a book by law professor Stephen Carter (1993), writing about Black achievement in academics and the workplace: "Like a flower blooming in winter, intellect is more readily noticed where it is not expected to be found" (p. 54).

At the same time, Carter (1993) recognized an opposite pattern of standard setting, in which members of devalued or negatively stereotyped groups are held to higher standards than members of valued or positively stereotyped groups: "Our parents' advice was true: We really do have to work twice as hard to be considered half as good [as Whites]" (p. 58). This idea is well-articulated in a theoretical perspective on double standards for evaluating competence (Foddy & Smithson, 1989; Foschi, 1992, 2000; Foschi & Foddy, 1988). According to this sociological perspective, gender and race (as well as other category memberships) are status characteristics that implicate different standards for evaluating competence:

> Those who are considered to be of lower status will have their performances scrutinized and then assessed by a stricter standard than those who are of higher status; the latter, on the other hand, will be given the benefit of the doubt and will be treated with a more lenient standard than the former. (Foschi, 1998, p. 63)

Furthermore, "the application of a more lenient standard to the higher status person ensures that more ability is assigned to him or her than to the lower status person with the same record" (Foschi, 2000, p. 26). In other words, holding lower status groups to higher standards of competence than high-status groups is conducive to assimilation effects in judgment.

My guess is that most readers of this chapter would agree, based on experience or intuition (or the research literature), that both patterns of standard setting are likely to occur. Stereotypes do mean that standards are lower for groups devalued on a given attribute, but stereotypes also lead us to require more evidence of an attribute if a target is stereotyped as not possessing the attribute. Indeed, the latter pattern is consistent with related findings that individuals are ready to perceive in others the attributes they expect (Brewer, 1988; Bruner, 1957; von Hippel, Sekaquaptewa, & Vargas, 1995), that information is sought in a way that may confirm stereotyped expectations (Trope & Thompson, 1997), and that expected behaviors are believed to have higher diagnostic value for inferring dispositions than unexpected behaviors (Trope & Liberman, 1996).

To recognize and reconcile the possibility that stereotypes can implicate both lower and higher standards for members of negatively stereotyped groups, Biernat and Kobrynowicz (1997) made a distinction between two types of standards: *minimum standards*—those indicating the low-end expectations about a group's standing on an attribute—and *confirmatory* (or ability) standards—those relevant for conclusively demonstrating that a group member has the attribute in question. When judges are asked to define minimum standards, these should be lower for groups stereotyped as deficient on the attribute in question (a prediction consistent with the shifting standards model).

When asked to define confirmatory standards, however, these should be higher for those same groups (as predicted by the double standards/status characteristics perspective). That is, a member of a negatively stereotyped group may be held to low minimum standards (consistent with low expectations) but high confirmatory standards (consistent with the idea that a judge will require stronger evidence that an unexpected outcome is due to an underlying disposition).

To test this prediction, Biernat and Kobrynowicz (1997) oriented judges toward either minimum or confirmatory standards and asked them to consider the resumé of a male or female (Study 1) or Black or White male (Study 2) job applicant. To measure standards, judges were asked to indicate the level of performance they would require of the applicant before considering him or her for a job. For example, in the minimum standards condition, judges were asked "how many examples [of job-relevant skills] would you require" for the applicant to "meet the *minimum standard* to perform the skill?" In the confirmatory standards condition, the question about examples concluded, "before feeling confident that [the applicant] *has the ability* to perform the skill?" Consistent with predictions, when minimum standards were assessed, women were held to lower standards than men, and Black applicants to lower standards than White applicants. Among those who indicated their confirmatory standards, however, the opposite pattern emerged—White women and Black men were held to higher standards to confirm their ability to perform job-related skills than White men.

A similar pattern emerged in research examining the standards for female and male targets to "qualify" as possessing a variety of personality attributes (Biernat, Ma, & Nario-Redmond, 2008). For example in one study, participants were provided with a list of 20 behaviors relevant to the trait "emotional." They were asked to consider a male or female target person, and to check off either (a) "the *minimum* number of behaviors necessary to detect whether or not the target is emotional; to *give you some inkling*" that the target is emotional, or (b) "the total number of behaviors that are necessary to *confirm* whether or not the target is emotional; to *demonstrate to you*" that the target is emotional. Because men are stereotyped as "deficient" in emotionality, the prediction was that they should be held to lower minimum emotionality standards, but higher confirmatory emotionality standards than women. The number of required behavioral examples checked was the index of the standard (minimum or confirmatory) the participant had in mind. Results confirmed that fewer behaviors were required to suspect that a man might be emotional (to meet minimum standards), but more behaviors were required to confirm that he was emotional relative to women (see also Biernat & Ma, 2005; Maass, Montalcini, & Biciotti, 1998).

In short, the minimum–confirmatory standards distinction seems useful for understanding how perceivers use and interpret trait terms. Perceivers apply different evidentiary rules depending on trait stereotypicality, target group membership, and the judgment standard (minimum or confirmatory) at hand. These different types of standards may be particularly relevant in decision-making contexts where, for example, one sets an initial screening standard (e.g., establishment of a "short list" of candidates for a job), followed by a final choice (e.g., a hiring decision). The short list may be akin to a minimum standard, and should potentially favor those group members who are stereotyped as deficient in job-related competence, whereas the hiring decision is akin to a confirmatory standard, and should favor those stereotyped as competent. In two studies involving simulated hiring decisions, female judges were indeed more likely to place female than male job applicants on short lists, but were also less likely to hire them (Biernat & Fuegen, 2001). These findings, like those based on distinctions between subjective and objective (or common rule) response scales, highlight the subtlety and complexity of the stereotyping process: Stereotypes can lead to either leniency or stringency in the evaluation of individual group members.

BEHAVING TOWARD MEMBERS OF STEROTYPED GROUPS

The shifting standards approach has highlighted the complex ways in which stereotypes guide our perceptions and judgments of individual members of stereotyped groups. Judgment is crucially important, but understanding whether and how that judgment translates into behavior matters as well. When and how do people act on their judgments of individual targets?

From a shifting standards perspective, this question becomes more complex because patterns of judgment vary depending on whether subjective or objective rating scales are used. For example, a woman might be subjectively judged as a "very good" candidate for an executive chief of staff position—better than a comparable man—but objectively judged as the less strong candidate (Biernat & Kobrynowicz, 1997). But whom would the judge hire in this situation? Would hiring behavior follow from the subjective sense of the female as strong, or the common rule judgment of the male as stronger than the female?

The shifting standards model suggests that the latter will be the case—that the hiring decision would favor the male candidate. One of the assumptions of the model is that judgments on objective scales, because they invoke a cross-category framework, better reflect perceivers' mental representations of target (see Figure 7.1). In this case, the male target is represented as the better of the two candidates, and a decision to hire calls for a cross-category choice; it will therefore reflect the representation. However, this is not to suggest that subjective judgments of individuals will never predict behavior. Indeed, consider the following scenario: You are the manager of a coed softball team, and one of your players steps up to bat and hits a single. How will you respond to this event? Will you cheer? Pat the player on the back? Do nothing in particular? Will your response depend on the gender of the player?

In research establishing precisely such a role-playing scenario, Biernat and Vescio (2002) found that female players were more likely than male players to be the recipients of effusive cheers and praise following a hit. This kind of behavioral response—praise, cheers, and so on—seemed not to follow from the stereotyped perception of men as better athletes than women, but rather from the subjective perception of a female hitting a single as "pretty good . . . for a woman." At the same time, role-playing managers favored male over female players on every other behavioral indicator: Male players were more likely than female players to be chosen for the team, placed in the top of the batting lineup, and assigned to valuable infield positions.

These two very different forms of behavior—team assignment and selections versus cheering and praise—capture an important distinction that may account for the different pattern of gender bias on each. Specifically, behavioral choices such as hiring decisions or position assignments can be characterized as having a *zero-sum* quality, in that behavior toward one individual constrains the behavioral options available toward another; scarce resources are involved. On the other hand, behaviors such as cheering, delivery of praise, and a variety of nonverbal acts have a *nonzero-sum* quality, in that they are in (relatively) endless supply and can be bestowed on any number of targets. Cheering Player 1 does not prevent me from cheering Player 2, but assigning Player 1 to shortstop means I cannot place Player 2 in that position (Biernat & Vescio, 2002; Biernat, Vescio, & Manis, 1998).

We have argued that zero-sum behaviors will tend to reveal assimilation to group stereotypes, whereas nonzero-sum behaviors will tend toward contrast (Biernat et al., 1998), and that objective judgments will better predict zero-sum behaviors, whereas subjective judgments will better predict nonzero-sum behaviors. The basis for these predictions lies in the fact that zero-sum behaviors require a cross-category frame of reference, comparable to the frame invoked when judgments are made on a common rule response scale (see Figure 7.1). To select the shortstop or hire the employee, one looks at the whole field of possible candidates. On the other hand, nonzero-sum behaviors such as provision of feedback or praise are likely made with reference to within-*category* expectations. Effusive praise, for example, may result when a target person exceeds expectations. If expectations are lower for one group than another (as is likely the case when considering the hitting power of female compared to male athletes), praise may be more likely in the former case. A similar finding can be seen in research on White judges' responses to Black versus White authors of poorly written essays (Harber, 1998). Feedback (marginal comments on these essays) was more favorable when White "graders" thought the author was Black than White. This positivity toward Blacks may have stemmed from low standards, compared to which the essays seemed "better" or more deserving of positive commentary. Not surprisingly, this pattern of praise (based on comparison to low expectations), is likely to be perceived as patronizing in nature (Foschi, 1992; Jackman, 1994).

The distinction between zero-sum and nonzero-sum behaviors can also be seen in a recent study by Vescio, Gervais, Snyder, and Hoover (2005, Study 1). Participants were placed in leadership roles and had authority over female and male subordinates in a work group described in masculine terms ("requiring strong strategic planning and competitive skills"). Leaders were asked to assign their subordinates to a number of valued tasks or roles (e.g., being the team captain or on the first string of a team competing in an "academic challenge" contest), a form of zero-sum behavior, and to offer comments to their "workers" (praise or criticism), a form of nonzero-sum behavior. Consistent with predictions derived from the shifting standards model, zero-sum behavioral choices favored male over female subordinates (assimilation to gender stereotypes), whereas praise (e.g., "Your answers during the first phase of the experiment were excellent!") was more likely to be offered to female than male subordinates. This pattern of behavior was not universal, however. It only occurred among male leaders, and only when these men had been oriented (through task instructions) to "avoid weaknesses" in their team. Among female leaders, and among men oriented to focus on strengths, gender bias on both types of behavior was reduced. Conditions invoking high-status group members' attention to stereotypical weaknesses of others may be particularly likely to instantiate assimilation to stereotypes in zero-sum behavioral choices, but contrast in nonzero-sum behaviors (e.g., a patronizing pattern of high praise).

COMPLEXITY AND MORE COMPLEXITY

If there is one theme apparent in the research generated by the shifting standards perspective, it is that stereotyping effects are complex and varied. Judgments of and behavior toward members of stereotyped groups may show evidence of assimilation or contrast—indeed the standards evoked by stereotypes may be conducive to assimilation or contrast—depending on the nature of the judgment or behavior at hand. The shifting standards research reviewed here has distinguished between judgments made in common rule and subjective units, standards based on confirmatory and minimum evidentiary criteria, and behaviors that have a zero-sum or nonzero-sum quality. In general, assimilation to stereotypes is more likely when judgments are made on common rule scales, with reference to confirmatory standards, and when the behaviors at hand are zero-sum. Contrast effects (or null effects) are more likely when judgments are made in subjective units, with reference to minimum standards, and when a judgment or a behavior is nonzero-sum in nature. This complexity means that we may sometimes underestimate the extent to which stereotypes guide judgment—we may be too quick to take an apparently null effect of a stereotype as evidence that the stereotype is no longer operative (e.g., Locksley, Borgida, Brekke, & Hepburn, 1980). When women and African Americans are placed on short lists in greater numbers, or when they are praised for their work, we may remark on the positively changing climate for these groups. However, if we recognize that at the same time, hiring or pay raises do not follow, we can continue to see evidence of stereotype operation in everyday life.

Certainly a large number of questions remain about when and why stereotypes will guide judgment and behavior in an assimilative versus contrastive direction, and the shifting standards model can provide only a partial perspective on these issues. For example, the model has little to say about the role of motivation in patterns of stereotyping effects, although it is clear that such factors matter (Fein & Spencer, 1997; Govorun, Fuegen, & Payne, 2006; Kunda & Sinclair, 1999). The model also says little about the normative context in which judgment occurs, although stereotyping and discrimination can be enhanced or reduced depending on situational factors and salient norms (Blanchard, Crandall, Brigham, & Vaughn, 1994; Gaertner & Dovidio, 1986; Pettigrew, 1959; Stangor, Sechrist, & Jost, 2001).

Some issues well within the realm of the shifting standards model seem important to address, however. One concerns the fact that people simultaneously belong to multiple categories, and thus which category standard will be activated in any given setting is an open question. In research in my lab, we have typically focused on one target group at a time (e.g., studying gender stereotyping of White targets, or racial stereotyping of male targets), although occasionally target race and gender have been crossed (e.g., Biernat & Manis, 1994). For example, in one study, judges rated the verbal ability of Black and White, male and female targets in either subjective or objective units (Biernat & Manis, 1994, Study 2). Two independent "shifting standards effects" emerged, such that White targets were judged more verbally able than Black targets in objective ratings, more so than subjective ratings, and women were judged more verbally able than men in objective but not subjective ratings. There was no evidence of a race and gender interaction, but perhaps this was the case because stereotypes about verbal skill exist with regard to both gender and race. One prediction might be that when a stereotype is relevant to one social category but not another, standards based on only the relevant category will be activated. Category expectations may also conflict, as they do for Black women on traits such as "aggressive" or "athletic" (Blacks are stereotyped as more aggressive and athletic than Whites, but women as less aggressive and athletic than men). It is unclear what standards might be invoked in these settings, although one category may dominate depending on context (e.g., Macrae, Bodenhausen, & Milne, 1995), or unique subtype standards may apply.

Additionally, standards may be determined by other features besides a target's category membership. Standards may be established by the context—either explicitly (as when criteria for hiring are specified), or implicitly (e.g., via priming effects; Mussweiler & Englich, 2005). Another commonly used standard for judging others is the *self* (Dunning & Cohen, 1992; Lambert & Wedell, 1991; Mussweiler, Epstude, & Rüter, 2005; Ross, Greene, & House, 1977). Additional work is clearly needed to identify which standards matter, and how different sources of standards are integrated to influence social judgment.

A final issue that research on the shifting standards model raises is whether the tendency to shift standards is a good or bad thing—more specifically, is the shifting standards effect a marker of prejudice? There is certainly reason to suspect that it may be. At the crux of the model is the assumption that perceivers hold stereotypes of social groups. Indeed, Biernat et al. (1991) found that standards did not shift on judgment dimensions (e.g., movie-going frequency, age) for which no gender stereotypes existed, and Biernat and Manis (1994) found that only individuals who explicitly endorsed the stereotype that women have greater verbal ability than men showed evidence of shifting standards in their judgments of individual men's and women's verbal ability. Endorsement of the stereotype that Blacks are more athletic than Whites was also associated with the tendency to shift athleticism standards for judging individual Blacks and Whites (Biernat & Manis, 1994, Study 3).

To the extent stereotypes are related to prejudice (albeit imperfectly), shifting standards may also be linked to prejudice. In several studies, Biernat and Manis (1994) examined whether racial and gender-role attitudes moderated the tendency to shift standards. Results were inconsistent. In one study only those high in racism showed evidence of shifting standards; in another, scores on the Modern Racism Scale (McConahay, Hardee, & Batts, 1981) had no effect on this tendency. Similarly, traditional attitudes toward women (Spence & Helmreich, 1972) were associated with shifting standards in judgments of male and female competence in one study, but not with judgments of verbal ability in another (Biernat & Manis, 1994).

This inconsistency may reflect, in part, the fact that sometimes using shifting standards can be nice. When I judge my 8-year-old's math skills relative to a lower standard than I use to judge the math skills of the college students in my classes, I am probably being appropriate and kind. When judging our assistant professor colleagues on their "service to the department" contributions, it may again be reasonable to use a lower standard than that used to judge our senior colleagues. When we consider the Verbal GRE scores of nonnative English speakers, we may be well advised to use a lower standard for evaluation than we do for native English speakers. In each of these examples, the use of shifting standards seems to suggest kindness, or even fairness, rather than prejudice. Of course, the use of lower standards for some groups may be patronizing in nature; it has the "benevolent" quality that may typify at least certain kinds of prejudice (Glick & Fiske, 2001; Jackman,

1994). Nonethless, the question of whether shifting standards is linked to indicators of prejudice is an open one.

In one recent line of research, we focused on racial attitudes and the tendency for individuals to shift standards when judging Black versus White targets on academic ability (Biernat, Collins, Katzarska-Miller, & Thompson, in press). A measure of individual differences in the tendency to shift standards was created by subtracting the race difference (White–Black) in subjective ratings of academic ability (very poor to very good) from the race difference in objective ratings of academic ability (estimated ACT scores). By this metric, individuals would score high in the tendency to shift standards if they judged Whites more academically competent than Blacks on the objective index and Blacks more competent than Whites on the subjective index. We then correlated this measure with an explicit measure of racial attitudes (the Pro-Black/Anti-Black Attitudes Questionnaire; Katz & Hass, 1988), and with a race implicit associations test (IAT) effect (Greenwald, McGhee, & Schwartz, 1998). We found little relationship between the tendency to shift standards and anti-Black attitudes ($r = .09$), pro-Black attitudes ($r = -.13$), or the IAT ($r = -.14$). Similarly, in two other studies, the tendency to shift standards was uncorrelated with an evaluative priming measure of prejudice and stereotyping (Wittenbrink, Judd, & Park, 1997; $rs = .02-.20$, ns). Thus, there was no indication that race-based shifting standards overlapped with commonly used indicators of explicit or implicit race prejudice.

However, there was some evidence that the indicator of shifting standards predicted an important behavioral outcome. Participants were asked to allocate funds to various student organizations, one of which was the "Black Student Union." This funding task was based on a procedure used by Haddock, Zanna, and Esses (1993), and required participants to cut the budget to all listed student organizations by 20% (from $10,000 to $8,000). In three studies, the tendency to shift race standards when judging academic ability predicted lower funding allocation to the Black Student Union. That is, shifting standards was associated with a more negative behavioral response to a Black organization, and this behavior was not consistently predicted by any other prejudice indicator.[3] Thus, although it may be unclear whether shifting standards can be conceptualized as a marker of prejudice, it seems to matter for at least one form of behavioral response. Interestingly, this behavior (funding allocation) can be conceptualized as zero-sum in nature—it involved allocation of a scarce resource in which behavior toward one group restricted the options available toward another. Further research is needed to examine the ability of the tendency to shift standards (for a variety of groups across a variety of domains) to predict a variety of behavioral responses. I suspect that the pattern of association will be complex and varied.

CONCLUSION

This chapter has provided an overview of questions and research generated from the perspective of the shifting standards model (Biernat et al., 1991). The basic idea behind the model is a simple one—that judgments of others are often based on a frame of reference provided by social category membership(s). It is because of group stereotypes that category memberships provide a frame of reference; stereotypes create a context of group expectations against which an individual group member is evaluated. The shifting standards model therefore suggests that instead of stereotypes solely guiding judgments in an *assimilative* fashion ("I expect that men are more aggressive than women and therefore I judge individual men as more aggressive than individual women"), they may lead to *contrast* effects, particularly on subjective rating scales or in the production of subjective language (Biernat, 2003).

---

[3] It was the shifting standards index and not its subcomponents (e.g., objective and subjective judgments of Blacks and Whites) that predicted funding decisions in all three studies. Additionally, the negative relationship between shifting standards and funding was strongest among those high in implicit prejudice.

One message that emerges from the work reviewed here is that whether stereotypes result in assimilative or contrastive effects depends in large part on the nature of the judgment or behavior at hand. As noted throughout this chapter, assimilation is the more likely outcome when judgments are rendered in common rule units, when confirmatory standards are invoked, and when behaviors are zero-sum in nature, whereas contrast effects or null effects are more likely in subjective judgments, when minimum standards are invoked, and when behaviors have a nonzero-sum quality. Thus, a female applicant for a masculine job may find herself judged favorably subjectively (largely because she is held to a lower minimum standard), but not objectively, compared to a comparable male applicant. More evidence will be required of her to meet confirmatory standards, and perhaps because of this, she is may be less likely to be hired. Nonetheless, she may find herself praised during her interview. In the event she is hired, she may find herself lauded for her work, but nonetheless assigned the less valuable tasks, positions, or resources. Stereotyping effects are complex, and perhaps downright confusing from the perspective of the recipient of these effects.

Of course, other factors may moderate the patterns predicted. For example, we assume equivalence in the qualifications of the female and male applicant in the preceding scenario. The shifting standards model has also typically assumed an "average" target—in this example, not extremely bad nor extremely good—as stereotyping effects are generally more evident when targets are "neutral," "ambiguous," or "average" in quality (e.g., Biernat & Vescio, 2002; Hodson, Dovidio, & Gaertner, 2002; Kunda & Thagard, 1996; Stapel & Winkielman, 1998). Strong motivations (e.g., to appear unprejudiced) may also overcome some of these tendencies. Nonetheless, *ceteris paribus,* stereotyping effects are likely to be revealed in the complex pattern of effects described in this chapter.

Research from the shifting standards model suggests a view of stereotyping beyond simple assimilation. A broader view of social stereotyping suggests a subtlety and complexity of effects that might be missed by studying judgment and behavior through a single lens or method.

REFERENCES

Biernat, M. (2003). Toward a broader view of social stereotyping. *American Psychologist, 58,* 1019–1027.

Biernat, M., Collins, E. C., Katzarska-Miller, I., & Thompson, E. R. (in press). Race-based shifting standards and racial discrimination. *Personality and Social Psychology Bulletin.*

Biernat, M., Crandall, C. S., Young, L. V., Kobrynowicz, D., & Halpin, S. M. (1998). All that you can be: Stereotyping of self and others in a military context. *Journal of Personality and Social Psychology, 75,* 301–317.

Biernat, M., & Eidelman, S. (2007). Translating subjective language in letters of recommendation: The case of the sexist professor. *European Journal of Social Psychology, 37,* 1149-1175.

Biernat, M., & Fuegen, K. (2001). Shifting standards and the evaluation of competence: Complexity in gender-based judgment and decision making. *Journal of Social Issues, 57,* 707–724.

Biernat, M., & Kobrynowicz, D. (1997). Gender- and race-based standards of competence: Lower minimum standards but higher ability standards for devalued groups. *Journal of Personality and Social Psychology, 72,* 544–557.

Biernat, M., Kobrynowicz, D., & Weber, D. (2003). Stereotyping and shifting standards: Some paradoxical effects of cognitive load. *Journal of Applied Social Psychology, 33,* 2060–2079.

Biernat, M., & Ma, J. E. (2005). Stereotypes and the confirmability of trait concepts. *Personality and Social Psychology Bulletin, 31,* 483–495.

Biernat, M., Ma, J. E., & Nario-Redmond, M. R. (2006). *Standards to suspect and diagnose stereotypical traits.* Manuscript submitted for publication.

Biernat, M., Ma, J. E., & Nario-Redmond, M. R. (2008). Standards to suspect and diagnose stereotypical traits. *Social Cognition, 26,* 288-313.

Biernat, M., & Manis, M. (1994). Shifting standards and stereotype-based judgments. *Journal of Personality and Social Psychology, 66,* 5–20.

Biernat, M., Manis, M., & Nelson, T. E. (1991). Stereotypes and standards of judgment. *Journal of Personality and Social Psychology, 60,* 485–499.

Biernat, M., & Vescio, T. K. (2002). She swings, she hits, she's great, she's benched: Implications of gender-based shifting standards for judgment and behavior. *Personality and Social Psychology Bulletin, 28,* 66–77.

Biernat, M., Vescio, T. K., & Manis, M. (1998). Judging and behaving toward members of stereotyped groups: A shifting standards perspective. In C. Sedikides, J. Schopler, & C. A. Insko (Eds.), *Intergroup cognition and intergroup behavior* (pp. 151–175). Hillsdale, NJ: Erlbaum.

Blanchard, F. A., Crandall, C. S., Brigham, J. C., & Vaughn, L. A. (1994). Condemning and condoning racism: A social context approach to interracial settings. *Journal of Applied Psychology, 79,* 993–997.

Breland, N. S. (1983). The use of letters of recommendation in undergraduate admissions. *Journal of College Student Personnel, 24,* 247–253.

Brewer, M. B. (1988). A dual process model of impression formation. In T. K. Srull & R. S. Wyer, Jr. (Eds.), *Advances in social cognition* (Vol. 1, pp. 1–36). Hillsdale, NJ: Erlbaum.

Bronstein, P., Black, L., Pfennig, J. L., & White, A. (1986). Getting academic jobs: Are women equally qualified—and equally successful? *American Psychologist, 41,* 318–322.

Bruner, J. S. (1957). On perceptual readiness. *Psychological Review, 64,* 123–152.

Campbell, J. T., Crooks, L. A., Mahoney, M. H., & Rock, D. A. (1973). *An investigation of sources of bias in the prediction of job performance: A six-year study* (Final Project Rep. No. PR-73-37). Princeton, NJ: ETS.

Carter, S. L. (1993). *Reflections of an affirmative action baby.* New York: Basic Books.

Colarelli, S. M., Hechanova-Alampay, R., & Canali, K. G. (2002). Letters of recommendation: An evolutionary psychological perspective. *Human Relations, 55,* 315–344.

Collins, E. C. (2006). *Shifting standards in making and interpreting subjective judgments: The subtle influence of stereotypes.* Unpublished doctoral dissertation, University of Kansas, Lawrence.

Dunning, D., & Cohen, G. L. (1992). Egocentric definitions of traits and abilities in social judgment. *Journal of Personality and Social Psychology, 63,* 341–355.

Fein, S., & Spencer, S. (1997). Prejudice as self-image maintenance: Affirming the self through derogating others. *Journal of Personality and Social Psychology, 73,* 31–44.

Foddy, M., & Smithson, M. (1989). Fuzzy sets and double standards: Modeling the process of ability inference. In J. Berger, M. Zelditch, Jr., & B. Anderson (Eds.), *Sociological theories in progress: New formulations* (pp. 73–99). London: Sage.

Foschi, M. (1992). Gender and double standards for competence. In C. L. Ridgeway (Ed.), *Gender, interaction, and inequality* (pp. 181–207). New York: Springer-Verlag.

Foschi, M. (1998). Double standards: Types, conditions, and consequences. *Advances in Group Processes, 15,* 59–80.

Foschi, M. (2000). Double standards for competence: Theory and research. *Annual Review of Sociology, 26,* 21–42.

Foschi, M., & Foddy, M. (1988). Standards, performances, and the formation of self–other expectations. In M. Foschi & M. Webster, Jr. (Eds.), *Status generalization: New theory and research* (pp. 248–260). Stanford, CA: Stanford University Press.

Gaertner, S. L., & Dovidio, J. (1986). The aversive form of racism. In J. Dovidio & S. L. Gaertner (Eds.), *Prejudice, discrimination, and racism* (pp. 61–89). New York: Academic.

Glick, P., & Fiske, S. T. (2001). Ambivalent stereotypes as legitimizing ideologies: Differentiating paternalistic and envious prejudice. In J. Jost & B. Major (Eds.), *The psychology of legitimacy* (pp. 278–306). Cambridge, UK: Cambridge University Press.

Govorun, O., Fuegen, K., & Payne, B. K. (2006). Stereotypes focus defensive projection. *Personality and Social Psychology Bulletin, 32,* 781–793.

Greenwald, A. G., McGhee, D. E., & Schwartz, J. L. K. (1998). Measuring individual differences in implicit cognition: The implicit association test. *Journal of Personality and Social Psychology, 74,* 1464–1480.

Haddock, G., Zanna, M. P., & Esses, V. M. (1993). Assessing the structure of prejudicial attitudes: The case of attitudes toward homosexuals. *Journal of Personality and Social Psychology, 65,* 1105–1118.

Harber, K. D. (1998). Feedback to minorities: Evidence of a positive bias. *Journal of Personality and Social Psychology, 74*(3), 622–628.

Hindle, M. (1985). *Introduction to Frankenstein.* New York: Penguin Classics.

Hodson, G., Dovidio, J. F., & Gaertner, S. L. (2002). Processes in racial discrimination: Differential weighting of conflicting information. *Personality and Social Psychology Bulletin, 28,* 460–471.

Hoessler, C., & Chasteen, A. L. (2008). Does aging affect the use of shifting standards? *Experimental Aging Research, 34,* 1–12.

Jackman, M. R. (1994). *The velvet glove: Paternalism and conflict in gender, class, and race relations.* Berkeley: University of California Press.

Judd, C. M., & Park, B. (1993). Definition and assessment of accuracy in social stereotypes. *Psychological Review, 100*(1), 109–128.

Katz, I., & Hass, R. G. (1988). Racial ambivalence and American value conflict: Correlational and priming studies of dual cognitive structures. *Journal of Personality and Social Psychology, 55,* 893–905.

Kelley, H. H. (1971). Causal schemata and the attribution process. In E. E. Jones, D. E. Kanouse, H. H. Kelley, R. E. Nisbett, S. Valins, & B. Weiner, *Attribution: Perceiving the causes of behavior* (pp. 151–174). Morristown, NJ: General Learning Press.

Kobrynowicz, D., & Biernat, M. (1997). Decoding subjective evaluations: How stereotypes provide shifting standards. *Journal of Experimental Social Psychology, 33,* 579–601.

Kraut, R. E., & Higgins, E. T. (1984). Communication and social cognition. In R. S. Wyer & T. K. Srull (Eds.), *Handbook of social cognition* (Vol. 3, pp. 87–127). Hillsdale, NJ: Erlbaum.

Kunda, Z., & Sinclair, L. (1999). Motivated reasoning with stereotypes: Activation, application, and inhibition. *Psychological Inquiry, 10,* 12–22.

Kunda, Z., & Thagard, P. (1996). Forming impressions from stereotypes, traits, and behaviors: A parallel-constraint satisfaction theory. *Psychological Review, 103,* 284–308.

Lambert, A. J., & Wedell, D. H. (1991). The self and social judgment: Effects of affective reaction and "own position" on judgments of unambiguous and ambiguous information about others. *Journal of Personality and Social Psychology, 61,* 884–897.

Locksley, A., Borgida, E., Brekke, N., & Hepburn, C. (1980). Sex stereotypes and social judgment. *Journal of Personality and Social Psychology, 39,* 821–831.

Lopez, S. J., Oehlert, M. E., & Moberly, R. L. (1997). Selection criteria for APA-accredited internships stratified by type of site and competitiveness. *Psychological Reports, 80,* 639–642.

Lunneborg, P. W., & Lillie, C. (1973). Sexism in graduate admissions: The letter of recommendation. *American Psychologist, 28,* 187–189.

Maass, A., Montalcini, F., & Biciotti, E. (1998). On the (dis-)confirmability of stereotypic attributes. *European Journal of Social Psychology, 28,* 383–402.

Macrae, C. N., Bodenhausen, G. V., & Milne, A. B. (1995). The dissection of selection in person perception: Inhibitory processes in social stereotyping. *Journal of Personality and Social Psychology, 69,* 397–407.

McConahay, J. B., Hardee, B. B., & Batts, V. (1981). Has racism declined in America? It depends on who is asking and what is asked. *Journal of Conflict Resolution, 25,* 563–579.

Mussweiler, T., & Englich, B. (2005). Subliminal anchoring: Judgmental consequences and underlying mechanisms. *Organizational Behavior and Human Decision Processes, 98,* 133–143.

Mussweiler, T., Epstude, K., & Rüter, K. (2005). The knife that cuts both ways: Comparison processes in social perception. In M. D. Alicke, D. A. Dunning, & J. I. Krueger (Eds.), *The self in social judgment* (pp. 109–130). New York: Psychology Press.

Parducci, A. (1963). Range-frequency compromise in judgment. *Psychological Monographs, 77,* 1–29.

Pettigrew, T. E. (1959). Regional differences in anti-Negro prejudice. *Journal of Abnormal and Social Psychology, 59,* 28–36.

Roberts, J. V., & Herman, C. P. (1986). The psychology of height: An empirical review. In C. P. Herman, M. P. Zanna, & E. T. Higgins (Eds.), *Physical appearance, stigma, and social behavior: The Ontario symposium* (Vol. 3, pp. 113–140). Hillsdale, NJ: Erlbaum Associates.

Ross, L., Greene, D., & House, P. (1977). The false consensus effect: An egocentric bias in social perception and attribution processes. *Journal of Experimental Social Psychology, 13,* 279–301.

Roth, P. L., Huffcutt, A. I., & Bobko, P. (2003). Ethnic group differences in measures of job performance: A new meta-analysis. *Journal of Applied Psychology, 88*(4), 694–706.

Spence, J. T., & Helmreich, R. (1972). The Attitudes Toward Women Scale: An objective instrument to measure attitudes toward the rights and roles of women in contemporary society. *JSAS: Catalog of Selected Documents in Psychology, 2,* 66.

Stangor, C., Sechrist, G. B., & Jost, J. T. (2001). Social influence and intergroup beliefs: The role of perceived social consensus. In J. P. Forgas & K. D. Williams (Ed.), *Social influence: Direct and indirect processes* (pp. 235–252). New York: Psychology Press.

Stapel, D. A., & Winkielman, P. (1998). Assimilation and contrast as a function of context–target similarity, distinctness, and dimensional relevance. *Personality and Social Psychology Bulletin, 24,* 634–646.

Trope, Y., & Liberman, A. (1996). Social hypothesis testing: Cognitive and motivational mechanisms. In A. Kruglanski & E. T. Higgins (Eds.), *Social psychology: Handbook of basic principles* (pp. 239–270). New York: Guilford.

Trope, Y., & Thompson, E. P. (1997). Looking for truth in all the wrong places? Asymmetric search of individuating information about stereotyped group members. *Journal of Personality and Social Psychology, 73,* 229–241.

Upshaw, H. S. (1962). Own attitude as an anchor in equal-appearing intervals. *Journal of Abnormal and Social Psychology.*

Vescio, T. K., Gervais, S. J., Snyder, M., & Hoover, A. (2005). Power and the creation of patronizing environments: The stereotype-based behaviors of the powerful and their effects on female performance in masculine domains. *Journal of Personality and Social Psychology, 88,* 658–672.

Volkmann, J. (1951). Scales of judgment and their implications for social psychology. In J. H. Rohrer & M. Sherif (Eds.), *Social psychology at the crossroads* (pp. 273–294). New York: Harper.

von Hippel, W., Sekaquaptewa, D., & Vargas, P. (1995). On the role of encoding processes in stereotype maintenance. In M. P. Zanna (Ed.), *Advances in experimental social psychology* (Vol. 27, pp. 177–254). Orlando, FL: Academic.

Wilson, T. D., & Brekke, N. (1994). Mental contamination and mental correction: Unwanted influences on judgments and evaluations. *Psychological Bulletin, 116,* 117–142.

Wittenbrink, B., Judd, C. M., & Park, B. (1997). Evidence for racial prejudice at the implicit level and its relationship with questionnaire measures. *Journal of Personality and Social Psychology, 72,* 262–274.

8 Stereotype and Social Identity Threat

Joshua Aronson
New York University

Matthew S. McGlone
University of Texas, Austin

In the 1994 race for governor of Texas, Ann Richards, the popular incumbent, was expected to easily win the debates and to go on to win the election. She was a brilliant debater whose public speaking earned her a reputation for being feisty, "silver tongued," and quick on her feet. Her underdog opponent, by contrast, was an undistinguished political newcomer; his résumé included many failed business ventures and a losing bid for Congress many years earlier. People were, therefore, naturally surprised when the newcomer turned out to be an artful debater—polished, articulate, and intelligent. In the debate he made Richards look awkward and defensive by comparison. The truly surprising thing about this is that the articulate newcomer was none other than George W. Bush, a man whose current reputation as a public speaker has inspired a cavalcade of ridicule: books cataloguing his frequent and embarrassing gaffes—with such titles as *The Bush Dyslexicon* and *Bushisms*—interview programs devoted to discussing the question "Is Bush an idiot?" and countless late-night talk show jokes on the subject of his inability to form a coherent sentence. Tapes of the 1994 debate show a Bush utterly unrecognizable to viewers a decade later:

> This Bush was eloquent. He spoke quickly and easily. He rattled off complicated sentences and brought them to the right grammatical conclusions. He mishandled a word or two ("million" when he clearly meant "billion"; "stole" when he meant "sold"), but fewer than most people would in an hour's debate. More striking, he did not pause before forcing out big words, as he so often does now, or invent mangled new ones. (Fallows, 2004)

The obvious question is to ask what happened. How does an articulate person become so decidedly bumbling and verbally maladroit? One observer of this 10-year difference, a doctor, concluded that Bush suffers from "pre-senile dementia," but other doctors dispute this, citing recent neurological exams Bush underwent that showed no sign of impairment. Although we cannot prove it, we believe the answer is both more complex and more interesting than dementia—and a good deal more relevant to the psychology of prejudice and discrimination. We believe that Bush suffers from an especially extreme case of what psychologists call stereotype threat, or social identity threat, a mental impairment arising from his negative reputation rather than a faulty brain. We return to exactly why we believe this later, but first we turn to a discussion of social identity threat phenomena and the research that has examined it. The research makes the general point that, like Bush, people who regularly display intellectual underperformance—African Americans, Latinos, and women in the domains of math and science—frequently are smarter than they appear and that many of their difficulties are rooted not in inferior intelligence, but rather in the more tractable social forces that confront them in their daily interactions.

SOCIAL IDENTITY THREAT DEFINED

Social identity threat is a state of psychological discomfort that people experience when confronted by an unflattering group or individual reputation in situations where that reputation can be confirmed by one's behavior (Aronson & Steele, 2005; Steele, 1997; Steele & Aronson, 1995; Steele, Spencer, & Aronson, 2002). A variety of cultural stereotypes refer to abilities of certain groups ("girls can't do math," "Jews are good with money," "White men can't jump," and so on), and people belonging to groups thus stereotyped tend to be as aware of their groups' reputation as anyone in the culture—whether or not they personally agree with the reputation (Devine, 1989).[1] Thus, in situations where such a reputation is relevant (e.g., taking a mathematics test) people negatively targeted by the stereotype (e.g., women) can experience an extra mental burden not experienced by people with a different social identity (e.g., men).

Once aroused, social identity threat can have a number of disruptive effects, among them, the short-term impairment of intelligent thought and performance on intelligence-related tests. Over time, social identity threat can prompt defensive adaptations that have far-reaching effects, such as disengaging from activities or domains where the stereotype is relevant, and, as a result, impaired intellectual development. Thus, social identity threat can result in a self-fulfilling prophecy whereby a person comes to resemble his or her reputation, living down to social expectations. Over the past dozen years, some 200 published studies have examined stereotype threat and demonstrated repeatedly how people confronted with this psychological predicament perform less well on various tests of intellectual ability than they do in situations where the threat is reduced. Thus stereotype threat has joined the list of environmental factors discussed in nature–nurture debates about race and gender gaps in mental test performance (e.g., Jencks & Phillips, 1998; Murray, 2005; Rushton & Jensen, 2005).

It has been frequently pointed out that social identity threats can take many forms and can manifest in different psychological experiences depending on the specifics of the situation, on individual differences the person brings to the situation (Aronson et al., 1999; Shapiro & Neuberg, 2007), and on the transient mindset he or she adopts in the situation (McGlone & Aronson, 2006; Shih, Pittinsky, & Ambady, 1999). As such, the term *stereotype threat* has become something of a catch-all used to describe a variety of situations that can make people perform or behave in a manner consistent with a negative stereotype. In a recent theoretical paper, Shapiro and Neuberg (2007) pointed out that there are at least six qualitatively distinct "stereotype threats" that can arise depending on whose performance or behavior is evaluated (one's self or the stereotyped group as a whole) and who is doing the evaluating (the self, others from one's group, or others from an outgroup). This list of threats grows larger still given that we define it to include cases such as that of George W. Bush, where the negative stereotype in question applies to a group of one.

That this phenomenon can take a variety of forms may partly explain why people may have heard of stereotype threat but appear unclear of its central tenets and range of application—who is susceptible, how it impairs performance, and what these effects mean in the "real world" of high-stakes testing or the classroom. In short, despite a good deal of coverage in the popular press, in college textbooks, and even in a Hollywood movie, people generally do not know how social identity threat works. This was highlighted in a recent survey of Stanford students, nearly all of whom failed a simple quiz about basic stereotype threat findings (Cherkasskiy, Glickman, & Steele, 2007). This is unfortunate, given that recent findings demonstrate that students with a clear understanding of how stereotype threat works are less susceptible to its effects on test performance (Aronson & Williams,

---

[1] People develop personal reputations that, like stereotypes, function as expectations about what they are like and how they are likely to behave or perform, and—as is the case with George W. Bush—these reputations are sometimes as known to the individual in question as to others. Because a group stereotype is not at issue in such instances, a better name for the phenomenon of confronting a negative personal reputation might be simply "identity threat." For the sake of simplicity, however, we include this under the same umbrella term—social identity threat.

2004; Johns, Schmader, & Martens, 2005; McGlone & Aronson, 2007). The complexity of the phenomenon is particularly acute at this writing, as the number of research studies, each with its own take on the phenomenon, has multiplied rapidly. We hope, therefore, to clearly lay out the most pertinent research findings in a way that can correct some common misunderstandings about stereotype and social identity threat. Rather than present an exhaustive cataloguing of all the studies, we focus most of our discussion on those studies most central to the issues of academic achievement problems, where the bulk of the research efforts have been made. However, we also briefly describe some of the most interesting applications of social identity threat to important domains beyond standardized test and school achievement.

INITIAL DEMONSTRATIONS OF SOCIAL IDENTITY THREAT

Steele and his students conducted the first studies of stereotype threat, examining the effects of stereotype threat on the standardized test performance of African Americans (Steele & Aronson, 1995) and the mathematics performance of women (Spencer, Steele, & Quinn, 1999). Steele and Aronson's first experiment tested the hypothesis that people who experience stereotype threat would experience less of it if they could be assured that their intelligence was not being evaluated, thus rendering the stereotype about their group irrelevant in the situation. African American and White college students were given a very difficult verbal exam comprised of difficult items culled from the Graduate Record Exam (GRE). In one study, half of the test-takers were informed that the test was being used much like an IQ test, to measure their abilities. This "diagnostic" condition was intended to create the psychological conditions people typically face when taking similar tests in the real world. That is, the African American test-takers were expected to experience a good deal of stereotype threat because the experimenter, a White man, was evaluating them on a dimension in which African Americans stereotypically are thought to be inferior. Their performance was compared to that of test-takers in a "nondiagnostic" condition of the experiment. In this condition, test-takers were assured that the study had nothing to do with intelligence and that their abilities would not be evaluated. In every other respect, the situation was identical. The main finding in this study was that African Americans performed dramatically better in the nondiagnostic condition. In a follow-up study, Steele and Aronson found that simply asking African Americans to indicate their race on a questionnaire prior to taking a test was enough to induce stereotype threat and undermine performance in an otherwise nondiagnostic (and presumably nonthreatening) situation; African American students asked to indicate their race solved roughly half as many items as their counterparts who were not asked to indicate their race. In both of these experiments the stereotype threat manipulations had negligible effects on the White test-takers (see Figure 8.1).[2]

Spencer et al. (1999) conducted similar studies in which the math abilities of women and men were tested. In the most intriguing of these studies, Spencer et al. gave men and women a difficult math test. In the control condition, men outperformed women to a significant degree, in line with the stereotype that men are better at math. In the experimental condition, the experimenter made a simple statement prior to administering the test: "This test does not show gender differences." Women in this condition performed significantly better—indeed their performance matched the performance of the men in the experiment.

---

[2] It is important to note that to reduce variability in these small studies, test-takers' verbal SAT scores were used as a covariate to equate students on verbal ability, preparation, and test-taking ability. Thus, the Black–White differences must be interpreted with caution. Specifically, equal mean performances between the Black and White students should not be interpreted to mean that reducing stereotype threat would eliminate the Black–White test score gap. However, the results do make clear that reducing stereotype threat improves the scores of Black test-takers significantly, an effect that is clear with or without the statistical correction for SAT.

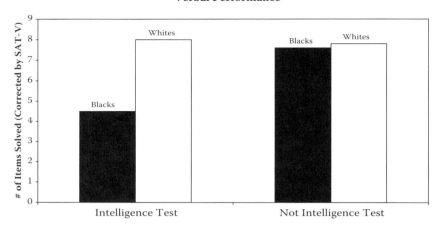

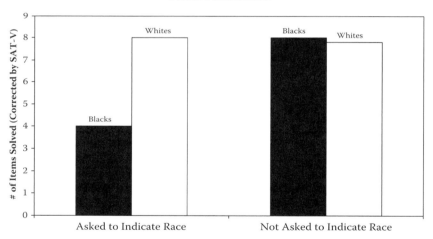

FIGURE 8.1   Effects of stereotype threat on verbal performance (Steele & Aronson, 1995).

GENERALITY OF SOCIAL IDENTITY THREAT EFFECTS

Social identity threat is not an experience limited to African Americans and women. For example, experiments have found performance decrements among Latinos (Aronson & Salinas, 1997; Gonzales, Blanton, & Williams, 2002; Schmader & Johns, 2003), Native Americans (Osborne, 2001), poor White college students in France (Croizet & Claire, 1998), students who are highly engaged and characterized by high aspirations (Aronson et al., 1999), and more average students (Aronson & Salinas, 1997; Brown & Day, 2006). Elderly individuals have been found to perform worse on memory tests when led to believe that memory deficits increase with age but perform better when such notions are debunked (Hess, Auman, Colcombe, & Rahhal, 2003). Although social identity threat may be most likely and most keenly felt among historically stigmatized groups it is a predicament that can beset anyone, not only because anyone can develop a negative personal reputation, but also because most groups can be compared to some other group that is reputed to be superior on some dimension (Aronson et al., 1999). Thus social identity threat can impair the performance of even those groups who are neither "minority" nor broadly stigmatized as intellectually inferior. White men at top-tier universities, for example, bear no historical stigma of being intellectually inferior. However, in select circumstances, comparisons with supposedly superior groups arise, effectively creating a situational threat. For example, in a simple experiment (Aronson et al., 1999), highly proficient White males were given a difficult math test. Two groups of these students were told that the test was aimed at determining their math abilities. For one of the groups, however, a stereotype threat was induced; they were told that a chief aim of the research was to understand the apparent superiority of Asians in mathematics ability. In this condition, these competent and confident males—most of them were mathematics or engineering majors with astronomical math SAT scores—performed nearly a full standard deviation worse than their equally talented counterparts in the control condition. Likewise, psychology students have been found to perform less well when they believe they will be compared to science students on tests of science ability (Croizet, Desprès, Gauzins, Huguet, Leyens, & Meot, 2004). Such studies refute any claim that stereotypes have impact only on those who have faced broad discrimination or prejudice, or who harbor persistent self-doubts about their group's abilities. Clearly, under the proper circumstances, just about anyone can perform poorly when confronted with a stereotype that puts their group at a disadvantage (see also Leyens, Désert, Croizet, & Darcis, 2000; Smith & White, 2002, for similar findings with White males).

THE PROCESS OF SOCIAL IDENTITY THREAT

We turn now to the social psychological process whereby a person confronted with a negative stereotype or individual reputation comes to perform more poorly and suffer both short- and long-term deficits in intellectual ability. This process is illustrated in Figure 8.2. The experience of social identity threat is thought to begin with the awareness that one has a negative reputation or belongs to a group that is negatively stereotyped. It has been assumed that this general awareness leads potential targets of stereotypes to approach situations vigilant for cues that the stereotype or reputation is confirmable (Kaiser, Vick, & Major, 2006; Inzlicht, Aronson, & Mendoza-Denton, in press; Steele, 1997; Steele, Spencer, & Aronson, 2002). Thus for the test-taker in Steele and Aronson's studies described earlier, the message that the researchers were interested in measuring their intelligence or that they wanted the test-takers to indicate their race offered clear and unambiguous cues that their group reputation (as unintelligent) was relevant. In many everyday cases, however, the cues are far less clear and individuals will experience ambiguity and uncertainty about whether they are being viewed through the lens of a stereotype or personal reputation. Such ambiguity appears to be commonplace for minority students, who in their social interactions wonder whether the feedback they receive or the outcomes they experience are mediated by prejudice (e.g., Crocker & Major, 1989).

THE ROLE OF INDIVIDUAL DIFFERENCES

The degree of vigilance for and the nature of one's reactions to potentially threatening cues depend importantly on individual differences. For example, difficult items on a test will mean different things to a highly proficient student than to a mediocre one. A presidential candidate with a reputation for putting his foot in his mouth may be particularly attuned to the political affiliation of his audiences and interviewers. Likewise, a White male experimenter administering an ability test may seem more racist to a Black student who has experienced a great deal of racism than an equally talented Black student who has not. Some individuals thus enter situations more alert than others to the "threat potential" of cues in the environment, to the prospect of bias or unfair treatment based on their social identity. Studies show that some students are particularly sensitive to any cues that signal racism or

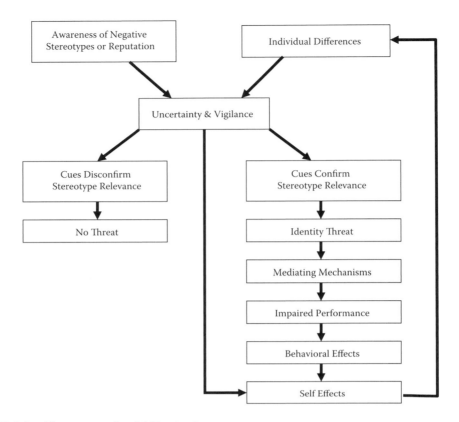

FIGURE 8.2. The process of social identity threat.

sexism (e.g., Pinel, 1999), and anxiously anticipate and react more intensely to such cues when they find them (Mendoza-Denton et al., 2002). Such individuals will be more likely to interpret ambiguous cues as instances of bias and therefore feel threatened. It is true that research points to benefits for self-esteem of attributing negative outcomes to prejudice; the individual can perform poorly without feeling dejected, for example, if he or she can blame the performance on a culturally biased test or a racially bigoted evaluator (e.g., Crocker & Major, 1989). With regard to academic performance, however, there are clear shortcomings to chronic expectations of bias and discrimination.

For example, Aronson and Inzlicht (2004) found that African Americans who measured high in expectations of racial prejudice performed more poorly on tests of their verbal abilities than equally intelligent African Americans with lower expectations of prejudice (see also Brown & Pinel, 2003; Massey, Charles, Lundy, & Fischer, 2003). Moreover, Aronson and Inzlicht found clear negative implications for students' academic self-confidence: Those who chronically expected prejudice had academic self-confidence that fluctuated wildly over time—as if they were riding on a roller-coaster of self-confidence and self-doubt—whereas those who expected less prejudice were far more stable in their confidence. Aronson and Inzlicht attributed this "unstable efficacy" to the fact that expectations of prejudice interfere with the process of assessing one's own abilities. Specifically, if one attributes academic outcomes to prejudice, it is more difficult to form clear knowledge about one's strengths and weaknesses and self-assessments are therefore more likely to be unduly influenced by one's most recent performances—to feel especially stupid after failure and especially smart after success—because academic self-concept typically helps people interpret their performances. People who expect less prejudice appear to have more internally grounded and less reactive assessments of their abilities. Perhaps as a result, minority college students who expect more prejudice appear to have greater difficulty adjusting to college (Mendoza-Denton et al., 2002). Thus, although self-esteem may remain protected despite perceptions of bias, academic performance and academic self-image appear to suffer consequences directly related to such perceptions.

Stereotype and social identity threat were initially discussed as purely situational phenomena, imposed on the person wholly from without (Aronson, Quinn, & Spencer, 1998; Steele, 1997; Steele & Aronson, 1995). Subsequent research, however, makes clear the role of both person and the situation. Situations vary in the degree to which they contain threatening cues, but individuals differ in the degree to which such cues are perceived and responded to. If such cues are not present or if they are actively nullified in the situation (say, by instructions that a test is unconcerned with measuring intelligence), most individuals, regardless of their individual vulnerability to stereotypes, will experience minimal social identity threat and performance will not suffer (as shown in the left side of Figure 8.2). By the same token, if the situational threat is strong enough, most individuals will probably perform less well on a difficult task, regardless of their chronic level of vulnerability, their "stigma consciousness" (Brown & Pinel, 2003), their "race-based rejection sensitivity" (Mendoza-Denton et al., 2002), or their level of racial or gender identity (C. Davis, Aronson, & Salinas, 2006; Schmader, 2002), all of which have been shown to predict underperformance in identity-threatening situations. As with personality traits and attitudes, the influence of such moderators is likely to be greatest when situational influences are ambiguous or weak (e.g., Brown & Pinel, 2003; Darley & Batson, 1973; Liberman, Samuels, & Ross, 2004).

Mediating Mechanisms of Short-Term Performance

When an individual experiences identity threat (right side of Figure 8.2), a number of psychological mechanisms have been proposed that impair performance and a score of experimental studies have found evidence for them.

Anxiety

A good deal of evidence suggests that trying to disprove a negative stereotype arouses anxiety. The early studies on stereotype threat studies tested for this by using self-report measures of test anxiety—and the evidence was spotty. Stereotype-threatened students sometimes reported heightened anxiety, but often did not (e.g., Osborne, 2001; Spencer et al., 1999; Steele & Aronson, 1995), despite a clear pattern of underperformance. Studies conducted since have employed more direct nonverbal measures and confirm that anxiety plays at least a partial role. Blascovich, Spencer, Quinn, and Steele (2001), for example, replicated the conditions of Steele and Aronson's studies; they had Black and White college students take a difficult verbal test under stereotype threat or no stereotype threat conditions (the diagnostic test was described as "racially fair" in the no stereotype threat condition). Blood pressure was monitored throughout the test in all conditions. The study yielded a typical pattern of stereotype threat effects on performance: Black test-takers performed least well when the test was represented as diagnostic of verbal ability and performed significantly better when it was represented as racially fair. Blacks in the stereotype threat condition showed a distinct pattern of blood pressure readings: Their blood pressure spiked sharply and significantly from their baseline levels, but for all other test-takers, it dropped. Importantly, questionnaires probing for anxiety found no differences, suggesting that people can experience disruptive physiological states like anxious arousal without necessarily reporting higher levels of anxiety than do less aroused people. This underscores the difficulty in relying on verbal reports to indicate internal states or causes of behavior and performance (e.g., Nisbett & Wilson, 1977).

A classic method of indicating anxiety and arousal is to compare the effects of testing conditions on complex versus simple tasks. Physiological arousal has long been known to boost performance on simple tasks but interfere with performance on complex tasks (Yerkes & Dodson, 1908). If stereotype threat impairs complex tasks but facilitates simple ones this strongly suggests that arousal is involved in stereotype threat. In a recent experiment, O'Brien and Crandall (2003) showed just this. Women under stereotype threat performed better on an easy math test than women under no stereotype threat but, replicating earlier stereotype threat studies (e.g., Spencer et al., 1999), performed worse on the hard math test.

Another approach to assessing anxiety is to observe individuals in stereotype-threatening situations and code their nonverbal behavior for signs of anxiety. In such a study, Bosson, Haymovitz, and Pinel (2004) found that homosexual men under stereotype threat displayed significantly greater levels of nonverbal anxiety than heterosexual or nonthreatened homosexual men when they were asked to interact with young students, a situation that made their identity as homosexuals problematic.

That stereotype threat arouses anxiety provides convergent evidence that students under stereotype threat are trying hard to not confirm the stereotype—adopting what are referred to as "performance avoidance goals" (Elliot & Church, 1997; Elliot, McGregor, & Gable, 1999; Smith, 2004), or "prevention goals" (Seibt & Förster, 2004)—where the individual's focus is on avoiding failure rather than achieving success. Brown and Josephs (1999) showed, for example, that women performed especially poorly when told a math test was designed to identify their weaknesses, but performed much better when told a test was designed to find their strengths.

Reduced Working Memory and Impaired Self-Regulation

The anxiety aroused by stereotype threat appears to interfere with cognitive functioning by reducing cognitive resources the test-taker needs to perform well. As anyone who has taken a high-stakes test knows, when anxious, a variety of extraneous thoughts and emotions can arise that can interfere with attention to the task and foil one's performance. Various researchers have examined this line of reasoning in the context of stereotype threat. Steele and Aronson (1995), for example, found that students under stereotype threat experienced greater cognitive activation of stereotype-related and self-doubt-related constructs. Others have found that students under stereotype threat report an abundance of negative thoughts and task-related worries (Beilock et al., 2007; Cadinu, et al., 2005; Keller & Dauenheimer, 2003; Marx & Stapel, 2006). Spencer, Iserman, Davies and Quinn (2001) found that people under stereotype threat actively try to suppress such thoughts and emotions, a process that appears to compound the problem and further undermine performance (see also Inzlicht & Gutsell, in press; McGlone & Aronson, 2007). Although theorists agree that all such intrusive processes impair performance by consuming mental resources, there is some disagreement about which resources are at issue. Schmader and her colleagues (2003; 2007) cast this impairment in terms of "reduced working memory capacity" and present evidence that such thoughts and emotions—in addition to direct effects of anxiety—simply reduce the amount of short-term memory available to solve intellectual problems. Consistent with this analysis, a recent study (Beilock, Rydell, & McConnell, 2007) found that women under stereotype threat performed worse on math problems that required short-term memory and because their short-term memory capacity was reduced, went on to perform poorly on a verbal task involving short-term memory. Such "spillover effects"—where impairments in a stereotyped domain deplete resources needed for performance in nonstereotyped domains—are particularly noteworthy, because they suggest that stigma exacts a more general toll than previously thought. For example, if a woman experiences stereotype threat during the math portion of the SAT, this can exert an extra burden on her performance on a subsequent verbal section of the test. Inzlicht and colleagues first documented this kind of spillover, finding that under stereotype threat, students were less adept than nonthreatened counterparts at performing any number of tasks that demand self-regulation—maintaining a tight squeeze on an exercise handgrip, resisting tempting food, performing well on a Stroop task, or staying focused during a standardized test (Inzlicht & Gutsell, 2007; Inzlicht, McKay, & Aronson, 2006). Stereotype threat thus appears to tax more than the process of remembering; it appears to put a burden on a broader set of "executive" functions. Whether it is more accurate or useful to distinguish a working memory explanation from a more general executive function explanation awaits research that pits the two explanations against one another in the same study. The general picture is clear, however: Stereotype threat undermines performance by depleting cognitive resources needed for all kinds of mental functions.

Expectations

A common misunderstanding about stereotype threat is that it undermines performance simply by lowering a person's performance expectations. One study did indeed find that inducing stereotype threat lowered performance expectations for an upcoming test (Stangor, Carr, & Kiang, 1998), but actual performance was not assessed in this study, so it is unclear whether these lowered expectations would have translated into lower performance. Other studies (e.g., Spencer et al., 1999; Stone, Lynch, Sjomeling, & Darley, 1999) find no such direct effect of stereotype threat on expectations, despite the fact that stereotype threat impaired performance. Still other studies (Steele & Aronson, 1995) find that raising performance expectations fails to undo the effects of stereotype threat on performance. The role of expectations in stereotype threat therefore appears to be complex. One reason for this is that on most sequential tasks like standardized tests, where items will differ in form and difficulty as one progresses, initial expectations based on situational cues that arouse or nullify stereotype threat can change as soon as one encounters success or difficulties while progressing from item to item. Blanket initial expectancies can thus be poor predictors of performance (e.g., Zigler & Butterfield, 1968).

Effort

Another misunderstanding of the literature on stereotype threat attributes the impaired performance to reduced effort. Sackett (2005), for example, argued that in the presence of stereotype threat cues, test-takers simply decide not to try because, in the context of a psychology experiment, there are no penalties for giving up. Were they in the real world taking a high-stakes test such as the SAT, where the penalties for withdrawing effort are real and severe, most test-takers would not reduce their effort, and the effect of stereotype threat on performance would evaporate. Sackett believed that this is why stereotype threat, although an interesting laboratory phenomenon, has little if any effect on test score gaps in the real world. Although this is certainly a plausible hypothesis, studies that have measured effort—how long people work on the test, how many problems they attempt, how much effort they report putting in, and so on—have revealed no clear pattern of effort withdrawal in response to stereotype threat. Still, effort withdrawal looms as a possible interpretation for the performance differentials in the real world, because in none of these laboratory studies were there any consequences imposed on test-takers for low performance or low effort. To examine whether inducing stereotype threat has effects in situations like high-stakes tests, where test-takers suffer consequences for giving up, Aronson and Salinas (2001) conducted an experiment in which meaningful consequences were attached to performance. Students took a difficult test with electrodes attached to their wrists that they were led to believe were monitoring the effort they expended on the test. The test-takers were further led to believe that there would be severe consequences for not trying hard to do well; they would have to retake the test—for up to 3 hours of testing—until an acceptable amount of effort was detected. Under such circumstances, only a masochist would simply give up on the test in the face of stereotype cues. The results clearly refuted the effort-withdrawal hypothesis; test-takers performed worst in the condition in which the stakes for not trying were imposed and when stereotype threat was induced. This strongly suggests that reduced effort is not a necessary mediator of stereotype threat effects on test performance. To be sure, this does not force the conclusion that effort withdrawal never mediates underperformance. Indeed, effort reduction appears to be a mediator of the longer term effects of social identity threat on academic achievement, as recent research with college students shows (e.g., Massey & Fischer, 2005). We discuss these effects shortly.

Priming Effects

The social cognition literature is replete with demonstrations of the behavioral effects of stereotype activation. These effects are typically assimilative; that is, behavior becomes consistent with the activated stereotype (Wheeler & Petty, 2001). For example, when people are subtly exposed to words associated with negative aging stereotypes (e.g., *senile*), they walk more slowly and exhibit poorer memory, but when the words cast aging in a positive light (e.g., *wise*), their walking pace quickens and their memories improve (Bargh, Chen, & Burrows, 1996; Hausdorff, Levy, & Wei, 1999). Researchers have characterized such priming effects as "ideomotor" phenomena in which behavior follows automatically from the activation of stereotypical trait schemas (Wheeler, Jarvis, & Petty, 2001). These effects are presumed to occur because our knowledge of stereotypes includes information about associated behaviors, which increase in action potential when the trait schema is highly accessible.

Stereotype threat theorists generally agree that the activation of a negative stereotype is a necessary condition for stereotype threat to occur. Is it sufficient? Investigations of stereotype priming and stereotype threat have proceeded separately for the most part, but have yielded some parallel findings. In particular, research has shown that stereotype activation can have a similar impact on stereotype targets and nontargets. Priming the African American stereotype can impair the intellectual performance of students both within (Steele & Aronson, 1995) and outside of (Wheeler et al., 2001) this ethnic group, and priming the female stereotype has a similar negative impact on men and women (Dijksterhuis, 2001). Although these parallel findings have been noted in the literature, theoretical explanations portray them as largely separate phenomena. For example, Dijksterhuis and Bargh (2001) suggested that self-relevant stereotypes can result in both stereotype threat and ideomotor effects, but the former may be stronger because they result from two sources of activation (knowledge of the stereotype plus one's social identity). Similarities notwithstanding, the hypothesized mechanisms underlying these effects are very different. As noted earlier, stereotype threat theorists typically characterize priming-based performance decrements as resulting from an affect-induced depletion of cognitive resources. In contrast, ideomotor theorists attribute priming effects to cognitive construct activation that can alter one's behavior without conscious awareness or affect (Wheeler & Petty, 2001).

Some researchers have suggested that the activation of negative stereotypes is sufficient to induce stereotype threat (Ambady et al., 2004; Dijksterhuis & Bargh, 2001; Oswald & Harvey, 2000; Wheeler et al., 2001; Wheeler & Petty, 2001), but others have argued that stereotype threat cannot be reduced to a simple priming effect. In particular, Marx and his colleagues have argued that priming will not produce stereotype threat unless the primed individuals harbor some concern about confirming a negative stereotype about their group (Marx, Brown, & Steele, 1999; Marx & Stapel, 2006a; Marx, Stapel, & Muller, 2005). Thus stereotype threat affects only those who know the stereotype (a requisite for priming it) and feel targeted by it (a requisite for it to be threatening). Stereotype priming may nevertheless exert assimilative effects on both targets and nontargets, but only the former should exhibit threat-based concerns.

To test this hypothesis, Marx and Stapel (2006a) had men and women take a difficult math test under stereotype threat (i.e., the test was portrayed as diagnostic of math ability) or neutral (nondiagnostic test) conditions. Prior to test administration, half of these participants were primed with the negative trait dumb and its semantic associates, and the other half were not primed. Priming this trait adversely affected the test performance of men and women alike in both the diagnostic and nondiagnostic test conditions (consistent with an ideomotor account). In addition, women underperformed relative to men when the test was portrayed as diagnostic, but not when it was portrayed as nondiagnostic (consistent with previous stereotype threat research). However, only women in the diagnostic test condition exhibited an increased concern about the relationship between their math ability and their gender; negative trait priming alone did not elevate women's threat-based concerns in the nondiagnostic condition. These results suggest that stereotype activation is not sufficient to induce stereotype threat. Targets must also make the connection between the stereotype and their performance in the testing context.

Most experiments that find some individual difference variable moderates the effects of stereotype activation on performance strengthen this argument. For example, Inzlicht, Aronson, Good, and McKay (2006) found that individuals low in "self-monitoring," the desire and ability to control one's self-expressions to cultivate a desired public image, were particularly vulnerable to a threatening environment—specifically in which their gender or racial group was outnumbered. Such situations typically result in lower performance among women on math tests (Inzlicht & Ben-Zeev, 2000). High self-monitors, however, were unaffected by being outnumbered, despite the fact that stereotypes were shown to be cognitively activated by this situation. A simple priming effect simply cannot explain these results.

LONGER TERM EFFECTS ON ACHIEVEMENT

Thus far we have sketched the process that spoils performance when people are confronted with social identity threat—anxiety about confirming a negative reputation consumes cognitive resources needed for intelligent thought. This is the short-term effect of social identity threat. Over time and in the face of failures of this sort, individuals are frequently apt to alter their behaviors in ways that reduce such threats. Studying harder, practicing more, and enrolling in test-prep courses could all reduce such vulnerability (see Beilock et al., 2007), and there is plenty of anecdotal evidence to suggest that individuals faced with stereotype threat sometimes respond to devaluation of their abilities by buckling down and working harder (Aronson, 2002). However, the literature also suggests that many individuals exposed to social identity threat frequently adopt defensive behaviors and strategies that lead to longer term deficits in ability, thus implicating negative stereotypes in producing not only test score gaps, but ability gaps as well.

Avoidance of Challenge

As the developmental theorist Judith Rich Harris (1998) has observed, students who start out just a little behind their peers in intellectual ability tend to avoid activities that could increase their intelligence. Meanwhile those who start out just a little bit ahead "are busy doing pushups with their brains." Thus an achievement gap between Blacks and Whites or girls and boys in math that starts out relatively small can widen dramatically over a span of years. This is an apt description of what occurs in American schools, where, for example, Blacks start school on average a year behind Whites, but fall increasingly behind as they make their way through school (e.g., Fryer & Levitt, 2004). It is an axiom of educational psychology that intellectual growth requires intellectual challenge. Yet under social identity threat, challenge can signal the potential for racial, gender, or personal devaluation—both in others' eyes and in one's own eyes as well. Aronson and Good (2001) have found, for example, that minority children respond to an evaluative—and thus identity threatening—setting by shying away from challenging problems in favor of easy, success-assuring ones. They found that in the sixth grade (but not before) students chose to work on easier problems on an evaluative test, but selected problems appropriate for their grade level when the test was framed as nondiagnostic of their abilities. This was true of both Latinos on a reading test and girls on a math test. Stone (2002) found conceptually similar results: Under stereotype threat, athletes were more likely to avoid practice that would have improved their likely performance on an upcoming test of golf ability. Similarly, Pinel (1998) showed that women most prone to stereotype threat actively avoided tests in domains in which women are stereotypically alleged to be inferior to men. Such avoidance tactics are related to "self-handicapping" (Jones & Berglas, 1978), wherein the individual interferes with his or her own performance to have a plausible excuse for failure—such as "I didn't practice," which although hardly flattering, is nonetheless preferable to "I lack ability." One can well imagine that in schools, when given the choice of a curriculum that varies in degree of difficulty, students' perceptions of potentially threatening circumstances may steer them toward alternatives with less threat potential, and as a result, they miss important opportunities to develop their intelligence.

Sociologist Douglas Massey and his associates (Massey et al., 2003; Massey & Fischer, 2005) conducted a longitudinal survey of more than 4,000 freshmen from different ethnic backgrounds attending more than 28 American colleges. Students were surveyed each year and their performance in college was monitored throughout their undergraduate careers. Unsurprisingly, Massey et al.

found the common achievement gaps observed between groups: Asians and Whites outperformed Blacks and Latinos, even when controlling for SAT scores, family income, and other important background factors. However, when students' responses to questions probing their degree of stereotype vulnerability were controlled, the grade gaps disappeared; the degree of stereotype threat they felt as freshmen was associated with lower grades. Moreover, the degree to which students endorsed the negative stereotypes about their group predicted the amount of effort they reported putting into their studies; the more they believed the stereotypes to be accurate, the less hard they worked and the lower grades they earned.

Disidentification

These dual effects—acceptance of the stereotype and reduced effort and engagement—may reflect a chronic defense referred to as "disidentification" (Steele, 1992), which involves detaching self-esteem from outcomes. Confronted with failure, people typically find ways of protecting their self-esteem. When a person fails a test and then claims the test was biased or that he or she does not really care about doing well—a response sometimes called "devaluing" (Major, Quinton, & McCoy, 2002)—this temporary response soothes the ego and reduces the dejection that typically accompanies failure. However, when such responses become chronic and the person adjusts his or her self-concept, divesting self-esteem from the domain, this can seriously thwart achievement. Stereotype threat on tests appears to be most acutely experienced by students who are most invested in doing well (Aronson et al., 1999; Steele, 1997), those who are highly identified with an intellectual domain. Thus one way to reduce the experience of threat is to psychologically divest from threatening domains. Although failure in and of itself is enough to prompt disidentification, stereotype threat appears to make it a far more common response among Blacks and Latinos because the stereotype suggests not only a lack of ability, but also limited belongingness in the domain (Cohen & Steele, 2002; Good, Dweck, & Rattan, 2006). In the long run, though, disengagement of this sort is counterproductive; some degree of psychological investment is necessary to sustain motivation for achievement (Osborne, 1997; Steele, 1992, 1997).

Thus, the endpoint of our model, after performance effects spur behavioral and attitudinal adaptations, is the modification of the self, which, as shown in Figure 8.1, feeds back to one's vulnerability to potentially threatening circumstances. In the case of disidentification, it is presumed that one will become less vulnerable to potentially threatening cues for the simple reason that devaluation in the domain requires one to care about the domain. However, other effects of social identity threat, such as chronic avoidance of challenge or evaluation, would presumably have the opposite effect, producing a vicious cycle that renders the individual less academically successful (e.g., Elliot & Church, 2003), more prone to negative affect (Zuckerman, Kieffer, & Knee, 1998), and more prone to self-doubt (e.g., Arkin & Oleson, 1998). George W. Bush, perhaps in response to his reputation as unintelligent, has adopted a pattern of avoiding press conferences, of accepting interviews only with politically sympathetic representatives of the press (i.e., Fox News), and of vetting audiences for his speeches to make sure they are supportive. This is functionally equivalent to the student who chooses easy problems to solve when under threat. Such a strategy is likely to increase one's vulnerability to social identity threat because it validates the fears that underlie it. By the same token, attributing one's difficulties to racial bias, as individuals often do (e.g., Major et al., 2002), can have a similarly spiraling effect: Each time one does it, one may become ever more prone to see bias in one's environment, thus rendering one's self more vulnerable to social identity threat (Aronson & Inzlicht, 2004; Mendoza-Denton et al., 2002). Shortly we describe adaptations that reduce threat without nurturing maladaptive tendencies.

THE PITFALLS AND PROMISE OF SOCIAL IDENTITY SALIENCE

As noted, the numerous demonstrations of social identity threat all hinge on cues—demographics questions about ethnicity or gender, a statement about how test results will be used, etc.)—that increase the salience of an individual's stigmatized identity in an evaluative context. Ascribed identities such as one's gender or ethnicity—the principal stigmatized identities investigated in stereotype threat research—are already well-formed, pivotal aspects of the self-concept before the age of 5 (Aboud, 1988). Children are not only cognizant of and conversant about these identities, but are also familiar with their associated stereotypes by the early elementary school years (Bigler, Jones, & Lobliner, 1997; Ruble & Martin, 1998). By adolescence, the centrality of gender and ethnicity to one's sense of self, combined with their stereotypical associations established during childhood ("Blacks aren't as smart as Whites," "Boys are better at math than girls," etc.) make college students with stigmatized ascribed identities especially vulnerable to stereotype threat, although its effects have been observed in much younger students as well (Aronson & Good, 2003; Good & Aronson, 2008; McKown & Weinstein, 2003).

This vulnerability is most evident in studies demonstrating the impact of social identity salience on intellectual performance. Prior to administering a mathematics test, Shih et al. (1999) presented their Asian American female participants with a brief questionnaire comprised of questions designed to make salient their identity as women (e.g., Do you prefer single-sex or coed college dormitories?), as Asian Americans (e.g., How many generations of your family have lived in America?), or as members of a test-irrelevant social category (cable TV subscribers). Participants primed to categorize themselves as women achieved the lowest performance of all three groups, consistent with the negative stereotype about women's math ability. In contrast, participants primed to categorize themselves as Asian American achieved the highest performance of all groups, consistent with the stereotype crediting this group with superior math ability. As noted earlier, Inzlicht and Ben-Zeev (2000) found that groups of women performed worse on a math (but not a verbal) test when a male test-taker was present, presumably because this made their female identity salient (see also Inzlicht & Ben-Zeev, 2003). These findings suggest that when students' multiple social identities are considered in an academic context, stereotype threat phenomena may be approached far more strategically than previously recognized. They also raise the intriguing possibility that subtle interventions designed to increase the salience of certain social identities but not others can improve students' test performance.

Nonascribed aspects of personal identity that emerge relatively late in adolescence may mitigate ego threat (Marcia, 1966). In particular, domains of identity predicated on interpersonal interaction (e.g., college student), religion (e.g., Roman Catholic), ideology (e.g., liberal), intellectual interests (e.g., psychology major), and occupational aspirations (e.g., prelaw) come to the fore as adolescents formulate a sense of self based on their own preferences, choices, and accomplishments (Patterson, Sochting, & Marcia, 1992; Waterman, 1982). These "achieved identities" are adaptive for any adolescent as she negotiates the spheres of independence and nonfamilial interdependence associated with adulthood. They also provide a potential substrate for female and ethnic minority adolescents to transcend the negative expectations associated with their stigmatized ascribed identities (Kobrynowicz & Biernat, 1998).

Shih et al.'s (1999) findings demonstrate that stereotype threat can be subdued by a subtle process of ascribed identity manipulation—in this case, focusing people's attention on an ascribed identity (Asian ethnicity) for which there is a positive test-relevant stereotype ("Asians are good at math") rather than one for which there is a negative stereotype ("females are bad at math"). McGlone and Aronson (2006) investigated the possibility that the manipulation of an individual's salient achieved identity (i.e., membership in social categories based on an individual's choices and achievements) can produce comparable benefits. With very few exceptions, the intellectual performance stereotypes associated with ascribed identities (gender and ethnicity) tend to be negative (e.g., "females are bad at math," "African Americans aren't good readers," etc.). Furthermore, the handful of positive performance stereotypes associated with ascribed identities (e.g., "Asians are good at math," "Jews are good at handling money," etc.) are often predicated on negative stereotypes about targets' habits (e.g., "Asian students don't have social lives") and motivation (e.g., "Jews are greedy"). The domain of achieved identities is broader than that of ascribed identities, and includes many positive performance

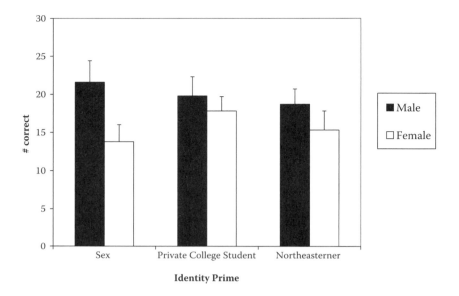

FIGURE 8.3. Spatial reasoning test performance by participant gender and identity prime condition (McGlone & Aronson, 2006).

stereotypes without negative motivational baggage. For example, consider the positive intellectual performance stereotype associated with the category of "private college students." Although this identity may be linked in some cases to ascribed characteristics (e.g., an individual who is born into a family with the means to afford a private college education), clearly an individual must choose a college and thus might contemplate the strong positive intellectual performance stereotype associated with this achieved identity (i.e., "private college students are academically gifted").

In a variant of Shih et al.'s (1999) methodology, McGlone and Aronson (2006) had undergraduates complete questionnaires designed to prime either their ascribed gender identity, achieved "private college student" identity, or a test-irrelevant identity prior to taking a spatial reasoning test. As shown in Figure 8.3, female participants who were primed to contemplate their identity as students at a selective private college performed better than those who were primed to contemplate their gender or a test-irrelevant identity. For males, priming their gender identity increased performance relative to the test-irrelevant or private college student primes. These results demonstrate that reminding students of their achieved identities (e.g., private college student) can subdue stereotype threat associated with their ascribed identities (e.g., female). They also add to the mounting evidence indicating that social identity can be both the vector and antidote of stereotype threat's ill effects. These results are important for a further reason: Spatial abilities are considered to be the most highly sex-linked abilities, those that are assumed to flow from biological differences. That the spatial abilities gap can be closed by a simple manipulation of social identity casts doubt on the notion that sex-linked differences are fixed and strongly suggests that they are remediable through intervention (e.g., Halpern, 2000; Newcomb, 2002).

BEYOND THE ACADEMIC CONTEXT

Investigations of social identity threat have focused principally on its impact on intellectual performance in laboratory and field-testing settings. Yet the predicament can in principle arise in any domain of human behavior for which there are identity-based stereotypic expectations about performance and any context in which this performance is evaluated. In recent years, researchers have demonstrated stereotype threat's operation in a variety of performance domains and populations beyond the academic context.

Athletic Performance

The overrepresentation of African Americans at the highest levels of certain amateur and professional sports has been a major source of racial stereotypes about athletic performance. Although the scientific evidence implicates class, cultural, and historical factors as primary causes for this phenomenon (Wiggins, 1997), mass media portrayals by some sportscasters (e.g., Jimmy "the Greek" Snyder) and filmmakers (e.g., Ron Shelton's 1992 film *White Men Can't Jump*) frame it as a consequence of Black athletes' alleged advantage in "natural ability" over White athletes. Several studies confirm that laypeople hold racial stereotypes about athletes consistent with this framing (Beilock & McConnell, 2004; Devine & Baker, 1991; Johnson, Hallinan, & Westerfield, 1999; Krueger, 1996; Sailes, 1996; Stone, Perry, & Darley, 1997). For example, Stone et al. (1997) observed that White college students listening to a radio broadcast of a men's basketball game were more inclined to attribute natural athletic ability to a successful target player when they thought he was Black, but attributed his performance to "court smarts" and "hustle" when they thought he was White.

Racial stereotypes can exert an influence not only on the perception of an athlete's performance, but also on the performance itself. Stone et al. (1999) invited Black and White college students to participate in a golf putting task that they characterized as a standardized measure of "natural athletic ability," "sports intelligence" (i.e., the ability to think strategically during an athletic performance), or "psychological factors associated with general sports performance." The two groups performed equally well when the task was framed as a measure of general sports performance. However, White participants performed worse than control participants when it was framed as diagnostic of natural athletic ability, and Black participants performed worse than the controls when it was framed as diagnostic of sports intelligence. These findings parallel the effects of diagnosticity framing in the intellectual performance domain: Frames that create the risk of confirming a negative group stereotype harm the performance of group members. The negative consequences of this framing may also have an impact on the way one approaches or prepares for the performance. In a subsequent study, Stone (2002) observed that when White participants were given the opportunity to practice prior to completing the aforementioned golf task, they practiced less when the task was framed as diagnostic of natural athletic ability than when it was purported to measure general sports performance. By self-handicapping themselves via reduced practice, the White athletes created ambiguity about the meaning of a potential poor performance. The irony of course is that withdrawing preparatory effort could provide evidence that others (competitors, audiences, and coaches) might interpret as confirmation of the negative stereotype.

Aging and Memory

Ageist stereotypes portraying older people as having memory problems are widespread, particularly in Western societies (Kite & Johnson, 1988; Nelson, 2002). Researchers have demonstrated a variety of negative memory outcomes associated with aging stereotype ideation. For example, Levy and Langer (1994) tested young and older groups of Americans and Chinese for their beliefs about aging and then assessed memory performance. They observed that age differences in memory were related to the degree to which individuals within these cultures displayed positive views of aging. Views toward aging were less positive among Americans than Chinese, and age differences in memory performance were larger in the former group. Levy (1996) found that older adults performed worse on a memory test when they were explicitly primed with negative rather than positive aging stereotypes. Stein, Blanchard-Fields, and Hertzog (2002) observed comparable effects induced by implicit stereotype activation.

Other researchers have explored the operation of stereotype threat among older adults more directly in studies manipulating the diagnosticity of memory tests or cues designed to highlight negative aging stereotypes. For example, Rahhal, Hasher, and Colcombe (2001) found that age differences in performance on a sentence memory task, obtained when participants were informed that the test was intended to examine their memory ability, were eliminated when the memory aspect of the task was deemphasized. Hess, Auman, Colcombe, and Rahhal (2003) administered a free recall test to younger and older adults after providing tutorials about positive or negative aspects of the relationship between aging and memory. Implicit measures of association (Banaji & Hardin, 1996) indicated that all participants exhibited higher activation of the negative aging stereotype in the negative than the positive information condition. However, only older adults' recall performance was significantly affected by the manipulation. They exhibited higher recall accuracy in the positive information condition and lower accuracy in the negative condition, relative to a control condition. Consistent with Steele and Aronson's (1995) claims regarding the role of ability identification in stereotype threat effects, the negative impact of aging stereotypes on recall performance was strongest among older adults who most valued their memory ability.

Political Knowledge

Political scientists and pollsters have long noted a significant gap between men and women's knowledge of basic civics as well as contemporary political figures and events. For example, data collected in the National Election Studies (NES) between 1947 and 1995 indicate that men achieved 20% to 35% higher accuracy in identifying the political party currently controlling the U.S. House of Representatives, the collective term used to refer to the first 10 amendments to the Constitution (Bill of Rights), or even a senator or representative from their home state (Delli-Carpini & Keeter, 1996). The persistence of the knowledge gap evident in NES data is consistent with findings of the Annenberg Survey Project (Jamieson, 1996; Jamieson et al., 2000; Jamieson & Kenski, 2000). Jamieson and her colleagues have also found that gender differences in political knowledge persist even when respondents are equated in terms of age, race, education, income, marital status, party identification, and exposure to news media. Their findings indicate that some mechanism beyond standard demographic factors is responsible for the knowledge gap. Conway (1985) suggested that women's apparent lack of political knowledge is due to their lack of interest in the domain. However, interest-based accounts are hard-pressed to explain why women have voted at an equal or higher rate than men since 1980 (Delli-Carpini & Fuchs, 1993). Graber (1988) hypothesized that women are under less social pressure to remember information than men and consequently forget information at a faster rate; if so, then the gender gap in political knowledge would be just one facet of a cross-domain retention gap. Although Graber's hypothesis has been embraced by some political scholars (Jamieson et al., 2000), to date there is no direct evidence directly supporting it. Moreover, the hypothesis is tenuous from a psychological standpoint, in that memory researchers have yet to document any domain-general gender differences in memory capacity or forgetting proclivity (Bourtchouladze, 2002).

Survey researchers have long been aware that people's desire to project a positive self-image can influence their reporting of attitudes and behaviors (e.g., Schumann & Converse, 1971). The concept of "social desirability bias" is routinely invoked when survey responses suggest a higher degree of awareness, affability, or resolve than less reactive measures indicate (Silver, Anderson, & Abramson, 1986; Welch, 1977). McGlone and Aronson (2006) explored the possibility that the desire to be positively regarded can influence not only women's reported political attitudes (Bennett & Bennett, 1989), but also their facility in drawing on the knowledge on which their attitudes are predicated (D. W. Davis & Silver, 2003). Specifically, they hypothesized that female respondents in a political knowledge survey would exhibit a performance decrement when threatened by the prospect of confirming a negative stereotype about their gender. They found that explicit reference to this prospect (i.e., a portrayal of the survey as diagnostic of gender differences in political knowledge) impaired women's survey performance, as did the more implicit cue of an interviewer's voice of the opposite sex. These cues exerted no appreciable influence on men's performance. This combination of findings suggests that the manipulated factors rendered the context of the survey an intellectually threatening environment for female respondents (Inzlicht & Ben-Zeev, 2000). These factors are operative in the methodology of the NES and other similar surveys, and thus may contribute to the gender gap in political knowledge.

Managerial Performance

Ethnic and gender stereotypes are widespread in the workplace. Numerous studies have demonstrated that Americans generally perceive the traits associated with successful managers as more likely to be held by White men than by women or members of any ethnic minority (Boyce & Herd, 2003; Brenner, Tomkiewicz, & Schein, 1989; Roberson & Block, 2001). This bias has been observed among both entry-level employees and managers themselves, and is magnified when the focus is on traits associated with higher levels (e.g., CEO) of management (Martell, Parker, Emrich, & Crawford, 1998). Such perceptions contribute to and are perpetuated by the underrepresentation of women and minorities at senior management levels, a phenomenon that has been the subject of numerous theories in the management literature. Among the most frequently advanced are discrimination theories, which assume that stereotyping and bias on the part of those in power are responsible for the slower progress of stigmatized groups in organizations (see Davison & Burke, 2000, for a review).

Until very recently, there has been scant research exploring the direct impact of stereotyping on stigmatized employees' performance. In a laboratory simulation, Bergeron, Block, and Echtenkamp (2006) had male and female participants perform a managerial decision-making task after priming stereotypically masculine (e.g., aggressive) or feminine (e.g., nurturing) traits. Although the men were not affected by the priming manipulation, women primed with masculine traits underperformed in the task relative to those primed with feminine traits. This effect was attenuated when women reported high identification with the masculine gender role, thus suggesting that women's susceptibility to threat in a managerial role hinges on their perceived fit into established gender roles (Fletcher, 1999).

In a survey of Black managers in the utility industry, Roberson, Deitch, Brief, and Block (2003) found a reliable relationship between solo status and reports of stereotype threat experiences: Managers who were the only Black employees in their workgroup were more likely to report feelings of stereotype threat than those who had one or more Black colleagues. Solo Black managers reported not only higher perceptions of threat, but also greater inclinations to seek indirect performance feedback (i.e., from peers rather than superiors) and also to discount feedback from superiors as motivated by racism and prejudice. Although correlational in nature, these findings point to the troubling possibility that stereotype threat may lead minority managers to develop suboptimal feedback strategies, thus depriving those who experience the threat of valuable information about their performance and recommendations for improvement.

THREAT-REDUCING INTERVENTIONS

Implicit in much of the preceding discussion is the fact that social identity threat can be reduced by attending to and modifying both the situational and personal influences that give rise to it. For example, reducing the degree of evaluative scrutiny in situations reliably improves performance across a number of studies (e.g., Croizet & Claire, 1998; Steele & Aronson, 1995), as does priming identities that facilitate performance (McGlone & Aronson, 2007; Shih et al., 1999). Yet such tactics are far less practicable in the real world than in the psychology laboratory, where conditions can be controlled and identities primed. Thus several lines of research have taken the approach of attempting to mitigate threats in situations more like the real world where ability evaluation is part and parcel of the environment, and where the cues that influence the salience of social identities are subject to myriad uncontrolled influences. The integrated classroom is a prime example of such an environment, increasingly so, in the current era of high standards and frequent tests. Several lines of research point to promising approaches to help students cope with the social identity threat frequently engendered in such environments.

FOREWARNING

A number of researchers have explored the possibility that awareness of one's susceptibility to processes such as stereotype threat can mitigate their ill effects. Give students an understanding of how anxiety can stem from stereotype threat, the reasoning goes, and they will feel less pressure, because an external attribution (I'm anxious because of stereotype threat) is less self-incriminating—and upsetting—than the internal one fostered by the stereotype itself (I'm anxious because I'm too dumb for this test). In one study (Aronson & Williams, 2004), prior to being tested in the Steele and Aronson paradigm described earlier, Black college students were sent and instructed to read a pamphlet describing either the stereotype threat effect, the phenomenon of test anxiety, or a completely unrelated topic. Those in the first two conditions performed just as well under stereotype threat as comparable students who were not forewarned but took the test under nonthreatening conditions. A similar study (Johns, Schmader, & Martens, 2004) found equally positive results among women taking difficult math tests. Also in the context of women and mathematics, McGlone and Aronson (2007) found that forewarning eliminated the male–female gap when test-takers were instructed to think of a positive social identity (private college student) to counter the stereotype, and widened the gap when they were instructed to suppress all stereotype-related thoughts. Thus, knowledge of the stereotype process can be helpful, particularly when individuals are given a specific cognitive strategy designed to counter the stereotype. The forewarning studies are not only important for those interested in interventions to boost achievement, but they also offer relief for those of us who worry that teaching their psychology students about the research might create rather than reduce a vulnerability to stereotypes.

REFRAMING THE NATURE OF ABILITY

Inspired by research on self-theories of intelligence (e.g., Dweck, 1999), Aronson (1999) reasoned that stereotype threat would be least problematic for students who conceived of their abilities as malleable rather than fixed. If stereotypes create anxiety by implying a lack of ability, stereotype threat should be less threatening if one sees or can be induced to see ability as expandable. To test this reasoning, students were given a GRE verbal test presented either as a test of an ability that was malleable or fixed. African Americans—and to a lesser degree the Whites—performed much better and reported lower performance anxiety when the test was said to diagnose an ability that could be expanded with practice.

Three field interventions built on these findings. Aronson, Fried, and Good (2002) employed numerous tactics of attitude change to induce college students to embrace a malleable-intelligence mindset. Attitudes toward academic achievement and actual performance were assessed 4 months later and at the end of the school year. The results were impressive. African American students in the malleable-intelligence condition raised their grades (overall grade point average) by four tenths of a grade point. In a second intervention study (Good, Aronson, & Inzlicht, 2003), low-income Latino and White junior high students participated in an intervention that taught and reinforced one of three different messages. One group learned that intelligence is expandable; another group of students were taught to attribute their academic difficulties to the normal process of adapting to junior high rather than any lack of ability, a conceptual replication of an intervention by Wilson and Linville (1982). These two groups of students were compared to a control group, which spent the same amount of time learning about the perils of drug use. The results were impressive; Latino students mentored in the two experimental groups received higher scores on the statewide standardized test of reading than their counterparts who received the antidrug message. Similar results were found for girls' math performance on the mathematics test; girls in the control group underperformed relative to boys, but those in the two intervention groups performed as well as boys. A recent study conceptually replicated these findings, boosting the grades and academic engagement among students making the transition from elementary to middle school by teaching the notion of expandable intelligence (Blackwell, Trzesniewski, & Dweck, 2007).

Role Models

Stereotypes gain power when objective reality confirms them. Thus when girls learn that they are not supposed to be as good at math as boys, this knowledge is reinforced by cues in the social environment, such as fewer women teaching math or held up as examples of mathematical prowess—or even just seeing women in stereotypically feminine roles (Davies, Spencer, Quinn & Gerhardstein, 2002). Thus, a number of studies have attempted to counter stereotype threat by increasing the salience of counterstereotypic individuals—and with good effects. Marx and Roman (2002), for example found that having a female experimenter, introduced as a math expert, administer an evaluative math test significantly boosted the performance of female test-takers. A similar study found that women performed better on a math test after merely reading about four individual women who had succeeded in architecture, law, medicine, and invention (McIntyre, Paulson, & Lord, 2003). Similarly positive effects have been found for African American students (Marx & Goff, 2005).

Self-Affirmations

A number of researchers have reasoned that if stereotype threat arouses anxiety because it poses a significant threat to self-esteem, then affirming the self-concept with self-affirmations—for example, getting students to reflect on central talents, values, and beliefs—may reduce threat and boost performance. Several studies support this line of reasoning, showing that affirmations improve test performance among the stereotype-threatened students. This has been demonstrated with women taking math tests (Martens, Johns, Greenberg, & Schimel, 2006) and low-income minority students in a field study (Cohen, Garcia, & Master, 2006). In one recent study, the affirmation procedure reduced the achievement gap in grades by 40%. It is important here to distinguish self-concept from self-esteem. These self-affirmations typically do not raise self-esteem; rather, they remind students of what matters to them, which has the effect of making them less susceptible to self-esteem threats—including stereotype threats alleging mathematics inferiority.

CONCLUSION: BUSH'S BRAIN

We began this chapter suggesting that there is probably nothing physically wrong with George W. Bush's brain to explain the apparent loss of IQ points he has experienced since his run for governor in 1994. Rather, two things happened that, in combination, provided ample grounds for a severe case of social identity threat, one strong enough to markedly impair his public speaking abilities. First, his job became much more difficult; the campaign for the presidency, like the presidency itself, is tremendously more demanding than running for—and even serving as—governor of Texas, a notoriously undemanding governorship. Second, he developed a reputation that portrayed him as unintelligent, one that reverberated, grew, and spread quickly in the media echo chamber. This reputation was very hard to find evidence of in the media prior to the 2000 presidential race. These two factors provide the necessary conditions for stereotype threat. As we have shown, the same process that confronts Bush often confronts the typical Black or Latino student taking a standardized test or being evaluated in an academic situation: A reputation of intellectual inferiority, a challenging task, and an evaluative context in which failure on the task will confirm the negative reputation all conspire to suppress intelligent thought. The good news is that although reputations, like stereotypes, can be hard to change, there are many ways to intervene to help individuals cope with social identity threat. Much of the research we have discussed shows how, with attention to the ways that situations are arranged and the mindsets that students can be taught, social identity threat need not compromise intellectual performance and growth. Acknowledging and acting on the fact that human intelligence is both fragile and malleable, we believe that schools and universities need not be the threatening environments they so often are for minority students, but instead, to quote Bush himself, can become the kind of places "where wings take dream."

REFERENCES

Aboud, F. E. (1988). *Children and prejudice.* New York: Blackwell.

Ambady, N., Paik, S. K., Steele, J., Owen-Smith, A., & Mitchell, J. P. (2004). Deflecting negative self-relevant stereotype activation: The effects of individuation. *Journal of Experimental Social Psychology, 40,* 401–408.

Ambady, N., Shih, M., Kim, A., & Pittinsky T. L. (2001). Stereotype susceptibility in children: Effects of identity activation on quantitative performance. *Psychological Science, 12,* 385–390.

Arkin, R. M., & Oleson, K. (1998). Self-handicapping. In J. M. Darley & J. Cooper (Eds.), *Attribution and social interaction: The legacy of Edward E. Jone*s (pp. 313–347). Washington, DC: American Psychological Association.

Aronson, J. (1999). *The effects of conceiving ability as fixed or improvable on responses to stereotype threat.* Unpublished manuscript, New York University, New York.

Aronson, J. (2002). Stereotype threat: Contending and coping with unnerving expectations. In J. Aronson (Ed.), *Improving academic achievement: Impact of psychological factors on education.* San Diego, CA: Academic.

Aronson, J., Fried, C., & Good, C. (2002). Reducing the effects of stereotype threat on African American college students by shaping theories of intelligence. *Journal of Experimental Social Psychology, 38,* 113–125.

Aronson, J., & Good, C. (2001). *Stereotype threat and the avoidance of challenging work.* Manuscript in preparation, New York University, New York.

Aronson, J., & Good, C. (2002). The development and consequences of stereotype vulnerability in adolescents. In F. Pajares & T. Urdan (Eds.), *Adolescence and education.* New York: Information Age.

Aronson, J., & Inzlicht, M. (2004). The ups and downs of attributional ambiguity: Stereotype vulnerability and the academic self-knowledge of African-American students. *Psychological Science, 15,* 829–836.

Aronson, J., Lustina, M., Good, C., Keough, K., Steele, C., & Brown, J. (1999). When white men can't do math: Necessary and sufficient factors in stereotype threat. *Journal of Experimental Social Psychology, 35,* 29–46.

Aronson, J., Quinn, D., & Spencer, S. J. (1998). Stereotype threat and the academic performance of minorities and women. In J. Swim & C. Stangor (Eds.), *Prejudice: The target's perspective.* San Diego, CA: Academic.

Aronson, J., & Salinas, M. F. (1997). Stereotype threat: *The role of effort withdrawal and apprehension on the, intellectual underperformance of Mexican-Americans.* Unpublished manuscript, University of Texas.

Aronson, J., & Salinas, M. F. (2001). *Stereotype threat, attributional ambiguity, and Latino underperformance.* Unpublished manuscript, New York University, New York.

Aronson, J. & Steele, C.M. (2005). Stereotypes and the fragility of human competence, motivation, and self-concept. In C. Dweck & E. Elliot (Eds.), *Handbook of Competence & Motivation.* New York, Guilford.

Aronson, J., & Williams, J. (2004). *Stereotype threat: Forewarned is forearmed.* Manuscript in preparation, New York University, New York.

Banaji, M., & Hardin, C. (1996). Automatic stereotyping. *Psychological Science, 7,* 136-141.

Bargh, J. A., Chen, M., & Burrows, L. (1996). Automaticity of social behavior: Direct effects of trait construct and stereotype activation on action. *Journal of Personality and Social Psychology, 71,* 230–244.

Beilock, S. L., Jellison, W. A., Rydell, R. J., McConnell, A. R., & Carr, T. H. (2006). On the causal mechanisms of stereotype threat: Can skills that don't rely heavily on working memory still be threatened? *Personality and Social Psychology Bulletin, 32,* 1059-1071.

Beilock, S. L., & McConnell, A. R. (2004). Stereotype threat and sport: Can athletic performance be threatened? *Journal of Sport & Exercise Psychology, 2004,* 597–609.

Beilock, S. L., Rydell, R. J., & McConnell, A. R. (2007). Stereotype threat and working memory: Mechanisms, alleviation, and spill over. *Journal of Experimental Psychology: General, 136,* 256–276.

Bennett, L. M., & Bennett, S. E. (1989). Enduring gender differences in political interest: The impact of socialization and political dispositions. *American Politics Quarterly, 17,* 105–122.

Bergeron, D. M., Block, C. J., & Echtenkamp, B. A. (2006). Disabling the able: Stereotype threat and women's work performance. *Human Performance, 19,* 133–158.

Bigler, R. S., Jones, L. C., & Lobliner, D. B. (1997). Social categorization and the formation of intergroup attitudes in children. *Child Development, 68,* 530–543.

Blackwell, L., Trzesniewski, K., & Dweck, C. S. (2007). Implicit theories of intelligence predict achievement across an adolescent transition: A longitudinal study and an intervention. *Child Development, 78,* 246–263.

Blascovich, J., Spencer, S. J., Quinn, D. M., & Steele, C. M. (2001). Stereotype threat and the cardiovascular reactivity of African-Americans. *Psychological Science, 12,* 225–229.

Bosson, J. K., Haymovitz, E. L., & Pinel, E. C. (2004). When saying and doing diverge: The effects of stereotype threat on self-reported versus non-verbal anxiety. *Journal of Experimental Social Psychology, 40,* 247–255.

Bourtchouladze, R. (2002). *Memories are made of this.* New York: Columbia University Press.

Boyce, L. A., & Herd, A. M. (2003). The relationship between gender role stereotypes and requisite military leadership characteristics. *Sex Roles, 49,* 365–378.

Brenner, O. C., Tomkiewicz, J., & Schein, V. E. (1989). The relationship between sex role stereotypes and requisite management characteristics revisited. *Academy of Management Journal, 32,* 662–669.

Brown, R. P., & Day, E. A. (2006). The difference isn't black and white: Stereotype threat and the race gap on Raven's Advanced Progressive Matrices. *Journal of Applied Psychology, 91,* 979–985.

Brown, R. P., & Josephs, R. A. (1999). A burden of proof: Stereotype relevance and gender differences in math performance. *Journal of Personality and Social Psychology, 76,* 246-257.

Brown, R. P., & Pinel, E. C. (2003). Stigma on my mind: Individual differences in the experience of stereotype threat. *Journal of Experimental Social Psychology, 39*(6), 626–633.

Cadinu, M., Maass, A., Rosabianca, A., & Kiesner, J. (2005). Why do women underperform under stereotype threat? *Psychological Science, 16,* 572-578.

Cherkasskiy, L. Glickman, A. & Steele, C. M. (2007). A survey of college student knowledge about stereotype threat. Presentation to the Annual Meeting of SPARC, San Jose California, May.

Cohen, G., Garcia, J., & Master, A. (2006). Reducing the racial achievement gap: A social-psychological intervention. *Science, 313,* 1307–1310.

Cohen, G. L., & Steele, C. M. (2002). A barrier of mistrust: How stereotypes affect cross-race mentoring. In J. Aronson (Ed.), *Improving academic achievement: Impact of psychological factors on education.* San Diego, CA: Academic.

Conway, M. M. (1985). *Political participation in the United States.* Washington, DC: Congressional Quarterly Press.

Crocker, J., & Major, B. (1989). Social stigma and self-esteem: The self-protective properties of stigma. *Psychological Review, 96,* 608–630.

Croizet, J. C., & Claire, T. (1998). Extending the concept of stereotype threat to social class: The intellectual underperformance of students from low socioeconomic backgrounds. *Personality and Social Psychology Bulletin, 24,* 588–594.

Croizet, J., Desprès, G., Gauzins, M; Huguet, P., Leyens, J., & Meot, A. (2004). Stereotype threat undermines intellectual performance by triggering a disruptive mental load. *Personality and Social Psychology Bulletin, 30,* 721-731

Darley, J. M., & Batson, C. D. (1973). From Jerusalem to Jericho: A study of situational and dispositional variables in helping behavior. *Journal of Personality and Social Psychology, 27,* 100–119.

Davies, P. G., Spencer, S. J., Quinn, D. M., & Gerhardstein, R. (2002). All consuming images: How demeaning commercials that elicit stereotype threat can restrain women academically and professionally. *Personality and Social Psychology Bulletin, 28,* 1615–1628.

Davis, C., Aronson, J., & Salinas, M. (2006). Shades of threat: Racial identity as a moderator of stereotype threat. *Journal of Black Psychology, 32,* 399–417.

Davis, D. W., & Silver, B. D. (2003). Stereotype threat and race of interviewer effects in a survey on political knowledge. *American Journal of Political Science, 47,* 33–45.

Davison, H. K., & Burke, M. J. (2000). Sex discrimination in simulated employment contexts: A meta-analytic investigation. *Journal of Vocational Behavior, 56,* 225–248.

Delli-Carpini, M. X., & Fuchs, E. (1993). The year of the woman: Candidates, voters, and the 1992 elections. *Political Science Quarterly, 108,* 29–36.

Delli-Carpini, M. X., & Keeter, S. (1996). *What Americans know about politics and why it matters.* New Haven, CT: Yale University Press.

Devine, P. G. (1989). Stereotypes and prejudice: Their automatic and controlled components. *Journal of Personality and Social Psychology, 56,* 5–18.

Devine, P. G., & Baker, S. M. (1991). Measurement of racial stereotype subtyping. *Personality and Social Psychological Bulletin, 17,* 44–50.

Dijksterhuis, A. (2001). Automatic social influence: The perception–behavior link as an explanatory mechanism for behavior matching. In J. Forgas & K. D. Williams (Eds.), *Social influence: Direct and indirect processes* (pp. 95–108). Philadelphia: Psychology Press.

Dijksterhuis, A., & Bargh, J. A. (2001). The perception–behavior expressway: Automatic effects of social perception on social behavior. *Advances in Experimental Social Psychology, 33,* 1–40.

Dweck, C. S. (1999). *Self-theories: Their role in motivation, personality, and development.* Philadelphia: Taylor & Francis.

Elliot, A. J., & Church, M. A. (1997). A hierarchical model of approach and avoidance achievement motivation. *Journal of Personality and Social Psychology, 72,* 218–232.

Elliot, A. J., & Church, M. A. (2003). A motivational analysis of defensive pessimism and self-handicapping. *Journal of Personality, 71,* 369–396.

Elliot, A. J., McGregor, H., & Gable, S. (1999). Achievement goals, study strategies, and exam performance: A mediational analysis. *Journal of Educational Psychology, 91,* 549–563.

Fallows, J. (2004, August). When George meets John. *The Atlantic, 294*(1), 39–44.

Fletcher, J. K. (1999). *Disappearing acts.* Cambridge, MA: MIT Press.

Fryer, R. G., & Levitt, S. D. (2004). Understanding the black–white test score gap in the first two years of school. *The Review of Economics and Statistics, 86,* 447–464.

Gonzales, P. M., Blanton, H., & Williams, K. J. (2002). The effects of stereotype threat and double-minority status on the test performance of Latino women. *Personality and Social Psychology Bulletin, 28,* 659–670.

Good, C., & Aronson, J. (2008). The development of stereotype threat: Consequences for educational and social equality. In C. Wainryb, J. G. Smetana, & E. Turiel (Eds.), *Social development, social inequalities, and social justice* (pp. 155-183). New York: Taylor & Francis.

Good, C., Aronson, J., & Inzlicht, M. (2003). Improving adolescents' standardized test performance: An intervention to reduce the effects of stereotype threat. *Journal of Applied Developmental Psychology, 24,* 645–662.

Good, C., Dweck, C. S., & Rattan, A. (2006). *The effects of perceiving fixed-ability environments and stereotyping on women's sense of belonging to math.* Manuscript under review, Barnard College, Columbia University, New York.

Graber, D. A. (1988). *Processing the news: How people tame the information tide.* New York: Longman.

Halpern, D. F. (2000). *Sex differences in cognitive abilities* (3rd ed). Mahwah, NJ: Erlbaum.

Harris, J. R. (1998). *The nurture assumption.* New York: Touchstone.

Hausdorff, J. M., Levy, B. R., & Wei, J. Y. (1999). The power of ageism on physical function of older persons: Reversibility of age-related gait changes. *Journal of the American Geriatrics Society, 47,* 1346–1349.

Herrnstein, R. J., & Murray, C. (1994). *The bell curve.* New York: Free Press.

Hess, T. M., Auman, C., Colcombe, S. J., & Rahhal, T. (2003). The impact of stereotype threat on age differences in memory performance. *Journals of Gerontology, 58*(1), 3–11.

Inzlicht, M., Aronson, J., Good, C., & McKay, L. (2006). A particular resiliency to threatening environments. *Journal of Experimental Social Psychology, 42,* 323-336.

Inzlicht, M., Aronson, J. & Mendoza-Denton, R. (in press). Contending and coping with minority status in school. In J. Levine & F. Buttera (Eds.) *Coping with Minority Status: Responses to Exclusion and Inclusion.* Cambridge UK: Cambridge University Press.

Inzlicht, M., & Ben-Zeev, T. (2000). A threatening intellectual environment: Why females are susceptible to experiencing problem-solving deficits in the presence of males. *Psychological Science, 11,* 365–371.

Inzlicht, M., & Ben-Zeev, T. (2003). Do high-achieving female students underperform in private? The implications of threatening environments on intellectual processing. *Journal of Educational Psychology, 95,* 796–805.

Inzlicht, M., & Gutsell, J. N. (2007). Running out of steam: Neural signals for ego-depletion and stereotype threat. Paper presented in T. Schmader (Chair), *A social neuroscience approach to understanding stereotype threat and psychological disengagement.* Symposium presented at the 8th annual conference of the Society for Personality and Social Psychology, Memphis, TN.

Inzlicht, M., & Gutsell, J. N. (in press). Running on empty: Neural signals for self-control failure. *Psychological Science.*

Inzlicht, M., McKay, L., & Aronson, J. (2006). Stigma as ego depletion: How being the target of prejudice affects self-control. *Psychological Science, 17,* 262–269.

Jamieson, K. H. (1996). *Presidential debate: The challenge of creating an informed electorate.* Oxford, UK: Oxford University Press.

Jamieson, K. H., Johnston, R., Hagen, M., Dutwin, D., Kenski, K., Kirn, K., et al. (2000). *The primary campaign: What did the candidates say, what did the public learn, and did it matter?* Annenberg Public Policy Center Working Paper No. 6. Philadelphia: University of Pennsylvania.

Jamieson, K. H., & Kenski, K. (2000). The gender gap in political knowledge: Are women less knowledgeable than men about politics? In K. Jamieson (Ed.), *Everything you think you know about politics and why you're wrong* (pp. 83–92). New York: Basic Books.

Jencks, C., & Phillips, M. (1998). *The Black–White test score gap.* Washington, DC: Brookings Institution Press.

Johns, M., Schmader, T., & Martens, A. (2005). Knowing is half the battle: Teaching stereotype threat as a means of improving women's math performance. *Psychological Science, 16,* 175–179.

Johnson, D. L., Hallinan, C. J., & Westerfield, R. C. (1999). Picturing success: Photographs and stereotyping in men's collegiate basketball. *Journal of Sport Behavior, 22,* 45-53.

Jones, E. E., & Berglas, S. (1978). Control of attributions of the self through self-handicapping strategies: The appeal of alcohol and the role of underachievement. *Personality and Social Psychology Bulletin, 4,* 200–206.

Kaiser, C. R., Vick, S. B., & Major, B. (2006). Prejudice expectations moderate preconscious attention to cues that are threatening to social identity. *Psychological Science, 17,* 332–338.

Keller, J., & Dauenheimer, D. (2003). Stereotype threat in the classroom: Dejection mediates the disrupting threat effect on women's math performance. *Personality and Social Psychology Bulletin, 29,* 371–381.

Kite, M. E., & Johnson, B. T. (1988). Attitudes toward older and younger adults: A meta-analysis. *Psychology and Aging, 3,* 233–244.

Kobrynowicz, D., & Biernat, M. (1998). Considering correctness, contrast, and categorization in stereotyping phenomena. In R. S. Wyer, Jr. (Ed.) *Stereotype activation and inhibition: Advances in social cognition* (Vol. 11, pp. 109–126). Mahwah, NJ: Erlbaum.

Krueger, J. (1996). Personal beliefs and cultural stereotypes about racial characteristics. *Journal of Personality and Social Psychology, 71,* 536–548.

Levy, B. R. (1996). Improving memory in old age by implicit self-stereotyping. *Journal of Personality and Social Psychology, 71,* 1092–1107.

Levy, B. R., & Langer, E. (1994). Aging free from negative stereotypes: Successful memory in China and among the American deaf. *Journal of Personality and Social Psychology, 66,* 989–997.

Leyens, J. P., Désert, M., Croizet, J. C., & Darcis, C. (2000). Stereotype threat: Are lower status and history of stigmatization preconditions of stereotype threat? *Personality and Social Psychology Bulletin, 26,* 1189–1199.

Liberman, V., Samuels, S. M., & Ross, L. (2004). The name of the game: Predictive power of reputations versus situational labels in determining prisoner's dilemma game moves. *Personality and Social Psychology Bulletin, 30,* 1175–1185.

Major, B., Quinton, W. J., & McCoy, S. K. (2002). Antecedents and consequences of attributions to discrimination: Theoretical and empirical advances. In M. Zanna (Ed.), *Advances in experimental social psychology* (Vol. 34). San Diego, CA: Academic.

Marcia, J. E. (1966). Development and validation of ego identity status. *Journal of Personality and Social Psychology, 21,* 551–559.

Martell, R. F., Parker, C., Emrich, C. G., & Crawford, M. W. (1998). Sex stereotyping in the executive suite: "Much ado about something." *Journal of Social Behavior and Personality, 13,* 127–138.

Martens, A., Johns, M., Greenberg, J., & Schimel, J. (2006). Combating stereotype threat: The effect of self-affirmation on women's intellectual performance. *Journal of Experimental Social Psychology, 42,* 236–243.

Marx, D. M., Brown, J. L., & Steele, C. M. (1999). Allport's legacy and the situational press of stereotypes. *Journal of Social Issues, 55,* 491–502.

Marx, D. M., & Goff, P. A. (2005). Clearing the air: The effect of experimenter race on target's test performance and subjective experience. *British Journal of Social Psychology, 44*(4), 645-657.

Marx, D. M., & Roman, J. S. (2002). Female role models: Protecting women's math performance. *Personality and Social Psychology Bulletin, 28*(9), 1183–1193.

Marx, D. M., & Stapel, D. A. (2006a). Distinguishing stereotype threat from priming effects: On the role of the social self and threat-based concerns. *Journal of Personality and Social Psychology, 91,* 243–254.

Marx, D. M., & Stapel, D. A. (2006b). It's all in the timing: Measuring emotional reactions to stereotype threat before and after taking a test. *European Journal of Social Psychology, 36,* 687–698.

Marx, D. M., Stapel, D. A., & Muller, D. (2005). We can do it: The interplay of construal orientation and social comparisons under threat. *Journal of Personality and Social Psychology, 88,* 432–446.

Massey, D. S., Charles, C. Z., Lundy, G. F., & Fischer, M. J. (2003). *The source of the river: The social origins of freshmen at America's selective colleges and universities.* Princeton, NJ: Princeton University Press.

Massey, D. S., & Fischer, M. J. (2005). Stereotype threat and academic performance: New data from the national survey of freshman. *The DuBois Review: Social Science Research on Race, 2,* 45–68.

McGlone, M., & Aronson, J. (2006). Social identity salience and stereotype threat. *Journal of Applied Developmental Psychology, 27,* 486–493.

McGlone, M. S., & Aronson, J. (2007). Forewarning and forearming stereotype-threatened students. *Communication Education, 56,* 119–133.

McGlone, M., Aronson, J. & Kobrynowicz, D. (2006). Stereotype threat and the gender gap in political knowledge. *Psychology of Women Quarterly, 30,* 392–398.

McIntyre, R. B., Paulson, R. M., & Lord, C. G. (2003). Alleviating women's mathematics stereotype through salience of group achievement. *Journal of Experimental Social Psychology, 39,* 83–90.

McKown, C., & Weinstein, R. S. (2003). The development and consequences of stereotype-consciousness in middle childhood. *Child Development, 74,* 498–515.

Mendoza-Denton, R., Purdie, V., Downey, G., Davis, A., & Pietrzak, J. (2002). Sensitivity to status-based rejection: Implications for African-American students' college experience. *Journal of Personality and Social Psychology, 83,* 896-918.

Murray, C. (2005, September). The inequality taboo. *Commentary.*

Nelson, T. D. (2002). *Ageism: Stereotyping and prejudice against older people.* Cambridge, MA:MIT Press.

Newcombe, N. (2002). Maximization of spatial competence: More important than finding the cause of sex differences. In A. McGillicuddy-De Lisi & R. De Lisi (Eds.), *Biology, society, and behavior: The development of sex differences in cognition: Advances in applied developmental psychology* (Vol. 21, pp. 183–206). New York: Ablex.

Nisbett, R. E., & Wilson, T. D. (1977). Telling more than we can know: Verbal reports on mental processes. *Psychological Review, 84,* 231–259.

O'Brien, L., & Crandall, C. (2003). Stereotype threat and arousal: Effects on women's math performance. *Personality and Social Psychology Bulletin, 29,* 782–789.

Osborne, J. W. (1997). Race and academic disidentification. *Journal of Educational Psychology, 89,* 728–735.

Osborne, J. W. (2001). Testing stereotype threat: Does anxiety explain race and sex differences in achievement? *Contemporary Educational Psychology, 26,* 291–310.

Oswald, D. L., & Harvey, R. D. (2000). Hostile environments, stereotype threat, and math performance among undergraduate women. *Current Psychology: Developmental, Learning, Personality, Social, 19,* 338–356.

Patterson, S., Sochting, I., & Marcia, J. (1992). The inner space and beyond: Women and identity. In G. Adams, T. Gullotta, & R. Montemayor (Eds.), *Adolescent identity formation* (pp. 9–24). Newbury Park, CA: Sage.

Pinel, E. C. (1999). Stigma consciousness: The psychological legacy of social stereotypes. *Journal of Personality and Social Psychology, 76,* 114–128.

Rahhal, T. A., Hasher, L., & Colcombe, S. J. (2001). Instructional manipulations and age differences in memory: Now you see them, now you don't. *Psychology and Aging, 16,* 697–706.

Roberson, L., & Block, C. J. (2001). Ratio ethnicity and job performance: A review and critique of theoretical perspectives on the causes of group differences. *Research in Organizational Behavior, 23,* 247–325.

Roberson, L., Deitch, E. A., Brief, A. P., & Block, C. J. (2003). Stereotype threat and feedback setting in the workplace. *Journal of Vocational Behavior, 62,* 176–188.

Ruble, D., & Martin, C. L. (1998). Gender development. In W. Damon & N. Eisenberg (Eds.), *Handbook of child psychology* (Vol. 3, pp. 933–1016).

Rushton, J. P., & Jensen, A. R. (2005). Thirty years of research on race differences in cognitive ability. *Psychology, Public Policy, and Law, 11,* 235–294.

Sackett, P. (2005). *High-stakes testing in higher education and employment: Appraising the evidence for validity and fairness.* Paper presented at the annual meeting of the American Psychological Association, Washington, DC.

Sailes, G. A. (1996). An investigation of campus stereotypes: The myth of Black athletic superiority and the dumb jock stereotype. In R. E. Lapchick (Ed.), *Sport in society: Equal opportunity or business as usual?* (pp. 193–202). Thousand Oaks, CA: Sage.

Schmader, T. (2002). Gender identification moderates the effects of stereotype threat effects on women's math performance. *Journal of Experimental Social Psychology, 38,* 194–201.

Schmader, T., & Johns, M. (2003). Converging evidence that stereotype threat reduces working memory capacity. *Journal of Personality and Social Psychology, 85,* 440–452.

Schmader, T., Johns, M., & Forbes, C. (2008). An integrated process model of stereotype threat effects on performance. *Psychological Review, 115,* 336-356.

Schumann, H., & Converse, J. M. (1971). The effects of black and white interviewers in black responses in 1968. *Public Opinion Quarterly, 35,* 44-68.

Seibt, B., & Förster, J. (2004). Stereotype threat and performance: How self-stereotypes influence processing by inducing regulatory foci. *Journal of Personality and Social Psychology, 87,* 38–56.

Shapiro, J. R., & Neuberg, S. L (2007). From stereotype threat to stereotype threats: Implications of a multi-threat framework for causes, moderators, mediators, consequences, and interventions. *Personality and Social Psychology Review, 11,* 107–130.

Shih, M., Pittinsky, T. L., & Ambady, N. (1999). Stereotype susceptibility: Identity salience and shifts in quantitative performance. *Psychological Science, 10,* 80–83.

Silver, B. D., Anderson, B. A., & Abramson, P. R. (1986). Who overreports voting? *American Political Science Review, 80,* 613–624.

Smith, J. L. (2004). Understanding the process of stereotype threat: A review of mediational variables and new performance goal directions. *Educational Psychology Review, 16,* 177–206.

Smith, J. L., & White, P. H. (2002). An examination of implicitly, explicitly activated and nullified stereotypes on mathematical performance: It's not just a women's issue. *Sex Roles, 47,* 179–191.

Spencer, S. J., Iserman, E., Davies, P. G., & Quinn, D. M. (2001). *Suppression of doubts, anxiety, and stereotypes as a mediator of the effect of stereotype threat on women's math performance.* Unpublished manuscript, University of Waterloo.

Spencer, S. J., Steele, C. M., & Quinn, D. M. (1999). Stereotype threat and women's math performance. *Journal of Experimental Social Psychology, 35,* 4–28.

Stangor, C., Carr, C., & Kiang, L. (1998). Activating stereotypes undermines task performance expectations. *Journal of Personality and Social Psychology, 75,* 1191–1197.

Steele, C. M. (1992, April). Race and the schooling of black Americans. *The Atlantic Monthly.*

Steele, C. M. (1997). A threat in the air: How stereotypes shape the intellectual identity and performance. *American Psychologist, 52,* 613–629.

Steele, C. M., & Aronson, J. (1995). Stereotype threat and the intellectual test performance of African Americans. *Journal of Personality and Social Psychology, 69,* 797–811.

Steele, C. M., Spencer, S., & Aronson, J. (2002). Contending with group image: The psychology of stereotype and social identity threat. In M. P. Zanna (Ed.), *Advances in Experimental Social Psychology* (Vol. 34, pp 379-440.). San Diego: Academic Press.

Stein, R., Blanchard-Fields, F., & Hertzog, C. (2002). The effects of age-stereotype priming on the memory performance of older adults. *Experimental Aging Research, 28,* 169–181.

Stone, J. (2002). Battling doubt by avoiding practice: The effects of stereotype threat on self-handicapping in White athletes. *Personality and Social Psychology Bulletin, 28,* 1667–1678.

Stone, J., Lynch, C. I., Sjomeling, M., & Darley, J. M. (1999). Stereotype threat effects on Black and White athletic performance. *Journal of Personality and Social Psychology, 77,* 1213–1227.

Stone, J., Perry, Z. W., & Darley, J. M. (1997). "White men can't jump": Evidence for the perceptual confirmation of racial stereotypes following a basketball game. *Basic and Applied Social Psychology, 19,* 291–306.

Waterman, A. (1982). Identity development from adolescence to adulthood: An extension of theory and a review of research. *Developmental Psychology, 18,* 341–358.

Welch, S. (1977). Women as political animals? A test of some explanations for male-female political participation differences. American Journal of Political Science, 21, 711–730.

Wheeler, S. C., Jarvis, B. G., & Petty, R. E. (2001). Think unto others: The self-destructive impact of negative racial stereotypes. *Journal of Experimental Social Psychology, 37,* 173–180.

Wheeler, S. C., & Petty, R. E. (2001). The effects of stereotype activation on behavior: A review of possible mechanisms. *Psychological Bulletin, 127,* 797–826.

Wiggins, D. K. (1997). "Great speed but little stamina": The historical debate over Black athletic superiority. In S. W. Pope (Ed.), *The new American sport history: Recent approaches and perspectives* (pp. 312–338). Urbana: University of Illinois Press.

Wilson, T. D., & Linville, P. W. (1982). Improving the academic performance of college freshmen: Attribution therapy revisited. *Journal of Personality and Social Psychology, 42*(2), 367-376.

Yerkes, R. M., & Dodson, J. D. (1908). The relationship of strength of stimulus to rapidity of habit-formation. *Journal of Comparative Neurology of Psychology, 18*, 459–482.

Zigler, E., & Butterfield, E. C. (1968). Motivational aspects of changes in IQ test performance of culturally deprived nursery school children. *Child Development, 39*, 1–14.

Zuckerman, M., Kieffer, S. C., & Knee, C. R. (1998). Consequences of self-handicapping: Effects on coping, academic performance, and adjustment. *Journal of Personality and Social Psychology, 74*, 1619–1628.

9 The Role of Entitativity in Stereotyping
Processes and Parameters

David L. Hamilton
University of California, Santa Barbara

Steven J. Sherman
Indiana University

Sara A. Crump
University of California, Santa Barbara

Julie Spencer-Rodgers
University of Victoria

We encounter a broad spectrum of groups in our daily lives. We all belong to families; we work closely with colleagues in our careers; we belong to social, sports, and religious organizations; and we are all members of multiple social categories based on gender, race, nationality, socioeconomic status, age, and occupation, among others. It is not surprising then that social psychology has long been dedicated to the study of groups (Allport, 1954; Campbell, 1958; Heider, 1958; Lewin, 1948; Tajfel & Turner, 1979). Over the decades, a large corpus of theoretical and empirical research has accumulated on how groups form and develop, how we categorize group-related information, and how we develop and rely on impressions of the groups that we encounter in everyday life.

Often those groups are large social categories reflecting groupings based on race, gender, nationality, religion, social class, and various aspects of lifestyle. As the chapters in this volume document, these large social categories have throughout history shaped the very nature of social life. Categorical distinctions impact how we think about, perceive, feel about, and interact with members of those categories, and they often determine the way the groups themselves relate to each other. Of particular relevance in this chapter, people develop belief systems—stereotypes—about those groups. In this chapter we explore some long-standing questions regarding the cognitive foundations of stereotypes, the conditions under which stereotypes are most likely to be formed and applied, and the types of groups about which stereotypes form.

A stereotype can be defined as a person's "knowledge, beliefs, and expectancies about some social group" (Hamilton & Trolier, 1986, p. 133). They are belief systems about groups, belief systems that represent the attributes, characteristics, behavior patterns, and so on, associated with a particular group. Once formed, that set of beliefs is applied to all members of the group, generalizing across individuals, despite the fact that those persons may show considerable variation in numerous respects. This generalization process leads to the perception of homogeneity among group members. This perception of homogeneity is inherent in stereotyping, and consequently, as Allport (1954) emphasized, stereotyping involves the overgeneralization of attributes to group members.

However, we do not form stereotypes of all groups. Members of the category "left-handed people" are homogeneous in their handedness, but we usually do not have stereotypes about them as a group. What are the constraints on stereotype formation? What are the preconditions that increase the tendency for stereotyping? What types of groups are most likely to be stereotyped? This chapter addresses some of these questions, and in doing so, we hope to specify some of the preconditions that underlie stereotypes of social groups.

ENTITATIVITY: THE GROUPNESS OF GROUPS

One fundamental way in which groups differ is the degree to which they may be viewed as coherent units or entities (Campbell, 1958; Hamilton & Sherman, 1996; Hamilton, Sherman, & Lickel, 1998; Lickel et al., 2000). Collections of individuals differ in the extent to which they possess the quality of "groupness." All would agree that a family, a work team, and a jury are likely to be viewed as highly interactive, interdependent, and meaningful social units. In contrast, the crowd of fans attending a baseball game and the people shopping in a grocery store are less likely to be perceived as highly uniform and cohesive groups of people. Campbell (1958) introduced the term *entitativity* to refer to the degree to which members of a group are bonded together in a coherent social unit. In recent years, theoretical and empirical work on the perception of group entitativity has significantly advanced our understanding of the construct (for reviews, see Brewer & Harasty, 1996; Brewer, Hong, & Li, 2004; Hamilton, Sherman, & Castelli, 2002; Hamilton et al., 1998; Hamilton, Sherman, & Rodgers, 2004; Sherman, Hamilton, & Lewis, 1999; Sherman & Johnson, 2003; Yzerbyt, Castano, Leyens, & Paladino, 2000; Yzerbyt, Rocher, & Schadron, 1997).

Much of the entitativity research has focused on identifying the perceptual cues that perceivers rely on when making entitativity judgments. These factors include group size, the degree of spatial proximity and amount of interaction among group members, the importance or social identity value of the group to its members, and perceived common goals and outcomes among group members (Campbell, 1958; Lickel et al., 2000). For instance, all other things being equal, numerical minorities may be perceived as higher in entitativity than majorities (Brewer & Harasty, 1996; Brewer, Weber, & Carini, 1995; although see McGarty, Haslam, Hutchinson, & Grace, 1995). Many researchers have emphasized the close relationship between the perceived homogeneity of a group and its degree of entitativity (Brewer et al., 1995; Dasgupta, Banaji, & Abelson, 1999; Yzerbyt, Rogier, & Fiske, 1998). Other antecedent factors that may elicit beliefs about entitativity include the level of interdependence, interpersonal bonds, organization, and behavioral influence among group members (Gaertner & Schopler, 1998; Hamilton et al., 1998; Welbourne, 1999).

Recent research has also emphasized the *consequences* of perceiving groups as cohesive entities. The extent to which groups are perceived to be unified entities strongly influences how people think about those groups, and consequently, has significant implications for a wide variety of judgment processes (Hamilton & Sherman, 1996; Yzerbyt et al., 1998). For instance, the degree of entitativity of a target influences perceptions of threat (Abelson, Dasgupta, Park, & Banaji, 1998), dispositional inferences (Yzerbyt et al., 1998), correspondence bias (Rogier & Yzerbyt, 1999), and the specific processing strategies that are used during impression formation (for a review, see Hamilton et al., 2002). When confronted with an entitative group, social perceivers overestimate the influence of group characteristics on a group member's behavior and they disregard the impact of situational forces. Moreover, high entitative targets evoke more integrative than memory-based processing, more spontaneous dispositional inferences, faster and more extreme judgements, and greater information recall than do low entitative targets (Hamilton & Sherman, 1996; Hamilton, Sherman, & Maddox, 1999; McConnell, Sherman, & Hamilton, 1994, 1997; Susskind, Maurer, Thakkar, Hamilton, & Sherman, 1999; Wyer, Bodenhausen, & Srull, 1984). Other consequences of entitativity for perceptions of groups, particularly regarding the relation to stereotyping, are the focus of later sections of this chapter.

As illustrated in our earlier examples, people continually encounter a diverse array of groups in the social environment (e.g., families, work groups, ethnic groups, social clubs, business organizations, etc.). There may be real and important systematic differences among the various groups that comprise this rich and complex social world. Therefore it is reasonable to expect that certain stimulus features will weigh more heavily than others as determinants of entitativity, depending, for example, on the type of group in question (Lickel et al., 2000). One fruitful approach to the study of entitativity would be to examine whether distinct perceptual cues are differentially important as predictors of "groupness" for different types of groups. A potentially useful framework for pursuing this question was offered by Brewer et al. (2004).

TYPES OF GROUPS

Although various authors have adopted several different strategies for distinguishing among different types of groups (Deaux, Reid, Mizrahi, & Ethier, 1995; Prentice, Miller, & Lightdale, 1994; Wilder & Simon, 1998), research by Lickel et al. (2000) has been particularly useful in empirically deriving a set of perceived group types and in determining their relation to perceptions of entitativity. Lickel et al. asked participants to rate 40 different groups on a wide range of attributes, including the size, permeability, and duration of the group; the similarity and level of interaction among group members; and the importance of the group to its members. Participants also completed a sorting task whereby they grouped the sample of 40 groups into "types" according to their own intuitive perceptions of the similarities and differences among the groups. Multivariate analyses of these data (factor analysis of ratings, clustering of sortings) identified four primary types of groups: intimacy groups (e.g., families, friends, support groups), task groups (e.g., a work group, a jury, the cast of a play), social categories (e.g., women, Jews, Americans), and loose associations (e.g., people living in the same neighborhood, students at a university, people in line at a bank). Moreover, the group types varied systematically with respect to their characteristic or defining features, based on participants' ratings of the groups. For instance, intimacy groups are perceived as small, impermeable, highly interactive units of long duration, which are very important to their members. Task-oriented groups are small in size, of relatively short duration, are relatively permeable (ease of joining or leaving the group), and their members share common goals. Social categories are large groups that are long lasting and impermeable, but fairly low in group member interaction. Thus, the participants' ratings generated distinct profiles or patterns of group features that are associated with each higher order group type.

An important finding in this research was that these group types differed significantly in their average perceived levels of entitativity. Intimacy groups were viewed as more entitative than task groups, which in turn, were regarded as more entitative than social categories. Loose associations were perceived as the least entitative type of group. These differences in entitativity among group types have been replicated by Pickett, Silver, and Brewer (2002). For purposes of this chapter, it is perhaps intriguing—and perhaps puzzling—that social categories—the groups about whom people have stereotypes, and that have been the focus of such an extensive research literature—were rated only moderately in entitativity. We return to this point later in the chapter.

The group typology manifested in Lickel et al.'s (2000) data was based on participants' ratings and sortings of 40 stimulus groups. Both of these tasks involve quite deliberative, intentional, and analytic cognitive processes. It may be, then, that the distinctions obtained in this study were the product, at least in part, of such processing and may not represent people's natural perceptions of groups in the social world. It is important, therefore, that Sherman et al. (2002) demonstrated (in a series of four experiments) that social perceivers spontaneously use these group types when encoding, organizing, and processing group-related information. For example, in a spontaneous categorization task (Sherman et al., 2002, Study 1), individuals made more within-type-of-group memory errors (e.g., between two social categories) than between-type-of-group errors (e.g., between a social category and a task group). For example, a face paired with the label "Frenchman" would later be more likely to be misidentified as "Presbyterian" (a within-type-of-group error) than as a jury member (a between-type-of-group error). Taken together, the Lickel et al. and Sherman et al. studies provide convergent evidence that intimacy groups, task groups, social categories, and loose associations are distinct, naturally occurring, psychologically meaningful, and widely used cognitive structures. These group types appear to reflect cognitive structures that people spontaneously use when processing information about groups and their members.

Given this accumulated evidence, then, entitativity may also be important for other aspects of group perception. We have already referred to work on perceptions of homogeneity in social categories and to the generalizations made about group members. How does entitativity relate to these phenomena? This question is the focus of the next two sections. We then turn specifically to the issue of entitativity's role in stereotyping.

PERCEPTIONS OF ENTITATIVITY AND HOMOGENEITY

One of the five cues that Lickel et al. (2000) found to be related to perceived entitativity—and the one cue that has been shown to play an important part in the stereotyping process—is the perception of similarity among group members. In essence, the perception of group members as homogeneous facilitates overgeneralizations being made about the group, which contributes directly to stereotyping. Research on the outgroup homogeneity effect has demonstrated just such a relationship between perceived similarity and stereotyping (Park & Hastie, 1987; Ryan, Judd, & Park, 1996).

THE OUTGROUP HOMOGENEITY EFFECT

The literature on the outgroup homogeneity effect has shown that people perceive outgroup members to be more similar to each other than one's ingroup members (Mullen & Hu, 1989; Ostrom & Sedikides, 1992; Park & Judd, 1990; Quattrone & Jones, 1980). A number of theories have been proposed to explain this finding. For example, according to social identity theory (Tajfel, 1978), ingroup members desire positive distinctiveness from outgroup members. One way they achieve such distinctiveness is by viewing members of the ingroup as unique and differentiated, whereas members of the outgroup are seen as "all the same." Another theory is that individuals perceive the outgroup to be more homogeneous because of less familiarity with members of the outgroup and greater familiarity with the ingroup (Linville, Fischer, & Salovey, 1989; Quattrone & Jones, 1980). Park and Judd (1990) reviewed the literature and compared the various methods used to assess outgroup homogeneity. Three common measures have assessed the extent to which (a) group members are perceived to possess stereotypic versus counterstereotypic traits, (b) group members are perceived to vary on a particular trait, and (c) ingroup members are perceived to be similar to one another. Evidence for outgroup homogeneity is found when members of the outgroup are perceived to possess more stereotypic traits than ingroup members, when outgroup members are judged to show less variability on various traits, and when outgroup members are rated to be more similar than members of one's ingroup.

Although the outgroup homogeneity effect has been observed in both minimal groups and naturally occurring groups (for a review see Ostrom & Sedikides, 1992), it does not generalize to every ingroup–outgroup comparison. In fact, as group size and status change, so do perceptions of group homogeneity. Specifically, members of majority groups are most likely to see members of minority groups as homogeneous. In contrast, minority group members tend to see their own ingroup as more homogeneous than the majority outgroup. This ingroup homogeneity effect has been demonstrated in a number of studies (Bartsch & Judd, 1993; Castano & Yzerbyt, 1998; Kelly, 1989; Simon & Pettigrew, 1990).

In more recent research, Guinote (2001) examined perceptions of both ingroup and outgroup homogeneity among minority and nonminority group members. In her study, Portuguese individuals living in Germany (a minority group) and Portuguese living in Portugal (a nonminority group) provided open-ended descriptions of both their ingroup and their outgroup. These responses were coded and the results showed that nonminority group members perceived their outgroup as homogeneous, whereas members of the minority perceived greater ingroup homogeneity. In addition, minority group members displayed a more complex and differentiated understanding of their nonminority outgroup (e.g., they used a greater number of attributes to describe the outgroup, used fewer redundant attributes, etc.). These results show that perceptions of group homogeneity depend on whether one is a member of a minority or majority group, and suggest that minority group members, being dependent on the majority group, are therefore motivated to attend carefully to information about them.

Finally, Judd, Park, Yzerbyt, Gordijn, and Muller (2005) conducted studies designed to assess people's perceptions of the extent to which their own ingroup and an outgroup endorsed outgroup homogeneity. In three studies examining a variety of ingroups and outgroups, participants were asked to provide their own perceptions of each group, in addition to predicting outgroup perceptions of each group (Study 1), and ingroup perceptions of each group (Studies 2 and 3). Across the three studies, the results showed that perceivers assumed that both ingroup and outgroup members perceived outgroups to be more homogeneous than ingroups. In contrast, individuals only showed evidence of the outgroup homogeneity effect when they were judging different nationalities, not when rating ethnic or gender outgroups.

In sum, a great deal of research has examined the perceptions of group homogeneity and how these perceptions are influenced by a variety of factors. Yet, what are some of the consequences of perceiving a group as homogeneous?

THE RELATION BETWEEN SIMILARITY AND STEREOTYPING

Regardless of its source, the perception that the members of an outgroup are homogeneous can lead to overgeneralizations about the outgroup members, and as a consequence, to stereotyping. For example, in a study by Wilder (1984), participants were separated into two groups and asked to rate the beliefs of members of both the ingroup and the outgroup on a variety of dimensions. Wilder found that participants tended to attribute a wide range of artistic and political beliefs to the ingroup, whereas members of the outgroup were thought to share similar artistic and political beliefs. In addition to the assumption that outgroup members have homogeneous beliefs, research by Howard and Rothbart (1980) showed that people have better memory for the negative behaviors of outgroup than of ingroup members. So, in addition to thinking that outgroup members share the same thoughts, individuals are also biased to remember that outgroup members have behaved in the same negative manner.

Yet on meeting a group member, do perceivers automatically generalize the characteristics of that individual to the group as a whole? Rothbart and Lewis (1988) found that perceivers are more likely to generalize from an individual to the rest of the group when the individual is prototypical or representative of the group. In their study, they provided participants with information about the voting behavior of a prototypical or an atypical fraternity member. The authors found that participants rated the fraternity as a whole as more liberal if a prototypical member voted for a Democrat, or more conservative if the prototypical candidate voted for a Republican. In contrast, participants were less likely to make generalizations about the fraternity as a whole when the individual member was less prototypical. In sum, the more similar an individual is to the rest of the group, the more likely perceivers will be to make generalizations from that individual to the group as a whole.

The work by Rothbart and Lewis (1988) focused on conditions under which people generalize from an individual group member to the group as a whole. Fiske and Neuberg (1990) proposed a model designed to outline conditions under which people move in the opposite direction; that is, making generalizations from the group to the individual. They theorized that perceivers automatically categorize others in terms of their group memberships, especially when the perceiver has little motivation or ability to make more accurate impressions. For example, a perceiver may meet a new person briefly and assume that they have characteristics that are similar to others of the same age, race, occupation, and so on. Those generalizations will be modified only when behavioral information does not fit with categorical preconceptions or when the perceiver is motivated toward accuracy, particularly when there is an interdependent relation with the target person.

More recent research has shown that people's lay theories influence their perception of group homogeneity and, as a consequence, stereotyping. Levy, Stroessner, and Dweck (1998) analyzed the perceptions of individuals who hold entity versus incremental theories of personality. Individuals who hold entity theories tend to view people's personalities as fixed and unchanging, whereas those who hold incremental theories of personality are more likely to accept that people's characteristics and attributes are malleable and may change over time. Given this understanding of people's lay theories, Levy et al. hypothesized that, in contrast to incremental theorists, entity theorists would perceive group members as all sharing the same traits and therefore view them as more similar. In one study, participants read a series of sentences describing behaviors performed by members of a fictitious group. After reading the sentences, participants provided an open-ended description of the group as a whole and judged the variability of the group. The results supported their hypothesis by showing that, compared to incremental theorists, entity theorists perceived members of the group to be more similar. In later research, Plaks, Stroessner, Dweck, and Sherman (2001) also found that entity theorists were more likely than incremental theorists to selectively attend to information that enhanced the perception of group homogeneity and as a consequence confirmed their stereotypes of the group.

The research reviewed here suggests that the perception of similarity among group members is an important contributor to the development of group stereotypes. Given their close relation, how might perceptions of similarity and entitativity differentially influence the perception of groups?

THE RELATION BETWEEN ENTITATIVITY AND SIMILARITY

Entitativity and homogeneity or similarity are intimately intertwined. The perception that a group is a meaningful, entitative unit is often based on the belief that the members share some form of similarity. Whether it is the appearances shared by members of a racial or ethnic group, the thoughts and beliefs held by members of the same political party, or the similar goals and concerns that unite members of a fundraising committee, the presence of some form of similarity is quite often an integral component of perceiving the entitativity of a group (Brewer et al., 1995; Castano, Yzerbyt, & Bourguignon, 2003; Dasgupta et al., 1999; Yzerbyt et al., 1998).

Research by Pickett (2001; Pickett & Perrott, 2004) has shown that the likelihood of making comparisons among group members depends on the level of group entitativity. When perceiving individual targets, comparisons tend to be made among individuals who are similar on the domain of interest (Festinger, 1954). For example, if a novice tennis player wants an accurate assessment of her ability, she should be more likely to compare her performance to that of another novice rather than to a highly skilled player. A similar comparison process may happen at the group level. Pickett (2001) predicted that comparisons among group members would be more likely when the group is perceived to be high in entitativity. In other words, the perception that a certain group of people is similar, shares common goals and outcomes, and so on, should facilitate comparisons between group members. In contrast, perceivers should make fewer comparisons among members of a group that is perceived to be lower in entitativity.

Pickett (2001) used a variant of the Ebbinghaus illusion to demonstrate that the knowledge that an individual is from a high- or low-entitativity group could influence even the most basic visual perceptions. The classic Ebbinghaus illusion is a demonstration of a perceptual contrast effect. In this illusion, the same-sized circle is perceived to be much larger when it is surrounded by smaller circles than when it is surrounded by larger circles. Pickett extended this illusion to the perception of faces. In two studies, participants were shown two faces. Participants were told that one of the individuals was in a fraternity or sorority and the other individual was born in the month of May. Each face was then shown surrounded by four other same-sex faces. These other faces shared fraternity membership (high-entitativity group) or birth month (low-entitativity group) with the central face. The participants' task was to judge the size of the face in the center. The results showed that, when the participants believed that the individual was part of a high-entitativity group, the face was judged to be much larger than when the face was described as a member of a low-entitativity group.

Pickett and Perrott (2004) extended these findings in a later study in which individuals were again described as members of either a high- or low-entitativity group. The participants first made entitativity and similarity ratings of each group. Participants were then given information about two of the members (e.g., "Bill received a C on his English exam" and "Mike received an A on his English exam") and were asked to make a comparison between the two members (e.g., who got the higher grade). The time taken for participants to make this comparison, as well as their level of accuracy, was assessed. The results showed that participants responded faster when the group was high versus low in entitativity, and there were no differences in accuracy between the conditions. Additionally, regression analyses revealed that both entitativity and similarity were significant predictors of facilitated comparisons among members, but that entitativity remained a predictor even when holding similarity constant. The results of this research suggest that, when a group is perceived to be highly entitative, perceivers will be more likely to make spontaneous comparisons between the members. In addition, similarity among the members is important, but there are additional properties characteristic of entitative groups that actually facilitate the comparison process.

Castano et al. (2003) analyzed the relations among entitativity, similarity, and identification. In one study they drew European participants' attention to either the similarities or the differences among the states of the European Union (EU). Participants were then asked to rate how entitative the EU was perceived as a group and also how much each participant identified with the EU. Castano et al. found that, among participants who were moderately identified with the EU, perceiving the states of the EU as similar led to increased identification with that group, and this relationship was mediated by perceptions of entitativity. In other words, greater similarity led to perceptions of higher entitativity, and this in turn led to high identification. In contrast, participants who noted differences between the states perceived the EU as less entitative and they were less identified with the EU.

Although entitativity and similarity are clearly related, we believe that they are not identical constructs and that the relationship between them is complex. In the next section we try to tease apart the differences and clarify the relation between them.

EMPIRICALLY DISTINGUISHING ENTITATIVITY AND SIMILARITY

In their research on entitativity, Lickel et al. (2000) found that perceptions of entitativity are influenced not only by group member similarity but also by how often the members interact, how important the group is to its members, and whether the members share common goals and outcomes. In other words, entitativity is not made up of similarity alone. Although similarity can enhance the perception of entitativity, entitativity may be based on other factors instead.

Because there has been a tendency to blend these two concepts, Crump, Hamilton, Sherman, Lickel, and Thakkar (2008) conducted a series of studies designed to differentiate between entitativity and similarity. In their research, participants made entitativity and similarity ratings of a variety of different groups. It was hypothesized that, regardless of the group in question, participants would rate their ingroup as more entitative than the outgroup and rate members of the outgroup as more similar than those of the ingroup. The second part of our hypothesis is simply a statement of the outgroup homogeneity effect. The first part of our hypothesis—perceived ingroup entitativity—was derived from Sherman et al. (1999), who argued that people derive more social identity value (the psychological benefits of group membership, such as self-esteem, self-concept, and optimal distinctiveness) from membership in highly entitative groups. In other words, because of the value placed on the groups to which one belongs, group members will perceive their ingroups as being higher in entitativity than groups to which they do not belong. In fact, Yzerbyt et al. (2000) showed that entitativity is seen as a desirable feature of the ingroup and that highly identified group members will often exclude undesirable members in an effort to maintain high entitativity.

In Crump et al.'s (2006) first study, participants made entitativity and similarity ratings of social categories, some of them being groups to which they belonged and others being groups to which they did not belong. As predicted, the results showed that participants rated their gender, religious, and political ingroups as higher in entitativity than the matched outgroup. In contrast, members of these outgroups were rated as more homogeneous than ingroup members. In the second study, participants recalled intimacy or task groups to which they belonged in high school and then rated them on the same measures. Again, participants rated members of both the intimacy and task outgroups as higher in similarity than ingroup members. In addition, participants rated their intimacy ingroups as higher in entitativity than the outgroup, but this difference was not significant for the task groups. Thus, across a variety of groups, individuals rate their ingroups as higher in entitativity and members of their outgroups as sharing greater similarity.

In a third study, participants learned about a fictitious group that was described as either high or low in entitativity, or as either high or low in similarity. Participants then completed entitativity and similarity measures about the group. The entitativity and similarity manipulations had different effects on group perceptions. Specifically, the entitativity manipulation influenced entitativity ratings, such that the high-entitativity group was rated higher in entitativity than the low-entitativity group. However, the entitativity manipulation had no significant effect on perceptions of group similarity. In contrast, when similarity was manipulated, participants rated members of the high-similarity group as more similar than members of the low-similarity group, but this similarity manipulation did not significantly influence perceptions of group entitativity. These findings are important in differentiating between entitativity and similarity. If entitativity and similarity were essentially the same construct, then manipulation of either one would have parallel effects on ratings of both. Their differing effects document the differential role of the two concepts in group perception.

Although perceptions of homogeneity and of entitativity are related, and although each one can serve as a cue to the other, the results of Crump et al.'s (2006) studies show that entitativity and similarity are distinct concepts in the perception of groups. Given this distinction, then, the two concepts may play meaningfully different roles in the stereotyping process.

ENTITATIVITY, STEREOTYPE DEVELOPMENT, GENERALIZATION, AND THE INTERCHANGEABILITY OF GROUP MEMBERS

As we have seen, the perception of entitativity for a group has important consequences, with many of these effects having relevance for stereotyping. In this section we discuss the idea that perceived entitativity leads to the perception of interchangeability among group members. Thus any inferences regarding traits, attributes, or abilities that are made about any group member are then transferred to all other members of a high-entitativity group. This occurs even when the other group members have not engaged in any behaviors that would warrant such trait or ability attributions. Interestingly, as we shall see, this perceived interchangeability of group members has the additional effect of decreasing strong and unique perceptions of the different individual members. All members of the group end up "looking alike," and the individuality and uniqueness of individuals is relatively diminished.

In this section we first examine how information about different individual members of a group is integrated to form an impression (or stereotype) of the group, and how, once formed, this impression is applied to all group members. We then use these ideas to analyze the phenomenon of collective responsibility.

ENTITATIVITY AND THE PROCESSES OF IMPRESSION FORMATION

Hamilton and Sherman (1996) presented a conceptual analysis of important differences in the way that impressions of individuals, low-entitativity groups, and high-entitativity groups are formed. According to their analysis, impressions of individuals and high-entitativity groups develop during online processing of information (Hastie & Park, 1986). Early information serves as the basis for an initial impression formed as that information is received, and later information is assimilated to and integrated into a coherent mental representation. On the other hand, impressions of low-entitativity groups are not formed online. Information about the group members is processed and stored separately until such time as a judgment of the group as a whole is needed. Thus, information is not integrated immediately into a coherent impression, and judgments are made in a memory-based fashion.

Studies by McConnell et al. (1994, 1997) supported these predictions. For individual targets and high group entitativity targets, there was evidence of good recall, primacy effects, a lack of any illusory correlation effect in judgments, and low recall–judgment correlations. These effects are all indications of online processing. For low-entitativity groups the opposite effects were seen, indicating memory-based judgments. Thus the processing of information about group members and the consequences of such processing are very different, depending on the level of perceived entitativity of the group.

ENTITATIVITY AND STEREOTYPE DEVELOPMENT

Definitions of stereotypes focus heavily on the overgeneralization that occurs in the perception of a group and its members (Allport, 1954; Hamilton & Sherman, 1994; Taylor, 1981). That is, certain traits and attributes are indiscriminately applied to all members of the group, even with little corroborating evidence provided by any particular individual member. Thus, to understand the development of stereotypes, we must understand the factors that foster overgeneralization in the perception of the members of a group. One key factor in this process is the degree to which the group is perceived as entitative. As we shall see, perceived entitativity is a precondition for inducing spontaneous trait inferences on the basis of a group member's behavior, and then for spontaneous trait transference of the inferred trait to the group as a whole and to all other group members.

The relation between perceived entitativity and stereotypes is strongly implied by some existing evidence in the literature. Research by Brewer and her colleagues (Brewer & Harasty, 1996; Welbourne, Harasty, & Brewer, 1997) indicated that high-entitativity groups were associated with prototypic representations, whereas low-entitativity groups were associated with exemplar-based representations. This work also suggested that perceived entitativity is involved in generalizing from individual members to a global representation of the group as a whole. When the group is perceived as entitative, members are more likely to be evaluated in terms of global expectancies. Thus, perceived entitativity is positively associated with expectancy strength and stereotyping, and perceived entitativity results in the assimilation of individuals to the group stereotype (Hilton & von Hippel, 1990).

Perhaps the strongest evidence for the sequence from perceived entitativity to trait inference to stereotype development to overgeneralization comes from recent work by Crawford, Sherman, and Hamilton (2002). The goal of this research was to provide information about how behavioral information about individual members of a high-entitativity group is integrated into a global representation, and how, once formed, this stereotype impression is applied to all group members as they are perceived as interchangeable parts. The model of this process is shown in Figure 9.1.

To test this model, Crawford et al. (2002) employed the savings-in-relearning inference paradigm (Carlston & Skowronski, 1994; Skowronski, Carlston, Mae, & Crawford, 1998). Participants read about behaviors performed by members of two different groups. For each group, half of the group members were described by behaviors that implied one trait (e.g., a lazy behavior) and half were described by behaviors that implied a different trait (e.g., an intelligent behavior). Thus, the

Members of a high entitativity group.

Each engages in a different behavior that is indicative of a different trait.

The perceiver makes a trait inference for each person based on his or her behavior.

The traits are applied to the group as a whole in the form of a stereotype.

The group stereotype is applied to all other members as members are interchangeable parts.

In the end, all members of the group are seen as characterized by all the traits.

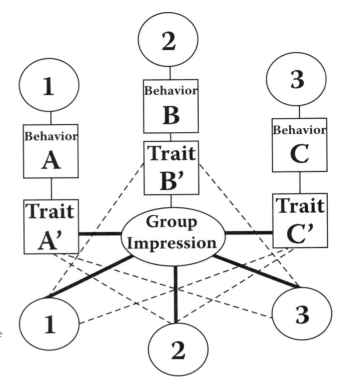

FIGURE 9.1   Model of group-level trait transference. Reprinted from Crawford, Sherman, and Hamilton (2002).

individual members of each group were described by two traits. In addition, the two groups were characterized in a way that made both of them appear to be highly entitative or both appear to be of low entitativity. In a later phase, each group member was either paired with a trait that was implied by the behavior that was originally paired with that target member (e.g., the trait term lazy) or with a trait that was implied by the behavior of other members of the group, but did not match the behavior of this particular individual (e.g., the trait term intelligent). The key measure was the ease with which participants learned these member–trait pairings. The first case (an individual paired with a behavior-implying trait) was called a *trait inference pairing,* as the trait matched the inference from that individual's previous behavior. The other case (an individual paired with a trait implied by another group member's behavior) was referred to as a *trait transference pairing.* In transference pairings the trait did not match the inference from that individual's previous behavior and therefore learning such pairs would be facilitated if spontaneous transference from the trait inferences about other group members had occurred.

The predictions of the Crawford et al. (2002) research were as follows. For high-entitativity groups, the trait implications of each member's behavior would be abstracted and transferred to all other group members. Thus, for high-entitativity groups (compared to low-entitativity groups) there should be greater ease of learning for trait transference trials. This transference would lay the groundwork for the interchangeability of group members. In addition, as this interchangeability results in the loss of individuality for members of a high-entitative group, the information for any given member would not be stored uniquely for that member. Thus, the trait inference trials should be more difficult in the case of high-entitativity groups.

Crawford et al.'s (2002) results strongly supported these predictions. For low-entitativity groups, trait inference trials were learned significantly better than were trait transference trials.

For high-entitativity groups, trait inference and trait transference trials were learned equally well, indicating that the members indeed were highly interchangeable and thus confusable.

In addition, these results emerged only when the entitativity information about the groups was received prior to exposure to the behavioral information. Thus, the effects of perceived entitativity are due to encoding rather than retrieval processes. That is, when a group is known to be highly entitative, behavioral information about group members leads to trait inferences and the formation of a group impression. This information is used to develop a stereotype about the group and is transferred to all members of that group. This kind of processing was further evidenced by the fact that, for high- (but not for low-)entitative groups, participants took significantly more time to process early behavioral information as opposed to later behavioral information. This result is important in establishing two points that are central to our interpretation. First, it takes time and resources to integrate the early information into a global impression of the group, but second, once a general impression of a highly entitative group is formed, new information is processed quickly and easily.

The Crawford et al. (2002) results demonstrate that, in the case of high-entitativity groups, the members are interchangeable in the sense that the attributes of any member of the group are spontaneously transferred to all other group members. These findings imply that one important effect of perceiving a high degree of group entitativity is the spontaneous comparison of group members. In fact, Pickett and her colleagues (Pickett, 2001; Pickett & Perrott, 2004) have shown exactly this. As described earlier in the chapter, Pickett has demonstrated that high perceived entitativity fosters the automatic comparison of group members, as indicated by a large perceptual contrast effect for group members during the Ebbinghaus illusion (Pickett, 2001) and by the fast response time in answering questions involving group member comparisons (Pickett & Perrott, 2004).

The findings of Crawford et al. (2002) and of Pickett (2001) have relevance for a more general question concerning the extent to which, and the conditions under which, any member of a group is perceived primarily in terms of his or her individual characteristics or in terms of the group category attributes. This distinction was central to both Brewer's (1988) dual-process model and to Fiske and Neuberg's (1990) continuum model. Both models distinguish between category-based and individuated processes, and they identify both individuated information and group categorical information as part of the impressions of individual group members. Work by Brewer et al. (1995) explored the effects of perceived entitativity on the extent to which information about group members is organized at the level of the individual or at the social category level. Participants viewed a videotaped discussion among six people, who were organized into two distinct groups of three members each. The two groups were either both high or both low in entitativity. After viewing the discussion, participants had to identify which particular person had made which comments. Recognition errors showed that participants made significantly more within-group errors (i.e., a different member of the same group was wrongly identified) than between-group errors (i.e., a member of the other group was wrongly identified). However, this difference between within- and between-group errors was significantly greater for high-entitative groups. Thus, the members of high-entitative groups are represented more in a category-based way than in a person-based way.

Putting together the work of Brewer et al. (1995) and Crawford et al. (2002), the evidence indicates that, for both impression formation and memory confusions, the members of highly entitative groups are more interchangeable and more confusable than are members of low-entitativity groups. It might be interesting to speculate about whether these kinds of confusions based on the interchangeability of group members would also apply to the perceptual level. That is, are people more likely to "mix up" or confuse photographs of members of high-entitativity rather than low-entitativity groups? Do people actually perceive the members of high-entitative groups as being physically more similar to each other than members of low-entitativity groups? Such a finding might not be all that surprising. After all, intimacy groups are reliably perceived as higher in entitativity than are task groups or social categories (Lickel et al., 2000). Families are the most frequently encountered intimacy groups, and of course, due to genetic similarity, family members actually do resemble each other physically more than do members of other groups. Thus, social perceivers may generalize physical similarity principles to all other groups of high perceived entitativity.

In sum, perceptions of high entitativity for a group cause information about individual members to be processed in an online fashion. This information is then integrated to form coherent, global impressions of the group as a whole, and it is then transferred to other group members. This process ensures that stereotypes of high-entitative groups are likely to form, that stereotypic traits and attributes are applied indiscriminately to all group members, and that, as this overgeneralization occurs, members are perceived and mentally represented as interchangeable elements in the group.

These ideas about the relation between entitativity and stereotyping have much in common with self-categorization theory (Haslam, Oakes, Turner, & McGarty, 1996; Turner, Hogg, Oakes, Reicher, & Wetherell, 1987). Self-categorization theory focuses on the operation of the categorization process as the cognitive basis of group behavior. This categorization process accentuates the similarities among members of an ingroup and the differences between the ingroup and some other outgroup as a contrast category. According to self-categorization theory, the metacontrast principle postulates that a group is most likely to be perceived as a single unit (in our terms, to have high perceived entitativity) to the extent that within-group similarities are high and between-group differences are also high. According to the theory, the end result of this categorization process is perceptual and behavioral depersonalization, or self-stereotyping (Hogg, 1996). Thus, self-categorization theory proposes strong links among the perceived entitativity of a group, the development of a stereotype of the group, and a perception of the interchangeability of the different members of that group. In particular, self-categorization theory suggests that perceived entitativity leads to an increase in the metacontrast ratio by minimizing the perception of intragroup differences and by maximizing the perception of intergroup differences. It is when the metacontrast ratio is high that the perception of the interchangeability of group members is most likely to occur.

Although there is agreement about the general effects of perceived entitativity on stereotype development, it is less clear what the strength of this relation is when we consider different group types (intimacy groups, task groups, and social categories). Research (Lickel et al., 2000; Pickett et al., 2002) has shown that social categories are perceived as having only moderate degrees of entitativity (less than intimacy and task groups), yet social categories such as gender, race, and ethnicity have the strong associated stereotypes (but see Spencer-Rodgers, Hamilton, & Sherman, 2007). Why might this be so? Self-categorization theory suggests that viewing groups as contrast categories is an important stimulus to stereotype development. Social categories are typically represented as competing contrast categories (e.g., men and women; Protestants, Jews, and Catholics; Irish and English). When groups are viewed as contrast categories, the metacontrast ratio is likely to be high and stereotype development becomes inevitable, even if the level of perceived entitativity of the groups is not especially high. It may be that it is the combination of high perceived entitativity and contrast categories that ultimately leads to the highest level of stereotyping.

ENTITATIVITY, STEREOTYPING, AND COLLECTIVE RESPONSIBILITY

Recently, Lickel, Schmader, and Hamilton (2003) studied another context in which high entitativity results in a reduced level of differentiation among group members, namely, the perception of collective responsibility. Collective responsibility occurs when members of a group are seen as having responsibility for another group member's negative behavior, even in the absence of any direct involvement in that act. Lickel et al. examined perceptions of collective responsibility in the context of the shootings at Columbine High School. Aside from the two student murderers, would there be collective responsibility assigned to other members of groups to which these two students belonged? In particular, Lickel et al. were concerned with attributions of responsibility to the killers' parents and to other members of the Trenchcoat Mafia (a school group to which the murderers belonged). Results indicated that the key to attributing collective responsibility to these group members was the perception of high entitativity for that group. Thus, participants who viewed the family or the

Trenchcoat Mafia as especially high in entitativity were more likely to assign responsibility to the parents or other members of the peer group for the murders. In a second study that investigated several other groups relevant to the incident, Lickel et al. found a strong relation between perceptions of entitativity of the various groups and the degree to which members of those groups were held collectively responsible for the murders.

Collective responsibility certainly implies a degree of interchangeability of group members; all members are seen as bearing some of the responsibility. The relation between perceived entitativity and collective responsibility is thus consistent with our idea that perceived entitativity fosters the perception that the members of a group are alike and are interchangeable.

Although Lickel et al. (2003) did not examine the stereotyping of the various groups, it is interesting to speculate about how stereotyping might enter into the relation between perceived entitativity and collective responsibility. Based on the findings of the Crawford et al. (2002) research, we might speculate that stereotyping actually serves as the mediator between perceived entitativity and collective responsibility. That is, perceived entitativity leads to the development of strong stereotypes (e.g., stereotypes of the Trenchcoat Mafia). These stereotypes then lead to the perception that all group members share the same traits, beliefs, values, and so on. Thus, any guilt must be shared because of this interchangeability.

ENTITATIVITY AND THE USE OF STEREOTYPES

The preceding sections have developed the argument that entitativity is a key element for some very important factors—perceptions of homogeneity, generalization through spontaneous trait inferences, and perceived interchangeability of group members—that lay the groundwork for the development of stereotypes. In this section we explore the relation between entitativity and the use of those stereotypes.

Stereotypes are cognitive structures containing a perceiver's knowledge and beliefs about a human group, and *stereotyping* involves the ascription of a set of psychological attributes to a group and its members. People are unlikely to have generalized knowledge and beliefs about a group of individuals unless those individuals are perceived as being united together in some type of coherent entity. That is, people may develop and use stereotypic knowledge only after they have come to see a group as a *group*—as a meaningful social unit. Moreover, if this is the case, then it also seems plausible that entitativity judgments may serve an important mediating function between other group properties (e.g., perceptions of homogeneity) and the strength of people's stereotypic beliefs. For example, perceived entitativity might mediate the association between homogeneity and stereotyping. Perceiving a group to be homogenous can foster stereotyping and permit generalizability of traits across group members, but the group must first be regarded as a bona fide entity.

Support for these ideas comes from the person perception literature showing that entity beliefs and judgments about individual targets are associated with greater stereotyping (Levy et al., 1998) and more elaborative information processing (Hamilton & Sherman, 1996; McConnell et al., 1997; Susskind et al., 1999). It seems reasonable to hypothesize that the same argument would hold for group targets. Consistent with this view, Rydell and colleagues (Rydell, Hugenberg, Ray, & Mackie, 2007) assessed people's implicit theories about groups and found that entity theorists (i.e., people who see group characteristics as fixed) stereotyped more than did incremental theorists (i.e., people who see them as malleable). Moreover, the perception of entitativity mediated the relationship between one's implicit theories and stereotypic group judgments. Groups that are more entitative also elicit stronger dispositional inferences (Yzerbyt et al., 1998) and greater correspondence bias (Rogier & Yzerbyt, 1999) than do less entitative groups. All of this research suggests that entitativity is a central precursor to stereotyping.

THE IMPORTANT ROLE OF ENTITATIVITY IN STEREOTYPING

To test the central hypothesis that the perception of "groupness" is an important precondition to stereotyping processes, we investigated the relationship of entitativity judgments and four other antecedent variables (i.e., homogeneity, essence, role differentiation, and agency) to people's generalized perceptions of two different types of groups: social categories and task groups (Spencer-Rodgers et al., 2007, Study 2). As outlined earlier in this chapter, people's beliefs about social groups are organized according to an intuitive group taxonomy, which includes social categories, task-oriented groups, intimacy groups, and loose associations (Lickel et al., 2000). If lay people hold qualitatively different intuitive theories about social categories, task groups, and so on, then this intuitive group taxonomy may have important implications for both entitativity judgments and stereotyping processes. For example, Sherman et al. (2002) showed that group-relevant information is spontaneously categorized in memory according to these group types. Therefore, to increase the generalizability of our findings, we included two types of groups (social categories, task groups) in our study.

In this research we set out to answer three interrelated questions: (a) What factors underlie stereotyping of different types of groups? (b) Does the perception of entitativity give rise to stereotypic group judgments? and (c) Does the perception of entitativity mediate the relationship between various group properties and stereotypic judgments?

The stereotyping literature has historically emphasized the role of perceived homogeneity and essence in underlying stereotypic judgments of social categories (Rothbart & Taylor, 1992; Yzerbyt et al., 1997). Social categories that are composed of members who are "all the same" are more strongly associated with specific psychological attributes than are those whose members are perceived to be highly dissimilar. Likewise, social groups that are viewed as having a deeply rooted "essential" nature (e.g., based on race, ethnicity, age, gender, etc.) are more apt to be stereotyped than are those that are based on less intrinsic factors such as occupation or geographical region of residence. A question that remains relatively unexplored in the stereotyping literature, however, is whether the same group properties underlie stereotypic judgments about other group types.

What factors lead social perceivers to form stereotypic beliefs about group types other than social categories? Perhaps for other types of groups, such as task-oriented groups, the extent to which the groups are perceived as possessing distinct psychological attributes depends more on patterns of role differentiation and agency than homogeneity or essence. For instance, the members of a closely knit work group may share many common goals and outcomes, they may be perceived as highly interactive, organized, and interdependent, and yet the group members may be very dissimilar in all other respects (e.g., in terms of race and ethnicity, age, beliefs, etc.). Thus, for task-oriented groups, the generalizability of psychological attributes across group members may depend more on the presence of common goals or fate and coordinated action than on the presence of shared, innate characteristics that are natural and stable.

A central purpose of our research was to explore these intriguing questions. In keeping with Brewer et al.'s (2004) "agency" versus "essence" theories of group perception, we hypothesized that different group properties would be differentially important in the stereotyping of different group types. Specifically, we predicted that agency (i.e., the group's ability to produce outcomes and achieve its goals) and role differentiation (i.e., the presence of clearly defined roles and tasks among group members) would be more potent predictors of stereotyping for task groups than for social categories. In contrast, perceptions of homogeneity and essence were expected to weigh more heavily for social categories.

In this study participants completed measures of entitativity, the four group property variables, and stereotyping. Perceptions of entitativity were assessed by eight items that indexed the perceived unity and organization of the group, as well as the level of interaction, importance, belongingness, cohesiveness, and interdependence among group members. Four items tapped the perceived homogeneity of the group in terms of overall similarity, physical appearance, behaviors, and personality characteristics. Our measure of agency reflected the extent to which the group and its members were perceived as being able to influence others, achieve their goals, act collectively, and produce outcomes. The role differentiation scale indexed the degree to which there were specific roles or functions, predictable behaviors, and tasks or duties associated with group membership. Essentialist beliefs were assessed with a modified seven-item version of Haslam, Rothschild, and Ernst's (2000) scale. Lastly, stereotyping was indexed as the strength of people's ratings on group-stereotypic attributes. In a preliminary study, participants generated free-response descriptors for each of the target groups, and the descriptors were used to identify attributes stereotypic of each target group. In the main study participants rated each of the target groups on those common attributes. The participants rated four social categories (Californians, Jews, elderly people, and Hispanics/Latinos) and four task groups (jury, environmental organization, student campus committee, and cast of a play) on all of the measures.

Our initial analyses focused on the mean levels of entitativity, homogeneity, role differentiation, agency, essence, and stereotyping among task groups and social categories. In accordance with prior research (Lickel et al., 2000; Pickett et al., 2002), perceptions of entitativity were significantly greater for task groups than for social categories. As we had expected, perceived role differentiation and agency were significantly higher for task groups than for social categories. In contrast, perceived homogeneity and essentialist beliefs were greater for social categories than for task groups. These findings make intuitive sense given that task groups are smaller social units that are noted for their coordinated action and productive outcomes (O'Laughlin & Malle, 2002), whereas social categories are large classifications of people who simply share a few psychologically meaningful characteristics.

In addition to differences in mean ratings on these four group properties, we found differences among these variables in the correlations between the predictors and stereotypic judgments for task groups and social categories. Although all four group property variables (i.e., role differentiation, agency, homogeneity, and essence) were significantly correlated with group stereotyping (as measured by participants' ratings on the group-stereotypic attributes), perceptions of homogeneity and essence were more strongly related to the stereotyping of social categories, whereas role differentiation and agency were more pertinent to the stereotyping of task groups. Thus, in answer to our first question, different factors do appear to underlie stereotyping of different types of groups.

In answer to our second question, regarding the relation of entitativity to stereotypic judgments, we determined the extent to which entitativity predicted stereotyping for each of the group types. We found that perceived entitativity was indeed strongly related to stereotypic group judgments for both types of groups. Moreover, the perception of entitativity was equally important to group impressions for social categories and task groups, pointing once again to the central role of entitativity in stereotyping processes. Regardless of group type, a stereotype cannot form and be applied unless and until a collection of individuals is perceived to be a uniform and cohesive social unit.

Our third, and most important, research question concerned whether perceptions of entitativity mediate the relationship between various group properties and stereotyping. To address this question we conducted a series of mediational analyses, following Baron and Kenny's (1986) procedures. Specifically, we examined whether entitativity mediated the relationship among each of the four group properties (homogeneity, essence, role differentiation, and agency) and group stereotyping. The analyses were conducted separately for social categories and task groups. Hence, altogether we performed eight mediational analyses. In almost all cases (seven of the eight), the observed associations between the four predictor variables and stereotypic group impressions were significantly reduced when entitativity judgments were controlled. That is, for both social categories and task groups, all four predictor variables were significantly related to the strength of participants' attribute ratings, and perceptions of entitativity played a substantial mediating role in the extent to which all of those variables were related to stereotypic group impressions. Moreover, in half of the cases, there was evidence of full mediation (i.e., the residual correlation between the predictor and stereotyping was no longer significant).

These analyses demonstrate that entitativity plays an important mediating role in the ability of these variables to predict stereotyping. Might it be, however, that these variables also mediate the prediction of stereotyping from entitativity? That is, one might wonder whether the four group property variables could function equally well as the mediator in a series of analyses in which perceived entitativity represented the *predictor* and stereotyping the outcome. To examine this possibility, we conducted a parallel set of mediational analyses in which entitativity served as the predictor variable and each of the four group properties (homogeneity, essence, role differentiation, and agency), separately, assumed the role of mediator. Importantly, these analyses yielded much weaker results. In half of the cases, there was no significant drop in the association between the predictor (entitativity) and the criterion (stereotyping) when we controlled for the mediator (e.g., perceptions of homogeneity). Moreover, in all cases the residual correlation between entitativity and stereotyping remained substantial and statistically significant (i.e., we did not obtain full mediation).

In sum, the perception of entitativity appears to play a central role in facilitating group impression formation. Most of the predictor variables in this study were moderately correlated with each other and all of them were significantly related to the outcome variable of stereotyping, suggesting that they are key constructs in stereotyping processes. However, the variables do have different functions in group perception. Homogeneity and essence are more pertinent to people's conceptions and beliefs about broad social categories, whereas role differentiation and agency are more relevant to dynamic task groups. Regardless of group type, the perception of entitativity is a potent predictor of people's stereotypic group impressions and it is a crucial mediating factor in group perception: A collection of individuals must be perceived as a unified and cohesive entity before stereotypic attributes will be ascribed to the group as a whole.

CONCLUSIONS

There are several important messages that we have tried to send in this chapter. These messages, we hope, advance our understanding of the concept of entitativity and especially the role of perceived entitativity in the development and use of stereotypes.

People perceive and spontaneously differentiate among types of groups, and these group types differ in their perceived entitativity. Intimacy groups have the highest level of perceived entitativity, task groups have somewhat less, and social categories have only a moderate level of perceived entitativity. We believe that different stimulus factors are likely to carry different weights in determining the level of perceived entitativity for the different group types.

An important consequence of perceived entitativity is the perception of similarity (homogeneity) among group members. This perception in turn facilitates overgeneralizations about the attributes characteristic of group members, leads to the perception that group members are interchangeable parts of the whole, and thus contributes to stereotype formation in highly entitative groups.

Entitativity and similarity, although conceptually related and often correlated, are not equivalent concepts and often function differently in group perceptions.

Entitativity plays a clear and direct role in stereotyping processes. In addition, the factors that are involved in these processes differ for the different types of groups. For social categories, perceived similarity and perceived essentialism of such groups are important for determining the degree to which groups are stereotyped. For task groups, however, agency and role differentiation are important factors for stereotype development and use. Importantly, for both social categories and task groups, perceived entitativity mediates the relations between the group properties (i.e., similarity, essentialism, agency, role differentiation) and stereotyping. Thus the perception of group entitativity functions in a central way in group stereotyping.

Although, in general, higher degrees of perceived entitativity may predict higher degrees of stereotyping, this relation is complex. For example, social categories are perceived as having only moderate levels of entitativity, yet these groups tend to have strongly associated stereotypes. We suggest that, because social categories are often represented as competing

contrast categories (e.g., men and women), the degree of ingroup versus outgroup differences is enhanced and stereotype development becomes more likely. Thus it may be a
combination of high perceived entitativity and the representation of groups as contrast
categories that most facilitates the development of strong stereotypes.

REFERENCES

Abelson, R. P., Dasgupta, N., Park, J., & Banaji, M. R. (1998). Perception of the collective other. *Personality and Social Psychology Review, 2,* 243–250.

Allport, G. W. (1954). *The nature of prejudice.* Garden City, NY: Doubleday/Anchor.

Baron, R. M., & Kenny, D. A. (1986). The moderator–mediator variable distinction in social psychological research: Conceptual, strategic and statistical considerations. *Journal of Personality and Social Psychology, 51,* 1173–1182.

Bartsch, R. A., & Judd, C. M. (1993). Majority–minority status and perceived ingroup variability revisited. *European Journal of Social Psychology, 23,* 471–483.

Brewer, M. B. (1988). A dual process model of impression formation. In T. K. Srull & R. S. Wyer (Eds.), *Advances in social cognition* (Vol. 1, pp. 1–36). Hillsdale, NJ: Erlbaum.

Brewer, M. B., & Harasty, A. S. (1996). Seeing groups as entities: The role of perceiver motivation. In R. M. Sorrentino & E. T. Higgins (Eds.), *Handbook of motivation and cognition* (Vol. 3, pp. 347–370). New York: Guilford.

Brewer, M. B., Hong, Y., & Li, Q. (2004). Dynamic entitativity: Perceiving groups as actors. In V. Yzerbyt, C. Judd, & O. Corneille (Eds.), *The psychology of group perception: Perceived variability* (pp. 25–38). New York: Psychology Press.

Brewer, M. B., Weber, J. G., & Carini, B. (1995). Person memory in intergroup contexts: Categorization versus individuation. *Journal of Personality and Social Psychology, 69,* 29–40.

Campbell, D. T. (1958). Common fate, similarity, and other indices of the status of aggregates of persons as social entities. *Behavioral Science, 3,* 14–25.

Carlston, D. E., & Skowronski, J. J. (1994). Savings in the relearning of trait information as evidence for spontaneous inference generation. *Journal of Personality and Social Psychology, 66,* 840–856.

Castano, E., & Yzerbyt, V. Y. (1998). The highs and lows of group homogeneity. *Behavioral Processes, 42,* 219–238.

Castano, E., Yzerbyt, V., & Bourguignon, D. (2003). We are one and I like it: The impact of ingroup entitativity on ingroup identification. *European Journal of Social Psychology, 33,* 735–754.

Crawford, M. T., Sherman, S. J., & Hamilton, D. L. (2002). Perceived entitativity, stereotype formation, and the interchangeability of group members. *Journal of Personality and Social Psychology, 83,* 1076–1094.

Crump, S. A., Hamilton, D. L., Sherman, S. J., Lickel, R., & Thakkar, V. (2008). *Group entitativity and similarity: Their differing perceptions of groups.* Manuscript under review.

Dasgupta, N., Banaji, M. R., & Abelson, R. P. (1999). Group entitativity and group perception: Associations between physical features and psychological judgment. *Journal of Personality and Social Psychology, 77,* 991–1003.

Deaux, K., Reid, A., Mizrahi, K., & Ethier, K. A. (1995). Parameters of social identity. *Journal of Personality and Social Psychology, 68,* 280–291.

Festinger, L. (1954). A theory of social comparison processes. *Human Relations, 7,* 117–140.

Fiske, S. T., & Neuberg, S. L. (1990). A continuum of impression formation, from category-based to individuat-
ing processes: Influences of information and motivation on attention and interpretation. In M. P. Zanna (Ed.), *Advances in experimental social psychology* (Vol. 23, pp. 1–74). New York: Academic.

Gaertner, L., & Schopler, J. (1998). Perceived ingroup entitativity and intergroup bias: An interconnection of self and others. *European Journal of Social Psychology, 28,* 963–980.

Guinote, A. (2001). The perception of group variability in a non-minority and a minority context: When adapta-
tion leads to out-group differentiation. *British Journal of Social Psychology, 40,* 117–132.

Hamilton, D. L., & Sherman, J. W. (1994). Stereotypes. In R. S. Wyer, Jr., & T. K. Srull (Eds.), *Handbook of social cognition* (2nd ed., Vol. 2, pp. 1–68). Hillsdale, NJ: Erlbaum.

Hamilton, D. L., & Sherman, S. J. (1996). Perceiving persons and groups. *Psychological Review, 103,* 336–355.

Hamilton, D. L., Sherman, S. J., & Castelli, L. (2002). A group by any other name: The role of entitativity in group perception. In W. Stroebe & M. Hewstone (Eds.), *European review of social psychology* (Vol. 12, pp. 139–166). Chichester, UK: Wiley.

Hamilton, D. L., Sherman, S. J., & Lickel, B. (1998). Perceiving social groups: The importance of the entitativity continuum. In C. Sedikides, J. Schopler, & C. A. Insko (Eds.), *Intergroup cognition and intergroup behavior* (pp. 47–74). Mahwah, NJ: Erlbaum.

Hamilton, D. L., Sherman, S. J., & Maddox, K. B. (1999). Dualities and continua: Implications for understanding perceptions of persons and groups. In S. Chaiken & Y. Trope (Eds.), *Dual process theories in social psychology* (pp. 606–626). New York: Guilford.

Hamilton, D. L., Sherman, S. J., & Rodgers, J. (2004). Perceiving the groupness of groups: Entitativity, homogeneity, essentialism, and stereotypes. In V. Yzerbyt, C. M. Judd, & O. Corneille (Eds.), *The psychology of group perception: Perceived variability, entitativity and essentialism.* (pp. 39–60). Philadelphia: Psychology Press.

Hamilton, D. L., & Trolier, T. K. (1986). Stereotypes and stereotyping: An overview of the cognitive approach. In J. F. Dovidio & S. L. Gaertner (Eds.), *Prejudice, discrimination, and racism* (pp. 127–163). San Diego, CA: Academic.

Haslam, N., Rothschild, L., & Ernst, D. (2000). Essentialist beliefs about social categories. *British Journal of Social Psychology, 39,* 113–127.

Haslam, S. A., Oakes, P. J., Turner, J. C., & McGarty, C. (1996). Social identity, self-categorization, and the perceived homogeneity of ingroups and outgroups: The interaction between social motivation and cognition. In R. M. Sorrentino & E. T. Higgins (Eds.), *Handbook of motivation and cognition* (Vol. 3, pp. 182–222). New York: Guilford.

Hastie, R., & Park, B. (1986). The relationship between memory and judgment depends on whether the judgment task is memory-based or on-line. *Psychological Review, 93,* 258–268.

Heider, F. (1958). *The psychology of interpersonal relations.* New York: Wiley.

Hilton, J. L., & von Hippel, W. (1990). The role of consistency in the judgment of stereotype-relevant behaviors. *Personality and Social Psychology Bulletin, 16,* 430–448.

Hogg, M. A. (1996). Social identity, self-categorization, and the small group. In E. H. Witte & J. H. Davis (Eds.), *Understanding group behavior: Vol. 2. Small group processes and interpersonal relations* (pp. 227–253). Hillsdale, NJ: Erlbaum.

Howard, J. W., & Rothbart, M. (1980). Social categorization and memory for in-group and out-group behavior. *Journal of Personality and Social Psychology, 38,* 301–310.

Judd, C. M., Park, B., Yzerbyt, V., Gordijn, E. H., & Muller, D. (2005). Attributions of intergroup bias and outgroup homogeneity to ingroup and outgroup others. *European Journal of Social Psychology, 35,* 677–704.

Kelly, C. (1989). Political identity and perceived intragroup homogeneity. *British Journal of Social Psychology, 28,* 239–250.

Levy, S. R., Stroessner, S. J., & Dweck, C. S. (1998). Stereotype formation and endorsement: The role of implicit theories. *Journal of Personality and Social Psychology, 74,* 1421–1436.

Lewin, K. (1948). *Resolving social conflicts.* New York: Harper.

Lickel, B., Hamilton, D. L., Wieczorkowska, G., Lewis, A., Sherman, S. J., & Uhles, A. N. (2000). Varieties of groups and the perception of group entitativity. *Journal of Personality and Social Psychology, 78,* 223–246.

Lickel, B., Schmader, T., & Hamilton, D. L. (2003). A case of collective responsibility: Who else is to blame for the Columbine High School shootings? *Personality and Social Psychology Bulletin. 29,* 194–204.

Linville, P. W., Fischer, G. W., & Salovey, P. (1989). Perceived distributions of the characteristics of in-group and out-group members: Empirical evidence and a computer simulation. *Journal of Personality and Social Psychology, 57,* 165–188.

McConnell, A. R., Sherman, S. J., & Hamilton, D. L. (1994). On-line and memory-based aspects of individual and group target judgments. *Journal of Personality and Social Psychology, 67,* 173–185.

McConnell, A. R., Sherman, S. J., & Hamilton, D. L. (1997). Target entitativity: Implications for information processing about individual and group targets. *Journal of Personality and Social Psychology, 72,* 750–762.

McGarty, C., Haslam, S. A., Hutchinson, K. J., & Grace, D. M. (1995). Determinants of perceived consistency: The relationship between group entitativity and the meaningfulness of categories. *British Journal of Social Psychology, 34,* 237–256.

Mullen, B., & Hu, L. (1989). Perceptions of ingroup and outgroup variability: A meta-analytic integration. *Basic and Applied Social Psychology, 10,* 233–252.

O'Laughlin, M. J., & Malle, B. F. (2002). How people explain actions performed by groups and individuals. *Journal of Personality and Social Psychology, 82,* 33–48.

Ostrom, T. M., & Sedikides, C. (1992). Out-group homogeneity effects in natural and minimal groups. *Psychological Bulletin, 112,* 536–552.

Park, B., & Hastie, R. (1987). Perception of variability in category development: Instance- versus abstraction-based stereotypes. *Journal of Personality and Social Psychology, 53,* 631–635.

Park, B., & Judd, C. M. (1990). Measures and models of perceived group variability. *Journal of Personality and Social Psychology, 59,* 173–191.

Pickett, C. L. (2001). The effects of entitativity beliefs on implicit comparisons between group members. *Personality and Social Psychology Bulletin, 27,* 515–525.

Pickett, C. L., & Perrott, D. A. (2004). Shall I compare thee? Perceived entitativity and ease of comparison. *Journal of Experimental Social Psychology, 40,* 283–289.

Pickett, C. L., Silver, M. D., & Brewer, M. B. (2002). The impact of assimilation and differentiation needs on perceived group importance and judgments of ingroup size. *Personality and Social Psychology Bulletin, 28,* 546–558.

Plaks, J. E., Stroessner, S. J., Dweck, C. S., & Sherman, J. (2001). Person theories and attention allocation: Preferences for stereotypic vs. counterstereotypic information. *Journal of Personality and Social Psychology, 80,* 876–893.

Prentice, D. A., Miller, D. T., & Lightdale, J. R. (1994). Asymmetries in attachments to groups and to their members: Distinguishing between common-identity and common-bond groups. *Personality and Social Psychology Bulletin, 20,* 484–493.

Quattrone, G. A., & Jones, E. E. (1980). The perception of variability within in-groups and out-groups: Implications for the law of small numbers. *Journal of Personality and Social Psychology, 38,* 141–152.

Rogier, A., & Yzerbyt, V. Y. (1999). Social attribution, correspondence bias, and the emergence of stereotypes. *Swiss Journal of Psychology, 58,* 233–240.

Rothbart, M., & Lewis, S. (1988). Inferring category attributes from exemplar attributes: Geometric shapes and social categories. *Journal of Personality and Social Psychology, 55,* 861–872.

Rothbart, M., & Taylor, M. (1992). Category labels and social reality: Do we view social categories as natural kinds? In G. R. Semin & K. Fiedler (Eds.), *Language, interaction, and social cognition* (pp. 11–36). London: Sage.

Ryan, C. S., Judd, C. M., & Park, B. (1996). Effects of racial stereotypes on judgments of individuals: The moderating role of perceived group variability. *Journal of Experimental Social Psychology, 32,* 71–103.

Rydell, R. J., Hugenberg, K., Ray, D. & Mackie, D. M. (2007). Implicit theories, entitativity, and stereotyping. *Personality and Social Psychology Bulletin, 33,* 549–558.

Sherman, S. J., Castelli, L., & Hamilton, D. L. (2002). The spontaneous use of a group typology as an organizing principle in memory. *Journal of Personality and Social Psychology, 82,* 328–342.

Sherman, S. J., Hamilton, D. L., & Lewis, A. C. (1999). Perceived entitativity and the social identity value of group memberships. In D. Abrams & M. A. Hogg (Eds.), *Social identity and social cognition* (pp. 80–110). Oxford, UK: Blackwell.

Sherman, S. J., & Johnson, A. L. (2003). Perceiving groups: How, what, and why? In G. V. Bodenhausen, & A. J. Lambert (Eds.), *Foundations of social cognition: A festschrift in honor of Robert S. Wyer, Jr.* (pp. 155–180). Mahwah, NJ: Erlbaum.

Simon, B., & Pettigrew, T. F. (1990). Social identity and perceived group homogeneity: Evidence for the ingroup homogeneity effect. *European Journal of Social Psychology, 20,* 269–286.

Skowronski, J. J., Carlston, D. E., Mae, L., & Crawford, M. T. (1998). Spontaneous trait transference: Communicators take on the qualities they describe in others. *Journal of Personality and Social Psychology, 74,* 837–848.

Spencer-Rodgers, J., Hamilton, D. L., & Sherman, S. J. (2007). The central role of entitativity in stereotypes of social categories and task groups. *Journal of Personality and Social Psychology, 92,* 369–388.

Susskind, J., Maurer, K., Thakkar, V., Hamilton, D. L., & Sherman, S. J. (1999). Perceiving individuals and groups: Expectancies, dispositional inferences, and causal attributions. *Journal of Personality and Social Psychology, 76,* 181–191.

Tajfel, H. (1978). Social categorization, social identity, and social comparison. In H. Tajfel (Ed.), *Differentiation between social groups: Studies in the social psychology of intergroup relations* (pp. 61–76). London: Academic.

Tajfel, H., & Turner, J. (1979). An integrative theory of intergroup conflict. In W. Austin & S. Worchel (Eds.), *The social psychology of intergroup relations* (pp. 33–47). Monterey, CA: Brooks/Cole.

Taylor, S. E. (1981). A categorization approach to stereotyping. In D. L. Hamilton (Ed.), *Cognitive processes in stereotyping and intergroup behavior* (pp. 83–114). Hillsdale, NJ: Erlbaum.

Turner, J. C., Hogg, M. A., Oakes, P. J., Reicher, S. D., & Wetherell, M. (1987). *Rediscovering the social group: Self-categorization theory.* Oxford, UK: Blackwell.

Welbourne, J. L. (1999). The impact of perceived entitativity on inconsistency resolution for groups and individuals. *Journal of Personality and Social Psychology, 55,* 738–748.

Welbourne, J. L., Harasty, A. S., & Brewer, M. B. (1997, May). *The impact of kindness and intelligence information on extremity ratings of groups and individuals.* Paper presented at the meeting of the Midwestern Psychological Association, Chicago.

Wilder, D. A. (1984). Predictions of belief homogeneity and similarity following social categorization. *British Journal of Social Psychology, 23,* 323–333.

Wilder, D., & Simon, A. F. (1998). Categorical and dynamic groups: Implication for social perception and intergroup behavior. In C. Sedikides, J. Schopler, & C. A. Insko (Eds.), *Intergroup cognition and intergroup behavior* (pp. 27–44). Mahwah, NJ: Erlbaum.

Wyer, R. S., Jr., Bodenhausen, G., & Srull, T. K. (1984). The cognitive representation of persons and groups and its effects on recall and recognition memory. *Journal of Experimental Social Psychology, 20,* 445–469.

Yzerbyt, V. Y., Castano, E., Leyens, J. P., & Paladino, M. P. (2000). The primacy of the ingroup: The interplay of entitativity and identification. *European Review of Social Psychology, 11,* 257–295.

Yzerbyt, V. Y., Rocher, S. J., & Schadron, G. (1997). Stereotypes as explanations: A subjective essentialistic view of group perception. In R. Spears, P. Oakes, N. Ellemers, & A. Haslam (Eds.), *The psychology of stereotyping and group life* (pp. 20–50). Oxford, UK: Blackwell.

Yzerbyt, V. Y., Rogier, A., & Fiske, S. T. (1998). Group entitativity and social attribution: On translating situational constraints into stereotypes. *Personality and Social Psychology Bulletin, 24,* 1089–1103.

10 The Unbearable Accuracy of Stereotypes

Lee Jussim, Thomas R. Cain, Jarret T. Crawford
Rutgers University–New Brunswick

Kent Harber
Rutgers University–Newark

Florette Cohen
Rutgers University–New Brunswick

Sixty years of empirical research has taught us much about stereotypes. Stereotypes can arise from, and sustain, intergroup hostility. They are sometimes linked to prejudices based on race, religion, gender, sexual orientation, nationality, and just about any other social category. They can serve to maintain and justify hegemonic and exploitative hierarchies of power and status. They can corrupt interpersonal relations, warp public policy, and play a role in the worst social abuses, such as mass murder and genocide. For all these reasons, social scientists—and especially social psychologists— have understandably approached stereotypes as a kind of social toxin.

Perhaps equally understandable, but scientifically untenable, is the corresponding belief that because stereotypes contribute to these many malignant outcomes, that they must also be—in the main—inaccurate. The tacit equation is, if stereotypes are associated with social wrongs, they must be factually wrong. However, the accuracy of stereotypes is an empirical question, not an ideological one. For those of us who care deeply about stereotypes, prejudice, and social harmony, getting to the truth of these collective cognitions should guide inquiry about them.

Unfortunately, this has not always been our experience. Because of his inquiries into stereotype accuracy, the first author has been accused by prominent social psychologists of purveying "nonsense," of living "in a world where stereotypes are all accurate and no one ever relies on them anyway," of calling for research with titles like "Are Jews really cheap?" and "Are Blacks really lazy?," of disagreeing with civil rights laws, and of providing intellectual cover for bigots.[1]

These reactions are understandable, if one remembers that social psychology has a long intellectual history of emphasizing the role of error and bias in social perception, and nowhere has this emphasis been stronger than in the area of stereotypes. To enter this zeitgeist and to argue for the need to take seriously the possibility that sometimes, some aspects of some stereotypes may have some degree of accuracy, therefore, is to risk making claims that are unbearable to some social scientists. However, science is about validity, not "bearability." It is about logic and evidence.

In this chapter we review conceptual issues and empirical evidence regarding the accuracy of stereotypes. By doing so we hope to correct some long-held beliefs about stereotypes, and to thereby remove some of the obstacles to the systematic investigation of stereotype accuracy and inaccuracy. The chapter has three main objectives: providing a logically coherent, defensible, and practical definition of "stereotype"; reviewing empirical research on stereotype accuracy; and considering the role of stereotypes in increasing or reducing accuracy in person perception.

ARE STEREOTYPES INACCURATE BY DEFINITION?

Given the frequency with which stereotypes are assumed to be inaccurate, both in popular culture and the social scientific literature, the first order of business is defining stereotype. The accuracy issue becomes "settled" if stereotypes are defined as inaccurate. In this section we explain why a more agnostic approach is needed.

We begin by seriously considering the consequences of defining stereotypes as inaccurate, as have so many researchers before us. When researchers define stereotypes as inherently inaccurate, or assume that stereotypes are inaccurate, there are only two logical possibilities regarding what they might mean: (a) All beliefs about groups are stereotypes and all are inaccurate; or (b) not all beliefs about groups are stereotypes, but stereotypes are the subset of all beliefs about groups that are inaccurate. We next consider the implications of each of these possibilities.

ALL BELIEFS ABOUT GROUPS CANNOT POSSIBLY BE INACCURATE

No social scientist has ever explicitly claimed that all beliefs about all groups are inaccurate. Thus, toppling the assertion that all stereotypes are inaccurate might appear to be refuting a straw assertion. Unfortunately, however, this straw assertion, even if it is merely an implicit rather than explicit assertion, appears to have an ardent scientific following. For decades, stereotypes were predominantly defined as inaccurate, with virtually no evidence demonstrating inaccuracy (e.g., Allport, 1954/1979; Aronson, 1999; Campbell, 1967; Schultz & Oskamp, 2000; see reviews by Ashmore & Del Boca, 1981; Brigham, 1971). Furthermore, among those who define stereotypes as inaccurate, statements regarding what sort of beliefs about groups are accurate (and, therefore, not stereotypes), almost never appear (for concrete examples, see, e.g., Aronson, 1999; Campbell, 1967; Devine, 1995; Jones, 1986; Schultz & Oskamp, 2000; Allport, 1954/1979, remains a lone exception). Accurate beliefs about groups, therefore, appeared to be an empty set.

Furthermore, in their empirical studies, the social sciences have considered people's beliefs about almost any attribute (personality, behavior, attitudes, criminality, competence, demographics) regarding almost any type of group (in addition to race, sex, class, occupation, dorm residence, sorority membership, college major, and many more) to be a stereotype (see, e.g., reviews by APA, 1991; Fiske & Neuberg, 1990; Kunda & Thagard, 1996; or the meta-analyses reviewed in Jussim, Harber, Crawford, Cain, & Cohen, 2005). It seems, then, that for all practical purposes, the social sciences consider any and all claims and beliefs about groups to be stereotypes.

Putting these points together: Stereotypes are defined (by some) as inaccurate. All beliefs about groups are stereotypes. Therefore, regardless of whether any researcher has explicitly made this claim, any perspective assuming that all beliefs about groups are stereotypes, and defining stereotypes as inaccurate, is logically compelled to reach the conclusion that all beliefs about groups are inaccurate.

This conclusion is untenable on purely logical grounds. It would mean that (a) believing that two groups differ is inaccurate and (b) believing two groups do not differ is inaccurate. Both these conditions are not simultaneously possible, and logical coherence is a minimum condition for considering a belief to be scientific. On logical grounds, alone, therefore, we can reject any claim stating or implying that all beliefs about groups are inaccurate.

Many researchers do not hold such an extreme view. Next, therefore, we consider the less extreme position. The only logical alternative (if one defines stereotypes as inaccurate) to claiming that all beliefs about groups are inaccurate is the following: Not all beliefs about groups are inaccurate, but stereotypes are the subset of beliefs about groups that are inaccurate.

If Stereotypes Are the Subset of Beliefs About Groups That Are Inaccurate, There Is No "Stereotype" Research

If all stereotypes are inaccurate by definition, then only inaccurate beliefs about groups can be considered stereotypes. *Accurate* beliefs about groups, then, must constitute a different phenomenon altogether. This is not a logical problem as long as those who subscribe to this view stick to their definition and live with its implications.

If Stereotypes Are Defined as Inaccurate Beliefs About Groups Then Only Empirically Invalidated Beliefs Constitute Stereotypes

Accurate beliefs about groups are not stereotypes. Beliefs about groups of unknown validity cannot be known to be stereotypes. This perspective has a major drawback: It invalidates nearly all existing research on "stereotypes." This is because so little of the stereotype research has assessed the accuracy of the beliefs under investigation. Without such an assessment, beliefs cannot be known to be stereotypes. No research on "stereotypes" has ever been framed as follows:

> Is this belief about that group a stereotype? We are going to figure out whether this belief about that group is a stereotype by assessing whether that belief is inaccurate. If this belief is inaccurate, we will conclude that it is a stereotype. If this belief accurately described that group, we will conclude that it is not a stereotype.

This, however, is precisely how research *must* be framed before one can know one is studying a stereotype, if stereotypes are the subset of beliefs about groups that are inaccurate. If the accuracy of a specific belief being researched has not been first determined, then it is impossible to know whether that belief is a stereotype. The nature, causes, and effects of beliefs of unknown accuracy cannot contribute to knowledge of stereotypes if only inaccurate beliefs are stereotypes.

Holding social psychology to this restrictive definition would mean discarding decades of research purportedly addressing stereotypes. Why? Because almost none of it has empirically established that the beliefs about groups being studied are in fact erroneous. There would be nothing left—no studies of the role of "stereotypes" in expectancy effects, self-fulfilling prophecies, person perception, subtyping, memory, and so on. Poof! We would have to throw out the baby, the bathwater, the tub, the bathroom, and indeed tear down the entire scientific and empirical house in which all our current understanding of "stereotypes" exists.

In the future, those researchers who define stereotypes as inaccurate, or even emphasize their inaccuracy, must provide clear answers to each of the following definitional questions: Do they consider all beliefs about groups to be stereotypes? Do they define all beliefs about groups as inaccurate? Or do they define stereotypes as the subset of beliefs about groups that are inaccurate? If the latter, how do they distinguish between accurate beliefs about groups that are not stereotypes and inaccurate beliefs about groups that are stereotypes?

A Neutral Definition of Stereotype

Fortunately, many modern definitions of stereotypes do not define stereotypes as inherently inaccurate, and are instead agnostic in terms of stereotype accuracy. One of the simplest of these definitions, and the one we use throughout this chapter, was provided by Ashmore and Del Boca (1981), who stated that "a stereotype is a set of beliefs about the personal attributes of a social group" (p. 21). Stereotypes, as defined by Ashmore and Del Boca, may or may not be accurate and rational, widely shared, conscious, rigid, exaggerations of group differences, positive or negative, or based on essentialist or biological rationales. Stereotypes may or may not be the cause or the effect of prejudice, or the cause of biases and self-fulfilling prophecies.

It is good that Ashmore and Del Boca's definition does not specify these things—that leaves these aspects of stereotypes open to the kinds of empirical investigation this topic deserves. One of the great values of truly believing in the neutral definition is that it does not presume that any time a person holds or uses a stereotype, something inherently bad (or good) is happening. Instead, it opens the door for understanding when stereotypes wreak damage, when they simply reflect social reality, and, possibly, when they actually perform a social good.

Our rejection of defining stereotypes as inaccurate is not equivalent to defining them as accurate. Accuracy is an empirical issue, which naturally raises a question: How (in)accurate are people's beliefs about groups?

ARE STEREOTYPES EMPIRICALLY INACCURATE?

This section reviews empirical investigations of stereotype accuracy. It includes a discussion of an important level of analysis issue with respect to understanding stereotype (in)accuracy, a brief review of common methods for assessing stereotype accuracy (and their limitations), and a discussion of the complexities and richness involved in assessing accuracy. After presenting an overview of those conceptual issues, this section then reviews the research that has assessed the accuracy of people's stereotypes.

STEREOTYPE ACCURACY AND LEVELS OF ANALYSIS

The following statement summarizes a class of criticisms of stereotype accuracy that has periodically appeared in the social psychological literature (e.g., APA, 1991; Fiske, 1998; Nelson, 2002; Schneider, 2004; Stangor, 1995):

> Even if it can be successfully shown that perceivers accurately judge two groups to differ on some attribute: (a) Perceivers should not assume that their stereotypes of the group automatically fit all members of the group; (b) perceivers cannot apply their beliefs about the group when judging individuals; and (c) if perceivers do apply their beliefs about the group when judging individuals, they are likely to be wrong much of the time because few members perfectly fit the stereotype.

According to this type of analysis, all stereotypes are already known to be largely inaccurate so there is no need to assess their accuracy.

There is merit to these points. Few, if any, members of a group are fully defined by stereotypes. Assessments of any individual based solely on stereotypes will generally be lacking. However, this logic implies nothing about stereotype accuracy. Instead, it is a claim about the accuracy of applying stereotypes of groups to specific group members.

Stereotype accuracy issues occur, therefore, at two different levels of analysis, each captured by a different question. First, how accurate are people's beliefs about groups? Just as a person might not accurately remember how many games Roger Clemens won in 2000 (inaccuracy in person perception) and still remember that the Yankees won the World Series that year (accurate belief about Clemens's group), inappropriate application of a stereotype does not mean that the stereotype is itself inaccurate. A person may correctly know that, on average, women earn about 70% of what men earn, but have no accurate knowledge whatsoever about how much Nancy earns.

Second, does people's use or disuse of stereotypes in judging individuals increase or reduce the accuracy with which they perceive differences between small groups of individuals with whom they have personally come into contact? This is the accuracy version of the "stereotypes and person perception" question. Do, for example, general stereotypes of male superiority in athletics lead the coach of a soccer team to erroneously view the particular boys on the team as better than the particular girls on the team, when they really have equal skill?

SOME PRELIMINARY CAVEATS

We next briefly summarize some key points made in previous research on accuracy that we need to draw on here, although space considerations preclude an extended discussion. First, stereotypes undoubtedly sometimes lead to errors, biases, self-fulfilling prophecies, and a variety of unfair and unjustified outcomes. The research on these topics, however, typically has provided little information about their accuracy (Funder, 1987, 1995; Jussim, 1991, 2005).

Second, methodological difficulties once plagued accuracy research. Those difficulties, however, have been resolved by statistical, methodological, and conceptual advances within the field of accuracy research over the last 20 years (e.g., Funder, 1987, 1995; Jussim, 1991, 2005; Kenny, 1994; Ryan, 2002). Accuracy is now a thriving area of research within social psychology.

Third, this chapter does not address the issue of how group differences originate. Why groups differ is a fundamentally different scientific question than whether people perceive those differences accurately. Whether group differences result from genetics, childhood environment, socialization, culture, or roles is beyond the scope of this chapter.

Fourth, the genesis of stereotypes is also irrelevant with respect to evaluating their accuracy. A belief's accuracy must be assessed on its merits, not on its sources. Assessing accuracy of beliefs is a different endeavor than assessing processes leading to those beliefs (Jussim, 2005).

DIFFERENT ASPECTS OF STEREOTYPE (IN)ACCURACY

TYPES OF STEREOTYPE ACCURACY

Stereotype accuracy has been commonly assessed in either of two ways in the scientific literature. *Discrepancy scores* assess how close to perfection people's beliefs come. The stereotype belief (e.g., "how tall [rich, aggressive, etc.] is the average woman in the United States") is compared to criteria (e.g., the average height [wealth, aggressiveness, etc.] of the average woman). The difference indicates how far people are from perfection. Smaller discrepancies equal greater accuracy.

Research on stereotype accuracy has also frequently used *correlations* to assess how well people's beliefs about groups correspond to what those groups are like. Stereotype beliefs are correlated with criteria (e.g., people's ratings of women's average height, wealth, and aggressiveness, could be correlated with criteria for women's height, wealth, and aggressiveness). Higher correlations indicate greater correspondence of the stereotype with criteria—that is, higher accuracy.

Discrepancy scores and correlations have been used to assess two types of stereotypes: cultural and personal stereotypes. *Cultural stereotypes* refer to the extent to which a stereotype is shared by the members of a culture, or a particular sample, and are usually assessed by sample means (e.g., the mean belief about women's height in a sample is the best estimate of the cultural stereotype for women's height for the group sampled). *Personal stereotypes* are simply any individual's beliefs about a group, regardless of whether that belief is shared by others.

WHAT IS A REASONABLE STANDARD FOR CHARACTERIZING A STEREOTYPIC BELIEF AS "ACCURATE"?

There is no objective gold standard with which to answer this question. Perfect or near perfect accuracy is reserved for a very select set of endeavors (e.g., moon landings, measuring atomic weights, etc.). Even when social scientists generate hypotheses that predict differences on some outcome between groups (whether experimental or demographic), they do not require a correlation of 1.0 between group and outcome to consider their hypotheses confirmed. Indeed, social psychologists are often quite satisfied with correlations of .2 or less (Richard, Bond, & Stokes-Zoota, 2003). So, the issue is, what is a reasonable standard for lay accuracy in stereotypes? Because there are two broad types of accuracy, discrepancy from perfection and correspondence with real differences, there must be two separate standards. Each is discussed next.

DISCREPANCIES

The Bull's-Eye

A bull's-eye is as good as it gets in target practice. Bull's-eyes are not microscopic geometric points. They usually have perceptible width, which means one can legitimately hit a bull's-eye without being Robin Hood, who could hit the target dead center, then split his own arrow on the next shot. Our standard is that, for the type of social perceptual phenomena usually studied by social psychologists, a bull's-eye is within 10% of dead center. There is nothing magic about 10%. Reasonable people may disagree about this standard, and it might not be always appropriate, but when judging proportions and probabilities, as is common in the study of stereotype accuracy, getting within 10% is doing pretty well.

Some studies, however, do not report their results as percentages. Most that do not, however, report their results as effect sizes or can be readily translated into effect sizes—real and perceived differences between groups in standard deviation units, which can be translated into percentages. If Kay perceives Group A as .25 SD higher on some attribute than Group B, this means that Kay perceives the average person in Group A to score higher on that variable than 60% of the people in Group B. Bingo! That is a 10% difference (we assume a normal distribution, so the average person in Group B scores at the 50th percentile, so the difference is 10%). Therefore, for studies assessing stereotype accuracy using effect sizes, we characterize a perceived difference as accurate if it is within .25 SD of the real difference.

Our standards often do not correspond to those used by the original authors. McCauley's research (see Tables 10.1 and 10.2) often used "less than 10% off" as his criteria for accuracy; we differ by a single percent, because we characterize 10% off as accurate. Others used statistical significance as their standard (e.g., if the perceived difference statistically exceeded or underestimated the real difference, they concluded it was not accurate). Although these standards have their own advantages and disadvantages, discussing them is beyond the scope of this chapter.

Near Misses

Accuracy is a matter of degree—it is not all or none (Jussim, 2005). Therefore, it does not seem reasonable to characterize a belief that is 10% off as "accurate" and one that is 10.1% off as "inaccurate." So how should we characterize near misses? As near misses. A near miss is not accurate, but it is not too far off. Continuing with the archery metaphor, one can still rack up some points if one hits the target, even if one does not hit the bull's-eye; not as many points as when one hits the bull's-eye, but more than if one misses the target completely.

What, then, is a reasonable standard for a near miss? We use more than 10% off, but no more than 20% off. Within 20% is certainly not a bull's-eye, but it is not completely out of touch with reality, either. It is certainly far more accurate, say, than being 40% off or more. Here, too, people can disagree about what reasonably constitutes a near miss.

Following the same rationale as for accuracy, when results are only reported in standard deviations, we use "more than .25 SD discrepancy (between belief and criterion) but no more than .50 SD discrepancy" as our standard for near misses. If Tom's belief is that Group A's mean is .5 SD higher than Group B's mean, when there really is no difference, he erroneously believes that the mean of Group A group exceeds the scores of about 70% of the members of Group B, when, in fact, it only exceeds the scores of 50% of Group B; again, this is a 20% difference.[2]

Types of Discrepancies

The literature has focused on two broad types of discrepancies. By far, the most interesting and important discrepancy involves perceiving differences between groups. Do people perceive a larger or smaller difference between groups than really exists, or do they perceive the difference accurately? These types of discrepancies directly test the exaggeration hypothesis that has been so long emphasized in the scholarly literature on stereotypes. It is also important for practical reasons. These discrepancies, when they show that people exaggerate real differences on socially desirable attributes, indicate whether people unjustifiably perceive one group as "better" than another (more intelligent, more athletic, etc.). When they show that people underestimate real differences on socially desirable attributes, they indicate that people unjustifiably see groups as more similar to one another than they really are.

There is a second type of discrepancy reported in the literature that is still relevant as "inaccuracy," but has considerably less theoretical or practical importance with respect to stereotypes. Independent of perceiving how two (or more) groups mutually differ on a given attribute (e.g., height), sometimes people have a general tendency to overestimate or underestimate the level of some attribute for all groups. For example, let's say men and women in the United States average 72 and 66 in. in height, respectively. Fred, however, believes that men and women average 74 and 68 in., respectively. He consistently overestimates height by 2 in. (this is a fairly meaningless "elevation" effect; see, e.g., Judd & Park, 1993; Jussim, 2005), but he does not exaggerate sex differences in height.

CORRESPONDENCE WITH REAL DIFFERENCES: HIGH ACCURACY

How much correspondence should be considered "accurate"? Again, this is a judgment call. Nonetheless, we advocate holding people to a high standard—the same standards to which social scientists hold themselves.

J. Cohen (1988), in his classic statistical treatise imploring social scientists to examine the size of the effects they obtained in their studies and not just the "statistical significance" of the results, suggested that effect sizes above .8 could be considered "large." Such an effect size translates into a correlation of about .4 (in the remainder of this article, effect sizes are discussed exclusively as correlations). By this standard, correlations of .4 and higher could be considered accurate because they represent a "large" correspondence between stereotype and reality.

This standard has been supported by two recent studies that have examined the typical effect sizes found in clinical and social psychological research. One recent review of more than 300 meta-analyses—which included more than 25,000 studies and over 8 million human participants—found that mean and median effect sizes in social psychological research were both about .2 (Richard et al., 2003). Only 24% of social psychological effects exceeded .3. A similar pattern has been found for the phenomena studied by clinical psychologists (Hemphill, 2003). Psychological research rarely obtains effect sizes exceeding correlations of. 3. Effect sizes of .4 and higher, therefore, constitute a strong standard for accuracy. Last, according to Rosenthal's (1991) binomial effect size display, a correlation of at least .4 roughly translates into people being right at least 70% of the time. This means they are right more than twice as often as they are wrong. That seems like an appropriate cutoff for considering a stereotype reasonably accurate.

CORRESPONDENCE WITH REAL DIFFERENCES: MODERATE ACCURACY

Moderate correspondence, of course, is less than high correspondence. It reflects a mix of accuracy and inaccuracy. Following the same standards as science (J. Cohen, 1988; Richard et al., 2003), we characterize correlations between people's beliefs and reality ranging from .25 to .40 as moderately accurate. Such correlations do not reflect perfect accuracy, nor do they reflect complete inaccuracy.

TABLE 10.1

Are Racial/Ethnic Stereotypes Inaccurate?

Study and Stereotype	Perceivers and Criteria	Personal Stereotype Accuracy Discrepancies	Consensual Stereotype Accuracy Discrepancies	Personal Stereotype Accuracy Correlations	Consensual Stereotype Accuracy Correlations
Ryan (1996); beliefs about differences in the personal characteristics (achievement, personality, athletic, intelligence, etc.) of African American and White University of Colorado students	Perceivers: Random samples of 50 African American and 50 White University of Colorado students Criteria: Self-reports from the same samples	Not available	African-Americans beliefs about: African-Americans: 5, 5, 7 White Americans: 5, 5, 7 Differences: 5, 5, 7 (errors tended to exaggerate real differences) White Americans' beliefs about: African-Americans: 5, 5, 7 White Americans: 5, 2, 10 Differences: 9, 4, 4 (no consistent pattern of exaggeration or underestimation)	African American perceivers: .42[a] White perceivers: .36[a]	African American perceivers: .73, .53, 77[b,c] White perceivers: .77, .68, .72[b,c]
McCauley and Stitt (1978); beliefs about demographic differences (high school degree, on welfare, etc.) between African Americans and other Americans	Perceivers: Five haphazard samples (church choir, union members, students, etc.), N = 62 Criteria: U.S. Census data	Not available	White American targets: 17, 13, 5 African-American targets: 17, 14, 4 Differences between African-Americans and Other Americans: 27, 8, 0 (all discrepancies underestimated the real differences)	Not available	Beliefs about:[a,b] AfricanAmericans: .60 Americans: .93 Differences between African Americans and other Americans: .88
Ashton and Esses (1999); beliefs about the achievement of nine Canadian ethnic groups	Perceivers: 94 University of Western Ontario students Criteria: Toronto Board of Education data	Accuracy: 36 of 94 Exaggeration: 33 of 94 Underestimation: 25 of 94[d]	Not Available	.69	Not available
Wolsko, Park, Judd, and Wittenbrink (2000) ; beliefs about differences between African Americans and White Americans on a variety of attributes (work ethic, intelligence, criminality, etc.)	83 White University of Colorado undergraduates Criteria: U.S. Census data and other reports	Not available	Accuracy in judging stereotypical attributes and near misses in judging counterstereotypical attributes. Perceivers overestimated counterstereotypical attributes more than stereotypical attributes, which means they underestimated how stereotypical each group was. They also underestimated real race differences, but by less than 10%, i.e., they were accurate	Not available	Not available

Note: Bold numbers represent accurate judgments, italicized numbers represent inaccuracies, and regular typeface numbers represent near misses. Accuracy means within 10% of the real percentage or within .25 SD. For discrepancy scores that were near misses and inaccuracies, parenthetical statements indicate the number of errors that exaggerated real differences, underestimated real differences, or were in the completely wrong direction (reversals). Not available means both that it was not reported and that we were unable to compute it from the data that were reported. See text for explanation of personal and consensual stereotype accuracy discrepancies and correlations. Ryan's (1996) results refer to her stereotypicality results, not her dispersion results.

a For simplicity, if the study reported more than one individual level (average) correlation, we simply averaged all their correlations together to give an overall sense of the degree of accuracy.

b These correlations do not appear in the original article, but are computable from data that were reported.

c For each group of perceivers, the first correlation is the correspondence between their judgments and the self-reports of their own groups; the second correlation is the correspondence between their judgments and the self-reports of the other group; and the third correlation is the correspondence between the perceived difference between the groups and the difference in the self-reports of the two groups.

d Ashton and Esses (1999) computed a personal discrepancy score for each perceiver, and then reported the number of perceivers who were within .2 SD of the criteria, the number that exaggerated real differences (saw a difference greater than .2 SD larger than the real difference) or underestimated real differences (saw a difference more than .2 SD smaller than the real difference). Ashton and Esses (1999) examined beliefs about nine different Canadian ethnic groups; and discrepancy results refer to the number of participants showing each pattern. The results reported here refer to their Table 2, which reports the number of perceivers within .2 SD of the real difference. They did not report results from which the number of perceivers within .25 SD of the real difference could be identified.

TABLE 10.2
Are Gender Stereotypes Inaccurate?

Study and Stereotype	Perceivers and Criteria	Personal Stereotype Accuracy Discrepancies	Consensual Stereotype Accuracy Discrepancies	Personal Stereotype Accuracy Correlations	Consensual Stereotype Accuracy Correlations
McCauley, Thangavelu, and Rozin (1988); McCauley and Thangavelu (1991); beliefs about the sex distribution into different occupations[a]	Perceivers: College students, high school students, rail commuters (N = 521 over the five studies) Criteria: U.S. Census	Not available	**56**, 28 (26 underestimates), 6 (all underestimations)	Not Available	.94–.98[b] across five studies
Swim (1994)[c]; beliefs about sex differences on 17 characteristics	Perceivers: Introductory psychology students (N = 293 over two studies) Criteria: Meta-analyses of sex differences	Not available	**18**, 7 (6 underestimations, 1 reversal), 7 (5 exaggerations, 2 underestimations)	Not Available	Study 1: .78 Study 2: .79
Briton and Hall (1995); beliefs about sex differences in nonverbal behavior	Perceivers: 441 introductory psychology students Criteria: Meta-analyses of sex differences in nonverbal behavior	Not available	Female perceivers: **9**, 0, 8 (5 exaggerations, 2 underestimations, 1 reversal) Male perceivers: **11**, 6 (3 underestimations, 1 exaggeration, 2 reversals), 0	Not Available	Female perceivers : .74 Male perceivers : .68
Hall and Carter (1999); beliefs about sex differences on 77 characteristics	Perceivers: 708 introductory psychology students Criteria: Meta-analyses of sex differences		Not available	.43	.70
Cejka and Eagly (1999); beliefs about the sex distribution into different occupations	Perceivers: 189 introductory psychology students Criteria: U.S. Census	Not available	Male-dominated occupations: Accuracy Female-dominated occupations: Near miss (underestimation)[d]	Not available	.91
Diekman, Eagly, and Kulesa (2002) beliefs about the attitudes of men and women[f]	Perceivers: 617 college students over three studies Criteria: Actual attitudes, as indicated in the General Social Survey, which is a recurring nationally representative survey of Americans	Near miss (on average, over all attitudes; they did not report results separately for each attitude)	Accuracy[e]	Male targets: .45[e] Female targets: .54[e] When judging sex differences: .60	Male targets: .66[e] Female targets: .77[e] When judging sex differences: .80

| Beyer (1999)[f]; beliefs about the sex distribution into different majors and mean grade point average of men and women in those majors | Perceivers: 265 college students

Criteria: College records regarding the majors and grade point averages of its attending students | Not Available | Majors
Male perceivers: **6**, 5 (3 underestimations, 2 reversals), *1 (1 underestimation)*

Female perceivers: **7**, 4 (1 underestimation, 1 exaggeration, 2 reversals), *1 (1 underestimation)*

Sex differences in grade point average
Male perceivers: **4**, 5 (3 underestimations, 2 reversals), *3 (2 underestimations, 1 reversal)*

Female perceivers: **1**, 7 (2 underestimations, 1 exaggeration, 4 reversals), *4 (1 underestimation, 3 reversals)* | Proportion:
Male perceivers: .48
Female perceivers: .52

Grade point average
Male targets: .22
Female targets: –.04 | Proportion:
Male perceivers: .80
Female perceivers: .79

Grade point average
Male targets: .35
Female targets: .34 |

Note: Bold numbers represent accurate judgments, italicized numbers represent inaccuracies, and regular typeface numbers represent near misses. Accuracy means within 10% of the real percentage or within .25 SD. For discrepancy scores that were near misses and inaccuracies, parenthetical statements indicate the number of errors that exaggerated real differences, underestimated real differences, or were in the completely wrong direction (reversals). Accuracy data are separated according to perceiver groups or target groups only when these data are reported in the original studies. "Not available," therefore, means both that it was not reported and that we were unable to compute it from the data that were reported. See text for explanation of personal and consensual stereotype accuracy discrepancies and correlations.

a These studies are grouped together because they were so similar.

b These correlations do not appear in the original article, but are computable from data that were reported.

c Swim (1994) sometimes reported more than one meta-analysis as a criterion for a perceived difference. In that case, we simply averaged together the real differences indicated by the meta-analyses to have a single criterion against which to evaluate the accuracy of the perceived difference.

d Cejka and Eagly (1999) examined beliefs about 80 occupations, but did not report results separately for each occupation. Instead, they simply reported overall discrepancies within male-dominated occupations and within female-dominated occupations. There was a slight overall tendency to underestimate the sex difference in distribution into male-dominated occupations (9.3%), which is accurate by our standards, and a somewhat stronger tendency to underestimate the sex difference in distribution into female-documented occupations (17.9%), which qualifies as a near miss by our standards.

e For Diekman et al. (2002) we have averaged several correlations together to give an overall assessment of accuracy. Unfortunately, Diekman et al. did not report their results separately for each attitude. Instead, they reported results averaged over all attitudes. They did, however, report results separately for men and women targets. Therefore, there were a total of six consensual stereotype accuracy discrepancies reported—three studies by men and women targets. All six were underestimates; that is, there was a general tendency to underestimate how much people supported the various positions. However, this tendency was not very large. All six consensual stereotype discrepancy results underestimated support by only 2% to 8%.

f For Beyer (1999), all results are reported separately for men and women perceivers, except the individual correlations for grade point average (GPA). Because there was no significant sex of perceiver difference in these correlations, Beyer reported the results separately for male and female targets. GPA is not given in percentages and Beyer did not report standard deviations. To determine whether a result was accurate, therefore, we used the conservative criteria of within .10 grade points for accuracy, and within .20 grade points for a near miss. There was an overall tendency to inaccurately overestimate students' GPA (which is most relevant to stereotyping anyway). There are many reversals in Beyer's data because, although the stereotype is, apparently, that men perform better in school than do women, women's GPAs were actually higher in every major, including the masculine ones (math, chemistry, etc.).

Using Rosenthal's (1991) binomial effect size display, a correlation of .3, for example, means that people are right almost two thirds of the time. Now, this also means they are wrong a little over one third of the time, but two out of three isn't bad.

CAVEATS AND CLARIFICATIONS

Systematic Errors

In social science research, "errors" are usually random. In contrast, in stereotypes, even if the stereotype has considerable accuracy, a major source of concern is the potentially nonrandom nature of the errors. In the preceding discussion on moderate accuracy, for example, a perceiver could be right two thirds of the time. There is, however, a big difference if the one third worth of errors are random versus systematically biased against one group. Fortunately, discrepancy score analyses were intentionally designed to assess systematic errors (Judd & Park, 1993; Jussim, 2005), and we report such errors in our review.

We Only Review Stereotype Accuracy Data

Many of the studies reviewed herein addressed many issues other than accuracy, However, we confine our discussion to those aspects that involve the accuracy of stereotypes. Other issues are beyond the scope of this chapter.

Differences in Terms

None of the studies described in this chapter use our exact terminology of personal and consensual stereotypes that can be evaluated using either discrepancies or correspondence with real differences (or both). Often, they simply discuss "stereotypes." Regardless, we do make that distinction and describe their results accordingly, regardless of whether they described their results this way.

Some researchers have distinguished between personal and consensual stereotypes, although they generally use somewhat different terminology than we do. For example, consensual stereotypes are sometimes discussed as "aggregated" results or stereotypes (because they aggregate across all perceivers). Personal stereotypes are sometimes discussed as "individual" stereotypes; and the Judd, Park, and Ryan group uses the phrase "within-subject sensitivity correlations" to refer to what we call personal stereotype correlations.

CRITERIA FOR INCLUSION

To be included here, the empirical studies assessing the accuracy of stereotypes needed to meet two major criteria. First, they had to compare perceivers' beliefs about one or more target groups with measures of what that group was actually like. Studies assessing social cognitive processes, even when those processes are widely presumed to be flawed and invalid, are not included here, because such studies provide no direct information about accuracy (Funder, 1987; Jussim, 2005).

Second, studies needed to use an appropriate target group. Sometimes, researchers have assessed people's beliefs about a group, and used as criteria the characteristics of a haphazard sample of members of the target group (e.g., Allen, 1995; Martin, 1987). These studies have an important disconnect between the stereotype they are assessing and the criteria they use. Consider, for example, a study in which perceivers provide their beliefs regarding men and women in general, and the criterion sample is a convenient but haphazard sample of college students (Allen, 1995). In this case, even if perceivers' stereotypes corresponded perfectly with men and women in general, they might not correspond to the characteristics of this criterion sample, if the criterion sample's characteristics differ from those of men and women in general. Consequently, such studies were not included in our review.

ACCURACY OF ETHNIC AND RACIAL STEREOTYPES

Table 10.1 summarizes the results of all studies assessing the accuracy of racial and ethnic stereotypes that met our criteria for inclusion. We review the most noteworthy of their results here. First, consensual stereotype discrepancies are a mix of accurate and inaccurate beliefs. Nonetheless, most judgments were either accurate or near misses. Only a minority were more than 20% off.

Second, people's consensual stereotype discrepancies for between group differences are consistently more accurate than are their consensual stereotype discrepancies for characteristics within groups. For example, in the Ryan (1996) study, Whites' consensual stereotypes regarding Whites and regarding African Americans each were accurate only 5 of 17 times (10 of 34, total). However, their judgments of differences between Whites and African Americans were accurate 9 times out of 17. A similar pattern occurred in the McCauley and Stitt (1978) study (see Table 10.1).

Third, these results provide little support for the idea that stereotypes typically exaggerate real differences. Exaggeration occurred, but it occurred no more often than did underestimation, with one exception. The only study to assess the accuracy of personal discrepancies found that a plurality of people was accurate, and that there was a slightly greater tendency to exaggerate real differences than to underestimate real differences (Ashton & Esses, 1999, summarized in Table 10.1).

Fourth, the extent to which people's stereotypes corresponded with reality was strikingly high. Consensual stereotype accuracy correlations ranged from .53 to .93. Personal stereotype accuracy correlations were somewhat lower, but still quite high by any standard, ranging from .36 to .69.

ACCURACY OF GENDER STEREOTYPES

Table 10.2 summarizes the results of all studies of gender stereotypes that met our criteria for inclusion. Results are broadly consistent with those for ethnic and racial stereotypes. In most cases, at least a plurality of judgments was accurate, and accurate plus near miss judgments predominate in every study. Inaccuracy constituted a minority of results. Again, some results showed that people exaggerated real differences. There was, however, no support for the hypothesis that stereotypes generally lead people to exaggerate real differences. As with race, underestimations counterbalanced exaggerations.

Again, consensual stereotype accuracy correlations were quite high, ranging from .34 to .98, with most falling between .66 and .80. The results for personal stereotypes were more variable. Once they were inaccurate, with a near-zero correlation with criteria (Beyer, 1999, perceptions of female targets). In general, though, they were at least moderately, and sometimes highly accurate (most correlations ranged from .40–.60; see Table 10.2).

STRENGTHS AND WEAKNESSES OF RESEARCH ON THE ACCURACY OF RACIAL, ETHNIC, AND GENDER STEREOTYPES

Several methodological aspects of these studies are worth noting because they bear on the generalizability of the results. First, although most of the studies only assessed the accuracy of undergraduates' stereotypes, several assessed the accuracy of samples of adults (McCauley & Stitt, 1978; McCauley & Thangavelu, 1991; McCauley, Thangavelu, & Rozin, 1988). Some of the highest levels of accuracy occurred with these adult samples, suggesting that the levels of accuracy obtained do not represent some artifact resulting from the disproportionate study of undergraduate samples. Nonetheless, additional research on the accuracy of noncollege samples is still needed.

Second, the studies used a wide variety of criteria: U.S. Census data, self-reports, Board of Education data, nationally representative surveys, locally representative surveys, U.S. government reports, and so on. The consistency of the results across studies, therefore, does not reflect some artifact resulting from use of any particular criteria.

Third, the studies examined a wide range of stereotypes: beliefs about demographic characteristics (McCauley & Stitt, 1978; Wolsko, Park, Judd, & Wittenbrink, 2000), academic achievement (Ashton & Esses, 1999; McCauley & Stitt, 1978; Wolsko et al., 2000), and personality and behavior (Ryan, 1996; Wolsko et al., 2000). The consistency of the results across studies, therefore, does not reflect some artifact resulting from the study of a particular type of stereotype.

Fourth, personal discrepancies were the least studied of the four types of accuracy. Thus, the studies do not provide much information about the extent to which individual people's stereotypes deviate from perfection.

INACCURATE STEREOTYPES

Despite the impressive and surprising evidence of the accuracy of stereotypes, there is some consistent evidence of inaccuracy in stereotypes. In the United States, political stereotypes tend to have little accuracy (e.g., Judd & Park, 1993). Many people in the United States seem to have little knowledge or understanding of the beliefs, attitudes, and policy positions of Democrats and Republicans.

A recent large-scale study conducted in scores of countries found that there is also little evidence of accuracy in national stereotypes regarding personality (Terracciano et al., 2005). It is probably not surprising that people on different continents have little accurate knowledge about one another's personality (e.g., that Indonesians do not know much about, say, Canadians, is not very surprising). However, somewhat more surprising is that people from cultures with a great deal of contact (various Western European countries; Britain and the United States) also have highly inaccurate beliefs about one another's personality characteristics.

Although the Terracciano et al. (2005) study was impressive in scope and innovative in topic, it suffers from one of the limitations that excluded several studies from this review. Specifically, the criteria samples were haphazard samples of convenience, rather than random samples obtained from target populations. The extent to which this explains their low level of accuracy is unknown until research is conducted on the same topic that obtains criteria from random samples. In general, why some stereotypes have such high levels of accuracy and others such low levels is currently unclear and is an important area of future research.

THE ROLE OF STEREOTYPES IN ENHANCING OR REDUCING THE ACCURACY OF PERSON PERCEPTION

WHAT SHOULD PEOPLE DO TO BE ACCURATE?

On the Use of Inaccurate Versus Accurate Stereotypes in Judging Individuals

Relying on an inaccurate belief to judge an individual will not increase accuracy, as can easily be seen with a nonsocial example. If Armand believes that Anchorage, Alaska is warmer than New York City, and he relies on that belief for making guesses about where it is going to be warmer, today, tomorrow, the next day, and so on, he will be wrong most of the time. Even though he may pick up an occasional hit on the rare days that Anchorage really is warmer than New York, he will be wrong far more often than he is right.

Stereotypes are no different. If Celeste believes that professional (American) football players are unusually tiny, and if she relies on that stereotype to guess their sizes, she will be very wrong. Relying on an inaccurate stereotype to judge an individual decreases the accuracy of that judgment.

But what happens when people rely on a largely accurate stereotype to judge an individual? Given that the prior section demonstrated moderate to high accuracy in many stereotype beliefs, this becomes a pressing question. It turns out that there are some conditions under which relying on an accurate stereotype can increase accuracy in judging an individual, and there are some conditions under which relying even on an accurate stereotype will not increase accuracy. Those conditions are the major focus of the next sections of this chapter.

Understanding the role of stereotypes in increasing or reducing accuracy involves understanding three different person perception situations. How perceivers should go about being as accurate as possible will be different in each of these three situations (because this discussion involves understanding the role of stereotypes in person perception, in all situations, perceivers know the target person's group membership). In each case, we first present an example involving nonsocial perception, in which the issues may, perhaps, be easier to understand, and which will certainly be less complicated by political correctness concerns.

Definitive Individuating Information

The first situation involves having vividly clear and relevant individuating information about a particular target. We refer to such individuating as "definitive" because it provides a clear, valid, sufficient answer to whatever question one has about a target. For example, when judging academic accomplishments, we might have standardized test scores and class rank and grade point average for a college applicant; when judging sales success, we might have 10 years of sales records for a salesperson; and when judging personality, we might have multiple expert judges' observations of, and well-validated personality test scores for, a particular individual. When we have this quality and quantity of information, how much should we rely on stereotypes?

If one discovers from a credible source (say, the Weather Channel) that it is 80 degrees today in much of Alaska, but only 60 in New York, what should one conclude? The fact that it is usually colder in Alaska is not relevant. Today, it is warmer in Alaska.

Professional basketball players tend to be tall—very tall. It is very rare to find one shorter than 6'4." It is, therefore, reasonable to expect all basketball players to be very tall.

Once in a while, though, a short player makes it into the National Basketball Association (NBA). Spud Webb was a starting player in the 1990s, and he was about 5'7." Once one knows his height, should one allow one's stereotype to influence one's judgment of his height? Of course not. His height is his height, and his membership in a generally very tall group—NBA players—is completely irrelevant.

In situations where one has abundant, vividly clear, relevant individuating information about a member of a group, the stereotype—its content, accuracy, and so on—becomes completely irrelevant. One should rely entirely on the individuating information.

Useful but Not Definitive Individuating Information

In many other situations, people may have some useful information, but not the definitive information presented in the first situation. Sometimes information is ambiguous, or limited in quality or degree.

Small Amounts of Information

When we meet a person for the first time, we might have only physical appearance cues (which will usually reveal sex, but which may or may not clue us in on race or ethnicity, attractiveness, neatness, wealth, concern with fashion, etc.). Or, although we might not be following the election for Town Council closely, we just happen to hear on the radio a 10-second sound bite from a candidate in which she claims that property taxes are too high.

Ambiguous Information

Some information is inherently ambiguous—its meaning and interpretation are unclear. Is a shove playful horsing around or assault? Is that a warm, friendly smile, or a superior sneer? Is that extreme compliment flattery or sarcasm? In these cases people have information, but its meaning or interpretation is unclear.

Inferences Versus Observations

Behavior can be observed directly. Most other aspects of psychology—beliefs, attitudes, motivations, personality, intentions, and so on—are not directly observable; they must be inferred on the basis of behavior. Whereas it is possible to definitively know (most of the time) whether David smiled, without lots of other information, it is not so easy to figure out whether David is a "happy" person. Whereas it is relatively easy to grade a student's test, without lots of other information, it is quite hard to know whether that high test score reflects the student's brilliance or the simplicity of the test. There is an inherent ambiguity in going from behavior to inferences about underlying attributes.

Predicting the Future Versus Evaluating the Past

The future is inherently ambiguous. It is not possible to know exactly what will happen in the future (history is littered with the inaccurate predictions of the holy, the greedy, the political, and the superstitious). Nonetheless, we must make predictions about the future all the time. Whenever we select people for admission to college, graduate school, or jobs, we are, essentially, making a prediction that the chosen person is the best for that position, or, at minimum, that he or she is likely to succeed reasonably well. Because the future is inherently unknowable, however, we can almost never have enough information to render such predictions definitive. So, with respect to making predictions about the future, nearly all information has some degree of ambiguity.

What Should People Do With Useful but Not Definitive Individuating Information?

Alaska Versus New York

You get one piece of information about each location. You learn that Jane, a lifelong resident of Anchorage, considers it "cold" today and Jan, a lifelong resident of New York, considers it "cold" today. Note that the "information" that you have is identical regarding the two places. Should you, therefore, predict that they have identical temperatures?

That would be silly. It ignores the wealth of information you already bring to bear on the situation: (a) It is usually much colder in Anchorage; (b) "cold" can mean lots of different things in different contexts; and (c) people usually adapt to their conditions, so, if it is usually 40 degrees in your neighborhood, you would probably judge 20 degrees as cold; but if it is usually 60 degrees in your neighborhood, 40 might be seen as quite cold. To ignore all this would be foolish, and, most of the time, doing so will lead you to an inaccurate conclusion about the weather in the two places.

In other words, in this situation, to the extent that your beliefs about the general characteristics of Alaska, Alaskans, New York, and New Yorkers are reasonably accurate, they should influence your interpretation of "cold" and your prediction regarding the weather in each place.

Stereotypes and Person Perception

The logic here is identical. Consider stereotypes of peace activists and al Qaeda members. You hear the same thing about an individual from each group: They have "attacked" the United States. Should you interpret this to mean that they engaged in identical behaviors? Not likely. The "attack" perpetrated by the peace activist is most likely a verbal "attack" on U.S. war policies; the al Qaeda attack is probably something far more lethal.

The same principles hold regardless of whether the stereotypes involve groups for whom stereotypes are deemed acceptable (e.g., peace activists or al Qaeda) or groups for whom stereotypes are deemed socially unacceptable (e.g., genders, nationalities, races, social classes, religions, ethnicities, etc.). For example, if we learn both Bob and Barb are regarded as "tall," should we conclude that they are exactly equal in height? Of course not. Undoubtedly, Bob is tall for a man, and Barb is tall for a woman, and, because men are, on average, taller than women, tall means different objective heights for men and women (implicit acceptance of these "shifting standards" has been thoroughly demonstrated; e.g., Biernat, 1995).

What about judgments about more socially charged attributes, such as intelligence, motivation, assertiveness, social skill, hostility, and so on? The same principles apply. If the stereotype is accurate and one only has a small bit of ambiguous information about an individual, using the stereotype as a basis for judging the person will likely enhance accuracy. For the statistically inclined, this is a very basic application of Bayes's theorem (e.g., McCauley, Stitt, & Segal, 1980) and principles of regression (Jussim, 1991). Let's assume for a moment that 30% of motorcycle gang members are arrested for violent behavior at some point in their lives, and 0.3% of ballerinas are arrested for violent behavior at some point in their lives. People who know this are being completely reasonable and rational if, on dark streets or at lonely train stations, they avoid the bikers more than ballerinas, in the absence of much other individuating information about them.

In all of these cases, the stereotype "biases" the subsequent judgments. At least, that is how such influences have nearly always been interpreted in empirical social psychological research on stereotypes (see, e.g., Devine, 1995; Fiske & Neuberg, 1990; Gilbert, 1995; Jones, 1986). It is probably more appropriate, however, to characterize such phenomena as stereotypes "influencing" or "informing" judgments. Such effects mean that people are appropriately using their knowledge about groups to reach as informed a judgment as possible under difficult and information-poor circumstances. If their knowledge is reasonably accurate, relying on the stereotype will usually increase, rather than decrease, the accuracy of those judgments (see also Jussim, 1991, 2005).

No Individuating Information
Alaska and New York

If you are given absolutely no information, and are asked to predict today's high temperature in Anchorage and New York, what should you do? If you know anything about the climate in the two places, you will predict that it will be warmer in New York. Indeed, you should predict this every time you are asked to do so. Would this mean your beliefs about climate are somehow irrationally and rigidly resistant to change? Of course not. All it means is that you recognize that, when two regions systematically differ and you are asked to predict the day's temperature, and are given no other information, it will always be better to guess that the place with the higher average temperature is warmer than the place with the lower average temperature.

Stereotypes and Person Perception

If you are given no information other than race, and you are asked to predict the income of Bill, who is African American, and George, who is White, what should you do? If you know about the average incomes of African Americans and Whites in the United States, you will predict that George is richer. Indeed, you should predict this every time you are asked to make a prediction about the income of an African American and White target about whom you have no other information. Would this mean your beliefs about racial differences in income are somehow irrationally and rigidly resistant to change? Of course not. All it means is that you recognize that, when the average income of two racial groups differs and you are asked to predict the income of an individual from those groups, and are given no other information, it will always be better to guess that the person from the group with the higher average income has more income.

What Do People Do When They Judge Individuals?

Process

People *should* primarily use individuating information, when it is available, rather than stereotypes when judging others. Do they? This area of research has been highly controversial, with many researchers emphasizing the power of stereotypes to bias judgments (Devine, 1995; Fiske &

Neuberg, 1990; Fiske & Taylor, 1991; Jones, 1986; Jost & Kruglanski, 2002) and others emphasizing the relatively modest influence of stereotypes and the relatively large role of individuating information (Jussim, Eccles, & Madon, 1996; Kunda & Thagard, 1996).

Fortunately, literally hundreds of studies have now been performed that address this issue, and, even more fortunately, multiple meta-analyses have been performed summarizing their results. Table 10.3 presents the results from meta-analyses of studies assessing stereotype bias in many contexts. It shows that the effects of stereotypes on person judgments, averaged over hundreds of experiments, range from 0 to .25. The simple arithmetic mean of the effect sizes is .10, which is an overestimate, because the meta-analyses with more studies yielded systematically lower effect sizes ($r = -.43$ between effect size and number of studies). The few naturalistic studies of the role of stereotypes in biasing person perception have yielded similarly small effects (e.g., Clarke & Campbell, 1955; Jussim et al., 1996; Madon et al., 1998).

How small is an effect of $r = .10$? It is small according to J. Cohen's (1988) heuristic categorization of effect sizes. It is among the smallest effects found in social psychology (Richard et al., 2003). An overall effect of .10 means that expectancies substantially influence social perceptions about 5% of the time (as per Rosenthal's [1991] binomial effect size display). This means that stereotypes do not influence perceptions 95% of the time.

In general, therefore, based on more than 300 experimental studies and a smaller number of naturalistic studies, stereotypes have only very modest influences on person perception. Of course,

---

TABLE 10.3
Meta-Analyses of the Role of Stereotypes in Person Perception

Meta-Analysis	Topic/Research Question	Number of Studies	Average Stereotype Effect
Swim, Borgida, Maruyama, and Myers (1989)	Do sex stereotypes bias evaluations of men's and women's work?	119	−.04[a]
Stangor and McMillan (1992)[b]	Do expectations bias memory?	65	.03
Sweeney and Haney (1992)	Does race bias sentencing?	19	.09
Mazella and Feingold (1994)	Does defendant social category affect mock juror's verdicts? Defendants':		
	Attractiveness	25	.10
	Race (African American or White)	29	.01
	Social class	4	.08
	Sex	21	.04[a]
Kunda and Thagard (1996)	Do stereotypes bias judgments of targets in the absence of *any* individuating information?	7	.25
Kunda and Thagard (1996)	Do stereotypes bias judgments of targets in the presence of individuating information?	40	.19

Note: Effect size is presented in terms of the correlation coefficient, *r*, between stereotype (or expectation) and outcome. All meta-analyses presented here focused exclusively on experimental research. Individuating information refers to information about the personal characteristics, behaviors, or accomplishments of individual targets. The effect size shown in the last column for each of the meta-analyses represents the overall average effect size obtained in that study. Effect sizes often varied for subsets of experiments included in the meta-analysis. Only meta-analyses of outcomes, not of moderators or mediators, are displayed.

[a] A negative coefficient indicates favoring men; a positive coefficient indicates favoring women.
[b] This meta-analysis is included here because many of the studies involved stereotypes.

there is always the possibility that researchers have not searched in the right places or in the right way for powerful stereotype biases in person perception. At minimum, however, the burden of proof (for the existence of widespread, powerful stereotype biases in person perception) has shifted to those emphasizing such powerful biases.

The existence of small stereotype effects, however, does not necessarily mean that people do generally rely heavily on individuating information. However, the empirical evidence shows, in fact, that they do. The one meta-analysis that has addressed this issue found that the effect of individuating information on person perception was among the largest effects found in social psychology, $r = .71$ (Kunda & Thagard, 1996). In other words, people seem to be generally doing the right thing—relying on individuating information far more than stereotypes.

But what about that .10 effect of stereotypes? Doesn't that demonstrate inaccuracy? It might, at least when the stereotype itself is clearly inaccurate. However, it does not necessarily demonstrate inaccuracy for two reasons: (a) Most of the studies examining these issues have examined experimentally created fictitious targets who had no "real" attributes, so that there was no criteria with which to assess accuracy; and (b) an influence of an accurate stereotype (typically characterized as "bias" in the literature) does not necessarily translate into inaccuracy. Indeed, some "biases" mean that people are being as accurate as possible under the circumstances (Jussim, 1991, 2005). Therefore, the next section reviews the very small handful of stereotype and person perception studies that have actually addressed the accuracy issue.

Accuracy

Accuracy in Perception of Small Group Differences

Madon et al. (1998) examined the accuracy of seventh-grade teachers' perceptions of their students' performance, talent, and effort at math about 1 month into the school year. Madon et al. assessed accuracy in the following manner. First they identified the teachers' perceptions of group differences by correlating teachers' perceptions of individual students with the students' race, sex, and social class. This correlation indicated the extent to which teachers systematically evaluated individuals from one group more favorably than individuals from another group. Next, Madon et al. assessed actual group differences in performance, talent, and effort by correlating individual students' final grades the prior year (before teachers knew the students), standardized test scores, and self-reported motivation and effort with students' race, sex, and social class. The teachers' accuracy was assessed by correlating the teachers' perceived differences between groups with the groups' actual differences.

Madon et al. (1998) found that teachers were mostly accurate. The correlation between teachers' perceived group differences and actual group differences was $r = .71$. The teachers' perceptions of sex differences in effort, however, were highly inaccurate—they believed girls exerted more effort than boys, but there was no sex difference in self-reported motivation and effort. When this outlier was removed, the correlation between perceived and actual group differences increased to $r = .96$.

We are aware of only two other studies that have addressed whether people systematically and unjustifiably favor or disparage individuals belonging to certain groups (Clarke & Campbell, 1955; Jussim et al., 1996). Both yielded evidence of accuracy accompanied by small bias.

All three studies (including Madon et al., 1998), however, were conducted in educational contexts—Jussim et al. (1996) addressed teachers' perceptions of students, and Clarke and Campbell (1955) addressed students' perceptions of one another. It remains an empirical question whether this pattern of accuracy and small bias in perceptions of demographic differences between individuals with whom one has extended contact is unique to classrooms, or characterizes social perception more broadly.

This pattern of moderate to high accuracy in perceptions of differences between small groups can occur for either of two reasons. First, perceivers might have jettisoned their stereotypes completely, and judged targets primarily on the basis of relevant individuating information. Second, perceivers might not have jettisoned their stereotypes. If their stereotypes (e.g., "girls perform slightly higher in math classes than do boys") were accurate (girls actually did perform slightly higher than boys), teachers could also have reached accurate perceptions of differences between boys and girls by applying their stereotype.

The research described thus far does not distinguish between these explanations. Regardless of the explanation, however, this research does lead to one clear conclusion: In the few studies that have examined stereotypes and person perception under naturalistic conditions, there is no evidence of stereotypes powerfully and pervasively distorting perception. There was some evidence of bias and distortion, but the far stronger pattern has been accuracy. The next section, therefore, reviews studies that have not only assessed accuracy, but have also assessed the sources of both accuracy and bias in person perception.

Does Relying on a Stereotype Increase or Reduce Accuracy in Person Perception?

What does empirical research indicate about whether people's reliance on stereotypes increases or reduces the accuracy of their judgments? Only a handful of studies provide data capable of addressing this issue, and they are discussed next.

Occupational Stereotypes: C. E. Cohen (1981)

C. E. Cohen (1981) examined whether people more easily remember behaviors and attributes that are consistent with a stereotype than those that are inconsistent with that stereotype. Perceivers in her study viewed a videotape of a dinner conversation between a husband and wife (they were actually husband and wife, but they were also experimental confederates trained by Cohen). Half of the time, this conversation led perceivers to believe the woman was a waitress; half of the time, the conversation led perceivers to believe the woman was a librarian. The remainder of the conversation conveyed an equal mix of librarian-like and waitress-like attributes and behaviors.

Perceivers were then given a series of choices regarding objective aspects of the woman in the videotape (e.g., wore glasses . . . did not wear glasses). Their task was to select the correct description. Perceivers consistently remembered 5% to 10% more behaviors or features that were consistent with the woman's supposed occupation than behaviors or features that were inconsistent with her supposed occupation. For example, they were more likely to accurately remember that the "librarian" wore glasses and liked classical music, whereas they were more likely to accurately remember that the "waitress" had a beer and no artwork in her house (even though the tape was identical, showing the woman wearing glasses, liking classical music, having a beer, and not having artwork in her apartment). This pattern occurred across two studies and regardless of whether the memory test occurred immediately after the videotape or up to 7 days later. Thus, it appeared that people selectively remembered stereotype-consistent information better than they remembered stereotype-inconsistent information.

C. E. Cohen (1981) also reported results regarding the accuracy of her perceivers' memories. Across the two studies, accuracy levels were quite high—ranging from a low of 57% to a high of 88% and averaging about 75% in the first study and about 66% in the second study. Overall, therefore, she found high (about 70%) accuracy and small (about 5%–10%) but real bias.

The results from her second study were particularly relevant with respect to understanding whether the stereotype increased or reduced accuracy. In this study, half of the perceivers learned of the woman's supposed occupation before viewing the tape (so the stereotype was activated prior to viewing); half learned of it after viewing the tape. In comparison to receiving the label after viewing the tape, when people received the label first, they more accurately remembered both stereotype-consistent and stereotype-inconsistent information. On average they correctly remembered 70% of the target's attributes (regardless of their degree of stereotype consistency) when they received the label first; they correctly remembered only about 63% of the target's attributes when they received the label last. The upshot here, therefore, is that, although the label biased memory in such a manner as to favor stereotype-consistent information, having the label up front also increased overall accuracy.

Why? Most likely, the label provided some sort of organizing scheme for perceivers, which facilitated their understanding and interpretation of both stereotype-consistent and stereotype-inconsistent attributes. Stereotypes may "bias" perception and, simultaneously, increase accuracy.

Residence Hall Stereotypes: Brodt and Ross (1998)

The utility of an accurate stereotype was also demonstrated by Brodt and Ross (1998). College students made predictions about the behaviors and preferences of other college students who lived in one of two dormitories. The students in the "preppie" dorm were widely seen as politically conservative, wealthy, and conventional. The students in the "hippie" dorm were widely seen as politically left wing with unconventional practices and preferences. Perceivers (other students who did not live in either dorm) viewed photographs of individual targets, were informed of each target's dorm, and then made predictions about each target's behaviors and attitudes. Perceivers' predictions were then compared to the targets' self-reports on these same preferences and attitudes.

When perceivers predicted targets to be consistent with their dorm (for a preppie dorm resident to have preppie attributes or for a hippie dorm resident to have hippie attributes), 66% of their predictions were correct (they matched the targets' self-reports). When perceivers jettisoned their dorm stereotypes, and predicted targets to be inconsistent with their dorm, 43% of their predictions were correct. Relying on the preppie–hippie dorm stereotypes enhanced the accuracy of person perception predictions.

Sex Stereotypes: Jussim et al. (1996) and Madon et al. (1998)

Both Jussim et al. (1996) and Madon et al. (1998) examined the accuracy of teacher expectations. (Madon et al., 1998, was described previously; Jussim et al., 1996, was similar, except that it was conducted in sixth grade rather than seventh grade, and it did not examine the accuracy of perceived differences between students from different demographic groups.) Both found that, when controlling for individuating information (motivation, achievement, etc.), student social class and race or ethnicity had little or no effect on teacher expectations. Thus, teachers essentially jettisoned their social class and ethnic stereotypes when judging differences between children from different social class and ethnic backgrounds. Although this finding is in many ways laudable, teachers relying entirely on individuating information does not help address the question of whether relying on a stereotype increases or reduces accuracy.

Both studies, however, found that sex stereotypes biased teachers' perceptions of boys' and girls' performance (standardized regression coefficients of .09 and .10 for performance, and .16 and.19 for effort, for Madon et al. and Jussim et al., respectively). In both studies, teachers perceived girls as performing higher and exerting more effort than boys. Because these effects occurred in the context of models controlling for individuating information, they are best interpreted as stereotypes influencing teacher perceptions—bias effects, in traditional social psychological parlance.

Did these sex stereotyping bias effects increase or reduce the accuracy of teachers' perceptions? They did both. In the case of performance, the sex stereotype effect increased teacher accuracy. The real performance difference, as indicated by final grades the prior year, was $r = .08$ and $r = .10$ (for the 1996 and 1998 studies, respectively, girls received slightly higher grades). The regression model producing the "biasing" effect of stereotypes yielded a "bias" that was virtually identical to the real difference. In other words:

> The small independent effect of student sex on teacher perceptions (of performance) accounted for most of the small correlation between sex and teacher perceptions (of performance). This means that teachers apparently stereotyped girls as performing slightly higher than boys, independent of the actual slight difference in performance. However, the extent to which teachers did so corresponded reasonably well with the small sex difference in performance. In other words, teachers' perceptions of differences between boys and girls were accurate because teachers relied on an accurate stereotype. (Jussim et al., 1996, p. 348)

The same conclusion, of course, also characterizes the results for the 1998 study.

On the other hand, the results regarding effort provided evidence of bias that reduced accuracy. There was no evidence that girls exerted more effort than boys. Therefore, the influence of student sex on teacher perceptions of effort (i.e., teachers' reliance on a sex stereotype to arrive at judgments of effort) led teachers to perceive a difference where none existed. This is an empirical demonstration of something that, logically, has to be true. Relying on an *inaccurate* stereotype when judging individuals can only harm one's accuracy.

SUMMARY AND CRITICAL EVALUATION

Our review has shown that it is logically incoherent to define stereotypes as inaccurate, that it is unusual (but not unheard of) for stereotypes to be highly discrepant from reality, that the correlations of stereotypes with criteria are among the largest effects in all of social psychology, that people rarely rely on stereotypes when judging individuals, and that, sometimes, even when they do rely on stereotypes, it increases rather than reduces their accuracy. Many scholars, scientists, and people of good will, we do not doubt, will find these conclusions unbearable.

Therefore, the next order of business is to identify important limitations and qualifications to these conclusions. We are going to (a) clearly state many of the things the stereotype literature does not show; (b) state what it does show; and (c) describe many of the limitations to existing research on stereotype accuracy. We hope that doing so reduces the extent to which some readers may misinterpret our claims about what the stereotype research does show, and what lessons can be learned from it.

WHAT THE STEREOTYPE RESEARCH DOES NOT SHOW

1. It does not show that all stereotypes are always perfectly 100% accurate. We know of no researcher who has ever made this claim.
2. It does not show that prejudice and discrimination do not exist, or are trivial and unimportant. Prejudice and discrimination are terribly important, and can be terribly destructive. The research reviewed in this chapter has not addressed prejudice and discrimination.
3. It does not show that people correctly explain why group differences exist. Inasmuch as social scientists do not agree as to why group differences exist, it is probably not possible to assess the accuracy of most lay explanations for group differences.
4. It does not show how people arrive at their stereotypes. There is very little research on where stereotypes come from. Much speculative discussion emphasizes hearsay, family socialization, and the media (e.g., Allport, 1954/1979; Katz & Braly, 1933; Pickering, 2001). The extraordinary levels of accuracy shown in many of the studies reviewed in this chapter, however, do suggest another source is the primary basis of stereotypes—social reality.
5. The amount of research that has addressed the accuracy of people's perceptions of differences between small groups of individuals they know personally (stereotypes and person perception) is quite modest, and does not yet provide a sufficiently broad foundation on which to reach any general conclusions. It appears as if relying on accurate stereotypes seems to mostly enhance accuracy, but that conclusion should be held tentatively, pending further studies.

WHAT THIS RESEARCH DOES SHOW

1. The claim that stereotypes, as beliefs about groups, are inherently inaccurate has been falsified.

2. A more modest claim, one that does not define stereotypes as inherently inaccurate, is that they are generally or frequently inaccurate. This also has been falsified. The scientific evidence provides more evidence of accuracy than of inaccuracy in social stereotypes. The most appropriate generalization based on the evidence is that people's beliefs about groups are usually moderately to highly accurate, and are occasionally highly inaccurate.

3. This pattern of empirical support for moderate to high stereotype accuracy is not unique to any particular target or perceiver group. Accuracy has been found with racial and ethnic groups, gender, occupations, and college groups.

4. The pattern of moderate to high stereotype accuracy is not unique to any particular research team or methodology. It has been found by a wide variety of American and Canadian researchers; by those using Judd and Park's (1993) componential methodology; by those using noncomponential methodologies; and regardless of whether the criteria are obtained through official government reports, meta-analyses, or the self-reports of members of the target group.

5. This pattern of moderate to high stereotype accuracy is not unique to the substance of the stereotype belief. It occurs for stereotypes regarding personality traits, demographic characteristics, achievement, attitudes, and behavior.

6. The strong form of the exaggeration hypothesis—either defining stereotypes as exaggerations or as claiming that stereotypes usually lead to exaggeration—is not supported by data. Exaggeration does sometimes occur, but it does not appear to occur much more frequently than does accuracy or underestimation, and may even occur less frequently.

7. The exaggeration hypothesis—as a *hypothesis*—can still be retained. Exaggeration sometimes does occur. Understanding when stereotypes are more likely to exaggerate real differences, more likely to underestimate real differences, and more likely to be accurate is an important question for future research.

8. In contrast to their reputation as false cultural myths perpetrated by exploitative hierarchies against the disenfranchised, consensual stereotypes were not only the most accurate aspect of stereotypes, not only more valid than nearly all social psychological hypotheses, but they were stunningly accurate by any standard. Correlations of $r = .70$ and higher are almost never repeatedly obtained in any area of social or psychological research. Using Rosenthal's (1991) binomial effect size display to translate correlations into intuitively meaningful relationships shows that correlations of .6 to .9 mean that consensual stereotypes are about 80% to 90% accurate.

Table 10.4 compares the frequency with which social psychological research produces effects exceeding correlations of $r = .30$ and $r = .50$, with the frequency with which the correlations reflecting the extent to which people's stereotypes correspond to criteria exceed $r = .30$ and $r = .50$. Only 24% of social psychological effects exceed correlations of $r = .30$ and only 5% exceed $r = .50$. In contrast, all 18 of the aggregate and consensual stereotype accuracy correlations shown in Table 10.1 and Table 10.2 exceed $r = .30$, and all but two exceed $r = .50$. Furthermore, 9 of 11 personal stereotype accuracy correlations exceeded $r = .30$, and 4 of 11 exceeded $r = .50$.

This is doubly important. First, it is yet another way to convey the impressive level of accuracy in laypeople's stereotypes. Second, it is surprising that so many scholars in psychology and the social sciences are either unaware of this state of affairs, unjustifiably dismissive of the evidence, or choose to ignore it (see reviews by Funder, 1987, 1995; Jussim, 1991, 2005; Ryan, 2002). When introductory texts teach about social psychology, they typically teach about phenomena such as the mere exposure effect (people like novel stimuli more after repeated exposure to it, $r = .26$), the weapons effect (they become more aggressive after exposure to a weapon, $r = .16$), more credible speakers are more persuasive ($r = .10$), and self-serving attributions (people take more responsibility for successes than failures, $r = .19$; correlations all obtained from Richard et al., 2003). How much time and space is typically spent in such texts reviewing and documenting the much stronger

TABLE 10.4

Ethnic and Gender Stereotypes Are More Valid Than Most Social Psychological Hypotheses

	Proportion of Social Psychological Effects Obtained in Research[a]	Proportion of Consensual Stereotype Accuracy Correlations[b]	Proportion of Personal Stereotype Accuracy Correlations[b]
Exceeding .30	24%	100% (18/18)	81% (9/11)
Exceeding .50	5%	89% (16/18)	36% (4/11)

[a] Data obtained from Richard, Bond, and Stokes-Zoota's (2003) review of meta-analyses including thousands of studies. Effects are in terms of the correlation coefficient, r.

[b] From Tables 10.1 and 10.2. Within parentheses, the numerator is the number of stereotype accuracy correlations meeting the criteria for that row (exceeding .30 or .50) and the denominator is the total number of stereotype accuracy correlations reported in Tables 10.1 and 10.2. Because Table 10.1 summarizes the results for five studies for McCauley, Thangavelu, and Rozin (1988), the .94–.98 figure is counted five times. These numbers probably *underestimate* the degree of stereotype accuracy, because all single entries in Tables 10.1 and 10.2 only count once, even though they often constitute averages of several correlations found in the original articles.

evidence of the accuracy of people's stereotypes? Typically, none at all. For a field that aspires to be scientific, this is a troubling state of affairs. Some might even say unbearable.

IMPORTANT LIMITATIONS

There are, of course, many important limitations to the existing work on the accuracy of stereotypes. First, the accuracy of two of the other major types of stereotypes—religion and social class—have, as far as we know, never been examined. Although we can think of no reason why patterns of accuracy should differ for these types of groups, we will never know until the research is actually conducted.

Second, the existing research has overwhelmingly examined the stereotypes held by college students, largely because those samples are convenient. Is this important? Maybe. Suggesting it may not be that important has been the research by McCauley and colleagues (see Tables 10.1 and 10.2), and by Clabaugh and Morling (2004) showing that the accuracy of noncollege groups is nearly identical to that of college students. Nonetheless, more research with noncollege samples is needed.

Third, there are many different types and aspects of accuracy, and few studies report results addressing all of them. Ideally, more research in the future will provide more comprehensive assessments of the various types of stereotype accuracy.

Fourth, most of the research on stereotype accuracy to date has been conducted in the United States and Canada. Perhaps stereotypes in other countries are less (or more) accurate.

ARE STEREOTYPES EVER HIGHLY INACCURATE?

The Evidence Reviewed in This Chapter

Evidence of major inaccuracy is rare but it is not entirely absent. First, even the studies that we have reviewed have shown that people are better at judging differences between groups, and at judging the rank order of attributes within a group, than they are at judging the exact level of particular attributes within a group. In other words, the analyses assessing correspondence, which correlated people's beliefs with group attributes or group differences, consistently found strong evidence of accuracy, whereas the analyses assessing discrepancies provided a more mixed picture, including a fair amount of bull's-eyes, a fair amount of near misses, and a fair amount of inaccuracy. Even when people do not exaggerate or underestimate real differences, the evidence we reviewed showed that, often, they either consistently over- or underestimate the level of an attribute in a group.

Second, on average, personal stereotypes corresponded well with groups' attributes (i.e., individual beliefs about groups correlated moderately to highly with criteria). Nonetheless, some personal stereotypes were highly inaccurate. Nearly all of the studies reporting personal stereotype accuracy correlations found at least some people with very low—near zero—correlations. Whether these are simply more or less random fluctuations and measurement error, or whether some people are systematically more accurate than others, is an important question for future research. Possible candidates for individual differences that would predict systematic variations in accuracy would be intelligence (are smarter people more accurate?), education (are more highly educated people more accurate?), exposure to and experience with groups (the "contact hypothesis"; e.g., Allport, 1954/1979, has long suggested that contact with a group reduces prejudice, in part, by disconfirming erroneous stereotypes), nonverbal sensitivity (actually, Hall & Carter, 1999, already showed that people lower in nonverbal sensitivity hold less accurate sex stereotypes, but it would be useful to see if this pattern replicates), and ideology/motivated egalitarianism/universalism (which, despite the intended benevolence of an egalitarian ideology, seems to lead people to hold less accurate stereotypes; Wolsko et al., 2000). Despite the existing evidence showing only weak relations between prejudice and stereotyping (Park & Judd, 2005), perhaps under the right (or wrong) conditions, deeply held prejudices and hostilities can sometimes lead to highly distorted stereotypes.

Speculations on Other Conditions of Inaccuracy

Studies that examined people's beliefs about groups and then used as criteria the self-reports of haphazard samples of members of the target group (Allen, 1995; Martin, 1987; Terracciano et al, 2005) consistently find more evidence of what those researchers interpret as "inaccuracy" than do researchers who used whole populations or random samples of targets (the research summarized in Tables 10.1–10.3). The disconnect between the stereotype and criteria, however, renders such results difficult to interpret.

The existence of so few clear and strong demonstrations of widespread stereotype inaccuracy does justify the conclusion that research on the accuracy of stereotypes usually finds evidence of moderate to high accuracy, and only rarely finds evidence of low accuracy. It does not, however, necessarily justify concluding that stereotypes are hardly ever inaccurate. Perhaps researchers have just not yet looked in the right places or in the right ways for stereotype inaccuracy.

For example, education and mass communication levels are so high in the United States and Canada, where most of the stereotype accuracy research has been conducted, that, perhaps, in general, people are more exposed to social reality in these places (and, probably, in other Western democracies) than in many other places around the world. Perhaps poverty and ignorance help breed stronger inaccurate stereotypes. Perhaps the propaganda of demagogues in authoritarian regimes helps perpetuate inaccurate stereotypes. The Jim Crow American South; South Africa under apartheid; the Indian caste system; the Nazis' racial beliefs; and beliefs about Christians, Jews, and Hindus held by 21st-century Islamists are a few examples where it seems plausible to speculate that stereotypes might be more inaccurate than found in the research reviewed here.

Unfortunately, because the powers that be under such systems are not likely to be open to challenges to their authority, it will probably be very difficult to perform studies of stereotype (in)accuracy in such contexts. If it is difficult to perform research in the contexts most likely to produce stereotype inaccuracy, the scientific literature will be skewed toward providing more evidence of stereotype accuracy than may be actually true of people in general, around the world.

THE SCIENTIFIC AND SOCIAL VALUE OF STEREOTYPE ACCURACY RESEARCH

Stereotypes can be accurate. Some scholars and lay people resist this conclusion, believing that crediting any accuracy to stereotypes is tantamount to endorsing prejudice. We argue that the opposite is more likely true—that acknowledging the accuracy of some stereotypes provides the epistemological clarity needed to more effectively address prejudice and bigotry, and to more effectively investigate the nature, causes, and moderators of stereotypes.

Distinguishing Accurate From Inaccurate Stereotypes

Not all stereotypes are accurate, and those that are inaccurate may be the most damaging. A special and important case is that of manufactured stereotypes, which are intentionally designed to despoil the reputation of particular social groups. A few notorious examples include 19th-century American stereotypes of indigenous peoples as uncivilized savages, stereotypes of civil rights workers as Communist fifth columnists, and the perpetual stereotype of Jews as seeking world domination. All these manufactured stereotypes served nefarious agendas, and all were (and are) patently false.

However, exposing the fallacious nature of these libelous stereotypes requires criteria and tools for assessing stereotype accuracy. These tools must be calibrated against a standard of authenticity, just as do the tools for demonstrating counterfeit and fraud in art and business. Whereas Jews do not seek world domination, it is not always absurd to believe that certain groups seek domination over, if not quite the world, at least large parts of it (consider, e.g., Rome, Nazis, Communists, Imperial Japan, the Mongolian Khans, and, possibly, some modern Islamic extremists, etc.). Without standards and methods for assessing (in)accuracy, it becomes impossible to reliably sort out valid from bogus beliefs.

Investigating the Dynamics of Stereotypes

Stereotypes are not static phenomenon, but shift with circumstance, policy, social contact, and other forces. To what degree do stereotypes map these changes? How responsive are they to social shifts, or to targeted interventions? Why do some stereotypes shift rapidly and others remain entrenched? Perhaps not surprisingly, if one makes the common assumption that stereotypes are inaccurate, and answers these questions by assumption, one is not likely to even consider such questions, let alone provide answers to them (e.g., see discussions of stereotypes in Aronson, 1999; Devine, 1995; Fiske, 1998; Gilbert, 1995; Jones, 1986). However, answers to some of these questions have indeed begun to be provided by researchers who make the alternative assumption, that stereotypes might be influenced by social reality (e.g., Eagly & Diekman, 2003; Oakes, Haslam, & Turner, 1994).

Generating a Coherent Understanding of Both Past and Future Research

The decades of research on the role of stereotypes in expectancy effects, self-fulfilling prophecies, person perception, subtyping, and memory, are jeopardized if all stereotypes are regarded as wholly inaccurate. This past research will be haunted by a definitional tautology; that is, that people who believe in stereotypes are in error because stereotypes are erroneous beliefs. On the other hand, accepting that stereotypes range in accuracy makes this past research coherent, and allows for more edifying interpretations of past and future research, such as "people in X condition, or of Y disposition, are more likely to believe in, subscribe to, and maintain false stereotypes, whereas people in A condition, or of B disposition are more likely to believe in, subscribe to, and maintain accurate stereotypes."

In sum, accepting that stereotypes can sometimes be accurate provides the means to distinguish innocent errors from motivated bigotry, assess the efficacy of efforts to correct inaccurate stereotypes, and reach a more coherent scientific understanding of stereotypes. We believe that this proposition can advance the depth, scope, and validity of scientific research on stereotypes, and thereby help improve intergroup relations.

NOTES

1 Some of these appear in print, some have occurred at a conference, and one was in a review of a manuscript submitted for publication. At the May 2004 American Psychological Society (now Association for Psychological Science) conference panel on Stereotyping, Discrimination, and the Law, "Nonsense" was Lee Ross's characterization of my description of Brodt and Ross (1998) as showing that relying on an

accurate stereotype can increase accuracy of person perception (he is the Ross on that study, which is discussed in some detail later in this chapter and is readily available to the general scholarly public because it was published in a widely circulated journal). Living "in a world where all stereotypes are accurate" was Susan Fiske's introductory comment as she began her talk at the same conference. "Disagreeing with civil rights" is also from Fiske (1998, p. 381), and refers specifically to McCauley, Jussim, and Lee's (1995) concluding chapter to their book, *Stereotype Accuracy* (in that chapter they argued that, in the absence of perfectly diagnostic individuating information, people would make more accurate person perception judgments if they relied on rather than ignored accurate stereotypes—exactly the result empirically found by Brodt and Ross, 1998). Stangor (1995) did not specifically accuse any particular person of "supporting bigots"; instead, he indicted the entire scientific attempt to assess the accuracy of stereotypes as potentially supporting bigotry. "Are Blacks really lazy?" and "Are Jews really cheap?" were a reviewer's comments on a draft of the article eventually published by *Psychological Review* (Jussim, 1991), which argued that, if social psychologists wanted to make claims about the inaccuracy of stereotypes (which, given the frequency of such claims they apparently wanted to do very much), it behooved them to perform research that actually empirically assessed the accuracy of stereotypes. Although this call was removed from that particular article, it appeared in many others, and, in fact, has been answered by many researchers over the last 15 years. This chapter reviews that evidence. It is, perhaps, worth noting that, of the scores of empirical studies and meta-analyses reviewed, not a single one is titled anything like "Are Blacks really lazy?" or "Are Jews really cheap?"

2. Standard deviations are not related to percentiles in a linear manner. Therefore, .52 SD comes closer to capturing a 20% difference than does .50 SD. But .50, is a round number, is easier to use and remember, and ease of use has its own value. A difference of .50 SD actually means the mean of one group is higher than the mean of 69.15% of the members of the other group, which is close enough to 70% for this chapter.

REFERENCES

Allen, B. P. (1995). Gender stereotypes are not accurate: A replication of Martin (1987) using diagnostic vs. self-report and behavioral criteria, *Sex Roles, 32,* 583–600.

Allport, G. W. (1979). *The nature of prejudice* (2nd ed.). (Original work published 1954). Reading, MA: Maddison-Wesley.

APA Brief (1991). In the Supreme Court of the United States: Price-Waterhouse versus Hopkins. *American Psychologist, 46,* 1061–1070

Aronson, E. (1999). *The social animal* (8th ed.). New York: Worth.

Ashmore, R. D., & Del Boca, F. K. (1981). Conceptual approaches to stereotypes and stereotyping. In D. L. Hamilton (Ed.), *Cognitive processes in stereotyping and intergroup behavior* (pp. 1–35). Hillsdale, NJ: Erlbaum.

Ashton, M. C., & Esses, V. M. (1999). Stereotype accuracy: Estimating the academic performance of ethnic groups. *Personality and Social Psychology Bulletin, 25,* 225–236.

Beyer, S. (1999). The accuracy of academic gender stereotypes. *Sex Roles, 40,* 787–813.

Biernat, M. (1995). The shifting standards model: Implications of stereotype accuracy for social judgment. In Y. T. Lee, L. Jussim, & C. R. McCauley (Eds.), *Stereotype accuracy* (pp. 87–114). Washington, DC: American Psychological Association.

Brigham, J. C. (1971). Ethnic stereotypes. *Psychological Bulletin, 76,* 15–38.

Briton, N. J., & Hall, J. A. (1995). Beliefs about female and male nonverbal communication. *Sex Roles, 36,* 79–90.

Brodt, S. E., & Ross, L. D. (1998). The role of stereotyping in overconfident social prediction. *Social Cognition, 16,* 225–252.

Campbell, D. T. (1967). Stereotypes and the perception of group differences. *American Psychologist, 22,* 817–829.

Cejka, M. A., & Eagly, A. H. (1999). Gender-stereotypic images of occupations correspond to the sex segregation of employment. *Personality and Social Psychology Bulletin, 25,* 413–423.

Clabaugh, A., & Morling, B. (2004). Stereotype accuracy of ballet and modern dancers. *Journal of Social Psychology, 144,* 31–48.

Clarke, R. B., & Campbell, D. T. (1955). A demonstration of bias in estimates of Negro of ability. *Journal of Abnormal and Social Psychology, 51,* 585–588.

Cohen, C. E. (1981). Personal categories and social perception: Testing some boundaries of the processing effects of prior knowledge. *Journal of Personality and Social Psychology, 40,* 441–452.

Cohen, J. (1988). *Statistical power analysis for the behavioral sciences.* New York: Academic.

Devine, P. (1995). Prejudice and outgroup perception. In A. Tesser (Ed.), *Advanced social psychology* (pp. 467–524). New York: McGraw-Hill.

Diekman, A. B., Eagly, A. H., & Kulesa, P. (2002). Accuracy and bias in stereotypes about the social and political attitudes of women and men. *Journal of Experimental Social Psychology, 38,* 268-282.

Eagly, A. H., & Diekman, A. B. (2003). The malleability of sex differences in response to changing social roles. In L. G. Aspinwall & U. M. Staudinger (Eds.), *A psychology of human strengths* (pp. 103–115). Washington, DC: American Psychological Association.

Fiske, S. T. (1998). Stereotyping, prejudice, and discrimination. In D. Gilbert, S. T. Fiske, & G. Lindzey (Eds.), *The handbook of social psychology* (4th ed., Vol. 2, pp. 357–411). New York: McGraw-Hill.

Fiske, S. T., & Neuberg, S. L. (1990). A continuum of impression formation, from category-based to individuating processes: Influences of information and motivation on attention and interpretation. *Advances in Experimental Social Psychology, 23,* 1–74.

Fiske, S. T., & Taylor, S. E. (1991). *Social cognition* (2nd ed.). New York: McGraw-Hill.

Funder, D. C. (1987). Errors and mistakes: Evaluating the accuracy of social judgment. *Psychological Bulletin, 101,* 75–90.

Funder, D. C. (1995). On the accuracy of personality judgment: A realistic approach. *Psychological Review, 102,* 652–670.

Gilbert, D. T. (1995). Attribution and interpersonal perception. In A. Tesser (Ed.), *Advanced social psychology* (pp. 99–147). New York: McGraw-Hill.

Hall, J. A., & Carter, J. D. (1999). Gender-stereotype accuracy as an individual difference. *Journal of Personality and Social Psychology, 77,* 350–359.

Hemphill, J. F. (2003). Interpreting the magnitudes of correlation coefficients. *American Psychologist, 58,* 78–79.

Jones, E. E. (1986). Interpreting interpersonal behavior: The effects of expectancies. *Science, 234,* 41–46.

Jost, J. T., & Kruglanski, A. W. (2002). The estrangement of social constructionism and experimental social psychology: History of the rift and prospects for reconciliation. *Personality and Social Psychology Review, 6,* 168–187.

Judd, C. M., & Park, B. (1993). Definition and assessment of accuracy in social stereotypes. *Psychological Review, 100,* 109–128.

Jussim, L. (1991). Social perception and social reality: A reflection-construction model. *Psychological Review, 98,* 54–73.

Jussim, L. (2005). Accuracy in social perception: Criticisms, controversies, criteria, components, and cognitive processes. *Advances in Experimental Social Psychology, 37,* 1–93.

Jussim, L., Eccles, J., & Madon, S. J. (1996). Social perception, social stereotypes, and teacher expectations: Accuracy and the quest for the powerful self-fulfilling prophecy. *Advances in Experimental Social Psychology, 29,* 281–388.

Jussim, L., Harber, K. D., Crawford, J. T., Cain, T. R., & Cohen, F. (2005). Social reality makes the social mind. *Interaction Studies, 6,* 85–102.

Katz, D., & Braly, K. (1933). Racial stereotypes of one hundred college students. *Journal of Abnormal and Social Psychology, 28,* 280–290.

Kenny, D. A. (1994). *Interpersonal perception: A social relations analysis.* New York: Guilford.

Kunda, Z., & Thagard, P. (1996). Forming impressions from stereotypes, traits, and behaviors: A parallel-constraint-satisfaction theory. *Psychological Review, 103,* 284–308.

Madon, S. J., Jussim, L., Keiper, S., Eccles, J., Smith, A., & Palumbo, P. (1998). The accuracy and power of sex, social class and ethnic stereotypes: Naturalistic studies in person perception. *Personality and Social Psychology Bulletin, 24,* 1304–1318.

Martin, C. L. (1987). A ratio measure of sex stereotyping. *Journal of Personality and Social Psychology, 52,* 489–499.

Mazella, R., & Feingold, A. (1994). The effects of physical attractiveness, race, socioeconomic status, and gender of defendants and victims on judgments of mock jurors: A meta-analysis. *Journal of Applied Social Psychology, 24,* 131–135.

McCauley, C., Jussim, L., & Lee, Y. T. (1995). Stereotype accuracy: Toward appreciating group differences. In Y. T. Lee, L. Jussim, & C. R. McCauley (Eds.), *Stereotype accuracy: Toward appreciating group differences* (pp. 293–312). Washington, DC: American Psychological Association.

McCauley, C., & Stitt, C. L. (1978). An individual and quantitative measure of stereotypes. *Journal of Personality and Social Psychology, 36,* 929–940.

McCauley, C., Stitt, C. L., & Segal, M. (1980). Stereotyping: From prejudice to prediction. *Psychological Bulletin, 87,* 195–208.

McCauley, C., & Thangavelu, K. (1991). Individual differences in sex stereotyping of occupations and personality traits. *Social Psychology Quarterly, 54,* 267–279.

McCauley, C., Thangavelu, K., & Rozin, P. (1988). Sex stereotyping of occupations in relation to television representations and census facts. *Basic and Applied Social Psychology, 9,* 197–212.

Nelson, T. (2002). *The psychology of prejudice.* Boston: Allyn & Bacon.

Oakes, P. J., Haslam, S. A., & Turner, J. C. (1994). *Stereotyping and social reality.* Cambridge, MA: Blackwell.

Park, B., & Judd, C. M. (2005). Rethinking the link between categorization and prejudice within the social cognition perspective. *Personality and Social Psychology Review, 9,* 108–130.

Pickering, M. (2001). *Stereotyping.* New York: Palgrave.

Richard, F. D., Bond, C. F., Jr., & Stokes-Zoota, J. J. (2003). One hundred years of social psychology quantitatively described. *Review of General Psychology, 7,* 331–363.

Rosenthal, R. (1991). *Meta-analytic procedures for social research* (2nd ed.). Newbury Park, CA: Sage.

Ryan, C. (1996). Accuracy of Black and White college students' in-group and out-group stereotypes. *Personality and Social Psychology Bulletin, 22,* 1114–1127.

Ryan, C. S. (2002). Stereotype accuracy. *European Review of Social Psychology, 13,* 75–109.

Schneider, D. J. (2004). *The psychology of stereotyping.* New York: Guilford.

Schultz, P. W., & Oskamp, S. (2000). *Social psychology: An applied perspective.* Upper Saddle River, NJ: Prentice-Hall.

Stangor, C. (1995). Content and application inaccuracy in social stereotyping. In Y. T. Lee, L. Jussim, & C. R. McCauley (Eds.), *Stereotype accuracy* (pp. 275–292). Washington, DC: American Psychological Association.

Stangor, C., & McMillan, D. (1992). Memory for expectancy-congruent and expectancy-incongruent information: A review of the social and social developmental literatures. *Psychological Bulletin, 111,* 42–61.

Sweeney, L. T., & Haney, C. (1992). The influence of race on sentencing: A meta-analytic review of experimental studies. *Behavioral Sciences and the Law, 10,* 179–195.

Swim, J. K. (1994). Perceived versus meta-analytic effect sizes: An assessment of the accuracy of gender stereotypes. *Journal of Personality and Social Psychology, 66,* 21–36.

Swim, J., Borgida, E., Maruyama, G., & Myers, D. G. (1989). Joan McKay vs. John McKay: Do gender stereotypes bias evaluations? *Psychological Bulletin, 105,* 409–429.

Terracciano, A., Abdel-Khalek, A. M., Ádám, N., Adamovová, L., Ahn, C.-K., Ahn, M., et al. (2005). National character does not reflect mean personality trait levels in 49 cultures. *Science, 310,* 96–100.

Wolsko, C., Park, B., Judd, C. M., & Wittenbrink, B. (2000). Framing interethnic ideology: Effects of multicultural and color-blind perspectives on judgments of groups and individuals. *Journal of Personality and Social Psychology, 78,* 635–654.

11 Downward and Upward Spirals in Intergroup Interactions
The Role of Egosystem and Ecosystem Goals

Jennifer Crocker
University of Michigan

Julie A. Garcia
Stanford University

Intergroup relations are notoriously difficult. When people with different social identities interact, tension and negative emotion often ensue (Stephan & Stephan, 1985). Frequently, tension escalates into seemingly intractable conflict, with destructive consequences (Prentice & Miller, 1999). We propose that interactions between people with different identities, one valued or nonstigmatized, and the other one devalued or stigmatized, are difficult in part because these interactions threaten the self-images of both participants. Self-image threats trigger a cascade of physiological, emotional, self-regulatory, and cognitive responses, which are at best unhelpful and at worst create downward spirals in these interactions. However, these responses are not inevitable; they depend on the goals of the participants. When participants have *egosystem goals,* focused on constructing, maintaining, and defending desired images of themselves and their groups, interactions with outgroup members tend to spiral downward. In contrast, we suggest that when participants have *ecosystem goals,* focused on what they can learn, contribute, or do to support others, interaction can create upward spirals of increased understanding, communication, and caring. Our analysis builds on and extends with new theory and research our earlier efforts to articulate the consequences of these different types of goals for intergroup interactions (Crocker & Garcia, 2006; Crocker, Garcia, & Nuer, 2008).

STIGMA AND SELF-IMAGE THREAT

SELF-IMAGE THREAT FOR TARGETS OF STIGMA

In ancient Greece, the term *stigma* referred to a sign, or mark, cut or burned into the body, that designated the bearer as a person who was morally defective and to be avoided—a slave, a criminal, or a traitor, for example (Goffman, 1963). Sociologist Erving Goffman (1963) used the term to refer to a deeply discrediting attribute that reduces a person "in our minds from a whole and usual person to a tainted, discounted one" (p. 3). Thus, stigma refers to a social identity, or membership in some social category, that calls into question a person's full humanity—the person is devalued, spoiled, or flawed in the eyes of others (Crocker, Major, & Steele, 1998; Jones et al., 1984). Whether an attribute connotes a spoiled identity depends on the context; for example, in some contexts, White male is a valued identity, whereas in other contexts it may be devalued (Crocker et al., 1998). Specifically, research has shown that White participants can experience stereotype threat effects in math domains when they are compared to Asians (Aronson & Lustina, 1999) and in athletic domains when compared to African Americans (Stone, Lynch, Sjomeling, & Darley, 1999). These examples highlight the situational variability of identity meanings, and consequently, potential social identity threat (Steele, Spencer, & Aronson, 2002).

Stigma poses a threat to the social self for the targets of stigma; it threatens desired self-images that one wants validated and acknowledged by others (see Crocker & Garcia, 2006, for a discussion). Intergroup interactions potentially thwart stigmatized peoples' efforts to maintain positive self-images as their devalued attribute could become a filter through which nonstigmatized others interpret their actions and qualities (Steele et al., 2002). Possession of a stigmatized attribute raises the possibility that one will be devalued, stereotyped, discriminated against, or dehumanized by others (Crocker et al., 1998). For example, women may fear being perceived as not being good at mathematics. Black men may be concerned that they will be seen as dangerous. Muslims may worry about being perceived as terrorists. These examples highlight how membership in devalued social groups may create an anxiety that, regardless of their personal qualities, others will view them as stereotypic. Negative media images further reinforce this possibility. Most generally, stigma threatens self-images of the stigmatized as good, competent, and worthy.

Despite the threat to desired self-images, stigma does not inevitably diminish self-esteem; many stigmatized people have self-esteem as high as, or even higher than the nonstigmatized (Crocker & Garcia, in press; Crocker & Major, 1989). For example, despite powerful negative stereotypes and pervasive prejudice and discrimination, African Americans on average have self-esteem that is significantly higher than the self-esteem of European Americans (Gray-Little & Hafdahl, 2000; Twenge & Crocker, 2002). Although many stigmatized individuals undoubtedly suffer from low self-esteem, this consequence of stigma is by no means inevitable or universal (Crocker & Garcia, in press; Crocker & Major, 1989; Major, McCoy, & Quinton, 2002). We argue that difficulties in intergroup interactions arise not from diminished self-esteem among the stigmatized, but in the threats to desired self-images they experience. Both stigmatized (Sigelman & Tuch, 1997) and nonstigmatized (Vorauer, Main, & O'Connell, 1998) people are aware that outgroup members could evaluate them negatively because of their social group. Thus, positive self-images are particularly at risk in intergroup interactions.

Self-Image Threat for People With Valued Identities

Stigma can also threaten the self-esteem of the nonstigmatized. Many people want to view themselves as unprejudiced (Monteith, 1993); their desired images include qualities such as fair, reasonable, unbiased, and benevolent. However, whether or not they personally agree with them, most people are aware of the cultural stereotypes associated with stigmatized identities (Devine, 1989). These cultural stereotypes may create biases in speech or behavior that operate outside of conscious awareness (e.g., Bazerman & Banaji, 2004). Thus, people who see themselves as nonprejudiced may unintentionally express biases, threatening their desired image as nonprejudiced (Cooper & Fazio, 1984; Devine, Plant, Amodio, Harmon-Jones, & Vance, 2002). Efforts to suppress or control prejudiced thoughts and expressions may backfire, leading to increased stereotyping under demanding conditions (Bodenhausen & Macrae, 1996). People with valued social identities may also fear being seen as benefiting from privilege or advantage conveyed by their identities, and consequently as undeserving.

Social Norms Against Prejudice

Social norms often shape behavior, including the expression of prejudiced opinions. American society espouses egalitarian norms, which are a powerful influence in suppressing the expression of prejudice (Katz & Hass, 1988; Katz, Wackenhut, & Hass, 1986). For example, students report their own prejudices only when they perceive prejudice against a group to be socially acceptable

(Crandall, Eshleman, & O'Brien, 2002). Furthermore, people suppress prejudicial responses when a social norm against prejudice is salient (Monteith, Deneen, & Tooman, 1996). Thus, egalitarian social norms play a powerful role in suppressing prejudice. Although egalitarian norms lead people to suppress expressions of prejudice, people still do express prejudice and discrimination, just in more covert ways (e.g., Beal, O'Neal, Ong, & Ruscher, 2000).

In sum, people with valued or nonstigmatized identities can experience self-image threat when interacting with stigmatized others. Either because of societal norms or personal values, the nonstigmatized might not want to be seen as prejudiced. Thus, intergroup interactions can pose a self-image threat for both stigmatized and nonstigmatized individuals. The stigmatized person faces potential devaluation because of his or her stigmatizing attribute, whereas the nonstigmatized person faces the possibility of being judged as prejudiced or bigoted. Neither wants these outcomes.

THE CONSEQUENCES OF SELF-IMAGE THREAT

Threats to desired self-images activate physiological, emotional, behavioral, self-regulatory, and cognitive responses that can derail intergroup interactions.

VIGILANCE

People tend to focus their attention on potentially hostile cues when they perceive threat (Pratto & John, 1991). Knowing that others may be prejudiced against them, the stigmatized may fear and expect rejection (Mendoza-Denton, Downey, Purdie, Davis, & Pietrzak, 2002). These concerns foster vigilance for evidence that one's desired self-images are indeed devalued (Mendoza-Denton et al., 2002; Steele et al., 2002). Vigilance can occur outside of conscious awareness; in two studies, chronic and situational expectations about being stigmatized predicted attention to subliminal cues that threatened women's social identities (Kaiser, Vick, & Major, 2006). Although most research has focused on vigilance among people with stigmatized identities, nonstigmatized people are also vigilant for threats to their social identities as nonprejudiced, fair, and good people (Vorauer, 2006; Vorauer & Turpie, 2004).

Vigilance for self-image threats shapes perceptions of events, so ambiguous events are interpreted as threatening. Vigilance can lead the stigmatized to interpret the intentions of their interaction partner as hostile (Kramer & Messick, 1998). African Americans who anxiously expect rejection tend to both perceive rejection more often and react to it more strongly (Mendoza-Denton et al., 2002). Ethnic minorities who expect Whites to be prejudiced have more negative experiences during interethnic interactions; this finding held whether the expectations were chronic or situationally induced (Shelton, Richeson, & Salvatore, 2005).

Of course, not all stigmatized individuals are equally vigilant for rejection, prejudice, or discrimination. Stigmatized people differ in *stigma consciousness,* or how much they expect to be stereotyped by others because of their stigma (Pinel, 1999). People who are high in stigma consciousness perceive and experience more stereotyping than those low in stigma consciousness. Previous experiences with devaluation of one's social identity can also increase subsequent vigilance for similar events (Major & O'Brien, 2005).

PHYSIOLOGICAL RESPONSES

Physiologically, perceived threats to desired images activate the self-preservation system, also called the fight-or-flight stress response (Henry & Wang, 1998). The self-preservation motivational system is evolutionarily very old and found in species from reptiles to humans (Henry & Wang, 1998). It evolved to enable organisms to mobilize resources in response to life-or-death threats to survival (Dickerson & Kemeny, 2004). Survival threats activate the hypothalamic–pituitary–adrenocortical (HPA) axis, raising levels of the hormone cortisol, which mobilizes energy and modulates other physiological systems to effectively respond to the short-term metabolic demands of fleeing or fighting the threat. In humans, threats to the social self, or to desired self-images, also activate the self-preservation system, raising cortisol levels and mobilizing energy to respond to the threat (Dickerson & Kemeny, 2004).

Flight Responses

Activation of the self-preservation physiological system prepares the person to fight or flee. Although conscious self-regulation processes may override these responses, a number of researchers have noted the tendency of people whose social identities are threatened to flee or withdraw. A study of the experiences of former mental patients in a three-wave panel study over a 2-year period showed that defensive strategies for coping with stigma such as secrecy or withdrawal from situations can backfire (Wright, Gronfien, & Owens, 2000). Former mental patients who had heightened concerns about rejection prior to discharge, and therefore implemented defensive strategies, reported more experiences of rejection a year after leaving the hospital. In addition, experiences with rejection were associated with defensive strategies at both times, suggesting that withdrawal and secrecy may create a self-fulfilling cycle. Implementing defensive strategies can result in greater experiences of rejection, and this rejection could, in turn, result in an increased usage of defensive strategies.

People may choose to withdraw from intergroup contact by exclusively interacting with ingroup members (Tatum, 1997). In so doing, members of stigmatized groups avoid potential devaluation by avoiding contact with people who could be biased against them. However, this prevents people from having positive interactions with outgroup members, which ultimately could foster constructive intergroup dynamics (Allport, 1954/1979; Brewer & Brown, 1998).

In addition to physical withdrawal, people might psychologically withdraw from threatening contexts by disengaging their self-esteem from or disidentifying with domains in which their group is negatively stereotyped (Crocker et al., 1998; Steele, 1997). Thus, when stigmatized people perceive potential discrimination, they might disengage self-esteem from success in that domain or not value that domain (Crocker & Major, 1989; Major & O'Brien, 2005).

The flight response is not exclusive to people with devalued identities. Although it has received less research attention, people with nonstigmatized or valued identities also may withdraw from interactions with outgroup members to reduce anxiety about intergroup interactions (Stephan & Stephan, 1985).

Fight Responses

Aggression is the flip side of flight responses to threats to desired images. Indeed, a review of the literature concluded that threatened egotism causes aggression and violence (Baumeister, Smart, & Boden, 1996). People with high but unstable self-esteem, who presumably experience self-image threats, tend to be high in defensiveness, anger, and hostility (Kernis, Grannemann, & Barclay, 1989). To our knowledge, few researchers have studied aggression in response to self-image threats of stigmatized or nonstigmatized participants in intergroup interactions; this would seem to be an important topic for research. Anecdotal evidence suggests that some hate crimes are motivated by self-image threats. For example, violence against gay men by straight men may be triggered by the perceived threats to masculinity.

EMOTIONAL RESPONSES

Self-image threats elicit self-relevant emotions, including shame, guilt, anger, and even narcissistic rage (Baumeister et al., 1996; Tangney, 1999). Whether the emotion is directed against the self, as in shame, guilt, and low self-esteem, or against others, as in anger or rage, depends on whether one perceives the event to be fair and deserved, or unfair and undeserved (Shaver, Schwarz, Kirson, & O'Connor, 1987; Smith & Ellsworth, 1985).

In the context of social interactions between stigmatized and nonstigmatized people, these potential self-threats can lead to mistrust, discomfort, anxiety, and even avoidance and withdrawal (Blascovich, Mendes, Hunter, Lickel, & Kowai-Bell, 2001; Monteith, Devine, & Zuwerink, 1993; Richeson, Trawalter, & Shelton, 2005; Stephan & Stephan, 1985). For the stigmatized, emotional reactions to negative experiences related to one's social identity depend on whether the stigmatized person believes the outcome was deserved, or was due to prejudice and discrimination (Crocker & Major, 1994; Major, Gramzow, et al., 2002).

When stigmatized people believe they deserve negative outcomes, because their stigma somehow disqualifies or discredits them, they experience depressed and anxious feelings, and their self-esteem suffers (Crocker, Cornwell, & Major, 1993). When the stigmatized believe that negative outcomes linked to their stigma are unfair, and due to prejudice and discrimination, their self-esteem is less likely to suffer, but they are likely to be angry, anxious, or sad (Major & Crocker, 1993; Major, Quinton, & McCoy, 2002).

For the nonstigmatized, discrepancies between how people believe they *should* act and how they *would* act with stigmatized others threaten desired self-images, with emotional consequences (Devine, Monteith, Zuwerink, & Elliot, 1991; Zuwerink, Devine, Monteith, & Cook, 1996). Specifically, when low-prejudice people act more prejudiced than their personal values dictate, they feel guilty and self-critical. Moreover, low-prejudice people internalize their nonprejudiced standards and try to act in accordance with those standards. In addition, high- and low-prejudice people react differently when confronted with their own prejudiced behavior (Czopp & Monteith, 2003). Low-prejudice people experienced more guilt than high-prejudice people when confronted with their gender bias. In contrast, both high- and low-prejudice people tended to react with greater levels of guilt and discomfort when confronted by racial bias.

Cognitive Responses

Ego threats affect cognitive capacity and processes. Intense arousal associated with perceived threat can disrupt thinking and behavior. As the perceived self-threat activates the fight-or-flight response in the older or "lower" parts of the brain, "higher" cognitive functions of abstract thinking and self-reflection shut down (Siegel, 1999). Flexible responses, including creativity, integration, planning, empathy, and perspective-taking are impaired. For example, social rejection, which threatens the fundamental human need to belong and constitutes an ego threat for nearly everyone, impairs intelligent thought (Baumeister, Twenge, & Nuss, 2002), distorts time perception and self-awareness, and increases feelings that life is meaningless (Twenge, Catanese, & Baumeister, 2003), increases costly entrapment in losing courses of action (Zhang & Baumeister, 2006), and decreases empathy for others' physical and emotional pain (DeWall & Baumeister, 2006).

The effect of ego threat on higher cognitive processes may account for the relatively poor performance of members of negatively stereotyped or stigmatized groups on difficult tests of intellectual ability (Schmader & Johns, 2003). It also suggests that the effects of self-image threats on both stigmatized and nonstigmatized interaction participants may be much broader than previously recognized. In a manner of speaking, people under threat quite literally "lose it," or lose many of their cognitive capacities. When desired self-images are threatened either by perceived devaluation or by accusations of prejudice, both stigmatized and nonstigmatized participants in these interactions may lose some of their abilities to reason, plan, and empathize.

Self-Regulation

Ego threat undermines the ability to self-regulate toward a goal, by depleting self-regulatory resources (Baumeister, 1997; Baumeister, DeWall, Ciarocco, & Twenge, 2005; Twenge, Catanese, & Baumeister, 2002). For stigmatized people, stigma concerns deplete resources for self-regulatory behavior (Inzlicht, McKay, & Aronson, 2006). Specifically, stigmatized and stigma-sensitive participants fare worse at academic, attentional, and physical self-regulation compared to nonstig-matized and less stigma-sensitive participants. Thus, when stigmatized persons are under ego threat, they were less able to sustain goal-directed behaviors.

Similarly, ego threat negatively influences self-regulation attempts for nonstigmatized people. Evaluative concerns disrupt nonstigmatized group members' ability to engage in intimacy-building behaviors, such as global responsiveness, reciprocal disclosure, novel self-disclosure, global positive regard, and eye contact, when interacting with stigmatized others, particularly for nonstigmatized group members with more favorable attitudes toward the outgroup (Vorauer & Turpie, 2004). Thus, nonstigmatized group members under the most ego threat, those who are nonprejudiced, have the most difficulty with behaviors that would foster a positive intergroup interaction. Conversely, other research has found that high-prejudice, not low-prejudice people, find it more difficult to engage in self-regulatory behaviors following an intergroup interaction (Richeson & Shelton, 2003). Taken together, these studies indicate that in intergroup interactions, both prejudiced and nonprejudiced individuals are motivated to not appear prejudiced, which ultimately depletes resources and pre-vents them from effectively engaging in self-regulation.

In sum, accumulating evidence indicates that self-image threats activate the fight-or-flight response, accompanied by a cascade of physiological, emotional, and cognitive, and self-regulatory consequences.

DOWNWARD SPIRALS

The consequences of self-image threats, and their effects on physiology, motivation, cognitive abili-ties and self-regulation, may become mutually reinforcing, and create downward spirals in these interactions. For example, a stigmatized person may worry that the other is prejudiced and hence may fear being devalued. These concerns may be based on previous experiences with that person, or with others in a similar context. Accuracy aside, these beliefs may trigger anxiety and vigilance, the desire to either exit the interaction (flee) or challenge the assumed devaluation (fight). The perceived self-image threat activates the stress response, diminishing self-control, the ability to reason about the accuracy of the belief, the capacity to take the perspective of the other person, and the ability to think through the consequences of various courses of action. Based on these internal events, the stigmatized person may act uncomfortable and mistrusting of the other person. The behaviors of the stigmatized person might be interpreted by the nonstigmatized person as evidence of dislike, mistrust, or hostility. Sensing that the stigmatized person mistrusts him , the nonstigmatized person might experience a self-image threat of his own. For example, he might worry that the other believes he is prejudiced. This self-image threat could trigger the fight-or-flight response in the nonstigma-tized person, with its accompanying stress response, emotions such as anxiety or anger, and preoc-cupation with how his behavior will be interpreted. Cognitive capacities such as the ability to take the perspective of the other and understand that the other may simply be anxious rather than hostile may be diminished. The nonstigmatized person could become nervous, distracted, or focused on suppressing inappropriate thoughts (Richeson & Shelton, 2003), which paradoxically can lead to a slip of the tongue (Macrae, Bodenhausen, Milne, & Jetten, 1994), and the unwanted expression of prejudice. The stigmatized person may respond with complicated emotions—on the one hand, her worst fears have come true. On the other hand, she may conclude that she was right to be vigilant and mistrusting. She may confront him about his behavior. He, thinking of himself as a good, fair, and nonprejudiced person, may react to this accusation either with rage, shame and humiliation, or both. He may become angry and defensive, and conclude that his good intentions are unappreciated. He may conclude that she is critical and judgmental, and never gives him the benefit of the doubt. He may respond with greater anxiety about being accused of prejudice, defending himself, counterat-tacking, withdrawing, or resisting. She, in turn, will feel misunderstood, judged, and disrespected, and this will reinforce her conclusion that he is prejudiced.

A similar negative dynamic may occur when we take the perception of the nonstigmatized per-son as the starting point of our analysis. Stereotypes often operate instantaneously and without awareness (Wittenbrink, Gist, & Hilton, 1997). When these stereotypes are activated, a nonstig-matized person might ultimately create a self-fulfilling prophecy (Word, Zanna, & Cooper, 1974). For example, when discussing a difficult topic such as racial profiling with a Black person, a White person might automatically or nonconsciously assume that the other is hostile (Devine, 1989), be afraid that he will say something that is perceived as prejudiced and anger the other, activating the desire to withdraw or flee from the interaction. Consequently, he may nonconsciously distance himself physically by sitting further away from a Black person in an interaction (Goff et al., 2008). As a result of these concerns, his nonverbal behaviors may seem unfriendly or uncomfortable to the Black person. The Black person might interpret these behaviors as indicating that the person is indeed prejudiced. Consequently, the Black person may act in a hostile manner. The Black person might think that she was right to be wary of interacting with a White person. The White person might feel like he is unjustly being treated badly. Thus, without intention, a nonstigmatized person could confirm both his or her and the other's fears.

Both of these examples highlight how people can behave in ways that ultimately confirm oth-ers' expectations (e.g., Sinclair, Hardin, & Lowery, 2006). People selectively attend to informa-tion that fits their stereotypes (Darley & Batson, 1973) or act in ways that confirm expectations (Snyder & Swann, 1978). Expectations often subtly influence intergroup perceptions. For example, research has shown that ambiguous cues are often viewed in line with stereotypic expectations (e.g., Eberhardt, Goff, Purdie, & Davies, 2004). People are more likely to interpret ambiguous figures as a gun when primed with a Black rather than a White face. Also, people who are sensitive to and vigilant for rejection often behave in ways that increase their likelihood of experiencing rejection (Downey, Freitas, Michaelis, & Khouri, 1998).

In this cycle, the behavior of both the stigmatized and the nonstigmatized person confirms the worst fears of each. He was right to be worried about being accused of prejudice, and she was right to worry that he is prejudiced. Neither sees how each contributes to this reality. Both are right, and both are wrongly accused. Both are innocent victims in their own minds, and both are perpetrators in the other person's mind. Consequently, talking about the dynamic can be counterproductive. In reality, each person in this interaction is both a victim and a perpetrator. After this interaction, each will approach the next interaction with more anxiety, mistrust, and suspicion, and create a new destructive cycle.

How can this cycle of suspicion, mistrust, and anxiety between stigmatized and nonstigmatized people be broken? Having a conversation about reality does not break the cycle, because both people have evidence that their behavior is simply a response to the other's behavior, and therefore change must begin with the other person. When both participants experience self-image threat, and the accompanying cascade of emotions, stress response, cognitive deficits, self-regulatory depletion, and desire to flee or fight, interaction is unlikely to bring understanding.

Although it is tempting to wait until the other person is doing his or her part also, one can be stuck in the cycle indefinitely waiting for the other to change. Each person in these interactions can change only the part of the cycle that he or she controls—his or her own thoughts and behavior. If people identify and takes responsibility for their own part of the cycle, recognizing that they are not only a victim in this cycle, but also a perpetrator, they may alter the cycle. Once the nonstigmatized person sees how his fear of being accused of prejudice leads him to behave in anxious, defensive ways that in the end make him appear prejudiced, he could break the cycle. Once the stigmatized person sees how her fear of being devalued leads her to become vigilant, leading the nonstigmatized person to feel uncomfortable, she could break the cycle.

Indeed, shifting one's perspective on negative events from a self-immersed to a distanced per-spective, and asking why events unfolded as they did rather than what happened can enable cooler, less emotionally intense, more reflective processing of emotions (Kross, Ayduk, & Mischel, 2005). Yet, people have difficulty achieving this distanced perspective in the midst of a self-image-threat-ening interaction (Richeson & Shelton, 2003; Shelton et al., 2005).

GOALS IN INTERGROUP INTERACTIONS

We propose that reducing the degree of self-image threat in intergroup interactions could break downward spirals. In our view, self-image threats in intergroup interactions are not inevitable; rather, they depend on the goals that people bring to these interactions. The notion that reactions to events depend on the goal relevance of those events is well established in research on emotions (Frijda, 1988) and self-regulation (Carver & Scheier, 1998; Scheier & Carver, 1988). Concerns about self-image reflect what we have called egosystem goals (Crocker & Garcia, 2006; Crocker, Garcia, & Nuer, 2008). The cognitive, emotional, and behavioral reactions that create downward spirals in intergroup interactions should depend on the degree to which participants in those interactions are motivated by egosystem goals.

In the egosystem framework, the direction of motivation is toward the self; people focus on satisfying their own wants, desires, and needs, giving them priority over the well-being of others. People can obtain what they want from others, at least some of the time, by constructing desired images of the self (Schlenker, 2003). Constructing desired images is a necessary and perhaps inevitable aspect of social life. People form impressions of one another without conscious effort, often on the basis of very little information (Ambady, Bernieri, & Richeson, 2000); extraneous information may influence their impressions (Chartrand, van Baaren, & Bargh, 2006; DeCoster & Claypool, 2004). When important resources are at stake, it behooves people to attend to and attempt to control the impressions that others form of them. When people have egosystem goals to construct, maintain, and defend desired self-images, being the target of prejudice or being accused of prejudice threatens the goal to construct, maintain, and defend a desired self-image, triggering the cascade of responses described previously. Although people often have egosystem goals in intergroup interactions, it is possible to have goals that do not focus on obtaining things for the self or constructing desired self-images. We have proposed ecosystem goals as an alternative to egosystem goals with fewer negative consequences (Crocker et al., 2008).

ECOSYSTEM GOALS

Drawing on the biological notion of an ecosystem, Crocker et al. (in press) used the term ecosystem motivation to refer to a motivational framework in which people see themselves as part of a larger whole, a system of individuals whose needs are equally important, and whose actions have consequences for others, with repercussions for the entire system. In the ecosystem framework, people recognize that satisfaction of needs is not a zero-sum proposition. Consequently, in ecosystem motivation people tend to focus on contributing to others, recognizing that doing so will not harm, and can ultimately benefit, the self.

Consequences of Ecosystem Goals

We propose that when people have ecosystem goals, awareness and concern for others' needs triggers a cascade of physiological, emotional, cognitive, and self-regulatory consequences.

Physiological Responses

Ecosystem goals are hypothesized to activate the species-preservation physiological system (Crocker et al., 2008). Concern for the well-being of others activates the species-preservation or tend-and-befriend response to stress (Brown & Brown, 2006; Henry & Wang, 1998; Taylor et al., 2000). The species-preservation motivational system is evolutionarily more recent than the self-preservation system, and found in all mammals (Henry & Wang, 1998). It evolved to support caregiving in organisms whose young are born too immature to survive on their own (Brown & Brown, 2006; Henry & Wang, 1998; Taylor et al., 2000). In this system, stress activates the caregiving system, raising levels of oxytocin and other hormones, which inhibits the fight-or-flight response so organisms can attend to the needs of others (Brown & Brown, 2006). For example, a recent study showed that nasal inhalation of oxytocin reduces cortisol levels in married couples discussing an area of conflict in their relationship (Ditzen, Bodenmann, Ehlert, & Heinrichs, 2006). Although research on the species preservation system in humans is very new, evidence suggests that the system is activated in response to vulnerability in others, which can also be interpreted as a sign of trust (Zak, Kurzban, & Matzner, 2005).

In interactions between stigmatized and nonstigmatized people, this research suggests that conveying trust through vulnerability could activate the species-preservation, rather than the fight-or-flight, response to stress. For example, expressing emotions or needs in a vulnerable, rather than demanding, defensive, or angry manner might elicit empathy rather than defensiveness in the other person (Rosenberg, 2003).

Caregiving Behavior

Activation of the species-preservation physiological system prepares the person to respond to the needs of others (Brown & Brown, 2006; Henry & Wang, 1998; Taylor et al., 2000). Although these responses have rarely been studied in social psychological research, anecdotal evidence indicates that people have the capacity to respond to outgroup members empathically. For example, the outpouring of support and contributions to victims of Hurricane Katrina suggests that vulnerability of outgroup members can elicit empathy and responsive behavior.

Emotional Responses

Emotionally, ecosystem goals are characterized by feelings of love, compassion, and empathy (Crocker & Canevello, in press). In other words, when people have ecosystem goals they experience positive, other-directed emotions. Threats to ecosystem goals do not elicit the same negative, self-relevant emotions as threats to egosystem goals. In a study of first-semester college students, students with ecosystem goals reported that setbacks toward their goals made them feel determined and realistic, rather than ashamed and confused (Moeller, Crocker, & Canevello, 2008). In the context of social interactions between stigmatized and nonstigmatized people, these findings suggest that ecosystem goals might foster positive, other-directed emotions such as empathy and compassion toward outgroup members.

Cognitive Responses

If ecosystem goals activate the species-preservation response to stress, which leads to reduction of the fight-or-flight response, we would expect that ecosystem goals would reduce the effects of perceived threat on disruptions to thinking and behavior. Furthermore, we hypothesize that people with ecosystem goals have more capacity for "higher" cognitive functions of abstract thinking and self-reflection under stress or threat. Flexible responses, including creativity, integration, planning, empathy, and perspective-taking should be fostered, or at least not reduced. Thus, we expect that people with ecosystem goals would experience decreases in the negative effects of social rejection on intelligent thought, distorted time perception, feelings that life is meaningless, and increased empathy for others' physical and emotional pain (DeWall & Baumeister, 2006).

This line of reasoning suggests that ecosystem goals could reduce the effect of ego threat on the performance of members of negatively stereotyped or stigmatized groups on difficult tests of intellectual ability. Furthermore, if ecosystem goals foster perspective-taking, empathy, planning, and other higher level cognitive processes under threat, or at least minimize the loss of these capacities under threat, then both stigmatized and nonstigmatized participants in interactions would have available greater access to cognitive resources and abilities that could foster constructive responses in these interactions.

Self-Regulation

Preliminary evidence indicates that ecosystem goals foster self-regulation toward goals. In a first examination of this hypothesis, students with self-improvement goals indicated how their self-improvement goal made them feel. The more students' goals caused them to feel positive, other-directed emotions (indicating that they had ecosystem goals), the more progress they reported toward their self-improvement goal over the next 2 weeks (Moeller, Crocker, & Canevello, 2008). A subsequent study assessed students' egosystem and ecosystem goals for friendships weekly for 10 weeks. For weeks when students were high in egosystem goals (compared to their own average), they reported more setbacks and less progress toward their most important friendship goals. In contrast, for weeks when students were high in ecosystem goals, they reported fewer setbacks and more progress toward their most important friendship goals. When asked how successfully they self-regulated in the domain of friendships (e.g., "focus on your most important relationship goals," "give your best effort to your friendships," and "resist distractions and focus on your friends"), for weeks when students were high in ecosystem goals (relative to their own average), they self-regulated better. Extending these findings to interactions between stigmatized and nonstigmatized people interacting, we would expect that interaction participants with ecosystem goals for the interaction would show improved self-regulation toward their goals for the interaction, and make more progress toward their goals.

In sum, accumulating evidence indicates that ecosystem goals activate the species-preservation system and the tend-and-befriend response to stress, accompanied by a cascade of physiological, emotional, cognitive, and self-regulatory consequences. Although the effects of egosystem and ecosystem goals in intergroup interactions has received very little empirical attention, the available research suggests that in contrast to egosystem goals, ecosystem goals may foster more positive outcomes in these interactions.

Evidence for the beneficial effects of ecosystem goals and costs of egosystem goals was provided by a study of 199 first-semester college freshmen, recruited for a study of goals and adjustment to college at the start of their freshman year of college (Crocker & Canevello, in press). Students completed a series of pretest questionnaires, then accessed a Web-based survey once each week for 10 weeks in the fall semester. The weekly survey included questions about their goals in the past week, their psychological well-being, their academic outcomes, and their relationships. Finally, participants completed a posttest survey. Egosystem goals were assessed in two domains (academics and friendships) by asking students how much over the past week they wanted or tried to construct desired images. Ecosystem goals were assessed by asking how much over the past week students wanted or tried to be supportive of others (e.g., have compassion for others' mistakes and weaknesses, be supportive of others, avoid being selfish or self-centered, avoid doing anything that would be harmful to others).

The design of this study provided multiple opportunities to examine the correlates and consequences of egosystem and ecosystem goals. Short-term within-person associations between weekly goals and weekly outcomes were examined using hierarchical linear modeling, entering weekly egosystem goals and weekly ecosystem goals simultaneously as within-person predictors of weekly outcomes. These analyses indicate whether changes in participants' goals led to changes in their outcomes, regardless of their average levels of the goals and outcomes. Individual differences in chronic egosystem and chronic ecosystem goals were assessed by computing average egosystem and average ecosystem goals scores across the 10 weekly reports, and regressing each outcome (averaged across the 10 weeks) on the two goals, gender, and social desirability. Relatively long-term changes in outcomes were assessed in regression analyses predicting posttest outcomes from chronic egosystem and ecosystem goals, controlling for pretest levels of the outcome, gender, and social desirability.

Relationships

Ecosystem goals foster feelings of closeness and social support, whereas egosystem goals foster feelings of loneliness and decreased social support. Both between- and within-person analyses indicate that egosystem goals are associated with increased loneliness, whereas ecosystem goals are associated with increased relationship closeness. Analyses of change over time suggest the egosystem goals undermine social support, whereas ecosystem goals increase social support.

Learning

Ecosystem goals fostered an orientation toward learning and growth. Both between- and within-person analyses of learning-oriented outcomes, and analyses of changes in achievement goals across the first semester of college, indicate that ecosystem goals are associated with increased learning orientations. Unexpectedly, egosystem goals were not related to any of the weekly measures of learning orientations. Egosystem goals did, however, predict increases in performance-focused achievement goals over the first semester of college.

Well-Being

Egosystem goals undermine well-being, whereas ecosystem goals improve well-being. Within-person analyses, between-person analyses, and analyses of changes over time all indicated that egosystem goals undermine psychological well-being, whereas ecosystem goals improve psychological well-being.

Egosystem and Ecosystem Goals and Disclosure of Concealable Stigmas

The egosystem–ecosystem framework may be useful to people with concealable stigmas such as depression as they consider whether to disclose their stigma to others. We proposed that the decision to disclose or conceal a concealable, potentially stigmatizing attribute can be guided either by egosystem motivation or by ecosystem motivation (Garcia & Crocker, 2008). Egosystem reasons to disclose a stigmatizing identity consider what disclosure means for the construction, protection, and enhancement of desired images, and how that affects one's ability to obtain desired outcomes and avoid unwanted outcomes. In the egosystem framework, people may ask themselves: What am I trying to prove or show about myself? What am I afraid will happen to me if I disclose? Will the other person accept me? Will they reject me? Will this person care about me after learning this? People with egosystem goals might disclose their stigma out of a sense of obligation or for foreseeable immediate benefits, like catharsis. Alternately, they may conceal their stigma when they believe they will be rejected or discriminated against.

Ecosystem goals for disclosing stigmatized identities include consideration of the needs and well-being of others, in addition to the self. For example, ecosystem goals might suggest disclosing when that disclosure will facilitate connection and growth, both for the self and others. Instead of focusing on inflating or protecting the self, in the ecosystem, people want to be supportive of others but not at the expense of their own well-being. They may ask themselves: What is at stake for other people? Would disclosure be good for both me and the other person? Will disclosing help the greater good? Unlike people with egosystem goals, they may be willing to risk possible rejection if disclosing would benefit others. Thus, people with ecosystem motivations might be willing to risk disapproval for the sake of creating authentic relationships with, educating, or supporting others.

A daily report study empirically examined the consequences of having egosystem and ecosystem motivations for disclosing a concealable stigma (Garcia, 2005). A total of 48 depressed college students and 50 sexual minority participants completed initial questionnaires designed to measure motivations to disclose or conceal, psychological well-being (i.e., depression, perceived stress, psychological well-being, and negative affect), and demographic variables. After the initial set of questionnaires, they completed daily reports on the Web for 2 weeks. At the end of each day they were asked if they had an opportunity to disclose their depression that day. If they did have an opportunity to disclose, they were asked to report their reasons for or against disclosure and their affect when they disclosed. After 2 weeks, they filled out additional questionnaires that were the same as the initial set of questionnaires.

We measured motivation to disclose or keep hidden a concealable stigma with a modified version of a scale developed by Derlega, Winstead, and Folk-Barron (2000). Seven subscales assessed reasons for disclosure: catharsis, seek help, duty to inform, educate, test other's reactions, emotionally close relationship, and similarity with the other person. Six subscales assessed reasons against disclosure: fear of rejection, privacy, self-blame or self-concept concerns, communication difficulties, conflict avoidance, and superficial relationship. We added three additional scales to assess identity and approval validation goals and growth goals. Approval validation goals included items such as, "It is important to me to confirm that others respect me." Identity validation goals included items such as, "It is important to me to confirm that others see me as a person with depression/nonheterosexual." Growth goals were assessed using Dykman's (1998) growth goals scale, which included items such as, "I look upon rejection as part of life since I know that such experiences will help me grow as a person in the long run."

A factor analysis confirmed that the motivations to disclose or conceal a concealable stigma loaded on the two hypothesized theoretical factors: egosystem and ecosystem goals. The egosystem factor included both reasons for and against disclosure: communication difficulty, conflict avoidance, fear of rejection, desire for others' approval, testing others' reactions, catharsis, and duty to inform. The ecosystem factor only included reasons to disclose: personal growth, educating the other, similarity with the other, and wanting to be seen as depressed (being authentic).

In daily disclosure decisions, people decide to disclose their depression based on a plethora of both egosystem and ecosystem motivations, including, but not limited to, obtaining support, avoiding discrimination, testing relationships, and supporting others. These reasons, in turn, influence whether or not they disclose and emotions when they disclose. Over time, these motivations could have a cumulative effect on psychological well-being. Using an experience sampling methodology enabled us to examine both the immediate and long-term effects of having egosystem and ecosystem motivations to disclose.

We explored the effect of initial egosystem and ecosystem motivations on disclosure and psychological well-being at the end of 2 weeks. Egosystem goals, despite including reasons for disclosure, predicted lower disclosure. For sexual minorities, only psychological well-being at pretest predicted psychological well-being at posttest. However, for depressed participants, ecosystem motivations predicted lower depressive symptoms at the end of 2 weeks, after controlling for initial disclosure levels. Next, we investigated the influence of initial egosystem and ecosystem motivations on daily disclosure and affect in daily disclosure decisions. Ecosystem goals predicted greater disclosure when participants had an opportunity to disclose. Also, when participants had ecosystem goals, they experienced more positive affect on days they disclosed. Thus, when participants had motivations to disclose that were beneficial to the self and others, they disclosed more and felt better when doing so.

CREATING UPWARD SPIRALS

Although preliminary, research and theory on ecosystem goals suggests that they can create or contribute to upward spirals in interactions between stigmatized and nonstigmatized people. Upward spirals in these interactions could be initiated by communicating in a constructive and vulnerable, rather than defensive or angry way, about one's emotions and goals for the relationship (e.g., "I'm afraid of being disrespected and I would like to create a relationship of mutual respect," rather than "I'm angry about being disrespected in the past and I don't want to be disrespected now"). For example, a nonstigmatized person could communicate a fear of being seen as prejudiced and a desire to understand and connect with the experience of the stigmatized person. Research suggests that expressing positive intentions and emotions in a vulnerable way communicates trust, which may trigger caregiving and compassion in the stigmatized person, raising oxytocin levels and inhibiting the fight-or-flight response.

With the suppression of the fight-or-flight response, the stigmatized person should have greater access to his or her capacities for perspective taking, empathy, logical thinking, planning, creativity, and flexible cognition. Consequently, even if the nonstigmatized person says something that could be interpreted as offensive or devaluing, he or she may have the capability to reflect on the intentions of the nonstigmatized person, consider several explanations for the other's comment, empathize with the anxiety of the nonstigmatized person, and respond in a constructive manner, perhaps exploring what the other is feeling rather than judging, criticizing, or withdrawing. These responses, in turn, communicate trust in the nonstigmatized person, which, according to our analysis, will further trigger tend-and-befriend responses in the nonstigmatized person. Thus, an upward spiral is created.

Similarly, the upward spiral could begin with the stigmatized person, who might express in a vulnerable and constructive manner her fears and intentions for the interaction (e.g., "I am uncomfortable because I'm afraid of being devalued in this interaction, and I would like to create a relationship of mutual respect.") This expression of vulnerability communicates a measure of trust in the nonstigmatized person, which may elicit a tend-and-befriend response in him, suppressing the fight-or-flight response.

Thus, either participant in the interaction could potentially initiate an upward spiral, by taking the risk to communicate in a vulnerable, constructive manner. Being the first to take this risk might be difficult, but the only alternative is to wait for the other to take a risk, which might never happen. Ecosystem goals encourage the person to be the starting point for creating a positive dynamic, or upward spiral, in the relationship, rather than waiting for the other person to demonstrate trustworthiness.

CONCLUSION

We have argued that egosystem goals contribute to downward spirals and ecosystem goals can create upward spirals in intergroup relations. One might object that setting aside vigilance and taking risks to create a more positive intergroup dynamic is too dangerous because past events demonstrate that the danger from outgroup members is real. Protective mechanisms based on dangerous past events feel necessary to survival, and they induce blind distrust of outgroup members. Vigilance for prejudice and discrimination can become a self-fulfilling prophecy, however, because it activates the fight-or-flight response. It is very difficult to be constructively vigilant.

One might object that, in urging people to focus on their own responsibility for downward spirals in intergroup relations, we are blaming the victim. Why should targets of prejudice and discrimination focus on their own egosystems when the perpetrators of prejudice and discrimination are truly at fault? Yet, as we have seen, in downward spirals of intergroup relations everyone believes they are the victim and the other is the perpetrator; if all victims wait for perpetrators to change their behavior, the downward spiral will continue unabated. The best possibility for creating change is starting with the self, at the places where one has responsibility, for those are the places where one has the leverage to create upward spirals in intergroup relations.

ACKNOWLEDGMENTS

Jennifer Crocker was supported by National Institute of Mental Health grant R01 MH58869–01, and Julie A. Garcia was supported by a National Science Foundation Minority Postdoctoral fellowship during the preparation of this chapter.

Jennifer Crocker and Julie A. Garcia contributed equally to this chapter; order of authorship is alphabetical.

We are grateful to Noah Nuer for his many contributions to our thinking on these issues.

REFERENCES

Allport, G. (1979). *The nature of prejudice.* New York: Doubleday/Anchor. (Original work published 1954)
Ambady, N., Bernieri, F. J., & Richeson, J. A. (2000). Toward a histology of social behavior: Judgmental accuracy from thin slices of the behavioral stream. In M. P. Zanna (Ed.), *Advances in experimental social psychology* (Vol. 32, pp. 201–271). San Diego, CA: Academic.

Aronson, J., & Lustina, M. J. (1999). When white men can't do math: Necessary and sufficient factors in ste-reotype threat. *Journal of Experimental Social Psychology, 35,* 29–46.

Baumeister, R. F. (1997). Esteem threat, self-regulatory breakdown, and emotional distress as factors in self-defeating behavior. *Review of General Psychology, 1,* 145–174.

Baumeister, R. F., DeWall, C. N., Ciarocco, N. J., & Twenge, J. M. (2005). Social exclusion impairs self-regulation. *Journal of Personality and Social Psychology, 88,* 589–604.

Baumeister, R. F., Smart, L., & Boden, J. M. (1996). Relation of threatened egotism to violence and aggression: The dark side of high self-esteem. *Psychological Review, 103,* 5–33.

Baumeister, R. F., Twenge, J. M., & Nuss, C. K. (2002). Effects of social exclusion on cognitive processes: Anticipated aloneness reduces intelligent thought. *Journal of Personality and Social Psychology, 83,* 817–827.

Bazerman, M., & Banaji, M. (2004). The social psychology of ordinary ethical failures. *Social Justice Research, 17,* 111–115.

Beal, D. J., O'Neal, E. C., Ong, J., & Ruscher, J. B. (2000). The ways and means of interracial aggression: Modern racists' use of covert retaliation. *Personality & Social Psychology Bulletin, 26,* 1225–1238.

Blascovich, J., Mendes, W. B., Hunter, S. B., Lickel, B., & Kowai-Bell, N. (2001). Perceiver threat in social interactions with stigmatized others. *Journal of Personality and Social Psychology, 80,* 253–267.

Bodenhausen, G. V., & Macrae, C. N. (1996). The self-regulation of intergroup perception: Mechanisms and consequences of stereotype suppression. In C. N. Macrae, C. Stangor, & M. Hewstone (Eds.), *Stereotypes and stereotyping* (pp. 227–253). New York: Guilford.

Brewer, M. B., & Brown, R. (1998). Intergroup relations. In D. T. Gilbert, S. T. Fiske, & G. Lindzey (Eds.), *The handbook of social psychology* (4th ed., pp. 554–594). Boston: McGraw-Hill.

Brown, S. L., & Brown, R. M. (2006). Selective investment theory: Recasting the functional significance of close relationships. *Psychological Inquiry, 17,* 1–29.

Carver, C. S., & Scheier, M. F. (1998). *On the self-regulation of behavior.* New York: Cambridge University Press.

Chartrand, T. L., van Baaren, R. B., & Bargh, J. A. (2006). Linking automatic evaluation to mood and infor-mation processing style: Consequences for experienced affect, impression formation, and stereotyping. *Journal of Experimental Psychology: General, 135,* 70–77.

Cooper, J., & Fazio, R. H. (1984). A new look at dissonance theory. *Advances in Experimental Social Psychology, 17,* 229–266.

Crandall, C. S., Eshleman, A., & O'Brien, L. (2002). Social norms and the expression and suppression of preju-dice: The struggle for internalization. *Journal of Personality & Social Psychology, 82,* 359–378.

Crocker, J. (2008). From egosystem to ecosystem: Implications for learning, relationships, and well-being. In H. Wayment & J. Brauer (Eds.), *Transcending self-interest: Psychological explorations of the quiet ego.* Washington, DC: APA. (63–72).

Crocker, J., & Canevello, A. (in press). Creating and undermining social support in communal relationships: The role of compassionate and self-image goals. *Journal of Personality and Social Psychology.*

Crocker, J., Cornwell, B., & Major, B. M. (1993). The stigma of overweight: Affective consequences of attri-butional ambiguity. *Journal of Personality and Social Psychology, 64,* 60–70.

Crocker, J., & Garcia, J. A. (2006). Stigma and the social basis of the self: A synthesis. In S. Levin & C. Van Laar (Eds.), *Stigma and group inequality: Social psychological perspectives* (pp. 287–308). Mahwah, NJ: Erlbaum.

Crocker, J., & Garcia, J. A. (in press). Social stigma and self-esteem: From internalized devaluation to situ-ational threat. In J. F. Dovidio, M. Hewstone, P. Glick, & V. Esses (Eds.), *Handbook of prejudice and discrimination.* Thousand Oaks, CA: Sage.

Crocker, J., Garcia, J. A., & Nuer, N. (2008). From egosystem to ecosystem in intergroup interactions: Implications for intergroup reconciliation. In A. Nadler, T. Molloy, & J. D. Fisher (Eds.), *The Social psychology of intergroup reconciliation* (pp. 171–194). Oxford, UK: Oxford University Press.

Crocker, J., & Major, B. M. (1989). Social stigma and self-esteem: The self-protective properties of stigma. *Psychological Review, 96,* 608–630.

Crocker, J., & Major, B. (1994). Reactions to stigma: The moderating role of justifications. In M. P. Zanna & J. M. Olson (Eds.), *The psychology of prejudice: The Ontario symposium* (Vol. 7, pp. 289–314). Hillsdale, NJ: Erlbaum.

Crocker, J., Major, B., & Steele, C. M. (1998). Social stigma. In D. Gilbert, S. T. Fiske, & G. Lindzey (Eds.), *The handbook of social psychology* (4th ed., Vol. 2, pp. 504–553). New York: McGraw-Hill.

Crocker, J., Nuer, N., Olivier, M.-A., & Cohen, S. (2006). Egosystem and ecosystem: Two motivational orienta-tions for the self.

Czopp, A. M., & Monteith, M. J. (2003). Confronting prejudice (literally): Reactions to confrontations of racial and gender bias. *Personality and Social Psychology Bulletin, 29,* 532–544.

Darley, J. M., & Batson, C. D. (1973). "From Jerusalem to Jericho": A study of situational and dispositional variables in helping behavior. *Journal of Personality and Social Psychology, 27,* 100–108.

DeCoster, J., & Claypool, H. M. (2004). A meta-analysis of priming effects on impression formation supporting a general model of informational biases. *Personality and Social Psychology Review, 8,* 2–27.

Derlega, V. J., Winstead, B. A., & Folk-Barron, L. (2000). Reasons for and against disclosing HIV-seropositive test results to an intimate partner: A functional perspective. In S. Petronio (Ed.), *Balancing the secrets of private disclosures* (pp. 53–69). Mahwah, NJ: Erlbaum.

Devine, P. G. (1989). Stereotypes and prejudice: Their automatic and controlled components. *Journal of Personality and Social Psychology, 56,* 5–18.

Devine, P. G., Monteith, M. J., Zuwerink, J. R., & Elliot, A. J. (1991). Prejudice with and without compunction. *Journal of Personality and Social Psychology, 60,* 817–830.

Devine, P. G., Plant, E. A., Amodio, D. M., Harmon-Jones, E., & Vance, S. L. (2002). The regulation of explicit and implicit race bias: The role of motivations to respond without prejudice. *Journal of Personality and Social Psychology, 82,* 835–848.

DeWall, C. N., & Baumeister, R. F. (2006). Alone but feeling no pain: Effects of social exclusion on physical pain tolerance and pain threshold, affective forecasting, and interpersonal empathy. *Journal of Personality and Social Psychology, 91,* 1–15.

Dickerson, S. S., & Kemeny, M. E. (2004). Acute stressors and cortisol responses: A theoretical integration and synthesis of laboratory research. *Psychological Bulletin, 130,* 355–391.

Ditzen, B., Bodenmann, J. G., Ehlert, U., & Heinrichs, M. (2006, June). *The effects of social support and oxytocin on psychological and physiological stress responses during martial conflict.* Paper presented at the International Conference of Neuroendoricrinology, Pittsburgh, PA.

Downey, G., Freitas, A. L., Michaelis, B., & Khouri, H. (1998). The self-fulfilling prophecy in close relationships: Rejection sensitivity and rejection by romantic partners. *Journal of Personality and Social Psychology, 75,* 545–560.

Dykman, B. M. (1998). Integrating cognitive and motivational factors in depression: Initial tests of a goal orientation approach. *Journal of Personality and Social Psychology, 74,* 139–158.

Eberhardt, J. L., Goff, P. A., Purdie, V. J., & Davies, P. G. (2004). Seeing black: Race, crime, and visual processing. *Journal of Personality and Social Psychology, 87,* 876–893.

Frijda, N. H. (1988). The laws of emotion. *American Psychologist, 43,* 349–358.

Garcia, J. A. (2005). *Motivations to disclose a concealable stigma: Exploring the antecedents and consequences of ego based and non-ego based goals.* Unpublished doctoral dissertation, University of Michigan, Ann Arbor.

Garcia, J. A., & Crocker, J. (2008). Coping with the stigma of depression: Egosystem and ecosystem goals. *Social Science and Medicine*, 67, 453-462.

Goff, P. A., Steele, C. M., & Davies, P. G. (2008). The space between us: Stereotype threat and distance in interracial contexts. *Journal of Personality and Social Psychology, 94,* 91-107.

Goffman, E. (1963). *Stigma: Notes on the management of spoiled identity.* Englewood Cliffs, NJ: Prentice-Hall.

Gray-Little, B., & Hafdahl, A. R. (2000). Factors influencing racial comparisons of self-esteem: A quantitative review. *Psychological Bulletin, 126,* 26–54.

Henry, J. P., & Wang, S. (1998). Effects of early stress on adult affiliative behavior. *Psychoneuroendocrinology, 23,* 863–875.

Inzlicht, M., McKay, L., & Aronson, J. (2006). Stigma as ego depletion: How being the target of prejudice affects self-control. *Psychological Science, 17,* 262–269.

Jones, E. E., Farina, A., Hastorf, A. H., Markus, H., Miller, D. T., & Scott, R. A. (1984). *Social stigma: The psychology of marked relationships.* New York: Freeman.

Kaiser, C. R., Vick, S. B., & Major, B. (2006). Prejudice expectations moderate preconscious attention to cues that are threatening to social identity. *Psychological Science, 17,* 332–338.

Katz, I., & Hass, R. G. (1988). Racial ambivalence and American value conflict: Correlational and priming studies of dual cognitive structures. *Journal of Personality and Social Psychology, 55,* 893–905.

Katz, I., Wackenhut, J., & Hass, R. G. (1986). Racial ambivalence, value duality, and behavior. In J. F. Dovidio & S. L. Gaertner (Eds.), *Prejudice, discrimination, and racism* (pp. 61–90). San Diego, CA: Academic.

Kernis, M. H., Grannemann, B. D., & Barclay, L. C. (1989). Stability and level of self-esteem as predictors of anger arousal and hostility. *Journal of Personality and Social Psychology, 56,* 1013–1023.

Kramer, R. M., & Messick, D. M. (1998). Getting by with a little help from our enemies: Collective para-
    noia and its role in intergroup relations. In C. Sedikides, J. Schopler, & C. A. Insko (Eds.), *Intergroup
    Cognition and Intergroup Behavior* (pp. 233-255). Mahwah, NJ: Lawrence Erlbaum.
Kross, E., Ayduk, O., & Mischel, W. (2005). When asking "why" does not hurt: Distinguishing rumination from
    reflective processing of negative emotions. *Psychological Science, 16,* 709–715.
Macrae, C. N., Bodenhausen, G. V., Milne, A. B., & Jetten, J. (1994). Out of mind but back in sight: Stereotypes
    on the rebound. *Journal of Personality and Social Psychology, 67,* 808–817.
Major, B., & Crocker, J. (1993). Social stigma: The consequences of attributional ambiguity. In D. M. Mackie
    & D. L. Hamilton (Eds.), *Affect, cognition, and stereotyping: Interactive processes in group perception*
    (pp. 345–370). New York: Academic.
Major, B., Gramzow, R., McCoy, S., Levin, S., Schmader, T., & Sidanius, J. (2002). Attributions to discrimina-
    tion: The role of group status and legitimizing ideology. *Journal of Personality and Social Psychology,
    82,* 269–282.
Major, B., McCoy, S. K., & Quinton, W. (2002). Antecedents and consequences of attributions to discrimina-
    tion: Theoretical and empirical advances. In M. P. Zanna (Ed.), *Advances in experimental social psychol-
    ogy* (Vol. 34, pp. 251–349). San Diego, CA: Academic.
Major, B., & O'Brien, L. T. (2005). The social psychology of stigma. *Annual Review of Psychology, 56,*
    393–421.
Major, B., Quinton, W. J., & McCoy, S. K. (2002). Antecedents and consequences of attributions to discrimina-
    tion: Theoretical and empirical advances. In M. P. Zanna (Ed.), *Advances in experimental social psychol-
    ogy* (Vol. 34, pp. 251–330). San Diego, CA: Academic.
Mendoza-Denton, R., Downey, G., Purdie, V. J., Davis, A., & Pietrzak, J. (2002). Sensitivity to race-based
    rejection: Implications for African-American students' college experience. *Journal of Personality and
    Social Psychology, 83,* 896–918.
Moeller, S., Crocker, J., & Canevello, A. (2008). Feeling clear and connected: Self-regulation in the warm
    system. Unpublished manuscript, Ann Arbor.
Moeller, S., Crocker, J., & Canevello, A. (2008). Perseverance in the face of failure: Feelings about goal set-
    backs shape guture goal progress. Unpublished manuscript.
Monteith, M. J. (1993). Self-regulation of prejudiced responses: Implications for progress in prejudice reduc-
    tion efforts. *Journal of Personality and Social Psychology, 65,* 469–485.
Monteith, M. J., Deneen, N. E., & Tooman, G. D. (1996). The effect of social norm activation on the expression
    of opinions concerning gay men and Blacks. *Basic & Applied Social Psychology, 18,* 267–288.
Monteith, M. J., Devine, P. G., & Zuwerink, J. R. (1993). Self-directed vs. other-directed affect as a conse-
    quence of prejudice-related discrepancies. *Journal of Personality and Social Psychology, 64,* 198–210.
Pinel, E. C. (1999). Stigma consciousness: The psychological legacy of social stereotypes. *Journal of Personality
    and Social Psychology, 76,* 114–128.
Pratto, F., & John, O. P. (1991). Automatic vigilance: The attention-grabbing power of negative social informa-
    tion. *Journal of Personality and Social Psychology, 61,* 380–391.
Prentice, D. A., & Miller, D. T. (Eds.). (1999). *Cultural divides: Understanding and overcoming group conflict.*
    New York: Russell Sage Foundation.
Richeson, J. A., & Shelton, J. N. (2003). When prejudice does not pay: Effects of interracial contact on execu-
    tive function. *Psychological Science, 14,* 287–290.
Richeson, J. A., Trawalter, S., & Shelton, J. N. (2005). African Americans' implicit racial attitudes and the
    depletion of executive function after interracial interactions. *Social Cognition, 23,* 336–352.
Rosenberg, M. (2003). *Nonviolent communication.* Encinitas, CA: Puddledancer Press.
Scheier, M. F., & Carver, C. S. (1988). A model of behavioral self-regulation: Translating intention into action.
    Advances in Experimental Social Psychology, 21, 303–346.
Schlenker, B. R. (2003). Self-presentation. In M. R. Leary & J. P. Tangney (Eds.), *Handbook of self and identity*
    (pp. 492–518). New York: Guilford.
Schmader, T., & Johns, M. (2003). Converging evidence that stereotype threat reduces working memory capac-
    ity. *Journal of Personality and Social Psychology, 85,* 440–452.
Shaver, P. R., Schwarz, J., Kirson, D., & O'Connor, C. (1987). Emotion knowledge: Further exploration of a
    prototype approach. *Journal of Personality and Social Psychology, 52,* 1061–1086.
Shelton, J. N., Richeson, J. A., & Salvatore, J. (2005). Expecting to be the target of prejudice: Implications for
    interethnic interactions. *Personality and Social Psychology Bulletin, 31,* 1189–1202.
Siegel, D. J. (1999). *The developing mind: Toward a neurobiology of interpersonal experience.* New York:
    Guilford.

Sigelman, L., & Tuch, S. A. (1997). Metastereotypes: Blacks' perceptions of Whites' stereotypes of Blacks. *Public Opinion Quarterly, 61,* 87–101.

Sinclair, S., Hardin, C. D., & Lowery, B. S. (2006). Self-stereotyping in the context of multiple social identities. *Journal of Personality and Social Psychology, 90,* 529–542.

Smith, C. A., & Ellsworth, P. C. (1985). Patterns of cognitive appraisal in emotion. *Journal of Personality and Social Psychology, 48,* 813–838.

Snyder, M., & Swann, W. B. (1978). Behavioral confirmation in social interaction: From social perception to social reality. *Journal of Experimental Social Psychology, 14,* 148–162.

Steele, C. M. (1997). A threat in the air: How stereotypes shape intellectual identity and performance. *American Psychologist, 52,* 613–629.

Steele, C. M., Spencer, S. J., & Aronson, J. (2002). Contending with group image: The psychology of stereotype and social identity threat. In M. P. Zanna (Ed.), *Advances in experimental social psychology* (Vol. 34, pp. 379–440). San Diego, CA: Academic.

Stephan, W. G., & Stephan, C. W. (1985). Intergroup anxiety. *Journal of Social Issues, 41,* 157–175.

Stone, J., Lynch, C. I., Sjomeling, M., & Darley, J. M. (1999). Stereotype threat effects on Black and White athletic performance. *Journal of Personality and Social Psychology, 77,* 1213–1227.

Tangney, J. P. (1999). The self-conscious emotions: Shame, guilt, embarrassment and pride. In T. Dalgleish & M. J. Power (Eds.), *Handbook of cognition and emotion* (pp. 541–568). Chichester, UK: Wiley.

Tatum, B. D. (1997). *Why are all the black kids sitting together in the cafeteria?* New York: Basic.

Taylor, S. E., Klein, L. C., Lewis, B. P., Gruenewald, T. L., Gurung, R. A. R., & Updegraff, J. A. (2000). Biobehavioral responses to stress in females: Tend-and-befriend, not fight-or-flight. *Psychological Review, 197,* 411–429.

Twenge, J. M., Catanese, K. R., & Baumeister, R. F. (2002). Social exclusion causes self-defeating behavior. *Journal of Personality and Social Psychology, 83,* 606–615.

Twenge, J. M., Catanese, K. R., & Baumeister, R. F. (2003). Social exclusion and the deconstructed state: Time perception, meaninglessness, lethargy, lack of emotion, and self-awareness. *Journal of Personality and Social Psychology, 85,* 409–423.

Twenge, J. M., & Crocker, J. (2002). Race, ethnicity, and self-esteem: Meta-analyses comparing Whites, Blacks, Hispanics, Asians, and Native Americans, including a commentary on Gray-Little and Hafdahl (2000). *Psychological Bulletin, 128,* 371–408.

Vorauer, J. D. (2006). An information search model of evaluative concerns in intergroup interaction. *Psychological Review, 113,* 862–886.

Vorauer, J. D., Main, K. J., & O'Connell, G. B. (1998). How do individuals expect to be viewed by members of lower status groups? Content and implications of meta-stereotypes. *Journal of Personality and Social Psychology, 75,* 917–937.

Vorauer, J. D., & Turpie, C. A. (2004). Disruptive effects of vigilance on dominant group members' treatment of outgroup members: Choking versus shining under pressure. *Journal of Personality and Social Psychology, 87,* 384–399.

Wittenbrink, B., Gist, P. L., & Hilton, J. L. (1997). Structural properties of stereotype knowledge and their influences on the construal of social situation. *Journal of Personality and Social Psychology, 72,* 526–543.

Word, C. D., Zanna, M. P., & Cooper, J. (1974). The nonverbal mediation of self-fulfilling prophesies in interracial interaction. *Journal of Experimental Social Psychology, 10,* 109–120.

Wright, E. R., Gronfien, W. P., & Owens, T. J. (2000). Deinstitutionalization, social rejection, and the self-esteem of former mental patients. *Journal of Health and Social Behavior, 41,* 68–90.

Zak, P. J., Kurzban, R., & Matzner, W. T. (2005). Oxytocin is associated with human trustworthiness. *Hormones and Behavior, 48,* 522–527

Zhang, L., & Baumeister, R. F. (2006). Your money or your self-esteem: Threatened egotism promotes costly entrapment in losing endeavors. *Personality and Social Psychology Bulletin, 32,* 881–893.

Zuwerink, J. R., Devine, P. G., Monteith, M. J., & Cook, D. A. (1996). Prejudice toward blacks: With and without compunction? *Basic & Applied Social Psychology, 18,* 131–150.

12 The Stereotypic Behaviors of the Powerful and Their Effect on the Relatively Powerless

Theresa K. Vescio, Sarah J. Gervais,
Larisa Heiphetz, and Brittany Bloodhart
The Pennsylvania State University

Power is often coveted, fought over, and fiercely protected. Some have suggested that power corrupts people (e.g., Lord Acton). Others have suggested that foolish people corrupt power (e.g., George Bernard Shaw). Regardless of whether power corrupts people or people corrupt power, inquiries typically have focused on who seeks and secures power over whom and with what adverse consequences.

Because power and social group membership historically have been and continue to be confounded in most societies, social scholars and commentators long have been interested in the potentially corruptive and status quo maintaining relation of power to stereotyping. In the United States, for instance, 36% of employed Whites are in management and professional positions, compared to only 26% of employed African Americans and 17% of Latinos. In addition, although women made up 46% of the U.S. labor force in 2004 and have higher salaries than in the past (e.g., women's median weekly earnings were a full 80% of men's; U.S. Department of Labor & Bureau of Labor Statistics, 2005), gender equity is confined to middle management positions in feminized or gender-neutral domains. Striking gender disparities remain among the ranks of the powerful in traditionally masculine domains, where the attributes predictive of success are stereotypically associated with men but not women. For example, only 23% of the chief executives, 6% of construction managers, and 6% of engineering managers are women (U.S. Department of Labor & Bureau of Labor Statistics, 2005). Thus, White men are more likely to hold positions of power than are women and minorities. In addition, if power corrupts people or foolish people corrupt power, stereotypes may influence the judgments and behaviors of the powerful in ways that effectively reinforce and maintain the status quo (e.g., Fiske, 1993; Jost & Banaji, 1994; Pratto, Sidanius, Stallworth, & Malle, 1994).

The goals of this chapter are twofold. First, we review prior theory and research on power and stereotyping to highlight core conceptualizations, foundational assumptions, classic findings, and the social contexts of interest. Our review and critique of prior theory and research, in the first half of this chapter, allows us to address a series of background questions. These include: What is power? Who traditionally has power? How does power shape thoughts and behaviors? How does power generally influence stereotyping and discrimination? Second, we present a broader theoretical perspective to elucidate both the causes and consequences of the stereotypic actions of powerful people. In the second half of the chapter, we link the basic human motives to belong and be legitimate to situations involving power differentials and note how this may shape the goals of high- and low-power people. After integrating considerations of basic human motives and situations with power differentials, we present theoretical propositions that provide the foundation for what we refer to as a goal-situated model of power and stereotyping.

POWER

Power has traditionally, and most frequently, been defined in social influence terms. Like others, we define power as the ability to influence other people in psychologically meaningful ways (Copeland, 1994; French & Raven, 1959) through the giving or withholding of rewards and punishments (Keltner, Gruenfeld, & Anderson, 2003). In this definition, psychologically meaningful influences include, but are not limited to, actions that affect the cognition, emotion, and behaviors of another. Importantly, dependence and power are inversely related (Emerson, 1964); those who depend on others for rewards and punishments are less powerful than those who do not. Of course, what constitutes a reward or punishment may vary across people in a given context or across contexts for a given person. Interpersonal pleasantries and incivilities, like praise or criticism, are sometimes meaningful rewards and punishments, as are the giving and withholding of limited resources like raises and demotions.

The social influence definition of power encompasses several kinds of power differentials. In fact, the definition includes four of the five types of power that French and Raven (1959) specified in their classic typology of power relations. We first define each of the four forms of power and then note their interrelations. First, *legitimate power* refers to influence associated with holding a position or role that confers authority and legitimates one's influence over another (e.g., the power bosses have over employees). Second, *reward power* refers to influence associated with distributing and withholding rewards (e.g., raises and promotions). Third, *punishment (or coercive) power* refers to influence associated with withholding or administering punishments (e.g., demotions or suspensions). Fourth, *informational power* refers to the influence associated with holding information needed or desired by another (e.g., the power of a car mechanic over a stranded driver). Interestingly, these four forms of power often co-occur. Professors, for instance, hold a role that legitimates and gives authority to their influence over students. They have achieved their role by obtaining information that students need to succeed (e.g., earning an advanced degree in a field of study) and they are expected to use their role to reward or punish students (e.g., with grades or assignments).

We refer to *role power* as the kind of power that combines legitimate power, reward power, punishment power, and informational power to create high power roles. High power roles, which are more likely to be held by White men than men who belong to ethnic minority groups or women of any ethnicity, legitimate one's influence over others by conferring on a person the right to give or withhold rewards and punishments and by formalizing his or her ability to convey important information.

Role power may be further exacerbated or attenuated by what French and Raven (1959) referred to as referent power. *Referent power* is the influence one has over others because of feelings of identification. Referent power is, for instance, the kind of influence that a cherished mentor has over the students, apprentices, or protégés who identify with and feel a sense of oneness with their teacher. Importantly, referent power is the only kind of power given up the hierarchy. Receiving referent power from a low-status person bestows one with an additional form of influence over and above the influence conferred by legitimate, reward, punishment, and informational power. Inversely, the impact that the behaviors of high-power people have on the self-concept of low-status people is minimized when low-power people withhold referent power by disidentifying with or devaluing a particular domain or a person of power (e.g., Steele & Aronson, 1995).

STEREOTYPING, POWER, AND THE MAINTENANCE OF THE STATUS QUO: PRIOR WORK

In this chapter, like others, we focus attention on situations where women and men of ethnic minority groups identify with stereotype-relevant domains, or domains where the attributes predictive of success are stereotypically associated with White men but not women or racial minorities (see also Steele & Aronson, 1995; Walton & Cohen, 2003, 2007). Traditionally valued achievement domains (e.g., science, technology, engineering, and mathematics, collectively referred to as STEM domains) have been of interest to researchers because gender and racial disparities in representation, status, and performance are particularly pronounced in these domains. As a result, White men often hold positions that confer power and legitimate their influence over others, including women and ethnic minorities. To the degree that high-power people initiate interactions with low-power people on the basis of stereotypes, they may behave in ways that elicit stereotypic behaviors from others (e.g., Snyder, Tanke, & Berscheid, 1977; Word, Zanna, & Cooper, 1974) and that reinforce existing power differentials (see, e.g., Fiske, 1993; Jost & Banaji, 1994; Pratto et al., 1994; Snyder & Miene, 1994).

Implicitly, power and stereotyping long have been assumed to be linked in status quo maintaining ways (e.g., Allport, 1954; Darley & Gross, 1983; Snyder et al., 1977; Tajfel, 1982; Word et al., 1974). The amassing body of contemporary literature on power and stereotyping, however, was inspired by Fiske's (1993) model of power as control. As a precursor to consideration of Fiske's theory and the research inspired by her work, we first note the commonalities across 1980s theories of stereotyping and contemporary prejudice. We then briefly review findings documenting the corruptive influences of power. Finally, we note how Fiske integrated those ideas and briefly review the body of literature inspired by her work. Findings in this literature suggest that powerful people often stereotype low-power people more strongly than the reverse. Importantly, however, powerful people do not stereotype uniformly. Stereotyping effects vary across situations and people. Thus, we conclude with a consideration of the situational factors and individual differences that influence stereotyping.

FOUNDATIONAL IDEAS OF RELEVANCE IN THE STEREOTYPING AND PREJUDICE LITERATURE

Often perceivers immediately and effortlessly categorize people, like objects, into groups (see Brewer, 1988; Fiske & Neuberg, 1990). The categorization of others into meaningful social groups (e.g., on the basis of gender, race, or age) allows people to both simplify complex social stimuli (Allport, 1954; Tajfel, 1978) and apply stereotypic knowledge to make inferences that go beyond what could be known solely on the basis of the information available (Bruner, 1973).

In the 1980s, several theories of racial prejudice were introduced to explain the more subtle (post-civil rights movement) face of American prejudice (e.g., aversive racism, Gaertner & Dovidio, 1986; ambivalent racism, Katz & Hass, 1988; modern or symbolic racism, Kinder & Sears, 1981; McConahay, 1982; McConahay, Hardee, & Batts, 1981). Toward that end, each theory integrated the notion that people process social information in the least effortful manner possible (e.g., category-based) unless sufficiently motivated to do otherwise (e.g., Brewer, 1988; Fiske & Neuberg, 1990) with findings that White Americans' endorsement of blatant racist statements had sharply declined.

Although theories of contemporary racism differ in several important ways, the commonalities across theories are relevant to this chapter. First, each theory considers White–Black relations in America and suggests that, as a result of shared socialization experiences, most White Americans are aware of the historic and ongoing antipathy toward, discrimination against, and stereotypes of Black Americans. Second, the theories share an assumption that White Americans have unwittingly internalized the pervasive cultural stereotypes and feelings of antipathy toward Black Americans and that Whites' unacknowledged negativity can influence perceptions, judgment, and behavior. Third, although both high- and low-prejudice Whites have internalized negative cognitions and feelings about Blacks, high- and low-prejudice Whites were suggested to critically differ in their blatant attitudes and controlled responses toward Black Americans. Unlike high-prejudice people, low-prejudice people (aversive, ambivalent, or modern and symbolic racists) presumably endorse personal beliefs (e.g., Devine, 1989), have self-concepts (e.g., Gaertner & Dovido, 1986), or cherish values (like egalitarianism; e.g., Katz & Hass, 1988) that explicitly *reject* the negative cultural stereotypes of Black Americans. As a result, unlike high-prejudice people, low-prejudice people tend to monitor, control, and squelch their conscious expressions of prejudice when they become aware that stereotypes are affecting judgment (e.g., when there are strong cues about appropriate interracial behavior in the environment: see Gaertner & Dovidio, 1986). However, both high-prejudice and low-prejudice Americans were still thought to unwittingly stereotype and discriminate against Black Americans as a result of automatic and nonconscious processes.

FOUNDATIONAL IDEAS OF RELEVANCE IN THE POWER LITERATURE

As noted at the outset, the assumption central to theorizing and research on power is the notion that power corrupts (Kipnis, 1972). Powerful people may not intend to abuse power or be aware of the fact that they have been corrupted by power, but power has been assumed to exert a primarily corruptive influence. Consistent with this notion, findings show that elevations in power are related to increases in the frequency of aggressive behavior (e.g., Haney, Banks, & Zimbardo, 1973), the tendency to take credit for the contributions of subordinates (Kipnis, 1972), and the likelihood that low-power women will be sexualized (Bargh, Raymond, Pryor, & Strack, 1995).

The corruptive influences of power may stem from a more general tendency for power to disinhibit behavior (Keltner et al., 2003). Compared to low-power people, for instance, high-power people talk more, interrupt more, and speak out of turn more often (DePaulo & Friedman, 1998). High-power people are also more likely than are low-power people to tease others in aggressive ways (Keltner, Capps, Kring, Young, & Heerey, 2001), bully their romantic partners (Howard, Blumstein, & Schwartz, 1986), and construe others in ways that increase the likelihood of sexual harassment (Studd, 1996; see also Bargh et al., 1995). Power does not, however, simply lead to negative and socially inappropriate behavior. Instead, high-power people, compared to low-power people, may sometimes engage in more nonconventional *prosocial* behaviors (e.g., offering unsolicited help, expressing affection; Chen, Lee-Chai, & Bargh, 2001; see also Keltner et al., 2001).

In other words, elevated power increases action, regardless of the particular actions available in a situation. Consistent with this idea, Galinsky, Gruenfeld, and Magee (2003) found that high-power people were more likely than low-power people to remove an annoying stimulus from an environment and to act in risky manners (e.g., take a hit on 16 when playing Blackjack). Galinsky et al. also found that powerful people were more likely to take from a common pool of resources when that was the action permitted in a situation. However, when the situation was altered such that the taking action involved donating to a common pool of resources, powerful people also contributed more to the common pool than did low-power people. Power, it seems, frees one from situational constraints (Overbeck, Tiedens, & Brion, 2006), such that high-power people act more (Galinsky et al., 2003) and behave more variably than do low-power people across situations as well as within situations (Guinote, 2001; Guinote, Judd, & Brauer, 2002).

CLASSIC THEORY AND RESEARCH ON POWER AND STEREOTYPING:
THE CONTEMPORARY STARTING POINT

The foregoing considerations point to core themes in the stereotyping and prejudice literature and the power literature. Theories of racial prejudice suggest that, unlike high-prejudice people, low-prejudice people inhibit discriminatory responding. Power is, however, inversely related to social inhibition; high-power people inhibit less and act more than do low-power people. Together, these ideas hint at the potentially problematic nature of the linkages between power and stereotyping.

First seeing the potentially problematic linkages between power and stereotyping, Fiske (1993) proposed that stereotyping should be stronger down than up the hierarchy. Consistent with the tenets of the broader models of impression formation (e.g., Brewer, 1988; Fiske & Neuberg, 1990) and dominant theories of prejudice (e.g., Devine, 1989; Gaertner & Dovidio, 1986; Katz & Hass, 1988), Fiske assumed that people process information about others in the least effortful manner (e.g., category-based perception). Extending this logic to consider the strength of stereotyping effects in situations involving power differentials, Fiske reasoned that low-power people should be relatively motivated to go beyond categorical knowledge and individuate those who have control over them; by individuating powerful people, low-power people may increase perceptions of the degree that high-power people are predictable, thereby enhancing feelings of personal control. By contrast, high-power people should stereotype low-power people either because they lack the motivation or cognitive resources to individuate those over whom they have power (e.g., stereotyping by default) or because they are motivated to maintain power differentials (e.g., stereotyping by design; Goodwin, Gubin, Fiske, & Yzerbyt, 2000).

Findings from several studies support the notion that stereotyping is often stronger down, rather than up, the hierarchy (Fiske, 1993). High- compared to low-power people pay more attention to and better remember stereotype-consistent information than stereotype-inconsistent information (Depret & Fiske, 1999; Goodwin et al., 2000; Rodríguez-Bailón, Moya, & Yzerbyt, 2000). In some situations, high-power people stereotype both high- and low-power others more than do low-power people, such that small, actual preexisting differences between high- and low-power people are exaggerated (Ebenbach & Keltner, 1998).

Automatic categorization and stereotyping processes are not, however, ubiquitous among people in general or high-power people in particular. Although several studies examined the core prediction forwarded by Fiske (1993)—that stereotyping was stronger down than up the hierarchy—Fiske also pointed to factors that should increase and decrease powerful people's tendency to stereotype. For instance, Fiske noted that stereotyping among the powerful should be stronger in some situations than others (e.g., when environments are cognitively taxing or when high-power people are less dependent on others). Fiske also posited that stereotyping among the powerful might be particularly strong among people motivated to maintain power differentials, such as those high in dominance.

Variability in Stereotyping as a Function of Situations

The socially meaningful groups to which people belong (e.g., gender of women and race of Blacks) may grab attention (Stroessner, 1996; Zárate & Smith, 1990) and set the stage for category-based perception (Brewer, 1988; Fiske & Neuberg, 1990). In addition, because stereotypes contain information about a group's relative social status and explanations for that status (Eagly & Karau, 2002; Vescio & Biernat, 1999; Wittenbrink, Gist, & Hilton, 1997), stereotypes are relevant to a wide array of achievement domains.

Importantly, however, stereotypic knowledge influences perceptions of others only when that knowledge is relevant to both the interpretation of a particular behavior and a component of the cultural stereotypes of the group to which a person belongs (Banaji, Hardin, & Rothman, 1993). For instance, the construct "dependence" might be activated in a situation and lead an observer to conclude that a woman behaving in an ambiguously dependent way is extremely dependent. However, the same observer would not necessarily rate a similarly behaving man as dependent, nor would primed dependence influence the interpretation of a woman's athletic behavior. Consistent with this notion, findings show that primed dependence influenced impressions of ambiguously dependent female (but not male) targets, whereas primed aggression affected appraisals of ambiguously aggressive male (but not female) targets (Banaji et al., 1993; see also Corneille, Vescio, & Judd, 2000). Recent findings have demonstrated that social applicability, or stereotype match, also determines whether people in high-power roles stereotype those in low-power roles (Vescio, Gervais, Heidenreich, & Snyder, 2006; Vescio, Gervais, Snyder, & Hoover, 2005; Vescio, Snyder, & Butz, 2003).

The responsibilities associated with high-power roles in a given situation can also affect stereotyping tendencies. For instance, Overbeck and Park (2001) assigned people to positions that gave authority to and legitimated the influence they had over others (e.g., the power a professor has over a student, or legitimate power; French & Raven, 1959). After creating legitimate power differentials, high- and low-power participants engaged in apparent interactions with one another. In this context, Overbeck and Park found that powerful people more strongly individuated (rather than stereotyped) low-power others than low-power people individuated high-power others. These findings were consistent with the suggestion that high-power roles confer both authority and responsibility, and to take responsibility and to do what is best for another one must attend to and be familiar with rather than stereotype the other.

VARIABILITY IN STEREOTYPING AS A FUNCTION OF INDIVIDUAL DIFFERENCES

A host of individual differences have been shown to be associated with increases in stereotyping and prejudice. Consistent with the suggestion that dominance may be a predictor of both who secures power and how much one endorses stereotypic beliefs (e.g., Fiske, 1993), findings show that members of high-power, high-social-status groups (e.g., men and White Americans) are more in-group favoring (e.g., Jost, 2001) and more social dominance oriented (i.e., prefer inequality among social groups) than are members of low-power, low-social-status groups (e.g., women and African Americans; e.g., Pratto et al., 1994). Social dominance orientation is also positively associated with employment in occupations that enhance group-based inequality (e.g., Pratto, Stallworth, Sidanius, & Siers, 1997), endorsement of reproductive behaviors that maintain gender inequality (e.g., multiple partners, avoidance of child care; Pratto & Hegarty, 2000), and belief in social and political ideology that supports the group-based hierarchy (e.g., meritocracy; Pratto et al., 1994), as well as implicit and explicit indicators of racism (e.g., Pratto & Shih, 2000; Sidanius, Pratto & Bobo, 1996).

As noted earlier, power has been suggested to free people from constraints, such that high-power people may be more likely than low-power people to act in line with their internal dispositions (Keltner et al., 2003; Overbeck et al., 2006). Consistent with this notion, Chen et al. (2001) found that individual differences in relationship orientation moderated stereotyping tendencies among people primed to think of power. In other words, communally oriented people were more equitable in their division of labor (or assignment of tasks to self vs. another) than were people who were exchange oriented. In addition, high-power people who were communally oriented endorsed more socially appropriate (i.e., less racist) beliefs than high-power people who were exchange oriented (Chen et al., 2001).

Importantly, the tendency for stereotypes to affect perceptions of and behavior toward others also varies as a function of differences in prejudice level. Findings point to meaningful differences in the content of high- and low-prejudice Whites' stereotypes of Blacks. The stereotypes held by both high- and low-prejudice Whites contain information about the relatively low social status of Black Americans (e.g., poor), but only the stereotypes held by high-prejudice Whites contain dispositional trait information (e.g., lazy; Vescio & Biernat, 1999; Wittenbrink & Henly, 1996). In addition, dispositional traits associated with the negative cultural stereotype of Blacks influence the judgments of high-prejudice (but not low-prejudice) Whites when racial category membership (e.g., "Black") is primed (Lepore & Brown, 1997). Thus, unlike high-prejudice Whites, low-prejudice Whites have not internalized the negative traits associated with Black Americans and the stereotypic traits of Black Americans are neither automatically activated nor influence judgments among low-prejudice Whites. Importantly, power seems to enhance these differences; for instance, findings show that racial biases in powerful people's evaluations and allocation of rewards to low-power Blacks are evident among Whites who are high in prejudice, but not low in prejudice (Vescio et al., 2006).

SUMMARY

The foregoing considerations highlight two important points. First, in many situations, stereotyping is stronger down than up the hierarchy (Fiske, 1993). Second, although high-power people often stereotype low-power people more than the reverse, stereotyping among the powerful is not ubiquitous. Various situational factors and individual differences moderate the relation between power and stereotyping (e.g., relationship orientation, Chen et al., 2001; focus on tasks vs. social responsibility, Overbeck & Park, 2001; prejudice level, Vescio et al., 2006).

A GOAL-SITUATED PERSPECTIVE ON POWER AND STEREOTYPING

In the remainder of this chapter we present theoretical propositions that integrate prior research and provide the basis for understanding both the causes and status quo maintaining consequences of the stereotypic actions of powerful people. Toward that end, we reiterate the situations of interest to our theorizing. We then note the characteristics of situations involving power differentials and consider the goals of high- and low-power people. Next, to refine and hone our consideration of the causes and consequences of the stereotypic acts of powerful people, we articulate three specific questions: (a) When do high-power people stereotype low-power people? (b) How do high-power people behave toward the low-power people they stereotype? and (c) What effects do the behaviors of high-power people have on the emotion, cognition, and performance of the low-power women and racial minorities who are stereotyped? Our answers to these questions provide the basis for several theoretical propositions. The core hypotheses and research relevant to these propositions are presented in the final portions of this section. These propositions provide a foundation for a goal-situated perspective on the relation between power and stereotyping.

DOMAINS OF INTEREST

We focus on traditionally valued achievement domains (STEM domains) because they are stereotype relevant. Women and ethnic minorities are stereotypically perceived as lacking attributes associated with success in STEM domains (e.g., rationality, logic). As a result, stereotypes may present a threat that can arouse anxiety and impede the performance of women and ethnic minorities (see Steele, 1997, 1998), contributing to persistent gender and racial disparities in representation, performance, and status in STEM domains.

We further narrow our focus to situations where low-power women and ethnic minorities are identified with STEM domains. These situations are important to understanding gender and ethnic disparities (Steele, 1997, 1998) but have received little theoretical and empirical attention in prior work on power and stereotyping. As a result, little is known about how powerful people perceive and behave toward low-power women and minority group members and how low-power women and minority group members respond to the behaviors of the powerful in such domains.

THE CORE HUMAN MOTIVES TO BELONG AND BE LEGITIMATE

As a starting point, we note that the need to belong is a core human motive (Baumeister & Leary, 1995). People deeply desire inclusion and want to belong, forming relationships with others quickly and easily (Brewer, 1979; Sherif, White, & Harvey, 1955) and experiencing distress when relationships dissolve (Hazan & Shaver, 1994). Conversely, social exclusion leads to threat and decreased self-esteem, control, and meaning (Williams, Shore, & Grahe, 1998). In fact, much of the meaning of people's lives derives from their relationships with groups, or social identity (Tajfel & Turner, 1986).

People are also motivated to see themselves as fair and principled. Principles of egalitarianism and equity are core to American ideology (e.g., Katz & Hass, 1988) and are endorsed cross-culturally (Bardi & Schwartz, 2003; Schwartz & Bardi, 2001). Findings also show that people genuinely value fairness, integrity, and rationality (e.g., Bierhoff, Cohen, & Greenberg, 1986; Folger, 1984; Greenberg & Cohen, 1982; Jost & Major, 2001; Lerner & Lerner, 1981).

GOAL-SHAPING FEATURES OF SITUATIONS INVOLVING DIFFERENTIALS IN ROLE POWER

The influences of the motives to belong and be legitimate (or fair and principled) in STEM contexts can be understood given a consideration of two important features of situations involving power differentials. First, there are clear objectives associated with these situations. People are awarded high-power roles (e.g., bosses, managers) because they are believed to be able to achieve the objectives associated with positions of power. Second, there are interdependencies among people high and low in role power, such that the efforts and contributions of all people are required to achieve those objectives. Thus, to achieve desired objectives, high-power people must work with and effectively influence low-power people to make efforts and contributions that facilitate rather than impede collective attempts to achieve desired outcomes. Simply stated, if the contributions of low-power people were not needed to secure desired outcomes, there would be no people assigned to those roles in a given context. A coach, for example, is hired to produce a winning season and to do so he or she must inspire winning performances from team members.

The Goals of High-Power People

Together, the foregoing considerations suggest that high-power people internalize the goals of their positions and are motivated to effectively and legitimately work with low-power people. In other words, we assume that people who accept high-power positions internalize the goals associated with those positions because doing so ensures belonging in a given context. In addition, like people in general, high-power people are motivated to effectively pursue their goals and to do so in legitimate, fair, and principled ways. Because the goals of high- and low-power people are interdependent, powerful people's desires to be effective and legitimate should become intertwined. To be effective, high-power people must attend to the goal-relevant skills, attributes, and abilities of the low-power people while ignoring goal-irrelevant characteristics. This suggestion is consistent with findings showing that high- (vs. low-) power people more quickly set and act on goals (Guinote, 2007a), are better able to inhibit goal-irrelevant information (Guinote, 2007b), and are more motivated and better able to process goal-related information about inconsistent others (Chen, Ybarra, & Kiefer, 2004). To be legitimate, high-power people must effectively pursue goals in ways that they perceive to be fair, unbiased, and principled.

The Goals of Low-Power People

Paralleling and complementing the goals of high-power people, low-power people who are domain identified also seek to belong. Desires to belong may, in fact, be higher for those low (compared to high) in power. People differ in the degree that they are prototypic members of in-groups (Tajfel, 1982). Those who embody the characteristics of a valued group or domain tend to be included and have more power, whereas those who less thoroughly embody the valued characteristics tend to be excluded and have less power (Emerson, 1964). As Tajfel (1978) noted, less prototypic, low-power people "constantly face the danger of being unmasked" (p. 15) and rejected by high-power people. In an effort to increase belongingness, low-power people should be motivated to effectively and legitimately perform the tasks that they are assigned by high-power people. Consistent with this notion, findings show that peripheral, low-power people (e.g., individuals who belong to groups that are negatively stereotyped) feel more belonging uncertainty than do higher power people (Walton & Cohen, 2007). In addition, because STEM domains are widely perceived to be meritocracies, low-power people may strive to appease belonging uncertainty by successfully completing tasks that contribute to the objectives valued in a particular domain (and powerful people's goals). This shows that they possess the attributes valued in a given domain and indicative of belonging.

WHEN DO HIGH-POWER PEOPLE STEREOTYPE LOW-POWER PEOPLE?

If powerful people are motivated to effectively and legitimately work with low-power people, then stereotyping should only occur when it slips by undetected. In other words, stereotyping should ensue when it seems effective and fair. Later we note when the processes of categorization and stereotyping come together in situations involving differentials in role power to permit the stereotyping tendencies of powerful people to slip by undetected.

The situations associated with STEM domains set the stage for the stereotyping of low-power women and ethnic minorities. As we have noted, there are gender and ethnic disparities in representation and status, such that White men are the normative people in STEM domains, similar to Western cultures more generally (Zárate & Smith, 1990). Importantly, nonnormative group memberships are attention-grabbing and provide a basis of categorization (e.g., race, gender, age; Brewer, 1988; Fiske & Neuberg, 1990). Women typically are categorized on the basis of their nonnormative gender and ethnic minority men are categorized on the basis of their nonnormative race; White men are not, however, immediately categorized (Zárate & Smith, 1990; see also Stroessner, 1996). Categorization is a necessary precondition of stereotyping, and cultural stereotypes contain information that implies that women and ethnic minorities have critical shortcomings that may impede success in STEM domains (e.g., emotional, illogical). In other words, stereotypes may provide information that is relevant to the goals of powerful people in STEM domains.

Stereotype-relevant STEM domains provide the necessary preconditions of stereotyping, but they do not provide sufficient conditions that assure stereotyping. Instead, once the situational preconditions of stereotyping are present, the tendencies of high-power people vary as a function of stereotype endorsement and how goal strivings are construed, as we note later.

The stereotyping tendencies of high-power people vary across and within groups as a function of the degree to which people endorse the cultural stereotypes of the groups to which low-power people belong. For instance, men and women differ in their endorsement of sexist ideologies and stereotypes. Men more strongly endorse both hostile and benevolent sexist attitudes (Glick & Fiske, 2001), view women as possessing fewer agentic traits (Diekman & Eagly, 2000; Spence & Buckner, 2000), and have less complex representations of women (Park & Judd, 1990) than do women. As noted earlier, findings from the prejudice literature also show that those who endorse stereotypes (e.g., high-prejudice people) have stronger links between the content of stereotypic representations and category labels (Lepore & Brown, 1997) and are less motivated to temper prejudiced responding (Plant & Devine, 1998) than people who reject stereotypes (e.g., low-prejudice people). Together, these findings suggest that those who endorse (vs. reject) negative stereotypes should more readily and frequently use stereotypes to make judgments about women and racial minorities. Consistent with this suggestion, findings show that in achievement domains powerful men (but not women) stereotype low-power women (Vescio et al., 2003), and powerful Whites who are high (but not low) in prejudice stereotype low-power Blacks (Vescio et al., 2006).

The stereotyping tendencies of powerful people also vary as a function of their *social influence strategies,* or plans about how to achieve goals that require the contributions of low-power people (Vescio et al., 2006; Vescio et al., 2005; Vescio et al., 2003). Social influence strategies can be manipulated across situations to take one of two forms. *Weakness-focused* social influence strategies are based on beliefs about how subordinates may impede goal strivings. As such, they are characterized by a heightened attention to contextually relevant weaknesses that low-power people possess and how those weaknesses impede goal strivings. *Strength-focused* social influence strategies are beliefs about how low-power people may enhance goal strivings. As a result, they are characterized by a heightened attention to contextually relevant strengths that low-power people possess and how those strengths enhance goal strivings.[1]

---

[1] Our distinction between strength- versus weakness-focused social influence strategies has some similarities to Higgins's (1997) articulation of promotion versus prevention self-regulatory focus. Like a promotion self-regulatory focus, strength-focused social influence strategies emphasize approach-related behavior and a heightened sensitivity to positive outcomes, and like a prevention self-regulatory focus, weakness-focused social influence strategies emphasize avoidance-related behavior and a heightened sensitivity to negative outcomes. However, Higgins's work dealt with the question of how people regulate their own goal-related activities and responses in light of salient self-images (e.g., "ideal" vs. "ought" self), whereas social influence strategies refer to how powerful people regulate interactions with others to promote or prevent particular subordinate outcomes. Additionally, we make no assumptions about self-involvement or self-focus of people in positions of power; strength-focused social influence strategies are not uniquely associated with the ideal self, nor are weakness-focused social influence strategies associated with the "ought self." For example, a powerful person may envision personal goals given reference to one's ideal self, positive outcomes, and a promotion focus but may adopt a weakness-focused social influence strategy (e.g., when subordinates are inexperienced).

Research from our lab shows that powerful people stereotype low-power people when the content of the cultural stereotypes of the groups to which low-power people belong matches and informs the social influence strategies powerful people have adopted. In STEM domains, cultural stereotypes of women and ethnic minorities match weakness-focused social influence strategies. In their efforts to secure goals, powerful people who are weakness focused seek to minimize impediments to goal strivings. As a result, they are attentive to and seek information about others that allows them to withhold valued tasks from those who lack the requisite skills. Cultural stereotypes of women and ethnic minorities match and inform weakness-focused social influence strategies. Stereotypes suggest that women and ethnic minorities have critical shortcomings that may compromise goal attainment (e.g., women are emotional, illogical and weak; African Americans are unintelligent and unmotivated), providing information of relevance. Thus, stereotypes of women and ethnic minorities match weakness-focused social influence strategies and stereotyping should ensue.

By contrast, stereotypes of women and ethnic minorities are mismatched with strength-focused social influence strategies in STEM domains. To enhance goal strivings, powerful people who are strength-focused seek information about others that allows them to assign valued tasks to those possessing requisite skills. Cultural stereotypes point to the strengths that women and ethnic minorities possess (e.g., women are caring and nurturing; African Americans are musical and athletic), but those strengths are irrelevant to goal strivings in STEM domains. As a result, stereotypes do not match strength-focused goal strivings and stereotyping should not ensue.

Together, the foregoing considerations provide the basis for predictions regarding when powerful people will stereotype low-power women and ethnic minorities in STEM domains. We predict that powerful people will stereotype low-power women and ethnic minorities when stereotypes of those groups (a) are endorsed by powerful people, and (b) match powerful people's social influence strategies. As noted, there are also variations in stereotype endorsement, between-group and within-group variations, such that stereotyping tendencies should be stronger among powerful men (vs. women) and powerful Whites who are high (vs. low) in prejudice. In addition, in STEM domains, stereotypes match weakness-focused social influence strategies.

Thus, powerful men (but not women) should stereotype low-power women in STEM domains and powerful Whites who are high (vs. low) in prejudice should stereotype low-power Blacks. Consistent with these suggestions, in STEM domains, across studies we have found that powerful men who were weakness-focused more strongly categorized low-power people according to gender and showed stronger antifemale biases in evaluations and the allocation of valued resources than did powerful men who were strength-focused and powerful women (regardless of social influence strategy; Vescio et al., 2005; Vescio et al., 2003). In academic domains, findings also showed that powerful Whites who were weakness-focused more negatively evaluated and allocated fewer valued resources to low-power Blacks than did powerful Whites who were strength-focused (Vescio et al., 2006).

HOW DO HIGH-POWER PEOPLE BEHAVE TOWARD THE LOW-POWER PEOPLE THEY STEREOTYPE?

If powerful people are motivated to effectively and legitimately work with low-power people such that stereotyping only occurs when it slips by undetected, then the stereotypic actions of powerful people must be more subtle and nuanced then typically thought. More specifically, people feel guilty and self-critical when confronted with evidence that their thoughts or behaviors have violated ideals of fairness (Czopp & Monteith, 2003; Devine, Monteith, Zuwerink, & Elliot, 1991; Monteith & Mark, 2005; Zuwerink, Devine, Monteith, & Cook, 1996; see also Winslow, 2004). As a result, most people are motivated (intrinsically, extrinsically, or both) to monitor and control their responses to avoid imputations of prejudice (from the self or others; Devine, Plant, Amodio, Harmon-Jones, & Vance, 2002). Presenting difficulty, however, is the fact that prejudicial acts are prototypically perceived to be hostile and direct (e.g., Inman & Baron, 1996; Inman, Huerta, & Oh, 1998). The implication is that attempts to monitor one's own behavior may be effective in limited contexts; namely, those in which one's behavior resembles what is prototypically perceived to be prejudice—blatant and hostile acts.

Gender-based and race-based inequities are, however, most typically and effectively maintained through the relatively more subtle and sweet persuasive influences of paternalism than through overt acts of hostility and disrespect (Jackman, 1994; Pratto & Walker, 2001). Like the all-knowing authoritarian father who makes decisions on behalf of others (e.g., his children) out of a belief that he is doing what is best for those over whom he has power, heterosexual relations are characterized by rituals and norms that involve men taking care of and protecting their women. Men are providers and protectors, with the assumption being that those they care for cannot provide for and protect themselves. As providers and protectors, men may act in ways that seem kind and derive from their seemingly sincere regard for women. Historically, race relations were characterized by similar paternalistic relations, whereby one group of people owned another to provide care for those whom they perceived to lack the capacity for self-care. As Jackman noted, however, the seemingly benign acts that derive from a sincere feeling of positive regard (e.g., praising, limiting activity for the welfare of others) may lubricate intergroup relations such that group-based inequities are concealed, reinforced, and maintained.

The notion that benevolence, or feelings of sincere positive regard, may coexist with deep-seated antipathy to mask group-based inequities is an implicit aspect of several theories of racial prejudice. Both aversive and ambivalent racism theories (Gaertner & Dovidio, 1986; Katz & Hass, 1988), for instance, posit that most White Americans endorse egalitarian values and are aware of the past injustices perpetrated against Black Americans. Egalitarian values and knowledge of the negative historical treatment of Black Americans presumably combine to produce a sincere positive regard for Black Americans. As a result, White Americans tend to discriminate against Black Americans only when there are clear situational justifications for negative behavior, such that racism is typically associated with attributional ambiguity.

Contemporary theories of gender stereotyping and sexism have also incorporated and extended the notion that group-based inequities are maintained through subtle acts of benevolence and paternalism, rather than overt hostility. Benevolent sexism (Glick & Fiske, 1996, 2001), for example, is characterized by beliefs of complementary gender roles (where communal female and agentic male partners create a whole), paternalism, and intimate heterosexual relations (e.g., sweet communal women adored and put on a pedestal). Although apparently positive, benevolently sexist beliefs are based on stereotypes that women are incompetent and childlike. Research testing the model of (often mixed) stereotype content (Fiske, Cuddy, Glick, & Xu, 2002) reveals that women, like the elderly and people with disabilities, are stereotyped as warm but incompetent. Perhaps not surprising given the content, stereotypes of traditional women elicit pity and benevolently sexist acts of condescension rather than respect. Likewise, social role theory (Eagly, 1987) notes that women are sometimes evaluated positively (even more positively than men). Women are adored, put on a pedestal, and flattered when appropriately communal and warm (e.g., the women are wonderful effect; Eagly & Mladinic, 1989), but punished and socially excluded when they are gender role violating and agentic (Rudman & Fairchild, 2004; Rudman & Glick, 1999, 2001). Importantly, however, even when women are adored and thought to be wonderfully gender appropriate, others' seemingly sweet acts of kindness are patronizing and insincere (Glick & Fiske, 2001); such acts imply women's inferiority.

What do the stereotypic and patronizing acts of benevolence look like? Our answer to this question focuses on gender stereotyping. In our initial theorizing and the research testing our hypotheses, we focused on gender stereotyping and sexism. We will, however, generalize our theory and findings to consider the implications for racial stereotyping in our concluding comments.

Patronizing behavior is a pattern of group-based inequity that is masked by trivial niceties (Vescio et al., 2005). More specifically, as Biernat and Vescio (2002) noted, patronizing behavior is characterized by a pattern of behaviors whereby women receive fewer valued resources than White men (e.g., raises, promotions), but more condescending flattery (e.g., praise, pats on the back). As noted earlier, traditional women are stereotyped as warm but incompetent (Fiske et al., 2002). The conflicting stereotype content may promote distinct kinds of behaviors from men. In masculine domains, stereotypes of women as warm and communal may promote positive verbal and nonverbal behaviors, like praise, encouragement, and pats on the back. By contrast, women's stereotypic incompetence may simultaneously inspire gender inequity in the allocation of valued resources, like raises and promotions (Vescio et al., 2005; see also Glick & Fiske, 2001). Thus, when powerful men stereotype low-power women, patronizing behavior may result, such that there are antifemale biases in the allocation of valued resources and profemale biases on praise.

Two findings from our lab support predictions. First, powerful men who were weakness-focused more strongly categorized their subordinates according to gender than did powerful men who were strength-focused (see Vescio et al., 2005; Vescio et al., 2003). Second, among powerful men who were weakness-focused, categorization was strongly correlated with patronizing behavior—including devalued position assignments and increased praise for women.

Ironically, although praise may mask gender inequities in the allocation of valued resources, powerful men who behaved in benevolently sexist ways perceive that their praise has stemmed from genuine and positive sentimentality toward women. Thus, as Jackman (1994) noted, subtle acts of sexism, like patronizing behavior, may not be viewed as sexist by male actors. Thus, powerful men can maintain goals of being effective and legitimate by behaving in patronizing ways. Patronizing behavior may, however, be keenly experienced as unfair by those who are patronized. Next we turn attention to the perspective of low-power people who are recipients of subtle prejudice.

How Do the Stereotypic and Patronizing Behaviors of the Powerful Affect Their Low-Power Recipients?

It is reasonable to expect that low-power people will be angered by the patronizing behaviors of those who have power over them. At minimum, patronizing behavior is duplicitous; one's apparently praiseworthy inputs are not met with equally valuable outputs. Importantly, anger is the emotion typically reported in response to perceptions of injustice (Mikula, 1986; Mikula, Scherer & Athenstaedt, 1998; Miller, 2001). Anger follows from perceptions that another person has committed a transgression against oneself (e.g., social rejection; Leary, Twenge, & Quinlivan, 2006) and that one has the coping mechanisms to fix the anger-inspiring situation (Lazarus, 1991).

Anger is also an approach-related emotion associated with the behavioral approach system (BAS; Harmon-Jones & Sigelman, 2001), which is the motivational system that activates approach behaviors in response to desired environmental stimuli (Gray, 1982, 1987). Importantly, however, when there are no actions that could ameliorate an anger-inspiring situation, irksome feelings persist while people remain in the anger-inspiring situation, but those feelings no longer inspire action (i.e., anger is no longer associated with asymmetric left midfrontal cortical activity, neural activity indicative of BAS; Harmon-Jones, Sigelman, Bohlig, & Harmon-Jones, 2003). In other words, anger can trigger and maintain sudden, direct, and focused bursts of attention and action (Sternberg & Campos, 1990), but only when people perceive control or think that their actions can fix the situation.

Low-power men and women who are treated in patronizing ways may experience anger because such behaviors seem unfair, but low-power men and women may differ in their behavioral expression of anger and perceptions of control. For instance, although men and women report anger at similar frequencies and intensities (Fischer, Rodriguez, Mosquera, van Vianen, & Manstead, 2004; Kopper & Epperson, 1991; Thomas, 1989), angry outbursts violate feminine gender roles, and there are social sanctions for gender-role violations (Rudman & Fairchild, 2004; Rudman & Glick, 1999, 2001). As a result, women may attempt to suppress behavioral expressions of anger, which is consistent with findings showing gender differences in the tendency to act on anger (for a review, see Shields, 2002). In addition, in STEM domains, women also have lower expectations for positive outcomes, less confidence, fewer perceptions of personal control, and worse performance relative to men (Meece, Parsons, Kaczala, & Goff, 1982; Parsons, Kaczala, & Meece, 1982; Ryckman & Peckham, 1987; Stipek, 1984).

We suggest that gender differences in the behavioral expression of anger may work together with gender differences in confidence and performance expectations in STEM domains to affect performance. Given our conceptualization of patronizing behavior (i.e., assigning devalued position but much praise), one may ameliorate anger by attempting to improve performance to assure belonging and avoid future patronization (if effort is associated with performance). In addition, as noted earlier, low-power people may strive to belong in valued STEM domains by successfully completing tasks that contribute to the objectives valued in a particular domain (and powerful people's goals). If women are less likely than men to be confident about their abilities in STEM domains and less likely to act on the basis of anger, then gender differences in performance should emerge.

To test the notion that the patronizing behaviors of high-power people create gender differences in performance among the relatively powerless where they would not otherwise exist, we have conducted several studies. In each, participants were assigned to low-power positions and received patronizing feedback from a male leader in a stereotypically masculine domain. To create patronizing feedback and appropriate comparison conditions, praise (high or low) and a position assignment (valued or devalued) were crossed. After receiving feedback and task assignments, people reported perceptions of control and anger. They also completed standardized logic and math problems in each of two rounds.

Three critical patterns of findings emerged across studies. First, in the patronizing conditions (devalued positions–high praise), both men and women reported more anger than in other conditions (Vescio et al., 2005, Study 2). Second, despite the fact that men and women were similarly angered as targets of patronizing behavior, there were gender differences in performance; women performed less well than did men in only one condition—the patronizing condition. In fact, women in the patronizing condition performed worse than women in other conditions, including women who received devalued positions but were not praised. By contrast, men in the patronizing condition performed better than men in the other three conditions.

Third, findings are consistent with the notion that, in patronizing conditions, gender differences in perceived control cause gender differences in performance. Gervais and Vescio (2007) conducted a series of studies that point to the import of perceptions of control. Findings show that, for instance, after being patronized by a powerful person, low-power men perceive that they have more control over their future ability to acquire such a position than do women. In addition, when control is manipulated (high control, low control, or ambiguous), gender differences in performance predictably vary. When performance is severed from outcomes, such that no participants (male or female) believe that their actions can fix the anger-inspiring situation, men underperform like women. By contrast, when perceptions of control are uniformly heightened (for women and men), gender differences in performance were no longer significant because women in the high-control condition perform as well as men.

Summary of Assumptions and Propositions

In the proceeding sections, we noted that the desires to belong and be legitimate are basic motives that are shaped by role power to determine high- and low-power people's goals. The *foundational assumptions* on which our prior and ongoing theory and research have been based are twofold. First, we assume that high-power people internalize the goals of their positions and are motivated to effectively and legitimately work with low-power people to achieve those goals. Second, we assume that low-power people are motivated to effectively and legitimately perform tasks that are valued in a given domain in an effort to increase or secure belonging.

Given these assumptions, the theory and research presented in this chapter addressed when, how, and with what consequences high-power people stereotype and discriminate against low-power women and minorities in STEM domains. We presented three propositions that, together, address this broad issue. The first two propositions address when high-power people stereotype low-power people and how they behave toward the low-power people they stereotype.

> *Proposition I:* High-power people stereotype low-power people when the stereotypes of the group to which low-power people belong:
>   are contextually relevant (e.g., gender and race stereotypes in STEM domains).
>   are endorsed by powerful people (e.g., seen as factual and therefore legitimate).
>   match powerful social influence strategies (e.g., effectively inform the situation).

Stereotyping lays the foundation for discriminatory behaviors, which we suggest are more subtle and nuanced than originally thought.

> *Proposition II:* The stereotypic acts of powerful people are often comprised of seemingly well-intentioned acts (like praise) that mask group-based inequities in the allocation of valued resources (e.g., raises, promotions).

From the perspective of high-power people, the niceties are believed to stem from sincere positive regard. From the perspective of low-power people, however, the behaviors of the powerful seem duplicitous and unfair. This leads to the final proposition, which addresses the question of the consequences that the stereotypic behaviors of high-power people have for their low-power recipients.

> *Proposition III:* Low-power people who are the targets of the stereotypic acts of powerful people typically will be angered by the duplicity of such behaviors. Anger should inspire effort and corrective actions when personal control is high, such that low-power people see acts that could ameliorate the adversity. If personal control is low, such that one fails to see potentially corrective actions, then effort should be withdrawn.

CONCLUDING COMMENTS

The foundational assumptions and ideas presented in Propositions I, II, and III represent a goal-situated perspective on the relation between power and stereotyping. At the heart of this perspective is the basic notion that the behaviors of high-power and low-power people can be understood given consideration of the way in which situations shape the expression of people's motives to belong and be legitimate. The propositions described note when high-power people stereotype low-power people and we consider these to be general theoretical statements. In other words, these are statements that are expected to apply to predictions about when low-power people from different social groups are stereotyped, as well as predictions that would be expected to predict stereotyping effects across diverse contexts. In this chapter, we focused on STEM domains and the relevance of stereotypes of women and ethnic minority groups to those domains. We would, however, expect similar patterns of effects when low-power people belong to other negatively stereotyped groups (e.g., Latinos, elderly).

Interestingly, in achievement domains, the groups that are negatively stereotyped are those groups stereotypically defined as incompetent. As Fiske and her colleagues (2002) noted, many groups are stereotypically perceived as incompetent but warm (e.g., traditional women, elderly people, and even entertaining but incompetent Black comedians and athletes). These groups are also the groups that are pitied and treated in paternalistic ways. Members of these pitied groups may be particularly like to be stereotyped in sugar-coated ways, such that trivial niceties (e.g., praise) mask underlying group-based inequities. There are, however, other negatively stereotyped groups that are stereotypically perceived to be competent but cold and cunning (e.g., feminist, Jewish people). These groups are respected for their capabilities, but disliked because of their lack of warmth. Members of these groups may be stereotyped in different contexts (e.g., caretaking situations) or subject to social incivilities rather than professional marginalization. Our ongoing work continues to test the predictions of our goal-situated perspective across target groups and contexts.

Regardless of the breadth of the statements outlined, our analysis is built on a dynamic social influence conceptualization of power. The propositions noted and the findings supporting the predictions demonstrate both the stereotypic tendencies of high-power people and their emotional and performance consequences for low-power people. As a result, our theory and research has pointed to important mechanisms that, together, contribute to gender disparities and racial disparities in achievement domains—anger and perceived control among the relatively powerless.

Our work has also pointed to a host of situational factors that can be altered to temper the status quo maintaining links between power and stereotyping. In particular, our theory and research point to factors that prevent the stereotyping of the powerful (e.g., situational manipulations of social influence strategies). Our theory and research also point to factors that can be altered such that low-power people's perceptions of their personal ability to control, or fix, an adverse situation are enhanced, such that anger leads to increased effort and improved performance rather than performance decrements. In sum, our theory and research point to tangible, efficient, and potential low-cost interventions that may temper the stereotyping among the powerful or increase perceptions of control among the relatively powerless, thereby minimizing the underperformance of women and ethnicity minorities in achievement domains.

REFERENCES

Allport, G. (1954). *The nature of prejudice.* Boston: Beacon Press.

Banaji, M. R., Hardin, C., & Rothman, A. J. (1993). Implicit stereotyping in person judgment. *Journal of Personality and Social Psychology, 65,* 272–281.

Bardi, A., & Schwartz, S. H. (2003). Values and behavior: Strength and structure of relations. *Personality and Social Psychology Bulletin, 29,* 1207–1220.

Bargh, J. A., Raymond, P., Pryor, J. B., & Strack, F. (1995). Attractiveness of the underling: An automatic power–sex association and its consequences for sexual harassment and aggression. *Journal of Personality and Social Psychology, 68,* 768–781.

Baumeister, R. F., & Leary, M. R. (1995). The need to belong: Desire for interpersonal attachments as a fundamental human motivation. *Psychological Bulletin, 117,* 497–529.

Bierhoff, H. W., Cohen, R. L., & Greenberg, J. (Eds.). (1986). *Justice in social relations.* New York: Plenum.

Biernat, M., & Vescio, T. K. (2002). She swings, she hits, she's great, she's benched: Shifting judgment standards and behavior. *Personality and Social Psychology Bulletin, 28,* 66–76.

Brewer, M. B. (1979). In-group bias in the minimal intergroup situation: A cognitive-motivational analysis. *Psychological Bulletin, 86,* 307–324.

Brewer, M. B. (1988). A dual process model of impression formation. In T. K. Srull & R. S. Wyer, Jr. (Eds.), *Advances in social cognition* (Vol. 1, pp. 1–36). Hillsdale, NJ: Erlbaum.

Bruner, J. S. (1973). *Beyond the information given: Studies in psychology of knowing.* Oxford, UK: Norton.

Chen, S., Lee-Chai, A. Y., & Bargh, J. A. (2001). Relationship orientation as a moderator of the effects of social power. *Journal of Personality and Social Psychology, 80,* 173–187.

Chen, S., Ybarra, O., & Kiefer, A. K. (2004). Power and impression formation: The effects of power on the desire for morality and competence information. *Social Cognition, 22,* 391–421.

Copeland, J. T. (1994). Prophecies of power: Motivation implications of social power for behavioral confirmation. *Journal of Personality and Social Psychology, 67,* 264–277.

Corneille, C., Vescio, T. K., & Judd, C. M. (2000). Incidentally activated knowledge and stereotype based judgments: A consideration of primed construct–target attribute match. *Social Cognition, 18,* 377–399.

Czopp, A. M., & Monteith, M. J. (2003). Confronting prejudice (literally): Reactions to confrontations of racial and gender bias. *Personality and Social Psychology Bulletin, 29,* 532–544.

Darley, J. M., & Gross, P. H. (1983). A hypothesis-confirming bias in labeling effects. *Journal of Personality and Social Psychology, 44*(1), 20–33.

DePaulo, B. M., & Friedman, H. S. (1998). Nonverbal communication. In D. T. Gilbert, S. T. Fiske, & G. Lindzey (Eds.), *The handbook of social psychology* (Vol. 2, pp. 3–40). New York: Oxford University Press.

Depret, E., & Fiske, S. T. (1999). Perceiving the powerful: Intriguing individuals versus threatening groups. *Journal of Experimental Social Psychology, 35,* 461–480.

Devine, P. (1989). Stereotypes and prejudice: Their automatic and controlled components. *Journal of Personality and Social Psychology, 56,* 5–18.

Devine, P. G., Monteith, M. J., Zuwerink, J. R., & Elliot, R. J. (1991). Prejudice with and without compunction. *Journal of Personality and Social Psychology, 60,* 817–830.

Devine, P. G., Plant, E. A., Amodio, D. M., Harmon-Jones, E., & Vance, S. L. (2002). The regulation of explicit and implicit racial bias: The role of motivations to respond without prejudice. *Journal of Personality and Social Psychology, 82,* 835–848.

Diekman, A. B., & Eagly, A. H. (2000). Stereotypes as dynamic constructs: Women and men of the past, present, and future. *Personality and Social Psychology Bulletin, 26,* 1171–1188.

Eagly, A. H. (1987). Reporting sex differences. *American Psychologist, 42,* 756–757.

Eagly, A. H., & Karau, S. J. (2002). Role congruity theory of prejudice toward female leaders. *Psychological Review, 109,* 573–598.

Eagly, A. H., & Mladinic, A. (1989). Gender stereotypes and attitudes toward women and men. *Personality and Social Psychology Bulletin, 15,* 543–558.

Ebenbach, D. H., & Keltner, D. (1998). Power, emotion, and judgmental accuracy in social conflict: Motivating the cognitive miser. *Basic and Applied Social Psychology, 20,* 7–21.

Emerson, R. M. (1964). Power-dependence relations: Two experiments. *Sociometry, 27,* 282–298.

Fischer, A. H., Rodriguez Mosquera, P. M., van Vianen, A. E. M., & Manstead, A. S. R. (2004). Gender and culture differences in emotion. *Emotion, 4,* 87–94.

Fiske, S. T. (1993). Controlling other people: The impact of power on stereotyping. *American Psychologist, 48,* 621–628.

Fiske, S. T., Cuddy, A. J. C., Glick, P., & Xu, J. (2002). A model of (often mixed) stereotype content: Competence and warmth respectively follow from perceived status and competition. *Journal of Personality and Social Psychology, 82,* 878–902.

Fiske, S. T., & Neuberg, S. L. (1990). A continuum of impression formation, from category-based to individuating processes: Influences of information and motivation on attention and interpretation. In M. Zanna (Ed.), *Advances in experimental social psychology* (Vol. 23, pp. 1–74). New York: Academic.

Folger, R. (Ed.). (1984). *The sense of injustice: Social psychological perspectives.* New York: Plenum.

French, J. R. P., & Raven, B. (1959). The bases of social power. In D. Cartwright (Ed.), *Studies in social power* (pp. 150–167). Oxford, UK: University of Michigan Press.

Gaertner, S. L., & Dovidio, J. F. (1986). The aversive form of racism. In S. L. Gaertner & J. F. Dovidio (Eds.), *Prejudice, discrimination, and racism* (pp. 61–89). San Diego, CA: Academic.

Galinsky, A. D., Gruenfeld, D. H., & Magee, J. C. (2003). From power to action. *Journal of Personality and Social Psychology, 85,* 453–466.

Gervais, S. J., & Vescio, T. K. (2007). *Patronizing behavior and control.* Manuscript submitted for publication.

Glick, P. & Fiske, S. (1996). The ambivalent sexism inventory: Differentiating hostile and benevolent sexism. *Journal of Personality and Social Psychology, 70,* 491-512.

Glick, P., & Fiske, S. T. (2001). Ambivalent sexism. In M. P. Zanna (Ed.), *Advances in experimental social psychology* (Vol. 33, pp. 115–188). San Diego, CA: Academic.

Goodwin, S. A., Gubin, A., Fiske, S. T., & Yzerbyt, V. Y. (2000). Power can bias impression processes: Stereotyping subordinates by default and by design. *Group Processes and Intergroup Relations, 3,* 227–256.

Gray, J. A. (1982). *The neuropsychology of anxiety: An inquiry into the functions of the septohippocampal system.* New York: Oxford University Press.

Gray, J. A. (1987). *The psychology of fear and stress.* Cambridge, UK: Cambridge University Press.

Greenberg, J., & Cohen, R. L. (Eds.). (1982). *Equity and justice in social behavior.* Philadelphia: Academic.

Guinote, A. (2001). Lack of control leads to less stereotypic perceptions of groups: An individual difference perspective. *Analise-Psicologica, 19,* 453–460.

Guinote, A. (2007a). Power and goal pursuit. *Personality and Social Psychology Bulletin, 33,* 1076–1087.

Guinote, A. (2007b). Power and the suppression of unwanted thoughts: Does control over others decrease control over the self? *Journal of Experimental Social Psychology, 43,* 433–440.

Guinote, A., Judd, C. M., & Brauer, M. (2002). Effects of power on perceived and objective group variability: Evidence that more powerful groups are more viable. *Journal of Personality and Social Psychology, 82,* 708–721.

Haney, C., Banks, C., & Zimbardo, P. (1973). Interpersonal dynamics in a simulated prison. *International Journal of Criminology & Penology, 1,* 69–97.

Harmon-Jones, E., & Sigelman, J. (2001). State anger and prefrontal brain activity: Evidence that insult-related left-prefrontal activation is associated with experienced anger and aggression. *Journal of Personality and Social Psychology, 80,* 797–803.

Harmon-Jones, E., Sigelman, J. D., Bohlig, A., & Harmon-Jones, C. (2003). Anger, coping, and frontal cortical activity: The effect of coping potential on anger-induced left frontal activity. *Cognition and Emotion, 17,* 1–24.

Hazan, C., & Shaver, P. R. (1994). Attachment as an organizational framework for research on close relationships. *Psychological Inquiry, 5,* 1–22.

Higgins, T. E. (1997). Beyond pleasure and pain. *American Psychologist, 52,* 1280-1300.

Howard, J. A., Blumstein, P., & Schwartz, P. (1986). Sex, power, and influence tactics in intimate relationships. *Journal of Personality and Social Psychology, 51,* 102–109.

Inman, M. L., & Baron, R. S. (1996). Influence of prototypes on perceptions of prejudice. *Journal of Personality and Social Psychology, 70,* 727–739.

Inman, M. L., Huerta, J., & Oh, S. (1998). Perceiving discrimination: The role of prototypes and norm violation. *Social Cognition, 16,* 418–450.

Jackman, M. R. (1994). *The velvet glove: Paternalism and conflict in gender, class and race relations.* Berkeley: University of California Press.

Jost, T. T. (2001). Outgroup favoritism and the theory of system justification: An experimental paradigm for investigating the effects of socio-economic success on stereotype content. In G. Moskowitz (Ed.), *Cognitive social psychology: On the tenure and future of social cognition* (pp. 89–102). Hillsdale, NJ: Erlbaum.

Jost, J. T., & Banaji, M. R. (1994). The role of stereotyping in system-justification and the production of a false consciousness. *British Journal of Social Psychology, 33,* 1–27.

Jost, J. T., & Major, B. (2001). Emerging perspectives on the psychology of legitimacy. In J. T. Jost & B. Major (Eds.), *The psychology of legitimacy* (pp. 3–32). Cambridge, UK: Cambridge University Press.

Katz, I., & Hass, R. G. (1988). Racial ambivalence and American value conflict: Correlational and priming studies of dual cognitive structures. *Journal of Personality and Social Psychology, 55,* 893–905.

Keltner, D., Capps, L. M., Kring, A. M., Young, R. C., & Heerey, E. A. (2001). Just teasing: A conceptual analysis and empirical review. *Psychological Bulletin, 127,* 229–248.

Keltner, D., Gruenfeld, D. H., & Anderson, C. (2003). Power, approach, and inhibition. *Psychological Review, 110,* 265–284.

Kinder, D. R., & Sears, D. O. (1981). Prejudice and politics: Symbolic racism versus racial threats to the good life. *Journal of Personality and Social Psychology, 40,* 414–431.

Kipnis, D. (1972). Does power corrupt? *Journal of Personality and Social Psychology, 24,* 33–41.

Kopper, A. A., & Epperson, D. L. (1991). Women and anger: Sex and sex-role comparisons in the expression of anger. *Psychology of Women Quarterly, 15,* 7–14.

Lazarus, R. S. (1991). Progress on a cognitive-motivational-relational theory of emotion. *American Psychologist, 46,* 819–834.

Leary, M. R., Twenge, J. M., & Quinlivan, E. (2006). Interpersonal rejection as a determinant of anger and aggression. *Personality and Social Psychology Review, 10,* 111–132.

Lepore, L., & Brown, R. (1997). Category and stereotype activation: Is prejudice inevitable? *Journal of Personality and Social Psychology, 72,* 275–287.

Lerner, M. J., & Lerner, S. C. (Eds.). (1981). *The justice motive in social behavior.* New York: Plenum.

McConahay, J. B. (1982). Self-interest versus racial attitudes as correlates of anti-busing attitudes in Louisville: Is it the buses or the blacks? *Journal of Politics, 44,* 692–720.

McConahay, J. B., Hardee, B. B., & Batts, V. (1981). Has racism declined in America? It depends on who is asking and what is asked. *Journal of Conflict Resolution, 25,* 563–579.

Meece, J. L., Parsons, J. E., Kaczala, C. M., & Goff, S. B. (1982). Sex differences in math achievement: Toward a model of academic choice. *Psychological Bulletin, 91,* 324–348.

Mikula, G. (1986). The experience of injustice: Toward a better understanding of its phenomenology. In W. W. Bierhoff, R. L. Cohen, & J. Greenberg (Eds.), *Justice in social relations* (pp. 223–244). New York: Plenum.

Mikula, G., Scherer, K. R., & Athenstaedt, U. (1998). The role of injustice in the elicitation of differential emotional reactions. *Personality and Social Psychology Bulletin, 24,* 769–783.

Miller, D. T. (2001). Disrespect and the experience of injustice. *Annual Review of Psychology, 52,* 527–553.

Monteith, M. J., & Mark, A. Y. (2005). Changing one's prejudiced ways: Awareness, affect, and self-regulation. *European Review of Social Psychology, 16,* 113–154.

Overbeck, J. R., & Park, B. (2001). When power does not corrupt: Superior individuation processes among powerful perceivers. *Journal of Personality and Social Psychology, 81,* 549–565.

Overbeck, J. R., Tiedens, L. Z., & Brion, S. (2006). The powerful want to, the powerless have to: Perceived constraint moderates causal attributions. *European Journal of Social Psychology, 36,* 479–496.

Park, B., & Judd, C. M. (1990). Measures and models of perceived variability. *Journal of Personality and Social Psychology, 59,* 173–191.

Parsons, J. E., Kaczala, C. M., & Meece, J. L. (1982). Socialization of achievement attitudes and beliefs: Classroom influences. *Child Development, 53,* 322–339.

Plant, E. A., & Devine, P. G. (1998). Internal and external motivation to respond without prejudice. *Journal of Personality and Social Psychology, 75,* 811–832.

Pratto, F., & Hegarty, P. (2000). The political psychology of reproductive strategies. *Psychological Science, 11,* 57–62.

Pratto, F., & Shih, M. (2000). Social dominance orientation and group context in implicit group prejudice. *Psychological Science, 11,* 515–518.

Pratto, F., Sidanius, J., Stallworth, L. M., & Malle, B. F. (1994). Social dominance orientation: A personality variable predicting social and political attitudes. *Journal of Personality and Social Psychology, 67,* 741–763.

Pratto, F., Stallworth, L. M., Sidanius, J., & Siers, B. (1997). The gender gap in occupational role attainment: A social dominance approach. *Journal of Personality and Social Psychology, 72,* 37–53.

Pratto, F., & Walker, A. (2001). Dominance in disguise: Power, beneficence, and exploitation in personal relationships. In A. Y. Lee-Chai & J. A. Bargh (Eds.), *The use and abuse of power: Multiple perspectives on the causes of corruption* (pp. 93–114). Philadelphia: Academic.

Rodríguez-Bailón, R., Moya, M., & Yzerbyt, V. (2000). Why do superiors attend to negative stereotypic information about their subordinates? *European Journal of Social Psychology, 30,* 651–671.

Rudman, L. A., & Fairchild, K. (2004). Reactions to counterstereotypic behavior: The role of backlash in cultural stereotype maintenance. *Journal of Personality and Social Psychology, 87,* 157–176.

Rudman, L. A., & Glick, P. (1999). Feminized management and backlash toward agentic women: The hidden costs to women of a kinder, gentler image of middle managers. *Journal of Personality and Social Psychology, 77,* 1004–1010.

Rudman, L. A., & Glick, P. (2001). Prescriptive gender stereotypes and backlash toward agentic women. *Journal of Social Issues, 57,* 743–762.

Ryckman, D. B., & Peckham, P. (1987). Gender differences in attributions for success and failure situations across subject areas. *Journal of Educational Research, 81,* 120–125.

Schwartz, S. H., & Bardi, A. (2001). Value hierarchies across cultures: Taking a similarities perspective. *Journal of Cross-Cultural Psychology, 32,* 268–290.

Sherif, M., White, B. J., & Harvey, O. J. (1955). Status in experimentally produced groups. *American Journal of Sociology, 60,* 370–379.

Shields, S. A. (2002). *Speaking from the heart: Gender and the social meaning of emotion.* Cambridge, UK: Cambridge University Press.

Sidanius, J., Pratto, F., & Bobo, L. (1996). Racism, conservatism, Affirmative Action, and intellectual sophistication: Matter of principled conservatism or group dominance? *Journal of Personality and Social Psychology, 70,* 476–490.

Snyder, M., & Miene, P. K. (1994). On the functions of stereotypes and prejudice. In M. P. Zanna (Ed.), *The psychology of prejudice: The Ontario symposium, Vol. 7* (pp. 33–54). Hillsdale, NJ: Erlbaum.

Snyder, M., Tanke, E. D., & Berscheid, E. (1977). Social perception and interpersonal behavior: On the self-fulfilling nature of social stereotypes. *Journal of Personality and Social Psychology, 35,* 656–666.

Spence, J. T., & Buckner, C. B. (2000). Instrumental and expressive traits, trait stereotypes, and sexist attitudes. *Psychology of Women Quarterly, 24,* 44–62.

Steele, C. M. (1997). A threat in the air: How stereotypes shape intellectual identity and performance. *American Psychologist, 52*(6), 613–629.

Steele, C. M. (1998). Stereotyping and its threat are real. *American Psychologist, 53*(6), 680–681.

Steele, C. M., & Aronson, J. (1995). Stereotype threat and the intellectual test performance of African Americans. *Journal of Personality and Social Psychology, 69,* 797–811.

Sternberg, C. R., & Campos, J. J. (1990). The development of anger expression in infancy. In N. L. Stein, B. Leventhal, & T. Trabasso (Eds.), *Psychological and biological approaches to emotion* (pp. 247–282). Hillsdale, NJ: Erlbaum.

Stipek, D. J. (1984). Sex differences in children's attributions for success and failure on math and spelling tests. *Sex Roles, 11,* 969–981.

Stroessner, S. J. (1996). Social categorization by race or sex: Effects of perceived non-normalcy on response times. *Social Cognition, 14,* 247–276.

Studd, M. V. (1996). Sexual harassment. In D. M. Buss & N. M. Malamuth (Eds.), *Sex, power, and conflict: Evolutionary and feminist perspectives* (pp. 54–89). New York: Oxford University Press.

Tajfel, H. (1978). *Differentiation between social groups: Studies in the social psychology of intergroup relations.* Oxford, UK: Academic.

Tajfel, H. (1982). Social psychology of intergroup relations. *Annual Review of Psychology, 33,* 1–39.

Tajfel, H., & Turner, J. C. (1986). The social identity theory of intergroup behavior. In S. Worchel & W. Austin (Eds.), *Psychology of intergroup relations* (pp. 7–24). Chicago: Nelson-Hall.

Thomas, S. P. (1989). Gender differences in anger expression: Health implications. *Research in Nursing and Health, 12,* 389–398.

U.S. Department of Labor & Bureau of Labor Statistics (2005). Retrieved August 9, 2008 from http://www.bls.gov/

Vescio, T. K., & Biernat, M. (1999). When stereotype-based expectations impair perceivers' performance: The effect of prejudice, race, and target quality on judgments and perceiver performance. *European Journal of Social Psychology, 29,* 961–969.

Vescio, T. K., Gervais, S. J., Heidenreich, S., & Snyder, M. (2006). The effects of prejudice level and social influence strategy on stereotypic responding to racial outgroups. *European Journal of Social Psychology, 36,* 435–450.

Vescio, T. K., Gervais, S. J., Snyder, M., & Hoover, A. (2005). Power and the creation of patronizing environments: The stereotype-based behaviors of the powerful and their effects on female performance in masculine domains. *Journal of Personality and Social Psychology, 88,* 658–672.

Vescio, T. K., Snyder, M., & Butz, D. A. (2003). Power in stereotypically masculine domains: A social influence strategy × stereotype match model. *Journal of Personality and Social Psychology, 85,* 1062–1078.

Walton, G. M., & Cohen, G. L. (2003). Stereotype lift. *Journal of Experimental Social Psychology, 39,* 456–467.

Walton, G. M., & Cohen, G. L. (2007). A question of belonging: Race, social fit, and achievement. *Journal of Personality and Social Psychology, 92,* 82–96.

Williams, K. D., Shore, W. J., & Grahe, J. E. (1998). The silent treatment: Perceptions of its behaviors and associated feelings. *Group Processes and Intergroup Relations, 1,* 117–141.

Winslow, M. P. (2004). Reactions to the imputation of prejudice. *Basic and Applied Social Psychology, 26,* 289–297.

Wittenbrink, B., Gist, P. L., & Hilton, J. L. (1997). Structural properties of stereotyping knowledge and their influences on the construal of social situations. *Journal of Personality and Social Psychology, 72,* 526–543.

Wittenbrink, B., & Henly, J. R. (1996). Creating social reality: Informational social influence and the content of stereotypic beliefs. *Personality and Social Psychology Bulletin, 22,* 598–610.

Word, C. O., Zanna, M. P., & Cooper, J. (1974). The nonverbal mediation of self-fulfilling prophecies in interracial interaction. *Journal of Experimental Social Psychology, 10*(2), 109–120.

Zárate, M. A., & Smith. E. R. (1990). Person categorization and stereotyping. *Social Cognition, 8,* 161–185.

Zuwerink, J. R., Devine, P. G., Monteith, M. J., & Cook, D. A. (1996). Prejudice toward blacks: With and without compunction? *Basic and Applied Social Psychology, 18,* 131–150.

13 Mechanisms Underlying the Malleability of Implicit Prejudice and Stereotypes
The Role of Automaticity and Cognitive Control

Nilanjana Dasgupta
University of Massachusetts

A central theme in contemporary social psychology is that people's attitudes, beliefs, and behavior are often shaped by factors that lie outside their awareness and cannot be fully understood by intuitive methods such as self-reflection (Bargh, 1997; Greenwald & Banaji, 1995; Nisbett & Wilson, 1977). In the last 20 years, experimental social psychology has discovered an important window into mental life by discovering that attitudes and beliefs can be activated in memory without perceivers' awareness or intention. Once activated, these cognitions and evaluations are difficult to suppress or inhibit in the moment and create prepotent action tendencies that facilitate evaluation-consistent behavior, judgments, and decisions. These subtle reactions have been variously labeled *implicit, automatic, unconscious,* or *nonconscious* (Bargh, 1994; Greenwald & Banaji, 1995; Kihlstrom, 1990). However, because it is rare for any psychological judgment or behavior to meet all of these criteria at the same time—lack of awareness, intention, effort, and control—any judgment that meets at least one of these criteria has been given these labels.

Implicit attitudes and beliefs are typically seen as conceptually distinct from *explicit, controlled, self-reported,* or *conscious* responses. As these terms suggest, attitudes are considered explicit when perceivers are aware of their evaluations, able to endorse them as personally held opinions, and when they have the capacity to learn and change their attitudes volitionally by expending effort. Whereas explicit attitudes are measured by directly asking people to consider how they feel about a particular object or issue and then report their thoughts in a deliberate fashion, implicit attitudes are inferred indirectly from people's performance on tasks that, at face value, seem unrelated to attitude measurement. For example, the speed with which people associate certain stimuli on speeded reaction time tasks or their choice of words on word completion tasks is used to infer implicit attitudes.

Much of the research on implicit attitudes and their effects on social behavior has been conducted in the domain of intergroup relations, particularly around issues of prejudice and stereotyping. Research has gravitated in this direction for two theoretical reasons. First, the socially sensitive nature of intergroup thoughts and evaluations typically raises concerns that people's voluntary responses toward in- and outgroups may be distorted by self-presentation and impression management concerns. In other words, people may not always be willing to report socially sensitive attitudes honestly, especially if those attitudes deviate from social norms. Second, when self-reporting their attitudes people sometimes make a strong distinction between their own personal attitudes and those circulating in the larger culture ("society at large is prejudiced against Group X, but I am not"). Yet, societal construals of particular groups may have been passively learned and incorporated into perceivers' own mental representations without their knowledge. In other words, when asked, people may not have complete introspective access to their attitudes and thus may not be able to report them fully and accurately (Banaji & Greenwald, 1994; Greenwald & Banaji, 1995; Nisbett & Wilson, 1977).

IMPLICIT ATTITUDES ARE MALLEABLE

The empirical evidence that implicit attitudes are automatically activated without awareness, and that they have the capacity to drive judgments and behavior regardless of explicit intention and control, had, for a long time, led to the conclusion that these attitudes are relatively immutable. Early theories of implicit social cognition argued that implicit attitudes and beliefs are learned early in life and that they change slowly across time only after the accrual of new associations and a great deal of training (Bargh, 1999; Devine, 1989; Petty, Tormala, Brinol, & Jarvis, 2006; Wilson, Lindsey, & Schooler, 2000). In other words, the assumption was that conventional persuasion techniques that change explicit attitudes by relying on perceivers' awareness of their attitudes, motivation to reconsider their stance, and willingness to expend effort to consider new information should leave implicit attitudes untouched.

As in the case of attitude change in general, prejudice reduction interventions that have been reported in the social science literature have typically assumed that conscious mental processes must be engaged for prejudicial attitudes to change. Specifically, the working assumption was that perceivers must: (a) be aware of their bias (Banaji, 2001; Dasgupta, 2004, in press); (b) be motivated to suppress negative thoughts (Macrae, Bodenhausen, Milne, & Jetten, 1994; Macrae, Bodenhausen, Milne, & Wheeler, 1996); (c) be motivated to change their responses toward outgroups because of personal values, feelings of guilt, compunction, or self-insight (Allport, 1954; Devine, Monteith, Zuwerink, & Elliot, 1991; Monteith, 1993; Monteith, Devine, & Zuwerink, 1993; Monteith, Zuwerink, & Devine, 1994; Myrdal, 1944); (d) exert effort to seek cognitive consistency between their general egalitarian values and attitudes toward specific groups (Gaertner & Dovidio, 1986; Katz & Hass, 1988; Katz, Wackenhut, & Hass, 1986; Rockeach, 1973); (e) develop and practice correction strategies to unlearn negative stereotypes (Gawronski, Deutsch, & Mbirkou, 2007; Kawakami, Dovidio, Moll, Hermsen, & Russin, 2000); and (f) be willing and motivated to engage in intergroup contact (Pettigrew & Tropp, 2006; Tropp & Bianchi, 2006; Tropp, Stout, Boatswain, Wright, & Pettigrew, 2006). Because changing intergroup attitudes was viewed as a self-conscious relearning process, the research just cited mostly focused on changing explicit attitudes. Until recently, few attempted to modify implicit forms of prejudice and stereotyping because these were seen as inescapable habits that are expressed despite attempts to bypass or ignore them (Bargh, 1999; Devine, 1989).

The advent of new data and new theories has cast doubt on the immutability of implicit attitudes and beliefs. The challenge has come from two sources. First, empirical evidence accumulating over the past 5 years has shown that implicit attitudes shift in response to various contextual and psychological factors (for reviews see Blair, 2002; Gawronski & Bodenhausen, 2006). Second, new theoretical models have begun to refine and modify the definition of implicit social cognition (Conrey, Sherman, Gawronski, Hugenberg, & Groom, 2005; Gawronski & Bodenhausen, 2006). These theories identify the mechanisms underlying rapid reactions to in- and outgroups that occur under time pressure. These mechanisms, in turn, may help clarify why particular social contexts, internal psychological states, or individual differences evoke changes in implicit attitudes and beliefs.

COGNITIVE CONTROL INFLUENCES THE MALLEABILITY OF IMPLICIT ATTITUDES

Two theoretical models have focused on the role of cognitive control in shaping attitude expressions that are typically thought of as "implicit" (see Conrey et al., 2005, for a description of the quadruple process model; see Payne, 2001, 2005; Payne, Lambert, & Jacoby, 2002, for a description of the process dissociation procedure [PDP] as applied to implicit attitude tasks). Conrey, Payne, and their colleagues have argued that although implicit attitudes may be activated without awareness (as demonstrated by subliminal priming studies in which perceivers are unaware of seeing in- and outgroup images) and expressed under time pressure (as demonstrated by studies using speeded reaction time tasks that constrain the time allowed to respond), such responses do not rule out the role of controlled processes. In other words, attitudes measured by seemingly implicit tasks are not "process pure"; rather, they are guided by a blend of automatic and controlled processes. For example, in the case of reaction time tasks that use the speed with which people associate social groups with particular attributes to indirectly infer attitude strength, part of those speeded responses is driven by the activation of automatic associations but another part is determined by individuals' ability to selectively attend to information that facilitates accurate responses and screen out unnecessary information that hinders accurate responses. By applying theories of cognitive control to the accumulated evidence demonstrating the malleability of implicit responses, one might ask this question: Do changes in cognitive control function as one mechanism responsible for the flexibility of implicit attitudes? Might particular social contexts or psychological states increase cognitive control and is this, in turn, responsible for the alleviation of implicit bias?

ACCESSIBILITY OF AUTOMATIC ASSOCIATIONS INFLUENCES THE MALLEABILITY OF IMPLICIT ATTITUDES

A different mechanism that may underlie the flexibility of implicit attitudes toward social groups has to do with changes in the automatic associations linking particular groups to particular attributes. Several theories have argued that automatic associations are learned through repeated exposure to certain group–attribute pairings in the larger society either via firsthand experience with group members who have certain characteristics or via mediated exposure from the mass media and information learned from peers and significant others (Gawronski & Bodenhausen, 2006; Smith & DeCoster, 2000; see also Rydell & McConnell, in press; Strack & Deutsch, 2004). For example, the associative-propositional evaluation model (APE model) proposes that once group–attribute associations are learned, they are likely to be activated automatically in the presence of a relevant target person irrespective of their perceived "truth value" (i.e., whether or not the perceiver considers these evaluations to be accurate). The implication here is that while repeated learning of counterstereotypic associations may change the original automatic associations, simply being told that the information one has learned about a target group is inaccurate (i.e., information about its truth value) should not change these associations (Gawronski & Bodenhausen, 2006).

Moreover, target groups may be associated with multiple attributes in memory. Which particular group–attribute association will become activated in the presence of a particular group member depends on the goodness of fit between preexisting mental associations and a particular set of external inputs. Thus, if a particular target group (e.g., Asians) is associated with two types of attributes (intelligent and nonathletic), which attribute will become activated in the presence of an Asian person will depend on the characteristics of that particular individual, the context in which he or she is encountered, and the goodness of fit between the external situation and the associations in memory. Seeing an Asian individual in a classroom is more likely to activate the "intelligent" association and influence subsequent judgments consistent with intelligence, whereas seeing the same individual on a soccer field is more likely to activate the "nonathletic" association and lead to different sorts of judgments. In other words, shifts in implicit attitudes about a particular group may be driven by the activation of different types of automatic associations that already exist in memory. In this example, encountering a particular person in a particular situation is the trigger that activates one of the underlying associations, making it rise to threshold and get expressed in a judgment or social behavior (see also Smith & DeCoster, 2000).

These new theories (QUAD, APE, and PDP models) offer refined descriptions of implicit social cognition (attitudes, beliefs, knowledge). They suggest that implicit responses are driven by a mixture of automatic associations rendered accessible in the moment and executive control driven by internal states (e.g., motivations, goals, emotions, individual differences, etc.). Moreover, they assume that these two processes work independently to influence social behavior.

GOALS OF THIS CHAPTER

This chapter revolves around a "why" question: Why do some social contexts, some internal psychological states, and some individual differences modulate implicit attitudes and beliefs about in- and outgroups? Is a single psychological mechanism responsible for it or are multiple mechanisms responsible? Put differently, the primary purpose of this chapter is to use the distinction between automaticity and cognitive control to shed light on the conditions under which, and the mechanisms by which, implicit attitudes and beliefs about social groups change temporarily or chronically.

For purposes of this chapter, I refer to rapid judgments and evaluations made under time pressure as "implicit" because these responses are clearly driven, at least in part, by automatic processes when cognitive resources are limited. At the same time we now know that implicit attitude expressions are influenced, to varying extents, by the exertion of control. As the influence of controlled processes increases, judgments and evaluations become more intentional, effortful, and conscious.

The rest of this chapter is organized around two possible mechanisms likely to be responsible for the attenuation or exacerbation of implicit intergroup bias: changes in cognitive control and changes in the accessibility of automatic associations. I review existing research showing modulations in implicit intergroup judgments by linking each research finding to one of the two mechanisms. These links, of course, are speculative and are proposed here as predictions that need to be empirically tested in future research. Acquiring a better understanding of why implicit bias against outgroups is alleviated by some situations but not others, and by some goals, motivations, and emotions but not others, promises to provide traction in designing future interventions that might effectively tackle these subtle forms of bias.

INCREASING THE SALIENCE OF GROUP MEMBERSHIP INCREASES IMPLICIT BIAS BY ACTIVATING AUTOMATIC ASSOCIATIONS

A number of studies have found that increasing the salience of in- and outgroups magnifies implicit preference for ingroups and bias against outgroups. Some of these studies manipulated category salience by drawing perceivers' attention to target individuals' social identity (Macrae, Bodenhausen, Milne, & Calvini, 1999; Macrae, Bodenhausen, Milne, Thorn, & Castelli, 1997) or by drawing attention to perceivers' own social identity (Bohner, Seibler, Gonzalez, Haye, & Schmidt, 2007; Sassenberg & Wieber, 2005). Similarly, the presence of sufficient attentional resources has been shown to increase the activation of racial stereotypes after exposure to Asian or Black individuals compared to the absence of attentional resources (Gilbert & Hixon, 1991; Spencer, Fein, Wolfe, Fong, & Dunn, 1998).

Other studies drew attention to ingroup–outgroup distinctions by manipulating task goals or varying the exemplars used to represent particular social groups. For instance, when White participants were instructed to attend to race (i.e., asked to classify White men and Black women along racial dimensions), they exhibited implicit preference for White men and bias against Black women. However, when participants were instructed to attend to gender (i.e., asked to classify the same individuals along the dimension of gender), they exhibited implicit preference for Black women and bias against White men (Mitchell, Nosek, & Banaji, 2003). In other words, attention to race or gender determined how individuals were categorized, which in turn influenced implicit evaluations of those individuals. The pervasive tendency to prefer White Americans only emerged when perceivers' attention was drawn to race, and a similar tendency to prefer women over men only emerged when perceivers' attention was drawn to gender. When an alternative social category membership was made salient, the same individuals were evaluated quite differently.

Category salience was also enhanced by varying individual representatives of a social group using stereotype-consistent versus stereotype-inconsistent members to represent the group. Implicit evaluations of outgroups tend to be significantly more negative if individual members fit the outgroup stereotype in terms of personality, social role, or physical appearance than if they are atypical. When individuals fit the stereotype or prototype of their group, more attention is drawn to category membership, which in turn evokes more implicit bias. For example, in the context of race, Mitchell et al. (2003) found that participants expressed strong implicit White preference when racial categories were represented with infamous Black individuals and famous White individuals. However, when the likeability of individual exemplars was reversed (famous Blacks and infamous Whites), implicit favoritism for Whites became nonsignificant (see Govan & Williams, 2004, for a similar effect). Similarly, individual outgroup members who fit the prototype of their group in terms of physical appearance tend to elicit more implicit negativity than others who do not fit the prototype. As a case in point, Black individuals with African facial features (darker complexion, fuller lips, broader nose) elicited more negative evaluations from White participants than Black individuals with less African facial features (light complexion, narrow lips and nose; Blair, Judd, & Fallman, 2004; Livingston & Brewer, 2002).

The effect of attention and category salience on implicit intergroup attitudes is not limited to known groups. A similar pattern of data emerges when fictitious groups are created in the laboratory. Drawing perceivers' attention to newly created groups produces implicit preference for individuals who are presented as ingroup members and bias against others who are presented as outgroup members (Ashburn-Nardo, Voils, & Monteith, 2001; Castelli, Zogmeister, Smith, & Arcuri, 2004; Otten & Wentura, 1999).

The common theme connecting all these studies is that they all drew participants' attention to particular types of category memberships (race, gender, etc.) which in turn probably activated default automatic evaluations associated with base categories (in the case of known groups) or created new associations (in the case of fictitious groups). Indirect evidence for this speculation comes from Payne et al. (2002), who found that drawing attention to the racial dimension of a speeded weapon identification task significantly increased race stereotypic errors compared to another condition where race was not emphasized prior to task performance. When participants' responses were disaggregated into automatic and controlled components (Jacoby, 1991), Payne and colleagues found that race-biased errors in identifying weapons were entirely driven by an increase in the automatic activation of racial stereotypes in the "race salient condition" compared to the "race not salient condition," whereas cognitive control did not change across the "race salient" versus "not salient" conditions. Taken together, this finding and the others already summarized suggest that increased attention to the social category membership of outgroup members and emphasis on ingroup–outgroup distinctions facilitate the activation of default automatic evaluations linked to ingroups versus outgroups: ingroup = good and outgroup = bad.

INCREASING THE SALIENCE OF COUNTERSTEREOTYPIC CUES DECREASES IMPLICIT BIAS BY ACTIVATING DIFFERENT POSITIVE ASSOCIATIONS

Social contexts that embody counterstereotypic or stereotypic cues have been known to significantly influence implicit evaluations and judgments of target group members seen in that context. For instance, exposure to African Americans in positive situations such as a family barbeque or church decreases implicit anti-Black bias relative to no-context controls, whereas exposure to the same individuals in negative situations such as a blighted inner-city street or in prison increases implicit anti-Black bias (Barden, Maddux, Petty, & Brewer, 2004; Rudman & Lee, 2002; Wittenbrink, Judd, & Park, 2001). Similarly, situations that make salient the positive cultural and historical contributions of Arab societies decrease implicit anti-Arab bias relative to a neutral context, whereas situations that make salient news about terrorism increase anti-Arab bias relative to a neutral context (Park, Felix, & Lee, 2007).

These effects are not limited to background features of social situations. Other cues in the foreground of social situations also modulate implicit evaluations and judgments. Situations that primed exposure to counterstereotypic members of disadvantaged groups prior to the measurement of implicit attitudes and beliefs revealed a substantial decline in implicit negativity against outgroups (e.g., elderly, African Americans, gay men; Dasgupta & Greenwald, 2001; Dasgupta & Rivera, 2008) and implicit stereotyping of ingroups (e.g., women; Dasgupta & Asgari, 2004). Such reduction of implicit bias was particularly evident for individuals whose everyday social environments provided little opportunity for close contact with outgroups. Others who had a great deal of prior contact showed less outgroup bias regardless of the situational manipulation in the laboratory (Dasgupta & Rivera, 2008). The influence of counterstereotypic individuals on the reduction of implicit bias has been shown to occur and endure even in year-long longitudinal studies (Asgari, Dasgupta, & Gilbert-Cote, 2008; Dasgupta & Asgari, 2004) and is not limited to a brief moment in the laboratory. There is, however, some sobering evidence suggesting that increased contact with outgroup members appears to elicit less of an impact on the attitudes of individuals who belong to high-status groups (White Americans in the United States and Christians in Lebanon) compared to those who belong to lower status groups (Black Americans in the United States and Muslims in Lebanon, respectively; Henry & Hardin, 2006).

Another situational cue that modulates implicit attitudes is perceivers' social role relative to their interaction partners. Specifically, White participants or male participants who anticipate an impending cross-race or cross-gender interaction where their interaction partner is in a superior (counterstereotypic) role exhibit less outgroup bias than others who anticipate interacting with an outgroup member who is in a subordinate (stereotypic) role (Richeson & Ambady, 2001, 2003). At the same time, however, cross-gender interactions with a woman in a superior (rather than subordinate) role cause men to implicitly compensate and stereotype themselves as more masculine (McCall & Dasgupta, 2007).

Such situation-driven changes in implicit bias are likely to be elicited by the activation of different mental associations linking social groups to counterstereotypic attributes (see Gawronski & Bodenhausen, 2006). Although stereotypic associations have greater accessibility in default situations or decontextualized experimental situations, the introduction of counterstereotypic cues (background features of situations, social roles of interaction partners, counterstereotypic individuals) enhances the accessibility of other (counterstereotypic) associations linked to target groups. Such cues may also suppress the accessibility of stereotypic associations if stereotypic and counterstereotypic attributes are perceived to be bipolar constructs that cannot be activated simultaneously (see Greenwald et al., 2002; Heider, 1958). Moreover, long-term immersion in counterstereotypic social contexts may reduce the default accessibility of stereotypes or enhance the chronic accessibility of counterstereotypes, thereby decreasing the likelihood of biased automatic judgments and evaluations in the future.

SPECIFIC MOTIVATIONS CAN INCREASE OR DECREASE IMPLICIT BIAS BY CHANGING IN COGNITIVE CONTROL

Although rapid evaluations and judgments under extreme time pressure have been typically assumed to bypass motivational processes, accumulating evidence has begun to reveal that chronic individual differences in motivation as well as situationally triggered motivation modulate implicit judgments of in- and outgroups. The specific source of motivation may be perceivers' emotional state, desire to protect self-esteem or group esteem, motivation to control prejudice, or a generalized capacity for executive control. Moreover, depending on the specific circumstance, motivation may decrease or increase implicit bias.

EMOTION AS A SOURCE OF MOTIVATION

In one program of research we have found that when people experience certain discrete emotions (e.g., anger, disgust) that are associated with motivations to aggress or avoid, the residue of the emotion spills over from the original source to bias implicit evaluations of real and fictitious groups, even when the emotion-inducing source is unrelated to social groups (Dasgupta, DeSteno, Pressman, Williams, & Hunsinger, Yogeeswaran, & Ashby, 2007; DeSteno, Dasgupta, Bartlett, & Cajdric, 2004). Interestingly, the biasing effect of emotion on outgroup evaluations only occurs for intergroup negative emotions (e.g., anger and disgust), not all negative emotions (e.g. sadness).

Moreover, although both anger and disgust are capable of creating implicit bias against previously neutral and unknown outgroups, these two emotions have differential effects on appraisals of known outgroups. Specifically, incidental feelings of anger (but not disgust) exacerbate implicit bias against Arabs and incidental feelings of disgust (but not anger) increase implicit bias against gays and lesbians (Dasgupta et al., 2007). We propose that because disgust is elicited by physical or moral contaminants, and because gays and lesbians are perceived to violate mainstream moral values about "appropriate" sexual behavior (Cottrell & Neuberg, 2005; Herek, 1996; Mosher & O'Grady, 1979; Nussbaum, 1999), incidental feelings of disgust are experienced as applicable to this group and thus have a spillover effect.

Similarly, because anger is elicited when people confront obstacles, and experience threats to their economic resources, freedoms, and rights (Cottrell & Neuberg, 2005; Fiske, Cuddy, Glick, & Xu, 2002; Mackie, Devos, & Smith, 2000; Smith, 1993), and because contemporary stereotypes of Arabs include anger-relevant attributes (Park et al., 2007), when people feel angry for incidental reasons, that emotion spills over into appraisals of Arabs. Our data showed that anger increased anti-Arab bias by depleting cognitive control (Dasgupta et al., 2007). Specifically, angry participants' erroneous evaluations were driven by a significant reduction in controlled processing compared to others who felt neutral or disgusted.

SELF-IMAGE THREAT AND SOCIAL IDENTITY THREAT AS A SOURCE OF MOTIVATION

Motivation to maintain a positive self-image or ingroup image also influences implicit attitudes toward outgroups. Self-threat and social identity threat have been found to increase implicit stereotyping and prejudice (Gonsalkorale, Carlisle, & von Hippel, 2007; Spencer et al., 1998) and to enhance collective self-esteem postjudgment (Gonsalkorale et al., 2007). The implication here is that threats to self-esteem and group esteem motivate people to derogate a target outgroup as a way of recovering positive self-regard or ingroup regard.

Similarly, criticism from an outgroup member increases implicit outgroup bias, whereas praise decreases outgroup bias. Specifically, White participants who had received praise from a Black or Asian person in a higher status role (e.g., manager, doctor, or experimenter) subsequently exhibited less implicit stereotypes about the relevant outgroup compared to others who had received criticism from the same person (Sinclair & Kunda, 1999). These data imply that praise validates perceivers' self-esteem and motivates them to like the praise-bearing messenger (outgroup member) and others in his or her group, whereas criticism invalidates their positive self-esteem and motivates them to dislike the criticism-bearing messenger and others in that outgroup.

In the studies mentioned earlier, self-esteem threat and social identity threat may have operated by modulating cognitive control. Specifically, threat may have decreased the motivation to be accurate by exerting control, which in turn increased stereotypic responses, whereas praise may have increased the motivation to be accurate by exerting control, which reduced stereotypic responses. In addition, self-threat and social identity threat may have also increased the accessibility of negative associations linked to the particular outgroup.

PROMOTION AND PREVENTION FOCUS AS A SOURCE OF MOTIVATION

Recent research has found that individuals' regulatory states (i.e., whether they are oriented toward accruing gains [promotion focus] or avoiding losses [prevention focus] influence their implicit attitudes toward groups that vary in power (Sassenberg, Jonas, Shah, & Brazy, 2007). Specifically, higher power ingroups are more likely to meet the regulatory needs of individuals with a promotion focus than a prevention focus because such ingroups give promotion-focused individuals the opportunity to pursue their ideals (e.g., to seek achievement, nurturance, etc.). Conversely, lower power ingroups meet the regulatory needs of individuals with a prevention focus more than a promotion focus because such ingroups allow their members to pursue behaviors that focus on safety and security to prevent losses. As predicted, Sassenberg and colleagues found that high-power ingroups were more implicitly favored by their members who had a promotion focus rather than a prevention focus, whereas lower power ingroups were more implicitly favored by their members who had a prevention focus rather than promotion focus.

Regulatory focus may have influenced cognitive control. Specifically, promotion focus may have increased individuals' motivation to attend to the desirable qualities of high-power ingroups, whereas prevention focus may have increased their motivation to attend to the positive qualities of lower power ingroups. In addition, changes in attention consistent with regulatory focus may have also changed the accessibility of particular attributes linked to in- and outgroups.

SOCIAL NORMS AS A SOURCE OF MOTIVATION

A classic finding in social psychology is that people tend to conform to norms in their social environment because they are motivated to be liked by, and be similar to, their peer group (Asch, 1955, 1956). As such, individuals who become aware that their opinions are out of sync with their peers tend to shift their attitudes toward the peer group. This normative influence is also apparent when it comes to implicit attitudes. Sechrist and Stangor (2001) found that participants' implicit beliefs about African Americans became less stereotypic if they discovered that their peer group was more egalitarian than themselves compared to a situation in which they had no information about peer opinion. However, participants' beliefs became more stereotypic if they discovered that their peer group was less egalitarian than themselves compared to "no information" controls. As in the case of Asch's famous conformity experiments, these shifts in implicit attitudes point to the role of normative influence; they suggest that awareness of social norms increased participants' motivation to be similar to their peers, which subsequently increased the degree to which they attempted to control and modify their outgroup evaluations to fit in.

MOTIVATION TO CONTROL PREJUDICE

Aside from situationally triggered motivations of the sort already described, individual differences in chronic motivation also affect implicit attitudes. For example, individual differences in motivation to control prejudice are known to moderate implicit racial attitudes in systematic ways.

Correlational research has found that people who are highly motivated to control prejudice show less implicit race bias than their less motivated peers. Moreover, although lower race bias is correlated with greater cognitive control, it is not correlated with race-biased automatic associations (Payne, 2005). Experimentally induced motivation (i.e., being reminded of one's past race-based transgressions) also decreases bias in subsequent behavior especially among people who are implicitly prejudiced yet explicitly egalitarian (i.e., aversive racists; Son Hing, Li, & Zanna, 2002; also see Son Hing, Chung-Yan, Grunfeld, Robichaud, & Zanna, 2005).

In some cases, however, high motivation to control prejudice can backfire and increase race bias if people are explicitly made aware that the task they are about to complete reveals racial prejudice for the majority of test-takers (Frantz, Cuddy, Burnett, Ray, & Hart, 2004; but see Nier, 2005). As Frantz and colleagues noted, this ironic effect may occur because individuals with high motivation to control prejudice are likely to be concerned about their own unintentional bias when made aware of the nature of the task; this concern in turn may interfere with their usual capacity to respond accurately (see Richeson, Baird, & Gordon, 2003; Richeson & Shelton, 2003). In addition to reduced cognitive control, concern about appearing prejudiced may also lead people to monitor stereotypic thoughts, which may inadvertently increase the accessibility of racial stereotypes revealed in subsequent judgments (see Wegner, 1994).

GLOBAL EXECUTIVE CONTROL AS A SOURCE OF ACCURACY MOTIVATION

Behavioral expressions of implicit stereotypes and prejudice may also be shaped by individual differences in people's capacity for executive control in general—this refers to basic attentional capacities that allow people to selectively attend to information that is relevant to the task goals at hand and simultaneously screen out other information that is irrelevant to those goals (Macrae, Bodenhausen, Schloerscheidt, & Milne, 1999; Payne, 2005). With one exception (Payne, 2005) there is little research examining the relationship between global executive control and implicit stereotypes and prejudice. Payne (2005) reported correlational evidence showing that individuals who exhibited better executive control on a task unrelated to social groups also showed more controlled processing and less bias against African Americans on a number of race-based speeded tasks (e.g., weapons identification task, evaluative priming task, and Implicit Association Test). Moreover, global executive control was uncorrelated with motivation to control prejudice.

Indirect evidence for the benefit of global executive control comes from research that examines the role of practice and training (i.e., improvement in executive control) on the accuracy of intergroup judgments. Specifically, Correll et al. (2007) compared police officers' and community members' decisions to shoot (or not shoot) Black and White men in a law enforcement simulation. They found that trained police officers outperformed community members in terms of overall speed and accuracy. Moreover, whereas community respondents used a relaxed decision criterion to shoot Black compared to White targets (thereby making more race-biased errors), police officers used a stricter criterion. However, both samples exhibited robust race bias in response speed. These data suggest that training (and presumably increased executive control as a result of it) encourages the selection of a stricter decision criterion before shooting, although it does not affect the speed with which stereotype-incongruent targets are processed.

Given the suggested benefit of global executive control, one avenue for future research is an investigation of whether such control moderates the effectiveness of social environments; that is, when immersed in counterstereotypic social environments, do individuals with better executive control exhibit a steeper decline in implicit bias compared to their peers who have less executive control?

THE INFLUENCE OF CONTEXTUAL CUES IS MODERATED BY INDIVIDUAL AND GROUP DIFFERENCES: THE COMBINED RULE OF AUTOMATIC ASSOCIATIONS AND COGNITIVE CONTROL

Initial research on the flexibility of implicit attitudes focused either on the role of social contexts or on the role of motivational processes, but not both. Collectively, this research illustrated that different types of situational cues and internal states change implicit appraisals of in- and outgroups. But what about the combined effect of social context and individual difference? Only a handful of studies have examined this question; they have found that the effect of social contexts on implicit attitudes is dependent on: (a) people's motivation to control prejudice (Maddux, Barden, Brewer, & Petty, 2005); (b) individual differences in social dominance (Pratto & Shih, 2000); (c) chronic beliefs in a dangerous world (Schaller, Park, & Mueller, 2003); and (d) perceivers' ingroup membership (Kühnen, Schießl,, and Bauer, 2001; Lowery, Hardin, & Sinclair, 2001).

For example, when African Americans and White Americans were seen in negative social contexts (e.g., jail, foggy road), White perceivers' reactions depended on individual differences in their motivation to control prejudice. Whereas individuals who were not motivated to control prejudice exhibited implicit ingroup preference for Whites, others who were highly motivated to control prejudice showed the reverse effect: they exhibited outgroup preference for Blacks (Maddux et al., 2005). These race-based evaluations were driven by slower reaction to stereotypic (Black-negative) associations. Analogously, Schaller and colleagues (2003) found that participants who harbored chronic beliefs that the world is a dangerous place showed more implicit bias against African Americans when placed in a potentially ominous situation (darkened room) compared to a less ominous situation (well-lit room), but others who did not share these chronic beliefs showed no changes in implicit attitudes as a function of context. Similarly, individual differences in social dominance modulated the magnitude of outgroup bias when perceivers' ingroup status was threatened. Individuals high in social dominance exhibited more ingroup favoritism and outgroup derogation than others who were low in social dominance, but only when the high status of their ingroup was called into question (Pratto & Shih, 2000).

Perceivers' group membership also moderates the effect of counterstereotypic social cues on implicit racial attitudes. For example, Lowery et al. (2001) found that whereas White participants exhibited substantially less implicit preference for Whites after interacting with a Black compared to a White experimenter, Asian participants' implicit racial attitudes did not vary as a function of experimenter race. Along the same lines, Kühnen et al. (2001) compared the impact of increasing the salience of ingroup identity on implicit intergroup attitudes. They predicted and found that when people's ingroup was positively stereotyped (e.g., being West German), increasing the salience of group identity exacerbated implicit ingroup favoritism but when people's ingroup was negatively stereotyped (e.g., being East German), increasing the salience of group identity attenuated ingroup favoritism.

The common theme running through these findings is that some individual- and group-level variables influence the degree of motivation and control people are willing or able to invest in ensuring that their rapid responses to in- and outgroups are accurate. Those who are highly motivated to control prejudice, those who do not believe that the world is a dangerous place, and those who belong to an advantaged group that historically has been the agent of discrimination, may all be particularly invested in monitoring and controlling their evaluative reactions in a racial context to override potentially biased automatic reactions. Thus, although stereotypic contextual cues enhance the accessibility of automatic stereotypes for everybody, increased motivation to control prejudice may trigger efforts to exert control, thereby overriding potential biases even in time-pressured situations.

LEARNING AND UNLEARNING IMPLICIT ATTITUDES: THE ROLE OF COGNITIVE CONTROL AND AUTOMATIC ASSOCIATIONS

Attitude change in general, and prejudice reduction in particular, requires unlearning old attitudes and learning new ones. Prejudice change is typically thought to occur when people consciously invest effort to reconsider old attitudes in light of new information or when they learn to suppress thoughts that are seen as invalid or inappropriate and replace them with new thoughts. To what extent do such conscious unlearning and learning strategies influence implicit attitudes toward social groups? If such strategies have an impact, do they change the accessibility of preexisting associations, change cognitive control, or both? Does the type of target group influence the effectiveness of learning and unlearning? Does expertise influence learning and unlearning? Recent research has begun to address some of these questions.

Learning and Unlearning Attitudes by Mere Instruction Versus Concrete Strategies

Research shows that even when people are made aware that their attitudes toward disadvantaged groups are being measured, and they are explicitly instructed to respond in an egalitarian manner, their implicit attitudes continue to exhibit bias against African Americans and gay men—although their explicit attitudes become less biased (Banse, Seise, & Zerbes, 2001; Kim, 2003). In fact, explicit instructions to suppress preexisting stereotypes have been known to produce an ironic effect in some studies by exacerbating the activation of implicit stereotypes (Galinsky & Moskowitz, 2000; Macrae et al., 1994). This is probably because bias suppression instructions actively draw people's attention to outgroup membership and enhance the accessibility of default stereotypic associations.

However, when instructions offer a concrete strategy that people can use to consciously override implicit bias, outgroup bias is attenuated. For example, participants who received a specific implementation intention to avoid gender stereotypes from biasing their judgments of an individual were able to control and reduce implicit stereotyping (Moskowitz, Gollwitzer, Wasel, & Schaal, 1999). Similarly, participants who received concrete instructions on how to modify their rapid race-based responses on a reaction time task were able to reduce implicit race bias (Kim, 2003). Likewise, others who were told to expect counterstereotypic information when they thought of women and men also showed reduced implicit gender stereotyping (Blair & Banaji, 1996).

Another type of concrete strategy that produces beneficial effects involves instructing people to mentally elaborate on the positive or counterstereotypic qualities of outgroups. Cognitive elaboration is likely to enhance the accessibility of counterstereotypic attributes associated with target groups that emerge with greater strength in subsequent implicit evaluations. For example, a number of studies have found that when people were instructed to imagine and describe women with counterstereotypic qualities they subsequently showed reduced implicit gender stereotyping compared with others who were not asked to engage in such cognitive elaboration or, alternatively, who were asked to describe women with stereotypic qualities (Blair, Ma, & Lenton, 2001; Carpenter, 2001). Cognitive elaboration also works somewhat indirectly by making salient the subjective ease of recalling well-liked members of an outgroup or the difficulty of recalling disliked members of the same group (Gawronski & Bodenhausen, 2005).

Just as instructions to think about the positive qualities of disfavored outgroups significantly attenuate previously ingrained implicit bias, the subsequent generation of negative thoughts increases outgroup bias again (Akalis & Banaji, 2008). Interestingly, the more skilled people are at mental discipline through yoga and meditation, the better they are at reducing implicit bias even when given a fairly open-ended instruction to reduce their prejudice "by whatever mental means possible" or to generate feelings of compassion and kindness toward a particularly disliked outgroup (Akalis & Banaji, 2008). Activating a creative mindset has a similar effect by reducing implicit stereotyping (Sassenberg & Moskowitz, 2005). In both these cases, experimental instructions may spontaneously increase elaboration about the positive qualities possessed by outgroup members;

alternatively, they may increase positive affect directed at the outgroup without elaboration about the specific reasons.

Other types of mental elaboration have been shown to attenuate implicit outgroup bias: People who read about multiculturalism and elaborated on the benefits of celebrating interethnic diversity subsequently exhibited less implicit race bias than others who read about color-blind values and elaborated on the benefits of ignoring group membership (Richeson & Nussbaum, 2004; but see Smyth & Nosek, 2007). Similarly, when college students thought about and elaborated on the benefits of diversity during a semester-long class on intergroup relations and diversity, they subsequently showed reduced implicit race bias in a pretest–posttest field study (Rudman, Ashmore, & Gary, 2001).

However, cognitive elaboration can sometimes backfire on perceivers who are ambivalently prejudiced. Specifically, Maio, Haddock, Watt, and Hewstone (in press) found that racially ambivalent participants (but not nonambivalent participants) who encountered antiracism advertisements exhibited an increase in implicit race bias when the ad presented weak arguments, suggesting that these participants were motivated to scrutinize the quality of the advertisement carefully and found it wanting.

Taken together, a common theme underlying the studies just mentioned is that when people engage in cognitive elaboration exercises that increase the salience of counterstereotypes or that encourage a different way of thinking, such directed thinking increases the accessibility of counterstereotypic associations linked to outgroups, which in turn temporarily alleviates implicit bias against outgroups. In other words, even when implicit judgments are made in highly time-pressured situations they can be debiased if people acquire concrete strategies that allow them to override and modify their automatic responses. These strategies function as detailed action plans on how to exert control whereas the mere instruction to avoid bias is clearly not sufficient and sometimes even counterproductive. The only time cognitive elaboration boomerangs and increases implicit prejudice is when perceivers are ambivalently biased to begin with and they encounter information that presents weak arguments in favor of egalitarianism.

So far, there appear to be two exceptions to the failure of "mere instruction" strategies: Mere instructions to decrease implicit bias appear to work for: (a) a group of participants with special training in mental discipline; and (b) fictitious attitude objects (social groups) created in the laboratory rather than real ones. In the first case, people who are skilled at mental discipline through the practice of yoga and meditation appear to be particularly good at decreasing implicit bias even when they are given a fairly open-ended instruction to reduce their prejudice "by whatever mental means possible" or when they are instructed to generate feelings of compassion and kindness toward a particularly disliked outgroup (Akalis & Banaji, 2008).

In the second case, the simple instruction to imagine a fictitious group as possessing positive (or negative) qualities appears to be sufficient to create new implicit attitudes that are consistent with the imagined quality (Gregg, Seibt, & Banaji, 2006). Although a mere suggestion can create implicit attitudes toward unknown groups from thin air, once these attitudes are formed they are more difficult to unlearn compared to their explicit counterparts. For example, Gregg and colleagues (2006) found that although implicit and explicit attitudes toward hypothetical social groups were influenced by the valence of information initially presented about these groups, when participants were later told that the initial information was false and the truth was actually the opposite of what they had initially learned, this new information either had no unlearning effect (Experiment 3) or a weak effect (Experiment 4) on implicit attitudes; however, it had a strong unlearning effect on explicit attitudes.

Conceptually similar results have been obtained for implicit attitudes toward unknown individuals (Petty et al., 2006; Rydell & McConnell, in press). For example, Petty and colleagues (2006) found that once initial attitudes had been formed about unfamiliar individuals, later invalidation of the initial information reversed explicit attitudes toward those individuals but could not reverse (albeit neutralized) implicit attitudes. The take-home message of these studies is that once people have acquired knowledge and opinions about groups and individuals, simply informing them that their knowledge is false does not allow them to reverse their responses through sheer willpower and control, nor does it change the accessibility of underlying mental associations (see Gawronski & Bodenhausen, 2006).

LEARNING AND UNLEARNING ATTITUDES BY EXTENDED TRAINING

An alternative way of modifying preexisting attitudes about known groups is to allow opportunities for extended training (rather than providing simple instruction) to enhance the accessibility of counterstereotypic associations about historically stereotyped groups. Several studies have found that when stimuli representing one social group (e.g., old people, African Americans, Asian, a fictitious group) were repeatedly paired with positive attributes, and stimuli representing a contrasting group were repeatedly paired with negative attributes (e.g., young people, White Americans, European), such extended training changed implicit intergroup evaluations (Gawronski, LeBel, Heilpern, & Wilbur, 2007, Experiment 2; Glaser, 1999, Experiment 2; Karpinski & Hilton, 2001; Olson & Fazio, 2006). Similarly, when participants were extensively trained to negate stereotypes (Kawakami et al., 2000) or affirm counterstereotypes (Gawronski et al., 2008) their implicit evaluations of target groups became less stereotypic compared to others who were trained to affirm stereotypes or who received no training at all. Recent research suggests that affirming counterstereotypes is a more effective way of reducing implicit stereotypes than negating stereotypes (Gawronski et al., 2007). Clearly, all these interventions work by temporarily changing the accessibility of underlying automatic associations about specific groups. However, they also require that perceivers be willing to engage in fairly effortful and intentional training processes and are thus quite different from situational interventions where incidental cues in the social context provide an indirect means of changing automatic associations about social groups.

CONCLUSION AND NEW DIRECTIONS

Although implicit prejudices and preferences are pervasive and reflective of stable societal inequalities, at an individual level these attitudes are remarkably flexible. Even when individuals' cognitive resources are depleted, their response time is tightly constrained, or they have limited awareness of the implications of their actions, individuals' behaviors continue to be remarkably pliable. This chapter highlighted two of the possible mechanisms that are likely to be responsible for driving the attenuation versus exacerbation of implicit bias depending on the situation: changes in automatic associations about social groups and changes in cognitive control over one's behavior. Generally speaking, situations that draw attention to social group membership, stereotypic or counterstereotypic group members, and status differences in social roles, and situations that offer extended training with counterstereotypic individuals are likely to change the magnitude of implicit bias by influencing the accessibility of particular group-related qualities. In comparison, situations that evoke specific motivations due to perceivers' emotions, normative influences, self-image or social identity threat, and particular individual differences are likely to modulate the magnitude of implicit bias via different route—by guiding the ebb and flow of cognitive control. Because little empirical research has directly pinpointed the underlying mechanisms driving specific shifts in implicit attitudes toward in- and outgroups, the goal of this chapter was to generate process-oriented hypotheses for future research based on indirect evidence. A deeper knowledge of the processes by which implicit intergroup attitudes change promises to inform other important questions such as how chronic versus temporary these changes are. And when might particular bias reduction strategies be translated from laboratory paradigms to real-world interventions?

REFERENCES

Akalis, S., & Banaji, M. R. (2008). *Do-it-yourself mental makeovers: Self-generated associations shift implicit references.* Manuscript in preparation, Harvard University, Cambridge, MA.

Allport, G. W. (1954). *The nature of prejudice.* Reading, MA: Addison-Wesley.

Asch, S. E. (1955). Opinions and social pressure. *Scientific American, 193,* 31–35.

Asch, S. E. (1956). Studies of independence and conformity: I. A minority of one against a unanimous majority. *Psychological Monographs, 70,* 70.

Asgari, S., Dasgupta, N., & Gilbert-Cote, N. (2008). *The influence of female leaders on women's implicit self-concept: Investigations in the lab and field.* Manuscript under review.

Ashburn-Nardo, L., Voils, C. I., & Monteith, M. J. (2001). Implicit associations as the seeds of intergroup bias: How easily do they take root? *Journal of Personality and Social Psychology, 81,* 789–799.

Banaji, M. R. (2001). Implicit attitudes can be measured. In H. L. Roediger, III & J. S. Nairne (Eds.), The nature of remembering: *Essays in honor of Robert G. Crowder* (pp. 117–150). Washington, DC: American Psychological Association.

Banaji, M. R., & Greenwald, A. G. (1994). Implicit stereotyping and prejudice. In M. P. Zanna & J. M. Olson (Eds.), *The psychology of prejudice: The Ontario symposium* (Vol. 7, pp. 55–76). Mahwah, NJ: Erlbaum.

Banse, R., Seise, J., & Zerbes, N. (2001). Implicit attitudes towards homosexuality: Reliability, validity, and controllability of the IAT. *Zeitschrift für Experimentelle Psychologie, 48,* 145–160.

Barden, J., Maddux, W. W., Petty, R. E., & Brewer, M. B. (2004). Contextual moderation of racial bias: The impact of social roles on controlled and automatically activated attitudes. *Journal of Personality and Social Psychology, 87,* 5–22.

Bargh, J. A. (1994). The four horsemen of automaticity: Awareness, intention, efficiency, and control in social cognition. In R. S. Wyer & T. K. Srull (Eds.), *Handbook of social cognition* (2nd ed., Vol. 1, pp. 1–40). Hillsdale, NJ: Erlbaum.

Bargh, J. A. (1997). The automaticity of everyday life. In R. S. Wyer, Jr. (Ed.), *The automaticity of everyday life: Advances in social cognition* (Vol. 10, pp. 1–61). Mahwah, NJ: Erlbaum.

Bargh, J. A. (1999). The cognitive monster: The case against the controllability of automatic stereotype effects. In S. Chaiken & Y. Trope (Eds.), *Dual-process theories in social psychology* (pp. 361–382). New York: Guilford.

Blair, I. V. (2002). The malleability of automatic stereotypes and prejudice. *Personality and Social Psychology Review, 6,* 242–261.

Blair, I. V., & Banaji, M. R. (1996). Automatic and controlled processes in stereotype priming. *Journal of Personality & Social Psychology, 70,* 1142–1163.

Blair, I. V., Judd, C. A., & Fallman, J. L. (2004). The automaticity of race and Afrocentric facial features in social judgments. *Journal of Personality and Social Psychology, 87,* 763–778.

Blair, I. V., Ma, J. E., & Lenton, A. P. (2001). Imagining stereotypes away: The moderation of implicit stereotypes through mental imagery. *Journal of Personality and Social Psychology, 81,* 828–841.

Bohner, G., Seibler, F., Gonzalez, R., Haye, A., & Schmidt, E. A. (2007). *Changing implicit group evaluations by priming social identities: The case of people with dual (Turkish/German) national identity.* Manuscript under review.

Carpenter, S. J. (2001). *Implicit gender attitudes.* Unpublished manuscript, Yale University, New Haven, CT.

Castelli, L., Zogmeister, C., Smith, E. R., & Arcuri, L. (2004). On the automatic evaluation of social exemplars. *Journal of Personality and Social Psychology, 86,* 373–387.

Conrey, F. R., Sherman, J. W., Gawronski, B., Hugenberg, K., & Groom, C. J. (2005). Separating multiple processes in implicit social cognition: The quad model of implicit task performance. *Journal of Personality and Social Psychology, 89,* 469–487.

Correll, J., Park, B., Judd, C. M., Wittenbrink, B., Sadler, M. S., & Keesee, T. (2007). Across the thin blue line: Police officers and racial bias in the decision to shoot. *Journal of Personality and Social Psychology, 92,* 1006–1023.

Cottrell, C. A., & Neuberg, S. L. (2005). Different emotional reactions to different groups: A sociofunctional threat-based approach to "prejudice." *Journal of Personality and Social Psychology, 88,* 770–789.

Dasgupta, N. (2004). Implicit ingroup favoritism, outgroup favoritism, and their behavioral manifestations. *Social Justice Research, 17,* 143–169.

Dasgupta, N. (in press). Color lines in the mind: Unconscious prejudice, discriminatory behavior, and the potential for change. In A. Grant-Thomas & G. Orfield (Eds.), *21st century color lines: Exploring the frontiers of America's multicultural future.*

Dasgupta, N., & Asgari, S. (2004). Seeing is believing: Exposure to counterstereotypic women leaders and its effect on automatic gender stereotyping. *Journal of Experimental Social Psychology, 40,* 642–658.

Dasgupta, N., DeSteno, D. A., Pressman, A., Williams, L., Yogeeswaran, K., Hunsinger, M., & Ashby, J. (2007). A tale of emotion specificity: *Behavioral and ERP evidence for the effect of incidental emotions in implicit prejudice.* Manuscript in preparation.

Dasgupta, N., & Greenwald, A. G. (2001). On the malleability of automatic attitudes: Combating automatic prejudice with images of admired and disliked individuals. *Journal of Personality and Social Psychology, 81,* 800–814.

Dasgupta, N., & Rivera, L. M. (2008). When social context matters: The influence of long-term contact and short-term exposure to admired outgroup members on implicit attitudes and behavioral intentions. *Social Cognition, 26,* 54–66.

DeSteno, D. A., Dasgupta, N., Bartlett, M. Y., & Cajdric, A. (2004). Prejudice from thin air: The effect of emotion on automatic intergroup attitudes. *Psychological Science, 15,* 319–324.

Devine, P. G. (1989). Stereotypes and prejudice: Their automatic and controlled components. *Journal of Personality and Social Psychology, 56,* 5–18.

Devine, P. G., Monteith, M. J., Zuwerink, J. R., & Elliot, A. J. (1991). Prejudice with and without compunction. *Journal of Personality and Social Psychology, 60,* 817–830.

Fiske, S. T., Cuddy, A. J. C., Glick, P., & Xu, J. (2002). A model of (often mixed) stereotype content: Competence and warmth respectively follow from perceived status and competition. *Journal of Personality and Social Psychology, 82,* 878–902.

Frantz, C. M., Cuddy, A. J. C., Burnett, M., Ray, H., & Hart, A. (2004). A threat in the computer: The race Implicit Association Test as a stereotype threat experience. *Personality and Social Psychology Bulletin, 30,* 1611–1624.

Gaertner, S. L., & Dovidio, J. F. (1986). An aversive form of racism. In J. F. Dovidio & S. L. Gaertner (Eds.), *Prejudice, discrimination, and racism* (pp. 61–89). New York: Academic.

Galinsky, A. D., & Moskowitz, G. B. (2000). Perspective-taking: Decreasing stereotype expression, stereotype accessibility, and in-group favoritism. *Journal of Personality and Social Psychology, 78,* 708–724.

Gawronski, B., & Bodenhausen, G. V. (2005). Accessibility effects on implicit social cognition: The role of knowledge activation and retrieval experiences. *Journal of Personality and Social Psychology, 89,* 672–685.

Gawronski, B., & Bodenhausen, G. V. (2006). Associative and propositional processes in evaluation: An integrative review of implicit and explicit attitude change. *Psychological Bulletin, 132,* 692–731.

Gawronski, B., Deutsch, R., Mbirkou, S., Seibt, B., & Strack, F. (2008). When "just say no" is not enough: Affirmation vs. negation training and the reduction of automatic stereotype activation. *Journal of Experimental Social Psychology, 44*(2), 370–377.

Gawronski, B., LeBel, E. P., Heilpern, K., & Wilbur, C. J. (2007). *Understanding the relative robustness of implicit and explicit attitudes: A test of the associative-propositional evaluation model.* Manuscript under review.

Gilbert, D. T., & Hixon, J. G. (1991). The trouble of thinking: Activation and application of stereotypic beliefs. *Journal of Personality and Social Psychology, 60,* 509–517.

Glaser, J. C. (1999). *The relation between stereotyping and prejudice: Measures of newly formed automatic associations.* Unpublished manuscript, Yale University, New Haven, CT.

Gonsalkorale, K., Carlisle, K., & von Hippel, W. (2007). Intergroup threat increases implicit stereotyping. *International Journal of Psychology and Psychological Therapy, 1,* 189–200.

Govan, C. L., & Williams, K. D. (2004). Changing the affective valence of the stimulus items influences the IAT by re-defining the category labels. *Journal of Experimental Social Psychology, 40,* 357–365.

Greenwald, A. G., & Banaji, M. R. (1995). Implicit social cognition: Attitudes, self-esteem, and stereotypes. *Psychological Review, 102,* 4–27.

Greenwald, A. G., Banaji, M. R., Rudman, L. A., Farnham, S. D., Nosek, B. A., & Mellott, D. S. (2002). A unified theory of implicit attitudes, stereotypes, self-esteem, and self-concept. *Psychological Review, 109,* 3–25.

Gregg, A. P., Seibt, B., & Banaji, M. R. (2006). Easier done than undone: Asymmetry in the malleability of implicit preferences. *Journal of Personality and Social Psychology, 90,* 1–20.

Heider, F. (1958). *The psychology of interpersonal relations.* Hoboken, NJ: Wiley.

Henry, P. J., & Hardin, C. D. (2006). The contact hypothesis revisited: Status bias in the reduction of implicit prejudice in the United States and Lebanon. *Psychological Science, 17,* 862–868.

Herek, G. M. (1996). Heterosexism and homophobia. In R. P. Cabaj & T. S. Stein (Eds.), *Textbook of homosexuality and mental health* (pp. 101–113). Washington, DC: American Psychiatric Association.

Jacoby, L. L. (1991). A process dissociation framework: Separating automatic from intentional uses of memory. *Journal of Memory and Language, 30,* 513–541.

Karpinski, A., & Hilton, J. L. (2001). Attitudes and the Implicit Association Test. *Journal of Personality and Social Psychology, 81,* 774–788.

Katz, I., & Hass, R. G. (1988). Racial ambivalence and American value conflict: Correlational and priming studies of dual cognitive structures. *Journal of Personality and Social Psychology, 55,* 893–905.

Katz, I., Wackenhut, J., & Hass, R. G. (1986). Racial ambivalence, value duality, and behavior. In J. F. Dovidio & S. L. Gaertner (Eds.), *Prejudice, discrimination, and racism* (pp. 35–60). New York: Academic.

Kawakami, K., Dovidio, J. F., Moll, J., Hermsen, S., & Russin, A. (2000). Just say no (to stereotyping): Effect of training in the negation of stereotypic associations on stereotype activation. *Journal of Personality and Social Psychology, 78,* 871–888.

Kihlstrom, J. F. (1990). The psychological unconscious. In L. A. Pervin (Ed.), *Handbook of personality: Theory and research* (pp. 445–464). New York: Guilford.

Kim, D.-Y. (2003). Voluntary controllability of the Implicit Association Test (IAT). *Social Psychology Quarterly, 66,* 83–96.

Kühnen, U., Schießl, M., & Bauer, N. (2001). How robust is the IAT? Measuring and manipulating implicit attitudes of East- and West-Germans. *Zeitschrift für Experimentelle Psychologie, 48,* 135–144.

Livingston, R. W., & Brewer, M. B. (2002). What are we really priming? Cue-based versus category-based processing of facial stimuli. *Journal of Personality and Social Psychology, 82,* 5–18.

Lowery, B. S., Hardin, C. D., & Sinclair, S. (2001). Social influence effects on automatic racial prejudice. *Journal of Personality and Social Psychology, 81,* 842–855.

Mackie, D. M., Devos, T., & Smith, E. R. (2000). Intergroup emotions: Explaining offensive action tendencies in an intergroup context. *Journal of Personality and Social Psychology, 79,* 602–616.

Macrae, C. N., Bodenhausen, G. V., Milne, A. B., & Calvini, G. (1999). Seeing more than we can know: Visual attention and category activation. *Journal of Experimental Social Psychology, 35,* 590–602.

Macrae, C. N., Bodenhausen, G. V., Milne, A. B., & Jetten, J. (1994). Out of mind but back in sight: Stereotypes on the rebound. *Journal of Personality and Social Psychology, 67,* 808–817.

Macrae, C. N., Bodenhausen, G. V., Milne, A. B., Thorn, T. M. J., & Castelli, L. (1997). On the activation of social stereotypes: The moderating role of processing objectives. *Journal of Experimental Social Psychology, 33,* 471–489.

Macrae, C. N., Bodenhausen, G. V., Milne, A. B., & Wheeler, V. (1996). On resisting the temptation for simplification: Counterintentional effects of stereotype suppression on social memory. *Social Cognition, 14,* 1–20.

Macrae, C. N., Bodenhausen, G. V., Schloerscheidt, A., & Milne, A. B. (1999). Tales of the unexpected: Executive function and person perception. *Journal of Personality and Social Psychology, 76,* 200–213.

Maddux, W. W., Barden, J., Brewer, M. B., & Petty, R. E. (2005). Saying no to negativity: The effects of context and motivation to control prejudice on automatic evaluative responses. *Journal of Experimental Social Psychology, 41,* 19–35.

Maio, G. R., Haddock, G., Watt, S. E., & Hewstone, M. (in press). Implicit measures and applied contexts: An illustrative examination of anti-racism advertising. In R. E. Petty, R. H. Fazio, & P. Brinol (Eds.), *Attitudes: Insights from the new wave of implicit measures.*

McCall, C., & Dasgupta, N. (2007). The malleability of men's gender self-concepts. *Self and Identity, 6*(2–3), 173–188.

Mitchell, J. P., Nosek, B. A., & Banaji, M. R. (2003). Contextual variations in implicit evaluation. *Journal of Experimental Psychology: General, 132,* 455–469.

Monteith, M. J. (1993). Self-regulation of prejudiced responses: Implications for progress in prejudice-reduction efforts. *Journal of Personality and Social Psychology, 65,* 469–485.

Monteith, M. J., Devine, P. G., & Zuwerink, J. R. (1993). Self-directed vs. other-directed affect as a consequence of prejudice-related discrepancies. *Journal of Personality and Social Psychology, 64,* 198–210.

Monteith, M. J., Zuwerink, J. R., & Devine, P. G. (1994). Prejudice and prejudice reduction: Classic challenges, contemporary approaches. In P. G. Devine, D. L. Hamilton, & T. M. Ostrom (Eds.), *Social cognition: Impact on social psychology* (pp. 323–345). San Diego, CA: Academic.

Mosher, D. L., & O'Grady, K. E. (1979). Homosexual threat, negative attitudes toward masturbation, sex guilt, and males' sexual and affective reactions to explicit sexual films. *Journal of Consulting and Clinical Psychology, 47,* 860–873.

Moskowitz, G. B., Gollwitzer, P., Wasel, W., & Schaal, B. (1999). Preconscious control of stereotype activation through chronic egalitarian goals. *Journal of Personality and Social Psychology, 77,* 167–184.

Myrdal, G. (1944). *An American dilemma; The Negro problem and modern democracy.* New York: Harper.

Nier, J. A. (2005). How dissociated are implicit and explicit racial attitudes? A bogus pipeline approach. *Group Processes and Intergroup Relations, 8,* 39–52.

Nisbett, R. E., & Wilson, T. D. (1977). Telling more than we can know: Verbal reports on mental processes. *Psychological Review, 84,* 231–259.

Nussbaum, M. C. (1999). "Secret sewers of vice": Disgust, bodies, and the law. In S. A. Bandes (Ed.), *The passions of law* (pp. 19–62). New York: New York University Press.

Olson, M. A., & Fazio, R. H. (2006). Reducing automatically activated racial prejudice through implicit evaluative conditioning. *Personality and Social Psychology Bulletin, 32,* 421–433.

Otten, S., & Wentura, D. (1999). About the impact of automaticity in the minimal group paradigm: Evidence from affective priming tasks. *European Journal of Social Psychology, 29,* 1049–1071.

Park, J., Felix, K., & Lee, G. (2007). Implicit attitudes toward Arab-Muslims and the moderating effects of social information. *Basic and Applied Social Psychology, 29,* 35–45.

Payne, B. K. (2001). Prejudice and perception: The role of automatic and controlled processes in misperceiving a weapon. *Journal of Personality and Social Psychology, 81,* 181–192.

Payne, B. K. (2005). Conceptualizing control in social cognition: How executive functioning modulates the expression of automatic stereotyping. *Journal of Personality and Social Psychology, 89,* 488–503.

Payne, B. K., Lambert, A. J., & Jacoby, L. L. (2002). Best laid plans: Effects of goals on accessibility bias and cognitive control in race-based misperceptions of weapons. *Journal of Experimental Social Psychology, 38,* 384–396.

Pettigrew, T., & Tropp, L. R. (2006). A meta-analytic test of intergroup contact theory. *Journal of Personality and Social Psychology, 90,* 751–783.

Petty, R. E., Tormala, Z. L., Brinol, P., & Jarvis, W. B. G. (2006). Implicit ambivalence from attitude change: An exploration of the PAST model. *Journal of Personality and Social Psychology, 90,* 21–41.

Pratto, F., & Shih, F. (2000). Social dominance orientation and group context in implicit group prejudice. *Psychological Science, 11*(6), 515–518.

Richeson, J. A., & Ambady, N. (2001). Who's in charge? Effects of situational roles on automatic gender bias. *Sex Roles, 44,* 493–512.

Richeson, J. A., & Ambady, N. (2003). Effects of situational power on automatic racial prejudice. *Journal of Experimental Social Psychology, 39,* 177–183.

Richeson, J. A., Baird, A. A., & Gordon, H. L. (2003). An fMRI investigation of the impact of interracial contact on executive function. *Nature Neuroscience, 6,* 1323–1328.

Richeson, J. A., & Nussbaum, R. J. (2004). The impact of multiculturalism versus color-blindness on racial bias. *Journal of Experimental Social Psychology, 40,* 417–423.

Richeson, J. L., & Shelton, J. N. (2003). When prejudice does not pay: Effects of interracial contact on executive function. *Psychological Science, 14,* 287–290.

Rockeach, M. (1973). *The nature of human values.* New York: The Free Press.

Rudman, L. A., Ashmore, R. D., & Gary, M. (2001). "Unlearning" automatic biases: The malleability of implicit prejudice and stereotypes. *Journal of Personality and Social Psychology, 81,* 856–868.

Rudman, L. A., & Lee, M. R. (2002). Implicit and explicit consequences of exposure to violent and misogynous rap music. *Group Processes and Intergroup Relations, 5,* 133–150.

Rydell, R. J., & McConnell, A. R. (in press). Understanding implicit and explicit attitude change: A systems of reasoning analysis. *Journal of Personality and Social Psychology.*

Sassenberg, K., Jonas, K. A., Shah, J. Y., & Brazy, P. C. (2007). Why some groups just feel better: The regulatory fit of group power. *Journal of Personality and Social Psychology, 92,* 249–267.

Sassenberg, K., & Moskowitz, G. B. (2005). Don't stereotype, just think different! Overcoming automatic stereotype activation by mindset priming. *Journal of Experimental Social Psychology, 41,* 506–514.

Sassenberg, K., & Wieber, F. (2005). Don't ignore the other half: The impact of ingroup identification on implicit measures of prejudice. *European Journal of Social Psychology, 35,* 621–632.

Schaller, M., Park, J. H., & Mueller, A. (2003). Fear of the dark: Interactive effects of beliefs about danger and ambient darkness on ethnic stereotypes. *Personality and Social Psychology Bulletin, 29,* 637–649.

Sechrist, G. B., & Stangor, C. (2001). Perceived consensus influences intergroup behavior and stereotype accessibility. *Journal of Personality and Social Psychology, 80,* 645–654.

Sinclair, L., & Kunda, Z. (1999). Reactions to a Black professional: Motivated inhibition and activation of conflicting stereotypes. *Journal of Personality and Social Psychology, 77,* 885–904.

Smith, E. R. (1993). Social identity and social emotions: Toward new conceptualizations of prejudice. In D. M. Mackie & D. L. Hamilton (Eds.), *Affect, cognition, and stereotyping: Interactive processes in group perception* (pp. 297–315). San Diego, CA: Academic.

Smith, E. R., & DeCoster, J. (2000). Dual-process models in social and cognitive psychology: Conceptual integration and links to underlying memory systems. *Personality and Social Psychology Review, 4,* 108–131.

Smyth, F., & Nosek, B. A. (2007, January). *The impact of multiculturalism versus color-blindness on racial bias revisited.* Paper presented at the annual meeting of the Society for Personality and Social Psychology, Memphis, TN.

Son Hing, L. S., Chung-Yan, G. A., Grunfeld, R., Robichaud, L. K., & Zanna, M. P. (2005). Exploring the discrepancy between implicit and explicit prejudice: A test of aversive racism theory. In J. P. Forgas, K. Williams, & S. Latham (Eds.), *Social motivation: Conscious and unconscious processes. Vol. 5. The Sydney Symposium of Social Psychology* (pp. 274–293). New York: Psychology Press.

Son Hing, L. S., Li, W., & Zanna, M. P. (2002). Inducing hypocrisy to reduce prejudicial response among aversive racists. *Journal of Experimental Social Psychology, 38,* 71–77.

Spencer, S. J., Fein, S., Wolfe, C. T., Fong, G., & Dunn, M. (1998). Automatic activation of stereotypes: The role of self-image threat. *Personality and Social Psychology Bulletin, 24,* 1139–1152.

Strack, F., & Deutsch, R. (2004). Reflective and impulsive determinants of social behavior. *Personality and Social Psychology Review, 8,* 220–247.

Tropp, L. R., & Bianchi, R. A. (2006). Valuing diversity and interest in intergroup contact. *Journal of Social Issues, 62,* 533–551.

Tropp, L. R., Stout, A. M., Boatswain, C., Wright, S., & Pettigrew, T. F. (2006). Trust and acceptance in response to references to group membership: Minority and majority perspectives on cross-group interactions. *Journal of Applied Social Psychology, 36,* 769–794.

Wegner, D. M. (1994). Ironic processes of mental control. *Psychological Review, 101,* 34–52.

Wilson, T. D., Lindsey, S., & Schooler, T. Y. (2000). A model of dual attitudes. *Psychological Review, 107,* 101–126.

Wittenbrink, B., Judd, C. M., & Park, B. (2001). Spontaneous prejudice in context: Variability in automatically activated attitudes. *Journal of Personality and Social Psychology, 81,* 815–827.

14 Intergroup Emotions Theory

Diane M. Mackie and Angela T. Maitner
University of California, Santa Barbara

Eliot R. Smith
Indiana University

> Men [sic] decide far more problems by hate, love, lust, rage, sorrow, joy, hope, fear, illusion, or some other inward emotion, than by reality, authority, any legal standard, judicial precedent, or statute.
>
> —Cicero (106 BC–43 BC)

When it comes to intergroup relations, we think Cicero had it right. For the last decade, we have argued that interactions between groups—often negative, but sometimes positive—cannot be understood without investigating the emotions that groups feel toward their own and other groups. We have argued that such emotions come with the psychological territory of group membership itself, and depend in some crucial ways on how psychologically deeply or centrally group membership is accepted. Like Cicero, we have argued that it is well worth distinguishing the possible effects of rage, sorrow, and fear, as well as other emotions, for understanding intergroup relations, and like Cicero, we see the power of positive as well as negative emotions in guiding behavior between groups. In step with his times, Cicero no doubt considered emotion an individual phenomenon, whereas we have argued for the essentially social underpinning of emotion, and thus that emotion is also interpersonal and intergroup in nature. Also in step with his times, Cicero referred to males when we hope he meant human beings, but we agree with his use of the plural term—we have argued that emotion is a shared product of group life and that it creates shared tendencies to act in common ways toward collective others.

We have formalized these ideas in intergroup emotions theory (IET; Mackie, Devos, & Smith, 2000; Mackie, Silver, & Smith, 2004; Mackie & Smith, 2002; E. R. Smith, 1993; E. R. Smith & Mackie, 2005, 2006). In this chapter we first describe the basic tenets of IET, focusing on the social categorization and identification processes that we believe make emotion an intergroup phenomenon, the similarities and differences between individual and intergroup emotion, and the consequences that intergroup emotion has for intergroup behavior. We then describe some of the empirical evidence relevant to IET that has accumulated from our own and others' research programs in the last decade. IET has been developed and extended several times, in particular to emphasize the functionally adaptive role of emotion in regulating intergroup reactions and interactions (Mackie et al., 2004) and the ability of IET to account for the variability in intergroup relations over time and context (E. R. Smith & Mackie, 2006). As our thinking about intergroup emotion has evolved, new lines of theoretical and empirical refinement and extension have suggested themselves, and we next describe and review some of the programs of research we currently have under development. Finally we note what we believe to be the distinctive features of the IET approach for the understanding of intergroup behavior, in the hope that this will also encourage others to extend the theory in new directions.

INTERGROUP EMOTION'S THEORY

IET claims emotions as fundamentally social phenomena. From the IET perspective, emotions are socially functional reactions to events and entities made psychologically consequential by the activation and acceptance of a social identity. Indeed the two most significant theoretical contributions made by IET are (a) to represent emotion as associated with a psychological identity rather than a biological entity, and (b) to provide for differentiated and nuanced, rather than only positive and negative, evaluative reactions to ingroups and outgroups. These insights were the product of E. R. Smith's (1993) integration of self-categorization and social identity theorizing about the consequences of group membership (Tajfel, 1982; Turner, Hogg, Oakes, Reicher, & Wetherell, 1987) with an appraisal theory view of the origins of distinct emotions (Frijda, 1986; Lazarus & Folkman, 1984; Roseman, 1984; Scherer, 1988; C. A. Smith & Ellsworth, 1985). There are two key antecedent conditions for the generation of intergroup emotions: the process of social categorization and the production of intergroup appraisals. The impact of the former on the latter is moderated by identification. Intergroup emotions have a privileged relation with intergroup behavioral tendencies and through them, with intergroup behavior (see Figure 14.1). In this section we explain the key antecedents of intergroup emotions, differentiate intergroup emotion from individual emotion, and describe the consequences of intergroup emotion for intergroup relations.

The foundational assumption of IET is that social categorization dictates intergroup emotional experience. In addition to being unique individuals, people are simultaneously members of multiple groups, whether face-to-face interacting groups (e.g., committees, sports teams, and work groups) or social categories (e.g., national, ethnic, gender, or religious groups). Certain circumstances impel people to consider themselves psychologically as members of a particular group, rather than as unique individuals. These circumstances typically involve cues or directions that make salient or accessible one of their many available memberships. Hearing one's school song, a foreign language, or an ethnic slur; donning a uniform, a yarmulke, or a stethoscope; finding oneself among fellow ingroup members or alone among members of the outgroup; engaging in cooperative interaction or competitive behavior; and so forth, can all subtly or not so subtly activate social categorization.

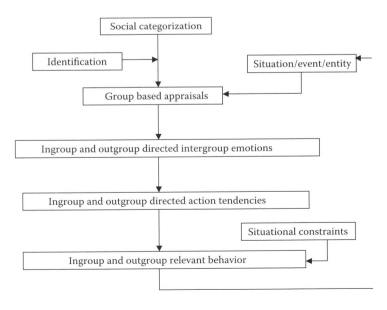

FIGURE 14.1   A model of intergroup emotions.

To the extent that group membership defines them, people do not think of themselves as unique individuals, but rather as relatively interchangeable members of the group (a process known as *depersonalization;* for a review, see Turner et al., 1987). Group members inevitably view the world through a group lens, so that social categorization entails intergroup appraisal. *Intergroup appraisal* is the construal or interpretation of events, entities (including the ingroup and outgroups and their members), and situations in terms of their implications for the ingroup, regardless of their personal relevance. Therefore events that negatively impact other members of the group (even if the self is unharmed), or circumstances that benefit the group as a whole (although not the self), or outgroup members who compete against fellow ingroup members (but not the self), are nevertheless psychologically significant.

Importantly, however, there are some individuals for whom the categorization process either occurs more fully (the group categorization is more central to the self) or assumes greater social and emotional significance (the group membership is more affectively laden or important to their positive view of the self). Thus individuals differ in their identification with any particular ingroup, with group membership more completely defining highly identified individuals both cognitively and emotionally. Because of this, individuals differ in the extent to which appraisal processes are group based. That is, identification moderates the impact of social categorization on intergroup appraisals, as reflected in Figure 14.1.

Borrowing broadly from appraisal theories, IET argues that perceiver and context factors combine to produce specific patterns of intergroup appraisals that trigger specific intergroup emotions. Our concern has never been with the ascendancy of any particular appraisal theory of emotion, but rather with the more general assumption of appraisal theories: that differentiated construal of events, entities, and situations (as beneficial vs. harmful, strong or weak, intended or unintended, justified or unjustifiable, etc.) results in the subjective experience of specific distinct emotions. For example, an action that harms the ingroup and is perpetrated by a strong outgroup (perhaps suggesting that the ingroup does not have the resources to cope with the threat) should invoke fear. On the other hand, when the ingroup is appraised as having the resources (in terms of numbers, power, or legitimacy) to deal with an outgroup's negative action, anger is the theoretically more likely emotion to be triggered. An ingroup-perpetrated action that violates a moral code might instigate guilt, whereas the same action appraised as justifiable might provoke satisfaction. The ability to predict differentiated emotional reactions to groups, rather than only positive or negative evaluation of them, gives IET a distinctive edge in the understanding of intergroup relations.

Nor is it theoretically crucial for IET what particular role the appraisal, construal, or interpretative process plays in generating emotion. For example, classic appraisal theories of emotion (e.g., Frijda, 1986; Roseman, 1984) hold that it is the configuration of appraisals (e.g., the perception that an action is a certain and unmanageable threat) that is necessary and sufficient to both generate and determine a particular emotion (and consequently all its cognitive, physiological, and behavioral implications). The crucial benefit of applying such theories to intergroup behavior is their assumption of the role of interpretative processes (appraisals) that lead to a number of finely differentiated and potentially intense evaluative reactions (emotions). However, IET is also broadly consistent with other theories of emotional experience that include similar elements. For example, the core affect model (Barrett, 2006; Russell, 2003; Russell & Barrett, 1999) holds that individuals experience certain levels of affect and arousal (as a result of internal or external events). Noticeable change in these levels triggers a categorization process that relies on input from the experienced affect and arousal, other physiological changes, behavior, cultural and personal knowledge, and interpretation of salient features of the current situation, event, or object. The result is that the episode is categorized based on similarity as an instance of fear (or anger, or joy). From the IET perspective, the internal and external events that contribute to core affect and arousal would be group rather than individually relevant, as would the interpretative processes. Regardless of the specifics of their generation, it is the experience and effects of differentiated emotions that is important to IET.

What are intergroup emotions like? We can say several things based on research and theory. First, we claim that intergroup emotions are conceptually and functionally distinct from individual emotions because they are experienced on behalf of the group as a function of group membership and intergroup appraisal. Because of this, we also see the experience of intergroup emotion as different from the experience of empathy: Empathy is feeling for others, whereas intergroup emotion is feeling as others, because the other and the self are psychologically one. People are not thrilled when their national team wins because the members of the team are feeling good; they are thrilled because they themselves won. Second, intergroup emotions can be acute or chronic. Appraisal of time-bounded events and situations produces acute intergroup emotions specific to that particular appraisal of that particular event or situation. However, repeated group-relevant events, situations, and interactions can also result in more stable profiles of intergroup emotion becoming associated with social entities, both ingroup and outgroup (Frijda, 1993; E. R. Smith & Mackie, 2006). Thinking about oneself in terms of a national identity might almost always generate pride, for example, compared to when one thinks of oneself as an individual or compared to when one considers a different identity, such as a school loyalty. Similarly, a particular ingroup identity might result in habitual generation of anger associated with a longtime rival outgroup, anger that would not be experienced if a different social identity or an individual identity was active. Third, target events or entities might induce multiple intergroup emotions both simultaneously and over time. Because every event or entity is multifaceted and because the particular way in which they are appraised might change, the same events and entities can invoke multiple intergroup emotions both simultaneously (e.g., different aspects of terrorist bombings might produce both fear and anger) and over time (the appraisals of a victory over a rival that originally produced joy might no longer be salient a decade or even a week after the event). Importantly, because identification moderates the impact of categorization on appraisal, and appraisal generates emotions, identification moderates the impact of social categorization on all aspects of the experience of intergroup emotions.

What are the consequences of experiencing intergroup emotions? One of the primary theoretical contributions of IET is the reliance on emotional differentiation as a means of predicting specificity in behavioral response to ingroups and outgroups. That benefit derives from the privileged association that particular emotions are thought to have with behavioral tendencies or impulses to act. That is, anger involves the impulse, desire, or tendency to take action against the source of the anger, just as fear involves the desire to move away from the source of the fear. Thus specific intergroup emotions produce specific intergroup action tendencies, allowing the prediction of which among a range of behavioral options—approach and affiliation, confrontation and attack, or avoidance and separation—group members are more likely to choose. In this view, the ability of any specific situational factors to produce particular behavioral tendencies derives from generation of emotion in that context: the impact of appraisals on behavioral tendencies is mediated by the experience of distinct intergroup emotions.

The value of being able to produce particular behavioral tendencies of course is that they create a readiness for, or increase the probability of, the associated actual behavior. Whereas the links between emotional experiences and the readiness to engage in certain types of action are fairly well established, the link between emotions and actual behaviors is more tenuous (Roseman, Wiest, & Swartz, 1994). One reason for this is that actual behaviors are more constrained by situational factors than are impulses or intentions (see Figure 14.1). Although group members may feel like confronting or aggressing against the outgroup, acting in line with these desires requires appropriate resources, no other pressing concerns, and so forth. On the other hand, affective responses have been shown to predict intergroup behaviors better than do some more cognitive assessments (Fiske, 1998) and normative pressures can sometimes facilitate rather than inhibit intergroup aggression (Insko et al., 1998). There have also been demonstrations in the intergroup emotion domain that actual behaviors associated with behavior tendencies are more likely to occur (Dumont, Yzerbyt, Wigboldus, & Gordijn, 2003). All else being equal then, the activation of a specific intergroup emotion and the action tendency associated with it makes the execution of relevant intergroup behavior more likely. People may or may not carry out such actions, but the potential for specific emotion-driven behaviors to occur is important theoretically and practically. Although an immediate opportunity to act may be suppressed because of other factors, it is perhaps still more likely that some other outlet for the tendency will be found.

The association of particular intergroup emotions with corresponding intergroup action tendencies is important evidence for the regulatory function of intergroup emotions: Intergroup emotions drive intergroup behavior, whether directed at the outgroup or the ingroup. Anger toward the outgroup motivates confrontation with them, whereas outgroup fear motivates moving away from their sphere of influence. At the same time, pride in the ingroup motivates affiliation with them, whereas ingroup guilt motivates apology and reparation. Because intergroup emotions serve a regulatory function, we also assume that the execution of motivated behaviors will have implications for the appraisals that generated the emotions that motivated them, an assumption reflected in the feedback loop between intergroup behavior and intergroup appraisals in Figure 14.1. For example, successfully implementing an emotionally induced behavior will dissipate the precipitating state because a new appraisal should signal that all is well, whereas failing to do so will intensify it.

In sum, social categorization dictates intergroup emotional experience. It does so because social categorization entails intergroup appraisal, and the occurrence of specific patterns of intergroup appraisals triggers specific intergroup emotions directed toward the ingroup and the outgroup. The impact of social categorization on intergroup emotion is moderated by identification. Specific intergroup emotions produce specific intergroup action tendencies, and the impact of appraisals on behavioral tendencies is mediated by the experience of distinct intergroup emotions. The functional role of intergroup emotion is to motivate intergroup behavior, and whether such motivated behavior occurs or not has iterative implications for experienced appraisals, emotions, and behavioral intentions.

EMPIRICAL SUPPORT FOR INTERGROUP EMOTIONS THEORY

Since IET was first proposed and developed, an impressive body of evidence supportive of its central tenets has emerged. This work has come both from our own programs of research and from many other relevant lines of investigation. In this section we briefly review support for the key assumptions of the theory, no doubt with a bias toward reporting our own work. We also note some aspects of the theory for which support is absent and other aspects that warrant further refinement, given the available empirical findings.

SOCIAL CATEGORIZATION DICTATES INTERGROUP EMOTIONAL EXPERIENCE

The fact that people experience different emotions depending on the currently accessible social identity provides compelling evidence for the foundational assumption of IET.

Some of the most elegant evidence for the idea that categorization dictates emotion comes from a series of studies that manipulated the salience of one of multiple possible group memberships available to individuals in a particular situation (Dumont et al., 2003; Gordijn, Wigboldus, & Yzerbyt, 2001; Gordijn, Yzerbyt, Wigboldus, & Dumont, 2006). For example, research participants were typically told about one group mistreating another group. Between-subjects salience manipulations led participants to categorize themselves with either the victim group or the perpetrator group. As expected, participants experienced more anger when they categorized themselves as members of the harmed group than when they did not. Thus social categorization dictated participants' emotional reaction to the situation.

Even more compelling evidence for the fact that social categorization determines emotion comes from a series of studies in which we manipulated social categorization within subject (E. R. Smith, Seger, & Mackie, 2008). For example after assessing a baseline individual emotional profile, we asked participants to think about themselves as a member of a particular available group membership ("Think about yourself as an American") and to report, as an American, the extent to which they felt 12 distinct emotions, both in general, and directed at either the ingroup or the outgroup. We then asked them to think about themselves in terms of a different categorization ("Think about yourself as a woman") and asked them again to convey the emotions they were experiencing, and so on. Over several different studies, with slightly varying means of activating group membership, and varying the order in which memberships were accessed, we asked people to report the emotions they felt when group memberships as varied as American, University of California at Santa Barbara (UCSB) student, male or female, Republican or Democrat, and smoker or nonsmoker were activated. The results across studies were reassuringly consistent: People report significantly different and distinct emotional profiles depending on the group membership currently activated. Thus the same participant might report considerable pride as a UCSB student compared to when other identities were activated; much more anger as an American; more fear as a Democrat; more guilt as a smoker, and so forth.

If social categorization dictates emotion, we might also expect people to share a certain emotional profile more when categorized as group members than when thinking about themselves as individuals. The study just described also provided support for this hypothesis (E. R. Smith et al., 2008). Comparing the emotional profiles that people reported as individuals with the emotional profiles the same people reported when thinking about themselves as group members revealed considerable convergence toward a group average in the latter case. That is, there was significantly more similarity in the amount of joy, fear, guilt, and so forth that participants reported feeling when thinking about themselves as Democrats, males, and so forth than in the joy, fear, and guilt they reported feeling when thinking about themselves as individuals. Thus social categorization produced considerable convergence in emotional experience, just as it produces convergence in self-perception, adherence to group norms, and so forth (Turner et al., 1987). Intergroup emotions are socially shared (see also Parkinson, Fischer, & Manstead, 2005).

SOCIAL CATEGORIZATION ENTAILS INTERGROUP APPRAISAL

Research showing that the same events can be appraised differently depending on which group membership is activated is fundamental to social psychology—the different appraisals and attributions Princeton and Dartmouth students made for the infamous 1951 football game being a prime example (Hastorf & Cantril, 1954). In a recent set of studies, we (Garcia-Prieto, Mackie, Tran, & Smith, 2007) asked Hispanic and White participants to review the application materials of an ethnic minority group member hired either through merit or a diversity recruitment procedure. Whites, especially highly identified Whites, appraised the hiring of a minority for diversity reasons as more harmful to the ingroup and beneficial to the outgroup, whereas Hispanics appraised the diversity hiring as more beneficial. Categorization similarly affected appraisals made about a proposal to raise tuition at the University of Colorado for nonresidents of the state (Gordijn et al., 2006). When categorized as students, participants appraised the proposal as more unfair than when they were categorized as Colorado residents. In addition, Brewer and Weber (1994) manipulated majority and minority group categorization and demonstrated membership-specific effects on self-ratings. When a member of the majority group performed, both majority and minority group members appeared to engage in individual social comparison, feeling worse when the performer did well and better when he or she poorly. But when a member of the minority group performed, assessments of the situation appeared to become group-based. Whereas majority group members had no reactions to the minority group performance, minority group members now felt better if their colleague performed well and worse if he or she performed poorly.

Presumably these different reactions reflect different appraisals of the situation for the self as an individual or group member. However, given its importance to our model, little research directly assessing the specifically group-based aspects of this crucial assumption has been collected. We know of only one study that assesses the presence versus absence of categorization on intergroup versus individually relevant appraisals. H. J. Smith and Spears (1996) found that when individual identity was primed, participants' evaluations of a situation reflected their personal concerns, whereas the activation of group identity led to evaluations that reflected both group and personal concerns. IET makes similar predictions. For example, from the IET perspective, an observer thinking about herself as a female will positively appraise the news that the lone female sales manager received the only bonus given out by management, whereas the news might be appraised negatively if the observer's individual identity were salient.

Despite the lack of direct evidence that categorization makes appraisals group based rather than individually based, there is plenty of evidence that people react to events that are relevant to their ingroup but do not affect them personally—group-representative sporting events (Cialdini, et al., 1976); historical misdeeds perpetrated by the ingroup (Doosje, Branscombe, Spears, & Manstead, 1998; Maitner, Mackie, & Smith, 2007); or events that happen to other ingroup members (Devos, Silver, Mackie, & Smith, 2002; Mackie, Silver, Maitner, & Smith, 2002). We have also shown that activation of social identity makes current members of a group carefully process information that will affect only future members of the group, even though such messages, being personally irrelevant, are virtually ignored when social categorization is not activated (Maitner, Claypool, Mackie, Smith, & Keeth, 2006). By inference then, an outcome objectively relevant to others must be appraised or interpreted in a way that makes an emotional experience possible; that is, it must be appraised in a group-relevant way.

SPECIFIC PATTERNS OF INTERGROUP APPRAISALS TRIGGER SPECIFIC INTERGROUP EMOTIONS

Once events are appraised in terms of outcomes for ingroups, they induce intergroup emotion. In close parallel with findings in the individual emotion domain, specific patterns of such appraisals produce quite different and distinct intergroup emotions. Threat from a weak outgroup produces more outgroup-directed anger than the same threat from a strong group (Mackie et al., 2000); severe harm to the ingroup produces more anger than less severe harm (Gordijn et al., 2006); ongoing harm that an outgroup refuses to rectify causes more anger than harm that is apologized for (Maitner, Mackie, & Smith, 2006); severe, unjustified harm done by the ingroup invokes more guilt and less satisfaction than less severe and less justifiable action (Branscombe, & Miron, 2004; Maitner et al., 2007; Schmitt, Behner, Montada, Muller, & Muller-Fohrbrodt, 2000); illegitimate ingroup privilege and unjust outgroup treatment provoke more ingroup guilt and outgroup sympathy than intergroup interactions perceived as legitimate and justified (Iyer, Leach, & Crosby, 2003; Maitner et al., 2007; Swim & Miller, 1999), and so forth. With rare exceptions (e.g., when anger and fear, or anger and disgust increase together) manipulations of how events are appraised affect only the specific emotion in intended ways. For example, Mackie et al. (2000) found that manipulations of intergroup appraisals of strength in the face of a threat to the ingroup increased reported experience of anger while decreasing fear. Far from producing generalized negative affect, specific appraisals generate quite different, quite separate, and quite specific negative emotions.

THE IMPACT OF SOCIAL CATEGORIZATION ON INTERGROUP
EMOTION IS MODERATED BY IDENTIFICATION

Two kinds of correlational evidence support this claim. First, the more group members identify with the group, the more they converge on their group's emotional average. So the joy, fear, and guilt reported by a single individual thinking about herself as an American are much more similar to the average joy, fear, and guilt reported by all Americans, if the individual is highly identified (E. R. Smith et al., 2007). Second, the evidence that highly identified group members feel intergroup emotions more intensely continues to mount (see earlier reviews in Devos et al., 2002; Mackie et al., 2004; Mackie & Smith, 2002). For example, Mackie et al. (2004) examined the relationship between identification and emotions in reaction to hypothetical terrorist attacks. The more strongly participants identified as Americans, the more anger and the more fear they reported about terrorist attacks on their country. Similarly, highly identified group members experience more satisfaction in response to acts of ingroup aggression (Maitner et al., 2007). That is, the acute emotional reactions highly identified group members had in response to group-relevant events were more intense than those reported by less identified participants. A similar relation between identification and anger experienced in the face of mistreatment was reported by Yzerbyt, Dumont, Wigboldus, and Gordijn (2003), Kessler and Hollbach (2005), Gordijn et al. (2006), and McCoy and Major (2003). The more participants identified with a victimized group, the more anger they experienced.

In the most comprehensive empirical test of this assumption to date, we examined the impact of identification on a wide variety not only of outgroup directed emotions but also ingroup directed emotions experienced by members of a wide variety of groups (E. R. Smith et al., 2007). The emotions measured in this study were not specifically in response to particular events or situations; we merely asked people to consider themselves in terms of a particular group membership and to report the emotions they were feeling, sometimes in general and sometimes with the ingroup or the outgroup specified as the target. We consistently found that identification was significantly and positively correlated with positive group emotions, such as joy and pride. In addition, we found strong positive relations between identification and outgroup directed anger, replicating the incident-specific outgroup anger found by Mackie et al. (2002) and Yzerbyt et al. (2003).

Overall, however, identification was only weakly and negatively related to ingroup anger and ingroup guilt. These results were inconsistent with our original ideas about identification and intensity of emotion, but consistent with other findings (including some from our own research) showing that highly identified group members feel less guilt on behalf of their ingroup than do less identified members (Doosje et al., 1998; Maitner et al., 2007). Why might identification increase the intensity of some emotions felt on behalf of a group and depress the intensity of others? The empirical evidence has led us to propose a more differentiated role of identification than we originally assumed, and we describe our current thinking about the issue in a later section of this chapter.

WHAT ARE INTERGROUP EMOTIONS LIKE?

Empirical evidence has now confirmed many of our claims regarding the nature of intergroup emotions. Perhaps most important, definitive evidence for the distinctiveness of intergroup and individual emotion comes from the study (E. R. Smith et al., 2006) in which people reported the extent to which they felt 12 different emotions as individuals before activating several available group memberships and reporting the emotions associated with each of those. As might be expected, reports of emotions at the individual and group level are correlated at around the .3 level (e.g., people who report feeling angrier as individuals also tend to report feeling angrier as group members). Despite this correlation, analyses showed that profiles of group emotions and individual emotions were not just quantitatively different—differing in the overall level or intensity of emotion reported—but qualitatively different, so that different emotions predominated when a social identity rather than individual identity was salient.

We also know that people can feel emotions at group-relevant outcomes even when they remain personally unaffected by those outcomes (Cialdini et al., 1976; Mackie et al., 2004; H. J. Smith & Kessler, 2004). For example, Yzerbyt et al. (2003) had participants read about an event that harmed another group with whom they shared a superordinate membership (as fellow students) but differed on another (as students at different universities). Only when a subtle manipulation made their common group membership with the victim salient did participants experience anger and unhappiness, reactions based on the collective self (group membership) shared with the victim. In addition, the wide variety of studies we have reported here demonstrates that intergroup emotions can be generated in response to specific events or as stable responses to social entities (e.g., E. R. Smith et al., 2007; Mackie et al., 2000) and that the same event can produce multiple intergroup emotions depending on what appraisal aspects are salient (Maitner et al., 2007).

Almost all of the research on intergroup emotions, from our own and from others' labs, has relied on self-report assessments. Beyond the general concerns that such a homogeneity in methods might raise, the exclusive use of self-report also gives rise to concerns that participants' responses in these studies might reflect at worst experimental demand and at best a more cognitive and less affective type of emotion than we were intending to study. We are reassured by the emergence of studies that show some very real consequences of intergroup emotions that suggest close parallels to individual emotions. First, the generation of intergroup anger appears to involve arousal in the same way as individually experienced anger. In one study (Rydell et al., in press) we successfully induced intergroup anger and pride by insulting or praising participants' ingroup. We then offered some participants a false but viable explanation for some of the consequences of emotion: Applying the classic misattribution paradigm, we told them that the cubicles in which they were working might be causing them to feel either positive excitement or negative arousal. Participants who read the insulting essay but who were not told anything about their work environment reported considerable anger, whereas those who read the insulting essay in a cubicle that supposedly might cause negative arousal reported significantly less anger. Such results are consistent with the inference that intergroup anger was indeed negatively arousing. Those who read the complimentary essay reported pride regardless of the conditions in which they worked.

Second, intergroup emotions can have processing effects that also parallel the well-established consequences of individual affect. For example, we (Rydell et al., in press) generated intergroup pride or happiness in some participants by praising their ingroup, whereas a matched group of participants merely read neutral descriptions about the ingroup (so each group had membership activated, but one group was feeling positive as well). Participants then read a persuasive essay about comprehensive exams that was composed of either weak or compelling arguments. Just as studies typically find that individually experienced happiness undermines careful processing of persuasive messages, we found that the induction of group-based happiness similarly undermined systematic processing of the information.

Although not definitely eliminating concerns about the self-report nature of our findings, such studies certainly suggest that intergroup emotions have many of the same hallmarks as do individually experienced emotions.

SPECIFIC INTERGROUP EMOTIONS PRODUCE SPECIFIC INTERGROUP ACTION TENDENCIES, AND THE IMPACT OF APPRAISALS ON BEHAVIORAL TENDENCIES IS MEDIATED BY THE EXPERIENCE OF DISTINCT INTERGROUP EMOTIONS

These two crucial aspects of IET are now well established. Consistent with the first point, we have shown that the distinct emotional profiles generated by activation of group memberships are related to distinct desires to approach and affiliate with the ingroup, and/or to confront and avoid the outgroup (E. R. Smith et al., 2007), or both. Three conclusions can be drawn from these results. First, again confirming their functional independence from individual emotions, intergroup emotions were vastly superior predictors of both intragroup and intergroup behavior compared to individual-level emotions across multiple emotions and across multiple group memberships. That is, it is the emotions that a person feels as a group member, and not as an individual, that dictate how the person wants to act toward both the ingroup and various outgroups.

Second, a range of positive emotions—pride, hope, gratitude—seem to predict affiliative action tendencies and intentions like displaying group symbols (E. R. Smith et al., 2007). Similarly, both respect for and pride in one's group have been shown to contribute positively to a wide range of good "citizenship" behaviors within family, work, university, and political contexts (Tyler, 1999, Tyler & Blader, 2000; Tyler, Degoey, & Smith, 1996; see also Esses & Dovidio, 2002, for emotional precursors of affiliation). It is not yet clear whether lack of differentiation among positive emotions is responsible for these results, or whether all these different emotions operate similarly but separately to increase ingroup affiliation.

Third, the effects of negative emotions are, as predicted by IET, more distinctly and differentially tied to particular patterns of behavior tendencies. In this regard outgroup-directed anger has proven to be a particularly potent and ubiquitous predictor of the desire to take action against the source of the emotion. For example, outgroup anger, but not outgroup fear or disgust, predicts ingroup bias, outgroup confrontation, defense of ingroup positions to the outgroup, and support for ingroup members criticizing the outgroup (Mackie et al., 2000; E. R. Smith et al., 2006). Similarly, outgroup-directed anger predicts willingness to take action against harmful and unfair action perpetrated by one group against another (Gordijn et al., 2006). Outgroup-directed anger also increased the desire to support and affiliate with the ingroup (E. R. Smith et al., 2007), findings consistent with previous research (Kessler & Hollbach, 2005) showing that this group emotion tends to increase ingroup identification.

A unique relation also exists between the experience of ingroup-directed guilt and the desire to undo harmful behavior. For example, group-based guilt is related to the commitment to apologize (McGarty et al., 2005) and support for policies reversing discrimination (Iyer et al., 2003; Schmitt et al., 2000; Swim & Miller, 1999). We have also found the experience of intergroup guilt in the face of ingroup aggression to suppress the desire for further conflict (Maitner et al., 2007). After reading about real acts of aggression committed by an ingroup, participants reported how those actions made them feel and how much they supported further acts of ingroup aggression. In three studies, experiencing intergroup satisfaction increased support for similar aggression, whereas experiencing intergroup guilt decreased support for further aggression. Other results showed that the experience of guilt versus satisfaction, and thus the desire for further aggression or not, depended on appraisals of the original aggression. Greater justification of intergroup aggression increased intergroup satisfaction and decreased guilt, and thus increased support for future aggression. Interestingly, greater identification with the ingroup was associated with greater desire for continued intergroup conflict (see also Jetten, Spears, & Manstead, 2001). This relation was mediated by appraisal and emotion. Highly identified group members were more likely to justify ingroup actions, feel intergroup satisfaction, and thus support further aggression. In an intriguing demonstration of the predictive specificity of intergroup emotion, Leach, Iyer, and Pedersen (2006) recently found that guilt explains support for reparations but only (ingroup-directed) anger explains willingness to actually take political action.

Other studies have shown that intergroup fear uniquely motivates desires to move away from the outgroup, seek information about the situation, and help and support victims, but not to confront or attack the offending outgroup (Dumont et al., 2003). For example, feelings of fear (but not anger) as Americans experienced in response to the attacks of September 11, 2001 predicted respondents' support for restrictions on civil liberties measured several months later (Skitka, Bauman, & Mullen, 2004). In contrast, anger at the outgroup makes Americans, Democrats, and Republicans less likely to avoid critical outsiders although it is associated with avoidance of media reports suspected of being biased toward the outgroup (E. R. Smith et al., 2007). Thus negative outgroup-directed emotions seem particularly powerful precursors of distinct outgroup-directed behavioral tendencies. A wealth of evidence now supports the idea that specific intergroup emotions produce specific intergroup action tendencies.

Findings also support the claim that the impact of situations on group members' desire for particular actions is mediated by the emotions experienced in those situations. For example, we (Mackie et al., 2000) arranged for members of groups to feel threatened by an outgroup described as either stronger or weaker, asked participants how they felt, and then asked them to indicate their desire to take a number of different kinds of actions. The actions ranged from leaving the outgroup alone (items like "I want to avoid/have nothing to do with/keep at a distance from/get away from them") to trying to hurt them (items such as "I want to confront/oppose/argue with/attack them"). Learning that the outgroup was weak led to appraisals of ingroup strength, outgroup-directed anger, and the desire to confront, oppose, argue with, and attack the outgroup. The relation between appraisals of strength and the desire to take action against the outgroup was significantly mediated by the emotion of outgroup-directed anger (see also Gordijn et al., 2006; Maitner et al., 2006).

Almost all of these studies asked individual participants to report their individual desires for action. Nevertheless, it might be expected that the generation of intergroup and the experience of group-level emotion would involve some privileged relation to the desire for group-based behavior, in addition to individual reactions. Two studies suggest the viability of such a hypothesis. Van Zomeren, Spears, Fischer, and Leach (2004) demonstrated that group-based anger strongly predicted support for collective action tendencies, especially if group support for such action was adequate. Similarly, Maitner et al. (2007) showed that intergroup satisfaction strongly predicted the desire for the ingroup to engage in similar aggression again. Although neither study provided data relevant to a preference for collective versus individual action, it appears that the role of intergroup emotions in predicting specifically group-level aspects of behavior warrants further attention (see also Simon et al., 1998).

REFLECTING THE REGULATORY FUNCTION OF INTERGROUP EMOTIONS, THE EXECUTION OF MOTIVATED BEHAVIORS WILL HAVE IMPLICATIONS FOR THE EMOTIONS THAT MOTIVATED THEM

If intergroup emotions are functional, successfully implementing an emotion-linked behavioral tendency should discharge the emotion, whereas impeding the behavioral tendency should intensify the emotion. The most compelling evidence for this aspect of IET comes from three studies in which we investigated the emotional consequences of satisfying or thwarting emotionally induced intergroup behavioral intentions (Maitner et al., 2006). The first study showed that if an attack on the ingroup produced anger, retaliation increased satisfaction, but if an attack produced fear, retaliation increased fear and guilt. Thus the execution of a behavior consistent with the experienced emotion (retaliation being consistent with anger) dissipated the emotion (anger was replaced by satisfaction) but if the behavior was inconsistent with the experienced emotion (retaliation being inconsistent with fear), that emotion was exacerbated. The second study showed that outgroup-directed anger instigated by outgroup insult dissipated when the ingroup successfully responded to the insult, but was exacerbated by an unsuccessful response. This study also showed the regulatory effect of emotion directed at the ingroup, and not just at the outgroup. When the ingroup failed to respond to the insult, anger directed at the ingroup was generated, as if to motivate the ingroup to engage in appropriate behavior. Study 3 demonstrated the regulatory function of intergroup guilt. Intergroup guilt following aggression was diminished when the ingroup made reparations, but was exacerbated when the ingroup aggressed again. Thus, as would be expected in a regulatory system, the achievement or failure to achieve a desired end state (the motivated behavior) initiates feedback to the motivating state (the intergroup emotion), either depressing it or increasing its motivational force. We measured this feedback loop returning to the emotion, but more formally we assume that it probably returns to change appraisals, which in turn produce the emotion.

NEW DIRECTIONS: REFINEMENTS AND EXTENSIONS OF INTERGROUP EMOTIONS THERAPY

The accumulating body of empirical evidence has generally supported our claims about the nature of intergroup emotions, as well as their key antecedents and consequences. In this section, we briefly mention several currently active lines of conceptual and empirical development that represent further refinement and extension of the IET model.

THE ROLE OF IDENTIFICATION

We noted earlier that identification with the group serves to intensify the valence of some group-based emotions but not others. Obviously the valence of the emotion (in conjunction with the target of the emotion) is key: Identification increases negative emotions about outgroups but depresses negative emotions about the ingroup. In this way identification appears to function to make the ingroup (and by association the self) good, and perhaps better than the outgroup. Theoretically, identification should be able to do so only because of its impact on appraisals, and there is evidence that this is the case. For example, highly identified members reminded of acts of intergroup aggression perpetrated by the ingroup appraised them as much more justifiable than less identified members, explaining the relation between increased identification and decreased guilt (Maitner et al., 2007). Thus identification biased appraisals (see also Doosje et al., 1998; Gordijn et al., 2006; Tiedens, Suttin, & Fong, 2004). Biasing appraisals, however, is quite a different function from the one assumed to operate in the original IET model. From the IET standpoint, social categorization entails depersonalization and depersonalization entails intergroup or group-based appraisals. What role does identification play? Note that we assumed that for some individuals the self-categorization and depersonalization process might occur more fully (the group categorization is more central to the self) or might assume greater social and emotional significance (the group membership is more affectively laden or important to their positive view of the self). These various aspects of identification are captured in different subscales of standard identification scales, and are often confounded in the measurement of group identification (Jackson & Smith, 1999). Given the empirical findings, we propose more closely assessing the role of self-overlap/centrality aspects of identification and affective/importance aspects of identification in the generation of intergroup appraisals and emotions. One possibility worth exploring is that overlap/centrality has an impact on the extent to which appraisals are group based, and thus the intensity of intergroup emotion, whereas affective/importance aspects of identification combine with situational factors to bias the nature of appraisals and thus what emotion is experienced, as proposed in Figure 14.2.

Quite independently of whether centrality and importance of identification have different effects, it is also possible that individuals have different kinds of affective ties with the group, which in turn may have consequences for their group-based emotions. Several theorists have suggested a distinction between those tied to the symbolic meaning of the group as a whole compared to those tied to the group through interpersonal affective bonds with members of the group (Brewer & Gardner, 1996). It has also been suggested that because of their differing social roles, for example, females

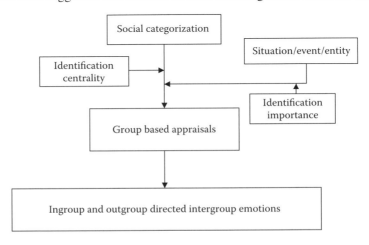

FIGURE 14.2   Possible roles for different components of identity.

are more likely to be interpersonally linked to others, whereas males are linked at the group or coalitional level (Gabriel & Gardner, 1999). One empirically verifiable implication of this is that the depersonalization model of self-categorization might be more consistent with male behavior than with female behavior. Another potential implication is for the nature of experienced group-based emotions. Some individuals, say females, or individuals interpersonally linked to the group, might be more likely to experience group-based emotion because they take the perspective of and individually experience the emotional outcomes of other individual group members. In contrast, males, say, or those coalitionally attached to the group, might chronically take the part of the group as a whole and experience its outcomes emotionally. In a situation in which the group and the individual group member's outcomes differ, people with different orientations would experience different emotions (Maitner, Claypool, Mackie, & Smith, 2006).

THE BASIS OF CONVERGENCE IN INTERGROUP EMOTIONS

The finding that group members converge on a common group profile of emotions provides some of the most compelling evidence for the group-based nature of emotion. What causes such convergence? From the IET perspective, shared emotion must result from shared appraisals. When group members react to the same event in the same way, convergence of emotion is inevitable. Recall, however, that we find convergence even when people report their emotions as group members rather than in reaction to specific events. This kind of group emotion convergence might occur because thinking about a group membership makes the same key group-relevant events salient to different perceivers, and evoke the same group-based appraisals, and thus the same emotions. For example, thinking about themselves as Americans might make many individual Americans bring to mind the same limited number of salient or accessible events or situations (e.g., attacks by militant anti-Americans, and decreased support from the international community). So many individuals might all report feeling angry as Americans because they are all responding to more or less the same salient events in more or less the same way. Research about the events, images, or concepts made accessible by the activation of group membership, and about how those events were appraised is necessary to know if this is a cognitive consequence of group membership that could explain within-group emotional convergence.

Other processes might also be responsible for this type of convergence, however. In interacting groups, emotional contagion (Neumann & Strack, 2000) would ensure that people took on the emotions displayed by fellow ingroup members. It is not as clear how contagion explains findings of convergence in isolated members of social categories, although contagion could occur if members were exposed to a group leader or prototype in the media, for example. Self-stereotyping of group norms would also produce converging group-level emotions. When an important group membership is made salient in a specific situation, group members tend to conform to group norms or move closer to the group prototype in their behaviors and their attitudes (Hogg & Turner, 1987; Simon & Hamilton, 1994). Although existing research has not considered emotions as a domain in which people move toward a group prototype, the same process could operate with emotions. Such a mechanism assumes widespread knowledge of a group emotional norm or stereotype, but such a notion does not appear far-fetched: Stereotypes of Scots as dour, men as stoic, Democrats as tender-hearted, or nurses as compassionate might be held by ingroup members as well as outside observers, for example. As these examples show, emotions can be part of stereotypes; the extent to which such stereotypes are accepted by group members and what role they might play in within-group emotional convergence is unknown. People also have more general theories about emotion sharing in groups in general. For example, people predict greater emotion (and mood) sharing among highly compared with moderately entitative groups, have theories about what dictates sharing in these groups, and have interactional tendencies toward a group that depends on the emotion they think the group is feeling and its entitativity (Mackie et al., 2006). Of course, all three of these processes (emotional contagion, self-stereotyping of emotion profiles that function as group norms or stereotypes, and shared reactions to salient group-relevant objects or events) may be important causes of group emotion convergence, either together, or under different circumstances.

THE ROLE OF DYNAMIC FEEDBACK LOOPS

The interplay of cognitive interpretation, emotional experience, and behavior regulation represented in the IET model allows for constant and iterative updating of the status of any given group vis-à-vis its environment. Scherer (2001) characterized the appraisal process as a continuously updating sequence of recursive chains between cognitive evaluations and suitable emotional responses that allow the individual to adapt to the ongoing situation. The situation with intergroup emotions is no different. We have shown, for example, that feelings of anger toward the outgroup in the face of an insult change in different ways depending on whether the ingroup mobilizes for a successful retaliation or slinks off in humiliation (Maitner et al., 2006). Outgroup-directed aggression dissipates the anger and increases satisfaction; failure to act directs anger at the ingroup as well. Although we investigated this feedback process empirically as an emotion-behavior-emotion regularity loop, it is probably more properly thought of as an emotion-intention-behavior-appraisal-emotion-intention-behavior loop. That is, behavior changes the situation, which changes appraisals, which change emotion, which changes behavioral intentions, and so forth.

Although we know of no studies that track the whole process, intriguing studies of iterative effects of some parts of the loop are emerging. For example, intergroup emotions can be predicted to influence future intergroup appraisals in an iterative way on the basis of findings showing similar effects with the impact of individual emotion on appraisals. Incidental emotions such anger, fear, or sadness can influence future judgments about objects or situations in ways that depend on appraisals specific to the emotion (Lerner & Keltner, 2000). For example, fear involves an appraisal that a negative event may possibly happen; that is, it involves an appraisal of uncertainty. When people are afraid, they judge many types of events to be relatively uncertain (Tiedens & Linton, 2001), perhaps making it more likely that they in turn feel fear following such appraisals. As another example, because anger involves an appraisal that someone else is responsible for a negative event, people feeling anger (for whatever reason) tend to judge other people as responsible. The relevance of such findings to intergroup situations is obvious. Ingroup members who are angry (even for reasons completely unrelated to an outgroup) might nevertheless be more likely to judge actions by an outgroup as involving deliberate intention and responsibility, precursors of aggression. In fact DeSteno, Dasgupta, Bartlett, and Cajdric (2004) hypothesized that anger would involve appraisals related to intergroup conflict and competition, so incidental anger should make people display more bias against an outgroup. This is just what they found: Induced anger (but not sadness) caused people to display prejudice against an outgroup in a minimal intergroup situation. Such emotion–appraisal chains reinforce the idea that the impact of specific emotions is likely to be quite specific (e.g., the uncertainty of fear is not true of other negative emotions for example) but also seem likely to intensify the experience of intergroup emotion: Anger toward an ingroup is even more likely to promote appraisals of that group's actions that result in more anger. Intriguingly, of course, given that this effect is linked to the emotion, and not the target, we could hypothesize that anger experienced toward one group also makes it more likely that the actions of other groups will be appraised in ways that promote anger toward them.

An iterative "strengthening" effect also seems a plausible outcome of feedback links among appraisals, emotions, and behaviors. Indeed both inwardly and outwardly directed behaviors produced by emotions might inherently affect the appraisal process in such a way as to strengthen the relations among them. Parkinson et al. (2005) suggested, for example, that greater group cohesion increases mutual influence, making it more likely that emotional events will be interpreted, responded to, and acted on, similarly. Thus we might predict that an event that prompts group pride (emotion) might promote greater interaction, cohesiveness, and influence (behavior) in a way that makes interpretation of a future event (appraisal) even more likely to result in group pride (emotion), and so forth. At least some of the consequences of iterative chaining among appraisals, emotions, and behavior seem likely to reinforce or exacerbate current reactions.

Despite this, perhaps the most critical implication of IET's focus on the continuous mutual feedback of appraisal, emotion, and behavior on one another is that it allows for change. In traditional views, both intragroup and intergroup perception, evaluation, and behavior are driven by stereotypes and prejudice. Whether directed toward the ingroup or outgroup, stereotypes and prejudice are regarded as highly stable—in fact, their resistance to change has motivated much research. In contrast, appraisals and the emotions they generate are labile, varying over time and in context (E. R. Smith & Mackie, 2006). Situations can change, evoking changed appraisals and changed emotions and thus changed interactions with groups. Emotions can change (both incidentally and integrally to the group situation), changing behavior (which changes situations and therefore appraisals), but also changing appraisals directly (even in an unchanged situation). Behavior can change, changing appraisals and emotions, and so forth. We are only just starting to explore the varied implications of the fluid view of intergroup relations that the IET approach contrasts with the much more static view inherent in stereotype and attitude approaches. Of these, the most significant consequence is the possibility for intervention, an issue we discuss in more detail later.

PREDICTIONS OF OUTGROUP EMOTION

If our emotions about other groups regulate our actions toward them, it makes sense both that other groups' emotions might regulate their behavior toward us, and that our beliefs about what the outgroup feels in turn might modulate our actual behavior toward them. Thus predictions of outgroup emotion may act as one of the moderators of the relation between intergroup emotions and intergroup behavior. For example, groups might expect an angry outgroup to be more likely to aggress than a happy, satisfied one; a guilty outgroup to be more likely to offer reparations than a satisfied one; a fearful outgroup more likely to back off than one that is angry, and so forth. Such theories might well affect the decision whether or when to retaliate a perceived slight, for example, independent of the ingroup's degree of antipathy toward the outgroup. This suggests the benefit of being able both to predict outgroup emotions and perhaps being able to manipulate them.

We have started to explore both people's theories about what outgroups feel and their ability to predict how other groups might react to particular events. In three studies, for example, we found that members of one group asked to predict the emotions that outgroup members felt (in general) demonstrated substantial, although imperfect accuracy (Seger, Smith, Kinias, & Mackie, 2006). That is, a Democrat could predict how much anger or pride Republicans feel with above chance accuracy, but their predictions were nevertheless significantly different from how Republicans actually said they were feeling. Accuracy is limited by specific biases that affected predictions, especially the projection of one's own ingroup emotions onto outgroups. Understanding this process requires answers to many questions. What relations between groups enhance or undermine predictive accuracy? What role does identification play in such processes? We found some cases in which stronger ingroup identification enhanced predictive accuracy, but these findings clearly need replication and extension. Are there circumstances under which ingroup emotions will be negatively projected onto outgroups—that is, that when the ingroup feels more satisfied the outgroup will be assumed to be less satisfied?

Other work is currently exploring the role of intergroup affective forecasting for particular events (Moons & Mackie, 2006). Management decisions might depend, for example, on projections of how employees would react emotionally to a cut in benefits rather than pay, how intense that reaction would be, and how long it might last. Cynically, perhaps, political decisions about granting voting privileges, tightening immigration rules, cracking down on freedom of the press, or forming a strategic alliance with a former enemy might equally be influenced by the same predictions. In preliminary work we have found that group stereotypes about emotion influence both outgroup and ingroup members' predictions of emotional reactions. For example, men were predicted to be more angry and women more sad in response to negative performance feedback, and these predictions in turn influenced participants' willingness to deliver the feedback. Other stereotypes will no doubt also affect such predictions (Leyens et al., 2001). Beyond the role of emotional stereotyping, it will be important to understand the role of factors such as group-level actor-observer biases, focusing on the causal event rather than the entire context, and relations of power and status among groups in this process. In these respects, the inclusion of prediction of outgroup intergroup emotion in the IET model is one important means of capturing the dynamic quality of intergroup relations.

The Impact of Group-Based Emotions on Other Cognitive Processes

In just the same way that individual emotion is self-regulatory in affecting self-knowledge, self-evaluation, and individual behavior, intergroup emotions regulate the cognitive, evaluative, and behavioral reactions that one group has regarding another. Although we have focused primarily on behavioral tendency consequences of intergroup emotions, we also expect intergroup emotions to drive generalized cognitive and evaluative reactions to groups. For example, we claim that the emotions one group feels toward another, especially over time, will change intergroup cognitions: Ingroup and outgroup stereotypes and images will derive from the intergroup emotions felt in interactions with those entities.

Similarly, we expect intergroup emotions to drive generalized evaluative reactions to groups as reflected in measures of prejudice and intergroup attitudes. We have demonstrated that the impact of factors like intergroup contact and general political predispositions on prejudice are mediated by intergroup emotions directed at the outgroup (Miller, Smith, & Mackie, 2004). In both studies, past intergroup contact and social dominance orientation predicted ratings of the outgroup as measured either by a feeling thermometer or the Modern Racism Scale. As expected, these effects were significantly mediated by intergroup emotions, above and beyond measures of stereotypes that were entered as alternative potential mediators. Thus intergroup emotions seem to determine generalized evaluative responses to groups as measured in attitude and prejudice scales (Esses & Dovidio, 2002; Fiske, 1998).

Nevertheless, we have yet to demonstrate direct effects of emotions on specific intergroup cognitions. Most obviously, if a specific emotion is experienced repeatedly over time in response to a particular group, this feeling can become associated with the mental representation of the group, through the process of classical conditioning. The emotion is then likely to be reactivated when group members are encountered or thought about, even in neutral contexts that do not involve any specific emotional events. Action tendencies may also become chronically accessible in the same way, so that the perceiver may feel impulses to attack or harm the group every time he or she thinks about them. The association of particular emotions or action tendencies with particular groups may lead over time to representations of those groups in ways that reflect the perceiver's emotional relationship with them. That is, group stereotypes should contain components that are directly relevant to the emotions that groups evoke. That is, we might predict that a group might be stereotyped as weak, foolish, or incapable because they evoke anger in us; as strong, domineering, or aggressive because they frighten us; as helpless and dependent because they evoke guilt; and so forth. Of course this means that an outgroup may be stereotyped in positive ways even though they generate negative emotions (as strong, but therefore frightening, or smart, and therefore threatening; e.g., Fiske, Cuddy, Glick, & Xu, 2002). In this view then, stereotypes can be usefully seen as end products of intergroup interactions, rather than only as antecedents of intergroup relations. Such views are consistent with the idea that stereotypes are often after-the-fact explanations or rationalizations of preexisting emotions about groups (Allport, 1954; Brewer & Alexander, 2002).

Interventions That Capitalize on the Crucial Role of Categorization and Identification

Social psychologists have long touted the potential benefits of changes in social categorization (Gaertner, Dovidio, Anastasio, Bachman, & Rust, 1993; Gaertner, Mann, Murrell, & Dovidio,

1989; Hewstone, 1996) as ways to reduce intergroup conflict. The emotional consequences of such changes, however, have been largely overlooked. In our view, it is because social categorization dictates intergroup emotional experience that changing categorization changes intergroup relations. Most obviously, individuals typically have multiple group memberships that may become salient under different circumstances. Although there is probably a degree of continuity between memberships (itself a topic worthy of research) each membership can produce a distinctive emotional profile, both chronically (E. R. Smith et al., 2007) and in reaction to a given event (Dumont et al., 2003; Gordign et al., 2001, 2006; Yzerbyt et al., 2003). Changing membership will change emotional reactions and thus intergroup relations. Recent work in our lab has investigated whether individuals react emotionally to the same target depending on their own group membership. For example, participants thinking about themselves as UCSB students had angrier reactions to "the police" than did those same participants when thinking about themselves as Americans (Ray, Rydell, Mackie, & Smith, 2008). In other cases, it appears that changing group membership may change the representation of the target, another way to undermine typical emotional reactions to outgroups.

Less obviously, but perhaps just as effective, individuals have personal selves and possibly several important relational selves as well (Sedikides & Brewer, 2001). Individual emotional reactions differ significantly from intergroup emotional reactions (E. R. Smith et al., 2006); although group memberships have perennial and sometimes unyielding appeal to individuals, disengaging group membership, and thus appraising events in personal terms, in any given case might be possible (H. J. Smith, Spears, & Oyen, 1994). A more frequent alternative might be to "switch" individuals to relational identities that compel them to react to events that impact, for example, another person rather than the group as a whole. The idea of encouraging the feeling of emotion experienced by an individual other in a negatively viewed outgroup seems closely consistent with Pettigrew's findings that individual friendships with outgroup others underpin the positive effects of intergroup contact (see Tropp & Pettigrew, 2005). We have shown that both natural inclinations and perspective-taking instructions can foster a focus on individual protagonists rather than an equally accessible ingroup or outgroup, even in intergroup situations, resulting in changes in emotion, prejudice, and behavior (Maitner, Claypool, Mackie, & Smith, 2006b; see also Batson et al., 1999; Batson, Klein, Highberger, & Shaw, 1995; Galinsky & Moskowitz, 2000). Although their boundaries have yet to be tested, such manipulations make potentially viable interventions. Given that people that people typically prefer feeling good to feeling bad, such shifts between one group membership and another, or between a group-level and interpersonal or individual-level self, might even be expected to occur spontaneously as part of an individual's own emotion regulation process (E. R. Smith & Mackie, 2006). Thus intervening in some directions (e.g., away from group memberships with negative connotations) will be easier than in others.

As our own and others' results show, not all group members have identical emotional reactions when group membership is salient. For some, group membership is either central or affectively important, or both. These highly identified group members both feel most group-based emotions more intensely and show more bias in appraisals that shield them from experiencing emotions that reflect poorly on their group. Thus one theoretically plausible way to undermine the consequences of intergroup emotion is to psychologically detach highly identified members from their groups. Practically, we suspect that this will be hard to accomplish, for the very reasons that made them highly identified in the first place. In addition, although manipulations of social categorization are common in the literature, successful manipulations of identity are not. Nevertheless, Kessler and Hollbach's (2005) finding that anger at the ingroup can loosen identity ties offers some pointers as to how this might be accomplished. If centrality versus importance do play different roles in heightened identity, as suggested earlier, undermining centrality will affect the degree to which group-based appraisals are made, and undermining importance will undermine, for example, a group justification bias in appraisals. If group-centered versus member-centered identification also have different effects, it might be possible to refocus the kinds of attachments people have to their groups to short-circuit the production of outgroup anger or enhance the production of ingroup guilt.

Again, if individuals can shift identities to help regulate the emotions they feel, people might be expected to more easily adopt identities associated with positive group emotions or disidentify from groups associated with negative group emotions. As these possibilities make clear, one of IET's unique contributions is to focus attention on the potential of emotional regulation theory and research (e.g., in contrast to stereotype or categorization change) to suggest fresh strategies for changing intergroup relations. For example, research might productively examine the effectiveness of categorization-based change strategies against appraisal-based change strategies or even suppression of group-based emotion (Gross, 1998).

CONCLUSIONS AND IMPLICATIONS FOR AMELIORATION OF INTERGROUP RELATIONS

When people think about themselves as members of a group, their emotional reactions reflect appraisals of the implications that events, situations, and perhaps especially, other social entities have for that group. Those distinct emotional reactions entail inclinations to act, perhaps especially toward the ingroup and outgroups, in equally distinct and specific ways. These two key ideas lie at the heart of the more detailed account of IET described in this chapter. The theory continues to enjoy considerable empirical support. In addition, it continues to generate theoretical refinements and extensions and provoke new lines of research investigation, including ones that suggest uniquely different approaches to ameliorating the all-too-often negative nature of intergroup relations. In this concluding section, we briefly highlight some of the ways in which the IET approach offers a distinct perspective on intergroup relations.

First, and perhaps most uniquely, IET claims that emotions are connected with categorizations and identities. Social categorization determines emotional reaction and identification moderates this relation. Because individuals might differentially identify with any of multiple group memberships and multiple interpersonal relations, individuals are capable of multiple emotional reactions to events and entities that have consequences for those social ties. Any or all of those emotional reactions might be quite different from the emotional reaction that would be provoked by the same event or entity if the individual was focused on his or her unique personal self.

Second, IET moves beyond a simple positive or negative evaluation of categorization of ingroups and outgroups to focus on the distinct and differentiated emotional reactions that ingroups and outgroups can provoke (Cottrell & Neuberg, 2005). IET allows prediction of when an outgroup will be feared, hated, or regarded with contempt, as well as when an ingroup will evoke pride, satisfaction, or guilt. Such a view requires a rethinking of traditional views of both ethnocentrism and prejudice.

Third, IET privileges action, or at least the proclivity toward, intention of, or inclination for action, toward or against other groups. IET's focus on emotion entrains the view of evaluation as readiness for action, as the embodied proclivity to strike out when angered, to shun when disgusted, to nurture when affectionate, or to flee when frightened. From this perspective, the theoretical focus is on what groups do to one another (rather than what they think of one another) and the generation of emotion predicts specific forms of discrimination (rather than generalized negative or positive behavior).

Fourth, IET encompasses the variability that characterizes intergroup relations. Whereas stereotypes and prejudice are regarded as stable over time and context, emotional reactions vary over both. The iterative chaining among appraisal, emotion, and behavior allows for similar situations and entities to be appraised and responded to differently depending on changes in the perceiver's categorization and identity, in the context and event, and in the number and intensity of emotions generated. Response variability also arises because of regulatory pressures at both the individual and group level: Individuals and groups may prefer and seek to experience some emotions rather than others, and individuals and groups will experience pressures to experience and display some emotions rather than others.

Fifth, IET takes a peculiarly social perspective on emotion. Not only does it see emotion as springing from social categorizations, but as socially influenced at all levels. The social influence that group membership entails may create changes in core affect, the causal attributions people make for such changes, the degree of emotional convergence they experience, the way they categorize those emotional experiences, and the types of actions that they may seek to performs as individuals or collectively, under the influence of emotional states. All of these aspects of the interplay among intergroup appraisals, emotions, and behavior are no doubt also influenced by the power and status relations among and between groups (Alexander, Brewer, & Hermann, 1999; Hermann & Fischerkeller, 1995; Kemper, 1990), making intergroup emotion equally dependent on social relations between as well as within groups.

Finally, IET sees emotion as functionally regulatory at the group level just as emotion is functionally regulatory at the individual level. Indeed, such group-level functionality is to be expected, for group living is evolutionarily ancient in humans as well as related primate species (Caporael, 1997). Just as emotion has changed from being seen as inherently disruptive of the best functioning of the individual to being understood as part of an intricate system that promotes adaptive functioning, so too do we view intergroup emotion as occurring for adaptive reasons and not merely as events inherently disruptive to intragroup or intergroup relations. The consequence of emotion at the individual or intergroup level is often disruptive and destructive but might also serve connectedness and self- or group-sustaining functions. The regulatory focus also suggests interventional strategies not immediately obvious from any other perspective on intergroup emotions. We believe that understanding the regulatory function of intergroup emotion regardless of its negative or positive consequences, will ultimately serve our discipline well in its attempt to ameliorate intergroup relations.

REFERENCES

Alexander, M. G., Brewer, M. B., & Hermann, R. K. (1999). Images and affect: A functional analysis of outgroup stereotypes. *Journal of Personality and Social Psychology, 77,* 78–93.

Allport, G. W. (1954). *The nature of prejudice.* Oxford, UK: Addison-Wesley.

Barrett, L. F. (2006). Solving the emotion paradox: Categorization and experience of emotion. *Personality and Social Psychology Review, 10,* 20–46.

Batson, C. D., Ahmad, N., Yin, J., Bedell, S. J., Johnson, J. W., Templin, C. M., et al. (1999). Two threats to the common good: Self-interested egoism and empathy-induced altruism. *Personality and Social Psychology Bulletin, 25*(1), 3–16.

Batson, C. D., Klein, T. R., Highberger, L., & Shaw, L. L. (1995). Immorality from empathy-induced altruism: When compassion and justice conflict. *Journal of Personality and Social Psychology, 68*(6), 1042–1054.

Branscombe, N. R., & Miron, A. M. (2004). Interpreting the ingroup's negative actions toward another group: Emotional reactions to appraised harm. In L. Z. Tiedens & C. W. Leach (Eds.), *The social life of emotions* (pp. 314–335). New York: Cambridge University Press.

Brewer, M. B., & Alexander, M. G. (2002). Intergroup emotions and images. In D. M. Mackie & E. R. Smith (Eds.), *From prejudice to intergroup emotions: Differentiated reactions to social groups* (pp. 209–226). New York: Psychology Press.

Brewer, M. B., & Gardner, W. (1996). Who is this "we"? Levels of collective identity and self representations. *Journal of Personality and Social Psychology, 71,* 83–93.

Brewer, M. B., & Weber J. G. (1994). Self-evaluation effects of interpersonal versus intergroup social comparison. *Journal of Personality and Social Psychology, 66,* 268–275.

Caporael, L. R. (1997). The evolution of truly social cognition: The core configurations model. *Personality and Social Psychology Review, 1,* 276–298.

Cialdini, R. B., Borden, R. J., Thorne, A., Walker, M. R., Freeman, S., & Sloan, L. R. (1976). Basking in reflected glory: Three (football) field studies. *Journal of Personality and Social Psychology, 34,* 366–375.

Cottrell, C. A., & Neuberg, S. L. (2005). Different emotional reactions to different groups: A sociofunctional threat-based approach to "prejudice." *Journal of Personality and Social Psychology, 88,* 770–789.

Desteno, D., Dasgupta, N., Bartlett, M. Y., & Cajdric A. (2004). Prejudice from thin air: The effect of emotion on automatic intergroup attitudes. *Psychological Science, 15,* 319–324.

Devos, T., Silver, L. A., Mackie, D. M., & Smith, E. R. (2002). Experiencing intergroup emotions. In D. M. Mackie & E. R. Smith (Eds.), *From prejudice to intergroup emotions* (pp. 111–134). New York: Psychology Press.

Doosje, B., Branscombe, N. R., Spears, R, & Manstead, A. S. R. (1998). Guilty by association: When one's group has a negative history. *Journal of Personality and Social Psychology, 75,* 872–886.

Dumont, M., Yzerbyt, V., Wigboldus, D., & Gordijn, E. H. (2003). Social categorization and fear reactions to the September 11th terrorist attacks. *Personality and Social Psychology Bulletin, 29,* 1509–1520.

Esses, V. M., & Dovidio, J. F. (2002). The role of emotions in determining willingness to engage in intergroup contact. *Personality and Social Psychology Bulletin, 28,* 1202–1214.

Fiske, S. T. (1998). Stereotyping, prejudice, and discrimination. In D. T. Gilbert, S. T. Fiske, & G. Lindzey et al. (Eds.), *The handbook of social psychology* (4th ed., Vol. 2, pp. 357–411). New York: McGraw-Hill.

Fiske, S. T., Cuddy, A. J. C., Glick, P., & Xu, J. (2002). A model of (often mixed) stereotype content: Competence and warmth respectively follow from perceived status and competition. *Journal of Personality and Social Psychology, 82,* 878–902.

Frijda, N. H. (1986). *The emotions.* Cambridge, UK: Cambridge University Press.

Frijda, N. H. (1993). Moods, emotion episodes and emotions. In M. Lewis & J. M. Haviland (Eds.), *Handbook of emotions* (pp. 381–403). New York: Guilford.

Gabriel, S., & Gardner, W. L. (1999). Are there "his" and "hers" types of interdependence? The implications of gender differences in collective versus relational interdependence for affect, behavior, and cognition. *Journal of Personality and Social Psychology, 77,* 642–655.

Gaertner, S. L., Dovidio, J. F., Anastasio, P. A., Bachman, B. A., & Rust, M. C. (1993). The common ingroup identity model: Recategorization and the reduction of intergroup bias. In W. Stroebe & M. Hewstone (Eds.), *European review of social psychology* (Vol. 4, pp. 1–26). Chichester, UK: Wiley.

Gaertner, S. L., Mann, J., Murrell, A., & Dovidio, J. F. (1989). Reducing intergroup bias: The benefits of recategorization. *Journal of Personality and Social Psychology, 57,* 239–249.

Galinsky, A. D. & Moskowitz, G. B. (2000). Perspective-taking: Decreasing stereotype expression, stereotype accessibility, and in-group favoritism. *Journal of Personality and Social Psychology, 78,* 708–724.

Garcia-Prieto, P., Mackie, D., Tran, V., & Smith, E. (2007). Intergroup emotions in workgroups: Some emotional antecedents and consequences of belonging. In M. A. Neale & C. Anderson (Eds.), *Affect and groups: Vol. 2. Research on managing groups and teams* (pp. 145–184). Amsterdam: Elsevier.

Gordijn, E. H., Wigboldus, D., & Yzerbyt, V. (2001). Emotional consequences of categorizing victims of negative outgroup behavior as ingroup or outgroup. *Group Processes and Intergroup Relations, 4,* 317–326.

Gordijn, E. H., Yzerbyt, V., Wigboldus, D., & Dumont, M. (2006). Emotional reactions to harmful intergroup behavior. *European Journal of Social Psychology, 36,* 15–30.

Gross, J. J. (1998). Antecedent- and response-focused emotion regulation: Divergent consequences for experience, expression, and physiology. *Journal of Personality and Social Psychology, 74,* 224–237.

Hastorf, A. H., & Cantril, H. (1954). They saw a game: A case study. *Journal of Abnormal & Social Psychology, 49,* 129–134.

Hermann, R. K., & Fischerkeller, M. (1995). Beyond the enemy image and spiral model: Cognitive-strategic research after the cold war. *International Organization, 49,* 415–450

Hewstone, M. (1996). Contact and categorization: Social psychology interventions to change intergroup relations. In C. N. Macraw, C. Stangor, & M. Hewstone (Eds.), *Stereotypes and stereotyping* (pp. 323–368). New York: Guilford.

Hogg, M. A., & Turner, J. C. (1987). Intergroup behavior, self-stereotyping and the salience of social categories. *British Journal of Social Psychology, 26,* 325–340.

Insko, C. A., Schopler, J., Pemberton, M. B., Wieselquist, J., McIlraith, S. A., Currey, D. P., et al. (1998). Long-term outcome maximization and the reduction of interindividual-intergroup discontinuity. *Journal of Personality and Social Psychology, 75,* 695–711.

Iyer, A., Leach, C. W., & Crosby, F. J. (2003). White guilt and racial compensation: The benefits and limits of self-focus. *Personality and Social Psychology Bulletin, 29,* 117–129.

Jackson, J. W., & Smith, E. R. (1999). Conceptualizing social identity: A new framework and evidence for the impact of different dimensions. *Personality and Social Psychology Bulletin, 25,* 120–135.

Jetten, J., Spears, R., & Manstead, A. S. R. (2001). Similarity as a source of differentiation: The role of group identification. *European Journal of Social Psychology, 31,* 621–640.

Kemper, T. D. (1990). Social relations and emotions: A structural approach. In T. D. Kemper (Ed.), *Research agendas in the sociology of emotions* (pp. 207–237). Albany: State University of New York Press.

Kessler, T., & Hollbach, S. (2005). Group-based emotion as determinants of ingroup identification. *Journal of Experimental Social Psychology, 41,* 677–685.

Lazarus, R. S., & Folkman, S. (1984). *Stress, appraisal, and coping.* New York: Springer-Verlag.

Leach, C. W., Iyer, A., & Pedersen, A. (2006). Anger and guilt about intergroup advantage explain the willingness for political action. *Personality and Social Psychology Bulletin, 32,* 1232–1245.

Lerner, J. S., & Keitner, D. (2000). Beyond valence: Toward a model of emotion-specific influences on judgment and choice. *Cognition & Emotion, 14,* 473–493.

Leyens, J. P., Rodriguez-Perez, A., Rodriguez-Torres, R., Gaunt, R., Paladino, M. P., Vaes, J., et al. (2001). Psychological essentialism and the differential attribution of uniquely human emotions to ingroups and outgroups. *European Journal of Social Psychology, 31,* 395–411.

Mackie, D. M., Devos, T., & Smith, E. R. (2000). Intergroup emotions: Explaining offensive action tendencies in an intergroup context. *Journal of Personality and Social Psychology, 79,* 602–616.

Mackie, D. M., Rydell, R. J., Sack, J. D., Claypool, H. M., Ryan, M. J., Schudel, K. M., et al. (2006). *Entitativity and beliefs about shared group emotions.* Unpublished manuscript, University of California, Santa Barbara.

Mackie, D. M., Silver, L. A., Maitner, A. T., & Smith, E. R. (2002). *Intergroup emotions in response to and as a predictor of intergroup aggression.* Unpublished manuscript, University of California, Santa Barbara.

Mackie, D. M., Silver, L. A., & Smith, E. (2004). Intergroup emotion: Emotion as an intergroup phenomenon. In L. Z. Tiedens & C. W. Leach (Eds.), *The social life of emotions* (pp. 227–245). New York: Cambridge University Press.

Mackie, D. M., & Smith, E. R. (2002). Intergroup emotions and the social self: Prejudice reconceptualized as differentiated reactions to outgroups. In J. P. Forgas & K. D. Williams (Eds.), *The social self: Cognitive, interpersonal, and intergroup perspectives* (pp. 309–326). Philadelphia: Psychology Press.

Maitner, A. T., Claypool, H. M., Mackie, D. M., & Smith, E. R. (2006a). *Comrade or company? Emotional consequences of events impacting a group member representing the group.* Unpublished manuscript, University of California, Santa Barbara.

Maitner, A. T., Claypool, H. M., Mackie, D. M., & Smith, E. R. (2006b). *Interpersonal and intergroup sources of emotion.* Unpublished manuscript, University of California, Santa Barbara.

Maitner, A. T., Claypool, H. M., Mackie, D. M., Smith, E. R., & Keeth, A. (2006). *Intergroup emotions impact information processing.* Unpublished manuscript, University of California, Santa Barbara.

Maitner, A. T., Mackie, D. M., & Smith, E. R. (2006). Evidence for the regulatory function of intergroup emotion: Emotional consequences of implemented or impeded intergroup action tendencies. *Journal of Experimental Social Psychology.*

Maitner, A. T., Mackie, D. M., & Smith, E. R. (2007). Antecedents and consequences of satisfaction and guilt following ingroup aggression. *Group Processes and Intergroup Relations.*

McCoy, S. K., & Major, B. (2003). Group identification moderates emotional responses to perceived prejudice. *Personality and Social Psychology Bulletin, 29,* 1005–1017.

McGarty, C., Pedersen, A., Leach, C. W., Mansell, T., Waller, J., & Bliuc, A. M. (2005). Group-based guilt as a predictor of commitment to apology. *British Journal of Social Psychology, 44,* 659–680.

Miller, D. A., Smith, E. R., & Mackie, D. M. (2004). Effects of intergroup contact and political predispositions on prejudice: Role of intergroup emotions. *Group Processes and Intergroup Relations, 7,* 221–237.

Moons, W. G., & Mackie, D. M. (2006). *I'll cry if he yells: A model of anticipated emotional interactions.* Unpublished manuscript. University of California. Santa Barbara.

Neumann, R., & Strack, F. (2000). "Mood contagion": The automatic transfer of mood between persons. *Journal of Personality and Social Psychology, 79,* 211–223.

Parkinson, B., Fischer, A. H., & Manstead, A. S. R. (2005). *Emotion in social relations: Cultural, group, and interpersonal processes.* New York: Psychology Press.

Ray, D., Rydell, R. J., Mackie, D. M., Smith, E. R. (2006). Changing categorization of self can change emotions about outgroups. *Journal of Experimental Social Psychology, 44,* 1210–1213.

Roseman, I. J. (1984). Cognitive determinants of emotion: A structural theory. *Review of Personality and Social Psychology, 5,* 11–36.

Roseman, I. J., Wiest, C., & Swartz, T. S. (1994). Phenomenology, behaviors, and goals differentiate discrete emotions. *Journal of Personality and Social Psychology, 67,* 206–221.

Russell, J. A. (2003). Core affect and the psychological construction of emotion. *Psychological Review, 110,* 145–172.

Russell, J. A., & Barrett, L. F. (1999). Core affect, prototypical emotional episodes, and other things called emotion: Dissecting the elephant. *Journal of Personality and Social Psychology, 76,* 805–819.

Rydell, R. J., Mackie, D. M., Maitner, A. T., Claypool, H. M., Ryan, M. J., Smith, E. R. (in press). Arousal, processing, and risk taking: Consequences of intergroup anger. *Personality and Social Psychology Bulletin.*

Scherer, K. R. (1988). Criteria for emotion-antecedent appraisal: A review. In V. Hamilton, G. H. Bower, & N. H. Frijda (Eds.), *Cognitive perspectives on emotion and motivation: Vol. 44, NATO ASI series D: Behavioral and social sciences* (pp. 89–126). Dordrecht, Netherlands: Kluwer.

Scherer, K. R. (2001). Appraisal considered as a process of multi-level sequential checking. In K. R. Scherer, A. Schorr, & T. Johnstone (Eds.), *Appraisal processes in emotion: Theory, methods, research* (pp. 92–120). New York: Oxford University Press.

Schmitt, M., Behner, R., Montada, L., Muller, L., & Muller-Fohrbrodt, G. (2000). Gender, ethnicity, and education as privileges: Exploring the generalizability of the existential guilt reaction. *Social Justice Research, 13,* 313–337.

Sedikides, C., & Brewer, M. B. (Eds.). (2001). *Individual self, relational self, collective self.* Philadelphia: Psychology Press/Taylor & Francis.

Seger, C. R., Smith, E. R., Kinias, Z., & Mackie, D. M. (2006). *Knowing how they feel: Predicting outgroup emotion.* Unpublished manuscript, Indiana University, Bloomington, Indiana.

Simon, B., & Hamilton, D. L. (1994). Self-stereotyping and social context: The effects of relative in-group size and in-group status. *Journal of Personality and Social Psychology, 66,* 699–711.

Simon, B., Loewy, M., Sturmer, S., Weber, U., Freytag, P., Habig, C., Kampmeier, C., & Spahlinger, P. (1998). Collective identification and social movement participation. *Journal of Personality and Social Psychology, 74,* 646–658.

Skitka, L. J., Bauman, C. W., & Mullen, E. (2004). Political tolerance and coming to psychological closure following the September 11, 2001 terrorist attacks: An integrative approach. *Personality and Social Psychology Bulletin, 30,* 743–756.

Smith, C. A., & Ellsworth, P. C. (1985). Patterns of cognitive appraisal in emotion. *Journal of Personality and Social Psychology, 48,* 813–838.

Smith, E. R. (1993). Social identity and social emotions: Toward new conceptualizations of prejudice. In D. M. Mackie & D. L. Hamilton (Eds.), *Affect, cognition, and stereotyping: Interactive processes in group perception* (pp. 297–315). San Diego, CA: Academic.

Smith, E. R., & Mackie, D. M. (2005). Aggression, hatred, and other emotions. In J. F. Dovidio, P. Glick, & L. A. Rudman (Eds.), *On the nature of prejudice: Fifty years after Allport* (pp. 361–376). Malden, MA: Blackwell.

Smith, E. R., & Mackie, D. M. (2006). It's about time: Intergroup emotions as time-dependent phenomena. In D. Capozza & R. Brown (Eds.), *Social identities: motivational, emotional, and cultural influences* (pp. 173–187). New York: Psychology Press.

Smith, E. R., Seger, C. R., & Mackie D. M. (2007). Can emotions be truly group-level? Evidence regarding four conceptual criteria. *Journal of Personality and Social Psychology, 93,* 431–446.

Smith, H. J., & Kessler, T. (2004). Group-based emotions and intergroup behavior: The case of relative deprivation. In L. Z. Tiedens & C. W. Leach (Eds.), *The social life of emotions* (pp. 292–313). New York: Cambridge University Press.

Smith, H. J., & Spears, R. (1996). Ability and outcome evaluations as a function of personal and collective (dis)advantage: A group escape from individual bias. *Personality and Social Psychology Bulletin, 22,* 690–704.

Smith, H. J., Spears, R., & Oyen, M. (1994). "People like us:" The influence of personal deprivation and group membership salience on justice evaluations. *Journal of Experimental Social Psychology, 30,* 277–299.

Swim, J. K., & Miller, D. L. (1999). White guilt: Its antecedents and consequences for attitudes toward affirmative action. *Personality and Social Psychology Bulletin, 25,* 500–514.

Tajfel, H. (1982). *Social identity and intergroup relations.* Cambridge, UK: Cambridge University Press.

Tiedens, L. Z., & Linton, S. (2001). Judgment under emotional certainty and uncertainty: The effects of specific emotions on information processing. *Journal of Personality and Social Psychology, 81,* 973–988.

Tiedens, L. Z., Sutton, R. I., & Fong, C. T. (2004). Emotional variation in work groups: Causes and performance consequences. In L. Z. Tiedens & C. W. Leach (Eds.), *The social life of emotions* (pp. 164–186). New York: Cambridge University Press.

Tropp, L. R., & Pettigrew, T. F. (2005). Differential relationships between intergroup contact and affective and cognitive dimensions of prejudice. *Personality and Social Psychology Bulletin, 31,* 1145–1158.

Turner, J. C., Hogg, M. A., Oakes, P. J., Reicher, S. D., & Wetherell, M. S. (1987). *Rediscovering the social group: A self-categorization theory.* Cambridge, MA: Basil Blackwell.

Tyler, T. R. (1999). Why people co-operate with organizations: An identity-based perspective. In R. I. Sutton & B. M. Staw (Eds.), *Research in organizational behavior* (Vol. 21, pp. 201–246). Greenwich, CT: JAI Press.

Tyler, T. R., & Blader, S. L. (2000). *Cooperation in groups: Procedural justice, social identity, and behavioral engagement.* New York: Psychology Press.

Tyler, T., Degoey, P., & Smith, H. (1996). Understanding why the justice of group procedures matters: A test of the psychological dynamics of the group-value model. *Journal of Personality and Social Psychology, 70,* 913–930.

Van Zomeren, M., Spears, R., Fischer, A. H., & Leach, C. W. (2004). Put your money where your mouth is! Explaining collective action tendencies through group-based anger and group efficacy. *Journal of Personality and Social Psychology, 87,* 640–664.

Yzerbyt, V., Dumont, M., Wigboldus, D., & Gordijn, E. (2003). I feel for us: The impact of categorization and identification on emotions and action tendencies. *British Journal of Social Psychology, 42,* 533–549.

15 How Our Dreams of Death Transcendence Breed Prejudice, Stereotyping, and Conflict

Terror Management Theory

Jeff Greenberg, Mark Landau
University of Kansas

Spee Kosloff
University of Arizona

Sheldon Solomon
Skidmore College

> Life is tragic simply because the earth turns and the sun inexorably rises and sets, and one day, for each of us, the sun will go down for the last, last time. Perhaps the whole root of our trouble, the human trouble, is that we will sacrifice all the beauty of our lives, will imprison ourselves in totems, taboos, crosses, blood sacrifices, steeples, mosques, races, armies, flags, nations, in order to deny the fact of death, which is the only fact we have.
>
> — James Baldwin (1963)

Seemingly intractable and escalating violent conflicts resulting from long-standing racial, religious, ethnic, and nationalistic prejudices—although by no means of recent origin in human history—are especially problematic at the outset of the 21st century. Lethal weapons of mass destruction (real and imagined), religious and political leaders (of nation-states or of their own lunatic fringes) with apocalyptic visions of eradicating evil (real and imagined), and media technology (Internet and satellite television) fostering rapid dissemination of information to incite hatred and provide explicit instructions for terrifying violence a toxic brew that appears to be close to boiling over. In light of these forces, humans becoming the first life form to extinguish itself seems more like a sober actuarial prediction than a science fiction prophecy. Surely then, understanding the psychological underpinnings of prejudice in hopes of fostering constructive efforts toward amelioration should be a high priority for social scientists of all stripes.

Allport (1954) made it abundantly clear in his classic *The Nature of Prejudice* that prejudice is a multifaceted phenomenon, and this *Handbook* undoubtedly provides excellent coverage of many of its causes and consequences. Terror management theory (TMT; Greenberg et al., 1986; Solomon, Greenberg, & Pyszczynski, 1991) and research offer a unique perspective by focusing specifically on the role of existential threat in prejudice, stereotyping, and intergroup aggression. In this chapter, we summarize the theory's core insights into the causes and consequences of prejudice and review substantial lines of research supporting these insights. We then consider how TMT complements other theoretical accounts of prejudice and offer some suggestions for further research and theoretical refinement. Finally, we briefly discuss the implications of this work for mitigating this grievous human predispostion.

TERROR MANAGEMENT: THEORY AND EVIDENCE

THEORY

Extensive presentations of TMT and the research supporting it, now consisting of more than 300 studies, can be found in Solomon et al. (1991), Pyszczynski, Solomon, and Greenberg (2003), and Greenberg, Solomon, and Arndt (2008). For current purposes, we present the theory and evidentiary base very concisely, and then focus on the theory's implications and research findings specifically pertinent to understanding prejudice, stereotyping, and intergroup conflict.

TMT is based on the writings of Becker (1971, 1973, 1975) and begins with the evolutionary assumption that humans, like other animals, have a wide range of biological systems oriented toward continuing our existence: "the obvious first priorities of a survival machine, and of the brain that makes the decisions for it, are individual survival and reproduction" (Dawkins, 1976/1989, p. 62). At the same time, unlike other animals, we humans have a cerebral cortex that make us smart enough to realize that we are vulnerable to all sorts of potentially lethal threats, and that inevitably, our efforts to continue existing will fail. Becker, as well as many before and since him, argued that because these realizations conflict with our many motivational systems geared toward survival, we cannot handle this existential truth; it has the potential to leave us paralyzed with anxiety: "Man . . . has an awareness of his own splendid uniqueness . . . and yet he goes back into the ground a few feet in order to blindly and dumbly rot and disappear forever. It is a terrifying dilemma to be in" (Becker, 1973, p. 26).

To manage the potential terror engendered by this awareness of one's own vulnerability and mortality, people rely on their cultures for psychological security. Cultures accomplish this by providing their members with meaningful views of reality and opportunities to feel enduringly significant. These internalized cultural worldviews provide psychological equanimity by allowing people to live out their lives in a world of meaning, values, purposes, and roles, fortifying a sense that they are more than mere animals fated only to obliteration upon death. This belief is buttressed by literal and symbolic forms of death transcendence provided by cultures. Literal immortality is provided by concepts such as an everlasting soul or spirit, heaven, and reincarnation. Symbolic immortality is obtainable by identification with larger groups and causes, offspring, and valued achievements in the arts and sciences. Based on the works of Otto Rank, Norman Brown and others, Becker (1975) summarizes the evolution of these immortality beliefs in this way:

> History . . . is the career of a frightened animal who must lie in order to live . . . societies are standardized systems of death denial; they give structure to the formulas for heroic transcendence. History can then be looked at as a succession of immortality ideologies, or as a mixture at any time of several of these ideologies. . . . For primitive man, who practiced the ritual renewal of nature, each person could be a cosmic hero of a quite definite kind: he could contribute with his powers and observances to the replenishment of cosmic life. Gradually . . . cosmic heroism became the property of special classes like divine kings and the military . . . And so the situation developed where men could be heroic only by following orders. . . . With the rise of money coinage one could be a money hero and privately protect himself and his offspring by the accumulation of visible gold-power. With Christianity something new came into the world: the heroism of renunciation of this world and the satisfactions of this life . . . It was a sort of anti-heroism by an animal who denied life in order to deny evil. . . . In modern times . . . a new type of productive and scientific hero came into prominence, and we are still living this today. And with the French Revolution . . . the revolutionary hero who will bring an end to injustice and evil once and for all, by bringing into being a new utopian society perfect in its purity. (pp. 153–155)

To boil these big ideas down to a simple theoretical formulation from which we could derive testable hypotheses, we developed TMT, which posits that to manage the potential terror engendered by the awareness of mortality, people must sustain faith in (a) an internalized cultural worldview that imbues subjective reality with order meaning and permanence, and bases of death transcendence to those who meet the culture's prescribed standards of value; and (b) the belief that they are meeting those prescribed standards of value (i.e., the feeling of self-esteem).

EVIDENCE

Research supporting TMT has shown that these two psychological constructs, cultural worldviews and self-esteem, protect people from anxiety and from death-related thought. These studies have used a variety of measures of anxiety and death thought accessibility. Research has also shown that reminders of death (mortality salience [MS]) instigate bolstering and defense of both faith in one's worldview and one's self-esteem (for recent reviews, see Greenberg Solomon, and Arndt, 2008; Solomon, Greenberg, & Pyszczynski, 2004).

In support of other hypotheses derived from the theory, MS has also been shown to increase: (a) distancing from reminders of one's animality (e.g., Goldenberg, Pyszczynski, Greenberg, & Solomon, 2000); (b) guilt after creative action (e.g., Arndt, Greenberg, Solomon, Pyszczynski, & Schimel, 1999); (c) desire for closeness to romantic partners (e.g., Mikulincer, Florian, & Hirschberger, 2003); and (d) preference for people, stimuli, and events that reinforce rather than challenge basic ways in which we view life as meaningful (e.g., Landau, Greenberg, et al., 2006). Finally, a great deal has been learned about the precise cognitive processes by which thoughts of death generate these effects, summarized by the dual defense model of conscious and unconscious defenses instigated by death-related thought (e.g., Arndt, Cook, & Routledge, 2004; Greenberg et al., 2003; Pyszczynski, Greenberg, & Solomon, 1999).

This body of work has employed a varied range of MS inductions to increase the accessibility of death-related thought, including open-ended items about one's death, death anxiety scales, accident footage, word search puzzles with death words embedded, proximity to funeral homes and cemeteries, and subliminal primes of the word "dead" or "death." In addition, the effects of these reminders of death have been compared to, and found to be different than, reminders of a wide array of other aversive concepts, including failure, uncertainty, dental pain, intense uncertain bouts of pain, paralysis, meaninglessness, general anxieties, worries after college, giving a speech in public, and social exclusion.[1]

TMT, PREJUDICE, STEREOTYPING, AND DISCRIMINATION

TMT AND PREJUDICE AS A RESPONSE TO THE THREAT OF ALTERNATIVE WORLDVIEWS

Although Becker (1971) was broadly concerned with explaining the motives that drive human behavior, "what makes people act the way they do" (p. vii), his most fervent concern was with intergroup aggression, which he saw as the primary way in which people contribute to human suffering. Becker's perspective on intergroup aggression is nicely summarized in his final book, *Escape from Evil*:

> What men have done is to shift the fear of death onto the higher level of cultural perpetuity; and this very triumph ushers in an ominous new problem. Since men must now hold for dear life onto the self-

---

[1] In well over 200 studies, MS has had different effects than these comparison inductions. Although a small number of researchers have reported a few similar effects with other inductions, heightened death thought accessibility may have played a role in these cases, and the alternative conceptualizations offered by these researchers have never been able to account for large proportions of the evidence supporting TMT (for more extensive discussions of these issues, see Greenberg, Solomon, & Arndt, 2008; Solomon et al., 2004).

transcending meanings of the society in which they live, onto the immortality symbols which guarantee them indefinite duration of some kind, a new kind of instability and anxiety are created. And this anxiety is precisely what spills over into the affairs of men. In seeking to avoid evil, man is responsible for bringing more evil into the world than organisms could ever do merely by exercising their digestive tracts. (Becker, 1975, p. 5)

Based on this analysis, the first implication of TMT we drew for understanding prejudice is that because people who subscribe to a worldview different from one's own are implicitly and often explicitly challenging the validity of one's own worldview, and one's worldview is the fundamental basis of one's psychological security, the individual must attempt to derogate, assimilate, or annihilate threatening others to restore faith in his or her worldview. We are sure the reader can think of many historical, often tragic, examples of such attempts. Harrington (1969) put it this way:

If those weird individuals with beards and funny hats are acceptable, then what about my claim to superiority? . . . Does he, that one, dare hope to live forever too—and perhaps crowd me out. I don't like it. All I know is, if he's right I'm wrong. So different and funny-looking. I think he's trying to fool the gods with his sly ways. Let's show him up. He's not very strong. For a start, see what he'll do if I poke him. (pp. 138–139)

If these efforts reflect a need to protect the worldview by which people ward off their terror of death, then reminders of mortality should increase negative reactions to others who subscribe to different worldviews. A variety of studies have supported this hypothesis. The first such study showed that MS increased American Christians' liking of a fellow Christian student and increased their disliking of a Jewish student (Greenberg et al., 1990). Harmon-Jones, Greenberg, Solomon, and Simon (1996) found that MS increased the minimal ingroup bias, but only to the extent that the basis for forming the two groups led participants to view their own group members as more similar to themselves than the outgroup members were. Nelson, Moore, Olivetti, and Scott (1997) found that gory accident footage led American viewers to recommend a more punitive monetary penalty to an auto manufacturer if they thought the manufacturer was Japanese, but only among Americans for whom the footage led to thoughts of their own death.

More recently, Castano, Yzerbyt, Paladino, and Sacchi (2002) found that MS increased Italians' bias in favor of fellow Italians and against Germans. He also found that this effect was mediated by ingroup identification and by perceptions of the ingroup as a real entity. Jonas, Fritsche, and Greenberg (2005) found that although Germans interviewed in front of a shopping area seemed to be equally favorable to German and foreign places and products, Germans interviewed in front of a cemetery a few blocks away from the shopping area strongly preferred the German things over the foreign ones. In the only reported MS study with children, Florian and Mikulincer (1998) found that although MS led 7-year-old Israelis to rate everyone negatively, it led 11-year-old Israelis to favor native-born Israelis over Russian immigrants. Although we cannot know definitively why the 7-year-olds did not display the typical ingroup favoritism and outgroup derogation after MS, two possibilities seem likely. One is that terror management defenses may not have been exhibited in the 7-year-olds because they lacked the cognitive maturity to understand the existential threat of their own mortality. The other is that this occurred because the 7-year-olds had yet to clearly distinguish their own worldview from that of Russian immigrants.

In these studies, the amplified derogation of the outgroup after MS presumably results from the challenge to the individual's faith in her or his own worldview posed by advocates of an alternative worldview. Although these studies provide no direct evidence that this is the case, other studies have supported the idea that worldview threat leads to MS-induced derogation. Indeed, the most common TMT finding is that after MS, people derogate others who directly criticize their worldview, whether these others are ingroup or outgroup members. As examples, after MS, Americans derogate American and foreign critics of the United States, Canadians derogate those who criticize

Canada, and liberal and conservative Americans derogate those who criticize their political orientation. Indeed, in three studies, McGregor et al. (1998) found that after MS, conservative and liberal Americans allocated high levels of painfully spicy hot sauce to another student who criticized conservatives and liberals, respectively. This is the one body of evidence to date that MS can instigate actual aggression against a different other.

Another way to interpret this substantial body of evidence is to suggest that it reflects MS-induced self-esteem defense and bolstering rather than worldview defense. As both TMT and social identity theory propose, people routinely base their self-esteem in part on their ingroup identifications. A variety of TMT studies have shown that MS increases self-esteem striving and defense (see, e.g., Pyszczynski, Greenberg, Solomon, Arndt, & Schimel, 2004). It therefore remains quite plausible that the sizable body of evidence supporting a role of TMT in prejudice reflects the need to bolster self-esteem rather than the worldview.

These two possibilities are difficult to tease apart because self-esteem is predicated on both faith in the culture's worldview that prescribes standards of value, and the individual's identification with his or her culture. For example, asserting that U.S. culture is sick and vile potentially undermines an American's self-esteem both because it calls into question the cultural bases of self-worth (e.g., American Express cards, nice cars, publications, etc.) and the use of simply being an American as a basis of self-worth. So whenever the validity or goodness of one's culture is implicitly or explicitly threatened, self-esteem is potentially undermined as well. MS-induced prejudice supports TMT either way, and this distinction probably matters little outside of an academic context, but it is a methodologically challenging problem that may warrant additional research.

One set of studies does hint at a role of group-identification-based self-esteem in MS-induced prejudice (Greenberg, Schimel, Martens, Pyszczynski, & Solomon, 2001). In a preliminary study, White participants viewed a White person who expressed racial pride more negatively than a Black person who did so. However, a second study showed that MS increased liking for the White pride advocate and reduced liking for the Black pride advocate. The final study conceptually replicated this effect assessing reactions to a White or Black employer who discriminated against an employee of the other race, and who justified his actions by claiming his own race has been victimized by "massive discrimination" in the workplace. Again, after MS the White participants became more sympathetic to the White bigot and less sympathetic to the Black bigot. It is highly unlikely that the White participants subscribed to a White supremacist worldview, but after MS they became significantly more sympathetic to Whites who "stood up for the White race."

TMT AND TWO SPECIAL KINDS OF PREJUDICE: SEXISM AND AGEISM

So far we have explored the idea that terror management needs incite prejudice because the outgroup represents a threat to faith in one's worldview and one's self-worth. However, some forms of prejudice are directed at groups that do not necessarily subscribe to a different worldview. Two such groups are women and the elderly. Both groups are part of every culture. Do terror management concerns contribute to prejudice against these groups? These prejudices, like all others, are undoubtedly multiply determined, but there is a reason to believe terror management does play a role, even though ingroup women and old people do not generally threaten a nonelderly male's worldview.

TMT sheds some light on the psychological roots of misogyny and violent tendencies toward women. Research conducted by Goldenberg et al. (2000) shows that people are often ambivalent about the body and the physical aspects of sex because of the link between the physical and the mortal: Physical creatures die, and our terror management depends on viewing ourselves as more than mere animals, as enduringly significant beings in a world of meaning. Building on this research, Landau, Goldenberg, et al. (2006) reasoned that men sometimes distance from attraction to women and generally devalue them because, by being reminded of their susceptibility to sexual arousal, men are confronted with their own animal and thus mortal nature. Thus, women who arouse carnal lust in men, especially outside the trappings of a symbolic conception of lust such as romantic love, may be viewed negatively.

This may at first seem far-fetched, but not if you consider the elaborate historical and cultural demonization and regulation of women's sexuality and animality across virtually every known culture. Indeed, according to the Bible it was that temptress Eve who got us into this existential mess in the first place by enticing Adam to taste the fruit of the tree of knowledge, which made awareness of mortality possible, and ambivalence toward the body probable. In one of six studies testing these ideas, MS led men to derogate a seductive woman, but this effect was eliminated when the same woman appeared more wholesome. Another study found that men reminded of death and subsequently asked to recall a time they were sexually aroused by a woman exhibited greater tolerance of aggression toward women when asked to choose a prison sentence for a man who assaulted his girlfriend. These findings suggest that the existential threat engendered by men's lust constitutes an important contributing factor to misogynistic tendencies.

What about the elderly? Well, to some extent, they may also represent the threat of reminding people of their animality, but even more directly, they remind us of our inevitable fate. We generally do not have to worry that we may transform into another gender or ethnicity, but we are fated to join this group, if we are lucky. But in the meantime, Martens, Greenberg, and Schimel (2004) argued that what we want to do is see ourselves as different from old people to minimize the extent to which they remind us of our own futures. To test this idea, in a first study, Martens et al. simply asked college students to look at pictures of old or young adults. In support of the idea that old people can serve as a reminder of death, pictures of elderly people increased death thought accessibility in the college students. In the second study, in response to MS, college students viewed the elderly more negatively and as dissimilar to themselves. In the final study, Martens et al. measured perceived similarity to the elderly during a mass survey and subsequently found that MS only increased negativity toward, and perceived dissimilarity to, the elderly among students who perceived themselves as relatively similar to elderly people in the mass survey. The fact that MS led to negative reactions to the elderly primarily in individuals who generally perceive some similarity to the elderly supports the idea that prejudice against the elderly is fueled by the self-threat of perceived similarity to the elderly combined with heightened salience of the threat of death.

TMT AND STEREOTYPING

Although TMT is clear that mortality concerns should spawn prejudice against members of outgroups, the theory is less straightforward about prejudice against minority groups within the individual's culture. Sometimes these minority groups may represent a different worldview; American Muslims may be such a minority group in the United States. However, generally minority groups share much of the worldview of the majority group; for example, like most White Americans, most Black, Hispanic, and homosexual Americans are patriotic, and most are Christians. The theory of symbolic racism (Sears, 1988) notes that some White Americans may still see these groups as threats to their own worldview (values, etc.), and this is surely true of White supremacists and other avowed racists. However, ever since we began doing TMT research, we felt that worldview threat was not the primary basis of contemporary prejudice and stereotyping against these minority groups, so we never felt that MS would simply increase White prejudice against these groups.

However, Schimel et al. (1999) suggested another way that terror management concerns could contribute to White attitudes toward members of these groups. As popularized by the classic Devine (1989) article, it seems quite clear that stereotypes of minority groups are deeply entrenched in mainstream American culture. According to TMT, reminders of mortality should increase reliance on the internalized cultural worldview and preference for those who reinforce that worldview. To the extent that stereotypes of stigmatized groups are part of the American worldview, MS should therefore increase stereotypic thinking and preference for minority group members who conform to the stereotype over those who call the stereotype into question.

Indeed, Greenberg et al. (1990) provided initial evidence consistent with this idea by showing that MS increased Christian students' endorsement of stereotypic traits in evaluating a Jewish student. However, it was unclear in this study whether this reflected an MS-induced desire to derogate or an MS-induced desire to bolster belief in the stereotype.

To assess this latter idea more directly, Schimel et al. (1999) conducted five studies, examining stereotypic thinking and preferences regarding women, Germans, African Americans, and male homosexuals. Although in the late 1990s, Germans were generally not targets of prejudice by Americans, and their current worldview was very compatible with the American worldview, MS led Americans to view Germans more stereotypically (e.g., more orderly and rigid). In a second study, MS led both males and females to offer more explanations for behaviors inconsistent with gender stereotypes than for behaviors consistent with gender stereotypes, suggesting a greater need among these participants to defend against threats to stereotypic beliefs.

In Study 3, White participants in a control condition preferred an African American confederate if he appeared counterstereotypic (a diligent student and chess club member) rather than stereotypic (a beer-guzzling gang banger). However, after MS, there was a strong preference for the stereotypic African American over the counterstereotypic one. Study 4 replicated this finding using gender stereotypes, finding that MS increased liking for gender-stereotypic job candidates and decreased liking for gender counterstereotypic ones. Finally, in Study 5, participants in a control condition preferred a masculine homosexual male over an effeminate homosexual male, whereas after MS the effeminate homosexual male was preferred over the masculine homosexual male. A three-way interaction in this study also showed that this two-way interaction was carried by people high in need for closure, suggesting that rigid stereotyping provides terror-assuaging meaning primarily to those predisposed to simple knowledge structures.

These studies showed that MS will not necessarily increase negativity toward minority groups within one's own culture or toward outgroups that do not threaten one's worldview (Germans). However, the work also shows that people like their minority group members and nonthreatening outgroupers best if they fit stereotypes of these groups. The dark side of this preference is that MS does lead to dislike of such outgroup individuals when they do not conform the stereotype, such as when an African American is a highly diligent student.

TMT AND THE ERADICATION OF THE EVIL OTHER: THE ULTIMATE FORM OF DISCRIMINATION

In *Escape from Evil,* Becker (1975) argued that no matter how potent our terror management defenses are, residual anxieties about death are likely to surface, and a potentially controllable source for them must be found:

> The fact is that self-transcendence via culture does not give man a simple and straightforward solution to the problem of death; the terror of death still rumbles underneath the cultural repression . . . . The result is one of the great tragedies of human existence, what we might call the need to "fetishize evil," to locate the treat to life in some special places where it can be placated and controlled. . . . [M]en make fantasies about evil, see it in the wrong places, and destroy themselves and others by uselessly thrashing about. (pp. 5, 148)

Therefore the most appealing worldviews for those in need of bolstered terror management are those that convince people that they are part of a special group that is heroically triumphing over evil. Unfortunately that evil to be heroically triumphed over tends to be some outgroup that can be viewed as the source of one's deepest fears and problems. In this way, people can falsely view the sources of their fears as controllable and eradicable, instead of having to face the deeper problem of their inevitable death, via cancer, heart disease, accident, or old age. For many centuries, charismatic leaders have been selling this grand vision of the ingroup heroically triumphing over the evil other and thereby setting up a paradise on earth. In this way, Becker, following Rank before him, made the ironic point that the effort to escape from evil by following such leaders is the primary way in which humans cause evil.

If this analysis is correct, reminding people of their mortality should increase the appeal of such good versus evil ideologies and those who espouse them. A recent series of studies supports this hypothesis. The first study to do so showed that MS increased the appeal of a hypothetical candidate for governor only if that candidate promoted a special vision that emphasized that he would lead the people to greatness (Cohen, Solomon, Maxfield, Pyszczynski, & Greenberg, 2004). Related research by Landau, Solomon, et al. (2004) and Cohen, Ogilvie, Solomon, Greenberg, and Pyszczynski (2005) examined the appeal of George W. Bush in the months prior to the 2004 American presidential election. In response to the attacks of September 11, 2001, Bush became a strong proponent of the heroic triumph over evil: "Our war that we now fight is against terror and evil. . . . Our struggle is going to be long and difficult. But we will prevail. We will win. Good will overcome evil" (Office of the White House Press Secretary, 2001).

In four studies, Landau, Solomon, et al. (2004) found that MS and reminders of terrorism led both conservative and liberal college students to become more favorable to Bush and his war on terrorism. In the last two of these studies, conducted in May and September of 2004, Bush's political opponent Senator John Kerry was preferred over Bush in the control condition, but this preference was completely reversed when mortality was made salient. When terror management needs are elevated, the decisive crusader against evil was consistently preferred over the candidate portrayed as a waffler and flip-flopper.

Of course Bush and Kerry varied on other qualities besides the penchant for using the rhetoric of heroically defeating evil, so we cannot be definitive about why MS increased Bush's appeal. What if we more directly assessed the impact of MS on the appeal of ideologies focused on killing the evil other? A great opportunity to do so was afforded us when Iranian social psychologist Abdolheissen Abdollahi joined our research team. Just as Bush has condemned Iran as a member of the "axis of evil," the United States has been disparaged by Iranian leaders as "the great satan." After an MS manipulation, Pyszczynski, Abdollahi et al. (2006) asked Iranian college students to react to interviews of two fellow students, one of whom expressed strong support for lethal martyrdom against Americans, and the other who advocated peaceful resolution to the Middle East conflict. In the control condition, the Iranian students preferred the anti-martyrdom student; however, after MS, the pro martyrdom student was highly preferred. Indeed, after MS the Iranian students actually indicated substantial interest in joining the martyrdom cause.

Before we jump to the conclusion that Iranians are an atypically violent lot, we should consider a second study in which Pyszczynski et al. asked conservative and liberal American college students how supportive they were of the use of extreme military violence to kill terrorists in the Middle East, including chemical and nuclear weapons and the collateral killing of thousands of innocent people. As with the Iranian students, in the control condition, there was very little support for violent measures regardless of political orientation. However, after MS, the conservative students strongly supported these extreme measures to eradicate "evil." Perhaps one could argue this was a matter of strategy in the war on terrorism rather than reflective of discrimination based on prejudice. However, it seems highly unlikely these same conservative students would have advocated the use of nuclear weapons and thousands of innocent deaths if terrorists were known to be somewhere in Chicago.

Although additional research is certainly needed, studies to date clearly support the idea that mortality concerns increase the appeal of efforts to kill members of outgroups designated as repositories of evil. In this way, TMT and research shed new light on the age-old dynamic of scapegoating, which has led to so many genocidal atrocities over the course of recorded history—and continues to do so to this day.

TMT AND THE PSYCHOLOGICAL CONSEQUENCES OF PREJUDICE

TMT has implications not only for understanding the causes of prejudice, but also for understanding the consequences for individuals within a culture who are targets of prejudice and discrimination. Such stigmatized individuals are likely to have difficulty sustaining a sense of self-worth because they are devalued within the prevailing mainstream culture. Although research suggests that such individuals use compensatory mechanisms to combat deficiencies in self-esteem, and self-report self-esteem measures generally fail to find lower self-esteem in stigmatized groups (Crocker & Major, 1989), TMT suggests that stigmatized individuals should have less stable and secure self-worth to the extent their self-worth is not well-validated within the context of the worldview to which they subscribe.

Furthermore, TMT (see, e.g., Solomon et al., 1991) posits that members of ethnic groups targeted by prejudice in the culture within which they reside typically are caught between two worldviews: the traditional worldview of their ancestral group and that of the prevailing culture. Under these circumstances, the individual is likely to have difficulty maintaining faith in both a meaningful worldview and a secure sense of enduring significance. In such contexts, three options seem possible to manage one's terror. Given that the traditional worldview and bases of self-worth are usually overshadowed by those of a prejudicial majority, one option is full assimilation. However, fully embracing the dominant worldview would require abandoning the traditional worldview and buying into a worldview that has treated one's group harshly for generations and that may still offer only limited bases of self-worth to members of one's group.

A second option is militancy, rejecting the mainstream worldview and attempting to sustain faith in and derive self-worth from the traditional worldview. However, this tends to be very difficult because the traditional worldview was adapted to different circumstances and is likely to be incompatible with aspects of the contemporary natural, social, and economic environment. Furthermore, such militant worldviews (e.g., The Black Panthers, the White Knights) are typically formed in reaction to a predominant worldview and therefore tend to be rigid and to offer limited bases of self-worth for their members.

The third option is pluralism, an attempt to construct a worldview that incorporates aspects of the traditional worldview and its bases of self-worth while participating in the larger stage and bases of self-worth of the predominant worldview. Although difficult to achieve, this alternative provides the best hope for deriving the meaning and significance likely to allow for effective terror management.

Salzman (2001) employed this TMT analysis to help understand the impact of colonization on indigenous groups around the world. He observed that in Alaska, other parts of North, Central, and South America, Hawaii, the South Pacific, and parts of Africa, colonization by Europeans has produced similar deleterious psychological effects on a genetically diverse range of peoples. The Yu'pik people of Alaska labeled this colonization experience as the "Great Death." The colonists brought deadly disease and pervasive cultural disruptions, wiping out up to 50% of the local population. In Australia, a wide range of means and interventions employed by White colonial settlers—including land dispossession, the theft of women, missionary activity, and slavery—severely undermined Aboriginal peoples' age-old sense of kinship and spirituality.

From a TMT perspective, such efforts undermined indigenous cultural belief systems, heightening anxieties and thus aiding the project of converting survivors to Christianity and instilling adherence to other aspects of the European worldview. Down to this day, relative to the ancestors of European settlers, the descendants of these indigenous peoples suffer from poverty, poor physical and mental health, alcohol and drug abuse, and anxiety (Manson et al., 1996; Salzman & Halloran, 2004). Salzman has labeled the experience of such colonization *cultural trauma* because the new culture arrives and shakes to its core the traditional culture that previously had been working fine for its people as a basis of psychological security.

Robbed of their traditional bases of terror management, members of these groups struggle to reconstruct a hybrid worldview in which they can sustain faith. Sometimes these efforts are successful. One example is the Hawaiian Renaissance, a cultural revival that helped reinstate many aspects of Hawaiian music, art, literature, and religion. Hawaiians have begun to regain a sense that they have distinctive, stimulating, and instructive contributions to make to the broader society, providing the promise of a successful model of cultural pluralism. This suggests the possibility that traditional views may still serve terror management despite their minority status, as long as the dominant cultural context is sufficiently supportive of accommodating aspects of the traditional worldview in a way that is validating and valuing. Unfortunately, however, in many if not most cases, the dominating culture manages to maintain the inferior status of the indigenous culture and offers its members limited opportunities for valued activity within the context of their worldview.

Although research testing hypotheses derived from the TMT analysis of the consequences of prejudice has been limited to date, studies have shown that MS can lead members of stigmatized groups to distance from their ingroup and conform to negative stereotypes of their group. The first evidence that MS leads people to reduce identification with negatively framed ingroups was reported by Dechesne, Greenberg, Arndt, and Schimel (2000). They found that among fans of a college football team anticipating the opening season game, MS increased optimism about the team's prospects; however, after the team lost that first game, fans presented with a reminder of mortality reported reduced identification with the team.

Arndt, Greenberg, Schimel, Pyszczynski, and Solomon (2002) then showed that a similar process happens with stigmatized groups. In each study, when a negative view of the stigmatized ingroup was made salient, MS led ingroup members to reduce identification or increase negative reactions to the ingroup. First, they showed that when anticipating a difficult math test (a domain in which women are negatively stereotyped), MS decreased women's identification with other women. In a second study, after reading about a Hispanic drug dealer, MS led Hispanic participants to derogate paintings when they were attributed to a Hispanic (but not Anglo-American) artist. In a final study, Arndt et al. showed that after the Hispanic drug dealer article, MS led Hispanic participants to view their own personality as especially different than the personality of a fellow Hispanic. These findings suggest that when facing a negative stereotypic view of their own group, concerns about mortality led members of the group to distance themselves from their ingroup.

Dechesne, Janssen, and van Knippenberg (2000) demonstrated that when an ingroup is criticized, both individual differences and salient features of the ingroup can affect whether group members distance from the group or defend it. They found that that MS led college students high in need for closure (who are likely to view group identification as closed and definitive; Shah, Kruglanski, & Thompson, 1998) to report greater disliking of a critic of their university after MS. In contrast, students low in need for closure who contemplated mortality responded to criticism o their ingroup by disidentifying from the group rather than degrading the critic. Similarly, a second study by Dechesne, Janssen, and van Knippenberg (2000) found that MS led to defense of the group when group identification was portrayed as impermeable, but led to disidentification when the group was portrayed as permeable (i.e., it is easy to transfer from one school to another). Minority group members may view their ethnic ingroup as permeable to the extent that they believe they can identify with the larger culture instead of their ingroup.

A recent study showed that in addition to reducing identification with a stigmatized ingroup, MS can lead members of such groups to conform to negative stereotypes of the group. Specifically, Landau, Greenberg, and Sullivan (2006) reasoned that because negative self-relevant group stereotypes become socially ingrained components of individuals' death-denying worldview, MS may heighten their influence over behavior, leading individuals to show lessened success on ego-relevant tasks for which their group is viewed as inferior. Indeed, mortality-primed women who were stereotyped to fare poorly on an academic test underperformed even when the task was quite easy.

Finally research by Halloran and Kashima (2004) suggests the possibility of pluralism functioning within the individual. They found that after MS, bicultural Aboriginal participants decreased their valuing of collectivism when the more individualistic Anglo-Australian worldview was made salient and decreased their valuing of individualism when the traditional Aboriginal worldview was made salient. Thus, minority group members may shift values as the context requires; however, TMT suggests that such biculturalism will work best for psychological equanimity if it stems from a well-integrated overarching hybrid worldview.

In sum, TMT posits that victims of prejudice face continual threats from the majority worldview to the meaning- and value-conferring structures that protect them from death concerns. Research testing this idea reveals, under some conditions, heightened mortality concerns lead stigmatized individuals to defensively disidentify from their ingroup and even conform to negative cultural stereotypes. However, research also shows that, under some conditions, prejudiced individuals can more constructively subscribe to hybrid worldviews that flexibly incorporate elements from their own culture and the broader culture. Additional research is necessary to gain a more complete understanding of the situational and personality factors that predispose members of stigmatized groups to pursue these different strategies.

TMT AND OTHER APPROACHES TO UNDERSTANDING OF PREJUDICE

Generally we believe the TMT perspective is quite compatible with other theoretical approaches to prejudice. TMT adds another level of understanding of many of these phenomena by addressing more basic *why* questions. However, TMT does not supplant these other perspectives because they are often informative in their own right by elucidating other macro- or microlevel factors that contribute to prejudice, stereotyping, and group conflict. Next we briefly consider how TMT can complement some of the other prominent theories of prejudice, each of which is undoubtedly considered in much greater detail elsewhere in this *Handbook*.

INDIVIDUAL DIFFERENCES

We begin with individual differences because any psychological theory of prejudice worth taking seriously should offer some insights into why in every culture and regardless of historical and socioeconomic circumstances, people vary in their levels of prejudice. Through various shaping influences, cultures tend to orient their members toward (a) particular outgroups within or outside the culture as designated inferiors and sources of evil; (b) particular stereotypic depictions of various groups; and (c) particular prejudice-fostering or prejudice-discouraging values such as tolerance, harmony, competitiveness, and order.

However, from a TMT perspective, people will differ in their levels of prejudice primarily because of the nature of the individualized, internalized version of the culturally derived worldview by which they imbue life with meaning and themselves with significance. Individuals form their own worldview based on how the broad cultural worldview is conveyed by their parents, other influential people in their lives, and the mass media, and their personal experiences, possibly in combination with genetically based propensities for hostility, conformity, structure, and reactance that may affect the appeal of particular aspects of the worldview-relevant concepts to which they are exposed. In addition, TMT suggests that the individuals' particular levels of self-worth and stability of self-worth, and the particular culturally based sources of self-worth on which they rely will also influence their levels of prejudice and the specific targets of their prejudice.

From this TMT perspective, individual difference variables associated with high levels of prejudice and stereotyping such as right-wing authoritarianism (Adorno, Frenkel-Brunswik, Levenson, & Sanford,, 1950; Altemeyer, 1994), religious orientation (Batson & Burris, 1994), personal need for structure (Schaller, Boyd, Yohannes, & O'Brian, 1995), and social dominance orientation (Pratto, Sidanius, Stallworth, & Malle, 1994) are indicators of worldviews that are rigid, simplistic, moralistic, and that emphasize status hierarchies and just world beliefs. These are precisely the kinds of worldviews that should lead people to be harsh toward those who are different and who are lower in socioeconomic status. Indeed, one of the first TMT studies showed that after MS high but not low authoritarians became especially unkind toward another individual who expressed very dissimilar attitudes. Similarly, after

MS, compared to politically liberal Americans, politically conservative Americans seem to become more negative toward people with different political beliefs and more supportive of extreme military violence against outgroup members (Pyszczynski et al., 2006).

Another individual difference factor that has received a good deal of attention in both prejudice and TMT research is personal need for structure (PNS)—the degree to which the person desires clear, certain, or unambiguous knowledge (Thompson, Naccarato, Parker, & Moskowitz, 2001). Research shows that high-PNS individuals are more likely to form simple impressions of others (Neuberg & Newsom, 1993) and rely on stereotypes about other groups (Schaller et al., 1995). TMT posits that high-PNS individuals buffer anxiety by pursuing simple and coherent interpretations of the world, whereas low-PNS individuals are more comfortable with uncertainty and a lack of structure, and may even derive meaning from novelty, accuracy, tolerance, and diversity. Accordingly, TMT studies show that individuals high, but not low, in PNS respond to MS with rigid defense of their social identity, preference for stereotypic others, devaluing of behaviorally inconsistent others, and victim derogation (see, e.g., Dechesne et al., 2000; Landau, Johns et al., 2004; Landau et al., 2006). The picture emerging from these findings is that high-PNS individuals' motivated efforts to seek terror-assuaging meaning in simple and well-structured interpretations of other people and social events can contribute to stereotyping and prejudice.

Research has also shown that threats to self-esteem (e.g., Fein & Spencer, 1997), insecure attachment (Mikulincer et al., 2003), and religious fundamentalism (Altemeyer & Hunsberger, 1992) are associated with high levels of prejudice. From a TMT perspective, these findings suggest that among those whose terror management defenses are unstable and highly vulnerable to threat, derogating different others serves to bolster both faith in one's own worldview and, through a social comparison process, in one's own self-worth. Consistent with this analysis, TMT research has shown that boosts to self-esteem, secure attachment, and intrinsic religiosity mitigate the effects of MS on outgroup bias (Harmon-Jones, Simon, Greenberg, Pyszczynski, & Solomon, 1997; Jonas & Fischer, 2006; Mikulincer & Florian, 2000). The one exception is if the different other attacks the basis of the individual's self-esteem boost (Arndt & Greenberg, 1999).

REALISTIC GROUP CONFLICT THEORY

Although individuals within a culture vary in their levels of prejudice, cultures clearly play a substantial role in determining the prevalent targets of prejudice for their members. Realistic group conflict theory (RCT) helps to explain the culture's particular choices of targets. The theory posits that feelings of hostility and prejudice arise when groups compete for scarce resources (e.g., Esses, Jackson & Armstrong, 1998). From this perspective, people derogate and even aggress against those perceived to be encroaching on valuable commodities such as jobs, education, and property. Partial support for RCT is provided by evidence that periods of downward mobility, job scarcity, and general economic frustration are positively correlated with prejudice and stereotypes (Dollard, Doob, Miller, Mowrer, & Sears, 1939; Hovland & Sears, 1940). Also, research in the laboratory (R. Brown, 1995; Jones, 1997) and the field (Sherif, Harvey, White, Hook, & Sherif, 1961) demonstrates that competing groups tend to derogate and stereotype each other.

RCT provides an intuitively sensible explanation of prejudice: People need to eat and survive and therefore feel contempt toward those perceived to threaten those basic goals. However, conflicting groups often seek resources far beyond what is necessary to sustain life; we therefore think it is important to consider psychological functions of procuring resources that RCT does not address. Many resources are sought at least in part for their symbolic value as bases of significance and immortality striving, above and beyond their pragmatic value for survival. The Israeli–Palestinian conflict provides an example of this. Although this is indeed largely a battle over lands, it is not just any lands that are sought, but rather lands that both groups consider holy, lands tied to the death-transcending ideologies of both groups:

Old Testament, Psalm 37:

If I do not remember thee, let my tongue cleave to the roof of my mouth;
If I prefer not Jerusalem above my highest joys.

The Hadith (sayings of the Prophet Mohammed):

. . . The dew which descends upon Jerusalem is a remedy from every sickness because it is from the gardens of paradise.

Based on extensive historical and anthropological evidence, Norman Brown (1959) and Becker (1975) proposed that land is not the only resource with symbolic value; gold, property, and other time-defying resources represent culturally sanctioned symbolic testimony to one's value, with the consequent assurance of safety and security in this life and literal or figurative immortality thereafter. TMT thus posits that procuring wealth serves (at least in part) to allay concerns about the finality of death. Accordingly, multiple studies demonstrate that MS increases consumerist and materialistic tendencies, even if they have negative implications for social and environmental well-being (see Arndt, Solomon, Kasser, & Sheldon, 2004, for review). In one study (Kasser & Sheldon, 2000, Study 2), mortality and control-primed participants engaged in a forest-management simulation and were told that although harvesting large amounts of timber would be personally profitable in the short term, it would have negative long-term consequences for the environment. Despite the awareness of these consequences, those reminded of their own mortality reported intending to harvest more of the available acres of forest than control-primed counterparts.

In short, TMT and research suggest that deep-seated needs for death-transcending value may contribute substantially to the intergroup conflicts central to RCT's analysis of prejudice. Furthermore, TMT provides a framework for understanding aspects of prejudice that are difficult to account for if we consider only the pragmatic advantages of resources. For one, it explains how conflicts can spring from efforts on the part of each group to assert its symbolic superiority even when material concerns are minimized or nonexistent. A TMT perspective also helps explain why in many cultures (e.g., the Mbuti in Zaire; Goldschmidt, 1990) valuable resources are deliberately wasted in the service of asserting the individual's or culture's symbolic prestige, a practice that would be difficult to explain from an RCT perspective.

Third, TMT explains why, both past and present, efforts by one group to conquer another group and appropriate their resources are carried out in the name of gods, political missions, and other ideological abstractions. For example, after starting the ball rolling on the enslavement and subsequent murder of millions of indigenous Americans, Christopher Columbus proclaimed "Let us in the name of the Holy Trinity go on sending all the slaves that can be sold" (quoted in Zinn, 1995, p. 3). More recently, both the 1991 Persian Gulf War and the 2003 invasion of Iraq were portrayed by the Presidents Bush to the public as efforts to defend freedom and goodness against forces of evil rather than as efforts to protect American resources in the region and benefit the American economy. Although in some cases, a concern with establishing the supremacy of one's worldview simply serves as a façade for a more basic desire to accumulate material wealth, ideological motives clearly often play a role at least in garnering public support for the actions, and also often acquire their own psychological significance, helping to perpetuate hostilities even after material issues may have been resolved or forgotten.

The key implication of TMT for RCT is that cultures compete not only for pragmatic resources like food and mates but also for symbolic resources that buttress faith in their worldview and significance, and thereby serve their terror management needs. Members of different cultures seek to conquer death in part by amassing resources that establish their symbolic superiority over other cultures.

SCAPEGOAT THEORY

Like RCT, scapegoat theory (Allport, 1954; Berkowitz & Green, 1962; Jones, 1997) posits that frustration over blocked goals can manifest in aggression and prejudice, but it goes further by suggesting that groups can also blame feelings of low status and moral inadequacy on a despised outgroup (i.e., the scapegoat). Allport (1954) discussed, for example, how Hitler solidified public support by blaming the Jews not only for Germany's postwar economic crisis, but also for undermining the purity and moral integrity of the German people. Because these tend to be convenient sources of blame rather than true competitors for resources, the choice of scapegoat can be quite arbitrary, but it is often a group maligned as different or holding an alternative worldview. This was expressed by one German leader: "The Jew is just convenient. . . . If there were no Jews, the anti-Semites would have to invent them" (quoted in Allport, 1954, p. 325).

As noted earlier, Becker (1973, 1975) proposed that even in the absence of a direct or external threat to the terror-assuaging worldview, there is residual death anxiety that is repressed and focalized onto a group either outside or inside the culture that is designated as the sole impediment to the realization of the culture's economic, moral, and religious superiority over others. Because the ultimate problem the worldview addresses is our animal mortal nature, something we cannot fully escape but that is disguised for us by our culture, an important aspect of derogating the scapegoat is viewing them as less than human, as animals—as though "we" are superior beings and true humans whereas "they" are mere animals unworthy of the rights afforded humans.

This can be seen very clearly in the Nazi equation of Jews with disease-spreading vermin, the American portrayal of blacks as animalistic, the Hutu reference to Tutsi as cockroaches, and the many dehumanizing names developed for despised outgroups such as krauts, nips, gooks, kikes, sandsharks, and wetbacks. By actively dehumanizing, humiliating, hating, and even eradicating the scapegoat, a group affirms its control over life and death and thereby symbolically secures itself against contingency and death—it is as if "they" perish so that "we" do not have to. In support of this analysis, Becker points to the cross-cultural ubiquity of human sacrifice as a means of symbolically cleansing the world of evil and assuring prosperity.

In this way, TMT addresses a deeper "why" question, rarely addressed by other theories of scapegoating, by positing that individuals and cultures sometimes attempt to cope with their existential anxieties by restoring faith in their worldview and their own significance through derogation, dehumanization, subjugation, and (in some cases) extermination of an outgroup perceived to be contaminating the group's enduring cultural legacy.

SOCIAL IDENTITY THEORY

Social identity theory (SIT; Tajfel & Turner, 1979) is based on the idea that people derive self-esteem in large measure from their membership in social groups and the perceived status and significance of those groups. The underlying motive to enhance self-esteem drives people to highlight the distinctive and positive qualities of their ingroup and to derogate outgroups. Empirical support for SIT is provided in part by evidence that identifying with positively evaluated ingroups enhances self-esteem (e.g., Hirt, Zillman, Erickson, & Kennedy 1992), and that those whose positive self-image has been threatened reaffirm their self-worth by evaluating their groups more favorably (Cialdini & Richardson, 1980) and denigrating outgroups (Fein & Spencer, 1997). Also, research using the minimal groups paradigm (see Brewer, 1979) has shown that feelings of ingroup solidarity and superiority can arise even when the basis of determining group membership is relatively trivial (e.g., preference for one of two abstract painters).

Central to both SIT and TMT is the idea that people seek self-esteem by associating themselves with certain groups and viewing their groups as superior to others. TMT goes one step further, however, in offering an account of what self-esteem is and what psychological function it serves. For TMT, self-esteem consists of the belief that one is a person of value in a world of meaning, and the primary function of self-esteem is to buffer anxiety stemming from the awareness of death. Through this perspective we can gain a deeper understanding of the psychological significance of specific functions of groups. For one, groups provide the individual with the broad consensual support necessary to sustain faith in a meaningful and enduring conception of reality. Also, groups prescribe what attributes and behaviors confer self-esteem and which result in social approbation, and provide the means to validate the individual's claims to certain achievements and identities, which confers a sense of enduring significance to their lives.

In addition to their role in self-esteem acquisition and maintenance, groups serve the terror management function of providing the individual with collective modes of immortality striving through identification with entities larger and longer lasting than the self. This function of groups was recognized by Rank (1930/1998), who proposed that people bolster faith in their continuance beyond death by merging with a death-transcending collective. This notion was echoed by Lifton (1979), who posited that in addition to seeking literal immortality (e.g., via an immaterial soul), people derive a symbolic sense of immortality by being a valued part of a larger collective such as a tribe or the nation that will live on in perpetuity. TMT converges with these perspectives in suggesting that people identify with and favor their own race, religion, and other social groups, and devalue outgroups, to perceive themselves as significant participants in a meaningful cultural reality instead of just nameless animals in a wholly material reality destined only to death and decay.

Combining insights from SIT and TMT, Castano and colleagues (2002) recently examined the effects of MS on the extent to which participants identify with and evaluate their ingroup. These researchers also reasoned that individuals motivated to seek symbolic immortality through their group identity would be more likely to view their group as high in entitivity; that is, as a real entity rather than as a loose assemblage of individuals (Campbell, 1958), so they included a measure of group entitivity to assess this possibility. The results showed that Italians primed with death identified more strongly with Italy, perceived Italy as more of an entity, and judged Italians, but not Germans, more positively. These findings add to the previously reviewed evidence from multiple studies that MS intensifies ingroup favoritism and outgroup prejudice (e.g., Greenberg et al., 2003; Greenberg et al., 1990; Harmon-Jones et al., 1996; Jonas et al., 2005; Nelson et al., 1997).

As just discussed, TMT posits that in addition to providing the basis for self-esteem, groups also provide people with a means of identifying with a larger and longer lasting entity that transcends the self. This raises the possibility that heightened mortality concerns would increase group identification even when doing so undermines rather than enhances one's self-esteem. In one set of studies assessing this possibility, Dechesne, Janssen, and van Knippenberg (2000) exposed mortality- and control-primed participants to a criticism of their university that had negative implications for their self-esteem. They found that under these conditions, participants with a low need for closure—who were not dispositionally inclined toward clear and stable meaning—readily disidentified from their university (see Arndt et al., 2002, for similar findings regarding gender and ethnic identifications). In contrast, participants with a high need for closure responded to MS and a criticism of their university by maintaining their university identification and derogating the source of the threat. Dechesne et al. also found that participants primed to think of their university identification as a stable and enduring identification maintained and defended their identification, whereas those primed to view such identifications are highly changeable and temporarily readily disidentified from their school when mortality was salient and their group was framed negatively.

In sum, TMT research demonstrates that MS increases group identification and favoritism. These results augment SIT's account of the self-esteem-conferring benefits of group identification by demonstrating that holding mortality concerns at bay is one important distal motivation for maintaining self-esteem. Furthermore, research shows that, at least for those inclined toward clear meaning and those led to conceive of groups as permanent and real, MS can strengthen group identification and heighten prejudicial reactions to outgroup threats even when one's social identity reflects negatively on self-worth. These findings extend SIT because they demonstrate that, in addition to providing a basis for self-esteem, groups confer the stable frameworks of meaning necessary to assuage existential concerns.

JUST WORLD AND SYSTEM JUSTIFICATION THEORIES

Lerner's (1980) just world theory postulates that people are fundamentally inclined to believe that the world is a just place where people get what they deserve and do not suffer unjustifiably. Confronting disadvantaged groups or victims of tragedy threatens to undermine this core belief and consequently motivates people to restore it by dissociating from innocent victims or attributing their misfortunes to their prior misdeeds or dispositional shortcomings. By believing, for example, that rape victims must have behaved seductively (Carli, 1999) and that poor people do not deserve better (Furnham & Gunter, 1984), more fortunate people can justify inequality and suffering and avoid the unsettling prospect that equally dire circumstances could befall them.

Similar to just world theory, system justification theory holds that prejudice helps justify the economic and social status quo, even if it means rationalizing the inferior status of one's ingroup (e.g., Jost & Banaji, 1994; Jost & Burgess, 2000). Therefore, threats to ideological beliefs that serve to justify the status quo should result in defensive efforts to reaffirm faith in those beliefs (e.g., with the use of stereotypes), even if it means justifying one's own disenfranchised position within that ideological system.

TMT shares with just world and system justification theories the broad notion that individuals are motivated to maintain faith in meaningful cultural beliefs and therefore react defensively toward people or events that threaten to undermine those beliefs. According to TMT, however, these beliefs serve a more distal psychological function of keeping death-related concerns at bay. Throughout this chapter we have reviewed evidence in support of this claim: MS exaggerates positive and negative evaluations of people and ideas that uphold or violate one's ideological beliefs. Furthermore, there is research that bears more specifically on just world and system justification theories.

From a TMT perspective, the belief that social events follow a just and benevolent order constitutes a fundamental building block of terror-assuaging meaning. By believing that people get what they deserve and deserve what they get, individuals can obscure the brute fact that they are perpetually susceptible to the threat of death at the hand of incalculable natural and social forces. In one study assessing this analysis, Landau, Johns et al. (2004, Study 5) primed high- and low-PNS participants with mortality or a control topic; then, in an ostensibly separate study, they read about a student whose face was disfigured in an attack and were given the opportunity to choose among information that cast the victim in either a positive or negative light. Results revealed that high-PNS individuals primed with mortality were especially interested in discovering negative information about the victim of a senseless tragedy, presumably because such information helped them restore their belief in a just world. A subsequent study tested the idea that, to the extent that just world beliefs serve the protective functions of keeping concerns about mortality at bay, compromising those beliefs should unleash such concerns. Accordingly, results showed that threatening just world beliefs by presenting positive information about the victim of a senseless tragedy heightened the accessibility of death-related thought among high-PNS participants. Hirschberger (2006) recently provided a conceptual replication of these findings (without measuring PNS); in these studies, MS led people to assign blame to an innocent victim of a paralyzing accident, and reading about such an individual increased death thought accessibility. These results provide converging evidence that just world beliefs serve a terror management function.

Regarding the relationship between system justification and terror management perspectives, Jost, Fitzsimons, and Kay (2004) posited that one existential motive that may prompt individuals to cling to ideology is the need to repress death anxiety. This notion would seem to make system justification and TMT quite compatible, yet Jost et al. saw as an important distinction the fact that TMT research has historically implied that support for one's worldview works in concert with shoring up self-esteem, whereas system justification theory holds that self-esteem is often sacrificed to shore up the system or worldview. However, we believe that TMT actually converges with system justification theory on this point because the worldview is the more fundamental component of terror management. The findings from the aforementioned studies by Landau et al. support this rapprochement by showing that MS does sometimes encourage people to sacrifice opportunities to boost self-esteem (e.g., performing well on a test) to maintain sources of cultural meaning (e.g., the exalted status of cultural icons; self-relevant stereotypes).

SOCIAL COGNITIVE APPROACHES

According to social cognitive approaches, stereotyped beliefs and prejudiced attitudes exist not only because of social conditioning and motivation, but also as by-products of normal thinking processes. These approaches are based on the idea that people simplify an otherwise overwhelming amount of information in the social world in part by spontaneously categorizing people (e.g., on the basis of salient features such as race, gender, and age) and applying schemas associated with those categories to form further inferences and judgments about their characteristics and behavior (e.g., Allport, 1954; Moskowitz, 2005). Although on the whole these processes are very useful, they can also yield systematic biases and errors that contribute to prejudice and stereotyping.

Although earlier social cognitive views placed almost exclusive emphasis on the role of cognition, researchers have become increasingly interested in the role of motivational states (e.g., goals, moods, needs) and dispositional propensities (e.g., personal need for structure) in people's use of simple structuring strategies (Kruglanski, 1996; Kunda, 1990; Pyszczynski & Greenberg, 1987). These and other lines of research assessing a motivated social cognition approach indicate that people rely on simple structuring processes to seek closure on confident and coherent judgments and minimize ambiguity. TMT complements this approach by addressing why people are fundamentally disposed to seek simple, well-structured representations of the world and respond adversely to ambiguity and incongruity.

As discussed earlier, TMT posits that to buffer the potential for anxiety inherent in the awareness of the inevitability of death, the individual subscribes to a worldview that imbues the world with stable meaning and order. Therefore, one important distal motivation for the maintenance of stereotypes, heuristics, and other cognitive processes designed to minimize ambiguity and approach subjective consistency is the need to maintain the epistemic clarity necessary to sustain faith in one's terror-assuaging conception of reality as meaningful and orderly. Without a secure epistemic foundation in simple knowledge structures—knowledge of how people behave, what characteristics are associated with different groups, and how interpersonal relations are structured—the individual would have difficulty sustaining faith in the stable, anxiety-buffering conceptions of reality that investment in a worldview provides.

To the extent that seeking simple, structured interpretations of social information serve a terror management function, MS should exaggerate the tendencies to perceive others in simple and schematic ways. Furthermore, based on the aforementioned analysis of individual differences, MS should exacerbate these structuring tendencies particularly among those dispositionally inclined to simple structure. These predictions were confirmed in Schimel et al.'s (1999) aforementioned findings that MS led participants with high need for closure to evaluate homosexual men more favorably when they behaved in a stereotype-consistent manner and more negatively when they behaved in a stereotype-inconsistent manner.

Building on these findings, Landau, Johns et al. (2004) tested whether MS heightens more general tendencies to seek simple structure and consequently devalue those who undermine that structure. In one study mortality-primed individuals were more likely to overlook objective statistical evidence in forming group membership judgments and assume that others belong to certain categories to the extent that they represent the category stereotype. Another study was based on Heider's (1958) claim that people maintain a coherent understanding of others by viewing their actions as stemming from clear causes and dispositions. Results show that high-PNS individuals primed with mortality were particularly disparaging of an individual who was portrayed in conversation as inconsistently displaying both introverted and extroverted behaviors.

In sum, TMT provides a unique existential perspective on the motivational underpinnings of epistemic clarity. These results are important in showing that stereotypes and other social cognitive structuring tendencies exist not only because of inherent cognitive limitations or the desire for closure, but also because of the more distal motive to maintain stable and orderly perceptions of reality to manage existential fears stemming from the awareness of death. Furthermore, as noted earlier, this research shows that there are important individual differences in the extent to which people derive terror-assuaging meaning from well-structured perceptions of others; therefore, these differences are likely to be important predictors of stereotyping and prejudice, particularly when people are reminded of their mortality.

SUMMARY

A general theme emerges from our discussion of how TMT complements other theoretical perspectives on prejudice. At a general level, many of these perspectives view prejudice as arising from the perception that some group or groups are preventing the achievement of certain goals, whether they be the needs to bolster individual and collective self-esteem, maintain clear and certain conceptions of the social world, or accumulate material goods. TMT supplements these approaches by explaining how each of these separate goals, although valid and interesting in their own right, serves a more distal terror management motive. A growing body of research supports this integrative approach by demonstrating the influence of mortality reminders (and their interaction with relevant individual differences) on diverse attitudinal and behavioral phenomena that contribute to prejudice, stereotyping, and discrimination, as well as by showing the effects of worldview threats on death-thought accessibility.

TMT AND THE AMELIORATION OF PREJUDICE AND INTERGROUP CONFLICT

> This is the great moral that Albert Camus drew from our demonic times, when he expressed the moving hope that a day would come when each person would proclaim in his own fashion the superiority of being wrong without killing [rather} than being right in the quiet of the charnel house. (Becker, 1975, p. 145)

The research reviewed so far portrays a very dark picture—our need for terror management in the face of awareness of our mortality clearly spawns prejudice, stereotyping, and intergroup aggression. And once intergroup aggression begins, the specter of mortality is likely to loom large, fueling more hostility, stereotypic depictions of the outgroup, and lethal conflict. There are, however, a few glimmers of hope that emerge out of the TMT literature.

Pyszczynski et al. (2003) proposed that the current conflicts in the Middle East and elsewhere have humanity stuck between a rock and hard place, two very different types of worldviews. The rock is a rigid worldview in which there are very decisive moral judgments of rights and wrongs, and very clear designations of good and evil. This is the type of worldview charismatic leaders typically espouse. The prominent negative emotion for those who subscribe to the rock is anger and there is strong prejudice against others who violate the moral prescriptions or who are designated evil. The rock provides a strong faith in a basis for terror management, typically with death transcendence taking the form of religious afterlife beliefs or collectivist identifications with the state and a futuristic myth of continuing revolution or evolution toward some vision of fascist or Marxist utopia (see e.g., Lifton, 1968)

The alternative, the hard place, is a relativistic worldview in which right and wrong, good and evil, are less certain and considered more a matter of one's perspective. In this type of worldview tolerance is valued, prejudice tends to be low, and the prominent negative emotion is anxiety. As a basis of terror management the hard place is shaky at best, and is often supplemented by the use of drugs such as alcohol, cannabis, Paxil, Zoloft, and so on, and ever-escalating consumerism. Often it seems that people who start out in the hard place end up latching onto a rock by idealizing some cult or cause such as environmentalism, animals rights, atheism, antiglobalization, and so on, as an ultimate raison d'etre.

Consistent with the idea that the hard place is better for nondefensive responses to different others, terror management research shows that people low in need for structure and authoritarianism, and, at least among Americans, people who self-identify as politically liberal, are generally less prone to respond to reminders of death with derogation or aggression against different others (e.g., Greenberg et al., 1990; Greenberg et al., 1992). Similarly, making the value of tolerance salient to Americans ameliorates reactions to different others (Greenberg et al., 1992). Recent findings (Pyszczynski, Maxfield, et al., 2006) also suggest that creating a sense of common humanity across cultures may have a similar function. Specifically, whereas participants who received MS showed elevated implicit anti-Arab prejudice on an implicit association test after being primed with images of American families or American people just hanging out in groups, being primed with pictures of families from all over the world led Americans who received MS to show decreased implicit anti-Arab prejudice.

In addition to a relativistic worldview, good psychological adjustment seems to be associated with less defensive reactions to reminders of death. MS is less likely to arouse defense in individuals low in neuroticism and depression and high in self-esteem and attachment security (e.g., Goldenberg et al., 2000; Harmon-Jones et al., 1997; Mikulincer et al., 2003; Simon, Arndt, Greenberg, Solomon, & Pyszczynski 1998). Boosts to self-esteem and self-affirmations also seem to eliminate the need for defense after MS (Harmon-Jones et al., 1997; Schmeichel & Martens, 2005). Recently, Weise, Pyszczynski, et al. (2008) also showed that MS reduced support for extreme military violence candidate when participants were primed to think of an unconditionally accepting interaction with an important person from their past.

A final possibility is that increased awareness of death, resulting from more conscious thoughtful contemplation of this problem, might make humans better able to accept their mortality without hostility, scapegoating, and the like. Janoff-Bulman and Yopyk (2004) recently summarized evidence of benefits along these lines for people who have faced life-threatening traumas (e.g., Calhoun & Tedeschi, 2001) and Cozzolino, Staples, Meyers, and Samboceti (2004) found that having extrinsically oriented individuals read an elaborate but concrete scenario in which their death occurs eliminated the greedy response exhibited after a more typical, subtle MS induction.

The picture that emerges from this evidence is that if we brought our children up to sustain faith in a relativistic worldview that places a high value on tolerance and provided them with stable bases of attachment security and self-esteem, and encouraged them to face the problem of death with careful deliberation, they would grow into adults who could face up to the existential threat of death without lashing out at others. The general guidelines for how to accomplish this have been laid out by humanistic (e.g., Rank, 1930/1998; Rogers, 1963) and existential (Becker, 1971; Yalom, 1980) psychologists, and more recently by Ryan and Deci (2002). Precisely how to accomplish this in a world in which children are brought up by adults who do not necessarily embrace relativistic worldviews or serve as reliable bases of security and self-worth, and who have their own terror with which to contend, although a difficult matter, should be a top priority for social scientists, practitioners, educators, and politicians.

REFERENCES

Adorno, T. W., Frenkel-Brunswik, E., Levenson, D. J., & Sanford, R. N. (1950). *The authoritarian personality.* New York: Harper & Row.

Allport, G. W. (1954). *The nature of prejudice.* Reading, MA: Addison-Wesley.

Altemeyer, B. (1994). Reducing prejudice in right-wing authoritarians. In M. P. Zanna & J. M. Olson (Eds.), *The psychology of prejudice* (Vol. 7, pp. 131–148). Hillsdale, NJ: Erlbaum.

Altemeyer, B., & Hunsberger, B. (1992). Authoritarianism, religious fundamentalism, quest, and prejudice. *International Journal for the Psychology of Religion, 2,* 113–133.

Arndt, J., Cook, A., & Routledge, C. (2004). The blueprint of terror management: Understanding the cognitive architecture of psychological defense against the awareness of death. In J. Greenberg, S. L. Koole, & T. Pyszczynski (Eds.), *Handbook of experimental existential psychology* (pp. 35–53). New York: Guilford.

Arndt, J., & Greenberg, J. (1999). The effects of a self-esteem boost and mortality salience on responses to boost relevant and irrelevant worldview threats. *Personality and Social Psychology Bulletin, 25,* 1331–1341.

Arndt, J., Greenberg, J., Schimel, J., Pyszczynski, T., & Solomon, S. (2002). To belong or not belong, that is the question: Terror management and identification with ethnicity and gender. *Journal of Personality and Social Psychology, 83,* 26–43.

Arndt, J., Greenberg, J., Solomon, S., Pyszczynski, T., & Schimel, J. (1999). Creativity and terror management: The effects of creative activity on guilt and social projection following mortality salience. *Journal of Personality and Social Psychology, 77,* 19–32.

Arndt, J., Solomon, S., Kasser, T., & Sheldon, K.M. (2004). The urge to splurge: A terror management account of materialism and consumer behavior. *Journal of Consumer Psychology, 14,* 198–212.

Baldwin, J. (1963). *The fire next time.* New York: Dial Press.

Batson, C. D., & Burris, C. T. (1994). Personal religion: Depressant or stimulant of prejudice and discrimination? In M. P. Zanna & J. M. Olson (Eds.), *The psychology of prejudice* (Vol. 7, pp. 149–169). Hillsdale, NJ: Erlbaum.

Becker, E. (1971). *The birth and death of meaning.* New York: The Free Press.

Becker, E. (1973). *The denial of death.* New York: The Free Press.

Becker, E. (1975). *Escape from evil.* New York: The Free Press.

Berkowitz, L., & Green, J. A. (1962). The stimulus qualities of the scapegoat. *Journal of Abnormal and Social Psychology, 64,* 293–301.

Brewer, M. B. (1979). In-group bias in the minimal intergroup situation: A cognitive–motivational analysis. *Psychological Bulletin, 86,* 307–324.

Brown, N. O. (1959). *Life against death: The psychoanalytic meaning of history.* Middletown, CT: Wesleyan.

Brown, R. (1995). *Prejudice: Its social psychology.* Cambridge, MA: Blackwell.

Calhoun, L. G., & Tedeschi, R. G. (2001). Posttraumatic growth: The positive lessons of loss. In R. A. Neimeyer (Ed.), *Meaning reconstruction and the experience of loss* (pp. 155–172). Washington, DC: American Psychological Association.

Campbell, D. T. (1958). Common fate, similarity, and other indices of the status of aggregates of persons as social entities. *Behavioral Science, 3,* 14–25.

Carli, L. L. (1999). Cognitive reconstruction, hindsight, and reactions to victims and perpetrators. *Personality and Social Psychology Bulletin, 25,* 966–979.

Castano, E., Yzerbyt, V., Paladino, M., & Sacchi, S. (2002). I belong, therefore, I exist: Ingroup identification, ingroup entitativity, and ingroup bias. *Personality and Social Psychology Bulletin, 28,* 135–143.

Cialdini, R. B., & Richardson, K. D. (1980). Two indirect tactics of image management: Basking and blasting. *Journal of Personality and Social Psychology, 39,* 406–415.

Cohen, F., Ogilvie, D. M., Solomon, S., Greenberg, J., & Pyszczynski, T. (2005). American roulette: The effect of reminders of death on support for George W. Bush in the 2004 presidential election. *Analyses of Social Issues and Public Policy, 5,* 177–187.

Cohen, F., Solomon, S., Maxfield, M., Pyszczynski, T., & Greenberg, J. (2004). Fatal attraction: The effects of mortality salience on evaluations of charismatic, task-oriented, and relationship-oriented leaders. *Psychological Science, 15,* 846–851.

Cozzolino, P. J., Staples, A. D., Meyers, L. S., & Samboceti, J. (2004). Greed, death, and values: From terror management to transcendence management theory. *Personality and Social Psychology Bulletin, 30,* 278–292.

Crocker, J., & Major, B. (1989). Social stigma and self-esteem: The self-protective properties of stigma. *Psychological Review, 96,* 608–630.

Dawkins, R. (1989). *The selfish gene.* New York: Oxford University Press. (Original work published 1976)

Dechesne, M., Greenberg, J., Arndt, J., & Schimel, J. (2000). Terror management and sports fan affiliation: The effects of mortality salience on fan identification and optimism. *European Journal of Social Psychology, 30,* 813–835.

Dechesne, M., Janssen, J., & van Knippenberg, A. (2000). Defense and distancing as terror management strategies: The moderating role of need for structure and permeability of group boundaries. *Journal of Personality and Social Psychology, 79,* 923–932.

Devine, P. G. (1989). Stereotypes and prejudice: Their automatic and controlled components. *Journal of Personality and Social Psychology, 56,* 5–18.

Dollard, J., Doob, L., Miller, N., Mowrer, O., & Sears, R. (1939). *Frustration and aggression.* New Haven, CT: Yale University Press.

Esses, V. M., Jackson, L. M., & Armstrong, T. L. (1998). Intergroup competition and attitudes toward immigrants and immigration: An instrumental model of group conflict. *Journal of Social Issues, 54,* 699–724.

Fein, S., & Spencer, S. J. (1997). Prejudice as self-image maintenance: Affirming the self through derogating others. *Journal of Personality and Social Psychology, 73,* 31–44.

Florian, V., & Mikulincer, M. (1998). Terror management in childhood: Does death conceptualization moderate the effects of mortality salience on acceptance of similar and different others? *Personality and Social Psychology Bulletin, 24,* 1104–1112.

Furnham, A., & Gunter, B. (1984). Just world beliefs and attitudes towards the poor. *British Journal of Social Psychology, 23,* 265–269.

Goldenberg, J., Pyszczynski, T., Greenberg, J., & Solomon, S. (2000). Fleeing the body: A terror management perspective on the problem of human corporeality. *Personality and Social Psychology Review, 4,* 200–218.

Goldschmidt, W. (1990). *The human career: The self in the symbolic world.* Cambridge, MA: Blackwell.

Greenberg, J., Martens, A., Jonas, E., Eisenstadt, D., Pyszczynski, T., & Solomon, S. (2003). Detoxifying thoughts of death: Eliminating the potential for anxiety eliminates the effects of mortality salience on worldview defense. *Psychological Science, 14,* 516–519.

Greenberg, J., Pyszczynski, T., & Solomon, S. (1986). The causes and consequences if the need for self-esteem: A terror management theory: In R.F. Baumeister (Ed.), *Public and private self* (pp. 189-212). New York: Springer-Verlag.

Greenberg, J., Pyszczynski, T., Solomon, S., Rosenblatt, A., Veeder, M., Kirkland, S., et al. (1990). Evidence for terror management theory II: The effects of mortality salience on reactions to those who threaten or bolster the cultural worldview. *Journal of Personality and Social Psychology, 58,* 308–318.

Greenberg, J., Schimel, J., Martens, A., Pyszczynski, T., & Solomon, S. (2001). Sympathy for the devil: Evidence that reminding whites of their mortality promotes more favorable reactions to white racists. *Motivation and Emotion, 25,* 113–133.

Greenberg, J., Solomon, S., & Arndt, J. (2008). A basic but uniquely human motivation: Terror management. In J. Shah & W. Gardner (Eds.). *Handbook of motivation science* (pp. 114–154). New York: Guilford.

Halloran, M. J., & Kashima, E. S. (2004). Social identity and worldview validation: The effects of ingroup identity primes and mortality salience on value endorsement. *Personality and Social Psychology Bulletin, 30,* 915–925.

Harmon-Jones, E., Greenberg, J., Solomon, S., & Simon, L. (1996). Terror management in the minimal ingroup paradigm. *European Journal of Social Psychology, 25,* 781–785.

Harmon-Jones, E., Simon, L., Greenberg, J., Pyszczynski, T., & Solomon, S. (1997). Terror management theory and self-esteem: Evidence that self-esteem attenuates mortality salience effects. *Journal of Personality and Social Psychology, 72,* 24–36.

Harrington, A. (1969). *The immortalist.* New York: Random House.

Heider, F. (1958). *The psychology of interpersonal relationships.* New York: Wiley.

Hirschberger, G. (2006). Terror management and attributions of blame to innocent victims: Reconciling compassionate and defensive responses. *Journal of Personality and Social Psychology, 91,* 832-844.

Hirt, E. R., Zillman, D., Erickson, G. A., & Kennedy, G. (1992). Costs and benefits of allegiance: Changes in fans' self-ascribed competencies after team victory versus defeat. *Journal of Personality and Social Psychology, 63,* 724–738.

Hovland, C. I., & Sears, R. (1940). Minor studies in aggression: VI: Correlation of lynchings with economic indices. *Journal of Psychology, 9,* 301–310.

Janoff-Bulman, R., & Yopyk, D. J. (2004). Random outcomes and valued commitments: Existential dilemmas and the paradox of meaning. In J. Greenberg, S. L., Koole, & T. Pyszczynski (Eds.), *Handbook of experimental existential psychology* (pp. 122–140). New York: Guilford.

Jonas, E., & Fischer, P. (2006). Terror management and religion: Evidence through intirnsic religiousness, mitigated worldview defense after mortality salience. *Journal of Personality and Social Psychology, 91,* 553–567.

Jonas, E., Fritsche, I., & Greenberg, J. (2005). Currencies as cultural symbols—An existential psychological perspective on reactions of Germans toward the Euro. *Journal of Economic Psychology, 26,* 129–146.

Jones, J. M. (1997). *Prejudice and racism* (2nd ed.). New York: McGraw-Hill.

Jost, J. T., & Banaji, M. R. (1994). The role of stereotyping in system-justification and the production of false consciousness. *British Journal of Social Psychology, 33,* 1–27.

Jost, J. T., & Burgess, D. (2000). Attitudinal ambivalence and the conflict between group and system justification motives in low status groups. *Personality and Social Psychology Bulletin, 26,* 293–305.

Jost, J. T., Fitzsimons, G., & Kay, A. C. (2004). The ideological animal: A system justification view. In J. Greenberg, S. L. Koole, & T. Pyszczynski (Eds.), *Handbook of experimental existential psychology* (pp. 263–283). New York: Guilford.

Kasser, T., & Sheldon, K. M. (2000). Of wealth and death: Materialism, mortality salience, and consumption behavior. *Psychological Science, 11,* 348–351.

Kruglanski, A. W. (1996). Motivated social cognition: Principles of the interface. In E. T. Higgins & A. W. Kruglanski (Eds.), *Social psychology: Handbook of basic principles* (pp. 493–520). New York: Guilford.

Kunda, Z. (1990). The case for motivated reasoning. *Psychological Bulletin, 198,* 480–498.

Landau, M. J., Goldenberg, J., Greenberg, J., Gillath, O., Solomon, S., Cox, C., et al. (2006). The siren's call: Terror management and the threat of men's sexual attraction to women. *Journal of Personality and Social Psychology, 90,* 129–146.

Landau, M. J., Greenberg, J., Solomon, S., Pyszczynski, T., & Martens, A. (2006). Windows into nothingness: Terror management, meaninglessness, and negative reactions to modern art. *Journal of Personality and Social Psychology, 90,* 879–892.

Landau, M., Greenberg, J., & Sullivan, D. (2006). *Managing terror when worldviews and self-worth collide: Evidence that mortality salience increases reluctance to excel beyond group stereotypes, one's parents, and canonized leaders.* Unpublished manuscript, Tucson, AZ.

Landau, M. J., Johns, M., Greenberg, J., Pyszczynski, T., Solomon, S., & Martens, A. (2004). A function of form: Terror management and structuring of the social world. *Journal of Personality and Social Psychology, 87,* 190–210.

Landau, M. J., Solomon, S., Greenberg, J., Cohen, F., Pyszczynski, T., Arndt, J., et al. (2004). Deliver us from evil: The effects of mortality salience and reminders of 9/11 on support for President George W. Bush. *Personality and Social Psychology Bulletin, 30,* 1136–1150.

Lerner, M. J. (1980). *The belief in a just world: A fundamental delusion.* New York: Plenum.

Lifton, R. J. (1968). *Revolutionary immortality: Mao Tse-tung and the Chinese cultural revolution.* New York: Random House.

Lifton, R. J. (1979). *The broken connection: On death and continuity of life.* New York: Simon & Schuster.

Manson, S., Beals, J., O'Neill, T., Piaseki, J., Bechtold, D., Keane, E., et al. (1996). Wounded spirits, ailing hearts: PTSD and related disorders among American Indians. In A. J. Marsella (Ed.), *Ethnocultural aspects of posttraumatic stress disorder: Issues, research, and clinical application* (pp. 251–282). Washington, DC: American Psychological Association.

Martens, A., Greenberg, J., & Schimel, A. (2004). Ageism and terror management: Effects of mortality salience and perceived similarity to elders on reactions to elderly people. *Personality and Social Psychology Bulletin, 30,* 524–536.

McGregor, H., Lieberman, J., Greenberg, J., Solomon, S., Arndt, J., Simon, L., et al. (1998). Terror management and aggression: Evidence that mortality salience motivates aggression against worldview threatening others. *Journal of Personality and Social Psychology, 74,* 590–605.

Mikulincer, M., & Florian, V. (2000). Exploring individual differences in reactions to mortality salience: Does attachment style regulate terror management mechanisms? *Journal of Personality and Social Psychology, 79,* 260–273.

Mikulincer, M., Florian, V., & Hirschberger, G. (2003). The existential function of close relationships: Introducing death into the science of love. *Personality and Social Psychology Review, 7,* 20–40.

Moskowitz, G. (2005). *Social cognition.* New York: Guilford.

Nelson, L. J., Moore, D. L., Olivetti, J., & Scott, T. (1997). General and personal mortality salience and nationalistic bias. *Personality and Social Psychology Bulletin, 23,* 884–892.

Neuberg, S. L., & Newsome, J. (1993). Personal need for structure: Individual differences in the desire for simple structure. *Journal of Personality and Social Psychology, 65,* 113–131.

Office of the White House Press Secretary. (2001, November 2). *Remarks by President Bush and President Obasanjo of Nigeria in Photo Opportunity.* Retrieved September 4, 2006, from http://www.whitehouse.gov/news/releases/2001/11/20011102–5.html

Pratto, F., Sidanius, J., Stallworth, L. M., & Malle, B. (1994). Social dominance orientation: A personality variable predicting social and political attitudes. *Journal of Personality and Social Psychology, 67,* 741–763.

Pyszczynski, T., Abdollahi, A., Solomon, S., Greenberg, J., & Weise, D. (2006). Mortality salience, martyrdom, and military might: The Great Satan versus the Axis of Evil. *Personality and Social Psychology Bulletin, 32,* 525–538.

Pyszczynski, T., & Greenberg, J. (1987). Toward an integration of cognitive and motivational perspective on social inference: A biased hypothesis-testing model. In L. Berkowitz (Ed.), *Advances in experimental social psychology* (Vol. 20, pp. 297–340). New York: Academic.

Pyszczynski, T., Greenberg, J., & Solomon, S. (1999). A dual process model of defense against conscious and unconscious death-related thoughts: An extension of terror management theory. *Psychological Review, 106,* 835–845.

Pyszczynski, T., Greenberg, J., Solomon, S., Arndt, J., & Schimel, J. (2004). Why do people need self-esteem? A theoretical and empirical review. *Psychological Bulletin, 130,* 435–468.

Pyszczynski, T., Maxfield, M., Cox, C., Seidel, A., Greenberg, J., & Solomon, S. (2006). *Priming a sense of common humanity reverses the effect of mortality salience on implicit anti-Arab prejudice.* Unpublished manuscript, University of Colorado, Colorado Springs.

Pyszczynski, T., Solomon, S., & Greenberg, J. (2003*). In the wake of September 11: The psychology of terror.* Washington, DC: American Psychological Association.

Rank, O. (1998). *Psychology and the soul* (G. C. Richter & E. J. Lieberman, Trans.). Baltimore: John Hopkins University Press. (Original work published 1930)

Rogers, C. R. (1963). The actualizing tendency in relation to "motives" and to consciousness. In M. R. Jones (Ed.), *Nebraska symposium on motivation* (Vol. 11, pp. 1–24). Lincoln: University of Nebraska Press.

Ryan, R. M., & Deci, E. L. (2002). Overview of self-determination theory: An organismic dialectical perspective. In E. L. Deci & R. M. Ryan (Eds.), *Handbook of self-determination research* (pp. 3–33). Rochester, NY: University of Rochester Press.

Salzman, M. B. (2001). Cultural trauma and recovery: Perspectives from terror management theory. *Trauma Violence and Abuse, 2,* 172–191.

Salzman, M. B., & Halloran, M. J. (2004). Cultural trauma and recovery: Cultural meaning, self-esteem, and the re-construction of the cultural anxiety-buffer. In J. Greenberg, S. L. Koole, & T. Pyszczynski (Eds.), *Handbook of experimental existential psychology* (pp. 231–246). New York: Guilford.

Schaller, M., Boyd, C., Yohannes, J., & O'Brian, M. (1995). The prejudiced personality revisited: Personal need for structure and formation of erroneous group stereotypes. *Journal of Personality and Social Psychology, 68,* 544–555.

Schimel, J., Simon, L., Greenberg, J., Pyszczynski, T., Solomon, S., Waxmonsky, J., et al. (1999). Stereotyping and terror management: Evidence that mortality salience increases stereotypic thinking and preferences. *Journal of Personality and Social Psychology, 77,* 905–926.

Schmeichel, B. J., & Martens, A. (2005). Self-affirmation and mortality salience: Affirming values reduces worldview defense and death-thought accessibility. *Personality and Social Psychology Bulletin, 31,* 658–667.

Sears, D. O. (1988). Symbolic racism. In P. A. Katz & D. A. Taylor (Eds.), *Eliminating racism: Profiles in controversy* (pp. 53–84). New York: Plenum.

Shah, J. Y., Kruglanski, A. W., & Thompson, E. (1998). Membership has its (epistemic) rewards: Need for closure effects on in-group bias. *Journal of Personality and Social Psychology, 68,* 247–260.

Sherif, M., Harvey, O. J., White, B. J., Hood, W. R., & Sherif, C. W. (1961). *Intergroup conflict and cooperation: The Robber's Cave experiment.* Norman: University of Oklahoma, Institute of Group Relations.

Simon, L., Arndt, J., Greenberg, J., Solomon, S., & Pyszczynski, T. (1998). Terror management and meaning: Evidence that the opportunity to defend the worldview in response to mortality salience increases the meaningfulness of life in the mildly depressed. *Journal of Personality, 66,* 359–382.

Solomon, S., Greenberg, J., & Pyszczynski, T. (1991). A terror management theory of social behavior: On the psychological functions of self-esteem and cultural worldviews. In M. P. Zanna (Ed.), *Advances in experimental social psychology* (Vol. 24, pp. 93–159). San Diego, CA: Academic Press.

Solomon, S., Greenberg, J., & Pyszczynski, T. (2004). The cultural animal: Twenty years of terror management theory and research. In J. Greenberg, S. Koole, & T. Pyszczynski (Eds.), *Handbook of experimental existential psychology* (pp. 13–34). New York: Guilford.

Tajfel, H., & Turner, J. C. (1979). An interactive theory of intergroup conflict. In W. G. Austin & S. Worchel (Eds.), *The social psychology of intergroup relations* (pp. 33–47). Monterey, CA: Brooks-Cole.

Thompson, M. M., Naccarato, M. E., Parker, K. C. H., & Moskowitz, G. B. (2001). The personal need for structure and personal fear of invalidity measures: Historical perspectives, current applications, and future directions. In G. B. Moskowitz (Ed.), *Cognitive social psychology: The Princeton Symposium on the legacy and future of social cognition* (pp. 19–39). Mahwah, NJ: Erlbaum.

Weise, D., Pyszczynski, T., Cox, C., Arndt, J., Greenberg, J., Solomon, S., & Kosloff, S. (2008). Interpersonal politics: The role of terror management and attachment processes in political preferences. Psychological Science, 19, 448-455.

Yalom, I. (1980). *Existential psychotherapy.* New York: Basic Books.

Zinn, H. (1995). *A people's history of the United States.* New York: Harper-Perennial.

16 You Were Always on My Mind
How Event-Related Potentials Inform Impression Formation Research

Jennifer T. Kubota and Tiffany A. Ito
University of Colorado

Face-to-face social interactions are such a common, everyday experience that the impressive array of processes that underlie them may typically go unnoticed. Although seemingly effortless, the act of forming impressions of an individual or group can be viewed as an unfolding, multistage process that relies on the deployment of visual attention, activation of stored beliefs and feelings, integration of multiple sources of information, and the generation of explicit behaviors, among others. Several interesting social psychological models of impression formation have been generated to explicate these processes, but some key assumptions have received less attention than others. This is due in part to methodological difficulties in studying processes that occur in quick temporal succession, as the component processes of impression formation likely do. In addition, many aspects of this process are thought to occur implicitly, requiring measures of processes about which perceivers may never be consciously aware. Finally, social norms and desirability concerns may obscure or alter some processes of interest.

Although social psychologists have developed measures to quantify implicit processing and circumvent social desirability (e.g., Fazio, Sanbonmatsu, Powell, & Kardes, 1986; Greenwald, McGhee, & Schwartz, 1998; Payne, 2001), these measures typically cannot assess the temporal ordering of multiple component processes. They also often lack the ability to directly measure the assumed underlying mechanisms. With the increasing application of neuroscience techniques to the study of social phenomena, a growing body of research now exists examining key aspects of social perception using neuroscience measures. These measures often allow for the assessment of phenomena with high temporal resolution, the assessment of implicit processing, and the circumvention of social desirability concerns, providing a useful complement to existing behavioral measures. The purpose of this chapter is to review what research using one neuroscience measure in particular—event-related brain potentials (ERPs)—reveals about various aspects of impression formation.

We begin with a brief methodological review for the recording and interpretation of ERPs. We then review ERP research associated with different aspects of impression formation, integrating these findings with extant models of impression formation.

UNDERSTANDING ERPS

ERPs reflect averaged electrical activity measured at the scalp, resulting from the synchronous and summated postsynaptic firing of neurons (Fabiani, Gratton, & Coles, 2000). When an individual views a stimulus or makes a response, groups of neurons fire and it is the electrical activity associated with these events that is quantified. The resulting waveform is comprised of positive- and negative-going deflections that occur across time, yielding a Voltage × Time function. The deflections in the waveform, referred to as components, are thought to reflect discrete information processing operations (Gehring, Gratton, Coles, & Donchin, 1992). Researchers typically quantify both the amplitude of a component, thought to reflect the extent to which a psychological process has been engaged, and the latency, thought to reflect the point in time at which the psychological operation has been completed.

A component's polarity reflects the polarity of the electrical potential at that point in time relative to the reference electrode(s). Several conventions are used in the literature to name the components. In one, components are named for both their polarity (either with an N for a negative-going component or a P for positive-going component) and latency after stimulus presentation (e.g., N100 indicates a negative-going component that peaks about 100 msec after stimulus onset). A similar convention sequentially orders the components without identifying their specific latency. As an example, the N1 would be the first negative-going component, and the N2 the second negative-going component. Other times, components are named for the psychological process they are assumed to capture (e.g., the error-related negativity is a negative-going component occurring during commission of an error).

ERPs provide several unique advantages for studying the process of impression formation. First, by using high sampling rates (e.g., 1,000 Hz), ERPs allow researchers to quantify ongoing responses with excellent temporal resolution (on the order of milliseconds). Second, ERPs do not require the explicit reporting of psychological operations, as some behavioral measures do; instead, neural activity associated with a stimulus can be recorded before a response is even made, or even in the absence of a response. In addition, research shows that some ERP components are insensitive to purposeful misrepresentation (Crites, Cacioppo, Gardner, & Berntson, 1995; Farwell & Donchin, 1991; Rosenfeld, Angell, Johnson, & Qian, 1991), making them useful in situations with social desirability concerns. Finally, ERPs can be used in identifying mechanisms relevant for many social psychological processes such as attention allocation, executive control, and affective responding. We next turn to a review of the way in which ERP research has refined or expanded what is known about some of the major aspects of impression formation.

SOCIAL CATEGORIZATION

Current models of person perception separate impression formation into discrete stages, which are implicitly if not explicitly ordered across time (Bodenhausen & Macrae, 1998; Brewer, 1988; Fiske & Neuberg, 1990). Each begins with encountering an individual, allowing for some act of identification and categorization that is tempered by attention allocation and self-relevance. It has long been suggested that we automatically categorize individuals along social categories such as age, race, and sex, based on visual cues as an efficient cognitive strategy for simplifying the world (Bodenhausen & Macrae, 1998; Brewer, 1988; Bruner, 1957; Fiske & Neuberg, 1990; Stangor, Lynch, Duan, & Glass, 1992). This tendency to quickly categorize has important implications because of the link among categorization, stereotyping, and prejudice. Although categorization may normally be a useful tool for processing the social world, it can sometimes result in unfair or incorrect inferences. Whereas the application and implicit nature of stereotyping and prejudice has been extensively examined, relatively little traditional social psychological research has been directed at examining when categorization occurs and how it may be moderated.

Many ERP studies have addressed the question of when processing of these primary social cues begins, finding that it occurs automatically and very rapidly, within milliseconds of viewing an individual (Caldara et al., 2003; Ito, Thompson, & Cacioppo, 2004; Ito & Urland, 2003, 2005; James, Johnstone, & Hayward, 2001; Kubota & Ito, 2007). One of the first studies to demonstrate these effects was by Mouchetant-Rostaing, Giard, Bentin, Aguera, and Pernier (2000), who showed participants pictures of faces or body parts (hands and torsos) that were blocked to contain either pictures from one gender group or from both. Participants performed one of two tasks. In the gender categorization task, participants judged the gender of the faces or body parts, and in the nongender categorization task, participants classified the presence of a target object (e.g., glasses on a face or a picture of a torso). While allowing for the comparison of responses to face and body parts, this paradigm also allowed for the comparison of explicit gender categorization (when participants were instructed to differentiate between genders in the mixed-gender blocks) with implicit gender categorization (when participants were instructed to categorize glasses or torsos). Results showed that after only about 145 msec of viewing the faces, and well before an explicit response was made, participants were sensitive to variations in gender. This was shown in a larger positive-going ERP component peaking at around 145 msec in blocks in which faces of both males and females were viewed as compared to single-gender blocks. This occurred in mixed-gender blocks both when participants were explicitly instructed to attend to gender and when they were simply instructed to attend to eyeglasses. By contrast, there was no effect of mixed versus same-gender block while viewing body parts, indicating that the sensitivity to gender cues was restricted to facial stimuli (see also Mouchetant-Rostaing & Giard, 2003, for a replication varying age). The rapid effect of gender on ERP responses (by 145 msec) and its effects under both task conditions support previous theorizing that social cues are processed quickly and implicitly.

The study by Mouchetant-Rostaing et al. (2000) is intriguing, and raises the question of whether other social categories are processed as quickly. Another issue is whether different targets within the same dimension (e.g., males vs. females) are processed in a similar way. In Mouchetant-Rostaing et al., responses were assessed as a function of whether mixed—and same—gender faces were seen without addressing possible attention differences to males versus females. Both issues were addressed by Ito and Urland (2003). In this study, participants, the majority of whom were White, viewed Black and White male and female faces while categorizing the faces in terms of either race or gender. This allowed for an examination of responses to both gender and race. In addition, this design allowed the researchers to assess implicit and explicit processing of both gender and race by varying which dimension participants were explicitly instructed to attend to, and to examine responses separately as a function of the two gender (male vs. female) and race (Black vs. White) categories.

Consistent with Mouchetant-Rostaing et al. (2000) and extant models of impression formation, target gender was processed very quickly. In this study, gender differences were observed in a positive-going component, occurring at approximately 180 msec after stimulus presentation. This component, which the researchers refer to as the P200, was larger to males than to females. Of importance, this occurred both when participants were explicitly categorizing by gender and when they were categorizing by race. Target race also quickly modulated processing, both when participants were instructed to attend to race as well as when they were instructed to attend to gender. Race effects occurred even more quickly than gender effects, occurring not only in the P200 but also in the preceding N100 component, which occurred with a mean latency of 122 msec. In both the N100 and P200, amplitudes were larger to Black than White faces. Subsequent research has further supported this finding (Correll, Urland, & Ito, 2006; Coulter & Ito, 2006; Ito & Urland, 2005; Kubota & Ito, 2007; Willadsen-Jensen & Ito, 2006; Willadsen-Jensen, Ito, & Park, 2007), suggesting that race cues are also processed very early and automatically. Given the association of the N100 and P200 with selective attention, with larger ERP responses indicative of greater attention, this greater attentional allocation to males and Blacks by predominantly White participants in these early components could reflect orienting to the more threatening or salient social group.

Moreover, there is evidence that the perceiver's own category membership can impact initial race perception. Recall that Ito and Urland (2003) included mostly White participants in their studies and found that the N100 as well as the P200 were greater to Black than White faces. This begs the question of whether this is true across perceivers of different races. That is, does this reflect an ingroup–outgroup effect in which more attention is directed to racial outgroup members regardless of the perceiver's racial identity, or does this reflect a target group effect in which greater attention is directed to Blacks by perceivers of all races? To address this question, Willadsen-Jensen and Ito (2006) had White and Asian American participants view pictures of Whites and Asians. For the White participants, the

P200 replicated past research with larger amplitudes to outgroup Asian than ingroup White faces. Interestingly, Asian participants showed the opposite pattern of results. Their P200s were larger to outgroup Whites than to ingroup Asians. These results therefore suggest that attentional processes reflected in the P200 are sensitive to ingroup–outgroup status, with greater attention directed to the outgroup target. This also supports the interpretation of the P200 as reflecting focus of attention on threatening or novel cues, both of which may be indicated by outgroup membership.

These studies illustrate how the application of social neuroscience methods produces evidence for understanding this initial stage of impression formation. First, processing of social category information does occur very early and automatically. Gender, age, and race all impact ERP amplitudes by at least 145 msec, even when the perceiver is attending to other social categories or to category-irrelevant cues such as the presence of eyeglasses. Interestingly, this differentiation is specific to the processing of faces and is absent for the processing of body parts (Mouchetant-Rostaing et al., 2000). Moreover, race effects occurred on average at around 120 msec, which was faster than the processing of both gender and age, which occurred between 145 msec and 180 msec. To offer speculation, the difference in the time course for race versus gender and age effects could be due to experience differences. That is, lack of exposure to racial outgroup members may make racial outgroup status a particularly potent cue for threat or salience. It could also be the case that race is more socially empathized than gender or age, speeding its processing. Alternatively, if the N100 and P200 are associated with threat, race may be more strongly associated with this concept than gender or age. It is important to note that the effects of race do not seem to be an artifact of some other visual cue that happens to covary with race. This is demonstrated by the fact that differentiation between races was found for both color and grayscale stimuli that were equated for luminance (Ito & Urland, 2003), indicating that these perceptual features were not responsible for the race effects. Additionally, race effects were not observed when the faces were blurred and inverted, rendering the facial cues imperceptible but leaving other physical differences such as color intact (Kubota & Ito, 2007). Finally, race processing is affected by the perceiver's group membership, demonstrated through the differentiation in P200 effects between White and Asian perceivers (Willadsen-Jensen & Ito, 2006), suggesting that the foundations of impression formation are built on the perceiver's identity in relation to those around them.

INDIVIDUATION

After an individual is quickly placed into visually derived categories, further information about that individual can be gathered as a means of individuating that person from the countless others in that same category. Like a taxonomical hierarchy, the process of individuating a face takes a stimulus object that is broadly categorized and sorts it into more specific and unique attributes. According to extant theories of impression formation, individuation is not assumed to occur for all targets. Instead, it is most likely in situations where the target is not easily categorizable or of high personal relevance (Bodenhausen & Macrae, 1998; Brewer, 1988; Fiske & Neuberg, 1990). In a broader sense, individuation is typically reserved for people we would benefit from gathering more information about, which often includes ingroup members. Supporting this claim, research has shown that ingroup members are spontaneously processed more deeply than other racial groups (Anthony, Cooper, & Mullen, 1992; Levin, 2000). Individuation is thought to involve effortful, relatively complex attribute analysis. Nevertheless, there may be rudimentary effects of individuation on attention. In particular, individuation may be supported by focusing more attentional resources on these individuals, helping to encode their personal characteristics.

Models of impression formation can be viewed as making two predictions readily testable with ERPs. First, processes related to individuation should be more likely for individuals who are more personally relevant, such as ingroup members. Second, because individuating ingroup members depends on knowing who is in the ingroup, individuated processing should occur after at least rudimentary processing of social category information. Each of these predictions is supported by extant ERP research examining the N200 component, which has been associated with individuation and deeper processing. For instance, this component is larger to pictures of one's own face than to other's faces (Tanaka, Curran, Porterfield, & Collins, 2006), and to famous as compared with unfamiliar faces (Bentin & Deouell, 2000). Studies assessing the N200 to different racial groups consistently find that White perceivers show larger N200s to ingroup White as compared to outgroup Black and Asian faces (Coulter & Ito, 2006; Ito & Urland, 2003, 2005; Kubota & Ito, 2007; Willadsen-Jensen & Ito, 2006). Moreover, these effects occur after the N100 and P200 effects discussed in the previous section (at around 250 msec). This suggests that although automatic vigilance mechanisms may make it adaptive to initially devote greater attentional resources to threatening or novel faces of racial outgroup members (as reflected in the N100 and P200), in the absence of any strong potential negative consequences, perceivers may subsequently devote more attentional resources to racial ingroup members because they are typically more desirable for greater individuation and are more approachable.

MODERATION OF EARLY VISUAL PROCESSING

Initial studies in which attention was affected by a social dimension such as race, even when attention was explicitly directed at another dimension such as gender, suggest that processing of social category information is unaffected by task. However, these studies all used some sort of social categorization task. Because participants were explicitly instructed to differentiate based on a social category, it could be argued that participants were primed to focus on all category distinctions. While Mouchetant-Rostaing and colleagues (2000) included a physical stimulus differentiation condition (presence or absence of eyeglasses), this detection still focused the perceivers on physical properties of the face.

Further information on the implicit nature of attention to social category information can be gleaned from studies examining how task instructions that focus attention away from race and gender affect reactions to these social category cues. Even when participants are performing more individuating tasks such as making a personality judgment or judging an individual's food preference, race and gender still affect P200 and N200 amplitudes (Ito & Urland, 2005). In addition, focusing attention away from the social nature of the stimuli by having participants attend to the presence or absence of a dot on a picture of a face similarly fails to affect P200 and N200 results (Ito & Urland, 2005). Thus, even when the goal is to process at a level deeper than the social category by making a personality or food preference judgment or when the goal is unrelated to the social nature of the stimuli, race and gender processing are still observed in a similar pattern to when individuals are asked to explicitly attend to race and gender information.[1]

In addition to manipulations of task factors, Kubota and Ito (2007) examined whether cues integral to the face that can themselves cue approach and withdrawal affect attention to race. They did this by having participants view pictures of Black and White males posing three facial expressions: angry, happy, and neutral. Across two blocks of trials, participants were instructed to explicitly categorize either based on race or facial expression. They found that race and emotion had largely independent effects; N100, P200, and N200 race results replicated Ito and Urland (2003) and were not moderated by emotional expression. These results further support the implicit nature of race perception, demonstrating that it occurs even when attention is directed to categorizing expression. Together, then, studies examining responses to race and gender in the context of varying task

---

[1] Interestingly, N100 race differences were eliminated in the food preference and dot detection tasks (but not the personality judgment task). The reason for this effect is unclear and could be the result of increased stimulus complexity required in these paradigms, more than task.

demands and the presences of other social cues converge in demonstrating the implicit nature of social category perception.

PERCEPTION OF RACIALLY AMBIGUOUS FACES

The studies reviewed to this point assessed reactions to individuals who could be readily categorized in terms of race, gender, and age. Although this is an important first step in understanding impression formation, individuals in real life can be categorized along multiple dimensions (e.g., race and gender), and a growing population is multiracial. According to Bodenhausen and Macrae (1998), social category ambiguity can potentially change how targets are processed. Although there exists a body of research on how the ambiguity of an individual can impact behavioral outcomes (Hugenberg & Bodenhausen, 2003, 2004), less is known regarding how individuals whose category membership is ambiguous are initially categorized. To address this, Willadsen-Jensen and Ito (2006) showed White participants faces of Whites, Asians, and computer-averaged Asian and White faces in one study and faces of Whites, Blacks, and computer-averaged White and Black faces in a second study. All faces were pretested for realism and equated on a series of other potentially confounding variables such as attractiveness. Interestingly, they found that at the P200 and N200, the racially ambiguous faces were differentiated from the 100% outgroup faces but not the White faces. That is, mixed Asian and White and Black and White faces were attended to similarly to White faces, but differentiated from Asians and Blacks, respectively. This suggested an overinclusion effect early in processing, such that faces containing any amount of ingroup features are attended similarly to that of 100% ingroup faces. Perhaps because of a White-processing norm (Smith & Zárate, 1992; Stroessner, 1996), perceivers use this group as a processing template on which other individuals are compared. When the face being considered contains many of the features of a White face, as these racially ambiguous faces did, they may be processed similarly to Whites. As we discuss later, it is not until later, more elaborative processing that the biracial faces are distinguished from both ingroup and outgroup members.

PREJUDICE AND STEREOTYPING

Processing in an individuated, person-based manner can be effortful, requiring attention on an attribute-by-attribute basis. As a result, it is generally assumed that not all individuals will be processed in an individuated manner. Instead, individuals who are easily categorized into an existing social group and for whom personal relevance is low are likely to activate category-based affect and beliefs (Bodenhausen & Macrae, 1998; Brewer, 1988; Fiske & Neuberg, 1990). In ERP research, activation of category-based affect has been examined with the P300 component. Numerous studies have shown that P300 amplitude increases as a function of the discrepancy between a given stimulus and preceding stimuli along salient dimensions (e.g., Cacioppo, Crites, Berntson, & Coles, 1993; Cacioppo, Crites, Gardner, & Berntson, 1994). This has led to the conclusion that P300 amplitude reflects working memory updates for maintaining an accurate mental model of the external environment (Donchin, 1981). To allow an examination of evaluative responses to members of different social groups, Ito et al. (2004) showed participants pictures of Black and White males that were embedded in a context of either positive items (e.g., cute puppies, appetizing foods) or negative items (e.g., dead animals, rotting food). Participants were instructed to report their liking of each image after viewing the picture. Additionally, participants completed the Modern Racism Scale (MRS), a self-report measure of prejudice (McConahay, Hardee, & Batts, 1981).

Ito et al. (2004) examined P300 amplitude to White and Black faces relative to positive and negative images. Two separate bias scores were computed for the P300s. In the first, a score was computed to reflect the degree to which P300s were larger to Black than White faces in the positive context, reflecting the degree to which Blacks are seen as discrepant with positive evaluations. In the second, a score was computed to reflect the degree to which P300s were larger to White than Black faces in a negative context, reflecting the degree to which Whites are seen as discrepant with negative evaluations. These scores were significantly correlated with MRS scores such that participants reporting more bias against Blacks also showed P300 responses indicative of greater negativity toward Blacks and greater positivity toward Whites. Bartholow and colleagues also used the P300 to examine the activation of category-based beliefs. This was done by having participants first read paragraphs that suggested a particular trait about a target individual (Bartholow, Fabiani, Gratton, & Bettencourt, 2001). They were then shown new behavioral descriptions that were either congruent or incongruent with this initial expectation. Just as a stimulus evaluatively incongruent with prior stimuli (e.g., an outgroup member seen in the context of positive images) elicited an enhanced P300 in Ito et al. (2004), sentences that violated the initial trait information produced a larger P300 than confirmatory information. Moreover, negative behavioral information that violated a prior expectation for positively valenced behavior produced larger P300s than positive information violating a prior expectation for negatively valenced behavior. This latter effect is consistent with a range of findings showing larger effects for negative than positive information (e.g., Bartholow & Dickter, 2008; Bartholow et al., 2001; Ito, Larsen, Smith, & Cacioppo, 1998; Peeters & Czapinski, 1990). Although these effects were obtained in response to newly formed behavioral expectations, stereotypes associated with different social groups may act similarly as prior expectations against which an exemplar's current behavior is compared, leading to similar behavioral incongruency effects in the P300.

In the studies reviewed in this section, the P300 peaked with a latency of approximately 500 msec. Although it is possible that subsequent studies will find earlier effects of prejudice and stereotyping, the time course of the present effects, occurring after the social categorization effects discussed earlier in the chapter, is consistent with sequential processing of social category information, followed by the activation of stereotyping and prejudice. Moreover, although studies using ERPs to assess the activation of prejudice and stereotypes are just beginning, and the studies reviewed here used explicit evaluative and semantic judgments, the sensitivity of the P300 to implicit evaluative and semantic judgments (Crites et al., 1995; Farwell & Donchin, 1991; Ito & Cacioppo, 2000; Rosenfeld et al., 1991) suggests this measure might also be useful in assessing implicit prejudice and stereotyping.

COGNITIVE CONTROL

In many instances, impression formation culminates in some sort of behavioral response. Because of the ease and speed with which individuals are categorized into different social groups, as supported by the research reviewed here, and the existence of biased beliefs and evaluations associated with many social groups, this can often result in a biased or discriminatory response. Behavior, however, may also be influenced by personal and societal motivations to control prejudiced responses (Devine, 1989). Bodenhausen and Macrae (1998), for instance, suggested a hierarchical control process in which the higher order structures of personal and societal motivations to control prejudice regulate or influence other, lower order aspects of impression formation, such as the application of stereotypic associations. They suggest a two-part system consisting of a comparator that assesses similarity between an actual and desired state, and an operator that tries to achieve the desired state if a discrepancy is detected.

The model suggested by Bodenhausen and Macrae (1998) is very similar to models of cognitive control that are frequently studied with ERPs (Botvinick, Braver, Barch, Carter, & Cohen, 2001; Carter et al., 1998). In these models, behavior regulation is also thought to involve a two-part system. The first system, the conflict-detection system, operates preconsciously to continuously monitor ongoing neural signals for conflicts between cognitions, such as between the desired outcome and an activated response tendency (Berns, Cohen, & Mintun, 1997; Nieuwenhuis, Ridderinkhof, Blom, Band, & Kok, 2001). When conflict is detected, the second regulatory system is signaled, engaging higher order attentional control to focus attention on the source of conflict, organizing behavior to resolve this conflict. If such a model characterizes the application of motivations to control prejudice, ERP studies should reveal operations of the conflict detection or cognitive control stages when nonprejudice intentions differ from an activated race-biased response.

Two initial studies seeking to understand behavior regulation examined conflict detection during stereotype activation. The first made use of the Weapons Identification Task (WIT; Payne, 2001) in which participants must identify guns and tools that are preceded by Black and White male face primes (Amodio et al., 2004). Participants were instructed to respond as fast and accurately as possible to the objects while using the face as a warning stimulus for the target. In addition, Amodio and colleagues made racial bias salient by telling participants that responding "gun" to a tool primed by a Black face would demonstrate racial prejudice. If we assume that participants would generally wish to avoid appearing prejudiced, this instruction should elevate conflict when such a response is made.

To investigate the neural mechanisms associated with this conflict, Amodio et al. (2004) quantified the error-related negativity (ERN), a negative-going, response-locked component occurring shortly after commission of an error (usually within 100 msec). Neural imaging and source localization studies have suggested that the ERN reflects activity in the dorsal regions of the anterior cingulate cortex (ACC), a region found to monitor for response competition, and once this conflict is detected, to engage executive control (Botvinick et al., 2001). As activity in this region increases, signals are sent to the dorsal lateral prefrontal cortex, an area associated with executive function and deliberate processing (Gehring & Fencsik, 2001; Kerns et al., 2004). Amodio et al. (2004) found that ERNs were larger when participants made errors on Black-tool than Black-gun trials, particularly for those who were internally motivated to be nonprejudiced, suggesting greater conflict during error commission of the more race-biased response (i.e., erroneously associating Blacks with guns), especially for those who were motivated to avoid such errors. Moreover, larger ERNs following errors on Black-tool trials were associated with longer reaction times and greater accuracy on trials following the error, which may be an indication of greater behavioral control following stereotype-based errors. Together, these results suggest that the process reflected in the ERN is an important mechanism for internal behavior regulation of stereotypes.

Although participants in Amodio et al. (2004) may have been influenced by their perceptions of external norms of behavior, their behavior was assessed under relatively private conditions (i.e., they made their responses alone), which may have dampened the evaluative aspect of normative egalitarian pressures. To explicitly assess the neural basis of behavior regulation in response to private versus public motivations, Amodio, Kubota, Harmon-Jones, and Devine (2006) instructed participants that their WIT responses would be entirely confidential or would be monitored to determine whether they were responding with bias. In this study, all participants were selected to be high in internal motivation to control prejudice while varying in level of external motivation, thus selecting participants who varied in the extent to which evaluations by others motivated their responding. Social psychological theory has emphasized a postconscious mechanism for eliciting behavioral control, such that an individual must first consciously recognize when his or her actions are out of line with intentions and then recruit corrective processes (Monteith, 1993; Wegener & Petty, 1997). To address this, Amodio et al. quantified not only the ERN, but also the error positivity (P_e), a positive-polarity deflection that immediately follows the ERN (Nieuwenhuis et al., 2001). Whereas the ERN is thought to reflect preconscious monitoring of conflict, the P_e is thought to reflect postconscious error perception. In neuroimaging studies, the P_e wave has been linked to activity of the rostral ACC (Kiehl, Liddle, & Hopfinger, 2001; van Veen & Carter, 2002), a brain region associated with affect and awareness in response to error commission (Bush, Luu, & Posner, 2000).

As in Amodio et al. (2004), ERNs were larger during error trials than during correct trials and were largest when errors were made on Black-tool trials. Additionally, the size of the ERNs on

Black-tool trials predicted behavioral control in the form of greater accuracy on Black-tool trials.[2] This occurred in both the private and public response conditions and for those high and low in level of external motivation. However, unlike the ERN, for those participants who were sensitive to external egalitarian pressures (i.e., who were high in external motivations to be nonprejudiced), P_e amplitude predicted response accuracy on Black-tool trials, but only in the public response condition. These findings complement Amodio et al. (2004) and additionally suggest that error perception, indexed by P_e, may depend not only on the individual's motivations but also on the context in which individuals find themselves while monitoring for response competition. Furthermore, a one-size-fits-all behavior regulation model is not sufficient to explain this complex system and instead a model that takes into account the interaction of individual differences and the activation of those goals can better allow researchers to explain and intervene in these behavior tendencies.

The WIT examines stereotypic associations by assessing object categorization. Similar racial stereotypes have also been examined in a paradigm measuring responses to individuals in a more externally valid situation (albeit in a controlled, laboratory context). Correll, Park, Judd, and Wittenbrink (2002) created a paradigm in which participants view pictures of Black and White men who are holding either guns or objects that do not pose a threat (e.g., wallets and cell phones). Participants' task is to decide as quickly as possible to "shoot" armed targets and to "not shoot" unarmed targets. Behavioral results show that participants are faster and more accurate in "shooting" armed Blacks as compared to Whites. Furthermore, they are faster and more accurate to "not shoot" unarmed Whites as compared with Blacks.

To assess the mechanisms responsible for behavior regulation in decisions to shoot, Correll, Urland, and Ito (2006) recorded ERPs while participants completed the shooter task. They examined the N200[3] component, which has been associated with the detection of conflict during successful behavior regulation (i.e., when correct behavior is implemented; Nieuwenhuis, Yeung, van den Wildenberg, & Ridderinkhof, 2003). Like the ERN quantified by Amodio et al. (2004) in the WIT, source modeling of the N200 implicates the ACC (Liotti, Woldorff, Perez, & Mayberg, 2000; Nieuwenhuis et al., 2003). N200s associated with conflict monitoring were larger to White targets than Black targets, with the largest N200s when viewing unarmed White targets. "Shoot" tends to be the dominant response in this task (e.g., participants are faster and more accurate in making shoot than not shoot decisions). Coupled with prevailing stereotypes more strongly linking Blacks than Whites with violence, deciding whether to shoot an unarmed White should result in more conflict than making the same decision about an unarmed Black, resulting in larger N200s to unarmed Whites. Moreover, this difference in conflict monitoring as a function of race predicted later race-bias differences in response latencies; those who showed larger race differences in the N200 also showed larger race differences in response latencies. The N200 effect also mediated the relationship between stereotype endorsement and biased response latencies, such that stronger neural signals of conflict monitoring in favor of Whites accounted for the link between more negative stereotypic associations toward Blacks as compared to Whites and biased responding.

The N200 has also been used to assess the psychological mechanism responsible for evaluative priming (Bartholow & Dickter, 2008). In this set of studies, the researchers adapted the Eriksen flanker task (Eriksen & Eriksen, 1974), in which a centrally presented, imperative stimulus is surrounded by either response compatible or incompatible stimuli. In this study, centrally presented Black and White faces were surrounded by positive White stereotypic words (e.g., rich, scholar, educated) and negative Black stereotypic words (e.g., rude, danger, lazy). Participants were asked to racially categorize the face and ignore the words.

---

[2] This differs slightly from Amodio et al. (2004), where behavioral control was indexed by accuracy on the trial following the error.

[3] Although they share a similar latency and scalp distribution, the N200 discussed here in the context of conflict detection (sometimes also referred to as an N2) and the N200 discussed in the context of social categorization effects have been treated as conceptually distinct.

This task yielded the expected flanker effect, with faster categorization of the faces on stereo-type-congruent than incongruent trials, implying conflict when faces were surrounded by words incongruent with the relevant racial stereotype. As expected, N200s were also larger for incongruent trials than congruent trials. Bartholow and Dickter (2008) also examined the lateralized readiness potential (LRP), a component quantified over motor cortices. Because movement is controlled contralaterally, comparing responses over the two motor cortices provides an indication of motor preparation of the responses associated with the two hands. Importantly, activity in the motor cortices begins prior to the appearance of actual movement (Coles, Smid, Scheffers, & Otten, 1995). In this way, the component is sensitive to responses that may be primed, even if they do not result in an overt response such as a button press. As expected, incongruent trials were associated with priming of the incorrect response (i.e., when the flankers were incongruent with the race of the face, the participants' initial motor response was to incorrectly categorize the race).

Of interest, whereas the N200 and LRP provide an indication of conflict detection and response priming on incongruent trials, respectively, only the LRP was correlated with response latency; as the tendency to initiate the incorrect response on incongruent trials increased, responding became slower. The authors suggest that this implicates conflict at the level of response output as opposed to stimulus evaluation as the source of incompatibility effects in this task. More generally, this study demonstrates how measures of multiple types of conflict can be used simultaneously to assess the mechanism through which an effect occurs.

These studies as a whole suggest that neural processes sensitive to the activation of stereotypic associations, and their degree of congruency with behavioral goals, are important in determining the influence of stereotypes on behavior. This research is relatively new but already shows promise in identifying specific mechanisms that may affect the influence of stereotypes on behavior (e.g., via conflict at the more abstract, representational level or at the level of the motor response). As we have reviewed, studies implicate both processes. It will be interesting in the future to determine if both processes contribute to behavior at the same time, or whether their relevance differs with the nature of the task.

CONCLUSION

The area of social psychological ERP research specifically and social neuroscience more broadly have already illuminated many aspects of impression formation and hold much promise for future research. These measures serve a complementary function to established explicit and implicit measures. By using social psychological theory to guide the application of such techniques, social neuroscience can assist in testing hypotheses that were previously difficult to assess and thereby expand social psychological theory. As we have demonstrated in this chapter, ERPs have a functional and valuable place in impression formation research. They help address areas of investigation in which social desirability is of concern, and also allow for a temporal evaluation of quickly occurring implicit and explicit processing.

When applied to the study of initial social categorization, ERP research has supported extant models of impression formation, finding that social cues such as age, gender, and race are processed fast and efficiently, and this processing is not dependent on explicit attention. Initially, perceivers appear to orient to threatening or salient and novel category members followed by a reorientation to ingroup members and approachable others. These early and automatic stages have not been moderated by task goals or other cues (facial expressions) that are integral to social processing.

ERPs have also been used to examine aspects of prejudice and stereotype activation, showing, for example, sensitivity to individual variability in group-based evaluative reactions (Ito et al., 2004) and violations of prior behavioral expectations (Bartholow & Dickter, 2008). Moreover, studies investigating how these feelings and beliefs affect behavior from the perspective of behavioral control are an excellent example of how ERPs can be applied to social psychological research. Although using ERPs to investigate conflict monitoring is a relatively recent development, this research has provided potential mechanisms for behavior regulation of bias. It has been shown that the associative link between targets and evaluations and stereotypes can be difficult to overcome and an individual's ability to monitor for potential discrepancies between intentions and responses can influence his or her ability to efficiently control for unwanted bias reactions. This filter can be achieved both at the level of continuous monitoring mechanisms, indexed via the N200, ERN, and P_e as well as at the level of a physical motor response, indexed via the LRP. Finally, it is important when considering the effectiveness of such mechanisms to take into account individual differences in motivation to respond in a nonbiased manner and the external forces that can trigger such motivations.

REFERENCES

Amodio, D. M., Harmon-Jones, E., Devine, P. G., Curtin, J. J., Hartley, S. L., & Covert, A. E. (2004). Neural signals for the detection of unintentional race bias. *Psychological Science, 15,* 88–93.

Amodio, D. M., Kubota, J. T., Harmon-Jones, E., & Devine, P. G. (2006). Alternative mechanisms for regulating racial responses according to internal versus external cues. *Social, Cognitive, and Affective Neuroscience, 1,* 26–36.

Anthony, T., Copper, C., & Mullen, B. (1992). Cross-racial facial identification: A social cognitive integration. *Personality and Social Psychology Bulletin, 18,* 296–301.

Bartholow, B. D., Fabiani, M., Gratton, G., & Bettencourt, B. A. (2001). A psychophysiological examination of cognitive processing of and affective responses to social expectancy violations. *Psychological Science, 12,* 197–204.

Bentin, S., & Deouell, L. Y. (2000). Structural encoding and identification in face processing: ERP evidence for separate mechanisms. *Cognitive Neuropsychology, 17,* 35–54.

Berns, G. S., Cohen, J. D., & Mintun, M. A. (1997). Brain regions responsive to novelty in the absence of awareness. *Science, 276,* 1272–1275.

Bodenhausen, G. V., & Macrae, C. N. (1998). Stereotype activation and inhibition. In J. R. Wyer (Ed.), *Advances in social cognition* (Vol. 11, pp. 1–52). Mahwah, NJ: Erlbaum.

Botvinick, M. M., Braver, T. S., Barch, D. M., Carter, C. S., & Cohen, J. D. (2001). Conflict monitoring and cognitive control. *Psychological Review, 108,* 624–652.

Brewer, M. B. (1988). A dual process model of impression formation. In T. K. Srull & R. S. Wyer (Eds.), *Advances in social cognition* (Vol. 1, pp. 1–36). Hillsdale, NJ: Erlbaum.

Bruner, J. S. (1957). On perceptual readiness. *Psychological Review, 64,* 123–151.

Bush, G., Luu, P., & Posner, M. I. (2000). Cognitive and emotional influences in anterior cingulate cortex. *Trends in Cognitive Science, 4,* 215–222.

Cacioppo, J. T., Crites, S. L., Jr., Berntson, G. G., & Coles, M. G. H. (1993). If attitudes affect how stimuli are processed, should they not affect the event-related brain potential? *Psychological Science, 4,* 108–112.

Cacioppo, J. T., Crites, S. L., Gardner, W. L., & Berntson, G. G. (1994). Bioelectrical echoes from evaluative categorizations: I. A late positive brain potential that varies as a function of trait negativity and extremity. *Journal of Personality and Social Psychology, 67,* 115–125.

Caldara, R., Thut, G., Servoir, P., Michel, C. M., Bovet, P., & Renault, B. (2003). Faces versus non-face objects perception and the "other-race" effect: A spatio-temporal event-related potential study. *Clinical Neurophysiology, 11,* 515–528.

Carter, C. S., Braver, T. S., Barch, D. M., Botvinick, M. M., Noll, D., & Cohen, J. D. (1998). Anterior cingulate cortex, error detection, and the online monitoring of performance. *Science, 280,* 747–749.

Coles, M. G. H., Smid, H. G. O. M., Scheffers, M. K., & Otten, L. J. (1995). Mental chronometry and the study of human information processing. In M. D. Rugg & M. G. H. Coles (Eds.), *Electrophysiology of the mind: Event-related brain potentials and cognition* (pp. 86–131). New York: Oxford University Press.

Correll, J., Park, B., Judd, C. M., & Wittenbrink, B. (2002). The police officer's dilemma: Using ethnicity to disambiguate potentially threatening individuals. *Journal of Personality and Social Psychology, 83,* 1314–1329.

Correll, J., Urland, G. R., & Ito, T. A. (2006). Event-related potentials and the decision to shoot: The role of threat perception and cognitive control. *Journal of Experimental Social Psychology, 42,* 120–128.

Coulter, H. M., & Ito, T. A. (2006, January). *Neural processes in racial categorization and individuation.* Poster presented at the 46th annual conference of the Society for Psychophysiological Research, Vancouver, BC,.

Crites, S. L., Cacioppo, J. T., Gardner, W. L., & Berntson, G. G. (1995). Bioelectrical echoes from evaluative categorizations: II. A late positive brain potential that varies as a function of attitude registration rather than attitude report. *Journal of Personality and Social Psychology, 68,* 997–1013.

Devine, P. G. (1989). Prejudice and stereotypes: Their automatic and controlled components. *Journal of Personality and Social Psychology, 56,* 5–18.

Dickter, C. L., & Bartholow, B. D. (2007). Racial ingroup and outgroup attention biases revealed by event-related brain potentials. *Social Cognitive and Affective Neuroscience, 2*(3), 189-198.

Dolcos, F., & Cabeza, R. (2002). Event-related potentials of emotional memory: Encoding pleasant, unpleasant, and neutral pictures. *Cognitive, Affective, and Behavioral Neuroscience, 2*(3), 252–263.

Donchin, E. (1981). Surprise! . . . Surprise? *Psychophysiology, 18,* 493–513.

Eimer, M., & Holmes, A. (2002). An ERP study on the timecourse of emotional face processing. *Neuroreport: For Rapid Communication of Neuroscience Research, 13*(4), 427–431.

Eimer, M., Holmes, A., & McGlone, F. P. (2003). The role of spatial attention in the processing of facial expression: An ERP study of rapid brain responses to six basic emotions. *Cognitive, Affective, & Behavioral Neuroscience, 3*(2), 97–110.

Eriksen B. A., & Eriksen, C. W. (1974). Effects of noise letters upon the identification of a target letter in a nonsearch task. *Perception and Psychophysics, 16,* 143–149.

Fabiani, M., Gratton, G., & Coles, M. G. H. (2000). Event-related brain potentials. In J. T. Cacioppo, L. G. Tassinary, & G. G. Berntson (Eds.), *Handbook of psychophysiology* (2nd ed., pp. 53–84). Cambridge, UK: Cambridge University Press.

Farwell, L. A., & Donchin, E. (1991). The truth will out: Interrogative polygraph ("lie detection") with event-related brain potentials. *Psychophysiology, 28,* 531–547.

Fazio, R. H., Sanbonmatsu, D. M., Powell, M. C., & Kardes, F. R. (1986). On the automatic activation of attitudes. *Journal of Personality and Social Psychology, 50,* 229–238.

Fiske, S. T., & Neuberg, S. L. (1990). A continuum of impression formation, from category-based to individuating processes: Influences of information and motivation on attention and interpretation. In M. Zanna (Ed.), *Advances in experimental social psychology* (Vol. 23, pp. 1–74). San Diego, CA: Academic.

Gehring, W. J., & Fencsik, D. E. (2001). Functions of the medial frontal cortex in the processing of conflict and errors. *Journal of Neuroscience, 21,* 9430–9437.

Gehring, W. J., Gratton, G., Coles, M. G. H., & Donchin, E. (1992). Probability effects on stimulus evaluation and response processes. *Journal of Experimental Psychology: Human Perception & Performance, 18,* 198–216.

Greenwald, A. G., McGhee, D. E., & Schwartz, J. L. K. (1998). Measuring individual differences in implicit cognition: The implicit association test. *Journal of Personality and Social Psychology, 74,* 1464–1480.

Hugenberg, K., & Bodenhausen, G. V. (2003). Facing prejudice: Implicit prejudice and the perception of facial threat. *Psychological Science, 14*(6), 640–643.

Hugenberg, K., & Bodenhausen, G. V. (2004). Ambiguity in social categorization: The role of prejudice and facial affect in race categorization. *Psychological Science, 15*(5), 342–345.

Ito, T. A., & Cacioppo, J. T. (2000). Electrophysiological evidence of implicit and explicit categorization processes. *Journal of Experimental Social Psychology, 36,* 660–676.

Ito, T. A., Larsen, J. T., Smith, N. K., & Cacioppo, J. T. (1998). Negative information weighs more heavily on the brain: The negativity bias in evaluative categorizations. *Journal of Personality and Social Psychology, 75,* 887–900.

Ito, T. A., Thompson, E., & Cacioppo, J. T. (2004). Tracking the timecourse of social perception: The effects of racial cues on event-related brain potentials. *Personality and Social Psychology Bulletin, 30*(10), 1267–1280.

Ito, T. A., & Urland, G. R. (2003). Race and gender on the brain: Electrocortical measures of attention to the race and gender of multiply categorizable individuals. *Journal of Personality and Social Psychology, 85,* 616–626.

Ito, T. A., & Urland, G. R. (2005). The influence of processing objectives on the perception of faces: An ERP study of race and gender perception. *Cognitive, Affective, and Behavioral Neuroscience, 5*(1), 21–36.

James, M. S., Johnstone, S. J., & Hayward, W. G. (2001). Event-related potentials, configural encoding, and feature-based encoding in face recognition. *Journal of Psychophysiology, 15*(4), 275–285.

Kerns, J. G., Cohen, J. D., MacDonald, A. W., Cho, R. Y., Stenger, V. A., & Carter, C. S. (2004). Anterior cingulate conflict monitoring and adjustments in control. *Science, 303,* 1023–1026.

Kiehl, K. A., Liddle, P. F., & Hopfinger, J. B. (2001). Error processing and the rostral anterior cingulate: An event-related fMRI study. *Psychophysiology, 37,* 216–223.

Kubota, J. T., & Ito, T. A. (2007). Multiple cues in social perception: The timecourse of processing race and facial expression. *Journal of Experimental Social Psychology, 43,* 738–752.

Levin, D. T. (2000). Race as a visual feature: Using visual search and perceptual discrimination tasks to understand face categories and the cross-race recognition deficit. *Journal of Experimental Psychology: General, 129*(4), 559–574.

Liotti, M., Woldorff, M. G., Perez, R., III, & Mayberg, H. S. (2000). An ERP study of the temporal course of the Stroop color-world effect. *Neuropsychologia, 38,* 701-711.

McConahay, J. B., Hardee, B. B., & Batts, V. (1981). Has racism declined in America? It depends on who is asking and what is asked. *Journal of Conflict Resolution, 25,* 563–579.

Monteith, M. J. (1993). Self-regulation of stereotypical responses: Implications for progress in prejudice reduction. *Journal of Personality and Social Psychology, 65,* 469–485.

Mouchetant-Rostaing, Y., & Giard, M. H. (2003). Electrophysiological correlates of age and gender perception on human faces. *Journal of Cognitive Neuroscience, 15,* 900–910.

Mouchetant-Rostaing, Y., Giard, M. H., Bentin, S., Aguera, P. E., & Pernier, J. (2000). Neurophysiological correlates of face gender processing in humans. *European Journal of Neuroscience, 12,* 303–310.

Nieuwenhuis, S., Ridderinkhof, K. R., Blom, J., Band, G. P. H., & Kok, A. (2001). Error-related brain potentials are differently related to awareness of response errors: Evidence from an antisaccade task. *Psychophysiology, 38,* 752–760.

Nieuwenhuis, S., Yeung, N., van den Wildenberg, W., & Ridderinkhof, K. R. (2003). Electrophysiological correlates of anterior cingulated function in a go/no-go task; Effects of response conflict and trial type frequency. *Cognitive, Affective, and Behavioral Neuroscience, 3,* 17–26.

Payne, B. K. (2001). Prejudice and perception: The role of automatic and controlled processes in misperceiving a weapon. *Journal of Personality and Social Psychology, 81,* 181–192.

Peeters, G., & Czapinski, J. (1990). Positive-negative asymmetry in evaluations: The distinction between affective and informational negativity effects. In W. Stroebe & M. Hewstone (Eds.), *European review of social psychology* (Vol. 1, pp. 33–60). Chichester, UK: Wiley.

Rosenfeld, J. P., Angell, A., Johnson, M., & Qian, J. (1991). An ERP-based, control-question lie detector analog: Algorithms for discrimination effects within individuals' average waveforms. *Psychophysiology, 28,* 319–335.

Schupp, H. T., Junghöfer, M., Weike, A. I., & Hamm, A. O. (2003). Attention and emotion: An ERP analysis of facilitated emotional stimulus processing. *Neuroreport: For Rapid Communication of Neuroscience Research, 14*(8), 1107–1110.

Smith, E. R., & Zárate, M. A. (1992). Exemplar-based model of social judgment. *Psychological Review, 99,* 3–21.

Stangor, C., Lynch, L., Duan, C., & Glass, B. (1992). Categorization of individuals on the basis of multiple features. *Journal of Personality and Social Psychology, 62,* 207–218.

Stroessner, S. J. (1996). Social categorization by race or sex: Effects of perceived non-normalcy on response times. *Social Cognition, 14*(3), 247–276.

Tanaka, J. W., Curran, T., Porterfield, A. L., & Collins, D. (2006). Activation of pre-existing and acquired face representations: The N250 ERP as an index of face familiarity. *Journal of Cognitive Neuroscience, 18,* 1488–1497.

van Veen, V., & Carter, C. S. (2002). The anterior cingulate as a conflict monitor: fMRI and ERP studies. *Physiological Behavior, 77,* 477–482.

Wegener, D. T., & Petty, R. E. (1997). The flexible correction model: The role of naïve theories of bias in bias correction. In M. P. Zanna (Ed.), *Advances in experimental social psychology* (Vol. 29, pp. 141–208). Mahwah, NJ: Erlbaum.

Willadsen-Jensen, E. C., & Ito, T. A. (2006). Ambiguity and the timecourse of racial perception. *Social Cognition, 24,* 580–606.

Willadsen-Jensen, E. C., Ito, T. A., & Park, B. (2007). *From perception to evaluation: How racially ambiguous faces affect early attention and automatic activation of bias.* Poster presented at the 7th annual conference of the Society for Personality and Social Psychology, Memphis, TN.

17 Pictures in Our Heads
Contributions of fMRI to the Study of Prejudice and Stereotyping

David M. Amodio and Matthew D. Lieberman
New York University and University of California, Los Angeles

In 1922, Walter Lippman famously referred to stereotypes as "pictures in our heads." His comment presaged nearly a century of research on how perceptions of stigmatized social groups are represented in the mind. In this chapter, we describe how the most recent addition to the prejudice researcher's methodological toolbox—functional magnetic resonance imaging (fMRI)—allows researchers to measure patterns of neural activity associated with prejudice, stereotyping, and discrimination (Figure 17.1). fMRI is a technique for measuring changes in blood flow in the brain. As neurons in the brain fire, their energy is depleted. Tiny capillaries throughout the brain deliver oxygenated blood supplies to replenish the neuron's energy stores. Oxygenated blood contains more ionized hemoglobin molecules, and changes in blood oxygen-dependent (BOLD) signal can be detected using magnetic resonance technology (see Huettel, Song, & McCarthy, 2004, for an in-depth description of fMRI methodology). The assumption in fMRI research is that increases in blood flow to a particular region of the brain are associated with a greater degree of neuronal activity in the preceding seconds. When placed in the hands of prejudice researchers, fMRI provides a way to study Lippman's "pictures in our heads" by examining patterns of activity in our brains (i.e., pictures of inside our heads).

In this chapter, we describe how neuroimaging methods have been used to study different components of racial bias, and how this research has contributed to theoretical advances in the field of intergroup bias. A second goal of this chapter is to present the extant findings on prejudice and stereotyping in a framework that emphasizes their role in the regulation of behavior. We begin with a brief review of the social cognition literature on prejudice and stereotyping to provide context for the body of recent fMRI studies in this area.

SOCIAL COGNITION RESEARCH ON PREJUDICE AND STEREOTYPING

In his book, *The Nature of Prejudice,* Allport (1954) observed that when it comes to race relations, many White Americans live in a state of conflict: On one hand, they may be ideologically opposed to prejudice, but on the other, they possess underlying tendencies to think and act in racially biased ways. More recent conceptualizations of Allport's "state of conflict" suggest that people may hold explicit egalitarian beliefs while possessing implicit racial associations that operate automatically in subconscious mental processes (e.g., Devine, 1989; see also Wilson, Lindsey, & Schooler, 2000). The interplay of implicit associations and explicit beliefs has captured the attention of social cognition researchers in recent years, as reviewed in more detail elsewhere in this volume, and the majority of fMRI investigations of racial bias have been designed to address central issues in the social cognition of prejudice. To set the stage for our review, we begin with a brief review of the key socio-cognitive mechanisms of prejudice that have been of particular interest to researchers taking a neuroscience approach.

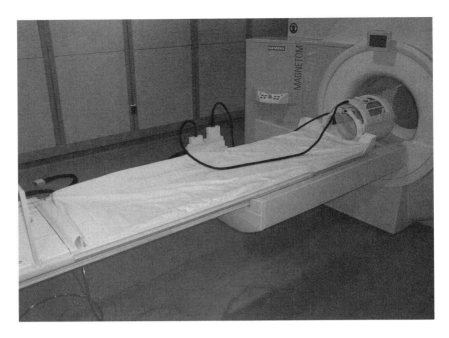

FIGURE 17.1   The MRI scanner. MRI scanning requires that the participant's head is centered inside the bore of a large electromagnet. Participants lie in a supine position on the scanner bed, and the bed is then moved into position. In addition, small movements may create problematic artifacts in the MR images. These restrictions of positioning and the need to remain extremely still during scans limits the types of tasks that can be used in experiments and may also affect the psychological experience of the participant. These limitations present special challenges for researchers interested in social behavior, such as prejudice researchers.

AUTOMATICITY OF BIAS

Automatic forms of race bias are typically described in a few different ways: as an instantaneous gut-level feeling about a person or group, or alternatively as thought that spontaneously pops into one's head when encountering a member of a stigmatized social group (Fiske, 1998; Greenwald & Banaji, 1995). Still others have focused on motor components of automaticity, such as spontaneously activated behaviors that are engaged when exposed to an outgroup member (Bargh, Chen, & Burrows, 1996; see also James, 1890). Although these different forms of implicit bias have been documented, very little research has distinguished them at a theoretical level, and thus the assumption has been they are learned, expressed, unlearned, and regulated through the same set of mechanisms (but see Amodio & Devine, 2006).

The proposition that automatic forms of racial bias could be dissociated from consciously held attitudes and beliefs was first demonstrated by Devine (1989). On the basis of research in cognitive psychology, Devine theorized that stereotypes were cognitive associations that could be overlearned through repeated exposure in one's cultural environment, such that they may be automatically activated in response to relevant stimuli (Meyer & Schvaneveldt, 1971; Shiffrin & Schneider, 1977). Her research showed that subconscious exposure to race-related words activated these stereotype constructs in participants' mental representations, which in turn biased participants' impressions of novel individuals in stereotype-consistent ways.

What was perhaps most interesting about her findings was that the automatic effects of stereotypes on behavior were not moderated by participants' level of explicit prejudice when they were unaware of the racial primes. Although implicit racial associations had been demonstrated in earlier work (Dovidio, Evans, & Tyler, 1986; Gaertner & McLaughlin, 1983), Devine (1989) suggested that Allport's (1954) "state of conflict" referred to a conflict between explicit beliefs and implicit stereotype associations.

Subsequent work focused on the automatic activation of negative evaluations of racial outgroups (i.e., implicit prejudices), such as in White people's responses to African Americans (Dovidio, Kawakami, Johnson, Johnson, & Howard, 1997; Fazio, Jackson, Dunton, & Williams, 1995). Whereas Devine (1989) examined the effects of subliminally primed stereotypes on social judgments, most of the work investigating evaluative effects of bias have focused on the relationship between reaction-time-based measures of bias with outcomes such as social behavior and self-reported attitudes. Implicit prejudice is typically indicated by greater facilitation of responses to negative words or objects following exposure to Black faces than White faces (and relative to responses to positive stimuli). Research using reaction-time measures has shown that implicit evaluations of Black people are generally unrelated to individuals' explicit attitudes, yet they predict biased patterns of nonverbal behaviors in actual and anticipated interracial interactions (Amodio & Devine, 2006; Dovidio, Kawakami, & Gaertner, 2002; Dovidio et al., 1997; Fazio et al., 1995; Henderson-King & Nisbett, 1996; McConnell & Leibold, 2001).

It is generally believed that implicit racial biases reflect exposure to biased patterns of racial associations in one's cultural milieu. Although little research has made direct connections between implicit bias and specific learning mechanisms (but see Olson & Fazio, 2006; Rydell & McConnell, 2006), research suggests that implicit racial biases are learned passively, without one's deliberative intention to learn (Gregg, Seibt, & Banaji, 2006; Rydell & McConnell, 2006). Indeed, much research examining associations between implicit and explicit racial responses have generally found modest relations (Blair, 2002), supporting the idea that automatic and consciously held attitudes and beliefs arise from independent processes (Devine, 1989; Wilson et al., 2000). As a result, implicit and explicit biases have been shown to predict different forms of discrimination (Dovidio et al., 1997; Fazio et al., 1995). Yet the underlying mechanisms for how different forms of bias affect different types of behaviors remain poorly understood, in part because different underlying forms of implicit bias are difficult to parse using behavioral measures.

REGULATING INTERGROUP RESPONSES

How are automatic biases controlled? For egalitarians—those who reject prejudiced ideology—intentional intergroup behavior requires the regulation of unwanted automatic biases (Devine, 1989). Regulation is accomplished through controlled processing: the effortful and deliberative implementation of an intended response that overrides the influences of unwanted automatic biases, such as implicit prejudices and stereotypes (Shiffrin & Schneider, 1977). Thus, egalitarians are expected to engage controlled processes in interracial interactions, whereas racists would not. Although numerous studies have demonstrated the effectiveness of controlled processing in regulating intergroup responses, the social psychology literature lacks a mechanistic model for how controlled processes accomplish intentional responses in the face of automatic biases (D. T. Gilbert, Fiske, & Lindzey, 1998). How do controlled processes interface with behavior? What is being controlled? Race-biased thoughts? Emotions? Behaviors? Are there multiple components of control? These important questions have been difficult to address using the traditional tools and theoretical models of social psychology, yet they are critical to our understanding of prejudice control, and of self-regulation more broadly.

AN fMRI APPROACH TO THE ACTIVATION AND REGULATION OF INTERGROUP RESPONSES

Over the past 15 years, a large body of accumulated findings attests to the power and pervasiveness of implicit racial biases as well as to humans' great capacity to regulate their effects on behavior (Blair, 2001). Interestingly, this body of research is largely descriptive. There have been several

TABLE 17.1

Independent Processes Involved in Intergroup Bias and Their Associated Neurocognitive Function and Neural Correlates

Role in Intergroup Bias	Neurocognitive Function	Candidate Structure(s)	Selected References
Implicit evaluative bias	Classical fear conditioning; arousal; vigilance	Amygdala	Phelps et al. (2000); Amodio et al. (2003); Cunningham et al. (2004)
Implicit stereotyping	Conceptual priming	Temporal cortex and left LPFC	Potanina et al. (2006)
Detecting bias and need for control	Conflict monitoring	Anterior cingulate cortex	Amodio et al. (2004); Cunningham et al. (2004)
Inhibition of implicit prejudice	Response inhibition; Affect inhibition	Ventral LPFC	Lieberman et al. (2005); Cunningham et al.(2004)
Implementation of intended response	Regulative control	Dorsal LPFC	Cunningham et al. (2004); Richeson et al. (2003)
Outgroup perception	Mentalizing; Theory of Mind	Dorsal MPFC (BA 9/32)	Mitchell, Macrae, & Banaji (2005, 2006); Amodio & Frith (2006)
Ingroup perception	Processing of self and similar others	MPFC (BA 10/32)	Gobbini et al. (2004); Harris & Fiske (2006); Mitchell et al. (2006)
Detecting external cues for engaging control	Regulating behavior to external social cues	MPFC, rostral paracingulate	Amodio et al. (2006)

Note. LPFC = lateral prefrontal cortex; MPFC = medial prefrontal cortex; BA = Brodmann's Area.

demonstrations of implicit biases and efforts to control one's racial responses. However, there has not been a clear, concrete theoretical explanation of what implicit bias is, what mechanisms facilitate its expression in behavior, and what mechanisms inhibit its expression. Without a strong theoretical model, efforts to predict the behavioral effects of implicit bias and to develop effective strategies for reducing implicit bias are limited. A major goal of the neuroscience approach to these enduring questions is to provide some theoretical scaffolding on which further advances in the understanding of intergroup behavior may be built. Our review of the neuroimaging literature on prejudice and stereotyping begins by highlighting the contributions of fMRI research to the central social cognitive mechanisms of racial bias outlined earlier (Table 17.1). We then describe some new directions in person perception that are relevant to issues of prejudice suggested by recent neuroimaging studies.

Neural Mechanisms of Implicit Prejudice

Some of the earliest mergers of social psychological and cognitive neuroscience approaches were aimed at identifying the neural underpinnings of implicit prejudice (for review, see Lieberman, 2007). Behavioral neuroscience investigations of classical conditioning in rodents had identified the amygdala—a small set of nuclei located bilaterally in the medial temporal lobes—as critical for fear conditioning (Figure 17.2; Davis, Hitchcock, & Rosen, 1987; but see Davis & Whalen, 2001; Fendt & Fanselow, 1999; LeDoux, 1992). When describing research on the amygdala, it is important to note that interpretations of amygdala function have evolved considerably over the years, and

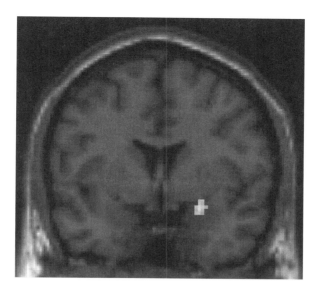

FIGURE 17.2   The amygdala comprises several small nuclei and is located bilaterally in the medial temporal lobe. The arrow on the left side indicates the anatomical image of the left amygdala.

although research continues to refine our understanding, functional explanations of the amygdala (as with most other brain structures) will likely undergo further revisions.

Early investigations of human amygdala function focused on the role of the amygdala in emotional processing, particularly as it pertains to the learning, perception, and expression of fear (Adolphs, Tranel, Damasio, & Damasio, 1995). Similarly, early neuroimaging studies found that presentations of fearful faces enhanced participants' amygdala activity, relative to neutral or happy facial expressions (Breiter et al., 1996; Morris et al., 1996). Later refinements to this body of work suggested that the amygdala serves as a low-level threat detector that is activated in response to stimuli that are potentially dangerous. Thus it was associated not just with fear, but also ambiguity, vigilance, arousal, and even uncertainty associated with positive outcomes (Whalen, 1998). Accumulating evidence continues to suggest that the amygdala responds to the emotional intensity of a stimulus (i.e., the arousal component of affect) rather than to the valence of a stimulus (Anderson et al., 2003; Cunningham, Raye, & Johnson, 2004), although intensity tends to be greater for negative stimuli on average (Lang, Bradley, & Cuthbert, 1990; Cacioppo, Gardner, & Berntson, 1999).

Despite changes in functional interpretations of amygdala response, neuropsychological and neuroimaging research have consistently demonstrated that the amygdala operates at an automatic and unconscious level of processing. A seminal study by Bechara et al. (1995) examined the ability of patients with bilateral amygdala damage to learn in a classical conditioning paradigm. In the task, participants viewed a series of colored shapes, some of which were paired with an aversive noise (a 100 dB blast of a boat horn). The researchers assessed learning in two ways, designed to test participants' implicit versus explicit processing. To assess explicit learning, participants were simply asked to report which stimulus was paired with the horn blast. To assess implicit learning, the researchers examined changes in participants' skin conductance levels when the condition stimulus appeared. Skin conductance reflects activity of the autonomic nervous system, and levels typically rise in anticipation of an aversive event. It was found that although the amygdala patients could correctly report the conditioned stimulus, they did not show the typical anticipatory rise in skin conductance, suggesting that the amygdala was important for implicit but not explicit processing. By contrast, a comparison group of patients with bilateral hippocampus damage were unable to report the conditioning contingency, yet their skin conductance levels displayed normal patterns of anticipatory autonomic responses when conditioned stimuli appeared, relative to stimuli that were not paired with the horn blast. Subsequent neuroimaging research showing that subliminal presentation of angry faces, masked by neutral faces, selectively activated the amygdala (Whalen et al., 1998), corroborating the notion that the amygdala operates at the implicit level of processing.

To prejudice researchers, the amygdala seemed like an excellent candidate for a neural substrate of implicit prejudice. Research in social psychology has long suggested that feelings of fear may underlie implicit or gut-level negative evaluations of African Americans (Mackie & Smith, 1998; Smith, 1993), so the amygdala seemed like an obvious choice. The first fMRI studies of prejudice measured brain activity while participants passively viewed faces of Black and White individuals. For example, Phelps et al. (2000) examined White American participants' neural responses to unfamiliar Black faces, in comparison with White faces. Although the authors did not observe a significant increase in amygdala activity to Black versus White participants, there was a trend toward this effect. In addition, they showed that the degree of difference in amygdala activity to Black versus White faces was correlated with participants' scores on a behavioral measure of implicit prejudice (the Implicit Associations Test [IAT]; Greenwald, McGhee, & Schwartz, 1998), as well as on a measure of startle-eye blink response to Black versus White faces that is known to be modulated by amygdala (Lang et al., 1990; see also Amodio, Harmon-Jones, & Devine, 2003). This pattern of correlations provided the first evidence that amygdala activity might underlie implicit prejudice.

In the same year of Phelps et al.'s seminal paper, Hart et al. (2000) published research examining White and African American participants' neural responses to faces of Black and White individuals. Hart et al. assessed neural activity to ingroup and outgroup faces in two blocks of trials (i.e., runs). Although amygdala activity to ingroup versus outgroup faces did not differ during the first block of trials, a difference emerged in the second block, such that amygdala responses to ingroup faces were lower than responses to outgroup faces. The authors' interpretation of this effect was that in the first block, all faces were unfamiliar to participants, and the amygdala was similarly active to the ingroup and outgroup. However, by the second block, participants had habituated to the ingroup faces, but not the outgroup faces. These effects were conceptually consistent with the findings of Phelps et al. (2000), in that they implicated the amygdala in implicit responses to race.

Significant differences in amygdala response to Black compared with White faces were initially reported by Amodio et al. (2003), who used the startle-eye blink method to infer the degree of amygdala activation, and this pattern has since been replicated several times in fMRI studies using a range of experimental tasks (Cunningham, Johnson, et al., 2004; Lieberman, Hariri, Jarcho, Eisenberger, & Bookheimer, 2005; Wheeler & Fiske, 2005). The strongest evidence to date that the amygdala may be involved in implicit prejudice was provided by Cunningham et al. (2004), in which participants were exposed to 30-msec presentations of Black and White faces (i.e., subliminal), masked by various shapes. The participants' task was to indicate whether the shape appeared on the left or right side of the screen. The authors found that subliminal presentations of Black faces elicited greater amygdala activity than White faces, and that the degree of increased amygdala activity to Black (vs. White) faces was associated with more anti-Black responses on an IAT assessing evaluative associations with Black versus White faces. Wheeler and Fiske (2005) also observed greater amygdala activity in response to Black versus White faces, but only when the participants' task was to categorize faces according to race. When the participants' task was to make an individuating inference from the face picture (e.g., guessing whether the target likes various vegetables) or when the task drew attention away from facial features of the target (e.g., when judging whether a small white dot was present in the picture), race effects for amygdala activity were not observed. On the surface, Wheeler and Fiske's (2005) finding that mere exposure to the faces did not activate the amygdala may appear to contradict the amygdala effects for subliminal pictures of Black faces observed by Cunningham et al. (2004). However, we speculate that the lack of amygdala activity during the dot-finding task and individuation tasks in the Wheeler and Fiske (2005) study may have been related to a redirection of attentional resources associated with task demands. By contrast, the task used by Cunningham et al. (2004) was less difficult, and although participants were not aware of having viewed a face, ample attentional resources were available for subconscious processing of faces.

Although most research examining the amygdala as a substrate of implicit prejudice has focused on White American participants, some theories of implicit race bias suggest that implicit prejudice is in part a cultural phenomenon learned by all members of the culture, regardless of their race (Devine, 1989; Greenwald & Banaji, 1995; Rudman, 2004). If this is true, then African American participants should also show greater amygdala activity toward Black faces than White faces, despite the obvious fact that they rarely (if ever) hold explicit anti-Black prejudices. In line with this prediction, Lieberman et al. (2005) found that exposure to Black versus White faces elicited greater amygdala activity among both White and African American participants. This finding is consistent with some behavioral research indicating anti-Black bias among African American participants (Correll, Park, Judd, & Wittenbrink, 2002).

Richeson et al. (2003) examined White Americans' neural responses to images of Black versus White faces and compared these responses with participants' scores on an IAT measure of racial evaluations. Interestingly, the authors did not find the typical pattern of enhanced amygdala activity in response to Black versus White faces, nor was change in amygdala activity associated with scores on the IAT. By contrast, regions of the prefrontal cortex (PFC) that are typically associated with executive function and working memory were more highly activated to Black than White faces and were positively correlated with implicit prejudice scores on the IAT. The authors interpreted this finding as reflecting participants' spontaneous attempt to control any prejudiced thoughts that may have been caused by the pictures, and suggested that individuals with strong implicit prejudice may have been more likely to engage in such attempts.

In summary, implicit prejudice has been the most studied component of intergroup bias in the fMRI literature. Across several studies using fMRI, greater amygdala activation has been observed while White participants viewed Black faces compared with White faces. Importantly, the interpretation that the difference in amygdala activity is associated with implicit prejudice has been validated in several studies through comparisons with behavioral and physiological assessments of implicit bias (e.g., Cunningham, Johnson, et al., 2004; Phelps et al., 2000) and by comparing patterns of amygdala activation with known individual differences associated with implicit bias (Amodio et al., 2003).

NEURAL CORRELATES OF IMPLICIT STEREOTYPING

Much research has focused on the role of the amygdala in evaluative and affective forms of implicit bias, but what about implicit stereotyping? Little, if any, research has yet explored these topics. However, recent theorizing by Amodio and Devine (2006) noted that implicit stereotyping relies on representations of conceptual knowledge and associations, which are supported by neurocognitive systems for implicit semantic memory (also referred to as conceptual priming; Gabrieli, 1998). According to neuroscientific models of memory systems (e.g., Squire & Zola, 1996), semantic memory processes are generally supported by regions of the neocortex and not the regions of subcortex associated with implicit prejudice. Results from neuroimaging research on semantic memory and conceptual priming are somewhat mixed, yet an emerging pattern of findings suggests that conceptual priming involves regions of lateral temporal lobe (LTL) and left lateral PFC (Rissman, Eliassen, & Blumstein, 2003; Wible et al., 2006; Wig, Grafton, Demos, & Kelley, 2005; see Figure 17.3). On the basis of this body of research, Amodio and Devine (2006) suggested that the mechanisms underlying implicit prejudice and implicit stereotyping are independent and dissociable, and are thus likely to be learned, expressed, regulated, and unlearned in somewhat different ways.

Research by Potanina, Pfeifer, Lieberman, and Amodio (2006) directly tested the hypothesis that implicit stereotyping should be uniquely associated with neural activity in the LTL and PFC (but not the amygdala), whereas implicit prejudice should be uniquely associated with activity in the amygdala (but not LTL or PFC). The task used by Potanina et al. (2006) was designed to engage participants in judgments of Black and White targets that relied on either basic affective or stereotypic information. The study was described as examining one's ability

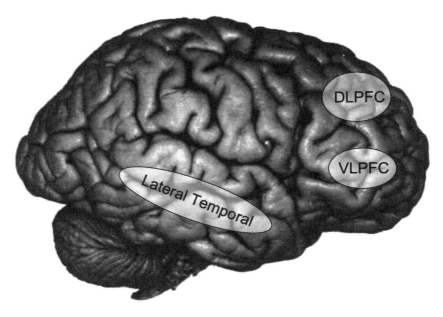

FIGURE 17.3 Lateral view indicating temporal lobe (LTL) and prefrontal cortex (PFC). Regions of dorsal and ventral lateral PFC (DLPFC) have been associated with the controlled processing, and left PFC has been linked to semantic processes that play a role in stereotyping.

to infer information about a target person based on a picture of the person's face. In particular, participants were told that the study was testing whether they could accurately infer a person's preferences for certain activities, such as sports, or the likelihood that the target individual is the type of person the participant would be friends with. To strengthen the cover story and to lead participants to believe that we could later assess the accuracy of their judgments, participants first filled out questionnaires assessing their personal preferences for various activities or hobbies and for qualities they preferred in a friend. They were then told they would make judgments of pictures of people who had reported the same information (on friendship and activity preferences), such that we could check the accuracy of their inferences. Next, participants learned they would view pairs of people's faces and decide which member of the pair was more likely to (a) be someone they would likely befriend (an affect-based judgment) or (b) prefer to engage in athletic activities (a more cognitive or stereotype-based judgment). Athletics was chosen because it is a central African American stereotype that is positive in valence and thus unlikely to involve negative affective processes (Devine & Elliot, 1995). Furthermore, the pair of faces presented on each trial was always of the same race (Black, White, or Asian), and therefore judgments could not be influenced by participants' concerns about responding with prejudice. That is, issues of prejudice control were irrelevant when judging which of two Black individuals is more likely to be athletic or more likely to be friendly.

Consistent with their hypotheses, Potanina et al. (2006) observed greater activity in the amygdala when participants judged Black face pairs on the basis of potential friendship, compared with White face pairs. Regions of neocortex associated with semantic processing were not observed for this contrast. On the other hand, the authors observed greater activity in the region of the left lateral temporal lobe and left PFC when participants judged Black versus White face pairs on the basis of athleticism. However, this comparison did not elicit amygdala activity. These results provide the first evidence that distinct neural mechanisms appear to be associated with implicit prejudice and implicit stereotyping, as suggested by the cognitive neuroscience literature on memory. With evidence that different memory systems underlie implicit prejudice and stereotyping, future research will be able to apply behavioral neuroscience models of learning to further our understanding of how implicit racial bias is learned and unlearned.

NEUROCOGNITIVE MECHANISMS OF CONTROL

Humans have a unique capacity for regulating their behaviors to act in line with one's intentions. Understanding the way in which the mind carries out the process of self-regulation is a central concern among prejudice researchers. Social neuroscientists' research on this issue has largely followed from the broader cognitive neuroscience literature on control. One influential theory from this literature is that successful control involves the concerted activity of two independent processes for (a) determining when control is needed and (b) implementing the desired behavior despite unwanted tendencies (Botvinick, Braver, Barch, Carter, & Cohen, 2001). This model is built on the assumption that representations of response tendencies (e.g., motor plans) are spontaneously activated in the brain. Occasionally, two or more representations with conflicting response implications are activated at the same time and create the potential for unintended behavior. Botvinick et al. (2001) proposed a solution to the crosstalk dilemma, whereby the degree of conflict in the system at any moment is represented in a *conflict monitoring* process. In a sense, activity of the conflict monitoring component serves as a barometer of response conflict. As the level of conflict rises, the conflict monitoring mechanism signals a second process referred to as the *regulative* component for top-down control. The regulative process is responsible for intervening in crosstalk and deciding which of the competing responses should be implemented. This model is unique because it posits a bottom-up process for detecting the need for control, thereby dispensing with the "homunculus" idea assumed by most social-cognitive models in which a "little man" inside our heads "just knows" when to engage control. An important feature of Botvinick et al.'s (2001) model of control is that the two components—conflict monitoring and regulation—are associated with distinct neural substrates. Across several fMRI and positron emission tomography (PET) studies, conflict monitoring has been associated with activity in the dorsal anterior cingulate cortex (DACC), a region of the cortex that is proximal to the supplementary motor cortex and has strong connections to a wide

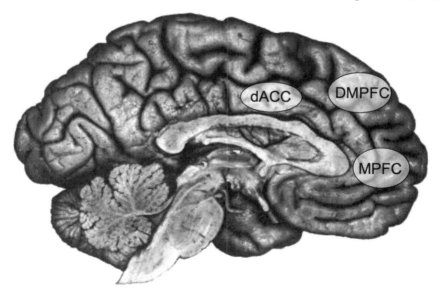

FIGURE 17.4 Medial view of the brain illustrating the dorsal ACC (dACC), dorsal medial prefrontal cortex (MPFC), and middle MPFC. The shaded areas of these regions are those typically activated in studies of prejudice control and person perception described in the text.

range of neural structures (Figure 17.4). The regulative mechanism has been associated with the lateral prefrontal cortex (LPFC), a region previously associated with executive control and working memory functions (see Figure 17.3; S. J. Gilbert et al., 2006).

Botvinick et al.'s (2001) model of control has been very influential among researchers interested in the neural mechanisms of prejudice control. It is widely assumed that the process of regulating intergroup responses involves general mechanisms of control (as opposed to specialized neural mechanisms for controlling racial biases). The role of the ACC as a conflict monitoring mechanism in the context of racial prejudice was first demonstrated using event-related potentials (ERPs; Amodio et al., 2004). Amodio et al. showed that ERP responses arising from the DACC were larger on trials that activated automatic stereotypes that conflicted with participants' intended response (see also Amodio, Devine, & Harmon-Jones, under review; Amodio, Kubota, Harmon-Jones, & Devine, 2006). Using ERPs, Amodio et al. (2004) observed an increase in DACC activity when a response required inhibition 100 msec before the response was made. Moreover, participants show-ing greater sensitivity of this conflict system on error trials were better at inhibiting stereotypes throughout the task. However, although ERP measures permit researchers to examine patterns of neural firing as it changes over the course of milliseconds, certain neuroanatomical factors render ERPs more sensitive to activity in some brain regions than others. ERPs tend to be very sensitive to changes in the DACC, but not very sensitive to changes in areas of the LPFC that are important for controlled processing. For this reason, fMRI has been a more useful tool for studying the regulative component of control.

fMRI STUDIES OF PREJUDICE CONTROL

fMRI provides much higher spatial resolution and coverage of frontal cortical processes than ERP measures, and therefore is a particularly useful tool for studying the control of prejudice. One of the first fMRI studies examining the control of prejudice was conducted by Cunningham et al. (2004). In their study, participants viewed faces of Black and White individuals and pictures of shapes. Their task was simply to indicate whether the stimulus appeared on the left or right side of their visual field. The authors observed greater amygdala activity to Black versus White faces when faces were presented subliminally (i.e., for 30 msec), as described previously. In contrast, when faces were presented for 525 msec and thus consciously perceived, activity in the DACC and LPFC—regions implicated in Botvinick et al.'s (2001) control network—were stronger in response to Black versus White faces. These results replicated the findings of Richeson et al. (2003), in which passive view-ing of Black versus White faces elicited ACC and PFC activity, and suggest that some element of control was more active among participants as they viewed Black faces. In addition, Cunningham et al. (2004) observed activity in the ventral region of LPFC. Whereas dorsal regions of LPFC have been primarily implicated in the implementation of an intended response, some theorizing suggests that the ventral LPFC may be involved in the inhibition of an unwanted behavioral or emotional response (Aron, Robbins, & Poldrack, 2004; Lieberman et al., in press; Ochsner, Bunge, Gross, & Gabrieli, 2002). Cunningham et al.'s (2004) results suggest that both forms of control may be involved when regulating prejudice.

The findings that viewing Black compared with White faces elicits activity in frontal cortical regions implicated in control raise important questions regarding the nature of "control" in the context of experimental studies. What exactly is being controlled? Given that these activations were observed when participants either viewed faces passively or simply decided on which side the screen the stimulus appeared, it is not clear whether these activations were associated with the intentional modulation of a thought, feeling, or behavior related specifically to responding without prejudice.

In an effort to begin to address some of the ambiguities of the fMRI literature on prejudice control, Amodio and Potanina (2006) recently used fMRI to examine participants' neural activity while they made decisions that could be influenced by explicit motivations to respond without preju-dice. The authors used the same paradigm as Potanina et al. (2006) described earlier, in which faces were judged according to the likelihood of friendship or athleticism, except that participants made decisions about mixed-race (i.e., Black vs. White) face pairs in addition to same-race pairs. When making judgments about mixed-race pairs, we expected that participants' concerns about appearing biased would become relevant, and thus they would be more deliberative in their ratings and try to respond in a way that did not reveal bias. In line with our hypotheses, we found that judgments of mixed-race pairs were generally associated with increased activity in the DACC and regions of dorsal LPFC, relative to judgments of same-race Black face pairs. In addition, an interesting pattern of activity appeared when comparing mixed-race judgments of athleticism with judgments of potential friendship. When judging whether a Black or a White individual was more athletic (vs. a potential friend), participants exhibited greater activity in dorsal and ventral regions of the LPFC, but little activity in the medial PFC, as in previous studies of prejudice control. By contrast, when judging between a Black versus White face as a potential friend (vs. being athletic), strong activations were observed in a region of the medial PFC that has been associated with processing of more familiar others and self-relevant stimuli. Although this area of medial PFC is often interpreted in terms of social information processing, recent work by Amodio et al. (2006; see also Amodio & Frith, 2006) suggests that activity in this region is important for regulating one's social behavior according to the expectations of social norms. The LPFC activations that were observed when judging athleticism of mixed-race face pairs are consistent with the idea that response regulation did not involve personal interest (as in the friendship judgments), but rather the control of objective, impersonal responses. Additional research will be needed to further unpack the possibility that medial and lateral regions of the PFC are involved in different aspects of self-regulation when making social judgments.

It is notable that recent advances in understanding the role of the LPFC in the regulation of prejudice have been made using EEG, and these findings may aid in interpreting the fMRI results already reviewed. A large body of literature has suggested that left versus right asymmetries in LPFC activity are associated with approach versus withdrawal motivation. Amodio, Devine, and Harmon-Jones (in press) used EEG to measure changes in the LPFC after participants realized they had responded in a prejudiced manner and while they were given an opportunity to engage in an activity designed to reduce their level of prejudice. Indeed, the authors observed a reduction in left LPFC when participants believed they had acted in a prejudiced way, and this reduction in activity was associated with high levels of guilt. However, when given a chance to make up for their transgression by reading magazine articles on how to reduce prejudice, LPFC activity in participants was increased. Importantly, participants' self-reported desire to engage in prejudice-reduction activities predicted their degree of LPFC activity, whereas their desire to engage in other activities that were not related to prejudice reduction was not related to PFC activity. Although this research did not use fMRI, it is the first study to provide direct evidence that changes in the LPFC are associated with self-regulation in the context of racial prejudice.

INHIBITION OF RACE-BIASED EMOTION

Most neuroscience research on control has focused on mechanisms involved in the regulation of behavior. More recently, researchers have begun to investigate mechanisms for regulating one's affective responses to race. Lieberman et al. (2005) used fMRI to examine the neural processes underlying the control of race-related affect. In this study, participants completed a matching task while their brains were scanned. In one condition, participants saw a target face at the top of the screen and two additional faces at the bottom of the screen (Figure 17.5, Panel A). Their task was to choose which of two faces most closely matched the target face. This condition was referred to as "perceptual encoding," because it involved matching one's visual image of the two faces. Target faces consisted of either White and Black male faces or colored shapes. In the case of faces, matches were determined on the basis of race. In a second "verbal encoding" condition, participants were presented with a target face at the top of the screen and the labels "Caucasian" and "African American" in the bottom of the screen (Figure 17.5, Panel B). Participants chose the label that best

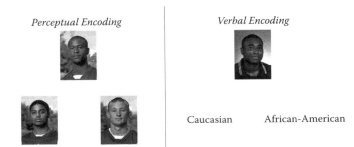

Perceptual Encoding   *Verbal Encoding*

                                          Caucasian   African-American

FIGURE 17.5   Stimuli used by Lieberman et al. (2005) in their matching task. Panel A shows a sample stimulus of the perceptual encoding task, in which participants match a face with two comparison faces. Panel B shows a sample stimulus of the verbal encoding task, in which participants match a face with a verbal label.

matched the target stimulus. Lieberman et al. (2005) reasoned that the process of encoding a face into a verbal representation involved the down-regulation of any emotional responses that might have been activated by the target stimulus (see Hariri, Bookheimer, & Mazziotta, 2000). As predicted, perceptual encoding of the targets produced greater amygdala activity to Black than White target faces, whereas this effect was absent in the verbal encoding condition. Instead, verbal encoding of the Black targets was associated with activity in ventrolateral PFC. The magnitude of this PFC response was inversely associated with amygdala activity, supporting the idea that ventrolateral PFC activity may play a role in regulating amygdala responses to Black targets and negative affect more generally (Lieberman, in press).

NEURAL BASIS OF INTERGROUP PERSON PERCEPTION

Most neuroscience studies of race bias from a social psychological approach have focused primarily on elucidating the automatic and controlled components of stereotyping and prejudice. However, researchers coming from a cognitive neuroscience perspective have emphasized the more basic role of person perception: How do we determine whether someone is part of our group? Neuroimaging research in this area suggests that medial regions of the PFC play an important role in several aspects of person perception and in the processing of social information (Amodio & Frith, 2006; Mitchell, Macrae, & Banaji, 2006).

NEURAL SUBSTRATES OF INGROUP VERSUS OUTGROUP PERCEPTION

The most basic form of social cognition involves determining whether an object is agentic (e.g., human) and distinct from the self. A large body of research has examined the neural correlates of *mentalizing:* the process of ascribing a unique perspective to another individual (Frith & Frith, 1999; Premack & Woodruff, 1978; Saxe, Carey, & Kanwisher, 2004). Theory of mind (ToM) refers to the ability to mentalize, and several different tasks have been used to study mentalizing and ToM processes. In ToM cartoon studies, participants view or read cartoons that require one to take a character's unique perspective into account. Compared with cartoons that do not require perspective taking, ToM cartoons typically elicit activity in a dorsal region of the medial PFC located in Brodmann's Area (BA) 9/32 (Fletcher et al., 1995; Gallagher et al., 2000). Across several studies using a range of tasks, the act of mentalizing has been associated with activity in the same general region of dorsal medial PFC (Saxe et al., 2004).

Mitchell and his colleagues have conducted several studies examining the neural substrates of social versus nonsocial aspects of person perception (Mitchell, Heatherton, & Macrae, 2002). Commonly used tasks in this line of research require participants to make judgments about an unfamiliar person that involves either social or nonsocial inferences. For example, in a study by Mitchell et al. (2002), participants viewed a series of noun–adjective pairs. Nouns were either names of people or inanimate objects, and adjectives could either describe a person (but not the object) or the object (but not the person). Mitchell et al. (2002) were interested in how patterns of brain activity differed on trials associated with a person-related judgment compared with judgments of inanimate objects. Across studies, social inferences were associated with increased activation in dorsal medial PFC compared with nonsocial judgments (Mitchell, Banaji, & Macrae, 2005; Mitchell, Macrae, & Banaji, 2005, 2006). The region of activity associated with social perception is similar to the region linked to mentalizing. Thus, the dorsal medial PFC appears to be involved in perceiving a person as a social being. Some have argued that this process may form the basis of prejudice (e.g., Qui, 2006)

Research examining neural correlates of self-reflection suggests that thinking about one's own personality traits, compared with traits of a familiar but unrelated person (e.g., the president), is linked to activity in the middle medial PFC (BA 10/32; Kelley et al., 2002). Subsequent work has shown that this region of medial PFC is more active when thinking about either the self or a similar other compared to a dissimilar other (Gobbini, Leibenluft, Santiago, & Haxby, 2004; Mitchell et al., 2006; but see Heatherton et al., 2006). By comparison, thinking about a dissimilar other is associated with activity in the dorsal medial PFC. Thus, these findings suggest potential differentiation in the neural correlates of ingroup versus outgroup perception. To date, fMRI research has not examined this effect within the context of racial prejudice, although there is reason to believe that similar effects would be observed.

Investigations of the social perception of similar versus dissimilar others indicates that there may be important differences in the way we process information about members of the ingroup versus the outgroup. However, additional research is needed to understand the meaning and implications of these different neural patterns. To date, research on person perception and social cognition have been rather descriptive, in that they have documented distinct patterns of brain activity for social and nonsocial judgments. As this line of work expands, researchers will begin to focus more on the functional properties of activations associated with social processes, such as their implications for the regulation of social behavior. Finally, it will be important for researchers to more fully integrate the findings from fMRI experiments with the rich body of theoretical and empirical work on intergroup processes in with social psychology literature. In all, fMRI research on person perception and mentalizing stands poised to make important contributions to our understanding of prejudice and intergroup relations.

NEURAL BASIS OF OUTGROUP EMPATHY

Most fMRI studies of social cognition have focused on the most basic process of perceiving a person as sentient entity with his or her own unique mental contents. Harris and Fiske (2006) have extended this line of inquiry to address how neural activity in these person perception areas relate to specific qualities ascribed to members of different social groups, as suggested by the stereotype content model (SCM; Fiske, Cuddy, Glick, & Xu, 2002). The SCM proposes that the perception of social groups is primarily driven by evaluations along two independent dimensions: warmth and competence. Fiske et al. (2002) argued that people's emotional reactions to different groups are associated with these factors. For example, groups defined by high warmth and high competence, such as middle-class Americans and Olympic athletes, are associated with pride. Groups defined by high levels of warmth but low competence, such as the elderly and disabled, are described as pitied. Highly competent but low-warmth groups, such as the wealthy, are met with envy. Most important for the present set of concerns, groups associated with low warmth and low competence—the homeless, the poor, African Americans, and Hispanics—are met with disgust (Fiske et al., 2002).

Harris and Fiske (2006) used fMRI to determine whether judgments of warmth and competence were related to neural activations in regions linked to mentalizing and person perception. During scans, participants viewed pictures of people belonging to groups from each of the four quadrants of the SCM model. The authors observed significant medial PFC activations relative to baseline when participants viewed pictures of groups associated with pride, envy, and pity. These activations were primarily in the middle region of the medial PFC, suggesting that these groups were processed similarly as the self. By contrast, groups associated with disgust did not elicit activity in this region. Harris et al. (2006) interpreted that lack of activity in this area as indicating *dehumanization* of these groups (see also Haslam, 2006). That is, low-warmth and low-competence groups were not being perceived as agentic human beings, but were rather perceived as inhuman objects, at least in terms of social emotional processing in the brain.

The results of Harris and Fiske (2006) suggest that prejudice and discrimination toward members of stigmatized social groups, such as African Americans, may be in part driven by a lack of "humanization" in some observers' social perceptions. However, the extant research suggests that the role of the medial PFC in racial prejudice is more complex. For example, Wheeler and Fiske (2005) found that the categorization of Black (vs. White) faces elicited activity in the amygdala as well as the insula, a region implicated in visceral states and disgust, yet no difference was observed in the medial PFC (L. Harris, personal communication). Thus, it appears that an understanding of the neural mechanisms of prejudiced person perception will require a consideration of a broad range of processes, of which mentalizing is just one. It is also worth noting that previous research has not been designed specifically to examine the role of mentalizing and racial prejudice—that is, to elicit mentalizing toward racial ingroups versus outgroups—so the jury is still out on this issue.

WHAT HAVE WE LEARNED ABOUT PREJUDICE FROM fMRI STUDIES?

Advances in neuroimaging methods have provided social psychologists with powerful new tools for studying the mechanisms of prejudice and discrimination. Has fMRI led to any significant new theoretical discoveries? This is a legitimate question often asked by social psychologists. fMRI research on social processes is valuable in two general ways. First, there is value in the basic endeavor of brain mapping to begin to understand the functions of different neural structures. The brain is a complex organ with much uncharted territory, and the only way to learn how it works is by observing activity as participants perform different types of tasks. Although there are caveats with this approach—neural operations are complex and specific structures often serve multiple and distributed functions (Poldrack, 2006)—it nevertheless serves an important role in cognitive neuroscience. Ultimately, brain mappers hope to build a catalog of task-related activations that, over time, show consistent and coherent patterns of mental function.

The second way in which fMRI research is valuable is in elucidating mechanisms involved in psychological processes that cannot be inferred from behavior or are difficult to distinguish using the traditional tools of social cognition. In addition, the use of fMRI permits researchers to connect the social psychology literature on humans with the vast neuroscience literature on animals, opening the door for crosstalk between fields and the application and integration of theoretical models from the two broad disciplines. From the prejudice researchers' perspective, the application of animal neuroscience models to questions of race bias may provide important information about how particular mechanisms involved in prejudice, stereotyping, and discrimination may be interconnected. It is through these applications that fMRI research has contributed to the literature in prejudice and stereotyping research. Here, we give a few examples of such contributions.

Patterns of behavior that would become known as implicit prejudice were first observed in the early 1980s (e.g., Devine, 1989; Dovidio et al., 1986; Gaertner & McLaughlin, 1983), and by the year 2000, implicit prejudice was a highly replicated and established phenomenon. Yet social psychology lacked a theoretical explanation for what it was. Was it a cognitive association? Was it an emotion? How could it actually be unconscious? How might it influence behavior? How was it learned? How could it be unlearned? Although much research was aimed at addressing these questions, there was not a theoretical foundation for how to conceptualize the process of implicit prejudice. The fMRI research linking implicit prejudice effects to the amygdala was groundbreaking in that it provided a concrete theoretical basis for the phenomenon. Through this work, we have learned that implicit prejudice likely involves a passive-learning memory system sensitive to affective cues (e.g., threats or punishments). It does not likely reflect conceptual representational networks as suggested by many social cognitive accounts. The social neuroscience research has shown that implicit prejudice is part of a subcortical response network that processes information rapidly and interfaces strongly with autonomic and behavioral systems. Moreover, linking implicit prejudice to the amygdala has allowed researchers to take the volumes of information gained from animal research on amygdala-based learning and memory and apply it to our understanding of how implicit prejudice may be learned and unlearned. For example, the unlearning of a classically conditioned response involves a very different process than those suggested by social cognition models that assume an associative learning process (e.g., Smith & DeCoster, 2000; see Amodio & Devine, 2006). These developments represent a major leap forward in our theoretical understanding of implicit prejudice.

A broader issue that is raised by the neuroscience approach to studying implicit prejudice concerns the meaning of the term. When implicit prejudice was first linked to amygdala activity, both prejudice and the amygdala were believed to reflect a fear response (Phelps et al., 2000). Over time, implicit prejudice still appears to be associated with amygdala activity. Yet researchers' interpretations of amygdala activity have changed. Currently, most researchers interpret patterns of amygdala activity as being associated with arousal or the emotional intensity of a stimulus, but not valence or fear per se (Anderson et al., 2002; Cunningham et al., 2004). To the extent that the amygdala is the primary neural substrate of implicit prejudice, these more recent findings suggest that implicit prejudice may be better conceived as reflecting the intensity of one's reaction to an outgroup (vs. ingroup) face. Furthermore, neuroscience analyses of the amygdala and implicit prejudice force researchers to take a closer look at what participants are thinking while viewing faces of Black and White individuals. Although social psychologists go to great lengths to hide the true nature of the study from participants, anyone who has completed more than a few trials on an implicit prejudice task, such as the IAT, knows that the study is examining prejudice toward Black people. Participants completing an implicit prejudice task may become more vigilant for the presentation of Black faces or have stronger reactions when Black faces appear simply because they know that their responses to Black (vs. White) faces are being monitored. Thus, it is unclear whether the amygdala activity is related to participants' prejudiced reaction to the face, as typically inferred, or their anxiety about being in a study of prejudice (although studies showing amygdala effects to subliminal pictures may argue against this alternative explanation). The role of anxiety in measures of implicit prejudice is an important one that needs to be resolved in future research.

As a second example, researchers have long distinguished between prejudice and stereotyping. Until recently, however, there was not a theoretical framework to specify the nature of their differences. It was unclear whether prejudice and stereotyping differed at the implicit level, and further unclear how either process might interface with behavior. A major obstacle to distinguishing between implicit prejudice and stereotyping is that they tend to operate in concert. That is, it is very difficult to design behavioral tasks capable of measuring these processes independently because they tend to be activated simultaneously. On the basis of neuroscience research regarding different regions of the brain involved in implicit affective versus semantic processing, we used fMRI to assess the activation of implicit prejudice and implicit stereotyping independently as they co-occurred (Potanina et al., 2006). By applying what is known about the different profiles of these neural regions, including their patterns of connectivity throughout the brain, we can develop a more concrete theoretical framework for how each process is learned, unlearned, expressed in behavior, and controlled. For example, our findings suggest that different prejudice reduction techniques are needed to target these two types of implicit bias, and that it may be best to use both types of reduction techniques in conjunction to most effectively diminish bias. Importantly, these advances were only possible through the integration of the social psychological and neuroscience literatures and the use of fMRI.

Finally, it is important to note that behavioral researchers can benefit from the advances made by fMRI research without using fMRI themselves. That is, new theoretical hypotheses about intergroup processes suggested by neuroimaging research can often be tested using behavioral methods (e.g., Amodio & Devine, 2006). Indeed, the range of behavioral tasks that may be used in the fMRI environment is limited, primarily due to the logistics of being confined to a small space and the need to keep one's head very still. Therefore, behavioral studies are often the preferred way to test hypotheses suggested by fMRI research, particularly when they pertain to social behavior that is best studied in real-life interpersonal interactions. A major goal of this chapter is to convince researchers who are not interested in doing their own fMRI studies that there is value in considering the neuroscience literature to enrich behavioral approaches to the study of social behavior.

CONCLUSION

As research on prejudice and intergroup relations continues to evolve, researchers are increasingly integrating theories and methods of traditionally disparate fields such as cognitive neuroscience. fMRI research is among the most recent approaches to be incorporated into the purview of prejudice research. Although relatively new, the fMRI approach to prejudice research is flourishing, and it has already begun to yield significant advances within social psychological theorizing. However, the advances described in this chapter are just the tip of the iceberg. Before long, the findings of fMRI studies on prejudice will be considered part of the canon, and fMRI will move from having the status of a new trend to being another valuable tool in the prejudice researchers' box.

REFERENCES

Adolphs, R., Tranel, D., Damasio, H., & Damasio, A. R. (1995). Fear and the human amygdala. *Journal of Neuroscience, 15,* 5879–5891.

Allport, G. W. (1954). *The nature of prejudice.* Reading, MA: Addison-Wesley.

Amodio, D. M., & Devine, P. G. (2006). Stereotyping and evaluation in implicit race bias: Evidence for independent constructs and unique effects on behavior. *Journal of Personality and Social Psychology, 91,* 652–661.

Amodio, D. M., Devine, P. G., & Harmon-Jones, E. (in press). A dynamic model of guilt: Implications for motivation and self-regulation in the context of prejudice. *Psychological Science.*

Amodio, D. M., Devine, P. G., & Harmon-Jones, E. (under review). Individual differences in responding without prejudice: The role of conflict detection and neural signals for control.

Amodio, D. M., & Frith, C. D. (2006). Meeting of minds: The medial frontal cortex and social cognition. *Nature Reviews Neuroscience, 7,* 268–277.

Amodio, D. M., Harmon-Jones, E., & Devine, P. G. (2003). Individual differences in the activation and control of affective race bias as assessed by startle eyeblink response and self-report. *Journal of Personality and Social Psychology, 84,* 738–753.

Amodio, D. M., Harmon-Jones, E., Devine, P. G., Curtin, J. J., Hartley, S. L., & Covert, A. E. (2004). Neural signals for the detection of unintentional race bias. *Psychological Science, 15,* 88–93.

Amodio, D. M., Kubota, J. T., Harmon-Jones, E., & Devine, P. G. (2006). Alternative mechanisms for regulating racial responses according to internal vs. external cues. *Social Cognitive and Affective Neuroscience, 1,* 26–36.

Amodio, D. M., & Potanina, P. V. (2006). *Roles of the medial and lateral prefrontal cortex in regulating intergroup judgments.* Manuscript in preparation.

Anderson, A. K., Christoff, K., Stappen, I., Panitz, D., Ghahremani, D. G., Glover, G., et al. (2003). Dissociated neural representations of intensity and valence in human olfaction. *Nature Neuroscience, 6,* 196–202.

Aron, A. R., Robbins, T. W., & Poldrack, R. A. (2004). Inhibition and the right inferior frontal cortex. *Trends in Cognitive Sciences, 8,* 170–177.

Bargh, J. A., Chen, M., & Burrows, L. (1996). Automaticity of social behavior: Direct effects of trait construct and stereotype activation on action. *Journal of Personality and Social Psychology, 71,* 230–244.

Bartholow, B. D., Dickter, C. L., & Sestir, M. A. (2006). Stereotype activation and control of race bias: Cognitive control of inhibition and its impairment by alcohol. *Journal of Personality and Social Psychology, 90,* 272–287.

Bechara, A., Tranel, D., Damasio, H., Adolphs, R., Rockland, C., & Damasio, A. R. (1995). Double dissociation of conditioning and declarative knowledge relative to the amygdala and hippocampus in humans. *Science, 269,* 1115–1118.

Blair, I. V. (2001). Implicit stereotypes and prejudice. In G. Moskowitz (Ed.), *Cognitive social psychology: On the tenure and future of social cognition* (pp. 359–374). Mahwah, NJ: Erlbaum.

Blair, I. V. (2002). The malleability of automatic stereotypes and prejudice. *Personality and Social Psychology Review, 6,* 242–261.

Botvinick, M., Braver, T., Barch, D., Carter, C., & Cohen, J. (2001). Conflict monitoring and cognitive control. *Psychological Review, 108,* 624–652.

Breiter, H. C., Rauch, S. L., Kwong, K. K., Baker, J. R., & et al. (1996). Functional magnetic resonance imaging of symptom provocation in obsessive-compulsive disorder. *Archives of General Psychiatry, 53,* 595–606.

Cacioppo, J. T., Gardner, W. L., & Berntson, G. G. (1999). The affect system has parallel and integrative processing components: Form follows function. *Journal of Personality and Social Psychology, 76,* 839–855.

Correll, J., Park, B., Judd, C. M., & Wittenbrink, B. (2002). The police officer's dilemma: Using ethnicity to disambiguate potentially threatening individuals. *Journal of Personality and Social Psychology, 83,* 1314–1329.

Cunningham, W. A., Johnson, M. K., Raye, C. L., Gatenby, J. C., Gore, J. C., & Banaji, M. R. (2004). Separable neural components in the processing of Black and White faces. *Psychological Science, 15,* 806–813.

Cunningham, W. A., Raye, C. L., & Johnson, M. K. (2004). Implicit and explicit evaluation: fMRI correlates of valence, emotional intensity, and control in the processing of attitudes. *Journal of Cognitive Neuroscience, 16,* 1717–1729.

Davis, M., Hitchcock, J. M., & Rosen, J. B. (Eds.). (1987). *Anxiety and the amygdala: Pharmacological and anatomical analysis of the fear-potentiated startle paradigm.* San Diego, CA: Academic.

Davis, M., & Whalen, P. J. (2001). The amygdala: Vigilance and emotion. *Molecular Psychiatry, 6,* 13–34.

Devine, P. G. (1989). Prejudice and stereotypes: Their automatic and controlled components. *Journal of Personality and Social Psychology, 56,* 5–18.

Devine, P. G., & Elliot, A. J. (1995). Are racial stereotypes really fading? The Princeton trilogy revisited. *Personality and Social Psychology Bulletin, 21,* 1139–1150.

Dovidio, J. F., Evans, N., & Tyler, R. B. (1986). Racial stereotypes: The contents of their cognitive representations. *Journal of Experimental Social Psychology, 22,* 22–37.

Dovidio, J. F., Kawakami, K., & Gaertner, S. L. (2002). Implicit and explicit prejudice and interracial interaction. *Journal of Personality and Social Psychology, 82,* 62–68.

Dovidio, J. F., Kawakami, K., Johnson, C., Johnson, B., & Howard, A. (1997). On the nature of prejudice: Automatic and controlled processes. *Journal of Experimental Social Psychology, 33,* 510–540.

Fazio, R. H., Jackson, J. R., Dunton, B. C., & Williams, C. J. (1995). Variability in automatic activation as an unobstrusive measure of racial attitudes: A bona fide pipeline? *Journal of Personality and Social Psychology, 69,* 1013–1027.

Fendt, M., & Fanselow, M. S. (1999). The neuroanatomical and neurochemical basis of conditioned fear. *Neuroscience & Biobehavioral Reviews, 23,* 743–760.

Fiske, S. T. (Ed.). (1998). *Stereotyping, prejudice, and discrimination.* New York: McGraw-Hill.

Fiske, S. T., Cuddy, A. J. C., Glick, P., & Xu, J. (2002). A model of (often mixed) stereotype content: Competence and warmth respectively follow from perceived status and competition. *Journal of Personality and Social Psychology, 82,* 878–902.

Fletcher, P. C., Happe, F., Frith, U., Baker, S. C., Dolan, R. J., Frackowiak, R. S., et al. (1995). Other minds in the brain: A functional imaging study of "theory of mind" in story comprehension. *Cognition, 57,* 109–128.

Frith, C. D., & Frith, U. (1999). Interacting minds: A biological basis. *Science, 286,* 1692–1695.

Gabrieli, J. D. E. (1998). Cognitive neuroscience of human memory. *Annual Review of Psychology, 49,* 87–115.

Gaertner, S. L., & McLaughlin, J. P. (1983). Racial stereotypes: Associations and ascriptions of positive and negative characteristics. *Social Psychology Quarterly, 46,* 23–30.

Gallagher, H. L., Happe, F., Brunswick, N., Fletcher, P. C., Frith, U., & Frith, C. D. (2000). Reading the mind in cartoons and stories: An fMRI study of "theory of the mind" in verbal and nonverbal tasks. *Neuropsychologia, 38,* 11–21.

Gilbert, D. T., Fiske, S. T., & Lindzey, G. (Eds.). (1998). *The handbook of social psychology* (Vol. 1, 4th ed.). New York: McGraw-Hill.

Gilbert, S. J., Spengler, S., Simons, J. S., Steele, J. D., Lawrie, S. M., Frith, C. D., et al. (2006). Functional specialization within rostral prefrontal cortex (Area 10): A meta-analysis. *Journal of Cognitive Neuroscience, 18,* 932–948.

Gobbini, M. I., Leibenluft, E., Santiago, N., & Haxby, J. V. (2004). Social and emotional attachment in the neural representation of faces. *Neuroimage, 22*(4), 1628–1635.

Greenwald, A. G., & Banaji, M. R. (1995). Implicit social cognition: Attitudes, self-esteem, and stereotypes. *Psychological Review, 102,* 4–27.

Greenwald, A. G., McGhee, D. E., & Schwartz, J. L. K. (1998). Measuring individual differences in implicit cognition: The implicit association test. *Journal of Personality and Social Psychology, 74,* 1464–1480.

Gregg, A. P., Seibt, B., & Banaji, M. R. (2006). Easier done than undone: Asymmetry in the malleability of implicit preferences. *Journal of Personality and Social Psychology, 90,* 1–20.

Hariri, A. R., Bookheimer, S. Y., & Mazziotta, J. C. (2000). Modulating emotional responses: Effects of a neocortical network on the limbic system. *Neuroreport: For Rapid Communication of Neuroscience Research, 11,* 43–48.

Harris, L. T., & Fiske, S. T. (2006). Dehumanizing the lowest of the low: Neuroimaging responses to extreme out-groups. *Psychological Science, 17,* 847–853.

Hart, A. J., Whalen, P. J., Shin, L. M., McInerney, S. C., Fischer, H. K., & Rauch, S. L. (2000). Differential response in the human amygdala to racial outgroup vs. ingroup face stimuli. *Neuroreport: For Rapid Communication of Neuroscience Research, 11,* 2351–2355.

Haslam, N. (2006). Dehumanization: An integrative review. *Personality and Social Psychology Review, 10,* 252–264.

Heatherton, T. F., Wyland, C. L., Macrae, C. N., Demos, K. E., Denny, B. T., & Kelley, W. M. (2006). Medial prefrontal activity differentiates self from close others. *Social Cognitive and Affective Neuroscience, 1,* 18–25.

Henderson-King, E. I., & Nisbett, R. E. (1996). Anti-Black prejudice as a function of exposure to the negative behavior of a single Black person. *Journal of Personality and Social Psychology, 71,* 654–664.

Huettel, S. A., Song, A. W., & McCarthy, G. (2004). *Functional magnetic resonance imaging.* Sunderland, MA: Sinauer Associates.

James, W. (1890). *The principles of psychology.* New York: Henry Holt.

Kelley, W. M., Macrae, C. N., Wyland, C. L., Caglar, S., Inati, S., & Heatherton, T. F. (2002). Finding the self? An event-related fMRI study. *Journal of Cognitive Neuroscience, 14,* 785–794.

Lang, P. J., Bradley, M. M., & Cuthbert, B. N. (1990). Emotion, attention, and the startle reflex. *Psychological Review, 97,* 377–395.

LeDoux, J. E. (1992). Emotion and the amygdala. In J. P. Aggleton (Ed.), *The amygdala: Neurobiological aspects of emotion, memory, and mental dysfunction* (pp. 339–351). New York: Wiley-Liss.

Lieberman, M. D. (2007). Social cognitive neuroscience: A review of core processes. *Annual Review of Psychology, 58,* 259–289.

Lieberman, M. D. (in press). Why symbolic processing of affect can disrupt negative affect: Social cognitive and affective neuroscience investigations. In A. Todorov, S. T. Fiske, & D. Prentice (Eds.), *Social neuroscience: Toward understanding the underpinnings of the social mind.* New York: Oxford University Press.

Lieberman, M. D., Eisengerger, N. I., Crockett, M. J., Tom, S. M., Pfeifer, J. H., & Way, B. M. (in press). Putting feelings into words: Affect labeling disrupts amygdala activity to affective stimuli. *Psychological Science.*

Lieberman, M. D., Hariri, A., Jarcho, J. M., Eisenberger, N. I., & Bookheimer, S. Y. (2005). An fMRI investigation of race-related amygdala activity in African-American and Caucasian-American individuals. *Nature Neuroscience, 8,* 720–722.

Lippman, W. (1922). *Public opinion.* New York: Macmillan.

Mackie, D. M., & Smith, E. R. (1998). Intergroup relations: Insights from a theoretically integrative approach. *Psychological Review, 105,* 499–529.

McConnell, A. R., & Leibold, J. M. (2001). Relations among the Implicit Association Test, discriminatory behavior, and explicit measures of racial attitudes. *Journal of Experimental Social Psychology, 37,* 435–442.

Meyer, D. E., & Schvaneveldt, R. W. (1971). Facilitation in recognizing pairs of words: Evidence of a dependence between retrieval operations. *Journal of Experimental Psychology, 90,* 227–234.

Mitchell, J. P., Banaji, M. R., & Macrae, C. N. (2005). The link between social cognition and self-referential thought in the medial prefrontal cortex. *Journal of Cognitive Neuroscience, 17,* 1306–1315.

Mitchell, J. P., Heatherton, T. F., & Macrae, C. N. (2002). Distinct neural systems subserve person and object knowledge. *Proceedings of the National Academy of Sciences, 99,* 15238–15243.

Mitchell, J. P., Macrae, C. N., & Banaji, M. R. (2005). Forming impressions of people versus inanimate objects: Social-cognitive processing in the medial prefrontal cortex, *NeuroImage, 26,* 251–257.

Mitchell, J. P., Macrae, C. N., & Banaji, M. R. (2006). Dissociable medial prefrontal contributions to judgments of similar and dissimilar others. *Neuron, 50,* 655–663.

Morris, J. S., Frith, C. D., Perrett, D. I., Rowland, D., & et al. (1996). A differential neural response in the human amygdala to fearful and happy facial expressions. *Nature, 383,* 812–815.

Ochsner, K. N., Bunge, S. A., Gross, J. J., & Gabrieli, J. D. E. (2002). Rethinking feelings: An fMRI study of the cognitive regulation of emotion. *Journal of Cognitive Neuroscience, 14,* 1215–1229.

Olson, M. A., & Fazio, R. H. (2006). Reducing automatically-activated racial prejudice through implicit evaluative conditioning. *Personality and Social Psychology Bulletin, 32,* 421-433.

Phelps, E. A., O'Connor, K. J., Cunningham, W. A., Funayama, E. S., Gatenby, J. C., Gore, J. C., et al. (2000). Performance on indirect measures of race evaluation predicts amygdala activation. *Journal of Cognitive Neuroscience, 12,* 729–738.

Poldrack, R. A. (2006). Can cognitive processes be inferred from neuroimaging data? *Trends in Cognitive Sciences, 10,* 59–63.

Potanina, P. V., Pfeifer, J. H., Lieberman, M. D., & Amodio, D. M. (2006). *Distinct neural substrates of implicit prejudice and stereotyping.* Manuscript in preparation.

Premack, D., & Woodruff, G. (1978). Does the chimpanzee have a theory of mind? *Behavioral and Brain Sciences, 1,* 515–526.

Qui, J. (2006). Neuroimaging: Peering into the root of prejudice. *Nature Reviews Neuroscience, 7,* 508–509.

Richeson, J. A., Baird, A. A., Gordon, H. L., Heatherton, T. F., Wyland, C. L., Trawalter, S., et al. (2003). An fMRI investigation of the impact of interracial contact on executive function. *Nature Neuroscience, 6,* 1323–1328.

Rissman, J., Eliassen, J. C., & Blumstein, S. E. (2003). An event-related fMRI investigation of implicit semantic priming. *Journal of Cognitive Neuroscience, 15,* 1160–1175.

Rudman, L. A. (2004). Sources of implicit attitudes. *Current Directions in Psychological Science, 13,* 79–82.

Rydell, B. J., & McConnell, A. R. (2006). Understanding implicit and explicit attitude change: A systems of reasoning analysis. *Journal of Personality and Social Psychology, 91,* 945–1008.

Saxe, R., Carey, S., & Kanwisher, N. (2004). Understanding other minds: Linking developmental psychology and functional neuroimaging. *Annual Review of Psychology, 55,* 87–124.

Shiffrin, R. M., & Schneider, W. (1977). Controlled and automatic human information processing: II. Perceptual learning, automatic attending and a general theory. *Psychological Review, 84,* 127–190.

Smith, E. R. (1993). Social identity and social emotions: Toward new conceptualizations of prejudice. In D. M. Mackie & D. L. Hamilton (Eds.), *Affect, cognition, and stereotyping: Interactive processes in group perception* (pp. 297–315). San Diego, CA: Academic.

Smith, E. R., & DeCoster, J. (2000). Dual-process models in social and cognitive psychology: Conceptual integration and links to underlying memory systems. *Personality and Social Psychology Review, 4,* 108–131.

Squire, L. R., & Zola, S. M. (1996). Ischemic brain damage and memory impairment: A commentary. *Hippocampus, 6,* 546–552.

Whalen, P. J. (1998). Fear, vigilance, and ambiguity: Initial neuroimaging studies of the human amygdala. *Current Directions in Psychological Science, 7,* 177–188.

Whalen, P. J., Rauch, S. L., Etcoff, N. L., McInerney, S. C., Lee, M. B., & Jenike, M. A. (1998). Masked presentations of emotional facial expressions modulate amygdala activity without explicit knowledge. *Journal of Neuroscience, 18,* 411–418.

Wheeler, M. E., & Fiske, S. T. (2005). Controlling racial prejudice: Social-cognitive goals affect amygdala and stereotype activation. *Psychological Science, 16,* 56–63.

Wible, C. G., Han, S. D., Spencer, M. H., Kubicki, M., Niznikiewicz, M. H., Jolesz, F. A., et al. (2006). Connectivity among semantic associates: An fMRI study of semantic priming. *Brain and Language, 97,* 294–305.

Wig, G. S., Grafton, S. T., Demos, K. E., & Kelley, W. M. (2005). Reductions in neural activity underlie behavioral components of repetition priming. *Nature Neuroscience, 8,* 1228–1233.

Wilson, T. D., Lindsey, S., & Schooler, T. Y. (2000). A model of dual attitudes. *Psychological Review, 107,* 101–126.

18 Measures of Prejudice

Michael A. Olson
University of Tennessee

Are you prejudiced? It is a simple question, but its many potential answers highlight the complexities underlying how prejudice is conceptualized and assessed. What do we mean by prejudice? Does being opposed to affirmative action mean I am prejudiced? Can I be prejudiced and be unaware of it? These are some of the many ambiguities inherent in conceptualizing, and hence, measuring prejudice, that must be addressed before posing some form of the "Are you prejudiced?" question.

Prejudice can take a variety of forms, and this basic feature of the phenomenon is reflected in the myriad measures of prejudice in use. The goal of this chapter is to review some of these measures. An exhaustive review would be impossible (detailed reviews of specific measurement types are available; e.g., indirect measures: Fazio & Olson, 2003; direct measures: Biernat & Crandall, 1999). However, I hope to have decided on the appropriate "major" measures, and I hope to have included illustrative studies. My intent is to summarize critical findings, debates, and problems associated with a variety of measures so that researchers can pursue the measure that is best suited to their research goals. In lieu of providing detailed psychometric information (which can be found in each scale's original location as noted), I highlight each scale's conceptual underpinnings, history, and applications.

OPENING OBSERVATIONS

Three observations are apparent on venturing into the annals in search of measures of prejudice. First, there are a lot. Second, reflecting the "great American dilemma," the majority of these measures assess Whites' prejudice toward Blacks in the United States. Third, a glimpse at the items of older compared to more contemporary measures highlights the constantly changing face of prejudice. For example, the "E-scale" measure of ethnocentrism from 1950 (Adorno, Frenkel-Brunswick, Levinson, & Sanford, 1950) included the following item: "There is something inherently primitive and uncivilized in the Negro, as shown in his music and his extreme aggressiveness," whereas Henry and Sears's (2002) Symbolic Racism 2000 Scale (SR2K) inquires more subtly, "Some say that Black leaders have been trying to push too fast. Others feel that they haven't pushed fast enough. What do you think?" Indeed, prejudice, particularly Whites' prejudice against Blacks, veiled itself throughout the 20th century, creating challenges for those interested its measurement.

It is the diverse theoretical approaches to prejudice that provide its diverse conceptualizations, and as this volume illustrates, there is no shortage of theories on the subject. With some exceptions, measures of prejudice are derived from these theories. Hence, it is important to connect prejudice measurement to prejudice theory. Many of these theories contrast two forms of prejudice that lie on the ends of a given dimension, such as "old-fashioned" versus "modern" prejudice (McConahay, 1986), or more controlled ("explicit") versus more automatic ("implicit") prejudice (Dasgupta, chap. 13, this volume). A transcending theme across many theories is that prejudice can take multiple forms not only between people, but within them. For example, a given individual can be characterized as having certain levels of both implicit and explicit prejudice. This theme manifests in contemporary prejudice research as the tendency for researchers to employ multiple measures of prejudice in a given study and assess the relationship of each with some sort of discriminatory behavior. With multiple measures in use, an understanding of what distinguishes them is critical to interpreting research findings.

SCOPE AND ORGANIZATION

Before delving into the measures, it is important to define what we mean by measures of prejudice. I have taken a broad scope, and count as a measure of prejudice any individual difference instrument designed to relate to discriminatory responding based on group membership. This means that in addition to measures designed to tap negative feelings and beliefs about a given group, measures that gauge one's motivation to inhibit the expression of prejudice are also included, as are measures that assess one's tendency to exhibit prejudice toward a variety of groups.

I could have organized this chapter in a number of ways, but one overarching distinction currently transcends other differences among measures of prejudice, and that is whether a given measure is explicit or implicit. However, these two terms have accumulated some unfortunate baggage in recent years, so I have opted to use the less loaded terms *direct* and *indirect* to refer to measures that either require participants to verbally report their prejudices, or that assess prejudice without requiring a verbal expression of one's prejudices, respectively (De Houwer, 2006; De Houwer & Moors, 2007). The importance of the direct–indirect distinction will become apparent as we progress.

DIRECT MEASURES

Direct measures are typically of the paper-and-pencil variety that require participants to verbally report their attitudes toward various groups (e.g., by indicating their liking or disliking for a given group on a Likert-type scale; e.g., McConahay's [1986] Modern Racism Scale). They share some common underlying assumptions, specifically, that people are aware of their responses on the measure and are at least somewhat willing to express them. These measures range from single items to lengthy, multifactor inventories. All can be administered and scored relatively easily and quickly. This convenience, particularly compared to indirect measures, contributes to their popularity despite some shortcomings.

Direct measures have a lineage that can be traced to a few specific influences (e.g., Bogardus, 1959; Woodmansee & Cook, 1967). One particularly ambitious early measure, the Multifactor Racial Attitudes Inventory (MRAI; Woodmansee & Cook, 1967), contained more than 100 items and 10 subscales, including Black Inferiority (e.g., "I think it is right that the black race should occupy a somewhat lower position socially than the white race"), Ease in Interracial Contacts (e.g., "If the blacks were of the same social class level as I am, I'd just as soon move into a black neighborhood as a white one" [reverse scored]), and Acceptance in Close Personal Relationships (e.g., "I would not take a black person to eat with me in a restaurant where I was well known"). The MRAI influenced the development of many later measures discussed here.

Owing to their datedness or limited use, some potential contenders are excluded from this review (see Biernat & Crandall, 1999). The measures reviewed next can be considered relatively current.

Racial Attitudes Scale (RAS; Sidanius, Pratto, Martin, & Stallworth, 1991)

This scale purports to assess what the authors call "classical racism," a more blatant and old-fashioned form of prejudice that is irrelevant to modern antiracist social norms. The items prompt respondents to indicate their positive or negative feelings toward a variety of race-related statements and issues, like "There are too many black students at the University," "Interracial dating should be avoided," "Affirmative action," "Racial equality," and "Foreigners."

It is important to note that the RAS assesses reactions to issues relating to a variety of racial minorities, not just Blacks. This is because the authors created the scale in the context of their theory of social dominance, which attempts to explain the general tendency to maintain current social hierarchies regardless of who happens to occupy high- and low-status positions (Sidanius & Pratto, 1993). It is also noteworthy that several of the items relate to political policies (e.g., affirmative action) that could be opposed based not on racial prejudice but on political conservativism (indeed, the scale is correlated with political conservatism; Sidanius et al., 1991). This debate—whether a measure of prejudice is confounded with conservatism—appears with respect to other direct measures as well.

Little is known about the RAS's relationships to other measures, but sensible known-groups effects have been reported. For example, Whites and Asians show more prejudice on the scale than do Hispanics and Blacks, and it is correlated with measures of nationalism (Sidanius, Feshbach, Levin, & Pratto, 1997). Consistent with the author's theorizing that people oriented toward more powerful positions in society are more likely to denigrate lower status groups, business students show greater prejudice on the scale than do students of other majors.

ATTITUDES TOWARD BLACKS (ATB), ATTITUDES TOWARD WHITES (ATW; BRIGHAM, 1993)

These two scales were designed as concise measures of attitudes toward Blacks and Whites, respectively, with primarily college student populations. The ATW has seen little use outside of the original publication, so we focus on the ATB. Many of the scale's items can be traced back to the MRAI (among others); hence, it features a diverse array of items tapping several aspects of prejudice, such as interracial contact ("I would rather not have blacks live in the same apartment building I live in"), misogyny ("Interracial marriage should be discouraged to avoid the 'who-am-I' confusion which the children feel"), and policy issues ("I worry that in the next few years I may be denied my application for a job or a promotion because of preferential treatment given to minority group members").

Although the ATB can be tied to a number of theoretical sources, it was not derived to test a particular theory of racial prejudice. Thus, the scale does not appear to have a "slant" toward specific components of prejudice, which makes it well suited for general use. In initial tests, the ATB correlated with respondents' ratings of the value of equality ($r = .33$) and self-reported contact with Blacks. Given the similarity in scale items, it is not surprising that it correlates strongly with other direct measures of racial prejudice (e.g., a short form of the MRAI, $r = .86$; the Modern Racism Scale (MRS), $r = .70$; Brigham, 1993).

The ATB sees some use in current research. Hodson, Dovidio, and Gaertner (2002) found that prejudice as assessed by the ATB related to greater discrimination against Black applicants to college, not when the applicants' credentials were clearly strong or weak, but only when they were mixed (both positive and negative), relative to a White applicant. This suggests that the ATB may tap relatively modern forms of prejudice that manifest more subtly than old-fashioned varieties. However, Plant, Devine, and Brazy (2003) reported a strong correlation ($r = .69$) of the ATB with a measure of one's internal motivation to respond without prejudice, suggesting that people who wish not to appear prejudiced will do so on the ATB, whether they genuinely harbor racial prejudice or not. So Although the ATB appears to be a good "all-purpose" direct measure of racial prejudice against Blacks, it may be influenced by motivational concerns, a drawback that probably besets all direct measures. Moreover, the ATB has seen less use than several other direct measures, and so relatively less is known about its validity.

PRO-BLACK/ANTI-BLACK ATTITUDES QUESTIONNAIRE (PAAQ; KATZ & HASS, 1988)

Ambivalence is the theme of the theory underlying this pair of measures. Katz and Hass (1988) argued that Whites' attitudes toward Blacks can be best characterized as both positive (e.g., they admire Blacks and feel sympathetic toward their continued disadvantages) and negative (e.g., they feel Blacks violate traditional American values). Pro-Black items include, "Too many blacks still lose out on jobs and promotions because of their skin color," and "Many whites show a real lack of understanding of the problems that blacks face." Anti-Black items include, "The root cause of most of the social and economic ills of blacks is the weakness and instability of the black family," and "On the whole, black people don't stress education and training."

Katz and Hass's theory of racial ambivalence led to the development of these scales as well as two others that they argue tap the underlying values that drive Whites' positive and negative views of Blacks: Humanitarianism-Egalitarianism (HE, which includes the values of equality and social justice) and the Protestant Ethic (PE, which includes the values of individualism and hard work), respectively. Correlational analyses performed by the authors verified that pro-black responses are relatively more correlated with HE ($r = .46$), whereas responses on anti-Black items are more correlated with PE ($r = .40$). An ambivalence score can be computed based on the cross-product of the standardized scores from each scale, which the authors use to test their hypothesis that ambivalent racial attitudes create "response amplification"; that is, more extreme responses to Blacks. In one study, for example, greater ambivalence was associated with more positive evaluations of a liked Black individual, but more negative evaluations of a disliked Black (Hass, Katz, Rizzo, Baley, & Eisenstadt, 1991).

These scales correlate in expected ways to other direct measures of prejudice like the MRS (e.g., .64 [reverse scored] and .58 for the Pro- and Anti-Black scales, respectively; Wittenbrink, Judd, & Park, 2001a, 2001b), and item comparisons indicate substantial overlap in content with the MRS and ABS. In addition to social desirability, the potential for artificially inflated orthogonality of the two scales is a concern. Items selected for each scale were deliberately uncorrelated with items from the other, and only two items from each scale are reverse scored, creating the potential for acquiescence bias. Thus, even though the scales' authors report nonsignificant correlations between the two, it is possible that they overestimate the incidence of ambivalence among respondents.

SUBTLE AND BLATANT PREJUDICE SCALES (PETTIGREW & MEERTENS, 1995)

In recognizing the many faces of prejudice, the Subtle and Blatant Prejudice Scales were developed to illuminate the different consequences of these two aptly named varieties. They speak to the way contemporary prejudice has become more subtle and still acknowledge that the old-fashioned variety is still around. The scales were developed in the context of the more diverse array of majority–minority tensions that characterize Western Europe, and so can be easily applied to a variety of racial and ethnic groups (the original scales tapped British prejudice against West Indians). Pettigrew (1998) described blatant prejudice as "hot, close, and direct," and subtle prejudice as "cool, distant, and indirect" (p. 83), and characterized subtle prejudice as more socially acceptable. The blatant scale includes both "threat/rejection" items (e.g., "West Indians come from less able races and this explains why they are not as well off as most British people") and "intimacy" items (e.g., "I would not mind if a suitably qualified West Indian person was appointed as my boss"; reverse scored). The Subtle scale includes items tapping "traditional values" (e.g., "West Indians living here should not push themselves where they are not wanted"), "cultural differences" (e.g., "How different or similar do you think West Indians living here are to other British people like yourself in their religious beliefs and practices"), and "positive emotions" (e.g., "How often have you felt admiration for West Indians living here?").

Meertens and Pettigrew (1997) reported a range of correlations from .48 to .70 between the two scales, and noted that the blatant scale trends toward a lower (i.e., less prejudiced) mean. More prejudiced scores on both scales relate to greater conservatism, less education, greater national pride, and less of a "European" identity; blatant prejudice shows a stronger relationship to perceived relative group deprivation, whereas subtle prejudice relates more (negatively) to having friends from the outgroup (see Pettigrew, 1998, for a review). Interestingly, although political conservatives tended to show more blatant prejudice, liberals and conservatives scored similarly on the subtle index. Scores on both measures have been used to identify people as "bigots" (high on both), "subtles" (low blatant, high subtle), and "egalitarians" (low on both), with few people being high subtle but low blatant (Pettigrew & Meertens, 1995). Compared to the MRS, these scales were better able to distinguish high- and low-prejudiced Dutch respondents in terms of the cultural stereotypes they held toward Moroccan and Surinamese people (Gordijn, Koomen, & Stapel, 2001), even though they were moderately correlated (as high as $r = .48$) and share similar items.

The Subtle and Blatant Prejudice Scales have the unique advantage of having been administered to a wide array of populations with similar results (Pettigrew & Meertens, 2001). However, although they have seen wide use in Europe, they have received little use in the United States. It might be the case that certain forms of prejudice are more "socially acceptable" to express in Europe than in the United States (particularly with respect to Blacks), and future research will tell whether, for example, White Americans are as willing as their European counterparts to express their prejudices.

THE MODERN RACISM SCALE (MCCONAHAY, HARDEE, & BATTS, 1981)

As the civil rights movement slowly wove its way through U.S. culture, publicly expressed prejudice against Blacks became increasingly less acceptable. According to the MRS's authors, old-fashioned racism had evolved into modern or "symbolic" prejudice, involving a belief that Blacks are unfairly demanding and violate "cherished values." The modern racist, in this view, does not actually believe he or she is racist. Aware that racism had "gone underground," researchers interested in prejudice desperately needed a nonreactive means of tapping more subtle prejudice, and the MRS seemed to deliver. The scale's popularity grew quickly, and despite repeated expressions that its age of over a quarter-century might render it "modern" no longer (e.g., Fazio, Jackson, Dunton, & Williams, 1995), it is still by far the most used direct measure of racial prejudice in social science. Its original form contains seven items focusing on beliefs about race-related public policies (e.g., "Discrimination against blacks is no longer a problem in the United States," "Blacks have more influence upon school desegregation plans than they ought to have," and "Blacks are getting too demanding in their push for equal rights").

Much information is available about the MRS's relationships with other variables (including those just mentioned). The MRS tends to be moderately correlated with measures of old-fashioned racism (rs = .30–.70; e.g., McConahay, 1982, 1986), patriotism, belief in the PE (negatively; Biernat, Vescio, Theno, & Crandall, 1996), and issues like opposition to busing in desegregation (McConahay, 1982).

The MRS has been used in many research contexts, and here I highlight only a few. Scores on the MRS have been associated with voting for a Black versus a White political candidate (McConahay & Hough, 1976). Devine (1989) demonstrated that although both high- and low-prejudiced individuals, according to the MRS, share knowledge of the cultural stereotypes of Blacks and automatic activation of the Black stereotype, only high-prejudiced individuals report more negative impressions of Blacks. Scores on the MRS have also been associated with impressions of Black targets (e.g., Biernat & Manis, 1994), personal standards about how one should react to Blacks (Devine, Monteith, Zuwerink, & Elliot, 1991), guilty verdicts and sentence judgments of Blacks (Wittenbrink & Henly, 1996), a tendency to categorize social targets by race (Blascovich, Wyer, Swart, & Kibler, 1997), more negative facial movements when exposed to Black targets (Vanman, Paul, Ito, & Miller, 1997), and subtle aggression against Blacks (Beal, O'Neal, Ong, & Ruscher, 2000).

Although there is no doubt a great deal of experimental evidence supporting the validity of the MRS, it has also been heavily criticized. First, critics have argued that the MRS confounds prejudice and conservativism, and repeated findings of correlations with measures of political ideology confirm it would be difficult for a political conservative to respond in a "pro-Black" direction on the MRS (Fazio et al., 1995; Sniderman & Tetlock, 1986). At the same time, it has also been argued that MRS implies a clearer distinction between old-fashioned and modern racism than might actually exist (Weigel & Howes, 1985; see Sears & Henry, 2005, for a review of these criticisms). Indeed, the MRS may increasingly resemble old-fashioned racism with age, and correlations between measures of the two were as high as .67 even in 1985 (Weigel & Howes). Its datedness may contribute to reports of its insensitivity (e.g., Gordijn et al., 2001, described earlier). Finally, despite early evidence to the contrary, the MRS has been shown to be reactive; that is, affected by social desirability and motivational concerns. McConahay and colleagues (1981) demonstrated that Whites do not attempt to appear less prejudiced on the MRS in the presence of a Black experimenter. However, by 1995 this was no longer the case: Fazio and colleagues demonstrated, indeed, that Whites adjust their responses in a less prejudiced direction with a Black experimenter present compared to a more anonymous mass-testing setting. Moreover, individuals motivated to control prejudiced reactions report less prejudice on the MRS (Fazio et al., 1995). Despite these serious concerns, the MRS remains in popular use, and has spawned a measure of sexism (Swim, Aikin, Hall, & Hunter, 1995), as well as adaptations for British populations (Lepore & Brown, 1997).

MORE RECENT MEASURES OF MODERN AND SYMBOLIC RACISM

Others have attempted to "modernize" the construct of symbolic racism by developing similar scales that address the growing datedness of the MRS. For example, the Racial Resentment Scale (RRS; Kinder & Sanders, 1996), includes some original MRS items, but focuses on feelings of anger and indignation on the part of Whites because of their perception that Blacks are not doing enough to improve their status. In National Election Survey studies, the RRS has shown reliable relationships to policy preferences (e.g., opposition to affirmative action), voting behavior, and feelings toward a variety of disadvantaged groups (e.g., gays, Palestinians; Kinder & Sanders, 1996).

The SR2K is also situated within the modern and symbolic racism tradition (Henry & Sears, 2002). The scale's authors argue that their version of modern racism entails "a blend of racial antipathy and traditional conservative values," and "is more than simply the sum of those parts" (p. 269). They report factor analyses in support of this view, and highlight their measure's ability to predict policy preferences and generalize across demographic groups. The scale overlaps considerably with the MRS and RRS, but avoids problems of earlier measures by balancing the items in terms of direction and avoiding mention of government involvement. Items include, "How much of the racial tension that exists in the United States today do you think blacks are responsible for creating?" and "It's really a matter of some people not trying hard enough; if blacks would only try harder they could be just as well off as whites."

Although relatively new, the SR2K appears to hold promise as a more contemporary means of assessing modern and symbolic prejudice. For example, the authors demonstrate that the SR2K better predicts attitudes toward various race-based government policies (e.g., federal assistance) than do several other measures of racial attitudes and political views (Sears & Henry, 2005).

OTHER MEASURES

Direct measures do more than merely assess prejudice through questionnaires, and readers should be aware of the variety of tools available. Thus, this section includes what might be called more "distal" measures of variables known to relate to prejudice, as well as measures of motivation to control it. It ends with a discussion of the various ways researchers create ad hoc measures of prejudice-related variables for specific research purposes.

Distal Measures

Although a full catalog of every psychological variable with known links to prejudice is beyond the scope of this chapter, there are a few that have been shown to relate in fundamental ways to prejudicial attitudes toward a variety of groups (and that have well-validated measures associated with them). Two additional measures, right-wing authoritarianism (RWA; Altemeyer, 1981) and social dominance orientation (SDO; Pratto, Sidanius, Stallworth, & Malle, 1994) are mentioned here.

The concept of RWA has a history extending back to at least Adorno et al. (1950), who advocated that a certain "type of man" is prone to develop prejudices towards Blacks, Jews, and many other groups perceived to be "deviant." Although this particular personality approach to prejudice was ignored by most social psychologists for many years, Altemeyer (1981, 1996) successfully exhumed it, modernized its measurement, and ensured it a stable place in prejudice research (e.g., Oyamot, Borgida, & Fisher, 2006). RWA is argued to consist of a cluster of traits conducive to prejudice development, including adherence to conventional (traditional) values, reverence to authority, and a willingness to aggress against those thought to threaten those values. The scale contains items like, "In these troubled times laws have to be enforced without mercy, especially when dealing with agitators and revolutionaries who are stirring things up."

SDO is not directly about prejudice so much as it is about a preference for making status distinctions between groups and maintaining the social hierarchies that support valuing some groups more than others (Sidanius & Pratto, 1993). Individuals high in SDO are argued to employ "legitimizing myths" that justify social and economic inequities between groups. The most commonly employed version of the scale (Pratto et al., 1994) includes 16 items like "Some people are just inferior to others," and "Sometimes other groups must be kept in their place."

These scales, RWA and SDO, tap related constructs, often appear together in published research, and are weakly to moderately correlated (e.g., Lambert, Payne, Ramsey, & Shaffer, 2005; Whitely, 1999). Both tap personality variables believed to result in prejudice toward outgroups of all kinds. However, they diverge in conceptually important ways. For example, whereas RWA is more strongly associated with authority-derived negativity toward perceived social deviants, SDO is more strongly associated with individual-derived negativity toward any low-status group (Whitely, 1999). Importantly, both have been used to help create and test more inclusive, general models of prejudice that incorporate a broad array of personality and socialization factors (e.g., Duckitt, Wagner, du Plessis, & Birum, 2002).

Measures of Motivation

Owing to the emphasis social cognitive models of prejudice place on relatively universal and less controllable aspects of prejudice (e.g., Devine, 1989), measures of one's motivation to curb those automatic prejudices have been developed. Two such measures frequently appear in the literature. Dunton and Fazio's (1997) Motivation to Control Prejudiced Reactions Scale (MCPR) includes items like, "It is important to me that others not think that I am prejudiced." It consists of two factors, concern for acting prejudice, which focuses on one's desire to not appear prejudiced to oneself or others, and restraint to avoid dispute, which relates more to wishing not to offend anyone or cause a dispute with or about Blacks. Plant and Devine's (1998) Internal (IMS) and External (EMS) Motivation to Respond Without Prejudice Scale is also widely used. Its two subscales, IMS and EMS, tap one's motivation to not be prejudiced for personal, self-derived reasons or because of external antiprejudice social norms, respectively.

These scales have seen relations with a variety of prejudice-related antecedents and outcomes (e.g., Plant & Devine, 2003). For example, both scales have shown links to different emotional consequences after a seemingly prejudiced response (e.g., Fazio & Hilden, 2001; Plant & Devine, 1998). Motivated individuals, according to scores on the MCPR, make efforts not to categorize others by race (e.g., Fazio & Dunton, 1997). High IMS in conjunction with low EMS scores have been linked to not only greater compunction upon exhibiting a prejudiced response, but also to the development of skills that, through practice, contribute to a reduction in racial prejudice over time (Devine, Plant, & Buswell, 2000). We saw earlier, perhaps not surprisingly, that internally motivated individuals tend to report less prejudice on direct measures, but interestingly, externally motivated individuals sometimes report more prejudice on direct measures, perhaps out of reactance (e.g., Plant & Devine, 1998). As we shall see later, coupling measures of automatic prejudice with measures that tap more controlled processes provides a more complete view of the determinants of discrimination.

Still More Measures

Although this review focuses on Whites' prejudice toward Blacks, there are a number of measures of prejudice toward other groups available. These include Blacks' attitudes toward Whites (e.g., Johnson

& Lecci, 2003), as well as prejudices toward a variety of other groups, including gays and lesbians (Larsen, Reed, & Hoffman, 1980) and Asians (Son Hing, Li, & Zanna, 2002), among others.

It is also important to acknowledge the important role that "unofficial" measures of prejudice play in the literature. These measures are often constructed for the aims of a specific study as dependent measures, but they are more flexible and, notably, more prolific than the "official" measures. Perhaps most common are semantic differentials, where a given group (or group member) is rated on a scale anchored by two opposing endpoints (e.g., unintelligent vs. intelligent), and trait ratings, where respondents indicate the extent to which they believe a given trait characterizes a group (e.g., Peffley, Hurwitz, & Sniderman, 1997). Simple Likert-type ratings of liking of groups are also used (e.g., Ford & Stangor, 1992). A variety of means of assessing the perceived homogeneity or variability of groups are available (e.g., Park & Judd, 1990), but these measures are rarely tied to other prejudice research (but see Lambert et al., 2005). Measures of "social distance" have a long history, and are used to assess the extent to which respondents would be comfortable sharing increasingly closer quarters with outgroup members (e.g., from living in the same town to sharing an office; Bogardus, 1959; e.g., von Hippel, Silver, & Lynch, 2000). Finally, a modest, single-item measure called the "feeling thermometer" deserves some recognition (e.g., Abelson, Kinder, Peters, & Fiske, 1982; Haddock, Zanna, & Esses, 1993). It invites respondents to indicate how "warmly" they feel toward a given group on a thermometer-like scale (typically ranging from 0 [cold] to 100 [warm]). This measure correlates with a remarkable number of other measures and is easily adapted to most any research purpose.

DIRECT MEASURES: SUMMARY

Clearly there is no shortage of direct measures of prejudice. This rich array of measurement tools provides flexibility for the researcher, but unfortunately, the extensive overlap between measures can feel both arbitrary and overwhelming when it comes to selecting a measure for one's own research. Moreover, the proliferation of measures creates the potential for "competition" between measures for validation and use, as well as redundant research findings. On the other hand, findings based on the use of a variety of direct measures continue to help devise, validate, and refine theories of prejudice. Compared to indirect measures that typically require respondents to be in front of a computer equipped with specialized software, practical considerations must be acknowledged: Direct measures require fewer resources to administer.

Direct measures do suffer, however, from some shortcomings. Foremost is the fact that by definition, they require verbal reports of one's attitude, and, by implication, assume both a willingness and an ability on the part of respondents to accurately report their attitudes. Many individuals are reluctant to report their prejudices, thus, direct measures cannot distinguish between respondents who appear to be low in prejudice based on motivational concerns from those who genuinely are low in prejudice. This has been demonstrated with the MRS in particular, but researchers who wish to distance themselves from the controversies surrounding the MRS should be aware that other direct measures likely suffer from similar problems. Also, attempts at creating more subtle measures can lead to questions that are circuitous or problematically ambiguous (e.g., that confound racial attitudes and political beliefs).

INDIRECT MEASURES

If you are prejudiced but are reluctant to admit it on a questionnaire, indirect measures may circumvent these barriers to direct attitude reporting and more accurately reveal your underlying racial sentiments. Indirect measures have derived from theories, not of prejudice, but of social cognition more generally. Such theories (e.g., Greenwald & Banaji, 1995) emphasize the role of spontaneous and uncontrollable cognitive processes, and indirect measures were developed as a means of tapping these processes. Thus, they not only provide a potential solution to the social desirability problems that affect direct measures, but indirect measures like priming and the Implicit Association Test (IAT) provide an index of the automaticity of one's attitudes through examinations of reaction times to stimuli.

A note about terminology is in order before we continue. The term *implicit* (as opposed to *explicit*) is nearly universally applied to the measures discussed in this section, so the terminology chosen here is a departure from orthodoxy. De Houwer (2006) gave good reason for the switch. First, the term implicit has been used in a number of inconsistent ways, with its most prevalent connotation also being its least tenable. Specifically, researchers have tended to use this word to describe attitudes tapped by indirect measures about which the perceiver is unaware (e.g., Richeson & Shelton, 2003; Rudman & Kilianski, 2000). Not only is there no evidence to support this claim, there is actually evidence against it (e.g., Olson, Fazio, & Hermann, 2007). "Implicit" has also been the label applied to claims that respondents are unaware that their attitudes are being assessed with a given indirect measure and that they cannot control their responses on the measure, and there is reason to question the accuracy of these uses of the term as well (e.g., Monteith, Voils, & Ashburn-Nardo, 2001). Moreover, some indirect measures might be implicit in one sense but not another. Hence, De Houwer (2006) advocates use of the term indirect because what is common to all such measures is that "participants are not asked to self-assess the extent to which they hold a certain attitude or cognition" (p. 20).

Indirect measures are a more recent addition to the prejudice measurement arsenal (see Gaertner & McLaughlin, 1983, for an early effort), but they have seen prolific use in the past decade, and much is now known about their validity and reliability. However, two measures in particular, the IAT (Greenwald, McGhee, & Schwartz, 1998) and variations on priming procedures (e.g., Fazio et al., 1995), have seen the lion's share of use, and thus receive the most focus in this review (see Fazio & Olson, 2003, for an extensive review).

PRIMING MEASURES

If one has a negative automatically activated attitude toward Blacks, perceiving a Black individual immediately and inescapably triggers negativity. Having such negativity activated should make it easier to respond to other negatively evaluated objects, and analogously, it should make responding to positive objects more difficult. This is the logic underlying priming measures. Such measures entail the presentation of a *prime,* which is the attitude object (e.g., a picture of a Black individual) for a brief duration (typically between 150 and 300 milliseconds) on a computer screen. The prime is immediately followed by a "target" that requires some kind of a response. Often the target is a positive or a negative adjective (e.g., *awesome, terrible*), and the respondent is required to identify its connotation by pressing one of two keys labeled "bad" and "good." Participants undergo many such trials, and in the case of a priming measure designed to assess Whites' attitudes toward Blacks, primes would include several Black and White primes as well as other race fillers, each presented multiple times followed by both positive and negative targets. The latency to respond to each target is recorded, and average response latencies across a 2 (prime: Black vs. White) × 2 (target: positive vs. negative) matrix are compared to arrive at an overall estimate of one's attitude toward Blacks relative to Whites. To the extent that one harbors automatic negativity toward Blacks, relatively quicker responses should be observed to negative targets following Black primes and positive targets following Whites primes. Indeed, the Prime × Target interaction is often computed on a per-participant basis to arrive at an estimate of automatically activated attitudes toward Blacks relative to Whites.

A variety of studies testify to the predictive validity of priming measures. For example, Fazio et al. (1995) found estimates of respondents' automatic racial prejudice based on a priming measure to predict a Black experimenter's impressions of the friendliness of respondents—those with more negative estimates were seen as less friendly. This measure also predicted attributions of responsibility for the 1992 riots in Los Angeles following the Rodney King verdict. In interracial interaction settings, individuals characterized by more negative priming estimates of racial prejudice tend to exhibit more negative nonverbal behavior (e.g., less eye contact, more speech errors, etc.; Dovidio, Kawakami, Johnson, Johnson, & Howard, 1997), more negative judgments of friendliness toward a Black interaction partner according to naive observers (e.g., Dovidio, Kawakami, & Gaertner, 2002), and less physical contact with a Black partner (Wilson, Lindsey, & Schooler, 2000). Respondents with more extreme racial attitude estimates tend to categorize social targets by race (Fazio & Dunton, 1997) and show different emotional responses to apparently prejudicial responses (e.g., Fazio & Hilden, 2001). Consistent with contemporary theories of social cognition, note that many of these studies focus on less monitored and less controllable prejudice-related behaviors. However, the automatic processes tapped by priming measures can influence more deliberate behaviors as well (Olson & Fazio, 2004b). For example, Towles-Schwen and Fazio (2006) found that a priming measure predicted the success of randomly assigned Black and White college freshmen dormmate relationships over the course of the students' first semester in college.

Several variations of priming measures of prejudice exist. Modifications have been applied to the nature of the primes and targets, as well as the type of judgment made. For example, Dovidio et al. (1997) utilized schematic Black and White faces as primes, Fazio and colleagues' research has employed actual photographs of Blacks and Whites, and Wittenbrink and colleagues have simply used the words "Black" and "White" as primes (Wittenbrink, Judd, & Park, 1997, 2001a). In terms of target judgment variations, the latter researchers have also shown that lexical decision tasks (i.e., word vs. nonword) are more sensitive to stereotype content, whereas connotation tasks (i.e., good vs. bad) are more sensitive to attitude activation. Payne, Cheng, Govorun, and Stewart (2005) employed Chinese symbols as targets and required participants to "guess" their meaning. The reasoning underlying their affect misattribution procedure (AMP) is that affect activated by the prime is misattributed to the symbol, thus influencing participants' impressions of it.

On the downside, priming measures have been criticized for their poor reliability (e.g., Cunningham, Preacher, & Banaji, 2001). As Wittenbrink and colleagues' research suggests, variations to primes, targets, or judgment task can tap different aspects of prejudice, and only a limited amount of research has investigated these issues. However, compared to other indirect measures, priming measures have a longer history of validation and their underlying mechanisms are better understood (Fazio & Olson, 2003).

IAT (GREENWALD ET AL., 1998)

Like priming measures, the IAT relies on response latencies to stimuli to gauge associations in memory. Unlike priming, it does so through forcing participants to classify four categories of stimuli using only two response keys (e.g., positive vs. negative stimuli and Black vs. White targets). On a given trial, one of the four types of stimuli appears, and respondents are instructed to categorize it as rapidly as possible. Two categories always share a response key assignment, and this assignment varies by "compatible" versus "incompatible" block. In the compatible block, respondents press one key to classify positive and White items, and the other key to classify negative and Black items. The key assignment is reversed in the incompatible block (i.e., positive and Black share a response key, and negative and White are assigned to the other). According to the measures' developers, to the extent that Black and negative share an association in memory, participants will be quicker to assign them to the same response key (and hence response times should, on average, be shorter during the compatible block relative to the incompatible block). Some form of a difference score is computed between average response latencies to the two block types, resulting in an index of automatic prejudicial associations to Black-negative and White-positive (for an overview, see Nosek, Greenwald, & Banaji, 2007).

Despite its widespread use, little was known about the mechanism underlying performance on the IAT until recently. De Houwer (2001) argued that stimulus features that are tangential to the categorization task can be used to solve the mapping problem posed by the IAT (see De Houwer, 2003, for a structural review of indirect measures). For example, although a Black stimulus is to be classified by race according to the task instructions, the negative valence associated with Blacks can be used to aid categorization in the compatible block. One need only note that an item is a member of the category "Black" to classify it as such. To test this relevant feature account, De Houwer conducted a British-foreigner IAT, but the exemplars used to represent each category were both positive and negative (e.g., foreigners included both Einstein and Hitler). He found that the exemplars did not matter: Participants (who were British) appeared to prefer British to foreigners regardless of whether individual Brits were liked or disliked. In other words, it is the responses to the categories, not the individual exemplars, that typically influence IAT performance.

Early IAT research focused on validation using a known groups approach (e.g., Jews vs. Christians tend to show a bias in favor of their own groups; Rudman, Greenwald, Mellott, & Schwartz, 1999; see also Greenwald et al., 1998). More recently, evidence has accumulated to suggest that the IAT relates reliably to behavior—particularly, and similarly to priming measures, to less controllable behavior. McConnell and Liebold (2001), for example, demonstrated correspondence between a racial prejudice IAT and naive judges' impressions of a White participant's behavior, as well as various nonverbal indicators such as speech errors and smiling, during an interracial interaction.

In addition to the prediction of discriminatory behavior, a variety of findings illustrate the IAT's ability to predict biases in perceptions of emotional expressions (Hugenberg & Bodenhausen, 2003), and cognitive impairment following interracial interactions (Richeson & Shelton, 2003). Richeson and her colleagues, in work on the contextual determinants of prejudice using the IAT as a dependent measure, have shown increased prejudice when Whites take a colorblind versus a multicultural perspective and when they are assigned a subordinate role to a Black (Richeson & Ambady, 2003; Richeson & Nussbaum, 2004). In prejudice reduction research, the IAT has proven sensitive to various forms of contact (Henry & Hardin, 2006) and diversity education (Rudman, Ashmore, & Gary, 2001). It has been adapted to many different populations, including children, who appear to develop prejudices at surprisingly young ages (Baron & Banaji, 2006), and has seen other unique prejudice-related applications, such as a measure of White identity (Knowles & Peng, 2005).

Clearly, since its presentation in 1998, an explosion of IAT-based research has resulted in an overwhelming literature, one that this review has only touched on. Although much research attests to its validity, other findings have stirred considerable controversy about just what the IAT measures. Compared to priming and other indirect measures, correspondence between the IAT and direct measures of prejudice has been observed with more regularity (e.g., McConnell & Liebold, 2001; Rudman et al., 1999). Some evidence suggests that respondents are at least somewhat aware of what the IAT measures (e.g., Monteith et al., 2001), and that more deliberate, motivated processes are related to IAT scores (Vanman, Saltz, Nathan, & Warren, 2004). Recent research also suggests that IAT performance can be faked (De Houwer, Beckers, & Moors, 2007). Other research has documented failures of the IAT to predict relevant behavior (e.g., Karpinski & Hilton, 2001), even behavior that other indirect measures do predict (e.g., Vanman et al., 2004). Others have questioned what any given IAT "score" actually indicates about a person's attitudes (Blanton & Jaccard, 2006).

Perhaps even more troubling is evidence that the IAT might be contaminated by "extrapersonal" information—associations that are available in memory but that do not contribute to one's attitudes (Han, Olson, & Fazio, 2006; Olson & Fazio, 2004a; see also Karpinski & Hilton, 2001). Extrapersonal associations can stem from knowledge of others' attitudes, cultural norms, or other sources. Han et al. (2006), for example, demonstrated that IAT-assessed attitude estimates were influenced by attitude-irrelevant sources respondents themselves deemed extraneous and incorrect, whereas a priming measure was not so contaminated. A modified (or "personalized") IAT involving subtle changes to the category labels (e.g., "Pleasant" was replaced with "I like") was sufficient to reduce the impact of extrapersonal associations in Han et al.'s research (see also Olson & Fazio, 2004a).

A variety of other modified IATs have also been developed. For example, Nosek and Banaji (2001) introduced the Go/No-go Association Task (GNAT) as a means of indirectly assessing attitudes without the need for two contrasting categories of attitude objects. Much research has also investigated specific psychometric parameters of the IAT such as the number of trials, exemplars, and various timing parameters (e.g., Greenwald, Nosek, & Banaji, 2003).

OTHER INDIRECT MEASURES

Owing to the popularity of the IAT (and, to some extent, priming), other indirect measures have probably not received the attention or use they merit. For example, word fragment completion measures are well understood and well validated (e.g., Dovidio et al., 1997; Son Hing et al., 2002), but rarely receive much attention in discussions of indirect measures. These measures are reviewed briefly here in the hope that researchers will not overlook them in choosing an indirect measure for their own research.

A subtle and perhaps unnoticed bias toward more abstract language tends to appear in descriptions of outgroup behavior that are consistent with negative expectancies about the group (Maass, Salvi, Arcuri, & Semin, 1989). Capitalizing on this phenomenon, von Hippel and colleagues (e.g., von Hippel, Sekaquaptewa, & Vargas, 1997) have prompted respondents to provide descriptions of behaviors performed by Blacks and others, and compare the use of abstract versus more concrete language to arrive at an estimate of prejudice they refer to as the stereotype explanatory bias (SEB). In recent work, an SEB measure related to a Black confederate's impressions of White participants: White participants who made external attributions for Black stereotype-incongruent behavior were viewed more negatively (Sekaquaptewa, Espinoza, Thompson, Vargas, & von Hippel, 2003).

Although social psychologists have been somewhat slow to incorporate them, physiological measures of prejudice are also becoming increasingly popular. Eye-blink startle responses to Black versus White faces have been used to predict various motivational orientations regarding race (Amodio, Harmon-Jones, & Devine, 2003). Other subtle facial reactions via electromyography (EMG) have been employed as indexes of affective reactions to Blacks versus Whites by Vanman and colleagues (Vanman, Paul, Ito, & Miller, 1997), and such measures predict race-related judgments (Vanman et al., 2004). Electroencephalography (EEG) approaches have also been used to illuminate the lack of intentionality often involved in race-biased responses (Amodio et al., 2004). Functional magnetic resonance imaging (fMRI) techniques have implicated the amygdala as being critically involved in affective responses to faces of differing races (Phelps et al., 2000; Wheeler & Fiske, 2005), and individual differences in amygdala activation relate to behavioral indicators of prejudice (Cunningham et al., 2004).

RELATIONSHIPS BETWEEN INDIRECT MEASURES

Several researchers report similar patterns of findings with priming and IAT measures in separate experiments (e.g., DeSteno et al., 2004), suggesting that similar processes are tapped by these measures. However, the simplistic assumption that indirect measures should correlate with one another because they all purport to assess more automatic forms of prejudice turns out to be incorrect. Although occasional correspondence between indirect measures has been observed (e.g., Rudman & Kilianaski, 2000; Wittenbrink et al., 1997), correlations near zero have been reported (Fazio & Olson, 2003). Moreover, although roughly half of White respondents appear prejudiced toward Blacks on priming measures, around three quarters do on the IAT (Olson & Fazio, 2003). Even more perplexing is the finding that Black respondents show a bias in favor of their own race on priming measures (Fazio et al., 1995), but often show a bias against Blacks on the IAT (Nosek, Banaji, & Greenwald, 2002).

The question, then, becomes one of how indirect measures diverge. Owing to the difficulty of incorporating multiple indirect measures in a single study, only a handful have systematically addressed the relationships between them. Cunningham et al. (2001) implicated their relatively poor reliabilities as the cause of their divergence, and across multiple data collection sessions and multiple IAT and priming measures, reported latent variable analyses that improve their correspondence substantially.

However, measurement error may be only part of the answer. Capitalizing on De Houwer's (2003) analysis suggesting that exemplars have little influence on typical IAT performance, Olson and Fazio (2003) demonstrated that the IAT assesses associations to the category (e.g., "Blacks"), whereas priming measures involving individual Black stimuli (typically images of faces) as primes tap automatic responses to individual members of the category. In a priming condition where respondents were led to perceive the exemplars as category members, the priming measure and the IAT showed greater convergence. Interestingly, a greater proportion of respondents appeared prejudiced when led to categorize the stimuli in terms of race on both priming and IAT measures. These findings suggest not only a potential for discordance between peoples' individual-level and group-level evaluations, but also that evaluative reactions to the category "Blacks" might be more negative than evaluative reactions to individual Blacks. These findings also suggest that a priming measure using the label "Blacks" as primes, as in Wittenbrink et al.'s (1997, 2001a) research, would correlate with the IAT better than a priming measure involving individual faces as primes, as most of Fazio and colleagues' research has employed.

Thus, in the same way that direct measures show imperfect convergence owing to different emphases within different measures, so too do indirect measures assess different aspects of prejudice. Some measures may emphasize stereotype content versus a more "pure" evaluative component (e.g., Wittenbrink et al., 2001a), or, as we have seen earlier, reactions to individuals versus categories. Physiological measures involving amygdala activation may best tap emotional reactions to groups, as might EMG measures. These assertions remain somewhat speculative, however, and future research (as arduous as it will be) will have to clarify the conceptual overlap among indirect measures.

MALLEABILITY OF INDIRECT MEASURES

Recent research suggests that responses on indirect measures can be malleable and context dependent (Wittenbrink et al., 2001b; for a review, see Blair, 2002). For example, exposure to positive Black and negative White exemplars (Dasgupta & Greenwald, 2001) and the presence of a Black experimenter (Lowery, Hardin, & Sinclair, 2001) have all been shown to decrease prejudice on indirect measures. This research has been interpreted as evidence that stable, enduring attitudes are unlikely to exist, and that, instead, attitudes are constructed as needed based on person variables and situational factors (e.g., Schwarz & Bohner, 2001). That this view has gained momentum in recent years is somewhat surprising given the wealth of research demonstrating both the tenacity and context-transcending nature of prejudice.

What is probably more likely is that many contextual manipulations affect not the attitude itself, but participants' construal of the attitude object. The manipulations involved in the malleability studies like those cited earlier often prompt participants to recategorize individuals about whom they harbor prejudices as members of liked groups or cause them to call up evaluations of liked subgroups, but underlying prejudicial associations probably remain intact in these cases. In other words, contexts are likely to produce "a change in the object of judgment" instead of a change "in the judgment of the object" (Asch, 1940). Researchers should consider the nature of the attitude object they have in mind in using indirect measures of prejudice, and recognize that contexts can have powerful effects on how those objects are construed and categorized.

RELATIONSHIPS BETWEEN DIRECT AND INDIRECT MEASURES

Several reviews have recently examined the interrelations of these two measurement types (e.g., Blair, 2001; Brauer, Wasel, & Niedenthal, 2000; Dovidio, Kawakami, & Beach 2001). Generally, correlations between direct and indirect measures of prejudice range from nonexistent (e.g., Dovidio et al., 2002; Fazio et al., 1995; Greenwald et al., 1998) to weak (e.g., Lepore & Brown, 1997; McConnell & Liebold, 2001; Wittenbrink et al., 1997). In a recent meta-analysis, Hoffman, Gawronski, Gschwendner, Le, and Schmitt (2005) reported increased IAT–direct measure correspondence to the extent that direct reports were made more spontaneously (and, hence, tapped more automatic processes) and when the two measurements corresponded conceptually. To these Nosek (2005) added the element of social sensitivity, among others. In domains like prejudice, where social forces often make the natural expression of one's attitudes contentious, direct and indirect measures are less likely to converge. Indeed, in less controversial domains, clear correspondence has been observed repeatedly (e.g., Fazio et al., 1986; Greenwald et al., 1998; Nosek et al., 2002; Olson & Fazio, 2001).

Thus, the question is a matter of when, not whether, direct and indirect measures are correlated. As we discuss next, it is the job of good theory to explain the interrelations among measures and the role each measurement type plays in predicting behavior.

THE BIGGER PICTURE

Social behavior is driven by both controlled and automatic processes, and the development and subsequent popularization of indirect measures was fed by a desire to examine the influence of the latter on social behavior in conjunction with the more controlled processes tapped by direct measures (even though no measure is "process pure"). Hence, researchers often employ both when trying to predict prejudicial behavior, and the overarching finding is that less controllable behaviors are better predicted by indirect measures, and more controllable behaviors are better predicted by direct measures. For example, in Dovidio et al.'s (1997) research, nonverbal behavior toward a Black person was predicted by a priming measure, but explicit ratings of liking were predicted by a direct measure of prejudice (see also Fazio et al., 1995).

Several theories on attitude–behavior relations, automatic social behavior, and impression formation are relevant to this work, and some research has attempted to integrate itself with these broader theories. For example, Wilson and colleagues' (2000) model of "dual attitudes" argues that individuals can have two attitudes toward the same object, one "implicit" (or automatic) and the other explicit, and that these two attitudes can coexist and independently influence behavior. One might, for example, have a negative automatic reaction to Blacks even though one holds positive views of Blacks explicitly. A related theory, Fazio's MODE model (Motivation and Opportunity as DEterminants of the attitude–behavior relation; Fazio & Towles-Schwen, 1999), does not assume that attitudes of the more automatic variety coexist with more "explicit" attitudes. Instead, automatically activated attitudes are those that are spontaneously activated on perception of the attitude object. These attitudes, assessed with indirect measures, will influence behavior in the absence of motivational concerns. If one is motivated and has opportunity to do otherwise, however, motivated processes will influence behavior. Motivation is typically assessed with Dunton and Fazio's (1997) MCPR, reviewed earlier. Thus, in the MODE model, direct measures map not onto "explicit attitudes," but motivation. For example, Whites' impressions of Blacks tend to be driven by their automatically activated attitudes in the absence of motivation, but Whites who are motivated to avoid appearing prejudiced will correct for the attitudes in reporting their impressions of Blacks (Olson & Fazio, 2004b). According to the MODE model, automatic responses can have "downstream" consequences in more controllable aspects of behavior as well (e.g., Towles-Schwen & Fazio, 2006), and other research also suggests that indirect measures can influence controllable behavior (Vanman et al., 2004). Thus, we should not expect a simple mapping of direct measures onto controllable behavior and indirect measures onto less controllable behavior.

Perhaps the discrepancy between these theories boils down to a definitional issue: Does one want to refer to a report on a direct measure an "attitude" in addition to the attitude revealed by an indirect measure? Wilson and colleagues would answer affirmatively, but Fazio and colleagues maintain that the opportunity for respondents to adjust how they present themselves on direct measures renders separating motivational influences from attitudes impossible. In other words, direct measures might reveal more about one's motives than one's attitudes.

Theories of attitudes have informed research on the measurement of prejudice, and these measures, in turn, have informed theories of prejudice. For example, Son Hing et al. (2002) used indirect and direct measures to identify "aversive racists" (Dovidio & Gaertner, 2004); that is, individuals who identify themselves as nonprejudiced (on a direct measure), but who still harbor hidden biases against Blacks (as revealed by an indirect measure). They found that aversive racists (as compared to other combinations of directly and indirectly measured prejudice) felt guilt and discomfort when writing about past prejudicial behavior. In a test of Fiske and Neuberg's (1990) continuum model of impression formation, Gawronski, Ehrenberg, Banse, Zukova, and Klauer (2003) demonstrated that more stereotypical impressions of women are formed only when respondents harbored strong gender stereotypes as assessed by an IAT. Impressions based on individual characteristics of the target, on the other hand, were formed in the relative absence of such stereotypes.

CONCLUSIONS

Clearly, prejudice has many forms and can stem from many sources. This means that no single measure can capture this multifaceted construct. I have attempted to illuminate the rich and diverse range of measures available. One conclusion that should be apparent is that the choice is not arbitrary. Direct measures tend to lend themselves toward more deliberate, controlled forms of prejudice along with some of its political undertones. Indirect measures, on the other hand, tap more automatic processes. Another apparent conclusion, ironically, might be that the choice of measures can feel somewhat arbitrary. Of the direct measures, should one select the MRS or ATB? If one aims for an indirect assessment, should it be the IAT or priming? The considerable overlap among measures notwithstanding, important differences do remain. For example, priming measures might suffer from reliability concerns, but the IAT appears to be contaminated by factors unrelated to prejudice.

Indirect measures have seen a tremendous surge in use, but much of their underlying mechanisms and the nature of the constructs they tap are in need of clarification. Some have even questioned whether these measures have lived up to their promise of accounting for variance in behavior for which direct measures cannot (Ajzen & Fishbein, 2005). Furthermore, research on more blatant forms of prejudice may risk being neglected in the face of the popularity of indirect measures. Hate crimes and genocide are rampant in this world, and one need not lift the rug to uncover the fact that old-fashioned forms of prejudice are everywhere. For example, a recent poll by Gallup (2006) indicated that nearly 40% of Americans are readily willing to admit publicly to "at least some prejudice" against Muslims, and nearly one third believe that Arabs should carry special identification cards.

To sum it all up, prejudice comes in many forms, and the "lens" one chooses to examine it affects what one finds. When selecting a measure, researchers should use relevant theory to inform their decision, with an eye toward the research history of each measure and the practical limitations of conducting the research.

ACKNOWLEDGMENTS

I thank Lowell Gaertner, P. J. Henry, and Ashby Plant for valuable feedback on an earlier version of this chapter.

REFERENCES

Abelson, R. P., Kinder, D. R., Peters, M. D., & Fiske, S. T. (1982). Affective and semantic components in political person perception. *Journal of Personality and Social Psychology, 42,* 619–630.

Adorno, T. W., Frenkel-Brunswick, E., Levinson, D. J., & Sanford, R. N. (1950). *The authoritarian personality.* New York: Harper.

Ajzen, I., & Fishbein, M. (2005). The influence of attitudes on behavior. In D. Albarracin, B. T. Johnson, & M. P. Zanna (Eds.), *The handbook of attitudes* (pp. 173–222). Mahwah, NJ: Erlbaum.

Altemeyer, R. A. (1981). *Right wing authoritarianism.* Winnipeg: University of Manitoba Press.

Altemeyer, R. A. (1996). *The authoritarian specter.* Cambridge, MA: Harvard University Press.

Amodio, D. M., Harmon-Jones, E., & Devine, P. G. (2003). Individual differences in the activation and control of affective race bias as assessed by startle eyeblink responses and self-report. *Journal of Personality and Social Psychology, 84,* 738–753.

Amodio, D. M., Harmon-Jones, E., Devine, P. G., Curtin, J. J., Hartley, S. L., & Covert, A. E. (2004). Neural signals for the detection of unintentional race bias. *Psychological Science, 15,* 88-93.

Asch, S. E. (1940). Studies in the principles of judgments and attitudes II: Determination of judgments by group and by ego standards. *Journal of Social Psychology, 12,* 433–465.

Baron, A. S., & Banaji, M. R. (2006). The development of implicit attitudes: Evidence of race evaluations from ages 6, 10 & adulthood. *Psychological Science, 17,* 53–58.

Beal, D. J., O'Neal, E. C., Ong, J., & Ruscher, J. N. (2000). The ways and means of interracial aggression. *Personality and Social Psychology Bulletin, 26,* 1225–1238.

Biernat, M., & Crandall, C. S. (1999). Racial attitudes. In J. Robinson, P. Shaver, & L. Wrightsman (Eds.), *Measures of political attitudes* (pp. 297–411). New York: Academic.

Biernat, M., & Manis, M. (1994). Shifting standards and stereotype-based judgments. *Journal of Personality and Social Psychology, 66,* 5–20.

Biernat, M., Vescio, T. K., Theno, S. A., & Crandall, C. S. (1996). Values and prejudice: Toward understanding the impact of American values on outgroup attitudes. In C. Seligman, J. M. Olson, & M. P. Zanna (Eds.), *The psychology of values: The Ontario symposium* (Vol. 8, pp. 153–189). Hillsdale, NJ: Erlbaum.

Blair, I. (2001). Implicit stereotypes and prejudice. In G. B. Moskowitz (Ed.), *Cognitive social psychology: The Princeton symposium on the legacy and future of social cognition* (pp. 359–374). Mahwah, NJ: Erlbaum.

Blair, I. (2002). The malleability of automatic stereotypes and prejudice. *Personality and Social Psychology Review, 6,* 242–260.

Blanton, H., & Jaccard, J. (2006). Arbitrary metrics in psychology. *American Psychologist, 61,* 27–41.

Blascovich, J., Wyer, N. A., Swart, L. A., & Kibler, J. L. (1997). Racism and racial categorization. *Journal of Personality and Social Psychology, 72,* 1364–1372.

Bogardus, E. S. (1959). *Social distance.* Yellow Springs, OH: Antioch Press.

Brauer, M., Wasel, W., & Niedenthal, P. (2000). Implicit and explicit components of prejudice. *Review of General Psychology, 4,* 79–101.

Brigham, J. C. (1993). College students' racial attitudes. *Journal of Applied Social Psychology, 23,* 1933–1967.

Cunningham, W. A., Johnson, M. K., Raye, C. L., Gatenby, J. C., Gore, J. C., & Banaji, M. R. (2004). Separable neural components in the processing of Black and White faces. *Psychological Science, 15,* 806–813.

Cunningham, W. A., Preacher, K. J., & Banaji, M. R. (2001). Implicit attitude measures: Consistency, stability, and convergent validity. *Psychological Science, 12,* 163–170.

Dasgupta, N., & Greenwald, A. G. (2001). On the malleability of automatic attitudes: Combating automatic prejudice with images of admired and disliked individuals. *Journal of Personality and Social Psychology, 81,* 800–814.

De Houwer, J. (2001). A structural and process analysis of the Implicit Association Test. *Journal of Experimental Social Psychology, 37,* 443–451.

De Houwer, J. (2003). A structural analysis of indirect measures of attitudes. In J. Musch & K. C. Klauer (Eds.), *Affective processes in cognition and emotion* (pp. 219-244). Mahwah, NJ: Erlbaum.

De Houwer, J. (2006). What are implicit measures and why are we using them. In R. W. Wiers & A. W. Stacy (Eds.), *The handbook of implicit cognition and addiction* (pp. 11–28). Thousand Oaks, CA: Sage.

De Houwer, J., Beckers, T., & Moors, A. (2007). Novel attitudes can be faked on the Implicit Association Test. *Journal of Experimental Social Psychology, 43*(6), 972–978.

De Houwer, J., & Moors, A. (2007). How to define and examine the implicitness of implicit measures. In B. Wittenbrink & N. Schwarz (Eds.), *Implicit measures of attitudes: Procedures and controversies* (pp. 179–194). New York: Guilford.

DeSteno, D., Dasgupta, N., Bartlett, M. Y., & Cajdric, A. (2004). Prejudice from thin air: The effect of emotion on automatic intergroup attitudes. *Psychological Science, 15,* 319–324.

Devine, P. G. (1989). Stereotypes and prejudice: Their automatic and controlled components. *Journal of Personality and Social Psychology, 56,* 5–18.

Devine, P. G., Monteith, M. J., Zuwerink, J. R., & Elliot, A. J. (1991). Prejudice with and without compunction. *Journal of Personality and Social Psychology, 60,* 817–830.

Devine, P. G., Plant, E. A., & Buswell, B. N. (2000). Breaking the prejudice habit: Progress and obstacles. In S. Oskamp (Ed.), *Reducing prejudice and discrimination* (pp. 185–208). Thousand Oaks, CA: Sage.

Dovidio, J. F., & Gaertner, S. L. (2004). Aversive racism. In M. P. Zanna (Ed.), *Advances in experimental social psychology* (Vol. 36, pp. 1–51). San Diego, CA: Academic.

Dovidio, J. F., Kawakami, K., & Beach, K. R. (2001). Implicit and explicit attitudes: Examination of the relationship between measures of intergroup bias. In R. Brown & S. Gaertner (Eds.), *Blackwell handbook of social psychology: Intergroup processes* (pp. 175–197). Malden, MA: Blackwell.

Dovidio, J. F., Kawakami, K., & Gaertner, S. L. (2002). Implicit and explicit prejudice and interracial interactions. *Journal of Personality and Social Psychology, 82,* 62–68.

Dovidio, J. F., Kawakami, K., Johnson, C., Johnson, B., & Howard, A. (1997). On the nature of prejudice: Automatic and controlled processes. *Journal of Experimental Social Psychology, 33,* 510–540.

Duckitt, J., Wagner, C., du Plessis, I., & Birum, I. (2002). The psychological basis of ideology and prejudice: Testing a dual process model. *Journal of Personality and Social Psychology, 83,* 75–93.

Dunton, B. C., & Fazio, R. H. (1997). An individual difference measure of motivation to control prejudiced reactions. *Personality and Social Psychology Bulletin, 23,* 316–326.

Fazio, R. H., & Dunton, B. C. (1997). Categorization by race: The impact of automatic and controlled components of racial prejudice. *Journal of Experimental Social Psychology, 33,* 451–470.

Fazio R. H., & Hilden, L. (2001). Emotional reactions to a seemingly prejudiced response. *Personality and Social Psychology Bulletin, 27,* 538–549.

Fazio, R. H., Jackson, J. R., Dunton, B. C., & Williams, C. J. (1995). Variability in automatic activation as an unobtrusive measure of racial attitudes: A bona fide pipeline? *Journal of Personality and Social Psychology, 69,* 1013–1027.

Fazio, R. H., & Olson, M. A. (2003). Implicit measures in social cognition research: Their meaning and use. *Annual Review of Psychology, 54,* 297–327.

Fazio, R. H., Sanbonmatsu, D. M., Powell, M. C., & Kardes, F. R. (1986). On the automatic activation of attitudes. *Journal of Personality and Social Psychology, 50,* 229–238.

Fazio, R. H., & Towles-Schwen, T. (1999). The MODE model of attitude-behavior processes. In S. Chaiken & Y. Trope (Eds.), *Dual process theories in social psychology* (pp. 97–116). New York: Guilford.

Fiske, S. T., & Neuberg, S. L. (1990). A continuum of impression formation, from category-based to individuating processes: Influences of information and motivation on attention and interpretation. In M. P. Zanna (Ed.), *Advances in experimental social psychology* (Vol. 32, pp. 1–74). New York: Academic.

Ford, T. E., & Stangor, C. (1992). The role of diagnosticity in stereotype formation: Perceiving group means and variances. *Journal of Personality and Social Psychology, 63,* 356-367.

Gallup Organization (2006). *Polling Report.* Retrieved July 1, 2006 from http://www.pollingreport.com/issues.htm

Gaertner, S. L., & McLaughlin, J. P. (1983). Racial stereotypes: Associations and ascriptions of positive and negative characteristics. *Social Psychology Quarterly, 46,* 23–30.

Gawronski, B., Ehrenberg, K., Banse, R., Zukova, J., & Klauer, K. C. (2003). It's in the mind of the beholder: The impact of stereotypic associations on category-based and individuating impression formation. *Journal of Experimental Social Psychology, 39,* 16–30.

Gordijn, E. H., Koomen, W., & Stapel, D. A. (2001). Level of prejudice in relation to knowledge of cultural stereotypes. *Journal of Experimental Social Psychology, 37,* 150–157.

Greenwald, A. G., & Banaji, M. R. (1995). Implicit social cognition: Attitudes, self-esteem, and stereotypes. *Psychological Review, 102,* 4–27.

Greenwald, A. G., McGhee, D., & Schwartz, J. L. K. (1998). Measuring individual differences in implicit cognition: The implicit association task. *Journal of Personality and Social Psychology, 74,* 1469–1480.

Greenwald, A. G., Nosek, B. A., & Banaji, M. R. (2003). Understanding and using the Implicit Association Test: I. An improved scoring algorithm. *Journal of Personality and Social Psychology, 85,* 197–216.

Haddock, G., Zanna, M. P., & Esses, V. M. (1993). Assessing the structure of prejudicial attitudes: The case of attitudes toward homosexuals. *Journal of Personality and Social Psychology, 65,* 1105–1118.

Han, H. A., Olson, M. A., & Fazio, R. H. (2006). The influence of experimentally-created extrapersonal associations on the Implicit Association Test. *Journal of Experimental Social Psychology, 42,* 259–272.

Hass, R. G., Katz, I., Rizzo, N., Baley, J., & Eisenstadt, D. (1991). Cross-racial appraisal as related to attitude ambivalence and cognitive complexity. *Personality and Social Psychology Bulletin, 17,* 83–92.

Henry, P. J., & Hardin, C. D. (2006). The contact hypothesis revisited: Status bias in the reduction of implicit prejudice in the United States and Lebanon. *Psychological Science, 17,* 862–868.

Henry, P. J., & Sears, D. O. (2002). The symbolic racism 2000 scale. *Political Psychology, 23,* 253–283.

Hodson, G., Dovidio, J. F., & Gaertner, S. L. (2002). Processes in racial discrimination: Differential weighting of conflicting information. *Personality and Social Psychology Bulletin, 28,* 460–471.

Hofmann, W., Gawronski, B., Gschwendner, T., Le, H., & Schmitt, M. (2005). A meta-analysis on the correlation between the Implicit Association Test and explicit self-report measures. *Personality and Social Psychology Bulletin, 31,* 1369–1385.

Hugenberg, K., & Bodenhausen, G. V. (2003). Facing prejudice: Implicit prejudice and the perception of facial threat. *Psychological Science, 14,* 640–643.

Johnson, J. D., & Lecci, L. (2003). Assessing anti-white attitudes and predicting perceived racism: The Johnson-Lecci Scale. *Personality and Social Psychology Bulletin, 29,* 299–312.

Karpinski, A., & Hilton, J. L. (2001). Attitudes and the Implicit Association Test. *Journal of Personality and Social Psychology, 81,* 774–778.

Katz, I., & Hass, R. G. (1988). Racial ambivalence and American value conflict: Correlational and priming studies of dual cognitive structures. *Journal of Personality and Social Psychology, 55,* 893–905.

Kinder, D. R., & Sanders, L. M. (1996). *Divided by color.* Chicago: University of Chicago Press.

Knowles, E. D. & Peng, K. (2005). White selves: Conceptualizing and measuring a dominant-group identity. *Journal of Personality and Social Psychology, 89,* 223–241.

Lambert, A. J., Payne, B. K., Ramsey, S., & Shaffer, L. M. (2005). On the predictive validity of implicit attitude measures: The moderating effect of perceived group variability. *Journal of Experimental Social Psychology, 41,* 114–128.

Larsen, K. S., Reed, M., & Hoffman, S. (1980). Attitudes of heterosexuals toward homosexuality: A Likert-type scale and construct validity. *Journal of Sex Research, 16,* 245–257.

Lepore, L., & Brown, R. (1997). Category and stereotype activation: Is prejudice inevitable? *Journal of Personality and Social Psychology, 72,* 275–87.

Lowery, B. S., Hardin, C. D., & Sinclair, S. (2001). Social influence effects on automatic racial prejudice. *Journal of Personality and Social Psychology, 81,* 842–855.

Maass, A., Salvi, D., Arcuri, L., & Semin, G. (1989). Language use in intergroup contexts: The linguistic intergroup bias. *Journal of Personality and Social Psychology, 57,* 981–993.

McConahay, J. B. (1982). Self-interest versus racial attitudes as correlates of anti-busing attitudes in Louisville: Is it the buses or the blacks? *Journal of Politics, 44,* 692–720.

McConahay, J. B. (1986). Modern racism, ambivalence, and the modern racism scale. In J. F. Dovidio & S. L. Gaertner (Eds.), *Prejudice, discrimination, and racism* (pp. 91–125). Orlando, FL: Academic.

McConahay, J. B., Hardee, B. B., & Batts, V. (1981). Has racism declined in America? It depends on who is asking and what is asked. *Journal of Conflict Resolution, 25,* 563–579.

McConahay, J. B., & Hough, J. C. (1976). Symbolic racism. *Journal of Social Issues, 32,* 23–45.

McConnell, A. R., & Liebold, J. M. (2001). Relations between the Implicit Association Test, explicit racial attitudes, and discriminatory behavior. *Journal of Experimental Social Psychology, 37,* 435–442.

Meertens, R. W., & Pettigrew, T. F. (1997). Is subtle prejudice really prejudice? *Public Opinion Quarterly, 61,* 54–71

Monteith, M. J., Voils, C. I., & Ashburn-Nardo, L. (2001). Taking a look underground: Detecting, interpreting, and reacting to implicit racial bias. *Social Cognition, 19,* 395–417.

Nosek, B. A. (2005). Moderators of the relationship between implicit and explicit evaluation. *Journal of Experimental Psychology: General, 134,* 565–584.

Nosek, B. A., & Banaji, M. R. (2001). The go/no-go association task. *Social Cognition, 19,* 625–666.

Nosek, B. A., Banaji, M. R., & Greenwald, A. G. (2002). Harvesting implicit group attitudes and beliefs from a demonstration website. *Group Dynamics, 6,* 101–115.

Nosek, B. A., Greenwald, A. G., & Banaji, M. R. (2007). The Implicit Association Test at age 7: A methodological and conceptual review. In J. A. Bargh (Ed.), *Social psychology and the unconscious: The automaticity of higher mental processes.* (pp. 265–292). New York: Psychology Press.

Olson, M. A., & Fazio, R. H. (2001). Implicit attitude formation through classical conditioning. *Psychological Science, 12,* 413-417

Olson, M. A., & Fazio, R. H. (2003). Relations between implicit measures of prejudice: What are we measuring? *Psychological Science, 14,* 36–39.

Olson, M. A., & Fazio, R. H. (2004a). Reducing the influence of extra-personal associations on the Implicit Association Test: Personalizing the IAT. *Journal of Personality and Social Psychology, 86,* 653–667.

Olson, M. A., & Fazio, R. H. (2004b). Trait inferences as a function of automatically activated racial attitudes and motivation to control prejudiced reactions. *Basic and Applied Social Psychology, 26,* 1–12.

Olson, M. A., Fazio, R. H., & Hermann, A. D. (2007). Reporting tendencies underlie discrepancies between implicit and explicit measures of self-esteem. *Psychological Science, 18*(4), 287–291.

Oyamot, C. M., Borgida, E., & Fisher, E. L. (2006). Can values moderate the attitudes of right-wing authoritarians? *Personality and Social Psychology Bulletin, 32,* 486–500.

Park, B., & Judd, C. M. (1990). Measures and models of perceived group variability. *Journal of Personality and Social Psychology, 59,* 173-191.

Payne, B. K., Cheng, C. M., Govorun, O., & Stewart, B. (2005). An inkblot for attitudes: Affect misattribution as implicit measurement. *Journal of Personality and Social Psychology, 89,* 277–293.

Peffley, M., Hurwitz, J., & Sniderman, P. M. (1997). Racial stereotypes and Whites' political views of Blacks in the context of welfare and crime. *American Journal of Political Science, 41,* 30–60.

Pettigrew, T. F. (1998). Reactions toward the new minorities of Western Europe. *Annual Review of Sociology, 24,* 77–103.

Pettigrew, T. F., & Meertens, R. W. (1995). Subtle and blatant prejudice in Western Europe. *European Journal of Social Psychology, 25,* 57–75.

Pettigrew, T. F, & Meertens, R. W. (2001). In defense of the subtle prejudice concept: A retort. *European Journal of Social Psychology, 31,* 299-309.

Phelps, E. A., O'Connor, K. J., Cunningham, W. A., Funayama, E. S., Gatenby, J. C., Gore, J. C., et al. (2000). Performance on indirect measures of race evaluation predicts amygdala activation. *Journal of Cognitive Neuroscience, 12,* 729–738.

Plant, E. A., & Devine, P. G. (1998). Internal and external motivation to respond without prejudice. *Journal of Personality and Social Psychology, 75,* 811–832.

Plant, E. A., & Devine, P. G. (2003). Antecedents and implications of interracial anxiety. *Personality and Social Psychology Bulletin, 29,* 790–801.

Plant, E. A., Devine, P. G., & Brazy, P. C. (2003). The bogus pipeline and motivations to respond without prejudice: Revisiting the fading and faking of racial prejudice. *Group Processes and Intergroup Relations, 6,* 187–200.

Pratto, F., Sidanius, J., Stallworth, L. M., & Malle, B. F. (1994). Social dominance orientation: A personality variable predicting social and political attitudes. *Journal of Personality and Social Psychology, 67,* 741–763.

Richeson, J. A., & Ambady, N. (2003). Effects of situational power on automatic racial prejudice. *Journal of Experimental Social Psychology, 39,* 177–183.

Richeson, J. A., & Nussbaum, R. J. (2004). The impact of multiculturalism versus color-blindness on racial bias. *Journal of Experimental Social Psychology, 40,* 417–423.

Richeson, J. A., & Shelton, J. N. (2003). When prejudice does not pay: Effects of interracial contact on executive function. *Psychological Science, 14,* 287–290.

Rudman, L. A., Ashmore, R. D., & Gary, M. L. (2001). "Unlearning" automatic biases: The malleability of implicit stereotypes and prejudice. *Journal of Personality and Social Psychology, 81,* 856–868.

Rudman, L. A., Greenwald, A. G., Mellott, D. S., & Schwartz, J. L. K. (1999). Measuring the automatic components of prejudice: Flexibility and generality of the Implicit Association Test. *Social Cognition, 17,* 437–465.

Rudman, L. A., & Kilianski, S. E. (2000). Implicit and explicit attitudes toward female authority. *Personality and Social Psychology Bulletin, 26,* 1315–1328.

Schwarz, N., & Bohner, G. (2001). The construction of attitudes. In A. Tesser & N. Schwarz (Eds.), *Blackwell handbook of social psychology: Intraindividual processes* (pp. 436–457). Malden, MA: Blackwell.

Sears, D. O., & Henry, P. J. (2005). Over thirty years later: A contemporary look at symbolic racism and its critics. *Advances in Experimental Social Psychology, 37,* 95–150.

Sekaquaptewa, D., Espinoza, P., Thompson, M., Vargas, P., & von Hippel, W. (2003). Stereotypic explanatory bias: Implicit stereotyping as a predictor of discrimination. *Journal of Experimental Social Psychology, 39,* 75–82.

Sidanius, J., Feshbach, S., Levin, S., & Pratto, F. (1997). The interface between ethnic and national attachment: Ethnic pluralism or ethnic dominance? *Public Opinion Quarterly, 61,* 103–133.

Sidanius, J., & Pratto, F. (1993). The inevitability of oppression and the dynamics of social dominance. In P. Sniderman & P. Tetlock (Eds.), *Prejudice, politics, and the American dilemma* (pp. 173–211). Stanford, CA: Stanford University Press.

Sidanius, J., Pratto, F., Martin, M., & Stallworth, L. (1991). Consensual racism and career track: Some implications of social dominance theory. *Political Psychology, 12,* 691–721.

Sniderman, P. M., & Tetlock, P. E. (1986). Symbolic racism: Problems of motive attribution in political analysis: *Journal of Social Issues, 42,* 129–150.

Son Hing, L. S., Li, W., & Zanna, M. P. (2002). Inducing hypocrisy to reduce prejudicial responses among aversive racists. *Journal of Experimental Social Psychology, 38,* 71-78.

Swim, J. K., Aikin, K. J., Hall, W. S., & Hunter, B. A. (1995). Sexism and racism: Old fashioned and modern prejudices. *Journal of Personality and Social Psychology, 68,* 199–214.

Towles-Schwen, T., & Fazio, R. H. (2006). Automatically-activated racial attitudes as predictors of the success of interracial roommate relationships. *Journal of Experimental Social Psychology, 42,* 698–705.

Vanman, E. J., Paul, B. Y., Ito, T. A., & Miller, N. (1997). The modern face of prejudice and the structural features that moderate the effect of cooperation on affect. *Journal of Personality and Social Psychology, 73,* 941–959.

Vanman, E. J., Saltz, J. L., Nathan, L. R., & Warren, J. A. (2004). Racial discrimination by low-prejudiced Whites: Facial movements as implicit measures of attitudes related to behavior. *Psychological Science, 15,* 711–714.

von Hippel, W., Sekaquaptewa, D., & Vargas, P. (1997). The Linguistic Intergroup Bias as an implicit indicator of prejudice. *Journal of Experimental Social Psychology, 33,* 490-509.

von Hippel, W., Silver, L. A., & Lynch, M. E. (2000). Stereotyping against your will: The role of inhibitory ability in stereotyping and prejudice among the elderly. *Personality and Social Psychology Bulletin, 26,* 523–532.

Weigel, R., & Howes, P. (1985). Conceptions of racial prejudice: Symbolic racism reconsidered. *Journal of Social Issues, 41,* 117–138.

Wheeler, M. E., & Fiske, S. T. (2005). Controlling racial prejudice and stereotyping: Social cognitive goals affect amygdala and stereotype activation. *Psychological Science, 16,* 56–63.

Whitely, B. E. (1999). Right-wing authoritarianism, social dominance orientation, and prejudice. *Journal of Personality and Social Psychology, 77,* 126–134.

Wilson, T. D., Lindsey, S., & Schooler, T. Y. (2000). A model of dual attitudes. *Psychological Review, 107,* 101–126.

Wittenbrink, B., & Henly, J. R. (1996). Creating social reality: Informational social influence and the content of stereotypic beliefs. *Personality and Social Psychology Bulletin, 22,* 598–610.

Wittenbrink, B., Judd, C. M., & Park, B. (1997). Evidence for racial prejudice at the implicit level and its relationship with questionnaire measures. *Journal of Personality and Social Psychology, 72,* 262–274.

Wittenbrink, B., Judd, C. M., & Park, B. (2001a). Evaluative versus conceptual judgments in automatic stereotyping and prejudice. *Journal of Experimental Social Psychology, 37,* 244–252.

Wittenbrink, B., Judd, C. M., & Park, B. (2001b). Spontaneous prejudice in context: Variability in automatically activated attitudes. *Journal of Personality and Social Psychology, 81,* 815–827.

Woodmansee, J. J., & Cook, S. W. (1967). Dimensions of racial attitudes: Their identification and measurement. *Journal of Personality and Social Psychology, 7,* 240–250.

19 Racism in the 21st Century

Michael A. Zárate
University of Texas at El Paso

Many of the world's problems are human made, including racism. Suffice it to say that racism is a long-standing problem—despite the tremendous scholarly investigation for at least the last 60 years. With so much attention, why then have researchers been unable to cure this problem? Simply put, racism is multiply determined. Some causes of racism predict an unwillingness to desire a cure or change. Other models of racism predict a lack of awareness of that racism—thereby avoiding change. Still other models and associated data suggest that racist beliefs are simply well engrained, making it difficult to change those beliefs even if one wants to. Because of these disparate reasons, once one attempts to produce some understanding of a complex behavior like racism, one is also left with the realization that we as a science are far from any real answer.

This chapter explores racism as it is occurring today. In the first section, racism is defined and the focus of this chapter is detailed. The second section presents current manifestations of racism. The third section describes the various models describing racism. Finally, potential solutions are described. When possible, each section highlights areas where research appears to lag behind the theories. The focus of this book precludes extensive discussion of many of the associated theories. For instance, this volume includes chapters on stereotype threat and the common ingroup identity model. Both of those chapters are covered by their original authors (Aronson and Gaertner, respectively). It seems prudent to avoid extensive review of those topics given their treatment by those authors in this volume.

DEFINING RACISM

Jones (1997) defined racism as a special form of prejudice. According to Jones, prejudice is the "positive or negative attitude, judgment, or feeling about a person that is generalized from attitudes or beliefs held about the group to which the person belong" (p. 10). Racism, however, adds to prejudice the following constructs.

> First, the basis of group characteristics is assumed to rest on biology—race is a biological construct. Second, racism has, as a necessary premise, the *superiority* of one's own race. Third, racism rationalizes institutional and culture practices that formalize the hierarchical domination of one racial group over another. (p. 11, italics in original)

Jones's definition brings together the concepts of perceived biological differences and apparent forms of competition and system justification, as well as feelings of self-superiority. Thus, the definition is broad enough that it encompasses most of the modern theories regarding racism.

RACISM AND ETHNICITY

The inclusion of a biological construct in the definition of racism provides room for expansion. Most geneticists and anthropologists agree that race is not a true biological construct (Smedley & Smedley, 2005). At the same time, social psychologists have long distinguished reality from the perceptions of reality. Race is a clear social and political construct, predictive of behavior and therefore worthy of scientific study. In a telephone survey of 600 respondents (Jayaratne et al., 2006), 27% of people reported that genetic influences accounted for some or most race differences across traits. Thus, "[r]ace, as people live and understand it, inhabits a dimension of reality that transcends biology and cannot be reduced to genes, chromosomes, or even phenotypes" (Smedley, 2006, p. 180). Because race as a biological construct is poorly defined, one is left with a much more ambiguous construct than first considered. What are layperson descriptions of race? If race does not exist as a biological construct, is it distinct from ethnicity?

This distinction between racism and ethnic discrimination, however, takes on added meaning in our new millennium. Using a layperson understanding of racism, many forms of racism are actually ethnic prejudice (Jayaratne et al., 2006). That only leads to a potentially diversionary discussion. Is it productive to distinguish racism as a biological construct from ethnicity as a cultural construct during discussions of racism (Helms & Telleyrand, 1997)? Within the context of racism and one chapter, those types of distinctions are probably less than helpful. Many of the pressing issues in the United States, for example, revolve around immigration from Mexico and Latin America and attitudes toward Arabs. In the historical categorization scheme of race, Latinos are probably most often classified as "Caucasian," and should therefore be considered part of the ingroup as far as most Whites are concerned. There has been little empirical research regarding the connections between racism and attitudes toward immigrants. Nevertheless, there is enough evidence to suggest that occasionally, ethnic prejudice is driving the debate regarding immigration. Accordingly, it is difficult to accurately discern what is driving that political debate. In addition, it is open to empirical test to see if people currently distinguish race from ethnicity. Thus, given the ways in which people think about race and ethnicity and the emerging issues in the United States, the two are treated similarly here. The issues are merged despite the realization that layperson distinctions between race and ethnicity might distinguish the types or quality of the associated stereotypes and prejudice.

IS RACISM STILL A PROBLEM?

It seems obvious that racism is alive and well—but also eroding (Dasgupta, McGhee, Greenwald, & Banaji, 2000). Any summary judgments like that, however, must be supported by data. Presented next are some basic indicators of race-based disparities, prejudices, and atrocities. The focus is on the current conditions in the United States, but some world data are also presented. One recognized problem with documenting the existence of racism, however, is the simple fact that many people lie about their attitudes. In fact, the recent explosion of implicit measures of racism (see Fazio & Olsen, 2003, for one review) was predicated partially on the realization that social desirability concerns cloud many self-report measures of racism. The other problem with documenting racism is that racism often goes unnoticed. Racism can influence all facets of life, yet it is hard to specifically identify as it is occurring (Bonilla-Silva, 2001). For instance, one can document the underrepresentation of minorities among elected and appointed officials (Bonilla-Silva, 2001, p. 101), but also find it virtually impossible to identify any specific instance of racism. For all these reasons, the first section focuses on basic indexes of racial disparities. Later sections identify the subtle ways in which prejudice is expressed.

DOES RACE PREDICT QUALITY OF LIFE?

One way to determine if racism still exists is to document any differences in quality of life across groups. Income is the easiest to document. The Census Bureau's most recent data (DeNavas-Walt, Procter, & Lee, 2006) show that in 2005, the median income for White non-Hispanics was $50,784, whereas the median income for Blacks was $30,858, and $35,967 for Hispanics. Thus, Blacks and Hispanics earn 61% and 71% of what Whites do, respectively. In contrast, the median income for Asians was $61,094, suggesting that more than just racism predicts income. Overall, these numbers differed little from 2004 and are only marginally better than in 1995. Thus, can race or ethnicity be a valid predictor of how much one earns? Yes. Is this a measure of racism or discrimination? It is certainly one measure, but income encompasses more than just racism in the workplace. Educational attainment is one predictor of income.

Regarding educational attainment, the U.S. Census Bureau (2005) reported that 91.5% of Whites between the ages of 20 and 24 have obtained a high school diploma. In contrast, only 82.5% of Blacks and 66.8% of Hispanics those same ages earned a high school diploma. Thus, maybe income is only a logical consequence of differential educational attainment. This begs the next question: Can we identify differences in the quality of the schools that Latinos, Blacks, and Whites attend, and can that predict differential educational paths? For example, can the makeup of the schools predict how much funding per student that school receives? Questions like this only highlight a never-ending cycle of issues. Nevertheless, it is fair to say that yes, race predicts quality of life in America, at least as quality of life is defined in the traditional American ways, which are income and education.

RACISM IN THE WORKPLACE

One obvious predictor of differential income across racial groups is workplace discrimination. Identifying workplace discrimination, however, is particularly difficult. One central goal within social psychology has been to document the implicit biases people have and the subtle ways in which people discriminate. Those efforts are particularly needed in workplace environments where individuals have two reasons to hide their racism. First, as with most situations, it is socially unacceptable to express ones' racist attitudes. Just as important, there are legal consequences for using race inappropriately in the workforce. Those increased motives make identifying workplace discrimination more difficult than usual.

Many treatments of workplace discrimination start out with the classic research by Word, Zanna, and Cooper (1974). Across two studies, Word et al. demonstrated that Black applicants are treated differently than White applicants (less eye contact, less interview time, etc.). Just as important, those differences translate into poorer interview performances later by Black and White interviewees. In effect, self-fulfilling prophecies produced poorer performance by Blacks in the interview situation. Because of the difficult nature of the study, true replications are hard to identify. Nevertheless, conceptually, the more critical components are readily replicated. Across at least three studies, data show that targets of racism are often good judges of the degree to which another person is racist or sexist (Dovidio, Kawakami, & Gaertner, 2002; Fazio, Jackson, Dunton, & Williams, 1995; McConnell & Leibold, 2001). For example, McConnell and Leibold (2001) demonstrated a positive relationship between explicit measures of prejudice and experimenters' evaluations of biased interactions with participants ($r = .33, p < .05$). Participants who reported favoring Whites over Blacks on an implicit measure of racism were rated as interacting more positively with a White experimenter than with a Black experimenter by the experimenters themselves. Thus, the experimenters who interacted with the prejudiced participants were able to identify prejudiced reactions from the participants. The multiple studies showing this effect demonstrate that this is a consistent phenomenon.

If people can identify racist attitudes in others, it must impact their overall job performance. Unfortunately, there is little research on this effect in the workplace. The existent research is often self-report evidence of discrimination, using samples with particularly low return rates. It seems that regarding the workforce, one is left to assume that the college students used in most of the published research are many of the same individuals who later become employees and managers.

Structural factors can also impact overall performance beyond any personal levels of racism or prejudice. For example, Niemann-Flores and Dovidio (1998) showed that in academic settings, minorities, and especially solo minorities, felt particularly stigmatized and less satisfied than their White counterparts. Being a solo minority produces a feeling of tokenism that can highlight group membership, which can then impair on-the-job performance. One test of that most specific hypothesis was offered by Roberson, Deitch, Brief, and Block (2003). Roberson et al. surveyed 166 African

American managers. As predicted, solo managers felt greater stereotype threat than did other managers. Here, stereotype threat was measured rather than manipulated. A sample item included "Some people feel I have less ability because of my race" (p. 181). The results were disturbing in that greater stereotype threat also predicted discounting workplace feedback. Managers who felt greater stereotype threat tended to dismiss feedback and doubted its accuracy and worried more about the motivations for the feedback.

CULTURAL INDICATORS OF QUALITY OF LIFE

In the modern world of "modern racism" (McConahay, 1986), the political issues have changed. Busing, school desegregation, and related topics are still relevant. In addition, new issues have taken hold and have sometimes taken the spotlight. Bilingual education, voting rights acts, and immigration are often the visible issues. These issues correlate with the changing demographics in the United States. Latinos are now the largest ethnic minority in the country. As groups become large enough to be perceived as a threat (Ruddell & Urbina, 2004), be it cultural or economic (Zárate, Garcia, Garza, & Hitlan, 2004), they become more salient targets of prejudice.

For instance, in the past few years, 30 states have adopted English as their official language (U.S. English Incorporated, 2008). Several more states have gone a step further, implementing specific English-on-the-job laws. A number of legal cases suggest that individuals feel excluded, ostracized, or offended when others in their work environment communicate with one another in a language other than English (*Garcia v. Spun Steak Co.*, 1994; *Jurado v. Eleven-Fifty Corp.*, 1987). The common theme running through these cases is that individuals were speaking Spanish, which offended others. In some cases, the persons speaking Spanish were having private conversations over lunch, yet others were bothered. Given the changing demographics and increased Latino presence in the United States (U.S. Census Bureau, 2007), it is expected that there will be a growing backlash against Latino immigrants.

The reaction toward the growing Latino population is consistent with other data supporting a national threat hypothesis. Ruddell and Urbina (2004) investigated incarceration rates across 140 nations. They investigated the relation between population heterogeneity and imprisonment rates across the countries. As nations become more diverse, they imprison a larger proportion of their population and are more likely to utilize the death penalty. Ruddell and Urbina utilized a measure of heterogeneity that also included ethnicity and religion, which further supports the argument that racism should be broadly defined. The underlying idea is that people often purport to enjoy diversity and new cultures, but only until they perceive that group to be a threat. Once a group becomes large enough, the group is viewed as a threat and others react in prejudiced fashions.

Disentangling well-meaning motives from racist motives in political decision making can be difficult. For instance, social psychologists seem to associate conservatism with racism, especially regarding attitudes toward affirmative action, and that probably unfairly characterizes a number of well-meaning individuals and their motives (cf. Reyna, Henry, Korfmacher, & Tucker, 2005; Sidanius, Pratto, & Bobo, 1996; Son Hing, Bobocel, & Zanna, 2002). Nevertheless, racism and conservatism are often confused. For instance, in 2004, Arizona passed Proposition 200, a state referendum designed to force proof of citizenship to register to vote. One can interpret that vote in any number of ways, many of which are nonracist. One thing is clear, however. The group that supported that referendum was partially directed by avowed racial separatists (the Protect Arizona Now initiative), clouding the issue tremendously. Thus, although some of the new issues surrounding immigration and politics are no doubt driven by well-meaning ideological differences, as with prior political issues, they might also reflect how racism is expressed in the modern world.

HEALTH AND STRESS

The U.S. Department of Health and Human Services details the many ways in which racial disparities are reflected in our health standards (National Center for Health Statistics, 2004). The effects of racism and the associated stress are evident early on (Giscombé & Lobel, 2005) and continue through the life span. The effects are seen in the mortality rates, incarceration rates, physical and mental health, health treatment options, and in seemingly every meaningful marker of health. It is virtually impossible to disentangle socioeconomic status from race in understanding health outcomes. One must also argue that those socioeconomic factors are indicators of racism in addition to predicting negative health outcomes. Nevertheless, the literature is clear that "the consistency of the finding that discrimination is associated with higher rates of disease is quite robust" (Williams, Neighbors, & Jackson, 2003, p. 202).

How might racism affect health? One avenue is through the added stress associated with dealing with racist behavior. Brondolo, Rieppi, Kelly, and Gerin (2003) reviewed the existing literature testing the explicit links among racism, blood pressure, and hypertension. They reported that while the evidence testing the link between racism and measures of blood pressure and hypertension is mixed, the lab evidence is clear. They concluded from their review that "acute exposure to racism is associated with increases in cardiovascular activation. In addition, past exposure to racism may influence current" reactions to stressors as well (p. 61). Future research will need to identify the specific mechanisms beyond cardiovascular response that are negatively influenced by racism.

IMPLICIT PREJUDICE

Possibly the most extensive evidence of prejudice has been developed by social cognitive researchers investigating implicit prejudice (Greenwald, McGhee, & Schwartz, 1998). Implicit attitudes are those attitudes that are either below conscious awareness or well practiced and therefore automatic. Implicit measures of attitudes are those measures that do not directly ask for the desired response. Rather, the measures are either indirect or subtle and prejudice is inferred. There are multiple motives for understanding implicit attitudes and implicit measures. One motive is purely theoretical. What is the structure of attitudes? Are they unidimensional (meaning that implicit attitudes should always correlate with explicit attitudes) or are they multifaceted? Are people even aware of their racist attitudes? What type of attitude best predicts discrimination? The second reason is equally important. Social desirability concerns obviously influence overt responses to prejudice measures. Thus, although it is fair to say that prejudice is eroding, it is also fair to say that some apparent reduction in prejudice is because participants consciously mask their true attitudes. It is no longer socially acceptable to express one's racist attitudes, and therein lies one motivation for developing implicit measures of prejudice.

The ways in which racism are measured have gone through a clear theoretical progression. Some of the first subtle measures included the Modern Racism measures (McConahay, 1986; McConahay & Hough, 1976). The measures were based on the recognition that many persons publicly reject or otherwise disavow themselves of traditionally racist beliefs. According to this type of model, racism is expressed symbolically (Sears, 1988) or indirectly through the endorsement of political and social attitudes that preserve racial inequalities.

More recently, however, the field has seen an explosion of even more subtle implicit measures of prejudice. One can identify any number of implicit measures, the most famous of which has been the Implicit Associations Test (IAT; Greenwald et al., 1998). The IAT measures the automatic or underlying associations between group labels (or faces, names, and other symbols of a group) with positive or negative evaluations. For example, Experiment 3 of Greenwald et al. (1998) asked participants to pair Black and White faces with positive and negative words. Participants are asked to respond to two sets of tasks. Often, they are asked to distinguish positive and negative words on one task, and Black and White faces on a supposedly unrelated but interlaced task. Thus, participants are required to respond with one hand to White and good, and the other hand to Black and bad (or vice versa). Bias is interpreted as the differential speed to respond with the same hand (associate) to the two race terms with positive or negative terms. In Greenwald et al., participants were clearly faster at associating White with positive than Black with positive. Moreover, their implicit responses were unrelated to their responses on explicit measures of prejudice. The IAT is impressive because it seems one can get the effect even if one warns the participants of what it measures. Moreover, responses show adequate reliability and validity (Cunningham, Preacher, & Banaji, 2001).

The IAT builds on previous literature using semantic priming methodologies to identify automatically activated attitudes (e.g., Dovidio, Evans, & Tyler, 1986; Zárate & Smith, 1990). It also reflects a developing theoretical perspective that suggests one can utilize well-practiced processes to identify tendencies participants might otherwise avoid expressing. Thus, participants often seem aware that prejudice is being measured. They are unaware of the fact that small response speed differences (e.g., 40 msec) can demonstrate racial bias with predictive utility. For instance, McConnell and Leibold (2001) demonstrated that more bias on an IAT predicted more negative interactions with a Black experimenter and more negative responses on an explicit measure of prejudice. The IAT identifies bias beyond any cultural-level associations between the color white and good versus the color black and bad (Smith-McAllen, Johnson, Dovidio, & Pearson, 2006). The effect occurs even if one controls for differential familiarity with Whites versus Blacks (Dasgupta et al., 2000). The explosive interest in the IAT as a methodological tool has earned some critical responses (cf. Blanton, Jaccard, Gonzales, & Christie, 2006; Olson & Fazio, 2004), but overall, the IAT has proven to be a valuable tool in understanding or identifying racism. Individuals consistently express more prejudice via the IAT than they do with more explicit measures of prejudice.

Implicit measures like the IAT are helpful in that they help identify many of the subtle ways that people stereotype others but are unable or unwilling to express. From a layperson's perspective, however, the measures are sometimes arcane. How can a few milliseconds actually predict later behavior? Towles-Schwen and Fazio (2006) demonstrated the predictive effects of implicit measures of racism. The participants of interest were students randomly paired in the dorms with either same-race or other-race living mates. The implicit measure of racism was given at the start of the semester. The main measure was if the participants were still living together at the end of the year. Participants were presented with photographs of Black, White, Asian, and Latino targets. The photos were used as primes within an evaluative judgment task. Following each face, participants were asked to respond to various positive and negative traits. Participants were asked to identify if each word was positive or negative, irrespective of the prime face. The relative degree to which the various faces facilitated responses to positive versus negative words served as the implicit measure. As expected, the best predictor of relationship status after the year was the implicit measure. Participants who demonstrated the greatest ingroup bias were the participants least likely to still be living with their other-race roommates.

The interest in the IAT coincides with a larger theoretical movement to identify multiple subtle or implicit ways in which racism is expressed. Many of these other measures are also more implicit in the sense that participants appear completely unaware of how racism is being measured or even that racism is being measured at all. One notable example is the stereotypic explanatory bias (SEB; Sekaquaptewa, Espinoza, Thompson, Vargas, & von Hippel (2003). The SEB occurs when individuals explain away or justify behavior when the behavior is inconsistent with their stereotype. Thus, if one assumes that all Latinos are lazy, for instance, one is more likely to explain why a particular Latino is not lazy than explain why a different Latino is lazy. The beauty of the methodology is that people appear unaware of how or when they produce the effect. This makes the measure particularly implicit. Sekaquaptewa et al. (2003) demonstrated that the tendency to explain Black-inconsistent events predicts more negative interactions with a Black partner. It is interesting to note that the SEB did not correlate with an IAT measure. This dissociation suggests that not all implicit measures are tapping into the same process. This type of dissociation is being investigated to fully disentangle the various processes.

ETHNIC CLEANSING

Probably the most compelling reason to merge together ethnic discrimination and racism is ethnic cleansing. Reports of ethnic cleansing continue, despite the horrible memory of the Nazi Holocaust. In Kosovo, Kosovar Albanians have been the victims of ethnic cleansing at the hands of Serbian forces. The very nature of the atrocities precludes accurate reports regarding the numbers of victims. The U.S. State Department reports that between 6,000 and 11,000 Albanians were killed. The atrocities do not stop there. Over 1.5 million Albanians were forcibly expelled from their homes, in multiple cities women were systematically raped, and thousands of homes were destroyed (U.S. State Department, 1999). Human Rights Watch (2006) described similar ethnic cleansing in West Dafur between two ethnically similar groups. The current fighting in Iraq between Sunni and Shiite Muslims is another example of ethnic cleansing. Thus, some of the worst forms of racial prejudice have been between ethnically similar groups. The one similarity among all of these conflicts is the correlation between small ethnic differences and religious differences. Thus, one argument is that researchers studying racism might attend more to religious prejudice as well. I do not know of any data supporting this, but it appears that people are more willing to express their religious prejudices than their racial prejudices. More important, it seems as if they are more willing to act on those beliefs. Thus, an analysis of the truly horrendous group conflicts suggests that too little attention has been paid to religious conflicts.

WHAT DRIVES RACISM?

Given the complex nature of racism and the multifaceted way it is expressed, it should not be surprising that there are any number of theories that predict racism. Each model or predictor has its own predictive utility. As with many predictors of any human behavior, however, most model building appears to have progressed with little attention to alternative models. Thus, although one can find tremendous evidence in support of any one model, one is left searching for answers regarding when each model is most predictive (Greenwald, Pratkanis, Leippe, & Baumgardner, 1986). Nevertheless, the types of theories one can bring to bear on racism are impressive.

Regarding the types of theories being tested, they fit well with Jones's definition of racism. In particular, most models appear based on essentialism, self-concepts, economic competition, and system-justifying motives. The models are diverse in origin and are rarely mutually exclusive. It also seems that some types of models can support or otherwise produce other effects, but at this stage, it is difficult to accurately determine what model drives what. Outlined next are a sampling of the diverse approaches toward understanding racism.

ESSENTIALISM

Jones's definition of racism includes a biological component that we suspect might drive many racist attitudes. Racist attitudes are presumed to derive from basic genetic differences between groups. Within an essentialist framework, differences between groups "are taken to represent human types, specifying that an individual is fundamentally a certain sort of person. Racism attempts to fix social groups in terms of essential, quasi-natural properties" (Verkuyten, 2003, p. 371). Thus, people perceive an essence or coherent structure underlying the different groups. Similarly, but within a different theoretical framework, Yzerbyt, Rocher, and Schadron (1997) contended that certain large social categories, like race, are perceived of as natural kinds that produce more group entitativity. Because these differences are fundamental properties of the person and the group to which they belong, they are also conceived of as natural and unavoidable. Because they are natural and unavoidable, more stable dispositional inferences are drawn regarding the behaviors of the person (Sekaquaptewa et al., 2003). Consistent with theorizing by Jayaratne et al. (2006), lay theories of essentialism are best characterized as "organized belief structures" (p. 79) that reflect a conceptualized framework for understanding group differences.

On an intuitive basis, a clear understanding of an essentialist approach seems paramount in understanding how people think about race. Nevertheless, there is surprisingly little empirical research on the topic. Jayaratne et al. (2006) showed that the more White participants endorsed a genetic model to explain race differences, the more bothered they would be if their son or daughter dated an African American. This effect held for more traditional measures (modern racism) of racism as well.

Haslam and colleagues (e.g., Bastian & Haslam, 2006; Haslam, Rothschild, & Ernst, 2002) developed a research program investigating essentialism and stereotyping. The basic idea rests on work by Levy, Stroessner, and Dweck on implicit person theories. Levy et al. (1998) found that some individuals they labeled entity theorists make more stereotypic judgments of others than those they labeled incremental theorists. Entity theorists believe that people change little over time and are the way they are because of human nature. Consistent with that general framework, Bastian and Haslam (2006) showed that the more one adheres to an essentialist framework, the more one endorses group differences. This endorsement was predicted after controlling for other forms of racism. Thus, essentialist beliefs appear to contribute unique variance to the predictability of stereotyping and prejudice. This general idea seems central to many definitions of racism and is an exciting new direction in racism research.

SOCIAL IDENTITY THEORY

Much of the modern social psychological theorizing has derived from social identity theory (SIT) as proposed by Tajfel and Turner (1986). SIT states that individuals attempt to achieve a positive social identity, and that this is accomplished partly through positive comparisons between the ingroup and relevant outgroups. The model includes both motivational and cognitive components. On the motivational side, people are theorized to desire a positive self-esteem. They do this by derogating relevant outgroups to make the ingroup appear more positive.

The cognitive component entails the process through which perceptions are driven by group memberships. Thus, the mere identification of differential group memberships is sufficient to produce ingroup favoritism. SIT predicts then, that the ability to differentiate groups is enough to produce prejudice. As such, person categorization has become one of the primary issues in social cognition. If true, this portends a never-ending racism in this country. Previous immigrant groups, for instance, assimilated relatively quickly, as least as compared to Blacks and Latinos. In the early 1900s, the immigrant groups were often from different European countries. Those groups provide fewer perceptual differences between the groups than do Europeans and most Latinos, African Americans, and Asians. The ability to differentiate the groups, then, should lead to a continued racism toward ethnic minorities. This general approach has dominated modern social psychology. Outlined next are some ramifications of the general approach.

SOCIAL CATEGORIZATION

Two of the most influential models in person perception, Brewer's (1988) dual-process model of impression formation and Fiske and Neuberg's (1990) continuum model, are parallel and serial process models, respectively. The ways in which person and group representations interact can have important consequences for stereotype change processes, yet this issue is somewhat understudied.

Fiske and Neuberg (1990) stated that

the [continuum] model proposes four general impression-formation processes: the rapid, "perceptual" initial categorization process that requires no attention to potentially individuating attributes, and three "thoughtful" processes— confirmatory categorization, recategorization, and piecemeal integration— that do require attention to and interpretation of potentially individuating target information. (p. 12)

Within the model, the first premise is that category-based processes "have priority over attribute-based processes" (p. 2). Depending on the target fit with any preexisting categories, perceiver motivation, and other social factors, the perceiver either stops at the categorical level, or proceeds to make attribute-based (which we interpret as person-based) inferences.

Brewer (1988) stated that "the primary distinction drawn in the model is that between processing states that are category-based and processing that is person-based (personalized). The two types of processing result in different representations of the same social information" (p. 5). This model is also more clearly a dual-process model (see Livingston & Brewer, 2002). In fact, at some levels, person identification is the primary process involved (Brewer, 1988, p. 5).

The common theme running through these highly influential models is the idea that the initial categorization should predict the types of inferences made about the person. To that end, the data strongly support that basic hypothesis. Dovidio et al. (1986) were the first to demonstrate this basic construct. Participants were presented with a series of race categories (Black, White) as primes. Following each prime, a test word was presented—some of which were stereotypic traits. Participants responded faster to the stereotypic terms when they matched the category label. Included in the terms were positive and negative traits as well. As predicted, participants also demonstrated an evaluative bias. Black primes produced faster responses to negative terms, and White primes produced faster responses to positive terms.

Zárate and Smith (1990) demonstrated a similar effect, but with pictures. In the main study of interest, they demonstrated that the faster White participants categorized targets by race, the more likely they were to ascribe race-stereotypic terms to others. Finally, Stroessner (1996) showed that African Americans are categorized faster as Black than White Americans are categorized as White. If speed of categorization predicts the degree of stereotyping, and Blacks are categorized fastest by race, it suggests that Blacks are much more likely to be stereotyped by race than are Whites.

Our own work on this topic suggests also that race- and person-based perception are antagonistic processes (Sanders, McClure & Zárate, 2004; Zárate, Sanders, & Garza, 2000). We have used visual field paradigms whereby faces are presented to either the left or right visual field. The information is then processed first by the contralateral hemisphere. Zárate et al. (2000) produced a series of related findings. One of the primary findings is that person and group information are processed differently. Ingroup and outgroup faces act as primes for positive and negative descriptors (respectively) only when presented to the left hemisphere. People demonstrate memory for the specific faces only in the right hemisphere. Current work is investigating the hypothesis that perceiving a person via group-based features inhibits the ability to perceive them as individuals. Later work has further delineated the neurocognitive underpinnings of social perception, all of which is reviewed elsewhere in this volume.

INDIVIDUAL DIFFERENCE VARIABLES

The social cognitive research cited earlier attempts to delineate the normal processes associated with stereotyping and prejudice. The underlying idea is that stereotyping and prejudice are normal by-products of our need to comprehend and interact with the social environment. In contrast to that approach are multiple types of individual difference factors that highlight seemingly motivational approaches to stereotyping and prejudice. Prejudice is no longer considered a normal by-product, but is something that is desired as a way to justify the status quo or to otherwise explain the current situation. Thus, stereotyping and prejudice are considered normal only in that most people hold some degree of motivation to justify the status quo. Prejudice is not, however, a necessarily expected outcome. The two models that have dominated the recent research domain are social dominance orientation and system justification approaches. Each is briefly outlined here.

One of the more influential theories has been social dominance orientation. Sidanius, Pratto, van Laar, and Levin (2004) conceptualized social dominance theory as a structural and psychological framework that identifies the ways in which societies develop group-based oppression strategies. Within this framework, racism is just one of the ways that people discriminate other groups to enhance their own group standing. Wealth is allocated to the powerful and actively kept from the less powerful groups. Within the theory is social dominance orientation, which is an active attempt to promote racism by the dominant group to enhance their overall standing. The individual difference factor derives from one's desire to enhance the group-based hierarchy. The degree to which people accept and promote the group-based hierarchy reflects their overall prejudice levels and reflects their overall orientation.

Similarly, the system justification approach (Jost & Hunyady, 2005; Jost, Kivetz, Rubini, Guermandi, & Mosso, 2005) posits that people develop an ideology or understanding of the world that supports the current status quo. According to the theory, people are motivated to justify the current situation or cultural system. One interesting aspect of the theory is that the motivation comes from disadvantaged groups as much as from individuals from advantaged groups. One way this occurs is to develop victim-enhancing stereotypes. Thus, disadvantaged ethnic groups often buy into statements such as "We may not be rich, but we are warm and happy" (Jost et al., 2005).

Summary

How do the various theories work together to produce the types of racism one sees at all levels of society? The nature of the models predicts few integrative programs of research. Thus, one can find studies whereby only those high in social dominance orientation, for example, produce particular implicit stereotyping effects consistent with the categorization view, but beyond that, the models appear to work in relative isolation. If one believes that racism is indeed multiply determined, however, this relative isolation makes perfect sense. I suspect that researchers will start to integrate the various models, particularly as we learn more about layperson theories of essentialism.

SOLUTIONS

When I am lecturing on racism, students sometimes ask me when I believe racism will stop. In my more pessimistic moments, I respond with "When Martians attack." My response reflects some well-known theories about racism (Sherif, Harvey, White, Hood, & Sherif, 1961). In this section, methods of combating racism are discussed. When possible, I focus on studies that have used race-based experimental groups. As already discussed, racism is possibly distinct from other forms of prejudice for a number of reasons. In particular, the essentialism discussed previously may provide more stable or otherwise distinct forms of prejudice that go beyond school affiliation or minimal group situations. Minimal group situations or school or political affiliation manipulations, however, provide still other problems. The most salient feature distinguishing the minimal group situation from race is the degree to which participants identify with the minimal group versus their own ethnic group. Degree of identification with the group is an important variable in intergroup interactions (Spears, Doosje, & Ellemers, 1997). Another important distinction between minimal groups or school affiliations versus ethnic groups is the degree to which the group memberships are permeable (Ellemers, van Knippenberg, & Wilke, 1990; Jackson, Sullivan, Harnish, & Hodge, 1996). Race, unlike minimal groups or even sports affiliations, is nonpermeable. One can choose to highlight racial identity, or even ignore it, but one cannot change the group, nor presume others will ignore the grouping. Because of the nonpermeable and salient nature of ethnic relationships, generalizations from minimal groups may prove misleading.

Regarding the targets of discrimination, what options do people have in reactions to racism? The options can be divided along personal reactions and group reactions. Regarding personal reactions, one can confirm the stereotype or confront the stereotype. One can also ignore the stereotype, which is probably rather common but also a relatively unstudied option (Crosby, 1984).

Group-level actions take on a different approach. With group-level actions, particular individuals or even actions are not necessary. Rather, the group acts as a collective to form a group identity or to combat institutional forms of racism. Specific people or racist actions are not always central. Regarding group actions, one can legally protest or form a group identity. One can also choose to highlight an assimilation view of intergroup relations, or a multicultural view of intergroup reactions (Berry, 1984). Those approaches are discussed last.

STEREOTYPE CONFIRMATION

This volume contains a chapter on stereotype threat processes (Steele, 1997; Steele & Aronson, 1995) that precludes extensive coverage in this chapter. Nevertheless, the importance of the effect warrants some discussion of the associated research. One way in which stereotypes are inadvertently confirmed is via stereotype threat, which occurs when a known stereotype influences stereotype-relevant task performance. A typical measure is to provide various Graduate Record Exam type questions to African Americans. The typical manipulation is to suggest to the students that the test measures intellectual performance or is unrelated to intellectual ability. When told it measures intellectual performance, students often perform worse. One common stereotype is that African Americans lack the same intellectual ability as Whites. Because of that, the performance inadvertently supports the very stereotype most people find offensive. The stereotype then becomes a self-fulfilling prophecy. The effect is particularly interesting given the fact that at least for gender stereotypes (Schmader, 2002), the more one identifies with the group, the more likely one is to confirm the stereotype. This becomes paradoxical in nature in that the more one opposes the stereotype, the more likely one is to support it.

Stereotypes are confirmed in a number of different ways, although as with other areas reviewed in this chapter, not all areas of research appear to attempt to disentangle when one process might predict behavior better than other processes. Wheeler and Petty (2001), however, disentangle ideomotor processes from stereotype threat processes regarding stereotype confirmation effects. Basically, simply activating stereotypes can then produce subsequent behavior in ways consistent with that general stereotype.

Ideomotor processes are reflected as behavioral priming effects. They are proposed to follow automatically once primed and without conscious awareness. They result from a simple semantic association between a stereotype and the associated behaviors. Because stereotypes are often associated with related behaviors, activation of the stereotype activates that behavior, making it more likely to be performed.

CONFRONTATIONAL APPROACHES

Either purposefully or nonconsciously supporting the stereotypes seems like a poor option given the fact that many if not most stereotypes are negative in character (Rothbart & Park, 1986). The clearest option, then, is to protest racism. That form of protest can also take multiple forms. Neither option studied, however, appears ideal.

In a particularly important study by Kaiser and Miller (2001), participants rated an African American male as more "hypersensitive, emotional, argumentative, irritating, trouble making, and complaining" when he attributed his failure on a test to discrimination rather than to the quality of his answers or to the difficulty of the test. This was found regardless of how much discrimination the participants were told the person actually faced. Most important, the study showed that the negative evaluation was not due to simply not taking blame for the failure. When the attribution was made to the difficulty of the test, also an external factor, the target was not rated negatively as when he attributed his failure to discrimination. Thus, the negative evaluations derived purely from identifying a racist situation.

In a later study, Kaiser and Miller (2003) further tested their hypothesis by allowing the participants to see the discrimination firsthand. In this study participants were told that they were going to be aiding in the evaluation of an employment interviewing process. They were handed the interviewer's notes where the interviewer expressed high, moderate, or low discriminatory comments, and were told that the interviewee attributed his failure to get the job to either discrimination, interview skills, or competition for the job. As in the first study, participants were rated as more hypersensitive, emotional, complaining, and so on, when they attributed their job rejection to discrimination, regardless of the degree of racism that the interviewer expressed in his or her comments. This study examined a more realistic setting in which discrimination may occur and allowed participants to directly witness the discrimination in the interviewers' notes. Despite the evidence, participants still evaluated the victim negatively when he attributed his job rejection to discrimination. Later work by Kaiser and colleagues (Kaiser, Dyrenforth, & Hagiwara, 2006) shows that individuals high in system-justifying belief ideologies are particularly punitive toward the victims of racism.

Thus, the consequences for complaining are real. The victims are derogated and seen negatively—even by observers who are privy to the racist information. It would be one thing for people to react negatively at being labeled a racist, but another for a casual observer to also react negatively toward the victim of racism. This is striking given the supposed social rules against expressing prejudice. One argument is that although openly expressing prejudice is against the social norms, there is a stronger social norm against identifying a racist act. This is particularly interesting in light of the already cited studies showing that perceivers can in fact accurately identify racist individuals.

A more confrontational form of protest against racism is to directly confront racist comments (Czopp, Monteith, & Mark, 2006). What are the effects of directly labeling behaviors as racist immediately after those behaviors occur in a conversation? The potential effects are tremendous. Aversive racism research demonstrates that people desire to be egalitarian (Dovidio & Gaertner, 2004). Aversive racism research also suggests that people are occasionally forced to reconcile their own racist attitudes with their desire to be egalitarian, and that this generally produces discomfort. In addition, given the strong social norms against racism, challenging individuals might also produce a sense of social challenge as opposed to just interpersonal challenge (assuming the victim is not then derogated by others in the conversation). The final avenue of change is that confrontations may make individuals more wary of future conversations (which, unfortunately, may simply increase racism), meaning there will be even less long-term change. Thus, for many reasons, openly challenging racist comments might very well prove to have long-term benefits.

Across three studies, Czopp et al. (2006) led participants to say sentences that could be easily construed as racist. Confederates then challenged those comments. The less threatening challenges produced more negative self-directed affect among the participants, which then reduced subsequent stereotyping. This effect was similar across Black and White confederates (confronters), suggesting that this effect can be readily used by minorities as well. Finally, confrontations also produced more negative evaluations of the confronter. Czopp et al. also reported contradictory evidence that White confronters can be more persuasive than Black confronters, and future research will need to empirically disentangle those divergent findings.

The problem with this methodology is reflected in how racist attitudes are usually expressed. The implicit social cognition measures are based on the realization that people rarely openly express their racist attitudes. Rather, racism is often expressed in very subtle forms. If one is to believe the studies by Dovidio et al. (2002), Fazio et al. (1995), and McConnell and Liebold (2001), people can accurately identify racist individuals, even when people are consciously masking their true attitudes. Intuition suggests that challenges toward subtle racism will produce far more reactance. Thus, this methodology is contingent on the idea that Whites will confront racist Whites to defend ethnic minorities. How often that will occur in the real world is open to empirical investigation.

Nevertheless, this is a promising line of research with a number of questions to be asked: What are the conditions for this to be effective? When are minorities effective and what are the repercussions? What are the conditions that would drive Whites to defend minorities? One particularly important question is this: What are the ramifications when minorities make claims of racism to subtle expressions of racism? A colleague of mine uses a great example. He is African American. He asks, "How do I respond if someone tells me 'You are very articulate'?" In this instance, the racism would be subtle. The person would be expressing surprise at meeting an articulate Black man. It is, however, a socially acceptable sentence and it is not explicitly racist. What would be the consequences of responding to that comment with a claim of racism?

COLLECTIVE APPROACHES TO PREJUDICE REDUCTION

The types of changes discussed next are psychological in nature, meaning the individual is driving the process. Nevertheless, these approaches also suggest a level of group identity and often reflect how groups of individuals react to the larger sociological context. Both approaches derive from the contact hypothesis, the simple idea that "contact between members of different groups will improve relations between them" (Hewstone, 1996, p. 327). Theoretically, stereotyping and prejudice are due to ignorance about the stereotyped group and its members, and contact reduces that ignorance (Stephan & Stephan, 1984). With enough contact with outgroup members, individuals learn to modify their previously held stereotypes and develop new and nonstereotypic attitudes.

Since Allport (1954), the idea has received extensive attention (Pettigrew, 1998; Wright, Aron, McLaughlin-Volpe, & Tropp, 1997). The subsequent research, however, has provided a number of limiting conditions necessary for contact to provide the most attitude change (Cook, 1978; Rothbart & John, 1985; Stephan, 1985). Contact assumes that over time, individuals learn to ignore group memberships and treat each other purely as individuals. Another possibility, however, is that contact might produce an appreciation of group differences that would then reduce prejudice. Outlined next are two distinct approaches that reflect that distinction.

COMMON INGROUP IDENTITY

When students ask about the end of racism, and I reply with "When Martians attack," I am responding with a common ingroup identity philosophy (Dovidio, Gaertner, & Validzic, 1998). The general idea is that one way to eliminate prejudice is to eliminate group boundaries. To do that, the most common process is to identify a common enemy or superordinate goal. One rarely expresses group-based prejudice against other ingroup members. The evidence supporting the common ingroup identity model is clear. Nier et al. (2001), for instance, recruited participants as they were entering a football game. There were two manipulations of interest. First, White fans were approached by either a White or Black experimenter. Second, the experimenter was wearing a cap from the same school as the football fan (identified via clothing worn by the fan) or from the opposing team. Participants were more compliant with the Black experimenter when the experimenter was from the same school as the fan. Thus, individuals were more positive toward individuals when they were from the same group. Even in the highly charged world of sports, a common identity overwhelms race. In the occasional brawl during games, never have the brawls been between the races. Invariably, brawls entail two teams going against each, not two races of players. That characterizes the common ingroup identity approach.

As a collective approach, it is consistent with an assimilation or melting pot model of intergroup relations. Thus, maybe everyone should simply label themselves as "American" rather than use any hyphenated labels and assimilate toward the norm (Berry, 1984; Berry, Poortinga, Segall, & Dasen, 2002). Berry identified a number of different ways in which groups merge. Within his framework are four distinct styles of intergroup relations—assimilation, integration, segregation-separation, and deculturation or marginalization. Assimilation, which appears intuitively appealing for many

Americans, entails a strategy whereby smaller minority groups relinquish their cultural identity and adopt the cultural ways of the dominant group. Within this assimilation type framework, one can assimilate in two ways. One can envision a "melting pot" whereby each group adds a distinct taste to the overall group culture and at any one time, the prevailing culture is a sort of weighted average of the constituent cultures. In practice, however, the norm is for new ethnic groups to simply relinquish their own identity and adopt the mainstream identity. Thus, the culture is essentially unchanged over time—even with the addition of new ethnic groups.

Consistent with that are societal pressures to make groups adapt to the dominant culture. For example, English-only laws are a relatively new phenomenon within the United States. Currently, there are 26 states with English-only laws, and all of them have been adopted since 1975, making them a new phenomenon. Language use is only one example, but a symbolically important example. Take, for example, the uproar in the summer of 2006 over a Spanish-language version of the U.S. national anthem. "The Star-Spangled Banner" was translated into Spanish and recorded and it received tremendous calls of protest. This was only one small but clear example of the constant pressures for groups to adapt particular cultural styles. Berry makes one point clear: Assimilation strategies are based on the assertion that there is a negative evaluation of the minority group. Thus, the attempts to sublimate the ethnic culture are from a conscious attempt to eradicate that cultural influence.

Under other conditions, however, it may be impossible to ignore group memberships. To the extent that persons develop self-esteem from that group identification, attempts to ignore or denigrate group identity can theoretically produce even greater prejudice. In summary and in principle, a common ingroup identity sounds appealing, but as stated by Crocker, Major, and Steele (1998),

> Despite the attractiveness of a society in which race, gender, disability, sexual orientation, or other social identities are irrelevant, it is rare (and perhaps impossible) for non-stigmatized individuals who are steeped in the cultural meaning of these identities to be truly "blind" to their significance in interactions with stigmatized individuals. (p. 539).

Accordingly, "it has become increasingly clear that attempts to emphasize integration and similarity can sometimes backfire by threatening group distinctiveness" (Spears et al., 1997, p. 545). Thus, alternative approaches exist that are designed to reduce racism.

MUTICULTURALISM: MAYBE GROUP DIFFERENCES ARE MEANT TO BE ENJOYED

SIT (Tajfel & Turner, 1986) postulates that one process driving prejudicial attitudes is the desire to identify positive differences between the ingroup and a relevant outgroup. Thus, "pressures to evaluate one's own group positively through ingroup/outgroup comparisons lead social groups to attempt to *differentiate* themselves from each other" (Tajfel & Turner, 1986, p. 16; italics added). Theoretically, ingroup distinctiveness reduces prejudice because it reduces the perceived competition between the two groups. Thus, highly similar outgroups are often perceived as a threat to the ingroup. To the extent that two groups are distinct (or are perceived as distinct), competition between the groups is reduced, and therefore, so is the prejudice.

As a collective approach to intergroup relations, this becomes a cultural pluralism model of prejudice reduction. If individuals actively identify between-group differences, one reduces the perceived competition between the groups, which acts to reduce the perceived threat posed by the outgroup. Accordingly, it may be more beneficial to the collective self-esteem to actively identify how the ingroup differs from relevant outgroups and to actively make conscious the ingroup identification. This model is in contrast to the common ingroup identity approach outlined earlier in that it represents a "salad bowl" approach rather than a melting pot approach to intergroup relations. Within U.S. culture, for example, assimilation models entail the notion that if persons of different ethnic groups stop using hyphenated labels (e.g., Mexican American), and refer to themselves only as American, all Americans will get along more peacefully. Thus, common or layperson theories of intergroup relations suggest that attention to group differences will increase prejudice, whereas this cultural pluralism model contends that attention to group differences can (under certain conditions) reduce prejudice.

In a series of studies we tested the effects of a cultural pluralism model on attitudes toward the outgroup (Carpenter, Zárate, & Garza, 2007; Zárate et al., 2004; Zárate & Garza, 2002). Across three sets of studies, participants were asked to make either similarity or difference comparisons between their ingroup and a relevant outgroup. Within each study, some participants made "similarity" comparisons, where they were asked to evaluate, on a scale ranging from 1 (*not at all similar*) to 7 (*extremely similar*) how similar their ingroup was to a salient outgroup. With a between-subject design, others were asked to evaluate how different their ingroup was to a relevant outgroup. These participants were asked to rate, on a scale ranging from 1 (*not at all different*) to 7 (*extremely different*), how different their ingroup was to the outgroup. Using this basic paradigm, multiple studies showed that Latino participants who made difference ratings expressed significantly less prejudice than participants who made similarity ratings.

Carpenter et al. (2007) also tested African American participants using the same basic manipulation. That manipulation did not, however, influence African American responses—although that is not surprising. That research was based on the assumption that subtle word manipulations can influence perceptions of differences between relatively similar groups. That manipulation may have been too subtle to influence perceptions of differences between Whites and African Americans, where there are greater perceptual differences between the groups. The effect, however, is conceptually replicated in other ways. In particular, Sellers and colleagues (Sellers, Copeland-Linder, Martin, & Lewis, 2006; Sellers & Shelton, 2003) have been investigating the relations between racial identity and psychological distress. Their studies encompass adult and adolescent African Americans. Their studies show convincingly that having a strong sense of racial identity acts as a buffer against the perceived discrimination felt by the participants. Thus, having a strong racial identity reduces the stress of racism.

The benefits of group diversity go beyond improved self-concepts for minorities. Group diversity also positively impacts multiple forms of group interaction. Polzer, Milton, and Swann (2002) reviewed the extensive literature on group decision making and diversity. Theoretically, a diverse decision-making team will provide more diverse ideas and perspectives, which should improve the problem-solving abilities of the group. Polzer et al. (2002) reviewed that literature to show general support for that broad hypothesis. Diversity does not, however, always facilitate group decision making. Polzer et al. posited that one moderating factor is the degree to which group members have high interpersonal congruence. Interpersonal congruence is the degree to which interacting individuals have some mutual agreement about their respective roles and skills. That agreement, or strong social identity, should then facilitate discussion and problem solving. Their research utilized masters of business administration (MBA) students assigned to work in study teams. Team assignments were developed to maximize within-group racial diversity. Consistent with their hypotheses, the diverse groups with high levels of interpersonal congruence consistently outperformed other groups. Thus, the degree to which groups recognized and respected the strengths and roles of other group members predicted their overall productivity.

Even in racially charged situations, diversity appears to be beneficial. Sommers (2006) used a jury deliberation paradigm to investigate the effects of diversity on discussion strategies. The defendant was Black, providing a potentially racially charged situation. Participants, White and Black, discussed more material and spoke more in diverse groups than in racially homogeneous groups.

Finally, the effects of diversity appear to extend beyond the immediate group decision-making situation. Simonton (1997) investigated the effects of foreign influence on national creative achievement. Simonton investigated the effects of outside immigration, eminent immigration, and travel on later national achievement. The analyses were limited to Japan because of the way Japan has closely moderated immigration to Japan over the centuries. Simonton reported a strong effect whereby the influx of immigrants and ideas stimulates creativity and achievement two generations later. One can only conjecture about why it takes two generations for diversity to have that positive effect. Perhaps some degree of negotiation and respect regarding the various roles was necessary?

How Does Multiculturalism Act in Real Life?

It is important to stress that a cultural pluralism approach need not be mutually exclusive from a melting pot approach (Pettigrew, 1976). Pettigrew (1976) suggested that attacks on ethnic pride might derive from "our failure to see how cultural diversity and richness can contribute to, rather than detract from, a stable, unified American society" (p. 15). Pettigrew further argued that ethnic pride and cultural pluralism are merely stages of the same ethnic assimilation processes that all immigrant groups have gone through throughout American history.

Collective action of this nature can be seen everywhere. At times, it is more confrontational, whereas at other times, the behaviors are clearly positive. How they are viewed, however, depends on the perspective of the individual. In November 2006, U.S. Representative Tom Tancredo, from Colorado, criticized Miami by saying "It has become a Third World country. You just pick it up and take it and move it someplace. You would never know you're in the United States of America" (CBS News, 2006). Later visits to Miami were cancelled, partially in response to reports of threats on his life. What instigated Tancredo's original comments? Tancredo originally complained that the non-English-speaking enclaves are proof that more control over immigration is needed. He then called for more control over immigration.

The Tancredo affair is not an isolated event. Representative Virgil Goode, Jr. (from Virginia) stated on Fox News that Representative-Elect Keith Ellison (from Minnesota) should use a Bible when taking the oath for office rather than the Koran Rep. Ellison had chosen to use. Goode then proceeded to say that the fact an elected Muslim was using the Koran poses a danger to traditional American values. Goode also stated that his using the Koran is evidence that the United States needs to control immigration or more Muslims will be elected to Congress. The interesting part is that Representative Ellison was born in the United States. Although both events offended particular groups, neither event earned widespread condemnation. Thus, calls for assimilation to a particular norm received condemnation, but they must have also received some level of support.

The remarks by Goode and Tancredo reflect a strong and possibly "aggressive" view of assimilation. It is one thing for groups to naturally assimilate, which may be the case under most circumstances. It is quite another to try to force groups to abandon important and beneficial self-concepts. To the best of my knowledge, the common ingroup identity manipulations have never "forced" participants to assimilate. Rather, the common ingroup identity manipulations provide an orthogonal (school affiliation) or superordinate categorization, which changes the group structure in a more subtle way. Thus, forcing people to change might actually produce reactance and more conflict rather than less conflict.

CONCLUSIONS

Is racism changing? Clearly it is (Dasgupta, 2004; Dovidio & Gaertner, 2000). How it is changing is the more interesting question. The expressed racism is becoming more subtle, and therefore harder to detect. Because of that, it leads to a different set of problems than before. This chapter did not cover attributional ambiguity and other daily stressors associated with racism. However, once racism is detected, the responses are less than optimal. One can ignore it, but then it will never change. One can complain, but that only provokes reactance. One can challenge racism. The idea is potentially groundbreaking, but one wonders how often people are willing to do so and if that will produce the desired consequences. From a minority perspective, it seems beneficial to simply accept the differences and to enjoy the diversity. Our work on that, however, has utilized primarily Latino participants, just as the somewhat contradictory common ingroup identity work has utilized primarily White participants. One wonders if the differing results are due to the different manipulations and perspectives, or if the participant pools dictate those differences. More research is needed regarding when and how racial identity (minority and White) produces antagonism versus when it produces improved intergroup relations.

REFERENCES

Allport, G. W. (1954). *The nature of prejudice.* Oxford, UK: Addison-Wesley.

Bastian, B., & Haslam, N. (2006). Psychological essentialism and stereotype endorsement. *Journal of Experimental Social Psychology, 42,* 228–235.

Berry, J. W. (1984). Cultural relations in plural societies: Alternatives to segregation and their sociopsychological implications. In N. Miller & M. B. Brewer (Eds.), *Groups in contact: The psychology of desegregation* (pp. 11–27). New York: Academic.

Berry, J. W., Poortinga, Y. H., Segall, M. H., & Dasen, P. R. (2002). *Cross cultural psychology: Research and applications* (2nd ed.). New York: Cambridge University Press.

Blanton, H., Jaccard, J., Gonzales, P. M., & Christie, C. (2006). Decoding the Implicit Association Test: Implications for criterion prediction. *Journal of Experimental Social Psychology, 42,* 192–212.

Bonilla-Silva, E. (2001). *White supremacy and racism in the post-civil rights era.* Boulder, CO: Rienner.

Brewer, M. B. (1988). A dual process model of impression formation. In T. K. Srull & R. S. Wyer (Eds.), *Advances in social cognition* (Vol. 1, pp. 1–36). Hillsdale, NJ: Erlbaum.

Brondolo, E., Rieppi, R., Kelly, K. P., & Gerin, W. (2003). Perceived racism and blood pressure: A review of the literature and conceptual and methodological critique. *Annals of Behavioral Medicine, 25*(1), 55-65.

Carpenter, S., Zárate, M. A., & Garza, A. (2007). Cultural pluralism and prejudice reduction. *Cultural Diversity and Ethnic Minority Psychology. 13*(2), 83–93.

CBS News (2006). GOP Rep. calls Miami 'Third World Country." Miami, Nov 30, 2006. Retrieved August 11, 2008, from http://www.cbsnews.com/stories/2006/11/30/politics/main2217944.shtml

Cook, S. W. (1978). Interpersonal and attitudinal outcomes in cooperating interracial groups. *Journal of Research & Development in Education, 12*(1), 97–113.

Crocker, J., Major, B., & Steele, C. (1998). Social stigma. In D. Gilbert, S. T. Fiske, & G. Lindzey (Eds.), *The handbook of social psychology* (Vol. 2, 4th ed, pp. 504–553). New York: McGraw-Hill.

Crosby, F. J. (1984). The denial of personal discrimination. *American Behavioral Scientist, 27,* 371–386.

Cunningham, W. A., Preacher, K. J., & Banaji, M. R. (2001). Implicit attitude measures: Consistency, stability, and convergent validity. *Psychological Science, 12,* 163–170.

Czopp, A. M., Monteith, M. J., & Mark, A. (2006). Standing up for a change: Reducing bias through interpersonal confrontation. *Journal of Personality and Social Psychology, 90,* 784–803.

Dasgupta, N. (2004). Implicit intergroup favouritism, outgroup favouritism, and their behavioural manifestations. *Social Justice Research, 17,* 143–169.

Dasgupta, N., McGhee, D. E., Greenwald, A. G., & Banaji, M. R. (2000). Automatic preference for White Americans: Eliminating the familiarity explanation. *Journal of Experimental Social Psychology, 36,* 316–328.

DeNavas-Walt, C., Procter, B. D., & Lee, C. H. (2006). *U.S. Census Bureau, Current Population Reports (P60–231): Income, poverty, and health insurance coverage in the United States: 2005.* Washington, DC: U.S. Government Printing Office.

Dovidio, J. F., Evans, N., & Tyler, R. B. (1986). Racial stereotypes: The content of their cognitive representations. *Journal of Experimental Social Psychology, 22,* 22–37.

Dovidio, J. F., & Gaertner, S. L. (2000). Aversive racism and selection decisions: 1989 and 1999. *Psychological Science, 11,* 315–319.

Dovidio, J. F., & Gaertner, S. L. (2004). Aversive racism. In M. P. Zanna (Ed.), *Advances in experimental social psychology* (Vol. 36, pp. 1–52). San Diego, CA: Academic.

Dovidio, J. F., Gaertner, S. L., & Validzic, A. (1998). Intergroup bias: Status, differentiation, and a common in-group identity. *Journal of Personality and Social Psychology, 75,* 109–120.

Dovidio, J. F., Kawakami, K., & Gaertner, S. L. (2002). Implicit and explicit prejudice and interracial interaction. *Journal of Personality and Social Psychology, 82*(1), 62–68.

Ellemers, N., van Knippenberg, A., & Wilke, H. (1990). The influence of permeability on group boundaries and stability of group status on strategies of individual mobility and social change. *British Journal of Social Psychology, 29,* 233–246.

Fazio, R. H., Jackson, J. R., Dunton, B. C., & Williams, C. J. (1995). Variability in automatic activation as an unobtrusive measure of racial attitudes: A bona fide pipeline? *Journal of Personality and Social Psychology, 69*(6), 1013–1027.

Fazio, R. H., & Olson, M. A. (2003). Implicit measures in social cognition research: Their meaning and uses. *Annual Review of Psychology, 54,* 297–327.

Fiske, S. T., & Neuberg, S. L. (1990). A continuum model of impression formation: Influences of information and motivation on attention and interpretation. In M. P. Zanna (Ed.), *Advances in experimental social psychology* (Vol. 23, pp. 1–74). New York: Academic.

Garcia v. Spun Steak Co., 998 F.2d 1480 (9th Cir. 1993), cert denied, 114 S.Ct 2726 (1994).

Giscombé, C. L., & Lobel, M. (2005). Exploring disproportionately high rates of adverse birth outcomes among African Americans: The impact of stress, racism, and related factors in pregnancy. *Psychological Bulletin, 131,* 662–683.

Greenwald, A. G., McGhee, D. E., & Schwartz, J. L. K. (1998). Measuring individual differences in implicit cognition. *Journal of Personality and Social Psychology, 74,* 1464–1480.

Greenwald, A. G., Pratkanis, A. R., Leippe, M. R., & Baumgardner, M. H. (1986). Under what conditions does theory obstruct research progress? *Psychological Review, 93,* 216–229.

Haslam, N., Rothschild, L., & Ernst, D. (2002). Are essentialist beliefs associated with prejudice? *British Journal of Social Psychology, 41,* 87–100.

Helms, J. E., & Talleyrand, R. M. (1997). Race is not ethnicity. *American Psychologist, 52,* 1246–1247.

Hewstone, M. (1996). Contact and categorization: Social psychological interventions to change intergroup relations. In N. Macrae, C. Stangor, & M. Hewstone (Eds.), *Stereotypes and stereotyping* (pp. 323–368). New York: Guilford.

Human Rights Watch (2006). *Darfur destroyed: Ethnic cleansing by government and militia forces in Western Sudan.* Retrieved from http://hrw.org/reports/2004/sudan0504/index.htm

Jackson, L. A., Sullivan, L. A., Harnish, R., & Hodge, C. N. (1996). Achieving positive social identity: Social mobility, social creativity, and permeability of group boundaries. *Journal of Personality and Social Psychology, 70,* 241–254.

Jayaratne, T. E., Ybarra, O., Sheldon, J. P., Brown, T. N., Feldbaum, M., Pfeffer, C. A., et al. (2006). White Americans' genetic lay theories of race differences and sexual orientation: Their relationship with prejudice toward Blacks, and gay men and lesbians. *Group Processes and Intergroup Relations*, 9, 77–94.

Jones, J. M. (1997). *Prejudice and racism* (2nd ed.). New York: McGraw-Hill.

Jost, J. T., & Hunyady, O. (2005). Antecedents and consequences of system-justifying ideologies. *Current Directions in Psychological Science, 14,* 260–265.

Jost, J. T., Kivetz, Y., Rubini, M., Guermandi, G., & Mosso, C. (2005). System-justifying functions of complementary regional and ethnic stereotypes: Cross-national evidence. *Social Justice Research, 18,* 305–333.

Jurado v. Eleven-Fifty Corp., 813 F.2d 1406 (9th Cir. 1987).

Kaiser, C. R., Dyrenforth, P. S., & Hagiwara, N. (2006). Why are attributions to discrimination interpersonally costly? A test of system- and group-justifying motivations. *Personality and Social Psychology Bulletin, 32*(11), 1523–1536.

Kaiser, C. R., & Miller C. T. (2001). Stop complaining! The social costs of making attributions to discrimination. *Personality and Social Psychology Bulletin, 27,* 254–263.

Kaiser, C. R., & Miller C.T. (2003). Derogating the victim: The interpersonal consequences of blaming events on discrimination. *Group Processes & Intergroup Relations, 6,* 227–237.

Levy, S. R., Stroessner, S. J., & Dweck, C. S. (1998). Stereotype formation and endorsement: The role of implicit theories. *Journal of Personality and Social Psychology, 74,* 1421–1436.

Livingston, R. W., & Brewer, M. B. (2002). What are we really priming? Cue-based versus category-based processing of facial stimuli. *Journal of Personality and Social Psychology, 82*(1), 5–18.

McConahay, J. B. (1986). Modern racism, ambivalence, and the modern racism scale. In J. F. Dovidio & S. L. Gaertner (Eds.), *Prejudice, discrimination, and racism* (pp. 91–125). Orlando, FL: Academic.

McConahay, J. B., & Hough, J. C. (1976). Symbolic racism. *Journal of Social Issues, 32,* 23–45.

McConnell, A. R., & Leibold, J. M. (2001). Relations among the Implicit Association test, discriminatory behavior, and explicit measures of racial attitudes. *Journal of Experimental Social Psychology, 37*(5), 435–442.

National Center for Health Statistics. Public Health Service. (2004). *With chartbook on trends in the health of Americans.* Hyattsville, MD:.

Niemann-Flores, Y., & Dovidio, J. F. (1998). Relationship of solo status, academic rank, and perceived distinctiveness to job satisfaction of racial/ethnic minorities. *Journal of Applied Psychology, 83*(1), 55–71.

Nier, J. A., Gaertner, S. L., Dovidio, J. F., Banker, B. S., Ward, C. M., & Rust, M. C. (2001). Changing interracial evaluations and behavior: The effects of a common group identity. *Group Processes and Intergroup Relations, 4,* 299–316.

Olson, M. A., & Fazio, R. H. (2004). Reducing the influence of extrapersonal associations on the Implicit Association Test: Personalizing the IAT. *Journal of Personality and Social Psychology, 86,* 653–667.

Pettigrew, T. F. (1976). Ethnicity in American life: A social psychological perspective. In A. Dashefsky (Ed.), *Ethnic identity in society* (pp. 13–23). Rand McNally: Chicago.

Pettigrew, T. F. (1998). Intergroup contact theory. *Annual Review of Psychology, 49,* 65–85.

Polzer, J. T., Milton, L. P., & Swann, W. B., Jr. (2002). Capitalizing on diversity: Interpersonal congruence in small work groups. *Administrative Science Quarterly, 47,* 296–324.

Reyna, C., Henry, P. J., Korfmacher, W., & Tucker, A. (2005). Examining the principles in principled conservatism: The role of responsibility stereotypes as cues for deservingness in racial policy decisions. *Journal of Personality and Social Psychology, 90,* 109–128.

Roberson, L., Deitch, E. A., Brief, A. P., & Block, C. R. (2003). Stereotype threat and feedback seeking in the workplace. *Journal of Vocational Behavior, 62,* 176–188.

Rothbart, M., & John, O. P. (1985). Social categorization and behavioral episodes: A cognitive analysis of the effects of intergroup contact. *Journal of Social Issues, 41*(3), 81–104.

Rothbart, M., & Park, B. (1986). On the confirmability and disconfirmability of trait concepts. *Journal of Personality and Social Psychology, 50*(1), 131–142.

Ruddell, R., & Urbina, M. G. (2004). Minority threat and punishment: A cross-national analysis. *Justice Quarterly, 21,* 903–931.

Sanders, J. D., McClure, K. A., & Zárate, M. A. (2004). Cerebral hemispheric asymmetries in social perception: Perceiving and responding to the individual and the group. *Social Cognition, 22*(3), 279–291.

Schmader, T. (2002). Gender identification moderates stereotype threat effects on women's math performance. *Journal of Experimental Social Psychology, 38,* 194–201.

Sears, D. O. (1988). Symbolic racism. In P. Katz & D. Taylor (Eds.), *Towards the elimination of racism: Profiles in controversy* (pp. 53–84). New York: Plenum.

Sekaquaptewa, D., Espinoza, P., Thompson, M., Vargas, P., & von Hippel, W. (2003). Stereotypic explanatory bias: Implicit stereotyping as a predictor of discrimination. *Journal of Experimental Social Psychology, 39*(1), 75–82.

Sellers, R. M., Copeland-Linder, N., Martin, P. P., & Lewis, R. L. (2006). Racial identity matters: The relationship between racial discrimination and psychological functioning in African American adolescents. *Journal of Research on Adolescence, 16*(2), 187–216.

Sellers, R. M., & Shelton, J. N. (2003). The role of racial identity in perceived racial discrimination. *Journal of Personality and Social Psychology, 84,* 1079–1092.

Sherif, M., Harvey, O. J., White, B. J., Hood, W. R., & Sherif, C. W. (1961). *Intergroup cooperation and competition: The Robbers Cave experiment.* Norman, OK: University of Oklahma Press.

Sidanius, J., Pratto, F., & Bobo, L. (1996). Racism, conservatism, affirmative action, and intellectual sophistication: A matter of principled conservatism or group dominance? *Journal of Personality and Social Psychology, 70*(3), 476–490.

Sidanius, J., Pratto, F., van Laar, C., & Levin, S. (2004). Social dominance theory: Its agenda and method. *Political Psychology, 25*(6), 845–880.

Simonton, D. K. (1997). Foreign influence and national achievement: The impact of open milieus on Japanese civilization. *Journal of Personality and Social Psychology, 72*(1), 86–94.

Smedley, A. (2006). On the confusion of "race" with biophysical diversity. *American Psychologist, 61*(2), 180–181.

Smedley, A., & Smedley, B. (2005). Race as biology is fiction, racism as a social problem is real: Anthropological and historical perspectives on the social construction of race. *American Psychologist, 60,* 16–26.

Smith-McAllen, A., Johnson, B. J., Dovidio, J. F., & Pearson, A. R. (2006). Black and White: The role of color bias in implicit race bias. *Social Cognition, 24,* 46–73.

Sommers, S. R. (2006). On racial diversity and group decision-making: Identifying multiple effects of racial composition on jury deliberations. *Journal of Personality and Social Psychology, 90,* 597–612.

Son Hing, L. S., Bobocel, D. R., & Zanna, M. P. (2002). Meritocracy and opposition to affirmative action: Making concessions in the face of discrimination. *Journal of Personality and Social Psychology, 83*(3), 493–509.

Spears, R., Doosje, B., & Ellemers, N. (1997). Self-stereotyping in the face of threats to group status and distinctiveness: The role of group identification. *Personality and Social Psychology Bulletin, 23,* 538–553.

Steele, C. M. (1997). A threat in the air: How stereotypes shape the intellectual identities and performance of
women and African-Americans. *American Psychologist, 52,* 613–629.

Steele, C. M., & Aronson, J. (1995). Stereotype vulnerability and the intellectual test performance of African-
Americans. *Journal of Personality and Social Psychology, 69,* 797–811.

Stephan, W. G. (1985). Intergroup relations. In G. Lindzey & E. Aronson (Eds.), *Handbook of social psychology* (3rd ed., Vol II, pp. 559–658). New York: Random House.

Stephan, W. G., & Stephan, C. (1984). The role of ignorance in intergroup relations. In N. Miller & M. Brewer
(Eds.). *Groups in contact: The psychology of desegregation* (pp. 229–255). New York: Academic Press.

Stroessner, S. J. (1996). Social categorization by race or sex: Effects of perceived non-normalcy on response
times. *Social Cognition, 14*(3), 247–276.

Tajfel, H., & Turner, J. C. (1986). The social identity theory of intergroup behavior. In S. Austin & W. G. Austin
(Eds.), *Psychology of intergroup relations* (pp. 7–24). Chicago: Nelson-Hall.

Towles-Schwen, T., & Fazio, R. (2006). Automatically activated racial attitudes as predictors of the success of
interracial roommate relationships. *Journal of Experimental Social Psychology, 42*(5), 698–705.

U.S. Census Bureau (2005). *Educational attainment in the United States: 2004.* Retrieved December 12, 2006,
from http://www.census.gov/population/www/socdemo/education/cps2004.html

U.S. Census Bureau (2007). *The American Community – Hispanic: 2004.* Retrieved September 14, 2007, from
http://www.census.gov/prod/2007pubs/acs-03.pdf

U.S. English Incorporated. (2008). Retrieved August 11, 2008, from http://www.us-english.org/view/13

U.S. State Department. (1999, December). *Ethnic cleansing in Kosovo: An accounting* (Report). Washington, DC.

Verkuyten, M. (2003). Discourses about ethnic group de-essentialism: Oppressive and progressive aspects.
British Journal of Social Psychology, 42, 371–391.

Wheeler, S. C., & Petty, R. E. (2001). The effects of stereotype activation on behavior: A review of possible
mechanisms. *Psychological Bulletin, 127*(6), 797–826.

Williams, D. R., Neighbors, H. W., & Jackson, J. S. (2003). Racial/ethnic discrimination and health: Findings
from community studies. *American Journal of Public Health, 93,* 200–208.

Word, C. O., Zanna, M. P., & Cooper, J. (1974). The nonverbal mediation of self-fulfilling prophecies in interracial interaction. *Journal of Experimental Social Psychology, 10*(2), 109–120.

Wright, S. C., Aron, A., McLaughlin-Volpe, T., & Tropp, S. A. (1997). The extended contact effect: Knowledge
of cross-group friendships and prejudice. *Journal of Personality and Social Psychology, 73,* 73–90.

Yzerbyt, V., Rocher, S., & Schadron, G. (1997). Stereotypes as explanations: A subjective essentialistic view
of group perception. In R. Spears, P. J. Oakes, N. Ellemers, & S Haslam (Eds.), *The social psychology of
stereotyping and group life* (pp. 20–50). Malden, MA: Blackwell Publishing.

Zárate, M. A., Garcia, B., Garza, A. A., & Hitlan, R. (2004). Cultural threat and perceived realistic group conflict as predictors of attitudes towards Mexican immigrants. *Journal of Experimental Social Psychology,
40,* 99–105.

Zárate, M. A., & Garza, A. A. (2002). In-group distinctiveness and self-affirmation as dual components of
prejudice reduction. *Self and Identity, 1,* 235–249.

Zárate, M. A., Sanders, J. D., & Garza, A. A. (2000). Neurological disassociations of social perception processes. *Social Cognition, 18,* 223–251.

Zárate, M. A., & Smith, E. R. (1990). Person categorization and stereotyping. *Social Cognition, 8,* 161–185.

20 Sexism

Janet K. Swim
The Pennsylvania State University

Lauri L. Hyers
West Chester University

Social psychological research on sexism has come a long way in the second half of the 20th century, from a mere page on sexism (termed antifeminism) in Allport's (1954) classic text *The Nature of Prejudice* to the current rate of thousands of pages of scholarly work published every year devoted exclusively to the topic. The accumulating knowledge of the significance of sexism is both a reflection of and reflected by dramatic changes in women's status. Women in Western countries have rejected second-class citizenship, obtaining rights to vote, hold property, seek divorce, run for public office, make choices about their personal health care and reproduction, wear pants, pursue higher education, develop careers of their choosing, and take legal action against abuse, sexual harassment, and rape. Although women's status is highly varied across cultures, efforts to resist sexist oppression can be found worldwide.

Still, at present, a pressing issue in the social sciences has been how to make the case that sexism exists in many different forms and that it produces measurable consequences. Documenting sexism and its consequences is important due to several myths about sexism. We use the term myth here, not as sacred stories, but as widely held cultural misnomers. One myth is that sexism is not that harmful (e.g., sexual harassment is just flirting; traditional gender-role divisions are good for women and men; "mild" domestic violence or emotional abuse is normal; using masculine pronouns or male-identified occupation titles are simply traditions; gendered career choices are functional; hostile sexism is balanced by benevolent caretakers; claims of antifemale sexism are blown out of proportion because both women and men experience sexism; women should not expect life to be easy; and women do not appreciate what has been done for them already). A second myth is that women enjoy their lesser status roles in society, freely choosing to comply with gender-role restrictions (e.g., wearing makeup, doing more domestic work than men, pursuing low-paying occupations, engaging in prostitution, living with abusers). Early psychological theory justified women's desire for their own oppression by characterizing them as masochistic or martyrs by nature (e.g., Deutsch, 1930). Although this early view is not likely to be currently widely accepted, the myth still exists when cultural context, social norms, and lesser social power are not fully acknowledged. Many religious and traditional beliefs continue to promote norms that reward women for embracing subservient roles. These two myths contribute to a third myth that sexism is rare. The prevalence of sexism is masked by restrictive definitions of what constitutes sexist beliefs and behavior; targets' lack of recognition, acknowledgment, or reporting of their experiences; and perpetrators' lack of awareness or willingness to admit their own sexist beliefs and behaviors.

In this chapter we examine evidence about the prevalence of sexism by examining different ways in which sexist beliefs can be manifested, evidence documenting sexist behaviors, and some of the consequences of sexism. We define sexism as individuals' attitudes, beliefs, and behaviors, and organizational, institutional, and cultural practices that either reflect negative evaluations of individuals based on their gender or support unequal status of women and men. Most of the chapter focuses on an individual level of analysis and antifemale sexism, as these represent most of the psychological research on sexism. However, it is important to acknowledge all levels of analyses are intertwined and both women and men experience sexism. We begin by placing research on sexism within the historical context of the study of gender differences.

GENDER DIFFERENCES

When the field of psychology was still in its infancy, some of the earliest research addressing sexism appeared, critical of a large body of pseudo-science "proving" that women were different and deficient (Caplin & Caplin, 1994). Research disputing innate gender differences represents a major chunk of the social scientific work on sexism, growing rapidly midcentury and continuing well into the 21st century. This research also spawned critiques of social scientific methods that lead to the refinement of nonsexist research practices and alternative methods of studying sexism.

Against a backdrop of historic social changes (e.g., the Industrial Revolution, the U.S. women's suffragist movement, and the major liberalizing social reforms following the French revolution and the antislavery movement), this research finds its roots in the "woman question," which inspired much debate about differences between women and men and whether women's lesser social status was fair. This was not a debate about "sexism" per se, for that term was not even coined until the 1960s (Lehrer, 1988; Shapiro, 1985). Arguments could be quite vicious, as is found in the "scientific" work of Mobius (1901), who declared that "all progress is due to man. Woman is like a dead weight on him" (p. 629).

Psychologists contributed to this debate. When psychology was just establishing itself, one could argue there was a fair amount of research pertaining to sexism. The majority of this work reinforced rather than questioned the sexist status quo (Caplin & Caplin, 1994; Shields, 1975). Antisexist scholars wishing to weigh in on the issue encountered some formidable foes, such as Freud who conjectured:

> It is really a stillborn thought to send women into the struggle for existence exactly as men. If for instance I imagined my gentle sweet girl as a competitor, it would only end in my telling her as I did 17 months ago, that I am fond of her and that I implore her to withdraw from the strife into the calm uncompetitive activity of my home. . . . Long before the age at which a man can earn a position in society, Nature has determined woman's destiny through beauty, charm, and sweetness. (Jones, 1961, p. 118).

G. S. Hall (1906) viewed the coeducation and shared workplace of women with men as "race suicide." On coeducation and menstruation, he questioned, "At a time when her whole future depends upon normalizing the lunar month, is there something not only unnatural and unhygienic, but a little monstrous of her having daily schooling with boys?" (p. 590). Much of this sexist work was invigorated by the popularity of Darwin's evolutionary theory.

For several decades, psychologists continued to "scientifically" demonstrate women's intellectual, moral, and mental health deficiencies, borrowing from a familiar racist formula of demonstrating deficiencies in non-White racial and ethnic groups (e.g., Guthrie, 2004). In fact, much of the sexist "scientific" theory was not merely similar to racism, but entangled with it in the belief that "more developed races" evolved to have greater sex differences. This is illustrated in the early work by Vogt (1864) who argued that "the male European excels much more than the female European, [more so] than the Negro and Negress" (p. 212), as part of his "woman-as-child-as-primitive argument" (Richards, 1983).

Early psychologists who might have disputed these sexist assumptions were up against decades of sexist "scientific" research against women (Shields, 1975). It is not surprising that antisexist researchers reacted by agreeing that women were different, but then offering alternative explanations (socialization and experience). For example, at the turn of last century, several women made scientific cases against sexist assumptions about the psychology of women. Helen Thompson and Mary Calkins refuted myths of women's inferior IQ and achievement; Mary Putnam Jacobi criticized views of menstruation as debilitating; and Karen Horney and Clara Thompson challenged sexist assumptions of psychoanalysis about gender differences in jealousy, self-esteem, and psychosexual development (Morantz-Sanchez, 1983; Quinne, 1987; Scarborough & Furumoto, 1987). Despite their efforts, sexism was more of the social scientific modus operandi than a social problem to be studied in itself. As a result, even emerging applied fields, such as educational intelligence testing and research on the clinical treatment of mental illness, resulted in further sexist oppression of women (e.g., Caplin & Caplin, 1994; Lupton, 1993; Schiebinger, 1989; Tavris, 1992).

Midcentury feminist research on gender differences set out to show that differences between women and men were unfounded. One strategy was to compare women and men on various tasks, abilities, and interests, with the expectation of documenting a lack of gender differences. However, this research sometimes revealed tangible gender differences, confirming gender stereotypes (e.g. women are more likely to be able to decode nonverbal messages [Hall, & Carter, 1999]; men are more likely to be physically aggressive [Swim, 1994]). Another strategy was to compare very young children and babies, again expecting few differences, especially because this young population would have had few socialization influences. This research, too, did not always come out as expected. A large body of studies examining gender differences developed. Summarizing this research was aided by the introduction of meta-analytic research techniques that corrected for some of the sampling and power issues inherent in narrative review articles. These meta-analyses allowed for assessment of the relative size of gender differences, the ability to examine contexts that accentuated and attenuated gender differences, and temporal changes in the size of these differences. These summaries, however, still left room for interpretation leading to debate about the political and practical meaning of gender differences (see Eagly, 1995; Hyde, 2005; and commentaries associated with these articles).

There were several responses to the documentation of gender differences. Some researchers moved toward a feminist version of essentialism, accepting the differences but arguing that these differences should be valued (Gilligan, 1982). Some looked at gender differences in process rather than in terms of raw skills or innate differences (e.g., differences in math confidence and choice rather than actual math skill [Hackett & Betz, 1981], gender differences in anticipated consequences of behaviors predicting gender differences in behavior [Eagly & Steffen, 1986], and concerns about confirming stereotypes interfering with women's math performance [Spencer, Steele, & Quinn, 1999]). Others emphasized the importance of comparing differences as a function of gender (the subjective state of being masculine or feminine) rather than sex (biological category; e.g., Lott, 1997). More recently, it has been argued that gender should not be considered an aspect of a person but should be examined as an emergent property of same-sex groups (Maccoby, 2002).

FEMINIST THEORIES OF GENDER SOCIALIZATION

A frequent framing of debates about gender differences is one where nature and nurture, and sometimes interactions between nature and nurture, are pitted against each other as alternative explanations for gender differences. Of particular importance to understanding sexism is not so much whether nature plays a role in gender differences, but documenting that sexism plays a role in developing or accentuating gender differences.

Behaviorism played a larger role in understanding the role that nurturing, and by extension sexism, plays in the emergence of gender differences. Behaviorist John B. Watson, not typically known as a feminist himself, denied the existence of maternal instinct, pointing out that, "We have observed the nursing, handling, bathing, etc. of the first baby of a good many mothers. . . . The instinctive factors are practically nil" (Watson, 1926, p. 54), thus, leaving room for the role of nurturing on gender-typed behaviors. Social learning theory, although broad in scope, was perhaps the most important springboard for what is now a common understanding of the role of learning on gender differences in behavior. Social learning theorists made the—now ridiculously obvious—claim that learning has something to do with the gender differences we observe. Likewise, social learning theory uncovers a major source of sexism in our culture, namely that we teach girls and boys to be different people. Such a concept is in stark contrast to the assumptions of the vast body of research that had come before that was used to argue that women were naturally different and inferior. Although social learning theory applies to more than just gender and sex differences, it was further elaborated on by three subsequent theories of gender.

Bem's (1981) gender schema theory provided a social-cognitive spin on social learning theory. Specifically, in teaching gendered behaviors to our girls and boys, we raise them to develop gender schemas, or stereotyped categories, by which they can judge all information about their own and others' gender-related behaviors that they encounter. Her theory offers important insight into the mechanisms by which women and men internalize sexism and come to perceive that they are choosing to perpetuate the status quo. It also provides some answers as to why some women and some men defy gender stereotypes and are critical of sexism, and others are not—those with more rigid gender schemas will be less concerned about what others may perceive to be sexism.

Eagly's (1987) social role theory is also consistent with the basics of social learning theory, exploring some of the cultural mechanisms that underlie gendered learning. This theory suggests that the appearance of sex-linked traits, skills, and interests are a result of women and men doing their best to live up to the roles in which they are placed. Because we have a sex-linked division of labor, women are directed toward different roles and tasks (e.g., babysitter, kindergarten teacher) than men (e.g., yard worker, soldier). In doing their best to live up to those roles, they develop traits that will help them perform well (e.g., nurturance vs. independence). Again, because of the basic desire to do well, women and men may not realize these subtle sexist forces they have internalized that operate on their skill development and interests.

Miller (1987) and Unger, Draper, and Pendergras (1986) introduced a more systemic explanation for sexism. Specifically, they argued that a larger patriarchal system serves to maintain sexist oppression. They make the case that there is not anything unique about sex, gender, and sexism, per se. Rather, sex and gender are the dimension on which society is stratified and sex differences are simply a manifestation of this sexist system on women and men. All that we associate as differences in gender or sex are really just differences due to women having less power. This theory is useful because it provides a means to link research on sexism to research on racism and other prejudices.

Feminist Methodological Critique

Whereas some continued to explore characteristics and sources of gender differences, others critiqued the methods and data used to document gender differences. Some explored how systemic bias in research methodology led to findings of spurious gender differences (e.g., looking at measurement strategies, sample characteristics, and study context, such as experimenter gender, how variables were manipulated or measured, and public or private nature of data collection). Others argued that feminists need to be vigilant of the implications of research on gender differences, such as research on evolutionary perspectives in psychology, for women's social status (Greene, 2004). Finally, others found the effort to study gender differences ultimately counterproductive and futile and switched to new ways of studying sexism.

Those who identified the social scientific methods themselves as the root of the problem in studying gender differences took two different approaches to critiquing these methods. The first group, feminist epistemologists, sought to critique and offer improved or alternative methods to standard scientific practice, all the while standing by the scientific method as a liberating force for women. They sought to improve scientific practice by making methods more true to the principles of objective and unbiased science (e.g., Denmark, Russo, Frieze, & Sechzer, 1988). The APA Task Force on Sexism identified several ways in which sexist bias contaminates scientific research. In reviewing the several decades of research in psychology, the task force revealed sexism in question formulation, methods, data analysis and interpretation, and conclusions. This work is a treatise on much of the sexism that feminist gender difference researchers were themselves tackling.

The second, methodological revisionists saw the idea of "objective" methods in and of themselves to be problematic and reifying of the oppressive status quo (Harding, 1993; Jagger, 2004; Keller, 1985). This other camp, although offering very different solutions (feminist standpoint, feminist postmodernist perspectives), are similar in their rejection of standard scientific practice as a systematic form of sexism was further oppressing disadvantaged groups (Brooks & Hesse-Biber, 2007). Problematic elements of objective science include the denial of the voice and authority of those being studied and the production of exclusive knowledge defined by and written for those with power. Feminist standpoint theorists focus more on the former two issues, valuing the unique perspective of the marginalized voice. Feminist postmodernists focus more on the power dynamics involved in the latter two issues, including how those with power have the privilege to define the terms used to articulate experience, and how all knowledge is situationally constructed and inextricable from one's place in the power hierarchy. Further, the androcentric and patriarchal bias of the scientific method itself has been argued to inhibit and even stifle the voices of those who might define their own experiences with sexism.

For the most part, this latter approach to studying sexism has not infiltrated much into mainstream research on sexism in psychology. However, the implications of both of these methodological critiques for the research on sexism have been vast. Some have sought to clean up the sexism in scientific research practice, to get on with the business of sexism as research topic instead of sexism as research practice. Some have developed research on topics such as violence against women, sexual harassment, the role of power on stereotyping, sexual objectification of women, sexist language, and interpersonal forms of discrimination into the field of research on sexism that may not have traditionally been considered part of the domain of research on prejudice. Others have sought to devise new methods to bring silenced perspectives into research. Still others have turned from an analysis of sexism in research methods, providing a much more complex analysis of the insidiousness of patriarchal control over all aspects of our self-understanding, our relationships, and our lives.

In the remainder of the chapter we describe research that illustrates the breadth of research on sexism, some of the underlying assumptions about what constitutes sexism, difficulties associated with different methodologies used to study sexism, and approaches that have been used to overcome some of the difficulties. We begin by examining various types of sexist beliefs. We then describe research that has documented sexist behaviors. We end by examining the consequences of sexism for women and men.

GENDER-RELATED BELIEFS AND IDEOLOGIES

Research on sexist beliefs has spawned a number of different theories, measures, and methodologies that help us better understand the nature of sexist beliefs and identify individuals who endorse sexist beliefs. This research reveals that people explicitly and implicitly endorse sexist beliefs, some of which most would agree are sexist and other beliefs that can be argued to be sexist.

GENDER STEREOTYPES

Stereotypes are expectations or beliefs about characteristics associated with different groups. Explicit and implicit measures have been used to assess gender stereotypes. Identifying stereotypes as sexist rests on the assumption that women and men should be seen similarly or that gender stereotypes, no matter how accurate, can lead to sexist behavior by inappropriately leading to differential treatment of women and men.

Explicit Stereotypes

Discussion of gender stereotypes and explicit assessment of gender stereotypes often examine expectations about personality traits. Communal traits (e.g., nurturing, expressive, warm) are associated with women and agentic traits (e.g., active, instrumental, competent) are associated with men

(Eagly, 1987; Fiske, Cuddy, Glick, & Xu, 2002; Spence, 1993). These different expectations are not, however, equally applicable to different subtypes of women. Housewives are characterized as warm but not competent and career women and feminists are thought of as competent and assertive but not warm (Fiske et al., 2002; Rudman & Glick, 1999; Twenge & Zucker, 1999). This no-win situation is not found for men; when working women become mothers they are perceived as warmer but less competent but when working men become fathers they are perceived as warmer and perceptions of their competence do not change (Cuddy, Fiske, & Glick, 2004).

The extent to which individuals perceive the association between these traits and gender is not historically stable. Eagly's (1987) social role model predicts that gender differences in behaviors and expectations about gender differences are derived from gender differences in social roles (Diekman & Eagly, 2008). Consistent with this analysis, changes in women's status from 1931 to 1993 are associated with changes in perceptions of women's assertiveness, increasing when social indicators point to increases in women's status and decreasing when social indicators point to a decrease in their status (Twenge, 2001). Cross-cultural data also support this analysis (e.g., Diekman, Eagly, Miadinic, & Ferreira, 2005; Wilde & Diekman, 2005).

It is important to remember that stereotypes about women and men include a wide variety of characteristics, not just those associated with personality traits (Ashmore, 1990; Twenge, 1999). Other attributes include beliefs about gender differences in abilities, occupations, roles, interests, physical appearance, nonverbal behavior, and emotional displays (Ashmore, 1990; Deaux & Lewis, 1984; Robinson, Johnson, & Shields, 1998; Twenge, 1999). It is important to examine these components because many are perceived to covary more with each other than with a gender label given to people (Deaux & Lewis, 1984).

Implicit Stereotypes

A variety of gender stereotypical characteristics have been assessed using implicit measures. These include testing associations between men and leadership, math, science, careers, and hierarchical structures relative to associations between women and caretaking, art, liberal arts, family, and egalitarian structures (Nosek, Banaji, & Greenwald, 2002; Rudman & Kilianski, 2000; Schmid, 2004). Comparisons between explicit and implicit stereotypes reveal a mismatch, with individuals, particularly women, being more likely to endorse gender stereotypes implicitly than explicitly (e.g., Rudman & Kilianski, 2000). An interesting aspect of implicit stereotypes is that they are malleable. For instance, women's tendency to associate leadership with men and supporters with women is diminished the more women are exposed to female leaders in their social environments including their exposure to female faculty (Dasgupta & Asgari, 2004).

Much research documenting implicit associations has used the Implicit Association Task to assess these differences. A limitation of this method is that it requires testing whether one characteristic is associated with men more than women, relative to an opposite characteristic being associated with women more than men. For instance, a tendency to associate careers with men more than women is compared with a tendency to associate families more with women than men. A better understanding of implicit stereotypes could emerge if other methods were used, such as the go/no-go task (Nosek & Banaji, 2001), to determine whether implicit gender stereotypes are a result of associating men more than women with masculine domains, associating women more than men with feminine domains, or both.

Stereotypes as Sexist Beliefs

Using endorsement of stereotypes to document sexism is based on an individualistic, gender-blind framework. Perceiving differences between women and men is considered sexist or potentially sexist when the stereotypes are applied to individuals. However, if stereotypes are accurate, they are not biased but reflect actual gender differences and may provide useful general knowledge. There is evidence that several general stereotypes about women and men are descriptively accurate (e.g., J. A. Hall & Carter, 1999; Swim, 1994). If stereotypes are described in terms of all women or men having certain attributes, they will be inaccurate. When stereotypes represent average beliefs about the size or direction of gender differences, then general stereotypes may still be generally accurate even with substantial variability within gender groups and even when a particular stereotype may not be accurately applied to particular women and men (Jussim, 2005). See also Chapter 10.

Yet, there are several reasons why gender stereotypes can be considered sexist even if descriptively accurate. First, people may oversimplify the characteristics associated with particular groups. For instance, although men do perform better on spatial tasks than women, the size of the difference depends on the test used (Hyde, 2005). Also, people may perceive women to be more emotional than men, but they still may perceive that men are more likely to display anger (Shields, 2002). Second, although there may be general tendencies to be accurate, there are individual differences in the tendency to be accurate (J. A. Hall & Carter, 1999). Third, people may essentialize gender differences, perceiving that differences are inevitable. If they perceive the differences to be inevitable, they may perceive that what is generally true should be true, thereby translating descriptive stereotypes into prescriptive stereotypes. Fourth, stereotypes justify the status quo (Jost & Kay, 2005), rationalize the distribution of women and men into social roles (Hoffman & Hurst, 1990), and can create differences through confirmatory biases (Deaux & Major, 1987). Fifth, essentializing gender differences overlooks, for example, behavioral confirmation processes, different situational constraints for women and men, and cultural or situationally primed social norms that differentially affect women and men (Deaux & Lafrance, 1998). These situational factors make it hard to determine how much variance is attributable to characteristics of women and men versus characteristics of the situations; what may be perceived as gender difference in traits or abilities may be a difference in reactions to social situations, selection into different situations, or how people in situations treat women and men. Finally, gender stereotypes can be problematic when they become self-limiting and self-destructive, or result in diminished confidence or underperformance.

TRADITIONAL GENDER ROLES

Another classic way of assessing sexist beliefs is to document that individuals perceive that women and men should occupy different social roles. One of the most frequently used measures of endorsement of traditional gender roles is the Attitudes Toward Women Scale. Respondents indicate the extent they believe, for instance, "The intellectual leadership of a community should be largely in the hands of men," and "In general, the father should have more authority than the mother in bringing up the children." Although not technically measures of attitudes toward women (Eagly & Mladinic, 1989), endorsement of such beliefs can be considered sexist because they reflect lack of support for those who do not occupy traditional roles, they limit people to particular roles, impart greater power and authority to men, and lead to women's dependency on men. Longitudinal data reveal a decrease in endorsement of traditional gender roles. This is true when examining changes over time in endorsement of beliefs assessed by scales such as the Attitudes Toward Women Scale (e.g., Spence & Hahn, 1997; Twenge, 1997) and in national opinion poll data (e.g., Swim & Campbell, 2001).

Other data, however, should be considered prior to concluding that there is a lack of endorsement of traditional gender roles. First, embedded within these trends remains a substantial number of individuals who endorse sexist beliefs. Certain populations are more likely to endorse such individuals in the southern part of the United States, those who are religious fundamentalists, and those from certain countries more so than other countries (e.g., Carter & Borch, 2005; Swim, Becker, Lee, & Pruitt, 2008; Twenge, 1997). Second, as reviewed later, people behave in ways that suggest that they endorse these roles by enacting gender roles in their domestic lives and backlash against those who violate gender roles. Third, changes in endorsement of gender roles could reflect dated phrasing in measures. Changes may only appear to occur because scales ask behaviors that are no longer relevant to gender roles. Plus, when phrased in benevolent terms, individuals may be more likely to endorse, for instance, paternalistic treatment of women and men, than if framed in terms of differential treatment of women and men (Glick & Fiske, 1996). Fourth, overall changes may not be reflected equally across different gender-role domains. Different domains that have been assessed across a variety of measures include marital, parental, employment, educational, and heterosexual relationship roles (Beere, 1990; King & King, 1997). There are also measures that focus on endorsement of gender roles for men, thereby providing a fuller picture of endorsement of gender-role ideology (e.g., Walker, Tokar, & Fischer, 2000). Examining trends within domains could shed more detailed light onto individuals' endorsement of traditional gender roles.

Modern Sexism and Neosexism

Following research on modern racism, the Modern Sexism and Neosexism scales were developed as alternatives to more blatant measures of sexist beliefs, such as those assessed in measures of endorsement of traditional gender roles (Swim, Aikin, Hall, & Hunter, 1995; Swim, Becker, & DeCoster, 2008; Tougas, Brown, Beaton, & Joly, 1995). For instance, the Neosexism scale was specifically designed to measure hidden negative attitudes toward women. Paralleling items found in the Modern Racism scale, both sexism scales assess: (a) denial of discrimination, (b) negative reactions to complaints about inequality, and (c) lack of support for efforts to reduce inequality. These beliefs are important because they relate to maintaining the status quo and, if gender inequity still exists, then endorsement of these beliefs relates to maintaining gender inequity.

Research using these scales supports their validity as measures of subtle or covert sexist beliefs. First, associations between beliefs about the prevalence of sexism and gender system justification beliefs support the assertion that denial of discrimination is related to maintaining the status quo (Swim et al., 2008). Second, factor analyses demonstrate that endorsement of Modern Sexist and Neosexist beliefs are related to but distinct from endorsement of traditional gender roles and stereotypes (Swim et al., 1995; Swim & Cohen, 1997; Tougas et al., 1995). Third, methodologically, these scales are more subtle measures of sexist beliefs than endorsement of traditional gender roles: Modern Sexism beliefs are less likely to be identified as sexist than are traditional gender role beliefs (Barreto & Ellemers, 2005b; Swim, Mallett, Russo-Devosa, & Stangor, 2005). Fourth, both scales demonstrate convergent validity. Endorsement of Modern or Neosexist beliefs are associated with less endorsement of egalitarian values; lesser likelihood of judging particular incidents as sexual harassment; more negative reactions to feminism, feminists, and women's rights; overestimating the extent to which there is gender equity in the workforce; greater endorsement of rape myths; adversarial sexual beliefs; hostility toward women, hostile sexism, and antigay beliefs and behaviors; more positive reactions to sexist language; greater use of sexist language; greater perceived threat to men's collective interests; men's greater likelihood of engaging in coercive sexual behavior and verbal aggression during interpersonal conflicts; men's greater perception of men's experiences with discrimination; and women's lesser perceptions of personal experiences with discrimination (Cameron, 2001; Campbell, Schellenberg, & Senn 1997; Cralley & Ruscher, 2005; Forbes and Adams-Curtis, 2001; Forbes, Adams-Curtis, & White, 2004; Glick & Fiske, 1996; Masser & Abrams, 1999, Morrison & Morrison, 2002; Swim et al., 1995; Swim & Cohen, 1997, Swim, Mallett, & Stangor, 2004; Tougas et al., 1995; Whitly, 2001). Finally, research has demonstrated cross-cultural support for the validity of both scales primarily in European countries (for a review, see Swim et al., 2007).

Despite the similarity in theoretical origins of the two scales, there are some important distinctions between them. The primary distinction is that most of the items in the Modern Sexism scale assess beliefs about the prevalence of sexism, whereas items in the Neosexism scale primarily assess lack of support for efforts to improve women's status (Swim et al. 2008). There is some evidence of higher reliability for the Neosexism scale than the Modern Sexism scale (Campbell et al. 1997), yet similar range in reliabilities can be found when looking across studies including studies using different age and ethnic groups. Revisions to both scales that highlight this distinction can improve their reliability (Swim et al., 2008).

REACTIONS TOWARD FEMINISM AND FEMINISTS

Another way to assess endorsement of sexist beliefs is to assess reactions to feminism and feminists. A goal of feminism is to address women's lack of social and economic power and thereby address gender inequality. Therefore, unfavorable attitudes toward feminism and feminists can be considered markers of lack of support of gender equity.

One way attitudes toward feminism have been assessed is by examining support for social policies supported by feminists. These policies include comparable worth policies, the equal rights amendment, affirmative action, and abortion (see Beere, 1990, for example scales). There are a number of reasons for not supporting these policies, not all of which directly relate to attitudes toward feminist or gender equality. Yet, a central viable reason that may be expressed is lack of support for efforts to achieve equality and, with regard to abortion, beliefs about women's rights to make decisions about their own bodies.

A second way to assess attitudes toward feminism is to assess attitudes at feminist organizations (e.g., the National Organization for Women), feminists (as representatives of those working to achieve gender equity), and about the feminist movement (e.g., Fassinger, 1994). Negative reactions to feminists are associated with feeling threatened by feminists (Cottrell & Neuberg, 2005) including believing that feminists threaten values (Haddock & Zanna, 1994).

When considering reactions to feminism and feminists as markers of sexist beliefs, it is important to recognize that there are a variety of types of feminists that may not be captured by general reactions to feminism (Henley, Spalding, & Kosta, 2000). Some feminists are what Sommers (1990) calls gender equity feminists, arguing that women and men should be treated the same. Yet other feminists argue that women and men should not be treated the same. Cultural feminists might argue that treating women and men the same will result in women's disadvantages because women and men are not the same; what needs to change is greater valuing of feminine attributes (e.g., Gilligan, 1982). Radical feminists might argue that treating women and men the same can be problematic because it does not take into account men's greater social power and will result in maintaining status differences (e.g., Mackinnon, 1987). There are also a variety of other types of feminism, including socialist feminism, lesbian feminism, and Black feminism. Running through these different feminist perspectives is the recognition of women's disadvantage relative to men, so general lack of support for feminism would reflect a general lack of concern about and willingness to address gender inequality. Yet, different types of feminists are associated with different beliefs about the cause of the disadvantages and what needs to be done to address women's disadvantages. Thus, it may take more to understand the relation between lack of support for feminism and sexist beliefs.

AMBIVALENT SEXISM

Beliefs about women and men are not uniformly positive or negative (Glick & Fiske, 1996). Benevolent sexist beliefs about women consist of (a) beliefs about the complementary nature of gender differences, (b) endorsement of paternalistic behavior, and (c) beliefs in heterosexual intimacy. Although the three components of benevolent sexism appear on the surface to be positive, they can be harmful to women because of the unspoken assumptions associated with the beliefs. For instance, complementary gender differences can be translated into believing that women are less competent than men. Paternalistic beliefs can be translated into believing that women are childlike. Heterosexual intimacy can be translated into believing that women control men through their sexuality. The negative sides to these beliefs are hostile sexist beliefs. Positive correlations between benevolent and hostile sexist beliefs support concerns about benevolent sexist beliefs. Consistent with the idea of ambivalent reactions to women, benevolent sexism is associated with endorsement of positive stereotypes about women and hostile sexism. These researchers also demonstrate similar benevolent and hostile beliefs about men, framed in terms of negative implications of benevolent belief about men for men rather than for women (Glick & Fiske, 1999).

The positive nature of benevolent sexist beliefs can make them particularly problematic. Women and men are less likely to identify benevolent than hostile sexist beliefs about women as sexist (Swim et al., 2005). Similarly, although women prefer egalitarian men to benevolent sexist men, benevolent sexist men are seen as less sexist than hostile sexist men because they are perceived as more likeable, even though the latter two are likely to be the same people (Killianski, & Rudman, 1998; Barreto & Ellemers, 2005a). Additionally, women who endorse benevolent sexist beliefs are more likely to respond more favorably to benevolently sexist explanations for discrimination from intimate partners (Moya, Glick, Expósito, de Lemus, & Hart, 2007).

A number of studies have demonstrated the importance of ambivalent sexist beliefs for understanding sexism against women. Cross-culturally, countries where individuals have been found to be more likely to endorse benevolent than hostile sexist beliefs also tend to be countries where there is greater gender inequality (Glick, Fiske, Mladinic, Saiz, Abrams, & Masser, et al., 2000). Benevolent sexist beliefs have been found to be important in understanding reactions to rape victims. Benevolent sexists are more likely to blame women than men for acquaintance rape, particularly when she is perceived to have behaved inappropriately (Abrams, Viki, Masser, & Bohner, 2003; Viki, Abrams, & Masser, 2004). In contrast, hostile sexism is related to rape proclivity for acquaintance rape (Abrams et al., 2003; Viki, Chiroro, & Abrams, 2006). Hostile sexism is also related to greater tolerance of sexism after hearing hostile humor about women (Ford & Ferguson, 2004).

Research on ambivalent sexism has not focused on ambivalence per se, but more on the usefulness of considering two forms or ways of framing sexist beliefs. Moreover, the research has not focused on the different components of benevolent sexism, although it may be useful in the future to consider the three different components of benevolent sexism.

BELIEFS SUPPORTING SEXUAL AGGRESSION AGAINST WOMEN

Brownmiller (1975) was one of the first to argue that sexism was a central cause of violence against women when she said that rape was a form of male dominance serving to keep women in a state of fear. Consistent with this, young women report that fear of rape is one of their most salient fears (Hickman & Muehlenhard, 1997).

A set of beliefs that support that has received much attention are rape myths. *Rape myths* are "attitudes and beliefs that are generally false but are widely and persistently held, and that serve to deny and justify male sexual aggression against women" (Lonsway & Fitzgerald, 1994, p. 134). The concept of rape myths was first introduced by sociologists (e.g., Schwendinger & Schwendinger, 1974) and feminists (e.g., Brownmiller, 1975) in the 1970s. Rape myths were theoretically tied to victim blaming and a belief in a just world (Payne, Lonsway, & Fitzgerald, 1999). Burt (1980) developed the first scale to assess rape myth acceptance and a number of others have since developed similar measures. Payne et al. (1999) developed one recent conceptually and methodologically strong measure that assesses beliefs such as blaming women for rape (e.g., she asked for it), denying rape (it wasn't really rape, she's lying, he did not mean to), and trivializing rape (rape is an infrequent and trivial event). Endorsement of rape myths is associated with, for instance, hostile beliefs about women, acceptance of interpersonal violence, and sex role stereotyping (Payne et al., 1999).

Going beyond rape myths, meta-analytic reviews have documented the association among several types of the beliefs about sexual violence and perceptions of and engaging in sexual aggression against women. *Perceptions* of specific incidents of rape and sexual coercion depend on the perceivers' beliefs about violence and sexuality (e.g., rape myth acceptance, acceptance of interpersonal violence against women, sexual callousness, and adversarial sexual beliefs) and their perception of the situation (e.g., whether the victim and perpetrator had a prior relationship, whether alcohol was involved, the extent to which a woman resisted; Emmers-Sommer & Allen, 1999). Research predicting men's sexual aggressive behavior reveals that similar beliefs, particularly those that direct men's behavior, also underlie sexual aggression against women. Masculine ideologies are some of the most important predictors of male sexual aggression (Murnen, Wright, & Kaluzny, 2002).

These masculine ideologies include belief in male dominance as a motive for sexual relationships, endorsement of hypermasculinity (e.g., violence is manly, any man who is a man needs sex regularly), and hostile masculinity (including beliefs that force and coercion are legitimate to use in sexual relationships, believing that relationships are fundamentally exploitive and each party is manipulative, and endorsement of rape myths). Measures more typically used to assess more general gender-related beliefs (e.g., describing oneself as instrumental, endorsement of traditional gender roles) have been found to be related to sexual aggression in men, but not as strongly as masculine ideologies. Research has also documented the role of implicit beliefs in sexual aggression against women. Men who endorse sexually aggressive attitudes are more likely to associate sex and power (Bargh, Raymond, Pryor, & Strack, 1995). Men who report more frequent and severe sexually coercive and aggressive behavior are more likely to associate women with sex and with hostility (Leibold & McConnell, 2004).

SEXIST BEHAVIORS

A wide range of types of sexist behaviors have been documented. One of the most frequent types of behaviors is judgments about identically described women versus men. The judgments consist of evaluations, resources given (e.g., jobs, salary), trait attributions, and attributions given for success or failures. It is likely that this method of documenting sexism is often used because it is well suited to empirical tests that cleanly compare the effects of a target's gender on others' behaviors. Yet, the reliance on this paradigm has some limitations. Because the studies often rely on fictitious people with minimal information given about them, rated by college students with little involvement with the target or situation, the studies are vulnerable to criticisms about their external validity (Copus, 2005). A related limitation is that this paradigm results in a restricted definition of the types of behaviors that one might consider as sexist and restricted contexts for studying sexist behaviors. In contrast, research outside of the laboratory setting has examined a wide range of other types of sexist behaviors. This includes research examining behavioral enactment of gender roles within families, research documenting interpersonal partner violence and sexual harassment, and research on everyday forms of discrimination. Although stronger in its external validity, this latter research also has its limitations, primarily in terms of the internal validity.

JUDGMENTS OF WOMEN AND MEN

The logic behind research testing for differential judgments of women and men as evidence of sexist behavior is based on a gender-blind philosophy, akin to a color-blind philosophy on race-relations. Antifemale sexism is illustrated when a woman is judged less favorably or to have more female stereotypical attributes than an identically described man. This illustrates that women and men were not being judged as individuals but being judged as a members of their gender groups. Individual characteristics such as the quality of a person's work could influence judgments, but in addition to these characteristics, the targets' gender-group membership influenced the judgments. Akin to research on the base-rate fallacy, some research suggests that people may underutilize their stereotypes in judgments relative to their general beliefs about women and men (e.g., Locksley, Borgida, Brekke, & Hepburn, 1980). Yet the concern in the literature is not whether gender stereotypes are underutilized or whether gender stereotypes are being used appropriately. Rather the concern from a gender-blind philosophy is that a target's gender group membership is used at all. Thus, the focus has been on whether gender influences judgments with the assumption that any influence of gender-category membership on judgments is problematic because individuals should be gender-blind in their judgments.

Historically, a perceived lack of fit between women's traditional roles, abilities, and traits was predicted to lead to judgments or attributions that did not favor women. Apart from predicting that some people would be more likely to judge women and men differently (e.g., those who endorse traditional gender roles), some domains might be more problematic than others (e.g., masculine domains for women), and some targets might be more likely to evoke negative gender stereotypes about abilities (e.g., attractive women), there was no discussion about the difference between, for instance, gender stereotype activation and application. Little attention was explicitly given to variables that would influence activation or suppression of stereotypes, whether activation of gender stereotypes could account for effects of a target's gender on a perceiver's judgments, the manner in which gender stereotypes influence judgments (e.g., contrast or assimilation effects), and variables that could attenuate or accentuate the relation between activation and application of gender stereotypes. As a result, although sometimes documenting differential treatment of women and men, these studies were not able to adequately account for heterogeneity of findings across studies.

In contrast, more recent research has paid much more attention to cognitive, affective, and motivational processes that influence the impact of target's category membership on judgments. There has been more theoretical consideration about the particular aspects of gender stereotypes (e.g., descriptive vs. prescriptive stereotypes; Gill, 2004) and the ways that treatment can be manifested (e.g., paternalistic behavior; Vescio, Gervais, Snyder, & Hoover, 2005). As a result researchers are better able to pinpoint why, when, and how another person's gender will influence judgments. Researchers are also beginning to attend more to intersections between category membership, such as the implications of both race and gender membership (e.g., Vescio, Judd, & Kwan, 2004). Research reviewing this literature is covered in detail in other sections of the *Handbook* (e.g., Biernat, chap. 7, this volume; Vescio, Gervais, Heiphetz, & Bloodhart, chap. 12, this volume). Therefore, we limit our review to two areas of research that have been of specific relevance to understanding judgments of women versus men.

Backlash

The concept of backlash against women was popularized by Faludi (1991) when she wrote a journalistic book arguing that there was an increasing negative reaction to women as they were gaining equality with men. Empirical data demonstrating backlash come from several different areas. For instance, the more women report attempts to access nontraditional careers, the more experiences with discrimination they report having. Plus, women's upward mobility may be more likely to increase endorsement of some forms of sexist beliefs, such as resentment toward efforts to improve women's status as assessed by Neosexist beliefs, than increase endorsement of traditional gender roles (Beaton, Tougas, & Joly, 1996; Tougas, Brown, Beaton, & St-Pierre, 1999).

Backlash can also be seen in greater negative evaluations of women than men in masculine domains (as documented by meta-analyses of evaluations of women and men; Bowen, Swim, & Jacobs, 2000; Eagly, Makhijani, & Klonsky, 1992; Swim, Borgida, Maruyama, & Myers, 1989) and in reactions to women in gender-atypical roles (e.g., Rudman & Glick, 1999). Negative evaluations of women in leadership positions are particularly characteristic of backlash because it is within the context of reacting against women in positions of power (Eagly et al., 1992). Backlash against women in positions of leadership is not necessarily because people doubt women's leadership skills. Another reason is that women who are leaders may be assumed to lack communal traits. For instance, when jobs require both agentic and communal traits, agentic women but not agentic men are less likely to be hired (Rudman & Glick, 1999). Another reason for backlash is that women in positions of power can threaten men's dominance (Beaton et al., 1996).

Consistent with the implication that backlash implies an extreme negative reaction, Rudman and Fairchild (2004) illustrated that participants sabotaged the future performance of a woman who had behaved in a gender-atypical manner in a masculine domain and a man who had behaved gender atypically in a feminine domain. Extreme negative reactions are also shown in the form of sexual aggression. It has been argued that sexual harassment or sexual assault can be used as a form of backlash against women threatening male dominance. Consistent with this argument, Maass, Cadinu, Guarnieri, and Grasselli (2003) found that highly identified men were more likely to sexually harass women by exposing women to pornography when women threatened men's gender identity and threatened the legitimacy of gender inequality (i.e., they were portrayed as a feminist).

Social Context

One particularly interesting context that can influence sexist behavior is whether or not the context suggests that sexism is permissible. This is nicely illustrated by Ford and Ferguson's (2004) prejudice norm theory. They argue that sexist humor increases tolerance for sexism, rather than, for instance, increased activation of sexist beliefs. Greater tolerance of sexism has the potential to increase the likelihood that individuals will engage in discriminatory behavior. Individuals may also try to create a situation that allows them to be sexist. When individuals demonstrate that they are not sexist, their subsequent judgments tend to be more sexist (Monin & Miller, 2001). This suggests that individuals are credentialing themselves as nonsexist individuals, thereby freeing themselves to be sexist. Contexts can also discourage sexist behavior, particularly for those who are motivated to be egalitarian. Those who are internally and externally motivated to not appear sexist have been found to rate sexist jokes more negatively when a situation indicated that it was not appropriate to be sexist but the type of situation did not influence those who did not report these motivations (Klonis, Plant, & Devine 2005).

TRADITIONAL GENDER ROLES

Although, as noted earlier, people are less likely to endorse traditional gender roles, data on gender division of labor suggest that many still support traditional gender roles. Unequal division of labor in the home is found for employed women including women in high-status and high-paying roles, not just women who depend completely on their partners' income. Full-time employed women do more unpaid work than full-time employed men (Craig, 2006; Gershuny, Bittman, & Brice, 2005). Although the amount of women's domestic work decreases as their earnings increase, this pattern alters when women earn more than 50% of the household income. The few women in this range seem to compensate for their higher earnings with a more traditional division of household work (Bittman, England, Sayer, Folbre, & Matheson, 2003). Although couples alter the amount of domestic work they do based on their partners' employment status, resulting in greater equity in domestic work as their employment status changes, some data indicate that the alterations have as much or even more to do with women doing less than men doing more (Bianchi, Milkie, Sayer, & Robinson, 2000). Other data indicate women are spending as much or more time with children as they did in 1965 (Sayer, Bianchi, & Robinson, 2004). Division of labor in child care is particularly prominent. The time that women spend with children is more demanding time than that spent by men. Time use diary data indicate that mothers not only spend two to three times more time with children than men, but women also assume more responsibility for managing child care, do more multitasking, more physical labor, more tasks that are based on rigid timetables (e.g., adjusting one's time to a child's schedule as opposed to interacting with children when the parent has time), and spend more time alone with children (Craig, 2006).

Inequity in relationships is also revealed by power differentials in heterosexual relationships. For example, in addition to inequitable division of domestic labor, women have less control over household income. Even when women bring home income, men tend to take control over household money (Kenney, 2006). Unequal power is especially prevalent when women earn less than men, which is characteristic of most of the population.

EVERYDAY EXPERIENCES AND INTERPERSONAL SEXISM

Another form of sexist behaviors that women experience are those embedded in their everyday lives that often emerge in interpersonal exchanges. These experiences include endorsement of traditional stereotypes and preference for gender roles, hostile comments directed at women, and unwanted sexual attention (Hyers, 2007; Swim, Hyers, Cohen, & Ferguson, 2001). The experiences also include general mistreatment in work and academic settings that are not necessarily identified as sexist but are experienced as incivility and are more often experienced by women than men (Lim & Cortina, 2005; Settles, Cortina, Malley, & Stewart 2006). The context and perpetrators for everyday experience with sexism are broader than just work and academic settings perpetrated by employers, teachers, and colleagues; they also include experiences in restaurants, bars, and stores perpetrated by employees directed at their customers, home and social gatherings perpetrated by friends and family members, and streets perpetrated by strangers, such as strangers engaging in what is called eve-teasing in India (Ramasubramanian & Oliver, 2003). Thus, these experiences include comments and behaviors that form hostile work environments, chilly classroom climates, and nonprosecutable comments and behaviors that intertwine within the fabric of women's public and private lives.

Evidence of these types of experiences are often documented with self-reports. Although one might worry about oversensitivity by reporters, one could also consider issues related to reporters not always knowing or admitting that they or others have been targets of sexism. Reasons for not reporting sexism include not noticing or defining incidents as sexist and not wanting to publicly report incidents (Becker & Swim, 2007; Stangor, Swim, Van Allen, & Sechrist, 2002). Not noticing and defining incidents as sexist can occur if the incidents are not prototypical (e.g., a woman treating another woman unfairly; Inman & Baron, 1996), incidents are perceived as normative or they are habitual (e.g. "ladies first" or sexist language, Benekraitus & Feagin, 1997; Swim et al., 2004), the incidents appear to be positive (e.g., stereotyping women as nicer than men, incidents that could be interpreted as involving sexual interest; Becker & Swim, 2007; Swim et al., 2004), or assuming one must know a perpetrator's beliefs and intent before identifying an experience as sexist (Swim, Scott, Sechrist, Campbell, & Stangor, 2003). Not wanting to publicly report incidents can occur for several reasons, including concerns about interpersonal and practical costs associated with confronting prejudice (Hyers, 2007; Swim & Hyers, 1999).

Not surprisingly then, the frequency with which women report experiencing everyday sexism is influenced by the ways in which these experiences are assessed. If women are asked how often they experience sexism, their estimates will be lower than if one sums across their reported experiences with a range of types of everyday sexist behaviors (Swim, Cohen, & Hyers, 1998). Women's recalled experiences with sexism are also lower than if they are asked to keep track of their experiences in a diary format. Plus, when asked to keep track of their experiences in a diary format, they will report more if they are given a list of possible behaviors to track than if they are not provided with such a list (Swim et al., 2001). If women are asked to publicly report whether they have experienced sexism, they are less likely to do so than if they can report it anonymously (Stangor et al., 2002). The focus here has been on antifemale sexism primarily reported by women, but it is also the case that people report antimale sexism, although the frequency of antimale sexism reported by women and men is lower than that of antifemale sexism (Swim et al., 2001).

Yet despite limitations associated with asking women about their experiences, much can be gained by examining the types of experiences individuals report. For instance, Benekraitus and Feagin (1997) conceptually identified and classified women's reported experiences with sexism into a large variety of types of sexist behaviors that provide insights into the ways that sexism is manifested in women's lives. Examples of such behaviors include condescending chivalry, tokenism, hostile humor about women, use of sexual innuendos or teasing as a way of intimidating women, fixating on women's gender or physical appearance rather than their work, making inferences that women are lesbians as a means to silence them, and encouraging women to be ambitious or successful but not following up this encouragement by misdirecting them into unchallenging positions, not rewarding them when they have nontraditional achievements, or giving them impressive titles without increases in salary or authority.

One prevalent type of everyday sexism is sexual or bodily objectification, which is experienced both indirectly, such as through media portrayals of women, and directly, such as through street remarks (Fredrickson & Roberts 1997). Women's bodies and body parts are often the target of attention. For instance, the media is more likely to portray only men's rather than only women's faces and less likely to portray men's than women's bodies. The objectification is most clear when body parts or functions are portrayed separate from a person's identity and are presented for the use or pleasure of others. Objectification can also occur from street remarks called or shouted out to women about their bodies or more generally through gaze, and specifically male gaze in the form of examining and presumably evaluating women's bodies. These portrayals and attention are often focused on sexual attractiveness of women. The connection between objectification and sexualization of women is made explicit in pornography.

VIOLENCE

Violence against women is vast both in terms of the multitude of forms it takes and in its prevalence. A report published by the U.S. Department of Justice for practitioners defines violence against women as "any physical, emotional, sexual, or psychological abuse or violence committed against women by intimate partners or acquaintances, including, current or former spouses, cohabiting partners, boyfriends, or dates" (Carlson, Worden, vanRyn, & Bachman, 2003, p. 2). They describe physical violence as both fatal and nonfatal physical assaults; sexual violence as various forms of rape and sexual assault; and emotional and psychological abuse as any act intended to denigrate, isolate, or dominate a partner. This report largely focuses on sexual assault, domestic abuse, and stalking, much of which can be described as forms of intimate partner violence. The concept of violence against women is broadened by the same behaviors committed by strangers and including sexual harassment, which has largely been studied within workplace and academic settings.

Estimates about the prevalence of violence against women vary according to the type of violence examined and the type of reports examined. Yet, the data point to the pervasiveness of male-per-petrated violence against women, especially when considered in cumulative form across different forms of violence. The American Psychological Association (1999) reported that in the United States alone, "By most conservative estimates, almost 1,000,000 women experience violent victimization by an intimate each year." Many also point to lifetime estimates of women experiencing violence. For instance, Carlson et al. (2003) reported that 25% of women experiencing intimate partner violence in their lifetime is a minimum estimate. The estimate is larger when one includes sexual harassment. The American Psychological Association (1999, p. 2) reported that nearly 50% of women are affected by sexual harassment during the course of their working lives.

Violence against women is seen as part of a larger picture of a sexist culture. Although recognizing multiple causal factors that lead to male violence against women, the American Psychological Association (1999, p. 3) noted this violence "remains fundamentally a learned behavior that is shaped by sociocultural norms and role expectations that support female subordination and perpetuate male violence."

One cultural source of support for male sexual aggression and beliefs about sex and violence that has gotten much research attention is pornography. One meta-analysis revealed that exposure to pornography is associated with endorsement of several beliefs that are associated with perceptions of and engagement of sexual aggression, including endorsement of rape myths (Oddone-Paolucci, Genuis, & Violato, 2000). A second meta-analysis revealed that nonexperimental exposure to pornography was not related to endorsement of rape myths but experimental exposure to violent and nonviolent pornography was associated with endorsement of rape myths (Allen, Emmers, Gebhardt, & Giery, 1995).

Although much attention has been given to interpersonal relationship violence against women, similar violence against men is also a problem, although not as prevalent. One representative U.S. national survey indicated that 17% of women and 3% of men reported experiencing rape in their lifetime, 8% of women and 2% of men experienced stalking, and 26% of women and 8% of men reported intimate partner violence (Tjaden & Thoeness, 2000). Insights into gender differences in these types of violence come from understanding differences in types of violence women and men experience. Johnson (2006) argued that there are four types of domestic abuse based on whether attempts to control one's partner are also part of the relationship. Control tactics included use of threat, economics, privilege and punishment, children, isolation, emotional abuse, and sex. The four types are (a) intimate terrorism where one partner is violent and controlling and the other is not; (b) mutual violent control where both partners are violent and controlling; (c) violent resistance where one partner is violent and not controlling with a partner who is violent and controlling; and (d) situational couple violence where there is violence by at least one partner but no attempts at control. Based on wives' descriptions of themselves and their husbands, Johnson found that intimate terrorism violence was more typical of husbands than wives, violent resistance is more typical of wives than husbands, and the remaining two types are found equally among wives and husbands.

Men experience more violence than women in other domains. Specifically, men report more experiences with physical assaults (e.g., being slapped or hit, pushed, grabbed or shoved, and being hit with an object) than women, with 52% of women and 66% of men reporting such experiences (Tjaden & Thoeness, 2000). This particular survey does not identify the gender of the perpetrator. Yet, even if the violence against men is perpetrated by a man, this violence can still be important for understanding sexism if it is part of a larger system of defining masculinity and establishing dominance hierarchies.

CONSEQUENCES OF SEXISM

The ability to detect the effects of sexism is not straightforward. There are direct, indirect, and secondary effects of sexism (Allison, 1998; Stangor et al., 2003). Direct effects include physical harm through, for instance, sexual violence, economic harm through loss of wages, and psychological harm through internalization of self-doubt and accumulated depression. Individuals may or may not be aware that sexism is directly affecting them. Indirect effects include those that are influenced by one's interpretation of incidents, sometimes attenuating and other times accentuating the negative consequences of stressful incidents (Major & O'Brien, 2005). Secondary effects are those that follow from direct or indirect effects. For instance, if sexism causes women to have lower income than men, they are more likely to be in poverty then men and experience a wide range of consequences associated with poverty. Here the consequences we focus on are violence, objectification, and internalization of gender stereotypes and roles (see also Major & Sawyer, Chapter 5 and Aronson, Chapter 8, this volume, for discussion of more effects).

VIOLENCE

Violence can be understood both as a consequence of sexism and as a type of sexist behavior causing other subsequent consequences. Violence against women results in some of the most extreme consequences of sexism for women. According to the U.S. Bureau of Justice, about 1,300 women in the United States in 1993 were murdered by partners or former partners, and this figure is likely an underestimate because in murders the relationship between victim and perpetrator is often not identified (American Psychological Association, 1999). There are also a number of subsequent consequences of violence against women, including those from sexual harassment. The American Psychological Association (1999, p. 2) summarized the following consequences:

> Victimized women suffer from depression, substance abuse, anxiety, and low self-esteem. Many exhibit negative cognitive and emotional after effects and consistently show among the highest rates of post-traumatic stress disorder (PTSD) associated with any type of traumatic event. Accordingly, PTSD is also a common diagnosis for many victims of violence. Violence against women has economic as well as psychological and physical costs. For example, the U.S. Merit Systems Protection Board (1995) estimated the cost of sexual harassment to the government over the course of the 2-year reporting period

of their study (from April 1992 through April 1994) at $327.1 million in job turnover, sick leave, individual productivity, and workgroup productivity. The same study also found that nearly 21% of sexual harassment victims reported suffering a decline in productivity. The average rape in the United States is estimated to cost $92,100 in tangible expenses, emotional distress, and lost quality of life.

OBJECTIFICATION OF WOMEN

One consequence of sexual objectification of women is that women tend to perceive that they are heavier than normal and become dissatisfied with their bodies. When women watch sexualized portrayals of women, they are more likely to want to be thinner (Lavine, Sweeney, & Wagner, 1999). Although body dissatisfaction in men is less common than in women, sexual portrayal of men can also influence men, for instance, by making them want to appear larger (Lavine et al., 1999).

A second consequence of objectification is self-objectification (Fredrickson & Roberts, 1997). Self-objectification involves having a third-party perspective on one's appearance, thinking about how others might view one's body rather than a first-party perspective about unobservable attributes such as one's thoughts and feelings. Self-objectification is argued to be an adaptive response, a type of pro-active strategy. This strategy is like other pro-active coping responses to discrimination that allow women to counteract or attenuate negative reactions to their bodies (Mallett & Swim, 2005). Despite its adaptive value, Fredrickson and Roberts (1997) argued that body objectification leads to body shame and depletion of attention resources that can influence performance on other tasks. Self-objectification leads to constant monitoring of one's body as to whether it fits cultural standards of beauty. Because these standards do not fit most women, most women will fail to meet them, resulting in shame and anxiety. The attention required to monitor one's body can lead to a split in attention between a task that one is working on and attention to one's body. It has also been associated with inattention to body cues, restrained eating, and disordered eating. Finally, it has been argued to be associated with other mental health risks such as depression and sexual dysfunction.

INTERNALIZATION OF SEXISM

Internalization of prescriptive gender-role behavior can undermine women's aspirations, undermine psychological well-being, and influence women's and men's behavior. For example, the more women endorse implicit beliefs that intimate male partners are "knights in shining armor" (i.e., men will take care of women and protect them), the less likely they are to aspire to higher education and high-status jobs (Rudman & Heppen, 2003). As another example, one prescriptive belief is that women should put other people's needs ahead of their own needs in relationships. This belief is at the center of what Jack (1991) calls self-silencing. Self-silencing is the tendency to endorse relationship beliefs that prescribe that one should not express one's thoughts and feelings in relationships to protect harmony of their relationships. Theoretically, these beliefs derive from gender-related beliefs about appropriate behavior for women in interpersonal interactions. The more women endorse these beliefs the more likely they are to have poorer psychological well-being, for instance, in the form of greater depression (Jack & Dill, 1992), and the less likely they are to confront everyday forms of sexism (Swim, Essell, Quinliven, & Ferguson, 2008).

Internalization of social role expectations can lead to gender differences in behaviors. The more women and men endorse stereotypical differences between women and men and the more situations prescribe expectations for gender differences in emotional expressivity, the greater the gender differences in self-reported and physiological measures of emotional intensity (Grossman & Wood, 1993). Similarly, although dominant women and men become leaders in same-sex dyads and in mixed-sex dyads doing a feminine task, in mixed sex dyads doing masculine or neutral tasks, less dominant men emerge as leaders (Ritter & Yoder, 2004). Ironically, this effect frequently occurs because more dominant women appoint the less dominant men. Conforming to gender-role norms can also be self-reinforcing. When individuals perceive social norms to be relevant to themselves, they feel better engaging in the norm-congruent behavior (Wood, Christensen, Hebl, & Rothgerber, 1997).

CONCLUSIONS

Research on sexism has developed much from its origins of defending women against sexist research on gender differences. Research has documented a variety of sexist beliefs and behaviors and the consequences of sexism for women and to some extent men as well. The research is not without its challenges including: (a) defining what types of beliefs and behaviors will be considered sexist; (b) detecting sexist beliefs when it is not politically correct to express them; (c) addressing the importance of beliefs when it is often the case that it is hard to make connections between beliefs and behaviors; (d) documenting sexist behaviors through self-reports when sexism may be unnoticed, may be noticed but people may differ in their interpretation of them, and even when interpreted as sexist some may not wish to report them; (e) limited external validity of some of the research, (f) acknowledging gender differences in traits, abilities, and behaviors, whatever their source, while still striving for fair and equitable treatment; (g) understanding the impact of interpretation of incidents on the consequences of incidents; and (h) making connections between individual levels of analysis and organizational, institutional, and cultural levels of analyses.

There are assumptions running through much of the literature that are worth considering. One assumption is that sexism exists and we can better understand and document it if we devise better and more precise ways of defining and measuring it. Different research might arise if one attempted to document changes that have resulted from decreases in sexism. Another assumption is a gender-blind society should be strived for and the resulting assumption that gender equity would be obtained if people saw and treated others as individuals and not as members of gender groups. Different research might emerge if one took an approach more akin to a multicultural perspective where striving to value differences that exist and thinking about gender as a property of groups rather than individuals. A third assumption is that it is profitable to assess manifestations and consequences of sexism at an individual level perhaps because these contribute to organizational, institutional, and cultural manifestations and consequences of sexism. Different research might emerge if one did not assume this connection existed. The research reviewed here has proven the value of taking these assumptions. Yet more might be gained if one thought about the implications of such assumptions and considered alternatives to them.

REFERENCES

Abrams, D., Viki, G. T., Masser, B., & Bohner, G. (2003). Perceptions of stranger and acquaintance rape: The role of benevolent and hostile sexism in victim blame and rape proclivity. *Journal of Personality and Social Psychology, 84*(1), 111–125.

Allen, M., Emmers, T., Gebhardt, L., & Giery, M. A. (1995). Exposure to pornography and acceptance of rape myths. *Journal of Communication, 45*(1), 5–26.

Allison, K. W. (1998). Stress and oppressed social category membership. In J. K. Swim & C. Stangor (Eds.), *Prejudice: The target's perspective* (pp. 145–170). San Diego, CA: Academic.

Allport, G. W. (1954). *The nature of prejudice.* Oxford, UK: Addison-Wesley.

American Psychological Association. (1999). Resolution on male violence against women reports. Retrieved January 6, 2007, from http://www.apa.org/pi/wpo/maleviol.html

Ashmore, R. D. (1990). Sex, gender, and the individual In L. A. Pervin (Ed.), *Handbook of personality theory and research* (pp. 486–526). New York: Guilford.

Bargh, J. A., Raymond, P., Pryor, J. B., & Strack, F. (1995). Attractiveness of the underling: An automatic power-sex association and its consequences for sexual harassment and aggression. *Journal of Personality and Social Psychology, 68,* 768–781.

Barreto, M., & Ellemers, N. (2005a). The burden of benevolent sexism: How it contributes to the maintenance of gender inequalities. *European Journal of Social Psychology, 35*(5), 633–642.

Barreto, M., & Ellemers, N. (2005b). The perils of political correctness: Men's and women's responses to old-fashioned and modern sexist views. *Social Psychology Quarterly, 68*(1), 75–88.

Beaton, A. M., Tougas, F., & Joly, S. (1996). Neosexism among male managers: Is it a matter of numbers? *Journal of Applied Social Psychology, 26*(24), 2189–2203.

Becker, J. C., & Swim, J. K. (2007*). Normalization of sexism: Differential effects of attending to sexism and its harm on reducing benevolent and modern sexist beliefs.* Manuscript under review.

Beere, C. A. (1990). *Gender roles: A handbook of tests and measures.* New York, NY: Greenwood Press.

Bem, S. L. (1981). Gender schema theory: A cognitive account of sex typing. *Psychological Review, 88*(4), 354–364.

Benekraitus, N. V., & Feagin, J. R. (1997). *Modern sexism.* Englewood Cliffs, NJ: Prentice-Hall

Bianchi, S. M., Milkie, M. A., Sayer, L. C., & Robinson, J. P. (2000). Is anyone doing the housework? Trends in the gender division of household labor. *Social Forces, 79*(1), 191–228.

Bittman, M., England, P., Sayer, L., Folbre, N., & Matheson, G. (2003). When does gender trump money? Bargaining and time in household work. *American Journal of Sociology, 109*(1), 186–214.

Bowen, C., Swim, J. K., & Jacobs, R. R. (2000). Evaluating gender biases on actual job performance of real people: A meta-analysis. *Journal of Applied Social Psychology, 30*(10), 2194–2215.

Brooks, A., & Hesse-Biber, S. H. (2007). An invitation to feminist research. In S. H. Hesse-Biber & P. L. Levy (Eds.), *Feminist research practice: A primer* (pp. 1–24). Thousand Oaks, CA: Sage.

Brownmiller, S. (1975). *Against our will: Men, women, and rape.* New York: Simon & Schuster.

Burt, M. R. (1980). Cultural myths and supports for rape. *Journal of Personality and Social Psychology, 38,* 217–230.

Cameron, J. E. (2001). Social identity, modern sexism, and perceptions of personal and group discrimination by women and men. *Sex Roles, 45*(11), 743–766.

Campbell, B., Schellenberg, E. G., & Senn, C. Y. (1997). Evaluating measures of contemporary sexism. *Psychology of Women Quarterly, 21*(1), 89–101.

Caplin, P. J., & Caplin, J. B. (1994). *Thinking critically about research on sex and gender.* New York: HarperCollins.

Carlson, B. E., Worden, A. P., VanRyn, M., & Bachman, R. (2003). *Violence against women: Synthesis of research for practitioners.* Retrieved January 8, 2007, from http://www.ncjrs.gov/pdffiles1/nij/grants/199577.pdf

Carter, J. S., & Borch, C. A. (2005). Assessing the effects of urbanism and regionalism on gender-role attitudes, 1974–1998. *Sociological Inquiry, 75*(4), 548–563.

Copus, D. (2005). *Out of bounds: The ecological invalidity of gender stereotypes research.* Paper presented at the Society of Industrial and Organizational Psychology annual conference in April 2005, Los Angeles.

Cottrell, C. A., & Neuberg, S. L. (2005). Different emotional reactions to different groups: A sociofunctional threat-based approach to "prejudice." *Journal of Personality and Social Psychology, 88*(5), 770–789.

Craig, L. (2006). Does father care mean fathers share? A comparison of how mothers and fathers in intact families spend time with children. *Gender & Society, 20*(2), 259–281.

Cralley, E. L., & Ruscher, J. B. (2005). Lady, girl, female, or woman: Sexism and cognitive busyness predict use of gender-biased nouns. *Journal of Language and Social Psychology, 24*(3), 300–314.

Cuddy, A. J. C., Fiske, S. T., & Glick, P. (2004). When professionals become mothers, warmth doesn't cut the ice. *Journal of Social Issues, 60*(4), 701–718.

Dasgupta, N., & Asgari, S. (2004). Seeing is believing: Exposure to counter stereotypic women leaders and its effect on the malleability of automatic gender stereotyping. *Journal of Experimental Social Psychology, 40,* 642–658.

Deaux, K., & Lafrance, M. (1998). Gender. In D. T. Gilbert, S. T. Fiske, & G. Lindzey (Eds.), *The handbook of social psychology* (Vol. 1, 4th ed., pp. 788–827). New York: McGraw-Hill.

Deaux, K., & Lewis, L. L. (1984). Structure of gender stereotypes: Interrelationships among components and gender label. *Journal of Personality and Social Psychology, 46,* 991–1004.

Deaux, K., & Major, B. (1987). Putting gender into context: An interactive model of gender-related behavior. *Psychological Review, 94*(3), 369–389.

Denmark, F., Russo, N. F., Frieze, I. H., & Sechzer, J. A. (1988). Guidelines for avoiding sexism in psychological research. *American Psychologist, 43,* 582–585.

Deutsch, H. (1930). The significance of masochism in the mental life of women. *International Journal of Psycho-Analysis, 11,* 48–60.

Diekman, A. B., & Eagly, A. H. (2000). Stereotypes as dynamic constructs: Women and men of the past, present, and future. *Personality and Social Psychology Bulletin, 26*(10), 1171-1188.

Diekman, A. B., Eagly, A. H., Mladinic, A., & Ferreira, M. C. (2005). Dynamic stereotypes about women and men in Latin America and the United States. *Journal of Cross-Cultural Psychology, 36*(2), 209–226.

Eagly, A. H. (1987). *Sex differences in social behavior: A social-role interpretation.* Hillsdale, NJ: Erlbaum.

Eagly, A. H. (1995). The science and politics of comparing women and men. *American Psychologist, 50*(3), 145–158.

Eagly, A. H., Makhijani, M. G., & Klonsky, B. G. (1992). Gender and the evaluation of leaders: A meta-analysis. *Psychological Bulletin, 111*(1), 3–22.

Eagly, A. H., & Mladinic, A. (1989). Gender stereotypes and attitudes toward men and women. *Personality and Social Psychology Bulletin, 15,* 543–558.

Eagly, A. H., & Steffen, V. J. (1986). Gender and aggressive behavior: A meta-analytic review of the social psychological literature. *Psychological Bulletin, 100*(3), 309–330.

Emmers-Sommer, T. M., & Allen, M. (1999). Variables related to sexual coercion: A path model. *Journal of Social and Personal Relationships, 16*(5), 659–678.

Faludi, S. (1991) *Backlash: The undeclared war against American women.* New York: Doubleday.

Fassinger, R. E. (1994). Development and testing of the attitudes toward feminism and the women's movement (FWM) scale. *Psychology of Women Quarterly, 18*(3), 389–402.

Fiske, S. T., Cuddy, A. J. C., Glick, P., & Xu, J. (2002). A model of (often mixed) stereotype content: Competence and warmth respectively follow from perceived status and competition. *Journal of Personality and Social Psychology, 82*(6), 878–902.

Forbes, G. B., & Adams-Curtis, L. E. (2001). Experiences with sexual coercion in college males and females: Role of family conflict, sexist attitudes, acceptance of rape myths, self-esteem, and the big-five personality factors. *Journal of Interpersonal Violence, 16*(9), 865–889.

Forbes, G. B., Adams-Curtis, L. E., & White, K. B. (2004). First- and second-generation measures of sexism, rape myths and related beliefs, and hostility toward women: Their interrelationships and association with college students' experiences with dating aggression and sexual coercion. *Violence Against Women, 10*(3), 236–261.

Ford, T. E., & Ferguson, M. A. (2004). Social consequences of disparagement humor: A prejudiced norm theory. *Personality and Social Psychology Review, 8*(1), 79–94.

Fredrickson, B. L., & Roberts, T. (1997). Objectification theory: Toward understanding women's lived experiences and mental health risks. *Psychology of Women Quarterly, 21*(2), 173–206.

Gershuny, J., Bittman, M., & Brice, J. (2005). Exit, voice, and suffering: Do couples adapt to changing employment patterns? *Journal of Marriage and Family, 67*(3), 656–665.

Gill, M. J. (2004). When information does not deter stereotyping: Prescriptive stereotyping can foster bias under conditions that deter descriptive stereotyping. *Journal of Experimental Social Psychology, 40*(5), 619–632.

Gilligan, C. (1982). *In a different voice: Psychological theory and women's development.* Cambridge, MA: Harvard University Press.

Glick, P., & Fiske, S. T. (1996). The ambivalent sexism inventory: Differentiating hostile and benevolent sexism. *Journal of Personality and Social Psychology, 70*(3), 491–512.

Glick, P., & Fiske, S. T. (1999). The ambivalence toward men inventory: Differentiating hostile and benevolent beliefs about men. *Psychology of Women Quarterly, 23*(3), 519–536.

Glick, P., Fiske, S. T., Mladinic, A., Saiz, J. L., Abrams, D., & Masser, B., et al. (2000). Beyond prejudice as simple antipathy: Hostile and benevolent sexism across cultures. *Journal of Personality and Social Psychology, 79*(5), 763–775.

Greene, S. (2004). Biological determinism: Persisting problems for the psychology of women. *Feminism and Psychology, 14,* 431–435.

Grossman, M., & Wood, W. (1993). Sex differences in intensity of emotional experience: A social role interpretation. *Journal of Personality and Social Psychology, 65*(5), 1010–1022.

Guthrie, R. V. (2004). *Even the rat was white: A historical view of psychology* (2nd ed.). Upper Saddle River, NJ: Pearson Education.

Hackett, G., & Betz, N. (1981). The relationship of career-related self-efficacy expectations to perceived career options in college women and men. *Journal of Counseling Psychology, 28,* 399–410.

Haddock, G., & Zanna, M. P. (1994). Preferring "housewives" to "feminists": Categorization and the favorability of attitudes toward women. *Psychology of Women Quarterly, 18*(1), 25–52.

Hall, G. S. (1906). The question of coeducation. *Munsey's Magazine, 34,* 588–592.

Hall, J. A., & Carter, J. D. (1999). Gender-stereotype accuracy as an individual difference. *Journal of Personality and Social Psychology, 77*(2), 350–359.

Harding, S. (1993). Rethinking standpoint epistemology: What is "strong objectivity"? In L. Alcoff & E. Potter (Eds.), *Feminist epistemologies* (pp. 49–82). New York: Routledge.

Henley, N. M., Spalding, L. R., & Kosta, A. (2000). Development of the short form of the feminist perspectives scale. *Psychology of Women Quarterly, 24*(3), 254–256.

Hickman, S. E., & Muehlenhard, C. L. (1997). College women's fears and precautionary behaviors relating to acquaintance rape and stranger rape. *Psychology of Women Quarterly, 21*(4), 527–547.

Hoffman, C., & Hurst, N. (1990). Gender stereotypes: Perception or rationalization? *Journal of Personality and Social Psychology, 58,* 197–208.

Hyde, J. S. (2005). The gender similarities hypothesis. *American Psychologist, 60*(6), 581–592.

Hyers, L. L. (2007). Resisting prejudice every day: Exploring women's assertive responses to anti-black racism, anti-semitism, heterosexism, and sexism. *Sex Roles, 56*(1–2), 1–12.

Inman, M. L., & Baron, R. S. (1996). Influence of prototypes on perceptions of prejudice. *Journal of Personality and Social Psychology, 70*(4), 727–739.

Jack, D. C. (1991). *Silencing the self: Women and depression.* Cambridge, MA: Harvard University Press.

Jack, D. C., & Dill, D. (1992). The silencing the self scale: Schemas of intimacy associated with depression in women. *Psychology of Women Quarterly, 16*(1), 97–106.

Jagger, A. (2004). Feminist politics and epistemology: The standpoint of women. In S. Harding (Ed.), *The feminst standpoint theory reader: Intellectual and political controversies* (pp. 55–66). New York: Routledge.

Johnson, M. P. (2006). Conflict and control: Gender symmetry and asymmetry in domestic violence. *Violence Against Women, 12*(11), 1003–1018.

Jones, E. (1961). *The life and work of Sigmund Freud.* New York: Basic Books.

Jost, J. T., & Kay, A. C. (2005). Exposure to benevolent sexism and complementary gender stereotypes: Consequences for specific and diffuse forms of system justification. *Journal of Personality and Social Psychology, 88*(3), 498–509.

Jussim, L. (2005). Accuracy in social perception: Criticisms, controversies, criteria, components, and cognitive processes. In M. P. Zanna (Ed.), *Advances in Experimental Social Psychology* (Vol. 37, pp. 1-93). San Diego, CA: Elsevier Academic Press.

Keller, E. F. (1985). *Reflections on gender and science.* New Haven, CT: Yale University Press.

Kenney, C. T. (2006). The power of the purse: Allocative systems and inequality in couple households. *Gender & Society, 20*(3), 354–381.

Killianski, S. E., & Rudman, L. A. (1998). Wanting it both ways: Do women approve of benevolent sexism? *Sex Roles, 39,* 333–352.

King, L. A., & King, D. W. (1997). Sex-role egalitarianism scale: Development, psychometric properties, and recommendations for future research. *Psychology of Women Quarterly, 21*(1), 71–87.

Klonis, S. C., Plant, E. A., & Devine, P. G. (2005). Internal and external motivation to respond without sexism. *Personality and Social Psychology Bulletin, 31*(9), 1237–1249.

Lavine, H., Sweeney, D., & Wagner, S. H. (1999). Depicting women as sex objects in television advertising: Effects on body dissatisfaction. *Personality and Social Psychology Bulletin, 25*(8), 1049–1058.

Lehrer, A. (1988). A note on the semantics of -ist and -ism. *American Speech, 63*(2), 181–185.

Leibold, J. M., & McConnell, A. R. (2004). Women, sex, hostility, power, and suspicion: Sexually aggressive men's cognitive associations. *Journal of Experimental Social Psychology, 40*(2), 256–263.

Lim, S., & Cortina, L. M. (2005). Interpersonal mistreatment in the workplace: The interface and impact of general incivility and sexual harassment. *Journal of Applied Psychology, 90*(3), 483–496.

Locksley, A., Borgida, E., Brekke, N., & Hepburn, C. (1980). Sex stereotypes and social judgment. *Journal of Personality and Social Psychology, 39*(5), 821–831.

Lonsway, K. A., & Fitzgerald, L. F. (1994). Rape myths: In review. *Psychology of Women Quarterly, 18*(2), 133–164.

Lott, B. (1997). The personal and social correlates of a gender difference ideology. *Journal of Social Issues, 53*(2), 279–297.

Lupton, M. J. (1993.) *Menstruation and psychoanalysis.* Urbana: University of Illinois Press.

Maass, A., Cadinu, M., Guarnieri, G., & Grasselli, A. (2003). Sexual harassment under social identity threat: The computer harassment paradigm. *Journal of Personality and Social Psychology, 85*(5), 853–870.

Maccoby, E. E. (2002). Gender and group process: A developmental perspective. *Current Directions in Psychological Science, 11*(2), 54–58.

Mackinnon, C. T. (1987) Difference and dominance. In *Feminism unmodified: Discourses on life and law* (pp. 32–45). Cambridge, MA: Harvard University Press.

Major, B., & O'Brien, L. T. (2005). The social psychology of stigma. *Annual Review of Psychology, 56,* 393–421.

Mallett, R. K., & Swim, J. K. (2005). Bring it on: Proactive coping with discrimination. *Motivation and Emotion, 29*(4), 411–441.

Masser, B., & Abrams, D. (1999). Contemporary sexism: The relationships among hostility, benevolence, and neosexism. *Psychology of Women Quarterly, 23*(3), 503–517.

Miller, J. B. (1987). *Toward a new psychology of women.* New York: Beacon Press.

Mobius, P. J. (1901). The physiological mental weakness of women (A. McCorn, Trans.). *Alienist and Neurologist, 22,* 624–642.

Monin, B., & Miller, D. T. (2001). Moral credentials and the expression of prejudice. *Journal of Personality and Social Psychology, 81*(1), 33–43.

Morantz-Sanchez, R. (1983). *Sympathy and science: Women physicians in American medicine.* Chapel Hill: University of North Carolina Press.

Morrison, M. A., & Morrison, T. G. (2002). Development and validation of a scale measuring modern prejudice toward gay men and lesbian women. *Journal of Homosexuality, 43*(2), 15–37.

Moya, M., Glick, P., Exposito, F., deLemus, S., & Hart, J. (2007). It's for your own good: Benevolent sexism and women's reactions to protectively justified restrictions. *Personality and Social Psychology Bulletin, 33*(10), 1421-1434.

Murnen, S. K., Wright, C., & Kaluzny, G. (2002). If "boys will be boys," then girls will be victims? A meta-analytic review of the research that relates masculine ideology to sexual aggression. *Sex Roles, 46*(11), 359–375.

Nosek, B. A., & Banaji, M. R. (2001). The go/no-go association task. *Social Cognition, 19*(6), 625–666.

Nosek, B. A., Banaji, M., & Greenwald, A. G. (2002). Harvesting implicit group attitudes and beliefs from a demonstration web site. *Group Dynamics: Theory, Research, and Practice, 6*(1), 101–115.

Oddone-Paolucci, E., Genuis, M., & Violato, C. (2000). A meta-analysis of the published research on the effects of pornography. In C. Violato, E. Oddone-Paolucci, & M. Genuis (Eds.), *International congress on the changing family and child development* (pp. 48–59). Aldershot, UK: Ashgate.

Payne, D. L., Lonsway, K. A., & Fitzgerald, L. F. (1999). Rape myth acceptance: Exploration of its structure and its measurement using the Illinois Rape Myth Acceptance Scale. *Journal of Research in Personality, 33,* 27–68.

Quinne, S. (1987). *A mind of her own: The life of Karen Horney.* New York: Summit Books.

Ramasubramanian, S., & Oliver, M. B. (2003). Portrayals of sexual violence in popular Hindi films, 1997–99. *Sex Roles, 48*(7), 327–336.

Richards, E. (1983). Darwin and the descent of women. In D. R. Oldroyd & I. Langham (Eds.), *The wider domain of evolutionary thought* (pp. 57–11). London: Reidel.

Ritter, B. A., & Yoder, J. D. (2004). Gender differences in leader emergence persist even for dominant women: An updated confirmation of role congruity theory. *Psychology of Women Quarterly, 28*(3), 187–193.

Robinson, M. D., Johnson, J. T., & Shields, S. A. (1998). The gender heuristic and the database: Factors affecting the perception of gender-related differences in the experience and display of emotions. *Basic and Applied Social Psychology, 20*(3), 206–219.

Rudman, L. A., & Fairchild, K. (2004). Reactions to counterstereotypic behavior: The role of backlash in cultural stereotype maintenance. *Journal of Personality and Social Psychology, 87*(2), 157–176.

Rudman, L. A., & Glick, P. (1999). Feminized management and backlash toward agentic women: The hidden costs to women of a kinder, gentler image of middle managers. *Journal of Personality and Social Psychology, 77*(5), 1004–1010.

Rudman, L. A., & Heppen, J. B. (2003). Implicit romantic fantasies and women's interest in personal power: A glass slipper effect? *Personality and Social Psychology Bulletin, 29*(11), 1357–1370

Rudman, L. A., & Kilianski, S. R. (2000). Implicit and explicit attitudes toward female authority. *Personality and Social Psychology Bulletin, 26,* 1315–1328.

Sayer, L. C., Bianchi, S. M., & Robinson, J. P. (2004). Are parents investing less in children? Trends in mothers' and fathers' time with children. *American Journal of Sociology, 110*(1), 1–43.

Scarborough, E., & Furumoto, L. (1987). *Untold lives: The first generation of American women psychologists.* New York: Columbia University Press.

Schiebinger, L. (1989). *The mind has no sex? Women in the origins of modern science.* Cambridge, MA: Harvard University Press.

Schmid, M. M. (2004). Men are hierarchical, women are egalitarian: An implicit gender stereotype. *Swiss Journal of Psychology—Schweizerische Zeitschrift für Psychologie—Revue Suisse de Psychologie, 63*(2), 107–111.

Schwendinger, J. R., & Schwendinger, H. (1974). Rape myths: In legal, theoretical, and everyday practice. *Crime and Social Justice, 1,* 18–26.

Settles, I. H., Cortina, L. M., Malley, J., & Stewart, A. J. (2006). The climate for women in academic science: The good, the bad, and the changeable. *Psychology of Women Quarterly, 30*(1), 47–58.

Shapiro, F. R. (1985). Historical notes on the vocabulary of the women's movement. *American Speech, 60,* 3-16.

Shields, S. (1975). Functionalism, Darwinism, and the psychology of women: A study in social myth. *American Psychologist, 30,* 739–754.

Shields, S. A. (2002). *Speaking from the heart: Gender and the social meaning of emotion.* New York: Cambridge University Press.

Sommers, C. H. (1994). *Who stole feminism? How women have betrayed women.* New York: Simon & Schuster.

Spence, J. T. (1993). Gender-related traits and gender ideology: Evidence for a multifactorial theory. *Journal of Personality and Social Psychology, 64*(4), 624–635.

Spence, J. T., & Hahn, E. D. (1997). The attitudes toward women scale and attitude change in college students. *Psychology of Women Quarterly, 21*(1), 17–34.

Spencer, S. J., Steele, C. M., & Quinn, D. M. (1999). Stereotype threat and women's math performance. *Journal of Experimental Social Psychology, 35*(1), 4–28.

Stangor, C., Swim, J. K., Van Allen, K. L., & Sechrist, G. B. (2002). Reporting discrimination in public and private contexts. *Journal of Personality and Social Psychology, 82,* 69-74.

Stangor, C., Swim, J. K., Sechrist, G. B., DeCoster, J., Van Allen, K. L., & Ottenbreit, A. (2003). Ask, answer and announce: Three stages in perceiving and responding to discrimination. In W. Stroebe & M. Hewstone (Eds.), *European review of social psychology* (Vol. 14, pp. 277–311). Hove, UK: Psychology Press/ Taylor & Francis.

Swim, J. K. (1994). Perceived versus meta-analytic effect sizes: An assessment of the accuracy of gender stereotypes. *Journal of Personality and Social Psychology, 66*(1), 21–36.

Swim, J. K., Aikin, K. J., Hall, W. S., & Hunter, B. A. (1995). Sexism and racism: Old-fashioned and modern prejudices. *Journal of Personality and Social Psychology, 68*(2), 199–214.

Swim, J. K., Becker, J. C., & Decoster, J. (2008). Higher order structures for contemporary measures of sexist beliefs. Manuscript under review.

Swim, J. K., Becker, J. C., Lee, L., & Pruitt, E. R. (2007). The interface between cultural and sexism and between gender and other social categories on the endorsement, expression and emergence of sexism. In H. Landrine & N. Russo (Eds.).

Swim, J. K., Becker, J. C., Lee, L., & Pruitt, E. R. (in press). Sexism reloaded: Worldwide evidence for its endorsement, expression, and emergence in multiple contexts. In H. Landrine & N Russo (Eds.), Bringing diversity to feminist psychology. New York, NY: Springer.

Swim, J., Borgida, E., Maruyama, G., & Myers, D. G. (1989). Joan McKay versus John McKay: Do gender stereotypes bias evaluations? *Psychological Bulletin, 105*(3), 409–429.

Swim, J. K., & Campbell, B. (2001). Sexism: Attitudes, beliefs, and behaviors. *The Handbook of Social Psychology: Intergroup Relations, 4,* 218–237.

Swim, J. K., & Cohen, L. L. (1997). Overt, covert, and subtle sexism: A comparison between the attitudes toward women and modern sexism scales. *Psychology of Women Quarterly, 21*(1), 103–118.

Swim, J. K., Cohen, L. L., & Hyers, L. L. (1998). Experiencing everyday prejudice and discrimination. In J. K. Swim & C. Stangor (Eds.), *Prejudice: The target's perspective* (pp. 37–60). San Diego, CA: Academic.

Swim, J. K., Eysell, K., Quinliven, E., & Fergusin, M. (2008). *Self-silencing to sexism.Manuscript under review.*

Swim, J. K., & Hyers, L. L. (1999). Excuse me—what did you just say?! Women's public and private responses to sexist remarks. *Journal of Experimental Social Psychology, 35*(1), 68–88.

Swim, J. K., Hyers, L. L., Cohen, L. L., & Ferguson, M. J. (2001). Everyday sexism: Evidence for its incidence, nature, and psychological impact from three daily diary studies. *Journal of Social Issues, 57*(1), 31–53.

Swim, J. K., Mallett, R., Russo-Devosa, Y., & Stangor, C. (2005). Judgments of sexism: A comparison of the subtlety of sexism measures and sources of variability in judgments of sexism. *Psychology of Women Quarterly, 29*(4), 406–411.

Swim, J. K., Mallett, R., & Stangor, C. (2004). Understanding subtle sexism: Detection and use of sexist language. *Sex Roles, 51*(3), 117–128.

Swim, J. K., Scott, E. D., Sechrist, G. B., Campbell, B., & Stangor, C. (2003). The role of intent and harm in judgments of prejudice and discrimination. *Journal of Personality and Social Psychology, 84*(5), 944–959.

Tavris, C. (1992). *The mismeasure of women.* New York: Touchstone.

Tjaden, P., & Thoeness, N. (2000). *Full report of the prevalence, incidents, and consequences of violence against women: Findings from the National Violence against Women Survey.* Retrieved January 8, 2007, from http://www.ncjrs.gov/pdffiles1/nij/183781.pdf

Tougas, F., Brown, R., Beaton, A. M., & Joly, S. (1995). Neosexism: Plus ça change, plus c'est pareil. *Personality and Social Psychology Bulletin, 21*(8), 842–849.

Tougas, F., Brown, R., Beaton, A. M., & St-Pierre, L. (1999). Neosexism among women: The role of personally experienced social mobility attempts. *Personality and Social Psychology Bulletin, 25*(12), 1487–1497.

Twenge, J. M. (1997). Attitudes toward women, 1970–1995: A meta-analysis. *Psychology of Women Quarterly, 21*(1), 35–51.

Twenge, J. M. (1999). Mapping gender: The multifactorial approach and the organization of gender-related attributes. *Psychology of Women Quarterly, 23*(3), 485–502.

Twenge, J. M. (2001). Changes in women's assertiveness in response to status and roles: A cross-temporal meta-analysis, 1931–1993. *Journal of Personality and Social Psychology, 81*(1), 133–145.

Twenge, J. M., & Zucker, A. N. (1999). What is a feminist? Evaluations and stereotypes in closed- and open-ended responses. *Psychology of Women Quarterly, 23*(3), 591–605.

Unger, R. K., Draper, R. D., & Pendergras, M. L. (1986). Personal epistemology and personal experience. *Journal of Social Issues, 42*(22), 67–79.

Vescio, T. K., Gervais, S. J., Snyder, M., & Hoover, A. (2005). Power and the creation of patronizing environments: The stereotype-based behaviors of the powerful and their effects on female performance in masculine domains. *Journal of Personality and Social Psychology, 88*(4), 658–672.

Vescio, T. K., Judd, C. M., & Kwan, V. S. Y. (2004). The crossed-categorization hypothesis: Evidence of reductions in the strength of categorization, but not intergroup bias. *Journal of Experimental Social Psychology, 40*(4), 478–496.

Viki, G. T., Abrams, D., & Masser, B. (2004). Evaluating stranger and acquaintance rape: The role of benevolent sexism in perpetrator blame and recommended sentence length. *Law and Human Behavior, 28*(3), 295–303.

Viki, G. T., Chiroro, P., & Abrams, D. (2006). Hostile sexism, type of rape, and self-reported rape proclivity within a sample of Zimbabwean males. *Violence Against Women, 12(8),* 789–800.

Vogt, C. (1864). *Lectures on man: His place in creation, and in the history of the earth.* London: Anthropological Society.

Walker, D. F., Tokar, D. M., & Fischer, A. R. (2000). What are eight popular masculinity-related instruments measuring? Underlying dimensions and their relations to sociosexuality. *Psychology of Men & Masculinity, 1*(2), 98–108.

Watson, J. B. (1926). *Studies on the growth of the emotions: Psychologies.* Worcester, MA: Clark University Press.

Whitly, B. E. J. (2001). Gender-role variables and attitudes toward homosexuality. *Sex Roles, 45*(11), 691–721.

Wilde, A., & Diekman, A. B. (2005). Cross-cultural similarities and differences in dynamic stereotypes: A comparison between Germany and the United States. *Psychology of Women Quarterly, 29*(2), 188–196.

Wood, W., Christensen, P. N., Hebl, M. R., & Rothgerber, H. (1997). Conformity to sex-typed norms, affect, and the self-concept. *Journal of Personality and Social Psychology, 73*(3), 523–535.

21 Ageism

Todd D. Nelson
California State University–Stanislaus

In and of itself, categorization is an adaptive feature of the brain, because it frees up cognition to perform more important tasks (Fiske & Neuberg, 1990). Once we know that this object before us is a table, we know what its purpose is and how to think about it, based on our earlier acquired information about tables and their features (Mervis & Rosch, 1981; Rosch, 1978). However, when we start applying this natural tendency to categorize objects in our environment to people, the categorization process is not nearly as accurate nor is it free of consequences. Miscategorizing a couch for a bed likely will not be a big deal under most circumstances. However, mistakenly categorizing a man as a woman might get you a punch in the face! Despite this and other risks, everyone tends to categorize other people on an innumerable array of dimensions.

In social perception, there are three primary dimensions on which we categorize other people on seeing them: race, gender, and age. This categorization process is so well learned that it becomes automatic rather early in life (Fiske & Neuberg, 1990; Hamilton & Sherman, 1994). The categorization along these dimensions is so fundamental to how we understand the rest of the individual that this process is often referred to as "primitive" or "automatic" categorization (Bargh, 1994; Brewer, 1988; Perdue & Gurtman, 1990). When we consider the influence of automatic categorization on social perception, attitude formation, and the formation and maintenance of prejudice, it becomes clear much of our understanding of social cognition processes must begin with an exploration of this primitive categorization process. How does automatic categorization along the lines of race, gender, and age influence the way we think about others? One prominent by-product of such thinking is that it facilitates the formation of simple rules of association between group membership and some characteristic. That is, this automatic categorization helps people start to think about everyone in that category as all sharing several of the same characteristics, to the extent that they should be grouped together and identified in a different way from other groups who show similarity along other dimensions. From this, we develop stereotypes about those groups. Stereotypes are "a set of beliefs about the personal attributes of a group of people" (Ashmore & Del Boca, 1981, p. 16). When we start thinking about others through the lens of stereotypes, we develop expectations for their behavior and certain stereotype-consistent interpretations of their behavior. We think, feel, and behave toward them on the basis of those stereotypes. In so doing, our behavior toward stereotyped groups and those within the group is heavily skewed, usually incorrect, and fraught with problematic perceptions of each other.

Stereotypes have been a focus of research in social psychology almost since the field began, because of the importance of understanding the strong influence they have on social behavior (G. W. Allport, 1954; Jones, 1998). Although social psychologists have learned much about prejudice and stereotyping based on race (racism; F. H. Allport, 1924; Katz & Braly, 1933; LaPiere, 1934) and on gender (sexism; Benokraitis & Feagin, 1986; Deaux & Kite, 1993; Eagly & Wood, 1991, 1999) we know comparatively little about the way people respond to another individual based on his or her age (ageism; Nelson, 2002). Why would one of the three major, automatic categories in which we think about another person be so underinvestigated by researchers throughout the decades? There are a number of possible reasons, and there is likely some validity for each, but one obvious reason is that our society has institutionalized ageism within nearly every aspect of its culture. People do not notice ageism because (a) it is institutionalized, and (b) the targets of the prejudice, older adults, largely buy into the stereotypes as reflecting a true state of the world, and therefore there is nothing wrong with being characterized along age stereotypes (Caporael, Lukaszewski, & Culbertson, 1983; Giles, Fox, Harwood, & Williams, 1994; Nelson, 2003; Neugarten, 1974). If there is "no outraged victim" protesting how they are stereotyped, does ageism simply not exist?

Unfortunately, ageism does indeed exist, and the purpose of this chapter is to discuss the nature of ageism, how it is perpetuated, and how to reduce it.

THE INSTITUTIONALIZATION OF AGEISM

Go into any greeting card store in the United States and in the birthday card section, peruse some of the cards. Almost immediately, you'll notice a common message: Sorry to hear you're another year older. Birthdays are seen as a decline, a step toward being in a group that is not respected and not valued in our society. Birthdays are a reminder of one's increasing physical and mental health issues as the years go by. Getting older is bad. Why would card makers put such a message on a card that ostensibly is meant for a celebration? That they do, and frequently print such overt and covert jokes about getting older, is one indicator of the degree to which aging is institutionalized in our culture. Try that same message with another stigmatized group, and you are likely to arouse not laughter in the card recipient, but anger: Sorry to hear you're overweight! Sorry to hear you're handicapped! Sorry to hear you're gay! I think you get the point. People spend billions of dollars every year to hide the physical signs that their body is aging: skin creams, face-lifts, tuck this, pull back that, hair dye (hide that gray), wigs, and makeup, all to conceal external signs of their age (National Consumer's League, 2004). Why? Because we are told, in innumerable ways throughout our life, that aging is bad. Young is good, and old is not good. This chapter explores some of the reasons why ageism is so institutionalized in America, and what that means for the lives of older adults.

EARLY AGEISM RESEARCH

Technically, *ageism* is defined as prejudice against anyone based on his or her age. Indeed, we do seem to have stereotypes for nearly every age group (teens, children, infants, those who are "middle-aged," and "old people"). Although some ageism research has focused on negative attitudes and stereotypes toward teens and children (termed "juvenile ageism"; e.g., Westman, 1991), most research on ageism has tended to focus on prejudice against older adults (Nelson, 2002, 2005). There are two major types of ageism: *malignant ageism* and *benign ageism* (Butler, 1980). In the former, the perceiver feels an extreme dislike toward the older person, and believes the older person is worthless. In the latter, the perceiver views the older person through prejudice and stereotypes due to their own fear of aging. We discuss this further when we talk about theories of ageism.

Research on ageism is still in its infancy, with only a couple of studies conducted on it prior to 1969, when the term was first coined by Butler (1969). One of the first studies on attitudes toward older people was conducted by Tuckman and Lorge (1953). Their research found that people in the United States tended to have a fairly negative attitude toward older adults. Indeed, later studies affirmed that Americans have negative attitudes toward older people and aging (Barrow & Smith, 1979; Falk & Falk, 1997; Nuessel, 1982). However, many other studies showed that people had very positive attitudes toward older adults (Bell, 1992; Crockett & Hummert, 1987; Green, 1981). What seems to account for these mixed findings on whether ageism even exists? A closer examination of the methods used in the studies reveals a significant difference in the way the questions are worded when asking questions about the respondent's attitude toward older adults. When one is asked "What is your attitude toward your grandparent (or older boss, or neighbor)?" one tends to answer with quite positive attitudes toward these specific older adults. However, when a respondent is asked about his or her attitudes toward "older people" in general, the response is typically fairly negative. Why might this occur? This is fairly typical in social perception. Many studies have shown that to the degree that one can individuate a member of a stereotyped outgroup, the less that the target's category status remains prominent in one's consideration of the target (Fiske, 1998; Fiske & Neuberg, 1990; Nelson, 2006). That is, the more you get to know the person as an individual, the less likely you will think of that person in terms of stereotypes. If we have negative views against "older people," how, exactly are we thinking about them? What is the content of ageist attitudes?

AGE STEREOTYPES

Younger people in society think about older adults not as a monolithic entity, but in many different ways. Researchers asked some young participants to sort personality trait cards into groups of traits that would be found within the same older person (Schmidt & Boland, 1986). Participants generated between 2 and 17 different groups, or different types of older persons. The researchers found that participants generated about twice as many negative subgroups (e.g., despondent, vulnerable, shrew or curmudgeon) as positive subgroups (e.g., liberal matriarch or patriarch, sage, perfect grandparent) for the concept of older person. Clearly, our conception of older people is much more complex than stereotypes might indicate, and younger adults have several ways of thinking about older persons, depending on their relationship and experiences with the older person.

POSITIVE INTENTIONS

Most people view older persons with a mixture of fondness and pity (Cuddy & Fiske, 2002). In their stereotype content model (SCM), Cuddy and Fiske (2002; Cuddy, Norton, & Fiske, 2005; Fiske, Cuddy, Glick, & Xu, 2002) suggest that people do not merely think about their stereotypes in uni-dimensional ways (e.g., one's attitude is either positive or negative toward the group). Rather, they say that stereotypes can be located along two intersecting dimensions of content: competence (able, independent) and warmth (trustworthy, friendly). The combination of these dimensions then yields three different types of stereotype: warm–incompetent, cold–incompetent, and competent–cold. According to Cuddy and Fiske (2002), people reserve the competent–warm category to describe their own ingroups. As mentioned earlier, when people think about older adults in the abstract, their attitude toward that group tends to be more negative. Yet, research finds that even when younger persons think of *specific* older persons in their life, their attitude toward those persons is, at best, described as "affectionate condescension" (Giles et al., 1994; Grainger, Atkinson, & Coupland, 1990). Cuddy and Fiske (2002) said that younger people view older persons as incompetent, but yet lovable (what they term "doddering but dear"), and there is empirical support for this idea (Fiske, Xu, Cuddy, & Glick, 1999; Heckhausen, Dixon, & Baltes, 1989).

The view of older people as dependent, incompetent, and in decline both physically and mentally (Lieberman & Peskin, 1992) tends to lead younger people to treat older persons as if they were children. This is referred to as *infantilization* (Gresham, 1973). Older people are shielded by younger persons from issues in the world or their own life that the younger person may deem "too complicated" or "too upsetting." Additionally, the opinions of the older person are not given the same importance as those of younger adults. Accompanying ageist behavior and infantilization is usually a marked difference in the way younger persons speak to elderly persons. Research on intergenerational communication has identified a particular ageist communication style termed *baby talk* (Caporael, 1981). Younger persons will speak to older adults more slowly, with exaggerated intonation, using simple words. Researchers have identified this speech style among nursing home caregivers (Kemper, 1994), and it has been found cross-culturally (Caporael & Culbertson, 1986). Caporael (1981) distinguished between two types of baby talk: primary and secondary. The former is used when younger adults speak to infants. The latter is used to address pets, inanimate objects, and older persons. Caporael (1981) filtered out the speech content, and asked participants to attempt to distinguish any differences in tone and pace (or any other aspects of speech) between two samples of speech: primary versus secondary baby talk. They were unable to accurately identify which type was which. This suggests that the way we speak to older adults is virtually identical to how we speak to babies.

INFLUENCE OF AGEISM ON OLDER PERSONS

Interestingly, not all older adults find this treatment insulting or prejudicial. Caporael et al. (1983) found that older people who had higher cognitive functioning and were overall in better health found secondary baby talk and infantilization behavior to be very insulting, and it made them angry. However, for those with diminished cognitive abilities or health problems, such ageist speech and behavior was perceived as comforting. The reason, the researchers speculated, is that this treatment connotes a dependency relationship, and that the elderly people will be taken care of by the younger individuals, so the older people need not worry about their own welfare—they have someone to look out for them.

Growing up in a culture that communicates directly and indirectly in many ways that, as one ages, cognitive and physical abilities will decline tends to lead older people to come to believe in the truth of those stereotypes. The stereotypes become a self-fulfilling prophecy (Levy, 2003) and this can in fact have a detrimental effect on the longevity of the older person. Levy, Slade, Kunkel, and Kasl (2003) found that older people who had a more positive view of aging lived an average of 7.5 years longer than those who had a negative view of getting older. Older people also appear to "instantly age" (speak, move, look, think slower) when younger persons direct baby talk toward them, compared to when others do not use baby talk with them (Giles, Fox, & Smith, 1993).

To the degree that older adults "buy into" or believe in the essential "truth" of the negativity of aging and stereotypes about elderly persons, they may be less likely to recognize ageist treatment directed toward them, or, if they do, they may be less likely to find it objectionable, because, the younger people are merely pointing out a "truth" about aging (Giles et al., 1994; Giles et al., 1993). In one study (Nelson, 2003), 850 older adults across the state of California were mailed a survey that was designed to measure their experiences with ageism. If they reported an experience of ageist treatment directed at themselves, the questionnaire asked the respondent to indicate how it made him or her feel. Results of the study are best interpreted through an important earlier analysis that Neugarten (1974) proposed. Neugarten said it is important to distinguish between two groups of older persons: the "young-old" (those aged 55–74) and the "old-old" (aged 75 and higher). The reason this distinction is important is that most of the negative stereotypes that people form about older persons are derived from their observations of the old-old (Hummert, Garstka, Shaner, & Strahm, 1995). The young-old are much less likely to feel physically or mentally "old" and as such, they dislike being associated with that stereotyped, less powerful group.

Coming back to the Nelson (2003) results, the data indicated that there was a marked difference in the way the young-old and the old-old responded to the question of whether they had ever experienced ageism. The young-old were much more likely to indicate that society has a negative view of older persons, that younger people do not respect older adults like they should, and that younger people believe that older adults do not contribute to society. On the other hand, the old-old were much more likely to agree with the idea that there are certain activities and interests that are not appropriate for older adults, and that there was no discrimination from health care workers directed at older adults. When asked how they would feel when they see examples of age prejudice, the young-old said they would be much more likely to feel sad, angry, and irritated, whereas the old-old were significantly more likely to say it would not bother them at all.

So what might explain the different results between these two different groups of older persons? The young-old do not think of themselves as "old," so it is perhaps easy to understand their negative reaction at being treated as if they were a member of a stigmatized group ("old person"). On the other hand, the reaction of the old-old to instances of age prejudice is a bit more complicated, and researchers have put forth some explanations as to why the old-old (a) often do not report experiencing ageism, and (b) when they see it directed at themselves, they are not bothered by it. First, the denial of discrimination directed at one's group may hold few (if any) psychological or emotional downsides for the individual, and indeed, may be an adaptive way of dealing with unfair treatment directed at oneself due to one's membership in a stigmatized group. Second, whether the old-old individual perceives the ageist treatment by the younger person is due in part to the older person's view of the upward mobility of individual group members. If he or she believes that people in the old-old group are able to do things to increase their status, then he or she is much less likely to see the behavior of younger persons as ageist. However, if the old-old person sees society as preventing old-old persons from moving up in status, he or she is much more likely to perceive ageism and other injustices related to age (Major, Gramzow, et al., 2002; Major, Quinton, & McCoy, 2002). Finally, the old-old person's decision about whether to perceive ageist treatment directed at him or her may also be due to his or her comfort with being perceived as "a complainer." Studies by Kaiser and Miller (2001, 2003) indicated that stigmatized persons who attribute the intergroup behavior of outgroup members to discrimination were less favorably regarded by others.

HISTORY OF AGEISM

Older people were not always regarded negatively by the young.[1] In Biblical times, people who lived a long time were regarded as favored by God to fulfill a divine purpose. As recent as the 1800s, older adults were regarded with much respect, and they held positions of power in their villages and towns. Older people were the historians of the village, they had the most life experience and the longest memories, and therefore their knowledge translated into power because everyone looked to older adults for guidance, wisdom, and help with decisions that will help their village flourish (Branco & Williamson, 1982). Two key historical developments served to change the way older people were regarded. First, the advent of the printing press meant that all the information and history that was formerly only contained in a few elders' memories could be written down, and mass-produced and distributed to everyone. Now everyone could have the power that comes with the information and memories that once were the sole province of the elders. The second development was the Industrial Revolution. In primitive, prehistoric, agrarian, and rural societies, it was fairly common for several generations of a family to all live under the same roof in the same house. The older adults were an important, welcome part of the family, and the contact they had daily with younger adults and children served to enhance the affection of the younger family members for the elders. However, the Industrial Revolution required that people be ready to move quickly if they were to obtain a job in one of the factories. People had to move to where the jobs were. Older people were not as keen to move about often or great distances merely because their sons or daughters got a job. As such, younger persons in the family began to resent their older family members as a burden who did not contribute much to the household (McCann & Giles, 2002). Families in the Industrial Revolution that were most mobile and able to move tended to do the best and thrive in that new economy. For millennia, what was important and valued was tradition and stability. However, the advent of the Industrial Revolution brought with it a different value: change. The ability to adapt one's skills to the demands of the workplace, and the mobility to pick up one's family and go to where the jobs were was critical to a family's survival.

WHY ARE PEOPLE AGEIST?

For decades, a search for a theory to best explain the origins of ageism left researchers frustrated. There simply was no good explanation for why people would be prejudiced against a group that they would someday join (if they were fortunate). However, recently a theory has come along that does an excellent job explaining ageism, and along with it, compelling empirical support provides confidence in its explanatory power. Ageism is driven in large part by our *gerontophobia,* defined as an irrational fear, hatred, or other hostility toward elderly people (Bunzel, 1972). Why would older people be feared by younger persons? What makes them threatening? Before we address this

---

[1] Here I am referring to older adults in the United States, and European, Western cultures, excluding Eastern cultures, where ageism is a very new phenomenon.

question, let's discuss the theory. Terror management theory (TMT; Greenberg, Pyszczynski, & Solomon, 1986; Pyszczynski, Greenberg, Solomon, Arndt, & Schimel, 2004; Solomon, Greenberg, & Pyszczynski, 1991b) says that culture and religion are human-created constructs that help us impose order on a chaotic universe. They help us feel a bit of control over what is uncontrollable. According to TMT, religion and culture help us avoid the frightening thought that what happens in the world is random, and that our time in the world is limited. We are mortal. Now, from childhood, we learn that being good and following the rules will be met with rewards, approval, and protection by our parents. The protection from our parents is another way we stave off thoughts of our mortality, and the chaotic random universe. Feeling good and self-esteem from doing good works then become anxiety buffers (against thoughts of mortality) after we leave the comfort of our parents' house and venture into the world. Research on TMT has shown that when the mortality of participants is made salient, experiment participants will feel anxious, and this will affect their cognition and behavior (Solomon, Greenberg, & Pyszczynski, 1991a).

Older people are a very poignant and salient reminder to younger people that they are mortal, that life is finite. Therefore, it seems reasonable to suggest that older people would make younger persons feel anxious out of their own fear of dying and thoughts of their own mortality. What purpose then would holding prejudiced attitudes about older persons serve for the younger person? By derogating elderly people, the younger person creates a defensive buffer out of their tendency to manage their mortality fears. Basically, the younger person is depersonalizing and objectifying the older adult and "blaming him for his low-status position in society and poor physical condition." In so doing, the younger person is trying to convince himself or herself "that (aging, getting old) won't happen to *me*" (Edwards & Wetzler, 1998). The negative image of aging is one that many would like to avoid. Yet it represents one possible future self for all of us (Markus & Nurius, 1986). The fear of this possible self drives younger persons to try to distance themselves from it by forming prejudices and stereotypes about older persons. Ageism is our own prejudice against our feared future self (Nelson, 2005). Experiments applying the TMT explanation for ageism have demonstrated support for hypotheses derived from TMT (Greenberg, Schimel, & Mertens, 2002; Martens, Goldenberg, & Greenberg, 2005; Martens, Greenberg, Schimel, & Landau, 2004). It is important to note that the theory rests on the fact that the individuals in a given society fear death and their own mortality. Is the TMT explanation of ageism applicable in countries or cultures where people do not fear death? Next, we explore the incidence of ageism in various cultures.

CROSS-CULTURAL DIFFERENCES IN AGEISM

Ageism is not prevalent all over the world. Indeed, even within the United States—perhaps the most ageist society in the world—ageism is not universal. In native Hawaiian families, for example, elders are held in high regard, respected as wise, and viewed with affection (Jensen & Oakley, 1982–1983). According to research by Slater (1964), older people are more likely to hold positions of respect and power in societies that are static, collectivistic, totalitarian, and authoritarian. In societies that value change and innovation, however, older people tend to not enjoy respect and prestige, and ageism is much more likely.

Perhaps the most obvious difference in the way that elders are regarded cross-culturally can be seen when contrasting Western versus Eastern cultures. Western societies value the individual, personal control, and innovation. Such values are less compatible with older persons who represent stability, roots, and yet who may require assistance from younger persons. Such dependency (for some older persons, not all) directly contradicts the value of personal control, leading younger persons to derogate the elder as weak and not contributing anything to society. Less emphasis is placed on tradition. Eastern cultures focus on the collectivist values of maintaining society, working for the good of everyone, the idea that one individual is not more important than another person, and taking care of everyone. In such cultures, older people are respected and revered (Levy & Langer, 1994). Another way these two cultures differ is how they regard death. Because Western cultures like that in the United States tend to put importance on individuality and personal control, death is feared because one has no control over when death will happen. That ultimate lack of control, and uncertainty about what happens to us after we die leads those in Western societies to fear death. Eastern cultures traditionally viewed the self, life, and death as all intertwined, and that death is a natural part of life. In fact, it is regarded as something to anticipate, because it meant joining one's revered ancestors (Butler, Lewis, & Sunderland, 1991). This may well account for why TMT explains ageism so well in Western cultures. The fear of one's mortality that permeates these cultures is what drives individuals in these cultures to try to distance themselves from older persons by forming stereotypes and prejudice about them. Research shows that this view of Eastern cultures is not entirely accurate. Studies by Ng (2002) and Williams et al (1997) have found a wide disparity of attitudes toward older persons among younger persons in Eastern cultures. In Japan, for example, there is a difference between what your culture dictates you do to show respect for older persons, and how one actually feels about older persons. So, although on the surface, Japanese may appear to be showing great respect, some will be secretly harboring negative attitudes, feelings of pity, and feelings of disgust toward their elderly citizens.

CONCLUSION

Although research on ageism is fairly nascent, there is much researchers have learned and, of course, many more questions yet to be addressed in future studies. With respect to reducing ageism, it is important that the message that aging is not something to fear be presented to children from a young age. Old persons are not scary, and being old is not something to dread. Programs that are designed to bring young children into contact with elders, such as foster grandparents, are an excellent way of breaking down those myths and fears about aging, and promoting positive attitudes toward older adults. Better training is needed in medical schools (Reyes-Ortiz, 1997) and for those training to be psychologists (Kastenbaum, 1964) to learn how to welcome older adults as patients and clients, and not to regard them through the lens of ageist stereotypes. These health professionals need specific and much more extensive training on the special needs and circumstances of older persons. Society needs to do a better job at recognizing the great contributions of older workers in the workplace, and show that recognition through continued employment (rather that forced retirement or buy-out programs) and other positions in the company designed to respect and welcome the years of experience the older employee has (Finklestein, Burke, & Raju, 1995). Similarly, programs designed to help the transition from being a worker to being a retiree are in great need. Older adults can then learn that not working does not mean one isn't a valuable, contributing member of society. There are many different ways people are valued and contribute within a community, and such programs designed to instruct new retirees about these postwork avenues and options go a long way to preventing older persons from "buying into" stereotypes about their age, and feeling depressed about their loss of an important part of their identity.

Research on ageism is just hitting its stride and it could not be more timely. The baby-boomers have just begun to retire, and will continue to do so over the next 10 to 15 years, in a demographic sea change (some refer to this as the "graying of America") in our society that will greatly change the composition and look of our population. According to the U.S. Census Bureau (2000), by the year 2030, the number of people over age 65 will double. To the degree that researchers can bring to bear their skills in addressing this pervasive, pernicious, and institutionalized form of prejudice to which we all will be subjected, we will be in a better position to understand its nature, and specific ways to reduce or eliminate it. In so doing, such ageism research will enhance the quality of life for all older adults, present and future.

REFERENCES

Allport, F. H. (1924). *Social psychology*. Boston: Houghton Mifflin.

Allport, G. W. (1954). *The nature of prejudice*. Reading, MA: Addison-Wesley.

Ashmore, R. D., & Del Boca, F. K. (1981). Conceptual approaches to stereotypes and stereotyping. In D. L. Hamilton (Ed.), *Cognitive processes in stereotyping and intergroup behavior* (pp. 1–35). Hillsdale, NJ: Erlbaum.

Bargh, J. A. (1994). The four horsemen of automaticity: Awareness, intention, efficiency, and control in social cognition. In R. S. Wyer & T. K. Srull (Eds.), *Handbook of social cognition* (Vol. 1, 2nd ed., pp. 3–51). New York: Guilford.

Barrow, G. M., & Smith, P. A. (1979). *Aging, ageism, and society*. New York: West.

Bell, J. (1992). In search of a discourse on aging: The elderly on television. *The Gerontologist, 32,* 305–311.

Benokraitis, N. V., & Feagin, J. R. (1986). *Modern sexism: Blatant, subtle, and covert discrimination*. Englewood Cliffs, NJ: Prentice-Hall.

Branco, K. J., & Williamson, J. B. (1982). Stereotyping and the life cycle: Views of aging and the aged. In A. G. Miller (Ed.), *In the eye of the beholder: Contemporary issues in stereotyping* (pp. 364-410). New York: Praeger

Brewer, M. B. (1988). A dual-process model of impression formation. In T. K. Srull & R. S. Wyer (Eds.), *Advances in social cognition* (Vol. 1, pp. 1–36). Hillsdale, NJ: Erlbaum.

Bunzel, J. (1972). Note on the history of a concept: Gerontophobia. *The Gerontologist, 12,* 116–203.

Butler, R. (1969). Age-ism: Another form of bigotry. *The Gerontologist, 9,* 243–246.

Butler, R. (1980). Ageism: A forward. *Journal of Social Issues, 36*(2), 8–11.

Butler, R., Lewis, M., & Sunderland, T. (1991). *Aging and mental health: Positive psychosocial and biomedical approaches*. New York: Macmillan.

Caporael, L. (1981). The paralanguage of caregiving: Baby talk to the institutionalized aged. *Journal of Personality and Social Psychology, 40,* 876–884.

Caporael, L., & Culbertson, G. (1986). Verbal response modes of baby talk and other speech at institutions for the aged. *Language and Communication, 6,* 31–34.

Caporael, L., Lukaszewski, M., & Culbertson, G. (1983). Secondary baby talk: Judgments by institutionalized elderly and their caregivers. *Journal of Personality and Social Psychology, 44,* 746–754.

Crockett, W. H., & Hummert, M. L. (1987). Perceptions of aging and the elderly. In K. Schaie & C. Eisdorfer (Eds.), *Annual review of gerontology and geriatrics* (Vol. 7, pp. 217–241). New York: Springer-Verlag.

Cuddy, A. J. C., & Fiske, S. T. (2002). Doddering but dear: Process, content, and function in stereotyping of older persons. In T. D. Nelson (Ed.), *Ageism: Stereotyping and prejudice against older persons* (pp. 3–26). Cambridge, MA: MIT Press.

Cuddy, A. J. C., Norton, M. I., & Fiske, S. T. (2005). This old stereotype: The pervasiveness and persistence of the elderly stereotype. *Journal of Social Issues, 61*(2), 267–285.

Deaux, K., & Kite, M. (1993). Gender stereotypes. In F. Denmark & M. Paludi (Eds.), *Psychology of women: A handbook of issues and theories* (pp. 107–139). Westport, CT: Greenwood.

Eagly, A. H., & Wood, W. (1991). Explaining sex differences in social behavior: A meta-analytic perspective. *Personality and Social Psychological Bulletin, 17*(3), 306–315.

Eagly, A. H., & Wood, W. (1999). The origins of sex differences in human behavior. *American Psychologist, 54*(6), 408–423.

Edwards, K., & Wetzler, J. (1998). *Too young to be old: The roles of self threat and psychological distancing in social categorization of the elderly*. Unpublished manuscript.

Falk, U., & Falk, G. (1997). *Ageism, the aged, and aging in America*. Springfield, IL: Charles Thomas.

Finklestein, L., Burke, M., & Raju, N. (1995). Age discrimination in simulated employment contexts: An integrative analysis. *Journal of Applied Psychology, 80*(6), 652–663.

Fiske, S. T. (1998). Stereotyping, prejudice and discrimination. In D. T. Gilbert, S. T. Fiske, & G. Lindzey (Eds.), *The handbook of social psychology* (Vol. 2, 4th ed., pp. 357–411). Boston: McGraw-Hill.

Fiske, S. T., Cuddy, A. J. C., Glick, P. S., & Xu, J. (2002). A model of (often mixed) stereotype content: Competence and warmth respectively follow from perceived status and competition. *Journal of Personality and Social Psychology, 82,* 878–902.

Fiske, S. T., & Neuberg, S. L. (1990). A continuum of impression formation, from category-based to individuating processes: Influences of information and motivation on attention and interpretation. In M. P. Zanna (Ed.), *Advances in experimental social psychology* (Vol. 23, pp. 1–74). New York: Academic.

Fiske, S. T., Xu, J., Cuddy, A. C., & Glick, P. (1999). (Dis)respecting versus (dis)liking: Status and interdependence predict ambivalent stereotypes of competence and warmth. *Journal of Social Issues, 55,* 473–489.

Giles, H., Fox, S., Harwood, J., & Williams, A. (1994). Talking age and aging talk: Communicating through the life span. In M. Hummert, J. Wiemann, & J. Nussbaum (Eds.), *Interpersonal communication in older adulthood: Interdisciplinary theory and research* (pp. 130–161). Thousand Oaks, CA: Sage.

Giles, H., Fox, S., & Smith, E. (1993). Patronizing the elderly: Intergenerational evaluations. *Research on Language and Social Interaction, 26*(2), 129–149.

Grainger, K., Atkinson, K., & Coupland, N. (1990). Responding to the elderly: Troubles-talk in the caring context. In H. Giles, N. Coupland, & J. Weimann (Eds.), *Communication health and the elderly* (pp. 192–212). Manchester, UK: Manchester University Press.

Green, S. K. (1981). Attitudes and perceptions about the elderly: Current and future perspectives. *International Journal of Aging and Human Development, 13,* 99–119.

Greenberg, J., Pyszczynski, T., & Solomon, S. (1986). The causes and consequences of a need for self-esteem. In R. F. Baumester (Ed.), *Public self and private self* (pp. 188–212). New York: Springer.

Greenberg, J., Schimel, J., & Martens, A. (2002). Ageism: Denying the face of the future. In T. D. Nelson (Ed.), *Ageism: Stereotyping and prejudice against older persons* (pp. 3–26). Cambridge, MA: MIT Press.

Gresham, M. (1973). The infantilization of the elderly. *Nursing Forum, 15,* 196–209.

Hamilton, D. L., & Sherman, J. W. (1994). Stereotypes. In R. S. Wyer & T. K. Srull (Eds.), *Handbook of social cognition* (Vol. 2, 2nd ed., pp. 1–68). Hillsdale, NJ; Erlbaum.

Heckhausen, J., Dixon, R. A., & Baltes, P. B. (1989). Gains and losses in development throughout adulthood as perceived by different adult age groups. *Developmental Psychology, 25,* 109–121.

Hummert, M., Garstka, T., Shaner, J., & Strahm, S. (1995). Judgments about stereotypes of the elderly: Attitudes, age associations, and typicality ratings of young, middle-aged, and elderly adults. *Research on Aging, 17*(2), 168–189.

Jensen, G. D., & Oakley, F. B. (1982–1983). Ageism across cultures and in perspective of sociobiologic and psychodynamic theories. *International Journal of Aging and Human Development, 15,* 17–26.

Jones, E. E. (1998). Major developments in five decades of social psychology. In D. T. Gilbert, S. T. Fiske, & G. Lindzey (Eds.), *The handbook of social psychology* (Vol. 1, 4th ed., pp. 3–57). Boston: McGraw-Hill.

Kaiser, C. R., & Miller, C. T. (2001). Stop complaining! The social costs of making attributions to discrimination. *Personality and Social Psychology Bulletin, 27*(2), 254–263.

Kaiser, C. R., & Miller, C. T. (2003). Derogating the victim: The interpersonal consequences of blaming events on discrimination. *Group Processes and Intergroup Relations 6*(3), 227–237.

Kastenbaum, R. (1964). The reluctant therapist. In R. Kastenbaum (Ed.), *New thoughts on old age* (pp. 139–145). New York: Springer.

Katz, D., & Braly, K. W. (1933). Racial stereotypes in one hundred college students. *Journal of Abnormal and Social Psychology, 28,* 280–290.

Kemper, S. (1994). Elderspeak: Speech accommodations to older adults. *Aging and Cognition, 1,* 17–28.

LaPiere, R. T. (1934). Attitudes versus actions. *Social Forces, 13,* 230–237.

Levy, B. R. (2003). Mind matters: Cognitive and physical effects of aging self-stereotypes. *Journal of Gerontology: Psychological Sciences, 58B*(4), 203–211.

Levy, B. R., & Langer, E. (1994). Aging free from negative stereotypes: Successful memory in China and among the American deaf. *Journal of Personality and Social Psychology, 66*(6), 987–989.

Levy, B. R., Slade, M. D., Kunkel, S. R., & Kasl, S. V. (2003). Longevity increased by positive self-perceptions of aging. *Journal of Personality and Social Psychology, 83*(2), 261–270.

Lieberman, M., & Peskin, H. (1992). Adult life crises. In J. Birren, R. Sloane, & G. Cohen (Eds.), *Handbook of mental health and aging* (2nd ed., pp. 119–143). San Diego, CA: Academic.

Major, B., Gramzow, R. H., McCoy, S. K., Levin, S., Schmader, T., & Sidanius, J. (2002). Perceiving personal discrimination: The role of group status and legitimizing ideology. *Journal of Personality and Social Psychology, 82*(3), 269–282.

Major, B., Quinton, W. J., & McCoy, S. K. (2002). Antecedents and consequences of attributions to discrimination: Theoretical and empirical advances. In M. Zanna (Ed.), *Advances in experimental social psychology* (Vol. 34, pp. 351–330). New York: Academic.

Markus, H., & Nurius, P. (1986). Possible selves. *American Psychologist, 41,* 954–969.

Martens, A., Goldenberg, J. L., & Greenberg, J. (2005). A terror management perspective on ageism. *Journal of Social Issues, 61*(2), 223–239.

Martens, A., Greenberg, J., Schimel, J., & Landau, M. J. (2004). Ageism and death: Effects of mortality salience and perceived similarity to elders on reactions to elderly people. *Personality and Social Psychology Bulletin, 30*(12), 1524–1536.

McCann, R., & Giles, H. (2002). Ageism in the workplace: A communication perspective. In T. D. Nelson (Ed.), *Ageism: Stereotyping and prejudice against older persons* (pp. 163–199). Cambridge, MA: MIT Press.

Mervis, C. B., & Rosch, E. (1981). Categorization of natural objects. *Annual Review of Psychology, 32,* 89–115.

National Consumer's League. (2004). New survey reveals consumers confused about, but overwhelmingly use, anti aging products and procedures. Retrieved February 2008, from http://www.nclnet.org/pressroom/antiaging.htm

Nelson, T. D. (Ed.). (2002). *Ageism: Stereotyping and prejudice against older persons.* Cambridge, MA: MIT Press.

Nelson, T. D. (2003). *Experiencing ageism: A survey of 850 older adults.* Paper presented at the 56th annual meeting of the Gerontological Society of America, San Diego, in November 2003, CA.

Nelson, T. D. (2005). Ageism: Prejudice against our feared future self. *Journal of Social Issues, 61*(2), 207–221.

Nelson, T. D. (2006). *The psychology of prejudice* (2nd ed.). New York: Allyn & Bacon.

Neugarten, B. (1974). Age groups in American society and the rise of the young-old. *Annals of the American Academy of Political and Social Science* (September), *415,* 187–198.

Ng, S. H. (2002). Will families support their elders? Answers from across cultures. In T. D. Nelson (Ed.), *Ageism: Stereotyping and prejudice against older persons* (pp. 295–309). Cambridge, MA: MIT Press.

Nuessel, F. (1982). The language of ageism. *The Gerontologist, 22*(3), 273–276.

Perdue, C. W., & Gurtman, M. B. (1990). Evidence for the automaticity of ageism. *Journal of Experimental Social Psychology, 26,* 199–216.

Pyszczynski, T., Greenberg, J., Solomon, S., Arndt, J., & Schimel, J. (2004). Why do people need self esteem? A theoretical and empirical review. *Psychological Bulletin, 130*(3), 435–468.

Reyes-Ortiz, C. (1997). Physicians must confront ageism. *Academic Medicine, 72*(10), 831.

Rosch, E. H. (1978). Principles of categorization. In E. Rosch & B. B. Lloyd (Eds.), *Cognition and categorization* (pp. 27–48). Hillsdale, NJ: Erlbaum.

Schmidt, D., & Boland, S. (1986). Structure of perceptions of other adults: Evidence for multiple stereotypes. *Psychology and Aging, 1*(3), 255-260.

Slater, P. E. (1964). Cross cultural views of the aged. In R. Kastenbaum (Ed.), *New thoughts on old age* (pp. 229–236). New York: Springer.

Solomon, S., Greenberg, J., & Pyszczynski, T. (1991a). Terror management theory of self esteem. In C. R. Snyder & D. R. Forsyth (Eds.), *Handbook of social and clinical psychology* (pp. 21–40). New York: Pergamon.

Solomon, S., Greenberg, J., & Pyszczynski, T. (1991b). A terror management theory of social behavior: The psychological function of self esteem and cultural worldviews. In M. Zanna (Ed.), *Advances in experimental social psychology* (Vol. 24, pp. 93–159). New York: Academic.

Tuckman, J., & Lorge, I. (1953). Attitudes toward old people. *Journal of Social Psychology, 37,* 249–260.

U.S. Census Bureau. (2000). *Projections of the total resident population by 5-year age groups, and sex with special age categories: Middle series, 2025–2045.* Washington, DC: Population Projections Program, U.S. Census Bureau.

Westman, J. (1991). Juvenile ageism: Unrecognized prejudice and discrimination against the young. *Child Psychiatry and Human Development, 21*(4), 237–256.

Williams, A., Ota, H., Giles, H., Pierson, H., Gallois, C., Ng, S., et al. (1997). Young people's beliefs about intergenerational communication: An initial cross-cultural comparison. *Communication Research, 24*(4), 370–393.

22 Sexual Prejudice

Gregory M. Herek
University of California, Davis

Social psychologists have been conducting research on racial, ethnic, and religious prejudices for nearly a century. By contrast, prejudice related to sexual orientation has only recently received systematic scientific scrutiny. Sexual prejudice manifests many of the same social psychological characteristics as other forms of prejudice with more extensive research pedigrees, as this chapter makes clear. Nevertheless, its relatively recent recognition by scientists and society is indicative of some of its distinctive features, notably that it is based on a concealable status and that it is not universally condemned. Indeed, it remains widespread in contemporary society.

This chapter considers these commonalities and differences in providing an overview of current theory and research on sexual prejudice, especially as it is manifested in the United States. The chapter is guided by a conceptual framework that integrates the constructs of stigma and prejudice, and provides a unified account of how they are experienced by sexual minorities and heterosexuals. After describing that framework, the chapter considers issues relevant to the definition of sexual prejudice as an attitude; its cognitive, affective, and behavioral sources; some of its key correlates; and its underlying motivations. The chapter concludes with a brief discussion of how cultural and psychological factors have combined to foster a reduction in sexual prejudice in recent years.

SEXUAL STIGMA AND PREJUDICE: A CONCEPTUAL FRAMEWORK

Although this chapter is about sexual prejudice, it is grounded in a conceptual framework that begins with the construct of stigma (earlier versions of this framework can be found in Herek, 2004, 2007; Herek, Chopp, & Strohl, 2007). As used here, *stigma* refers to the negative regard, inferior status, and relative powerlessness that society collectively accords to people who possess a particular characteristic or belong to a particular group or category. Inherent in this definition is the fact that stigma constitutes shared knowledge about which attributes and categories are valued by society, which ones are denigrated, and how these valuations vary across situations. Whereas lay definitions of stigma tend to focus on the condition or attribute that discredits the individuals who manifest it—marking them as diverging in an undesirable way from society's understanding of normalcy—social psychological accounts have emphasized the social processes through which a stigmatized condition acquires its meaning in different situations (Goffman, 1963; see also Crocker, Major, & Steele, 1998; Jones et al., 1984). These culturally constructed meanings are grounded in society's power relations so that individuals who inhabit a stigmatized role enjoy less access to valued resources, less influence over others, and less control over their own fate than the nonstigmatized (Link & Phelan, 2001).

Sexual stigma is the stigma attached to any nonheterosexual behavior, identity, relationship, or community. It constitutes socially shared knowledge about homosexuality's devalued status in society—that is, its denigration and discrediting relative to heterosexuality (for other discussions of sexual stigma, see Herek, 2004, 2007; Herek et al., 2007). Like other stigmas, sexual stigma creates roles and expectations for conduct that are shared and understood by the members of society. Regardless of their own sexual orientation or personal attitudes, people in the United States (and many other countries) know that homosexual desires and behaviors are widely regarded in negative terms relative to heterosexuality. They are also aware of the malevolent stereotypes that are routinely attached to individuals whose personal identities are based on same-sex attractions, behaviors, relationships, or membership in a sexual minority community.

Although same-sex and different-sex behaviors are ubiquitous in human societies and other species, notions of "the homosexual" and "the heterosexual"—and the idea that individuals can be defined in terms of their sexual attractions and behaviors—emerged in medical discourse relatively recently (e.g., Chauncey, 1982–1983). The stigmatization process was apparent in the very construction of these categories during the 19th century. The modern term *homosexuality* (*Homosexualität*), appears to have been first used in 1869 by Karl Maria Benkert in a German-language pamphlet (Feray & Herzer, 1990; Herzer, 1985).[1] It was not the only term in use at that time to refer to the phenomenon of same-sex attraction and love, but it represented an attempt to cast them in more positive terms. Nevertheless, homosexuality's inferior status is evident in the fact that Benkert contrasted it with "normal sexuality" (*Normalsexualität*). *Heterosexuality* (*Heterosexualität*) came into usage as the counterpart to homosexuality only later (see also J. N. Katz, 1995). Thus, the stigmatization of homosexuality has historically been inherent in the differentiation of sexual behaviors and desires in Western thought.

As with other social groupings that create majority and minority statuses, sexual orientation is a socially constructed category. Our contemporary understanding of it as a binary heterosexual–homosexual system (with the status of bisexuality often ambiguous) is historically recent. Thus, sexual stigma is a product of cultural forces, although the various social categories linked to homosexuality over the past century (including categories related to disease, predation, and immorality) may resonate with cultural universals of stigma (Cottrell & Neuberg, 2005; Kurzban & Leary, 2001). As sexual stigma becomes increasingly delegitimized, homosexuality may cease to be associated with these categories.

Stigma-derived differentials in status and power are legitimated and perpetuated by society's institutions and ideological systems in the form of *institutional* or *structural stigma* (e.g., Link & Phelan, 2001). As a product of sociopolitical forces, structural stigma "represents the policies of private and governmental institutions that restrict the opportunities of stigmatized groups" (Corrigan et al., 2005, p. 557). Structural sexual stigma is referred to here as *heterosexism*. Adapting Link and Phelan's (2001) definition of institutional racism, heterosexism can be understood as a cultural ideology that is embodied in institutional practices that work to the disadvantage of sexual minority groups even in the absence of individual prejudice or discrimination. It comprises the organizing rules that enforce and perpetuate sexual stigma in society's institutions. As with institutional and individual racism, distinguishing between heterosexism and individual sexual prejudice facilitates the analysis of structural policies and individual attitudes as separate albeit interrelated phenomena.

By embedding sexual stigma in society's institutions, including religion, the law, and medicine, heterosexism has historically justified the differential status of sexual minorities relative to heterosexuals. It is noteworthy, however, that as lesbian, gay, and bisexual people have increasingly come to be recognized as a minority group whose members deserve recognition not simply as human beings but also as well-functioning members of society who are entitled to full citizenship and equal rights, discriminatory practices and policies against them have begun to lose their claims to moral righteousness. In other words, heterosexism's legitimacy in the United States and elsewhere is increasingly contested (e.g., Kelman, 2001). In some arenas, such as the mental health professions and behavioral sciences, heterosexism is now completely delegitimized, as signaled by the American Psychiatric Association's removal of homosexuality from its *Diagnostic and Statistical Manual of Mental Disorders* in 1973, and the American Psychological Association's subsequent commitment to "take the lead in removing the stigma of mental illness that has long been associated with homosexual orientations" (Conger, 1975, p. 633).

---

[1] It has been argued that *Homosexualität* should be translated as "homosexual" rather than "homosexuality" (Bech, 1998).

Nevertheless, heterosexism remains strong in many societal institutions, notably in most religious denominations and in much of the U.S. legal system (Herek et al., 2007). In these domains, it legitimizes and perpetuates power differentials between heterosexuals and sexual minority individuals through at least two general processes. First, it promotes a heterosexual assumption (i.e., all people are presumed to be heterosexual) and thereby renders gay, lesbian, and bisexual people invisible in most social situations. Second, when people with a nonheterosexual orientation become visible, heterosexism problematizes them. Nonheterosexuals, homosexual behavior, and same-sex relationships are presumed to be abnormal and unnatural and, therefore, are regarded as inferior, as requiring explanation, and as appropriate targets for hostility, differential treatment, and even aggression. By contrast, heterosexuals are regarded as prototypical members of the category *people,* and heterosexual behavior and different-sex relationships are presumed to be normal and natural (Hegarty & Pratto, 2004; for a more detailed discussion of institutional stigma and specific aspects of heterosexism, see Herek et al., 2007).

INDIVIDUAL MANIFESTATIONS OF SEXUAL STIGMA

Heterosexism provides the institutional context for individual manifestations of sexual stigma, including sexual prejudice. As elaborated later, sexual prejudice is conceived here as the internalization and acceptance of sexual stigma. Before addressing it, two other individual manifestations of stigma—enacted stigma and felt stigma—are briefly discussed.

ENACTED SEXUAL STIGMA

Enacted sexual stigma refers to the overt behavioral expression of sexual stigma through actions such as the use of antigay epithets, shunning and ostracism of sexual minority individuals, and explicit discrimination and violence against them. Sexual minority adults and adolescents routinely encounter such enactments (Badgett, Lau, Sears, & Ho, 2007; D'Augelli, Grossman, & Starks, 2006; Herek, in press). For example, criminal victimization of sexual minorities is widespread (e.g., Berrill, 1992; Herek & Sims, 2008). A study reporting data from a national probability sample of self-identified lesbian, gay, and bisexual adults found that 21% of the respondents had experienced violence or a property crime based on their sexual orientation at least once during their adult life (Herek, in press). Using data from the National Crime Victimization Survey (NCVS), an ongoing national survey with a large population-based sample, the U.S. Bureau of Justice Statistics estimated that more than 37,800 hate crime victimizations motivated by the victim's sexual orientation occurred in the United States between July 2000 and December 2003 (Harlow, 2005). Most of them (about 58%) were not reported to police authorities (Harlow, 2005; Herek & Sims, 2008; see also Herek, Cogan, & Gillis, 2002). In addition to physical harm, suffering violence because of one's sexual orientation appears to inflict greater psychological trauma on victims than other kinds of violent crime (Herek, Gillis, & Cogan, 1999; see also Mills et al., 2004; Szymanski, 2005).

Although enactments of sexual stigma typically target sexual minority individuals, they also are directed at heterosexuals. The close associates of sexual minorities—friends, family members, and "allies" (heterosexuals who take a public stand against sexual stigma)—are at risk for such enactments through what Goffman (1963) called a *courtesy stigma* (Neuberg, Smith, Hoffman, & Russell, 1994; Sigelman, Howell, Cornell, Cutright, & Dewey, 1991). Moreover, by virtue of sexual orientation's concealable nature, any heterosexual can be mistakenly labeled homosexual or bisexual and is thus potentially vulnerable to enactments of sexual stigma. This fact has important implications for understanding another facet of sexual stigma, namely, felt stigma.

FELT SEXUAL STIGMA

People need not be the targets of enacted stigma for it to affect their lives. Indeed, the knowledge that enacted stigma is likely to occur under certain circumstances often motivates people to modify their behavior to avoid being a victim. This is the essence of *felt stigma,* an individual's expectations about the probability that stigma will be enacted in different situations and under various circumstances (Scambler & Hopkins, 1986). Felt stigma derives from individuals' awareness of the existence of sexual stigma and their beliefs about how and when society condones expressions of it. Because virtually anyone, regardless of his or her sexual orientation, can be a target for enactments of sexual stigma, and because people generally wish to avoid being such a target, felt stigma often affects behavior.

Among stigmatized individuals, felt stigma can be manifested as a high level of *stigma consciousness;* that is, a stigmatized individual's chronic self-consciousness of her or his own stigmatized status and expectations of being stereotyped by others because of it (Pinel, 1999). It also can appear in more subtle ways, as when *stereotype threat* impairs a lesbian, gay, or bisexual individual's performance in situations where negative stereotypes about sexual minorities become salient (Bosson, Haymovitz, & Pinel, 2004).

Felt stigma also motivates stigmatized individuals to engage in preemptive, protective coping behaviors to avoid situations in which stigma enactments are possible (Scambler & Hopkins, 1986). Such behaviors include, for example, attempting to pass as a member of the nonstigmatized majority and isolating oneself from that majority. Although these coping strategies can reduce one's risks for discrimination and attack, they can also significantly disrupt a stigmatized individual's life, restrict her or his options, and heighten her or his psychological distress (Herek, 1996; R. J. Lewis, Derlega, Griffin, & Krowinski, 2003). For example, chronically concealing one's sexual orientation utilizes cognitive resources in a way that can negatively affect well-being (Pachankis, 2007; Smart & Wegner, 2000; see also R. J. Lewis, Derlega, Clarke, & Kuang, 2006) and often reduces opportunities for social support (Herek, 1996). These factors help to explain why concealment of one's gay identity has been linked to psychological distress and health problems, whereas being out of the closet has been found to correlate with positive psychological and physical states (Cole, 2006; Morris, Waldo, & Rothblum, 2001; Strachan, Bennett, Russo, & Roy-Byrne, 2007; Ullrich, Lutgendorf, & Stapleton, 2003; but see Frable, Wortman, & Joseph, 1997). Thus, although concealing one's sexual orientation can protect an individual from enacted stigma, it also creates stress and may have deleterious effects on psychological and physical well-being.

Like sexual minority individuals, most heterosexuals learn about the negative consequences of being labeled a homosexual during childhood and adolescence (Phoenix, Frosh, & Pattman, 2003; Poteat, Espelage, & Green, 2007; G. W. Smith, 1998). However, sexual stigma tends not to be salient to heterosexuals unless sexual orientation becomes personally relevant, as occurs when they knowingly encounter a gay, lesbian, or bisexual person, or in situations where their own sexual orientation might be questioned. On those occasions, felt stigma can motivate them to ensure that their nonstigmatized status is readily evident to others, thereby avoiding the possibility that they will be inaccurately perceived as stigmatized (and thus become a target of enacted stigma). Self-presentation strategies are especially important for males, who are continually called on to affirm their heterosexual masculinity by avoiding stereotypically feminine behaviors (Bosson, Prewitt-Freilino, & Taylor, 2005; Bosson, Taylor, & Prewitt-Freilino, 2006) and, sometimes, by enacting sexual stigma against others to prove to their peers that they are "real men" (Herek, 1986b; Kimmel, 1997).

INTERNALIZED SEXUAL STIGMA

Internalization is the process whereby individuals adopt a social value, belief, regulation, or prescription for conduct as their own and experience it as a part of themselves (e.g., Kelman, 1961; Ryan & Connell, 1989). When someone internalizes stigma, she or he embraces society's denigration and discrediting of the stigmatized group. Thus, internalized stigma refers to an individual's personal acceptance of stigma as a part of her or his own value system and self-concept.

Stigma can be internalized by minority and majority group members alike. A stigmatized individual's internalization of stigma, whereby her or his self-concept is congruent with the stigmatizing responses of society, is referred to here as *self-stigma* (Corrigan & Watson, 2002; Jones et al., 1984). For sexual minorities, self-stigma involves accepting society's negative evaluation of homosexuality as warranted, and consequently harboring negative attitudes toward oneself and one's own homosexual desires. Such attitudes may be manifested as a wish to deny or renounce one's homosexuality and become heterosexual (e.g., Herek, Cogan, Gillis, & Glunt, 1998). Self-stigma among sexual minorities has been labeled *internalized homophobia* (Shidlo, 1994; Weinberg, 1972), *internalized heterosexism* (Szymanski & Chung, 2003), and *internalized homonegativity* (Mayfield, 2001). It often has important negative consequences for physical and psychological well-being (Herek & Garnets, 2007; Meyer, 2003).

Whereas the internalization of stigma is manifested among the stigmatized in the form of negative attitudes toward the self, it is manifested among members of the nonstigmatized majority as negative attitudes toward the stigmatized, that is, prejudice. Thus, *sexual prejudice* is internalized sexual stigma that results in attitudes toward sexual minorities that are congruent with the stigmatizing responses of society. The remainder of the chapter focuses mainly on sexual prejudice.

SEXUAL PREJUDICE: DEFINITIONAL CONSIDERATIONS AND DISTINCTIONS

Sexual prejudice is conceptualized here as an *attitude;* that is, a category-based evaluative tendency to respond to groups or to individuals on the basis of their group membership (Albarracin, Zanna, Johnson, & Kumkale, 2005; Duckitt, 1992; Eagly & Chaiken, 1993). As psychological phenomena, attitudes can be highly idiosyncratic and may be harbored toward anyone and anything. Thus, in a strictly psychological sense, anyone can manifest prejudice against another person because of the latter's sexual orientation. For example, sexual minority individuals can be prejudiced against heterosexuals, just as heterosexuals can be prejudiced against lesbian, gay, and bisexual people. Although both manifestations of negative attitudes can appropriately be labeled prejudice, the conceptual framework described earlier helps to clarify why they are not equivalent.

As the internalization of sexual stigma, prejudice against sexual minorities is part of a larger cultural complex. It represents an individual's endorsement of an ideological system that disempowers sexual minorities, creates institutional barriers to their full participation in society, and fosters enactments of stigma against them, including extreme violence. By contrast, heterosexuals do not constitute a socially devalued and disempowered minority group whose members routinely encounter discrimination, hostility, and bias because of their sexual orientation. Lacking institutional and societal support, prejudice against heterosexuals is simply an expression of individual attitudes.

This is not to suggest that sexual minority individuals cannot harbor prejudice that represents the internalization of sexual stigma. Self-stigma among sexual minorities is inner-directed sexual prejudice. It may be manifested not only as negative feelings toward oneself, but also as negative feelings toward others who share one's stigma. Moreover, individuals in one segment of the sexual minority population can manifest prejudice against those in other segments, as when gay men or lesbians express prejudice against bisexuals, or when sexual minority individuals of one gender express negative attitudes toward their counterparts of the other gender (e.g., Kristiansen, 1990; Mohr & Rochlen, 1999; Rust, 1993). Such attitudes may combine self-stigma with other intergroup attitudes (e.g., gender-based prejudice). Although they represent an understudied and interesting topic, this chapter focuses on sexual prejudice as a heterosexual person's negative attitude toward sexual minority individuals or toward homosexuality.

DISTINGUISHING SEXUAL PREJUDICE FROM OTHER
SEXUAL ORIENTATION ATTITUDES

Although a variety of attitudes implicate sexual orientation, it is useful to distinguish sexual prejudice from two related types of attitude. First, sexual prejudice is distinct from attitudes toward policies that enforce or implement sexual stigma; that is, attitudes toward heterosexism. Examples of such policies include the U.S. government's exclusion of open sexual minorities from military service (Herek, 1993) and laws prohibiting marriage equality for same-sex couples (Herek, 2006). Although researchers have often treated positive attitudes toward such policies as direct expressions of sexual prejudice (Herek, 2008), empirical research highlights the potential utility of considering them separately from heterosexuals' attitudes toward sexual minorities as a group.

One example that demonstrates the value of this distinction is the consistent finding that much of the U.S. public condemns homosexual behavior as immoral while simultaneously endorsing civil liberties for homosexuals (Loftus, 2001). Indeed, some public opinion survey questions about basic rights for homosexuals and other stigmatized minorities were originally conceived as measures of tolerance for unpopular groups. Underlying the notion of tolerance is the idea that one can support basic civil rights for groups that one personally dislikes (Jackman, 1977; Stouffer, 1955). Further support for a distinction between prejudice and policy attitudes can be found in empirical research showing that feelings toward sexual minorities played a decreasingly important role in determining public opinion about gay rights over the course of the 1990s while egalitarian values became more important (P. R. Brewer, 2003), and in studies indicating that heterosexuals' attitudes toward gay men and lesbians do not fully account for the variation in their attitudes toward policies implicating sexual minorities (Strand, 1998; see also Wood & Bartkowski, 2004). For example, in a 2005 national telephone survey, with sexual prejudice statistically controlled, heterosexuals' antigay policy attitudes were predicted significantly by their egalitarian values, moral traditionalism, and political conservatism (Herek, 2008).

Thus, although sexual prejudice is an important predictor of policy attitudes, the latter are also shaped by political and moral attitudes and values that are conceptually distinct from the internalization of sexual stigma. This suggests that policy attitudes may be amenable to change even in the absence of a widespread reduction in the heterosexual public's sexual prejudice. If these structural manifestations of stigma are perceived as intolerant and antiegalitarian, for example, public support for them might erode independently of changes in individual heterosexuals' prejudice.

A second distinction is between sexual prejudice and attitudes that, although ostensibly directed at another attitude object, are fueled largely by sexual prejudice. A prime example of such symbolic expressions of prejudice can be found in public attitudes toward people with HIV/AIDS and AIDS-related policies. In the United States and many other countries, the HIV epidemic has had a devastating impact on gay and bisexual men, and AIDS was often equated with homosexuality in the early years of the epidemic. Even though the epidemiology of HIV changed in the 1990s, with gay and bisexual men constituting a shrinking portion of U.S. AIDS cases, much of the American public continues to equate AIDS with homosexuality (Herek & Capitanio, 1999a; Kaiser Family Foundation, 2006). Because of this association, AIDS has served as a vehicle for many heterosexuals to express sexual prejudice (Herek, 1997; Herek & Capitanio, 1999a; Herek & Glunt, 1991; Pryor, Reeder, & Landau, 1999; Pryor, Reeder, Vinacco, & Kott, 1989). Thus, a better understanding of sexual prejudice can also assist in understanding public attitudes toward groups and issues that are symbolically linked with homosexuality. Nevertheless, the latter are not synonymous with the former. Attitudes toward people with HIV/AIDS can also be based on concerns about risks of infection for oneself or loved ones (e.g., Herek, 2000b; Pryor, Reeder, & McManus, 1991) or on attitudes toward other stigmatized groups, such as injecting drug users (Capitanio & Herek, 1999).

SIMILARITIES TO AND DIFFERENCES FROM OTHER FORMS OF PREJUDICE

Sexual prejudice has much in common with racial, ethnic, religious, and other prejudices. All are understood as attitudes that are founded on the target's group membership. As attitudes, they are all based on information that individuals derive from their beliefs, affective responses, and past behaviors. In each case, the attitude object is a socially devalued minority group whose members routinely encounter discrimination, hostility, and bias. Each type of prejudice can be operationally defined and measured with similar explicit and implicit techniques. And, as discussed later, many of the same variables predict all of these forms of prejudice.

As noted at the outset of the chapter, however, sexual prejudice differs from many other forms of prejudice in at least two noteworthy respects (see also Fiske & Taylor, 2007). One difference results from the previously noted fact that an individual's sexual orientation is not usually apparent during social interactions. Indeed, sexual minority individuals themselves only recognize, discover, or construct an identity based on their sexual orientation over the course of development, sometimes not until they are adults. From the minority individual's perspective, this means that one is likely to grow up in a heterosexual environment with an expectation of being heterosexual as an adult. He or she must develop an awareness or recognition of her or his homosexual orientation and then disclose it to others, often without guidance from a sympathetic adult or a sexual minority role model. Sexual minority individuals are also likely to have internalized sexual stigma before first recognizing their nonheterosexual orientation.

The concealability of sexual orientation also has important implications for heterosexuals. As discussed earlier, because anyone can be labeled as nonheterosexual, enacted stigma and felt stigma can be experienced by heterosexuals as well as by sexual minorities. This fact motivates many heterosexuals to assert their sexual orientation in social settings, sometimes even by enacting sexual stigma against others. In addition, the concealability of sexual orientation means that heterosexuals can unknowingly interact with lesbian, gay, and bisexual individuals. As discussed later, this has important implications for the effects of intergroup contact on sexual prejudice.

A second important difference between sexual prejudice and many other forms of contemporary prejudice is the extent to which the former is considered acceptable by much of society. Although the legitimacy of sexual stigma (and, therefore, sexual prejudice) is increasingly contested, contemporary social norms do not uniformly condemn discrimination, bias, and hostility against sexual minorities. Indeed, as previously noted, many societal institutions favor differential treatment of sexual minorities and negative attitudes toward homosexuality remain widespread. In response to a General Social Survey question about sexual relations between two adults of the same sex, for example, a majority (57% in 2004) has consistently regarded homosexual behavior as "always wrong." In the American National Election Studies (ANES), the average feeling thermometer ratings for "gays and lesbians" have remained below the neutral score of 50 (the mean score was 49 in 2004) and, compared to the public's feelings toward other groups, feeling thermometer scores for "gays and lesbians" have ranked near the bottom of the list. It is also noteworthy that the number of respondents assigning gays and lesbians a zero—the coldest possible score—tends to be larger than for other groups (Sherrill & Yang, 2000).[2] Other national surveys have consistently shown that substantial numbers of heterosexuals regard gay men and lesbians as disgusting and consider homosexuality to be wrong and unnatural (e.g., Herek, 1994; Herek, 2002a).

Despite the persistence of sexual prejudice, U.S. public opinion data reveal trends toward less condemnation and dislike. The size of the majority considering homosexual relations to be always wrong, for example, has declined since the 1970s and 1980s, when it was as high as 75% (Yang, 1997). The mean ANES thermometer ratings for "gays and lesbians" have increased from 39 in

---

[2] My discussion of polling data relies on my own examination of the data in publicly available archives (especially the Roper Center at the University of Connecticut), as well as the published sources cited here.

1996. In Gallup polls, a majority of respondents (57% in 2007) now consider homosexuality an acceptable lifestyle, compared to 34% in 1982 (Saad, 2007).

The willingness of much of the U.S. public to express negative attitudes toward gay people is in sharp contrast to racial and ethnic prejudice, which are socially proscribed in most settings. Indeed, the latter fact has fostered the development of theories and methods to explain and assess subtle, hidden, and ambivalent manifestations of prejudice (e.g., Gaertner & Dovidio, 2005b; I. Katz, 1981; McConahay, 1986). The need for similar approaches to sexual prejudice has been less apparent, especially outside of tolerant social settings such as many college campuses (e.g., Morrison & Morrison, 2002). Important insights can nevertheless be gained from approaches such as the Implicit Association Test (IAT; e.g., Banse, Seise, & Zerbes, 2001; Dasgupta & Rivera, 2006; Jellison, McConnell, & Gabriel, 2004; Steffens, 2005; Steffens & Buchner, 2003; Tsang & Rowatt, 2007), but their role in the study of sexual prejudice has not yet been developed to the same extent as for other forms of prejudice.

COGNITIVE, AFFECTIVE, AND BEHAVIORAL SOURCES OF SEXUAL PREJUDICE

In contemporary social psychology, attitudes are understood as entities based on cognitive, affective, and behavioral information. Attitudes can both influence and be inferred from those three sources, but are nevertheless distinguishable from them (e.g., Albarracin et al., 2005; Fabrigar, MacDonald, & Wegener, 2005; Haddock, Zanna, & Esses, 1993). In this chapter's conceptual framework, for example, heterosexuals' internalization of sexual stigma (i.e., sexual prejudice) is distinguished from stigma enactment (i.e., negative behaviors toward sexual minority individuals). Stigma enactments are often motivated by prejudice (e.g., Bernat, Calhoun, Adams, & Zeichner, 2001; Franklin, 2000; Parrott & Zeichner, 2005; San Miguel & Millham, 1976) but this is not always the case. For example, some heterosexuals who perpetrate antigay hate crimes nevertheless express favorable attitudes toward gay people as a group (Franklin, 1998). As in other domains (Ajzen & Fishbein, 2005), patterns of antigay behavior are likely to be correlated with sexual prejudice, but only moderately so. Across several empirical studies, correlations between measures of sexual prejudice and self-reported negative behaviors toward sexual minorities have ranged from $r = .25$ to $r = .40$ (Franklin, 2000; Herek, 2008; Patel, Long, McCammon, & Wuensch, 1995; Roderick, McCammon, Long, & Allred, 1998).

Sexual Prejudice and Beliefs About Sexual Minorities

Research on the cognitive sources of sexual prejudice has focused mainly on three types of beliefs: stereotypes, beliefs about values, and essentialist beliefs. Each is discussed briefly here.

Whereas psychological stereotyping is a product of normal cognitive categorization processes and can be relatively benign, it usually derives its content from cultural stereotypes of sexual minorities. Those stereotypes, grounded as they are in sexual stigma, generally portray sexual minorities in negative terms as outsiders. Like stereotypes of other historically stigmatized groups, they are often malevolent and dehumanizing—characterizing group members as predatory, animalistic, hypersexual, overvisible, heretical, conspiratorial, and diseased (Adam, 1978; Gilman, 1985; Herek, 1991). Belief in such stereotypes both fuels sexual prejudice and provides a justification for antipathy toward sexual minorities. For example, the stereotype that gay men (and, to a lesser extent, lesbians) prey on children has been widespread in the United States at least since the World War II era (Chauncey, 1993; Freedman, 1989). Although most heterosexual Americans today recognize that this stereotype is baseless (Herek, 2002a), it continues to be invoked in antigay discourse as a strategy for promoting and justifying hostility toward sexual minorities and discrimination against them (e.g., Family Research Institute, 2006).

Perhaps because these inflammatory stereotypes of sexual minorities are not widely believed in settings such as college campuses, much of the social psychological research on this topic (which typically relies on college students as participants) has examined more innocuous stereotypes. Nevertheless, such research has documented the role that stereotypes can play in perceptions of gay men and lesbians and in sexual prejudice. For example, early research found that heterosexuals attributed stereotypically "gay" characteristics to an individual who was labeled gay or lesbian, but not to the same individual when he or she was not labeled (Gross, Green, Storck, & Vanyur, 1980; Gurwitz & Marcus, 1978). Similar processes appear to operate in retrospectively recalling the characteristics of a lesbian or gay person (McGann & Goodwin, 2007; Snyder & Uranowitz, 1978).

Sexual prejudice can potentiate the negative effects of stereotypes about sexual minorities by, for example, impairing heterosexuals' ability to suppress stereotypical thoughts (Monteith, Spicer, & Tooman, 1998) or differentiate among sexual minority individuals (Walker & Antaki, 1986). It also can bias heterosexuals' perceptions of sexual minority individuals and influence their assimilation of new information, which can perpetuate their stereotypical beliefs (e.g., Munro & Ditto, 1997; Sherman, Stroessner, Conrey, & Azam, 2005). Even when heterosexuals perceive intragroup variability among sexual minorities, they may assimilate this information by recategorizing the latter into stereotype-consistent subgroups. For example, Clausell and Fiske (2005) found that heterosexual undergraduates cognitively organized subgroups of gay men according to the latter's ostensible conformity to traditional gender roles. Moreover, none of the subtypes were regarded as both competent and warm—attributes that typically are associated with one's ingroup or valued reference groups and are linked to positive emotions (Clausell & Fiske, 2005).

In addition to stereotypes, prejudiced heterosexuals may harbor the belief that sexual minorities support or embody values that conflict with their own (Esses, Haddock, & Zanna, 1993; Haddock & Zanna, 1998; Haddock et al., 1993; Jackson & Esses, 1997). Such beliefs have become especially salient in the United States since the advent of the so-called "culture wars" in the 1980s, when sexual minorities came to be widely portrayed as embodying values that are antithetical to conservative Christianity (Herman, 1997). Strong associations have been observed between measures of sexual prejudice and traditionalist values concerning sexuality, gender roles, and family structure in both correlational studies and laboratory experiments (e.g., Herek, 1988; Kite & Whitley, 1998; Vescio & Biernat, 2003). Moreover, policy issues in which sexual orientation and family structure intersect (e.g., marriage equality for same-sex couples, adoption and parenting by sexual minority adults) are viewed by many Americans mainly in terms of conservative religious values (P. R. Brewer, 2003; P. R. Brewer & Wilcox, 2005; Price, Nir, & Cappella, 2005).

A third type of belief that is relevant to understanding sexual prejudice relates to essentialism. Allport (1954) proposed that a "belief in essence" (p. 174) develops as a consequence of the principle of least effort in cognitions about social groups, and is often associated with prejudice. In the domain of sexual prejudice, the role played by subjective essentialism is complex. Some components of essentialist beliefs—especially the notions that sexual orientations are discrete categories and that gay and lesbian people are fundamentally different from heterosexual men and women—are reliably associated with sexual prejudice. Other components, however, such as beliefs that sexual orientation is immutable and a universal characteristic of human beings, are associated with lower levels of prejudice, at least in the United States (Haslam & Levy, 2006; Haslam, Rothschild, & Ernst, 2002; Hegarty, 2002; Hegarty & Pratto, 2001).

Beliefs about whether or not sexual orientation is immutable and whether or not it is freely chosen have played a prominent role in public debate about policies related to sexual minorities in the United States. A growing number of American adults—in some recent polls, a plurality—now believe that homosexuality is "something a person is born with" (Saad, 2007). Compared to such individuals, those who believe that homosexuality is chosen tend to manifest higher levels of sexual prejudice (Herek & Capitanio, 1995; Jayaratne et al., 2006; Saad, 2007; Schneider & Lewis, 1984).[3]

---

[3] The fact that most discussion in this area centers on the origins of homosexuality but not heterosexuality illustrates how the former is routinely problematized whereas the latter is assumed to be natural and not requiring explanation.

This pattern has often been explained with reference to attribution theory (e.g., Whitley, 1990). From this perspective, the belief that a person is responsible for acquiring a stigmatized characteristic such as homosexuality leads to more negative attitudes toward the person, less sympathy, and less desire to assist the individual (Weiner, 1993). Conversely, it is assumed that heterosexuals will become less prejudiced if they become convinced that being gay is not a choice.

Because of the correlational nature of the data about choice beliefs and sexual prejudice, however, a causal relationship cannot be assumed. Hegarty (2002; Hegarty & Golden, 2008) argued that expressing the belief that homosexuality is chosen may be a consequence of sexual prejudice rather than a cause. He contended that in a society like the United States, where assertions as to whether or not homosexuality is a choice have become symbolic expressions of prejudice, heterosexuals may construct their beliefs about choice "to fit their sexual politics rather than the reverse" (Hegarty, 2002, p. 163). In support of this argument, he found that choice beliefs were correlated with prejudice only among those respondents who also perceived that tolerant attitudes toward sexual minorities are signified by statements that homosexuality is unchangeable and not chosen (Hegarty, 2002).

It is also possible that the choice–prejudice correlation may result from the causal influence of a third factor, such as heterosexuals' personal contact with sexual minority people. In one survey with a national U.S. sample, Whites (but not Blacks) harbored less sexual prejudice and were less likely to regard homosexuality as a choice if they personally knew one or more gay people. Those relationships may have reduced their prejudice while also affording them an opportunity to learn their friend or relative's ideas about the origins of her or his own sexual orientation.

Thus, although the link between immutability beliefs and sexual prejudice has been reliably observed in the U.S. public, the underlying reasons for this association are not well understood. Immutability beliefs may reflect attributions of responsibility and thus cause heightened prejudice, or they may be justifications for the expression of preexisting prejudice. Alternatively, immutability beliefs and prejudice may both result from interpersonal contact or some other variable.

AFFECTIVE SOURCES OF SEXUAL PREJUDICE

As with beliefs, sexual prejudice is related to but distinct from negative affect toward sexual minorities. Nevertheless, it is clear that emotions play an important role in sexual prejudice, as well as in enactments of extreme forms of sexual stigma, such as hate crimes. For example, substantial proportions of national probability samples—in many cases majorities—have expressed disgust at male or female homosexuality in telephone interviews (e.g., Herek, 2002a; Herek & Capitanio, 1999b; Herek & Glunt, 1993). Other research has shown that anger can form the basis for attitudes in some cases, and may mediate the relationship between sexual prejudice and enactments of stigma (e.g., Parrott & Zeichner, 2005; Parrott, Zeichner, & Hoover, 2006). Indeed, emotional factors may contribute more strongly to sexual prejudice than do stereotyping and other cognitive influences (Fiske & Taylor, 2007).

The first conceptualization of sexual prejudice to achieve widespread attention focused on affect. Weinberg (1972) coined the word *homophobia* and defined it as "the dread of being in close quarters with homosexuals" (p. 4; see Herek, 2004, for an extended discussion of Weinberg's work). By labeling these attitudes a phobia, Weinberg suggested they were based on irrational fears. Although this assumption is theoretically problematic and lacks empirical support (Herek, 2004), homophobia has attained widespread usage. Thus, fear is popularly presumed to be at the heart of antigay prejudice.

Different authors, however, have identified different targets for that fear. Whereas Weinberg's definition seems to clearly link heterosexuals' fears to gay people themselves, two activist colleagues of Weinberg characterized homophobia in a 1969 article as heterosexuals' fear that others will think they are homosexual (Nichols & Clarke, 1969, cited in Herek, 2004). Kimmel (1997) extended this analysis, arguing that

Homophobia is more than the irrational fear of gay men, more than the fear that we might be perceived as gay. . . . Homophobia is the fear that other men will unmask us, emasculate us, reveal to us and the world that we do not measure up, that we are not real men. (p. 233)

The actual role played by fear in sexual prejudice has been difficult to assess, especially in light of the different objects proposed for that fear, and empirical data on the importance of fear versus other emotions is mixed. Shields and Harriman (1984) assessed the heart rates of heterosexual male undergraduates as they viewed slides of male–female, male–male, and female–female sexual activity. Of the men who had scored high on a self-administered measure of sexual prejudice, only some displayed a physiological response consistent with fear (heart-rate acceleration to the male–male slides; Shields & Harriman, 1984). Bernat and his colleagues found that heterosexual male undergraduates who scored high on a measure of sexual prejudice also reported more negative affect, anxiety, and anger after viewing a video depicting male–male sexual acts, compared to their low-scoring counterparts (Bernat et al., 2001). Although fear was included in their measure of negative affect, so were shame, guilt, hostility, and other feelings. Thus, their findings do not permit conclusions about the role of fear in sexual prejudice.

Mahaffey and her colleagues found that undergraduate men's self-reported discomfort around gay men was significantly associated with levels of startle eye-blink responses in conjunction with viewing photographs of nude and seminude male couples (Mahaffey, Bryan, & Hutchison, 2005a; see also Mahaffey, Bryan, & Hutchison, 2005b). Meier and his colleagues compared heterosexual male undergraduates on the basis of their scores on measures of discomfort with gay men and defensive self-enhancement. Compared to other participants, those who scored high on both measures (whom the researchers labeled *defensive homophobics*) spent less time viewing computer screen images of kissing or embracing male couples than of similarly engaged heterosexual couples (Meier, Robinson, Gaither, & Heinert, 2006). The same group also manifested more negative associations with gay men on an implicit attitude measure. The findings of both research groups suggest that negative affect is present among heterosexual males who express discomfort about social contact with gay men, but do not indicate whether that affect consists of fear, disgust, anger, or some other negative emotion.

All of the studies just described focused on heterosexual males' responses to images of two men (often at least partially unclothed) engaged in affectionate or explicit sexual activity. Thus, they assessed reactions to a rather narrowly defined stimulus, and may reveal more about heterosexual men's responses to male–male sexual activity than their attitudes toward gay men in routine social situations. To the extent that heterosexuals tend to think of gay people largely or entirely in sexual terms, however, these reactions may be highly relevant to understanding sexual prejudice.

A somewhat different approach was used by Bosson and her colleagues. They focused on the aspect of "homophobia" discussed by Kimmel (1997) and others, namely, heterosexuals' fears of being incorrectly labeled homosexual. They found that engaging in tasks that might cause them to be perceived as gay evoked discomfort among heterosexuals; this discomfort was alleviated, however, when the research participants were given the opportunity to assert their heterosexuality (Bosson et al., 2005; Bosson et al., 2006). Within this chapter's conceptual framework, the heterosexuals' discomfort can be understood as the product of felt stigma.

KEY CORRELATES OF SEXUAL PREJUDICE

Empirical research has identified a group of demographic, psychological, and social variables that are reliably correlated with heterosexuals' attitudes toward gay men and lesbians, and many of these correlates are also common to racial, ethnic, religious, and other prejudices (Duckitt, 1992). Heterosexuals with high levels of sexual prejudice are more likely than their nonprejudiced counterparts to be older, less well-educated, and residing in geographic areas where negative attitudes are the norm (e.g., rural areas of the midwestern or southern United States). They are also more likely to be men, a fact that is discussed later. In terms of social attitudes, they are less likely to be sexually permissive (e.g., unlikely to condone sexual activity outside a heterosexual marriage) and they generally express traditional attitudes concerning gender roles. They are more likely to be highly religious, to hold orthodox or fundamentalist religious beliefs, and to identify themselves as politically conservative rather than liberal or moderate. They tend to display higher levels of psychological authoritarianism, dogmatism, and intolerance for ambiguity. They are also more likely to believe that a homosexual orientation is freely chosen and are less likely to have had close personal friends or family members who are openly lesbian or gay (for reviews, see Herek, 1984, 1994; Loftus, 2001; Simon, 1998; Whitley & Lee, 2000; see also Ellison & Musick, 1993; Haeberle, 1999; Herek & Capitanio, 1995, 1996; Herek & Glunt, 1993; G. B. Lewis & Rogers, 1999). Although research on heterosexuals' attitudes toward bisexual men and women is fairly limited, many of the same variables have been shown to be correlated with those attitudes as well (Herek, 2002b; Mohr & Rochlen, 1999). Of these many correlates, three types of variables have proved to be especially important for understanding sexual prejudice. Each of them is discussed briefly in the next sections.

GENDER

Some of the earliest available data on heterosexuals' attitudes toward sexual minorities revealed a gender gap, with men manifesting more negative attitudes than women toward gay people. In the mid-20th century, for example, Alfred Kinsey and his colleagues found that White college-educated females were less likely to disapprove of homosexual sex than were their male counterparts; the former's attitudes were also less disapproving than those of college-educated Blacks of both genders as well as White respondents with no college (Gebhard & Johnson, 1979).[4] In what was perhaps the first national survey to assess attitudes toward homosexuality, a 1965 Harris poll found that 82% of male respondents believed that homosexuals were "more harmful than helpful to American life," compared to 58% of female respondents (Harris, 1965).

Since these early studies, empirical research conducted in the United States has found that heterosexual men and women differ reliably in their attitudes toward homosexuality and gay people, and these gender differences display three principal patterns. First, women tend to express more favorable and less condemning attitudes than men toward gay people. Second, in the aggregate, attitudes toward gay men tend to be more hostile than attitudes toward lesbians. Third, the most negative attitudes are those expressed by heterosexual men toward gay men (e.g., Herek, 2002a; Kite, 1994; Kite & Whitley, 1996, 1998). Across studies, the magnitude of the gender gap in attitudes toward homosexuality varies depending on whose attitudes are being measured and which attitude domain is being assessed. In some domains the differences are strikingly large, whereas some issues related to policies affecting sexual minorities have not elicited gender differences in attitudes (Kite & Whitley, 1996). Most of the relevant data are derived mainly from non-Hispanic White samples of U.S. adults, but the limited available evidence suggests that gender gaps may also occur in some facets of the attitudes of African American (Herek & Capitanio, 1995; G. B. Lewis, 2003) and U.S. Hispanic adults (Herek & Gonzalez-Rivera, 2006; Sherrod & Nardi, 1998).

Research also suggests that heterosexual men tend to respond to sexual minorities in terms of gender, whereas heterosexual women tend to respond in terms of orientation group. In a U.S. national telephone survey in which respondents provided separate feeling thermometer ratings for gay men, lesbians, bisexual men, and bisexual women, the heterosexual female respondents rated bisexuals significantly less favorably than they rated homosexuals, regardless of gender. By contrast, heterosexual men rated sexual minority males less favorably than sexual minority females,

---

[4] The sample did not include a sufficient number of Blacks with less than a college education to permit their inclusion in the comparison.

regardless of whether the target was bisexual or homosexual (Herek, 2000a). A similar pattern has been observed in Germany (Steffens & Wagner, 2004).

In addition to revealing attitudinal differences between men and women, empirical research has consistently yielded a significant correlation between attitudes toward homosexuality and gender-related attitudes. Negative attitudes toward gay men and lesbians have been reliably associated with support for traditional gender roles and heightened concern about gender-role conformity, especially among males (Herek, 1994; Jellison et al., 2004; Kilianski, 2003; Kite & Whitley, 1998; Parrott, Adams, & Zeichner, 2002).

Gender differences have also been observed in the cognitive dynamics underlying attitudes toward homosexuality. In national surveys with probability samples of English-speaking U.S. adults, heterosexual men's self-reported attitudes toward gay people—especially lesbians—were dramatically affected by the order in which the questions were asked, whereas women's responses largely were not (Herek, 2002a; Herek & Capitanio, 1999b). These surveys used the three-item parallel versions of the Attitudes Toward Gay Men (ATG) and Attitudes Toward Lesbians (ATL) scales, which are reliable measures of sexual prejudice (Herek, 1994). When the ATL questions followed the identically phrased ATG items in a 1997 survey, for example, 54% of the men agreed with the ATL item "I think female homosexuals are disgusting." By contrast, of the men who were randomly assigned to answer the ATL items first, only 36% agreed with the same statement, a difference of 18 points (Herek & Capitanio, 1999b). Similarly, in a 1999 survey, for the ATL item, "Sex between two women is just plain wrong," the difference was 17 points: When it was administered after the ATG items, 59% agreed with this statement, but only 42% agreed when ATL items came first (Herek, 2002a; see Steffens, 2005, for discussion of a similar context effect with an implicit measure of sexual prejudice in a German student sample). In addition, in the 1999 survey, response latencies for the first attitude item in the lesbian and gay male series ("Sex between two women [men] is just plain wrong") differed significantly between men who were low in sexual prejudice and those who were high in it. Highly prejudiced men had significantly longer response latencies for the lesbian version than the gay male version regardless of the order in which items were presented. By contrast, men with lower levels of sexual prejudice took longer to answer whichever item version came first, a pattern that probably reflects a normal practice effect (Herek, 2002a).

These patterns indicate that heterosexual men's attitudes toward lesbians are strongly influenced by contextual cues. They are substantially more negative when a respondent is primed to think about lesbians in relation to gay men than when the context encourages him to think about lesbians independently (i.e., if the lesbian questions are asked first in the sequence). By contrast, heterosexual women's survey responses generally have shown only minimal effects of item order, or none at all. Thus, not only do quantitative gaps exist between heterosexual men's and women's attitudes toward lesbians and gay men, but heterosexual men's attitudes toward gay men also may be more accessible and fully formed than their attitudes toward lesbians.

RELIGIOUS BELIEFS AND AFFILIATIONS

Public opinion data and laboratory research show that antigay prejudice is strongly correlated with multiple indicators of religiosity. More frequent attendance at religious services is associated with higher levels of antigay attitudes, especially among members of more fundamentalist denominations, and heterosexuals tend to be more prejudiced against sexual minorities to the extent that they say their religion is an important source of guidance in their daily lives (Fisher, Derison, Polley, & Cadman, 1994; Herek, 1984, 1994; Herek & Capitanio, 1996; Loftus, 2001; Scott, 1998).

This pattern is reminiscent of findings in early studies of racial and ethnic prejudice. Although religiosity would seem to be antithetical to such prejudice, researchers observed that they were often correlated (e.g., Duckitt, 1992; Stark & Glock, 1973). This led Allport (1954, 1966) to propose that an individual's way of being religious determined her or his propensity for prejudice. Those for whom religion served primarily as a means to obtaining social status and personal security (which

Allport termed an *extrinsic* religious orientation) were likely to be prejudiced, whereas those for whom religion serves as an end in itself (an *intrinsic* orientation) were likely to be unprejudiced. Because intrinsics use religious teachings to inform their everyday interactions with others, Allport believed, for them "there is no place for rejection, contempt, or condescension" toward other human beings (Allport & Ross, 1967, p. 441). The extrinsically motivated, by contrast, are religious mainly so they can enjoy social acceptance and integration. Religion provides them with "security, comfort, status, or social support" (Allport & Ross, 1967, p. 441). Because prejudice often provides similar benefits (as was especially the case in mid-20th-century America), extrinsics were often prejudiced (Allport, 1966).

Research on racial and ethnic prejudice among U.S. Christians tended to support Allport's hypothesis that individuals with an extrinsic orientation would tend to score higher on self-report measures of prejudice (Batson, Schoenrade, & Ventis, 1993). However, this pattern was not observed in studies that employed indirect measures (Batson, Naifeh, & Pate, 1978; see generally Batson & Stocks, 2005).

Studies of prejudice and religious orientation generally focused on forms of prejudice that are proscribed by religious denominations, such as racism. As noted earlier, sexual prejudice is strongly endorsed by some religious denominations. Research that has examined the link between Christians' religious orientation and sexual prejudice has shown that an intrinsic orientation is correlated with prejudice against lesbians and gay men (Burris & Jackson, 1999; Duck & Hunsberger, 1999; Griffiths, Dixon, Stanley, & Weiland, 2001; Herek, 1987b; McFarland, 1989; Tsang & Rowatt, 2007). This association is typically reduced to a nonsignificant level when religious fundamentalism is statistically controlled. Similarly, Hunsberger and his colleagues found fundamentalism was significantly correlated with sexual prejudice among Christians and non-Christians in Canada and Ghana (Hunsberger, 1996; Hunsberger, Owusu, & Duck, 1999). Jackson and Esses (1997) found that higher levels of fundamentalism were correlated with more negative judgments of homosexuals among Canadian college students, and this relationship was mediated by students' perception that gay people threatened their values.[5] A third type of religious orientation, *quest* (an open-ended, questioning approach to religion; Batson et al., 1993), has generally been found to be negatively correlated with various forms of prejudice, including sexual prejudice (Fisher et al., 1994; Kirkpatrick, 1993; McFarland, 1989, 1998).

Some religious believers separate their attitudes toward acts and toward actors, as expressed in the maxim, "Love the sinner but hate the sin." Applied to homosexuality, this distinction suggests that the individual holds positive regard for the gay or lesbian individual even while condemning her or his sexual behavior. However, social psychological research has failed to produce evidence for it. Fulton, Gorsuch, and Maynard (1999) found that fundamentalists rejected people who were described as homosexual even if the latter were characterized as celibate. Moreover, their rejection of noncelibate homosexuals tended to be greater than their rejection of heterosexuals who engage in sex outside of marriage (Fulton et al., 1999). In a laboratory experiment, Batson and his colleagues led religious undergraduate students to believe their actions would help or hinder another student of the same sex in winning a raffle. The other student was described variously as a lesbian who wanted to use the raffle money to finance a trip to a gay pride rally, a lesbian or gay man who would use the money to visit grandparents, or a presumed heterosexual (sexual orientation not stated) who would use the raffle prize to visit grandparents. The researchers hypothesized that a philosophy of "loving the sinner but hating the sin" would be expressed in not helping the student who wanted to attend a gay rally (because that would constitute "promoting" homosexuality) but helping the student who wanted to visit grandparents, regardless of the student's sexual orientation. This pattern was observed for students who scored low on intrinsic religious orientation; however, those scoring

---

[5] Presumably, most of the students were heterosexual. However, the published paper does not report information about the participants' sexual orientation.

high on intrinsic orientation were less likely to help the lesbian or gay student, regardless of how she or he planned to spend the money (Batson, Floyd, Meyer, & Winner, 1999).[6]

PERSONAL EXPERIENCE AND RELATIONSHIPS

Heterosexuals who report personally knowing gay men or lesbians reliably express significantly more favorable attitudes toward gay people as a group than do heterosexuals who lack such contact (Herek & Capitanio, 1996; Herek & Glunt, 1993; G. B. Lewis, 2006; Pettigrew & Tropp, 2006). Contact appears to be most likely to reduce sexual prejudice when heterosexuals know multiple sexual minority individuals, when those contacts include emotionally close relationships, and when the relationships include open discussion of what it means to be a sexual minority (Herek, 2008; Herek & Capitanio, 1996).

Although the correlation between contact and prejudice can be partly explained by the fact that gay people are more likely to disclose their sexual orientation to heterosexuals whom they expect to be supportive, there are both empirical and theoretical indications that contact reduces prejudice. Longitudinal data indicate that heterosexuals' contact experiences predict subsequent prejudice reduction to a greater extent than initially low levels of prejudice predict having subsequent contact experiences (Herek & Capitanio, 1996). In addition, when heterosexuals are matched on other relevant characteristics, those reporting personal contact have significantly lower levels of sexual prejudice and are more supportive of policies benefiting sexual minorities than those without contact (G. B. Lewis, 2007).

At a theoretical level, the contact hypothesis predicts that prejudice will be reduced by contact between majority and minority group members in the pursuit of common goals (Allport, 1954). Allport (1954) noted that contact's beneficial effects are enhanced to the extent that it is "sanctioned by institutional supports" and "leads to the perception of common interests and common humanity between members of the two groups" (p. 281). A large body of empirical research supports the contact hypothesis and indicates that, although the four conditions specified by Allport (equal group status, common goals, intergroup cooperation, institutional support) are not essential for contact to decrease intergroup hostility, their presence typically leads to even greater prejudice reduction (Pettigrew & Tropp, 2006).

Pettigrew (1998) suggested that contact situations fostering the development of friendship between group members are the most likely to reduce prejudice, in part because intergroup friendship potentially invokes all four of the facilitative factors identified by Allport (Pettigrew, 1998). Applied to heterosexuals' experiences with sexual minorities, such contact is likely to increase the former's knowledge, foster greater empathy, and reduce anxieties about interacting with the latter group, all of which are likely to be associated with decreases in prejudice (Pettigrew, 1998; Stephan & Finlay, 1999; Stephan & Stephan, 1985; Vonofakou, Hewstone, & Voci, 2007). These beneficial effects of contact should be even greater to the extent that heterosexuals have multiple lesbian or gay friends or relatives. Knowing multiple members of a stigmatized group is also more likely to foster recognition of that group's variability than is knowing only one group member (Wilder, 1978) and may reduce the likelihood that nonstereotypical behavior is discounted as atypical (Rothbart & John, 1985).

The concealable nature of sexual orientation creates different dynamics for interactions between majority and minority group members than is the case with, for example, race and ethnicity. Whereas the participants' respective category memberships are usually immediately salient in contact between people of different racial or ethnic groups, heterosexuals often have contact with

---

[6] Another experiment used a similar design to assess whether individuals scoring high on quest would distinguish between an individual and his or her behavior. In that study, the student peer was characterized as intolerant of gay people. In one condition, participants believed she would use the raffle winnings to promote intolerance, but not in the other condition. High-quest participants were less likely to help the peer only when doing so would promote intolerance (Batson, Eidelman, Higley, & Russel, 2001).

sexual minority individuals without being aware of it. Such contact even includes long-standing friendships and family relationships that predate the sexual minority individual's recognition of her or his own orientation.

Thus, instead of involving strangers whose respective group memberships constitute some of the first information available, contact between heterosexual people and sexual minority individuals often involves revelation of the latter's status within the context of an already established relationship. When heterosexuals learn about a friend or relative's homosexuality or bisexuality, an intergroup relationship is imposed on the preexisting interpersonal relationship. To the extent that the qualities of that personal relationship—including positive affect, individuation, and personalization—are carried over to the new intergroup relationship, it is likely that the heterosexual individual will be able to generalize from her or his feelings toward the sexual minority individual to a more positive attitude toward lesbians and gay men as a group (M. B. Brewer & Miller, 1984; Brown & Hewstone, 2005).

This dynamic is perhaps most likely to occur in the case of close friendships (Herek & Capitanio, 1996; Pettigrew, 1998; Vonofakou et al., 2007). Having a close lesbian or gay friend may lead a heterosexual person to reconceptualize her or his most important group affiliations, such that she or he feels a common group membership with sexual minorities (e.g., Gaertner & Dovidio, 2005a). In this process of recategorization, the ingroup may become more broadly defined so that it now includes nonheterosexuals. It is important that the heterosexual person not perceive the new information about her or his friend's sexual orientation as calling into question all of her or his prior knowledge about and impressions of the friend, which could lead to a negative recategorization of the individual (e.g., Fiske, Lin, & Neuberg, 1999) rather than a positive recategorization of the outgroup. This outcome is less likely to occur when the heterosexual and the sexual minority person openly discuss the latter's experiences (Herek, 2008).

MOTIVATIONS FOR SEXUAL PREJUDICE

The fact that sexual prejudice is reliably correlated with a range of other variables is consistent with the notion that it has multiple underlying motivations. One framework for understanding how these different motivations operate is the functional approach to attitudes, which has been applied to a variety of attitude domains (D. Katz, 1960; Maio & Olson, 2000; Pratkanis, Breckler, & Greenwald, 1989; M. B. Smith, Bruner, & White, 1956), including heterosexuals' attitudes (positive and negative) toward sexual minorities and homosexuality (Herek, 1986a, 1987a). It has also been used to understand the motivations underlying behavioral enactments of sexual stigma (Franklin, 2000; Herek, 1992). The functional approach posits that attitudes are formed and maintained because they serve a psychological need for the individual, and that the function served by an attitude differs among individuals and, within any individual, can vary across situations and attitude objects. Thus, according to the functional approach, heterosexuals' attitudes toward lesbians and gay men are shaped by a combination of personal needs, situational factors, and perceptions of the cultural meanings attached to sexual minorities and to homosexuality.

Although no definitive list of attitude functions has been compiled, four functions have received the most attention in regard to heterosexuals' attitudes toward sexual minorities and homosexuality. First, such attitudes can mediate one's interpersonal relations and strengthen bonds with valued groups (commonly labeled a *social adjustment* or *social expressive* function). Examples of this function (discussed earlier) include expressions of sexual prejudice by heterosexual men as a means of gaining (or avoiding the loss of) acceptance by heterosexual peers (e.g., Herek, 1986b; Kimmel, 1997) and expressions of prejudice by extrinsically religious individuals as a way of cementing their social relationships with fellow religionists (Griffiths et al., 2001; Herek, 1987b). This function is also evident in attitudes that derive from ongoing concerns about self-presentation and acceptance by others (Herek, 1987a).

Second, heterosexuals' attitudes can provide a vehicle for expressing values important to their self-concept. The operation of this *value-expressive* function is evident in expressions of attitudes that derive from an intrinsic religious orientation or from fundamentalist religious beliefs (Griffiths et al., 2001; Herek, 1987a, 1987b). Such attitudes provide the heterosexual individual with a means for affirming her or his self-concept as a religious and moral person. In addition, as noted earlier, many attitudes toward policies affecting sexual minorities appear to fit this function in that they are based mainly on political or religious values such as egalitarianism or moral traditionalism (e.g., P. R. Brewer, 2003; Herek, 2008; Price et al., 2005).

Third, heterosexuals' attitudes can be a strategy for warding off or coping with perceived threats to self-esteem (a *defensive* function). Such threats can derive from a variety of sources, including anxieties about one's ability to meet cultural or personal standards associated with one's gender role (Glick, Gangl, Gibb, Klumpner, & Weinberg, 2007; Herek, 1986b, 1987a; Lippa & Arad, 1999), concerns about one's own heterosexuality (Adams, Wright, & Lohr, 1996),[7] a felt need to distinguish oneself from a disliked outgroup (Haslam & Levy, 2006), and poor performance on tasks unrelated to sexuality or gender (Fein & Spencer, 1997; Mikulincer & Shaver, 2001). A defensive function can also be associated with stable personality characteristics, such as general externalizing or self-enhancing tendencies (Herek, 1987a; Meier et al., 2006).

Finally, heterosexuals' attitudes can assist them in making sense of their past experiences with sexual minority individuals (an *object-appraisal* or *schematic* function). This function is especially likely to be associated with attitudes that are based on one's personal relationships with sexual minority individuals (e.g., Herek, 1987a; Herek & Capitanio, 1996; Pettigrew & Tropp, 2006).

In theory, an attitude's function is independent of its valence. However, the social construction of stigma and the groups it targets are likely to affect how attitude functions are actually manifested (Herek, 2000b). In the case of heterosexuals' attitudes toward sexual minorities, it appears that defensive attitudes are generally negative, whereas attitudes based on personal relationships with sexual minority individuals (*object appraisal* or *schematic* attitudes) tend to be positive. Within the category of value-expressive attitudes, those that derive from religious beliefs tend to be associated with sexual prejudice, whereas those that are based on political values related to egalitarianism tend to be associated with positive attitudes toward sexual minorities.

CONCLUSION

As noted throughout this chapter, the foundations of sexual stigma in the United States have come to be increasingly contested, a development that can be traced to a variety of societal changes during the latter half of the 20th century. These include a more highly educated populace, growing sensitivities to minority groups of all kinds as a result of the civil rights movements of the 1950s and 1960s, changes in popular views of gender and sexuality as a consequence of the feminist movement and advances in contraceptive technologies, and greater endorsement of the belief that sexual privacy is a basic right. Against this backdrop, a political movement emerged that ultimately established gay men, lesbians, and bisexuals as a quasi-ethnic minority group capable of challenging society's hostility. Responding to these changes, the mental health profession reversed its long-standing position that homosexuality constituted a psychopathology, and pledged itself to helping to eradicate the stigma associated with sexual minority status. Sexual minority rights came to be seen as a legitimate political issue, and gay, lesbian, and bisexual people increasingly came out to their heterosexual friends and family. These historical events have many important implications for

---

[7] Adams et al. (1996) found that high-prejudice males evidenced greater penile tumescence than low-prejudice males while viewing a videotape of explicit male–male sexual activity. Although the researchers proposed that this response pattern indicated repressed homosexual desires among the high-prejudice men, it may also have been a product of anxiety (e.g., Barlow, Sakheim, & Beck, 1983) due to other factors, such as concerns about the experimenters' judgments about the participant's sexuality. In this conceptual framework, such concerns are understood as a manifestation of felt stigma.

understanding the current status of sexual prejudice in the United States, two of which are noted here (see Herek, 2008, for a more extensive discussion).

First, social norms concerning homosexuality and sexual minorities have changed. Many heterosexuals now perceive sexual prejudice to be incompatible with their personal value systems, and thus are subject to feelings of discomfort and guilt when they detect prejudice in their own thoughts or actions (Devine, Monteith, Zuwerink, & Elliot, 1991). Yet, because well-learned aspects of stigma are manifested as immediate, reflexive responses to the stigmatized group (e.g., Pryor, Reeder, Yeadon, & Hesson-McInnis, 2004), overcoming the entrenched habits of prejudiced thinking is often a difficult task (e.g., Devine, 1989, 2005; Monteith, Sherman, & Devine, 1998). Individuals can learn how to be unprejudiced, however, provided they have sufficient motivation to do so (Dunton & Fazio, 1997; Plant & Devine, 1998; Ratcliff, Lassiter, Markman, & Snyder, 2006).

Whereas shifts in social norms might lead a heterosexual person to feel compunction about sexual prejudice, they may not be enough to motivate that individual to engage in the long-term cognitive work necessary to change her or his fundamental patterns of thinking about sexual minorities. What might push heterosexuals to exert the effort required to disavow their sexual prejudice?

This question highlights a second important consequence of recent historical developments. Heterosexuals' opportunities for having a close personal relationship with an openly lesbian, gay, or bisexual friend or family member have expanded significantly in the past few decades. As noted earlier, having such relationships is negatively correlated with sexual prejudice. It seems likely that the emotional bonds associated with them can motivate heterosexuals to reexamine their preexisting prejudices and change their ways of thinking about sexual minorities, much as sexual minority individuals are themselves motivated to challenge their own internalized sexual stigma when they first acknowledge or recognize their sexual orientation.

This discussion illustrates the complex interrelationships that exist between sexual stigma and prejudice. It also highlights the importance of considering sexual prejudice not only in terms of its commonalities with other forms of prejudice, but also with an appreciation for its distinctive social history and its roots in societal institutions. The framework described in this chapter facilitates such an approach by conceptualizing sexual prejudice and stigma from a cultural as well as a psychological perspective. By attending to both perspectives, social scientists will enhance our prospects for gaining new theoretical insights into the nature of sexual prejudice and generating effective strategies for eliminating it.

ACKNOWLEDGMENTS

I express my sincere thanks to Aaron Norton and Thomas Allen for their helpful comments on an earlier version of this chapter.

REFERENCES

Adam, B. D. (1978). *The survival of domination: Inferiorization and everyday life.* New York: Elsevier.

Adams, H. E., Wright, L. W., Jr., & Lohr, B. A. (1996). Is homophobia associated with homosexual arousal? *Journal of Abnormal Psychology, 105,* 440–445.

Ajzen, I., & Fishbein, M. (2005). The influence of attitudes on behavior. In D. Albarracin, B. T. Johnson, & M. P. Zanna (Eds.), *The handbook of attitudes* (pp. 173–221). Mahwah, NJ: Erlbaum.

Albarracin, D., Zanna, M. P., Johnson, B. T., & Kumkale, G. T. (2005). Attitudes: Introduction and scope. In D. Albarracin, B. T. Johnson, & M. P. Zanna (Eds.), *The handbook of attitudes* (pp. 3–19). Mahwah, NJ: Erlbaum.

Allport, G. W. (1954). *The nature of prejudice.* Garden City, NY: Doubleday.

Allport, G. W. (1966). The religious context of prejudice. *Journal for the Scientific Study of Religion, 5,* 447–457.

Allport, G. W., & Ross, J. M. (1967). Personal religious orientation and prejudice. *Journal of Personality and Social Psychology, 5,* 432–443.

Badgett, M. V. L., Lau, H., Sears, B., & Ho, D. (2007). *Bias in the workplace: Consistent evidence of sexual orientation and gender identity discrimination.* Retrieved June 26, 2007, from http://www.law.ucla.edu/williamsinstitute/publications/Policy-Discrimination-index.html

Banse, R., Seise, J., & Zerbes, N. (2001). Implicit attitudes towards homosexuality: Reliability, validity, and controllability of the IAT. *Zeitschrift Fuer Experimentelle Psychologie, 48*(2), 145–160.

Barlow, D. H., Sakheim, D. K., & Beck, J. G. (1983). Anxiety increases sexual arousal. *Journal of Abnormal Psychology, 92,* 49–54.

Batson, C. D., Eidelman, S. H., Higley, S. L., & Russel, S. A. (2001). "And who is my neighbor?" II: Quest religion as a source of universal compassion. *Journal for the Scientific Study of Religion, 40,* 39–50.

Batson, C. D., Floyd, R. B., Meyer, J. M., & Winner, A. L. (1999). "And who is my neighbor?:" Intrinsic religion as a source of universal compassion. *Journal for the Scientific Study of Religion, 38,* 445–457.

Batson, C. D., Naifeh, S. J., & Pate, S. (1978). Social desirability, religious orientation, and racial prejudice. *Journal for the Scientific Study of Religion, 15,* 29–45.

Batson, C. D., Schoenrade, P., & Ventis, W. L. (1993). *Religion and the individual: A social-psychological perspective.* New York: Oxford University Press.

Batson, C. D., & Stocks, E. L. (2005). Religion and prejudice. In J. Dovidio, P. Glick, & L. Rudman (Eds.), *On the nature of prejudice: Fifty years after Allport* (pp. 413–427). Malden, MA: Blackwell.

Bech, H. (1998). A dung beetle in distress: Hans Christian Andersen meets Karl Maria Kertbeny, Geneva, 1860: Some notes on the archaeology of homosexuality and the importance of tuning. *Journal of Homosexuality, 35*(3–4), 139–161.

Bernat, J. A., Calhoun, K. S., Adams, H. E., & Zeichner, A. (2001). Homophobia and physical aggression toward homosexual and heterosexual individuals. *Journal of Abnormal Psychology, 110,* 179–187.

Berrill, K. T. (1992). Antigay violence and victimization in the United States: An overview. In G. M. Herek & K. T. Berrill (Eds.), *Hate crimes: Confronting violence against lesbians and gay men* (pp. 19–45). Thousand Oaks, CA: Sage.

Bosson, J. K., Haymovitz, E. L., & Pinel, E. C. (2004). When saying and doing diverge: The effects of stereotype threat on self-reported versus non-verbal anxiety. *Journal of Experimental Social Psychology, 40,* 247–255.

Bosson, J. K., Prewitt-Freilino, J. L., & Taylor, J. N. (2005). Role rigidity: A problem of identity misclassification? *Journal of Personality and Social Psychology, 89,* 552–565.

Bosson, J. K., Taylor, J. N., & Prewitt-Freilino, J. L. (2006). Gender role violations and identity misclassification: The roles of audience and actor variables. *Sex Roles, 55,* 13–24.

Brewer, M. B., & Miller, N. (1984). Beyond the contact hypothesis: Theoretical perspectives on desegregation. In N. Miller & M. B. Brewer (Eds.), *Groups in contact: The psychology of desegregation* (pp. 281–302). Orlando, FL: Academic.

Brewer, P. R. (2003). Values, political knowledge, and public opinion about gay rights: A framing-based account. *Public Opinion Quarterly, 67,* 173–201.

Brewer, P. R., & Wilcox, C. (2005). Trends: Same-sex marriage and civil unions. *Public Opinion Quarterly, 69,* 599–616.

Brown, R., & Hewstone, M. (2005). An integrative theory of intergroup contact. In M. P. Zanna (Ed.), *Advances in experimental social psychology* (Vol. 37, pp. 255–343). San Diego, CA: Elsevier Academic.

Burris, C. T., & Jackson, L. M. (1999). Hate the sin/love the sinner, or love the hater? Intrinsic religion and responses to partner abuse. *Journal for the Scientific Study of Religion, 38,* 160–174.

Capitanio, J. P., & Herek, G. M. (1999). AIDS-related stigma and attitudes toward injecting drug users among black and white Americans. *American Behavioral Scientist, 42,* 1148–1161.

Chauncey, G., Jr. (1982–1983). From sexual inversion to homosexuality: Medicine and the changing conceptualization of female deviance. *Salmagundi, 58–59,* 114–146.

Chauncey, G., Jr. (1993). The postwar sex crime panic. In W. Graebner (Ed.), *True stories from the American past* (pp. 160–178). New York: McGraw-Hill.

Clausell, E., & Fiske, S. T. (2005). When do subgroup parts add up to the stereotypic whole? Mixed stereotype content for gay male subgroups explains overall ratings. *Social Cognition, 23,* 161–181.

Cole, S. W. (2006). Social threat, personal identity, and physical health in closeted gay men. In A. M. Omoto & H. S. Kurtzman (Eds.), *Sexual orientation and mental health: Examining identity and development in lesbian, gay, and bisexual people* (pp. 245–267). Washington, DC: American Psychological Association.

Conger, J. J. (1975). Proceedings of the American Psychological Association, Incorporated, for the year 1974: Minutes of the annual meeting of the Council of Representatives. *American Psychologist, 30,* 620–651.

Corrigan, P. W., & Watson, A. C. (2002). The paradox of self-stigma and mental illness. *Clinical Psychology: Science and Practice, 9,* 35–53.

Corrigan, P. W., Watson, A. C., Heyrman, M. L., Warpinski, A., Gracia, G., Slopen, N., et al. (2005). Structural stigma in state legislation. *Psychiatric Services, 56,* 557–563.

Cottrell, C. A., & Neuberg, S. L. (2005). Different emotional reactions to different groups: A sociofunctional threat-based approach to "prejudice." *Journal of Personality and Social Psychology, 88,* 770–789.

Crocker, J., Major, B., & Steele, C. (1998). Social stigma. In D. T. Gilbert, S. T. Fiske, & G. Lindzey (Eds.), *The handbook of social psychology* (Vol. 2, 4th ed., pp. 504–553). Boston: McGraw-Hill.

Dasgupta, N., & Rivera, L. M. (2006). From automatic antigay prejudice to behavior: The moderating role of conscious beliefs about gender and behavioral control. *Journal of Personality and Social Psychology, 91,* 268–280.

D'Augelli, A. R., Grossman, A. H., & Starks, M. T. (2006). Childhood gender atypicality, victimization, and PTSD among lesbian, gay, and bisexual youth. *Journal of Interpersonal Violence, 21,* 1462–1482.

Devine, P. G. (1989). Stereotypes and prejudice: Their automatic and controlled components. *Journal of Personality and Social Psychology, 56,* 5–18.

Devine, P. G. (2005). Breaking the prejudice habit: Allport's "inner conflict" revisited. In J. Dovidio, P. Glick, & L. Rudman (Eds.), *On the nature of prejudice: Fifty years after Allport* (pp. 327–342). Malden, MA: Blackwell.

Devine, P. G., Monteith, M. J., Zuwerink, J. R., & Elliot, A. J. (1991). Prejudice with and without compunction. *Journal of Personality and Social Psychology, 60,* 817–830.

Duck, R. J., & Hunsberger, B. (1999). Religious orientation and prejudice: The role of religious proscription, right-wing authoritarianism and social desirability. *International Journal for the Psychology of Religion, 9,* 157–179.

Duckitt, J. H. (1992). *The social psychology of prejudice.* New York: Praeger.

Dunton, B. C., & Fazio, R. H. (1997). An individual difference measure of motivation to control prejudiced reactions. *Personality and Social Psychology Bulletin, 23,* 316–326.

Eagly, A. H., & Chaiken, S. (1993). *The psychology of attitudes.* Fort Worth, TX: Harcourt Brace Jovanovich.

Ellison, C. G., & Musick, M. A. (1993). Southern intolerance: A fundamentalist effect? *Social Forces, 72,* 379–398.

Esses, V. M., Haddock, G., & Zanna, M. P. (1993). Values, stereotypes, and emotions as determinants of inter-group attitudes. In D. M. Mackie & D. L. Hamilton (Eds.), *Affect, cognition and stereotyping: Interactive processes in intergroup perception communication* (pp. 137–166). San Diego, CA: Academic.

Fabrigar, L. R., MacDonald, T. K., & Wegener, D. T. (2005). The structure of attitudes. In D. Albarracin, B. T. Johnson, & M. P. Zanna (Eds.), *The handbook of attitudes* (pp. 79–125). Mahwah, NJ: Erlbaum.

Family Research Institute. (2006). *Getting the facts: Same-sex marriage.* Retrieved May 7, 2007, from http://familyresearchinst.org/

Fein, S., & Spencer, S. J. (1997). Prejudice as self-image maintenance: Affirming the self through derogating others. *Journal of Personality and Social Psychology, 73,* 31–44.

Feray, J.-C., & Herzer, M. (1990). Homosexual studies and politics in the 19th-century: Karl Maria Kertbeny. *Journal of Homosexuality, 19*(1), 23–47.

Fisher, R. D., Derison, D., Polley, C. F., & Cadman, J. (1994). Religiousness, religious orientation, and attitudes towards gays and lesbians. *Journal of Applied Social Psychology, 24,* 614–630.

Fiske, S. T., Lin, M., & Neuberg, S. L. (1999). The continuum model: Ten years later. In S. Chaiken & Y. Trope (Eds.), *Dual-process theories in social psychology* (pp. 231–254). New York: Guilford.

Fiske, S. T., & Taylor, S. E. (2007). *Social cognition: From brains to culture.* New York: McGraw-Hill.

Frable, D. E. S., Wortman, C., & Joseph, J. (1997). Predicting self-esteem, well-being, and distress in a cohort of gay men: The importance of cultural stigma, personal visibility, community networks, and positive identity. *Journal of Personality, 65,* 599–624.

Franklin, K. (1998). Unassuming motivations: Contextualizing the narratives of antigay assailants. In G. M. Herek (Ed.), *Stigma and sexual orientation: Understanding prejudice against lesbians, gay men, and bisexuals* (pp. 1–23). Thousand Oaks, CA: Sage.

Franklin, K. (2000). Antigay behaviors among young adults: Prevalence, patterns and motivators in a noncriminal population. *Journal of Interpersonal Violence, 15,* 339–362.

Freedman, E. (1989). "Uncontrolled desires": The response to the sexual psychopath, 1920-1960. In K. Peiss & C. Simmons (Eds.), Passion and power: Sexuality in history (pp. 195-225). Philadelphia: Temple University Press.

Fulton, A. S., Gorsuch, R. L., & Maynard, E. A. (1999). Religious orientation, antihomosexual sentiment, and fundamentalism among Christians. *Journal for the Scientific Study of Religion, 38,* 14–22.

Gaertner, S. L., & Dovidio, J. F. (2005a). Categorization, recategorization, and intergroup bias. In J. Dovidio, P. Glick, & L. Rudman (Eds.), *On the nature of prejudice: Fifty years after Allport* (pp. 71–88). Malden, MA: Blackwell.

Gaertner, S. L., & Dovidio, J. F. (2005b). Understanding and addressing contemporary racism: From aversive racism to the Common Ingroup Identity model. *Journal of Social Issues, 61,* 615–639.

Gebhard, P. H., & Johnson, A. B. (1979). *The Kinsey data: Marginal tabulations of the 1938–1963 interviews conducted by the Institute for Sex Research.* Bloomington: Indiana University Press.

Gilman, S. L. (1985). *Difference and pathology: Stereotypes of sexuality, race, and madness.* Ithaca, NY: Cornell University Press.

Glick, P., Gangl, C., Gibb, S., Klumpner, S., & Weinberg, E. (2007). Defensive reactions to masculinity threat: More negative affect toward effeminate (but not masculine) gay men. *Sex Roles, 57,* 55–59.

Goffman, E. (1963). *Stigma: Notes on the management of spoiled identity.* Englewood Cliffs, NJ: Prentice-Hall.

Griffiths, B., Dixon, C., Stanley, G., & Weiland, R. (2001). Religious orientation and attitudes towards homosexuality: A functional analysis. *Australian Journal of Psychology, 53*(1), 12–17.

Gross, A. E., Green, S. K., Storck, J. T., & Vanyur, J. M. (1980). Disclosure of sexual orientation and impressions of male and female homosexuals. *Personality and Social Psychology Bulletin, 6,* 307–314.

Gurwitz, S. B., & Marcus, M. (1978). Effects of anticipated interaction, sex, and homosexual stereotypes on first impressions. *Journal of Applied Social Psychology, 8,* 47–56.

Haddock, G., & Zanna, M. P. (1998). Authoritarianism, values, and the favorability and structure of antigay attitudes. In G. M. Herek (Ed.), *Stigma and sexual orientation: Understanding prejudice against lesbians, gay men, and bisexuals* (pp. 82–107). Thousand Oaks, CA: Sage.

Haddock, G., Zanna, M. P., & Esses, V. M. (1993). Assessing the structure of prejudicial attitudes: The case of attitudes toward homosexuals. *Journal of Personality and Social Psychology, 65,* 1105–1118.

Haeberle, S. H. (1999). Gay and lesbian rights: Emerging trends in public opinion and voting behavior. In E. D. B. Riggle & B. L. Tadlock (Eds.), *Gays and lesbians in the democratic process: Public policy, public opinion, and political representation* (pp. 146–169). New York: Columbia University Press.

Harlow, C. W. (2005). *Hate crime reported by victims and police.* Washington, DC: U.S. Department of Justice. Retrieved July 4, 2006, from http://www.ojp.usdoj.gov/bjs/pub/pdf/ hcrvp.pdf

Harris, L. (1965, September 27). Public registers strong disapproval of nonconformity. *Washington Post,* p. A2.

Haslam, N., & Levy, S. R. (2006). Essentialist beliefs about homosexuality: Structure and implications for prejudice. *Personality and Social Psychology Bulletin, 32,* 471–485.

Haslam, N., Rothschild, L., & Ernst, D. (2002). Are essentialist beliefs associated with prejudice? *British Journal of Social Psychology, 41,* 87–100.

Hegarty, P. (2002). "It's not a choice, it's the way we're built": Symbolic beliefs about sexual orientation in the US and Britain. *Journal of Community and Applied Social Psychology, 12,* 153–166.

Hegarty, P., & Golden, A. M. (2008). Attributional beliefs about the controllability of stigmatized traits: Antecedents or justifications of prejudice? *Journal of Applied Social Psychology, 38,* 1023-1044.

Hegarty, P., & Pratto, F. (2001). Sexual orientation beliefs: Their relationship to anti-gay attitudes and biological determinist arguments. *Journal of Homosexuality, 41*(1), 121–135.

Hegarty, P., & Pratto, F. (2004). The differences that norms make: Empiricism, social constructionism, and the interpretation of group differences. *Sex Roles, 50,* 445–453.

Herek, G. M. (1984). Beyond "homophobia": A social psychological perspective on attitudes toward lesbians and gay men. *Journal of Homosexuality, 10*(1–2), 1–21.

Herek, G. M. (1986a). The instrumentality of attitudes: Toward a neofunctional theory. *Journal of Social Issues, 42*(2), 99–114.

Herek, G. M. (1986b). On heterosexual masculinity: Some psychical consequences of the social construction of gender and sexuality. *American Behavioral Scientist, 29,* 563–577.

Herek, G. M. (1987a). Can functions be measured? A new perspective on the functional approach to attitudes. *Social Psychology Quarterly, 50,* 285–303.

Herek, G. M. (1987b). Religious orientation and prejudice: A comparison of racial and sexual attitudes. *Personality and Social Psychology Bulletin, 13,* 34–44.

Herek, G. M. (1988). Heterosexuals' attitudes toward lesbians and gay men: Correlates and gender differences. *Journal of Sex Research, 25,* 451–477.

Herek, G. M. (1991). Stigma, prejudice, and violence against lesbians and gay men. In J. C. Gonsiorek & J. D. Weinrich (Eds.), *Homosexuality: Research implications for public policy* (pp. 60–80). Newbury Park, CA: Sage.

Herek, G. M. (1992). Psychological heterosexism and anti-gay violence: The social psychology of bigotry and bashing. In G. M. Herek & K. T. Berrill (Eds.), *Hate crimes: Confronting violence against lesbians and gay men* (pp. 149–169). Thousand Oaks, CA: Sage.

Herek, G. M. (1993). Sexual orientation and military service: A social science perspective. *American Psychologist, 48,* 538–549.

Herek, G. M. (1994). Assessing heterosexuals' attitudes toward lesbians and gay men: A review of empirical research with the ATLG scale. In B. Greene & G. M. Herek (Eds.), *Lesbian and gay psychology: Theory, research, and clinical applications* (pp. 206–228). Thousand Oaks, CA: Sage.

Herek, G. M. (1996). Why tell if you're not asked? Self-disclosure, intergroup contact, and heterosexuals' attitudes toward lesbians and gay men. In G. M. Herek, J. Jobe, & R. Carney (Eds.), *Out in force: Sexual orientation and the military* (pp. 197–225). Chicago: University of Chicago Press.

Herek, G. M. (1997). The HIV epidemic and public attitudes toward lesbians and gay men. In M. P. Levine, P. Nardi, & J. Gagnon (Eds.), *In changing times: Gay men and lesbians encounter HIV/AIDS* (pp. 191–218). Chicago: University of Chicago Press.

Herek, G. M. (2000a). Sexual prejudice and gender: Do heterosexuals' attitudes toward lesbians and gay men differ? *Journal of Social Issues, 56,* 251–266.

Herek, G. M. (2000b). The social construction of attitudes: Functional consensus and divergence in the US public's reactions to AIDS. In G. R. Maio & J. M. Olson (Eds.), *Why we evaluate: Functions of attitudes* (pp. 325–364). Mahwah, NJ: Erlbaum.

Herek, G. M. (2002a). Gender gaps in public opinion about lesbians and gay men. *Public Opinion Quarterly, 66,* 40–66.

Herek, G. M. (2002b). Heterosexuals' attitudes toward bisexual men and women in the United States. *Journal of Sex Research, 39,* 264–274.

Herek, G. M. (2004). Beyond "homophobia": Thinking about sexual stigma and prejudice in the twenty-first century. *Sexuality Research and Social Policy, 1*(2), 6–24.

Herek, G. M. (2006). Legal recognition of same-sex relationships in the United States: A social science perspective. *American Psychologist, 61,* 607–621.

Herek, G. M. (2007). Confronting sexual stigma and prejudice: Theory and practice. *Journal of Social Issues, 63,* 905–925.

Herek, G. M. (2008). Understanding sexual stigma and sexual prejudice in the United States: A conceptual framework. In D. Hope (Ed.), *Contemporary perspectives on lesbian, gay & bisexual identities*: The 54th Nebraska Symposium on Motivation. New York: Springer.

Herek, G. M. (in press). Hate crimes and stigma-related experiences among sexual minority adults in the United States: Prevalence estimates from a national probability sample. *Journal of Interpersonal Violence.*

Herek, G. M., & Capitanio, J. P. (1995). Black heterosexuals' attitudes toward lesbians and gay men in the United States. *Journal of Sex Research, 32,* 95–105.

Herek, G. M., & Capitanio, J. P. (1996). "Some of my best friends": Intergroup contact, concealable stigma, and heterosexuals' attitudes toward gay men and lesbians. *Personality and Social Psychology Bulletin, 22,* 412–424.

Herek, G. M., & Capitanio, J. P. (1999a). AIDS stigma and sexual prejudice. *American Behavioral Scientist, 42,* 1130–1147.

Herek, G. M., & Capitanio, J. P. (1999b). Sex differences in how heterosexuals think about lesbians and gay men: Evidence from survey context effects. *Journal of Sex Research, 36,* 348–360.

Herek, G. M., Chopp, R., & Strohl, D. (2007). Sexual stigma: Putting sexual minority health issues in context. In I. Meyer & M. Northridge (Eds.), *The health of sexual minorities: Public health perspectives on lesbian, gay, bisexual, and transgender populations* (pp. 171–208). New York: Springer.

Herek, G. M., Cogan, J. C., & Gillis, J. R. (2002). Victim experiences in hate crimes based on sexual orientation. *Journal of Social Issues, 58,* 319–339.

Herek, G. M., Cogan, J. C., Gillis, J. R., & Glunt, E. K. (1998). Correlates of internalized homophobia in a community sample of lesbians and gay men. *Journal of the Gay and Lesbian Medical Association, 2,* 17–25.

Herek, G. M., & Garnets, L. D. (2007). Sexual orientation and mental health. *Annual Review of Clinical Psychology, 3,* 353–375.

Herek, G. M., Gillis, J. R., & Cogan, J. C. (1999). Psychological sequelae of hate-crime victimization among lesbian, gay, and bisexual adults. *Journal of Consulting and Clinical Psychology, 67,* 945–951.

Herek, G. M., & Glunt, E. K. (1991). AIDS-related attitudes in the United States: A preliminary conceptualization. *Journal of Sex Research, 28,* 99–123.

Herek, G. M., & Glunt, E. K. (1993). Interpersonal contact and heterosexuals' attitudes toward gay men: Results from a national survey. *Journal of Sex Research, 30,* 239–244.

Herek, G. M., & Gonzalez-Rivera, M. (2006). Attitudes toward homosexuality among U.S. residents of Mexican descent. *Journal of Sex Research, 43,* 122–135.

Herek, G. M., & Sims, C. (2008). Sexual orientation and violent victimization: Hate crimes and intimate partner violence among gay and bisexual males in the United States. In R. J. Wolitski, R. Stall, & R. O. Valdiserri (Eds.), *Unequal opportunity: Health disparities among gay and bisexual men in the United States* (pp. 35–71). New York: Oxford University Press.

Herman, D. (1997). *The antigay agenda: Orthodox vision and the Christian Right.* Chicago: University of Chicago Press.

Herzer, M. (1985). Kertbeny and the nameless love. *Journal of Homosexuality, 12*(1), 1–26.

Hunsberger, B. (1996). Religious fundamentalism, right-wing authoritarianism, and hostility toward homosexuals in non-Christian religious groups. *International Journal for the Psychology of Religion, 6,* 39–49.

Hunsberger, B., Owusu, V., & Duck, R. (1999). Religion and prejudice in Ghana and Canada: Religious fundamentalism, right-wing authoritarianism and attitudes toward homosexuals and women. *International Journal for the Psychology of Religion, 9,* 181–194.

Jackman, M. R. (1977). Prejudice, tolerance, and attitudes toward ethnic groups. *Social Science Research, 6,* 145–169.

Jackson, L. M., & Esses, V. M. (1997). Of scripture and ascription: The relation between religious fundamentalism and intergroup helping. *Personality and Social Psychology Bulletin, 23,* 893–906.

Jayaratne, T. E., Ybarra, O., Sheldon, J. P., Brown, T. N., Feldbaum, M., Pfeffer, C. A., & Petty, E. M. (2006). White Americans' genetic lay theories of race differences and sexual orientation: Their relationship with prejudice toward blacks, and gay men and lesbians. *Group Processes and Intergroup Relations, 9,* 77-94.

Jellison, W. A., McConnell, A. R., & Gabriel, S. (2004). Implicit and explicit measures of sexual orientation attitudes: Ingroup preferences and related behaviors and beliefs among gay and straight men. *Personality and Social Psychology Bulletin, 30,* 629–642.

Jones, E. E., Farina, A., Hastorf, A. H., Markus, H., Miller, D. T., & Scott, R. A. (1984). *Social stigma: The psychology of marked relationships.* New York: Freeman.

Kaiser Family Foundation. (2006). *2006 Kaiser Family Foundation survey of Americans on HIV/AIDS.* Retrieved September 22, 2006, from http://www.kff.org/kaiserpolls/upload/7513.pdf

Katz, D. (1960). The functional approach to the study of attitudes. *Public Opinion Quarterly, 24,* 163–204.

Katz, I. (1981). *Stigma: A social psychological analysis.* Hillsdale, NJ: Erlbaum.

Katz, J. N. (1995). *The invention of heterosexuality.* New York: Dutton.

Kelman, H. C. (1961). Processes of opinion change. *Public Opinion Quarterly, 25,* 57–78.

Kelman, H. C. (2001). Reflections on social and psychological processes of legitimization and delegitimization. In J. T. Jost & B. Major (Eds.), *The psychology of legitimacy: Emerging perspectives on ideology, justice, and intergroup relations* (pp. 54–73). New York: Cambridge University Press.

Kilianski, S. E. (2003). Explaining heterosexual men's attitudes toward women and gay men: The theory of exclusively masculine identity. *Psychology of Men and Masculinity, 4,* 37–56.

Kimmel, M. S. (1997). Masculinity as homophobia: Fear, shame and silence in the construction of gender identity. In M. M. Gergen & S. N. Davis (Eds.), *Toward a new psychology of gender* (pp. 223–242). New York: Routledge.

Kirkpatrick, L. A. (1993). Fundamentalism, Christian orthodoxy, and intrinsic religious orientation as predictors of discriminatory attitudes. *Journal for the Scientific Study of Religion, 32,* 256–268.

Kite, M. E. (1994). When perceptions meet reality: Individual differences in reactions to lesbians and gay men. In B. Greene & G. M. Herek (Eds.), *Lesbian and gay psychology: Theory, research, and clinical applications* (pp. 25–53). Thousand Oaks, CA: Sage.

Kite, M. E., & Whitley, B. E., Jr. (1996). Sex differences in attitudes toward homosexual persons, behaviors, and civil rights: A meta-analysis. *Personality and Social Psychology Bulletin, 22,* 336–353.

Kite, M. E., & Whitley, B. E., Jr. (1998). Do heterosexual women and men differ in their attitudes toward homosexuality? A conceptual and methodological analysis. In G. M. Herek (Ed.), *Stigma and sexual orientation: Understanding prejudice against lesbians, gay men, and bisexuals* (pp. 39–61). Thousand Oaks, CA: Sage.

Kristiansen, C. M. (1990). The symbolic value-expressive function of outgroup attitudes among homosexuals. *Journal of Social Psychology, 130*(1), 61–69.

Kurzban, R., & Leary, M. R. (2001). Evolutionary origins of stigmatization: The functions of social exclusion. *Psychological Bulletin, 127,* 187–208.

Lewis, G. B. (2003). Black–white differences in attitudes toward homosexuality and gay rights. *Public Opinion Quarterly, 67,* 59–78.

Lewis, G. B. (2006, September 2). *Personal relationships and support for gay rights.* Paper presented at the meeting of the American Political Science Association, Philadelphia.

Lewis, G. B. (2007, August). *The friends and family plan: Knowing LGBs and supporting gay rights.* Paper presented at the annual meeting of the American Psychological Association, San Francisco.

Lewis, G. B., & Rogers, M. A. (1999). Does the public support equal employment rights for gays and lesbians? In E. D. B. Riggle & B. L. Tadlock (Eds.), *Gays and lesbians in the democratic process: Public policy, public opinion, and political representation* (pp. 118–145). New York: Columbia University Press.

Lewis, R. J., Derlega, V. J., Clarke, E. G., & Kuang, J. C. (2006). Stigma consciousness, social constraints, and lesbian well-being. *Journal of Counseling Psychology, 53,* 48–56.

Lewis, R. J., Derlega, V. J., Griffin, J. L., & Krowinski, A. C. (2003). Stressors for gay men and lesbians: Life stress, gay-related stress, stigma consciousness, and depressive symptoms. *Journal of Social and Clinical Psychology, 22,* 716–729.

Link, B. G., & Phelan, J. C. (2001). Conceptualizing stigma. *Annual Review of Sociology, 27,* 363–385.

Lippa, R. A., & Arad, S. (1999). Gender, personality, and prejudice: The display of authoritarianism and social dominance in interviews with college men and women. *Journal of Research in Personality, 33,* 463–493.

Loftus, J. (2001). America's liberalization in attitudes toward homosexuality. *American Sociological Review, 66,* 762–782.

Mahaffey, A. L., Bryan, A., & Hutchison, K. E. (2005a). Sex differences in affective responses to homoerotic stimuli: Evidence for an unconscious bias among heterosexual men, but not heterosexual women. *Archives of Sexual Behavior, 34,* 537–545.

Mahaffey, A. L., Bryan, A., & Hutchison, K. E. (2005b). Using startle eye blink to measure the affective component of antigay bias. *Basic and Applied Social Psychology, 27,* 37–45.

Maio, G. R., & Olson, J. M. (Eds.). (2000). *Why we evaluate: Functions of attitudes.* Mahwah, NJ: Erlbaum.

Mayfield, W. (2001). The development of an internalized homonegativity inventory for gay men. *Journal of Homosexuality, 41*(2), 53–76.

McConahay, J. B. (1986). Modern racism, ambivalence, and the Modern Racism Scale. In J. F. Dovidio & S. L. Gaertner (Eds.), *Prejudice, discrimination, and racism* (pp. 91–125). Orlando, FL: Academic.

McFarland, S. G. (1989). Religious orientations and the targets of discrimination. *Journal for the Scientific Study of Religion, 28,* 324–336.

McFarland, S. G. (1998). Communism as religion. *International Journal for the Psychology of Religion, 8,* 33–48.

McGann, K. J., & Goodwin, K. A. (2007). Gay men remembered: The biasing role of stereotypes in memory. *Current Research in Social Psychology, 12*(7), 91–119.

Meier, B. P., Robinson, M. D., Gaither, G. A., & Heinert, N. J. (2006). A secret attraction or defensive loathing? Homophobia, defense, and implicit cognition. *Journal of Research in Personality, 40,* 377–394.

Meyer, I. H. (2003). Prejudice, social stress, and mental health in lesbian, gay, and bisexual populations: Conceptual issues and research evidence. *Psychological Bulletin, 129,* 674–697.

Mikulincer, M., & Shaver, P. R. (2001). Attachment theory and intergroup bias: Evidence that priming the secure base schema attenuates negative reactions to out-groups. *Journal of Personality and Social Psychology, 81,* 97–115.

Mills, T. C., Paul, J., Stall, R., Pollack, L., Canchola, J., Chang, Y. J., et al. (2004). Distress and depression in men who have sex with men: The Urban Men's Health Study. *American Journal of Psychiatry, 161,* 278–285.

Mohr, J. J., & Rochlen, A. B. (1999). Measuring attitudes regarding bisexuality in lesbian, gay male, and heterosexual populations. *Journal of Counseling Psychology, 46,* 353–369.

Monteith, M. J., Sherman, J. W., & Devine, P. G. (1998). Suppression as a stereotype control strategy. *Personality and Social Psychology Review, 2,* 63–82.

Monteith, M. J., Spicer, C. V., & Tooman, G. D. (1998). Consequences of stereotype suppression: Stereotypes on AND not on the rebound. *Journal of Experimental Social Psychology, 34,* 355–377.

Morris, J. F., Waldo, C. R., & Rothblum, E. D. (2001). A model of predictors and outcomes of outness among lesbian and bisexual women. *American Journal of Orthopsychiatry, 71,* 61–71.

Morrison, M. A., & Morrison, T. G. (2002). Development and validation of a scale measuring modern prejudice toward gay men and lesbian women. *Journal of Homosexuality, 43*(2), 15–37.

Munro, G. D., & Ditto, P. H. (1997). Biased assimilation, attitude polarization, and affect in reactions to stereotyped-relevant scientific information. *Personality and Social Psychology Bulletin, 23,* 636–653.

Neuberg, S. L., Smith, D. M., Hoffman, J. C., & Russell, F. J. (1994). When we observe stigmatized and "normal" individuals interacting: Stigma by association. *Personality and Social Psychology Bulletin, 20,* 196–209.

Pachankis, J. E. (2007). The psychological implications of concealing a stigma: A cognitive-affective-behavioral model. *Psychological Bulletin, 133,* 328–345.

Parrott, D. J., Adams, H. E., & Zeichner, A. (2002). Homophobia: Personality and attitudinal correlates. *Personality and Individual Differences, 32,* 1269–1278.

Parrott, D. J., & Zeichner, A. (2005). Effects of sexual prejudice and anger on physical aggression toward gay and heterosexual men. *Psychology of Men and Masculinity, 6,* 3–17.

Parrott, D. J., Zeichner, A., & Hoover, R. (2006). Sexual prejudice and anger network activation: Mediating role of negative affect. *Aggressive Behavior, 32,* 7–16.

Patel, S., Long, T. E., McCammon, S. L., & Wuensch, K. L. (1995). Personality and emotional correlates of self-reported antigay behaviors. *Journal of Interpersonal Violence, 10,* 354–366.

Pettigrew, T. F. (1998). Intergroup contact theory. *Annual Review of Psychology, 49,* 65–85.

Pettigrew, T. F., & Tropp, L. R. (2006). A meta-analytic test of intergroup contact theory. *Journal of Personality and Social Psychology, 90,* 751–783.

Phoenix, A., Frosh, S., & Pattman, R. (2003). Producing contradictory masculine subject positions: Narratives of threat, homophobia and bullying in 11–14 year old boys. *Journal of Social Issues, 59,* 179–195.

Pinel, E. C. (1999). Stigma consciousness: The psychological legacy of social stereotypes. *Journal of Personality and Social Psychology, 76,* 114–128.

Plant, E. A., & Devine, P. G. (1998). Internal and external motivation to respond without prejudice. *Journal of Personality and Social Psychology, 75,* 811–832.

Poteat, V. P., Espelage, D. L., & Green, H. D., Jr. (2007). The socialization of dominance: Peer group contextual effects on homophobic and dominance attitudes. *Journal of Personality and Social Psychology, 92,* 1040–1050.

Pratkanis, A. R., Breckler, S. J., & Greenwald, A. G. (Eds.). (1989). *Attitude structure and function.* Hillsdale, NJ: Erlbaum.

Price, V., Nir, L., & Cappella, J. N. (2005). Framing public discussion of gay civil unions. *Public Opinion Quarterly, 69,* 179–212.

Pryor, J. B., Reeder, G. D., & Landau, S. (1999). A social-psychological analysis of HIV-related stigma: A two-factor theory. *American Behavioral Scientist, 42,* 1193–1211.

Pryor, J. B., Reeder, G. D., & McManus, J. (1991). Fear and loathing in the workplace: Reactions to AIDS-infected co-workers. *Personality and Social Psychology Bulletin, 17,* 133–139.

Pryor, J. B., Reeder, G. D., Vinacco, R., Jr., & Kott, T. L. (1989). The instrumental and symbolic functions of attitudes toward persons with AIDS. *Journal of Applied Social Psychology, 19,* 377–404.

Pryor, J. B., Reeder, G. D., Yeadon, C., & Hesson-McInnis, M. (2004). A dual-process model of reactions to perceived stigma. *Journal of Personality and Social Psychology, 87,* 436–452.

Ratcliff, J. J., Lassiter, G. D., Markman, K. D. , & Snyder, C. J. (2006). Gender differences in attitudes toward gay men and lesbians: The role of motivation to respond without prejudice. *Personality and Social Psychology Bulletin, 32,* 1325–1338.

Roderick, T., McCammon, S. L., Long, T. E., & Allred, L. J. (1998). Behavioral aspects of homonegativity. *Journal of Homosexuality, 36*(1), 79–88.

Rothbart, M., & John, O. P. (1985). Social categorization and behavioral episodes: A cognitive analysis of the effects of intergroup contact. *Journal of Social Issues, 41*(3), 81–104.

Rust, P. C. (1993). Neutralizing the political threat of the marginal woman: Lesbians' beliefs about bisexual women. *Journal of Sex Research, 30,* 214–228.

Ryan, R. M., & Connell, J. P. (1989). Perceived locus of causality and internalization: Examining reasons for acting in two domains. *Journal of Personality and Social Psychology, 57,* 749-761.

Saad, L. (2007). *Tolerance for gay rights at high ebb.* Gallup Poll News Service. Retrieved May 29, 2007, from http://www.gallup.com

San Miguel, C. L., & Millham, J. (1976). The role of cognitive and situational variables in aggression toward homosexuals. *Journal of Homosexuality, 2*(1), 11–27.

Scambler, G., & Hopkins, A. (1986). Being epileptic: Coming to terms with stigma. *Sociology of Health and Illness, 8,* 26–43.

Schneider, W., & Lewis, I. A. (1984, February–March). The straight story on homosexuality and gay rights. *Public Opinion,* 16–20, 59–60.

Scott, J. (1998). Changing attitudes to sexual morality: A cross-national comparison. *Sociology, 32,* 815–845.

Sherman, J. W., Stroessner, S. J., Conrey, F. R., & Azam, O. A. (2005). Prejudice and stereotype maintenance processes: Attention, attribution, and individuation. *Journal of Personality and Social Psychology, 89,* 607–622.

Sherrill, K., & Yang, A. (2000). From outlaws to in-laws: Anti-gay attitudes thaw. *The Public Perspective, 11*(1), 20–23.

Sherrod, D., & Nardi, P. M. (1998). Homophobia in the courtroom: An assessment of biases against gay men and lesbians in a multiethnic sample of potential jurors. In G.M. Herek (Ed.), *Stigma and sexual orientation: Understanding prejudice against lesbians, gay men, and bisexuals* (pp. 24–38). Thousand Oaks, CA: Sage.

Shidlo, A. (1994). Internalized homophobia: Conceptual and empirical issues in measurement. In B. Greene & G. M. Herek (Eds.), *Lesbian and gay psychology: Theory, research, and clinical applications* (pp. 176–205). Thousand Oaks, CA: Sage.

Shields, S. A., & Harriman, R. E. (1984). Fear of male homosexuality: Cardiac responses of low and high homonegative males. *Journal of Homosexuality, 10*(1–2), 53–67.

Sigelman, C. K., Howell, J. L., Cornell, D. P., Cutright, J. D., & Dewey, J. C. (1991). Courtesy stigma: The social implications of associating with a gay person. *Journal of Social Psychology, 131,* 45–56.

Simon, A. (1998). The relationship between stereotypes of and attitudes toward lesbians and gays. In G. M. Herek (Ed.), *Stigma and sexual orientation: Understanding prejudice against lesbians, gay men, and bisexuals* (pp. 62–81). Thousand Oaks, CA: Sage.

Smart, L., & Wegner, D. M. (2000). The hidden costs of hidden stigma. In T. F. Heatherton, R. E. Kleck, M. R. Hebl, & J. G. Hull (Eds.), *The social psychology of stigma* (pp. 220–242). New York: Guilford.

Smith, G. W. (1998). The ideology of "fag": The school experience of gay students. *Sociology Quarterly, 39,* 309–335.

Smith, M. B., Bruner, J. S., & White, R. W. (1956). *Opinions and personality.* New York: Wiley.

Snyder, M., & Uranowitz, S. W. (1978). Reconstructing the past: Some cognitive consequences of person perception. *Journal of Personality and Social Psychology, 36,* 941–950.

Stark, R., & Glock, C. Y. (1973). Prejudice and the churches. In C. Y. Glock (Ed.), *Religion in sociological perspective: Essays in the empirical study of religion* (pp. 88–101). Belmont, CA: Wadsworth.

Steffens, M. C. (2005). Implicit and explicit attitudes towards lesbians and gay men. *Journal of Homosexuality, 49*(2), 39–66.

Steffens, M. C., & Buchner, A. (2003). Implicit Association Test: Separating transsituationally stable and variable components of attitudes toward gay men. *Experimental Psychology, 50,* 33–48.

Steffens, M. C., & Wagner, C. (2004). Attitudes toward lesbians, gay men, bisexual women, and bisexual men in Germany. *Journal of Sex Research, 41,* 137–149.

Stephan, W. G., & Finlay, K. (1999). The role of empathy in improving intergroup relations. *Journal of Social Issues, 55,* 729–743.

Stephan, W. G., & Stephan, C. W. (1985). Intergroup anxiety. *Journal of Social Issues, 41*(3), 157–175.

Stouffer, S. A. (1955). *Communism, conformity, and civil liberties: A cross-section of the nation speaks its mind.* Garden City, NY: Doubleday.

Strachan, E. D., Bennett, W. R. M., Russo, J., & Roy-Byrne, P. P. (2007). Disclosure of HIV status and sexual orientation independently predicts increased absolute CD4 cell counts over time for psychiatric patients. *Psychosomatic Medicine, 69,* 74–80.

Strand, D. A. (1998). Civil liberties, civil rights, and stigma: Voter attitudes and behavior in the politics of homosexuality. In G. M. Herek (Ed.), *Stigma and sexual orientation: Understanding prejudice against lesbians, gay men, and bisexuals* (pp. 108–137). Thousand Oaks, CA: Sage.

Szymanski, D. M. (2005). Heterosexism and sexism as correlates of psychological distress in lesbians. *Journal of Counseling and Development, 83,* 355–360.

Szymanski, D. M., & Chung, Y. B. (2003). Feminist attitudes and coping resources as correlates of lesbian internalized heterosexism. *Feminism and Psychology, 13,* 369–389.

Tsang, J.-A., & Rowatt, W. C. (2007). The relationship between religious orientation, right-wing authoritarianism, and implicit sexual prejudice. *International Journal for the Psychology of Religion, 17,* 99–120.

Ullrich, P. M., Lutgendorf, S. K., & Stapleton, J. T. (2003). Concealment of homosexual identity, social support and CD4 cell count among HIV-seropositive gay men. *Journal of Psychosomatic Research, 54,* 205–212.

Vescio, T. K., & Biernat, M. (2003). Family values and antipathy toward gay men. *Journal of Applied Social Psychology, 33,* 833–847.

Vonofakou, C., Hewstone, M., & Voci, A. (2007). Contact with out-group friends as a predictor of meta-attitudinal strength and accessibility of attitudes toward gay men. *Journal of Personality and Social Psychology, 92,* 804–820.

Walker, P., & Antaki, C. (1986). Sexual orientation as a basis for categorization in recall. *British Journal of Social Psychology, 25,* 337–339.

Weinberg, G. (1972). *Society and the healthy homosexual.* New York: St. Martin's.

Weiner, B. (1993). On sin versus sickness: A theory of perceived responsibility and social motivation. *American Psychologist, 48,* 957–965.

Whitley, B. E., Jr. (1990). The relationship of heterosexuals' attributions for the causes of homosexuality to attitudes toward lesbians and gay men. *Personality and Social Psychology Bulletin, 16,* 369–377.

Whitley, B. E., Jr., & Lee, S. E. (2000). The relationship of authoritarianism and related constructs to attitudes toward homosexuality. *Journal of Applied Social Psychology, 30,* 144–170.

Wilder, D. A. (1978). Reduction of intergroup discrimination through individuation of the out-group. *Journal of Personality and Social Psychology, 36,* 1361–1374.

Wood, P. B., & Bartkowski, J. P. (2004). Attribution style and public policy attitudes toward gay rights. *Social Science Quarterly, 85,* 58–74.

Yang, A. S. (1997). Trends: Attitudes toward homosexuality. *Public Opinion Quarterly, 61,* 477–507.

23 Anti-Fat Prejudice

Christian S. Crandall
Angela Nierman
University of Kansas

Michelle Hebl
Rice University

Prejudice against heavyweight people is prevalent, powerful, and potent. As with many other prejudices, the stereotyping, prejudice, and discrimination aimed at people on the basis of their weight can have a powerful effect on their lives. In this chapter, we review evidence revealing that differential treatment on the basis of weight occurs in all the major domains of heavyweight people's lives, with strong consequences for achievement, self-esteem, career opportunities, friendships, and physical and mental health (see Brownell, Puhl, Schwartz, & Rudd, 2005, for a book-length review of many of these issues). Prejudice against heavyweight people is much like other prejudices—it limits opportunities; is associated with a negative stereotype; and prototypically involves the domination of powerful, unstigmatized individuals or groups over stigmatized, less powerful individuals or groups. In many ways, however, prejudice against heavyweight people is different, special, and relatively unusual when compared to the more commonly discussed and researched prejudices of race and gender. There are simply a wide range of phenomena and practices associated with many prejudices that are not applicable to anti-fat prejudice, and there are aspects of anti-fat prejudice that often do not appear when considering racism and sexism. In this chapter, we consider some of the ways in which anti-fat prejudice is both similar to and different from the prejudices of race and gender.

We begin by reviewing research that shows the relative disadvantage of heavyweight people compared to leaner people. This review begins with some of the traditional dimensions examined in race and gender research (e.g., adverse effects on mental health, discrimination in the workplace). After making a case that anti-fat prejudice is a significant and important prejudice, we then discuss a variety of topics associated with anti-fat prejudice that are critical to consider, some of which are different from those associated with the prejudices of race and gender.

EFFECTS ON MENTAL HEALTH

Mistreatment on the basis of weight begins at an early age. Rejection of heavyweight people has been documented consistently among 3-year-olds (Cramer & Steinwert, 1998), elementary school children (Latner & Stunkard, 2003; Richardson, Goodman, Hastorf, & Dornbusch, 1961), and 7- to 9-year-old boys and girls (Kraig & Keel, 2001). Heavyweight children are less often nominated as friends (Staffieri, 1967), much less likely to be chosen as a best friend, and more likely to receive few or no friendship choices than leaner peers (Strauss & Pollack, 2003). There are a number of domains in which heavyweight children experience negative outcomes on a daily basis, the sum of which may have strong associations with deficits in mental health.

TEASING

Teasing by peers is alienating and leads to negative self-images, and poorer relations with one's peers (Troop-Gordon & Ladd, 2005). In one study, 96% of heavyweight girls reported being the subject of hurtful comments or weight-related teasing (Neumark-Sztainer & Eisenberg, 2005). In another study, heavyweight children were more than 15 times as likely to be ganged up on and victimized by peers than were leaner children (Lagerspetz, Kjorkvist, Nerts, & King, 1982). In a sample of more than 4,700 middle and high school adolescents, nearly 30% of girls, and nearly 20% of boys reported being teased about their weight more than a few times a year (Neumark-Sztainer et al., 2002). However, 45% of heavyweight girls and 50% of heavyweight boys reported being teased much more often.

What are the repercussions or associations with this teasing? Teens who were teased were more likely to use diet pills, abuse laxatives, and binge eat than were those who did not experience teasing. Such teens were also more likely to report depression, suicidal thoughts, and suicide attempts; the effects seemed to be worse for girls than boys. That is, heavyweight girls who had been teased reported twice the level of suicidal ideation than did girls who had not been teased (51% vs. 25%). Although boys reported fewer suicidal thoughts overall, boys who had been teased reported more than three times the level of suicidal thoughts (13% vs. 4%; Eisenberg, Neumark-Sztainer, Haines, & Wall, 2006; Haines, Neumark-Sztainer, Eisenberg, & Hannan, 2006) than did those who had not been teased, even after controlling for body weight.

SELF-ESTEEM

The relationship between stigmatization and self-esteem is complex. Although many theories strongly connect negative physical characteristics (e.g., being heavyweight) with a negative self-view, this is often not the case (Crocker & Major, 1989). Thus, it is not surprising to learn that the body of empirical evidence examining the relationship between self-esteem and weight is not simple or clear. In the domain of body-related self-esteem, heavyweight adults have lower esteem than their leaner adult counterparts (French, Story, & Perry, 1995). This lower body-related esteem seems to be in part caused by the teasing (Thompson, Herbozo, Himes, & Yamamiya, 2005).

Despite the effects we have discussed thus far, the effects on global self-esteem do not seem to be as consistent or strong. For instance, in a meta-analysis conducted by Miller and Downey (1999), they found a reliable, significant, but modest correlation of $r = -.12$ between actual weight and self-esteem. This relationship is weak, but it is notable in that several studies have found no such significant correlation (see Crocker & Major, 1989). Miller and Downey also found a correlation between self-perceived weight and self-esteem ($r = -.34$), suggesting that low self-esteem may affect just how heavy a person may see himself or herself as.

The self-esteem of heavyweight people can suffer from discrimination, depending on other attitudes. Women who are both heavyweight and have anti-fat attitudes have significantly more negative self-esteem than do women who are heavyweight and do not have such attitudes (Crandall & Biernat, 1990). When rejected by a fellow student as a dating partner, heavyweight women tended to attribute this rejection to their weight, and they felt depressed, hostile, and anxious, and had lower appearance-based self-esteem than average-weight women, and women who were not rejected (Crocker, Cornwall, & Major, 1993).

One important source of self-esteem is the development of a social identity based on group membership (e.g., Brewer, 1991; Hogg & Abrams, 1990). One's identity is flexible, and is typically constructed in such a way as to maximize one's own positive distinctiveness (Tajfel & Turner, 1979). As a result, people tend to have positive views of their own groups, which, in turn, enhance their self-esteem. This ingroup bias is a pervasive and highly dependable research finding (Aberson, Healy, & Romero, 2000; Brewer, 1979; Crocker & Luhtanen, 1990). In a surprising set of findings, however, heavyweight people do not seem to show ingroup bias; hence, heavyweight people are cut off from one important source of self-esteem. Across seven different samples of college students, Crandall

(1994) found no significant correlation between high levels of body mass index (BMI) and positive ratings of heavyweight people ($r = -.01$, $N = 1,384$). The same pattern was found in two separate samples of college students collected by Crandall and Biernat (1990), and across separate samples of students from six nations on five continents. That is, there was no sign of a positive ingroup bias among heavyweight people. It is remarkable that heavyweight people do not show such a bias, as it is one of the most widespread and reliable of all social psychological phenomena (Scheepers, Spears, Doosje, & Manstead, 2006).

It is critical, in discussing issues surrounding mental health, to point out that research does not show that obesity results from poor mental health (Britz et al., 2000). That is, heavyweight people do not suffer unduly from mental disorders (e.g., van Hanswijck, de Jonge, van Furth, Lacey, & Walker, 2003), nor is there evidence that mental disorders lead to obesity. The psychological consequences of mistreatment of heavyweight people are real (see Brownell et al., 2005), but there is no reason to believe that heavyweight people are any more disordered than their leaner counterparts. Two exceptions to this include disorders related to body image and dieting (e.g., Hudson, Hiripi, Pope, & Kessler, 2007) and the fact that antipsychotic medicines often generate significant weight gains (Allison & Casey, 2001).

EDUCATION

Education is often described as the single most important factor in occupational and social class advancement (e.g., Argyle, 1994). At nearly every educational level, the heavier the student, the fewer the opportunities that he or she has. In the preteen years, heavyweight students primarily experience discrimination and harassment at school (e.g., Neumark-Sztainer, Story, & Faibisch, 1998). Across all grades, teachers exhibit anti-fat attitudes toward their students (Neumark-Sztainer, Story, & Harris, 1999).

Is weight associated with lower cognitive skills? The research evidence is very mixed. For instance, Datar, Sturm, and Magnabosco (2004) found that heavyweight kindergarteners and first graders scored lower on math and reading skills than their leaner peers. This relationship disappeared when social-class-relevant variables were controlled for, suggesting that weight may be more of a marker of socioeconomic class than a measure of lesser abilities. Crandall (1995), however, found no relation between BMI and high school grade point average in a U.S. national sample. Furthermore, Kuo et al. (2006) found that BMI was positively associated with a variety of cognitive skills among older adults, including reasoning tasks and visual-spatial processing speed. At best, then, the literature reveals that weight is not a reliable predictor of lower cognitive skills.

Canning and Mayer (1966) showed that despite equal grades, standardized test scores, and high school quality, heavyweight adolescents were underrepresented at several prestigious colleges and universities in the Northeast. Similarly, Pargman (1969) and Crandall (1991, 1995) found a significant underrepresentation of heavyweight students at Boston University and the University of Florida, respectively. Interestingly, in both cases, the universities that were examined did not require face-to-face interaction or photos for admissions, suggesting that the biasing factor is not a straightforward denigration of the heavyweight applicants. Once admitted, there is evidence that heavyweight students are sometimes judged more harshly and that they are more likely to be dismissed from college than are their leaner counterparts (Weiler & Helms, 1993).

Based on a nationally representative sample of high school seniors, Crandall (1995) showed that weight had no relationship to the enjoyment of the academic component of high school, high school grades, or the desire to attend college. The barriers to attending college do not seem to be in the academic preparation or motivation of the students. Rather, it seems that they may involve demographic correlates such as low socioeconomic status (SES) or the reliance on pernicious stereotypes that limit heavyweight individuals. Crandall (1995) showed that parents are significantly less likely to give financial support to their heavyweight children than their average-weight children for college (regardless of ability to pay), and this effect was particularly striking among daughters.

WORKPLACE

Heavyweight individuals face a great deal of prejudice and discrimination in the workplace (i.e., Fikkan & Rothblum, 2005; Rothblum, Brand, Miller, & Oetjen, 1990). These biases emerge across the entire employment cycle—from being recruited initially to being promoted among the ranks—and these effects are particularly detrimental for women (see Roehling, 1999 for a review). We consider, in some detail, how such biases affect three different contexts: hiring paradigms, promotion and pay scales, and customer service (treatment of customers).

Hiring Paradigms

A number of studies have examined perceptions and ratings of job applicants as well as the specific hiring recommendations that are made. This research shows that heavyweight applicants are perceived to have more negative work-related attributes (Polinko & Popovich, 2001) than those who are leaner. Additional research has shown a similar pattern with actual hiring decisions; that is, heavyweight job applicants are recommended for hire much less often than are their thinner counterparts, even when the credentials of both sets of candidates are equal (Larkin & Pines, 1979; Pingitore, Dugoni, Tindale, & Spring, 1994). In fact, the anti-fat stigma in hiring paradigms is so strong at times that it even seems to affect job applicants who are simply in physical proximity to heavyweight individuals. Hebl and Mannix (2003) found that a male job applicant was rated much more negatively and recommended for hire significantly less when he was seen with a heavyweight woman compared to an average weight woman, even if there was no relationship or association between the two beyond physical proximity.

Promotion and Pay Scales

Promotions are often based on the evaluations that employees receive and the opportunities that they are given. A number of studies show that heavyweight employees are evaluated much more negatively and receive more limited workplace opportunities than employees who are leaner. For instance, heavyweight salespeople were rated as being less punctual, enthusiastic, productive, competent, well-mannered, and trustworthy than were average-weight salespersons (Jasper & Klassen, 1990; Larkin & Pines, 1979; Zemank, McIntyre, & Zemanek, 1998) and they are assigned to less important and desirable sales territories (Bellizi & Hasty, 1998). Such differences emerge at higher levels of employment, too; for instance, research reveals that heavyweight managers are rated as less desirable and worthy of recognition than are managers who are leaner (Decker, 1987). There may be some truth to the fact that heavyweight individuals are not performing as well as their thinner counterparts; however, research testing this idea shows that part of the performance decrement arises from differences in training that heavyweight versus average weight individuals receive from others. That is, Shapiro, King, and Quinones (2007) found that the size (heavyweight or not) of individuals assigned to play the role of trainee significantly increased negative expectations held—and evaluations given—by trainers. Trainer attitudes and behaviors created a self-fulfilling prophecy, whereby trainers actually showed decrements in performance in some conditions.

Given these differences in evaluations—clearly linked to promotion decisions—it would make sense that strong differences be observed between the salaries that heavyweight and average-weight individuals earn. Such salary differences seem to exist for women alone (Pagan & Davila, 1997; Register & Williams, 1990; Sargent & Blanchflower, 1994; Sobal & Stunkard, 1989). In a study examining consequences of weight in adolescence and young adulthood, women who were heavyweight as adolescents or young adults ultimately had lower household incomes ($6,710 less per year) than did women who were leaner (Gortmaker, Must, Perrin, Sobol, & Dietz, 1993). For men, the relationship was not significant.

CUSTOMER SERVICE

Another area in which prejudice and discrimination has been documented against heavyweight individuals is in the customer service that they receive. Recently, King, Shapiro, Hebl, Singletary, and Turner (2006) conducted three studies in which they examined the treatment from store personnel that heavyweight versus leaner individuals received when they entered retail stores. All three studies revealed that heavyweight individuals did not receive more overt forms of discrimination (i.e., there were no differences in being greeted, actually receiving help) but that they did receive significantly more subtle, interpersonal discrimination (i.e., less eye contact, less friendliness) than leaner individuals. These subtle and seemingly small amounts of discrimination still have severe consequences (Martel, Lane, & Willis, 1996; Valian, 1998). Furthermore, King and colleagues showed that such discrimination against heavyweight individuals also has negative ramifications for the organizations that are discriminating. That is, heavyweight individuals who have experienced such discrimination report spending less money at the store than they intended to, and that they are less willing to recommend the store to others and less likely to return for future patronage.

As a whole, then, there is consistent and discouraging evidence that heavyweight individuals face a great deal of discrimination in the workplace. Although we focused our review on only some aspects of the workplace, it is again important to note that they emerge across virtually every aspect of the employment cycle (see Roehling, 1999).

MARRIAGE, RELATIONSHIPS, AND FAMILY

Anti-fat bias has been well documented in a wide array of public domains, including the workplace, education, and health care institutions. Consequently, antidiscrimination policies have been implemented to discourage the unfair treatment of heavyweight individuals. Although outside the realm of legal regulation, anti-fat bias also enters into the private domain of personal relationships. This section focuses on the consequences of anti-fat bias in the areas of friendship, dating, and marriage.

FRIENDSHIP

Heavyweight people have fewer friends, are less popular, are less liked, have fewer social skills, and are lonelier than their leaner counterparts (e.g., Davison & Birch, 2004; Harris, Harris, & Bochner, 1982). Strauss and Pollack (2003) found that heavyweight adolescents were more likely to be socially marginalized and to be peripheral to social networks than were leaner adolescents. Other studies, however, find that heavyweight people are rated as being just as friendly, or even friendlier, than leaner people (Tiggemann & Rothblum, 1988). Friendships seem to be based in part on weight, with leaner men and women forming friendships with other lean people, and heavier women and men forming friendships with other heavy people (Crandall, Schiffhauer, & Harvey, 1997).

Heavyweight individuals may learn to compensate for their appearance by developing effective social skills (Miller, Rothblum, Felicio, & Brand, 1995). Miller et al. (1995) found that heavyweight women were able to compensate for the anti-fat prejudice of their conversation partners when they were aware that they were visible, and in these conditions were judged no differently in social competence than leaner women. New research is sorely needed to disentangle subjective biases (i.e., the negative stereotypes about heavyweight individuals) from objective differences (i.e., differences in social skills and talents as a function of weight).

DATING

In addition to the stereotypes that heavyweight people are unpopular and socially unskilled, heavyweight individuals are less preferred as sexual partners than leaner individuals (Chen & Brown, 2005). They also are rated as less attractive, less likely to be in a dating relationship, and less deserving of an attractive romantic partner than their leaner counterparts (Cossrow, Jeffrey, & McGuire, 2001; Harris, 1990; Pearce, Boergers, & Prinstein, 2002). This is not to say that heavy-weight people do not date, but rather that they begin dating later as adolescents, date less often, and date less attractive partners than do leaner individuals (Cawley, Joyner, & Sobal, 2006; Pearce et al., 2002). Because social standards often equate physical attractiveness with thinness, it is espe-cially difficult for heavyweight individuals, particularly women, to enter into romantic relationships (Regan, 1996). As with friendship, dating relationships reveal that anti-fat bias does not prevent heavyweight individuals from having successful, romantic relationships, but it does mean that they must overcome stereotypes, prejudice, and discrimination.

MARRIAGE

Considering that the onset of dating is often delayed for heavyweight individuals given the difficulty they experience in entering into intimate relationships, it is not surprising that heavyweight indi-viduals also might get married later in life relative to leaner individuals. There is some evidence to suggest that heavyweight adults have lower marriage rates than do their leaner counterparts; how-ever, this may be limited to marriage rates among young adults (Fu & Goldman, 1996; Gortmaker et al., 1993). Once married, however, the quality of the marital relationship does not seem to be any different for heavyweight versus leaner individuals. Sobal, Rauschenbach, and Frongillo (1995) found no significant relationships between weight and marital satisfaction, conflict, or problems.

Some studies report greater marital instability in heavier than leaner people (Macías, Leal, López-Ibor, Rubio, & Caballero, 2004), but others show that a marriage may be more stable when one or both of the partners are heavyweight; obese women report less marital unhappiness (Sobal et al., 1995).

It is likely that there is as much variability in marriage success among heavyweight as leaner couples; partners' weight does not seem to be the determining factor in relationship success. Rand, Kowalske, and Kuldau (1984) found marital improvement in some couples following surgery for extreme obesity and marital deterioration in others. Surgery may simply accentuate the existing quality of the marriage; when weight is changed by surgery, good marriages improve and bad mar-riages fail (Macías et al., 2004; Marshall & Neill, 1977).

Just as in friendship choice, lean people marry lean partners and heavy people marry heavy partners. Allison et al. (1996) found a significant correlation between the relative weight of each partner that cannot be otherwise explained by cohabitation, age similarity, or selective survival of marriages between couples more similar in relative weight. For some couples, one or both partners being heavyweight may serve a stabilizing or protective function in the marriage (Marshall & Neill, 1977). Some men say they prefer heavier women because the heaviness of their wives protects them from competition with other males and the possibility of abandonment (Marshall & Neill, 1977). Married heavyweight women may report less unhappiness than unmarried heavyweight women because they feel less pressure to lose weight than when they were seeking a partner, and because the affection in the marriage is less contingent on weight and appearance (Marshall & Neill, 1977; Sobal et al., 1995).

Forming and maintaining meaningful relationships is typically a challenge for everyone, regard-less of weight. Being heavyweight can make the experience of meeting new friends and finding suitable dating partners even more difficult, especially for women. However, the final word on inti-mate relationships is not as dismal as in the public domain of anti-fat bias, nor as definitive. Despite stereotypes, heavyweight people often are socially skilled and well liked. They do find compatible dating partners, participate in romantic relationships, get married, and enjoy satisfaction with their partners.

HEALTH CARE

Much research has documented prejudice and discrimination in the health care system by examining the attitudes and behaviors of physicians, residents, medical students, and nurses. Many of the studies are 20 years old or more, but they converge in showing that all of these individuals tend to hold negative attitudes toward and discriminate against those who are heavyweight. Physicians hold heavyweight individuals responsible for their condition and attribute their failures at weight loss to gluttony and a general lack of cooperation and discipline (DeJong, 1980; Price, Desmond, Krol, Snyder, & O'Connell, 1987; Price, Desmond, Ruppert, & Stelzer, 1989; Young & Powell, 1985). Although one recent study showed that physicians and other health professionals may be somewhat less likely to show overt forms of anti-fat bias toward heavy patients than are nonhealth professionals, this study simultaneously revealed that physicians are equally likely to exhibit cognitive biases and deep-rooted stereotypes against heavyweight individuals (Teachman & Brownell, 2001). Such biases may be strengthened in physicians during their training, as they realize that heavier people often require more space, more surgery time, increased recovery times, and nonstandard sizes of equipment (Gallagher, 1996, 1998). Indeed, medical residents have reported liking their heavyweight patients less and believing that they are more emotional than their leaner patients (Blumberg & Mellis, 1985). Similarly, responses from medical students reveal that they believe heavyweight patients are not as likely to benefit from medical help, are more depressed and nervous, and would benefit from seeing a psychiatrist or a clinical psychologist more than would patients who are leaner (Bretytspraak, McGee, Conger, Whatley, & Moore, 1977).

Physicians not only perceive patients differently on the basis of weight, they also discriminate against those who are heavyweight (Hebl & Xu, 2001). For instance, when asked to make medical recommendations, physicians indicated that they would spend less time (approximately 9 minutes fewer) and would display more negative behaviors (i.e., having less desire to help, being less patient, displaying less positivity) toward heavyweight patients than those who were leaner. Fewer than 50% of physicians recommended responses (e.g., weight loss, nutrition counseling, exercise counseling) that would seem to be relevant for heavier individuals, recommendations that some health experts believe are the critical foundation for obesity health care (Galuska, Will, Serdula, & Ford, 1999; Wee, McCarthy, Davis, & Phillips, 1999).

In a study examining whether heavyweight patients detect this discrimination, Hebl, Xu, and Mason (2003) had patients exiting their appointments complete a brief questionnaire describing the physician–patient interaction they had just had. A gender difference emerged such that heavyweight women tended to feel that the quality of care they received was equal or better than that reported by women who were leaner; however, heavyweight men reported that the quality of their care was equal or worse than that reported by average-weight patients. Heavyweight patients are less likely to receive warm, friendly, and caring treatment by physicians. Because a friendly physician–patient relationship improves medical care, and an unfriendly one harms care (Gawande, 2007; Groopman, 2007), it is critical that heavyweight patients pay careful attention to the quality of their relationship with caregivers.

GENDER, ETHNICITY, CULTURE, AND SOCIAL CLASS

Weight matters for everyone, but the degree of importance differs according to its social context. Because prejudice of any sort depends on cultural categories, definitions, boundaries, and values, one must understand the pattern of prejudice across locations and targets.

GENDER

There is no doubt that weight is much more important to the self and social perception for women than for men. Women are more body conscious, are more concerned about (and dissatisfied with) body shape and size, diet more often, and feel that their weight interferes with their social life more than men (e.g., Brownell et al., 2005; Harris, Walters, & Waschull, 1991; Rodin, Silberstein, & Striegel-Moore, 1984; Stake & Lauer, 1987; Tiggemann & Rothblum, 1988). Women's dissatisfaction with their own bodies and a concomitant sense of unattractiveness in comparison to men is both reliable and increasing (Feingold & Mazzella, 1998). Concerns about weight and dieting are an important factor in the etiology of eating disorders, which disproportionately affect women (Cachelin & Regan, 2006; Striegel-Moore & Franko, 2006).

The social costs of weight, in terms of dating and marriage, affect women more than men (Cawley et al., 2006; Regan, 1996), and relational aggression is more common toward heavyweight girls than heavyweight boys (Pearce, et al., 2002). Salary differences associated with weight are mostly for women; men do not experience wage penalties until they exceed their ideal standard by more than 100 pounds (Maranto & Stenoien, 2000; cf. Frieze, Olson, & Good, 1990). The cost of weight to self-esteem is also significantly greater for women than for men (Miller & Downey, 1999; see also Crandall & Biernat, 1990).

Overall, the research consistently shows that weight affects women more strongly than men. The interpersonal costs (e.g., jobs, dating, friendship) and the intrapersonal costs (e.g., self-esteem, mental health, eating disorders) are all significantly greater for women than for men.

ETHNICITY AND CULTURE

The research focusing on anti-fat bias and different ethnic groups tends to find prejudice against most heavyweight people of all colors, although there are some important exceptions and variations. Most of the research on ethnicity and race focuses on the Black–White comparison, but there is also a growing literature on attitudes of Latinos, from Mexico, Central and South Americas. (There is a significant debate about the meaning of ethnicity and its relation to culture, and here we finesse the issue by conflating the distinction in this section.)

Black individuals tend to be more satisfied with their own body shape (Hebl & Turchin, 2005), rate heavyweight women as more attractive (Hebl & Heatherton, 1998), and are less likely to reject heavyweight women as dating partners (Harris, Walters, & Waschull, 1991) than are White individuals. The wage penalties for mildly obese White women (20% over ideal weight) appear to be more severe than those for severely obese (100% over ideal weight) Black men (Maranto & Stenoien, 2000). Black men have a larger acceptable standard for women's weight than White men, and in ratings studies, large Black men are stigmatized less than large White men (Hebl & Turchin, 2005). Although White women rate heavyweight women lower on a variety of dimensions, Black women generally do not show the same denigration of heavyweight women, especially when rating heavyweight Black women (Hebl & Heatherton, 1998).

For Mexican Americans, acculturation to the dominant cultural view is associated with greater concern about weight and more anti-fat attitudes (e.g., Ayala, Mickens, Galindo, & Elder, 2007; Olvera, Suminski, & Power, 2005). Hispanic parents appear to be tolerant of their heavyweight children (Rich et al., 2005) and are more accepting of obesity in adults than are White Americans (e.g., Anderson, Hughes, Fisher, & Nicklas, 2005).

There is evidence of body dissatisfaction, distorted body image, and dislike of fatness for both self and others in Mexico (Gomez-Peresmitre, Griselda, Liliana-Moreno, Sugey-Saloma, & Gisela-Pineda, 2001). In a comparison between students in Mexico City and students in the United States (in Florida and Kansas), the Mexican students reported more positive attitudes toward heavyweight people than the Americans did (Crandall & Martinez, 1996).

Crandall and colleagues (Crandall et al., 2001) compared anti-fat attitudes in six nations, three representing individualistic countries (Australia, Poland, and the United States) and three representing collectivist countries (India, Turkey, and Venezuela). Overall, fatness was seen as highly negative (e.g., "In our culture, being fat is considered a bad thing" and "In our culture, being thin is an important part of being attractive") in the individualistic countries, but was significantly more positive in the collectivist countries.

In a review of the connection between SES and obesity, Sobal and Stunkard (1989) found that obesity in women was associated with low SES in developed societies, but by contrast obesity was associated with high SES in developing nations. They reported that a "review of social attitudes toward obesity and thinness reveals values congruent with the distribution of obesity by SES in different societies" (p. 260). People in developing societies are significantly more positive toward obesity, and under many circumstances find it highly desirable (Brown & Konner, 1987). In general, one must argue that anti-fat prejudice is deeply embedded in the values, ideologies, and cultural norms and mores of a society (Crandall & Schiffhauer, 1998; De Garine, 1995).

THEORETICAL ACCOUNTS OF ANTI-FAT PREJUDICE

There are few theories specifically designed to account for anti-fat stigma. Such theories might clarify why anti-fat stigma is particularly severe, help predict contexts in which individuals are especially vulnerable to the stigma, and ultimately work to avoid or remediate the pernicious effects associated with being heavyweight. In this section, we briefly summarize modern theories of stigma and their potential applications to anti-fat stigma. For an extended discussion of many of these theories, we point interested readers to a recent chapter by King, Hebl, and Heatherton (2005).

STEREOTYPE CONTENT MODEL

This theory proposes that the content of stereotypes varies along two dimensions of more and less socially desirable traits: warmth and competence (Fiske, Cuddy, Glick, & Xu, 2002). For example, the stereotype of Asian American individuals is high on the competence dimension but low on the warmth dimension. The point at which a particular stereotype falls on the dimensions of warmth and competence is associated with specific affective reactions (i.e., prejudices). Across a large number of participants and multiple samples, Fiske et al. (2002) showed that the content of stereotypes for feminists, housecleaners, gay men and lesbians, and other stigmatized groups fell into four clusters along the dimensions of warmth and competence.

Although not originally included, this model could be extended to include anti-fat stigma. The stigma of obesity may be particularly negative because it is both visible and perceived to be controllable (Weiner, Perry, & Magnusson, 1988) and numerous studies show that being heavyweight is associated with perceptions of being lazy, undisciplined, and gluttonous (DeJong & Kleck, 1981; Harris, Harris, & Bochner, 1982; Hebl & Kleck, 2002). Such findings suggest that stereotypes about heavyweight individuals are likely to be low in both warmth and competence dimensions, a combination that results in the worst amount of stigmatization (Fiske et al., 2002). As a result of these dimensions, it is likely that affective reactions to heavyweight individuals consist of disgust and contempt.

INTERGROUP EMOTIONS THEORY

This theory proposes that emotions are central to the process of stigmatization and draws on appraisal and self-categorization theories (see Mackie, Devos, & Smith, 2000; Smith & Henry, 1996). More specifically, this theory suggests that prejudice is driven by specific emotional reactions to an outgroup that are generated by appraisals of the outgroup. When individuals feel that their ingroup is more powerful than an outgroup, their emotional response (i.e., anger) may lead to action tendencies that are manifested in discrimination toward members of that outgroup.

Although not originally developed to explain anti-fat stigma, this theory is useful in understanding potentially negative reactions toward heavyweight individuals. Societal ideals reveal that thinness has greater status in our society than does heaviness. Identification with the high-status group (i.e., thin individuals) may trigger specific emotions (i.e., anger) toward the low-status group (i.e., heavyweight individuals) and ultimately result in both overt and subtle forms of prejudice and discrimination.

Predictions regarding anti-fat stigma that follow from an intergroup emotions approach may be contradictory to those made by the stereotype content model. Although both theories predict negative emotional reactions to heavyweight individuals, intergroup emotions theory predicts anger as the outcome, whereas the stereotype content model predicts disgust as the outcome. Although both emotions are negative in valence, these two emotions may have different sets of implications for remediating anti-fat stigma; strategies targeted to diminish anger might differ significantly from strategies designed to lessen disgust. Future research might consider which of these emotions—anger or disgust—are most salient in response to heavyweight individuals (see also Cottrell & Neuberg, 2005).

EVOLUTIONARY APPROACHES

There are a number of evolutionary approaches (i.e., sociofunctional, biocultural, disease) that focus even more intensely than the previously discussed theories on addressing why stigmatization occurs. Such approaches are grounded in the assumption that stigmatizing others can serve meaningful purposes to the stigmatizer (Neuberg, Smith, & Asher, 2000). For instance, Neuberg and his colleagues argue that stigmatization is rooted in an inherent biological need to live in effective groups to promote the survival of their genetic makeup. Individuals or groups who are perceived to threaten the survival of one's ingroup will be stigmatized. Neuberg et al. argued that individuals will attempt to minimize perceived threat from stigmatized outgroups with specific emotional (i.e., prejudice) and behavioral (i.e., discrimination) responses. Thus, the process of stigmatization arose as a by-product of evolution, in which the stigmatizing individuals successfully minimized threat by rejecting others (see also Kurzban, Tooby, & Cosmides, 2001)

The renewed interest in evolutionary explanations for psychological phenomena encourages exploration of the biological functionality of the stigmatization of heavyweight individuals. On the one hand, proponents of this approach might argue that obesity is often genetically based and has been linked with severely negative health outcomes (see Wadden, Brownell, & Foster, 2002); thus, it may be functionally adaptive to avoid heavyweight individuals in the process of mate selection. Consistent with this approach, heavyweight individuals could arguably consume more resources than other individuals, making it more difficult to support the interests of the group as a whole. On the other hand, Kurzban and Leary (2001) suggested that a biocultural approach cannot explain the anti-fat stigma. They suggested that obesity is a relatively new condition in evolutionary terms in that it is only within the last several hundred years that leisure has been coupled with excess food. Thus, evolutionary theories may have limited value in understanding anti-fat stigma.

Park, Schaller, and Crandall (2007) suggested that humans possess a behavioral pathogen avoidance mechanism that allows them to avoid contagious disease. To the extent that this mechanism may be biased in favor of perceiving disease (and thus be overinclusive in the perception of threats), people might avoid others with a deviant weight (e.g., obese people). In a series of studies, they showed that people who are chronically concerned about infectious disease had more negative attitudes toward fat people, and that making infectious disease salient enhanced the rejection of obese targets.

SYSTEM JUSTIFICATION APPROACH

System justification theory (SJT) suggests that individuals of both high- and low-status groups are motivated to reinforce and justify the status quo, or existing social arrangements. There are both cognitive reasons (e.g., need for cognitive closure, uncertainty reduction) and motivational reasons (e.g., belief in a just world, illusion of control) for participating in system justification (Jost & Banaji,

1994; Jost, Pelham, & Carvallo, 2002). SJT may explain why heavyweight individuals perceive their weight negatively. That is, unlike members of some stigmatized groups (e.g., African American individuals) who maintain high self-esteem despite their stigma (Crocker & Major, 1989), heavyweight individuals tend to share the thoughts and feelings of their stigmatizers, view themselves negatively, and have low self-esteem (Crandall & Biernat, 1990; Crocker, Cornwell, & Major, 1993). This is probably because the attitudes, beliefs, and values that explain and justify anti-fat prejudice are fundamental and ubiquitous values, such as Protestant ethic, individualism, and belief in a just world (Crandall, 1994), which are socialized and internalized without regard to weight status. These ideologies, adopted as a part of socialization into the dominant value culture, in turn prohibit escape from justification beliefs that excuse and normalize anti-fat prejudice. One step toward remediation of anti-fat stigma may be to change the reinforcing thoughts, feelings, and values of heavyweight people themselves.

JUSTIFICATION SUPPRESSION MODEL

The justification suppression model (JSM) by Crandall and Eshleman (2003) proposes that individuals face two conflicting demands: (a) wanting to express their emotions and (b) wanting to maintain egalitarian values and self-image. The JSM suggests that prejudice is expressed as a function of three processes: genuine prejudice, suppression, and justification. The core emotional component of prejudice—genuine prejudice—is pure, original, and unmanaged negative feelings toward members of a devalued group. Because the expression of prejudice is at odds with an egalitarian self-image, suppression—motivated processes that seek to reduce the expression of prejudice—moderate this expression. However, affect has strong motivational properties, and the suppression of this motivation creates tension and discomfort, and hijacks attention and depletes energy. As a result, people will engage justification processes—any process that allows the expression of genuine prejudice, without internal guilt or anxiety, or other external punishments as a release for the pent-up emotion.

According to the JSM, the expression of prejudice is decreased when suppression is maximized and justification is minimized, and prejudice is most likely to be expressed when suppression is minimized and justifications are maximized. Prejudice suppression can be enhanced by extensive practice, egalitarian goal commitment, and having many cognitive resources (e.g., time, attention, energy).

The JSM suggests that genuine prejudice on the basis of weight can come from many sources—media effects, categorization of weight into ingroups and outgroups, competition over scarce resources, classical conditioning of emotions, direct tuition by families and peers, and so on. It is not particularly well-suited to asking "Why is there prejudice based on weight?" Instead, the JSM is best applied to anti-fat prejudice in examining suppression and justifications. Egalitarian values, which are negatively correlated with anti-fat attitudes (e.g., Crandall, 1994), are associated with motives to suppress prejudice (Crandall, Eshleman, & O'Brien, 2002; Katz & Hass, 1988). By contrast, factors that are associated with higher levels of anti-fat attitudes (e.g., Protestant ethic, attributions of responsibility, belief in a just world, negative stereotypes) are associated with greater expressions of anti-fat attitudes. The expression of prejudice and discrimination is complex, and any full account of prejudice on the basis of weight must look not only at the affective state of prejudice, but also the moderators, suppressors, and justifications of that prejudice.

WHAT IS REMARKABLE, UNUSUAL, OR UNIQUE ABOUT WEIGHT-BASED PREJUDICE?

Prejudice against heavyweight people is similar to gender and ethnic prejudice in many important ways. All of these characteristics are visible, almost immediately perceived, and usually central to the perception of the target (Schneider, 2004). There are powerful stereotypes about all of these groups, and across a wide range of contexts—workplace, friendships, education, health care—there are many potential disadvantages to being a member of these groups. In all of these cases, the relative position of groups is closely connected to cultural values—the prejudice and discrimination against these groups is closely connected to religion, fundamental cultural values about work, pleasure, and justice. None of these prejudices can be understood alone, but rather must be understood as part of a complex cultural worldview and social ideology.

PEOPLE ARE RESPONSIBLE FOR THEIR WEIGHT

The stigma of weight differs from many other stigmas in important and interesting ways. Perhaps the most important difference is that weight is seen as mutable—the afflicted are seen as responsible for their condition (e.g., Tiggemann & Rothblum, 1997), and capable of becoming significantly leaner (e.g., Price et al., 1987). This kind of perception leads to attributions of responsibility, a circumstance that is highly predictive of anti-fat attitudes (Crandall, 1994; Crandall et al., 2001; Crandall & Horstman Reser, 2005; Weiner, Perry, & Magnusson, 1988). The fact that adiposity and body shape are mostly biologically determined, with a very large genetic contribution and a substantial cultural environment component, has not yet reached most members of the Western public (see Kolata, 2007). People are rarely personally blamed for their gender or race.

WEIGHT IS ESCAPABLE

Although people rarely leave their gender or ethnic groups, many people actively seek to lose weight and their heavyweight status—in the United States, dieting and weight loss is a $55 billion-a-year industry (Marketdata Enterprises, 2006). One of the most important buffers against prejudice and discrimination for racial, religious, and ethnic minorities, and also for women is to identify strongly with their group, to connect with other members of their group, and build a positive and stable sense of self, connected to their group membership (e.g., Branscombe, Schmitt, & Harvey, 1999; McCoy & Major, 2003; Noel, 1964). However, when people are members of low-status or devalued groups, but see their status as malleable, with the availability of social mobility through permeable boundaries into a higher status group, they fail to identify with their own group, avoid identification with the group, and do not pursue strategies of social change and group improvement (Ellemers, 1991; Ellemers, van Knippenberg, de Vries, & Wilke, 1988). Although diets rarely work, and are not a realistic strategy for individual improvement, the belief that they could work cuts heavyweight people off from one of the most effective strategies for well-being—they do not show ingroup bias and do not strongly identify with their group (see Crandall, 1994).

SOCIAL NORMS ABOUT EXPRESSION

There are powerful social norms in the United States and Canada that suppress the overt expression of prejudice against women and racial minorities (e.g., Devine, Plant, Amodio, & Harmon-Jones, 2002; Legault, Green-Demers, Grant, & Chung, 2007). These norms exist for anti-fat attitudes as well, but they are significantly weaker (see Crandall et al., 2002, Table 1). In some ways, research about anti-fat prejudice is more straightforward, in that it is not as hard to find people who will overtly agree with negative statements such as "I really don't like fat people much" (Crandall, 1994). Comparable items measuring racial, ethnic, and gender items lost this unsubtle content many years ago (Biernat & Crandall, 1999). Although much of the research on racial prejudice—and plenty on gender as well—in the current century has focused on subtle and implicit biases and neurological phenomena (e.g., Nosek, 2007; Richeson, et al., 2003), and some of this has been applied to weight prejudice (Bessenoff & Sherman, 2002), it is still possible to study overt and unsubtle prejudice against fat people. Some prejudices seem to have gone underground, whereas others remain in plain sight. The field of stereotyping and prejudice needs a theory of social change—a focus many decades ago that seems to have been lost (Bettelheim & Janowitz, 1964).

Is Obesity Related Research Biased Against the Null Hypothesis?

When one reviews the kinds of effects discrimination researchers look at, we find education, employment, and marriage in many of them. Certainly there is discrimination in employment with respect to gender and race—these literatures are vast, reporting a wide range of effects. This chapter reviews some of these areas for weight-based prejudice, and reports many of the same effects. However, there is a kind of confirmation bias in these studies—researchers sensibly set out to locate effects that seem likely to be present. Common sense and past history guide researchers, as they should. In addition, however, there is also a confirmation bias that may be based in stereotyping—researchers look for differences among groups (based on gender, ethnicity, or weight) that are stereotype relevant. This reveals effects on employment and education, but we found surprisingly few decrements in personal relationships for heavyweight participants—this finding is interesting in part because it seems counterstereotypic.

However, stereotyping and prejudice researchers should not be so affected by stereotypes in defining the domains they study. We know very little about whether heavyweight people have different rates of drug use, alcohol abuse, crime, auto accidents, work, and farm-related accidents. Do we research areas where stigmatized groups are likely to excel? Do we define, a priori, those areas that matter to people's lives, and then study them regardless of our preconceived notions of whether the domain is relevant? We suggest that scientists do not follow such a strategy, but that much could be learned by exercising it.

SUMMARY AND CONCLUSIONS

Prejudice based on weight affects an ever-growing body of people across many of the most important dimensions of life. It rivals all other prejudices in terms of breadth of impact, the number of people affected, and the lack of group-based strategies for social change. Any understanding of prejudice as a phenomenon must look across the wide range of targets of prejudice, and weight-based prejudice helps reveal the complexity and texture of prejudice.

REFERENCES

Aberson, C. L., Healy, M., & Romero, V. (2000). Ingroup bias and self-esteem: A meta-analysis. *Personality and Social Psychology Review, 4,* 157–173.

Allison, D. B., & Casey, D. E. (2001). Antipsychotic-induced weight gain: A review of the literature. *Journal of Clinical Psychiatry, 62*(Suppl. 7), 22–31.

Allison, D. B., Neale, M. C., Kezis, M. I., Alfonso, C., Heshka, S., & Heymsfield, S. B. (1996). Assortative mating for relative weight: Genetic implications. *Behavior Genetics, 26*(2), 103–111.

Anderson, C. B., Hughes, S. O., Fisher, J. O., & Nicklas, T. A. (2005). Cross-cultural equivalence of feeding beliefs and practices: The psychometric properties of the child feeding questionnaire among Blacks and Hispanics. *Preventive Medicine, 41,* 521–531.

Argyle, M. (1994). *The psychology of social class.* London: Routledge.

Ayala, G. X., Mickens, L., Galindo, P., & Elder, J. P. (2007). Acculturation and body image perception among Latino youth. *Ethnicity and Health, 12,* 21–41.

Bellizzi, J. A., & Hasty, R. W. (1998). Territory assignment decisions and supervising unethical selling behavior: The effects of obesity and gender as moderated by job-related factors. *Journal of Personal Selling and Sales Management, 18,* 35–49.

Bessenoff, G.R. & Sherman, J.W. (2000). Automatic and controlled components of prejudice toward fat people: Evaluation versus stereotype activation. *Social Cognition, 18*, 329–353.

Bettelheim, B., & Janowitz, M. (1964). *Social change and prejudice.* New York: Collier-Macmillan.

Biernat, M., & Crandall, C. S. (1999). Racial attitudes. In J. Robinson, P. Shaver, & L. Wrightsman (Eds.), *Measures of political attitudes* (2nd ed., pp. 297–411). New York: Academic.

Blumberg, P., & Mellis L. P. (1985). Medical students' attitudes toward the obese and the morbidly obese. *International Journal of Eating Disorders, 4,* 169–175.

Branscombe, N. R., Schmitt, M. T., & Harvey, R. D. (1999). Perceiving pervasive discrimination among African Americans: Implications for group identification and well-being. *Journal of Personality and Social Psychology, 77,* 135–149.

Bretytspraak, L. M., McGee, J., Conger, J. C., Whatley, J. L., & Moore, J. T. (1977). Sensitizing medical students to impression formation processes in the patient interview. *Journal of Medical Education, 52,* 47–54.

Brewer, M.B. (1979). In-group bias in the minimal intergroup situation: A cognitive motivational analysis. *Psychological Bulletin, 86,* 307–324.

Brewer, M. R. (1991). The social self: On being the same and different at the same time. *Personality and Social Psychology Bulletin, 17,* 475–482.

Britz, B., Siegfried, W., Ziegler, A., Lamertz, C., Herpertz-Dahlmann, B. M., Remschmidt, H., et al. (2000). Rates of psychiatric disorders in a clinical study group of adolescents with extreme obesity and in obese adolescents ascertained via a population based study. *International Journal of Obesity, 24,* 1707–1714.

Brown, P. J., & Konner, M. (1987). An anthropological perspective on obesity. *Annals of the New York Academy of Sciences, 499,* 29–46.

Brownell, K.D., Puhl, R.M., Schwartz, M.B. & Rudd, L. (Eds.) (2005). *Weight bias: Nature, extent, and remedies.* New York: Guilford Press.

Cachelin, F. M., & Regan, P. C. (2006). Prevalence and correlates of chronic dieting in a multi-ethnic U.S. community sample. *Eating and Weight Disorders, 11,* 91–99.

Canning, H., & Mayer, J. (1966). Obesity: Its possible effect on college acceptance. *New England Journal of Medicine, 275,* 1172–1174.

Cawley, J., Joyner, K., & Sobal, J. (2006). Size matters: The influence of adolescents' weight and height on dating and sex. *Rationality and Society, 18,* 67–94.

Chen, E. Y., & Brown, M. (2005). Obesity stigma in sexual relationships. *Obesity Research, 13,* 1393–1397.

Cossrow, N. H., Jeffrey, R. W., & McGuire, M. T. (2001). Understanding weight stigmatization: A focus group study. *Journal of Nutrition Education, 33,* 208–214.

Cottrell, C. A., & Neuberg, S. L. (2005). Different emotional reactions to different groups: A sociofunctional threat-based approach to "prejudice." *Journal of Personality and Social Psychology, 88,* 770–789.

Cramer, P., & Steinwert, T. (1998). Thin is good, fat is bad: How early does it begin? *Journal of Applied Developmental Psychology, 19,* 429–451.

Crandall, C.S. (1991). Do heavyweight students have more difficulty paying for college? *Personality and Social Psychology Bulletin, 17,* 606-611.

Crandall, C. S. (1994). Prejudice against fat people: Ideology and self-interest. *Journal of Personality and Social Psychology, 66,* 882–894.

Crandall, C. S. (1995). Do parents discriminate against their own heavyweight daughters? *Personality and Social Psychology Bulletin, 21,* 724–735.

Crandall, C. S., & Biernat, M. (1990). The ideology of anti-fat attitudes. *Journal of Applied Social Psychology, 20,* 227–243.

Crandall, C. S., D'Anello, S., Sakalli, N., Lazarus, E., Nejtardt, G. W., & Feather, N. T. (2001). An attribution-value model of prejudice: Anti-fat attitudes in six nations. *Personality and Social Psychology Bulletin, 27,* 30–37.

Crandall, C. S., & Eshleman, A. (2003). A justification-suppression model of the expression and experience of prejudice. *Psychological Bulletin, 129,* 414–446.

Crandall, C. S., Eshleman, A., & O'Brien, L. T. (2002). Social norms and the expression and suppression of prejudice: The struggle for internalization. *Journal of Personality and Social Psychology, 82,* 359–378.

Crandall, C. S., & Horstman Reser, A. (2005). Attributions and weight-based prejudice. In K. D. Brownell, R. M. Puhl, & M. B. Schwartz (Eds.), *Weight bias: Nature, consequences and remedies* (pp. 83–96). New York: Guilford.

Crandall, C.S. & Martinez, R. (1996). Culture, ideology, and anti-fat attitudes. Personality and Social Psychology Bulletin, 22, 1165-1176.

Crandall, C.S. & Schiffhauer, K.L. (1998). Anti-fat prejudice: Beliefs, values and American culture. *Obesity Research, 6,* 458-461.

Crandall, C. S., Schiffhauer, K. L., & Harvey, R. (1997). Friendship pair similarity as a measure of group value. *Group Dynamics, 1,* 133–143.

Crocker, J., Cornwell, B., & Major, B. (1993). The stigma of overweight: Affective consequences of attributional ambiguity. *Journal of Personality and Social Psychology, 60,* 218–228.

Crocker, J., & Luhtanen, R. (1990). Collective self-esteem and ingroup bias. *Journal of Personality and Social Psychology, 58,* 60–67.

Crocker, J., & Major, B. (1989). Social stigma and self-esteem: The self-protective properties of stigma. *Psychological Review, 96,* 608–630.

Datar, A., Sturm, R., & Magnabosco, J. L. (2004). Childhood overweight and academic performance: National study of kindergartners and first-graders. *Obesity Research, 12,* 58–68.

Davison, K. K., & Birch, L. L. (2004). Predictors of fat stereotypes among 9-year-old girls and their parents. *Obesity Research, 12,* 86–94.

Decker, W. H. (1987). Attributions based on managers' self-presentation, sex, and weight. *Psychological Reports, 61,* 175–181.

De Garine, I. (1995). *Social aspects of obesity.* New York: Routledge.

DeJong, W. (1980). The stigma of obesity: The consequences of naive assumptions concerning the causes of physical deviance. *Journal of Health and Social Behavior, 21,* 75–87.

DeJong, W., & Kleck, R. E. (1981). The social psychological effects of overweight. In C. P. Herman, M. P. Zanna, & E. T. Higgins (Eds.), *Physical appearance, stigma, and social behavior* (pp. 65–87). Hillsdale, NJ: Erlbaum.

Devine, P. G., Plant, E. A., Amodio, D., & Harmon-Jones, E. (2002). The regulation of explicit and implicit race bias: The role of motivations to respond without prejudice. *Journal of Personality and Social Psychology, 82,* 835–848.

Eisenberg, M. E., & Neumark-Sztainer, D. (2005). Weight-teasing and emotional well-being in young adults: Longitudinal findings from Project EAT. *Journal of Adolescent Health, 36,* 100–101.

Eisenberg, M. E., Neumark-Sztainer, D., Haines, J., & Wall, M. (2006). Weight-teasing and emotional well-being in adolescents: Longitudinal findings from Project EAT. *Journal of Adolescent Health, 38,* 675–683.

Ellemers, N. (1991). *Identity management strategies: The influence of socio-structural variables on strategies of individual mobility and social change.* Gronigen, The Netherlands: Rijkuniversiteit Gronigen.

Ellemers, N., van Knippenberg, A., de Vries, N., & Wilke, H. (1988). Social identification and permeability of group boundaries. *European Journal of Social Psychology, 18,* 497–513.

Feingold, A., & Mazzella, R. (1998). Gender differences in body image are increasing. *Psychological Science, 9,* 190–195.

Fikkan, J., & Rothblum, E. (2005). Weight bias in employment. In K. D. Brownell, R. M. Puhl, M. B. Schwartz, & L. Rudd (Eds.), *Weight bias: Nature, consequences, and remedies* (pp. 15–28). New York: Guilford.

Fiske, S. T., Cuddy, A. J. C., Glick, P., & Xu, J. (2002). A model of (often mixed) stereotype content: Competence and warmth respectively follow from perceived status and competition. *Journal of Personality and Social Psychology, 82,* 878–902.

French, S. A., Story, M., & Perry, C. L. (1995). Self-esteem and obesity in children and adolescents: A literature review. *Obesity Research, 3,* 479–490.

Frieze, I. M., Olson, J. E., & Good, D. C. (1990). Perceived and actual discrimination in the salaries of male and female managers. *Journal of Applied Social Psychology, 20,* 46–67.

Fu, H., & Goldman, N. (1996). Incorporating health into models of marriage choice: Demographic and sociological perspectives. *Journal of Marriage and the Family, 58,* 740–758.

Gallagher, S. M. (1996). Meeting the needs of the obese patient. *American Journal of Nursing, 96,* 1S–12S.

Gallagher S. M. (1998). Caring for obese patients. *Nursing, 43,* 32HN1–32HN3.

Galuska, D. A., Will, J. C., Serdula, M. K., & Ford, E. S. (1999). Are health care professionals advising obese patients to lose weight? *Journal of the American Medical Association, 282,* 1576–1578.

Gawande, A. (2007). *Better: A surgeon's notes on performance.* New York: Metropolitan Books.

Gomez-Peresmitre, G., Griselda, A. H., Liliana-Moreno, E., Sugey-Saloma, G., & Gisela-Pineda, G. (2001). Trastornos de la alimentacion: factores de riesgo en tres diferentes grupos de edad: Pre-puberes, puberes y adolescentes [Eating disorders: Risk factors in three different age groups: Prepubescent, pubescent and adolescent]. *Revista Mexicana de Psicologia, 18,* 313–324.

Gortmaker, S. L., Must, A., Perrin, J. M., Sobol, A. M., & Dietz, W. H. (1993). Social and economic consequences of overweight in adolescence and young adulthood. *New England Journal of Medicine, 329,* 1008–1012.

Groopman, J. (2007). *How doctors think.* New York: Houghton Mifflin.

Haines, J., Neumark-Sztainer, D., Eisenberg, M. E., & Hannan, P. J. (2006). Weight-teasing and disordered eating behaviors in adolescents: Longitudinal findings from Project EAT (Eating Among Teens). *Pediatrics, 117,* 209–215.

Harris, M. B. (1990). Is love seen as different for the obese? *Journal of Applied Social Psychology, 20,* 1209–1224.

Harris, M. B., Harris, R. J., & Bochner, S. (1982). Fat, four-eyed, and female: Stereotypes of obesity, glasses, and gender. *Journal of Applied Social Psychology, 12,* 503–516.

Harris, M. B., Walters, L. C. & Waschull, S. (1991). Gender and ethnic differences in obesity-related behaviors and attitudes in a college sample. *Journal of Applied Social Psychology, 21,* 1545-1566.

Hebl, M. R., & Heatherton, T. F. (1998). The stigma of obesity in women: The difference is black and white. *Personality and Social Psychology Bulletin, 24,* 417–426.

Hebl, M. R., & Kleck, R. E. (2002). Acknowledging one's stigma in the interview setting: Effective strategy or liability? *Journal of Applied Social Psychology, 32,* 223–249.

Hebl, M. R., & Mannix, L. M. (2003). The weight of obesity in evaluative others: A mere proximity effect. *Personality and Social Psychology Bulletin, 29,* 28–38.

Hebl, M. R., & Turchin, J. M. (2005). The stigma of obesity: What about men? *Basic and Applied Social Psychology, 27,* 267–275.

Hebl, M. R. & Xu, J. (2001). Weighing the care: Physicians' reactions to the size of a patient. International *Journal of Obesity, 25,* 1246-1252.

Hebl, M. R., Xu, J. & Mason, M. F. (2003). Weighing the care: patients' perceptions of physician care as a function of gender and weight. *International Journal of Obesity and Related Metabolic Disorders, 27,* 269–275.

Hogg, M. A., & Abrams, D. (1990). *Social identifications: A social psychology of intergroup relations and group processes.* London: Routledge.

Hudson, J. I., Hiripi, E., Pope, H. G., Jr., & Kessler, R. C. (2007). The prevalence and correlates of eating disorders in the National Comorbidity Survey Replication. *Biological Psychiatry, 61,* 348–358.

Jasper, C. R., & Klassen, M. L. (1990). Perceptions of salespersons' appearance and evaluation of job performance. *Perceptual and Motor Skills, 71,* 563–566.

Jost, J. T., & Banaji, M. R. (1994). The role of stereotyping in system justification and the production of false consciousness. *British Journal of Social Psychology, 33,* 1–27.

Jost, J. T., Pelham, B. W., & Carvallo, M. R. (2002). Non-conscious forms of system justification: Implicit and behavioral preferences for higher status groups. *Journal of Experimental Social Psychology, 83,* 586–602.

Katz, I., & Hass, R. G. (1988). Racial ambivalence and American value conflict: Correlational and priming studies of dual cognitive structures. *Journal of Personality and Social Psychology, 55,* 893–905.

King, E., Hebl, M., & Heatherton, T. F. (2005). Theories of stigma: Limitations and needed direction. In K. D. Brownell, R. M. Puhl, & M. B. Schwartz (Eds.), *Bias, stigma, discrimination, and obesity* (pp. 109–120). New York: Guilford.

King, E., Shapiro, J. L., Hebl, M., Singletary, S., & Turner, S. (2006). The stigma of obesity in customer service: A mechanism for remediation and bottom-line consequences of interpersonal discrimination. *Journal of Applied Psychology, 91,* 579–593.

Kolata, G. (2007). *Rethinking thin: The new science of weight loss—and the myths and realities of dieting.* New York: Farrar, Straus & Giroux.

Kraig, K.A. & Keel, P.K. (2001). Weight-based stigmatization in children. *International Journal of Obesity, 25,* 1661-1666.

Kuo, H. K., Jones, R. N., Milberg, W. P., Tennstedt, S., Talbot, L., Morris, J. N., et al. (2006). Cognitive function in normal-weight, overweight, and obese older adults: An analysis of the Advanced Cognitive Training for Independent and Vital Elderly cohort. *Journal of the American Geriatrics Society, 54,* 97–103.

Kurzban, R., & Leary, M. R. (2001). Evolutionary origins of stigmatization: The functions of social exclusion. *Psychological Bulletin, 127,* 187–208.

Kurzban, R., Tooby, J., & Cosmides, L. (2001). Can race be erased? Coalitional computation and social categorization. *Proceedings of the National Academy of Sciences, 98,* 15387–15392.

Lagerspetz, K. M., Kjorkvist, K. A. J., Nerts, M., & King, E. (1982). Group aggression among schoolchildren in three schools. *Scandinavian Journal of Psychology, 23,* 45–52.

Larkin, J. E. & Pines, H. A. (1979). No fat persons need apply. *Sociology of Work and Occupations, 6,* 312–327.

Latner, J. D. & Stunkard, A. J. (2003). Getting worse: the stigmatization of obese children. *Obesity Research, 11,* 452–456.

Legault, L., Green-Demers, I., Grant, P., & Chung, J. (2007). On the self-regulation of implicit and explicit prejudice: A self-determination theory perspective. *Personality and Social Psychology Bulletin, 33,* 732–749.

Macías, J. A. G., Leal, F. J. V., López-Ibor, J. J., Rubio, M. A., & Caballero, M. G. (2004). Marital status in morbidly obese patients after bariatric surgery. *Journal of Psychiatry, 7*(3), 22–27.

Mackie, D. M., Devos, T., & Smith, E. R. (2000). Intergroup emotions: Explaining offensive action tendencies in an intergroup context. *Journal of Personality and Social Psychology, 79,* 602–616.

Maranto, C. L. & Stenoien, A. F. (2000). Weight discrimination: A multidisciplinary analysis. *Employee Responsibilities and Rights Journal, 12,* 9–24.

Marketdata Enterprises. (2006). *The U.S. weight loss and diet control market* (9th ed.). Tampa, FL: Author.

Marshall, J. R., & Neill, J. (1977). The removal of a psychosomatic symptom: Effects on the marriage. *Family Practice, 16,* 273–280.

Martel, R., Lane, D. M., & Willis, C. (1996). Male–female differences: A computer simulation. *American Psychologist, 51,* 157–158.

McCoy, S. K., & Major, B. (2003). Group identification moderates emotional responses to perceived prejudice. *Personality and Social Psychology Bulletin, 29,* 1005–1017.

Miller, C. T., & Downey, K. T. (1999). A meta-analysis of heavyweight and self-esteem. *Personality and Social Psychology Review, 3,* 68–84.

Miller, C. T., Rothblum, E. D., Felicio, D., & Brand, P. (1995). Compensating for stigma: Obese and nonobese women's reactions to being visible. *Personality and Social Psychology Bulletin, 21,* 1093–1106.

Neuberg, S. L., Smith, D. M., & Asher, T. (2000). Why people stigmatize: Toward a biocultural framework. In T. F. Heatherton, R. E. Kleck, M. R. Hebl, & J. G. Hull (Eds.), *The social psychology of stigma* (pp. 31–61). New York: Guilford.

Neumark-Sztainer D. & Eisenberg, M. E. (2005). Weight bias in a teen's world. In K.D. Brownell, R.M. Puhl, M.B. Schwartz & L. Rudd (Eds.) (2005). *Weight bias: Nature, extent, and remedies.* New York: Guilford Press, pp. 68-79.

Neumark-Sztainer, D., Falkner, N., Story, M., Perry, C., Hannan, P., Mulert, S. (2002). Weight-teasing among adolescents: Correlations with weight status and disordered eating behaviors. *International Journal of Obesity, 1,* 123-131.

Neumark-Sztainer, D., Story, M., & Faibisch, L. (1998). Perceived stigmatization among overweight African-American and Caucasian adolescent girls. *Journal of Adolescent Health, 23,* 264–270.

Neumark-Sztainer, D., Story, M., & Harris T. (1999). Beliefs and attitudes about obesity among teachers and school health care providers working with adolescents. *Journal of Nutrition Education, 31,* 3–9.

Noel, D. L. (1964). Group identification among Negroes: An empirical analysis. *Journal of Social Issues, 20,* 71–84.

Nosek, B. A. (2007). Implicit–explicit relations. *Current Directions in Psychological Science, 16,* 65–69.

Olvera, N., Suminski, R., & Power, T. G. (2005). Intergenerational perceptions of body image in Hispanics: Role of BMI, gender, and acculturation. *Obesity Research, 13,* 1970–1979.

Pagan, J. A., & Davila, A. (1997). Obesity, occupational attainment, and earnings. *Social Science Quarterly, 78,* 756–770.

Pargman, D. (1969). The incidence of obesity among college students. *Journal of School Health, 29,* 621-627.

Park, J. H., Schaller, M. & Crandall, C. S. (2007) Pathogen-avoidance mechanisms and the stigmatization of obese people. *Evolution and Human Behavior, 28,* 410-414.

Pearce, M. J., Boergers, J., & Prinstein, M. J. (2002). Adolescent obesity, overt and relational peer victimization, and romantic relationships. *Obesity Research, 10,* 386–393.

Pingitore, R., Dugoni, B. L., Tindale, R. S., & Spring, B. (1994). Bias against overweight job applicants in a simulated employment interview. *Journal of Applied Psychology, 79,* 909–917.

Polinko, N. K., & Popovich, P. M. (2001). Evil thoughts but angelic actions: Responses to overweight job applicants. *Journal of Applied Social Psychology, 31,* 905–924.

Price, J. H., Desmond, S. M., Krol, R. A., Snyder, F. F., & O'Connell, J. K. (1987). Family practice physicians' beliefs, attitudes, and practices regarding overweight. *American Journal of Preventative Medicine, 3,* 339–345.

Price, J. H., Desmond, S. M., Ruppert, E. S., & Stelzer, C. M. (1989). Pediatricians' perceptions and practice regarding childhood overweight. *American Journal of Preventative Medicine, 5,* 95–103.

Rand, C. S., Kowalske, K., & Kuldau, J. M. (1984). Characteristics of marital improvement following obesity surgery. *Psychosomatics, 25,* 221–226.

Regan, P. C. (1996). Sexual outcasts: The perceived impact of body and gender on sexuality. *Journal of Applied Social Psychology, 26,* 1803–1815.

Register, C. A., & Williams, D. R. (1990). Wage effects of obesity among young workers. *Social Science Quarterly, 71,* 130–141.

Rich, S. S., DiMarco, N. M., Huettig, C., Essery, E. V., Andersson, E., & Sanborn, C. F. (2005). Perceptions of health status and play activities in parents of overweight Hispanic toddlers and preschoolers. *Family and Community Health, 28,* 130–141.

Richardson, S. A., Goodman, N., Hastorf, A. H., & Dornbusch, S. M. (1961). Cultural uniformity in reaction to physical disabilities. *American Sociological Review, 26,* 241-247.

Richeson, J. A., Baird, A. A., Gordon, H. L., Heatheron, T. F., Wyland, C. L., Trawalter, S., et al. (2003). An fMRI investigation of the impact of interracial contact on executive function. *Nature Neuroscience, 6,* 1323–1328.

Rodin, J., Silberstein, L., & Striegel-Moore, R. (1984). Women and weight: A normative discontent. *Nebraska Symposium on Motivation, 32,* 267–307.

Roehling, M. V. (1999). Weight-based discrimination in employment: Psychological and legal aspects. *Personnel Psychology, 52,* 969–1016.

Rothblum, E., Brand, R. A., Miller, C. T., & Oetjen, H. A. (1990). The relationship between obesity, employment discrimination, and employment-related victimization. *Journal of Vocational Behavior, 37,* 251–266.

Sargent, J. D., & Blanchflower, D. G. (1994). Obesity and stature in adolescence and earning in young adulthood. *Archives of Pediatric Adolescent Medicine, 148,* 681–687.

Scheepers, D., Spears, R., Doosje, B., & Manstead, A. S. R. (2006). Diversity in in-group bias: Structural factors, situational features, and social functions. *Journal of Personality and Social Psychology, 90,* 944–960.

Schneider, D. J. (2004). *The psychology of stereotyping.* New York: Guilford.

Shapiro, J. R., King, E. B., & Quiñones, M. A. (2007). Expectations of obese trainees: How stigmatized trainee characteristics influence training effectiveness. *Journal of Applied Psychology, 92,* 239-249.

Smith, E. R., & Henry, S. (1996). An in-group becomes part of the self: Response time evidence. *Personality and Social Psychology Bulletin, 22,* 635–642.

Sobal, J., Rauschenbach, B. S., & Frongillo, E. A., Jr. (1995). Obesity and marital quality. *Journal of Family Issues, 16,* 746–764.

Sobal, J., & Stunkard, A. J. (1989). Socioeconomic status and obesity: A review of the literature. *Psychological Bulletin, 105,* 260–275.

Staffieri, J.R. (1967). A study of social stereotype of body image in children. *Journal of Personality and Social Psychology, 7,* 101-104.

Stake, J. & Lauer, M.L. (1987). The consequences of being overweight: A controlled study of gender differences. *Sex Roles, 17,* 31-47.

Strauss, R. S., & Pollack, H. A. (2003). Social marginalization of overweight children. *Archives of Pediatric and Adolescent Medicine, 157,* 746–752.

Striegel-Moore, R. H., & Franko, D. L. (2006). Adolescent eating disorders. In C. A. Essau (Ed.), *Child and adolescent psychopathology: Theoretical and clinical implications* (pp. 160–183). New York: Routledge/ Taylor & Francis.

Tajfel, H., & Turner, J. C. (1979). An integrative theory of intergroup conflict. In W G. Austin & S. Worchel (Eds.), *The social psychology of intergroup relations* (pp. 33-47). Monterey, CA: Brooks/Cole.

Teachman, B. A., & Brownell, K. D. (2001). Implicit anti-fat bias among health professionals: Is anyone immune? *International Journal of Obesity and Metabolic Disorders, 25,* 1525.

Thompson, J.K., Herbozo, S., Himes, S. & Yamamiya, Y. (2005). Effects of weight-related teasing in adults. In K.D. Brownell, R.M. Puhl, M.B. Schwartz & L. Rudd (Eds.) (2005). *Weight bias: Nature, extent, and remedies.* New York: Guilford Press, pp. 137-148.

Tiggemann, M., & Rothblum, E. D. (1988). Gender differences in social consequences of perceived overweight in the United States and Australia. *Sex Roles, 18,* 75–86.

Tiggemann, M., & Rothblum, E. D. (1997).Gender differences in internal beliefs about weight and negative attitudes towards self and others. *Psychology of Women Quarterly, 21,* 581–593.

Troop-Gordon, W., & Ladd, G. W. (2005). Trajectories of peer victimization and perceptions of the self and school-mates: Precursors to internalizing and externalizing problems. *Child Development, 76,* 1072–1091.

Valian, V. (1998). *Why so slow?: The advancement of women.* Cambridge, Massachusetts: The MIT Press.

van Hanswijck de Jonge, P., van Furth, E. F., Lacey, J. H., & Waller, G. (2003). The prevalence of *DSM–IV* personality pathology among individuals with bulimia nervosa, binge eating disorder and obesity. *Psychological Medicine, 33,* 1311–1317.

Wadden, T. A., Brownell, K. D., & Foster, G. D. (2002). Obesity: Responding to the global epidemic. *Journal of Consulting and Clinical Psychology, 70,* 510–525.

Wee, C. C., McCarthy, E. P., Davis, R. B., & Phillips R. S. (1999). Physician counseling about exercise. *Journal of the American Medical Association, 282,* 1583–1588.

Weiler, K., & Helms, L. B. (1993). Responsibilities of nursing education: The lessons of *Russell v. Salve Regina. Journal of Professional Nursing, 9,* 131–138.

Weiner, B., Perry, R. P., & Magnusson, J. (1988). An attributional analysis of reactions to stigmas. *Journal of Personality and Social Psychology, 55,* 738–748.

Young, L. M., & Powell, B. (1985). The effects of overweight on the clinical judgments of mental health professionals. *Journal of Health and Social Behavior, 26,* 233–246.

Zemank, J. E., McIntyre, R. P., & Zemanek, A. (1998). Salespersons' weight and ratings of characteristics related to effectiveness of selling. *Psychological Reports, 82,* 947–952.

24 A Common Ingroup Identity
A Categorization-Based Approach for Reducing Intergroup Bias

Samuel L. Gaertner
University of Delaware

John F. Dovidio
Yale University

One direct or indirect benefit of exploring the intricacies of prejudice, stereotyping, and discrimination is the potential to learn how to reduce, eliminate, or reverse the processes that initiate and maintain these manifestations of intergroup conflict. Although psychologists have learned much about the intricacies of these phenomena, current events compellingly demonstrate that researchers still have much to learn about reducing intergroup hostility.

The place to begin may well involve those processes implicated in the origins of intergroup conflict and bias. Indeed, the causes of prejudice have been traced theoretically to many forces, including intraindividual, psychodynamic (Adorno, Frenkel-Brunswik, Levinson, & Sanford, 1950), cognitive (Doise, 1978; Tajfel, 1969), cognitive-motivational (Tajfel & Turner, 1979; Turner, 1975), interpersonal (Dovidio & Gaertner, 2004), institutional (Feagin, 2006), and cultural (Jones, 1997) factors.

In addition to the varied causes of prejudice, the actual nature of prejudice itself may be complex and varied. Whereas traditional forms of prejudice are direct and overt, contemporary forms may be indirect and subtle. For example, aversive racism is a modern form of prejudice that characterizes the racial attitudes of many White adults who genuinely regard themselves as nonprejudiced, but who have not completely escaped cultural, cognitive, and motivational forces that promote racial bias (Dovidio & Gaertner, 2004; Gaertner & Dovidio, 1986; see also Kovel, 1970).

One basic assertion we have made in our research on aversive racism is that the negative feelings that develop toward other groups may be rooted, in part, in fundamental, normal psychological processes. One such process, identified in the classic work of Allport (1954) and Tajfel (1969) and others, is the categorization of people into ingroups and outgroups—"we" and "they." People respond systematically more favorably to others whom they perceive to belong to their group than to different groups. Thus, if prejudice is linked to fundamental, normal psychological processes that operate consistently, then attempts to ameliorate it should be directed not at eliminating the process but rather at redirecting the forces to produce more harmonious intergroup relations. By shifting the basis of categorization from race to an alternative dimension shared by African Americans and European Americans who may be interacting, it might be possible to alter who is a "we" and who is a "they" through recategorization, and thereby undermine a potentially contributing force to intergroup biases.

In this chapter, we summarize research on a prejudice reduction strategy, the common ingroup identity model (Gaertner & Dovidio, 2000; Gaertner, Dovidio, Anastasio, Bachman, & Rust, 1993), which has guided our work on the reduction of intergroup bias. This work has found converging evidence across a variety of laboratory and field experiments, as well as cross-sectional and longitudinal surveys involving participants ranging in age from elementary school children to corporate executives who experienced a corporate merger. In this chapter, we first discuss the impact of social categorization on adults' and children's attitudes toward members of other groups.

SOCIAL CATEGORIZATION

One facet of human thinking essential for efficient functioning, which is critical for all age groups, including infants (see Kelly et al., 2007; Kelly et al., 2005), is the ability to sort the many different objects, events, and people encountered quickly and effectively into a smaller number of meaningful categories (Hamilton & Trolier, 1986; Hamilton & Sherman, 1994). Categorization enables decisions to be made quickly about incoming information because the instant an object is categorized, it is assigned the properties shared by other category members. Time-consuming consideration of each new experience is forfeited because it is usually wasteful and unnecessary. Categorization often occurs spontaneously on the basis of physical similarity, proximity, or shared fate (Campbell, 1958).

Social categorization not only produces greater reliance on heuristic, relative to more detailed and elaborative processing, but also it produces systematic social biases in evaluations of others. Attraction and prejudice are fundamentally related to social categorization and to the perception of intergroup boundaries that define who is included in one's own group (a "we") and who is excluded (a "they").

CATEGORIZATION AND BIAS

When people or objects are categorized into groups, actual differences between members of the same category tend to be perceptually minimized (Tajfel, 1969) and are often ignored in making decisions or forming impressions. Members of the same category seem to be more similar than they actually are, and more similar than they were before they were categorized together. In addition, although members of a social category may be different in some ways from members of other categories, these differences tend to become exaggerated and overgeneralized. Thus, categorization enhances perceptions of similarities within groups and differences between groups are emphasized, leading to distorted perceptions of social difference and group distinctiveness. For social categorization, this process becomes more ominous because these within- and between-group distortions have a tendency to generalize to additional dimensions (e.g., character traits) beyond those that differentiated the categories originally (Allport, 1954).

Moreover, in the process of categorizing people into two groups, people typically classify themselves into one of the social categories and out of the other. The insertion of the self into the social categorization process increases the emotional significance of group differences and thus leads to further perceptual distortion and evaluative biases that reflect favorably on the ingroup (Sumner, 1906), and consequently on the self (Tajfel & Turner, 1979). In social identity theory, Tajfel and Turner (1979) proposed that a person's need for positive self-identity may be satisfied by one's own accomplishments as well as by membership in prestigious social groups. This need for positive distinctiveness motivates social comparisons that favorably differentiate the self from others, as well as ingroups from outgroups. In addition, individuals frequently derive material benefit, receive valuable information, and experience a sense of belonging and security from the ingroup (Correll & Park, 2005). Perhaps one reason ethnocentrism is so prevalent is because these biases operate even when the basis for the categorization is quite trivial, such as when group identity is assigned randomly on the basis of unfamiliar, fictitious personality dimensions (Billig & Tajfel, 1973).

On social categorization of people as members of the ingroup and of outgroups, people favor ingroup members in reward allocations (Tajfel, Billig, Bundy, & Flament, 1971), esteem (Rabbie, 1982), and the evaluation of the products of their labor (Ferguson & Kelley, 1964). Also, ingroup membership decreases psychological distance and facilitates the arousal of promotive tension or empathy (Hornstein, 1976). Moreover, empathy has a more significant impact for helping ingroup than outgroup members (Stürmer, Snyder, & Omoto, 2005). Also, prosocial behavior is offered more readily to ingroup than to outgroup members (Piliavin, Dovidio, Gaertner, & Clark, 1981). In addition, people are more likely to be cooperative and exercise more personal restraint when using endangered common resources when these are shared with ingroup members than with others (Kramer & Brewer, 1984).

In terms of information processing, people retain more information in a more detailed fashion for ingroup members than for outgroup members (Park & Rothbart, 1982), have better memory for information about ways ingroup members are similar and outgroup members are dissimilar to the self (Wilder, 1981), and remember less positive information about outgroup members (Howard & Rothbart, 1980). In addition, people are more generous and forgiving in their explanations for the behaviors of ingroup relative to outgroup members. Positive behaviors and successful outcomes are more likely to be attributed to internal, stable characteristics (the personality) of ingroup than outgroup members, whereas negative outcomes are more likely to be ascribed to the personalities of outgroup members than of ingroup members (Hewstone, 1990; Pettigrew, 1979). Relatedly, observed behaviors of ingroup and outgroup members are encoded in memory at different levels of abstraction (Maass, Salvi, Arcuri, & Semin, 1989). Undesirable actions of outgroup members are encoded at more abstract levels that presume intentionality and dispositional origin (e.g., she is hostile) than identical behaviors of ingroup members (e.g., she slapped the girl). Desirable actions of outgroup members, however, are encoded at more concrete levels (e.g., she walked across the street holding the old man's hand) relative to the same behaviors of ingroup members (e.g., she is helpful).

These cognitive biases help to perpetuate social biases and stereotypes even in the face of countervailing evidence. For example, because positive behaviors of outgroup members are encoded at relatively concrete levels, it becomes less likely that counterstereotypic positive behaviors would generalize across situations or other outgroup members (see also Karpinski & von Hippel, 1996). People do not remember that an outgroup member was "helpful," but only the very concrete descriptive actions. Thus, outgroup stereotypes containing information pertaining to traits, dispositions, or intentions are not likely to be influenced by observing counterstereotypic outgroup behaviors.

Language plays another role in intergroup bias through associations with collective pronouns. Collective pronouns such as we or they that are used to define people's ingroup or outgroup status are frequently paired with stimuli having strong affective connotations. As a consequence, these pronouns may acquire powerful evaluative properties of their own. These words (we, they) can potentially increase the availability of positive or negative associations and thereby influence beliefs about, evaluations of, and behaviors toward other people, often automatically and unconsciously (Perdue, Dovidio, Gurtman, & Tyler, 1990).

Whereas social categorization can initiate intergroup biases, the type of bias due largely to categorization primarily represents a pro-ingroup orientation (i.e., preference for ingroup members) rather than an anti-outgroup orientation usually associated with hostility or aggression. Nevertheless, disadvantaged status due to preferential treatment of one group over another can be as pernicious as discrimination based on anti-outgroup orientations (Murrell, Dietz-Uhler, Dovidio, Gaertner, & Drout, 1994). Pro-ingroup biases can also provide a foundation for generating hostility and conflict that can result from intergroup competition for economic resources and political power.

Because categorization is a basic process that is also fundamental to intergroup bias, social psychologists have targeted this process as a place to begin to improve intergroup relations. In the next section we explore how the forces of categorization can be harnessed and redirected toward the elimination of intergroup bias.

CATEGORIZATION-BASED MODELS OF BIAS REDUCTION

The process of social categorization is not completely unalterable. Categories are hierarchically organized, and higher level categories (e.g., university) are more inclusive of lower level ones (e.g., psychology department). By modifying a perceiver's goals, motives, past experiences, expectations, factors within the immediate perceptual field and the situational context more broadly, there is opportunity to alter the level of category inclusiveness that will be primary in a given situation (see Wilder, 1981). That is, it may be possible to encourage *decategorization* in which the salience of group boundaries weakens and people from different groups regard one another primarily as distinct individuals and interact in interpersonal (i.e., me and you) rather than group-based (e.g., we vs. they) modes of relating to one another (e.g., see Fiske, Lin, & Neuberg, 1999; Miller & Brewer, 1984; Tajfel & Turner, 1979). In addition, if decategorization occurs through personalized interactions, in which information about each other's unique qualities is exchanged, intergroup bias will be further reduced by undermining the validity of the outgroup stereotypes (Brewer & Miller, 1984; Miller, 2002; Miller, Brewer, & Edwards, 1985).

Brewer and Miller (1984) offered a conceptually unifying theoretical framework that proposed that the features specified by the contact hypothesis (e.g., equal status, cooperative interaction, self-revealing interaction, and supportive norms) share the capacity to decategorize group boundaries and to promote more differentiated and personalized conceptions, particularly of outgroup members. With a more differentiated representation of outgroup members, there is the recognition that there are different types of outgroup members (e.g., sensitive as well as tough professional hockey players), thereby weakening the effects of categorization and the tendency to perceptually minimize and ignore differences between category members. When personalized interactions occur, ingroup and outgroup members slide even further toward the individual side of the self as individual–group member continuum. Members "attend to information that replaces category identity as the most useful basis for classifying each other" (Brewer & Miller, 1984, p. 288).

During personalization, members focus on information about an outgroup member that is relevant to the self (as an individual rather than self as a group member). Repeated personalized interactions with a variety of outgroup members should over time undermine the value of the category stereotype as a source of information about members of that group. Thus, the effects of personalization would be expected to generalize to new situations as well as to heretofore unfamiliar outgroup members. For the benefits of personalization to generalize, however, it is of course necessary for outgroup members' group identities to be salient, although not primary, during the interaction to enable the group stereotype to be weakened.

A number of experimental studies provide evidence supporting this theoretical perspective (Bettencourt, Brewer, Croak, & Miller, 1992; Marcus-Newhall, Miller, Holtz, & Brewer, 1993; Miller et al., 1985). In Miller et al. (1985), for example, contact that permitted more personalized interactions (e.g., when interaction was person focused rather than task focused) resulted not only in more positive attitudes toward those outgroup members present, but to other outgroup members viewed on video. Thus, these conditions of intergroup contact reduced bias in both an immediate and generalizable fashion.

Although there are similarities between perceiving ingroup and outgroup members as "separate individuals" and having "personalized interactions" with outgroup members, these are related but theoretically distinct concepts. Personalization involves receiving self-relevant, more intimate information about members of the outgroup, such that each can be differentiated from the others in relation to comparisons with the self. In contrast, perceiving either outgroup members (see Wilder, 1986) or both memberships structurally as "separate individuals" denotes perceiving them as individuals, not as groups. It does not necessarily imply that this perception is based on information exchange. For example, strangers waiting for a bus may regard themselves as separate individuals, as opposed to a group. Thus, increasing the perception that outgroup members are separate individuals by revealing variability in their opinions or having outgroup members respond as individuals rather than as a group renders each member more distinctive and thus potentially blurs the prior categorization scheme (Wilder, 1978). Another decategorization strategy of repeatedly criss-crossing category memberships, by forming new subgroups each composed of members from former subgroups, changes the pattern of who is "in" and who is "out" (Brewer, Ho, Lee, & Miller, 1987;

Commins & Lockwood, 1978; Deschamps & Doise, 1978; Vanbeselaere, 1987) and can also render the earlier categorization less salient (Brown & Turner, 1979).

Whereas personalization and crossed categorization (see Crisp & Hewstone, 2006) strategies are designed to degrade group boundaries, another approach acknowledges the difficulty of eliminating perceptions of group identities and instead focuses on changing perceptions of the relationship between the groups while emphasizing the positive distinctiveness of each group.

Brown and Hewstone (2005; see also Hewstone & Brown, 1986) posited that intergroup relations will be harmonious when group identities remain mutually differentiated, rather than threatened by extinction, but maintained in the context of cooperative intergroup interaction. From the perspective of social identity theory, threats to group distinctiveness associated with high degrees of similarity between groups or attempts to degrade intergroup boundaries motivates members to reestablish positive group distinctiveness, a goal that is achieved by regarding one's ingroup as better than the other group. Thus, relative to the personalization or the purely one-group strategies, this mutual intergroup differentiation perspective proposes that maintaining group distinctiveness within a cooperative intergroup relationship would be associated with low levels of intergroup threat and, consequently, with lower levels of intergroup bias. In addition, the salience of intergroup boundaries provides an associative mechanism through which changes in outgroup attitudes that occur during intergroup contact can generalize to the outgroup as a whole.

Alternatively, it may be possible to promote a recategorization of group boundaries such that people from different groups conceive of themselves as members of the same more inclusive group, and thus see themselves as people with a common ingroup affiliation. In particular, Allport (1954) proposed that shifting the focus from membership at a more differentiated level, such as racial groups, to a more inclusive level, such as national or human identity, could undermine the type of categorization that leads to violence between racial or ethnic groups.

For recategorization and decategorization, reducing the salience of the original group boundaries is expected to decrease intergroup bias. With recategorization as proposed by the common ingroup identity model (Gaertner & Dovidio, 2000), if members of different groups are induced to conceive of themselves as a single more inclusive, superordinate group, rather than just as two completely separate groups, attitudes toward former outgroup members should become more positive through processes involving pro-ingroup bias. In terms of decategorization, if these memberships are induced to conceive of themselves or others as separate individuals (Wilder, 1981) or to have more personalized interactions with one another, intergroup bias should also be reduced (Brewer & Miller, 1984), but in ways that possibly degrade these pro-ingroup biases.

Theoretically, the rationale for these changes in intergroup bias rests on two conclusions from Brewer's (1979) analysis that relate nicely to social identity theory (Tajfel & Turner, 1979; Turner, 1975) and self-categorization theory (Turner, 1985). First, intergroup bias often takes the form of in-group enhancement rather than out-group devaluation. Second, the formation of a group brings ingroup members closer to the self, whereas the distance between the self and non-ingroup members remains relatively unchanged. Thus, on ingroup formation or when an individual assumes a group-level identification, the egocentric biases that favor the self are transferred to other ingroup members. Thus, increasing the inclusiveness of group boundaries enables some of those cognitive and motivational processes that contributed initially to intergroup bias to be redirected or transferred to former outgroup members. If ingroup and outgroup members are induced to conceive of themselves as separate individuals rather than as group members, former ingroup members would no longer benefit from the egocentric biases transferred to the group on self-identification as a group member.

The recategorization and decategorization strategies and their respective means of reducing bias were directly examined in a laboratory study (Gaertner, Mann, Murrell, & Dovidio, 1989). In this experiment members of two separate laboratory-formed groups were induced through various structural interventions (e.g., seating arrangement) either to recategorize themselves as one superordinate group or to decategorize themselves and to conceive of themselves as separate individuals. Supportive of the value of altering the level of category inclusiveness, these changes in the perceptions of intergroup boundaries reduced bias. Furthermore, as expected, these strategies reduced bias in different ways. Recategorizing ingroup and outgroup members as members of a more inclusive group reduced bias by increasing the attractiveness of former outgroup members, whereas decategorizing members of each group reduced bias by decreasing the attractiveness of former ingroup members. Nearly identical patterns of findings were obtained by Guerra, Rebelo, and Monteiro (2004) and by Rebelo, Guerra, and Monteiro (2004) among 9- and 10- year-old children in Portugal. These studies varied the cognitive representations of three-person groups of African Portuguese (lower status) and European Portuguese (higher status) fourth graders similar to those of Gaertner et al. (1989). The results of these studies involving conditions of categorization, recategorization, and decategorization converge on a common conclusion. Consistent with self-categorization theory, "the attractiveness of an individual is not constant, but varies with the ingroup membership" (Turner, 1985, p. 60).

These ideas about recategorization and decategorization have also provided explanations for how the apparently loosely connected diverse features specified by the contact hypothesis may operate psychologically to reduce bias. Allport's (1954) revised contact hypothesis proposed that for contact between groups to be successful, certain prerequisite features must be present (see Dovidio, Gaertner, & Kawakami, 2003). These include equal status between the groups, cooperative (rather than competitive) intergroup interaction, opportunities for self-revealing personal acquaintance between the members, especially with those whose personal characteristics do not support stereotypic expectations, and supportive norms by authorities within and outside of the contact situation. Whereas this prescription has been easier to write than to implement, there is evidence to support the efficacy of this formula when these conditions are present, particularly for changing intergroup attitudes (Cook, 1984; Johnson, Johnson, & Maruyama, 1983).

THE COMMON INGROUP IDENTITY MODEL

In contrast to the decategorization approach described earlier, recategorization is not designed to reduce or eliminate categorization but rather to structure a definition of group categorization at a higher level of category inclusiveness in ways that reduce intergroup bias and conflict. Specifically, we hypothesize that if members of different groups are induced to conceive of themselves within a single group rather than as completely separate groups, attitudes toward former outgroup members will become more positive through processes involving pro-ingroup bias (Gaertner & Dovidio, 2000; Gaertner et al., 1993).

This model identifies potential antecedents and outcomes of recategorization, as well as mediating processes. Figure 24.1 summarizes the general framework and specifies the causes and consequences of a common ingroup identity. Specifically, it is hypothesized that the different types of intergroup interdependence and cognitive, perceptual, linguistic, affective, and environmental factors (listed on the left) can either independently or in concert alter individuals' cognitive representations of the aggregate. These resulting cognitive representations (i.e., one group, two subgroups with one group, two groups, or separate individuals) are then proposed to result in the specific cognitive, affective, and overt behavioral consequences (listed on the right). Thus, the causal factors listed on the left (that include features specified by the contact hypothesis) are proposed to influence members' cognitive representations of the memberships (center) that in turn mediate the relationship, at least in part, between the causal factors (left) and the cognitive, affective, and behavioral consequences (on the right). In addition, we proposed that common ingroup identity may be achieved by increasing the salience of existing common superordinate memberships (e.g., a school, a company, a nation) or by introducing factors (e.g., common goals or fate) that are perceived to be shared by the memberships.

Once outgroup members are perceived as ingroup members, it is hypothesized that they would be accorded the benefits of ingroup status heuristically and in stereotyped fashion. There would likely be more positive thoughts, feelings, and behaviors (listed on the right) toward these former

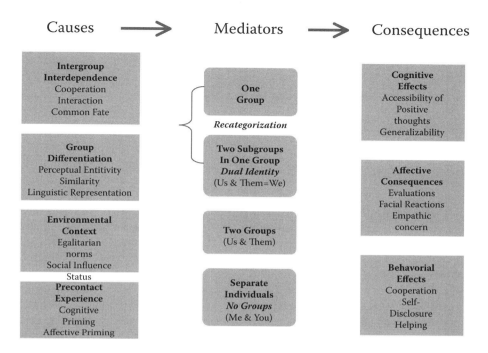

FIGURE 24.1 The common ingroup identity model.

outgroup members by virtue of categorizing them now as ingroup members. These more favorable impressions of outgroup members are not likely to be finely differentiated, at least initially (see Mullen & Hu, 1989). Rather, we suggest that these more elaborated, personalized impressions can soon develop within the context of a common identity because the newly formed positivity bias is likely to encourage more open communication and greater self-disclosing interaction between former outgroup members. Thus, over time a common identity is proposed to encourage personalization of outgroup members and thereby initiate a second route to achieving reduced bias.

Also we propose that the development of a common ingroup identity does not necessarily require each group to forsake its less inclusive group identity completely. Social identities are complex; every individual belongs to multiple groups simultaneously (Brewer, 2000). Thus, depending on their degree of identification with different categories and contextual factors that make particular identities more salient, individuals may activate one or more of these identities simultaneously (Roccas & Brewer, 2002) as well as sequentially (Turner, 1985). As depicted by the subgroups within one group (i.e., a dual identity) representation, we believe that it is possible for members to conceive of two groups (e.g., parents and children) as distinct units within the context of a superordinate (i.e., family) identity. When group identities and the associated cultural values are central to members' functioning or when they are associated with high status or highly visible cues to group membership, it would be undesirable or impossible for people to relinquish these group identities or, as perceivers, to be "colorblind." Indeed, demands to forsake these group identities or to adopt a colorblind ideology would likely arouse strong reactance and result in especially poor intergroup relations (see Schofield, 1986). If, however, people continued to regard themselves as members of different groups all playing on the same team or as part of the same superordinate entity, intergroup relations between these subgroups would be more positive than if members only considered themselves as "separate groups" (see Brewer & Schneider, 1990). In addition, because a dual identity representation maintains associate links to the former outgroup categories as well as the superordinate connection between the subgroups, any positive effects of intergroup contact may generalize to outgroups as a whole, beyond those present in the contact situation. Thus, a dual identity representation is partially aligned with the mutual differentiation approach because of its emphasis on original subgroup identities, but within the context of a more inclusive common ingroup identity. In the next section, we examine empirical tests of the common ingroup identity model.

COMMON IDENTITY AND THE REDUCTION OF INTERGROUP BIAS

Among the antecedent factors proposed by the common ingroup identity model are the features of contact situations (Allport, 1954) that are necessary for intergroup contact to be successful (e.g., interdependence between groups, equal status, equalitarian norms). From this perspective, cooperative interaction, for example, enhances positive evaluations of outgroup members, at least in part, because cooperation transforms members' representations of the memberships from separate groups to one group.

From the recategorization perspective, cooperation among Sherif and Sherif's (1969) groups of summer campers increased positive attitudes toward outgroup members because it changed members' perceptions of one another from "us" and "them" to a more inclusive "we." To test this mediation hypothesis directly, we conducted a laboratory experiment (Gaertner, Mann, Dovidio, Murrell, & Pomare, 1990) that brought two three-person laboratory groups together under conditions designed to vary independently the members' representations of the aggregate as one group or two groups (by varying factors such as seating arrangement) and the presence or absence of intergroup cooperation interaction. In the absence of cooperative interaction, participants induced to feel like one group relative to those whose separate group identities were emphasized reported that the aggregate did feel more like one group. They also had lower degrees of intergroup bias in their evaluations (likable, cooperative, honest, and trustworthy) of ingroup and outgroup members. We regard this as an important preliminary finding because it helps to establish the causal relation between the induction of a one-group representation and reduced bias, even in the absence of intergroup cooperation.

Supportive of the hypothesis concerning how cooperation reduces bias, among participants induced to feel like two groups, the introduction of cooperative interaction increased their perceptions of one group and also reduced their bias in evaluative ratings relative to those who did not cooperate during the contact period. Also supportive of the common ingroup identity model, reduced bias associated with introducing cooperation was due to enhanced favorable evaluations of outgroup members. Consistent with Brewer's (1979) analysis, cooperation appeared to move the new ingroup members closer to the self.

Consistent with our mediation hypothesis, cooperation induced group formation among members of the two groups and also reduced bias. In addition, more direct support for the mediation hypothesis was revealed by the multiple regression mediation approach, a form of path analysis (see Baron & Kenny, 1986). This analysis indicated that the influence of the introduction of cooperation on more positive evaluations of outgroup members was substantially reduced when the mediating effects of group representations and perceptions of cooperation and competition were considered. Furthermore, consistent with our model, among these potential mediators, only the "one group" representation related independently to evaluations of outgroup members.

The advantage of the experimental design is that we know that cooperation preceded changes in participants' representations of the aggregate from two groups to one group and also changes in intergroup bias. Also, when we manipulated only the representations of the aggregate (i.e., in the absence of cooperation), we know that the one group representation preceded changes in intergroup bias. Such confidence regarding the direction of causality is not afforded by our subsequent three survey studies, using a correlational approach of the effects of contact hypothesis variables on intergroup bias that we conducted involving more natural contexts. However, we can rely on the results of the experimental study to support the plausibility of the direction of causality proposed by our model as it is applied to the study of the effects of cooperation as well as the other features specified by the contact hypothesis on intergroup harmony in more natural contexts.

The three survey studies conducted in natural settings across different domains of intergroup life offered converging support for the idea that features specified by the contact hypothesis increase intergroup harmony, in part, because they transform members' representations of the memberships from separate groups to one more inclusive group. Participants in these studies included students attending a multiethnic high school (Gaertner, Rust, Dovidio, Bachman, & Anastasio, 1996), banking executives who had experienced a corporate merger involving a wide variety of banks across the United States (Bachman, 1993), and college students who are members of blended families whose households are composed of two formerly separate families trying to unite into one (Banker & Gaertner, 1998; see also Banker, 2002).

These surveys included items (specifically designed for each context) to measure participants' perceptions of the conditions of contact (i.e., equal status, self-revealing interaction, cooperation, equalitarian norms), their representations of the aggregate (i.e., one group, two subgroups within one group, two separate groups and separate individuals), and a measure of intergroup harmony or bias. For example, contact hypothesis items measuring participants' perceptions of equal status between the groups included items such as, "Teachers at this school are fair to all groups of students." Participants' cognitive representations of the aggregate as "one group" were measured by items such as, "Within the merged organization it feels like one group." Although the measures of intergroup bias or harmony were different across the three contexts, each study included some measure of affective reactions (e.g., feeling good, respectful, happy, awkward) to ingroup and outgroup members. Within each setting composite indexes were created for each of the major components of our model; that is, the conditions of contact, the representations, and intergroup harmony or bias.

In general, the more favorable participants reported the conditions of contact between the groups (e.g., cooperation), the more the school (or company or family) felt like one group. Supportive of the model, the more it felt like one group, the lower the bias in affective reactions in the high school, the less the intergroup anxiety among the banking executives, and the greater the amount of stepfamily harmony. Recently, a longitudinal study of stepfamilies found evidence supportive of the direction of causality between the constructs proposed by our model across time (Banker, 2002). Thus, across a variety of intergroup settings and methodological approaches we have found reasonably strong and consistent support for the common ingroup identity model. In the next section, we explore whether a common ingroup identity can make an even more fundamental change in the behavior of Whites during interracial interactions.

To directly determine whether a common ingroup identity can increase positive reactions to racial outgroup members, we executed two additional studies. In a laboratory experiment (Nier, Gaertner, Dovidio, Banker, & Ward, 2001, Study 1) White participants involved in the same session with a Black or White confederate were induced to perceive themselves as separate individuals with no functional connection participating in an experiment or as members of the same team who would compete against a team from another university. The results revealed that the evaluations of the other White confederate were virtually equivalent in the individual and team conditions, whereas the evaluations of the Black confederate were reliably more positive when they were teammates than when they were just individuals without a common group connection.

Additionally, a field experiment (Nier et al., 2001, Study 2) conducted at the University of Delaware football stadium prior to a game between the University of Delaware and Westchester State University demonstrates how a salient superordinate identity can increase behavioral compliance with a request for assistance from a person of a different race. In this experiment, Black and White, male and female students approached fans of the same sex as themselves from both universities just before the fans entered the stadium. These fans were asked if they would be willing to be interviewed about their food preferences. Our student interviewers systematically varied whether they were wearing a University of Delaware or Westchester State University hat. By selecting fans who wore similar clothing that identified their university affiliation, we systematically varied whether fans and our interviewers had common or different university identities in a context where we expected these identities to be particularly salient. Although we planned to oversample Black fans, the sample was still too small to yield any informative findings.

Among White fans, however, sharing common university identity with the Black interviewers significantly increased their compliance (59%) relative to when they did not share common identity with the Black interviewer (36%). When the interviewers were White, however, there was no significant difference in their levels of compliance as a function of their university identity. They gained slightly, but not reliably higher levels of compliance when they shared common university identity with the fan (44%) as when they appeared to be affiliated with the rival university (37%). These findings together with those of the preceding study offer support for the idea that racial outgroup members will be treated more favorably in terms of evaluations and prosocial behavior when they are perceived to also share a more inclusive, common ingroup affiliation. Although it is puzzling why fellow Whites in Study 1 or Study 2 were not accorded more positive behavior when they shared a common team affiliation, we suspect that participants may have perceived some level of common group membership with the White confederate or surveyor regardless of the experimental manipulation. In an experiment described in the next section, we consider the reciprocal relations between recategorization and decategorization.

In another laboratory experiment we obtained support for the prediction that a common ingroup identity would reduce intergroup bias in helping and self-disclosure (Dovidio et al., 1997). First, members of two three-person laboratory groups ("Over- and Under-estimators") were induced to conceive of themselves as either one group or two groups (as in Gaertner et al., 1990; Gaertner et al., 1989). Then, some participants were given an opportunity to help or to engage in a self-disclosing interaction with an ingroup or an outgroup member. For helping, participants listened individually to an audio recording of another student (described as either an over- or underestimator, from a previous session) describe how illness had prevented her from completing an important survey of student life for a committee on which she served. Subsequently, participants received a note ostensibly from this person that contained an appeal to help her by placing posters recruiting volunteers to participate in the survey in various locations across campus. The other participants were engaged in a self-disclosure task in which they were asked to discuss the topic, "What do I fear most?" During this task, participants interacted with either an ingroup or outgroup member who participated earlier in their session.

The results for the helping and self-disclosure measures converged to support predictions from our model. In each case, the bias favoring ingroup members that was present in the two-groups condition was reduced (and actually reversed) for those induced to regard the aggregate as one group. That is, in the one-group condition, more positive behaviors were directed to outgroup members than toward ingroup members, albeit by an amount that was not statistically significant. These findings are important for at least two reasons. First, the finding that outgroup members in the one-group condition received especially positive reactions for both self-disclosure and helping parallels the amplified compliance accorded Black interviewers who shared common university affiliation in the football stadium study as well as the more positive evaluations of the Black teammates in the laboratory study.

One important aspect of this pattern of change across these different studies is that it suggests that on recognition of a superordinate group connection, newly regarded ingroup members are initially accorded especially positive reactions compared to when they were only regarded as outgroup members. Also, these reactions to newcomers are even more extreme compared to the reactions accorded original ingroup members. If indeed, superordinate connection motivates initially amplified positive reactions to "newcomers," this emotional reaction can perhaps be leveraged to promote more harmonious long-term relationships.

A second important aspect of these findings is that they demonstrate that common ingroup membership can initiate more personalized interactions between former outgroup members. This consequence can thereby activate an additional, independent pathway for increasing intergroup harmony. Similarly, in an additional experiment (Gaertner, Rust, & Dovidio, 1997), we observed that the capacity of personalized, self-disclosing interactions to bring ingroup and outgroup members psychologically closer also transformed their perceptions of the aggregate from two groups to one group. Thus, common ingroup identity and personalized interactions seem to reciprocally share the capacity to facilitate each other.

In addition to a common superordinate identity increasing positive evaluations, compliance, helping, self-revealing interactions and cooperative behavior toward people who would otherwise be regarded as outgroup members, we are encouraged by some recent independent evidence demonstrating its capacity also to reduce subtle linguistic biases that serve to perpetuate stereotypes (Maass, Ceccarelli, & Rudin, 1996, Study 2). In this laboratory experiment, northern and southern Italians living in Switzerland received messages that emphasized the differentiation between northern and southern Italians (in a two-group condition), or between Italians and the Swiss (in a superordinate "Italian" condition). These participants were then shown cartoons depicting northern and southern Italians performing positive and negative behaviors. Participants were then asked to choose one of four response alternatives corresponding to the four levels of abstraction. When the distinction between northern and southern Italians was emphasized, the results replicated the linguistic bias effect. Higher levels of abstraction were used to describe positive behaviors of ingroup members (e.g., she is helpful) when compared with outgroup members (e.g., she walked with the old lady). Also, higher levels of abstraction were used to describe undesirable behavior of outgroup members than were used for ingroup members. This linguistic bias was not evident in the superordinate identity condition. Thus, a superordinate identity fundamentally changed the way behavioral information about ingroup and outgroup members was processed and, importantly, in a way that reduced this subtle bias in information processing. In addition, recent research by Karpinski and von Hippel (1996) reveals that this linguistic bias mediates the extent to which people maintain stereotypic expectancies in the face of disconfirming information. Thus, the development of a common ingroup identity cannot only reduce general intergroup prejudice, but also, by reducing intergroup linguistic bias, can help to change intergroup stereotypes.

THE VALUE OF A DUAL IDENTITY

Earlier, we discussed the possibility that acceptance of a superordinate identity does not require members to forsake their ethnic or racial group identity (Gaertner et al., 1989), and our own research on dual identity seems to support this idea. In addition, two studies further suggest that the intergroup benefits of a strong superordinate identity remain relatively stable even when the strength of the subordinate identity becomes equivalently high (Huo, Smith, Tyler, & Lind, 1996; Smith & Tyler, 1996). This suggests that social cohesion does not require individuals to deny their ethnic identity.

For example, in a survey study of White adults, Smith and Tyler (1996, Study 1) measured the strength of respondents' superordinate identity as "American" and also the strength of their identification as "White." Following Berry's (1984) strategy of creating four groups on the basis of a median split on each measure, the investigators identified four groups of respondents that varied in terms of the relative strength of their superordinate and subgroup identities. The results revealed that regardless of whether they strongly identified with being White, those respondents with a strong American identity were more likely to base their support for affirmative action policies that would benefit Blacks and other minorities on relational concerns regarding the fairness of congressional representatives than on whether these policies would increase or decrease their own well-being. However, for the group who identified themselves more strongly with being White than being American, their position on affirmative action was determined more strongly by concerns regarding the instrumental value of these policies for themselves.

This pattern of findings suggests that a strong superordinate identity allows individuals to support policies that would benefit members of other racial subgroups without giving primary consideration to their own instrumental needs. Furthermore, once people identify with the superordinate entity, the relative strength of their subgroup identities does not strongly change the basis for determining their support for policies that will benefit other groups within the superordinate collective. An additional laboratory similarly demonstrates the value of a dual identity in which each group remains distinctive within a superordinate identity.

As our earlier work on the conditions specified by the contact hypothesis suggests, equal status would be expected to facilitate the development of a common ingroup identity. However, bringing different groups together, particularly when they are similar on an important dimension (such as task-relevant status) might arouse motivations to achieve "positive distinctiveness" (Tajfel & Turner, 1979), which could exacerbate rather than alleviate intergroup bias (Brown & Wade, 1987). In this respect, establishing a common superordinate identity while maintaining the salience of subgroup identities (i.e., developing a dual identity as two subgroups within one group) would be particularly effective because it permits the benefits of a common ingroup identity to operate without arousing countervailing motivations to achieve positive distinctiveness. We conducted two experiments investigating this hypothesis.

In one study (Dovidio, Gaertner, & Validzic, 1998) groups of three students were given feedback indicating that, based on their performance on an earlier task, their group was higher, lower, or equal in status to another group with which they were about to cooperate. This status manipulation was crossed factorially with whether the groups were assigned identical or different task perspectives in preparation for their cooperative interaction. The discussions involved the Winter Survival Problem (Johnson & Johnson, 1975), and when the groups had different task perspectives, the members of one group were told to assume that they would hike to safety whereas the members of the other group were asked to assume that they would stay put to await search parties. As predicted, the analyses revealed that when the groups were of equal status and task perspectives were different, intergroup bias was lower and the representation of the aggregate feeling like one group was higher than in each of the other three conditions (i.e., equal status–same task, unequal status–different task, and equal status–same task). In addition, the one-group representation mediated the relation between the experimental manipulations of status and task perspective on intergroup bias. These findings are consistent with the proposed value of equal status, primarily, as Hewstone and Brown (1986) proposed, when the distinctiveness between groups is maintained.

In another study we varied relative group status among actual employees of many different companies by asking them to imagine that their current organization was about to merge with another (Mottola, 1996). In one condition, their present company was described as higher in status than the other in terms of generating greater sales and greater profits. In another condition, their company was lower in status on both dimensions. In a third condition, both companies were described as having equal status in terms of both sales and profit. In a fourth condition, their company was described as higher in status on one dimension (e.g., profit), but the other company was higher on the other dimension. Consistent with Hewstone and Brown's (1986) ideas about the benefits of maintaining the mutual distinctiveness of groups working together, participants in the fourth condition in which one company had higher profit and the other higher sales anticipated that they would more strongly identify with the merged organization than did participants in each of the other three conditions (which did not differ from one another). Thus, when each group can maintain positive distinctiveness, we can anticipate greater acceptance of a superordinate identity from the members of both groups.

In general, when we present this work people frequently question whether the development of a common ingroup identity is a useful or practical strategy for combating intergroup biases. Our evaluation study of an elementary school anti-bias education intervention provides an encouraging answer to this question.

THE GREEN CIRCLE ELEMENTARY SCHOOL ANTI-BIAS EDUCATION PROGRAM

Several years ago, we became aware of the Green Circle elementary school-based intervention program, which is now run by the National Conference of Community and Justice of Northern Delaware, which is practically and theoretically compatible with the common ingroup identity model. The guiding assumption of Green Circle is that helping children bring people from different groups conceptually into their own circle of caring and sharing fosters appreciation of their common humanity as well as respect for their differences.

In the program, a Green Circle facilitator visits each class for about 40 minutes per session four times over a 4-week period and shows children a small green circle on a felt board. The facilitator states, "Whenever you see the green circle, you should think about your world of people; the people who you care about and the people who care about you." A stick figure is added to the circle and the students are told that the figure represents themselves. The facilitator explains that each person has "a big job of deciding who is going to be in your circle, how to treat people, and how big your circle will grow," and engages children in a variety of exercises designed to expand the circle. The facilitator points out that, "All of us belong to one family—the human family." Paralleling the common ingroup identity model, Green Circle assumes that an appreciation of common humanity will increase children's positive attitudes toward people who would otherwise remain outside of their circle of inclusion.

This collaboration with the Green Circle staff provided an applied opportunity to test the general principles of the common ingroup identity model and also offered the Green Circle program an evaluation of their intervention's effectiveness (see Houlette et al., 2004). On the basis of the goals of the Green Circle program and the principles of the common ingroup identity model, we expected that children receiving the program would be more inclusive of others who are different than themselves in playing and sharing following the implementation of the program relative to pretest levels and also relative to children in a control condition who did not yet receive the program. To evaluate attitudes toward children similar and different in sex, race, and weight, children were asked about their willingness to share with and play with each of eight different children depicted in drawings in which sex, race (Black and White), and weight were systematically varied.

Overall, our results revealed that first- and second-grade children in fairly well-integrated classrooms still had a general preference for playing and sharing with children of the same race than those of a different race. Nevertheless, we also found that the Green Circle intervention did lead children to be more inclusive in terms of their most preferred playmate. Specifically, compared to children in the control condition who did not participate in Green Circle activities, those who were part of Green Circle showed a significantly greater increase in willingness to select the child from the eight drawings who was different from them (in terms of race, sex, and weight) as the child they "would most want to play with." These changes involve greater willingness to cross group boundaries in making friends—a factor that is one of the most potent influences in producing more positive attitudes toward the outgroup as a whole (Pettigrew, 1998).

Conceptually, the Green Circle findings illustrate that it is realistic to operationalize the primary theme underlying the common ingroup identity model. These findings also demonstrate also how interpersonal and intergroup routes toward reducing intergroup biases can involve complementary processes that reciprocally facilitate one another. That is, changes in intergroup boundaries can facilitate the occurrence of positive interpersonal behaviors across group lines such as self-disclosure and helping in college students (see also Dovidio et al., 1997) and, as the Green Circle study illustrates, preferred playmates in children.

CONCLUSION

We have reviewed some evidence suggesting that a common ingroup identity partially mediates the effects of contact hypothesis variables, increasing positive feelings and behaviors toward specific outgroup members. Also, it seems to have some potential to increase positive attitudes toward outgroup members more generally. Furthermore, we are optimistic because a superordinate identity can initiate more self-disclosing, personalized interactions as well as more cooperative, prosocial orientations toward outgroup members. Although the cognitive representation of a superordinate identity may itself often be fleeting and unstable, it seems to be capable of initiating behaviors that call forth reciprocity and can thus have more permanent intergroup consequences. Also, some of these behaviors can initiate processes that can reduce bias through additional, independent pathways. Thus, we regard the major strength of inducing a common identity to be its capacity to temporarily change the course of intergroup interactions and to initiate constructive intergroup and interpersonal processes and exchanges in a fashion that can have more long-lasting effects for producing more positive relations between groups.

ACKNOWLEDGMENTS

This research reported in this chapter was supported largely by National Institute of Mental Health Grant MH 48721 and the preparation of this chapter has been facilitated by National Science Foundation Grant # 0613218.

REFERENCES

Adorno, T. W., Frenkel-Brunswik, E., Levinson, D. J., & Sanford, R. N. (1950). *The authoritarian personality.* New York: Harper.
Allport, G. W. (1954). *The nature of prejudice.* New York: Addison-Wesley.
Bachman, B. A. (1993). *An intergroup model of organizational mergers.* Unpublished doctoral dissertation, Department of Psychology, University of Delaware, Newark.
Banker, B. S. (2002). *Intergroup conflict and bias reduction in stepfamilies: A longitudinal examination of intergroup relations processes.* Unpublished doctoral dissertation, Department of Psychology, University of Delaware, Newark.
Banker, B. S., & Gaertner, S. L. (1998). Achieving stepfamily harmony: An intergroup relations approach. *Journal of Family Psychology, 12,* 310–325.
Baron, R. M., & Kenny, D. A. (1986). The moderator–mediator variable distinction in social psychological research: Conceptual, strategic, and statistical considerations. *Journal of Personality and Social Psychology, 51,* 1173–1182.
Berry, J. W. (1984). Cultural relations in plural societies. In N. Miller & M. B. Brewer (Eds.), *Groups in contact: The psychology of desegregation* (pp. 11–27). Orlando, FL: Academic.
Bettencourt, B. A., Brewer, M. B., Croak, M. R., & Miller, N. (1992). Cooperation and the reduction of intergroup bias: The roles of reward structure and social orientation. *Journal of Experimental Social Psychology, 28,* 301–319
Billig, M. G., & Tajfel, H. (1973). Social categorisation and similarity in intergroup behavior. *European Journal of Social Psychology, 3,* 27–52.
Brewer, M. B. (1979). Ingroup bias in the minimal intergroup situation: A cognitive-motivational analysis. *Psychological Bulletin, 86,* 307–324.
Brewer, M. B. (2000). Reducing prejudice through crosscategorization: Effects of multiple social identities. In S. Oskamp (Ed.), *Claremont symposium on applied social psychology: Reducing prejudice and discrimination* (pp. 165-183). Thousand Oaks, CA: Sage.
Brewer, M. B., Ho, H., Lee, J., & Miller, N. (1987). Social identity and social distance among Hong Kong school children. *Personality and Social Psychology Bulletin, 13,* 156–165.
Brewer, M. B., & Miller, N. (1984). Beyond the contact hypothesis: Theoretical perspectives on desegregation. In N. Miller & M. B. Brewer (Eds.), *Groups in contact: The psychology of desegregation* (pp. 281–302). Orlando, FL: Academic.
Brewer, M. B., & Schneider, S. (1990). Social identity and social dilemmas: A double-edged sword. In D. Abrams & M. Hogg (Eds.), *Social identity theory: Constructive and critical advances* (pp. 169–184). London: Harvester Wheatsheaf.
Brown, R., & Hewstone, M. (2005). An integrative theory of intergroup contact. In M. P. Zanna (Ed.), *Advances in experimental social psychology* (Vol. 37, pp. 255–343). San Diego, CA: Academic.
Brown, R. J., & Turner, J. C. (1979). The criss-cross categorization effect in intergroup discrimination. *British Journal of Social and Clinical Psychology, 18,* 371–383.
Brown, R. J., & Wade, G. (1987). Superordinate goals and intergroup behavior: The effect of role ambiguity and status on intergroup attitudes and task performance. *European Journal of Social Psychology, 17,* 131–142.

Campbell, D. T. (1958). Common fate, similarity and other indices of the status of aggregates of persons as social entities. *Behavioral Science, 3,* 14–25.

Commins, B., & Lockwood, J. (1978). The effects of intergroup relations of mixing Roman Catholics and Protestants: An experimental investigation. *European Journal of Social Psychology, 8,* 218–219.

Cook, S. W. (1984). Cooperative interaction in multiethnic contexts. In N. Miller & M. B. Brewer (Eds.), *Groups in contact: The psychology of desegregation* (pp. 291–302). Orlando, FL: Academic.

Correll, J., & Park, B. (2005). A model of the ingroup as a social resource. *Personality and Social Psychology Review, 9,* 341–359.

Crisp, R. J., & Hewstone, M. (Eds.). (2006). *Multiple social categorization: Processes, models, and applications.* Philadelphia: Psychology Press.

Deschamps, J. C., & Doise, W. (1978). Crossed-category membership in intergroup relations. In H. Tajfel (Ed.), *Differentiation between social groups* (pp. 141–158). London: Academic.

Doise, W. (1978). *Groups and individuals: Explanations in social psychology.* Cambridge, UK: Cambridge University Press.

Dovidio, J. F., & Gaertner, S. L. (2004). Aversive racism. In M. P. Zanna (Ed.), *Advances in experimental social psychology* (Vol. 36, pp. 1-51). San Diego, CA: Academic Press.

Dovidio, J. F., Gaertner, S. L., & Kawakami, K. (2003). The contact hypothesis: The past, present, and the future. *Group Processes and Intergroup Relations, 6,* 5–21.

Dovidio, J. F., Gaertner, S. L., Niemann, Y. F., & Snider, K. (2001). Racial, ethnic, and cultural differences in responding to distinctiveness and discrimination on campus: Stigma and common group identity. *Journal of Social Issues, 57,* 167–188.

Dovidio, J. F., Gaertner, S. L., & Validzic, A. (1998). Intergroup bias: Status, differentiation, and a common ingroup identity. *Journal of Personality and Social Psychology, 75,* 109–120.

Dovidio, J. F., Gaertner, S. L., Validzic, A., Matoka, K., Johnson, B., & Frazier, S. (1997). Extending the benefits of re-categorization: Evaluations, self-disclosure and helping. *Journal of Experimental Social Psychology, 33,* 401–420.

Feagin, J. R. (2006). *Systemic racism: A theory of oppression.* New York: Routledge.

Ferguson, C. K., & Kelley, H. H. (1964). Significant factors in over-evaluation of own groups' products. *Journal of Abnormal and Social Psychology, 69,* 223–228.

Fiske, S. T., Lin, M., & Neuberg, S. L. (1999). The continuum model: Ten years later. In S. Chaiken & Y. Trope (Eds.), *Dual process theories in social psychology* (pp. 211–254). New York: Guilford.

Gaertner, S. L., Bachman, B. A., Dovidio, J. D., & Banker, B. S. (2001). Corporate mergers and stepfamily marriages: Identity, harmony, and commitment. In M. A. Hogg & D. Terry (Eds.), *Social identity in organizations* (pp. 265–288). Oxford, UK: Blackwell.

Gaertner, S. L., & Dovidio, J. F. (1986). The aversive form of racism. In J. F. Dovidio & S. L. Gaertner (Eds.), Prejudice, discrimination, and racism (pp. 61-89). Orlando, FL: Academic Press.

Gaertner, S. L., & Dovidio, J. F. (2000). *Reducing intergroup bias: The common ingroup identity model.* Philadelphia: Psychology Press.

Gaertner, S. L., Dovidio, J. F., Anastasio, P. A., Bachman, B. A., & Rust, M. C. (1993). The common ingroup identity model: Recategorization and the reduction of intergroup bias. In W. Stroebe & M. Hewstone (Eds.), *European review of social psychology* (Vol. 4. pp. 1–26). New York: Wiley.

Gaertner, S. L., Mann, J. A., Dovidio, J. F., Murrell, A. J., & Pomare, M. (1990). How does cooperation reduce intergroup bias? *Journal of Personality and Social Psychology, 59,* 692–704.

Gaertner, S. L., Mann, J., Murrell, A., & Dovidio, J. F. (1989). Reducing intergroup bias: The benefits of recategorization. *Journal of Personality and Social Psychology, 57,* 239–249.

Gaertner, S. L., Rust, M. C., & Dovidio, J. F. (1997). *The value of a superordinate identity for reducing intergroup bias.* Unpublished manuscript, Department of Psychology, University of Delaware. Newark, DE.

Gaertner, S. L., Rust, M. C., Dovidio, J. F., Bachman, B. A., & Anastasio, P. A. (1996). The contact hypothesis: The role of a common ingroup identity on reducing intergroup bias among majority and minority group members. In J. L. Nye & A. M. Brower (Eds.), *What's social about social cognition?* (pp. 230–360). Newbury Park, CA: Sage.

Guerra, R., Rebelo, M., & Monteiro, M. B. (2004, June). *Changing intergroup relations: Effects of recategorization, decategorization and dual identity in the reduction of intergroup discrimination.* Paper presented at Change in Intergroup Relations: 7th Jena Workshop on Intergroup Processes, Friedricht Schiller University, Jena, Germany.

Hamilton, D. L., & Sherman, J. W. (1994). Stereotypes. In R. S. Wyer & T. K. Srull (Eds.), *Handbook of social cognition* (Vol. 2, pp. 1–68). Hillsdale, NJ: Erlbaum.

Hamilton, D. L., & Trolier, T. K. (1986). Stereotypes and stereotyping: An overview of the cognitive approach. In J. F. Dovidio & S. L. Gaertner (Eds.), *Prejudice, discrimination, and racism* (pp. 127–163). Orlando, FL: Academic.

Hewstone, M. (1990). The "ultimate attribution error"? A review of the literature on intergroup causal attribution. *European Journal of Social Psychology, 20,* 311–335.

Hewstone, M., & Brown, R. J. (1986). Contact is not enough: An intergroup perspective on the "contact hypothesis." In M. Hewstone & R. Brown (Eds.), *Contact and conflict in intergroup encounters* (pp. 1–44). Oxford, UK: Basil Blackwell.

Hornstein, H. A. (1976). *Cruelty and kindness: A new look at aggression and altruism.* Englewood Cliffs, NJ: Prentice Hall.

Houlette, M., Gaertner, S. L., Johnson, K. M., Banker, B. S., Riek, B. M., & Dovidio, J. F. (2004). Developing a more inclusive social identity: An elementary school intervention. *Journal of Social Issues, 60,* 35–56.

Howard, J. M., & Rothbart, M. (1980). Social categorization for in-group and out-group behavior. *Journal of Personality and Social Psychology, 38,* 301–310.

Huo, Y. J., Smith, H. H., Tyler, T. R., & Lind, A. E. (1996). Superordinate identification, subgroup identification, and justice concerns: Is separatism the problem? Is assimilation the answer? *Psychological Science, 7,* 40–45.

Johnson, D. W. & Johnson, F. P. (1975). *Joining together: Group theory and group skills.* Englewood Cliffs, NJ: Prentice-Hall.

Johnson, D. W., Johnson, F. P., & Maruyama, G. (1983). Interdependence and interpersonal attraction among heterogeneous and homogeneous individuals: A theoretical formulation and a meta-analysis of the research. *Review of Educational Research, 52,* 5–54.

Jones, J. M. (1997). *Prejudice and racism* (2nd ed.). New York: McGraw-Hill.

Karpinski, A., & von Hippel, W. (1996). The role of the linguistic intergroup bias in expectancy maintenance. *Social Cognition, 14,* 141–163.

Kelly, D. J., Liu, S., Ge, L., Quinn, P. C., Slater, A. M., Lee, K., et al. (2007). Cross-race preferences for same-race faces extend beyond the African versus Caucasian contrast in 3-month-old infants. *Infancy, 11,* 87–95.

Kelly, D. J., Quinn, P. C., Slater, A. M., Lee, K., Gibson, A. Smith, M., et al.. (2005). Three-months-olds, but not newborns, prefer own-race faces. *Developmental Science, 8,* F31–F36.

Kovel, J. (1970). *White racism: A psychohistory.* New York: Pantheon.

Kramer, R. M., & Brewer, M. B. (1984). Effects of group identity on resource utilization in a simulated commons dilemma. *Journal of Personality and Social Psychology, 46,* 1044–1057.

Maass, A., Ceccarelli, R., & Rudin, S. (1996). Linguistic intergroup bias: Evidence for in-group-protective motivation. *Journal of Personality and Social Psychology, 71,* 512–526.

Maass, A., Salvi, D., Arcuri, L., & Semin, G. R. (1989). Language use in intergroup contexts: The linguistic intergroup bias. *Journal of Personality and Social Psychology, 57,* 981–993.

Marcus-Newhall, A., Miller, N., Holtz, R., & Brewer, M. B. (1993). Cross-cutting category membership with role assignment: A means of reducing intergroup bias. *British Journal of Social Psychology, 32,* 125–146.

Miller, N. (2002). Personalization and the promise of contact theory. *Journal of Social Issues, 58,* 29–44.

Miller, N., & Brewer, M. B. (1984). (Eds.). *Groups in contact: The psychology of desegregation.* Orlando, FL: Academic Press.

Miller, N., Brewer, M. B., & Edwards, K. (1985). Cooperative interaction in desegregated settings: A laboratory analog. *Journal of Social Issues, 41*(3), 63–75.

Mottola, G. (1996). *The effects of relative group status on expectations of merger success.* Unpublished doctoral dissertation, University of Delaware, Newark.

Mullen, B., & Hu, L. T. (1989). Perceptions of ingroup and outgroup variability: A meta-analytic integration. *Basic and Applied Social Psychology, 10,* 233–252.

Murrell, A. J., Dietz-Uhler, B. L., Dovidio, J. F., Gaertner, S. L., & Drout, C. E. (1994). Aversive racism and resistance to affirmative action: Perceptions of justice are not necessarily colorblind. *Basic and Applied Social Psychology, 5,* 71–86.

Nier, J. A., Gaertner, S. L., Dovidio, J. F., Banker, B. S., & Ward, C. M. (2001). Changing interracial evaluations and behavior: The effects of a common group identity. *Group Processes and Intergroup Relations, 4,* 299–316.

Park, B., & Rothbart, M. (1982). Perception of out-group homogeneity and levels of social categorization: Memory for the subordinate attributes of in-group and out-group members. *Journal of Personality and Social Psychology, 42,* 1051–1068.

Perdue, C. W., Dovidio, J. F., Gurtman, M. B., & Tyler, R. B. (1990). "Us" and "them": Social categorization and the process of intergroup bias. *Journal of Personality and Social Psychology, 59,* 475–486.

Pettigrew, T. F. (1979). The ultimate attributional error: Extending Allport's cognitive analysis of prejudice. *Personality and Social Psychology Bulletin, 55,* 461–476.

Pettigrew, T. F. (1998). Intergroup contact theory. *Annual Review of Psychology, 49,* 65–85.

Piliavin, J. A., Dovidio, J. F., Gaertner, S. L., & Clark, R. D., III. (1981). *Emergency intervention.* New York: Academic.

Rabbie, J. M. (1982). The effects of intergroup competition and cooperation on intragroup and intergroup relationships. In V. J. Derlega & J. Grzelak (Eds.), *Cooperation and helping behavior: Theories and research* (pp. 128–151). New York: Academic.

Rebelo, M., Guerra, R., & Monteiro, M. B. (2004, June). *Reducing prejudice: Comparative effects of three theoretical models.* Paper presented at the Fifth Biennial Convention of the Society for the Psychological Study of Social Issues, Washington, DC.

Roccas, S., & Brewer, M. (2002). Social identity complexity. *Personality and Social Psychology Review, 6,* 88–106.

Schofield, J. W. (1986). Causes and consequences of the colorblind perspective. In J. F. Dovidio & S. L. Gaertner (Eds.), *Prejudice, discrimination and racism* (pp. 231–253). Orlando, FL: Academic.

Sherif, M., & Sherif, C. W. (1969). *Social psychology.* New York: Harper & Row

Smith, H. J., & Tyler, T. R. (1996). Justice and power: When will justice concerns encourage the advantaged to support policies which redistribute economic resources and the disadvantaged to willingly obey the law? *European Journal of Social Psychology, 26,* 171–200.

Stürmer, S., Snyder, M., & Omoto, A. M. (2005). Prosocial emotions and helping: The moderating role of group membership. *Journal of Personality and Social Psychology, 88,* 532–546.

Sumner, W. G. (1906). *Folkways.* New York: Ginn.

Tajfel, H. (1969). Cognitive aspects of prejudice. *Journal of Social Issues, 25*(4), 79–97.

Tajfel, H., Billig, M. G., Bundy, R. F., & Flament, C. (1971). Social categorisation and intergroup behavior. *European Journal of Social Psychology, 1,* 149–177.

Tajfel, H., & Turner, J. C. (1979). An integrative theory of intergroup conflict. In W. G. Austin & S. Worchel (Eds.), *The social psychology of intergroup relations* (pp. 33–48). Monterey, CA: Brooks/Cole.

Turner, J. C. (1975). Social comparison and social identity: Some prospects for intergroup behavior. *European Journal of Social Psychology, 5,* 5–34.

Turner, J. C. (1985). Social categorization and the self-concept: A social cognitive theory of group behavior. In E. J. Lawler (Ed.), *Advances in group processes* (Vol. 2, pp. 77–122).Greenwich, CT: JAI.

Vanbeselaere, N. (1987). The effects of dichotomous and crossed social categorization upon intergroup discrimination. *European Journal of Social Psychology, 17,* 143–156.

Wilder, D. A. (1978). Reducing intergroup discrimination through individuation of the outgroup. *Journal of Personality and Social Psychology, 36,* 1361–1374.

Wilder, D. A. (1981). Perceiving persons as a group: Categorization and intergroup relations. In D. L. Hamilton (Ed.), *Cognitive processes in stereotyping and intergroup behavior* (pp. 213–257). Hillsdale, NJ: Erlbaum.

Wilder, D. A. (1986). Social categorization: Implications for creation and reduction of intergroup bias. In L. Berkowitz (Ed.), *Advances in experimental social psychology* (Vol. 19, pp. 291–355). Orlando, FL: Academic.

25 The Self-Regulation of Prejudice

Margo J. Monteith
Purdue University

Aimee Y. Mark
University of Southern Indiana

All in all, we are forced to conclude that prejudice in a life is more likely than not to arouse some compunction, at least some of the time. It is almost impossible to integrate it consistently with affiliative needs and human values. (Allport, 1954, p. 329)

Prejudice during the past 20 years has been conceptualized in social psychological theories most often as involving some form of conflict or ambivalence (e.g., Devine, 1989; Dovidio & Gaertner, 1998; Katz & Hass, 1988; Sears & Henry, 2003). Many factors contribute to a propensity toward bias and prejudice toward outgroups, ranging from natural cognitive (e.g., categorization) and motivational (ingroup favoritism) underpinnings (Tajfel & Turner, 1986); value orientations (e.g., individualism) that support attitudinal prejudice (e.g., Biernat, Vescio, Theno, & Crandall, 1996); personality tendencies that foster dislike of outgroups (Sidanius & Pratto, 1999); and socialization processes that contribute to the learning and maintenance of bias (e.g., Katz, 2003). At the same time, people often are uncomfortable with their prejudices. As the opening quote from Allport (1954) underscores, prejudice is fundamentally incompatible with humanitarian precepts, egalitarian values, and internalized personal standards calling for the unbiased treatment of others.

What do people do about this conflict? How do they live with it? One process for handling conflict is to maintain one's prejudices but justify them on seemingly nonprejudiced grounds. For example, according to symbolic and modern racism theories, Whites express negative affect toward Blacks in ways that justify and rationalize their prejudices (Sears & Henry, 2003). Aversive racism theory maintains that Whites often avoid Blacks so that their underlying negativity may remain unacknowledged, or they express their negativity only when it can be justified with nonracial explanations (Dovidio & Gaertner, 1998). Still another possibility, found in the ambivalent theory of prejudice, is that people vacillate between positive and negative responses, and through a process of response amplification, assert the appropriateness of their response and excuse themselves from experiencing the threat to self-integrity that would follow from recognition of their ambivalence (Hass, Katz, Rizzo, Bailey, & Eisenstadt, 1991).

In sum, people appear to be able to live comfortably with their prejudices through rationalization, justification, denial, and just plain ignoring and avoiding outgroups. All of these processes contribute to the maintenance of prejudice rather than to its change.

Another possibility, however, is that people recognize and confront their prejudiced tendencies and work toward prejudice reduction. This pathway to change has been the focus of research on the self-regulation of prejudice. In this chapter, we review strategies that involve the self-regulation of stereotyping and prejudice and their consequences for the reduction of bias. In addition, we consider the emerging literature that takes a neuroscientific approach to understanding bias reduction through self-regulation. Finally, we consider consequences of the self-regulation of prejudice that occur in the specific context of intergroup interactions.

507

SELF-REGULATION

Self-regulation has been an important construct in psychological theory and research since the beginnings of psychology (James, 1890/1950). Generally speaking, the act of self-regulation involves setting goals and working toward the achievement of those goals. Both daily life and the accomplishment of long-term objectives require the ability to engage in self-regulation. For example, a goal on a certain day may be to avoid eating chocolate, and the long-term goal may be to lose 10 pounds. With respect to prejudice, a daily goal may be to avoid stereotypic thoughts, and the long-term goal may be to live consistently with one's egalitarian self-image. Central to the process of self-regulation is the exertion of self-control, or attempts by the self to control the self so as to achieve desired outcomes (Mischel, 1996).

Self-regulation has been studied at many levels, from more macroscopic approaches (e.g., cultural analyses) to the neural level. A general model for understanding how individuals go about self-regulation is the cybernetic model (Carver & Scheier, 1990). This model includes four phases in a test, operate, test, exit (TOTE) sequence. The test phase involves a determination of whether there is a discrepancy between one's standards and desired states. In the operate phase, behaviors are initiated and enacted for reaching one's goal. The test phase is then performed again to check on progress, and if the desired goal has been met, one may exit and discontinue concerted self-regulatory efforts. However, if a discrepancy still exists, further self-regulation occurs to adjust and monitor behavior for goal attainment.

An important factor affecting people's ability to engage in self-regulation, particularly for executing action in the operate phase, is self-control strength. Muraven and Baumeister (2000) argued that self-control is a limited resource resembling a muscle. Although self-control strength is necessary for the executive functioning that is involved in self-regulation (e.g., initiating appropriate actions and inhibiting inappropriate ones), self-control resources can be weakened and depleted by having multiple regulatory demands or stressors (Muraven, Baumeister, & Tice, 1999). Like a muscle, self-control apparently can also be strengthened by exercising it across time (Muraven et al., 1999).

Obviously, for people to engage self-regulatory efforts, they need to be motivated to do so. There are a variety of factors that affect people's motivation and thus likelihood of attempting to regulate their prejudiced tendencies. One critical factor is people's personal attitudes and standards. People who hold low-prejudice attitudes or standards for responding to members of stereotyped groups are personally motivated to try to respond in egalitarian ways (e.g., Devine, 1989). Nonetheless, much research indicates that people with low-prejudice attitudes are prone to automatic activation of stereotypes and implicit biases that result in prejudiced responses. That is, without conscious bidding or the intent to have biased thoughts, feelings, or actions, stereotypes can be activated and applied when responding to the relevant outgroup (see Bargh, 1999; Dasgupta, 2004) and sometimes even in relation to one's ingroup (i.e., in the case of low-status groups; Ashburn-Nardo, Knowles, & Monteith, 2003; Jost, Pelham, & Carvallo, 2002). Thus, low-prejudice individuals are often faced with the need to self-regulate their responses and, as will be seen throughout this chapter, much research has focused on this group of people. They are often identified with the use of standard attitudinal questionnaires (e.g., Whites who score low on the Attitudes Toward Blacks scale; Brigham, 1993). Another way to conceptualize and operationalize this group of people is in terms of their high internal motivation to control prejudice (Dunton & Fazio, 1997; Plant & Devine, 1998).

People who hold more prejudiced beliefs also can be motivated to self-regulate their prejudiced responses. This motivation can stem from a strong concern with social pressures to respond without prejudice, or being high in the external motivation to control prejudice (Plant & Devine, 1998). It can also stem more generally from factors that create normative pressures to respond without bias (although highly externally motivated individuals are likely to respond most strongly to these pressures). For example, the actual or expected presence of a peer or authority figure who is believed to reprove prejudice leads to reductions of prejudiced self-reports and behaviors (Blanchard, Lilly, &

Vaughn, 1991; Monteith, Deneen, & Tooman, 1996; Plant, Devine, & Brazy, 2003), and we would argue that these reductions often involve self-regulatory processes.

When people are sufficiently motivated to self-regulate their prejudiced responses, precisely how do they do it? Two main strategies have been studied in connection with the exertion of self-control over stereotyping and prejudice. The first involves the suppression of stereotypic thoughts and biases, and the second involves the "unlearning" of prejudiced biases through processes of monitoring, inhibition, and the exertion of control. We turn now to a review of each of these strategies.

SELF-REGULATION THROUGH SUPPRESSION

One method of self-regulating prejudice involves suppression, or the attempt to banish stereotypic and biased thoughts from the mind. Stereotype suppression involves quite simply trying not to have stereotypic thoughts and instead focusing on "distracter" thoughts. For example, a heterosexual attempting to avoid stereotypic thoughts about a gay person with whom he or she is interacting might try to avoid thinking about the fact that the person is gay, try not to attend to what might be perceived as stereotype-consistent traits, and so on.

The active effort involved in attempting to banish stereotypic thoughts from the mind has often been shown to backfire and result in a rebound effect. For example, in the classic demonstration of this effect, Macrae, Bodenhausen, Milne, and Jetten (1994, Study 1) asked participants to spend 5 minutes writing about a typical "day in the life" of a person shown in a photograph, and that person was a skinhead. Half of the participants were instructed to avoid stereotypic thoughts while writing their passage, and others were given no special instructions. Participants then wrote another passage, again about a skinhead, but this time none of them were instructed to suppress stereotypes. Results indicated that participants who had initially suppressed stereotypes showed a rebound effect on the second passage they wrote, such that they used stereotypes even more than participants who never received suppression instructions. This rebound effect was also replicated with behavioral (Study 2) and stereotype accessibility (Study 3) measures. The theoretical explanation for the stereotype rebound effect relates to Wegner's (1994) model of mental control. This model posits that, as individuals engage in a controlled operating process so as to successfully regulate their thoughts by identifying appropriate distracters, an ironic monitoring process continually searches consciousness for evidence of the unwanted thoughts. Unfortunately, this has the effect of priming the unwanted thoughts (Macrae et al., 1994), and when the conscious monitoring process is taxed or relaxed, the suppressed thought will return with a vengeance.

Many studies have further demonstrated the paradoxical effects of stereotype suppression. They occur not only with blatant experimenter instructions to avoid stereotyping, but also when more subtle situational cues prompt suppression attempts (Macrae, Bodenhausen, & Milne, 1998). They are manifested in superior memory for stereotypical behaviors and impaired memory for nonstereotypic individuating information (Macrae, Bodenhausen, Milne, & Wheeler, 1996; Sherman, Stroessner, Loftus, & Deguzman, 1997). Also, the effortful nature of stereotype suppression depletes regulatory resources and results in a generalized increase in stereotyping (Gordijn, Hindriks, Koomen, Dijksterhuis, & van Knippenberg, 2004).

This body of research thus suggests that self-regulating one's stereotypic thoughts through suppression will be not only unsuccessful, but will have counterproductive outcomes. However, researchers have also identified important boundary conditions to the stereotype rebound effect (Monteith, Sherman, & Devine, 1998), finding it is a consistently successful strategy for some people and for others it can be successful under some conditions. Using the same "day in the life" paradigm as Macrae et al. (1994), Monteith, Spicer, and Tooman (1998) found that low-prejudice individuals were less prone to the rebound effect. Gordijn et al. (2004) similarly found that individuals who are high in internal motivation to suppress stereotypes did not reveal the typical rebound effect. They further showed that these individuals did not show a depletion of regulatory resources following stereotype suppression, whereas people low in suppression motivation did. The act of suppression thus does not appear to be as taxing for internally motivated people, perhaps because egalitarian thoughts provide ready replacements (see Monteith, Spicer, & Tooman, 1998).

Even high-prejudice people do not show the stereotype rebound effect if social norms call for continual avoidance of the use of stereotypes after the initial suppression period and cognitive resources are sufficient for continued suppression (Monteith, Spicer, & Tooman, 1998; see also Wyer, Sherman, & Strossner, 2000). Furthermore, if self-control is strengthened for high-prejudice individuals even in a domain unrelated to stereotype use, stereotype rebound can be avoided. This was recently demonstrated by Gailliot, Plant, Butz, and Baumeister (2007). Their participants were low in their motivation to control prejudice and had to exert quite a lot of self-control to suppress stereotypes initially, as evidenced in impairment in executive functioning following stereotype suppression (measured by Stroop and anagram task performance). However, after they had completed 2 weeks of self-regulation exercises in a stereotype-unrelated domain (e.g., refraining from cursing), the act of stereotype suppression no longer depleted regulatory resources.

In sum, stereotype suppression may sometimes prove successful and not result in rebound. Nonetheless, we believe that this strategy has a potentially important limitation beyond the possibility of producing rebound effects. Because it does not create a positive goal that one works toward but rather places a focus on avoidance of unwanted thoughts and outcomes, this strategy alone is not likely to prove effective in producing long-term changes to the stereotypic and evaluative underpinnings of prejudiced responses even among low-prejudice individuals. Furthermore, research has indicated that encouraging people to comply with proegalitarian pressures when their personal preference is for prejudiced responding can lead to anger and backlash (Plant & Devine, 2001).

THE SELF-REGULATION OF PREJUDICE MODEL

Other chapters in this volume (see Dasgupta, chap. 13, this volume; Devine & Sharp, chap. 4, this volume) provide compelling and comprehensive reviews of the implicit and automatic nature of stereotypic and evaluative intergroup biases, and also of the cognitive, motivational, and social processes that contribute to the automatic aspects of prejudice. The critical question for our purposes in this section, given the automatic and implicit processes underlying many people's prejudiced responses, is, How can self-regulation enable people to respond consistently with their egalitarian self-image (or, in some cases as will be discussed, with low-prejudice standards for responding that are imposed by others)? In other words, how can people learn to deautomatize their "habit" of responding in prejudiced ways (Devine, 1989) and reautomatize less prejudiced ways of responding?

Monteith and colleagues (Monteith, 1993; Monteith, Ashburn-Nardo, Voils, & Czopp, 2002; for reviews, see Monteith & Mark, 2005; Monteith & Voils, 2001) have developed and tested the self-regulation of prejudice model (SRP model) for understanding this process of change (see Figure 25.1). The model starts with the now well-documented fact that stereotypes and implicit evaluative biases can be automatically activated and used as a basis for responding (Devine, 1989). For people who hold low-prejudice attitudes, such responses result in the occurrence of a discrepant response, or a response that is more prejudiced than one's personal standards suggest is appropriate. If people become aware that they have engaged in a prejudiced response that is discrepant from their standards, the model specifies a variety of consequences that will be critical to subsequent self-regulatory efforts. First, arousal should be momentarily increased, and there should be a brief interruption of ongoing responding, or *behavioral inhibition*.

Second, awareness of the discrepancy should elicit negative self-directed affect, such as guilt and self-disappointment. Third, the model holds that individuals will engage in retrospective reflection to identify indicators of the discrepant response, such as features of the situation, the environment, and the self. Such attention results in the identification of stimuli that predict the occurrence of the discrepant response. With these consequences comes the natural development of *cues for control,* or the building

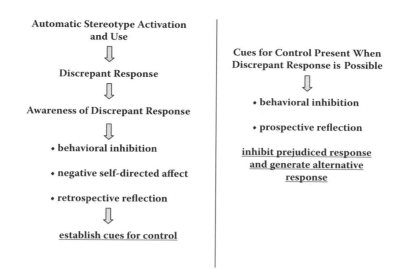

FIGURE 25.1 The self-regulation of prejudice model.

of associations between stimuli that predict the occurrence of a discrepant response, the discrepant response itself, and the negative self-directed affect resulting from awareness of one's discrepancy.

For example, a White woman (call her Elaine) might find herself clutching her purse as she passes a Black man while walking down the street. She might wonder at her reaction, knowing full well that she had passed several White men on the street without clutching her purse, and realize that her behavior is inconsistent with her personal standards for responding without bias in relation to Black people. Awareness of the discrepant response should result in a momentary pausing in Elaine's behavior, heightened self-directed negative affect, and noting of stimuli present or in some way related to the discrepant response (e.g., where Elaine was; where she going; which purse she carried; and features of the man, such as his race). These consequences should work in concert to establish cues for control, or the building of associations among the prejudiced response (in this case, clutching the purse), the negative affect, and related stimuli (e.g., the man's race). Theoretically, this process should take only milliseconds.

These initial consequences of becoming aware of a discrepant response should be critical for the self-regulation of prejudiced responses in the future. Specifically, the presence of cues for control in subsequent situations when a prejudiced response is possible should trigger behavioral inhibition that allows one to engage in *prospective reflection*. In other words, the detection of a situation where a biased response may occur should interrupt ongoing responding and allow for a more careful consideration of how to respond. This enables one to inhibit a prejudiced response and generate a nonbiased response instead. Theoretically, with practice, this process of self-regulation should result in the deautomatization of prejudiced responses and the consistent generation of less biased responses. In the preceding example with Elaine, her previously established cues for control should trigger self-regulation so that she can interrupt the process of automatic bias and experience greater success responding in low-prejudice ways.

The theoretical basis for expecting these types of consequences when people become aware of prejudice-related discrepant responses arises from several lines of research. For example, the idea that awareness that violation of an important self-standard should result in the experience of negative self-directed affect, such as feeling guilty and disappointed with the self, is consistent with Higgins's (1987) self-discrepancy theory. In addition, Gray's (1982; Gray & McNaughton, 1996) theoretical account of motivation and learning is central to the theoretical account described by the SRP model. Gray described the behavioral inhibition system (BIS) as the seat of self-regulation. This system, which is linked to the operation of particular brain structures, initially functions as a comparator, checking for mismatches between expected and actual events. Applying this to the self-regulation of prejudiced responses, the BIS responds to the detection of prejudice-related discrepant responses. Gray's analysis goes on to posit that detection of mismatches results in increased arousal, interruption of ongoing behavior, retrospective reflection, and building of cues for control (referred to by Gray, 1982, as cues for punishment)—the types of consequences adapted in the SRP model. Finally, this theoretical account explains how the BIS is triggered again in the presence of stimuli that have come to be associated with an unwanted response and the aversive consequences of that response so that prospective reflection and response inhibition may occur.

The process of conflict monitoring, detection, and exerting control over automatic processes can also be approached from a neuroscientific perspective by drawing on theory that posits two separate neural systems that operate when intended behavior conflicts with other inclinations (e.g., Botvinick, Braver, Barch, Carter, & Cohen, 2001). One system involves conflict detection and the other involves regulation. We discuss recent empirical developments relevant to this neuroscientific approach after summarizing research that tests the pathways hypothesized in the SRP model.

PREJUDICE-RELATED DISCREPANCIES

A first step in investigating the SRP model involved determining the extent to which people are aware of their prejudice-related discrepancies. Although the model suggests that across time and with practice regulatory control may be routinized and initiated spontaneously in the presence of cues for control (see Monteith et al., 2002), an initial awareness of the experience of discrepant responses is essential to cue development and subsequent self-regulation. An empirical method for examining awareness of prejudice-related discrepancies that has been used successfully in many studies (e.g., Devine, Monteith, Zuwerink, & Elliot, 1991; Monteith, Devine, & Zuwerink, 1993; Monteith & Voils, 1998; see Monteith & Mark, 2005, for a review) involves administration of the Should-Would Discrepancy Questionnaire. Participants are asked to consider various situations in which biased responses are possible, and they make two types of ratings in connection with each situation. First, they report the extent to which they *would* have the biased responses. Second, they report the extent to which they *should* have the biased response based on their personable standards for responding, defined as what they personally consider appropriate based on their beliefs. For example, White participants report the extent to which they would feel uncomfortable when shaking the hand of a Black person, and the corresponding should item asks about the extent to which they should feel uncomfortable doing so. Discrepancy scores are then generated by subtracting each should (belief) rating from the corresponding would rating and summing the resulting difference scores. This research has revealed that the vast majority of participants (approximately 80%) report positive discrepancies, suggesting that they are aware that they are prone to responding in ways that are more prejudiced than their personal standards suggest are appropriate.

Of course, an important issue is whether these self-reported discrepancies are authentic. This question was investigated by Monteith and Voils (1998, Study 3) in a study that participants were told concerned psychological aspects of humor. The White participants and a White confederate were supposedly randomly assigned roles as the joke teller or the joke evaluator, and the procedure was rigged so that the actual participants always evaluated the jokes. Four of the jokes told played on negative stereotypes of Blacks, and interest centered on how the low-prejudice participants would evaluate these jokes as a function of their proneness to prejudice-related discrepancies (explicit prejudice and discrepancy proneness were assessed in an earlier screening session). Furthermore, participants were either induced to experience low or high cognitive load while they evaluated the jokes, because generating prejudiced responses is more likely when cognitive resources are taxed (e.g., Pratto & Bargh, 1991).

The results indicated that the low-prejudice participants who self-reported larger discrepancies did indeed experience difficulty responding without bias under high cognitive load. That is, these participants evaluated the jokes relatively favorably when they were cognitively taxed, although they were able to generate less favorable evaluations when they were free of distraction. The low-prejudice participants whose discrepancies were smaller (i.e., who reported that they would and should respond with little bias across the situations included in the discrepancy questionnaire) generated unfavorable evaluations of the racial jokes, even when they were cognitively taxed. Thus, these results indicate that participants' reports of their degree of difficulty in controlling prejudiced responses, as indexed by should–would discrepancies, corresponded with their behavioral responses to the racial jokes.

Discrepancy-Related Affect

> Self-insight, however, does not automatically cure prejudice. At best it starts the individual wondering. And unless one questions the truth of his convictions, he certainly is unlikely to alter them. If he begins to suspect that they are not in conformity with facts, he may then enter a period of conflict. If the dissatisfaction is great enough, he may be driven to a reorganization of beliefs and attitudes. (Allport, 1954, pp. 328–329)

Allport's (1954) seminal writing on the experience of prejudice with compunction suggests that people must be dissatisfied with their prejudice to be motivated to change. The SRP model likewise posits that awareness of one's discrepant responses must give rise to feelings of negative self-directed affect if such awareness is to be useful for ultimately learning to inhibit and change one's prejudiced patterns of responding. These affective consequences of discrepancy awareness have been examined in many studies (see Monteith & Mark, 2005, for a review) by having participants report their current feelings immediately after they complete the Should-Would Discrepancy Questionnaire. To the extent that participants report prejudice-related discrepancies on the questionnaire, these inconsistencies should be primed and have affective consequences. Results have consistently indicated that low-prejudice individuals with larger discrepancy scores report greater general discomfort and also self-directed negative affect when they have just had their discrepancy proneness brought to mind. In contrast, as high-prejudice individuals' proneness to discrepancies increase, they report more general discomfort but not feelings suggesting that they are disappointed with themselves. This difference as a function of prejudice level is to be expected because low-prejudice individuals' personal standards for responding are well internalized and involve strong feelings of moral obligation, whereas this is less the case for high-prejudice individuals (e.g., Monteith et al., 1993; Monteith & Walters, 1998).

The affective consequences of awareness of prejudice-related discrepancies have also been investigated experimentally. These studies often induce participants to believe they have engaged in prejudiced responses or not, thus creating the benefits of control achieved through experimental manipulations. For example, Monteith (1993) led heterosexual participants who evaluated the credentials of a supposed law school applicant to believe that their negative evaluation of him was based on his being gay. In another series of investigations (Monteith et al., 2002), low-prejudice White participants were given false physiological feedback suggesting that they had negative reactions when viewing racial pictures (e.g., an interracial couple). Such experimental research has consistently shown that low-prejudice participants report significantly more negative self-directed affect when they believe they are having prejudiced responses that conflict with their personal standards than when they do not.

In an intriguing recent investigation, Amodio, Devine, and Harmon-Jones (2007) tested a dynamic conceptualization of discrepancy-associated guilt, hypothesizing that it initially functions as a negative reinforcement cue and reduces approach motivation, but then it transforms into approach-motivated behavior when one has the opportunity for reparation. Whereas the initial reduced approach motivation helps one to interrupt ongoing behavior and process the transgression to learn from mistakes, the transformation of guilt into approach responses facilitates more personally acceptable responding in the future. Because frontal EEG has been validated as an index of motivation orientation in past research (Hagemann, Naumann, Thayer, & Bartussek, 2002), Amodio et al. reasoned that an EEG measure of frontal cortical asymmetry could capture changes in approach and withdrawal orientations linked with the two functions of guilt.

This conceptualization was tested among low-prejudice Whites who initially viewed faces of Whites, Asians, and Blacks while EEG recordings were made. Then they were given bogus feedback suggesting that they had moderately negative reactions when viewing faces of Blacks but more positive reactions to the other faces, and a postfeedback assessment of guilt indicated that it was indeed elevated relative to participants' earlier baseline levels. Participants were then asked to evaluate stimuli for a future, supposedly unrelated study. Specifically, participants were shown 19 magazine article titles and instructed to indicate how much they would be interested in reading each article. Three titles were relevant to prejudice reduction ("10 ways to reduce prejudice in everyday life"). The results showed that elevated guilt levels were associated with a reduction (relative to baseline) in left-sided frontal asymmetry, indicating a reduction in approach motivation. In contrast, when the opportunity for pursuing a prejudice-reducing activity was introduced, guilt was associated with greater self-reported interest in the activity and also with increased left-frontal asymmetry, indicating an increase in approach motivation.

BEHAVIORAL INHIBITION AND RETROSPECTIVE REFLECTION

The momentary interruption of ongoing behavior that the SRP model posits occurs when discrepant responses are detected has been indexed with reaction times in computer-controlled experiments. For instance, in the false physiological feedback experiments mentioned earlier (Monteith et al., 2002, Studies 1 and 2), a variety of racial and nonracial pictures were presented to participants on a computer screen one at a time, and each one was followed by a graph that supposedly depicted participants' level of negative arousal. Participants were instructed to press the spacebar after seeing each graph to move on to the next picture. The time taken to press the spacebar was measured (in milliseconds) and served as an indicator of behavioral inhibition. As expected, participants who received physiological feedback suggesting that they were having negative reactions to the racial pictures took longer to press the spacebar than participants who received the same type of feedback for the nonracial pictures. The nonracial pictures were not obviously disturbing; rather, they were somewhat odd images, and participants had no reason to expect that their reactions to these pictures would be negative. Nevertheless, the pattern of observed findings suggested that participants' ongoing behavior was interrupted following the negative physiological feedback only when they believed their negative reactions were occurring in relation to their reactions to Blacks.

In contrast to behavioral inhibition, which is a mere interruption of ongoing behavior, retrospective reflection involves paying attention to features of the discrepancy situation and processing information that may help to predict similar discrepant responses in the future. This aspect of the SPR model has been tested primarily in thought-listing tasks following the induction of a prejudice-related discrepancy. For example, in the same false physiological feedback studies noted earlier, participants were asked to list their thoughts about the experiment at the conclusion of the experimental session. Among participants who believed they had negative reactions to the racial pictures, approximately 25% of the listed thoughts reflected a preoccupation with their reactions to the pictures. In contrast, virtually none of the thoughts indicated such a preoccupation among participants who believed they had negative reactions to the nonracial pictures. Similar findings were obtained by Monteith (1993, Study 1), in that the low-prejudice participants were especially preoccupied with their negative evaluations of a law school applicant when they believed that their evaluations reflected a heterosexist bias.

PROSPECTIVE REFLECTION AND PREJUDICE REGULATION IN THE PRESENCE OF CUES FOR CONTROL

The discrepancy consequences discussed thus far should be functional in that they serve to establish cues for control that can trigger an interruption of ongoing responding (prospective reflection) and a more careful generation of responses in the future. In other words, future regulation should improve. In one study relevant to these hypotheses (Monteith, 1993, Study 2), low-prejudice heterosexual participants received feedback on a (bogus) test of subtle prejudice suggesting that they were prone to subtle prejudice in relation to gays. This constituted the initial prejudice-related discrepancy experience. The critical test of the prospective reflection and inhibition of prejudiced responses then occurred in a supposedly separate second study about humor, where 2 of 12 jokes that participants evaluated played on stereotypes of gays. The results indicated that participants given discrepancy feedback took longer (in milliseconds) to evaluate these anti-gay jokes and evaluated them less favorably than participants assigned to a control condition who had not been given feedback suggesting that they were prone to subtle prejudice.

In another study that tested the cues for control idea in a different way (Monteith et al., 2002), low-prejudice participants took a racial implicit association test (IAT) that involved the dual categorization of traditionally Black and White names and pleasant and unpleasant words. They were given a summary of their performance suggesting that they could more easily pair White names with pleasant words and Black names with unpleasant words than the reverse. Participants then completed a measure of their affect. Later in the study, as part of a supposedly unrelated task, participants were presented with words one at a time on the computer and were asked to indicate their first reaction to each word: Was it something they liked or disliked? Some of the words were the traditionally Black names from the IAT. Results indicated that participants paused longer when these names were presented in the like–dislike task to the extent that their performance on the IAT had elicited negative self-directed affect. Furthermore, the more guilt participants had experienced in relation to their IAT performance, the more positively they evaluated the traditionally Black names in the like–dislike task. These results suggest that the more participants were disappointed with themselves following the initial discrepancy task, the more the race-related stimuli from that task triggered an interruption of responding when they might again demonstrate bias by negatively evaluating traditionally Black names.

APPLICATION TO HIGH-PREJUDICE INDIVIDUALS

Although the SPR model applies most directly to self-regulatory activity among individuals who are internally motivated to try to control their prejudice, it can be adapted to apply to high-prejudice individuals. Even if one's conscious attitudes are negative toward a particular group, pressures to respond with less prejudice and punishments for failures to do so (e.g., social rejection) likely prompt the development and operation of cues for control among high-prejudice individuals. Just like their low-prejudice counterparts, high-prejudice people often report being prone to prejudice-related discrepancies (e.g., Monteith et al., 1993), particularly if they want to see themselves as egalitarian and this desire is linked to a sense of moral obligation (Monteith & Walters, 1998). This was evident in a recent study where White participants were led through a guided interview designed to gather information about the development and operation of cues for control (Monteith, Mark, Ashburn-Nardo, & Czopp, 2008). For example, one high-prejudice participant reported:

> My roommate's Black and sometimes when we're watching shows they kinda like make the Blacks look trashy, you know like on Jerry Springer. . . . I was laughing at it but he wasn't really and it kind of automatically made me feel like I had done something wrong so I felt bad . . . I didn't want him to think, "Well he looks like some kind of racist."

When asked whether this experience affected the participant in the future, he responded:

> If something on TV comes up that's like shady you know it's like I think about it . . . you know I think
> about it to make sure that it doesn't happen again in case he actually was mad about it. I wouldn't laugh
> out loud if I thought maybe it would be offensive to someone else. I'm just a little more careful now.

In sum, both high- and low-prejudice individuals seem to put the "brakes" on their prejudices (Allport, 1954) through the development and operation of cues for control, although this process is driven more by fear of punishment from others and external concerns for highly prejudiced people.

Neuroscientific Evidence for the Self-Regulation of Prejudice

The work discussed thus far examined various aspects of the self-regulation of prejudice using measures of affect, cognition (based on reaction times and expressed thoughts), and behaviors. Recent developments applying cognitive neuroscientific models have provided insight into regulatory processes at the neural level, and this work brings exciting new advances to our understanding of the self-regulation of prejudice.

One line of research has identified the neural components that appear to be involved in automatic and controlled race-related evaluation. Cunningham et al. (2004) presented Black and White faces to low-prejudice White participants during event-related functional magnetic resonance imaging (fMRI). When faces were presented for just 30 msec, evidence of heightened amygdala activity was found for presentation of the Black relative to the White faces, suggesting greater emotional processing occurred for Black faces (see also Phelps et al., 2000). Furthermore, the extent to which amygdala activity increased for the Black versus the White faces was significantly correlated with participants' racial IAT scores, which strengthens the argument that evaluative processing occurs in the amygdala. Relevant to self-regulation, activity in different areas of the brain was evident when Black versus White faces were presented at longer intervals (525 msec). Specifically, the longer presentation of Black faces was associated with activity in areas of the prefrontal cortex and the anterior cingulate cortex (ACC). These areas are associated with inhibition, conflict, and control (MacDonald, Cohen, Stenger, & Carter, 2000; Ochsner, Bunge, Gross, & Gabrieli, 2002). Cunningham et al. (2004) further found that activity in these brain regions was correlated with a reduction in amygdala activity during long versus short presentations of the Black versus White faces, suggesting that controlled processing was modulating automatic processing. These results suggest that there are areas of the brain involved in regulation and executive functioning that may help in overriding racially biased responses that would otherwise result from automatic processing.

Other research has implicated the ACC in the regulation of racial bias as well. Amodio et al. (2004; see also Bartholow, Dickter, & Sestir, 2006) monitored electroencephalographic activity while White participants completed the weapons identification task (Payne, 2001), a measure of implicit racial bias. Although participants were not preselected to be low in prejudice, the population from which the sample was drawn led the researchers to suggest that this likely was the case. The researchers were particularly interested in the error-related negativity (ERN) wave, which appears to originate from activity in the ACC (Dehaene, Posner, & Tucker, 1994). The ERN is a component of the event-related potential that is sensitive to the conflict-detection process and especially conflicts that can result in failures to implement control (Gehring & Fencsik, 2001; Van Veen & Carter, 2002). Amodio et al. (2004) reasoned that ERNs would be larger (suggesting greater conflict-detection activity) when participants made racial bias errors on the weapons task (i.e., when they mistakenly "shot" Blacks holding tools) relative to when they made errors on comparison trials (i.e., on White-tool trials). The results confirmed this prediction. As noted by the researchers, this finding suggests that "unintentional race-based responses may occur despite the activation of neural systems that detect the need for control" (p. 88), and they posited that processing resources during the fast-paced weapons task likely were not sufficient for overcoming the bias. In addition, however, process dissociation procedures were used to separate the extent to which participants' performance on the weapons task was due to automatic versus controlled processing, and the researchers found that the greater participants' ERNs to race-biased responses, the greater their control as they completed the task.

Taking individual differences in motivations to control prejudice into account in this type of work has also proved to be important for understanding regulatory processes at the neural level and how successful individuals are in implementing control. Amodio, Devine, and Harmon-Jones (2008) examined such individual differences in the ability to detect and regulate race-biased conflict. They noted that people who are highly internally motivated to control prejudice but low in external motivation appear to be particularly adept at responding in low-prejudice ways (Devine, Plant, Amodio, Harmon-Jones, & Vance, 2002). The individuals' motives for responding without bias are not driven by external concerns but rather are highly internalized, well rehearsed, and implemented consistently across situations as a dominant response set. Amodio et al. (2008) reasoned that these high internal motivation, low external motivation participants would show greater evidence of control than high internal motivation, high external motivation participants when responses required stereotype inhibition due to conflict-monitoring activity. Using the paradigm described earlier of assessing ERN during the weapons identification task, these researchers found support for their hypothesis. That is, participants with high internal motivation and low external motivation exhibited better control at stereotype inhibition (i.e., on Black-tool trials), which was associated with ERN activity.

Another study further extended this examination of the role of individual differences by investigating whether internal and external motivations to control prejudice are related to different areas of brain activity. Specifically, Amodio, Kubota, Harmon-Jones, and Devine (2006) reasoned that whereas the conflict-monitoring processes involved in race-bias regulation among individuals high in internal motivation are related to activity in the dorsal regions of the ACC, externally motivated individuals should show a different pattern of neural activity, and particularly when there are strong external cues for controlling prejudiced responses. The rostral subregions of the ACC appear to be responsive to perception of response errors and the processing of external goal contingencies (e.g., Garavan, Ross, Kaufman, & Stein, 2003), and so Amodio et al. (2006) anticipated that this region would be related to stereotype inhibition among participants with high external motivation when they were responding in public. This was indeed the case.

In sum, a variety of studies have demonstrated that the control of automatic racial bias is linked to neural activity in the ACC and prefrontal cortex. As Amodio et al. (2008) argued, this neurocognitive research provides a "nonhumuncular" explanation for how the need for control can be signaled. Furthermore, the assumption is that these detection and control processes operate below conscious awareness and do not require the conscious intention to implement (Amodio et al., 2004). One should keep in mind, however, that the operation of executive control processes is taxing and thus may have less than desirable effects when one moves beyond an examination of whether prejudiced responses occur. We turn now to a review of how these taxing effects have been studied in the context of intergroup interactions.

SELF-REGULATION IN INTERGROUP INTERACTIONS

Intergroup interactions can be stressful and anxiety provoking (Plant, 2004), particularly if one is attempting to self-regulate one's responses to avoid responding in prejudiced ways or being perceived as biased. Evidence for the taxing effects of interracial interactions stems from research reported by Blascovich, Mendes, Hunter, Lickel, and Kowai-Bell (2001). These researchers found that nonstigmatized individuals experienced greater levels of threat (as measured via self-report, behaviorally, and physiologically) during an intergroup interaction than during an intragroup interaction. In a study that focused specifically on interracial interactions (White participants interacting with a Black vs. White confederate), threat responses were especially evident to the extent that the participants had little prior intergroup contact experience (Blascovich et al., 2001, Study 3). These results underscore the taxing nature of intergroup interactions.

Intergroup interactions can also take a toll on executive functioning. Building on the idea that executive function is a limited resource that can be depleted with effortful self-regulation (Muraven & Baumeister, 2000), Richeson and Shelton (2003) provided an elegant test of the idea that self-regulation during interracial interactions can be cognitively depleting. White participants in their research first completed a racial IAT as a measure of proneness to implicit racial bias. Participants then interacted with a White or a Black experimenter who asked for their thoughts on two rather controversial topics. After this, participants completed a Stroop task as a measure of cognitive interference. The results indicated that the greater participants' implicit prejudice scores, the greater interference they experienced on the Stroop task following their interaction with the Black experimenter. In contrast, cognitive interference was unrelated to implicit prejudice following an interaction with the White experimenter. Another finding from this research was that, during the interracial interaction, participants who scored higher on implicit bias moved their body less, looked around the room less, and moved their hands less than participants with lower implicit bias scores. This suggests that participants were attempting to regulate and control their behavior more during the interracial interaction, although additional tests did not reveal that such control mediated the effect of racial bias on cognitive interference.

Although the Richeson and Shelton (2003) study did not specifically establish that it was efforts at self-regulation and control among higher implicit prejudice participants that were responsible for undermining cognitive performance, this issue was pursued in subsequent research. Richeson, Shelton, and colleagues (Richeson et al., 2003) conducted a two-session study with White participants. The first session involved a replication of the Richeson and Shelton (2003) procedures. The results were consistent with the previous findings, indicating that the greater participants' implicit racial bias, the more cognitive interference was evident on the Stroop task following the interracial interaction. In a second session with the same White participants, fMRI data of the right dorsolateral prefrontal cortex (DLPFC) and the ACC were collected while participants viewed pictures of unfamiliar Black and White faces. Richeson et al. (2003) reasoned that because these brain regions support executive control processes such as response monitoring, inhibition, and conflict detection (e.g., Cohen, Botvinick, & Carter, 2000), they should be activated on viewing Black faces to the extent that participants were more prone to implicit racial bias. That is, because participants in this study were assumed to hold egalitarian self-standards and to be concerned about inhibiting their automatically activated biases, viewing Black faces should activate brain regions associated with exercising control. Results indicated that this was indeed the case.

Furthermore, analysis of the relation between data collected in Sessions 1 and 2 indicated that neural activity was related to interference on the Stroop task. The critical test in this research then involved an examination of whether the extent of activity in the brain regions thought to be critical to executive control mediated the relation between implicit racial bias and Stroop interference. The results supported the mediational test (in particular, for activity in the DLPFC). These findings suggest that the interracial interaction was cognitively depleting for participants who were prone to implicit racial biases because it taxed limited executive control resources. This resource depletion account has also been supported in investigations that manipulated the self-regulatory demands of interracial interactions (Richeson & Trawalter, 2005). For example, in one study (Study 1), White participants' concerns about being prejudiced were manipulated prior to a dyadic interaction by having participants complete the racial IAT and telling them that "most people are more prejudiced than they think they are." Other participants were given prejudice-unrelated feedback after completing the IAT. Later, participants in the prejudice concern condition showed greater impaired Stroop performance if they had interacted with a Black confederate than if they had interacted with a White confederate. In contrast, less Stroop interference was evident as a function of race of interaction partner among participants whose prejudice concerns had not been heightened.

Despite the cognitive burden that appears to result from the regulation of implicit prejudice, other research indicates that efforts at self-regulation can ultimately have positive effects on how individuals are perceived by outgroup members. Recall that Richeson and Shelton (2003) found that bodily control (less eye, hand, and body movement) during an interracial interaction increased as proneness to implicit racial bias increased. Another study (Shelton, 2003) similarly revealed that White participants who were instructed to try not to appear prejudiced during an interaction with a Black participant fidgeted less than participants who were not given this instruction. Also, Black participants reported more favorable evaluations of White participants who were asked to try to control their prejudice. Given these findings, Shelton, Richeson, Salvatore, and Trawalter (2005) reasoned that the behavioral control exerted by Whites who are prone to implicit racial biases might lead Black individuals to perceive them as quite engaged during interracial interactions, which may lead to greater liking. To test this hypothesis, White participants first completed the racial IAT. Then they interacted either with a White or Black partner, and partners subsequently reported how engaged the White participants were in the interaction and how favorably they felt toward these individuals. The results revealed that Whites who were more prone to implicit racial bias were perceived more favorably by Black (but not White) interaction partners. Furthermore, this relation was mediated by the extent to which the Black interaction partners perceived the White participants to be engaged in the interaction.

Vorauer and Turpie (2004) reported another line of research that suggests that individuals who are higher in explicit prejudice are more likely to engage in positive interracial behaviors out of concerns about appearing prejudiced. White Canadian participants prepared a videotaped message that supposedly would be shown to another participant who was identified either as a White or a First Nations Canadian student. In addition to varying the ethnicity of participants' supposed partner (i.e., the person who would view the videotape), the researchers examined the effects of participants' evaluative concerns. For example, in one study (see Study 3), high evaluative concern was created by telling participants that they should "watch themselves" while recording their message. Vorauer and Turpie reasoned that high evaluative concerns would lead participants to exhibit certain behaviors when recording their videotaped message. Specifically, the videotapes were coded on various dimensions related to intimacy-building behaviors (e.g., self-disclosure) or behaviors that, theoretically, convey positive feelings and foster closeness. The findings indicated that participants who were higher in explicit prejudice "shined" in their behaviors; in other words, they were more likely to engage in intimacy-building behaviors to the extent that they were concerned about how they would be evaluated by their supposed partner. In contrast, people who were lower in explicit prejudice "choked," such that they were less likely to engage in the intimacy-building behaviors to the extent that they were concerned about their appearance in their partner's evaluations.

In sum, the literature examining self-regulation during intergroup interactions suggests that it can have beneficial outcomes for the quality of the interaction, but nonetheless will have a depleting effect for the regulator.

CONCLUSIONS AND FUTURE DIRECTIONS

The research we have discussed in this chapter suggests that people often are motivated to self-regulate their prejudice, and that they may do so with two main strategies. Whereas suppression has the possibility of producing an ironic effect of increasing biased responses, regulation through the processes described by the SRP model, along with related neuroscientific evidence of self-regulation, suggests that people can learn to inhibit and control unwanted prejudiced biases. Nonetheless, the self-regulation of prejudice is not an easy solution to the problem of intergroup bias. It requires self-insight, effort, and vigilance among other things, and as we saw from the work on regulation during intergroup interactions, it can be depleting. This should come as no surprise, as controlling and changing any automatized response pattern is difficult, much less patterns that find reinforcement in culture and an array of intergroup and intrapersonal processes.

Much of the research we have reviewed constitutes recent advances, and we believe that this relatively new body of work will provide a gateway for making considerable additional progress in the scientific understanding of the self-regulation of prejudice. Some research questions arise quite directly from the completed research. For example, an important issue to examine in connection with the SRP model is whether previously developed cues for control can signal the need for control and the recruitment of executive resources preconsciously. Theoretically, the process of monitoring and exerting control should be able to be routinized and occur without the need for attentional resources (cf. Monteith et al., 2002). With respect to the neuroscientific approach to understanding the self-regulation of prejudice, a multitude of questions remain given this work is only now in its infancy. In the case of the examination of the self-regulation of prejudice in intergroup interactions, it will be important to determine whether practice at self-regulation during such interactions helps to diminish the cognitive depletion effects that have been observed. These and a host of other questions represent natural and essential follow-ups to what we currently know about the self-regulation of prejudice.

We also believe that other less straightforward research questions can be formulated and theoretical advances can be made given recent advances in the understanding of the self-regulation of prejudice. Interestingly, when Bargh (1999) reviewed the extant literature on stereotyping and the possibility of controlling automatically activated stereotypes, his ultimate conclusion was not optimistic. Bargh likened stereotypes to a "cognitive monster" and concluded that "Hoping to stop the cognitive monster by trying to control already activated stereotypes is like mowing dandelions; they just sprout up again" (p. 378). The body of research now available makes the possibility of control through self-regulation seem much more likely.

Nonetheless, there are both caveats to this more optimistic conclusion and the need for additional research and theoretical development. The self-regulation of prejudice is strongly situation dependent for some individuals, such as when it occurs publicly but not privately and requires ample cognitive resources (Plant et al., 2003). In addition, we believe that key questions for future research concern what exactly changes through self-regulation, and also through other avenues of bias reduction. Considerable research indicates that self-regulation involves conflict monitoring, inhibition, and replacement. Sometimes this replacement may result in overcorrection (Harber, 1998; Wegener & Petty, 1997). We also do not know exactly how effective self-regulation is in changing the underlying processes that can give rise to bias. Can self-regulation result in the modification of the neural underpinnings of automatic bias, or does its influence cease with the replacement process? If self-regulation can become automatized (see Amodio et al., 2004), it may be feasible as a permanent means to reducing automatic bias. However, if the automatic processes that underlie prejudice continue to be imprinted on the brain (much like riding a bike, one never seems to forget), then other strategies of change most certainly are necessary in addition to self-regulation for the maintenance of nonprejudiced responding. For example, close and meaningful intergroup contact that links outgroups to the self may be a candidate for the complete elimination of the roots of automatic bias.

ACKNOWLEDGMENT

Preparation of this chapter was supported in part by Grant MH56536 from the National Institute of Mental Health to Margo Monteith.

REFERENCES

Allport, G. W. (1954). *The nature of prejudice.* Reading, MA: Addison-Wesley.
Amodio, D. M., Devine, P. G., & Harmon-Jones, E. (2007). A dynamic model of guilt: Implications for motivation and self-regulation in the context of prejudice. *Psychological Science, 18,* 524–530.
Amodio, D. M., Devine, P. G., & Harmon-Jones, E. (2008). Individual differences in the regulation of intergroup bias: The role of conflict monitoring and neural signals for control. *Journal of Personality and Social Psychology, 94,* 60–74.
Amodio, D. M., Harmon-Jones, E., Devine, P. G., Curtin, J. J., Hartley, S. L., & Covert, A. E. (2004). Neural signals for the detection of unintentional race bias. *Psychological Science, 15,* 88–93.

Amodio, D. M., Kubota, J. T., Harmon-Jones, E., & Devine, P. G. (2006). Alternative mechanisms for regulating racial responses according to internal vs. external cues. *Social Cognitive and Affective Neuroscience, 1,* 26–36.

Ashburn-Nardo, L., Knowles, M. L., & Monteith, M. J. (2003). Black Americans' implicit racial associations and their implications for intergroup judgment. *Social Cognition, 21,* 61–87.

Bargh, J. A. (1999). The cognitive monster: The case against the controllability of automatic stereotype effects. In S. Chaiken & Y. Trope (Eds.), *Dual process theories in social psychology* (pp. 361–382). New York: Guilford.

Bartholow, B. D., Dickter, C. L., & Sestir, M. A. (2006). Stereotype activation and control of race bias: Cognitive control of inhibition and its impairment by alcohol. *Journal of Personality and Social Psychology, 90,* 272–287.

Biernat, M., Vescio, T. K., Theno, S. A., & Crandall, C. S. (1996). Values and prejudice: Understanding the impact of American values on outgroup attitudes. In C. Seligman, J. M. Olson, & M. P. Zanna (Eds.), *The psychology of values* (pp. 153–189). Mahwah, NJ: Erlbaum.

Blanchard, E. A., Lilly, T., & Vaughn, L. A. (1991). Reducing the expression of racial prejudice. *Psychological Science, 2,* 101–105.

Blascovich, J., Mendes, W. B., Hunter, S. B., Lickel, B., & Kowai-Bell, N. (2001). Perceiver threat in social interactions with stigmatized others. *Journal of Personality and Social Psychology, 80,* 253–267.

Botvinick, M. M., Braver, T. S., Barch, D. M., Carter, C. S., & Cohen, J. D. (2001). Conflict monitoring and cognitive control. *Psychological Review, 108,* 624–652.

Brigham, J. C. (1993). College students' racial attitudes. *Journal of Applied Social Psychology, 23,* 1933–1967.

Carver, C. S., & Scheier, M. F. (1990). Origins and functions of positive and negative affect: A control-process view. *Psychological Review, 97,* 19–35.

Cohen, J. D., Botvinick, M., & Carter, C. S. (2000). Anterior cingulated and prefrontal cortex: Who's in control? *Nature Neuroscience, 3,* 421–423.

Cunningham, W. A., Johnson, M. K., Raye, C. L., Catenby, J. C., Gore, J. C., & Banaji, M. R. (2004). Separable neural components in the processing of Black and White faces. *Psychological Science, 15,* 806–813.

Dasgupta, N. (2004). Implicit ingroup favouritism, outgroup favouritism, and their behavioural manifestations. *Social Justice Research, 17,* 143–169.

Dehaene, S., Posner, M. I., & Tucker, D. M. (1994). Localization of a neural system for error detection and compensation. *Psychological Science, 5,* 303–305.

Devine, P. G. (1989). Stereotypes and prejudice: Their automatic and controlled components. *Journal of Personality and Social Psychology, 56,* 5–18.

Devine, P. G., Monteith, M. J., Zuwerink, J. R., & Elliot, A. J. (1991). Prejudice with and without compunction, *Journal of Personality and Social Psychology, 60,* 817–830.

Devine, P. G., Plant, E. A., Amodio, D. M., Harmon-Jones, E., & Vance, S. L. (2002). The regulation of explicit and implicit race bias: The role of motivations to respond without prejudice. *Journal of Personality and Social Psychology, 82,* 835–848.

Dovidio, J. F., & Gaertner, S. L. (1998). On the nature of contemporary prejudice: The causes, consequences, and challenges of aversive racism. In J. L. Eberhardt & S. T. Fiske (Eds.), *Confronting racism: The problem and the response* (pp. 3–32). Thousand Oaks, CA: Sage.

Dunton, B. C., & Fazio, R. H. (1997). An individual difference measure of motivation to control prejudiced reactions. *Personality and Social Psychology Bulletin, 23,* 316–326.

Gailliot, M. T., Plant, E. A., Butz, D. A., & Baumeister, R. F. (2007). Increasing self-regulatory strength can reduce the depleting effect of suppressing stereotypes. *Personality and Social Psychology Bulletin, 33,* 281–294.

Garavan, H., Ross, T. J., Kaufman, J., & Stein, E. A. (2003). A midline dissociation between error-processing and response-conflict monitoring. *Neuroimage, 20,* 1132–1139.

Gehring, W. J., & Fencsik, D. E. (2001). Functions of the medial frontal cortex in the processing of conflict and errors. *Journal of Neuroscience, 21,* 9430–9437.

Gordijn, E. H., Hindriks, I., Koomen, W., Dijksterhuis, A., & van Knippenberg, A. (2004). Consequences of stereotype suppression and internal suppression motivation: A self-regulation approach. *Personality and Social Psychology Bulletin, 30,* 212–224.

Gray, J. A. (1982). *The neuropsychology of anxiety: An enquiry into the functions of the septo-hippocampal system.* New York: Oxford University Press.

Gray, J. A., & McNaughton, N. (1996). The neuropsychology of anxiety: Reprise. In D. A. Hope (Ed.), *Nebraska symposium on motivation, 1995: Perspectives on anxiety, panic, and fear. Current theory and research in motivation* (Vol. 43, pp. 61–134). Lincoln: University of Nebraska Press.

Hagemann, D., Naumann, E., Thayer, J. F., & Bartussek, D. (2002). Does resting EEG asymmetry reflect a trait? An application of latent state-trait theory. *Journal of Personality and Social Psychology, 82,* 619–641.

Harber, K. D. (1998). Feedback to minorities: Evidence of positive bias. *Journal of Personality and Social Psychology, 74,* 622–628.

Hass, R. G., Katz, I., Rizzo, N., Bailey, J., & Eisenstadt, D. (1991). Cross-racial appraisal as related to attitude ambivalence and cognitive complexity. *Personality and Social Psychology Bulletin, 17,* 83–92.

Higgins, E. T. (1987). Self-discrepancy theory: A theory relating self and affect. *Psychological Review, 94,* 319–340.

James, W. (1950). *The principles of psychology.* New York: Dover. (Original work published 1890).

Jost, J. T., Pelham, B. W., & Carvallo, M. R. (2002). Nonconscious forms of system justification: Implicit and behavioral preferences for higher status groups. *Journal of Experimental Social Psychology, 38,* 586–602.

Katz, I., & Hass, R. G. (1988). Racial ambivalence and American value conflict: Correlational and priming studies of dual cognitive structures. *Journal of Personality and Social Psychology, 55,* 593–905.

Katz, P. A. (2003). Racists or intolerant multiculturalists? How do they begin? *American Psychologist, 58,* 897–909.

MacDonald, A. W., Cohen, J. D., Stenger, V. A., & Carter, C. S. (2000). Dissociating the role of dorsolateral prefrontal cortex and anterior cingulated cortex in cognitive control. *Science, 288,* 1835–1837.

Macrae, C. N., Bodenhausen, G. V., & Milne, A. B. (1998). Saying no to unwanted thoughts: Self-focus and the regulation of mental life. *Journal of Personality and Social Psychology, 74,* 578–589.

Macrae, C. N., Bodenhausen, G. V., Milne, A. B., & Jetten, J. (1994). Out of mind but back in sight: Stereotypes on the rebound. *Journal of Personality and Social Psychology, 67,* 808–817.

Macrae, C. N., Bodenhausen, G. V., Milne, A. B., & Wheeler, V. (1996). On resisting the temptation for simplification: Counterintentional effects of stereotype suppression on social memory. *Social Cognition, 14,* 1-20.

Mischel, W. (1996). From good intentions to willpower. In P. M. Gollwitzer & J. A. Bargh (Eds.), *The psychology of action: Linking cognition and motivation to behavior* (pp. 197–218). New York: Guilford.

Monteith, M. J. (1993). Self-regulation of prejudiced responses: Implications for progress in prejudice reduction efforts. *Journal of Personality and Social Psychology, 65,* 469–485.

Monteith, M. J., Ashburn-Nardo, L., Voils, C. I., & Czopp, A. M. (2002). Putting the brakes on prejudice: On the development and operation of cues for control. *Journal of Personality and Social Psychology, 83,* 1029–1050.

Monteith, M. J., Deneen, N. E., & Tooman, G. D. (1996). The effect of social norm activation on the expression of opinions concerning gay men and Blacks. *Basic and Applied Social Psychology, 18,* 267–287.

Monteith, M. J., Devine, P. G., & Zuwerink, J. R. (1993). Self-directed versus other-directed affect as a consequence of prejudice-related discrepancies. *Journal of Personality and Social Psychology, 64,* 198–210.

Monteith, M. J., & Mark, A. Y. (2005). Changing one's prejudice ways: Awareness, affect, and self-regulation. *European Review of Social Psychology, 16,* 113–154.

Monteith, M. J., Mark, A. Y., Ashburn-Nardo, L., & Czopp, A. M. (2008). *Taking a "cue" from the real world: A qualitative analysis of cues for the control of prejudiced responses.* Manuscript in preparation.

Monteith, M. J., Sherman, J., & Devine, P. G. (1998). Suppression as a stereotype control strategy. *Personality and Social Psychology Review, 2,* 63–82.

Monteith, M. J., Spicer, C. V., & Tooman, G. (1998). Consequences of stereotype suppression: Stereotypes on AND not on the rebound. *Journal of Experimental Social Psychology, 34,* 355–377.

Monteith, M. J., & Voils, C. I. (1998). Proneness to prejudiced responses: Toward understanding the authenticity of self-reported discrepancies. *Journal of Personality and Social Psychology, 75,* 901–916.

Monteith, M. J., & Voils, C. I. (2001). Exerting control over prejudiced responses. In G. Moskowitz (Ed.), *Cognitive social psychology: The Princeton symposium on the legacy and future of social cognition* (pp. 375–388). Mahwah, NJ: Erlbaum.

Monteith, M. J., & Walters, G. L. (1998). Egalitarianism, moral obligation, and prejudice-related personal standards. *Personality and Social Psychology Bulletin, 24,* 86–199.

Muraven, M., & Baumeister, R. F. (2000). Self-regulation and depletion of limited resources: Does self-control resemble a muscle? *Psychological Bulletin, 126,* 247–259.

Muraven, M., Baumeister, R. F., & Tice, D. M. (1999). Longitudinal improvement of self-regulation through practice: Building self-control strength through repeated exercise. *Journal of Social Psychology, 139,* 446–457.

Ochsner, K. N., Bunge, S. A., Gross, J. J., & Gabrieli, J. D. E. (2002). Rethinking feelings: An fMRI study of the cognitive regulation of emotion. *Journal of Cognitive Neuroscience, 14,* 1215–1229.

Payne, B. K. (2001). Prejudice and perception: The role of automatic and controlled processes in misperceiving a weapon. *Journal of Personality and Social Psychology, 81,* 181–192.

Phelps, E. A., O'Connor, K. J., Cunningham, W. A., Funayama, E. S., Gatenby, J. C., Gore, J. C., et al. (2000). Performance on indirect measures of race evaluation predicts amygdale activitation. *Journal of Cognitive Neuroscience, 12,* 729–738.

Plant, E. A. (2004). Responses to interracial interactions over time. *Personality and Social Psychology Bulletin, 30,* 1458–1471.

Plant, E. A., & Devine, P. G. (1998). Internal and external motivation to respond without prejudice. *Journal of Personality and Social Psychology, 75,* 811–832.

Plant, E. A., & Devine, P. G. (2001). Responses to other-imposed pro-Black pressure: Acceptance or backlash? *Journal of Experimental Social Psychology, 37,* 486–501.

Plant, E. A., Devine, P. G., & Brazy, P. C. (2003). The bogus pipeline and motivations to reduce prejudice: Revisiting the fading and faking of racial prejudice. *Group Processes and Intergroup Relations, 6,* 187–200.

Pratto, F., & Bargh, J. A. (1991). Stereotyping based on apparently individuating information: Trait and global components of sex stereotypes under attention overload. *Journal of Experimental Social Psychology, 27,* 26–47.

Richeson, J. A., Baird, A. A., Gordon, H. L., Heatherton, T. F., Wyland, C. I., Trawalter, S., et al. (2003). An fMRI investigation of the impact of interracial contact on executive function. *Nature Neuroscience, 6,* 1323–1328.

Richeson, J. A., & Shelton, J. N. (2003). When prejudice does not pay: Effects of interracial contact on executive function. *Psychological Science, 14,* 287–290.

Richeson, J. A., & Trawalter, S. (2005). Why do interracial interactions impair executive function? A resource depletion account. *Journal of Personality and Social Psychology, 88,* 934–947.

Sears, D. O., & Henry, P. J. (2003). The origins of symbolic racism. *Journal of Personality and Social Psychology, 85,* 259–275.

Shelton, J. N. (2003). Interpersonal concerns in social encounters between majority and minority group members. *Group Processes and Intergroup Relations, 6,* 171–186.

Shelton, J. N., Richeson, J. A., Salvatore, J., & Trawalter, S. (2005). Ironic effects of racial bias during interracial interactions. *Psychological Science, 16,* 397–402.

Sherman, J. W., Stroessner, S. J., Loftus, S. T., & Deguzman, G. (1997). Stereotype suppression and recognition memory for stereotypical and nonstereotypical information. *Social Cognition, 15,* 205–215.

Sidanius, J., & Pratto, F. (1999). *Social dominance: An intergroup theory of social hierarchy and oppression.* New York: Cambridge University Press.

Tajfel, H., & Turner, J. C. (1986). The social identity theory of intergroup behavior. In W. G. Austin & S. Worchel (Eds.), *Psychology of intergroup relations* (2nd ed., pp. 7–27). Chicago: Nelson-Hall.

Van Veen, V., & Carter, C. S. (2002). The timing of action-monitoring processes in the anterior cingulated cortex. *Journal of Cognitive Neuroscience, 14,* 593–602.

Vorauer, J. D., & Turpie, C. (2004). Disruptive effects of vigilance on dominant group members' treatment of outgroup members: Choking versus shining under pressure. *Journal of Personality and Social Psychology, 87,* 384–399.

Wegener, D. T., & Petty, R. E. (1997). The flexible correction model: The role of naïve theories of bias in bias correction. In M. P. Zanna (Ed.), *Advances in experimental social psychology* (Vol. 29, pp. 141–208). New York: Academic.

Wegner, D. M. (1994). Ironic processes of mental control. *Psychological Review, 101,* 34–52.

Wyer, N. A., Sherman, J. W., & Stroessner, S. J. (2000). The roles of motivation and ability in controlling the consequences of stereotype suppression. *Personality and Social Psychology Bulletin, 26,* 13–25.

26 The Future of Research on Prejudice, Stereotyping, and Discrimination

*Susan T. Fiske, Lasana T. Harris, Tiane L. Lee,
and Ann Marie Russell*
Princeton University

In July 1999, the Oxford meeting of the European Association of Experimental Social Psychology witnessed, out of 33 total symposia, 13 focused on stereotyping, prejudice, and discrimination. In October 1999, the St. Louis meeting of the American Society for Experimental Social Psychology witnessed, out of 18 symposia, 6 on the same topics. At the 2007 Memphis meeting of the Society for Personality and Social Psychology, the numbers had decreased, from a third to about a sixth, but still a sizable number. Now this volume and one or two others focus exclusively on these topics. Certainly, social psychologists have been busy with bias.

At the seam between the centuries, Western social psychologists enthusiastically stitched away, trying to mend intergroup tears in the fabric of society and to embroider intragroup patterns of identity. The same social wear and tear motivated our forebears in the early part of the last century, so perhaps a turn-of-the-century assessment and prognosis is in order. This chapter focuses on the interpersonal level of bias: one person responding to another, based on that person's perceived social category.

To examine where we are going, we need to consider where we are now. (Stangor has admirably described where we have been, in his opening chapter on history.) In the present, how are social psychologists approaching this patchwork quilt of categorical thoughts, feelings, and behavior? What are we doing now, and what might we do in the future?

For the better part of a century, researchers in stereotyping, prejudice, and discrimination have focused on the mind, in both a cognitive and motivational sense. This volume's distribution of chapters accordingly reflects this concentration on cognition: The cognitive processes section is the largest, compared to sections on targets, measurement, affect, prejudice reduction, and neurobiology.

The 21st century may continue to emphasize mind, augmented by (one hopes) a focus on differentiated emotions, behavior, cultural sensitivity, and altogether new links to the brain. Doubtless, individuals will continue to stereotype, prejudge, and discriminate against each other on the basis of perceived category membership, so social psychologists are unlikely to go out of the mending business any time soon.

WHAT WILL WE BE DOING?

Predicting the future is a fool's task, and like the weather forecast, maybe the safest prediction is "more of the same." For intellectual entertainment, we offer three directions that move outward, from issues central in social psychology to those farther from the core. This speculation is necessarily brief, because the future is yet to come, but nonetheless urgent, as current events indicate.

Behavior: Remember Discrimination?

Social psychologists have learned a lot, at century's turn, about the complex interplay of motivation and cognition in reactions to outgroup members. By this logic, now we should be happily combining motivation and cognition to produce behavior, which we are beginning to do, but not enough. Early examples include the work (Bargh, Dijksterhuis, and colleagues) on mimicking the behavior of primed outgroup members. Arguably, social identity theory or self-categorization theory does an adequate job of addressing discrimination, but the intergroup level of analysis does not necessarily reflect one-on-one-discrimination. And we are not yet doing enough. Thoughts and feelings do not exclude, oppress, and kill people; behavior does.

Ten years ago, one might have worried that social psychologists have overslept. The stereotyping literature needed a wake-up call, on the order of the attitude–behavior wake-up call two or three decades ago, to get serious about predicting behavior (S. T. Fiske, 1998). The alarm was urgent. We then could not say enough, with enough authority, about what does and does not produce one-on-one discrimination. For example, dissociations among stereotyping, prejudice, and discrimination are frequent (Mackie & Smith, 1998).

Scattered accounts already suggest that prejudice will do a better job than stereotyping at predicting discriminatory behavior. Meta-analysis (Dovidio, Brigham, Johnson, & Gaertner, 1996; Stangor, Sullivan, & Ford, 1991; Talaska, Fiske, & Chaiken, in press; Tropp & Pettigrew, 2005) indicates that stereotyping correlates only modestly with discrimination, whereas prejudice does about twice as good a job of predicting discrimination. As a specific example, emotional measures predict behavior as well as behavioroid (intent) measures do (Talaska et al., in press) in 50 years of racial prejudice studies.

A pessimist would argue that our neglect of behavior has been a disgrace. An optimist would predict that social psychologists over the next decades will understand better the relationships among stereotypes, prejudice, and actual discrimination. Besides, we already have certain leads from the stereotyping literature and from the attitudes literature. From the stereotyping literature, we know that people can be motivated by core social motives (belonging, understanding, controlling, self enhancing, and trusting) to express or not to express stereotypes. Surely the same moderators motivate discrimination and tolerance. But we do not completely know yet. From the attitudes literature, we know that the attitude–behavior relation depends, among other factors, on the nature of (a) the attitude (read: stereotype or prejudice), that is, its strength, coherence, accessibility, and centrality; (b) the person (e.g., sensitivity to norms vs. self, chronic motivations, values), and (c) the context (e.g., salient norms, accountability, roles, relationships). Stereotyping researchers need to test our assumptions about generalizability from thoughts and feelings to behavior.

Social psychologists are beginning to wake up to behavioral issues. After a decades-spanning lull, the new century has witnessed significant progress in the study of the behavioral consequences of prejudice. We are developing new and important insights into the social cognitive and motivational factors that produce, predict, and moderate discriminatory behavior. Importantly, we are even beginning to understand the variables that attenuate it.

One area of study reveals that whereas explicit attitudes may not reliably predict behavioral outcomes, implicit attitudes predict certain kinds of behaviors. Implicit attitudes can lead to automatic and unintentional discrimination, particularly when conscious cognitive control is impaired by factors such as distraction, inebriation (Bartholow, Dickter, & Sestir, 2006), and poor executive functioning (Payne, 2005). Disturbingly, we now know that intergroup contact alone is enough to trigger cognitive impairment. Richeson and Shelton's (2003) findings indicate that cross-race interpersonal interactions often trigger self-regulatory demands (i.e., trying not to appear prejudiced, trying not to behave in a stereotypical manner) that exhaust the cognitive capacity of interactants from both majority and minority groups.

Other research links cognitions to specific discriminatory behaviors. For example, when we view outgroups as less human than our ingroup we are more likely to both deprive them and directly act against them (Vaes, Paladino, Castelli, Leyens, & Giovanazzi, 2003). Employment research shows that implicit attitudes lead to discrimination in the workplace. In one of the first studies to demonstrate the predictive value of the implicit association test (IAT), implicit racist attitudes were shown to interact with a racist corporate environment to predict discrimination in the evaluation and hiring of job candidates (Ziegert & Hanges, 2005).

Discrimination can have direct consequences in a variety of real-world contexts. In the criminal justice system, one provocative study found that prison sentences show a pattern of discrimination on the basis of Afrocentric features. Both Black and White inmates with more Afrocentric facial features received harsher sentences than other inmates with equivalent criminal records (Eberhardt, Davies, Purdie-Vaugh, & Johnson, 2006). Another study, inspired by the police shooting of an unarmed Amadou Diallo, revealed the disturbing finding that stereotyping can lead to potentially deadly results (Correll, Park, Judd, & Wittenbrink, 2002). In an investigation of the shooter bias phenomenon, participants played a videogame that presented targets who were either unarmed or armed and either Black or White and required the played to shoot at the armed targets. As the researchers hypothesized, participants fired more rapidly at armed Black targets than armed White targets in general, and were more likely to mistakenly fire at an unarmed target if he was Black.

Not only are people punished based on stereotypes associated with their category, they can also be punished for deviating from the stereotypic expectations of their category. The backlash effect shows that people sabotage women who violate prescribed gender roles (Rudman & Fairchild, 2004), and hiring discrimination targets agentic females unless they moderate their agency with niceness (Rudman & Glick, 2001).

On a more hopeful note, recent research has begun to show that change is possible. Automatic attitudes are malleable (Dasgupta & Asgari, 2004; Dasgupta & Greenwald, 2001; Wittenbrink, Judd, & Park, 2001) and so are the automatic behaviors that derive from them (Dasgupta & Rivera, 2006). Automatic and unconscious biases can be countered by the activation of conscious processes. In a study of anti-gay prejudice, Dasgupta and Rivera (2006) recently showed that activating conscious egalitarian beliefs as well as the motivation to control behavior can significantly reduce the expression of discrimination and can even eliminate it. The employment discrimination study referenced earlier (Ziegert & Hanges, 2005) manipulated the presence of racist culture in a simulated office environment. The encouraging findings showed that the absence of a racist culture in the office significantly reduced discriminatory hiring practices compared to the racist condition. Therefore the prospect of reducing and eliminating discrimination is more hopeful than some might think.

The verdict is in. In the 21st century—because discrimination is still alive, pervasive, dangerous, and sometimes fatal—social psychologists are asking good behavioral questions and are beginning to understand why and when this behavior occurs. Where there was once a gap in the study of cognition and behavior, there is now at least a bridge. More and more work on consequential behavior will probably continue. However, attenuation is the ultimate goal, and future research will doubtless guide our understanding of how to achieve it.

CULTURE

Doubtless, in the 21st century, moderator variables will strongly support the importance of cultural and local norms in predicting discriminatory behavior. Culture channels stereotyping and prejudice, by defining who constitutes "us" and "them." A critic might argue that each stereotype is unique, reflecting a unique cultural history, and because it does, psychologists have mostly ignored the contents of stereotypes. If the contents are arbitrary, why bother expending scientific resources on them?

Recently, we have suggested that the content of stereotypes may be systematic, and indeed may respond to universal principles of social structure. That is, a typology of prejudice suggests (a) paternalistic prejudice toward the incompetent but nice, subordinate outgroup; (b) envious prejudice toward the competent but cold, higher status outgroup; (c) contemptuous prejudice toward the incompetent, exploitative, not warm, low-status outgroup that cannot be trusted; and (d) admiration for the ingroup (S. T. Fiske, 1998; Glick & Fiske, 2001). In our data, the ambivalent kinds of outgroup stereotypes apparently predominate: those that are incompetent but maybe warm, and those that are competent but cold. Comparable clusters appear across the United States (S. T. Fiske, Glick, Cuddy, & Xu, 2002; S. T. Fiske, Xu, Cuddy, & Glick, 1999), in Europe (Phalet & Poppe, 1997), and in Asia (Cuddy, Fiske, Kwan, et al., in press). Moreover, status predicts which groups will be seen as competent, implying a just world in which groups get what they deserve (Caprariello, Cuddy, & Fiske, 2007). And competition with other groups predicts which groups are seen as not warm. Principles such as these can explain cultural differences in stereotype content, depending on social structure in that culture.

Besides content, culture determines acceptable levels of expressed bias, from subtle to overt. Cultures differ in norms for describing perceived differences between social categories, as either inherent and traditional differences between categories, or as unacceptable and controllable. For example, one kind of sexism, ambivalent sexism (Glick & Fiske, 1996, 2001a,b), appears in a similar form across a range of varied cultures (Glick et al., 2000). Nevertheless, degrees of its expression differ in cultures defined by United Nations gender indexes as more progressive (Australia, the Netherlands) or more traditional (South Korea, Turkey).

Other possibly fertile avenues include pursuing the role of stereotyping, prejudice, and discrimination in relatively individualistic and collectivistic cultures. In collectivistic cultures, ingroup harmony is key, and ingroup loyalty, favoritism, and conformity motivate social behavior. People belong to fewer groups, and distance from outgroups is considerable. On the one hand, this kind of context would seem to exaggerate bias against the outgroup, but on the other hand, contact with the outgroup would be limited, thereby minimizing the expression of bias. In more individualistic cultures, where people belong to many groups, and have contact with a variety of outgroup members, their opportunities for expressing bias may be more frequent. These speculations aside, collaboration between cultural and stereotyping researchers would benefit both lines of work.

One challenge will be the balance between cultural differences and cultural stereotypes. Several antidotes are prescribed. First, active collaboration with social psychologists from the relevant cultures inhibits a one-sided perspective. Second, cultural differences overlap with affirmed cultural identities, again based on groups' own images of themselves. Third, of course, variability within cultures undercuts stereotypic overgeneralization. Fourth, overlap between cultures teaches us about minority trends within our own cultures of origin, trends that might otherwise go undetected. Finally, some general principles cut across cultural variation and show similar processes operating on different content. Cultural similarities are useful generalities, and cultural differences may be of intrinsic interest, as well as predictable by broad, measurable cultural variables. The trend to study culture in social psychology (A. Fiske, Kitayama, Markus, & Nisbett, 1998) has yet to address stereotyping and prejudice in full force, but doubtless it will. We neglect culture at our peril, and cross-national (especially cross-hemispheric) collaboration will prove crucial to scientific progress in the 21st century.

In creating a balance between cultural differences and cultural stereotypes, social psychologists have been most successful with two research strategies. First, more and more researchers focus on prejudice targeted not at traditionally salient groups and categories (e.g., race, gender) but now examine less visible research targets, namely (a) subgroups, and (b) local culture (intragroup dynamics) in creating or exaggerating group differences. Second, research aims to understand change as it relates to social cognition: shifts in stereotype content over time, or the changes in groups themselves over different contexts.

Researchers are increasingly interested in social cognition about subgroups, ranging from women (Cuddy, Fiske, & Glick, 2004; Eckes, 2002), to homosexuals (Clausell & Fiske, 2005), and specific immigrant groups (Lee & Fiske, 2006). Prior to the latter work, for example, research investigated primarily the stereotype content of "immigrants" (Cuddy, Fiske, Kwan, et al., in press; Eckes,

2002). As researchers themselves become more aware of the nuances in perceivers' attitudes toward subgroups, it remains a matter of time before subgroups will highlight variability within groups.

Related to subgroups, researchers are also interested in how group members react to subtypes and fellow group members who violate norms. Recent work on the backlash effect understands punishing counternormative behaviors as a means for stereotype maintenance (Rudman & Fairchild, 2004). Likewise, researchers could more aggressively study discrimination directed at those who deviate from cultural expectations of the group. Although the black-sheep concept (see Marques, Yzerbyt, & Leyens, 1988) has been around for a while, more work is needed on the roles that various intragroup factors play in stereotype maintenance; group identification (Jetten, Postmes, & McAuliffe, 2002) and auto-stereotyping (Kashima & Kostopoulos, 2004; Prentice & Miller, 2002) are but two examples. Investigating intragroup dynamics allows researchers to step away from using traditionally salient group categories as the unit of analysis, thereby lessening the overlap between group boundaries and group differences.

Along with subgroup and subtype targets, researchers have increasingly looked at the different kinds of stereotypes that specifically impact particular subgroups and differentially produce discrimination. The most striking example is the way in which descriptive and prescriptive stereotypes function to produce different (but unequal) outcomes (Burgess & Borgida, 1999; Heilman, 2001). More specifically, prescriptive stereotypes of women as nice encourages the punishment of agentic women who violate the communal female stereotype (Rudman & Glick, 2001).

Another fruitful strategy in culture and prejudice research is to examine change, in stereotype content and in target groups. In the first line of research, researchers could illuminate the malleability of social attitudes as a function of shifting societal relations, by tracking the correspondence between attitude content and the historical interrelationships between groups. Three examples come to mind. First, a series of studies conducted at Princeton (Gilbert, 1951; Karlins, Coffman, & Walters, 1969; Katz & Braly, 1933; Leslie, Constantine, & Fiske, 2007) over 50 years are helpful in understanding the evolution of different ethnic groups, concomitant with historical and political changes. The same can be said of national stereotypes: Given that stereotypes reflect political economic factors (Linssen & Hagendoorn, 1994; Peabody, 1985; Salazar & Marin, 1977), researchers can systematically track how they correspond with real changes in the relationship between target and perceiver groups, as did Poppe (2001) and Poppe and Linssen (1999). Likewise, people increasingly attribute masculine traits to women, attendant with increased female representation in traditionally male-dominated contexts (Diekman & Eagly, 2000). In all these cases, changes in stereotype content are examined in relation to actual changes in group relations.

Another set of research investigates and documents differences between members of the same group across contexts. One prominent example stands out: Self-esteem rates vary among Asian participants as a function of exposure to North American culture. Third-generation immigrants, who are most exposed to and, therefore, socialized into the culture, report the highest self-esteem rates, on par with European Canadians, whereas Japanese who had never been abroad report the lowest (Heine, Lehman, Markus, & Kitayama, 1999). Studies such as this illustrate the variability of group differences as a function of context, not group membership. Within-group analyses on the culture of honor in the American South (Vandello & Cohen, 1999) and individualism in Hokkaido (Kitayama, Ishii, Imada, Takemura, & Ramaswamy, 2006) demonstrate that culture varies not necessarily by static group categories, but by historical context. Further, the latter study illustrates intergroup overlap (individualism in traditionally collectivistic Japan resembles European American individualism), minimizing the exaggeration of between-group differences.

Researchers tend to interpret intergroup differences as reflecting cultural differences of those groups without sufficiently implicating a cultural variable (Betancourt & Lopez, 1993). The field could counteract this trend by understanding group differences in relation not only to historical development as in the preceding studies, but also along robust cultural dimensions or principles. Some suggestions are to investigate how group differences relate to cultural dimensions (Hofstede, 1983), universal values (Schwartz, 1992), social relationships (A. P. Fiske, 1992), or cultural axioms

(Leung et al., 2002). To the extent that cultures rely on these dimensions to varying degrees, researchers could examine how group differences align with differences along these dimensions.

BRAIN

After the U.S. Decade of the Brain in the 1990s left social psychology relatively untouched, suddenly interest in social neuroscience is sprinkled across universities. A variety of initial data sets indicate that racial categorization occurs in unique neural locations closely linked to emotion. People apparently process Black and White faces with different patterns of activation (Golby, Gabrieli, Chiao, & Eberhardt, 2001). Cross-racial identification by both Black and White respondents shows more activation in the amygdala, hippocampus, and insular cortex, regions associated with the processing of emotional stimuli (Hart, Whalen, Shin, McInerney, Fischer, & Rauch, 2000). Similarly, amygdala activation occurred in Whites identifying Black faces, and that activation correlated with potentiated startle response, as well as racial bias, as measured by the Implicit Attitude Test (Phelps et al., 2000). Amygdala activation was not correlated with a conscious measure of racial attitudes (Modern Racism Scale), and it was eliminated in judgments regarding familiar and positively regarded Black individuals. The role of the emotionally attuned amygdala urges even more attention to prejudice as well as stereotyping measures in basic research.

On a more cognitive note, functionally independent and anatomically distinct slow learning and fast learning memory systems may respectively store general schemas (stereotypes) and specific individuating details (Smith & DeCoster, 2000). Moreover, the memory systems that specify specific sources differ from those for stereotypes, and they correlate with performance tests for different areas of the brain (Mather, Johnson, & De Leonardis, 1999). As people age, for example, their ability to recall specific details declines faster than their memory for general categories. These types of findings lend converging physiologically based evidence for categorizing and individuating processes (S. T. Fiske, Lin, & Neuberg, 1999; S. T. Fiske & Neuberg, 1990).

The budding interest in social neuroscience analyses, whatever their ultimate particulars, does not in itself constitute theory. Geography is not inherently theoretical. However, theory-based accounts of psychologically meaningful brain regions allied to responses of social importance could provide encouraging evidence for existing theories (i.e., dual process theories, as just noted) and could facilitate theory development. For example, cross-racial identification apparently links with emotion centers of the brain, which fits together with early indications that prejudice may predict discrimination better than stereotypes do. The role of midrange, not necessarily grand, theories will be crucial as at least some stereotyping and prejudice researchers seek the neural regions associated with biased responses.

Social neuroscience is now forging a reciprocal relationship between social psychology and cognitive neuroscience, wherein social psychological theory informs neuroscience and neuroscience findings inform social psychology. The early studies looking at prejudice and the amygdala just discussed led to social psychological predictions for neuroscience data. Is it possible to reduce amygdala activation via traditional social psychological treatments such as individuation? What other types of implicit perceptions did the amygdala track besides fear conditioning and IAT scores? Do participants without intact amygdala and temporal cortex due to lesions show IAT effects? Given that intergroup emotion models argue for ambivalent affect beyond pure antipathy, what brain regions track other types of prejudice? This wealth of research questions translated into additional data (see Cunningham et al., 2004; Harris & Fiske, 2004; Lieberman, Hariri, Jarcho, Eisenberger, & Bookheimer, 2005; Wheeler & Fiske, 2005). However, each study added more information about the psychological process.

Black participants as well as Whites show increased amygdala activity to Black faces (Lieberman et al., 2005), evidence that this is not an ingroup–outgroup effect. Frontal regions come online after 525 msec that correlate inversely with amygdala activity (Cunningham et al., 2004), suggesting signs of a conscious control mechanism.

Finally, prejudice is more diverse and involves regions of the brain other than the amygdala. An area of medial prefrontal cortex shows reduced activation to social group actors who elicit disgust, a basic emotion, as opposed to a more complex social emotion like pride, envy, or pity (Harris & Fiske, 2006, 2007). This research results from applying social psychological theory, in this case the stereotype content model (SCM; S. T. Fiske et al., 2002) of intergroup emotion to an area of the brain that reliably activates in social cognition tasks (the medial prefontal cortex; Amodio & Frith, 2006). The reduced activation is interpreted as a form of dehumanization or less-human perception because of the necessity of the area of the brain in thinking about people.

Converging evidence shows categorizing and individuating processes across different types of prejudice. Immediate preference judgments facilitate individuation, eliminating the difference between Black and White faces in amygdala and insula activation (Harris & Fiske, 2004; Wheeler & Fiske, 2005), and reactivating the medial prefrontal cortex for disgust-eliciting social groups.

Future research must attend to the goal of the participant and the functioning of brain areas. If the task can have these effects on the brain, then do they have corresponding behavioral effects? A number of social neuroscience studies of prejudice have again followed the lead of the initial studies and correlate neural activity with behavioral data.

Social psychological theory has been informed by social neuroscience. The reciprocal nature of the field requires an understanding of each field. Researchers who study prejudice find neuroscience a useful tool for dissociating processes, implicit affective assessment, and insight into control processes. Social neuroscience sits in the enviable position of being in conversation with strong theory and useful measures that have just begun to come together. Judging from the recent explosion in progress, the future possibilities for prejudice research seem better than ever.

CONCLUSION

Social psychologists laid out the pattern of research on stereotyping, prejudice, and discrimination 70 years ago, inspired by Lippmann (1922), and commencing with the initial work of Bogardus (1927) on social distance and of Katz and Braly (1933) on stereotype contents. Since then, given what we have done (intraindividual and contextual analyses, first motivational, then cognitive, now joint), we came to the current activity, which integrates motivational and cognitive features of interpersonal bias. Future prospects suggest we have much yet to do, in studying behavior, culture, and brain. The state of the world suggests that such expertise will continue to be sorely needed in the 21st century.

ACKNOWLEDGMENTS

Portions of this chapter are reprinted and adapted with permission from Fiske, S. T. (2000). Stereotyping, prejudice, and discrimination at the seam between the centuries: Evolution, culture, mind, and brain. *European Journal of Social Psychology, 30,* 299–322. Those original portions copyright © 2000 John Wiley & Sons, Ltd.

We would like to thank, for their rapid and perceptive comments on the original EJSP article, Stephanie Goodwin, Jacques Philippe Leyens, Charles Stangor, Roos Vonk, Vincent Yzerbyt, and an extremely helpful anonymous reviewer.

REFERENCES

Amodio, D. M., & Frith, C. D. (2006). Meeting of minds: The medial frontal cortex and social cognition. *Nature Reviews Neuroscience, 7,* 268–277.

Bartholow, B. D., Dickter, C. L., & Sestir, M. A. (2006). Stereotype activation and control of race bias: Cognitive control of inhibition and its impairment by alcohol. *Journal of Personality and Social Psychology, 90,* 272–287.

Betancourt, H., & Lopez, S. R. (1993). The study of culture, ethnicity, and race in American psychology. *American Psychologist, 48,* 629–637.

Bogardus, E. S. (1927). Race friendliness and social distance. *Journal of Applied Sociology, 11,* 272–287.

Burgess, D., & Borgida, E. (1999). Who women are, who women should be: Descriptive and prescriptive gender stereotyping in sex discrimination. *Psychology, Public Policy, and the Law, 5,* 665–692.

Caprariello, P. A., Cuddy, J. C., & Fiske, S. T. (2007). *Beliefs about social structure cause variations in stereotypes, and emotion: A causal test of the stereotype-content model.* Unpublished manuscript.

Clausell, E., & Fiske, S. T. (2005). When do subgroup parts add up to the stereotypic whole? Mixed stereotype content for gay male subgroups explains overall ratings. *Social Cognition, 23,* 161–181.

Correll, J., Park, B., Judd, C. M., & Wittenbrink, B. (2002). The police officer's dilemma: Using ethnicity to disambiguate potentially threatening individuals. *Journal of Personality and Social Psychology, 83,* 1314–1329.

Cuddy, A. J. C., Fiske, S. T., & Glick, P. (2004). When professionals become mothers, warmth doesn't cut the ice. *Journal of Social Issues, 60,* 701–718.

Cuddy, A. J. C., Fiske, S. T., & Glick, P. (2007). The BIAS map: Behaviors from intergroup affect and stereotypes. *Journal of Personality and Social Psychology, 92,* 631–648.

Cuddy, A. J. C., Fiske, S. T., Kwan, V. S. Y., Glick, P., Demoulin, S., Leyens, J.-Ph., et al. (in press). Is the stereotype content model culture-bound? A cross-cultural comparison reveals systematic similarities and differences. *British Journal of Social Psychology.*

Cunningham, W. C., Johnson, M. K., Raye, C. L., Gatenby, J. C., Gore, J. C., & Banaji, M. R. (2004). Separable neural components in the processing of Black and White faces. *Psychological Science, 15,* 806–813.

Dasgupta, N., & Asgari, S. (2004). Seeing is believing: Exposure to countersterotypic women leaders and its effect on automatic gender stereotyping. *Journal of Experimental Social Psychology, 40,* 642–658.

Dasgupta, N., & Greenwald, A. G. (2001). On the malleability of automatic attitudes: Combating automatic prejudice with images of admired and disliked individuals. *Journal of Personality and Social Psychology, 81,* 800–814.

Dasgupta, N., & Rivera, L. M. (2006). From automatic antigay prejudice to behavior: The moderating role of conscious beliefs about gender and behavioral control. *Journal of Personality and Social Psychology, 91,* 268–280.

Diekman, A. B., & Eagly, A. H. (2000). Stereotypes as dynamic constructs: Women and men of the past, present, and future. *Personality and Social Psychology Bulletin, 26,* 1171–1188.

Dovidio, J. F., Brigham, J. C., Johnson, B. T., & Gaertner, S. (1996). Stereotyping, prejudice, and discrimination: Another look. In C. N. Macrae, C. Stangor, & M. Hewstone (Eds.), *Stereotypes and stereotyping* (pp. 276–319). New York: Guilford.

Eberhardt, J. L., Davies, P. G., Purdie-Vaughns, V. J., & Johnson, S. L. (2006). Looking deathworthy: Perceived stereotypicality of black defendants predicts capital-sentences outcomes. *Psychological Science, 17,* 383-386.

Eckes, T. (2002). Paternalistic and envious gender stereotypes: Testing predictions from the stereotype content model. *Sex Roles, 47,* 99–114.

Fiske, A. P. (1992). The four elementary forms of sociality: Framework for a unified theory of social relations. *Psychological Review, 99,* 689–723.

Fiske, A. P., Kitayama, S., Markus, H. R., & Nisbett, R. E. (1998). The cultural matrix of social psychology. In D. T. Gilbert, S. T. Fiske, & G. Lindzey (Eds.), *The handbook of social psychology* (4th ed., Vol. 2, pp. 915–981). New York: McGraw-Hill.

Fiske, S. T. (1998). Stereotyping, prejudice, and discrimination. In D. T. Gilbert, S. T. Fiske, & G. Lindzey (Eds.), *The handbook of social psychology* (4th ed., Vol. 2, pp. 357–411). New York: McGraw-Hill.

Fiske, S. T., Cuddy, A. J., Glick, P., & Xu, J. (2002). A model of (often mixed) stereotype content: Competence and warmth respectively follow from perceived status and competition. *Journal of Personality and Social Psychology, 82,* 878–902.

Fiske, S. T., Lin, M. H., & Neuberg, S. L. (1999). The continuum model: Ten years later. In S. Chaiken & Y. Trope (Eds.), *Dual process theories in social psychology* (pp. 231–254). New York: Guilford.

Fiske, S. T., & Neuberg, S. L. (1990). A continuum model of impression formation: From category-based to individuating processes, as a function of information, motivation, and attention. In M. P. Zanna (Ed.), *Advances in experimental psychology* (Vol. 23, pp. 1–108). San Diego, CA: Academic.

Fiske, S. T., Xu, J., Cuddy, A. C., & Glick, P. (1999). (Dis) respecting versus (dis)liking: Status and interdependence predict ambivalent stereotypes of competence and warmth. *Journal of Social Issues, 55*(3), 473-489.

Gilbert, G. M. (1951). Stereotype persistence and change among college students. *Journal of Abnormal and Social Psychology, 46*, 245–254.

Glick, P., & Fiske, S. T. (1996). The ambivalent sexism inventory: Differentiating hostile and benevolent sexism. *Journal of Personality and Social Psychology, 70*, 491–512.

Glick, P., & Fiske, S. T. (2001a). An ambivalent alliance: Hostile and benevolent sexism as complementary justifications of gender inequality. *American Psychologist, 56*, 109–118.

Glick, P., & Fiske, S. T. (2001b). Ambivalent sexism. In M. P. Zanna (Ed.), *Advances in experimental social psychology* (Vol. 33, pp. 115–188). New York: Academic.

Glick, P., Fiske, S. T., Mladinic, A., Saiz, J. L., Abrams, D., Masser, B., et al. (2000). Beyond prejudice as simple antipathy: Hostile and benevolent sexism across cultures. *Journal of Personality and Social Psychology, 79*, 763–775.

Golby, A. J., Gabrieli, J. D. E., Chiao, J. Y., & Eberhardt, J. L. (2001). Differential responses in the fusiform region to same-race and other race faces. *Nature Neuroscience, 4*, 845-850.

Harris, L. T., & Fiske, S. T. (2004). *Amygdala and insula activations to Black faces affected by social context.* Unpublished manuscript, Princeton University, Princeton, NJ.

Harris, L. T., & Fiske, S. T. (2006). Dehumanizing the lowest of the low: Neuro-imaging responses to extreme outgroups. *Psychological Science, 17*, 847–853.

Harris, L. T., & Fiske, S. T. (2007). Social groups that elicit disgust are differentially processed in mPFC. *Social Cognitive and Affective Neuroscience, 2*, 45–51.

Hart, A. J., Whalen, P. J., Shin, L. M., McInerney, S. C., Fischer, H., & Rauch, S. L. (2000). Differential response in the human amygdala to racial outgroup vs ingroup face stimuli. *Neuroreport, 11*, 2351–2355.

Heilman, M. E. (2001). Description and prescription: How gender stereotypes prevent women's ascent up the organizational ladder. *Journal of Social Issues, 57*, 657–674.

Heine, S. J., Lehman, D. R., Markus, H. R., & Kitayama, S. (1999). Is there a universal need for positive self-regard? *Psychological Review, 106*, 766–794.

Hofstede, G. (1983). National cultures revisited. *Behavior Science Research, 18*, 285–305.

Jetten, J., Postmes, T., & McAuliffe, B. J. (2002). We're all individuals: Group norms of individualism and collectivism, levels of identification and identity threat. *European Journal of Social Psychology, 32*, 189–207.

Karlins, M., Coffman, T. L., & Walters, G. (1969). On the fading of social stereotypes: Studies in three generations of college students. *Journal of Personality and Social Psychology, 13*, 1–16.

Kashima, Y., & Kostopoulos, J. (2004). Cultural dynamics of stereotyping: Interpersonal communication may inadvertently help maintaining auto-stereotypes too. *Current Psychology of Cognition, 22*, 445–461.

Katz, D., & Braly, K. (1933). Racial stereotypes of one hundred college students. *Journal of Abnormal and Social Psychology, 28*, 280–290.

Kitayama, S., Ishii, K., Imada, T., Takemura, K., & Ramaswamy, J. (2006). Voluntary settlement and the spirit of independence: Evidence from Japan's "Northern Frontier." *Journal of Personality and Social Psychology, 91*, 369–384.

Lee, T. L., & Fiske, S. T. (2006). Not an outgroup, not yet an ingroup: Immigrants in the stereotype content model. *International Journal of Intercultural Relations, 30*, 751–768.

Leslie, L. M., Constantine, V. S., & Fiske, S. T. (2007). *The Princeton quartet: Does private ambivalence moderate modern stereotype content?* Unpublished manuscript.

Leung, K., Bond, M. H., de Carrasquel, S. R., Munoz, C., Hernandez, M., Murakami, F., et al. (2002). Social axioms: The search for universal dimensions of general beliefs about how the world functions. *Journal of Cross-Cultural Psychology, 33*, 286–302.

Lieberman, M. D., Hariri, A., Jarcho, J. M., Eisenberger, N. I., & Bookheimer, S. Y. (2005). An fMRI investigation of race-related amygdala activity in African-American and Caucasian-American individuals. *Nature Neuroscience, 8*, 720–722.

Linssen, H., & Hagendoorn, L. (1994). Social and geographical factors in the explanation of the content of European nationality stereotypes. *British Journal of Social Psychology, 33*, 165–182.

Lippmann, W. (1922). *Public opinion.* Harcourt Brace: New York.

Mackie, D. M., Smith, E. R. (1998). Intergroup relations: Insights from a theoretically integrative approach. *Psychological Review, 105*, 499–529.

Marques, J. M., Yzerbyt, V. Y., & Leyens, J.-Ph. (1988). The "black sheep effect": Extremity of judgments towards ingroup members as a function of group identification. *European Journal of Social Psychology, 18*, 1–16.

Mather, M., Johnson, M. K., & De Leonardis, D. M. (1999). Stereotype reliance in source monitoring: Age differences and neuropsychological test correlates. *Cognitive Neuropsychology, 16,* 437–458.

Payne, B. K. (2005). Conceptualizing control in social cognition: How executive functioning modulates the expression of automatic stereotyping. *Journal of Personality and Social Psychology, 89,* 488-503.

Peabody, D. (1985). *National characteristics.* New York: Cambridge University Press.

Phalet, K., & Poppe, E. (1997). Competence and morality dimensions of national and ethnic stereotypes: A study in six eastern European countries. *European Journal of Social Psychology, 27,* 703–723.

Phelps, E. A., O'Connor, K. J., Cunningham, W. A., Funayama, E. S., Gatenby, J. C., Gore, J. C., et al. (2000). Performance on indirect measures of race evaluation predicts amygdala activation. *Journal of Cognitive Neuroscience, 12,* 729–738.

Poppe, E. (2001). Effects of changes in GNP and perceived group characteristics on national and ethnic stereotypes in Central and Eastern Europe. *Journal of Applied Social Psychology, 31,* 1689–1708.

Poppe, E., & Linssen, H. (1999). In-group favouritism and the reflection of realistic dimensions of difference between national states in Central and Eastern European nationality stereotypes. *British Journal of Social Psychology, 38,* 85–102.

Prentice, D. A., & Miller, D. T. (2002). The emergence of homegrown stereotypes. *American Psychologist, 57,* 352–359.

Richeson, J. A., & Shelton, J. N. (2003). When prejudice does not pay: Effects of interracial contact on executive function. *Psychological Science, 14,* 287-290.

Rudman, L. A., & Fairchild, K. (2004). Reactions to counterstereotypical behavior: The role of backlash in cultural stereotype maintenance. *Journal of Personality and Social Psychology, 87,* 157–176.

Rudman, L. A., & Glick, P. (2001). Prescriptive gender stereotypes and backlash toward agentic women. *Journal of Social Issues, 57,* 743–762.

Salazar, J., & Marin, G. (1977). National stereotypes as a function of conflict and territorial proximity. *Journal of Social Psychology, 101,* 13–19.

Schwartz, S. H. (1992). The universal content and structure of values: Theoretical advances and empirical tests in 20 countries. In M. Zanna (Ed.), *Advances in experimental social psychology* (Vol. 25, pp. 1–65). New York: Academic.

Smith, E. R., & DeCoster, J. (2000). Dual-process models in social and cognitive psychology: Conceptual integration and links to underlying memory systems. *Personality and Social Psychology Review, 4,* 108–131.

Stangor, C., Sullivan, L. A., & Ford, T. E. (1991). Affective and cognitive determinants of prejudice. *Social Cognition, 9,* 59–80.

Talaska, C. A., Fiske, S. T., & Chaiken, S. (in press). Legitimating racial discrimination: A meta-analysis of the racial attitude–behavior literature shows that emotions, not beliefs, best predict discrimination. *Social Justice Research.*

Tropp, L. R., & Pettigrew, T. F. (2005). Differential relationships between intergroup contact and affective and cognitive dimensions of prejudice. *Personality and Social Psychology Bulletin, 31,* 1145–1158. Erratum. *Personality and Social Psychology Bulletin, 31,* 1456.

Vaes, J., Paladino, M., Castelli, L., Leyens, J., & Giovanazzi, A. (2003). On the behavioral consequences of infrahumanization: The implicit role of uniquely human emotions in intergroup relations. *Journal of Personality and Social Psychology, 85,* 1016–1034.

Vandello, J. A., & Cohen, D. (1999). Patterns of individualism and collectivism across the United States. *Journal of Personality and Social Psychology, 77,* 279–292.

Wheeler, M. E., & Fiske, S. T. (2005). Controlling racial prejudice and stereotyping: Social cognitive goals affect amygdala and stereotype activation. *Psychological* Science, *16,* 56–63.

Wittenbrink, B., Judd, C. M., & Park, B. (2001). Spontaneous prejudice in context: Variability in automatically activated attitudes. *Journal of Personality and Social Psychology, 81,* 815-827.

Ziegert, J. C., & Hanges, P. J. (2005). Employment discrimination: The role of implicit attitudes, motivation, and a climate for racial bias. *Journal of Applied Psychology, 90,* 553-562.

Subject Index

Note: Page numbers with "n" after them indicate a note.
      Page number in **bold** refer to figures or tables.

A

A (automatic bias) parameter, 116
Abdollahi, Abdolheissen, 316
Academic context, 166–169
Academic performance, 163–164
Academic self-confidence, 158–159
ACC (anterior cingulate cortex), 79, 340, 516
Accessibility of discrimination, 95
Accuracy
    ambiguous information, 213
    beliefs about groups, 201
    of ethnic and racial stereotypes, 211
    of gender stereotypes, 211
    high, 205
    inaccurate stereotypes, 212
    individuating information, 213
    inferences vs. observations, 214
    judging individuals, 212–213, 217–218
    moderate, 205–210
    near misses, 204
    no individuating information, 215
    partial information received, 214
    predicting future vs. evaluating past, 214
    small amounts of information, 213
    social psychology, 203
    of stereotypes, 199n1
    stereotypes and person perception, 214–215
Accuracy/inaccuracy, 222–223
ACT (American College Testing) scores, 142, 148
Action and behavioral tendencies, 293–295
Actions, 234
Activation of biased associations, 117–119
Activation of mental associations, 111
Activation of negative stereotypes, 162
Activation of social identity, 291
Activation/regulation of intergroup responses, 349–350
Affect, 96. *See* Prejudice
Affect, Cognition, and Stereotyping (Mackie), xix
Affective/cognitive consequences of control, 124–125
Affective sources of sexual prejudice, 450–451
Affect misattribution procedure (AMP), 376
Affect predicts attitudes, 4
African Americans
    athletic performance, 167
    children's racial attitudes, 27
    discrimination views, 92
    and GRE, 397
    intellectual performance, 162
    manipulation, 401
    minimum–confirmatory standards, 144
    mortality rates, 7
    perceived rejection, 231
    and PRAM, 27

self-esteem, 100
    standardized test performance, 155
Ageism
    age stereotypes, 433
    categorization process, 431
    cross-cultural differences, 436–437
    early ageism research, 432–433
    history of, 435
    influence on older persons, 434–435
    institutionalization of, 432
    positive intentions, 433
    prejudice, xx
    research, 437
    views of elderly, 314
    why are people ageist, 435–436
Agency vs. essence theories, 192
Agentic and distinct object, 358
Age stereotypes, 433
Aggression, 232
Aggressive views, 402
aggressive views
    Assimilation, 402
Aging, 432
Aging and memory, 167–168
Ambiguous information, 213
Ambiguous Pictures Task, 25
Ambivalence, 369
Ambivalent sexism, 415–416
Amelioration of intergroup emotions theory (IET),
      302–303
Amelioration of prejudice/intergroup conflict, 326–327
American College Testing (ACT) scores, 142
American National Election Studies (ANES), 447–448
American Society for Experimental Social Psychology,
      525
AMP (affect misattribution procedure), 376
Amplified derogation after MS, 312–313
Amygdala, 378, 530
ANES (American National Election Studies), 447–448
Anger, 258
Annenberg Survey Project, 168
Antagonistic processes, 395
Antecedents and consequences, 90–91
Antecedents of threat, 45
Antecedent variables, 191
Anterior cingulate cortex (ACC), 79, 340, 516
Anti-bias education program, 500–501
Anti-Black, 126
Antifat, xx
Anti-fat attitudes, 471, 476–477
Anti-fat bias, 473, 474, 476
Anti-fat prejudice
    dating, 473–474
    education, 471
    ethnicity and culture, 476–477
    evolutionary approach, 478
    friendship, 473

Author Index

Monteith, M.J., 510
Monteith, M. J., 512, 513, 514
Monteith, M.J., 515
Monteith, M. J., 515, 520
Monteith, M. J., & Mark, A. Y., 256, 510, 512, 513
Monteith, M.J. & Mark, chap. 25, this volume, 75
Monteith, M. J., & Voils, C. I., 510, 512
Monteith, M. J., & Walters, G. L., 513, 515
Monteith, M. J., Deneen, N. E., & Tooman, G. D., 5, 231, 509
Monteith, M. J., Devine, P. G., & Zuwerink, J. R., 233, 268, 512
Monteith, M. J., Sherman, J., & Devine, P. G., 509
Monteith, M. J., Sherman, J. W., & Devine, P. G., 73, 117, 458
Monteith, M. J., Spicer, C. V., & Tooman, G., 509, 510
Monteith, M. J., Spicer, C. V., & Tooman, G. D., 73, 449
Monteith, M. J., Zuwerink, J. R., & Devine, P. G., 268
Monteith and Mark, xx
Moons, W. G., & Mackie, D. M., 299
Moore, J.T., 475
Moors, A., 377
Morantz-Sanchez, R., 409
Morera, M. D., Dupont, E., Leyens, J. P., & Desert, M., 94
Morling, B., 222
Morris, J. F., Waldo, C. R., & Rothblum, E. D., 444
Morris, J. S., 351
Morrison, K.R., xix
Morrison, K.R., & Ybarra, 54, 58
Morrison, M. A., & Morrison, T. G., 414, 448
Mosher, D. L., & O'Grady, K. E., 273
Moskalenko, S., McCauley, C., & Rozin, P., 54
Moskowitz, G., 325
Moskowitz, G. B., 67, 74, 79, 119, 120
Moskowitz, G. B., Gollwitzer, P. M., Wasel, W., & Schaal, B., 67, 120
Moskowitz, G. B., Gollwitzer, P., Wasel, W., & Schaal, B., 277
Moskowitz, G. B., Salomon, A. R., & Taylor, C. M., 67, 120
Moskowitz, G. B., Wasel, W., Schaal, B., & Gollwitzer, P. M., 6
Mottola, G., 500
Mouchetant-Rostaing, Y., 334, 335, 336, 337
Mouchetant-Rostaing, Y., & Giard, M. H., 335
Moya, M., Glick, P., Exposito, F., deLemus, S., & Hart, J., 416
Mullen, B., 51, 336
Mullen, B., & Hu, L., 182
Mullen, B., & Hu, L. T., 495
Mullen, B., & Johnson, C., 9
Muller, L., 291
Muller-Fohrbrodt, G., 291
Mummendey, A., 3
Munro, G. D., & Ditto, P. H., 449
Münte, T.F., 116
Muraven, M., 117, 508, 518
Murnen, S. K., Wright, C., & Kaluzny, G., 416
Murray, C., 154
Murrell, A., 11
Murrell, A. J., 11
Murrell, A. J., Dietz-Uhler, B. L., Dovidio, J. F., Gaertner, S. L., & Drout, C. E., 491
Mussweiler, T., & Englich, B., 147

Mussweiler, T., Epstude, K., & Rüter, K., 147
Myrdal, G., 268

N

Naifeh, S.J., 454
Nario-Redmond, M.R., 144
National Center for Health Statistics. Public Health Service., 391
National Consumer's League, 432
Navarrete, C. D., & Fessler, D. M. T., 47
Neely, J. H., 62, 120
Nelson, xx
Nelson, C., 7
Nelson, L. J., 323
Nelson, L. J., Moore, D. L., Olivetti, J., & Scott, T., 312
Nelson, T., 202
Nelson, T. D., 1, 167, 431, 432, 433, 434, 436
Nelson, T.E., 137
Nesdale, D., 34, 37
Nesdale, D., Maass, A., Durkin, K., & Griffiths, J., 34
Neuberg, S. L., 9, 11
Neuberg, S.L., 47, 51, 273, 302, 415, 442, 478
Neuberg, S. L., & Fiske, S. T., 9, 72
Neuberg, S. L., & Newsome, J., 320
Neuberg, S. L., Smith, D. M., & Asher, T., 478
Neuberg, S. L., Smith, D. M., Hoffman, J. C., & Russell, F. J., 443
Neugarten, B., 432, 434
Neumann, R., & Strack, F., 297
Neumark-Sztainer, D., 470
Neumark-Sztainer, D., Story, M., & Faibisch, L., 471
Neumark-Sztainer, D., Story, M., & Harris T., 471
Neumark-Sztainer D. & Eisenberg, M.E., 470
Newcombe, N., 27, 166
Newman, L.S., 7
Ng, S. H., 437
Nicklas, T.A., 476
Niedenthal, P., 6, 379
Niemann-Flores, Y., & Dovidio, J. F., 389
Nier, J. A., 275, 399, 497
Nieuwenhuis, S., 340, 341
Nieuwenhuis, S., Ridderinkhof, K. R., Blom, J., Band, G. P. H., & Kok, A., 339
Nieuwenhuis, S., Yeung, N., van den Wildenberg, W., & Ridderinkhof, K. R., 341
Nisbett, R. E., & Wilson, T. D., 159, 267, 268
Noel, D. L., 480
Norman, D. A., & Shallice, T., 116, 117
Norton, M. I., 127
Norton, M. I., Sommers, S. R., Apfelbaum, E. P., Pura, N., & Ariely, D., 127
Nosek, B. A., 6
Nosek, B.A., 8, 66, 271, 376, 377, 378
Nosek, B. A., 380
Nosek, B.A., 380, 412
Nosek, B. A., 480
Nosek, B.A. et al., 2007, 6
Nuer, N., 229, 236
Nuessel, F., 432
Nuss, C.K., 233
Nussbaum, M. C., 273
Nystrom, L.E., 79

van Veen, V., & Carter, C. S., 340
Van Veen, V., & Carter, C. S., 516
Van Zomeren, M., Spears, R., Fischer, A. H., & Leach, C. W., 295
Vaughn, L.A., 146, 508–509
Ventis, W.L., 454
Verkuyten, M., 127, 127n3, 393
Vescio, T.K., 5, 7, 139, 145, 149, 251
Vescio, T. K., 252
Vescio, T.K., 252
Vescio, T. K., 255, 256
Vescio, T.K., 257
Vescio, T. K., 257, 258, 259
Vescio, T.K., 371, 449, 507
Vescio, T. K., Gervais, S. J., Heidenreich, S., & Snyder, M., 251
Vescio, T.K., Gervais, S.J., Heiphetz, L., & Bloodhart, B., chap. 12, this volume, 418
Vescio, T. K., Gervais, S. J., Snyder, M., & Hoover, A., 146, 251, 418
Vescio, T. K., Judd, C. M., & Kwan, V. S. Y., 418
Vescio, T. K., Sechrist, G. B., & Paolucci, M. P., 121
Vescio, T. K., Snyder, M., & Butz, D. A., 251
Vescio and her colleagues, xx
Viki, G.T., 416
Voci, A., & Hewstone, M., 49
Voelkl, K., 7, 89, 90, 93
Vogt, C., 408
Voils, C.I., 71, 75, 120, 271, 375, 510
Volkmann, J., 138
von Hippel, W., & Gonsalkorale, K., 116
von Hippel, W., Sekaquaptewa, D., & Vargas, P., 143, 378
von Hippel, W., Silver, L. A., & Lynch, M. E., 374
Vonofakou, C., 456
Vonofakou, C., Hewstone, M., & Voci, A., 455
Vorauer, J. D., 12, 122, 231
Vorauer, J. D., & Kumhyr, S. M., 91
Vorauer, J. D., & Sakamoto, Y., 12
Vorauer, J. D., & Turpie, C., 123, 519
Vorauer, J. D., & Turpie, C. A., 231, 234
Vorauer, J. D., Hunter, A., Main, K., & Roy, S., 122
Vorauer, J. D., Main, K., & O'Connell, G., 124
Vorauer, J. D., Main, K. J., & O'Connell, G. B., 230

W

Wadden, T.A., 478
Wade, G., 500
Walker, D. F., Tokar, D. M., & Fischer, A. R., 414
Walker, P., & Antaki, C., 449
Walther, E., 70
Walther, E., Nagengast, B., & Trasselli, C., 112
Walton, G.M., 8, 248, 254
Wanke, M., 3
Ward, B., 43
Ward, C.M., 497
Warren, J.L., 7
Wasel, W., 6, 379
Waterman, A., 165
Watkins, C., Terrell, F., Miller, F. S., & Terrell, S. L., 7
Watson, A.C., 445
Watson, J. B., 409
Weber, D., 140
Weber, J.G., 180

Weber, R., 10, 11
Weber J.G., 290
Wee, C. C., McCarthy, E. P., Davis, R. B., & Phillips R. S., 475
Wegener, D. T., & Petty, R. E., 72, 121
Wegener, D. T., & Petty, R. E., 121
Wegener, D. T., & Petty, R. E., 340, 520
Wegner, D. M., 73, 117, 118, 275, 509
Wegner, D. M., & Erber, R., 118
Weigel, R., & Howes, P., 371
Weiler, K., & Helms, L. B., 471
Weinberg, G., 445, 450
Weiner, B., 99, 450
Weiner, B., Perry, R. P., & Magnusson, J., 94, 477, 480
Weiner, M. J., & Wright, F. E., 29
Weise, D., Pyszczynski, T., 327
Welbourne, J. L., 180
Welbourne, J.L., 187
Welch, S., 168
West, T.L., 25, 30, 36
Westman, J., 432
Whalen, P., 97
Whalen, P. J., 351, 352
Whatley, J.L., 475
Wheeler, M. E., & Fiske, S. T., 117, 352, 360, 378, 530, 531
Wheeler, S. C., 162
Wheeler, S. C., & Petty, R. E., 9, 161, 162, 397
Wheeler, S. C., Jarvis, B. G., & Petty, R. E., 162
Whitely, B. E., 373
Whitley, B. E., Jr., 450
Whitley, B. E., Jr., & Lee, S. E., 452
Whitly, B.E.J., 414
Wible, C. G., 353
Wicklund, R. A., 115
Wig, G. S., Grafton, S. T., Demos, K. E., & Kelley, W. M., 353
Wiggins, D. K., 167
Wilcox, C., 449
Wilde, A., & Diekman, A. B., 412
Wilder, D., & Simon, A. F., 181
Wilder, D. A., 1, 51, 183, 455, 491, 492, 493
Willadsen-Jensen, E. C., & Ito, T. A., 335, 336, 337, 338
Willadsen-Jensen, E. C., Ito, T. A., & Park, B., 335
Williams, A., 437
Williams, D. R., 7
Williams, D. R., & Rucker, T. D., 7
Williams, D. R., & Williams-Morris, R., 7
Williams, D. R., Neighbors, H. W., & Jackson, J. S., 391
Williams, D. R., Spencer, M. S., & Jackson, J. S., 7
Williams, J., 154–155, 170
Williams, J. E., Best, D. L., & Boswell, D. A., 24
Williams, K. D., Shore, W. J., & Grahe, J. E., 253
Williams, K.J., 156
Williams & Edwards, 1969, 27
Williamson, J.B., 435
Wilson, T. D., 349, 380
Wilson, T. D., & Brekke, N., 72, 121, 142
Wilson, T. D., Lindsey, S., & Schooler, T. Y., 70, 268, 347, 376
Wilson, T.D., & Linville, P.W., 170
Winner, A.L., 455
Winslow, M. P., 251, 256
Wittenbrink, B., 12, 66, 74, 77, 81, 117, 341, 353, 378, 379, 527